OXFORD LIBRARY OF PSYCHOLOGY

Editor in Chief PETER E. NATHAN

Editor, Organizational Psychology STEVE W. J. KOZLOWSKI

The Oxford Handbook of Organizational Psychology

Edited by

Steve W. J. Kozlowski

VOLUME 1

OXFORD
UNIVERSITY PRESS

OXFORD
UNIVERSITY PRESS

Oxford University Press, Inc., publishes works that further
Oxford University's objective of excellence
in research, scholarship, and education.

Oxford   New York
Auckland   Cape Town   Dar es Salaam   Hong Kong   Karachi
Kuala Lumpur   Madrid   Melbourne   Mexico City   Nairobi
New Delhi   Shanghai   Taipei   Toronto

With offices in
Argentina   Austria   Brazil   Chile   Czech Republic   France   Greece
Guatemala   Hungary   Italy   Japan   Poland   Portugal   Singapore
South Korea   Switzerland   Thailand   Turkey   Ukraine   Vietnam

Copyright © 2012 by Oxford University Press, Inc.

Published by Oxford University Press, Inc.
198 Madison Avenue, New York, New York 10016
www.oup.com

Library of Congress Cataloging-in-Publication Data
The Oxford handbook of organizational psychology / edited by Steve W.J. Kozlowski.
     p. cm. — (Oxford library of psychology)
  ISBN-13: 978–0–19–992830–9 (acid-free paper)
  1. Psychology, Industrial—Handbooks, manuals, etc.
  2. Organizational behavior—Handbooks, manuals, etc.   I. Kozlowski, Steve W. J.
  HF5548.8.O94 2012
  302.3′5—dc23
  2011037047

9 8 7 6 5 4 3 2
Printed in the United States of America
on acid-free paper

SHORT CONTENTS

OXFORD LIBRARY OF PSYCHOLOGY

The *Oxford Library of Psychology*, a landmark series of handbooks, is published by Oxford University Press, one of the world's oldest and most highly respected publishers, with a tradition of publishing significant books in psychology. The ambitious goal of the *Oxford Library of Psychology* is nothing less than to span a vibrant, wide-ranging field and, in so doing, to fill a clear market need.

Encompassing a comprehensive set of handbooks, organized hierarchically, the *Library* incorporates volumes at different levels, each designed to meet a distinct need. At one level are a set of handbooks designed broadly to survey the major subfields of psychology; at another are numerous handbooks that cover important current focal research and scholarly areas of psychology in depth and detail. Planned as a reflection of the dynamism of psychology, the *Library* will grow and expand as psychology itself develops, thereby highlighting significant new research that will impact on the field. Adding to its accessibility and ease of use, the *Library* will be published in print and, later on, electronically.

The *Library* surveys psychology's principal subfields with a set of handbooks that capture the current status and future prospects of those major subdisciplines. This initial set includes handbooks of social and personality psychology, clinical psychology, counseling psychology, school psychology, educational psychology, industrial and organizational psychology, cognitive psychology, cognitive neuroscience, methods and measurements, history, neuropsychology, personality assessment, developmental psychology, and more. Each handbook undertakes to review one of psychology's major subdisciplines with breadth, comprehensiveness, and exemplary scholarship. In addition to these broadly-conceived volumes, the *Library* also includes a large number of handbooks designed to explore in depth more specialized areas of scholarship and research, such as stress, health and coping, anxiety and related disorders, cognitive development, or child and adolescent assessment. In contrast to the broad coverage of the subfield handbooks, each of these latter volumes focuses on an especially productive, more highly focused line of scholarship and research. Whether at the broadest or most specific level, however, all of the *Library* handbooks offer synthetic coverage that reviews and evaluates the relevant past and present research and anticipates research in the future. Each handbook in the *Library* includes introductory and concluding chapters written by its editor to provide a roadmap to the handbook's table of contents and to offer informed anticipations of significant future developments in that field.

An undertaking of this scope calls for handbook editors and chapter authors who are established scholars in the areas about which they write. Many of the nation's and world's most productive and best-respected psychologists have agreed to edit *Library* handbooks or write authoritative chapters in their areas of expertise.

For whom has the *Oxford Library of Psychology* been written? Because of its breadth, depth, and accessibility, the *Library* serves a diverse audience, including graduate students in psychology and their faculty mentors, scholars, researchers, and practitioners in psychology and related fields. Each will find in the *Library* the information they seek on the subfield or focal area of psychology in which they work or are interested.

Befitting its commitment to accessibility, each handbook includes a comprehensive index, as well as extensive references to help guide research. And because the *Library* was designed from its inception as an online as well as a print resource, its structure and contents will be readily and rationally searchable online. Further, once the *Library* is released online, the handbooks will be regularly and thoroughly updated.

In summary, the *Oxford Library of Psychology* will grow organically to provide a thoroughly informed perspective on the field of psychology, one that reflects both psychology's dynamism and its increasing interdisciplinarity. Once published electronically, the *Library* is also destined to become a uniquely valuable interactive tool, with extended search and browsing capabilities. As you begin to consult this handbook, we sincerely hope you will share our enthusiasm for the more than 500-year tradition of Oxford University Press for excellence, innovation, and quality, as exemplified by the *Oxford Library of Psychology*.

Peter E. Nathan
Editor-in-Chief
Oxford Library of Psychology

ABOUT THE EDITOR

Steve W. J. Kozlowski

Dr. Kozlowski is a recognized authority in human learning, team effectiveness, and multilevel theory. His research is focused on the design of active learning systems and the use of "synthetic experience" to train adaptive skills, the development of systems to enhance team learning and team effectiveness, and the critical role of team leaders in the development of adaptive teams. The goal of his programmatic research is to generate actionable theory, research-based principles, and deployable tools to facilitate the development of adaptive individuals, teams, and organizations. His work has generated over $7 million in funded research. He has published over 80 books, chapters, and articles and has delivered over 200 refereed and invited presentations. Dr. Kozlowski is the Editor (and a former Associate Editor) for the *Journal of Applied Psychology* and serves as the Editor for the *Oxford Series in Organizational Psychology*. He serves on the Editorial Boards of *Current Directions in Psychological Science* and the *Journal of Management*, and he has previously served on the Editorial Boards of the *Academy of Management Journal, Human Factors*, the *Journal of Applied Psychology*, and *Organizational Behavior and Human Decision Processes*. He is a Fellow of the American Psychological Association, the Association for Psychological Science, the International Association for Applied Psychology, and the Society for Industrial and Organizational Psychology. Dr. Kozlowski received his B.A. in psychology from the University of Rhode Island, and his M.S. and Ph.D. degrees in organizational psychology from The Pennsylvania State University.

CONTRIBUTORS

Linda Argote
Tepper School of Business
Carnegie Mellon University
Pittsburgh, PA

Tammy D. Allen
Department of Psychology
University of South Florida
Tampa, FL

Zeynep Aycan
Department of Psychology
Koc University
Istanbul, Turkey

Bradford S. Bell
Department of Human Resource Studies
Cornell University
Ithaca, NY

Sabrina Blawath
School of Management
University of St. Gallen
St. Gallen, Switzerland

Walter C. Borman
PDRI
University of South Florida
Tampa, FL

Daniel J. Brass
LINKS Center for Social Network Analysis
University of Kentucky
Lexington, KY

Laura L. Koppes Bryan
School of Psychological and Behavioral Sciences
University of West Florida
Pensacola, FL

Daniel M. Cable
Kenan-Flagler Business School
University of North Carolina at Chapel Hill
Chapel Hill, NC

John P. Campbell
Department of Psychology
University of Minnesota
Minneapolis, MN

Georgia T. Chao
The Eli Broad Graduate School of Management
Michigan State University
East Lansing, MI

Gilad Chen
Department of Management and Organization
University of Maryland
College Park, MD

Adrienne J. Colella
A. B. Freeman School of Business
Tulane University
New Orleans, LA

Jason A. Colquitt
Terry College of Business
University of Georgia
Athens, GA

John Cordery
UWA Business School
University of Western Australia
Perth, Australia

Reeshad S. Dalal
Department of Psychology
George Mason University
Fairfax, VA

Shanna R. Daniels
A. B. Freeman School of Business
Tulane University
New Orleans, LA

David V. Day
UWA Business School
University of Western Australia
Perth, Australia

Richard P. DeShon
Department of Psychology
Michigan State University
East Lansing, MI

Deborah DiazGranados
Department of Psychology
University of Central Florida
Orlando, FL

Lillian T. Eby
Department of Psychology
University of Georgia
Athens, GA

J. Kevin Ford
Department of Psychology
Michigan State University
East Lansing, MI

Stephen M. Fiore
Department of Philosophy and Institute for
Simulation and Training
University of Central Florida
Orlando, FL

Pennie Foster-Fishman
Department of Psychology
Michigan State University
East Lansing, MI

Michael Frese
NUS Business School
National University of Singapore
Singapore
Leuphana University of Lueneburg
Lueneburg, Germany

Michele J. Gelfand
Department of Psychology
University of Maryland
College Park, MD

Cristina B. Gibson
Management and Organisations
The University of Western Australia
Crawley, WA

Lucy L. Gilson
School of Business
Department of Management
University of Connecticut
Storrs, CT

Jonathan Grudin
Microsoft Research
Redmond, WA

Paul J. Hanges
Department of Psychology
University of Maryland
College Park, MD

Jerry W. Hedge
Survey Research Division
RTI International
Research Triangle Park, NC

David A. Hofmann
Kenan-Flagler Business School
University of North Carolina at Chapel Hill
Chapel Hill, NC

John R. Hollenbeck
The Eli Broad Graduate School of Management
Michigan State University
East Lansing, MI

Charles L. Hulin
Department of Psychology
University of Illinois
Champaign, IL

Timothy A. Judge
Mendoza College of Business
University of Notre Dame
Notre Dame, IN

Ruth Kanfer
School of Psychology
Georgia Institute of Technology
Atlanta, GA

Kwanghyun Kim
Korea University Business School
Korea University
Seoul, Korea

Bradley L. Kirkman
Mays Business School
Texas A&M University
College Station, TX

Alex Kirlik
Departments of Computer Science, Psychology,
and the Beckman Institute
University of Illinois at Urbana-Champaign
Urbana, IL

Steve W. J. Kozlowski
Department of Psychology
Michigan State University
East Lansing, MI

Manuel London
College of Business
State University of New York at
Stony Brook
Stony Brook, NY

John E. Mathieu
School of Business
Department of Management
University of Connecticut
Storrs, CT

Patrick F. McKay
School of Management and Labor Relations
Rutgers University
Piscataway, NJ

Cheri Ostroff
Department of Psychology
University of Maryland
College Park, MD

Sharon K. Parker
UWA Business School
University of Western Australia
Perth, Australia

José M. Peiró
Department of Social Psychology
University of Valencia
Valencia, Spain

Robert E. Ployhart
The Moore School of Business
Department of Management
University of South Carolina
Columbia, SC

Steven E. Poltrock
Bellevue, WA and Padova, Italy

Quinetta M. Roberson
School of Business
Villanova University
Villanova, PA

Michael A. Rosen
Department of Psychology
University of Central Florida
Orlando, FL

Ann Marie Ryan
Department of Psychology
Michigan State University
East Lansing, MI

Sara L. Rynes
Tippie College of Business
University of Iowa
Iowa City, IA

Paul R. Sackett
Department of Psychology
University of Minnesota
Minneapolis, MN

Eduardo Salas
Institute for Simulation & Training and
Department of Psychology
University of Central Florida
Orlando, FL

Marissa L. Shuffler
Department of Psychology
University of Central Florida
Orlando, FL

Sloane M. Signal
A. B. Freeman School of Business
Tulane University
New Orleans, LA

James W. Smither
School of Business
Department of Management
La Salle University
Philadelphia, PA

Scott A. Snell
Darden School of Business
University of Virginia
Charlottesville, VA

Charles C. Snow
Department of Management and Organization
The Pennsylvania State University
University Park, PA

Sabine Sonnentag
Department of Psychology
University of Mannheim
Mannheim, Germany

Matthias Spitzmuller
The Eli Broad Graduate School of Management
Michigan State University
East Lansing, MI

Paul Tesluk
Department of Management and Organization
University of Maryland
College Park, MD

Lois E. Tetrick
Department of Psychology
George Mason University
Fairfax, VA

Andrew J. Vinchur
Department of Psychology
Lafayette College
Easton, PA

Mo Wang
Warrington College of Business Administration
University of Florida
Gainesville, FL

Sallie J. Weaver
Department of Psychology
University of Central Florida
Orlando, FL

Kang Yang Trevor Yu
College of Business (Nanyang Business School)
Nanyang Technological University
Singapore

Dov M. Zohar
William Davidson Faculty of Industrial
    Engineering and Management
Technion – Israel Institute of Technology
Technion City, Haifa, Israel

CONTENTS

An Introduction to Organizational Psychology

The Nature of Organizational Psychology

Steve W. J. Kozlowski

Abstract

Organizational psychology is *the science of psychology applied to work and organizations*. This field of inquiry spans more than a century and covers an increasingly diverse range of topics as the nature of work and organizations continue to evolve. The purpose of this chapter is to provide a concise overview of organizational psychology as a field of inquiry and the topics covered in this handbook, which endeavors to encapsulate key topics of research and application, summarize important research findings, and identify innovative directions for research and practice. The chapter is organized around four sections. First, it begins with a brief overview of the evolution of the concept of work and the changing career model to provide a backdrop to our examination of the psychology of organizations. Second, it describes several dialectic tensions—industrial *and* organizational psychology, employee well-being *and* organizational effectiveness, basic *and* applied science, science *and* practice activities, and individual *and* organizational levels—that characterize organizational psychology as an applied, translational science. The tensions are a source of challenges that require a dynamic balance, but they also create important synergies for the field. Third, I highlight important trends over the last 35 years in the evolution of the field—it is increasingly multilevel, encompassing teams, studying dynamic phenomena, and expanding its breadth of coverage—that are shaping the field, as well as its future. Finally, I close with a tour of the structure of the volume and the topics that illustrate the breadth and diversity of this field that studies the science of psychology applied to work and organizations.

Key Words: introduction to organizational psychology; the evolution of work; dialectic tensions; evolutionary themes

> "Work is the inescapable starting point for all social inquiry."
> —(*Heilbroner*, 1985, p. 9)

The Centrality of Work and Organizations
Organizations Are Ubiquitous

People working together in organizations are the primary means by which contemporary societies accomplish the ordinary, mundane, but very important basics of everyday life which include providing food, water, clothing, shelter, and safety; managing the engines of economics, commerce, and trade; linking us via media for communication, entertainment, and enrichment; moving us by far-flung air transportation systems; and pushing the boundaries of the extraordinary by cracking the atom, putting men on the moon, and planning missions to more distal heavenly bodies. Work is central to modern culture, to the societies in which we live, and to the well-being of the people who comprise global cultures and societies. Those of you reading this chapter spent a substantial portion of your lives preparing for a career and have spent or will spend an even greater portion of your life building that career. Most people develop their careers by filling a series of roles in a single organization or across a set of different organizations. As they gain experience and enhanced competence, they seek to progress to roles with greater responsibility and concomitant material rewards. Other people depart from this typical pattern and define their own roles, and even their own organizations, as entrepreneurs. However, whether we work in an organization or create our own, we will interact with and accomplish many of our life goals in and through organized institutions. Organizations are ubiquitous in our world and in our lives.

Work Is Central to Life

Aside from the many material benefits provided by work and organizations, work is also an important source of identity and psychological well-being. Work structures time and activity, it provides opportunities for social interaction and exchange, and it is a foundation for self-identity and self-esteem (Jahoda, 1988). We invest on the order of 20 to 25 years in educational preparation in elementary school and high school, and occupational pre-socialization in college and post-graduate study. Work is a vehicle for career striving for the pursuit of achievement, power, and material rewards as well as a means to satisfy psychological needs. In contemporary society, a career trajectory will span roughly 40 or more years. By retirement, nearly half of one's waking life will have been spent preparing for and engaging in work, career, and organizational life. When work and careers are satisfying, they enhance our sense of well-being and are a major source of fulfillment. When our work life is troubled, or when it conflicts with other important life roles, it becomes a major source of tension, stress, and psychological and even physical dysfunction. Thus, the effects of work extend well beyond the bounds of the organizations in which work is embedded; work is central to adult fulfillment and well-being in most societies.

Overview

This chapter is designed to provide a broad overview of the field of organizational psychology—the psychology of human cognition, affect, behavior, and performance applied to work and organizations. Understanding the nature of organizational psychology necessitates an understanding of work as a fact of life, its cultural juxtaposition, and its evolution from ancient to modern times. An important aspect of this evolution is the shift from work as basic subsistence for maintaining existence to modern forms of work in organizations where the meaning of work is more abstract and where the outcomes—money, power, status—go beyond mere subsistence. Another purpose for tracing the evolution of work is to make salient the fact that work and organizations are not fixed "givens"; rather, they are socially constructed concepts, and they change and evolve as the societies and cultures around them advance. Hence, factors that are important research foci in different historical epochs change as society changes and the nature of work and organizations evolve (Koppes-Bryan & Vinchur, chapter 2 of this handbook).

This introductory chapter is structured into four sections. First, I begin with a concise tracing of *the evolution of work*. Work has been a central fact of human history, but its existential meaning has changed over time, and our modern conceptions, which are also in flux, are no more fixed or "real" than were ancient views of work. With continued advances in technology and culture, our conceptions of work and organizations will continue to evolve. Second, I consider several *core dialectic tensions* that underlie industrial and organizational (I/O)[1] psychology: industrial *and* organizational psychology, employee well-being *and* organizational effectiveness, basic *and* applied science, science *and* practice activities, and individual *and* organizational levels. I discuss how a dynamic balance among the contrasting poles of these tensions creates positive synergies for the field. Third, I describe what I view as four important *evolutionary trends in organizational psychology* over the last 35 years: (1) the rise of multilevel theory and research that encompass the individual, group, and organizational levels; (2) the surge of interest in team effectiveness, with teams at the juncture of the individual and organizational levels; (3) the nascent interest in dynamic processes; and (4) the expanding breadth of topics covered by the field. The fourth section, which provides an overview of the organization, structure, and coverage of the handbook, illustrates this latter trend.

In designing the structure of this handbook, I was careful to represent the foundation and the core of the field, but I also attended to areas that are expanding and to areas where organizational psychology needs to build stronger linkages. Authors of the chapters in this handbook are top scholars in each of their respective topic areas. You will find each of their contributions to provide a solid overview of the topic, a deep summary of key findings, and insightful directions for future research progress.

The Evolution of Work
Work, Ancient and Modern

Any effort to briefly sketch the etiology of work over the course of human history is doomed to oversimplify and gloss over complexities in a rich and varied tapestry. However, this risk is offset by the value in realizing that conceptions of work have evolved considerably and, hence, future conceptions of work are likely to be quite different from the current views we take for granted. For those interested in a deeper treatment of this evolution, Applebaum's *Concept of Work* (1992)—on which this brief sketch is based—is highly recommended.

"Work is basic to the human condition, to the creation of the human environment, and to the context of human relationships" (Applebaum, 1992, p. ix). Although one can certainly trace back further in time, work in ancient Greece and Rome was woven into the fabric of life and community. In Greece, the aristocratic *oikos* was a household that comprised an extended family group, with a landed estate and considerable accumulated wealth (primarily from plunder and gifts). These large estates needed "workers" in the form of slaves, hired help, and craftsmen. Even with the strong class distinctions of that time, based on wealth, power, and one's type of work, everyone engaged in different forms of productive activity.

Of course, those differences could be pretty big. As Applebaum (1992) noted, Aristotle distinguished *praxis,* activity that has no purpose other than its intrinsic enjoyment, and *poiesis,* activity for a specific end state or product. The latter was viewed as a form of dependence that was not fit for a free man, who should not be burdened with labor in order to engage in a more contemplative and rewarding intellectual life. The nature of work conferred social status. Does this sound familiar? This distinction is still viewed as important in motivational terms. Heckhausen & Kuhl (1985) describe activity for its own sake as *action goals* that are intrinsically motivating, whereas activity in the service of outcomes is described as *consequence goals* that motivate extrinsically.

> The human necessity to work was part of the religious myths and philosophies of the ancient world. Just as in the Old Testament, Adam and Eve were thrust out of the garden of bliss for the sin of eating the apple, so in the Greek myths, Zeus punished mankind for the sins of Prometheus.[2] In both cases, the result was that mankind had to earn its living through work. He could no longer attain the wherewithal for life for free or without cost. The products of nature would henceforth yield themselves up to humankind only in pure form. They would be unusable unless welded to the fire of work, unformed unless molded into new shapes through the use of tools, and unconsumable unless they were cooked with fire. (Applebaum, 1992, p. 168)

During the Middle Ages, more than 90% of the European population lived in small villages and worked the land. Before the relentless invasions began, peasants owned or rented the land. Later, they needed protection, which was exchanged for social obligations. They were obliged to work the land for the king or lord and to exchange labor or products. Work was communal and, although entailing more complex social structures, was still closely connected to the rhythm of daily life. In addition, craft guilds and the apprenticeship system developed, serving as a source of both social organization and social mobility.

And, essentially, so it went for hundreds of years. The rise of market-based economies and the use of currency begin to separate work from its intimacy with the fabric of life. The basic activities of growing food, raising animals for food and clothing, potting, and so on, are all related to agricultural-based economies. Separating work from direct sustenance made it more of an abstraction: the exchange of effort in return for compensation.

> The Protestant attitude toward work is the beginning of the modern concept of work, and it is convenient to locate this great change with the ideas of Luther. This new attitude toward work has also been merged with the notion that Protestantism and its perspectives on work were also the ideological precursors for capitalism and its work ethic. This latter notion was created by Max Weber in his seminal essay on the *Protestant Ethic and the Spirit of Capitalism* (1950). (Applebaum, 1992, p. 321)

This view was, and remains, controversial.

The revolutionary aspect of Luther (he did not support commerce, since it was not real work, or profit, since the purpose of work was just maintenance) was the notion that one should work within one's social niche (the trade, profession, or station into which one was born) doing best that which one was "called" to do, with no desire to advance in the social hierarchy. The revolutionary part was that it rejected the "three orders" and the notion that the lower orders had to "work for the benefit of the higher orders, nobles, and clerics who were to have leisure to pursue the contemplative and spiritual life" (Applebaum, 1992, p. 322). (The roots of this notion go back to Aristotle, as noted previously.) It rejected the "...double standard of the higher and lower callings and it also shifted the concept of calling or work—from the...emphasis on the penal quality of work, especially in its manual aspects, to the positive and creatively enjoyable aspects of work" (Applebaum, 1992, p. 323).

With Calvinism came a new view toward work. All must work, even the rich. Hard work stems from religious conviction. Idleness, luxury, anything soft is to be shunned. Hard work to cleanse the soul is taken as a religious duty. "Puritanism—which developed from Calvinism—goes further, teaching that it is one's duty to extract the greatest possible gain from work. Success, which is proven by profit, is the certain indication that the chosen profession is pleasing to God" (Applebaum, 1992, p. 325). Calvin also taught that it was one's duty to strive for social advancement. The view of work was one as "mobile, fluid, man-made rather than God-given, and rationalized...If this sounds very modern, it is. It is also possibly the first ideological wind of the modern spirit of entrepreneurship and profit-seeking" (Applebaum, 1992, p. 325). Subsequent reformation efforts by the Puritans coupled their ethics with the principles of modern capitalism. And so we marry up with more contemporary views of work prevalent in the latter half of the twentieth century.

Recent Views of Work and Careers

In many ways, contemporary views of work and careers and their relationship to organizations are bound within this historical perspective. The evolution of work provides the base, but our conception is largely rooted in recent history that has unfolded over the last half century or so. Following the destruction wrought by World War II, developed societies, including those devastated by the conflict, embarked on a period of economic expansion unparalleled in human history. In exchange for their effort, loyalty, and hard work, people were rewarded with material benefits and career opportunities as companies

grew. This has contributed to a "traditional" view of work in which work roles, career progression, and the nature of organizations have conformed to a set of assumptions that were largely taken for granted for many years: A person prepared for a single job or career (the person here was typically a white male—this was the normative model), worked for a single company (or at least very few companies), and got ahead by working hard in his chosen specialty (people were rewarded for their individual merit). There have been, to be sure, some incremental changes in this traditional perspective as historically disenfranchised groups of people sought, and continue to seek, more inclusion in this model. The basic nature of the exchange relationship between individuals and organizations, however, remained intact from post–World War II up to the mid-1980s and 1990s. That traditional model, if it ever was truly descriptive of career development, is now in the midst of dramatic revision.

A revolution is taking place in the world of work in which this traditional model is unlikely to survive. There are a multitude of environmental forces operating to change organizations in ways that will upend the traditional views of work as well. Organizations are increasingly multinational, cutting across what used to be impenetrable cultural, political, and economic system barriers. Indeed, the political and economic barriers between capitalism and Marxism erected in the aftermath of World War II have mostly fallen by the wayside. Competition is increasingly global, creating pressures for firms to meet higher standards of efficiency, quality, and flexibility. Technological innovation in both product (what is made) and process (how it is made) continues to accelerate rapidly, contributing to the obsolescence of work skills, technical knowledge, and jobs, and even to the decline of companies and entire industries.

Organizations attempt to respond to these forces in a number of different ways. They merge or acquire other organizations in an effort to eliminate competitors or to purchase specific kinds of expertise that they need to compete effectively. They reorganize their structure in an effort to enhance responsiveness, flexibility, and efficiency. They shut down obsolete manufacturing plants and invest in advanced manufacturing technologies to improve product quality and consistency. They may even move jobs to other parts of the world where labor costs are low. These efforts to respond oftentimes result in workforce reductions as organizations close manufacturing plants, reduce layers of management, and lay off surplus personnel. Many companies reduce their workforces as part of a general retrenchment process in response to poor economic performance. As a consequence of these different organizational responses, organizational downsizing became a common phenomenon, beginning in the 1980s, accelerating in the 1990s, and continuing into the new millennium (Cascio & Wynn, 2004). These economic disruptions, as growth in the developed world has slowed and expansion in the developing world has gained momentum, continue in the present day. The recent economic dislocation has exacerbated these effects.

These organizational changes have begun to affect the traditional career and work model. First, the career model is changing. It is less and less likely that individuals will be able to develop satisfying careers in a single organization. Not only will advancement opportunities be more restricted as organizations reduce layers of management, but the continuing threat of downsizing will tend to undercut loyalty to any one organization. People will tend to exhibit more mobility as they move from company to company to enhance or protect their careers. Moreover, it is less and less likely that individuals will be able to pursue a single career path. Technological obsolescence may require people to prepare for significant career shifts throughout their productive work lives. At the very least, most people will have to continually update their knowledge and skills through continuing, lifelong education and training just to keep up with advances in knowledge (London, chapter 35 of this handbook; Molloy & Noe, 2010). People will need to be increasingly flexible in career management.

Second, the model of work is also changing. As organizations streamline to enhance innovation and agility, job responsibilities expand. With fewer levels of management, decision making moves lower in the organization to put decisions closer to the work. In addition, broad-based skills become more important because jobs have to be more dynamic and flexible; they are likely to be revised and redesigned more frequently. Emphasis on product quality and customer service fosters attention to continuous improvement in product and process. This requires continuous improvements in worker skills and knowledge (London, chapter 35 of this handbook). It also places a premium on teamwork as organizations worldwide have shifted their work designs from individual to team-based systems over the last two decades (Devine, Clayton, Phillips, Dunford, & Melner, 1999).

Finally, workers are changing as well. The traditional models of work and careers are also a product of the culture, societal values, and the people that comprise the society. The traditional models are linked to a time when work and careers were predominantly the province of men, and family lifestyles were more uniform. As the culture changes, however, so does the view of work. In our culture, lifestyles have become far more diverse than they were in the immediate postwar era. In addition, over the next several decades, our society will experience a variety of demographic changes that will affect the nature of the workforce. There will be more women in the workforce, particularly at the higher decision-making levels of corporations (http://www.dol.gov/wb/stats/main.htm). There will be more "minorities" and fewer white males as a percentage of the workforce. Indeed, white males will constitute a "minority" group in the latter half of the twenty-first century (Lee & Mather, 2008).[3] And there will be greater distinctions between well-educated and highly skilled workers and those who are lacking education, work skills, or basic literacy. This diversity of the workforce, combined with the changes in organizations and careers, will revolutionize the nature of work and how we think about it.

Although it is easy to be pessimistic about change—and, indeed, change is often resisted—I am optimistic about the future. The changes in careers, work, and cultural values create challenges for government, for organizations, and for all of us. At the same time, they provide an opportunity to redefine work and careers so that they are more fulfilling for more people. This is the province and the challenge of organizational psychology: *to understand the psychology of organizations and people, and to apply that basic psychological science to help people become more fulfilled and to help organizations become more effective.*

Foci of Organizational Psychology
Dialectic Tensions

The abbreviated definition of organizational psychology highlighted above is characterized by an underlying set of core dialectic tensions illustrated in Figure 1.1: industrial *and* organizational psychology, employee well-being *and* organizational effectiveness, basic *and* applied science, science *and* practice activities, and individual *and* organizational levels. I do not mean to describe these foci as forces in strong opposition or conflict, but they do tug the field in different directions, creating tension and

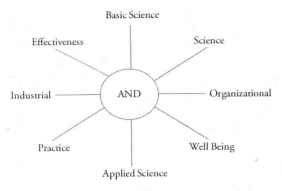

Figure 1.1 Dialectical Tensions of Industrial and Organizational Psychology. Note: Orientation of the axes is arbitrary and not intended to be meaningful.

flux between the poles, and necessitating a dynamic balance among the tugs and pulls. The tensions are sometimes, perhaps often, viewed as problems that are bifurcating I/O psychology and that have the potential to cleave it at its joints. However, I think that is an extreme and pessimistic viewpoint. Rather, I think that the tensions are endemic in the origin, nature, and evolution of the field, and that the dialectic flux is healthy so long as we actively endeavor to maintain a dynamic balance between the poles and among the collective tensions. In the sections that follow, I will briefly highlight the nature of these tensions and the value that the field of organizational psychology gains by maintaining a dynamic balance.

Industrial and Organizational

The industrial and organizational foci represent domains of research and application that have evolved historically and that together span the richness of human characteristics, behavior, and performance in organizations. The earliest principles and tools of psychology applied to work and organizations centered on individual differences, assessments and tests that captured them, and applied that technology to selecting employees. In addition, there were applications to job design, employee performance assessment, and training. For example, Galton and Cattell contributed to the development of differential psychology and the assessment of individual differences in abilities; Münsterberg used work samples and early forms of work simulations for selection and training; and World War I stimulated the application of ability testing to large-scale selection and classification by the army. Testing,

selection, and training were obviously also applicable to industry, and the techniques quickly diffused for application in organizations. These applications were primarily focused on enabling basic human resource management (HRM) functions and, consistent with terminology of the era, characterized an "industrial" psychology. Subsequent development of research interest on worker attitudes and productivity from the Hawthorne Studies in the 1920s and 1930s; the post–World War II focus on leadership and motivation; and the rise of organizational systems theory with its focus on organizational development, change, and effectiveness led to a characterization of an "organizational" psychology, which was added to the industrial psychology label in 1973 (Koppes-Bryan & Vinchur, chapter 2 of this handbook).

Although the distinction between the "I" "slash" "O" is sometimes viewed as a fracture, the field firmly remains I *and* O. It is not bifurcated, it is connected. This is noteworthy because in management, human resources management (HRM; a.k.a. industrial psychology) and organizational behavior (OB; a.k.a. organizational psychology) are treated as distinct sub-specialties. Contemporary interest in strategic HRM necessitates spanning I *and* O psychology, HRM *and* OB, and leveraging synergies across the micro-macro divide to understand how organizational strategy shapes worker requirements and how the emergence of human capital shapes organizational strategy, capabilities, and effectiveness (Ployhart, chapter 8 of this handbook; Snow & Snell, chapter 30 of this handbook).

Employee Well-being and Organizational Effectiveness

From its earliest inception, organizational psychology has been concerned with the application of psychological principles to improving the experience and well-being of workers and the effectiveness of organizations. There is a tension between these two foci such that improving organizational effectiveness *could* come at the expense of employee well-being, or that improvements in employee well-being are costly to the organization. For example, an organizational restructuring and streamlining that also downsized the workforce could prompt feelings of guilt and increased work stress for surviving employees (Kozlowski, Chao, Smith, & Hedlund, 1993). Conversely, a lavish organizational benefits package might be viewed as detrimental to the bottom line or the creation of shareholder value by some observers. Google, for example, offers a very favorable employee benefits package:

> The goal is to strip away everything that gets in our employees' way. We provide a standard package of fringe benefits, but on top of that are first-class dining facilities, gyms, laundry rooms, massage rooms, haircuts, carwashes, dry cleaning, commuting buses—just about anything a hardworking employee might want. Let's face it: programmers want to program, they don't want to do their laundry. So we make it easy for them to do both.
> (Eric Schmidt, CEO Google)[4]

As inherent in the Google example, the goal is to manage the tension so as to achieve mutual benefit to all parties. Indeed, the mission statement for the Society for Industrial and Organizational Psychology (SIOP) states in part: "The Society's mission is to enhance human well-being and performance in organizational and work settings by promoting the science, practice, and teaching of industrial-organizational psychology."[5]

Basic and Applied Science

Psychological science studies a wide range of basic phenomena. For example, cognitive neuroscience maps brain function to psychological phenomena such as decision making, mood, and disorders. Developmental psychology examines psychological functioning across the life span—child, adolescent, and adult development. Social psychologists study basic personality, attitudes, values, and interpersonal interactions. Basic psychological science seeks to discover generalizable principles of human behavior that cut across a wide range of situations.

What makes organizational psychology somewhat unique is that it is focused on psychological functioning in a particular context, the workplace—a context that entails some very potent motivators, including achievement, power, and money. "Work is like the spine which structures the way people live, how they make contact with material and social reality, and how they achieve status and self-esteem" (Applebaum, 1992, p. ix). The work context grounds organizational psychology and the phenomena of interest. The context constrains the range of behavior to focus primarily on the functioning of normal adults. The context also limits the range of potential situational or environmental influences that are of interest to factors such as organizational features, leadership, and group processes and behavioral outcomes such

as job performance, attitudes, and other reactions. The context allows organizational psychologists to examine psychological phenomena within a more tightly focused range, with better grounding, and greater precision. The intent is to apply basic science to the work setting.

Basic and applied sciences are often depicted as opposite poles conceptually similar to Aristotle's *praxis* (basic) and *poiesis* (applied): basic discovery of knowledge for its own sake versus application of knowledge to achieve a specific purpose. However, basic and applied sciences are not necessarily opposite ends of a continuum. In his seminal book, *Pasteur's Quadrant*, Donald Stokes (1997) juxtaposes the quest for *fundamental understanding* and *considerations of use* as orthogonal dimensions that create four quadrants characterizing three meaningful classes of research. A quest for fundamental understanding with no consideration of use is pure basic research, as exemplified by the physics of Niels Bohr or Albert Einstein. A focus on use with no consideration for fundamental understanding is pure applied research, as exemplified by the inventions of Thomas Edison. The quest for fundamental understanding *and* consideration is use-inspired basic research: Pasteur's Quadrant. The remaining quadrant – no consideration for understanding or use—is null. Rigorous and relevant organizational psychological research targets Pasteur's Quadrant: it seeks to generate basic scientific knowledge that can be applied to solve important problems in organizations.

Science and Practice

As in the previous discussion of Pasteur's Quadrant, I/O psychological science is targeted on fundamental understanding that has implications for solving applied problems. The tools of our science include the development of meta-theories that help explain important phenomena; systematic research to investigate more specific models drawn from these theories; research summaries and meta-analyses that help to codify knowledge and provide a basis for validated principles for understanding important classes of work behavior; and the development of "tools" to influence, shape, and enhance human performance.

In the science-practice model, practitioners draw on scientific theories, principles, and tools, but tailor them with sensitivity to the local context and conditions of the organization. Theory and research-based principles at a higher level of generality *cannot* encompass every important contingency that operates in a given organizational setting. The art and experience of seasoned practitioners are necessary components of the translation of applied science to effective application.

The science-practice model is important because it merges the content areas of OB and HR, and distinguishes the practice of I/O psychology from related disciplines in management. Anyone with any disciplinary background whatsoever can be a consultant to organizations. What distinguishes the practice of I/O psychology from other disciplines is that it is fundamentally based in the *science of psychology* applied to organizations. Maintaining a tight coupling between science and practice is increasingly a challenge as the unique aspects of each role tug science and practice in different directions (Rynes, chapter 13 of this handbook). However, in I/O psychology, the linkage between science and evidence-based practice is critical if we are to remain rigorous *and* relevant.

Individual and Organizational

The roots of organizational psychology go to the role of individual differences in ability, personality, and other characteristics in predicting human behavior in the workplace. The formative history of the field was firmly focused on individuals as the level of primary interest and the appropriate level of explanation. The primary focus on the individual characterized the field for much of its development, although the Hawthorne studies conducted in the 1920s and 1930s began to spark nascent interest in characteristics of groups and settings in the workplace (Koppes-Bryan & Vinochur, chapter 2 of this handbook). Post–World War II interests in the nature and effects of leadership, the role of organizational climate as a representation of organization contextual factors like technology and structure, and systems theory which viewed elements of the organization as linked together in complex and dynamic patterns of ongoing influence brought more attention to the characteristics of the context—the organization—and their effects on individuals (Katz & Kahn, 1978). Subsequent development of multi-level theory (MLT) pushed the level of explanation beyond the individual to encompass the group and organizational levels, to consider the interplay across levels, and to appreciate the ways in which higher level—group and organizational—phenomena *emerge* from individuals interacting over time in a work setting (Kozlowski & Klein, 2000; Rousseau, 1985). The levels of explanation are individual,

group, and organizational; micro, meso, and macro; I *and* O.

Evolutionary Trends in Organizational Psychology
Complexities and Challenges

The dialectics undergirding organizational psychology are merely reflective of the complexities and challenges of studying organizations and the behavior that occurs within them. Complexities, and the theoretical and research challenges that they create, force a field of study to evolve as it seeks to better capture and explain complex phenomena. Some of the evolution of the field since its inception is inherent in the dialectics described previously. The evolution of organizational psychology, more generally, is captured in its history and development (Koppes Bryan & Vinochur, chapter 2 of this handbook). However, there are, I think, some key developments that have occurred during the last 35 years that are having a substantial influence on the evolution of the field. These trends include: (a) the rise of multilevel theory, research, and methods; (b) the related surge of theory and research focused on team effectiveness; (c) nascent interest in developmental processes and the dynamics of behavior; and (d) increased breadth of research encompassed by organizational psychology as represented in the topics covered by this handbook (wider, deeper, more multidisciplinary).

This is, not coincidentally, a strongly personal perspective. I began graduate studies in I/O psychology shortly after publication of the first *Handbook of Industrial and Organizational Psychology* (Dunnette, 1976). As a graduate student, I was exposed to that Handbook and it serves as my point of entry to the field and my benchmark for new developments and the evolution of I/O psychology. I do not mean to imply that these are the only important trends in the field. It is simply that I see their influence as pervasive and growing. I will highlight the first three related trends—multilevel theory, the rise of work teams, and dynamics—in this section. Breadth of the field is addressed in the next section, which lays out the organization, structure, and topics covered in this handbook.

Organizations Are Multilevel Systems

Organizations are socially constructed systems. They are abstract, rather than concrete, systems in that their strategy, design, structure, and processes are enacted by the people who compose them (Katz & Kahn, 1978). They are embedded in a shifting and often unpredictable environment. Organizations are in exchange with the external environment, importing resources, transforming them, and exporting something "value added" that enables continued energy importation. As environments shift, organizations change, evolve, and adapt—or die. This view of organizations as systems of interacting elements, in exchange with a changing external environment, and adapting dynamically to maintain homeostasis, has been a dominant theoretical framework for understanding organizational behavior for over 70 years; it is traceable back to the Hawthorne Studies (Roethlisburger & Dickson, 1939). It is a very useful perspective, but it has limitations.

The problem has been that it is more of a metaphor than a theory, it has not been useful for developing testable propositions, and it has not advanced research. To accomplish those aims, one needs a set of theoretical principles that can be used to meaningfully decompose "holistic" systems phenomena, measurement principles to specify constructs that can represent different levels of phenomena, and analytical tools that can deal with phenomena that unfold over time and at multiple levels (Kozlowski & Klein, 2000). The advent of multilevel theory, coupled with the development of multilevel analytical systems, has provided the means to resolve these issues.

For much of its history, I/O psychology was primarily focused on individuals. Even during the 1950s and 1960s, when systems theory was taking hold and there was growing interest in the effects of organizational factors on human behavior, the level of explanation stayed fixed on the individual. This individual-centric focus began to change in the late 1970s and early 1980s. Although there are many formative influences, the publication of a book entitled *Building an Interdisciplinary Science of Organizations* (Roberts, Hulin, & Rousseau, 1978) signaled the beginning of a shift in the field that would ultimately result in a more balanced theoretical, research, and application focus on individuals, groups, and organizations as integrated—rather than distinct—levels of explanation. A key observation made by Roberts and colleagues (1978) is that the disciplines comprising organizational science had sliced the organizational system into distinct layers. They selected four exemplar paradigms, or *four worlds of organizational science:* I/O psychology (the individual), human factors (tasks), social psychology (groups), and sociology (organization)—to make their point.

In the years that followed, many scholars highlighted the ways in which a more integrated perspective that encompassed the multiple, nested levels of the organizational system could push the field forward (Klein, Dansereau, & Hall, 1994; Mossholder & Bedeian, 1983; Rousseau, 1985). However, the challenges were many. Researchers routinely misunderstood the implications of data aggregation (Robinson, 1950; Thorndike, 1939). Researchers routinely evoked theoretical explanations that spanned levels, but failed to measure, appropriately represent, or analyze them at commensurate levels (Klein et al., 1994). There were controversies surrounding the justification for aggregating data (James, Demaree, & Wolf, 1984, 1993; Kozlowski & Hattrup, 1992; Schmidt & Hunter, 1989) and conducting multilevel analyses (George, 1990; George & James, 1993; Yammarino & Markham, 1992). There was interest in multilevel research, but the complexities were many and the persistent controversies over theory and method sowed confusion and wariness. Multilevel and cross-level research was rare.

In 2000, Klein and Kozlowski produced an edited book for the SIOP Frontiers Series, *Multilevel Theory, Research, and Methods in Organizations: Foundations, Extensions, and New Directions,* that was intended to bring order to this chaos and to advance multilevel theory and research. The opening chapter (Kozlowski & Klein, 2000) synthesized a set of theoretical principles for developing multilevel models;[6] formulated methodological principles and a measurement framework for aligning the levels of constructs and data; and developed a theoretically based typology of emergence to help researchers appropriately represent higher level phenomena that emerge from individual cognition, affect, behavior, and other person characteristics. Chapters were commissioned to apply multilevel theory to topics that had traditionally been rooted solely at the individual level—selection, performance appraisal, and training—or largely at more macro levels—culture, HRM strategy, and inter-organizational relations. Finally, there were thorough treatments of the issues of aggregation and non-independence, analytic systems (i.e., cross-level operator approaches, within and between analysis [WABA], and hierarchical linear modeling [HLM]), and—importantly—a direct comparison among the analytic techniques analyzing a common data set. The book was largely successful in its goals of providing a solid theoretical foundation for multilevel research, clarifying measurement and analytic issues, and pointing toward the many potential areas where multilevel theory could extend research effectiveness.

In addition, during the 1990s and especially since the turn of the century, there have been substantial developments in multilevel modeling techniques. Multilevel random coefficient modeling has clearly established superiority over alternative analysis methods (i.e., analysis of variance and covariance [ANOVA, ANCOVA], ordinary least squares regression, and within and between analysis [WABA]), and it has become widely available in a variety of statistical software analysis packages. Publication of multilevel research—better integrating across levels in the organizational system—has increased significantly in volume in the major organizational psychology, HRM, and OB journals. Multilevel research has moved from the periphery of organizational research to its center. Since the turn of the century, multilevel research has flourished.

The Rise of Work Teams

One area of scholarly activity that well illustrates this ongoing evolution of multilevel research is the growth of work on team effectiveness in organizational psychology. As I noted previously, for much of its history I/O psychology has been centered on the individual as its focal level. However, competitive pressures on organizations to be more adaptive, to push decision making closer to the source of problems, and to harness diverse expertise sparked a worldwide shift from individual-based work structures to team-based work systems in organizations during the late 1980s and 1990s (Devine et al., 1999). Since at least the 1930s, research on small group behavior has been the province of social psychology, but the evolution in work structure prompted a change in the locus of research focused on small groups and work teams. As Kozlowski and Bell (2003, p. 333) noted:

> Over the last 15 years...group and team research
> has become increasingly centered in the fields
> of organizational psychology and organizational
> behavior. Indeed, Levine and Moreland (1990)
> in their extensive review of small group research
> concluded that, "Groups are alive and well, but
> living elsewhere...The torch has been passed to (or,
> more accurately, picked up by) colleagues in other
> disciplines, particularly organizational psychology."
> (p. 620)

As go organizations, so goes I/O psychology. The increasing interest in teams, teamwork, and team effectiveness was concurrent with the evolving interest in multilevel theory, methods, and analyses. Teams are at the juncture of the person and the broader organizational system. The person is *micro*. The organizational system is *macro*. Work teams are *meso*. They provide the most proximal social context for the experiences that impinge on employees—experiences that are frustrating, fulfilling, or enervating. They are also the unit that most proximally captures the synergies of good teamwork, collaboration, and coordination that emerge to influence higher level performance. Teams are the juncture that links layers of the organization—top-down and bottom-up—together into an integrated system. Teams increasingly represent an important focus for organizational psychology theory and research (Bell, Kozlowski, & Blawath, chapter 26 of this handbook; Chen & Tesluk, chapter 24 of this handbook; Hollenbeck & Spitzmuller, chapter 23 of this handbook; Kirkman, Gibson, & Kim, chapter 25 of this handbook; Kozlowski & Ilgen, 2006; Mathieu & Gilson, chapter 27 of this handbook).

Dynamics

Whether increasing interest in the *dynamics* of human cognition, affect, and behavior in organizations is a clear trend is debatable, but—whether it is a trend or not—it *should be* represented in our theory, research, and practice. In the 100+ year history of the field, we have learned much about work and behavior in organizations; much of that knowledge is captured in this handbook. However, it is also the case that the vast majority of our evidence and knowledge are based on relationships observed in static correlational designs—results from cross-sectional data collections in the field—or in lab studies that can establish causal relations, but within limited time frames and often with little or no attention to process dynamics. We need to do better.

There are, nonetheless, several areas of inquiry where the influence of dynamic processes unfolding over time as developmental progression, growth, or the persistence of a phenomenon; processes characterized by cycles or episodes; or phenomena that exhibit intra- or inter-individual (or higher level units) variance are receiving theoretical and research attention. This is an important nascent trend since virtually every phenomenon of interest has at its core a psychological process which, by definition, is dynamic. This list is by no means intended to be a comprehensive sampling, but just a simple illustration to demonstrate that there is a lot more research that entails temporal dynamics than you might think at first blush. For example, socialization researchers began conducting longitudinal studies in the late 1980s and early 1990s, which led to major advances in that topic area (Chao, chapter 18 of this handbook). In the 1990s, researchers in the area of learning and skill acquisition began examining cycles of learning and self-regulation processes and their linkages to knowledge, performance, and adaptation outcomes (Salas, Weaver, & Shuffler, chapter 11 of this handbook). During the early part of the twenty-first century, researchers stimulated by affective events theory (Weiss & Cropanzano, 1996) began using experience sampling methods to examine variability in mood, emotions, and affect over days and weeks (Judge, Hulin, & Dalal, chapter 15 of this handbook).

Moreover, more complex dynamics are explicitly addressed in several chapters in this handbook. For example, Hanges and Wang (chapter 3 of this handbook) discuss how treating organizations as complex adaptive systems necessitates a focus on dynamics in research design. DeShon (chapter 4 of this handbook) characterizes the increasing interest in dynamic phenomena, the complex longitudinal data structures needed to represent these processes, and the sophisticated analytical techniques required to model them. Ryan and Sackett (chapter 5 of this handbook) consider intra- and interindividual variability on individual difference characteristics and their implications for making predictive inferences. Sonnentag and Frese (chapter 17 of this handbook) review the research on job performance as a dynamic process and develop a taxonomy to advance understanding of performance dynamics. Bell, Kozlowski, and Blawath (chapter 26 of this handbook) examine theory and research on team learning, specifically treating team learning as a process that is distinct from team knowledge outcomes. They describe several models of team learning that incorporate cyclical process dynamics. Mathieu and Gilson (chapter 27 of this handbook) close their chapter with a discussion of four temporal phenomena that can be harnessed to advance research on team effectiveness. There are other examples as well, sprinkled throughout the handbook. Serious interest in the dynamics of phenomena is beginning to emerge in organizational psychology theory and research.

Organization, Structure, and Coverage of the Handbook
Overview
This handbook joins several others that have characterized and summarized I/O psychology.

Dunnette (1976) produced the first such handbook, a single volume with 37 chapters covering basic topics to emerging trends—many that are still relevant today. Dunnette and Hough (1990) updated that first effort with a comprehensive four-volume revision that is characterized by its greatly expanded coverage. Borman, Ilgen, and Klimoski (2003) developed the next iteration of an I/O handbook as volume 12 of a compendium designed to capture of the entire domain of psychology. Their topic coverage was more in line with Dunnette (1976), although it included updates to capture the evolution of the field. That iteration is currently under revision with new editors (Schmitt and Highhouse). The American Psychological Association is also producing a multivolume handbook edited by Zedeck (2010). This handbook is a volume of the *Library of Psychology* series published by Oxford University Press. It is at the top level of an organizational psychology handbook hierarchy; more narrowly focused second- and third-tier handbooks, designed to expand topic areas in more depth, are under development.

It is challenging to represent the field of organizational psychology in a handbook. A single volume cannot be as expansive as a multivolume work and thus must be more selective about the topics that are covered. There is a need to represent the foundation and core of the field, but to also capture the breadth of the field and those topic areas that are ascendant. Ultimately, the handbook is organized around my perspective of the field of organizational psychology and where it is heading; my sincere apologies for those topics that I was not able to incorporate.

Part I: An Introduction to Organizational Psychology
The handbook begins with, well, this chapter, "The Nature of Organizational Psychology", which provides an overview of the field. My intent is to convey a sense of the evolution of the concept of work to provide a backdrop for our study of the psychology of the workplace, characterize key dialectic tensions that permeate I/O psychology as an applied science, and highlight trends in its evolution and breadth of its coverage.

The next chapter in this part, "A History of Organizational Psychology," by Koppes-Bryan and Vinchur, provides sweeping coverage of the history of the field's development. Beginning with its inception in the late nineteenth century to its current breadth and diversity, Koppes-Bryan and Vinchur interweave the context of the historical era with developments in the field. The chapter illustrates well how the evolution of the nature of organizations and the human problems they encounter in different epochs has shaped the development of I/O psychology.

Part II: The Foundation

With the background in place, the next part focuses on what I regard as foundational aspects of the field: strong grounding in rigorous research methods, use of sophisticated data analytic systems, central focus on individual differences, and concerted and systematic efforts to characterize important job behaviors and job performance. This is the core of organizational psychology.

The first chapter in this part, "Seeking the Holy Grail in Organizational Science: Establishing Causality Through Research Design," by Hanges and Wang, surveys the research design challenges that have to be resolved to establish causal relations. As a science that has a strong field research component, organizational psychology faces many impediments in its effort to go beyond descriptive, correlational relations and to build a scientific foundation based on causal relations. Hanges and Wang consider different perspectives for establishing causality (i.e., Campbell Causal Model, Rubin Causal Model) and, in particular, several quasi-experimental designs (e.g., regression discontinuity, longitudinal designs) that can be used to help map causal linkages in organizational psychology research.

The second chapter in this part, "Multivariate Dynamics in Organizational Science," by DeShon, highlights the increased research interest in dynamic phenomena, complex multivariate data structures needed to capture the dynamics, and sophisticated data analytic techniques necessary to model the dynamics of behavior. He describes data structures, techniques, and examples appropriate for linear dynamic systems (e.g., leadership, dynamic mediation, loosely coupled systems, and motivational feedback) and stochastic linear dynamic systems (e.g., self-efficacy and performance).

The next chapter, "Individual Differences: Challenging Our Assumptions," by Ryan and Sackett, shifts to a core content focus in organizational psychology. Differential psychology makes strong assumptions about the stability of individual difference characteristics (e.g., abilities, personality traits, and interests)—assumptions that are critical to measurement, prediction, and explanation. Ryan and Sackett examine evidence for variability between and within individuals on these

characteristics in the work setting, challenge some of the assumptions, and highlight important implications for science and practice.

The primary "criterion" in I/O psychology is typically a set of job behaviors that underlie job performance that is of value to the organization. The last chapter in this part, "Behavior, Performance, and Effectiveness in the Twenty-first Century," by Campbell, examines the conceptual convergence in the latent structure of job performance that has developed in the field over the last quarter century. He concludes that the structure of the job performance construct is invariant across occupations, organizational levels, contexts, and time. Given the overarching concern with the "criterion problem" (James, 1973) in the 1960s, this is an important achievement for the field.

Part III: Aligning Person and Job Characteristics

Whereas the prior part focused on the core of our methods, analytics, and substantive focus, the next part of the handbook focuses on core applications concerned with aligning person characteristics and the job setting. At a broad conceptual level it is useful to recognize that some person characteristics are fixed and others are malleable and, by the same token, some job setting characteristics are essentially fixed while others can be adapted to the person. The core logic of most I/O and HRM applications is achieving a good "fit" between person characteristics and job requirements, and the range of techniques available provide several options for achieving a good fit. Topics covered in this part are functional in the HRM sense, addressing recruitment, selection, work design, performance management, training, and conceptions of "fit," as well as some challenging gaps between science and practice in the use of these applications.

The first chapter in this part, "Recruitment and Competitive Advantage: A Brand Equity Perspective," by Yu and Cable, applies a strategic perspective to recruitment practices in organizations. Applying a resource-based view, their premise is that carefully designed recruitment practices can differentially attract a workforce that can build sustained competitive advantage for a firm.

Once desirable applicants are attracted, hiring decisions have to be made that maximize the talent pool for the organization. The next chapter by Ployhart, "Personnel Selection: Ensuring Sustainable Organizational Effectiveness Through the Acquisition of Human Capital," also adopts an

RBV to craft a vision regarding the future of personnel selection. From his perspective, selection has to re-orient from an emphasis on individually focused person-job fit to acquiring human capital to ensure sustained organizational effectiveness. Realizing this vision necessitates shifts in the focal level—from the individual to higher units—and consideration of time—from single point estimates to longitudinal—in personnel selection theory and research.

Once workers are hired, it is important to have jobs and roles that are designed to engage employee motivation and commitment. In the next chapter, "Work Design: Creating Jobs and Roles That Promote Individual Effectiveness," Cordery and Parker consider recent evolution in the nature of job tasks and work roles. They address the ways in which this evolution is broadening perspectives on work design, going beyond the traditional focus on task features to encompass social considerations, to enlarge the traditional focus on individual jobs to teamwork, and to consider a broader set of relevant psychological processes that engage employee motivation and engagement.

Once employees are fit to a position that is motivating, the focus shifts to managing their performance so as to continually improve their effectiveness. The next chapter, "Performance Management," by Smither, focuses on the core elements of this process: setting goals, providing feedback, developing employee skills, evaluating performance, and providing rewards. Performance management as an active process is distinguished from the more traditional and narrow focus of performance appraisal, which focuses primarily on the measurement and evaluation of job performance.

Learning and development, both formal and informal, are a critical aspect of building an effective workforce, and continuous knowledge and skill improvement is an important part of maintaining good employee fit. In their chapter on "Learning, Training, and Development in Organizations," Salas, Weaver, and Shuffler take a broad perspective on classic, formal training techniques, but also review the many forms of informal development that help maintain a continuously improving workforce.

All these prior chapters, albeit indirectly, are concerned with applications that address the broad concept of fit—fitting employees to the job and context. The next chapter, "Person-Environment Fit in Organizational Settings," by Ostroff, addresses notions of fit directly. Although the concept of fit is simple, pervasive, and intuitively appealing, it is actually quite diverse (i.e., there are many different perspectives of fit), conceptually complex (i.e., different levels of fit, different reference points), and in some areas it is ambiguous and muddled (i.e., misfit). Ostroff provides a comprehensive review, framework, and points the way forward.

Finally, in "The Research-Practice Gap in I/O Psychology and Related Fields: Challenges and Potential Solutions," Rynes examines the gap between the applied science and practice of I/O psychology, HRM, and OB on the one side and the consumers of our science—HRM professionals and practicing managers—on the other. This is different from the dialectic tension between science and practice within the discipline. Rather, it is about the failure to apply the science because of lack of awareness, disbelief, or faith in intuitive knowledge. A strong case is made for the importance of promoting and facilitating evidence-based practice in management and organizational behavior.

Part IV: Motivation, Job Attitudes and Affect, and Performance

The prior part of the handbook explicated core applications for fitting people to the workplace. This part shifts focus to the *core processes* of work motivation, job attitudes and affect, and performance that underlie behavior at work. Motivation sets the direction and magnitude of effort invested at work, job attitudes and affect are appraisals of different work foci and support (or detract from) motivation, and performance is a desired outcome of motivation and supportive appraisals. I describe these psychological processes as *core* because they underlie virtually all other topics to some extent or another. Motivation, attitudes and affect, and performance thread through nearly everything!

In "Work Motivation: Theory, Practice, and Future Directions," Kanfer characterizes the broad sweep and substantial progress in this basic line of inquiry. Her chapter is organized into four sections. The first section examines basic constructs, processes, and content underlying the study of work motivation. The second section describes the substantial research progress that has been accomplished and highlights new conceptualizations that have the potential to enhance our understanding of behavior and performance at work. The third section considers key determinants of motivation structured around content (person), context (situation), and change (time); and the final section closes with knowledge gaps, practical issues, and promising research directions.

The next chapter, "Job Satisfaction and Job Affect," by Judge, Hulin, and Dalal, reviews the broad sweep of research on job satisfaction, considers its affective nature, and develops an integrative theoretical model of job attitudes. Their review places particular emphasis on distinguishing research on job satisfaction, which has tended to focus on cognitive appraisals, from research on social attitudes that entail cognitive, affective, and behavioral foci. The emerging emphasis on affect in organizational psychology necessitates changes to the treatment of job satisfaction. Newer approaches that touch on engagement, affective events, personality, and satisfaction as a unit-level construct are considered. In addition, the authors present a multilevel model of core self-evaluations.

We then shift focus a bit to consider research on "Organizational Justice" by Colquitt. This topic, which can be regarded as a specific type of motivation, has emerged to become an active and pervasive area of research activity over the last quarter century. Colquitt organizes his review around three themes—differentiation (justice dimensions), cognition (justice calculations), and exogeneity (justice as an antecedent)—and argues that future progress can be gained by relaxing or reversing these themes to focus on combining justice concepts, incorporating affects, and surfacing antecedents of justice perceptions.

Finally, the last chapter in this part focuses on job performance. Unlike most traditional treatments that focus on the dimensionality underlying job performance, in "Dynamic Performance," Sonnentag and Frese consider theory and research that are focused on performance change and variability over time. This is consistent with the more process-oriented perspectives emerging in the motivation arena, and is one of the evolutionary themes in the field. The authors develop a taxonomy of dynamic performance processes and map a research agenda for future progress.

Part V: Informal Learning, Meaning Creation, and Social Influence

With core processes in place, the next part of the handbook addresses several phenomena that informally assimilate, shape, and develop employees (socialization and mentoring); influence sense-making and meaning creation (culture and climate); and capture the ways in which social interconnections, key contextual factors, and leaders (networks and leadership) shape behavior in organizations.

In the first chapter of this part, "Organizational Socialization: Background, Basics, and a Blueprint for Adjustment at Work," Chao examines socialization as a learning and adjustment process that helps to align the individual and the organization in a mutual process of fit. Chao takes a broad perspective, first reviewing basic theoretical foundations for socialization (i.e., uncertainty reduction theory, the need to belong, social exchange theory, and social identity theory), then examining the basic components of organizational socialization (i.e., processes, content, and outcomes), and finally closing with a "blueprint" for future research that calls for a more balanced perspective that integrates organizational and individual orientations.

Whereas socialization assimilates newcomers and role changers, mentoring considers the longer term, career-enhancing effects of having a seasoned, well-placed insider guide a younger protégé on the path to career success. In "Workplace Mentoring: Past, Present, and Future Perspectives," Eby examines factors that influence this special relationship, its positive *and* negative aspects, and the role of the organizational context in shaping the relationship. The chapter closes with attention to methodological challenges and important directions for research.

Next, in "Organizational Culture and Climate," Zohar and Hofmann reconcile and integrate two distinctive constructs and literatures used to understand how employees "make sense" of the organization. They provide a state-of-the-art review, dissect the similarities and differences, and develop an integration of culture and climate that has the potential to substantially influence research that will pull these central, important, yet distinctive construct domains together.

Shifting to processes of social influence, Brass applies "A Social Network Perspective on Organizational Psychology." Unlike the individual differences perspective that is at the core of I/O psychology, social networks focus on relationships that link actors together in a social structure that provides both opportunities and constraints on action. The chapter introduces network concepts, reviews antecedents and consequences of networks, and applies the framework to topics of recruitment and selection, performance, power, and leadership.

Finally, this part closes with a chapter by Day on "Leadership." Leaders are arguably at the core of social influence processes in organizations, responsible for shaping and harnessing individual efforts to accomplish goals at multiple levels of the system. Leadership as a topic is broad, diverse, and multifaceted. It encompasses multiple levels, sources of origin, and distinctive outcomes such as leader emergence and leader effectiveness. Day organizes the diverse array of theories and research findings and identifies promising directions for future work to expand our understanding of this important topic.

Part VI: Work Teams in Organizations

As I described previously in this chapter, teams have emerged as an important theoretical and research focus in organizational psychology over the last couple of decades, supplementing the field's primary focus on the individual level. This shift has largely been driven by the push from organizations to restructure work around team workflows rather than individual jobs. With the explosion of research on work teams, this part is designed to highlight key factors including team structure, participation and empowerment, distributed or "virtual teams," team learning, and team effectiveness.

One of the key challenges in studying teams is addressing the duality of individuals as meaningful psychological entities and the team as a collective unit with its own distinct identity. Hollenbeck and Spitzmuller characterize this as a figure-ground paradox, which they examine in "Team Structure: Tight Versus Loose Coupling in Task-Oriented Groups." They develop a four-dimensional framework of structural interdependence to help unravel this paradox. Whereas structural interdependence is a "hard" mechanism for linking team members, they are also linked by more psychological and behavioral attributes.

The next chapter, "Team Participation and Empowerment: A Multilevel Perspective," by Chen and Tesluk, develops a multilevel model that integrates participation—a concept long examined in the literature—with the more recent concept of work engagement. Their conceptualization treats engagement as an overarching concept, with participation oriented toward its psychological aspects and empowerment oriented toward its behavioral aspects. Their model incorporates individual-, team-, and organizational-level antecedents and outcomes and provides a road map for extending our knowledge of how to engage teams and their members.

One key reason that organizations use teams is that it gives them the ability to leverage diverse expertise. Increasingly, those experts are distributed in space and time, making their teams virtual rather than face-to-face social entities. Kirkman, Gibson, and Kim, in "Across Borders and Technologies:

Advancements in Virtual Teams Research," review the voluminous research on this emerging form of global teamwork. Their detailed review captures eleven meaningful areas of research and they highlight five themes—virtuality, team development, leadership, levels of analysis, and multidisciplinarity—as overarching themes for future research on virtual teams.

Teams are often used to perform complex, cognitively demanding tasks that individuals cannot perform on their own. An important aspect of team effectiveness is how teams—not just individual members—learn, create knowledge, and apply their capabilities to accomplish goals, make decisions, and solve complex problems. In "Team Learning: A Theoretical Integration and Review," Bell, Kozlowski, and Blawath examine this large but diverse and messy literature with the goal of developing an integrated conceptualization. They emphasize three theoretical foci for their examination of team learning, treating it as multilevel (individual *and* team, not individual *or* team), dynamic (iterative and progressive; a *process*, not an *outcome*), and emergent (outcomes of team learning can manifest in different ways over time). Their review framework distinguishes team learning process theories, supporting emergent states, team knowledge representations, and respective influences on team performance and effectiveness.

Finally, this part on teams closes with "Criteria Issues and Team Effectiveness," by Mathieu and Gilson. Team effectiveness is what theory and research seek to understand, but as the authors note, the conceptualization and measurement of team effectiveness has received relatively little attention. They distinguish two general classes of effectiveness criteria: tangible outputs (i.e., productivity, efficiency, and quality) and member reactions (i.e., individual attitudes, reactions, behaviors, and person development; team emergent states). Importantly, they consider assessment approaches for the different criteria and close with a focus on how an understanding of temporal factors applied to these criteria can enhance our understanding of team effectiveness.

Part VII: Organizational Learning, Development, and Adaptation

In this part, we continue our move upward across levels of the organizational system to consider learning, development, and strategic adaptation as macro-level phenomena. In "Organizational Learning and Knowledge Management," Argote examines the research in these topic areas that has accumulated over the last two decades and summarizes primary findings about the creation, retention, and transfer of organizational knowledge. She highlights gaps in our research knowledge and identifies directions for future research to advance theory and practice.

The next chapter, "Organizational Development and Change: Linking Research from the Profit, Nonprofit, and Public Sectors," by Ford and Foster-Fishman, examines factors that influence the success or failure of organizational change interventions. Drawing from organizational psychology, community psychology, and organizational behavior literatures, they review the history of the field, key change theories, and empirical findings. The chapter highlights conceptual and methodological advances and concludes with targets for future research.

Finally, Snow and Snell conclude this part with their chapter on "Strategic Human Resource Management" (SHRM), which forms the underpinnings for organizational adaptation. They distinguish two perspectives on SHRM. The systemic fit perspective focuses on ensuring an adaptive fit of the organization to its external environment, aligning the system internally, and fitting human resources to accomplish organizational strategy; strategy drives SHRM. The strategic resources and capability perspective is future oriented, with the goal of harnessing unique human resource capabilities to achieve competitive advantage through organizational learning and innovation; SHRM "propels" strategy formulation and gives the organization a range of adaptive options.

Part VIII: Managing Differences Within and Across Organizations

The next part of the handbook shifts perspective to examine the challenges of managing differences within and across organizations, covering the topics of diversity, discrimination, and cross-cultural psychology. In the previous section of this chapter that reviewed the evolution of work and organizations, I observed that the dominant career model for much of the twentieth century was one dominated by white males in Western societies. That model has changed as workforces have become more diverse and global.

This part begins with a chapter by Roberson on "Managing Diversity," which, while seemingly straightforward, is actually a complex and complicated research literature. Her review encompasses conceptualizations of diversity, theoretical views on its effects examined across levels of analysis, and the

evolution of diversity management. Research gaps are identified, and profitable directions for research are highlighted.

The next chapter, by Colella, McKay, Daniels, and Signal, examines the voluminous literature on "Employment Discrimination," which has been an important aspect of HRM research and practice across the latter half of the twentieth century and into the new millennium. Their review is truly comprehensive and focuses on targets, causes, forms, and the impact of employment discrimination. The chapter identifies future research that cuts across levels of analysis, disciplines, and science/practice.

Finally, this part concludes with a chapter on "Cross-Cultural Organizational Psychology." As the history chapter documents, the development of organizational psychology was largely based on North American and, to some extent, European interests in work psychology. However, with the globalization of organizations, interest in cross-cultural organizational psychology burgeoned in the latter part of the twentieth century. Aycan and Gelfand provide a comprehensive review on the key substantive topics (i.e., recruitment and selection, performance criteria, motivation, attitudes, teamwork, leadership, and conflict and negotiation), discuss methodological challenges, and map future research directions based on a "historical projection" of the evolution of this field of inquiry. Since work is global and cross-cultural, so too should be I/O psychology research.

Part IX: The Interface of Work and Life

The opening to this introductory chapter highlighted the centrality of work to identity, esteem, and well-being in modern society, and the extraordinary amount of time and effort devoted toward preparation, socialization, and striving across a career or series of careers. Work is quite simply an important part of modern life—so much so that work spills over to influence the quality and nature of our non-work lives. Allen, in "The Work and Family Interface," takes a broad perspective to consider the intersection of work and family life, examining research from individual, family, organization, and global perspectives. An agenda for future research is presented.

In addition to work being central, it is also the case that contemporary careers necessitate continuous learning and updating of skills. In "Lifelong Learning," London examines the workplace trends that push the importance of continuous learning across the span of a career, considering theories of learning, factors that influence it, organizational supports, and technological advances. He concludes with an agenda for advancing research and practices for lifelong learning.

Work can be an important source of well-being. The other side of this, of course, is that work can be a source of stress, accidents, and injuries that undermine health and well-being. Tetrick and Peiró, in "Occupational Safety and Health," review research on workplace safety, focusing on safety training, regulatory focus, safety climate, leadership, and job design. They also examine occupational health, with a strong focus on stress, and consider the implications of psychological contracts, climate for sexual harassment, collective burnout, recovery, and programs for organizational wellness. Finally, they document interventions designed to enhance employee safety, health, and well-being.

One occupational trend in the twenty-first century is that we live longer and work longer. In addition, older workers often have developed valuable knowledge and skills that are difficult for organizations to easily replicate, making it desirable to retain, maintain, or attract older workers. On the other hand, there are well-documented cognitive declines with aging, so there are also challenges for managing and accommodating older workers. In "Work and Aging," Hedge and Borman adopt individual, organizational, and societal perspectives to examine aging and the workforce. They conduct a comprehensive review and develop an ambitious agenda for research and practice on this topic of emerging importance. We are all getting older!

Part X: Technology, System Design, and Human Performance

The Industrial Revolution was driven by machines, and one could argue that technology is at the core of work psychology. The increasing penetration of technology systems into all aspects of work, the powerful influence of technology on the nature of work and work processes, and the way that technology systems can transcend organizational boundaries to create large-scale, complex, and critical systems (e.g., NextGen Air Traffic Control, digitized medicine, home health care) make the intersection of disciplines that study the interface of technology and human cognition, behavior, and performance—human factors (HF) psychology, cognitive engineering, human-systems integration (HSI), computer-supported cooperative work (CSCW), and naturalistic decision making (NDM)—with organizational psychology

much more important that it has been in the past. The perspectives and methods of these disciplines focused on technology in the workplace provide opportunities for complementarities and synergies with organizational psychology.

In the opening chapter, "An Overview of Human Factors Psychology," Kirlik presents the origins, core research foci, methodologies, and cutting-edge research on three technology-driven topics that intersect with I/O psychology, including human-automation interaction; situation awareness; and distraction, multitasking, and interruption. He closes the chapter by highlighting the forces pushing HF and I/O together and discussing the potential for a stronger symbiotic relationship between our fields.

The next chapter, "Cognition and Technology: Interdisciplinarity and the Impact of Cognitive Engineering Research on Organizational Productivity," by Fiore, examines the development and evolution of cognitive engineering, a field of inquiry at the intersection of cognition and human-technology interaction. He defines cognitive engineering as a holistic approach that combines concepts and methodologies drawn from cognitive psychology, computer science, and engineering. The chapter closes with a vision for the future that stresses the importance of harmonizing basic and applied science to advance organizational performance.

Another interdisciplinary area of inquiry, CSCW, has focused specifically on computer-based technology and its influence on facilitating human interaction and collaboration. In "Taxonomy and Theory in Computer-Supported Cooperative Work" (CSCW), Grudin and Poltrock trace the development and evolution of this area of inquiry, which blends social scientists and technologists. One of the challenges of CSCW is that the technology has been, and continues to be, a moving target, making it somewhat difficult for the science to flourish. Grudin and Poltrock survey the applications of theory and taxonomies drawn from social science that have been used to facilitate an understanding of this important topic.

Finally, this part closes with "Decision Making in Naturalistic Environments," by Salas, Rosen, and DiazGranados. NDM is about decision making in real-world settings. It often involves critical tasks and high stakes, time pressure, uncertainty, individuals and teams, and is usually technology enabled. Research on NDM encompasses the topics covered in this part. Salas and his colleagues define the domain, highlight key theories, sketch methodologies, summarize findings, discuss applications to improve NDM, and map future research opportunities.

Postscript: *On the Horizon*

Having toured the breadth, depth, and diversity of organizational psychology—and related disciplines with shared interests—the handbook closes with some of my parting thoughts about emerging challenges and opportunities for organizational psychology in the twenty-first century. I advocate four *desirable evolutionary trends* that I believe will enhance the potential, relevance, and impact of the field: it should strengthen its scientific foundation, increase its multi- and interdisciplinary linkages, focus on multilevel system dynamics as core capabilities, and improve the translation of I/O psychological science into evidence-based practice.

And, now, without further ado—delve into the handbook! I think you will find it informative, intellectually stimulating, and valuable for outlining the future directions of the field of organizational psychology—the science of psychology applied to work and organizations.

Acknowledgment

I would like to express my appreciation to Bradford S. Bell, Chu-Hsiang (Daisy) Chang, and Georgia T. Chao for their helpful comments on drafts of this chapter. I also gratefully acknowledge the Office of Naval Research (ONR), Command Decision Making Program (N00014-09-1-0519, S. W. J. Kozlowski and G. T. Chao, Principal Investigators) and the National Aeronautics and Space Administration (NASA, NNX09AK47G, S. W. J. Kozlowski, Principal Investigator) for support that, in part, assisted the composition of this chapter. Any opinions, findings, and conclusions or recommendations expressed are those of the authors and do not necessarily reflect the views of ONR or NASA.

Notes

1. It is important to acknowledge that the historical label for the field is "industrial and organizational" psychology. However, I am among many who think "organizational psychology" is shorter, sweeter, and superior. I will use the labels interchangeably, but with a decided preference for "organizational psychology" as the name for our field.

2. Prometheus stole fire from the gods.

3. http://www.prb.org/pdf08/63.2uslabor.pdf.

4. http://www.google.com/support/jobs/bin/static.py?pa.ge=benefits.html#hw.

5. http://www.siop.org/mission.aspx.

6 I use the label "multilevel" generically to refer variously to homologous multilevel models, cross-level models, and models of emergence.

References

Applebaum, H. (1992). *The concept of work: Ancient, medieval, and modern.* Albany: State University of New York Press.

Borman, D. R. Ilgen, & R. J. Klimoski. (2003). *Handbook of psychology: Organizational psychology* (Vol. 12). London: Wiley.

Cascio, W. F., & Wynn, P. (2004). Managing a downsizing process. *Human Resource Management, 43,* 425–436.

Devine, D. J., Clayton, L. D., Phillips, J. L., Dunford, B. B., & Melner, S. B. (1999). Teams in organizations: Prevalence, characteristics, and effectiveness. *Small Group Research, 30,* 678–711.

DOL. Women workforce stats. Available at http://www.dol.gov/wb/stats/main.htm.

Dunnette, M. D. (1976). *Handbook of industrial and organizational psychology.* Chicago: Rand McNally.

Dunnette, M. D., & Hough, L. M. (1990). *Handbook of organizational psychology.* Palo Alto, CA: Consulting Psychologists Press.

George, J. M. (1990). Personality, affect, and behavior in groups. *Journal of Applied Psychology, 75,* 107–116.

George, J. M., & James, L. R. (1993). Personality, affect, and behavior in groups revisited: Comment on aggregation, levels of analysis, and a recent application of within and between analysis. *Journal of Applied Psychology, 78,* 798–804.

Google Benefits. Available at http://www.google.com/support/jobs/bin/static.py?page=benefits.html#hw.

Heckhausen, H., & Kuhl, J. (1985). From wishes to action: The dead ends and short cuts on the long way to action. In M. Frese & J. Sabini (Eds.), *Goal directed behavior: The concept of action in psychology* (pp. 134–160). Hillsdale, NJ: Erlbaum.

Heilbroner, R. L. (1985). *The act of work.* Washington, DC: Library of Congress.

Jahoda, M. (1988). Economic recession and mental health: Some conceptual issues. *Journal of Social Issues, 44,* 13–23.

James, L. R. (1973). Criterion models and construct validity for criteria. *Psychological Bulletin, 80,* 75–83.

James, L. R., Demaree, R. G., & Wolf, G. (1984). Estimating within group interrater reliability with and without response bias. *Journal of Applied Psychology, 69,* 85–98.

James, L. R., Demaree, R. G., & Wolf, G. (1993). r_{wg}: An assessment of within group interrater agreement. *Journal of Applied Psychology, 78,* 306–309.

Katz, D., & Kahn, R. L. (1978). *The social psychology of organizations.* New York: Wiley.

Klein, K. J., Dansereau, F., & Hall, R. J. (1994). Levels issues in theory development, data collection, and analysis. *Academy of Management Review, 19,* 195–229.

Kozlowski, S. W. J., & Bell, B. S. (2003). Work groups and teams in organizations. In W. C. Borman, D. R. Ilgen, & R. J. Klimoski (Eds.), *Handbook of industrial and organizational psychology* (Vol. 12, pp. 333–375). London: Wiley.

Kozlowski, S. W. J., Chao, G. T., Smith, E. M., & Hedlund, J. A. (1993). Organizational downsizing: Strategies, interventions, and research implications. In C. L. Cooper & I. T. Robertson (Eds.), *International review of I/O psychology* (Vol. 8, pp. 263–332). New York: Wiley.

Kozlowski, S. W. J., & Hattrup, K. (1992). A disagreement about within-group agreement: Disentangling issues of consistency versus consensus. *Journal of Applied Psychology, 77,* 161–167.

Kozlowski, S. W. J., & Ilgen, D. R. (2006). Enhancing the effectiveness of work groups and teams (Monograph). *Psychological Science in the Public Interest, 7,* 77–124.

Kozlowski, S. W. J., & Klein, K. J. (2000). A multilevel approach to theory and research in organizations: Contextual, temporal, and emergent processes. In K. J. Klein & S. W. J. Kozlowski (Eds.), *Multilevel theory, research and methods in organizations: Foundations, extensions, and new directions* (pp. 3–90). San Francisco, CA: Jossey-Bass.

Lee, M. A., & Mather, M. (2008). U.S. labor force trends. *Population Bulletin, 63*(2). Washington, DC: Population Reference Bureau.

Levine, J. M., & Moreland, R. L. (1990). Progress in small group research. *Annual Review of Psychology, 41,* 585–634.

Molloy, J. C., & Noe, R. A. (2010) "Learning" a living: Continuous learning for survival in today's talent market. In S. W. J. Kozlowski & E. Salas (Eds.), *Learning, training, and development in organizations* (pp. 333–361). New York: Routledge Academic

Mossholder, K. W., & Bedeian, A. G. (1983). Cross-level inference and organizational research: Perspectives on interpretation and application. *Academy of Management Review, 8,* 547–558.

Roberts, K. H., Hulin, C. L., & Rousseau, D. M. (1978). *Developing an interdisciplinary science of organizations.* San Francisco: Jossey-Bass.

Roethlisberger, F. J., & Dickson, W. J. (1939). *Management and the worker.* Cambridge, MA: Harvard University Press.

Robinson, W. S. (1950). Ecological correlations and the behavior of individuals. *American Sociological Review, 15,* 351–357.

Rousseau, D. M. (1985). Issues of level in organizational research: Multi-level and cross-level perspectives. In L. L. Cummings & B. M. Staw (Eds.), *Research in organizational behavior* (Vol. 7, pp.1–37). Greenwich, CT: JAI Press.

Schmidt, F. L., & Hunter, J. E. (1989). Interrater reliability coefficients cannot be computed when only one stimulus is rated. *Journal of Applied Psychology, 74,* 368–370.

SIOP Mission. Available at http://www.siop.org/mission.aspx. Accessed October 25, 2011.

Stokes, D. (1997). *Pasteur's Quadrant: Basic science and technological innovation.* Washington, DC: The Brookings Institution.

Thorndike, E. L. (1939). On the fallacy of imputing the correlations found for groups to the individuals or smaller groups composing them. *American Journal of Psychology, 52,* 122–124.

Weiss, H. M., & Cropanzano, R. (1996). Affective events theory: A theoretical discussion of the structure, causes and consequences of affective experiences at work. *Research in Organizational Behavior, 18,* 1–74.

Yammarino, F. J., & Markham, S. E. (1992). On the application of within and between analysis: Are absence and affect really group-based phenomena? *Journal of Applied Psychology, 77,* 168–176.

Zedeck, S. (2010). *APA Handbook of organizational psychology.* Washington, DC: American Psychological Association.

A History of Industrial and Organizational Psychology

Laura L. Koppes Bryan *and* Andrew J. Vinchur

Abstract

This chapter is a historical overview of the evolution of industrial and organizational (I/O) psychology both in the United States and abroad, from the late nineteenth century to its current incarnation as a complex, wide-ranging scientific and applied discipline. Contextual background is integrated with the development of science and practice from a chronological perspective, partitioning this history into seven somewhat arbitrary time periods. Following a discussion of pre-1900 precursors, we discuss the genesis of the field from 1900 to 1914, when dynamic cultural, economic, and other external forces influenced early efforts in areas such as advertising, fatigue, and selection. Industrial psychology became established from 1915 through 1919, due in large part to the work of the Division of Applied Psychology at the Carnegie Institute of Technology and to psychologists' efforts in World War I. The period of 1920 to 1939 included the influential Hawthorne Studies and the maturation of industrial psychology, while 1940 to 1959 saw considerable expansion during World War II and its aftermath. This expansion continued during the period of 1960 to 1979, with "industrial" psychology now "industrial-organizational" psychology. We close with an overview of developments from 1980 to the present day.

Key Words: History of Psychology, industrial-organizational psychology

In comparison to the early years of a broad science of work in Europe, industrial and organizational (I/O) psychology in the United States was a narrowly defined technical discipline focused on individual level differences (i.e., selection), which then evolved into a complex, wide-ranging scientific and applied discipline emphasizing individual and organizational issues for achieving both individual and organizational goals. I/O psychology evolved into a recognizable subdiscipline of psychology in the early years of the twentieth century. As this psychology subdiscipline emerged, it was labeled *economic psychology* (Münsterberg, 1914), or *business psychology* (Kingsbury, 1923; Münsterberg, 1917) initially in the United States. Another label was *employment psychology* (Burtt, 1926). *Industrial psychology* was used infrequently before World War

I but became more common after the war (Viteles, 1932). In Europe, an early label was *psychotechnology* (Jenkins, 1935)[1]. *I/O psychology* was not used in the United States until fairly recently, and was never used in other countries, but more commonly, the terms *work psychology* or *organizational psychology* describe the science and practice of psychology in work and organizational settings outside the US. To be consistent with the title of this handbook, we use the terms *industrial psychology* and *I/O psychology* to encompass the science and practice of psychology in work and organizational settings in the United States as well as other countries.

Throughout the world today, the objectives of I/O psychology are to increase individual and organizational efficiency and to facilitate goal attainment by theorizing, researching, and applying psychology in the workplace, with consideration for individual and organizational factors. The genesis and evolution of I/O psychology were the result of confluences of dynamic external (cultural, societal, philosophical, economic, legal, military, technological, psychological) and internal forces (individuals, theories, scientific investigations, applications). Examining our historical roots will help us more clearly understand present-day I/O psychology.

The purpose of this chapter is to provide a historical overview that integrates a contextual background with I/O developments from a chronological perspective, which sets the stage for the other chapters in this handbook. Our approach is to expand upon an extensive timeline created by Koppes (2007) by briefly describing the context of each time period and describing key contributors and major developments. The organizing scheme of the chapter is presented in Table 2.1. While a

Table 2.1 Overview of the Chronological History of Industrial and Organizational Psychology

Year	Developments
	Psychology Applied to Work: Period of Precursors
Prior to 1900	I-O psychology did not emerge in a vacuum but evolved from a confluence of precursors and roots. This was a period of formation for psychology as it broke away from philosophy in Europe, and was established in the United States. I-O was not a formalized discipline.
	• American Psychological Association founded in 1892.
	• Kraeplin's studies of physical and mental fatigue and work performance were conducted.
	• Formation of psychotechnics occurred, first in Europe, then in the U.S.
	• Personal history inventory introduced in 1894.
	• Skills of professional telegraphers are investigated in 1897.
	• Great man theory introduced in 1894.
	• A group is more than a sum of its parts, in 1895.
	Other: psychology and advertising, psychological testing included the U.S. Army testing for surgeons as early as 1814, initial work on Civil Service Examinations.
1900–1914	**Industrial Psychology: Period of Genesis**
	The first 15 years of the 20th century was a time when industrial psychology began to come into its own both in the United States and abroad. The study of work was part of the desire to place all life on an orderly and scientific basis. An emphasis on measurement and quantification continued in the rise of Psychology.
	• Formation of scientific management to study work occurred.
	• Early selection studies by Pizzoli, Lahy, Meriam were conducted.
	• Studies on the acquisition of typing skills were conducted.
	• *The Theory of Advertising* published by W. D. Scott, 1903.
	• *Increasing Human Efficiency in Business* published by W. D. Scott, 1911.
	• *Influencing Men in Business* by published W. D. Scott, 1911.
	• *Psychology and Industrial Efficiency* published by H. Münsterberg, 1913.
	• First record of a job analysis was documented.
	Other: selection of streetcar motormen/drivers, ship officers, stenographers, telephone operators, aviators; vocational guidance and counseling; shift from apprenticeship programs to business' factory schools.

(Continued)

Table 2.1 (Continued)

Year	Developments
1915–1919	**Industrial Psychology: Period of Establishment**

Psychologists were compelled to legitimize their science and to address society's skepticism of the profession by placing great emphasis on empirical methods. Significant progress was made in establishing industrial psychology as a recognizable subfield of psychology.

- Division of Applied Psychology, Carnegie Institute of Technology (CIT) established.

- W. D. Scott appointed first professor of applied psychology at CIT.

- Psychologists' participation in the World War I war effort: development of Army Alpha and Army Beta under Yerkes; Committee on Classification of Personnel under Scott.

- The Scott Company, the first personnel consulting organization, formed.

- *Journal of Applied Psychology* began publication in 1917.

- Henry Link, first full-time Ph.D.-level psychologist was documented as working in industry.

- Industrial Fatigue Research Board in Great Britain established 1918, later named the Industrial Health Research Board.

- Life Insurance Sales Research Bureau (LISRB) founded in 1919.

- R. H. Macy and Company hires female psychologist Elsie Oschrin Bregman, 1919.

- Four-step method of instruction of "show-tell-do-check" for training purposes is implemented.

- Relevant publications: *Vocational Psychology*; *Aids in the Selection of Salesmen*; *Applied Psychology*; *Employment Psychology*.

- Activities in other countries: aptitude testing for radio operators, pilots, and drivers; selection research for submarine detection operators, selection and training of armed forces; a series of lectures on industrial psychology delivered in Sydney, Australia, 1916.

1920–1939	**Industrial Psychology: Period of Development**

Applications used in the war were expanded and other applications were developed. Corporate leaders focused on finding the right employee for the job; businesses created personnel departments. Social philosophy of workers shifted from a policy of noninterference to one that emphasized employees' welfare. The Depression's adverse effects on individuals led to heightened sensitivity to and concern for the human condition and the humanization of work. Unemployment and adjustment of workers became prevalent, resulting in the genesis of a human relations movement.

- International Association of Psychotechnics formed in 1920 during the International Congress of Psychotechnology; in 1955 this association was renamed the International Association of Applied Psychology (IAAP).

- Bruce V. Moore earns Ph.D. in applied psychology at CIT.

- The Psychological Corporation established, 1921.

- National Institute for Industrial Psychology (NIIP) formed, 1921.

- Personnel Research Federation founded, 1921.

- Graphic rating scale introduced, 1922.

- Hawthorne Studies begin in 1924 (Hawthorne effect).

- Myers authored *Industrial Psychology* (1925) and *Industrial Psychology in Great Britain* (1926).

Table 2.1 (Continued)

Year	Developments
	• New York State Association of Consulting Psychologists (founded in 1921) went national as the Association of Consulting Psychologists (ACP) in 1930.
	• *Industrial Psychology*, first comprehensive textbook published by Viteles, 1932.
	• U.S. Employment Service developed the General Aptitude Test Battery (GATB) and published the *Dictionary of Occupational Titles*.
	• American Association of Applied Psychology (AAAP) formed in 1937. Four sections: clinical, consulting, educational, and industrial and business (Section D).
	• *Journal of Personnel Research* (later *Personnel Journal*) published, 1922.
	• Minnesota Employment Stabilization Research Institute established, 1931.
	• Studies conducted on job satisfaction and morale; motivation research focused on attitudes.
	• Organizational interventions at the Harwood Pajama Factory were implemented.
	• O. Tead (1935) introduced ten desirable qualities of a leader.
	• Academy of Management formed, 1936.
	• Publications: *Psychological Tests in Business; The Psychology of Selling and Advertising; Principles of Employment Psychology; Applied Psychology: Its Principles and Methods*.
	Other: validity and criterion emerged as concepts; analysis of variance development; the job psychograph as a job analysis method; automotive industry research at Ohio State; Paterson provided 12 principles of psychological ratings; Kornhauser (1926–1927) reported three empirical studies of ratings and discussed the reliability of ratings, rater comparison, and comparison of ratings on different traits; a self-help book on leadership by Kleiser (1923); Mary Parker Follett's essay on leadership and participation in 1927; examination of leader qualities proposed by Craig and Charters; development of personnel counseling; the KR-20 reliability coefficient; the Scanlon plan; Ringelman role-pull task study.
1940–1959	**Industrial Psychology: Period of Expansion**
	A significant expansion of applications and research occurred. World War II created an opportunity for psychologists to apply their techniques. This era saw the genesis of an organizational psychology with the increased emphasis on human relations.
	• Military research centers established.
	• *Ethical Principles of Psychologists Technical Recommendations of Psychological Tests and Diagnostic Techniques* published.
	• Army General Classification Test to assess cognitive abilities of military personnel was introduced.
	• Aviation Psychology Unit of the Army Air Forces in 1941; 19 volumes published, known as the "Blue Books."
	• Applied Psychology Panel formed in 1942 to work on problems associated with selection and classification.
	• *Assessment of* Men describes selection of agents for Office of Strategic Services (OSS); assessment tools were forerunners of situational tests and assessment centers.
	• APA Division 14 founded; Bruce V. Moore as the first president in 1946.
	• American Institutes for Research (AIR) formed, 1946.

(*Continued*)

Table 2.1 (Continued)

Year	Developments
	• The National Training Laboratory for Group Development (NTL) formed, development of t-groups, 1946–1947.
	• Tavistock Institute of Human Relations in London formed, 1946–1947.
	• *Human Relations* journal published, 1947.
	• Robert Thorndike's book on *Personnel Selection* was published in 1949.
	• Wherry's Theory of Ratings introduced in 1950 and 1952.
	• AT&T Management Progress Study began in 1956.
	• McGregor's formulation of Theory Y and Theory X introduced.
	• Herzberg's two-factory theory or motivation-hygiene theory described.
	• The Ohio State Leadership Studies; Leader Behavior Description Questionnaire Research Center for Group Dynamics at the Massachusetts Institute of Technology; then, in 1948, the Research Center joined the Michigan Survey Research Center, the University of Michigan Institute for Social Research (ISR) was formed.
	• Research groups were created within private companies (e.g., General Electric, Standard Oil of New Jersey) and consulting firms were established, such as the Richardson, Bellows, Henry & Company and the Life Insurance Agency Management Association (LIAMA), a merging of Association of Life Agency Offices, founded in 1916, and the Life Insurance Sales Research Bureau, founded in 1919.
	• Publications: *Personnel and Industrial Psychology; Group Dynamics in Industry; Overcoming Resistance to Change; Handbook of Applied Psychology; Motivation and Morale; Organizations; Personnel Psychology* journal; *Administrative Science Quarterly* journal.
	Other: expansion and refinement of selection methods (interview, application blank, biodata, tests for managerial selection); critical incident technique; coefficient alpha for estimating reliability; conceptualization of construct validity and synthetic validity; concepts of criterion deficiency, contamination, and relevance; multitrait-multimethod matrix; utility analysis; supervisor training; on-the-job training; off-the-job training (human relationships training, case studies, role plays, simulators, sensitivity training, televisions and films); training evaluation (trainee reactions, learning, behavior back on the job, and results); forced choice rating procedure; quality circles.
1960–1979	**Industrial and Organizational Psychology: Period of Modernization**
	Industrial psychology evolved into the modern discipline of industrial AND organizational psychology as it is known today. The previous work on organizational issues continued and strengthened, and an emphasis was placed on theory construction and theory-related research of organizational psychology. The birth of organization development (OD) was observed as an attempt to better understand the process of group dynamics. A focus on worker well-being emerged. I-O psychologists well-trained in experimental methods turned to laboratory and field experiments to provide rigorous analysis of phenomena that had been identified in correlational and case studies.
	• In 1962, "Business" dropped from APA Division 14 label, to become APA Division 14 Industrial Psychology.
	• Organizational psychology achieved recognition in industrial psychology when APA Division 14 changed its name to the Division of Industrial-Organizational Psychology in 1973.
	• McGregor's seminal book, *The Human Side of Enterprise,* published in 1960.
	• Book on *Organizational Psychology* published, 1965.
	• *Handbook of Industrial and Organizational Psychology,* published in 1976.

Table 2.1 (Continued)

Year	Developments
	• Job Descriptive Index and Minnesota Satisfaction Questionnaire introduced.
	• "Topeka System" implemented in Gaines dog food plant in Topeka, KS.
	• Supreme Course decisions issued (e.g., *Griggs v. Duke Power*, 1971; *Albermarle v. Moody*, 1975; *Washington v. Davis*, 1976).
	• First comprehensive book on job analysis published in 1979.
	• Validity generalization research resulted in meta-analysis procedure.
	• *Principles for the Validation and Use of Personnel Selection Procedures* published in 1975.
	• Behaviorally Anchored Rating Scales, Mixed Standard Scales, Behavioral Expectation Scales, Behavioral Observation Scales introduced.
	• *Training in Business and Industry* described the three-step training needs assessment process.
	• In training, instructional systems design (ISD) model; training methods including on-the-job training, job rotation, coaching, behavior modification, lectures, films, television, business games, in-baskets, case studies, role playing, simulations, and team training.
	• Internationalization of I-O psychology proliferated.
	• *Journal of Occupational Psychology*, published in 1975
	Other: job enrichment theory, expectancy theory, equity theory, behavior modification in work settings; goal setting theory; social learning or social cognitive theory; contingency theories of leadership (situational theory, path-goal, vertical dyad linkage); leadership perceptions as key components of the leadership process (performance cue studies and implicit leadership theories); input, process, output (IPO) model; the formation of teams; t-groups provided for team building; quality circles, groupthink; functional job analysis approach; the Position Analysis Questionnaire.
1980–Present Day	**Industrial and Organizational Psychology: Period of Refinement and Adaptability**
	I-O psychology has grown rapidly with an emphasis on refinement and adaptability. Old techniques have been applied to new problems, and new solutions have been developed for traditional problems. New topics of interest surfaced.
	• APA Division 14 incorporated as the Society for Industrial and Organizational Psychology (SIOP) in 1982.
	• Research on levels of analysis conducted.
	• Meta-analysis; hierarchical linear modeling (HLM); structural equation modeling (SEM); confirmatory factor analyses (CFA); item response theory used in research.
	• Strategic human resource management emerged.
	• Serious attention given to utility analysis.
	• Project A: The U.S. Army Selection and Classification Research Project conducted.
	• Occupational Information Network (O*Net) developed.
	• *Principles for the Validation and Use of Personnel Selection Procedures* revised in 1980, 1987, and 2003.
	• Occupational Analysis Inventory; the Generalized Work Inventory; Common Metric Questionnaire (CMQ); Fleishman Job Analysis Survey (F-JAS) published.

(Continued)

Table 2.1 (Continued)

Year	Developments

- *The Job Analysis Handbook for Business, Industry, and Government* published in 1988.

- The *International Journal of Selection and Assessment,* published in 1993.

- Strategic learning era; models of training effectiveness; models of the transfer of training; instructor-led training; corporate university and technology-delivered instruction (e.g., self-directed learning activities such as CD-ROM and web-based training); organizational learning, knowledge management, intellectual capital.

- Cognitive processes involved in performance appraisals; social context in which performance appraisals operate; rater training; employee reactions; supervisor-subordinate relationships; organizational politics; multisource rating and feedback systems, also known as 360-degree ratings; employee participation.

- Cognitive processes of leaders and followers; shared leadership in teams; implicit leadership theory; transformational leadership and neo-charismatic leadership cross-cultural leadership. Global Leadership and Organizational Behavior Effectiveness (GLOBE) study; leader-member exchange theory; leadership substitutes; strategic leadership; followership; gender and leadership; leadership knowledge, skills, and ability; redux of leadership trait theory; leadership development.

- How teams form, evolve, and perform; team taxonomies and classifications; self management work teams; knowledge in teamwork; shared cognition and shared mental models; team maturation; hierarchical team decision making; team performance and effectiveness; team training and development; team performance measurement; distributed and virtual teams; team member individual differences; expansion of work teams and groups; fluidity of work teams; expansion of virtual teams; selection of team members.

- Work, family and health issues; worker stress, health, and well-being; quality of work life; work and family (work-life) balance and/or conflict; work-family enrichment, perceived organizational support; behaviors of leadership and/or supervisors supportive of work-life effectiveness; flexibility in the workplace; models of stress; psychological effects of job loss; workplace violence; counterproductive work behaviors.

- Increased focus on measurement, antecedents, and consequences of job satisfaction, organizational commitment, job involvement, organizational citizenship behaviors, and emotions at work.

- The *Journal of Occupational Behavior* (now known as *Journal of Organizational Behavior*) was first published in 1980. It was renamed the British Psychological Society's *Journal of Occupational and Organizational Psychology* in 1992 to reflect a wider coverage of the field.

- First volume in the SIOP Frontiers Service, *Careers in Organizations,* published in 1986.

- First volume of the SIOP Practice Series, *Working with Organizations and Their People,* published in 1991.

- Second edition of the *Handbook of Industrial, Work, and Organizational Psychology* published (1992).

- Top I-O psychology journals: *Journal of Applied Psychology, Personnel Psychology, Academy of Management Journal, Academy of Management Review, Organizational Behavior and Human Decision Processes, Administrative Science Quarterly, Journal of Management, Journal of Organizational Behavior, Organizational Research Methods,* and *Journal of Vocational Behavior.*

- In 2009, SIOP joined forces with the International Association of Applied Psychology (IAAP) and the European Association of Work and Organizational Psychology (EAWOP) to form the Alliance of Organizational Psychology.

- Other: individual assessment (assessment centers, computerized adaptive testing, use of biodata, structured interviews, situational interview technique); attraction-selection-attrition model; revival of research on personality characteristics (five-factor model of personality as a valid predictor of performance); general cognitive ability tests as valid predictors of performance; integrity tests; computer and Internet-based recruitment, assessment, and testing; organizational justice theory; theory of the high-performance cycle (HPC).

complete and comprehensive account of the history of I/O psychology is not possible in just one chapter, we include those individual contributions, activities, and events that we believe were most important to the development of the field or are illustrative of the types of developments during each time period.

Overview of Historical Accounts

Scholarship on the history of psychology has evolved considerably since Watson's call for such scholarship in 1960. More specifically, the history of I/O psychology has enjoyed serious attention by scholars, especially in the past 20 years. These historical accounts of I/O psychology vary in emphasis, orientation, and detail.

Morris Viteles (1932) documents an early history of industrial psychology through the description of independent investigators whose work comprised the field during the early years, in both the United States and abroad. Much later, Baritz (1960) provides a great deal of information about early industrial psychology, although his view is highly critical of industrial psychologists as servants to those in power (i.e., management). Leonard Ferguson's (1962–1965) series of pamphlets is viewed as a primary source for the early historical developments within the discipline in the United States, while McCollom (1968) gives a summary of the early years of the field both inside and outside America. Napoli (1981) includes aspects of I/O psychology in his history of the psychological profession, and a chapter by Hilgard (1987) concentrates on the history of I/O psychology in the United States. Katzell and Austin (1992) offer a more comprehensive overview using a contextual approach to the U.S. I/O psychology history, as does Koppes (2003). A recent chapter by Vinchur and Koppes (2011) examines the history of I/O psychology and organizational behavior both here and abroad. The edited book by Koppes (2007) takes a topical approach to I/O history (e.g., job analysis, selection, training and development, work motivation, leadership) and provides contextual influences on history development as well. While much of this text focuses on developments in the United States, Warr's chapter provides an overview of developments outside the United States (Warr, 2007). Many other histories of I/O psychology exist that focus on specific content areas, individuals, or time periods (e.g., Austin & Villanova, 1992; Benjamin, 1997a, 1997b; Capshew, 1999; Colarelli, 1998; de Wolff & Shimmin, 1976; Farr & Tesluk, 1997; Ferguson, 1952, 1961; Highhouse, 1999; Koppes, 1997; Landy, 1992, 1997; Sokal, 1987; Stagner, 1981; Thayer, 1997; Van de Water, 1997; van Strien, 1998; Zickar, 2001). To the extent possible, we will refer to these sources as we trace the evolution of I/O psychology in this chapter.

Pre-1900s
Contextual Background

During this first period in our chronological timeline, an applied psychology in work and organizations did not exist. However, it is possible to trace predecessors of modern day I/O psychologists to antiquity.[2] In fact, Katzell and Austin (1992) identify several early efforts that attended to worker issues, such as Plato in *The Republic*, when he initiated a program for managerial selection and development as well as methods for selecting and training workers, and the Chinese who used a multiple-hurdle selection system for bureaucrats over 3,000 years ago (DuBois, 1965, 1970). We will begin with more recent, directly relevant antecedents.

As noted previously, I/O psychology did not emerge in a vacuum but evolved from a confluence of precursors. For example, Viteles (1932) notes economic (e.g., emphasis on efficiency), societal, and psychological (e.g., experimental psychology, study of individual differences) factors that served as the foundations of then industrial psychology. Other relevant precursors are the blossoming of science, the rise of evolutionary theory, the emergence of an industrial revolution, and the separation of psychology from philosophy as a scientific discipline, resulting in new approaches and thought (e.g., differential psychology, experimental psychology, functionalism; Katzell & Austin, 1992; Koppes, 2003; Koppes & Pickren, 2007).

Koppes and Pickren (2007) provide an overview of the philosophical thought that established the basis for a psychological science generally and, more specifically, for an applied psychology. They note that explanations of the world in naturalistic terms beginning in the early modern period (fourteenth and fifteenth centuries) provided the foundation for science. The English philosopher John Locke (1632–1704), who was influenced by Francis Bacon (1561–1626), pioneered an "experimental, incremental approach to science" (Boorstin, 1992, p. 566; see Pickren, 2000). The late eighteenth century saw the flowering of science (Roback, 1952) and an intellectual climate characterized by positivism, materialism, and empiricism (Zickar & Gibby,

2007). In addition, with rapid population growth, the spread of the Industrial Revolution across Europe, and the need of nation-states to have greater control over the lives of their citizens, it became even more important to understand one's self and abilities in relation to other individuals (Koppes & Pickren, 2007). Thus, science, or systematic knowledge, had increasing appeal.

Later in the nineteenth century, the theory of evolution by natural selection put forth by Charles Darwin (1809–1882) and Alfred Russel Wallace (1823–1913) stands as a punctuation mark in the establishment of scientific naturalism as the dominant worldview. Their theories emphasized the role of "function." Variations in function, Darwin argued, were the key to adaptation and species change. Darwin firmly placed man in the natural order, thus subject to natural law (Darwin, 1859). But it was his emphasis on the variability among species that underlies natural selection and served as one of the foundations for a science of psychology.

In the hands of Darwin's cousin Francis Galton (1822–1911), individual differences and their functions were seen as important to understanding and reforming society. Galton believed that these individual differences were due to heredity. Although the claims of Galton's eugenics had more benign effects in Britain than in the United States, eugenics found one expression in the rise of mental testing, especially intelligence testing (Koppes & Pickren, 2007). The idea that tests could expose unobserved and underlying abilities and character traits was advantageous to the rising field of an applied psychology. Galton, along with William Stern and James McKeen Cattell, is considered one of the founders of differential psychology, the study of individual differences. Galton also did pioneering work in quantification and measurement; he coined the term co-relation in 1888 and developed the precursor to the correlation coefficient. This coefficient was further developed by, among others, F. Y. Edgeworth and Karl Pearson (Cowles, 2001).

As science blossomed toward the end of the nineteenth century, the inception of psychology as a scientific discipline separate from philosophy occurred. Psychologists were interested in empirically investigating the mind and behavior using experiments and psychometric methods. The laboratory became the primary place to search for truth, and the "experiment" became the primary method for finding truth. In an early example related to work, Angelo Mosso (1846–1910), a physiologist,

approached the problem of fatigue through laboratory experimentation (1906 [1891]). With the use of an ergograph, Mosso showed how the contraction time of a muscle grows as the muscle becomes fatigued, with the result that work potential is reduced. In using this technique, Mosso borrowed from Wilhelm Wundt's (1832–1920) physiological psychology to graphically show a physiological process that had psychological implications. Wundt, a German psychologist often referred to as the founder of modern scientific psychology, established the psychological laboratory at the University of Leipzig to distinguish psychology from philosophy. He used the experimental method to control observations for objectively studying mind and behavior. A number of graduates of Wundt's doctoral program, such as James McKeen Cattell, Hugo Münsterberg, and Walter Dill Scott, played major roles in the development of I/O psychology.

Although psychology was initially taught within traditional philosophy departments, several psychology laboratories were established in the U.S. universities, the first at Johns Hopkins in 1884 (Fryer & Henry, 1950). To formalize psychology as a discipline in America, the American Psychological Association (APA) was founded in 1892 by G. Stanley Hall and others. New psychological journals were established: *Pedagogical Seminary* (1891), *Psychological Review* (1894), *Psychological Monographs* (1894), and *Psychological Index* (1894; Benjamin, n.d.); and William James published his landmark textbook, *Principles of Psychology,* in 1890 (James, 1950).

The prevailing school of psychological thought in Germany focused on the structure of conscious thought, this *structuralism* was most identified with Edwin B. Titchener at Cornell University. In the United States, a shift to a functional psychology, based on Darwinism and differential psychology, was formulated to challenge the structuralist view. Functionalism emphasized how and why the mind adapts the individual to the environment (Angell, 1907). This functional perspective provided a foundation for the mental testing movement that took place at the turn of the twentieth century and served as an orientation for psychologists interested in studying work behavior.

As psychology was emerging as a scientific discipline, rapid changes were occurring across Europe and in the United States, including industrialization, immigration, a high birth rate, education reform, and urban growth. Dramatic technological changes, such as the development and widespread use of the telephone, telegraph, and typewriter, sped up communication. The expansion and standardization of railroads increased travel volume. Other changes included the introduction of mass production, expansion of organizations, growth of corporations, and innovations in engineering. This Industrial Revolution created a prevailing faith in capitalism (Katzell & Austin, 1992). Businesses emphasized the improvement of efficiency, increase of productivity, and decrease of costs through standardization and simplification (Koppes, 2003). The intellectual, social, cultural, and economic milieu was supportive of the formation of an applied psychology in work settings.

PSYCHOLOGY APPLIED TO WORK: PERIOD OF PRECURSORS

Whether they called themselves economic psychologists, business psychologists, psychotechnicians, or simply applied psychologists, those individuals who pioneered the application of psychological principles, theories, and techniques in business and industry in the early 1900s were building on the previous work of the earlier experimental psychologists. James McKeen Cattell, for example, was not an industrial psychologist, nor did he conduct research or practice in applied psychology. Nevertheless, his influence on the field was significant.

Cattell (1860–1944) completed an 1886 doctorate with Wundt at the University of Leipzig and followed this with a brief period of teaching in the United States. He went to Cambridge University, where he was strongly influenced by Galton, who inspired Cattell to use the experimental techniques he developed in his doctoral work to quantitatively measure individual difference characteristics (Sokal, 1987). Thus, Cattell did some of the earliest research on individual differences. He was a strong advocate for a quantitative, measurement-based approach to psychology and was credited with coining the term *mental test* in 1890. He spent 29 years in academe at the University of Pennsylvania and Columbia University.[3] Throughout his career, Cattell saw the potential of applied psychology and promoted it through his activities, and the journals and magazines he created or acquired. As we will discuss later, he founded one of the first applied psychology consulting firms, the Psychological Corporation. Cattell took a leadership role in the American Association for the Advancement of Science and also purchased and edited the journal *Science* (Coon & Sprenger, 1998).[4]

Two strands of activity in the late 1800s, the work on psychology and advertising in the United

Figure 2.1 James McKeen Cattell.

States and research, primarily in Europe, on worker fatigue, led to more expansive industrial psychology work in the early twentieth century. Psychologists Edward W. Scripture (1895) and Harlow Gale (1896) applied psychology to advertising, ushering in what came to be called business psychology. This work continued in the early 1900s, most notably by Walter Dill Scott, whose story we will pick up in the next section.

European researchers such as E. J. Marey, Angelo Mosso, Gustav Fechner, Emil Kraepelin, and Hugo Münsterberg conducted experimental research on worker fatigue and work potential (Fryer & Henry, 1950; Koppes & Pickren, 2007; Münsterberg, 1913). Among those in Europe who pursued the psychological aspects of fatigue, Kraepelin (1856–1926), a psychiatrist who also had training with Wundt in psychology, examined both physical and mental fatigue. Although he first worked with school children measuring fatigability on various cognitive tasks (Kraepelin, 1896), Kraepelin's core construct was work performance. He argued that there were few differences between mental and physical fatigue in work performance. He interpreted the results in terms of work curves, which showed a decline in production over time. Kraepelin (1896) believed that his research showed that fatigue could be reduced through practice and training. He also sought to eliminate the subjective aspects of work, such as feelings of tiredness and satisfaction. Where Kraepelin (1896) sought to remove these subjective aspects from the study of fatigue, Münsterberg (1913) studied them. Beginning in Germany (and later at Harvard), Münsterberg's (1913) experimental research on labor, fatigue, and training was focused on improving the output of each worker in industry. He later wrote that work pauses and increases in free time would make workers more efficient and would reduce accidents (Münsterberg, 1913). Furthermore, in contrast to Kraepelin's (1896) belief that psychological characteristics of the individual were not important, Münsterberg (1913) emphasized individual differences and claimed that understanding them was critical to a successful "psychotechnics." Each worker, Münsterberg (1913) wrote, brought to the work situation a unique pattern of fatigability, training, intellectual capacity, attitude, and personality. Although some of Münsterberg's early psychotechnical work was in the United States, this field developed more rapidly in Germany. The German applications of psychotechnics ranged widely. These included various applications for personnel tasks (van Drunen, 1997), training railroad engineers (see Hacker & Echterhoff, 1997), and selecting streetcar conductors, military drivers, and pilots during World War I (see Gundlach, 1997; Hacker & Echterhoff, 1997; van Drunen, 1997). We will provide a more detailed look at Münsterberg in the next section.

In addition to work on advertising and fatigue, there was early activity in other areas of what came to be I/O psychology, not all of it conducted by psychologists. Work on psychological testing included the U.S. Army testing for surgeons as early as 1814, initial work on Civil Service Examinations (DuBois, 1970; Hale, 1992), and Cattell's (1890) individual difference tests. Bryan and Harter (1897) researched skill development in telegraphers and businesspersons. Thomas Peters of the Washington Life Insurance Company introduced a precursor of the selection tool, the personal history inventory, in 1894 (Ferguson, 1961). The field of leadership was dominated by studies of the characteristics of notable leaders, an emphasis that did not change in psychology until well into the twentieth century (Day & Zaccaro, 2007). The emphasis in the United States on measuring individual differences and using paper-and-pencil tests was in contrast with European industrial psychologists, who used either standard psychological

laboratory apparatus, or modified versions of that apparatus, for various applications (see van Drunen, 1997). They were concerned with a broad range of factors that could influence the efficiency of workers, such as methods of work, training, effects of rest periods and working conditions on productivity, monotony and fatigue, selection, and human relations (Baritz, 1960; Myers, 1929). An early laboratory of work psychology was founded in 1889 by L. O. Patrizi in Modena, Italy (deWolff & Shimmin, 1976). Pioneering French sociologist Emile Durkheim (1895) noted that a group is more than the sum of individual group members (Salas, Priest, Stagl, Sims, & Burke, 2007), a precursor of the science and practice of teams in the workplace.

1900 to 1914
Contextual Background

As noted previously, at the turn of the century, rapid changes ensued, including industrialization, immigration, high birth rate, education reform, urban growth, and technology changes. Hilgard (1987) noted that many changes occurred in the United States society during this time, as it "moved from an essentially agrarian society before the Civil War to the modern, urban industrial society..." (p. 700). To manage such change, the generation of Americans known as Progressives wanted to make American society a better and safer place to live and work; to do so, they sought to rationalize society and rebuild the social order. A Progressive drive for reform prevailed (Minton, 1988). Examples of such rational approaches included the standardization of goods and measures and the creation of new bureaucratic structures (e.g., the U.S. Food and Drug Administration) to ensure orderly change (Haber, 1964). This search for a new social order created a demand for new forms of expertise, that is, specific knowledge-based disciplinary experts such as political scientists, sociologists, and psychologists (Minton, 1988). Americans were ready for the practical and useful, and society looked toward science for practical solutions. Technological advancements led to a focus on workplace efficiency. In addition, as Zickar and Gibby (2007) stated, "The public turned to populist politicians...to reduce social problems, to reduce the power of business monopolies and trusts, and to reduce corruption in government. One of the main targets of the progressives was the world of work" (p. 62). Kraiger and Ford (2007) noted that moving from craft to mass production resulted in major work design and control changes.

Zickar and Gibby (2007) observed that the intellectual climate was an exciting time for science generally and psychology specifically. Intellectual debates continued about schools of thought, such as James's functionalism, Freud's psychodynamism, and Wundt's and Titchener's structuralism. American functional psychology was formalized at the University of Chicago and Columbia University. In 1913, Watson published his behaviorist manifesto, *Psychology as the Behaviorist Views It*.

Within the discipline of psychology, institutional pressures to justify psychology departments and resources encouraged psychologists to popularize their science and to demonstrate the value of psychology in solving problems and helping society (Burnham, 1987; Goodwin, 1999). Taking psychology outside academic laboratories and increasing psychological research on practical applications in education, medicine, business, and industry were expressions of psychologists' intense desire for social recognition and support (Camfield, 1973). Although some psychologists opposed the application of psychology during this time, other proponents of applied research viewed that the development of an applied psychology offered "the hope of seeing greater socio-economic values placed upon the science in American community life" (Camfield, 1973, p. 75).

Measurement and quantification continued to be emphasized in psychology. Cattell's anthropomorphic measures of physiological and sensory characteristics proved inadequate for predicting achievement, as illustrated by his student Clark Wissler's (1901) failure to find relationships between these measures and academic performance.[5] These anthropometric measures were being replaced by cognitive tests by around 1910 (Sokal, 1984). In 1903 Binet laid the foundation for the Binet-Simon intelligence test with the publication of his *Étude experimentale de l'intelligence* (Fryer & Henry, 1950). The Binet scale was translated in America in 1908 by Henry Herbert Goddard working at the Vineland Training School; and early roots of test validation were proposed by Binet and Simon as early as 1905 (Benjamin, n.d.). Spearman introduced factor analysis in 1904 and first used the term *reliability coefficient* in 1907 (DuBois, 1970). In addition, around this time it was becoming standard to evaluate the predictive accuracy of a test by its correlation with a measure or standard of success, which later became known as the *validity* of

the test (Rogers, 1995). An early example of the use of this method was Meriam (1906), who correlated elementary schoolteacher normal school grades and city examination results with superintendent and principal ratings.

STUDYING WORK IN ORGANIZATIONS: SCIENTIFIC MANAGEMENT

The timing was right in America for industrial engineer Frederick Winslow Taylor's new systematic management approach, known as scientific management. His ideas meshed with the prevalent Progressivism, and his rational approach addressed the prevailing business objectives of efficiency, productivity, and costs. Taylor, working as a manager, became interested in how to influence workers to be productive. He developed and/or recommended several procedures for increasing production, including the improvement of work methods and the provision of effective tools (Taylor, 1911). Taylor argued that his approach was "scientific" because he emphasized the use of the scientific method and empirical measurements to evaluate the effects of changes. In addition to Taylor, Frank and Lillian Gilbreth, also known as scientific management experts, used time and motion studies to investigate and design

Figure 2.2 Lillian Moller Gilbreth. Courtesy of Purdue University Libraries, Karnes Archives & Special Collections.

work to improve efficiency. In 1915, Lillian Moller Gilbreth (1878–1972), a psychologist, was one of the first individuals to complete an industrial psychology–themed doctoral dissertation on the application of psychology to the work of classroom teachers (Koppes, 1997).[6]

Although American psychologists initially embraced Taylor's ideas, his program eventually came under scrutiny for neglecting human welfare and the worker's well-being (Baritz, 1960; Viteles, 1932). Viteles (1932) even argued that "Taylor contributed little to the theory and procedures of psychology as applied in industry" (p. 16). The primary importance of Taylor's and the Gilbreths' work, however, was a foundation for the scientific investigation of work behavior and the establishment of a precedent for scientists to enter organizations to carry out such investigations. Their work also set an economic criterion for industrial psychology (Viteles, 1932). Scientific management influenced the development of human factors (also known as ergonomics), which was considered to be part of early industrial psychology.

AN INDUSTRIAL PSYCHOLOGY:
PERIOD OF GENESIS

The first 15 years of the twentieth century was a time when industrial psychology began to come into its own, both in the United States and abroad. From the previous discussion, one can surmise that an applied psychology reflected Americans' demand for a "useful" science, such as psychology (James, 1892), indicative of the Progressive Era. The study of work was part of the desire to place all life on an orderly and scientific basis. Early psychologists advocated that psychology could improve business and operations and argued that the results of industrial psychology would benefit workers as well as employers. In 1913, Hugo Münsterberg stated, "Our aim is to sketch the outlines of a new psychology which is to intermediate between the modern laboratory psychology and the problems of economics: the psychological experiment is systematically placed at the service of commerce and industry" (Münsterberg, 1913, p. 3). Later, Viteles (1932) stated "Industry can expect a definite return from an investigation and analysis of human behavior" (p. 18).

The application of psychology to advertising and marketing continued in the United States in the early 1900s by Columbia University Ph.D. Harry Levi Hollingworth (1880–1956), whose 1911 investigation of the behavioral effects of caffeine in Coca-Cola led to an extensive career in consulting

(Benjamin, 1996); and University of Iowa Ph.D. Daniel Starch (1883–1979), who published *Principles of Advertising: A Systematic Syllabus* in 1910 and four years later *Advertising, Its Principles, Practice, and Technique* (1914), which established him as a leader in the new field (Schumann & Davidson, 2007). Advertising was also Walter Dill Scott's entrée into applied work. Scott's contributions went well beyond advertising, however. Along with Hugo Münsterberg, Scott can legitimately be considered a founder of the field (Ferguson, 1962–1965; Hilgard, 1987).

Scott (1869–1955) received his doctorate with Wundt at Leipzig. In 1901, while working as a professor at Northwestern University, he was contacted by advertising manager Thomas L. Balmer to give a talk at Chicago's Agate Club on how psychology could be useful in advertising. Scott was reluctant, mindful of the stigma attached to applied work by academic psychologists and aware that Münsterberg, E. L. Thorndike, and Northwestern's George A. Coe had already turned Balmer down. Scott did eventually agree to give the talk, and subsequently published two books on advertising: *Theory of Advertising* (1903) and *The Psychology of Advertising* (1908). Scott subsequently broadened his scope to publish *Increasing Human Efficiency in Business* (1911), which Hilgard (1987) saw "...as the beginning of serious industrial psychology in

Figure 2.3 Walter Dill Scott.

America" (p. 703). Scott's subsequent contributions to industrial psychology, discussed in the next section, include his work at the Carnegie Institute of Technology's (CIT) Division of Applied Psychology, his leadership role in applying industrial psychology in World War I, and his founding of the first industrial psychology consulting firm, the Scott Company, in 1919. Scott's career as an industrial psychologist effectively ended in 1920, when he was appointed president of Northwestern University, a position he held until 1939 (Jacobson, 1951).

The other major figure in the genesis of industrial psychology is Hugo Münsterberg (1863–1916). Initially quite hostile toward applied psychology (Benjamin, 2000), he came to embrace application and made notable contributions not only to industrial psychology, but also to educational, forensic, and clinical psychology. Following a doctorate with Wundt in 1885 and an M.D. degree in 1887 from the University of Heidelberg, Münsterberg taught at the University of Freiburg until 1892, when William James recruited him for Harvard University. In 1909 he published an article in *McClure's Magazine* on psychology and business, which led to the consulting opportunities that formed the basis for his landmark book *Psychology and Industrial Efficiency* (1913; published in German in 1912; Benjamin, 2000). Münsterberg's vision for industrial psychology delineated in this book has proven to be very influential.[7]

Figure 2.4 Hugo Münsterberg.

Notable was Münsterberg's (1913) work on selecting streetcar motormen, ship officers, and telephone operators. In the latter case, the skeptical phone company embedded experienced operators in the trainee pool without Münsterberg's knowledge; fortunately for Münsterberg, these workers tested at the top of the list. Other developments include the first record of a job analysis in the United States at the Dennison Manufacturing Company in 1914 (Wilson, 2007). In Germany, William Stern (1871–1938), a pioneer in differential psychology, had anticipated much of Münterberg's work by 1900 (Hale, 1980). Along with Otto Lipmann (1880–1933), Stern founded *Zeitschrift für angewandte Psychologie* (Journal for Applied Psychology) in 1907 (Viteles, 1932).[8] A year earlier, Lipmann founded and financially supported the Institute of Applied Psychology in Berlin (Stern, 1934). He developed the first selection tests for aviators in Germany, worked on selection tests for industrial apprentices, telegraphers, and typesetters, and introduced vocational guidance to that country (Baumgarten, 1934). Other early work on employee selection took place in Italy, where in 1901 Uzo Pizzoli used tests to select apprentices (Salgado, 2001) and in France, where Jean Marie Lahy selected stenographers by 1905 (Viteles, 1923) and streetcar drivers by 1908 (Fryer & Henry, 1950).

While selection was the predominant activity for industrial psychologists, there was activity in other areas. Selection's mirror image, vocational counseling, or finding the best job for the individual, was pioneered in the 1909 book by Boston University law professor Frank Parsons, although that field can trace its roots to earlier counseling work done after the Civil War by the Young Men's Christian Association (Savickas & Baker, 2005).[9] In Cincinnati in 1914, H. L. Wooley founded the first vocational guidance bureau in a public school system (Fryer & Henry, 1950). In the area of training, businesses began to move from apprenticeship programs to their own factory schools (Kraiger & Ford, 2007). American Steel and Wire Company's formal training program, for example, was instituted in 1912 (Baritz, 1960). Münsterberg (1913) began to go beyond scientific management's emphasis on monetary incentives to look at other factors such as "mental monotony," that could affect worker performance.

The genesis of an industrial psychology was observed during this time period. By 1915, both scientists and practitioners had discovered ways to apply psychology to address issues in the workplace, which set the stage for establishing the discipline in the next several years.

1915 to 1919
Contextual Background

The Progressive Era and the Industrial Revolution continued; the appearance of capitalism and an emphasis on efficiency forced companies to determine how to hire the most qualified employees. Also, a developing specialization of the labor market required a system in which individual differences in ability could be identified (Minton, 1988). Psychology's popularity increased, and many individuals not trained in psychology began practicing to gain financial rewards. Consequently, skepticism about the legitimacy of psychology as a science surfaced. Images of psychology as common sense or as occultism and superstition and society's stereotype of the psychologist as an "absent-minded professor, preoccupied with abstruse manners" (Burnham, 1987, p. 92) were widespread in American society. Psychologists were compelled to legitimize their science and to address society's skepticism of the profession by placing great emphasis on empirical methods. A response was to use experimentation to invalidate the claims of pseudo-scientists, including the use of case studies, laboratory experiments, and quasi-experiments. Other developments included Lewis Terman's version of the Binet scale: the Stanford-Binet in 1917 (Benjamin, n.d.). To further the professionalization of the discipline, the Society for Applied Psychology and the Economic Psychology Association were formed in 1915 (Benjamin, n.d.).

When the United States declared war on Germany in 1917, an occasion appeared for psychologists to further demonstrate psychology's value to society (e.g., Capshew, 1999). Consequently, the war was a significant impetus for an applied psychology, particularly mental testing and abnormal psychology. G. Stanley Hall first suggested the use of psychology in the military in 1916 while addressing a joint session of the APA and the American Association for the Advancement of Science (Hergenhahn, 1997). Then a group of psychologists led by Robert M. Yerkes (then president of APA) and others (from the National Academy of Sciences, the American Association for the Advancement of Science, and the APA) formed the Psychology Committee of the National Resource Council to evaluate a psychological examining program for recruits (von Mayrhauser, 1987). At the same time, W. D. Scott and W. V. Bingham, faculty at Carnegie Institute

of Technology (CIT), formed the Committee on Classification and Personnel to aid the army in the selection of officers (von Mayrhauser, 1987). Douglas Fryer worked with a small program in the Morale Branch of the Surgeon General's Office to ease the adjustment of soldiers to army life, and psychologists were stationed at 40 army hospitals during the war. Activities relevant to industrial psychology during the war are discussed in the next section.

INDUSTRIAL PSYCHOLOGY: PERIOD OF ESTABLISHMENT

Two events occurred in the five-year period from 1915 through 1919 that were of signal importance for the establishment of an industrial psychology. The first was the formation of the first graduate program in industrial psychology, the Division of Applied Psychology, at CIT. The second was psychologists' participation in the World War I war effort, particularly in Great Britain, Germany, and the United States. In this period, significant progress was made in establishing industrial psychology as a recognizable subfield of psychology, viewed by managers and the military as having at least the potential to be useful.

What eventually became the Division of Applied Psychology (DAP)[10] was the brainchild of CIT president Arthur A. Hamerschlag, who initially recruited Dartmouth professor Walter Van Dyke Bingham to write a report on the benefits that psychology might provide for the young Pittsburgh institution. Impressed by Bingham's ideas, Hamerschlag offered him an appointment at CIT; Bingham accepted and began work as DAP director in 1915. The DAP included the Bureau of Salesmanship Research, a cooperative venture between CIT and a number of Pittsburgh businessmen, who provided financial support. Walter Dill Scott, on leave from Northwestern, served as director of that bureau and also became the first person in the United States with the title of professor of applied psychology. Scott and his colleagues did pioneering work in employee selection on such procedures as interviews, application blanks, and various tests. Other DAP divisions included the Bureau of Retail Training, which conducted attitude research, and the Bureau of Personnel Research, which focused on vocational guidance (Ferguson, 1962–1965).

Walter Van Dyke Bingham (1880–1952) received his Ph.D. from the University of Chicago in 1908, where he was exposed to the functionalist orientation of that psychology department. After a trip to Europe

Figure 2.5 Walter Van Dyke Bingham. Courtesy of the Archives of the History of American Psychology, the University of Akron.

where he met psychologists prominent in Gestalt psychology (e.g., Kurt Koffka and Wolfgang Köhler), quantitative methods (e.g., Charles Spearman and Cyril Burt), and industrial psychology (e.g., Charles S. Myers), Bingham completed a philosophy minor at Harvard with William James. While at Harvard he became acquainted with Münsterberg (Bingham, 1952). Bingham was prominent among the contingent of psychologists who contributed his services in World War I, as discussed below. Following the war, he returned to CIT until that program's early demise in 1924.[11] Highlights of Bingham's subsequent career include serving as director of the Personnel Research Federation, founding and editing the *Journal of Personnel Research*, and serving as Chief Psychologist in the war department's Adjutant General's Office during World War II.

Despite its short lifespan, there are a number of reasons that the CIT program was so important in the development of industrial psychology. Although only four students received doctorates from the program,[12] the DAP was the first graduate program to focus on industrial psychology. It provided a model for cooperation between business and academia, providing training and research to companies that contributed to its coffers. The program was an incubator for industrial psychology talent; many of the students and staff associated with the

program went on to make important contributions to industrial psychology. In addition to Bingham and Scott, a partial list includes Marion A. Bills, Max Freyd, Arthur W. Kornhauser, Grace Manson, Bruce V. Moore, James B. Miner, Beardsley Ruml, Edward K. Strong, Jr., Louis Leon Thurstone, Guy Montrose Whipple, and Clarence Stone Yoakum.[13] Marion A. Bills (1890–1970), for example, was an early female applied psychologist who had a highly successful career after working at DAP with Bingham. She worked for several years at Aetna Life Insurance Company, where her studies were considered to be at the forefront of selection research. She conducted long-term research on selection and retention of clerical and sales personnel for the life insurance industry, which was viewed as one of the first cooperative partnerships between managers and psychologists (Ferguson, 1952; Koppes & Bauer, 2006; Vinchur & Koppes, 2007).

There was also the innovative work produced by these individuals while at CIT, as illustrated by a few examples. Early work on the measurement of vocational interests was done by Yoakum's doctoral students, Moore, Manson, Freyd, and M. J. Ream—work that Strong, after moving to Stanford University and in collaboration with Karl Cowdery, developed into the well-known Strong Vocational

Figure 2.6 Marion A. Bills . Photo courtesy of Bentley Historical Library, University of Michigan.

Interest Blank. Scott and his colleagues' work on employee selection procedures such as biographical data, various tests, and rating scales, including Scott's man-to-man rating system (Ferguson, 1961), were later adapted for military use in World War I.

Bingham, Scott, and a number of other individuals associated with the CIT program offered their services to the military. Scott vehemently disagreed with the approach advocated by APA president Robert Yerkes, who proposed putting psychology's efforts into developing standardized group intelligence tests. Scott favored using the techniques developed at CIT for selection and classification. Each went his own way; Yerkes' group, working under the Surgeon General, developed the Army Alpha and Beta tests, group intelligence tests appropriate for literate and illiterate individuals, respectively. These tests were eventually given to over 1.7 million recruits (Ferguson, 1962–1965). Despite the army's tepid response to the tests, the effort was deemed a great success by Yerkes and the general public, fueling a postwar boom in psychological testing. One unfortunate consequence of the Army Alpha and Beta testing program was the misinterpretation of group differences in test results by Brigham (1923) and others as evidence that these differences were solely due to hereditary factors (see Samuelson, 1977).

Scott and Bingham, working under the Adjutant General, established the Committee on Classification of Personnel to adapt and apply the selection procedures pioneered in the DAP to the military. Their efforts were successful. They adapted rating scales, developed indices of occupations and occupational needs, and developed trade specifications. Approximately 130,000 soldiers received the standardized trade tests developed by the Committee (Bingham, 1919; Strong, 1918). For his efforts, Scott was the only psychologist awarded the Distinguished Service Medal, and in 1919, he was elected president of APA. In February of that year Scott, along with Robert Clothier, Joseph W. Hayes, L. B. Hopkins, Stanley B. Mathewson, and Beardsley Ruml, founded the Scott Company, the first personnel consulting organization. The company took a broader approach to staffing than was common at the time, advocating an approach, developed by Ruml, of looking at both the worker and the job as a unit, each able to change in response to the other. One notable achievement of the Scott Company Laboratory was the graphic rating scale, which replaced Scott's man-to-man rating scale (Freyd, 1923). Another achievement of note was the

employment of one of the first female applied psychologists, Mary Holmes Stevens Hayes. Despite its success, the Scott Company only lasted a few years, possibly due to turnover, as its employees found other opportunities (Katzell & Austin, 1992), and/or a recession in 1921–1922 (Ferguson, 1961).

The war spurred industrial activity in other countries as well. German psychologists were involved in aptitude testing for radio operators, pilots, and drivers (Sprung & Sprung, 2001). Great Britain saw selection research for submarine detection operators, most notably by Charles S. Myers, who would become that country's preeminent industrial psychologist. In 1915 the Health of Munitions Workers Committee, an organization that trained a number of future industrial psychologists (McCollom, 1968), was created, and in 1918, the Industrial Fatigue Research Board (later, in 1927, the Industrial Health Research Board) was established. During World War I, Lahy and his colleagues in France were involved with the selection and training of armed forces (Warr, 2007).

Other notable developments in this time period include a series of lectures on industrial psychology delivered in Sydney, Australia, in 1916 by Bernard Muscio and published in 1917 (Hearnshaw, 1964). In the United States, the *Journal of Applied Psychology*, an outlet for a great deal of industrial psychology research, began publication in 1917 by G. Stanley Hall, and in 1918 Geissler published an article in that journal on training for consulting psychologists. Henry Link, believed to be the first full-time Ph.D.-level psychologist in industry, was the director of Training and Psychological Research at the Winchester Repeating Arms Company in 1917. He introduced a portable testing lab at Winchester that same year (Fryer & Henry, 1950). R. H. Macy and Company in New York hired Elsie Oschrin Bregman in 1919, who, with Mary H. S. Hayes was one of the first female applied psychologists. In the same year, the Life Insurance Sales Research Bureau (LISRB) was founded. Notable publications during this period included *Vocational Psychology* (Hollingworth, 1916), *Aids in the Selection of Salesmen* (Scott, 1916; cited in Ferguson, 1962–1965), *Applied Psychology* (Hollingworth & Poffenberger, 1917) and *Employment Psychology* (Link, 1919). In Germany, Curt Piorkowski and Walter Moede began publication of the psychotechnics journal *Praktiske Psychologie* (Salgado, 2001). During World War I, the United States Shipping Board introduced an early training model: the four-step method of instruction of "show-tell-do-check" (Kraiger & Ford, 2007). Lahy continued as an important contributor to the development of work psychology in France. During this period, he was involved with the establishment of l'Institute d'Orientation Professionnelle for vocational guidance, and the creation of psychology departments in the Puegeot and Renault automotive companies, as well as in the Paris transportation system and the French railways (Warr, 2007).

Psychologists in general, including industrial psychologists, were establishing a professional identity during this period. The perceived success of psychologist's efforts in World War I, particularly in testing and selection, was a key in establishing industrial psychology's bona fides in the public eye.

1920 to 1939
Contextual Background

After World War I, euphoria and prosperity swept the United States. Despite a short recession in 1921–1922, the gross national product rose 39% between 1919 and 1929 (Cashman, 1989), which resulted in a growth of employment that provided opportunities for industrial psychologists as full-time employees or consultants in industry (Arthur & Benjamin, 1999; Katzell & Austin, 1992). Corporate leaders were primarily concerned with finding the right employee for the job. They became interested in the psychological applications used during the war (e.g., in selection and placement) and, consequently, research on these personnel issues in organizations flourished during the early to mid-1920s (e.g., Bregman, 1922; Pond, 1927). Businesses also created personnel departments to centralize hiring and job placement activities, and employment management as a discipline grew.

Viteles (1932) noted a shift in the social philosophy of workers from the first part of the twentieth century through the 1920s, from a policy of noninterference to one that emphasized employees' welfare. The latter policy was reinforced during the economic depression, when 25% of the workforce was unemployed (Manchester, 1973–1974). The depression's adverse effects on individuals led to heightened sensitivity to and concern for the human condition and the humanization of work; social issues such as unemployment and adjustment of workers became prevalent. Because the greatest need was to find jobs for people to fill, there was less interest in personnel selection and training.

During the Great Depression, the U.S. government under Franklin Roosevelt strengthened its influence by creating New Deal legislation and programs to help the downtrodden employee. The U.S. Employment Service (USES), founded in 1917, was renewed with the Wagner-Peyser Act of 1933 (Lowenberg & Conrad, 1998). The USES tried to eliminate the large gaps between the unemployed and limited job opportunities. The USES is known for developing the General Aptitude Test Battery (GATB) and completing the first large-scale systematic analysis of jobs, the *Dictionary of Occupational Titles*, published in 1939 (United States Employment Service, 1939). Other Federal legislation during this period generated funding for public training in handicrafts such as leatherwork, weaving, and chair caning. Furthermore, Roosevelt's reform programs provided a favorable climate for organized labor; thus, corporate America had to respond to new labor laws and the growing muscle of unions. In 1935, the National Labor Relations Act (Wagner Act) was passed, which was the first law to give workers the right to collective bargaining. Then, in 1938, The Fair Labor Standards Act was passed, which identified those jobs that were exempt versus those jobs that were not exempt from working hour requirements and overtime, based on work activities.

During the 1920s, several changes were observed in the discipline of psychology. Structuralism disappeared after the death of Titchener in 1927; behaviorism became a dominant system of psychology. Debates ensued over nature-nurture, and Gestalt psychology ideas crossed the Atlantic. The APA established a certification program for consulting psychologists, and in 1924, G. Allport published his text, *Social Psychology*. This was a decade of great public popularity for psychology, and the first popular psychology magazines were published, including one on industrial psychology titled *Industrial Psychology Monthly*.

In contrast to the 1920s, psychology's public popularity was at a low point in the 1930s. Social psychology, child psychology, and behaviorism became prevalent, while grand theories of personality (Allport, Murray) and neobehaviorism (Tolman, Hull, Guthrie, Skinner) were introduced (Benjamin, n.d.). Attitude measurement was refined by L. L. Thurstone and Rensis Likert. The Psychometric Society was formed in 1935 and the Society for the Psychological Study of Social Issues was established in 1936. Due to dissatisfaction by applied psychologists with the APA's emphasis on academic psychology, in 1930 the New York State Association of Consulting Psychologists (founded in 1921) went national as the Association of Consulting Psychologists (ACP), under the leadership of Douglas Fryer. Again under Fryer, in 1937 a new national organization, the American Association of Applied Psychology (AAAP), was formed. Clinical, consulting, educational, and industrial and business (Section D) psychology were the four sections of AAAP (Benjamin, 1997a), with Harold Burtt as the first president of Section D. The *Journal of Consulting Psychology* (1937) was introduced during this decade.

Between 1916 and 1938, the number of APA members in teaching positions increased more than fivefold, from 233 to 1,299; however, the number of members in applied psychology positions grew even more dramatically, from 24 to 694 (Finch & Odoroff, 1939).

INDUSTRIAL PSYCHOLOGY: PERIOD OF DEVELOPMENT

This time period can be characterized as an expansion of applications used in the war, as well as further development of applications for other aspects of work. The early 1920s particularly were full of activity, including the publication of the *Journal of Personnel Research* (later *Personnel Journal*), an outlet for much industrial psychology research (e.g., Pond, 1927), founded by Bingham in 1922 (Hilgard, 1987). Behaviorism was a catalyst for conducting objective studies of behavior, developing practical applications, and including environmental or situational variables in theories of work behavior.

The perceived success of the Army group testing program in World War I precipitated a postwar boom in demand for these tests in industry and education. This surge was short-lived, however, with a decline evident by the mid-1920s. Possible reasons for this decline were the upturn in the economy and corresponding reduction in turnover (Hale, 1992), but the major factor was probably the overselling of the tests and the failure of testing to deliver on its promise (Hale, 1992; Sokal, 1984). As testing became something of a fad, there were unqualified individuals pushing tests, and a number of psychologists (e.g., Kornhauser & Kingsbury, 1924) urged caution. Industrial psychology, like psychology in general, needed to establish itself as a legitimate profession. In part, this was accomplished, according to Brown (1992), by appropriating metaphors from the more established disciplines of medicine and engineering to describe psychology. Industrial

psychologists also needed to separate themselves from purveyors of pseudoscientific selection procedures such as palmistry, phrenology, graphology, and physiognomy (the latter the use of physical characteristics such as hair color and face shape to determine personality characteristics and fitness for employment; see, for example, Blackford & Newcomb, 1914). Psychologists conducted empirical studies to refute these nonscientific procedures (see Cleeton & Knight, 1924; Dunlap, 1923; Kornhauser, 1922; Paterson & Ludgate, 1922–1923).[14]

By the early 1920s, tests were being evaluated using a strategy recognizable as today's *criterion-related validation* (Guion, 1976). The term *validity* to describe the procedure for evaluating the predictive capacity of a test was in common use (Rogers, 1995); and *criterion* was beginning to be used to mean a job standard (Austin & Villanova, 1992; Bingham, 1926; Burtt, 1926). Hull (1928) anticipated the concept of selection *utility* with his Index of Forecasting Efficiency (Taylor & Russell, 1939).

An important development for industrial psychology was the founding in 1920 of the International Association of Psychotechnics by Swiss psychologists Edward Claperáde and Pierre Bovet at a congress held in Geneva (Pickren & Fowler, 2003). In 1955 this association was renamed the International Association of Applied Psychology (IAAP; see Fleishman, 1979, 1992; Pickren & Fowler, 2003); it is now the largest international association of individual members, representing more than 80 countries and encompassing all fields of applied psychology.

In the United States, Cattell organized the Psychological Corporation in 1921.[15] Twenty influential psychologists were directors, and approximately 170 psychologists held stock. This consulting firm operated as a holding company for psychologists whose purpose was to advance psychology through research and "...the promotion of the useful applications of psychology" (Cattell, 1923, p. 165). According to Burnham (1987), the Psychological Corporation was created to popularize psychology, and the founders tried to set standards for an applied psychology. The corporation failed under Cattell's leadership, however. Although Cattell espoused the application of psychology, he had never himself been an applied psychologist. Consequently, he provided little direction to those who worked under him (Sokal, 1981). Sokal (1981) noted that both Cattell's ineffective leadership and the context in which the corporation existed explain the company's failure. While initially unprofitable, a reorganization by Paul S. Achilles and Bingham turned the Psychological Corporation around (Sokal, 1981).

The landmark group of studies in human relations, the iconic Hawthorne Studies, began in the 1920s. The Hawthorne Studies are a touchstone for many facets of organizational psychology and its more interdisciplinary cousin, organizational behavior. Work on group processes, motivation, job satisfaction, leadership, and other topic areas can all find some roots in these studies. For some (e.g., Roethlisberger, 1941) they appeared to augur a sea change in thinking about organizations, away from a mechanistic view of employees to greater concern with employee attitudes and feelings. Predictably, the more well-known these studies and their conclusions became, the more minutely they were examined, with an inevitable backlash that questioned the researchers' methods and conclusions (see, for example, Highhouse, 2007, and Landsberger, 1958). Despite criticisms that Hawthorne researchers failed to consider alternative hypotheses or drew conclusions beyond the scope of their findings, what endures is the belief of the primacy of employee motivation, attitudes, and group interactions.

While influenced by psychologists such as Münsterberg and Scott (Highhouse, 2007), the main researchers who conducted the studies at the Western Electric plant in Hawthorne, Illinois, were not themselves psychologists. The first studies (1924–1927) were supervised by C. E. Snow, who was head of the electrical engineering department at the Massachusetts Institute of Technology (MIT; cited in Highhouse, 2007). They were conducted by the Committee on Industrial Lighting of the gas and electric lighting industry, who wanted to demonstrate that better illumination would improve productivity and job satisfaction (Highhouse, 2007). No such simple relationship was demonstrated; productivity increased whether or not the illumination level increased, decreased, or stayed the same.

Intrigued by these results, in 1927 Hawthorne managers invited researchers from the Harvard Graduate School of Administration to the plant. Their initial study examined the effects of variation in breaks, day and week length, and wage incentives on monotony and fatigue on a small group of women who assembled telephone relays. Similar to the earlier illumination study, productivity increased, regardless of the variation used. Mayo[16] (1933) explained the increased productivity as the result of increased attention given to the women, the so-called *Hawthorne effect*. In a subsequent study,

a group of 14 men who wired telephone banks were examined. The observer noted that workers restricted output to a group norm, despite the fact that their pay was based on a financial incentive system. Violators of this socially imposed norm were subject to increasing aversive pressure from the group members, ranging from verbal and then physical harassment to social isolation (Vecchio, 1995). The researchers also conducted company-wide interviews (1928–1931) gauging employee attitudes on working conditions and in 1936 initiated a personnel counseling program that lasted until 1956 (Hilgard, 1987).

While the human relations message of the Hawthorne Studies proved very influential, it is important to note that concern for worker well-being by industrial psychologists predated these studies, particularly outside the United States. This was true in Germany, as illustrated by Otto Lipmann's emphasis on worker motivation and satisfaction (Hausmann, 1931; Viteles, 1932). This was also true in Great Britain in the early 1920s, where there was considerable emphasis on worker satisfaction (Myers, 1920) and criticism of scientific management (Farmer, 1958; Pear, 1948). Prominent among industrial psychologists in Great Britain was Charles S. Myers (1873–1946). Myers earned his A.B. (1895), A.M. (1900), M.D. (1901), and

Figure 2.7 Charles S. Myers. Courtesy of the London School of Economics and Political Science, National Institute of Industrial Psychology (NIIP) collection.

Sc.D. (1909) from Cambridge University, where he taught experimental psychology, directed the psychology laboratory, and authored the *Textbook in Experimental Psychology* (1909), for years the standard British text on the subject (Burt, 1947). He developed an interest in industrial psychology while serving as a consultant psychologist and psychiatrist to the British army in World War I, where he conducted selection research in addition to his duties treating shell shock (Myers, 1936). Finding Cambridge unsupportive of his new interests, with businessman H. J. Welch he founded the National Institute for Industrial Psychology (NIIP) in 1921 (Welch & Myers, 1932) and served as its director (1921–1930) and principal (1930–1938). Myers was the author of *Industrial Psychology* (1925) and *Industrial Psychology in Great Britain* (1926).

Moore and Hartmann (1931) noted that European countries, such as England and Germany, were further advanced than the United States in industrial psychology during the 1920s, and that U.S. psychology suffered from a lack of centers organized around various research objectives. In England, Germany, Russia, Czechoslovakia (the present-day Czech Republic and Slovakia), Italy, and Japan, centers or institutes were established to study work (Bringmann, Lück, Miller, & Early, 1997; Shimmin & van Strien, 1998; Viteles, 1932). For example, in 1920 the Institute for Vocational and Business Psychology in Berlin, the Central Institute of Labor in Moscow (Tagg, 1925), and the Psychotechnic Institute and Center for Vocational Counseling in Prague (Warr, 2007) were created. By 1926, 11 similar institutes existed in Czechoslovakia, and by 1931, the Central Institute of Labor had approximately 1,000 branches throughout Russia (Viteles, 1932, 1938). In 1920, a Psychological Institute was formed at the Sorbonne University by Henri Piéron. The purpose of this institute was to train psychologists to work in the areas of clinical, school, and work psychology (Warr, 2007). In 1921 the Division of Applied Psychology at Berlin University (Sprung & Sprung, 2001) was formed. The Kurashiki Institute of the Science of Labor in Japan (McCollom, 1968) was established in 1921, when psychotechnical investigations expanded after the war. In 1924 the Institute of Industrial Psychology in Zurich was formed (Heller, 1929–1930), and in 1927, the Australian Institute of Industrial Psychology was established (Warr, 2007). In Spain, psychotechnic centers were established in Madrid and Barcelona to focus on practical issues, such as rehabilitation of disabled workers, vocational guidance, and personnel selection. Psychology took root in Holland, with positions established in several universities (Warr, 2007).

Bingham (1929) observed that the United States was "relatively backward in certain essential respects" (p. 399) when compared to industrial nations in Europe. Furthermore, Viteles (1928) stated, "...That the European psychologist continues to preempt a major portion of the research field turned over to industrial engineers in this country [U.S.] is evidenced in the number of articles on motion study, on the effect of illumination, ventilation, and other conditions of work, on rest pauses, etc." (pp. 324–325).

Other activity relevant for industrial psychology included the development of analysis of variance in 1926; Viteles' (1923) introduction of the job psychograph as a job analysis method; automotive industry research at Ohio State; Strong's (1925) publication of *The Psychology of Selling and Advertising*; Paterson's 12 principles of psychological ratings in 1923; and Kornhauser's (1926–1927) reporting of three empirical studies of ratings and his discussion of the reliability of ratings, rater comparison, and comparison of ratings on different traits. Early work on the topic of leadership included a self-help book on leadership by Kleiser (1923); Mary Parker Follett's essay on leadership and participation in 1927; and an examination of leader qualities proposed by Craig and Charters (1925).

Throughout this time period, private organizations hired psychologists. For example, Harry Hepner was at the Kaufman Department Store, Ruml at Macy's, Marion Bills at Aetna, H. G. Kenagy at Procter & Gamble, and Sadie Myers Shellow at Milwaukee Electric Railway. By the end of the 1920s, approximately 50 full-time psychologists in industry were identified (Katzell & Austin, 1992). Psychologists with I/O interests were hired at universities, including Viteles at the University of Pennsylvania, Kingsbury at the University of Chicago, Paterson at the University of Minnesota, and Fryer at New York University. Universities that now offered industrial-oriented psychology doctorates included Ohio State University, the University of Minnesota, and Stanford University (Lowman, Kantor, & Perloff, 2007).

During the 1930s, industrial psychology underwent further development. For example, the Minnesota Employment Stabilization Research Institute was established in 1931. There a theory of worker adjustment was developed and occupational aptitude patterns were identified. The year 1932 saw the publication of *Industrial Psychology* by Morris S. Viteles (1898–1996). Viteles pulled together the various aspects of industrial psychology and provided a detailed treatment of methods and research results (Hilgard, 1987). Called the "Bible" by generations of students (Thompson, 1998), this text, in keeping with Viteles' lifelong international orientation, gave extensive coverage to research abroad as well as in the United States. The book was organized into three major sections. The first section covered economic, social, and psychological foundations of industrial psychology, along with the field's history and a discussion of individual differences. The second section focused on employee selection, job analysis, and various tests and procedures. The third, "Maintaining Fitness at Work," covered topics such as safety, training, fatigue, motivation, and supervision.

Viteles spent his entire academic career at the University of Pennsylvania, where he was an advocate for and an example of a scientist-practitioner. In addition to his academic career he consulted with and conducted research in industry (e.g., Viteles, 1925–1926). Among his accomplishments were the establishment of the first vocational guidance program based in a university (Thompson, 1998) and his pioneering job analysis work with the job

Figure 2.8 Morris S. Viteles.

psychograph. Viteles was a strong advocate of maintaining international relations in psychology. Early in his career he traveled throughout Europe, meeting with psychologists, including Lipmann and Stern in Germany, Lahy in France, and Myers in England. Viteles was the first American psychologist elected president of the International Association of Applied Psychology; he served a ten-year term from 1958 to 1968.

Katzell and Austin (1992) noted that more than 16% of the companies that had used personnel tests dropped them during the Great Depression. The emphasis on employee welfare during the Depression led to the development of personnel counseling as a popular organizational intervention for helping employees solve personal problems (Highhouse, 1999). Studies were conducted on employee attitudes such as job satisfaction (Hoppock, 1935) and morale, some at large corporations such as Kimberly-Clark and Procter & Gamble (Uhrbrock, 1934). Motivation research focused on attitudes (Latham & Budworth, 2007). In the late 1930s, organizational interventions were initiated by Kurt Lewin and his associates at the Harwood Pajama Factory (Coch & French, 1948). In leadership activity, O. Tead (1935) introduced ten desirable qualities of a leader. The increased awareness of employee welfare that resulted from the Hawthorne Studies was the genesis of a human relations movement. For example, Kraiger and Ford (2007) noted that this period was the beginning of a humanistic approach to training.

Additional noteworthy developments included the formation of the Academy of Management in 1936 and the offering of industrial-oriented degrees at Pennsylvania State College, Purdue University (home of the Occupational Research Center, first established as the Division of Educational and Applied Psychology), Columbia University, and the University of Pennsylvania (Lowman, Kantor, & Perloff, 2007). The KR-20 reliability coefficient was introduced by Kuder and Richardson in 1937. Lewin, Lippitt, and White (1939) published their comparison of democratic and authoritarian leadership. The National Research Council formed the Committee on Aviation Psychology in 1939. The Scanlon plan was introduced as part of the evolution of work teams (Salas et al., 2007).

In Germany the economy expanded during the early 1930s, primarily due to the buildup of armaments under National Socialist control. While psychology flourished, after 1933 selection decisions were influenced by ethnic background and preferences. According to Warr (2007), "Nearly a third of Germany's leading psychologists lost their jobs for political, racial, or religious reasons, and a substantial number left the country. However, many others remained and psychology as a discipline was encouraged" (p. 84). Psychologists worked for railway and other companies, as well as the military; training studies expanded; and psychometric applications became commonplace (Warr, 2007).

In Eastern European Countries, applied psychology research and practice were banned in 1936 by the Soviet government. As Warr (2007) explained: "Distinguishing between people on the basis of their psychological characteristics conflicted with Marxist ideology and the interests of the communist party..." (p. 85). This ban lasted until the end of the 1950s, and throughout this period, communication with Western psychologists was prohibited. In Spain, the Spanish Civil War (1936–1939) disrupted psychological research and practice, and many scientists left the country.

In 1932, Lahy published the journal *Le Travail Humain*, for which he served as editor in chief until his death (Warr, 2007). During these early years in France, work psychology focused on two primary areas. Numerous studies centered on sensation, vision, memory, and other processes, which spurred research on ergonomic issues. In addition, there was a focus on personnel issues, accidents, and working conditions. Although there was some early academic interest in I/O psychology in the 1920s, the first Chinese text in industrial psychology was published in 1935 (Wang, 1994). Studies focused on working conditions, as well as the traditional areas of personnel selection and vocational guidance.

By the end of the 1930s, industrial psychology in the United States and other countries had further developed through scientific studies and practical applications. This era saw the very early beginnings of an organizational psychology with the attention to human relations in the workplace.

1940 to 1959
Contextual Background

World War II was fought during this period. Immediately following World War II, the economy provided for prosperity, affluence, education, and a heightened awareness of the good life in the United States. This prosperity continued through the 1950s. The nation's manufacturing-based economy evolved into a service-based economy, changing the economic/business objective from efficiency to one of quality or customer service. By the late 1950s, more than 50% of the workforce consisted of service employees (Katzell & Austin, 1992). In addition, the economic and political division of the world along capitalist-communist lines, the emergence of the Soviet Union as a superpower, and the threat of nuclear war increased military spending (Dipboye, Smith, & Howell, 1994). The civil rights movement began in the United States when the separate-but-equal doctrine in education was struck down in the case of *Brown v. Board of Education* (1954).

These economic, political, and societal changes shaped a new generation of American workers who valued non-economic outcomes and personal rewards (satisfaction, personal growth, self-fulfillment, actualization, self-expression) instead of traditional bread-and-butter rewards (Katzell, 1958). Changing values and salient attention to discriminatory and unfair practices consequently led to societal unrest, which began to demand more equitable practices in organizations.

A tremendous growth of psychology was observed during these decades. Like World War I, World War II created an opportunity for psychologists to apply their techniques. The U.S. Army, in particular, sought the assistance of psychologists who were ready to be involved (e.g., Capshew, 1999). The National Research Council (NRC), a quasi-governmental agency that supported research for military applications, sponsored an Emergency Committee in Psychology to mobilize psychologists for the war effort (Samuelson, 1977). The purpose of this committee was to provide communication to the psychological community about opportunities for applied research and practice (Salas, DeRouin, & Gade, 2007). Psychologists performed exceptionally in areas of military equipment design, psychological warfare, conducting therapy, personnel selection, and training. As previously noted, after the war, the military increased its spending, and was especially interested in behavioral strategies to improve the effectiveness of the armed forces. Military research centers were established, such as the Personnel Research Section (PRS) of the Army Adjutant General's Office, which was the forerunner of the Army Research Institute, and the Air Force Personnel and Training Research Center (AFPTRC).

Behaviorism was peaking in experimental psychology with the efforts of B. F. Skinner (1953) but then began to decline as interest in modern cognitive psychology strengthened and provided a foundation for significant developments in years to come. Social psychology gained in prominence as interest in group processes, teams, and attitudes increased. Other areas of emphasis were human factors, physiological psychology, development across the lifespan, and statistics; new subfields that emerged included space psychology, psychopharmacology, and the use of computers (Benjamin, n.d.). The first professional school of psychology at Adelphi University was founded.

The APA reorganized by merging several groups (particularly AAAP).In 1945 a central office was established in Washington, D.C., and its flagship journal, *American Psychologist,* was introduced in 1946. The *Minnesota Multiphasic Personality Inventory* (*MMPI*) was published in 1942, and the 1949 Boulder Conference established the scientist-practitioner model of training for clinical psychologists. Moreover, as attention about the licensing of psychologists increased, APA published its first code of ethics, the *Ethical Principles of Psychologists* (American Psychological Association, 1953). Congressional hearings on civil rights led to publications dealing with standards of testing, including the *Technical Recommendations of Psychological Tests and Diagnostic Techniques* (American Psychological Association, 1954).

INDUSTRIAL PSYCHOLOGY: PERIOD OF EXPANSION

By the early 1940s, organizations were paying increasing attention to the importance of worker attitudes and motivation. Simultaneously, the role of the supervisor continued to evolve with the rise of a formalized personnel management function. Supervisors were no longer fully responsible for hiring workers, and they were not expected to have technical knowledge of all the jobs of their subordinates (Kraiger & Ford, 2007). I/O psychologists were highly engaged in various activities associated with the war, with an emphasis on the traditional areas of selection and training, including aptitude and intelligence tests (Harrell & Churchill, 1941). For example, the Army General Classification Test was developed for purposes of assessing cognitive abilities of military personnel in 1940 (Samuelson, 1977).

The U.S. Navy established a new branch of the Medical Corps for psychologists and other experts in 1940 to focus on test development. Specifically, in June 1942, the Applied Psychology Panel was formed to work on problems associated with selection and classification. By 1943, five new tests were administered at all the naval training stations, and by the end of the war more than 250 tests had been developed (Napoli, 1981).

The NRC received funding from the Civil Aeronautics Authority to conduct research on pilot selection, and subsequently, formed the Committee on Selection and Training of Aircraft Pilots (Capshew, 1999). From 1940 to 1947, this committee funded research projects to investigate the problems and difficulties with pilot selection and training. Particularly noteworthy was the NRC-funded project with the Medical Division of the Air Corps to form a psychological research agency. John C. Flanagan, who earned his Ph.D. in educational psychology from Harvard, was recruited to develop the Aviation Psychology Program for the U.S. Army Air Forces in 1941. This program investigated applied problems that were broad and varied and served as a foundation for future research and practice in I/O psychology. Examples included use of new types of tests, examination of methodological difficulties associated with test batteries, use of sophisticated statistical techniques to evaluate effectiveness of measures, and development of performance criteria (Salas, DeRouin, & Gade, 2007). One notable outcome was a test for classifying aircrew cadets, titled the Aviation Cadet Qualifying Examination (Capshew, 1999). This program employed over 150 psychologists, many with doctoral degrees, and many others (over 1,400) who had psychological training as assistants (Meyer, 2007; Most, 1993). Flanagan published 19 volumes describing the Aviation Psychology Program, also known as the "Blue Books" (Flanagan, 1948).

Another psychologically related activity within the military was the assessment of individuals who would be involved with covert operations, known as military operatives, of the Office of Strategic Services (OSS). Using methods created by British and German psychologists, Harvard psychologist Henry Murray joined the U.S. Army Medical Corps to develop assessment tools for selection and classification of intelligence agents. Specifically, Murray used "situational tests" in which prospective agents had to participate in realistic settings. Information about the selection of special agents can be found in the text *Assessment of Men* (United States Office of Strategic Services, 1948). These assessment tools were the forerunners of situational tests and assessment centers later used in the Central Intelligence Agency and corporations such as AT&T (described later) and Standard Oil Company (Bray & Grant, 1966; Highhouse, 2002; Murray & MacKinnon, 1946).[17]

As in the aftermath of World War I, techniques and methods used during World War II were further researched and extended to business, industry, and governmental agencies. When Flanagan resigned as a colonel in the Air Corps, he established the highly successful nonprofit organization American Institutes for Research (AIR) to conduct scientific research on human resources (Flanagan, 1984). Several I/O psychologists served on the board of directors and also spearheaded numerous research projects. In 1947, the General Aptitude Test Battery was released by the U.S. Department of Labor's Employment Service. This assessment instrument consisted of cognitive, perceptual, and psychomotor ability tests.

Applied research from the 1940s provided a basis for expanding and refining selection methods. During the 1950s, the interview, application blank, and biodata were popular selection procedures, with an increased use of tests for managerial selection (Hale, 1992). Cronbach (1951) introduced coefficient alpha for estimating reliability, and with Paul Meehl provided the conceptual foundation for construct validity (Cronbach & Meehl, 1955). Lawshe originated the concept of synthetic validity in 1952, which generated much discussion for companies who did not have enough workers to conduct criterion-related validation studies (Mossholder & Arvey, 1984). In the late 1950s, Campbell and Fiske (1959) offered the multitrait-multimethod matrix for establishing the construct validity of measures. The first large-scale factor analyses identifying abilities in the psychomotor performance domain were conducted (Fleishman, 1954), and Robert Thorndike's book on *Personnel Selection* was published in 1949.

The evaluation of criteria was emphasized in the 1940s and 1950s due to a heightened awareness by industrial psychologists of the difficulty in assessing these standards: the "criterion problem." Thorndike (1949) classified criteria into ultimate, intermediate, and immediate levels, and Flanagan (1954) published the critical incident technique to identify specific examples of successful and unsuccessful job performance. The concepts of criterion deficiency, contamination, and relevance generated a fair amount of interest (Austin & Villanova, 1992). Following from Taylor and Russell's (1939) work, Brogden introduced additional ideas about the economic utility of a selection test, and along with Taylor, introduced the Dollar Criterion in 1950 (Brogden & Taylor, 1950). Despite this increased interest in criteria, Wallace and Weitz (1955) stated

"The criterion problem continues to lead all other topics in lip service and trail most in terms of work reported" (p. 218).

The Bell System's Management Progress Study, begun in 1956 under the direction of Douglas Bray, was a milestone in demonstrating the value of an assessment center for managerial selection (Bray & Campbell, 1968; Bray & Grant, 1966). Various assessment techniques were used to assess candidates, including biodata, interviews, paper-and-pencil tests, and work simulations such as the in-basket test. A 30-year follow-up was published by Ann Howard and Bray in 1988, which contains details about this large-scale project (Howard & Bray, 1988).

Supervisor training for influencing and motivating employees emerged, as the role of the supervisor shifted to a more "human relations" approach (Kraiger & Ford, 2007). During the war years, the Training Within Industry (TWI) program was formed by the War Production Board of the U.S. government to implement training programs to over 2 million supervisors and training officers on topics such as job instruction, job relations, job methods, and job safety (Kraiger & Ford, 2007; Steinmetz, 1967). One of the first organizations to implement supervisor training was the International Harvester Company (Fleishman, Harris, & Burtt, 1955). Job rotation was introduced (Tiffin, 1942), and while on-the-job training continued to be the dominant training method, off-the-job training increased in popularity (Kraiger & Ford, 2007). By 1960, training methods included the use of human relationships training, case studies, role plays (Maier, 1952), simulators (Miller, 1953), sensitivity training (Highhouse, 2002), and televisions and films. A training profession began to surface when the American Society of Training Directors was established in 1945 (later known as American Society of Training and Development). The emphasis on supervisory training and the formalization of off-the-job training methods crystallized the need for trainers and the job of training specialist in the 1950s. Scant attention was given to needs assessment or evaluation until Mahler and Monroe discussed needs assessment in 1952. In 1959, Donald Kirkpatrick identified his four categories of training evaluation: the measurement of trainee reactions, learning, behavior back on the job, and results in light of organizational objectives.

In the area of performance appraisal, a new method was introduced in the mid-1940s. The forced choice rating procedure was intended to overcome problems with the existing rating system and to provide a foundation for personnel decisions in the U.S. Army (Sisson, 1948). This sparked a great deal of interest and research activity. Another contribution from World War II was the research that produced Wherry's Theory of Ratings in 1950 and 1952. Wherry introduced a mathematical model to specify the factors affecting a performance rating. Initially, Wherry's work had little impact because of its limited availability in a U.S. Army technical report. Thirty years later, at the encouragement of his graduate student C. J. Bartlett, Wherry published his now highly regarded theory (Wherry, 1983; Wherry & Bartlett, 1982).

This era saw the genesis of an organizational psychology; the shift from manufacturing to service created changes in organizational structure and the nature of work, raising awareness of organizational characteristics and their impact on employee attitudes and behaviors. A focus on workers' attitudes and motivations inspired researchers and practitioners to investigate topics other than those directly tied to bottom-line performance, including the effects of work on individuals, motivation, job satisfaction, leadership, and intergroup and intragroup relations. The emphasis was on both fitting people for the job and fitting the job for people (Katzell & Austin, 1992).

According to Latham and Budworth (2007), "The concept of motivation was now being explicitly discussed in the I-O literature" (p. 358). T. A. Ryan noted, along with Patricia Cain Smith, that motivation is the main issue of industrial psychology (Ryan & Smith, 1954). Viteles published his book *Motivation and Morale* (1953), which became a definitive textbook on motivation for the next 30 years. He postulated that motivation is equated with employee performance and morale. Attitude surveys became the focal point for studying motivation. Patricia Cain Smith published studies on the measurements of monotony and boredom in the workplace. Brayfield and Crockett's (1955) seminal article challenged the prevailing belief that motivation and job performance are linked to employee attitudes, such that "the worker who is highly productive is a worker who has positive attitudes toward the job" (cited in Latham & Budworth, 2007, p. 359). Brayfield and Crockett argued that little or no relationship existed between employee attitudes and performance.

Maslow's need hierarchy theory was introduced in 1943; this theory greatly influenced McGregor's formulation of Theory Y and Theory X, presented during a key speech in 1957. McGregor introduced these concepts to distinguish between an inappropriate view of employees as resistant and passive (Theory X) and, in his opinion, a correct view of employees as self-directed and responsible (Theory Y). With Theory Y, McGregor (1960) argued for a new kind of motivation that is based on the appropriate assumptions of human nature. McGregor (1960) referred to a book written in 1959 by Frederick Herzberg and colleagues (Herzberg, Mausner, & Snyderman, 1959). It was in this publication that Herzberg's two-factory theory, or motivation-hygiene theory, was introduced. This theory identified two types of needs, hygiene factors and motivators, as characteristics of the job. Herzberg et al. (1959) postulated that substandard hygiene factors (pay, benefits) leads to dissatisfaction, whereas motivators that make the job intrinsically interesting will lead to satisfaction and motivation. Argyris presented a similar view in his book *Personality and Organization: The Conflict Between the System and the Individual* (1957).

Although a few early publications discussed leadership (see Day & Zaccaro, 2007, for examples), the first industrial psychology text to devote one chapter to leadership was Blum's text in 1949. A shift in focus away from leader trait theory occurred in the 1940s after several authors criticized the trait approach (Bird, 1940; Gibb, 1947; Jenkins, 1947; Stogdill, 1948). A major program of the Personnel Research Board (PRB) at Ohio State University was the Ohio State Leadership Studies, which began in 1945 and aimed to shift research from a focus on leadership traits to identifying leadership behaviors. PRB was an interdisciplinary research group whose goal was to scientifically study organizational behavior for military, industry, and governmental organizations (Meyer, 2007). John Hemphill, using subordinate descriptions of leaders, first developed a Leader Behavior Description Questionnaire that listed 100 behaviors, scored on 10 dimensions. Additional data were collected and factors analyzed, resulting in the identification of two major underlying leadership dimensions: "consideration" and "initiating structure" (see Fleishman et al., 1955, for details about this research). This behavioral research shaped the direction and focus of future leadership research in several ways, including the development of questionnaires and assessment instruments, a focus on the leadership episode noting the importance of followers, and the inadequacy of the trait approach. A similar research program was implemented at the University of Michigan (Katz, Maccoby, & Morse, 1950).

Another shift occurred in the leadership research from investigating lower level leaders to considering executive leaders from a psychological viewpoint (Browne, 1951; Shartle, 1949). According to Day and Zaccaro (2007), the "real change in focus to examining middle and upper level leaders came about as a result of the AT&T studies of progression into middle management" (p. 385; described earlier in the chapter, and see Bray, Campbell, & Grant, 1974).

Several significant landmark events occurred during this era that greatly impacted the human relations movement and focus on groups and teams. In 1944, Kurt Lewin (1890–1947) formed the Research Center for Group Dynamics at the Massachusetts Institute of Technology (MIT; Salas et al., 2007). In their historical review of work teams, Salas et al. (2007) stated "Kurt Lewin's research has profoundly affected the domains of leadership, experiential learning, action research, and group dynamics" (p. 415). They further note that Lewin's center concentrated on group productivity, communication, social perception, intergroup relationships, group membership, and group leader training. After Lewin's death, in 1948 the Research Center joined the Michigan Survey Research Center, and the University of Michigan Institute for Social Research (ISR) was formed. ISR was originally established in 1946 as the Michigan Survey Research Center, following the discontinuation of the Division of

Program Survey, founded by Rensis Likert for the U.S. Department of Agriculture. Although not intended to be an I/O organization, a major component of the research was organizational behavior. Daniel Katz joined the group in 1947 and, along with Likert, initiated a research program in 1953 on organizational effectiveness called the Organization Behavior and Human Relations Program. In addition, during the 1950s, Likert formed relations with European research organizations, which led to collaborations with groups in Europe, Africa, Japan, and Australia (Meyer, 2007).

The National Training Laboratory for Group Development (NTL) was formed in 1947 to continue Lewin's work on using groups as a technique for communicating feelings and attitudes (Benne, 1964; Highhouse, 2007). Their work eventually led to the development of the *t-group*, "a method aimed at gaining personal insight by focusing on the immediate behavior of the group members" (Highhouse, 2007, p. 340). In another development from the late 1940s, Hemphill introduced 15 group dimensions, and their measurement scales, for the description and differentiation of numerous types of groups (Hemphill, 1949).

One outcome of World War II was the widespread exchange of resources on a global level. In 1946, the Rockefeller Foundation funded a grant that established the Tavistock Institute of Human Relations in London. Through the British army, several scholars (including psychologists, psychiatrists, and anthropologists) were brought together to conduct scientific research on health and well-being, conflict, self-regulating groups, and organizations as open, "socio-technical" systems (Trist, Emory, Murray, & Trist, 1997), emphasizing the social relationship aspects of psychoanalysis in this research (Warr, 2007). The Tavistock coal-mining studies (Trist & Bamforth, 1951) are the most famous examples of this research. They raised an awareness of the importance of building positive social relationships within teams, noted the dangers of focusing only on an engineering perspective, and led to research on group-based rather than individual work (Warr, 2007). The Tavistock researchers found that their conceptualization of a broad form of psychiatrically based social science did not mesh well with traditional academic frameworks; consequently, they established a new journal, *Human Relations*, in 1947 to communicate their ideas and findings (Warr, 2007).

Another important development in Great Britain was the establishment of the War Office Selection

Figure 2.9 Kurt Lewin

Board (WOSB). Initially developed for officer selection in 1942, it was later used in the British civil service as the Civil Service Selection Board, and then the procedures were further developed into assessment center techniques (Warr, 2007). In other developments in Great Britain, the Medical Research Council (MRC) supported psychological research through the formation of research centers. In 1944, the Unit for Research in Applied Psychology (later known at the Applied Psychology Unit, APU) was established at the University of Cambridge to advance science. Topics included skills and information processing, human-machine interface, noise and performance, and other important issues related to cognitive psychology. The Council also started the Industrial Psychology Research Unit, which operated between 1947 and 1969 in London, and the Unit for Research in Occupational Aspects of Ageing, which operated between 1955 and 1970 in Liverpool. In 1950, the professional category of Psychologist was established in the Civil Service of Great Britain (Warr, 2007).

Additional examples of the internationalization of I/O psychology include work done in Japan, where psychologists employed by the army and navy conducted studies on personnel selection and placement. Additional topics of interest included aptitude testing, vocational guidance, fatigue, accidents, human engineering, time and motion studies, and transportation issues (Warr, 2007). As in the United States, job satisfaction and motivation were researched in the 1940s and 1950s. In Australia, the Commonwealth Department of Labour and National Service was established to implement practices relating to labor policy, industrial training and welfare, and postwar rehabilitation (Bucklow, 1977). The Industrial Welfare Division, in particular, promoted the value of psychological applications to address various industrial problems (Cook, 1949). The State of Israel, established in 1948, needed industrial psychologists to help in developing a new labor force. In 1947, Louis Guttman established the behavioral unit of the military, which evolved into the Israel Institute of Applied Social Research. Guttman contributed to factor analysis, multidimensional scaling analysis, and Facet Theory (Warr, 2007). In 1957, the first department of psychology in Israel was founded at Hebrew University, and the Israel Psychological Association was formed.

Unlike these countries, Germany stopped industrial psychology activity around 1943, when institutions were destroyed and military psychology was cut back. When the country divided in 1949, academic psychologists within West Germany were primarily influenced by the work of contemporaries in the United States, whereas those psychologists in East Germany were largely influenced by work in the Soviet Union (Warr, 2007).

In the United States, several small research-oriented groups surfaced, based on personal contacts. An informal group of psychologists began meeting in 1947 at an APA meeting, known as the Psychologists Full-time in Industry. This group met each year for half-day meetings when APA met, and consisted of psychologists who were full-time members of personnel departments in organizations. According to Meyer (2007), "…for the first 10 or 15 postwar years, this group probably did stimulate a wider variety of I/O research and applications activities in industry than would have been the case without the structured exchange these annual meetings provided" (p. 161). Eventually, the group was phased out, as it became too large for volunteers to handle.

The Dearborn Conference Group first met in 1950 at an American Management Association meeting when personnel representatives from several companies met at the Dearborn Inn near Detroit. An organizing meeting was sponsored by Douglas McGregor, then president of Antioch College, and was held at the College in 1951. Discussions focused around challenges in companies, as well as general issues and problems related to human resource management. McGregor played an active role in the early years of these meetings. Some members believed that a concentrated discussion about worker productivity and morale may have contributed to McGregor's development of Theory X and Theory Y (Meyer, 2007). Additionally, a powerful conversation on challenges with performance-appraisal policies and programs may have led to McGregor's article titled "An Uneasy Look at Performance Appraisal," published in the *Harvard Business Review* (McGregor, 1957; Meyer, 2007). Shortly after the Dearborn Group was founded, another group was established in 1954 that restricted membership to I/O psychologists involved in personnel research of large companies. Because members could not reach consensus on a name, they agreed upon the "No-Name Group" (Meyer, 2007).

The expansion of industrial psychology was apparent through a variety of other activities, events, and developments. The AAAP Section D merged with APA; consequently, Division 14 was founded, with Bruce V. Moore (1891–1977) as the first president in 1946. The new Industrial and Business

Figure 2.10 Bruce V. Moore. Courtesy of Penn State University Archives, Pennsylvania State University Libraries.

Psychology Division consisted of 130 members. Research groups were created within private companies (e.g., General Electric, Standard Oil of New Jersey) and consulting firms were established, such as the Richardson, Bellows, Henry & Company and the Life Insurance Agency Management Association (LIAMA). LIAMA was a merging of Association of Life Agency Offices, founded in 1916, and the Life Insurance Sales Research Bureau, founded in 1919 (Meyer, 2007).

In 1948, Ghiselli and Brown published their seminal book *Personnel and Industrial Psychology*, and the journal *Personnel Psychology* began publication. Other important publications from the 1940s and 1950s were Marrow's *Group Dynamics in Industry* (1948)and *Overcoming Resistance to Change* by Coch and French (1948). The *Handbook of Applied Psychology*, edited by Fryer and Henry, was published in 1950, the *Administrative Science Quarterly* journal was first published in 1955, and March and Simon's influential text *Organizations* appeared in 1958.

The number of graduate programs in I/O psychology, including terminal master's degree programs, grew during this time period (Lowman et al., 2007). Moreover, the evolution toward a scientific focus in management education was initiated

by the publication of two reports sponsored by the Ford Foundation (Gordon & Howell, 1959) and Carnegie Foundation (Pierson, 1959), which would later prove to have significant implications for the employment of academic I/O psychologists. Further, in large part as a result of the exponential growth of military applications and research, the field of human factors or engineering psychology emerged as an entity distinct from I/O psychology. The APA Division 21, Society of Engineering Psychology, was created in 1956. In 1958, the Human Factors Society was formed and the *Human Factors* journal was first published.

The 1940s and 1950s allowed for a significant expansion of applications and research, which provided a foundation for the next several decades. In 1959, McCollom found at least 1000 psychologists who were employed full-time in industry in the United States (McCollom, 1959).

1960 to 1979
Contextual Background

In the United States, this era saw changes in societal values, enhanced attention to discriminatory and unfair practices, large numbers of "babyboomers" entering the workforce, increased international competition, and the assassinations of John and Robert Kennedy, Martin Luther King, and Malcolm X. According to Dipboye et al. (1994), the fabric of American society seemed to be breaking down. A new generation of employees emerged who questioned the authority of organizations, consequently creating increased interest in democracy and autonomy in the workplace. America's involvement in Vietnam and the Watergate scandal resulted in additional challenges to tradition and authority. The increase in Americans' levels of affluence and education after World War II carried over into these decades, which contributed to interest in work motivation, attitudes, and quality of work life as Americans sought new and better ways to find meaning and fulfillment (Katzell & Austin, 1992). Technological innovations that affected daily lives became more visible (e.g., video games, barcodes, the artificial heart).

The civil rights movement that had begun in the 1950s strengthened, leading to the passage of the Civil Rights Act (CRA) of 1964, Title VII, which prohibits employment discrimination based on race, color, religion, sex, or national origin. Other legislation during this time included the 1963 Equal Pay Act (EPA), and in 1967, the Age Discrimination in Employment Act (ADEA). Consequently, the social and legal emphasis was on ensuring that employers did not blatantly discriminate against minorities and women. For example, in the case of *Griggs v. Duke Power Co.* (1971), the Supreme Court ruled that selection tools must be job-related to minimize discrimination due to non-job-related factors. The federal government established the Equal Employment Opportunity Commission (EEOC), which, along with the Civil Service Commission and Departments of Justice and Labor, issued discrimination guidelines for employers in 1978 (*Uniform Guidelines on Employee Selection Procedures,* Equal Employment Opportunity Commission, 1978). In 1972, the CRA was amended to include educational institutions and state and federal agencies (Gutman, Koppes, & Vodanovich, 2011). Moreover, in 1971, the Occupational Safety and Health Administration (OSHA) was established to monitor safety in the workplace.

Flagging productivity, in conjunction with shifting societal views, motivated some American companies to rethink their methods of interacting with and managing employees. They examined their foreign competitors' successes and consequently changed from highly bureaucratic authoritarian structures to more open systems, and an emphasis was placed on how the organization could best serve the individual. Later in this time period, as worker alienation became a buzzword, greater concern was given to the impact of the workplace on employee mental health (Highhouse, 2007). In addition, under Presidents Nixon and Carter, the Department of Health, Education and Welfare transitioned from focusing on civil rights and community development to reform in the workplace (Highhouse, 2007; Kleiner, 1996). Organizations began to adopt more humanistic values as attitudes changed, so employees were no longer "just interchangeable cogs in the organizational wheel" (Salas et al., 2007, p. 421).

On the global front, many countries, especially in Eastern Europe, remained under a communist system and showed little advancement in I/O psychology. It is beyond the scope of this chapter to discuss communism in relation to I/O psychology; readers are referred to Warr (2007) and Roe (1995).

The cognitive revolution dramatically impacted the field of psychology. The journal *Cognitive Psychology* was first published in 1970. Humanistic psychology began, the behavior modification movement continued, and Albert Bandura introduced social learning theory in 1977. American psychologists discovered Piagetian ideas, especially in education (Benjamin, n.d.). The history of psychology became

a specialty field, and the Archives of the History of American Psychology (AHAP) was founded at the University of Akron in 1965.[18] In 1966, the first edition of the *Standards for Educational and Psychological Tests and Manuals* was published (APA, 1966). With the establishment of the American Association of State Psychology Boards in 1961, increased attention was placed on professional psychology. The majority of states passed laws for licensure of psychologists, a process completed in the 1970s. The issue of licensure for I/O psychologists has been one of controversy, both then and now. The journal *Professional Psychology* was created in 1969. Additionally, a debate over professional training models led to a Vail Conference in 1974 and the development of the doctorate of psychology (PsyD), which engendered subsequent growth of professional schools in many subfields, including I/O psychology.

As noted earlier, some organizations shifted from authoritative bureaucracies to open structures that allowed for participative management. Kraiger and Ford (2007) noted that Drucker's (1954) management by objectives (MBO), in which managers and employees negotiated performance objectives, grew in applications in the 1960s. Moreover, there was the widespread use of several participative management techniques (quality circles, self-directed work teams, total quality management) from Scandinavia and Japan. Katz and Kahn (1966) published their classic text about socio-technical systems and introduced organizational open systems theory.

INDUSTRIAL AND ORGANIZATIONAL PSYCHOLOGY: PERIOD OF MODERNIZATION

Throughout these two decades, industrial psychology evolved into the modern discipline of industrial *and* organizational psychology as we know it today. The previous work on organizational issues, begun in previous decades, continued and strengthened, and an emphasis was placed on theory construction and theory-related research on organizational psychology topics such as motivation, leadership, group/team development, and refinement of job attitude measurement. For example, organization development (OD) began as an attempt to better understand the process of group dynamics. The assumption that developing people would create healthier and more effective organizations changed to the assumption that developing organizations would create healthier and more effective people (Mirvis, 1988). The increased attention to worker well-being was apparent from a joint Division 13 and Division 14 symposium entitled "Humanizing Organizational Psychology," which was held several times during APA conventions in the early 1970s (Highhouse, 2007). These decades saw the beginning of a movement known as quality of work-life (QWL). Additionally, I/O psychologists well-trained in experimental methods turned to laboratory and field experiments to provide rigorous analysis of phenomena that had been identified in correlational and case studies (Latham & Budworth, 2007).

In 1962, "Business" was dropped from the APA Division 14 label, and it became APA Division 14 Industrial Psychology. Organizational psychology achieved recognition in industrial psychology when APA Division 14 changed its name to the Division of Industrial-Organizational Psychology in 1973. Schein and Bass published separate books on *Organizational Psychology* in 1965. In 1976 Marvin Dunnette edited the first *Handbook of Industrial and Organizational Psychology*, which captured the topics important in this time period.

Numerous theories were developed on the topic of work motivation, primarily resulting from Douglas McGregor's seminal book, *The Human Side of Enterprise*, in 1960. As we noted previously, in a 1957 speech McGregor introduced the idea that it was time to make human organizations effective through the application of the social sciences, which he reinforced in his book with a more thorough conceptualization of Theory X and Theory Y. McGregor was influenced by Herzberg's two-factor theory (Herzberg, Mausner, & Snyderman, 1959). Although heavily criticized in the 1960s (Vroom, 1964), Herzberg's theory raised awareness that the intrinsic nature of work could be enhanced through job enrichment. Later, another job enrichment theory was developed by Hackman and Oldham (1975, 1976), which took into account individual differences in relation to five job characteristics.

J. Stacey Adams proposed another motivation theory, equity theory, which was largely influenced by Festinger's 1957 cognitive dissonance theory. Adams postulated that workers examine the ratio of their outcomes (pay) relative to their inputs (effort, education, experience). If the ratio is unequal, then the person feels tension, which motivates the individual to react in one of several ways in order to reduce the inequity. Equity theory was criticized for a lack of precision (see Latham & Budworth, 2007), and psychologists shifted their attention to another new theory, expectancy theory. This theory is viewed as the "first cognitive, broad-range theory of motivation developed by an I/O psychologist"

(Latham & Budworth, 2007, p. 364) and was formally introduced by Victor Vroom in 1964. Based upon the work of Tolman and Lewis, Vroom theorized that the amount of effort exerted results from a person's expectancies, valences, choices, and instrumentalities. In other words, an employee will be motivated if she expects that her efforts will lead to performance, and her performance will lead to outcomes that she values. Additionally, B. Skinner's operant conditioning model was researched in organizational settings and evolved into a methodology called behavior modification in work settings (Luthans & Kreitner, 1975). This approach declined in popularity, however, and two additional theories took precedence: goal-setting theory and social learning or social cognitive theory.

Edwin Locke initially formulated the basic propositions of goal-setting theory while completing his doctoral dissertation (Locke, 1968); "...goals have the effect of directing attention and action (choice), mobilizing energy expenditure (effort), prolonging effort over time (persistence), and motivating the individual to develop relevant strategies (cognition) for goal attainment" (Latham & Budworth, 2007, p. 366; Locke, Shaw, Saari, & Latham, 1981). By the mid-1970s, two literature reviews were completed of the extensive empirical studies on goal setting (Latham & Yukl, 1975; Steers & Porter, 1974), and by the end of the twentieth century, goal setting was considered to be a practical and valid motivational technique (Latham & Budworth, 2007). In 1977, Albert Bandura, a social psychologist, published his social learning theory, which was renamed social cognitive theory, in the *Psychological Review*. This theory includes components from both cognitive and behaviorist views, such that behavior is a reciprocal function of environmental consequences, as well as an individual's conscious intentions or goals (Bandura, 2001).

Although studies of leadership behaviors based upon survey research from the 1950s continued, a shift occurred from a behavioral focus to a situational or contingency approach (Day & Zaccaro, 2007). In 1967, Fred Fiedler presented his contingency theory, which emphasized situational factors that affect leader effectiveness. Additional contingency theories developed during this time were the situational theory of leadership (Hersey & Blanchard, 1969), path-goal theory (House, 1971), and vertical dyad linkage theory (Graen, 1976). As noted by Day and Zaccaro (2007), "These theories dominated the discussion of leadership in the 1960s and 1970s" (p. 393) and "...were described and viewed as in contraposition to the classic trait models" (p. 393). In 1969, Hollander and Julian offered the idea that leadership perceptions are a key component of the leadership process. Almost a decade later, researchers followed up on this idea from a theoretical viewpoint. Relying on attribution theory as a framework for explaining leadership perceptions (Calder, 1977; Pfeffer, 1977), leadership was defined as "...a social construction of observers (followers) that is used to understand causal relations in social systems (i.e., make sense of the events taking place in the world)" (Day & Zaccaro, 2007, p. 394). Lord (1977) proposed an alternative approach to understanding leadership perceptions with a foundation in social cognitive theory and research, which was considered to be pioneering work (Day & Zaccaro, 2007). Toward the end of the 1970s, performance cue studies and implicit leadership theories (ILT) were introduced (Lord, Binning, Rush, & Thomas, 1978; Rush, Thomas, & Lord, 1977).

Salas et al. (2007) described notable research on teams and groups in the 1960s and 1970s. Examples include McGrath's (1964) introduction of the input, process, output (IPO) model, which advanced a framework for group and team effectiveness. The participative work practices that were emerging during this time period gave way to the use of work teams. Team researchers began to investigate the distinctions between teams and groups, and team characteristics and task characteristics (e.g., Briggs & Johnston, 1967, cited in Salas et al., 2007), as well as the formation of teams (Tuckman, 1965). For example, t-groups provided for team building, although this approach received considerable criticism in the 1970s (Salas et al., 2007). Moreover, quality circles, or process improvement groups, emerged from Japan's total quality control movement in 1962 (Glassop, 2002). The Crew Consortium Research Laboratory of the Air Force Personnel Research and Training Center in San Antonio was established to study group formation and functions, team performance, and team effectiveness. Janis (1972) introduced the concept of "groupthink" from his research on social conformity in groups. Salas et al. (2007) acknowledged the importance of technology on teamwork in the 1970s. Due to the complexity of ways in which work was completed, decisions were made, and employees communicated, teamwork was necessary to develop innovative solutions. Beginning in the 1970s and later, Salas et al. (2007) noted, "A wide range of [team] research was undertaken to investigate everything from sociopsychological constructs

to the deeper cognitions that permeate information processing in groups" (p. 421).

Advancements were made with the measurement of job satisfaction. For example, Smith, Kendall, and Hulin (1969) introduced the Job Descriptive Index (JDI) in their highly influential publication *The Measurement of Satisfaction in Work and Retirement*. The JDI measures satisfaction along five dimensions: type of work, pay, promotion opportunities, supervision, and coworkers, and continues to be used today as the "gold standard" for measuring job satisfaction (Balzer, Locke, & Zedeck, 2008). Also in 1969, Lofquist and Dawis introduced a theory of worker adjustment, which postulated that employees would like their work to fulfill their needs and wants. The Minnesota Satisfaction Questionnaire was developed from this theory, which measures 20 facets of satisfaction.

Highhouse (2007) described a number of interesting applications of organizational theory and research, including the reorganization of the U.S. State Department using t-groups as reported by Chris Argyris in 1967. Theory Y management was implemented in a reorganization of Non-Linear Systems, Inc., which Gray (1978) called one of the most noteworthy field experiments since the Hawthorne Studies. The "Topeka System" was implemented in a Gaines dog food plant as a strategy to reduce worker alienation, and consisted of self-managing work teams responsible for the production. Although the Topeka plant is frequently viewed as the prototype of humanized workplaces, Highhouse (2007) provides another perspective of the problems that surfaced with this and other landmark organizational interventions.

While organizational psychology increased in popularity throughout these decades, research and practice in the traditional areas of industrial psychology continued, primarily driven by employment legislation and case law. Supreme Court decisions in the 1970s greatly influenced the practice of personnel selection (e.g., *Griggs v. Duke Power*, 1971; *Albermarle v. Moody*, 1975; *Washington v. Davis*, 1976). Psychologists focused on ethnic and gender differences in the validity and fairness of employment tests, resulting in increased attention to methodology for conducting job analyses. Fine and Wiley (1971) introduced the Functional Job Analysis approach, and McCormick and colleagues introduced the Position Analysis Questionnaire in 1972 (McCormick, Jeanneret, & Meacham, 1972). McCormick also presented the first comprehensive book on job analysis in 1979.

In selection, Frank Schmidt and John Hunter (1977) found that validity is more generalizable than previously believed. Their validity generalization research resulted in their meta-analysis procedure, the standard operating procedure in selection research for evaluating predictors (Vinchur & Koppes, 2011). Selection interviews became routine for screening and selecting employees (Hakel, 1986). Behavior measures replaced output measures and personal traits, resulting in increased attention to criteria research (Austin & Villanova, 1992). Personality testing was heavily criticized in the late 1950s and early 1960s, both by the general public and within the profession. Guion and Gottier (1965) in a review noted that research on personality was flawed, and the common view subsequently was that personality tests were not valid or practical predictors. Work began on the theoretical underpinnings of selection instruments due to innovations such as structural equation modeling and item response theory (Hakel, 1986). Several professional standards and guidelines were published, as mentioned earlier, and Division 14 published the first edition of *Principles for the Validation and Use of Personnel Selection Procedures* in 1975. Additional books on selection were published during the 1960s and 1970s, including the notable text on personnel testing by Guion in 1965.

According to Farr and Levy (2007), the 1960s and 1970s were marked by a return to measurement issues, with a new emphasis on behavioral measurement, as well as better articulation of the role of feedback in the development of employees. Performance rating scales reflected a shift from rating individual traits and qualities to rating employees on behavior dimensions. This shift was particularly evident when Smith and Kendall (1963) forged new ground with the development of the Behaviorally Anchored Rating Scales (BARS). An important aspect of these rating scales was the participation of raters in developing the dimensions and anchors, which was consistent with the participative management practices surfacing at that time (Farr & Levy, 2007; Likert, 1961; McGregor, 1960). Behavioral measurement led to additional measures, such as the Mixed Standard Scale (Blanz & Ghiselli, 1972), Behavioral Expectation Scales (BES; Smith & Kendall, 1963), and Behavioral Observation Scales (BOS, Latham & Wexley, 1977). Farr and Levy (2007) stated, "Using rating scales as a source of performance-related information that supervisors could provide to their subordinates became frequent in the 1960s and has continued to be a major use of ratings" (p. 320). Particularly noteworthy during this time was the empirical performance appraisal field research conducted by Herb Meyer at General Electric. Several useful findings resulted from this research. For example, Meyer and his coworkers concluded that one session should be held to address the developmental needs of an individual, and a separate second session should be held to address salary issues (Meyer, Kay, & French, 1965).

Although cognitive psychology was surfacing in other aspects of I/O psychology, a behavioral perspective prevailed in training (Kraiger & Ford, 2007). A landmark text, *Training in Business and Industry* (McGehee & Thayer, 1961), described the three-step training needs assessment process, which continues to dominate training research and practice today. In the early 1970s, pessimism dominated views of training research. As quoted in Kraiger and Ford (2007), Campbell (1971) in his Annual Review chapter wrote that the field of training "is voluminous, non-empirical, non-theoretical, poorly written, and dull" (p. 565). In the mid-1970s, systems thinking became part of training research when Goldstein (1974) presented an instructional systems design (ISD) model. Diverse training methods in use included on-the-job training, job rotation, coaching, behavior modification, lectures, films, television, business games, in-baskets, case studies, role playing, simulations, and team training. With time, psychologists gradually became less interested in researching these training methods and focused on assessment and design, training transfer, and evaluation methods following training. Other developments included an increased emphasis on managerial training, such as situational leadership, and some movement to more self-directed learning such as programmed instruction and computer-assisted instruction (Kraiger & Ford, 2007).

This era saw advances in I/O psychology outside the United States. In Holland, for example, I/O psychology surfaced in the 1920s, but it was not until the 1960s that a quantitative empirical approach was accepted, statistical and methodological rigor became valued, and American scholarship was monitored more closely. In comparison to Americans, Dutch psychologists focused less on management issues because of communal European laws and national norms. Organizational psychology was visible in Belgium in the 1960s, but was taught within broader courses of psychology (Warr, 2007). In Spain, when a shift to constitutional monarchy occurred after General Francisco Franco's death in

1975, scientific advancements rapidly grew as new I/O centers were created and themes beyond traditional ones were expanded, with attention to economic and social pressures to change (Warr, 2007). In China, I/O developments were halted because of the Cultural Revolution (1966–1976). Psychology was viewed as a pseudoscience, and academic psychologists were required to leave their jobs to undertake manual jobs (Warr, 2007). In 1978, after Mao's death, China launched an economic reform to open itself to the world; consequently, new institutions were established and psychologists had to learn about recent innovations. In that year, the Chinese Psychological Society formed a national committee of industrial psychology with two branches: engineering psychology and organizational psychology (Wang, 1990, 1994).

According to Warr (2007), in Great Britain, a widespread concern for the quality of work and industrial democracy emerged; however, "occupational psychology was held in low esteem within the British academic community" (p. 99) throughout the 1960s. Although the number of psychology departments had grown since the 1940s, students were rarely taught about the methods and findings of applied research. Academics preferred rigorous laboratory experimentation to examine issues from previous laboratory experiments. Business had limited interest in the field, and therefore an interchange between researchers and practitioners was almost nonexistent. The country's first and only department of occupational psychology was established at Birkbeck College of the University of London in 1962. The Medical Research Council in 1968 founded a Social and Applied Psychology Unit (SAPU) at Sheffield University to conduct research on attitudes, perceptions, and decision making in organizations (Warr, 1999, 2001). The SAPU worked in many organizations until its closure in 1996, with a focus on well-being and effectiveness. The National Institute of Industrial Psychology focused on projects about career counseling, personnel selection, occupational stress, and accidents, but was forced to close in 1973 because of financial difficulties. NIIP's journal, *Occupational Psychology*, was taken over by the British Psychological Society as the *Journal of Occupational Psychology*, an international journal of research.

In the United States, several organizations and groups were formed to advance research and practice in I/O psychology (Meyer, 2007). The Human Resources Research Office (HumRRO), originally formed in 1951 to conduct human resources research for the army, began to take on non-military clients in 1967. Although the army moved its research operations in-house in the 1970s, HumRRO continues today as a viable research organization. The Army Research Institute (ARI) rapidly developed during the 1960s and 1970s to conduct basic and applied research in response to the army's needs (Salas, DeRouin, & Gade, 2007; Zeidner & Drucker, 1983). The Navy Personnel Research and Development Center (NPRDC) was organized in the 1970s in San Diego; it was one of the largest agencies to support personnel and organizational research, though it is no longer in existence (Salas, DeRouin, & Gade, 2007). Many of the survey and selection projects of NPRDC were shifted to the Naval Personnel Research, Studies, and Technology unit (NPRST) in Tennessee. The Personnel Decisions Research Institute (PDRI), an offshoot of Personnel Decisions Incorporated (PDI), was established in 1975 to investigate personnel procedures such as job analysis, predictors, performance-rating scales, and test validation. The Center for Creative Leadership was formed in 1970 as an international, nonprofit, educational institution devoted to leadership research and training (Meyer, 2007). Development Dimensions International (DDI), a human resources consulting company, was created in 1970 to help organizations use the assessment center method in the selection and development of managers. An informal group, the Mayflower Group was organized in 1971 by professionals from large private-sector companies to discuss and collaborate on organizational surveys.

I/O educational programs proliferated, with excellent financial support from U.S. business and government; doctoral programs in I/O were established at Bowling Green State University, North Carolina State University, and the University of Akron, among others (Lowman et al., 2007). APA Division 14 guidelines for I/O doctoral training were issued in 1965. The *Journal of Occupational Psychology* was created in 1975. Additionally, the APA Division of Consumer Psychology (Division 23) was founded in 1960, officially separating advertising and consumer psychology from its early ties to industrial psychology.

Since the beginning of I/O psychology, critics of the discipline have accused I/O psychologists of being responsive to management concerns only (i.e., *Servants of Power* by Baritz, 1960) and for being atheoretical or primarily data-driven researchers. By the end of the 1970s, however, these criticisms began to disappear as the death of "dust bowl empiricism" was observed and extensive theoretical advancements and research were generated.

1980 to the Present Day
Contextual Background

The U.S. social and economic environment of the last two decades of the twentieth century and the beginning of this century has been turbulent, with a roller-coaster financial economy, globalization of markets and foreign competition, rapid changes in technology, the emergence of the internet and e-commerce, demographic changes and increased cultural diversity, significant growth of an information-oriented economy, and an increased awareness of environmental issues. A global and diverse marketplace and workforce became commonplace with the fall of Soviet Bloc communism and the end of the Cold War, the passage of NAFTA, and the formation of the European Union. The terrorist attacks that destroyed the World Trade Center in New York on September 11, 2001, and the subsequent anthrax scares had a global impact, leading to a heightened awareness of national security, workplace violence, and worker stress. To protect the country from further attacks, the United States formed the Department of Homeland Security.

Since the 1960s, the birth rate in the United States has declined, creating a shortage in the supply of skilled workers in the 1990s (Cascio, 1995; Cohen, 1995). In addition, minority group members increased as a proportion of the workforce. The bulk of the workforce was getting older as the baby boomers aged and life expectancies increased (Briggs, 1987: Cohen, 1995). Although workers retired earlier because of the prosperous economy during the 1990s, more recently retirement-age workers are postponing retirements because of the economic recession in 2008–2009. In Shultz's and Adams' (2007) edited book, several advantages of recruiting and employing older workers are noted. Due to the recent economic recession, unemployment was unusually high at the beginning of 2010, resulting in a surplus of skilled and professional workers.

Interest in fair employment practices declined during the 1980s, but was renewed in the 1990s with the passage of the American with Disabilities Act in 1990 and the Civil Rights Act of 1991, which prohibited quota hiring. The Family and Medical Leave Act was signed in 1993, and the first U.S. executive order of the twenty-first century, issued by President Bill Clinton, forbade federal departments and agencies from discriminating in personnel decisions based on protected genetic information. President Barack Obama signed the Ledbetter Fair Pay Act of 2009 into law on January 29 of that year, which overturned the Supreme Court's ruling in *Ledbetter v. Goodyear Tire and Rubber Co.* (2007), and applies to Title VII, the ADEA, the ADA, and the Rehabilitation Act of 1973. It is a narrow statute designed to cover the single issue of compensation and to treat pay discrimination as a continuing violation. A historical overview and the impact on human resources practices of U.S. legislation and court rulings can be found in Gutman et al. (2011).

A factor that affected all aspects of society and the economy during this era was technological advancement. The extraordinary reliance on technology has transformed organizations, work, and processes. Craiger (1997) described two paradigm shifts in the history of computer technology and organizations. The first shift occurred from the 1950s to the 1980s when computers used for military purposes were converted to business purposes. The second paradigm shift occurred in the early 1980s, when computer technology was installed throughout organizations. The ubiquity of computer technology inspired organizational leaders to reevaluate their business practices and organizational structures (Craiger, 1997). Then, local area network (LAN) and client-server networks were introduced, allowing workers to share hardware, software, and information. The primary work unit transformed from individuals and typical department work groups to empowered work teams (Tapscott & Caston, 1993). Personal computers became standard, which resulted in increased availability of sophisticated software, including statistical analysis software. The advent of the Internet has had an enormous impact on organizations. These technological advancements led to the development of high-performance organizations that place extensive emphasis on defining, monitoring, and constantly improving organizational performance.

Capturing all developments in the discipline of psychology during this era is beyond the scope of this chapter; however, a few relevant events are worth noting. The cognitive revolution permeated all psychological subfields throughout this period. For example, instrumental conditioning models of learning were transformed by the inclusion of cognitive elements, such that "learning theory moved from postulating how thought mediated stimulus-response relations to the study of an internal world that seemingly acted on its own but influenced decision making, behavior, and performance" (Kraiger & Ford, 2007, p. 291). There was increased attention paid to positive psychology that aimed "...to begin to catalyse a change in the focus of psychology from preoccupation only with repairing the worst things in life to also building positive qualities" (Seligman & Csikszentmihalyi, 2000, p. 5). In 1988, due to the heavy clinical and applied emphases of APA, many psychologists formed a new professional organization, the American Psychological Society, now known as the Association for Psychological Science. APS attracted science-oriented researchers, including I/O psychologists, to advance and promote the science of psychology. In 1984, Lillian Gilbreth became the only American psychologist ever to appear on a U.S. postage stamp. The *Standards for Educational and Psychological Testing* were revised in 1999 (American Educational Research Association, American Psychological Association, & National Council on Measurement in Education, 1999).

Beginning in the 1980s, sluggish productivity and threats to economic well-being heightened concerns about productivity and quality, especially in the United States. To survive these tumultuous decades and to be competitive, strategies for managing change and for creating a committed and satisfied workforce became crucial to the survival of organizations. Flexible organizational responses include restructuring, mergers and acquisitions, downsizing or "rightsizing," job re-engineering, and new product lines or services. One of the most consistent trends was the flattening of the organizational structure. "Organizations have pursued leaner structures to control costs, increase flexibility, and increase communication internally and with customers" (Wilson, 2007, p. 228). These changes, however, created an increasing turbulence in the person-organization interface, resulting in workers feeling less embedded and committed to the same organization and/or career.

INDUSTRIAL-ORGANIZATIONAL PSYCHOLOGY: PERIOD OF REFINEMENT AND ADAPTABILITY

Since the 1980s, the field of I/O psychology has grown rapidly with an emphasis on refinement and adaptability. Old techniques have been applied to new problems, and new solutions have been developed for traditional problems. The participative management approach started in the 1970s continued through the 1980s. The cognitive movement swept the discipline, and legal requirements and court decisions that emerged during the past 45 years greatly affected I/O psychology's evolution.

Additionally, as American society's unrest and questioning raised consciousness about many social issues and the field became internationalized, new topics of interest surfaced.

Because of numerous elaborations and expansions, Marvin Dunnette and Leaetta Hough edited a second edition of the *Handbook of Industrial and Organizational Psychology*, expanding the one-volume book published in 1976 to four volumes (Dunnette & Hough, 1990–1993). Borman, Ilgen, and Klimoski (2003) provide a review of developments in the 1990s in *Industrial and Organizational Psychology*, volume 12 of the *Handbook of Psychology* (Weiner, 2003). An examination of these two sources reveal that research and practice ensued in conventional areas (selection, performance appraisal, motivation, leadership) as well as in new and innovative areas (e.g., item response theory, organizational commitment, stress in organizations, strategic decision making, diversity in organizations).

Borman et al. (2003) described advances in four areas that resulted from extending previous work of I/O psychologists. One category consists of research on levels of analysis. Historically, theory and practice had focused on individuals; however, when I/O psychologists began to examine the broader organizational context, it became essential to conceptualize and analyze behavioral phenomena at different levels and at cross-levels of individuals, groups, and organizations (Rousseau, 1985). Multilevel theory moved mainstream in the mid- to late 1990s, and then really took off after the book *Multilevel Theory, Research, and Methods in Organizations: Foundations, Extensions, and New Directions* was published in 2000 (Klein & Kozlowski, 2000a). A second advance was a renewed interest in viewing workers as individuals, with a look at the needs and expectations of applicants and employees. Using this perspective, psychologists studied questions about organizational entry, the psychological contract, issues of fairness and justice, selection, training, performance appraisal, and career management. The third category is the development and refinement of methods, models, and theories. Meta-analysis (Hunter & Schmidt, 1990) and other major methodological advances, such as hierarchical linear modeling (HLM), structural equation modeling (SEM), and confirmatory factor analyses (CFA), have facilitated the interface between theory and data, as scholars specify the theory underlying their empirical work. These methods have created a shift away from depending solely on statistical significance testing (Borman et al., 2003; Schmidt, 1996), which continues to be the standard approach. Other statistical methods developed were item response theory (Drasgow & Hulin, 1990) and methods to study change (Collins & Horn, 1991). Finally, the fourth category is strategic human resource management. According to Borman et al. (2003), this view is a major shift in the thinking of I/O researchers and practitioners: "...it is increasingly recognized that our theories and models need to add value in the view of society for us to have the luxury of pursuing our scholarship" (Borman et al., p. 10). Although the foundations for utility analysis had been offered earlier (e.g., Brogden, 1946), it was not until the 1980s that serious attention to utility analysis surfaced (Cascio, 1991). Wright and McMahan (1992) offer this definition of strategic management: "the pattern of planned human resource deployments and activities intended to enable the firm to achieve its goals" (p. 298). One specific approach resulting from this shift is greater involvement with strategic planning.

In addition to extensions of previous work, Borman et al. (2003) elaborate on other advances. One area of advancement was the development of theory and models of performance with an emphasis on criteria (Campbell, 1999; Campbell, Gasser, & Oswald, 1996; Campbell, McCloy, Oppler, & Sager, 1993). Additionally, work was completed to identify predictors of performance ratings (e.g., Borman, White & Dorsey, 1995; Borman, White, Pulakos, & Oppler, 1991). Two additional large-scale developments affected thinking and practice: Project A, the U.S. Army Selection and Classification Project; and the Occupational Information Network (O*Net). The U.S. Army Project A was a seven-year project spearheaded by the U.S. Army Research Institute, partnering with a group of private research firms to overhaul the army's selection and classification system and to enhance the system for enlisted entry-level positions (Campbell, 1990; Campbell & Knapp, 2001). Possibly the largest-scale personnel research project ever conducted, this effort resulted in a 12-hour test predictor battery that measures a broad array of individual differences (e.g., cognitive abilities, personality, biographical information), and the development of extensive criterion measures. According to Borman et al. (2003), "the Project A research program provided industrial and organizational psychologists with an unprecedented opportunity to study relationships between a broad array of individual differences and job performance constructs. Perhaps most noteworthy was the specification of job performance, resulting in a replicable

multidimensional model of performance" (p. 5). Another noteworthy large-scale development was the Occupational Information Network (O*Net), created to replace the *Dictionary of Occupational Titles* (DOT). The U.S. Department of Labor formed a group of I/O psychologists to develop the plan for this database, which was presented in 1995, and then released in 1998 with a database of 1,100 occupations (Peterson, Mumford, Borman, Jeanneret, & Fleishman, 1999; Peterson et al., 2001). Positive characteristics of this database include that it is primarily based on earlier model developments of taxonomies, that it is flexible and useful, and that it relies on a common nomenclature for describing different jobs (Borman et al., 2003).

In addition to the advancements described above, other developments were observed throughout this era in the industrial side of the field. Legislation and case law emphasized fairness in personnel decisions (e.g., employment, promotion, compensation). The Americans with Disabilities Act (ADA) called attention to the importance of identifying essential job functions and physical requirements and redesigning jobs to accommodate employees. The ADA is perhaps the most significant law to influence the work of I/O psychologists since the CRA of 1964 (see Guttman et al., 2011). The *Principles for the Validation and Use of Personnel Selection Procedures,* first published in 1975, were revised in 1980, 1987, and 2003 (Society for Industrial and Organizational Psychology, 1975, 1980, 1987, 2003).

The increased emphasis on fairness in personnel decisions led to greater interest in job analysis (Harvey, 1991), validation strategies (Guion, 1991) and validity generalization (Hunter & Schmidt, 1990). In his historical overview of job analysis, Wilson (2007) labeled this period "At a Crossroads: Job Analysis in the Information Age (1981–2003)" (p. 227) because it was during this time that disputes developed about the use, evaluation, and level of detail needed for job analysis. Developments in job analysis included the Occupational Analysis Inventory and the Generalized Work Inventory (Cunningham, Boese, Neeb, & Pass, 1983). Gael published *The Job Analysis Handbook for Business, Industry, and Government* in 1988. Harvey created The Common Metric Questionnaire (CMQ) in 1991, while Fleishman developed the Fleishman Job Analysis Survey (F-JAS) in 1992.

Selection and assessment research and practice focused on individual assessment, assessment centers, computerized adaptive testing, use of biodata, structured interviews, and the situational interview technique. The attraction-selection-attrition model was proposed by Benjamin Schneider in 1987 to explain the fit between individuals and organizations. A revival of research on personality characteristics emerged, and personality testing in industry increased with the conclusion that the five-factor model of personality is a valid predictor of performance (Barrick & Mount, 1991). Moreover, general cognitive ability tests were confirmed as a valid predictor of performance (Schmidt & Hunter, 1998), and integrity tests were developed, validated, and implemented. The *International Journal of Selection and Assessment* was first published in 1993. Recently, increasing importance has been placed on computer and Internet-based recruitment, assessment, and testing.

In training, there was optimism about the future of training research as advances in cognitive and educational psychology provided a foundation to expand training research (Kraiger & Ford, 2007). There was a focus on cognitive theory and information-processing models and learning (Ford & Kraiger, 1995; Howell & Cooke, 1989; Lord & Maher, 1991) with a greater emphasis on the acquisition of knowledge, skills, and core competencies as the fundamental building blocks of jobs and training programs. J. P. Campbell (1989) advocated for a paradigm shift from focusing on training methods to training objectives. A primary development was the institutionalization of methods for needs assessment and training evaluation. The 1990s became the strategic learning era, "named for the coupling of knowledge management and organizational initiatives that promote system-wide learning behaviors, thus enabling long-term adaptive capacity" (Kraiger & Ford, 2007, p. 294) and linking training to the broader issue of individual, team, and organization development. Major advances were made in models of training effectiveness (Cannon-Bowers, Salas, Tannenbaum, & Mathieu, 1995; Noe, 1986) and models of the transfer of training (Baldwin & Ford, 1988). Instructor-led training was prominent, but other forms of training surfaced, such as the corporate university and technology-delivered instruction (e.g., self-directed learning activities such as CD-ROM and web-based training). Additionally, the concepts of organizational learning, knowledge management, and intellectual capital were introduced (Kraiger & Ford, 2007). In 1997, the *International Journal of Training and Development* was first published.

Two threads in performance appraisal research were evident in the 1980s and 1990s. One was a major focus on the cognitive processes involved in performance appraisals, resulting from two seminal articles that had substantial impact on future performance appraisal research (Farr & Levy, 2007). Landy and Farr (1980) along with Feldman (1981) inspired a paradigm shift from an emphasis on rating formats toward understanding the cognitive processes involved with performance appraisals (Austin & Villanova, 1992). Since then, frameworks have been developed (e.g., DeNisi, Cafferty, & Meglino, 1984; Wexley & Klimoski, 1984) and a plethora of research studies were conducted to examine both cognitive processes and ways to improve performance appraisals (e.g., Ilgen, Barnes-Farrell, & McKellin, 1993). The second thread was the focus on the social context in which performance appraisals operate. In 1991, Murphy and Cleveland introduced a social-psychological view that acknowledged the importance of the social context on the effectiveness of the performance appraisal process. Other contemporary developments include work on rater training (Hauenstein, 1998); employee reactions (Findley, Giles, & Mossholder, 2000); supervisor-subordinate relationships (Kacmar, Witt, Zivnuska, &Gully, 2003); organizational politics (Hochwarter, Witt, & Kacmar, 2000); multisource rating and feedback systems, also known as 360-degree ratings (Fletcher & Baldry, 1999); employee participation in the rating process (Korsgaard & Roberson, 1995); and knowledge of the appraisal system or perceived system knowledge (Levy & Williams, 1998).

The cognitive revolution also influenced organizational psychology in areas of motivation, leadership, and work teams. Special attention was given to cognitive factors involved with motivational processes in the workplace. Extensive empirical research on goal-setting theory had shown that setting specific, difficult goals increases performance (Locke & Latham, 1990, 2002), and by the end of the twentieth century, goal-setting theory was supported as a valid and practical theory of worker motivation. In 1987, Greenberg introduced organizational justice theory to address fairness and trust in the workplace. "Greenberg's theory supplanted Adam's equity theory as a central role in promoting organizational well-being" (Latham & Budworth, 2007). Locke and Latham (1990) introduced the theory of the high-performance cycle (HPC) to explain how a person's performance and job satisfaction can be increased. Latham and Budworth (2007) stated that cognitive theories of motivation will likely be integrated with affective processes (Brief & Weiss, 2002), with clinical psychology about the unconscious (Latham & Heslin, 2003; Locke & Latham, 2004) and with personality theory (Judge & Ilies, 2002).

Avolio, Sosik, Jung, and Berson (2003) provide a review of leadership models, methods, and applications, and offer projections about emerging areas in leadership theory and research. They noted a significant transition in leadership research because of new theoretical perspectives introduced in the 1980s and 1990s. A change in focus occurred from an emphasis on contingency models and an extensive examination of initiation of structure and consideration behaviors, to the development of new leadership theories and streams of research (e.g., cognitive processes of leaders and followers; shared leadership in teams) in the 1990s and beyond. Avolio et al. (2003) note that a cognitive revolution in the leadership field began with Calder's (1977) work, which directed new research and theories, such as the implicit leadership theory (Lord, Foti, & DeVader, 1984; Lord & Maher, 1991).

Lowe and Gardner (2000), in their published review of leadership research conducted during the 1990s, noted several trends that influenced the field of leadership, including attention to transformational leadership (Avolio, 1999; Bass, 1985, 1998; Bass & Avolio, 1993, 1994) and neo-charismatic leadership derived from House's (1977) charismatic leadership theory. Lowe and Gardner (2000) observed that while most leadership research was conducted by American scholars, a renewed interest on cross-cultural leadership emerged. Particularly noteworthy was a major research project to identify universal and cultural-specific leadership behaviors in 60 different countries. Results from the Global Leadership and Organizational Behavior Effectiveness (GLOBE) study revealed attributes that were universally endorsed by middle-level managers across these countries (Chhokar, Brodbeck, & House, 2007). In addition, Avolio et al. (2003) stated that another driving force in leadership research was the introduction of levels of analysis in theory building, research design, and measurement (e.g., Dansereau, Alutto, & Yammarino, 1984; Klein & House, 1995). According to Avolio et al.(2003), "A levels-of-analysis frame of reference provided a huge leap toward more sophisticated multilevel models of leadership that now include the context in which leadership is embedded" (p. 279). During this era, work continued on leader-member exchange theory (Gertsner & Day, 1997; Graen,

Novak, & Sommerkamp, 1982; Lord, 2000); leadership substitutes (Meindl, Ehrlich, & Dukerich, 1985); strategic leadership (House & Aditya, 1997); gender and leadership (Rosener, 1995); leadership knowledge, skills, and ability (Mumford, Zaccaro, Harding, Jacobs, & Fleishman, 2000); and a redux of leadership trait theory (Day & Zaccaro, 2007). In the past decade, leadership researchers have examined leadership development, strategic leadership, e-leadership, authentic leaders, visionary leaders, moral and ethical leaders, green or organic leaders, and leadership in new organizational contexts.

Rapidly developing research on teams became programmatic and central to the fields of organizational psychology and organizational behavior (Kozlowski & Bell, 2003), with particular attention to ways in which teams form, evolve, and perform (Salas et al. 2007). In their review, Kozlowski and Bell (2003) provide theory and research on work groups and teams in organizations representative of work throughout these decades, noting "an ongoing shift from work organized around individual jobs to team-based work structures" (p. 333). Salas et al. (2007) identified several developments in their historical review of work teams in organizations. In the 1980s, team taxonomies and classification emerged, and by the mid-1980s, quality circles became common in the American workplace and were considered to be one of the most promising team-related strategies in industry (Bettenhausen, 1991; Salas et al., 2007). Self-management work teams become a prominent part of organizations. For example, Volvo implemented empowered teams to improve job satisfaction, improve productivity and quality, and to achieve organizational objectives (Salas et al., 2007). Cognitive psychology permeated team research beginning in the 1980s through recent years. An emphasis has been placed on Knowledge, Skills, and Abilities (KSAs) as well as continued interest in teamwork skills (Salas et al., 2007). Research on a shared cognition has progressed, with attention to shared mental models (SMM; Orasanu & Salas, 1993) and their role in team performance and effectiveness (e.g., Marks, Sabella, Burke, & Zaccaro, 2002; Stout, Cannon-Bowers, Salas, & Milanovich, 1999).

In the 1990s and beyond, team researchers targeted team maturation (e.g., Ancona & Chong, 1999; Kozlowski, Gully, Nason, & Smith, 1999); team types and taxonomies (e.g., Fleishman & Zaccaro, 1992); hierarchical team decision making (e.g., Hollenbeck, Ilgen, LePine, Colquitt, & Hedlund, 1998); team performance and effectiveness (e.g., Campion, Medsker, & Higgs, 1993; DeShon, Kozlowski, Schmidt, Milner & Wiechmann, 2004); team training and development (e.g., the U.S. Navy Tactical Decision Making Under Stress [TADMUS] project); crew resource management [CRM]; team-building (e.g., Campbell & Kuncel, 2001; Salas &Cannon-Bowers, 2001); team performance measurement (Day & Lance, 2004; Klein & Kozlowski, 2000b); distributed and virtual teams (e.g., Bell & Kozlowski, 2002; Driskell, Radtke, & Salas, 2003; Zaccaro, Ardison, & Orvis, 2004); and team member individual differences (e.g., LePine, 2003; Neuman & Wright, 1999). In recent years, greater emphasis has been placed on the expansion of work teams and groups, the fluidity of work teams, the expansion of virtual teams, and the selection of team members (Sundstrom, McIntyre, Halfhill, & Richards, 2000).

As noted earlier, societal and economic events raised awareness of organizational and worker issues, expanding research in organizational psychology beyond the traditional topics of motivation, leadership, and teamwork. To explore these issues from the 1980s and early 1990s, Lynn Offerman and Marilyn Gowing (1990) edited a special issue in *American Psychologist*, which included emerging topics such as work, family, and health issues. The 1980s were known as the health decade, and research was initiated to study worker stress, health, and well-being (e.g., Ilgen, 1990). Peter Warr conducted numerous studies to understand the environmental determinants of individual well-being in the workplace (Warr, 1987, 1990, 1999). Increased attention was given to quality of work life, as well as work and family (work-life) balance and/or conflict (Allen, 2001; Major & Cleveland, 2007; Thompson, Beauvais, & Lyness, 1999; Zedeck, 1992). This activity influenced family leave policies, child care benefits, elder care assistance, flexible work arrangements, and other valued work-life support and programs. Research on work-family issues has evolved into an integrated science and practice (see Koppes & Swanberg, 2008). Recently, scholars have examined work-family enrichment (Greenhaus & Powell, 2006), perceived organizational support (Rhoades & Eisenberger, 2002), behaviors of leadership and/or supervisors supportive of work-life effectiveness (Hammer, Kossek, Yragui, Bohner, & Hanson, 2009; Koppes, Schneider, & Linnabery, 2009), flexibility in the workplace (Baltes, Briggs, Huff, Wright, & Neuman, 1999), and issues of the sandwich generation (parents who simultaneously have child care and elder care responsibilities) in relation to various outcomes, including life and job satisfaction, absenteeism, turnover, and job stress (Neal & Hammer, 2007).

Because of terrorist attacks, the global war on terror, and the economic recession, workplace stress has become a focal point for research and practice. Models of stress were constructed (Cartwright & Cooper, 1997), the psychological effects of job loss were investigated (Keita & Hurrell, 1994), and workplace violence (O'Leary-Kelly, Griffin, & Glew, 1996) and counterproductive work behaviors (Motowidlo, 2003; Sackett, 2002) were given increased emphasis by organizations and researchers. Moreover, this era saw an increased focus on measurement, antecedents, and consequences of job satisfaction, organizational commitment, job involvement, organizational citizenship behaviors, and emotions at work.

Finally, a rapprochement between industrial and organizational approaches was observed throughout these decades. It is evident from Borman et al.'s (2003) handbook volume that a third category of research and practice focuses on the work environment, which requires the integration of individual, team, and organizational issues. The topic of organizational culture (Schein, 1983, 1985; Schneider, 1990) became prominent in the 1980s as a result of several best-selling trade books (Deal & Kennedy, 1982; Ouchi, 1981; Peters & Waterman, 1982) that emphasized the importance of strong organizational cultures for organizational effectiveness (Ostroff, Kinicki, & Tamkins, 2003). Since then, a large number of practice and research publications on culture have been published (e.g., Barley, Meyer, & Gash, 1988).

While it is beyond the scope of this chapter to review all of the global developments in I/O psychology since 1980, a few representative examples are provided. In the last three decades, Spain achieved greater prominence in the field. For example, the 1994 Congress of the International Association of Applied Psychology was held in Madrid, and the XIV European Congress of Work and Organizational Psychology met in 2009 in Santiago. I/O psychology continued to evolve in China; by 1981, it had become a priority and was being taught in many Chinese universities (Warr, 2007). The discipline became firmly established in universities, government, and business organizations in Great Britain. Although neglected earlier by academic departments, studies of occupational psychology were accepted for both academic and practical value, with graduate-level courses in more than 20 universities. Also, numerous consulting groups flourished due to an increased demand for expertise (Warr, 2007).

Publications of I/O psychology research and practice proliferated. The *Journal of Occupational Psychology* was first published in 1975. It was renamed the British Psychological Society's *Journal of Occupational and Organizational Psychology* in 1992 to reflect a wider coverage of the field. The first volume in the SIOP Frontiers Service, *Careers in Organizations,* edited by Douglas T. Hall, was published in 1986. In 1991, the first volume of the SIOP Practice Series, *Working with Organizations and Their People,* by Douglas Bray, was published. A second edition of the *Handbook of Industrial, Work, and Organizational Psychology* (1992) was published to reflect the field's cross-cultural diversity (Anderson, Ones, Sinangil, & Viswesvaran, 2001). In 2003, a *Handbook of Psychology* was published, with a chapter devoted to the history of I/O psychology in Volume I (Koppes, 2003), and an entire volume dedicated to I/O psychology (Vol. 12, Borman et al., 2003). An *Encyclopedia of Industrial and Organizational Psychology* also appeared (Rogelberg, 2006). Recently, the following were named as the top I/O psychology journals by Oliver, Blair, Gorman, and Woehr (2005) and Zickar and Highhouse (2001): *Journal of Applied Psychology, Personnel Psychology, Academy of Management Journal, Academy of Management Review, Organizational Behavior and Human Decision Processes, Administrative Science Quarterly, Journal of Management, Journal of Organizational Behavior, Organizational Research Methods,* and *Journal of Vocational Behavior.*

Educational and training programs continued to proliferate in the 1980s with the expansion of professional psychology schools offering doctoral training in I/O psychology, such as the California School of Professional Psychology (Lowman et al., 2007). Less expansion of traditional I/O programs occurred in the 1990s, but a new program that focused on humanistic values was established at the Saybrook Institute. Business schools offered studies in I/O psychology or organizational behavior, as well as other programs in industrial and labor relations and public administration (Lowman et al., 2007). Terminal master's degree programs grew exponentially as organizations valued the competences of these graduates (Lowe, 1993, 2000). Subsequently, SIOP issued guidelines for master's training and education. According to the SIOP directory, as of 2009, 111 active doctoral programs and 123 active master's degree programs are currently listed (Lori Peake, Society for Industrial and Organizational

Psychology, personal communication, October 29, 2009).

The discipline has seen changes in professional employment. SIOP reported in 2004 that employment in academic positions had remained steady (39% in 2004), primarily because of I/O psychologists being hired by business schools in recent years. As compared to earlier years, the greatest change is the shift from employment in private organizations (20%) to consulting firms (35%; Levy, 2006). Meyer (2007) noted that the evolution of consulting firms in the 1980s is an interesting story of adaptation for I/O psychologists. With restructuring and downsizing in corporations, fewer positions were available; thus, many I/O psychologies ventured into consulting. Some I/O psychologists (6%) work in public organizations, including the military and government agencies.

To achieve independence from APA, APA Division 14 incorporated as the Society for Industrial and Organizational Psychology (SIOP) in 1982 (Hakel, 1979). In 1945, when APA Division 14 was formed, there were 130 members (fellows and associates). By the end of 2009 there were 3,817 professional members (fellows, members, associates, international affiliates, retired) and 2,792 student members, for a total of 6,609 (Lori Peake, Society for I/O Psychology, personal communication, October 29, 2009). The international membership has risen over the years, with 8.5% of professional members living outside the United States in 2009. Most recently, SIOP joined forces with the International Association of Applied Psychology (IAAP) and the European Association of Work and Organizational Psychology (EAWOP) to form the Alliance of Organizational Psychology. The mission "is envisioned as supporting and advancing the science and practice of organizational psychology in the global world and expanding its scope of application and contribution to society to improve the quality of working life" (Peiró, 2009, October).

Past Is Prologue: What Does History Tell Us About Our Science and Practice?

In this chapter, we attempted to provide over 100 years of history on the science and practice of I/O psychology by identifying individuals, events, and developments representative of various time periods. To do so, we acknowledged the importance of the contextual forces that influenced the field including the two world wars, economic prosperity, recessions and depressions, government investment policies, investment in higher education, private-sector investment (Campbell, 2007), as well as legislation and court rulings, and recently, the economic recession and the global war on terror. Upon review of these 100+ years, what can we conclude about our science and practice?

In 1992, Katzell and Austin provided several lessons from their 100-year historical account of I/O psychology in the United States. For example, they noted that while there may be a lack of appreciation or understanding of I/O psychology's contributions, the field had become a viable scientific discipline that has contributed greatly to knowledge about work behavior and to the general well-being of Americans. It has also been an important contributor to the practice of management. Katzell and Austin (1992) observed that the content had undergone much development over time, with science exceeding some areas of practice, and vice versa. They opined that laboratory experimentation was on the rise, while quasi-experimentation was used too little. They noted that conflict continues between scientist and practitioner, but that the industrial and organizational sides are merging to solve problems.

Fifteen years later, several scholars provide lessons learned from reviewing histories of various subfields of I/O psychology (Farr & Levy, 2007; Highhouse, 2007; Kraiger & Ford, 2007; Salas et al., 2007; Vinchur, 2007; Wilson, 2007). Meyer (2007) noted that "...research and development in I/O psychology have become more of a team rather than an individual activity" (p. 165), which has coincided with the proliferation of organized groups of I/O psychologists in the last 50 years. These groups "have provided stimulation, cross-fertilization, and individual development that have resulted in much greater volume, diversity, and the importance of the contributions of I-O psychologists..." (p. 165, Meyer, 2007).

As mentioned earlier, critics over the years stated that I/O psychologists simply serve only those in power and heavily rely on theory and research from other disciplines to address workplace issues and problems. Although these criticisms may have been legitimate in the early years, the discipline has evolved to the extent that we "own" several contributions. Campbell (2007) identified achievements in the following areas made by I/O psychologists throughout a century of research and practice: leadership, training design, performance theory, human motivation, the high-performance work team, assessment methods, the nature of human judgments of performance, attitude (job satisfaction) assessment, and quantitative modeling.

We have learned from studying our history that our future should be one of adaptation and growth in the nature of research questions, influence of other specialties, the values of science and practice, and the education and training of I/O psychologists (Campbell, 2007). For in the twenty-first century, organizations are undergoing a radical transformation, nothing less than a new Industrial Revolution (Cascio, 2003). According to Cascio:

This time around, the revolution is reaching every corner of the globe and, in the process, rewriting the rules laid down by Alfred P. Sloan, Jr. (the legendary chairman of General Motors), Henry Ford, and other Industrial-Age giants. The twenty-first-century organizations that emerge will, in many ways, be the polar opposite of the organizations that helped shape them. (Cascio, 2003, p. 416)Cascio (2003) believes that important workplace factors for now and in the future are Internet technologies; flat organizational structures; individualized products and services; intellectual capital; globalization; and new forms of organizations (virtual organization, modular corporation). An emphasis on speed will require new technology and restructuring; training will be delivered when and where it is needed; rewards and incentives are likely to be team-based and organization-wide; work environments will need to be fostered in which creativity and innovation can thrive; and effective leaders who can inspire employees to commit to the vision and mission will be necessary. Additionally, as the demographics of the workforce change and generational values shift, organizations will need to be cognizant of the interface with work and life outside work, with special attention to deployment-related issues of active duty military, veterans, and their family members (Cascio, 2003).

As an applied science and as scientists-practitioners, we have learned that a constant key challenge within the discipline is to maintain an identity as a rigorous scientific discipline while providing a growing range of professional services and applications. We believe that good professional practice is based on good theories, models, and data, and that good theories must be connected to organizational realities. Upon reflection of our history, we have learned that I/O psychologists are capable and willing to embrace an ever-changing society and economy, and the discipline will continue to evolve, expand, and thrive.

Author Note

We thank Bianca Falbo and Kim Robert Bryan for assisting with this chapter. We dedicate this chapter to Frank J. Landy, who inspired many industrial and organizational psychologists to understand the importance of knowing and studying history.

Notes

1. The term *psychotechnik* was coined by the German psychologist William Stern (1871–1938 in 1903 (Salgado, 2001).

2. See, for example, Kaiser, 1989.

3. Students who received their doctorates from Columbia during this period and made important contributions to industrial psychology include Harry Hollingworth, James B. Miner, Edward K. Strong, Jr., and Edward L. Thorndike.

4. Surprisingly, there is no book-length biography of Cattell. Sokal (1971, 1981, 1984, 1987, 1995, 2009) has been active in chronicling Cattell's life and work. See Vinchur and Koppes (2007) for a short biography of Cattell along with many of the other early industrial psychology pioneers mentioned in this chapter.

5. Wissler's study was one of the first to use the correlation coefficient as a measure of the predictive accuracy of a test (von Mayrhauser, 1992).

6. E. K. Strong, Jr.'s 1911 dissertation is another example of an early dissertation on a business theme (Hansen, 1987).

7. Münsterberg during his lifetime was one of the best-known and most influential psychologists in the United States; however, his influence waned following his death in 1916 at age 53. A German national, Münsterberg was an ardent supporter of Germany, an extremely unpopular position on the eve of America's entry into World War I. Hale (1980) provides a book-length biography of Münsterberg.

8. Salgado (2001) notes that Leo Engel first used the term *work psychology* in this journal in 1912.

9. By the 1930s, psychologists interested in career guidance began to split from mainstream industrial psychology, and by the 1950s, this activity was increasingly identified with counseling psychology (Savickas & Baker, 2005).

10. Beginning in the year 1916–1917, the Division of Applied Psychology consisted of the Department of Psychology and Education, the Bureau of Mental Tests, the Department for Training of Teachers, the Department of Psychology and Education in the Margaret Morrison Carnegie School, and the Department of Psychology and Pedagogy in the School of Applied Industries (Ferguson, 1962–1965).

11. CIT graduate Richard S. Uhrbock offered possible reasons for closing the DAP, including a new CIT president who was less supportive of the program, difficulty in regaining corporate sponsorship, and Bingham's increasing interest in directing the Personnel Research Federation (Hilgard, 1987).

12. Bruce V. Moore received his doctorate from the CIT program in 1921, the first Ph.D. specifically in industrial psychology. Ph.D.s were also awarded to Max Freyd, Grace Manson, and Merrill Ream (Ferguson, n.d.).

13. Ferguson (n.d., 1962–1965) provides information about these and other CIT staff and students. Others involved in the program include L. Dewey Anderson, Eugene Benge, W. W. Charters, Glen Cleeton, Daivd Craig, Thelma Gwinn Thurstone, C. F. Hansen, Dwight and Newman Hoopingamer, H. G. Kenagy, Franklyn Meine, Merrill Ream, and Edward S. Robinson.

14. Not that industrial psychology was immune to the use of practices that would be considered questionable or worse today. Examples include judgments of applicant characteristics based on anatomical characteristics (Shelton, 1927–1928) or ethnic group membership (e.g., Frost, 1920).

15. Following his dismissal from Columbia University in 1917, Cattell sued the university. He settled with Columbia in 1921 and used the proceeds to start the Psychological Corporation (Sokal, 2009).

16. (George) Elton Mayo (1880–1949) emerged as the chief spokesperson and interpreter of the Hawthorne Studies. Mayo immigrated to American in 1922 from Australia and held positions at the University of Pennsylvania and at Harvard Business School (Griffin, Landy, & Mayocchi, 2002; Miner, 2002). Other prominent researchers included Fritz J. Roethlisberger, a protégé of Mayo's, Clair Turney, a professor of public health at MIT, and W. J. Dickson, an employee of Western Electric. Mayo (1933) popularized the studies, while Roethlisberger and Dickson (1939) presented a detail analysis of the data (Hilgard, 1987).

17. For additional industrial psychology activity arising out of World War II, see Capshew (1999); Salas, DeRouin, and Gade (2007); and Samuelson (1977).

18. AHAP is the depository of APA Division 14 (now SIOP) archival records, along with the records of several prominent I/O psychologists.

References

Albermarle v. Moody (1975). 422 U.S. 405.

Allen, T. (2001). Family-supportive work environments: The role of organizational perceptions. *Journal of Vocational Behavior, 58*(3), 414–435.

Allport, G. (1924). *Social psychology*. Boston: Houghton Mifflin.

American Educational Research Association, American Psychological Association, & National Council on Measurement in Education. (1999). *Standards for educational and psychological testing*. Washington, DC: American Educational Research.

American Psychological Association. (1953). *Ethical principles of psychologists*. Washington, DC: Author.

American Psychological Association. (1954). *Technical recommendations of psychological tests and diagnostic techniques*. Washington, DC: Author.

American Psychological Association. (1966). *Standards for educational and psychological tests and manuals*. Washington, DC: Author.

Ancona, D., & Chong, C. L. (1999). Cycles and synchrony: The temporal role of context in team behavior. In R. Wageman (Ed.), *Research on managing groups and teams: Groups in context* (Vol. 2, pp. 33–48). Stamford, CT: JAI Press.

Anderson, N., Ones, D. S., Sinangil, H. K., & Viswesvaran, C. (Eds.). (2001). *Handbook of industrial, work, and organizational psychology* (Vol. 2). London: Sage.

Angell, J. R. (1907). The province of functional psychology. *Psychological Review, 14*, 61–91.

Argyris, C. (1957). *Personality and organization: The conflict between the system and the individual*. New York: Harper & Row.

Argyris, C. (1967). Some causes of organizational ineffectiveness within the Department of State. *Occasional papers, Department of State*. Washington, DC: U.S. Government Printing Office.

Arthur, W., Jr., & Benjamin, L. T., Jr. (1999). Psychology applied to business. In A. M. Stec & D. A. Bernstein (Eds.), *Psychology: Fields of application* (pp. 98–115). Boston: Houghton Mifflin.

Austin, J. T., & Villanova, P. (1992). The criterion problem: 1917–1992. *Journal of Applied Psychology, 77*, 836–874.

Avolio, B. J. (1999). *Full leadership development: Building the vital forces in organizations.* Thousand Oaks, CA: Sage.

Avolio, B. J., Sosik, J. J., Jung, D. I., & Berson, Y. (2003). Leadership models, methods, and applications. In W. C. Borman, D. R. Ilgen, & R. J. Klimoski (Eds.), *Handbook of psychology:* Vol. 12, *Industrial and organizational psychology* (pp. 277–307). Hoboken, NJ: Wiley.

Baldwin, T. T., & Ford, J. K. (1988). Transfer of training: A review and directions for future research. *Personnel Psychology, 41*, 63–105.

Baltes, B. B., Briggs, T. E., Huff, J. W., Wright, J. A., & Neuman, G. A. (1999). Flexible and compressed workweek schedules: A meta-analysis of their effects on work-related criteria. *Journal of Applied Psychology, 84*, 496–513.

Balzer, W. K., Locke, E., & Zedeck, S. (2008). Patricia Cain Smith (1917–2007). *American Psychologist, 63*(3), 198.

Bandura, A. (1977). Self-efficacy: Toward a unifying theory of behavioral change. *Psychological Review, 84*, 191–215.

Bandura, A. (2001). Social cognitive theory: An agentic perspective. *Annual Review of Psychology, 52*, 1–26.

Baritz, L. (1960). *The servants of power: A history of the use of social science in American industry.* Middletown, CT: Wesleyan University Press.

Barley, S. R., Meyer, G. W., & Gash, D. C. (1988). Cultures of culture: Academics, practitioners and the pragmatics of normal control. *Administrative Science Quarterly, 33*, 24–60.

Barrick, M. R., & Mount, M. K. (1991). The big five personality dimensions and job performance: A meta-analysis. *Personnel Psychology, 44*, 1–26.

Bass, B. M. (1965). *Organizational psychology.* Boston: Allyn & Bacon.

Bass, B. M. (1985). *Leadership and performance beyond expectations.* New York: Free Press.

Bass, B. M. (1998). *Transformational leadership: Industry, military, and educational impact.* Mahwah, NJ: Erlbaum.

Bass, B. M., & Avolio, B. J. (1993). Transformational leadership: A response to critiques. In M. M. Chemers & R. Ayman (Eds.), *Leadership research and theory: Perspectives and directions* (pp. 49–80). New York: Academic Press.

Bass, B. M., & Avolio, B. J. (1994). *Improving organizational effectiveness through transformational leadership.* Thousand Oaks, CA: Sage.

Baumgarten, F. (1934). Otto Lipmann—Psychologist. *Personnel Journal, 12*, 324–327.

Bell, B. S., & Kozlowski, S. W. J. (2002). A typology of virtual teams: Implications for effective leadership. *Group & Organization Management, 27*, 14–49.

Benjamin, L. T., Jr. (1996). Harry Hollingworth: Portrait of a generalist. In G. A. Kimble, C. A. Boneau, & M. Wertheimer (Eds.), *Portraits of pioneers in psychology* (Vol. 2, pp. 119–135). Washington, DC: American Psychological Association, and Mahwah, NJ: Lawrence Erlbaum Associates.

Benjamin, L. T., Jr. (1997a). Organized industrial psychology before Division 14: The ACP and the AAAP (1930–1945). *Journal of Applied Psychology, 82*, 459–466.

Benjamin, L. T., Jr. (1997b). A history of Division 14 (Society for Industrial and Organizational Psychology). In D. A. Dewsbury (Ed.), *Unification through division: Histories of the divisions of the American Psychological Association* (Vol. 2, pp. 101–126). Washington, DC: American Psychological Association.

Benjamin, L. T., Jr. (2000). Hugo Münsterberg: Portrait of an applied psychologist. In G. A. Kimble & M. Wertheimer (Eds.), *Portraits of pioneers in psychology* (Vol. 4, pp. 113–129). Washington, DC: American Psychological Association, and Mahwah, NJ: Lawrence Erlbaum Associates.

Benjamin, L. T., Jr. (n.d.). *The first century of psychological science and practice in America.* Unpublished manuscript.

Benne, K. D. (1964). History of the t group in the laboratory setting. In L. P. Bradford, J. R. Gibb, & K. D. Benne (Eds.), *T-group theory and laboratory method* (pp. 80–135). New York: Wiley.

Bettenhausen, K. L. (1991). Five years of group research: What we have learned and what needs to be addressed. *Journal of Management, 17*, 345–381.

Bingham, W. V. (1919). Army personnel work: With some implications for education and industry. *Journal of Applied Psychology, 3*, 1–12.

Bingham, W. V. (1926). Measures of occupational success. *Harvard Business Review, 5*, 1–10.

Bingham, W. V. (1929). Industrial psychology in the United States: An appraisal. *Annals of Business Economics and Science of Labour, 3*, 398–408.

Bingham, W. V. (1952). Walter Van Dyke Bingham. In E. G. Boring, H. S. Langfeld, H. Werner, & R. M. Yerkes (Eds.), *A history of psychology in autobiography* (Vol. 4, pp. 1–26). New York: Appleton-Century-Crofts.

Bird, C. (1940). *Social psychology.* New York: Appleton-Century.

Blackford, K. M. H., & Newcomb, A. (1914). *The job, the man, the boss.* Garden City, NY: Doubleday, Page.

Blanz, F., & Ghiselli, E. E. (1972). The mixed standard scale: A new rating system. *Personnel Psychology, 25*, 185–200.

Blum, M. L. (1949). *Industrial psychology and its social foundation.* New York: Harper.

Boorstin, D. J. (1992). *The creators: A history of the heroes of the imagination.* New York: Random House.

Borman, W. C., Ilgen, D. R., & Klimoski, R. J. (Vol. Eds.). (2003). *Handbook of psychology:* Vol. 12: *Industrial and organizational psychology.* Hoboken, NJ: Wiley.

Borman, W. C., White, L. A., & Dorsey, D. W. (1995). Effects of ratee task performance and interpersonal factors on supervisor and peer performance ratings. *Journal of Applied Psychology, 80*, 168–177.

Borman, W. C., White, L. A., Pulakos, E. D., & Oppler, S. H. (1991). Models of supervisory job performance ratings. *Journal of Applied Psychology, 76*, 863–872.

Bray, D. W., & Campbell, R. J. (1968). Selection of salesmen by means of an assessment center. *Journal of Applied Psychology, 52*, 36–41.

Bray, D. W., Campbell, R. J., & Grant, D. L. (1974). *Formative years in business: A long term AT&T study of managerial lives.* New York: Wiley.

Bray, D. W., & Grant, D. L. (1966). The assessment center in the measurement of potential for business management. *Psychological Monographs, 80*, 1–27.

Brayfield, A. H., & Crockett, W. H. (1955). Employee attitudes and employee performance. *Psychological Bulletin, 62*, 396–424.

Bregman, E. O. (1922). Studies in industrial psychology. *Archives of Psychology, 9*, 1–60.

Brief, A. P., & Weiss, H. M. (2002). Organizational behavior: Affect in the workplace. *Annual Review of Psychology, 53*, 279–307.

Briggs, V. M., Jr. (1987). The growth and composition of the U.S. labor force. *Science, 238*, 176–180.

Briggs, G. E., & Johnston, W. A. (1967). *Team training* (NAVRADEVCEN-1327-4, AD-660019). Orlando, FL: Naval Training Device Center.

Brigham, C. C. (1923). *A study of American intelligence.* Princeton, NJ: Princeton University Press.

Bringmann, W. C., Lück, H. E., Miller, R., & Early, C. E. (Eds.). (1997). *A pictorial history of psychology.* Carol Stream, IL: Quintessence.

Brogden, H. E. (1946). On the interpretation of the correlation coefficient as a measure of predictive efficiency. *Journal of Educational Psychology, 37,* 64–76.

Brogden, H. E., & Taylor, E. K. (1950). The dollar criterion: Applying the cost accounting concept to criterion construction. *Personnel Psychology, 3,* 133–154.

Brown v. Board of Education. (1954). 347 U.S. 483.

Brown, J. (1992). *The definition of a profession: The authority of metaphor in the history of intelligence testing, 1890–1930.* Princeton, NJ: Princeton University Press.

Browne, C. G.(1951). Study of executive leadership in business. *Journal of Applied Psychology, 35,* 36–37.

Bryan, W. L., & Harter, N. (1897). Studies in the physiology and psychology of the telegraphic language. *Psychological Review, 4,* 27–35.

Bucklow, M. (1977). Applied psychology is Australia—The history. In M. Nixon & R. Taft (Eds.), *Psychology in Australia: Achievements and prospects* (pp. 23–34). Rushcutters Bay, NSW, Australia: Pergamon.

Burnham, J. C. (1987). *How superstition won and science lost: Popularizing science and health in the United States.* New Brunswick, NJ: Rutgers University Press.

Burt, C. (1947). Charles Samuel Myers. *Occupational Psychology, 21,* 1–6.

Burtt, H. (1926). *Principles of employment psychology.* New York: Harper.

Calder, B. J. (1977). An attribution theory of leadership. In B. M. Staw & G. R. Salancik (Eds.), *New directions in organizational behavior* (pp. 179–204). Chicago: St. Clair Press.

Camfield, T. (1973). The professionalization of American psychology, 1870–1917. *Journal of the History of Behavioral Sciences, 9,* 66–75.

Campbell, J. P. (1971). Personnel training and development. *Annual Review of Psychology, 22,* 565–602.

Campbell, J. P. (1989). An agenda for theory and research. In I. L. Goldstein & Associates (Eds.), *Training and development in organizations* (pp. 457–468). San Francisco: Jossey-Bass.

Campbell, J. P. (1990). An overview of the Army Selection and Classification Project (Project A). *Personnel Psychology, 43,* 231–239.

Campbell, J. P. (1999). The definition of measurement of performance in the new age. In D. R. Ilgen & E. D. Pulakos (Eds.), *The changing nature of performance* (pp. 399–430). San Francisco: Jossey-Bass.

Campbell, J. P. (2007). Profiting from history. In L. L. Koppes (Ed.), *Historical perspectives in industrial and organizational psychology* (pp. 441–457). Mahwah, NJ: Erlbaum.

Campbell, D. T., & Fiske, D. W. (1959). Convergent and discriminant validation by the multitrait-multimethod matrix. *Psychological Bulletin, 56,* 81–105.

Campbell, J. P., Gasser, M. B., & Oswald, F. L. (1996). The substantive nature of performance variability. In K. R. Murphy (Ed.,), *Individual differences and behavior in organizations* (pp. 258–299). San Francisco: Jossey-Bass.

Campbell, J. P., & Knapp, D. J. (Eds.). (2001). *Exploring the limits in personnel selection and classification.* Mahwah, NJ: Erlbaum.

Campbell, J. P., & Kuncel, N. R. (2001). Individual and team training. In N. Anderson, D. S. Ones, H. K. Sinangil, & C. Viswesvaran (Eds.), *Handbook of industrial, work and organizational psychology: Personnel psychology* (Vol. 1, pp. 278–312). London: Sage.

Campbell, J. P., McCloy, R. A., Oppler, S. H., & Sager, C. E. (1993). A theory of performance. In N. Schmitt & W. C. Borman (Eds.), *Personnel selection in organizations* (pp. 35–70). San Francisco: Jossey-Bass.

Campion, M. A., Medsker, G. J., & Higgs, A. C. (1993). Relations between work group characteristics and effectiveness: Implications for designing effective work groups. *Personnel Psychology, 46,* 823–850.

Cannon-Bowers, J. A., Salas, E., Tannenbaum, S. I., & Mathieu, J. E. (1995). Toward theoretically based principles of training effectiveness: A model and empirical investigations. *Military Psychology, 7,* 141–164.

Capshew, J. H. (1999). *Psychologists on the march: Science, practice, and professional identity in America, 1929–1969.* Cambridge: Cambridge University Press.

Cartwright, S., & Cooper, C. L. (1997). *Managing workplace stress.* Thousand Oaks, CA: Sage Publications.

Cascio, W. F. (1991). *Costing human resources: The financial impact of behavior in organizations* (3rd ed.). Boston: PWS-Kent.

Cascio, W. F. (1995). Whither industrial and organizational psychology in a changing world of work? *American Psychologist, 50,* 928–939.

Cascio W. F. (2003). Changes in workers, work, and organizations. In W. C. Borman, D. R. Ilgen, & R. J. Klimoski (Eds.), *Comprehensive handbook of psychology: Vol. 12: Industrial and organizational psychology* (pp. 401–422). New York: Wiley.

Cashman, S. D. (1989). *America in the twenties and thirties.* New York: New York University Press.

Cattell, J. M. (1890). Mental tests and measurements. *Mind, 15,* 373–381. Reprinted in *James McKeen Cattell: Man of science,* Vol. 1: *Psychological research* (1947). Lancaster, PA: Science Press.

Cattell, J. M. (1923). The Psychological Corporation. *Annals of the Academy of Political and Social Science, 110,* 165–171.

Chhokar, J. S., Brodbeck, F. C., & House, R. J. (2007). *Culture and leadership across the world: The GLOBE book of in-depth studies of 25 societies.* Mahwah, NJ: Erlbaum.

Cleeton, G. U., & Knight, F. B. (1924). Validity of character judgment based on external criteria. *Journal of Applied Psychology, 8,* 215–231.

Coch, L., & French, J. R. P., Jr. (1948). Overcoming resistance to change. *Human Relations, 1,* 512–532.

Cohen, M. S. (1995). *Labor shortages as America approaches the twenty-first century.* Ann Arbor: University of Michigan Press.

Colarelli, S. M. (1998). Psychological interventions in organizations: An evolutionary perspective. *American Psychologist, 53,* 1044–1056.

Collins, L. M., & Horn, J. L. (Eds.). (1991). *Best methods for the analysis of change.* Washington, DC: American Psychological Association.

Cook, P. H. (1949). The work of psychologists in Australian industry. *Occupational Psychology, 23,* 38–46.

Coon, D. J., & Sprenger, H. A. (1998). Psychologists in service to science: The American Psychological Association and the American Association for the Advancement of Science. *American Psychologist, 53*, 1253–1269.

Cowles, M. (2001). *Statistics in psychology: A historical perspective* (2nd ed.). Mahwah, NJ: Erlbaum.

Craig, D. R., & Charters, W. W. (1925). *Personal leadership in industry*. New York: McGraw-Hill.

Craiger, P. (1997). Technology, organizations, and work in the 20th century. *Industrial-Organizational Psychologist, 34*(3), 89–96.

Cronbach, L. J. (1951). Coefficient alpha and the internal structure of tests. *Psychometrika, 6*, 671–684.

Cronbach, L. J., & Meehl, P. E. (1955). Construct validity in psychological tests. *Psychological Bulletin, 52*, 281–302.

Cunningham, J. W., Boese, R. R., Neeb, R. W., & Pass, J. J. (1983). Systematically derived work dimensions: Factor analyses of the Occupation Analysis Inventory. *Journal of Applied Psychology, 68*, 232–252.

Dansereau, F., Alutto, J. A., & Yammarino, F. J. (1984). *Theory testing in organizational behavior: The variant approach.* Englewood Cliffs, NJ: Prentice Hall.

Darwin, C. (1859). *On the origins of species by means of natural selection.* London: John Murray.

Day, D. V., & Lance, C. E. (2004). Modeling leader growth and development. In D. V. Day, S. J. Zaccaro, & S. M. Halpin (Eds.), *Leadership development for transforming organizations* (pp. 41–69). Mahwah, NJ: Erlbaum.

Day, D., & Zaccaro, S. (2007). Leadership: A critical historical analysis of the influence of leader traits. In L. L. Koppes (Ed.), *Historical perspectives in industrial and organizational psychology* (pp. 383–405). Mahwah, NJ: Erlbaum.

Deal, T. E., & Kennedy, A. A. (1982). *Corporate cultures: The rites and rituals of corporate life.* Reading, MA: Addison-Wesley.

DeNisi, A. S., Cafferty, T., & Meglino, B. (1984). A cognitive view of the performance appraisal process: A model and research propositions. *Organizational Behavior and Human Performance, 33*, 360–396.

DeShon, R. P., Kozlowski, S. W. J., Schmidt, A. M., Milner, K. R., & Wiechmann, D. (2004). Multiple goal feedback effects on the regulation of individual and team performance in training. *Journal of Applied Psychology, 89*, 1035–1056.

de Wolff, C. J., & Shimmin, S. (1976). The psychology of work in Europe: A review of a profession. *Personnel Psychology, 29*, 175–195.

Dipboye, R. L., Smith, C. S., & Howell, W. C. (1994). *Understanding industrial and organizational psychology: An integrated approach.* New York: Harcourt Brace College Publishers.

Drasgow, R., & Hulin, C. L. (1990). Item response theory. In M. D. Dunnette & L. M. Hough (Eds.), *Handbook of industrial and organizational psychology* (2nd ed., Vol. 1, pp. 577–636). Palo Alto, CA: Consulting Psychologists Press.

Driskell, J. E., Radtke, P. H., & Salas, E. (2003). Virtual teams: Effects of technological mediation on team performance. *Group Dynamics, 7*, 297–323.

Drucker, P. (1954). *The practice of management.* New York: Harper.

DuBois, P. H. (1965). A test-dominated society: China, 1115 B.C.–1905 A.D. In *Proceedings of the 1964 invitational conference on testing problems* (pp. 3–11). Princeton, NJ: Educational Testing Service.

DuBois, P. H. (1970). *A history of psychological testing.* Boston: Allyn & Bacon.

Dunlap, K. (1923). Fact and fable in character analysis. *Annals of the Academy of Political and Social Science, 110*, 74–80.

Dunnette, M. D. (Ed.). (1976). *Handbook of industrial and organizational psychology.* Chicago: Rand McNally.

Dunnette, M. D., & Hough, L. M. (Eds.). (1990–1993). *Handbook of industrial and organizational psychology.* Palo Alto, CA: Consulting Psychologists Press.

Durkheim, E. (1895). *Rules of sociological method.* New York: Free Press.

Equal Employment Opportunity Commission. (1978). Uniform guidelines on employee selection procedures. *Federal Register, 43*, 38290–38315.

Farmer, E. (1958). Early days in industrial psychology: An autobiographical note. *Occupational Psychology, 32*, 264–267.

Farr, J. L., & Levy, P. E. (2007). Performance appraisal. In L. L. Koppes (Ed.), *Historical perspectives in industrial and organizational psychology* (pp. 311–327). Mahwah, NJ: Erlbaum.

Farr, J. L., & Tesluk, P. E. (1997). Bruce V. Moore: First president of Division 14. *Journal of Applied Psychology, 82*(4), 478–485.

Feldman, J. M. (1981). Beyond attribution theory: Cognitive processes in performance appraisal. *Journal of Applied Psychology, 66*, 127–148.

Ferguson, L. W. (n.d.). *A new light of the history of industrial psychology.* Unpublished manuscript. Ferguson Collection, Carnegie Mellon University.

Ferguson, L. W. (1952). A look across the years 1920–1950. In L. L. Thurstone (Ed.), *Applications of psychology: Essays to honor Walter V. Bingham* (pp. 7–22). New York: Harper.

Ferguson, L. W. (1961). The development of industrial psychology. In B. V. Gilmer (Ed.), *Industrial psychology* (pp. 18–37). New York: McGraw-Hill.

Ferguson, L. W. (1962–1965). *The heritage of industrial psychology* [14 pamphlets]. Hartford, CT: Finlay Press.

Festinger, L. (1957). *A theory of cognitive dissonance.* Oxford: Row, Peterson.

Fiedler, F. E. (1967). *A theory of leadership effectiveness.* New York: McGraw-Hill.

Finch, F. H., & Odoroff, M. E. (1939). Employment trends in applied psychology. *Journal of Consulting Psychology, 3*, 118–122.

Findley, H. M., Giles, W. F., & Mossholder, K. W. (2000). Performance appraisal process and system facets: Relationships with contextual performance. *Journal of Applied Psychology, 85*(4), 634–640.

Fine, S. A., & Wiley, W. W. (1971). *An introduction to functional job analysis.* Washington, DC: The Upjohn Institute.

Flanagan, J. C. (1948). *The aviation psychology program in the army air forces* (Rep. No. 1). Washington, DC: U.S. Government Printing Office.

Flanagan, J. C. (1954). The critical incident technique. *Psychological Bulletin, 51*, 327–358.

Flanagan, J. C. (1984). The American Institutes for Research. *American Psychologist, 39*(11), 1272–1276.

Fleishman, E. A. (1954). Dimensional analysis of psychomotor abilities. *Journal of Experimental Psychology, 48*, 437–454.

Fleishman, E. A. (1979). The new applied psychology: An international perspective. *International Review of Applied Psychology, 28*, 67–74.

Fleishman, E. A. (1992). *The Fleishman-Job Analysis Survey (F-JAS).* Palo Alto, CA: Consulting Psychologists Press.

Fleishman, E. A., Harris, E. F., & Burtt, H. E. (1955). *Leadership and supervision in industry: An evaluation of a supervisory training program*. Columbus: Ohio State University, Bureau of Educational Research.

Fleishman, E. A., & Zaccaro, S. J. (1992). Toward a taxonomy of team performance functions. In R. W. Swezey & E. Salas (Eds.), *Teams: Their training & performance* (pp. 31–56). Norwood, NJ: Ablex.

Fletcher, C., & Baldry, C. (1999). Multi-source feedback systems: A research perspective. *International Review of Industrial and Organizational Psychology, 14*, 149–193.

Follett, M. P. (1927). Leader and expert. In H. C. Metcalf (Ed.), *The psychological foundations of management* (pp. 220–243). Chicago: Shaw.

Ford, J. K., & Kraiger, K. (1995). The application of cognitive constructs and principles to the instructional systems of model training: Implications for needs assessment, design, and transfer. In C. L. Cooper & I. T. Robertson (Eds.), *International review of industrial and organizational psychology* (Vol. 10, pp. 1–48). Chichester, England: Wiley.

Freyd, M. (1923). The graphic rating scale. *Journal of Educational Psychology, 14*, 83–102.

Friedman, T. L. (2006). *The world is flat: A brief history of the twenty-first century*. New York: Farrar, Straus, and Giroux.

Frost, E. (1920). What industry wants and does not want from the psychologist. *Journal of Applied Psychology, 4*, 18–25.

Fryer, D. H., & Henry E. R. (Eds.). (1950). *Handbook of applied psychology* (2 vols.). New York: Rinehart.

Gael, S. (1988). *The job analysis handbook for business, industry, and government*. New York: Wiley.

Gale, H. (1896). On the psychology of advertising. In H. Gale (Ed.), *Psychological studies* (pp. 39–69). Minneapolis, MN: Author.

Geissler, L. R. (1918). A plan for the technical training of consulting psychologists. *Journal of Applied Psychology, 2*, 77–83.

Gertsner, C. R., & Day, D. V. (1997). Meta-analytic review of leader-member exchange theory: Correlates and construct issues. *Journal of Applied Psychology, 82*(6), 827–844.

Ghiselli, E. E., & Brown, C. W. (1948). *Personnel and industrial psychology*. New York: McGraw-Hill.

Gibb, C. A. (1947). The principles and traits of leadership. *Journal of Abnormal and Social Psychology, 42*, 267–284.

Glassop, L. I. (2002). The organizational benefits of teams. *Human Relations, 55*, 225–249.

Goldstein, I. L. (1974). *Training: Program development and evaluation*. Monterey, CA: Brooks/Cole.

Goodwin, C. J. (1999). *A history of modern psychology*. New York: Wiley.

Gordon, R. A., & Howell, J. E. (1959). *Higher education for business*. New York: Columbia Press.

Graen, G. (1976). Role-making processes within complex organizations. In M. D. Dunnette (Ed.), *Handbook of industrial and organizational psychology* (pp. 1201–1245), Chicago: Rand McNally.

Graen, G. B., Novak, M. A., & Sommerkamp, P. (1982). The effects of leader-member exchange and job design on productivity and job satisfaction: Testing a dual attachment model. *Organizational Behavior and Human Performance, 30*, 109–131.

Gray, E. R. (1978, February). The non-linear systems experience: A requiem. *Business Horizons, 21*, 31–37.

Greenberg, J. (1987). A taxonomy of organizational justice theories. *Academy of Management Review, 12*, 9–22.

Greenhaus, J. H., & Powell, G. N. (2006). When work and family are allies: A theory of work-family enrichment. *Academy of Management Review, 31*, 72–92.

Griffin, M. A., Landy, F. J., & Mayocchi, L. (2002). Australian influences on Elton Mayo: The construct of revery in industrial society. *History of Psychology, 5*, 356–375.

Griggs v. Duke Power (1971). 401 U.S. 424.

Guion, R. M. (1965). *Personnel testing*. New York: McGraw-Hill.

Guion, R. M. (1976). Recruiting, selection, and job placement. In M. D. Dunnette (Ed.), *Handbook of industrial and organizational psychology* (pp. 777–828). Chicago: Rand McNally.

Guion, R. M. (1991). Personnel assessment, selection, and placement. In M. D. Dunnette & L. M. Hough (Eds.), *Handbook of industrial and organizational psychology* (2nd ed., Vol. 2, pp. 327–397). Palo Alto, CA: Consulting Psychologists Press.

Guion, R. M., & Gottier, R. F. (1965). Validity of personnel measures in personnel selection. *Personnel Psychology, 18*, 135–164.

Gundlach, H. U. K. (1997). The mobile psychologist: Psychology and the railroads. In W. G. Bringmann, H. E. Lück, R. Miller, & C. E. Early (Eds.). *A pictorial history of psychology* (pp. 506–509). Chicago: Quintessence.

Gutman, A., Koppes, L. L., & Vodanovich, S. (2011). *EEO Law and Personnel Practices* (3rd ed.). New York: Taylor and Francis, Inc.

Haber, S. (1964). *Efficiency and uplift: Scientific management in the progressive era 1890–1920*. Chicago: University of Chicago Press.

Hacker, H., & Echterhoff, W. (1997). Traffic psychology. In W. G. Bringmann, H. E. Lück, R. Miller, & C. E. Early (Eds.), *A pictorial history of psychology* (pp. 503–505). Chicago: Quintessence.

Hackman, J. R., & Oldham, G. R. (1975). Development of the job diagnostic survey. *Journal of Applied Psychology, 60*, 159–170.

Hackman, J. R., & Oldham, G. R. (1976). Motivation through the design of work: Test of a theory. *Organizational Behavior and Human Performance, 16*, 250–279.

Hakel, M. (1979). Proposal to incorporate as the Society for Industrial and Organizational Psychology. *Industrial-Organizational Psychologist, 16*, 4–5.

Hakel, M. (1986). Personnel selection and placement. In M. R. Rosenzweig & L. W. Porter (Eds.), *Annual review of psychology* (pp. 351–380). Palo Alto, CA: Annual Reviews.

Hale, M. (1992). History of employment testing. In A. Widgor & W. R. Garner (Eds.), *Ability testing: Uses, consequences, and controversies* (pp. 3–38). Washington, DC: National Academy Press.

Hale, M., Jr. (1980). *Human science and the social order: Hugo Münsterberg and the origins of applied psychology*. Philadelphia: Temple University Press.

Hammer, L. B., Kossek, E. E., Yragui, N. L., Bohner, T., & Hanson, G. C. (2009). Development and validation of a multidimensional measure of family supportive supervisor behaviors (FSSB). *Journal of Management, 35*(4), 837–856.

Hansen, J. C. (1987). Edward Kellogg Strong, Jr.: First author of the Strong Interest Inventory. *Journal of Counseling and Development, 66*, 119–125.

Harrell, T. W., & Churchill, R. D. (1941). The classification of military personnel. *Psychological Bulletin, 38*, 331–353.

Harvey, R. J. (1991). *The Common Metric Questionnaire (CMQ): A job analysis system*. San Antonio, TX: Psychological Corporation.

Hauenstein, N. M. A. (1998). Training raters to increase the accuracy of appraisals and the usefulness of feedback. In J. W. Smither (Ed.), *Performance appraisal: State of the art in practice* (pp. 404–442). San Francisco: Jossey-Bass.

Hausmann, M. F. (1931). Otto Lipmann and industrial psychology in Germany [Review of *Grundriss der arbeitswissenschaft und ergebnisse der arbeitswissenschaftlichen statistik*]. *Personnel Journal, 9*, 417–420.

Hearnshaw, L. S. (1964). *A short history of British psychology 1840–1940*. Westport, CT: Greenwood Press.

Heller, W. J. (1929–1930). Industrial psychology and its development in Switzerland. *Personnel Journal, 8*, 435–441.

Hemphill, J. K. (1949). *Situational factors in leadership*. Columbus: Ohio State Bureau of Educational Research.

Hergenhahn, B. R. (1997). *An introduction to the history of psychology* (3rd ed.). Pacific Grove, CA: Brooks/Cole.

Hersey, P., & Blanchard, K. H. (1969). Life cycle theory of leadership. *Training and Development Journal, 23*, 26–34.

Herzberg, F., Mausner, B., & Snyderman, B. S. (1959). *The motivation to work*. New York: Wiley.

Highhouse, S. (1999). The brief history of personnel counseling in industrial-organizational psychology. *Journal of Vocational Behavior, 55*, 318–336.

Highhouse, S. (2002). Assessing the candidate as a whole: A historical and critical analysis of individual psychological assessment. *Personnel Psychology, 55*, 363–396.

Highhouse, S. (2007). Applications of organizational psychology: Learning through failure or failure to learn. In L. L. Koppes (Ed.), *Historical perspectives in industrial and organizational psychology* (pp. 331–352). Mahwah, NJ: Erlbaum.

Hilgard, E. R. (1987). *Psychology in America: A historical survey*. San Diego, CA: Harcourt, Brace, Jovanovich.

Hochwarter, W. A., Witt, L. A., & Kacmar, K. M. (2000). Perceptions of organizational politics as a moderator of the relationship between conscientiousness and job performance. *Journal of Applied Psychology, 85*(3), 472–478.

Hollander, E. P., & Julian, J. W. (1969). Contemporary trends in the analysis of leadership processes. *Psychological Bulletin, 71*, 387–397.

Hollenbeck, J. R., Ilgen, D. R., LePine, J. A., Colquitt, J. A., & Hedlund, J. (1998). Extending the multilevel theory of team decision making: Effects of feedback and experience in hierarchical teams: *Academy of Management Journal, 41*, 269–282.

Hollingworth, H. H. (1916). *Vocational psychology: Its problems and methods*. New York: Appleton.

Hollingworth, H. H., & Poffenberger, A. T. (1917). *Applied psychology*. New York: Appleton.

Hoppock, R. (1935). *Job satisfaction*. Oxford, England: Harper.

House, R. J. (1971). A path-goal theory of leader effectiveness. *Administrative Science Quarterly, 16*, 321–338.

House, R. J. (1977). A 1976 theory of charismatic leadership. In J. G. Hunt & L. L. Larson (Eds.), *Leadership: The cutting edge* (pp. 189–207). Carbondale: Southern Illinois University.

House, R. J., & Aditya, R. N. (1997). The social scientific study of leadership: Quo Vadis? *Journal of Management, 23*, 409–473.

Howard, A., & Bray, D. W. (1988). *Managerial lives in transition: Advancing age and changing times*. New York: Guilford Press.

Howell, W. C., & Cooke, N. J. (1989). Training the human information processor: A review of cognitive models. In I. L. Goldstein & Associates (Eds.), *Training and development in organizations* (pp. 121–182). San Francisco: Jossey-Bass.

Hull, C. L. (1928). *Aptitude testing*. Yonkers-on-Hudson, NY: World Book.

Hunter, J. E., & Schmidt, F. L. (1990). *Methods of meta-analysis: Correcting error and bias in research findings*. Newberry Park, CA: Sage.

Ilgen, D. R. (1990). Health issues at work: Opportunities for industrial/organizational psychology. *American Psychologist, 45*, 273–283.

Ilgen, D. R., Barnes-Farrell, J. L., & McKellin, D. B. (1993). Performance appraisal process research in the 1980s: What has it contributed to appraisals in use? *Organizational Behavior and Human Decision Processes, 54*, 321–368.

Jacobson, J. Z. (1951). *Scott of Northwestern*. Chicago: Louis Mariano.

James, W. (1892). *Psychology: Briefer course*. New York: Henry Holt.

James, W. (1950). *The principles of psychology* (2 vols.). New York: Dover (Original work published in 1890).

Janis, I. L. (1972). *Victims of groupthink: A psychological study of foreign-policy decisions and fiascoes*. Boston: Houghton Mifflin.

Jenkins, J. G. (1935). *Psychology in business and industry: An introduction to psychotechnology*. New York: Wiley.

Jenkins, W. O.(1947). A review of leadership studies with particular reference to military problems. *Psychological Bulletin, 44*, 54–79.

Judge, T. A., & Ilies, R. (2002). Relationship of personality to performance motivation: A meta-analytic review. *Journal of Applied Psychology, 87*, 797–807.

Kacmar, K. M., Witt, L. A., Zivnuska, S., & Gully, S. M. (2003). The interactive effect of leader-member exchange and communication frequency on performance ratings. *Journal of Applied Psychology, 88*(4), 764–772.

Kaiser, A. E. (1989). A chronology of the theoretical developments in organizational behavior. In J. S. Ott (Ed.), *Classic readings in organizational behavior* (pp. 10–26). Pacific Grove, CA: Brooks/Cole.

Katz, D., & Kahn, R. L. (1966). *The social psychology of organizations*. New York: Wiley.

Katz, D., Maccoby, N., & Morse, N. (1950). *Productivity, supervision, and morale in an office situation*. Ann Arbor, MI: Institute for Social Research.

Katzell, R. A. (1958). Looking around: Is individualism disappearing? *Harvard Business Review, 36*, 139–143.

Katzell, R. A., & Austin, J. T. (1992). From then to now: The development of industrial-organizational psychology in the United States. *Journal of Applied Psychology, 77*, 803–835.

Keita, G. P., & Hurrell, J. J., Jr. (Eds.). (1994). *Job stress in a changing workforce: Investigating gender, diversity, and family issues*. Washington, DC: American Psychological Association.

Kingsbury, F. A. (1923). Applying psychology to business. *Annals of the American Academy of Political and Social Sciences, 110*, 2–12.

Kirkpatrick, D. L. (1959). Techniques for evaluating training programs. *Journal of the ASTD, 13*, 3–9.

Klein, K. J., & House, R. J. (1995). On fire: Charismatic leadership and levels of analysis. *Leadership Quarterly, 6*, 183–198.

Klein, K., & Kozlowski, S. W. J. (2000a). *Multilevel theory, research, and methods in organizations: Foundations, extensions, and new directions*. San Francisco: Jossey-Bass.

Klein, K., & Kozlowski, S. W. J. (2000b). A multilevel approach to theory and research in organizations: Contextual, temporal, and emergent processes. In K. J. Klein &

S. W. J. Kozlowski (Eds.), *Multilevel theory, research, and methods in organizations: Foundations, extensions, and new directions* (pp. 3–90). San Francisco: Jossey-Bass.

Kleiner, A. (1996). *The age of heretics: Heroes, outlaws, and the forerunners of corporate change.* New York: Doubleday.

Kleiser, G. (1923). *Training for power and leadership.* New York: George H. Doran.

Koppes, L. L. (1997). American female pioneers of industrial and organizational psychology during the early years. *Journal of Applied Psychology, 82,* 500–515.

Koppes, L. L. (2003). Industrial-organizational psychology. In I. B. Weiner & D. K. Freedheim (Eds.), *Comprehensive handbook of psychology* (Vol. 1, pp. 376–389). New York: Wiley.

Koppes, L. L. (Ed.). (2007). *Historical perspectives in industrial and organizational psychology.* Mahwah, NJ: Erlbaum.

Koppes, L. L., & Bauer, A. M. (2006). Marion Almira Bills: Industrial psychology pioneer bridging science and practice. In D. A. Dewsbury, L. T. Benjamin, Jr., & M. Wertheimer (Eds.), *Portraits of pioneers in psychology* (Vol. 6, pp. 103–116). Washington, DC: American Psychological Association.

Koppes, L. L., & Pickren, W. (2007). Industrial and organizational psychology: An evolving science and practice. In L. L. Koppes (Ed.), *Historical perspectives in industrial and organizational psychology* (pp. 3–37). Mahwah, NJ: Erlbaum.

Koppes, L. L., Schneider, S., & Linnabery, E. (2009, April). What managers' behaviors support employees and their work-life effectiveness? In L. L. Koppes (Chair), *Work-Life effectiveness: Bridging research and practice.* Symposium for the Annual Conference of the Society for Industrial and Organizational Psychology. New Orleans, LA.

Koppes, L. L., & Swanberg, J. (Eds.). (2008). Work-Life effectiveness: Implications for organizations [Special Issue]. *The Psychologist-Manager Journal.* New York: Taylor & Francis.

Kornhauser, A. W. (1922). The psychology of vocational selection. *Psychological Bulletin, 19,* 192–229.

Kornhauser, A. W. (1926–1927). What are rating scales good for? *Journal of Personnel Research, 5,* 189–193, 309–317, 338–344, 440–446.

Kornhauser, A. W., & Kingsbury, F. A. (1924). *Psychological tests in business.* Chicago: University of Chicago Press.

Korsgaard, M. A., & Roberson, L. (1995). Procedural justice in performance evaluation: The role of instrumental and non-instrumental voice in performance appraisal discussions. *Journal of Management, 21,* 657–669.

Kozlowski, S. W. J., & Bell, B. S. (2003). Work groups and teams in organizations. In W. C. Borman, D. R. Ilgen, & R. J. Klimoski (Eds.), *Comprehensive handbook of psychology: Vol. 12: Industrial and organizational psychology* (pp. 333–375). New York: Wiley.

Kozlowski, S. W. J, Gully, S. M., Nason, E. R., & Smith, E. M. (1999). Developing adaptive teams: A theory of compilation and performance across levels and time. In D. R. Ilgen & E. D. Pulakos (Eds.), *The changing nature of work and performance: Implications for staffing, personnel actions, and development* (1st ed., pp. 240–292). San Francisco: Jossey-Bass.

Kraepelin, E. (1896). A measure of mental capacity. *Appleton's Popular Science Monthly, 49,* 756–763.

Kraiger, K., & Ford, J. K. (2007). The expanding role of workplace training: Themes and trends influencing training research and practice. In L. L. Koppes (Ed.), *Historical

perspectives in industrial and organizational psychology* (pp. 281–309). Mahwah, NJ: Erlbaum.

Kuder, G. F., & Richardson, M. W. (1937). The theory of estimation of test reliability. *Psychometrika, 2,* 151–166.

Landsberger, H. A. (1958). *Hawthorne revisited: Management and the worker, its critics, and developments in human relations in industry.* Ithaca, NY: Cornell University Press.

Landy, F. J. (1992). Hugo Münsterberg: Victim or visionary. *Journal of Applied Psychology, 77,* 787–802.

Landy, F. J. (1997). Early influences on the development of industrial and organizational psychology. *Journal of Applied Psychology, 82,* 467–477.

Landy, F. J., & Farr, J. L. (1980). Performance rating. *Psychological Bulletin, 87,* 72–107.

Latham, G. P., & Budworth, M. H. (2007). The study of work motivation in the 20th century. In L. L. Koppes (Ed.), *Historical perspectives in industrial and organizational psychology* (pp. 353–381). Mahwah, NJ: Erlbaum.

Latham, G. P., & Heslin, P. A. (2003). Training the trainee as well as the trainer: Lessons to be learned from clinical psychology. *Canadian Psychology, 44,* 218–231.

Latham, G. P., & Wexley, K. N. (1977). Behavioral observation scales for performance appraisal purposes. *Personnel Psychology, 30,* 225–268.

Latham, G. P., & Yukl, G. A. (1975). A review of research on the application of goal setting in organizations. *Academy of Management Journal, 18,* 824–845.

Lawshe, C. H. (1952). Employee selection. *Personnel Psychology, 5,* 31–34.

Ledbetter v. Goodyear Tire & Rubber Co. (2007). 550 U.S. 618.

LePine, J. A. (2003). Team adaptation and postchange performance: Effects of team composition in terms of members' cognitive ability and personality. *Journal of Applied Psychology, 88,* 27–39.

Levy, P. E. (2006). *Industrial/Organizational psychology: Understanding the workplace* (2nd ed.). Boston: Houghton Mifflin.

Levy, P. E., & Williams, J. R. (1998). The role of perceived system knowledge in predicting appraisal reactions, job satisfaction, and organizational commitment. *Journal of Organizational Behavior, 19,* 53–65.

Lewin, K., Lippitt, R., & White, R. K. (1939). Patterns of aggressive behavior in experimentally created social climates. *Journal of Social Psychology, 10,* 271–301.

Likert, R. (1961). *New patterns of management.* New York: McGraw-Hill.

Link, H. C. (1919). *Employment psychology.* New York: Macmillan.

Locke, E. A. (1968). Toward a theory of task motivation and incentives. *Organizational Behavior & Human Decision Processes, 3,* 157–189.

Locke, E. A., & Latham, G. P. (1990). *A theory of goal setting and task performance.* Englewood Cliffs, NJ: Prentice-Hall.

Locke, E. A., & Latham, G. P. (2002). Building a practically useful theory of goal setting and task motivation: A 35-year odyssey. *American Psychologist, 57,* 705–717.

Locke, E. A, & Latham, G. P. (2004). What should we do about motivation theory? Six recommendations for the 21st century. *Academy of Management Review, 29,* 388–403.

Locke, E. A., Shaw, K. M., Saari, L. M., & Latham, G. P. (1981). Goal setting and task performance: 1969–1980. *Psychological Bulletin, 90,* 125–152.

Lofquist, L. H., & Dawis, R. V. (1969). *Adjustment to work: A psychological view of man's problems in a work-oriented society.* New York: Appleton-Century-Crofts.

Lord, R. G. (1977). Functional leadership behavior: Measurement and relation to social power and leadership perceptions. *Administrative Science Quarterly, 22,* 114–133.

Lord, R. G. (2000). Leadership. In A. E. Kazdin (Ed.), *Encyclopedia of psychology* (Vol. 3, pp. 775–786). Washington, DC: American Psychological Association.

Lord, R. G., Binning, J. F., Rush, M. C., & Thomas, J. C. (1978). The effect of performance cues and leader behavior on questionnaire ratings of leadership behavior. *Organizational Behavior and Human Performance, 21,* 27–39.

Lord, R. G., Foti, R. J., & De Vader, C. L. (1984). A test of leadership categorization theory: Internal structure, information processing, and leadership perceptions. *Organizational Behavior and Human Performance, 34,* 343–378.

Lord, R. G., & Maher, K. J. (1991). Cognitive theory in industrial/organizational psychology. In M. D. Dunnette & L. M. Hough (Eds.), *Handbook of industrial and organizational psychology* (2nd ed., Vol. 2, pp. 1–62). Palo Alto, CA: Consulting Psychologists Press.

Lowe, R. (1993). Master's programs in industrial-organizational psychology: Current status and call for action. *Professional Psychology, 24,* 27–34.

Lowe, R. (2000). The silent conversation: Talking about the master's degree. *Professional Psychology, 31,* 339–345.

Lowe, K. B., & Gardner, W. L. (2000). Ten years of the *Leadership Quarterly*: Contributions and challenges for the future. *Leadership Quarterly, 11,* 459–514.

Lowenberg, G., & Conrad, K. A. (1998). *Current perspectives in industrial/organizational psychology.* Needham Heights, MA: Allyn & Bacon.

Lowman, R. L., Kantor, J., & Perloff, R. (2007). A history of I-O psychology educational programs in the United States. In L. L. Koppes (Ed.), *Historical perspectives in industrial and organizational psychology* (pp. 111–137). Mahwah, NJ: Erlbaum.

Luthans, F., & Kreitner, R. (1975). *Organizational behavior modification.* Glenview, IL: Scott, Foresman.

Mahler, W. R., & Monroe, W. H. (1952). *How industry determines the need for and effectiveness of training.* New York: Psychological Corporation.

Maier, N. R. F. (1952). *Principles of human relations.* New York: Wiley.

Major, D. A., & Cleveland, J. (2007). Strategies for reducing work-family conflict: Applying research and best practices from industrial and organizational psychology. In G. P. Hodgkinson & J. K. Ford (Eds.), *International review of industrial and organizational psychology* (Vol. 22, pp. 111–140). Chichester, England: Wiley.

Manchester, W. (1973–74). *The glory and the dream* (2 vols.). Boston: Little, Brown.

March, J. G., & Simon, H. A. (1958). *Organizations.* New York: Wiley.

Marks, M. A., Sabella, M. J., Burke, C. S., & Zaccaro, S. J. (2002). The impact of cross-training on team effectiveness. *Journal of Applied Psychology, 87,* 3–13.

Marrow, A. (1948). Group dynamics in industry—Implications for guidance and personnel workers. *Occupation, 26,* 472–476.

Maslow, A. H. (1943). A theory of human motivation. *Psychological Review, 50,* 370–396.

Mayo, E. (1933). *The human problems of an industrial civilization.* New York: Viking.

McCollom, I. N. (1959). Psychologists in industry in the United States. *American Psychologist, 14,* 704–708.

McCollom, I. N. (1968). Industrial psychology around the world: Part One: America and Western Europe. Part Two: Eastern Europe, Africa, Asia, and Australasia. *International Review of Applied Psychology, 17,* 3–19; 137–148.

McCormick, E. J. (1979). *Job analysis: Methods and applications.* New York: AMACOM.

McCormick, E. J., Jeanneret, P. R., & Meacham, R. C. (1972). A study of job characteristics and job dimensions as based on the Position Analysis Questionnaire (PAQ). *Journal of Applied Psychology, 56,* 347–368.

McGehee, W., & Thayer, P. (1961). *Training in business and industry.* New York: McGraw-Hill.

McGrath, J. (1964). *Social psychology: A brief introduction.* New York: Holt, Rinehart & Winston.

McGregor, D. M. (1957). The human side of enterprise. *Management Review, 46,* 22–28.

McGregor, D. M. (1960). *The human side of enterprise.* New York: McGraw-Hill.

Meindl, J. R., Ehrlich, S. B., & Dukerich, J. M. (1985). The romance of leadership. *Administrative Science Quarterly, 30,* 521–551.

Meriam, J. L. (1906). *Normal school education and efficiency in teaching.* New York: Columbia University, Teachers College Contributions to Education, 152.

Meyer, H. H. (2007). Influence of formal and informal organizations on the development of I-O psychology. In L. L. Koppes (Ed.), *Historical perspectives in industrial and organizational psychology* (pp. 139–168). Mahwah, NJ: Erlbaum.

Meyer, H. H., Kay, E., & French, J. R. (1965). Split roles in performance appraisal. *Harvard Business Review, 43*(1), 123–129.

Miller, R. B. (1953). *Handbook of training and training equipment design.* Pittsburgh: The American Institute of Research.

Miner, J. B. (2002). *Organizational behavior: Foundations, theories, and analyses.* New York: Oxford University Press.

Minton, H. L. (1988). Charting life history: Lewis M. Terman's study of the gifted. In J. G. Morawski (Ed.), *The rise of experimentation in American psychology* (pp. 138–162). New Haven and London: Yale University Press.

Mirvis, P. H. (1988). Organizational development. Part I: An evolutionary perspective. In W. A. Pasmore & R. A. Woodman (Eds.), *Research in organizational change and development* (Vol. 2, pp. 1–57). Greenwich, CT: JAI Press.

Moore, B. V., & Hartmann, G. W. (Eds.). (1931). *Readings in industrial psychology.* New York: Appleton-Century.

Mossholder, K. W., & Arvey, R. D. (1984). Synthetic validity: A conceptual and comparative review. *Journal of Applied Psychology, 69,* 322–333.

Mosso, A. (1906 [1891]). *Fatigue* (M. Drummond & W. B. Drummond, Trans.). London: Allen & Unwin.

Most, R. (1993). John C. Flanagan: The power of planning. *The Industrial-Organizational Psychologist, 30,* 44–49.

Motowidlo, S. J. (2003). Job performance. In W. C. Borman, D. R. Ilgen, & R. J. Klimoski (Eds.), *Handbook of psychology: Industrial and organizational psychology* (Vol. 12, pp. 39–53). New York: Wiley.

Mumford, M. D., Zaccaro, S. J., Harding, F. D., Jacobs, T. O., & Fleishman, E. A. (2000). Leadership skills for a changing world: Solving complex social problems. *Leadership Quarterly, 11,* 11–35.

Münsterberg, H. (1913). *Psychology and industrial efficiency.* Boston: Houghton Mifflin.

Münsterberg, H. (1914). *Psychology: General and applied.* New York and London: Appleton.

Münsterberg, H. (1917). *Business psychology.* Chicago: La Salle Extension University.

Murphy, K. R., & Cleveland, J. N. (1991). *Performance appraisal: An organizational perspective.* Boston: Allyn & Bacon.

Murray, H. A., & MacKinnon, D. W. (1946). Assessment of OSS personnel. *Journal of Consulting Psychology, 10*, 76–80.

Myers, C. S. (1909). *A textbook of experimental psychology.* London: Arnold.

Myers, C. S. (1920). Psychology and industry. *The British Journal of Psychology, 10*, 177–182.

Myers, C. S. (1925). *Industrial psychology.* New York: People's Institute.

Myers, C. S. (1926). *Industrial psychology in Great Britain.* London: Cape.

Myers, C. S. (Ed.). (1929). *Industrial psychology.* London: Thornton Butterworth.

Myers, C. S. (1936). Charles Samuel Myers. In C. Murchinson (Ed.), *A history of psychology in autobiography* (Vol. 3, pp. 215–230). Worcester, MA: Clark University Press.

Napoli, D. S. (1981). *Architects of adjustment: The history of the psychological profession in the United States.* Port Washington, NY: Kennibat Press.

Neal, M. B., & Hammer, L. B. (2007). *Working couples caring for children and aging parents: Effects on work and well-being.* Mahwah, NJ: Erlbaum.

Neuman, G. A., & Wright, J. (1999). Team effectiveness: Beyond skills and cognitive ability. *Journal of Applied Psychology, 84*, 376–389.

Noe, R. A. (1986). Trainees' attributes and attitudes: Neglected influences on training effectiveness. *Academy of Management Review, 11*, 736–749.

Offerman, L. R., & Gowing, M. K. (Eds.). (1990). Organizational psychology [Special issue]. *American Psychologist, 45*, 95–283.

O'Leary-Kelly, A. M., Griffin, R. W., & Glew, D. J. (1996). Organization-motivated aggression: A research framework. *Academy of Management Review, 21*(1), 225–253.

Oliver, J., Blair, C. A., Gorman, C. A., & Woehr, D. J. (2005). Research productivity of I-O psychology doctoral programs in North America. *Industrial-Organizational Psychologist, 43*(1), 55–63.

Orasanu, J., & Salas, E. (1993). Team decision making in complex environments. In G. A. Klein, J. Orasanu, R. Calderwood, & C. E. Zsambok (Eds.), *Decision making in action: Models and methods* (pp. 327–345). Stamford, CT: Ablex.

Ostroff, C., Kinicki, A. J., & Tamkins, M. M. (2003). Organizational culture and climate. In W. C. Borman, D. R. Ilgen, & R. J. Klimoski (Eds.), *Handbook of psychology: Industrial and organizational psychology* (Vol. 12, pp. 565–593). New York: Wiley.

Ouchi, W. G. (1981). *Theory Z: How American business can meet the Japanese challenge.* Reading, MA: Addison-Wesley.

Parsons, F. (1909). *Choosing a vocation.* Boston: Houghton-Mifflin.

Paterson, D. G. (1923). Methods of rating human qualities. *Annals of the American Academy of Political and Social Science, 110*, 81–93.

Paterson, D. G., & Ludgate, K. E. (1922–1923). Blond and brunette traits: A quantitative study. *Journal of Personnel Research, 1*, 122–127.

Pear, T. H. (1948). Industrial psychology as I have seen it. *Occupational Psychology, 22*, 107–117.

Peiró, J. (2009, October). Division news...Division 1-Organizational Psychology. *The IAAP Bulletin, 21*(4), 12.

Peters, T. J., & Waterman, R. (1982). *In search of excellence.* New York: Harper & Row.

Peterson, N. G., Mumford, M. D., Borman, W. C., Jeanneret, P. R., & Fleishman, E. A. (Eds.). (1999). *The occupation information network (O*NET).* Washington, DC: American Psychological Association.

Peterson, N. G., Mumford, M. D., Borman, W. C., Jeanneret, P. R., Fleishman, E. A., Levin, K. Y., Campion, M. A., Mayfield, M. S., Morgeson, F. P., Pearlman, K., Gowing, M. K., Lancaster, A. R., Silver, M. B., & Dye, D. M. (2001). Understanding work using the Occupational Information Network (O*NET): Implications for practice and research. *Personnel Psychology, 54*, 451–492.

Pfeffer, J. (1977). The ambiguity of leadership. *Academy of Management Review, 2*, 104–112.

Pickren, W. E. (2000). European psychology. In G. B. Ferngren (Ed.), *The history of science and religion in the Western tradition* (pp. 495–501). New York: Garland Publishing.

Pickren, W. E., & Fowler, R. D. (2003). Professional organizations. In Freedheim, D. K. (Vol. Ed.) & I. B. Weiner (Ed.-in-Chief), *Handbook of psychology: Vol. 1: History of psychology* (pp. 535–554). Hoboken, NJ: Wiley.

Pierson, F. C. (1959). *The education of the American businessmen.* New York: McGraw-Hill.

Pond, M. (1927). Selective placement of metalworkers. *Journal of Personnel Research, 5*, 345–368, 405–417, 452–466.

Rhoades, L., & Eisenberger, R. (2002). Perceived organizational support: A review of the literature. *Journal of Applied Psychology, 87*(4), 698–714.

Roback, A. A. (1952). *A history of American psychology.* New York: Collier-Macmillan.

Roe, R. A. (1995). Developments in eastern Europe and work and organizational psychology. In C. L. Cooper & I. T. Robertson (Eds.), *International review of industrial and organizational psychology* (pp. 275–349). Chichester, England: Wiley.

Roethlisberger, F. J. (1941). *Management and morale.* Cambridge, MA: Harvard University Press.

Roethlisberger, F. J., & Dickson, W. J. (1939). *Management and the worker: An account of a research program conducted by the Western Electric Company, Hawthorne Works, Chicago.* Cambridge, MA: Harvard University Press.

Rogelberg, S. G. (Ed.). (2006). *Encyclopedia of industrial-organizational psychology.* Thousand Oaks, CA: Sage.

Rogers, T. B. (1995). *The psychological testing enterprise: An introduction.* Pacific Grove, CA: Brooks/Cole.

Rosener, J. B. (1995). *America's competitive secret: Utilizing women as management strategy.* New York: Oxford University Press.

Rousseau, D. (1985). Issues of level in organizational research: Multi-level and cross-level perspectives. In L. L. Cummings & B. M. Staw (Eds.), *Research in organizational behavior* (Vol. 7, pp. 1–38). Greenwich, CT: JAI Press.

Rush, M. C., Thomas, J. C., & Lord, R. G. (1977). Implicit leadership theory: A potential threat to the internal validity of leader behaviors. *Organizational Behavior and Human Performance, 20*, 93–110.

Ryan, T. A., & Smith, P. C. (1954). *Principles of industrial psychology.* New York: Ronald Press.

Sackett, P. R. (2002). The structure of counterproductive work behaviors: Dimensionality and relationships with facets of job performance. *International Journal of Selection and Assessment, 10*, 5–11.

Salas, E., & Cannon-Bowers, J. A. (2001). The science of training: A decade of progress. *Annual Review of Psychology, 52*, 471–499.

Salas, E., DeRouin, R. E., & Gade, P. A. (2007). The military's contribution to our science and practice: People, places, and things. In L. L. Koppes (Ed.), *Historical perspectives in industrial and organizational psychology* (pp. 169–189). Mahwah, NJ: Erlbaum.

Salas, E., Priest, H. A., Stagl, K. C., Sims, D. E., & Burke, C. S. (2007). Work teams in organizations: A historical reflection and lessons learned. In L. L. Koppes (Ed.), *Historical perspectives in industrial and organizational psychology* (pp. 407–438). Mahwah, NJ: Erlbaum.

Salgado, J. F. (2001). Some landmarks of 100 years of scientific personnel selection at the beginning of the new century. *International Journal of Selection and Assessment, 9*, 3–8.

Samuelson, F. (1977). World War I intelligence testing and the development of psychology. *Journal of the History of the Behavioral Sciences, 13*, 274–282.

Savickas, M. L., & Baker, D. B. (2005). The history of vocational psychology: Antecedents, origin, and early development. In W. B. Walsh & M. L. Savickas (Eds.), *Handbook of vocational psychology: Theory, practice, research* (3rd ed., pp.15–50). Mahwah, NJ: Erlbaum.

Schein, E. H. (1965). *Organizational psychology.* Englewood Cliff, NJ: Prentice-Hall.

Schein, E. H. (1983). The role of the founder in creating organizational culture. *Organizational Dynamics, 12*, 13–28.

Schein, E. H. (1985). *Organizational culture and leadership.* San Francisco: Jossey-Bass.

Schmidt, F. L. (1996). Statistical significance testing and cumulative knowledge in psychology: Implications for training researchers. *Psychological Methods, 1*, 115–129.

Schmidt, F. L., & Hunter, J. E. (1977). Development of a general solution to the problem of validity generalization. *Journal of Applied Psychology, 62*, 529–540.

Schmidt, F. L., & Hunter, J. E. (1998). The validity and utility of selection methods in personnel psychology: Practical and theoretical implications of 85 years of research findings. *Psychological Bulletin, 124*, 262–274.

Schneider, B. (1987). The people make the place. *Personnel Psychology, 40*, 437–453.

Schneider, B. (Ed.). (1990). *Organizational climate and culture.* San Francisco: Jossey-Bass.

Schumann, D. W., & Davidson E. (2007). Early influences of applied psychologists on consumer response: 1895–1925. In L. L. Koppes (Ed.), *Historical perspectives in industrial and organizational psychology* (pp. 265–280). Mahwah, NJ: Erlbaum.

Scott, W. D. (1903). *Theory of advertising.* Boston: Small, Maynard.

Scott, W. D. (1908). *The psychology of advertising.* Boston: Small, Maynard.

Scott, W. D. (1911). *Increasing human efficiency in business.* New York: Macmillan.

Scripture, E. W. (1895). *Thinking, feeling, doing.* New York: Flood & Vincent.

Seligman, M. E. P., & Csikszentmihalyi, M. (2000). Positive psychology: An introduction. *American Psychologist, 55*, 5–14.

Shartle, C. L. (1949). Leadership and executive performance. *Personnel, 25*, 370–380.

Shelton, W. H. (1927–28). Social traits and morphologic types. *Personnel Journal, 6*, 47–55.

Shimmin, S., & van Strien, P. J. (1998). History of the psychology of work and organization. In P. J. D. Drenth, H. Thierry, & C. J. de Wolff (Eds.), *Handbook of work and organizational psychology* (2nd ed., pp. 71–99). Hove, UK: Psychology Press.

Shultz, K. S., & Adams, G. A. (Eds.). (2007). *Aging and work in the 21st century.* Mahwah, New Jersey: Lawrence Erlbaum Associates.

Sisson, E. D.(1948). Forced choice: The new army rating. *Personnel Psychology, 1*, 365–381.

Skinner, B. F. (1953). *Science and human behavior.* New York: Macmillan.

Smith, P. C. (1955). The prediction of individual differences in susceptibility to industrial monotony. *Journal of Applied Psychology, 39*, 322–329.

Smith, P. C.,& Kendall, L. M. (1963). Retranslation of expectations: An approach to the construction of unambiguous anchors for rating scales. *Journal of Applied Psychology, 47*, 149–155.

Smith, P. C., Kendall, L. M., & Hulin, C. L. (1969). *Measurement of satisfaction in work and retirement.* Chicago, IL: Rand McNally.

Society for Industrial and Organizational Psychology. (1975). *Principles for the validation and use of personnel selection procedures.* College Park, MD: Author.

Society for Industrial and Organizational Psychology. (1980). *Principles for the validation and use of personnel selection procedures* (2nd ed.). College Park, MD: Author.

Society for Industrial and Organizational Psychology. (1987). *Principles for the validation and use of personnel selection procedures* (3rd ed.). College Park, MD: Author.

Society for Industrial and Organizational Psychology. (2003). *Principles for the validation and use of personnel selection procedures* (4th ed.). Bowling Green, OH: Author.

Sokal, M. M. (1971). The unpublished autobiography of James McKeen Cattell. *American Psychologist, 26*, 626–635.

Sokal, M. M. (1981). The origins of the Psychological Corporation. *Journal of the History of the Behavioral Sciences, 17*, 54–67.

Sokal, M. M. (1984). James McKeen Cattell and American psychology in the 1920s. In J. Brozek (Ed.), *Explorations in the history of psychology in the United States* (pp. 273–323). Lewisburg, PA: Bucknell University Press.

Sokal, M. M. (Ed.). (1987). *Psychological testing and American society, 1890–1930.* New Brunswick, NJ: Rutgers University Press.

Sokal, M. M. (1995). Stargazing: James McKeen Cattell, American men of science, and the reward structure of the scientific community. In F. Kessel (Ed.), *Psychology, science, and human affairs: Essays in honor of William Bevan* (pp. 64–86). Boulder, CO: Westview.

Sokal, M. M. (2009). James McKeen Cattell, Nicholas Murray Butler, and academic freedom at Columbia University, 1902–1923. *History of Psychology, 12*, 87–122.

Spearman, C. (1904). "General intelligence," objectively determined and measured. *American Journal of Psychology, 15*, 201–293.

Sprung, L., & Sprung, H. (2001). History of modern psychology in Germany in 19th and 20th century thought and society. *International Journal of Psychology, 36*, 364–376.

Stagner, R. (1981). Training and experiences of some distinguished industrial psychologists. *American Psychologist, 36*, 497–505.

Starch, D. (1910). *Principles of advertising*. Madison, WI: University Cooperative Co.

Starch, D. (1914). *Advertising: Its principles, practice and technique*. New York: Appleton.

Steers, R. M., & Porter, L. W. (1974). The role of task-goal attributes in employee performance. *Psychological Bulletin, 81*, 434–452.

Steinmetz, C. S. (1967). The evolution of training. In R. L. Craig & L. R. Bittel (Eds.), *Training and development handbook* (pp. 1–15). New York: McGraw-Hill.

Stern, W. (1934). Otto Lipmann: 1880–1933. *American Journal of Psychology, 46*, 152–154.

Stogdill, R. M. (1948). Personal factors associated with leadership: A survey of the literature. *Journal of Psychology, 25*, 35–71.

Stout, R. J., Cannon-Bowers, J. A., Salas, E., & Milanovich, D. M. (1999). Planning, shared mental models, and coordinated performance: An empirical link is established. *Human Factors, 41*, 61–71.

Strong, E. K., Jr. (1918). Work of the Committee of Classification of Personnel. *Journal of Applied Psychology, 2*, 130–139.

Strong, E. K., Jr. (1925). *The psychology of selling and advertising*. New York: McGraw-Hill.

Sundstrom, E., McIntyre, M., Halfhill, T., & Richards, H. (2000). Work groups: From the Hawthorne Studies to work teams of the 1990s and beyond. *Group Dynamics: Theory, Research, and Practice, 4*(1), 44–67.

Tagg, M. (1925). Industrial psychology in Russia. *Journal of the Institute of Industrial Psychology, 2*, 359–364.

Tapscott, D., & Caston, A. (1993). *Paradigm shift: The new promise of information technology*. New York: McGraw-Hill.

Taylor, F. W. (1911). *Principles of scientific management*. New York: Harper.

Taylor, H. C., & Russell, J. T. (1939). The relationship of validity coefficients to the practical effectiveness of tests in selection. *Journal of Applied Psychology, 23*, 565–578.

Tead, O. (1935). *The art of leadership*. New York: McGraw-Hill.

Thayer, P. W. (1997). Oh! For the good old days! *Industrial-Organizational Psychologist, 34*(3), 17–20.

Thompson, A. S. (1998). Morris S. Viteles. *American Psychologist, 53*, 1153–1154.

Thompson, C. A., Beauvais, L. L., & Lyness, K. S. (1999). When work-family benefits are not enough: The influence of work-family culture on benefit utilization, organizational attachment, and work-family conflict. *Journal of Vocational Behavior, 54*, 392–415.

Thorndike, L. L. (1949). *Personnel selection*. New York: Wiley.

Tiffin, J. (1942). *Industrial psychology*. New York: Prentice-Hall.

Trist, E. L, Emory, F., Murray, H., & Trist, B. (Eds.). (1997). *The social engagement of social science: A Tavistock anthology: The socio-ecological perspective*. Philadelphia: University of Pennsylvania Press.

Trist, E. L., & Bamforth, K. W. (1951). Some social and technical consequences of the long-wall method of coal-getting. *Human Relations, 4*, 6–38.

Tuckman, B. W. (1965). Personality, structure, group composition, and group functioning. *Sociometry, 27*, 469–487.

Uhrbrock, R. S. (1934). Attitudes of 4430 employees. *Journal of Social Psychology, 5*, 365–377.

U.S. Employment Service. (1939). *Dictionary of occupational titles*. Washington, DC: U.S. Government Printing Office.

U.S. Office of Strategic Services. (1948). *Assessment of men: Selection of personnel for the office of strategic services*. Lanham, MD: Rinehart Publishing.

Van de Water, T. (1997). Psychology's entrepreneurs and the marketing of industrial psychology. *Journal of Applied Psychology, 82*(4), 486–499.

van Drunen, P. (1997). Psychtechnics. In W. G. Bringmann, H. D. Lück, R. Miller, & C. E. Early (Eds.). *A pictorial history of psychology* (pp. 480–484). Chicago: Quintessence.

van Strien, P. J. (1998). Early applied psychology between essentialism and pragmatism: The dynamics of theory, tools, and clients. *History of Psychology, 1*, 208–234.

Vecchio, R. P. (1995). *Organizational behavior* (3rd ed.). Fort Worth, TX: Dryden.

Vinchur, A. J. (2007). A history of psychology applied to employee selection. In L. L. Koppes (Ed.), *Historical perspectives in industrial and organizational psychology* (pp. 193–218). Mahwah, NJ: Erlbaum.

Vinchur, A. J., & Koppes, L. L. (2007). Early contributors to the science and practice of industrial psychology. In L. L. Koppes (Ed.), *Historical perspectives in industrial and organizational psychology* (pp. 37–58). Mahwah, NJ: Erlbaum.

Vinchur, A. J., & Koppes, L. L. (2011). A historical survey of research and practice in industrial and organizational psychology. In S. Zedeck (Ed.), *Handbook of industrial and organizational psychology*. Washington, DC: American Psychological Association.

Viteles, M. S. (1923). Psychology in business—In England, France, and Germany. *Annals of the American Academy of Political and Social Science, 110*, 207–220.

Viteles, M. S. (1925–1926). Research in the selection of motormen. Part I. Survey of the literature. II. Methods devised for the Milwaukee Electric Railway and Light Company. *Journal of Personnel Research, 4*, 100–115; 173–199.

Viteles, M. S. (1928). Psychology in industry. *Psychological Bulletin, 25*, 309–340.

Viteles, M. S. (1932). *Industrial psychology*. New York: Norton.

Viteles M. S. (1938). Industrial psychology in Russia. *Occupational Psychology, 12*, 1–19.

Viteles, M. S.(1953). *Motivation and morale in industry*. New York: Norton.

von Mayrhauser, R. (1987). The manager, the medic, and the mediator: The clash of professional psychological styles and the wartime origins of group mental testing. In M. M. Sokal (Ed.), *Psychological testing and American society* (pp. 128–157). New Brunswick, NJ: Rutgers University Press.

von Mayrhauser, R. (1992). The mental testing community and validity: A prehistory. *American Psychologist, 47*, 244–253.

Vroom, V. H.(1964). *Work and motivation*. New York: Wiley.

Wallace, S. R., & Weitz, J. (1955). Industrial psychology. In C. P. Stone & Q. McNemar (Eds.), *Annual review of psychology* (pp. 217–250). Stanford, CA: Annual Review.

Wang, Z. M. (1990). Recent developments in ergonomics in China. *Ergonomics, 33*, 853–865.

Wang, Z. M. (1994). Culture, economic reform, and the role of industrial and organizational psychology in China. In H. C. Triandis, M. D. Dunnette, & L. M. Hough (Eds.), *Handbook of industrial and organizational psychology* (Vol. 4, pp. 689–725). Palo Alto, CA: Consulting Psychologists Press.

Warr, P. B. (1987). *Work, unemployment, and mental health*. Oxford: Oxford University Press.

Warr, P. B. (1990). The measurement of well-being and other aspects of mental health. *Journal of Occupational Psychology, 63*, 193–210.

Warr, P. B. (1999). Well-being and the workplace. In D. Kahneman, E. Diener, & N. Schwartz (Eds.), *Wellbeing: The foundations of hedonic psychology* (pp. 392–412). New York: Russell Sage Foundation.

Warr, P. B. (2001). *Psychology in Sheffield: The early years.* Sheffield, UK: Sheffield Academic Press.

Warr, P. (2007). Some historical developments in I-O psychology outside the United States. In L. L. Koppes (Ed.), *Historical perspectives in industrial and organizational psychology* (pp. 81–107). Mahwah, NJ: Erlbaum.

Washington v. Davis (1976). 426 U.S. 229.

Watson, J. B. (1913). Psychology as the behaviorist views it. *Psychological Review, 20*, 158–177.

Watson, R. I. (1960). The history of psychology: A neglected area. *American Psychologist, 15*, 251–255.

Weiner, I. B. (Editor-in-Chief). (2003). *Handbook of psychology* (Vol. 12, pp. 1–12). Hoboken, NJ: Wiley.

Welch, H. J., & Myers, C. S. (1932). *Ten years of industrial psychology: An account of the first decade of the National Institute of Industrial Psychology.* London: Pitman.

Wexley, K. N., & Klimoski, R. (1984). Performance appraisal: An update. In K. Rowland & G. Ferris (Eds.), *Research in personnel and human resources* (Vol. 2, pp. 35–79). Greenwich, CT: JAI.

Wherry, R. J.(1983). Appendix: Wherry's theory of rating. In F. J. Landy & J. L. Farr (Eds.), *The measurement of work performance* (pp. 283–303). New York: Academic Press.

Wherry, R. J., & Bartlett, C. J. (1982). The control of bias in ratings: A theory of rating. *Personnel Psychology, 35*, 521–551.

Wilson, M. A. (2007). A history of job analysis. In L. L. Koppes (Ed.), *Historical perspectives in industrial and organizational psychology* (pp. 219–241). Mahwah, NJ: Erlbaum.

Wissler, C. (1901). The correlation of mental and physical tests. *Psychological Review, 3*, 1–63.

Wright, P. M., & McMahan, C. C. (1992). Theoretical perspectives for strategic human resource management. *Journal of Management, 18*, 295–320.

Zaccaro, S. J., Ardison, S. D., & Orvis, K. L. (2004). Leading virtual teams. In D. Day, S. J. Zaccaro, & S. M. Halpin (Eds.), *Leader development for transforming organizations* (pp. 267–292). Mahwah, NJ: Erlbaum.

Zedeck, S. (1992). *Work, families, and organizations.* San Francisco: Jossey-Bass.

Zeidner, J., & Drucker, A. J. (1983). *Behavioral science in the Army: A corporate history of the Army Research Institute.* Alexandria, VA: U.S. Army Research Institute for the Behavior and Social Sciences.

Zickar, M. J. (2001). Using personality inventories to identify thugs and agitators: Applied psychology's contribution to the war against labor. *Journal of Vocational Behavior, 59*, 149–164.

Zickar, M. J., & Gibby, R. E. (2007). Four persistent themes throughout the history of I-O psychology in the United States. In L. L. Koppes (Ed.), *Historical perspectives in industrial and organizational psychology* (pp. 61–80). Mahwah, NJ: Erlbaum.

Zickar, M. J., & Highhouse, S. (2001). Measuring prestige of journals in industrial-organizational psychology. *Industrial-Organizational Psychologist, 38*(4), 29–36.

PART 2

The Foundation

Seeking the Holy Grail in Organizational Science: Uncovering Causality through Research Design

Paul J. Hanges*, *and* Mo Wang

Abstract

In this chapter, we focus on the importance of establishing causal relationships in the organizational sciences. Specifically, we provide an explicit definition of a causal relationship, identify several different forms that have been explored in the scientific literature, and discuss the conditions under which causality can be established. Specifically, we discuss the Campbell Causal Model (CCM), which emphasizes threats to causal interpretations and the elimination of these threats, as well as the Rubin Causal Model (RCM), which emphasizes the biasing effect of non-random assignment of participants to conditions (i.e., selection bias) and how to overcome this bias in observational research. A variety of quasi-experimentation designs (e.g., regression discontinuity approaches, longitudinal designs) that enable organizational science researchers to study phenomena in the field are discussed. We finish our chapter by considering the recent trend conceptualizing organizations as complex systems, and we argue that this perspective may change the kinds of causality questions that researchers ask in the future.

Key Words: Research design, causality, Campbell Causal Model, Rubin Causal Model, Quasi-experimentation, threats to validity, regression discontinuity design, person-centered methods

Empirical research holds the promise of answering age-old questions and/or identifying effective solutions to the problems of individuals, groups, organizations, and societies. Instead of endless debate on some issue, systematic and rigorous research promises definitive resolutions to questions or conflicts. For example, consider the following questions:

• What causes people to act unethically and what can be done to minimize such behavior?

• Why do some teams structure themselves so that information and power are shared equally across members, whereas other teams restrict the flow of information and power to a subset of members?

• What interventions can change shared perceptions regarding the importance of an organization's goals?

• Can the average educational level of a national workforce improve if a school voucher program is implemented?

These are examples of questions at different levels of analysis that social scientists hope might be susceptible to the scientific method.

In this chapter, we focus on the importance of establishing causal relationships for empirical research in the organizational sciences. Specifically, we provide an explicit definition of a causal relationship and identify several different forms of causal relationships that have been discussed in the scientific literature. We discuss the conditions under which causality can be established and discuss the two main models—Campbell Causal Model (CCM) and Rubin Causal Model (RCM)—by

* The first authors' work on this chapter was supported by the U. S. Army Research Laboratory and the U. S. Army Research Office under grant number W911NF-08–1-0144.

which causality is evaluated in empirical research. These two models emphasize different issues: CCM emphasizes research design and threats to causal interpretations; RCM emphasizes statistical adjustment of biasing factors for studies in which conditions were not randomly assigned to participants. We finish our chapter by considering the recent trends (i.e., conceptualizing organizations as complex systems and focusing on person-centered phenomena and processes). We argue that these perspectives may change the kinds of causality questions that researchers ask in the future.

Types of Empirical Research

Before discussing causation, we first note that Brewer (2000) identified three broad classes of empirical research—demonstration research, causation research, and explanation research—to help clarify the type of research that is the focus of this chapter. According to Brewer, the purpose of demonstration research is to establish the existence of some phenomenon or some relationship. For example, the work of Farman, Gardiner, and Shanklin (1985) documenting the hole in the ozone layer of the upper atmosphere is a perfect example of this type of research. Another example is criterion-related validation studies conducted by personnel psychologists. Personnel psychologists conduct such studies to demonstrate that test scores used to make personnel decisions are related to important job-related outcomes. A final example can be obtained from the cross-cultural literature in which researchers might be interested in demonstrating that a particular relationship established in one culture might also hold in a different culture. In this final example, cross-cultural researchers are trying to demonstrate whether culture is a moderator of a previously established finding or relationship.

Demonstration research is intended to establish facts and aims to be descriptive (Brewer, 2000). Although such studies are most frequently conducted in the field, they can also be done in the lab as well. For example, the classic Stanford prison study, which demonstrated that social situations can shape and transform behavior (Haney, Banks, & Zimbardo, 1973), took place in a controlled simulated setting. The second class of research identified by Brewer focuses on the establishment of causal relationships. Causality refers to a special relationship between two or more variables such that changes in the value of one set of variables—called the antecedent(s), cause(s), predictor(s), or the independent variable(s)—create changes in another set of variables—called the

consequent(s), effect(s), or dependent variable(s). Before the scientific method was developed, people regularly relied on supernatural or mythological explanations to understand the cause of some phenomenon. The scientific method surpassed these other methods because of its demonstrated superiority in differentiating useful from spurious causal relationships. Indeed, this utilitarian approach to research is usually adopted to understand why causation plays such a central role in the scientific endeavor (Cook & Campbell, 1979; Mackie, 1974). Establishing causal relationships allows the identification of potential agents that can be manipulated to change important outcome variables. Imagine the economic benefit that would accrue if the causal relationships accounting for the 2008–2011 global recession were completely identified and if the important causal agents could be controlled.

The third type of empirical study, according to Brewer (2000), is an explanatory study. In these studies, the purpose is not to establish causal relationships but rather to explain why these causal relationships exist. In other words, this final class of studies might ask questions such as:

• Why does a training intervention result in better performance than a control group?
• Why do authentic leaders have more dedicated followers than other types of leaders?

In other words, explanatory studies assess the accuracy of theories or, at the very least, attempt to identify the mediating variables that move the influence of the antecedents to the dependent variable. In addition, these types of studies also seek to understand why relationships vary as a function of particular moderators (e.g., culture, age).

All of these different types of empirical studies can benefit from the techniques specified in this chapter. Specifically, we discuss research design in this chapter. That is, we discuss methodology that was primarily designed for Brewer's (2000) second type of empirical study. However, even when one is concerned with simply demonstrating that a relationship exists (Brewer's first type of empirical study) or explaining why a relationship exists (Brewer's third type of study), the techniques discussed in this chapter will help researchers eliminate alternative explanations for their results. For example, if a negative relationship is found between a new self-report measure of integrity and counterproductive behavior on the job (e.g., stealing, sabotage), how can one tell whether that relationship is artificial (i.e., due to some third variable such as common method bias)? While research design is important for all kinds of research, other techniques that will not be covered in this chapter, such as structural equation modeling (explanatory research) or data mining approaches (demonstration studies) such as neural network methodology (Hanges, Lord, Godfrey, & Raver, 2002), were established to address issues primarily raised in Brewer's demonstration and explanation studies. In the next section, we focus on causality and the different underlying models.

Causation

While it may seem counterintuitive, there has been serious debate among philosophers and some scientists questioning the utility of the entire notion of causation in science. In particular, the positivist school of philosophy is often cited with challenging the scientific credentials of the causation construct. However, the most extreme form of the challenge really came from the logical positivists (Cook & Campbell, 1979). According to positivists, all knowledge is based on one's own senses and positive verification. One famous positivistic philosopher is John Locke ([1690] 1894) who is attributed with coining the phrase that the mind is a "blank slate," or a tabula rasa, at birth. Locke believed that causation was uncovered by our perceptual processes as we observe covariation among phenomena. While Locke never went so far as to declare that causation was an attribution that people assume is real, David Hume, another famous philosopher from the logical positivist school, did. While agreeing with Locke that true knowledge is rooted in the perceptual processes, David Hume argued that causality is an illusion. Hume believed that causality is an attribution imposed on the data by the observer to account for repeated co-occurrence of events.

Following on the positivist roots, Bertrand Russell (1913) argued that science—in particular, physics—was concerned with establishing functional relationships between variables and *not* causation. A functional relationship is a specification of a set of variables that relate to one another. It could be as simple as saying that behavior is a function of environment and genetics (i.e., *behavior = f (environment, genetics)* in which the manner by which environment and genetics combine to produce behavior is unspecified. Or it can also be slightly more specific as seen in the classic physics example:

$$velocity_t = gt + velocity_o \tag{1}$$

which predicts the velocity of an object falling freely in a vacuum as a function of the gravitational constant (g), the amount of time that has passed

(t) since the observation period started, and the velocity of the object at the start of the observation period (velocity$_0$). Note that in Equation 1, none of the variables on the right side of that equation has any causal connection to *velocityt*. Both g and *velocity$_o$* are constants and cannot account for any variability in *velocity$_t$*. The only variable on the right of Equation 1 that varies is time (*t*). While time does determine *velocity$_t$*, time does not have a causal influence on it (or, indeed, anything else).

Thus, Russell claimed that we should not be concerned with causation but, like physics, we should be concerned with establishing functional relationships. Functional relationships imply reversibility (Cook & Campbell, 1979) which means that any of the three variables in Equation 1 can be moved to the left side of that equation and thus a meaningful equation could be created. So we could convert Equation 1 to obtain the gravitational constant:

$$g = \frac{velocity_t - velocity_o}{t} \tag{2}$$

and the new equation would still be proper and meaningful. Thus, Russell argued, we should not worry about causation.

Today, however, belief in the utility of causal relationships has made a comeback in philosophy (Bunge, 2009). While there are times when all we are interested in is establishing functional relationships, as stated by Russell, there are other times when causation is extremely useful to establish. The most direct and cogent argument against Russell was provided by Suppes in 1970 when he noted that while not all functional relationships imply cause, many do. For example, when the ideal gas law (PV= nRT)[1] was specified, careful experimentation verified what happened to volume and pressure when temperature was deliberately varied. Thus, Russell's depiction of physics as unconcerned with causation was simply incorrect.

Forms of Causation

As discussed earlier, causality refers to a special relationship between two or more variables such that changes in the value of one set of variables—hereafter called the causal agent(s)—create changes in another set of variables—hereafter referred to as the dependent variable(s). While this definition appears to be somewhat simple, we can use it to make a major distinction among the causal models explored by researchers: unidirectional (i.e., recursive) and non-directional (i.e., non-recursive) causal models. Most of the empirical assessment of social science models has focused on unidirectional models (see Kozlowski, Chapter 1 of this handbook). Examples of three such causal models are shown in Figure 3.1. All of the relationships shown in this figure are unidirectional because the causal influence among the variables flows in only one direction. Specifically, the causal influence flows from the variables on the left to those on the right. In the simplest model, Figure 3.1A, a single variable—Goal Difficulty—influences the state of the dependent variable—Task Performance. Assuming that Figure 3.1A shows a positive relationship, increases in goal difficulty are expected to cause task performance to increase. The causal agent, goal difficulty, is referred to as an exogenous variable in this model, because the causal source(s) of this variable is not specified in Figure 3.1A. In contrast, at least one causal source of task performance is identified in this figure, and so task performance is referred to as an endogenous variable.

Compare this model to the one shown in Figure 3.1B. Figure 3.1B shows a model in which there are multiple causal agents that influence a single dependent variable. This is also a unidirectional causal model in that the flow of causation goes in one direction—from the multiple causes (i.e., multiple exogenous variables) to the single dependent variable (i.e., a single endogenous variable). The relative contributions of the multiple causes in affecting the dependent variable probably differ; but they do not have to. Figure 3.1C shows another unidirectional causal chain model, but this time there are multiple causes (exogenous variables) and multiple dependent (endogenous) variables. Even though the model is more complicated than the previous models, it is important to recognize that the causal flow is still unidirectional.

Causal chain models, such as the one shown in Figure 3.1C, are illustrations of Brewer's (2000) third type of research study (i.e., explanatory studies) mentioned earlier. Structural equation modeling and mediation testing are examples of statistical approaches by which the explanatory paths in such chains can be assessed. In contrast to statistical approaches to test such explanatory models, Spencer, Zanna, and Fong (2005) and Stone-Romero and Rosopa (2008) have strongly argued that tests of mediation, or what we call causal chain models, truly require experimental research, and weak evidence is provided by non-experimental data using statistical mediation testing. For example, Spencer et al. (2005) proposed that one could test a causal chain model by conducting two experiments. Namely, the first experiment demonstrates that manipulating the extraneous causal agent affects the mediator (e.g., goal difficulty affects task performance in Figure 3.1C). The second experiment would be designed to show that manipulating the mediator

Figure 3.1 Three Possible Directional Causal Models

affects the final dependent variable (e.g., task performance affects contingent reward). Spencer et al. (2005) call this approach a moderation-of-process design. Stone-Romero and Rosopa (2008) indicated that experiments provide the strongest evidence for the mediation-causal chain model, whereas a non-experimental research in which the causal chain was tested statistically would produce the weakest support for the proposed model. It should be noted, however, that if one really wants to test the causal nature of the chain, one might combine the research design methodology discussed in this chapter with the aforementioned statistical techniques (Stone-Romero & Rosopa, 2010).

In contrast to unidirectional causal models, the causal process can also be circular or reciprocal in nature. These kinds of models are called bidirectional or non-recursive. Figure 3.2 shows examples of two such models. As can be seen in this figure, these models have feedback loops or simultaneous causal paths. Such models have been discussed in the social science literature for decades. However, it was the introduction of general systems theory

(e.g., Katz & Kahn, 1978; von Bertalanffy, 1950, 1956) that provided a serious challenge to the unidirectional causal model. As the father of general systems theory, von Bertalanffy, wrote in 1968:

> The only goal of science appeared to be analytical, i.e., the splitting up of reality into ever smaller units and the isolation of individual causal trains.... Correspondingly, causality was essentially one-way: one sun attracts one planet in Newtonian mechanics, one gene in the fertilized ovum produces such and such inherited character, one sort of bacterium produces this or that disease, mental elements are lined up, like the beads in a string of pearls, by the law of association.... We may state as characteristic of modern science that this scheme of isolable units acting in one-way causality has provided to be insufficient. Hence the appearance, in all fields of science, of notions like wholeness, holistic, organismic, gestalt, etc., which all signify that, in the last resort, we must think in terms of systems of elements in mutual interaction. (p. 45)

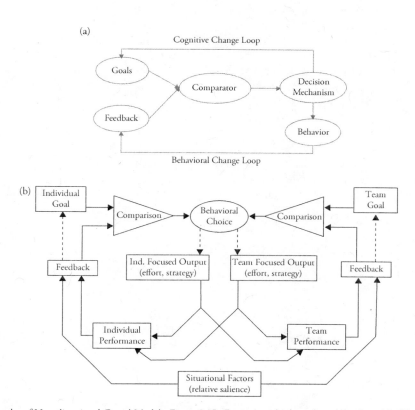

Figure 3.2 Examples of Non-directional Causal Models. Figure 3.2B. From: A multiple goal, multilevel model of feedback effects on the regulation of individual and team performance. *Journal of Applied Psychology, 89*, 1035–1056. Published by the American Psychological Association. Reprinted with permission

One question is how to establish non-recursive relationships. Research designs such as cross-lagged panel designs or time series research designs may fulfill this purpose. Specifically, when adopting cross-lagged designs, both predictors and outcomes are measured at Time 1 and Time 2. As such, the predictor-outcome relationships can be examined over time while covarying out the stability in the variables (e.g., Kelloway, Gottlieb, & Barham, 1999). In particular, outcome variables at Time 2 are regressed on both predictors at Time 1 and outcome variables at Time 1 (i.e., controlling for the stability in outcome variables). Similarly, reverse causality is tested by regressing predictors at Time 2 on both outcome variables at Time 1 and predictors at Time 1. Statistical methodology such as two-stage least squares models, indirect least squares, and structural equation modeling were developed to analyze data from such research designs to be able to determine whether the non-recursive relationships existed.

Another research design to establish non-recursive relationships is to model both predictors and outcome variables as parallel time series (Rosel & Plewis, 2008). In other words, both predictors and outcome variables are measured simultaneously over multiple time points. As illustrated in Figure 3.3, with this type of data, the relationships between predictors and outcome variables can be modeled as crossed effects (i.e., feedback loops) among parallel autoregressive models (i.e., linear prediction models that attempt to predict values of variables based on their previous values). Moving beyond this basic model, one could test for different orders (i.e., first order, second order, etc.) of both the autoregressive effects as well as the hypothesized non-recursive effects in different directions. One advantage of this type of model is that it provides a useful form of

modeling when the available theory does not permit a precise specification of the appropriate lag between predictors and outcomes. Within the constraints imposed by the number and timing of measurement occasions, researchers could test hypothesized non-recursive relationships across various lags.

Recent discussions in social science definitely appear to have supported von Bertalanffy's position in that researchers are increasingly using dynamical systems terminology, logic, and approaches to conceptualize and explain psychological and organizational phenomena (e.g., DeShon, Chapter 4 of this handbook; Hanges, Lord, & Dickson, 2000; Lord, Hanges, & Godfrey, 2003; Hanges, Lord, Godfrey, & Raver, 2002; Vallacher & Nowak, 1994). A dynamical system is one in which the units of the system (e.g., people if the system is a team/organization, concepts or neurons if the system is the brain) are richly interconnected, and through these connections, each unit has the potential to influence the state of all other units in the system. Using the causal forms language just specified, dynamic systems have very tangled feedback loops and, within the system, causal influence flows in all directions. With such systems, the utility of using classic experimental design to determine the causal structure among the units within the dynamic system is clearly suspect. Indeed, researchers and others have even written that you destroy the very phenomena that you want to study by using reductionist science. We will discuss at the end of this chapter how the science of complexity theory and emergent properties can help researchers model with these type of causal phenomena.

Definition of Causation

In the previous section, we identified two types of causal relationships: unidirectional and

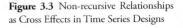

Figure 3.3 Non-recursive Relationships as Cross Effects in Time Series Designs

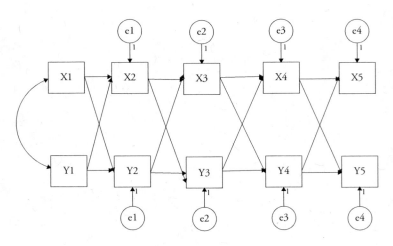

non-directional. While useful, this distinction only provides a vague conceptualization of a causal relationship. More specificity about causal relationships needs to be provided. As we indicated earlier, a causal relation refers to a relationship between two or more variables such that changes in the value of one set of variables create changes in another set of variables (Bunge, 2009). The causal relationship can be interpreted as one in which some form of energy is transferred from the antecedent to the dependent variable (Bunge, 2009).

According to Bunge (2009), the best way to represent a causal relationship is to compare the behavior of the dependent variable when it is under the influence of the antecedent variable to the behavior of the dependent variable when it is not under the influence of the antecedent variable. More specifically, the behavior of the dependent variable, Y, can be recorded at a single time period or at multiple time periods over time. The behavior of Y over the recorded time periods is called the history of Y and is denoted as h(Y) when Y is independent of the influence of the antecedent variable, X. The history of Y is denoted as h(Y|X) when Y is influenced by changes in X.

The history of Y can be geometrically represented by using something called a phase space. A phase space is a multidimensional space that represents all possible values that Y might take (Nowak & Lewenstein, 1994). The actual values that Y could take as a function of other variables (i.e., the actual history of Y) are shown as a line or trajectory through this phase space. For example, in Figure 3.4 we show two dimensions: one dimension represents the possible values that the dependent variable, Y, could take, and the other dimension is X. Figure 3.4A shows the history of the dependent variable recorded for some time period when the dependent variable, Y, is independent of the influence of X (i.e., h(Y)). In contrast, Figure 3.4B represents the history of Y when it was under the influence of X. The change in the two trajectories is a geometric representation of Bunge's (2009) definition of a causal effect. Specifically, the causal effect of X on Y is the difference between the trajectory of Y when X is influencing it from the free trajectory of Y. More formally:

$$Causal\_Effect = \delta_{Y \bullet X} = h(Y|X) - h(Y) \quad (3)$$

The use of this definition of a causal effect has two advantages. First, Bunge's connection to the geometric interpretation of a causal effect connects the classic discussion of causal forms (i.e., unidirectional vs. non-directional) with recent discussions of dynamical systems in which units/variables are so richly interconnected that the reductionist tendency to specify each individual causal relationship misses the interesting and unique systems-level behavior. Indeed, complexity scientists frequently use phase space diagrams to obtain a conceptual understanding of the behavior of their dynamical system.

Second, Bunge's causal effect definition highlights the fact that causal relationships can only be truly detected and understood when they are compared to conditions in which the influence of the antecedent is controlled. This important comparison condition is what is called a counterfactual, and it is only by comparing the behavior of the dependent variable under the counterfactual condition that the causal effect of X on Y can truly be deduced.

Counterfactuals

Discussions of the need for counterfactual information can be traced back to the birth of experimental design (Cochran & Cox, 1950; Fisher, 1935). Discussions can also be found in the economics literature (e.g., Heckman, 1974; Roy, 1951), as well as in the philosophy of science literature. In a series of papers, Rubin (e.g., 1974, 1981, 1990) explored the utility of the counterfactual argument for observational research and outlined a formal procedure for using it to draw causal inferences.

The basic discussion of counterfactuals proceeds as follows. Assume that we have conducted a simple study in which participants are assigned to either a treatment (X = 1) or a control condition (X = 0). If a particular participant (p_i) was assigned to the treatment condition, then assume that p_i's value on the dependent variable would be Y_i^1. However, if p_i was assigned to the control condition, then assume that p_i's value on the dependent variable would be Y_i^0. The difference in the value of the dependent variable across these two conditions is the magnitude of the treatment's causal effect on this participant. More formally:

$$\delta_i = Y_i^1 - Y_i^0 \quad (4)$$

In this equation, δ_i represents the causal effect for the participant. Note the exact structural similarity between this formula and Bunge's causal effect formula provided earlier. Specifically, Y_i^1 is the value of the dependent variable when the participant, or system, is under the influence of X (i.e., the treatment) and Y_i^0 is the value of the dependent variable when the participant/system is not influenced by X (i.e., control). When the participant is assigned to

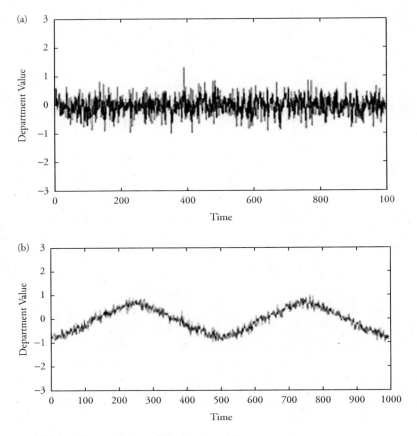

Figure 3.4 Phase Space Diagrams Showing History of Y as Function of X

the treatment condition, then the dependent variable in the control condition is the counterfactual. If the participant was assigned to the control condition, then the dependent variable in the treatment condition is the counterfactual. Either way, the causal effect is only defined when both conditions are known.

Of course, we cannot observe both of these states of the dependent variable for a particular participant (Morgan & Winship, 2007). If we assign the participant to the treatment condition and measure the dependent variable, we immediately lose the ability to assign the exact same participant (i.e., in the same naïve mental state) to the control condition to obtain a value of the dependent variable. Thus, much like Schrödinger's Cat[2] discussed in quantum physics, before conducting our experiment, the possibility of measuring the causal effect for an individual exists. However, once the experiment occurs, that possibility is shattered.

Researchers try to get around the issue of an indefinable causal effect at the individual level by trying to solve the problem at the group level of analysis.

Multiple people are assigned to the treatment and control groups. In this way, we have information about the average dependent variable in the treatment condition (i.e., $\overline{Y}_\bullet^1$) and information about the average dependent variable in the control condition (i.e., $\overline{Y}_\bullet^0$). We can then estimate Equation 1 more directly by:

$$E(\delta) = E(Y^1) - E(Y^0) \qquad (5)$$

In this equation, $E(\delta)$ represents the average causal effect, $E(Y^1)$ represents the average dependent variable in the treatment condition, and $E(Y^0)$ represents the average dependent variable in the control condition.

What is not often realized is that the aggregation of the causal effect issue to group averages does not eliminate the problem of counterfactuals (Morgan & Winship, 2007). The simple experiment that we described above actually has two hidden counterfactual conditions that are not often discussed. The first counterfactual condition is how the same kinds of people who were originally assigned to the treatment condition would do in the control condition.

The second counterfactual condition is how the same kinds of people who were originally assigned to the control condition would do in the treatment condition.

In a classic experiment, in which conditions are assigned to participants[3] and in which there are sufficient numbers of participants, the randomization process should equalize the two groups of participants, on average. Thus, in an experiment in which conditions are randomly assigned to participants, the two counterfactual conditions are equivalent with the two observed conditions. Thus, the magnitude of the causal effect can be obtained. However, in experiments in which the randomization process did not work (e.g., there are significant differences between the participants in the treatment and control conditions on some meaningful variable) or in observation studies, this collapse of the counterfactual conditions with the observed conditions does not occur.

To illustrate why this is true, let us assume that we were hired by an international training firm to evaluate the effectiveness of its cross-cultural competence training program for middle managers. We develop a measure of job performance and gather data from a sample of middle managers who completed the training program three months earlier, as well as a sample of typical middle managers who did not take the training program. Typically, the data would be analyzed by comparing the training group's performance ($\bar{Y}^1$) to the control group's performance ($\bar{Y}^0$). If we assume that $\bar{Y}^1 = 6$ and $\bar{Y}^0 = 2$, applying Equation 3 would yield a causal effect estimate of 4. However, this is an inappropriate estimate of the causal effect in this study because we ignored the factor that, unlike in a classic random experiment, the training and control groups are probably different at the start of the study. Perhaps the middle managers who registered for the training course are more motivated to succeed in a foreign assignment than a typical middle manager. The managers who attended the training course had to spend money to attend the course. Depending upon cost and length of time required for the completion of the course, attendance could differentiate the two initial groups from each other.

Thus, there are two counterfactual conditions in this example. First, there is the counterfactual condition of middle managers who are identical in motivation to the ones who took the training course but who were not given the opportunity to take the training. For argument's sake, assume that these middle managers have an average job performance measure of 4.5 as a result of their motivation to improve their cross-cultural competence and perhaps attain experiences or information via sources (e.g., books, movies, interacting with people from diverse groups) other than the training in question (i.e., $\bar{Y}^{(0|1)} = 4.5$). The second counterfactual condition consists of middle managers identical to the control group but who completed the training in question. Given that the training literature has found that pre-training motivation is an important factor influencing actual learning and subsequent training transfer (Beier & Kanfer, 2010; Naquin & Baldwin, 2003; Noe, 1986), we can assume that these managers have a subsequent job performance score of 3.0 (i.e., $\bar{Y}^{(1|0)} = 3.0$) after completing the training.

When the value of the dependent variable in these two counterfactual conditions is taken into account, it can be seen that our estimate of 4.0 for the training program's causal effect is a biased estimate. Considering all people who were highly motivated to improve their cross-cultural competence (i.e., treatment group and first counterfactual group), the causal effect attributable to the training program is only 1.5 ($\bar{Y}^1 - \bar{Y}^{(0|1)}$). On the other hand, when one considers all the people who have an average level of motivation with regard to improving their cross-cultural competence (i.e., control group and second counterfactual group), the causal effect estimate was only 1.0 ($\bar{Y}^{(1|0)} - \bar{Y}^0$). Clearly, the causal implications of the cross-cultural competence training are not as clear as the simple contrast between the training group and the control group would lead one to believe in this scenario.

Establishing Causal Relationships

John Stuart Mill (1843) argued that the viability of causal statements depends upon scientists being able to argue for or demonstrate the following three conditions: (a) time precedence of changes in the hypothesized causal agent over changes in the dependent variable; (b) establishment of a relationship between the hypothesized causal agent and the dependent variable; and (c) isolation of the causal agent–dependent variable relationship from other potential causal agents. The first condition, time precedence, simply means that changes in the status of the causal agent of interest need to occur before the predicted changes in the variable of interest (i.e., dependent variable) occurred. This condition is well reflected in the cross-lagged designs and time series designs that we mentioned earlier. While this criterion might seem somewhat obvious in unidirectional causal models, it becomes more complicated once we consider non-directional models.

For example, assume that we are interested in the relationship between task performance and self-efficacy. Does self-efficacy cause task performance, or does task performance cause self-efficacy? It seems reasonable that a person's success at performing some difficult task should affect his or her self-efficacy. Indeed, Bandura (1982) indicated that mastery of a challenging task is an important determinant of self-efficacy. However, both self-efficacy and task performance influence each other on an ongoing basis all the time. Research has also shown that self-efficacy determines whether someone persists at trying to learn a challenging task (Bandura, 1982). So which is the cause and which the effect, task performance or self-efficacy? It turns out that in this kind of cyclical situation, involving ongoing processes that interact, that both task performance and self-efficacy may cause and be affected by each other. This makes it very hard to establish a causal relationship in this situation.

The second condition, relationship, refers to the fact that variations in the causal agent have to be associated with variations in the dependent variable. John Stuart Mill identified two methods by which a relationship between two variables can be established. His first method for establishing a relationship was called method of agreement. According to this method, the effect had to be present when the cause is present. His second method was called the method of difference and it states that the effect had to be absent when the cause is absent.

These two methods lead to the idea that causal relationships can be described as necessary and/or sufficient. The term *necessary* refers to the situation in which the causal agent has to be present for the effect to occur. In other words, *necessary* is consistent with Mill's method of difference in that the effect will be absent if the causal agent is absent. The term *sufficient* refers to the situation in which the causal agent by itself is all that is necessary to produce the effect. In other words, *sufficient* is consistent with Mill's method of agreement.[4] The establishment of a relationship between two variables is usually determined statistically, although it can be qualitatively seen as we demonstrated with the comparison of the two Phase Spaces in Figure 3.4.

Finally, isolation refers to the elimination of any other possible alternative explanation for why the causal agent and the dependent variable are related. In other words, if one could remove or control the influence of all other possible causal agents and variables, manipulating the value of the causal agent would result in a change in the value of the dependent variable, after some time had passed. It is these three conditions laid out by Mill that are the cornerstone to experimental design.

The isolation criterion is very critical for determining causation. To understand why, remember that when we discussed causal flow and illustrated three unidirectional models in Figure 3.1, we differentiated between exogenous and endogenous variables. The isolation condition enables the causal agent of interest to remain exogenous in our experiment. If we do not meet the isolation condition, then other variables can influence the causal agent as well as the dependent variable. In other word, the causal agent of interest (goal difficulty in Figure 3.1A) is no longer exogenous: it is caused by other variables in our experiment. Regardless of how we have drawn our model, the reality is that the causal agent being tested is endogenous in our experiment. The consequence of violating Mill's isolation criteria and making our causal agent endogenous in our experiment is that the results provide ambiguous evidence regarding the causal relationship between goal difficulty and task performance.

Unfortunately, this last criterion can be very difficult to achieve. When designing an experiment, one must think about all the potential variables that might influence the dependent variable. After identifying the list of potential variables, the researcher needs to differentiate the variables into two categories: those variables that are of interest and those variables that are not of interest (usually referred to as nuisance variables) in the present study. It is important to realize, however, that there is nothing intrinsic about this categorization process and, indeed, one researcher's nuisance variable can be another researcher's variable of interest. After identifying the list of nuisance variables, the researcher needs to identify a subset of nuisance variables that could realistically influence the dependent variable in the present study and thus would violate Mill's isolation criterion.

There are four strategies by which the influence of a nuisance variable on the dependent variable can be isolated. You can: (a) randomize over it, (b) hold it constant, (c) incorporate the nuisance variable into the experiment, or (d) statistically control its effect on the dependent variable (Kirk, 1995). We have already discussed the efficacy of the first strategy (i.e., randomization) for isolating the effect of nuisance variables on the dependent variable. However, we have not discussed the downside of using this strategy: namely, the introduction of additional noise into the variance of the dependent variable. As more variables that can affect the dependent variable are allowed to vary in an experiment, the dependent variable will exhibit greater variance. The good news is that as long as the random assignment strategy works, the effect of the treatment of interest can be cleanly separated (i.e., isolated) from the effects of all these other variables. The downside is that it becomes harder to see the influence of the treatment of interest when more variables influence the dependent variable. For example, radar uses electromagnetic waves to detect the speed, direction, and altitude of various objects. To the extent that the radar can separate the desired object's signal (e.g., aircraft) from the background noise of other electromagnetic waves is called the signal-to-noise ratio. It is harder to detect the desired object (e.g., some treatment) as background noise increases. Researchers who have used the first strategy to control nuisance variables in their experiment need to consider the signal-to-noise ratio of their experiment and take steps (e.g., increase their sample size, change precision/direction of hypothesis) to increase their power to detect their treatment.

The second strategy, holding the nuisance variable constant, also called experimental control, basically means that you permit only one value of the nuisance variable to be represented in your study. For example, in 1988, the results of a large-scale study exploring the effectiveness of aspirin for reducing heart attacks was made public. This study's results convinced thousands of doctors to recommend to their patients that they start taking one aspirin every morning. However, it turns out that the original study only included male participants. The researchers did this because of the well-known gender effect on heart attack rates (i.e., in the 1980s, females had a substantially lower rate of heart attacks than males). By holding gender constant, the influence of this variable was isolated and removed from the study. Gender differences could not add variance to the dependent variable in the study because there simply were no gender differences in the study. While effective at removing the influence of the nuisance variable, there is, of course, a downside to this strategy: it limits the generalizability of the study's results. It was only after a subsequent replication consisting of only female participants was published that doctors had evidence that aspirin therapy generalized to female patients.

The third strategy, incorporating the nuisance variable into the experiment, literally means that the variable becomes a treatment in the experiment. If the nuisance variable is something that can be manipulated, then it is treated like any other treatment condition in the experiment. However, if the nuisance variable cannot be manipulated (e.g., gender, SES, eye color), then the level of the nuisance variable is noted and an equal number of participants in the levels of the nuisance variable is sought so that the effect of this variable can be isolated from the effect of the initial treatment of interest. This strategy is also referred to as a matching strategy. Its downside is that it is impractical with more than 2 or 3 nuisance variables controlled in this fashion. We will discuss a solution to this impracticality problem when we discuss propensity scores and the Ruben causal model.

The final strategy, statistical control, referred to as covarying the influence of nuisance variables (a.k.a. covariates), is different from the other strategies in that this approach can be employed after the experimental data have been collected. The only requirement is that some measure of the covariates has to been obtained. The technique consists of regressing the dependent variable onto the covariates and examining the effect of the treatment of interest on the regression's residuals. The usual documented downside to this strategy is that it is limited to controlling for linear effects of the covariates on the dependent variable; however, this is not quite correct. Some forms of nonlinear relationships can also be controlled using this approach. A real limitation is that to fulfill Mill's isolation criterion, the same covariate regression equation has to hold across levels of the experimental treatment (i.e., there can be no treatment by covariate interaction).

As we mentioned earlier, the isolation condition for establishing causation is the one that poses the most difficulties and has to do with the *exogeneity* of x (i.e., that x is not caused by other variables). Our review of research design is essentially concerned with the isolation and time precedence conditions; these conditions, particularly the isolation condition, have less to do with theoretical arguments and more to do with design and analysis issues.

Experimental Design: Campbell Causal Model and Rubin Causal Model

The typical experimental design chapter in our field focuses on Campbell's causal model and discusses his typology of four types of validity as well as a sample of the growing list of possible threats to each type of validity. The heart of Campbell's approach to experimental design is a consideration of possible threats to each validity type as a potential alternative explanation for the effect of the treatment on the dependent variable. Thus, the role of experimental design is to rule out as many alternative explanations as possible over the course of multiple studies. In this way, Campbell's approach is similar in heart to Popper's (1959) philosophy of science. Popper emphasized the importance of falsification over confirmation of a theory as the main driving force in science. Thus, Campbell's approach basically has the researcher generate alternative hypotheses that could account for the relationship between the treatment and the dependent variable and then design a study that potentially rejects these alternative hypotheses. This approach was first outlined in a journal article (Campbell, 1957) and then was expanded upon over the years (Cook & Campbell, 1976, 1979; Campbell & Stanley, 1963; Shadish, Cook, & Campbell, 2002).

In contrast to Campbell's causal model, Rubin's model is more statistical in nature and focuses on the notions of counterfactuals and their effect on estimation of the magnitude of the causal relationship. He explicitly focused on field experiments in which random assignment to conditions is inhibited or not possible, and his writings have resulted in a technique known as propensity scores (Guo & Fraser, 2010), which is used to match participants in field studies to allow bias-free estimates of causal relationships. Rubin started publishing his work in the 1970s and expanded his ideas through the decades that followed (e.g., 1974, 1981, 1990, 2010). However, he frequently notes that the roots of his ideas can be traced back to the 1920s with the work of Neyman (Shadish, 2010).

In the present chapter we will discuss both causal models and their utility for designing effective research designs. We will start with Campbell's causal model.

Campbell's Causal Model

As Shadish highlighted, Campell's Causal Model originally focused on two central inferences made by scientists (Shadish, 2010; Shadish, Cook & Campbell, 2002). First, did the intervention included in their study actually change the value of the dependent variable? Second, does this effect generalize to different variables, settings, and populations? Campbell called the first inference one of internal validity and the second one of external validity (Shadish, 2011). While this two-inference CCM typology appeared to be simple, it generated some confusion, and subsequent work

sought to clarify the issue by expanding the original two inferences into four (Cook & Campbell, 1979; Shadish et al., 2002). These are:

1. *Statistical conclusion validity:* This validity questions the adequacy of the statistical evidence used to establish the existence of covariation among one or more antecedents and one or more dependent variables (Cook & Campbell, 1979).

2. *Internal validity:* This validity questions the appropriateness of labeling the observed covariation between an antecedent and a dependent variable as a causal relationship (Cook & Campbell, 1979).

3. *Construct validity:* This concerns the appropriateness of generalizing conclusions from one measure of some underlying concept (e.g., House et al.'s (2004) uncertainty avoidance societal culture measure) or operationalization of a treatment to another set of measures (e.g., Hofstede's [1980] uncertainty avoidance societal culture measure) or treatment operationalization (Cook & Campbell, 1979).

4. *External validity:* This validity questions the appropriateness of generalizing inferences from one sample (i.e., characteristics of people and setting) to another sample.

Statistical conclusion validity and internal validity touch upon the first central scientific inference mentioned earlier—did the intervention change the value of the dependent variable? Construct validity and external validity touch upon the second—does the obtained effect generalize? While helping to reduce confusion, the reader should note that the boundary conditions among the four validity types are fuzzy (Shadish, 2011): so, it would be unproductive to argue and spend much time trying to pigeonhole an issue into one and only one validity type. At the very least, such arguments are a misapplication of CCM. The main focus of CCM is to identify and eliminate threats to appropriate inferences, and a particular issue may touch upon multiple validities and thereby be affected by multiple threats.

A threat to validity is simply another way of saying that there are plausible alternative explanations for a research finding. For example, assume that we conducted a field study in which we obtained empirical support for some intervention (e.g., we found that a particular motivation seminar improved group performance compared to a control group). Perhaps the improved performance was not due to the beneficial effects of the seminar. Maybe the differences between the seminar and control group were due to a factor called "resentful demoralization." This occurs when the control group participants know that they are being treated differently and they lose their motivation. Thus, perhaps the difference in performance that we observed was not a result of the motivation seminar improving the intervention group's performance but rather the control group's performance falling. Resentful demoralization is a threat to the construct validity of an intervention (Shadish et al., 2002).

Another possibility is that the performance difference between the seminar group and the control group was due to something called "selection" bias. This threat results when there are initial differences in the kinds of people assigned to the seminar and control conditions. Perhaps only people nominated by their managers are sent to the seminar, and it is possible that managers nominated only high performers to attend the desirable seminar. The reader can see how such initial differences in the sample can cause differences in the dependent variable even when the seminar was completely worthless. Selection bias is typically listed as a threat to internal validity (Shadish et al., 2002).

According to the CCM approach, the main role of research design is to identify potential threats to validity and to design a study or a series of studies to minimize the influence of these threats on the research findings. In this way, as noted earlier, CCM is consistent with Popper's (1959) emphasis on falsification over confirmation of a theory as the main driving force in science. CCM emphasizes the importance of ruling out threats to validity in order to increase the likelihood of appropriate inferences being made.

We will discuss each of the four validities and some potential threats in more detail. For convenience, we divide the threats to validity into three categories. The first involve the single group threats—alternative hypotheses that might explain your results when a single group is explored. The second consists of the multiple group threats—alternative hypotheses that might explain your results when several groups are explored in a study (e.g., a program and a comparison group). Finally, we will consider social threats to internal validity—threats that arise because our research is conducted in real-world human contexts in which people react to what affects them as well as what is happening to others around them.

STATISTICAL CONCLUSION VALIDITY

As we defined previously, statistical conclusion validity centers on issues of drawing proper inferences about the existence of covariation between causal agent(s) and dependent variable(s) in a population from sample data (Austin, Boyle, & Lualhati, 1998; Cook & Campbell, 1979). To draw proper inferences, a researcher has to make two related inferences. First, do the causal agent and dependent variable actually covary in the population of interest, and, second, what is the best estimate of the strength of that relationship (Shadish et al., 2002)?

Table 3.1 shows the threats to statistical conclusion validity that have been identified in the latest version of CCM (Shadish et al., 2002). As can be seen by reviewing this table, these threats cover a variety of topics, such as statistical power, violation of assumptions for statistical tests, unreliability of measurement, and range restriction problems. The scope of this chapter prevents a complete discussion of all these threats, and the reader is strongly encouraged to see Shadish et al. (2002) for a very complete discussion of these issues. We will focus on only a few threats to statistical conclusion validity in this chapter.

Statistical power.

One of the first threats listed in Table 3.1 is inadequate statistical power. To understand what statistical power is, we must first describe the logic behind Null Hypothesis Significance Testing (NHST) as well as Type 1 and Type II errors. The process of testing hypotheses known as NHST was developed by Ronald Fisher, Jerzy Neyman, and Egon Pearson at the turn of the last century (Austin et al, 1998; McGrayne, 2011). Basically, NHST requires the researcher to specify two hypotheses about the value of some population parameter (e.g., mean, standard deviation, kurtosis). The first hypothesis is called the null hypothesis (H_o) and the second is called the alternative hypothesis (H_a). The null hypothesis is set to a particular value (e.g., $H_o: \mu = 100$) enabling the generation of a sampling distribution used to estimate the probability of obtaining a statistic as extreme as the one observed in a researcher's sample. The alternative hypothesis (H_a) usually reflects the researcher's hypothesis of interest, although it is typically specified as a range of possible alternative hypotheses (e.g., Nondirectional $H_a: \mu \neq 100$; Directional $H_a: \mu > 100$; Directional $H_a: \mu < 100$).

A Type I error rate (a.k.a. α) is the conditional probability of rejecting the null hypothesis given that the null hypothesis is true [i.e., $\alpha = P(H_a | H_o)$]. A Type II error rate (a.k.a. β) is the conditional probability of failing to accept the alternative hypothesis given that the alternative hypothesis is true

Table 3.1 Threats to Statistical Conclusion Validity

Low statistical power	Study may incorrectly conclude that there is no relationship between causal agent and dependent variable when there truly is a relationship.
Assumptions of statistical tests not met	Violations of statistical test assumptions can lead to either overestimating or underestimating the size and significance of an effect.
Error rate problems due to fishing for significance	Repeated tests for significance, if uncorrected, can artificially inflate statistical significance.
Measurement unreliability	Unreliability weakens relationship between two variables. However, it can weaken or strengthen the relationships among three or more variables.
Range restriction	Systematically excluding certain ranges of a variable from observations tends to reduce relationships between two variables. However, it can weaken and even reverse the sign (and thereby strengthen) the relationships among three or more variables.
Implementation problems of intervention/ manipulation	If manipulation or intervention is only partially given for some participants, effects will be underestimated.
Extraneous variance in study	An aspect of the study inflates noise in the dependent variable, thereby increasing the difficulty of detecting an effect.
Heterogeneity of units	Increased variability on the dependent variable within experimental conditions increases noise. Increase in noise makes it more difficult to find a true relationship.
Inaccurate estimation of effect size	Some statistics systematically overestimate or underestimate the size of an effect.

[i.e., $\beta = P(H_o | H_a)$]. To give another perspective on Type I and Type II errors, imagine a radar operator on a submarine whose task is to determine if there is a real object in front of the submarine. The null hypothesis (H_o) for the radar operator would be that there is no object, whereas the alternative hypothesis (H_a) would be that there is some object (e.g., rock, another submarine) in front of the submarine. Table 3.2 presents a 2 by 2 table illustrating the relationship between Type I and Type II error rates in terms of this example. Statistical power is the probability that the radar operator will decide that there is a real object in front of the submarine given that there really is something there. More technically, statistical power is the probability of choosing the alternative hypothesis given that the alternative hypothesis is true (i.e., $1-\beta$).

We used the submarine and radar operator example in Table 3.2 to emphasize that statistical power is really an issue of signal-to-noise ratios. The signal comes from the alternative hypothesis (i.e., a real object is sending a signal to the operator), whereas the random noise comes from the null (i.e., background noise) hypothesis. Given this metaphor, it can be shown that a number of factors affect statistical power. For example, the reliability of the causal agents and the dependent variable measures affects statistical power. Reliability reflects the degree to which a measure is free from random noise. So the lower the reliability (i.e., more random noise) in the causal agents or dependent variables, the lower statistical power (i.e., the harder it is to detect a true signal). In addition, choosing a more sensitive research design (e.g., repeated measures versus a between-subject design) or statistical analysis approach (Bliese & Hanges, 2004) will increase the power to detect an alternative hypothesis. More sensitive research designs control random noise and so they have more statistical power. Further, a measurement scale can also be said to have more or less sensitivity for a given purpose. For example, using a truck weight scale to measure the weight difference between three or four potatoes is an example of an inappropriate use of a scale that creates considerable noise—and a subsequent loss of statistical power—in any study that would use that

Table 3.2 Illustration of Relationship Between Type I and Type II Error Rates

	True State of World	
Decision	Ho is true: Nothing	Ha is true: Real Object
Ho is not rejected: False Alarm	Correct Decision	Type II error
Ha is accepted: Real Object	Type I error	Correct Decision

scale to measure potato differences. In social sciences, examples of using inappropriate scales occur when measures designed to assess broad differences (e.g., cultural differences at the societal level) are used in studies analyzing differences between organizational cultures. The strength of the effect being sought (a.k.a., effect size) affects statistical power. It is easier to detect a stronger effect (more signal) than a weaker effect (less signal). Also, the more observations included in a study, the better the statistical power. Simply put, as we collect and average more observations, the doubt we may have had earlier regarding whether we truly saw a signal or random noise decreases, thereby increasing statistical power.

Finally, the decision criterion that the researcher is using also affects statistical power. The Type I error rate (α) set by the researcher affects the statistical power (i.e., larger α yields greater statistical power), as does the direction of the alternative hypothesis. There is greater statistical power with directional, rather than non-directional, alternative hypotheses.

In general, the recommendation is for a study to have a probability between 80 to 90 percent for statistical power (Cohen, 1979; Meehl, 1991). Further, researchers need to conduct a power analysis before conducting their study to ensure that they have sufficient power to detect their alternative hypothesis (Hedges & Pigott, 2004). Indeed, Rosenthal (1994) has argued that it is unethical to conduct studies with insufficient power because they waste the time of participants with a poorly designed study, potentially giving these participants a poor impression of social science research, and if the study somehow gets published, it has the potential to add confusion to the literature. In 1962, after reviewing the literature in abnormal and social psychology, Cohen reported that the median statistical power was 0.48 for a medium effect. Unfortunately, subsequent reports of statistical power have been low for medium effects (Austin et al., 1998) although

Mone, Mueller, and Mauland (1996) report statistical power of 0.74 for a medium effect size in the management literature, so there appears to be some improvement.

Null Hypothesis Significance Testing (NHST). Another issue that has generated debate is the use of NHST in the social sciences. For example, Rozeboom (1997) described NHST as "the most bone-headedly misguided procedure ever institutionalized in the rote training of science students" (p. 335). Carver (1978) described it as "a corrupt form of the scientific method" (p. 378), and Lakatos (1978) questioned whether the role of statistical procedures such as NHST in the social sciences were not to "primarily provide a machinery for producing phony corroborations and thereby a semblance of 'scientific progress' where, in fact, there is nothing but an increase in pseudo-intellectual garbage" (p. 88). Given these sentiments, it is not surprising that some researchers have called for a ban on the use of NHST (Cohen, 1994; Schmidt, 1996).

What is the problem with the use of NHST in the social sciences? Meehl (1967; 1990) argued that the precision of theories in the social sciences are insufficient to effectively use it. As we noted previously, in the social sciences, we associate our theories with the alternative hypothesis. However, Meehl (1967, 1990) pointed out that the theories in physics are sufficiently precise to generate numerical predictions, and so theories are associated with the null hypothesis in this science. This difference concerning which hypothesis is associated with scientific theories actually is critical, and Meehl conjectures that it accounts for the differential rates of progress in these two branches of sciences. Specifically, rejecting the null hypothesis supports a social science theory, whereas it refutes a theory in physics. Therefore, it becomes easier for social scientists but harder for physicists to support their theories as research becomes more rigorous.

Other classic arguments against NHST have been that it is logically flawed—specifically, it violates the *modus tollens* rule of syllogistic reasoning (Cohen, 1994; Meehl, 1990; Schmidt, 1996). However, Cortina and Landis (2011) convincingly argued that this critique is a minor issue. Another classic criticism is that NHST sets up a "straw man" comparison. In particular, when the H$_0$ is set to "no effect," it is never true. As such, rejecting H$_0$ is just a function of whether the researcher has a sufficient sample size and not a function of the quality of the researcher's theory. To a large extent, this issue can be addressed by setting what Meehl (1990) referred to as "crud" levels, although we prefer the term *ambient noise level* used by Lykken (1968). In this approach, the researcher sets a range of values for the H_o that represents inconsequential effects from a theoretical perspective (Cortina & Dunlap, 1997; Edwards & Berry, 2010; Murphy, 1990). If a researcher follows this advice, then rejecting the H_o would imply substantive support for a theory, as opposed to trivial rejection of a patently false no effect H_o. Finally, Nickerson (2000) has pointed out that many researchers have argued that NHST should be banned because it has been misinterpreted/misused (e.g., incorrectly interpreting the p-value as the probability that the H_o is true). The recommended alternative to NHST is to estimate the relationship magnitude (e.g., provide the correlation, d-statistic, η^2) and set a confidence interval around this estimate. With regard to this alternative, Cortina and Landis (2011) point out that the belief that researchers who have misinterpreted and misused NHST will now suddenly interpret and use confidence intervals correctly is a dream. These authors point out that NHST has a well-specified set of rules that help researchers determine whether their data support their hypotheses. There are no comparable set of rules for the confidence interval approach. Thus, Cortina and Landis raise a reasonable question: If researchers misinterpret and misuse a process in which rules are well specified and stated, why would switching to a process with fewer rules lead to less misinterpretation and misuse?

As shown above, the classic critiques of NHST have attacked the inherent logic of the system. However, either the damage of the critiques has been overblown (e.g., logical inconsistency) or there are procedural fixes to the identified problems (e.g., setting ambient noise levels). So the question remains, how should our science address Meehl's (1967, 1990) critique that the theories in social science lack sufficient precision to use NHST effectively and that this imprecision has slowed the progress of our science? Edwards and Berry (2010) indicate that we need to address Meehl not by attacking NHST but by increasing the precision of our theories. In a review of articles published in the *Academy of Management Review* between 1985 to 2009, Edwards and Berry identified 183 propositions and described these propositions as follows:

> Regarding the magnitude of the relationships predicted by these propositions, 19 (10.4%) simply stated that a relationship would exist, 164 (89.6%)

described the direction of the relationship, and none of the propositions predicted a point value or range of values. With respect to the form of the relationship, 177 (96.7%) of the propositions were silent on this issue. Of the 6 propositions that addressed form, 3 (1.6%) described the shape of the relationship, and an additional 3 (1.6%) articulated specific features of the relationship, referring to peaks or turning points in curvilinear functions. Finally, 44 (24.0%) of the propositions included conditions that influence the predicted relationship, most of which were cast as moderator variables, whereas 139 (76.0%) propositions stated predictions without reference to conditions. (p. 670)

Clearly, this analysis demonstrates that Meehl (1967, 1990) correctly described the state of affairs in the organizational sciences literature. To improve precision in organizational sciences, Edwards and Berry (2010) recommended that we: (a) predict upper and lower limits for our parameters; (b) develop studies that test competing models or theories, as opposed to seeking confirmatory support for a single model or theory; (c) follow the example used in physics and set the H_o to a value specified by theory or obtained from previous findings (e.g., meta-analyses); (d) specify the shape of the relationship (e.g., linear, quadratic, discontinuous); and (e) propose and test for moderators. The reader is strongly encouraged to read Edwards and Berry because they provide specific advice about how to accomplish each of these steps for improving the precision of our theories.

Finally, before moving on to the next validity topic in CCM, one issue that has recently been leveled against NHST, in particular, but is a concern for statistical conclusion validity, in general, needs to be discussed. In particular, this issue concerns the use of Bayesian statistical techniques as opposed to more traditional statistical methods. Traditional statistical methods interpret probability as a long-run relative frequency (Dienes, 2011)—that is, probability is viewed as the percentage of times that a particular outcome will occur when an experiment is repeated over a substantial number of trials. As such, probability is not descriptive of individual phenomenon (e.g., whether a particular coin landed heads or tails), but rather it is descriptive of collections of phenomena or events (e.g., the percentage of times that an event—exactly two heads—appears when a coin is flipped twice and the coin flip experiment is repeated 20,000 times). In the same way, a theory or a particular hypothesis—which are individual phenomena—are either true or false, and thus probability estimates from traditional statistics do not directly apply to particular theories or particular hypotheses (Dienes, 2011). NHST provides a set of decision criteria that we can use to estimate the probability of a particular value for a statistic given certain assumptions as specified by a hypothesis (e.g., null hypothesis) or theory. In contrast to traditional statistics, what we want to know is the probability that a hypothesis or theory is true given a data set. This is exactly what the Bayesian approach provides (Dienes, 2011). It accomplishes this by using prior knowledge about an event's likely outcomes to adjust probability estimates for future events.

The Bayesian argument against NHST is that the probability estimates obtained from NHST depend upon the behavior and intentions of the researcher, which is exactly what a carefully designed research study is supposed to prevent (Kruschke, 2011a, 2011b). For example, suppose we are interested in determining whether there is gender bias in the perception of leadership ability. If there was no gender bias, there should be a 50 percent chance of choosing a male versus a female candidate as one's leader given that the two gender candidates were of equal leadership ability. Suppose we run a study in which we have people read the resumes of two candidates (one male and one female) and pick one as a leader. We observe that of 22 people, only 8 picked the female leader. Is that evidence of gender bias? In the situation where the experimenter intended to ask 22 people (i.e., number of people asked (n) is fixed to 22) and if eight people were found who chose the female leader (i.e., x is a random variable and it is the number of people choosing a female leader), the binomial distribution would be used to compute the probability for this study, and the p-value would not be sufficient to reject the null hypothesis ($p = 0.143$). There does not appear to be support for the gender bias hypothesis.

However, if the experimenter intended to stop the data collection after finding a certain number of people who chose the female leader (i.e., x is fixed), and it turned out that 22 people had to be sampled (i.e., N is random) before the eighth female-leader supporter was found, then the Pascal (a.k.a., negative binomial) distribution is used to compute the probability for this study. This time the p-value would be sufficient to reject the null hypothesis ($p = 0.041$). Even though we are using the exact same data as before, we now reject the null hypothesis and conclude that gender bias exists. In other words, we either rejected or failed to reject the null hypothesis

using NHST based upon the experimenter's intentions! Interestingly, the experimenter's intentions are irrelevant when a Bayesian approach to hypothesis testing is taken (Kruschke, 2011b). Unfortunately, the founders of NHST were strong opponents of Bayesian approaches, and Fisher's vitriolic attack against Bayesian statistics made it virtually off-limits for statisticians for decades (McGrayne, 2011).

In summary, many factors affect statistical conclusion validity. Table 3.1 provides the formal list of threats, and we have gone into detail regarding only a few of these. The reader is strongly encouraged to consult Shadish et al. (2002) as well as Austin et al. (1998) for a more complete discussion of statistical conclusion validity and the factors that affect whether one can conclude whether a causal agent and a dependent variable have a relationship or not.

INTERNAL VALIDITY

As defined earlier, the central issue in internal validity is whether observed changes in the dependent variable can be attributed to the hypothesized causal agent or intervention and *not* to other possible causes (Cook & Campbell, 1979). Of the four types of validity, Campbell emphasized internal validity (Shadish, 2011). Indeed, he wrote that "internal validity is the prior and indispensable condition" (Campbell, 1957, p. 310) and that it was "the *sine qua non*" (Campbell & Stanley, 1963, p. 175) of experimental work. However, other scholars, such as Lee Cronbach, disagreed with this position (Shadish, 2011). As we mentioned at the beginning of this chapter, Brewer (2000) classified research into three different categories. Of the three types of research, internal validity would be less important for studies focused on establishing phenomena (i.e., demonstration studies) than for studies focusing on establishing causation or providing explanation for relationships.

If a researcher focused on only internal validity to the exclusion of the other three types of validity, then the question focused on whether causality could be established in the researcher's specific study. In other words, internal validity can be thought of as a "zero generalizability" concern. If internal validity is established to the exclusion of the other three validity types, then the only conclusion that can be reached is that the causal agent used in that particular study caused a particular dependent variable to change. The researcher could not say whether what was manipulated (i.e., the actual intervention) was a function of the intended latent construct. Nor could the researcher say whether the measured dependent variable actually was consistent with the broader latent dependent variable construct that s/he wanted to measure—both of these are construct validity concerns.

It is possible to have internal validity in a study and not have construct validity. For example, suppose you are interested in assessing the claims of a company that their new computerized tutoring program will improve math performance of elementary students about to move into middle school. Imagine that one major aspect of the tutoring program is the computer game simulation component. You hypothesize that the gaming component is what actually improves math performance. However, it turns out that your hypothesis is wrong. While math performance does improve at the end of the experiment, the improvement was not due to the tutorial computer program. It turns out that the organization hires an adult tutor to work with the students as they interact with the computer program. It is the individual attention from the adult tutor that made the difference in final math learning—the computer program did not make any difference. This study would have internal validity because something in the intervention affected the dependent variable—the manipulation did cause *something* to happen. But the study would not have construct validity, specifically, the label "computer math program" does not accurately describe the actual cause (perhaps better described as "personal adult attention").

In the recent version of CCM (Shadish et al., 2002), nine different threats to internal validity have been identified (see Table 3.3 for a list of these threats). For example, ambiguous temporal precedence is directly concerned with Mill's first condition for determining causality: the causal agent must precede the dependent variable. The strength of the causal inference that can be gleaned from a study is diminished if the causal variables and dependent variables are collected simultaneously or if the dependent variable is actually collected before the hypothesized causal variable(s), perhaps due to convenience. Table 3.3 shows that another threat is called "selection." This refers to systematic differences in the characteristics of participants in the various conditions before an experiment. If there are characteristic differences in the participants (knowledge differences, interest differences, motivation differences), then it is ambiguous whether the intervention causes any changes in the dependent variable at the end of

Table 3.3 Threats to Internal Validity

Temporal precedence ambiguity	Lack of clarity about which variable occurred first results in confusion about which variable is truly the causal agent and which one is the dependent variable.
Selection	Differences in participants' characteristics among treatment conditions that potentially can account for intervention effect.
History	Events occurring concurrently with intervention might have caused the change in the dependent variable.
Maturation	The observed change in the dependent variable might have been due to naturally occurring changes over time.
Regression	If participants are selected to be in a study because their score on some measure was extreme (i.e., extremely higher or lower than group mean), participants will often have less extreme scores when measure (or other variables) is taken again.
Attrition	Loss of participants to treatment or to measurement can produce biased effects if participant loss is systematically related to conditions.
Testing	A pretest measure might positively affect subsequent scores on the test. This increase in subsequent scores can yield a false impression that the intervention worked.
Instrumentation	If a measure changes over the course of a study (i.e., measure changes over time or different measure in different conditions), score differences could be confused with an intervention effect.
Additive and interactive effects of threats to internal validity	The impact of a threat can be added to that of another threat or may depend on the level of another threat.

the experiment or whether the differences in the dependent variable were a function of the initial differences between people. In other words, selection bias speaks directly to the presence of third variable explanations.

Random assignment of participants to conditions directly eliminates the selection bias threat (Shadish et al., 2002) and might reduce the plausibility of some of the other internal validity threats (Shadish et al., 2002). However, random assignment to conditions does not eliminate all the potential threats to internal validity. For example, participants can still be sensitized by pretest measures, or the change in instrumentation could destroy the ability to detect true treatment effects. In sum, all of these factors affect the interpretation of the study.

CONSTRUCT VALIDITY

Construct validity is concerned with the extent to which our measures as well as laboratory manipulations or field interventions are really reflections of some targeted theoretical concept/construct (Shadish et al., 2002). This validity focuses on the extent to which a particular study is connected to the overarching theory that drove the study in the first place. For example, a theory specifies a set of abstract constructs that are usually separated into a subset of causal agents (e.g., leadership, organizational culture) and a subset of dependent variables (e.g., task performance, intrinsic motivation). The theory then specifies how the variables in the causal relationship subset relate to the variables in the dependent variable subset.

To assess the viability of this theory, researchers design studies in which the directly unobservable (i.e., latent) constructs are made manifest through either measurement (e.g., the Multifactor Leadership Questionnaire is used to measure leadership perceptions) or by manipulation (e.g., an actor enacts either participative or authoritarian leadership). The extent that the study's findings are relevant to the veracity of the theory depends upon the strength of the connections between the manifest measures/manipulations to the latent constructs they were intended to assess.

The most recent list of CCM threats to construct validity is shown in Table 3.4. The first threat listed in this table is *inadequate explication of the construct*. While this may seem an obvious and easy threat to avoid, the time and effort required to clearly specify a latent construct should not be underestimated and is well taken. Indeed, specification of a construct requires building what Cronbach and Meehl (1955)

called a nomological network. A good nomological network specifies the theoretical framework supporting the constructs, as well as specifying how to measure these constructs. Finally, the nomological network specifies the relationships between the theoretical constructs, the relationships between the manifest measures, and the measurement relationships between the latent constructs and manifest measures.

One mistake in defining latent constructs is that they are sometimes specified too broadly (Shadish et al., 2002), without any qualifiers or without sufficient detail (e.g., happiness, attractiveness, pornography). The consequence of this error is that it leads to confusion regarding whether a particular measure or manipulation is an appropriate manifestation of the latent construct. Another mistake in defining latent constructs is that they can be defined too narrowly. That is, the definition of the construct is overly specified with unnecessary restrictions in terms of pertinent populations, settings, and even measurement tools. This error was frequently committed during the 1930s to 1960s, when the operationalism philosophy of measurement was influential (Michell, 1990). During this time, researchers equated their latent constructs to their measures—as exemplified by Boring's (1945) often-quoted definition of the construct of intelligence (i.e., "Intelligence is what tests test," p. 244).

Once a construct has been defined, manifest measures of it are identified. Unfortunately, there is no one perfect measure or manipulation of any particular construct (Shadish et al., 2002). All measures are deficient in two ways. The first is *construct underrepresentation* (Messick, 1995), which means that a manifest measure only assesses a portion of a construct's definitional domain. Important aspects of the intended construct are not reflected in any specific measure. The second deficiency inherent in all measures is *construct-irrelevant variance,* which indicates that all manifest measures are influenced by multiple factors (e.g., an intelligence test could be influenced by student's intelligence, SES of parents, quality of education, degree of dyslexia in student, family value placed on education, English language facility). Some of these factors are theoretically meaningful constructs (of which, intelligence, our intended construct is one) and, for our research purposes, others are not (e.g., English language facility, dyslexia).

Confusion in the nomological network will occur if researchers rely on only a single measure or manipulation of constructs across multiple studies.

Table 3.4 Threats to Construct Validity

Inadequate explication of constructs	Constructs not fully defined, resulting in inappropriate inferences about the connection between the construct and the measure/manipulation
Construct confounding	Measures/manipulations tend to be influenced by more than one construct. Failure to understand all the constructs may result in inadequate inferences about construct.
Mono-operation bias	Inferences are complicated because any measure/manipulation of a construct both underrepresents the full construct of interest and measures irrelevant constructs.
Mono-method bias	When all variables in a study use the same method (e.g., self-report), the method is potentially confounded with the construct.
Confounding constructs with levels of constructs	Inferences about the constructs that best represent study operations may fail to describe the limited levels of the construct that were actually studied.
Treatment sensitive factorial structure (a.k.a. Measurement Equivalence)	The structure of a measure may change as a result of some intervention or condition.
Reactive self-report changes	Self-reports can be affected by participant motivation to be in a treatment condition, motivation that can change after assignment is made.
Reactivity to the experimental situation	Participant responses reflect not just intervention and measures but also participants' perceptions of the study. Perceptions of study are part of the treatment being tested
Researcher expectancies	The researcher influences participant responses by conveying expectations about desired responses. These expectations are part of the treatment being tested
Novelty and disruption effects	Participants may respond unusually well or unusually poorly to a novel innovation. Response must be included as part of the treatment description
Compensatory equalization	When intervention provides desirable goods or services, administrators, staff, or constituents may provide compensatory goods or services to those not receiving treatment. This action must be included as part of the treatment description.
Compensatory rivalry	Participants not receiving treatment may be motivated to show they can do as well as those receiving treatment. This must be included as part of the treatment description.
Resentful demoralization	Participants not receiving a desirable treatment may be resentful or demoralized so that they respond more negatively than otherwise. This must be included as part of the treatment description.
Treatment diffusion	Participants may receive some benefit from an experimental treatment that they were not assigned. This makes construct descriptions of intervention conditions difficult.

For example, assume that an observed relationship between two manifest variables is observed repeatedly across multiple studies because the same two manifest variables are used in all of these studies. Unfortunately, this relationship was not predicted by the original nomological network. The researcher must decide if the nomological network must be adjusted given this consistent evidence—perhaps the original theoretical framework was faulty. Or perhaps the results can be ignored and there is no need to change the theory—perhaps the unpredicted relationships were due to secondary factors in the measures and not the primary constructs of interest. Unfortunately, there is no information to help the researcher decide until new studies are conducted with different manifest measures of these latent constructs. This confusion is what Messick (1981) called nomological noise, and it is caused by consistently using a single manifestation of a construct. Relying on a single manifestation of a construct and the subsequent confusion it causes is the third threat to construct validity in Table 3.4.

Multilevel issues in establishing construct validity.

When developing nomological networks of a construct, it is important to consider whether the meaning of the construct and its nomological networks may replicate across different levels of research interest. For example, when researchers are interested in understanding the construct of collective team efficacy, it is natural to ask the question of whether the construct would have the same meaning as individual members' perceived team efficacy and would share the same functional relationships with other variables. Therefore, different composition models should be considered to specify the functional relationships among phenomena or constructs at different levels of analysis (e.g., individual level, team level, and organizational level) that reference essentially the same content but that are qualitatively different at different levels (Chan, 1998a; Kozlowski & Klein, 2000). Specifying the functional relationships among constructs at different levels provides a systematic framework for mapping the transformation across levels, which offers conceptual precision in the target construct and aids in the derivation of hypotheses regarding the nomological networks across levels.

According to Chan (1998a), five basic forms of composition models are: (a) additive, (b) direct consensus, (c) referent-shift consensus, (d) dispersion, and (e) process composition. In the additive composition models, the meaning of the higher level variable is a summation of lower level units, regardless of the variance among these units. Further, this summation-based variable is descriptive in nature (Kozlowski & Klein, 2000). Direct consensus composition model uses within-group consensus of the lower level units as the functional relationship to specify how the construct conceptualized and operationalized at the lower level is functionally isomorphic to another form of the construct at the higher level. The typical operational combination process

is using within-group agreement and/or reliability of scores to index consensus and/or consistency at the lower level and to justify aggregation of lower level scores to represent scores at the higher level.

Referent-shift consensus composition model is similar to direct consensus composition in that within-group consensus is used to compose the lower level construct to the higher level construct. But, in referent-shift consensus composition models, the lower level attributes being assessed for consensus are conceptually distinct, though derived from the original individual-level construct. That is, there is a shift in the referent prior to consensus assessment, and it is the new referent that is actually being combined to represent the higher level construct. In the case of referent-shift consensus, composition proceeds with the researcher beginning with a conceptual definition and operationalization of the focal construct at the lower level. While maintaining the basic content of the construct, the researcher then derives a new form of the construct at the same level by shifting the referent of the basic content. The new form of the construct then is aggregated to the higher level construct based on within-group consensus.

Dispersion models focus on the use of within-group variance or agreement to specify the functional relationship in composition of a group-level construct. Dispersion is by definition a group-level characteristic because it refers to the variability within a group, and a variance statistic is indexing an attribute of a group, as opposed to an attribute of any individual-level response. In other words, dispersion is used to refer to variance (or homogeneity) of scores on any lower level units or attributes (e.g., individual cognitive ability, individual climate perceptions). Recently, Harrison and Klein (2007) have further distinguished dispersion composition (they termed it as "separation") from variety and disparity compositions. Specifically, they argue that the dispersion composition is only appropriate to use in deriving higher level construct-to-index differences in position or opinion among lower level units, such as values, beliefs, or attitudes. They propose that a variety composition be used to derive higher level construct-to-index differences in kind, source, or category of relevant knowledge or experience among lower level units and that a disparity composition be used to derive higher level construct-to-index differences in differences in proportion of socially valued assets or resources held among lower level units.

Process composition models are concerned with composing some process or mechanism from the lower level of conceptualization to the higher level.

In these models, a process or mechanism is first specified at the lower level, explicating the essential or critical parameters and their interrelationships. The process then is composed to the higher level by identifying critical higher level parameters, which are higher level analogues of the lower level parameters, and describing interrelationships among higher level parameters, which are homologous to the lower level parameter relationships. In essence, process composition models specify parallel nomological networks among similar constructs across levels of analysis. Testing and establishing process composition models can add to the parsimony and breadth of the construct in question. Further, if the process composition model does not hold, it signals a boundary condition and a need to refine the conceptualization of the construct to better understand how the nomological network of the construct operates at each distinct level. For interested readers, Chen, Bliese, and Mathieu (2005) provide a detailed discussion regarding how to test process composition models and DeShon, Kozlowski, Schmidt, Milner, and Wiechmann (2004) provide an empirical research example for such test.

EXTERNAL VALIDITY

External validity refers to the extent to which the results from a scientific study can generalize to other populations, settings, or contexts. Specifically, inferences based on research findings are said to possess external validity if they may be generalized from the unique and idiosyncratic settings, procedures, and participants to the populations and conditions that are of interest (Shadish et al., 2002). One important factor that often influences a study's external validity is the representativeness of the research sample. The representativeness of the sample is critical when the study aims to answer research questions about a specific, well-defined population of interest (Highhouse & Gillespie, 2008). For example, a researcher who is specifically interested in studying the group process among firefighters could not sample from any population other than the population of firefighter to answer his/her research question. To achieve the representativeness of the sample, random sampling procedure is often used. It involves selecting people by chance from a clearly defined population. Following this procedure, a sample that matches the population on all attributes (e.g., mean and variance) is generated, thus eliminating the possibility that some members of the population may be oversampled or undersampled (Shadish et al., 2002). This way, the data from this sample can be used to draw statistical conclusions about its target population, thus providing the generalizability of the statistical findings to the target population. Unfortunately, random sampling is often too costly and is rarely used in conducting organizational science research (for some exceptions, see Frone [2008] and Wang [2007]).

A random sampling procedure should not be confused with random assignment procedure. The latter is often used to improve internal validity in studies with experimental design, involving randomly assigning participants into experimental conditions. Given that each participant has an equal and independent chance of being assigned to every condition, the groups are expected to be equal with respect to any and all potential participant-associated confounding variables. Thus, using random assignment helps to rule out the potential confounding effects due to individual differences. Obviously, random assignment happens after a sample of participants is selected, and thus has no impact on the representativeness of the sample.

Highhouse (2009) cautioned about judging a sample's representativeness merely based on the superficial similarity between the sample and the target population. For example, researchers often prefer using field samples rather than using college student samples in studying organizational phenomena. A typical argument for this preference is that workers from field samples are more generalizable to "people" in organizations than are college student samples. However, scrutinizing this argument, it certainly does not apply universally. The superior generalizability of field samples depends on whether the specific work experiences of the research sample would influence the phenomena being studied in a way that would confound the results of the study (Campbell, 1986). If there is no good reason to expect the confounding effect of work experience, college student samples would be just as generalizable as field samples in answering the research question (Highhouse, 2009). In other words, if the constructs and processes are essentially the same across field and student samples (i.e., maintaining the psychological fidelity), then using student samples should render the same generalizability as using field samples.

It is also important to note that social science researchers, including organizational science researchers, are typically more interested in theoretical generalizability than statistical generalizability (Highhouse & Gillespie, 2008; Sackett & Larson, 1990). In other words, they are more interested in whether a causal relationship, but not the particular effect size of that causal relationship, may hold across populations. Therefore, to achieve the theoretical generalizability, it is not necessary to use samples that are strictly representative of the population, but only necessary to use samples that do not systematically differ from the population in a way that would interact with the causal relationship. Often times, we see researchers who used samples from non-Western cultures/countries apologetically note in the limitation sections of their papers that findings from their samples may not generalize to Western populations. However, before hastily reaching that conclusion, they should scrutinize whether their samples provide adequate theoretical generalizability or psychological fidelity. Studies using samples from Western cultures/countries should not be immune to this scrutiny either. For example, to the extent that the differences between a sample of American participants and a sample of Chinese participants (e.g., in their cultural values) would not interact with the causal effect of job experience on job performance, using either the American sample or the Chinese sample in the study should provide the same theoretical generalizabilty of this causal relationship to both American and Chinese populations. Given that true random sampling is rarely used in applied behavioral research (Shadish et al., 2002), scrutinizing the theoretical generalizability of the research sample is particularly important in ensuring the external validity of a study. Threats to external validity are shown in Table 3.5.

In summary, we have discussed the four types of validity covered by CCM. We have listed the various threats that have currently been identified for each validity type and have discussed more recent debates regarding these threats. The heart of the CCM approach to experimental design is for the experimenter to consider and design studies that rule out various alternative explanations for the effect of the causal agent on the dependent variable. As we discussed previously, CCM is similar in spirit to Popper's (1959) emphasis of falsification over confirmation as the main driving force in science. Before discussing the Rubin Causal Model, we do not want the reader to believe that the CCM approach leads to stagnation because a perfect research design that rules out all possible threats to validity cannot be designed. Rather, the elimination of alternative explanations for an effect can unfold across multiple studies as different threats are controlled for in different studies.

Quasi-Experimentation and the Rubin Causal Model (RCM)

In this section, we discuss the Rubin Causal Model (RCM) and explain how it differs from as well as complements CCM. RCM was designed specifically to eliminate a threat to validity that occurs when researchers conduct research in the field. Thus, before we discuss RCM, we will introduce the concept of quasi-experimentation and will explain how these types of experiments differ from traditional experimental work.

As discussed earlier, our focus in this chapter was to discuss the methods used by scientists to evaluate causal relationships. We reviewed the concept of causation and the equation that specifies the causal effect magnitude for individuals (see Equation 4). Unfortunately, causal effects cannot be estimated for individuals because this equation requires

Table 3.5 Threats to External Validity

Interaction of the causal relationship with participants	An effect found with certain kinds of participants might not hold if other kinds of participants had been studied.
Interaction of the causal relationship over treatment variations	An effect found with one treatment variation might not hold with other variations of that treatment, or when that treatment is combined with other treatments, or when only part of that treatment is used.
Interaction of the causal relationship with dependent variable	An effect found on one kind of dependent variable may not hold if a different dependent variable was used.
Interactions of the causal relationship with settings	An effect found in one kind of setting may not hold if other kinds of settings were to be used.
Context-dependent mediation	An explanatory mediator of a causal relationship in one context may not mediate in another context.

knowledge of the participant's outcome in the control as well as in the treatment condition, provided that the participant is in the same naïve mental state in both experimental conditions. As we discussed, this cannot be done. Instead, researchers estimate the causal effect at the group level (see Equation 5). However, this equation can only be solved when empirical data are collected in such a way that the two hidden counterfactual conditions are equivalent to the two observed conditions. The data collection method that permits solution to Equation 5 is randomization—specifically, random assignment of conditions to participants. This is one reason that methodologists pick randomized experiments as the design of choice when testing hypotheses about causation (West, Biesanz, & Pitts, 2000).

Randomized experimentation has typically been used in controlled, laboratory settings. However, some researchers have successfully conducted randomized experiments in the field. For example, Dvir, Eden, and Banjo (1995) told officers in the Israeli Defense Force that psychological testing had revealed that a portion of their male and female cadets were poised to excel in the coming months. Of course, the male and female cadets identified as having the potential to excel were randomly selected into these conditions. The Dvir et al. field experiment demonstrated the causal effect of expectations on performance of a real job with an adult population.

While successful randomized experiments can occur in the field, more often than not, factors arise that make the implementation of classic experimental control problematic. For example, it is understandable that organizational management might be reluctant to release its authority as well as its liability to an experimenter who wants to randomize employees into various experimental conditions. What are the potential disruptions to the business operation due to the random assignment of employees to experimental conditions? What legal implications are there if a group of employees miss promotion opportunities or do not receive raises simply because their supervisors were not randomly selected to be informed that those employees were "primed to excel"? Further, Argyris (1975) pointed out that, even though it is not discussed in the literature, the traditional controlled research study has its own unique culture. In a traditional controlled experiment, participants are unempowered individuals who are subjected to conditions or assigned tasks by a powerful other—the experimenter. To what extent will organizations welcome experimenters who want to conduct traditional experiments if the organization's culture (e.g., empowered workforce) is inconsistent with the implicit culture of the traditional randomized experiment? To what extent will the results of such an experiment generalize to a company with a completely different culture? Can an experiment that has an implicit culture that is inconsistent with the culture of the broader organization successfully be completed, or will the organization find itself with an angry and discontented workforce?

Finally, the process of randomly assigning conditions to participants itself can be problematic when studying certain phenomena in the field. For example, if the researcher was interested in determining the effectiveness of a certain training intervention (e.g., sensitivity training) but there have been reports that some people who undergo such interventions experience psychological harm, then random assignment of people to conditions creates the ethical dilemma for the experimenter in that s/he is directly responsible for negatively affecting the long-term health of participants (Grant & Wall, 2009; Shadish et al., 2002).

Quasi-experimentation is a collection of techniques that permit researchers to explore questions about causation in the field when random assignment of conditions to participants does not occur (Grant & Wall, 2009; Shadish et al., 2002; West et al., 2000). The first use of this term was by Campbell and Stanley in 1963. While randomization to conditions does not occur in quasi-experiments, the hypothesized causal agents are manipulated in these research designs (Shadish et al., 2002; West et al., 2000). However, also unlike traditional experiments, the manipulation of the causal agent is not necessarily under the control of the experimenter. The manipulation of the hypothesized causal agents might be determined by management or other organizational factors.

With regard to estimating causal effects, the lack of randomization means that the counterfactual conditions for the causal effect are probably not equivalent in quasi-experimentation. That is, in all likelihood, the people in the different intact groups probably differ on a multitude of factors, and thus the selection threat to internal validity for any empirical study is a viable alternative hypothesis. Quasi-experimentation will produce a biased causal effect estimate (Equation 5) unless the researcher takes extreme care in designing the research study and also takes additional steps to reduce the selection threat as much as possible. Specifically, the Rubin Causal Model (RCM) was developed as a way to reduce preexisting differences that exist in intact groups to bring the quasi-experiment back in line with a true randomized experiment (Shadish & Cook, 2009). RCM attempts to build a mathematical equation that will statistically account for the selection threat to internal validity inherent in quasi-experiments.

In RCM, the problem of not being able to estimate the causal effect at the individual level (Equation 4) is conceptualized as a missing data problem (West & Thoemmes, 2010). Rubin solved this "missing data" problem by first estimating the conditional probability of each participant being in the treatment condition (Guo & Fraser, 2010; Morgan & Winship, 2007). A number of different techniques can be used to establish this conditional probability: for example, logistic regression, probit analysis, multinomial logit regression (Guo & Fraser, 2010). Regardless of the specific statistical technique, the researcher scans his/her data set and identifies a set of variables collected before the experimental manipulation was delivered that might influence to which particular intact group the participant belonged. For example, individual differences in interests, personality, motivation, and values might account for selection into different intact groups (Schneider, 1987; Dickson, Resick, & Goldstein, 2008). An analysis is then performed (e.g., logistic regression analysis) in which the identified variables are used to predict the binary outcome of whether the participant is in a treatment or control condition (e.g., outcome variable can be coded 0= control, 1=treatment). The analysis yields propensity scores which provide the probability that a participant will receive the treatment, conditioned on the state of the variables used in the equation (Guo & Fraser, 2010; Morgan & Winship, 2007).

The second step of this procedure is for the researcher to match participants in the treatment condition with participants in the control condition as a function of their propensity score. Of course, it is possible that the researcher will not be able to find a direct match for each and every participant's propensity score, and so some participants will be dropped from further analysis. However, a number of different techniques have been developed (e.g., greedy matching, Mahalanobis metrix distance matching, optimal matching) to assist the researcher in finding participants across the experimental conditions that sufficiently match on the propensity scores (Guo & Fraser, 2010). Provided that the logistic equation adequately explains the differential selection into groups (Rubin, 1977), the selection threat to validity will have been removed

in the reduced matched sample (Guo & Fraser, 2010). In other words, the quasi-experiment will now be as close as possible to the classic randomized experiment for determining causal effects. Indeed, Equation 5 can now be solved because, like randomization, the propensity score matching will have isolated the proposed causal agent from any third variable and thus satisfy Mill's third criteria for determining causation (West et al., 2000; West & Thoemmes, 2010).

Rubin's propensity score matching procedure is similar in logic to the classic experimental matching approach discussed earlier in this chapter as a technique for controlling the influence of nuisance variables in a study. As noted when we initially discussed the classic matching strategy, an equal number of participants for each level of a nuisance variable are found, and these participants are assigned across all experimental conditions, thereby isolating the effect of the nuisance variable from the causal agent of interest. We noted that the classic matching strategy is only practical when used with one or two variables. However, Rubin's propensity score-matching approach solved this limitation by taking multiple external variables and using a statistical procedure (e.g., logistic regression) to convert them into a single propensity score. Thus, rather than trying to simultaneously match participants on multiple variables, the propensity score approach requires the researcher to match participants on only one score (Guo & Fraser, 2010), thereby solving one classic problem with the matching strategy.

Comparing CCM with RCM, the reader should note that the two approaches are very compatible. Both CCM and RCM agree that the classic randomized experiment yields an unbiased estimate of the causal effect. CCM emphasizes pre-experimental design improvements to minimize threats to validity, whereas RCM emphasizes analytic adjustments for specific threats once data has been collected (West et al., 2000). As far as we can tell, these two approaches are complementary and the quality of the research done in the organizational sciences will be strengthened by considering both approaches.

Research Designs

Many different quasi-experimental research designs have been developed to test causal hypotheses in the field. Discussion of these various designs is beyond the scope of this chapter. The reader is encouraged to consult Shadish et al. (2002) to gain information about the multitude of quasi-experimental designs as well as their strengths and weaknesses. In the next section, we will discuss only two quasi-experimental designs—the regression discontinuity and longitudinal designs.

Regression Discontinuity Design

One research design that deserves more attention from organizational researchers is the regression discontinuity design (RDD), also known as the cutoff research design (Shadish & Cook, 2009). The RDD, originally brought to the attention of the scientific community by Thistlewaite and Campbell in 1960, is a useful quasi-experimental design when there are concerns about using random assignment in the field (Shadish et al., 2002). For example, consider a school board that has limited financial assets but wants to evaluate the effectiveness of a promising mathematics acceleration program. One way that the school board could design its study is to randomly assign the experimental conditions (i.e., math acceleration program or control) to a subset of students from its district. However, random assignment implies that the school district probably would be spending money sending students not interested in math to the expensive acceleration program. Another way to design this study is to first evaluate students' motivation to learn math and then assign the experimental conditions to the students as a function of their motivation to learn math. The school board could set the motivation cutoff score at the mean on this test, and only those students who have motivation scores higher than the mean are sent to acceleration program. The students at or below the cutoff score on the motivation test would be in the control condition. In this version of the research design, the school board is spending its money on students who are interested in learning math. The question is whether anything meaningful can be learned from this second research design. The surprising answer is yes, and this second design describes exactly how an RDD would be designed.

As illustrated in the school board example, the RDD assigned conditions to participants on the basis of some measured assignment variable, as opposed to random assignment (Shadish & Cook, 2009). The researcher can use any measure as an assignment variable, as long as it was assessed before the experimental manipulation or intervention occurred. The assignment variable could be an important predictor of the dependent variable, or it could even be a pretest measure of the dependent variable. Interestingly, the assignment variable can even be completely uncorrelated with the dependent variable (Shadish et al., 2002). The most important

factor is that the researcher sets a cutoff score on the assignment variable of choice and assigns the experimental conditions to participants strictly as a function of the participants' score on the assignment variable. All participants scoring at or below the assignment variable's cutoff score are in one condition, whereas participants scoring above the cutoff score are in another condition.

Unlike studies using random assignment, the process of assigning conditions to participants in the RDD is perfectly replicable. Unlike quasi-experiments, the experimenter retains control over the assignment of conditions to participants in the RDD. The explanation for why the RDD produces meaningful results is that the assignment process is precise and mathematically describable, enabling this process to be incorporated into the statistical analyses[5] of the data (Antonakis, Bendahan, Jacquart, & Lalive, 2010). The RDD produces unbiased causal effect estimate only when researchers strictly use the assignment variable scores and the set cutoff score to determine the experimental condition for the participants (Shadish & Cook, 2009).

The results one should see from RDD when there is no effect or when there is an effect for the manipulation can be seen in Figures 3.5 and 3.6, respectively. Figure 3.5 shows a continuous regression line that does not break or change its slope at the assignment variable's cutoff score. Continuing with our school board example, this result would indicate that the math acceleration program had no effect on the dependent variable (i.e., performance on a standardized mathematics test at the end of the school year). Figure 3.6, however, shows that the regression line discontinuously breaks at the cutoff score of the assignment variable. This reflects that

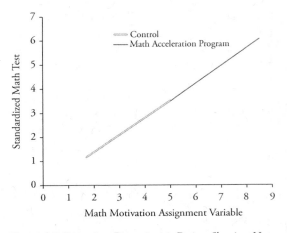

Figure 3.5 Regression Discontinuity Design Showing Nonsignificant Treatment Effect

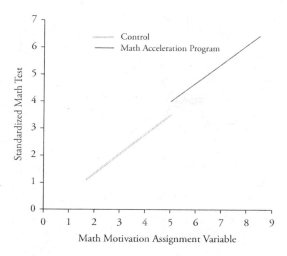

Figure 3.6 Regression Discontinuity Design Showing Significant Treatment Effect

the acceleration program had an effect and significantly improved the mathematics performance of the motivated students who attended the program.

In terms of the statistical power of this research design, the RDD requires more observations than a randomized experiment to yield comparable amounts of statistical power. However, there are modifications that one can do to enhance the power of the RDD. For example, setting the cutoff score at the mean of the assignment variable improves the power of the test. Also, choosing an assignment variable that is correlated with the dependent variable reduces noise in the dependent error and thus enhances statistical power.

In terms of statistical conclusion validity, it is critical that the researcher using RDD correctly specify the nature of the relationship between the assignment variable and the dependent variable (Shadish et al., 2002). The RDD causal effect estimate is unbiased only when the correct form of the assignment-dependent variable relationship is used in the regression analysis (Shadish & Cook, 2009). If the true relationship between these variables is nonlinear and the researcher models a linear assignment-dependent variable relationship, the estimate of the causal effect will be biased and the design could indicate a significant effect when there is none (Shadish & Cook, 2009).

Longitudinal Design

The ultimate goal of scientific research is to understand the underlying causal processes between variables. There are typically three steps to building a causal case in conducting field studies: establishing a correlation, establishing time sequence, and ruling out feasible alternative explanations. Employing a longitudinal design could significantly help researchers to fulfill these three steps. Specifically, like cross-sectional designs, the variables measured in longitudinal designs can be correlated to establish relations. Further, using a longitudinal design incorporates the time component into the research, which helps establish time sequence. When the aim is to establish time sequence to infer a causal effect, researchers usually pay less attention to how the exact amount of time lag between data collections influences the causal effect, but rely on the ordering of time to draw the causal inference. However, simply measuring variable A at Time 1 before measuring variable B at Time 2 is not sufficient in drawing causal inference that the correlation between A and B represents the causal effect of A on B. To examine the causal effect, it is important to test whether A at Time 1 has a relation with the change in B from Time 1 to Time 2. Statistically, this could be done by controlling for Time 1 measure of B as a baseline in a regression equation where B at Time 2 is regressed on A and B at Time 1. In addition, to rule out the possibility of reversed causality, it is also important to measure A at Time 2, and to test the effect of B at Time 1 in predicting the change in A from Time 1 to Time 2. Therefore, the ideal longitudinal design to help in establishing causal inference is to measure both independent and dependent variables in multiple time points, as we mentioned earlier in the cross-lagged designs and time series designs (Singer & Willett, 2003). Readers should also be cautioned that, although it is time ordering that helps the inference here, it is also important to select a meaningful time lag between two measurement points for the research design. For example, for detecting a training effect, the research literature has shown that the effect is stronger immediately after the training (e.g., two weeks), but weaker when longer time has passed (e.g., a half year). As such, researchers should make an informed decision (e.g., based on pilot studies or previous literature) in choosing the most meaningful time lag in their longitudinal design to detect the lagged effect (see Wang, Zhan, McCune, & Truxillo, 2011, for an example).

In some other research scenarios, longitudinal designs are used to depict and understand how variables (e.g., job satisfaction, job performance, and psychological well-being, etc.) change over time. The change characteristics that are of interest typically include the average change pattern of the variable across individuals (e.g., increase or decrease in average job performance from a sample over time), as well as individual differences in the starting point of change (e.g., initial job performance when entering a job) and the speed of change (e.g., how fast job performance improves over time). Therefore, studying variables as functions of time is the central research goal for these research scenarios. These longitudinal designs typically measure the variables of interest at multiple time points, in order to provide a relatively comprehensive survey of the entire change process of the variables. Statistical techniques that have been applied to analyze such data to achieve estimations of change trajectories include latent growth modeling (LGM; e.g., Willett & Sayer, 1994) and hierarchical linear modeling (HLM; e.g., Curran, 2003). Regarding research design, it should be noted that when using LGM, the time intervals between two consecutive measurements for all participants need to be the same. In contrast, HLM does not impose such constraints on data collection, which appears to be more flexible. Nevertheless, both statistical techniques could incorporate time-variant (e.g., job attitudes) and time-invariant (e.g., ethnicity) predictors to further understand the static and dynamic factors that influence the change trajectories of the interested variables (Singer & Willett, 2003). Interested readers can refer to Chan (1998b, 2001) for detailed discussions of the relative advantages of each modeling approach in organizational research.

Recently, latent mixture modeling techniques (i.e., statistical techniques that model and identify unobserved subpopulations in an observed population distribution) have been incorporated into the LGM framework in analyzing longitudinal data. In addition to estimating change trajectories of variables, these new techniques (e.g., growth mixture modeling [GMM] and latent class growth analysis [LCGA]; Muthén, 2004; Wang & Bodner, 2007) can also examine whether multiple change patterns exist for the variables of interest (e.g., for different subpopulations of retirees, their psychological adjustment to retirement may follow different change patterns over time; Wang, 2007). Accordingly, unobserved subpopulations corresponding to different change patterns can be identified and predicted. Therefore, these techniques help to address an important question in organizational research regarding longitudinal change: "Is the change to be considered unitary or multipath?" (Chan, 1998b, p. 425). Addressing this question has both theoretical and practical implications (Wang, 2007). Theoretically, examining the existence of different

latent trajectories in the target population may be the focus of theory testing, as it directly examines the generalizability of the theory. Further, it could help resolve inconsistent research findings by testing the possibility for the coexistence of different change patterns. Practically, it could inform policy making and intervention design by reaching appropriate matches between practices and indentified subpopulations. For example, for expatriates who enter an unfamiliar country, giving culture-related training to those who have little previous international assignment experience and higher levels of learning-goal orientation may be far more effective in improving their adjustment to the foreign work environment than providing the same training to those veterans with abundant international assignment experience and lower levels of learning-goal orientation (Wang & Takeuchi, 2007)

It should be noted that when studying changes in variables over time, organizational researchers have typically focused on the changes in continuous variables, such as job performance (e.g., Ployhart & Hakel, 1998), work stress (e.g., Garst, Frese, & Molenaar, 2000), psychological well-being (e.g., Wang, 2007), and newcomer adaptation (e.g., Chan & Schmitt, 2000). There has been a lack of application of statistical methods (e.g., latent Markov modeling [LMM] and latent transition analysis [LTA]) to adequately describe and assess the changes in *qualitative* status over time in organizational science research (Wang & Chan, 2011). Some meaningful longitudinal change phenomena in organizational science research are clearly not continuous. For example, people's qualitative employment status may change over time (e.g., at each time point, it could simply be dichotomized into two qualitative [discrete] statuses: being employed vs. not being employed). Therefore, for organizational researchers who are interested in studying long-term issues related to career change, it is important to statistically capture and summarize these qualitative changes over time into meaningful trends and patterns. Serving this type of research purpose, LMM and LTA could be used to analyze the data by modeling the current qualitative state of an individual/subject as being predicted by the previous qualitative state of the same individual/subject via a multinomial regression function (Langeheine & Van de Pol, 2002; Wang & Chan, 2011). In other words, the qualitative change over time could be estimated as odds ratios (or likelihood in percentage) of directional shift between two qualitative states. In addition, both LMM and LTA take into account the possible measurement error in observed indicator(s) of the unobservable latent qualitative states (e.g., in the career development literature, it is not uncommon for participants to report wrong employment status in surveys; Wang & Chan, 2011). The difference between LMM and LTA lies in the type of observed indicators in model specification: latent qualitative states modeled in LMM usually only have observed qualitative states as indicators, whereas the latent qualitative states modeled in LTA could be based on either continuous or discrete indicators (e.g., whether a person passes critical skill threshold to perform a job could be indicated by the person's performance on a work sample test or by the person's educational and professional qualifications). Readers can refer to Kaplan (2008) and Wang and Chan (2011) for more detailed introduction of statistically modeling longitudinal qualitative changes.

In some other research scenarios, longitudinal designs are used to study how likely it is that an event/behavior may occur over time. For example, organizations may be interested in knowing the likelihood of employee turnover over time (e.g., Morita, Lee, & Mowday, 1989). To answer this type of research question, the event/behavior of interest for each participant needs to be monitored over a time period before it occurs. Survival analysis is the statistical method typically used to analyze the data generated from this research design. We have no intention to dive into the statistical details for survival analysis here (for interested readers, please refer to Collett [2003] and Elandt-Johnson and Johnson [1999]), but we will present an overview for the research design issues in this type of research. Specifically, this type of research design requires a meaningful selection of assessment interval (i.e., the frequency at which the event/behavior should be monitored). On the one hand, the smaller the assessment interval is (e.g., daily), the more precision researchers will have in pinpointing exactly when the event/behavior occurred. On the other hand, using a small assessment interval could be costly, as it means that the assessment will be carried out more frequently. Further, this type of design also requires a meaningful selection of the total length of the monitoring period. For example, likelihood estimates for employees to turn over during the first three months on their jobs may not be able to extrapolate to the second three months on their jobs. A related issue is to choose the starting and ending time points of the monitoring for the sample. Ideally, the monitoring should start at the same time that the process of interest starts. For the employee turnover example, the monitoring should start when the employees are hired. When the monitoring starts at an arbitrary time point after the process of interest starts, the data generated from the monitoring are said to be left-censored. Similarly, when the monitoring ends at a time point that the event/behavior still has not occurred for some participants, the data from these participants are said to be right-censored. The family of survival analysis methods provides means for handling the censored-data situations, but researchers need to be clear regarding the type of data generated by their research design in order to select the correct method for analyzing the data.

Over the last decade, researchers also increasingly have used experience sampling methods (ESM) as a longitudinal design strategy to examine a wide variety of research questions in organizational sciences and related fields (e.g., Judge, Woolf, & Hurst, 2009; Liu, Wang, Zhan, & Shi, 2009; Trougakos, Beal, Green, & Weiss, 2008; Wang, Liao, Zhan, & Shi, 2011; Wang, Liu, Zhan, & Shi, 2010). Basically, the ESM approach aims at assessing people's experiences and behaviors as well as everyday events and situational conditions in situ—or, as Bolger, Davis, and Rafaeli (2003) stated it, "capturing life as it is lived" (p. 579).

In an ESM study, a person is typically asked to respond to survey questions multiple times either within a day or over several days; participants provide data over multiple days, sometimes even over several weeks. By asking a person about his or her feelings and certain situational factors at the very moment, ESM studies provide the advantage that memory biases (e.g., recency of effects), different salience of experiences, and the problem that ratings may be influenced by momentary affective states are minimized. In addition, the ecological validity of ESM studies is considered to be very high, as participants can be asked in their natural environments, for example at their workplace or at home. As multiple measures are collected from the participants of ESM studies, researchers are able to investigate variation between persons as well as variation within persons. For example, using an ESM design, Wang et al. (2010) examined how within-person daily fluctuations in work-family conflict might be associated with the within-person differences in workers' daily alcohol use. They further demonstrated that between-person differences in peer drinking norms, coworker support, and family support could moderate the strength of the within-person association between daily work-family conflict and alcohol use.

The most common statistical method to examine both within- and between-variation is hierarchical linear modeling (also often referred to as multilevel modeling). But ESM data can also be analyzed using other approaches (e.g., time series analysis).

Although all ESM studies aim at collecting multiple measures per person, there are three different types of data collecting protocols (Wheeler & Reis, 1991): (a) interval-contingent protocols, (b) signal-contingent protocols, and (c) event-contingent protocols. In interval-contingent protocols, participants are instructed to report to the surveys at regular, predetermined intervals (e.g., every four hours). The length of the intervals should represent "theoretically or logically meaningful units of time" (Reis & Gable, 2000, p. 198). For example, in the study of Totterdell and Parkinson (1999), participants responded every two hours to surveys assessing their current mood and the affect regulation strategies they had used over the last two hours. In signal-contingent protocols, participants respond to surveys when a signal (e.g., the alarm of a handheld computer or cell-phone) is delivered. Signals can follow fixed or random schedules, or a combination of the two (e.g., random within a certain time interval, such as every two hours). For example, in the classical study of Csikszentmihalyi and LeFevre (1989), participants received signals randomly within two-hour periods within a time interval from 7:30 A.M. to 10:30 P.M. to answer questions about their quality of experiences and performed activities. Event-contingent protocols require participants to respond to questions whenever a certain event (which has to be defined for participants) occurs. For example, in the study of Wheeler and Nezlek (1977), participants were instructed to fill in a survey whenever they encountered a social interaction.

Reis and Gable (2000) provide a comparison of the different data collection protocols and situations favoring a certain protocol. Interval-contingent protocols are recommended when the time interval is inherently meaningful (e.g., one working day), when susceptibility to retrospection bias is low, and when participants' burden has to be minimized (e.g., Liu et al., 2009; Wang et al., 2011). Signal-contingent protocols are advised when researchers aim at describing and comparing "different domains of activity or mental states during different activities" (Reis & Gable, 2000, p. 200). This protocol should be used when susceptibility to retrospection bias is high and it is important to verify the time of recording. Event-contingent protocols should be used when researchers aim at investigating "a specific class of events or states, especially rare, clearly defined states" and comparing relatively infrequent variations within a class of events (Reis & Gable, 2000, p. 200). This protocol is also advised when susceptibility to retrospection bias is high and when it is important to obtain many episodes of the event or state in question.

In summary, although employing longitudinal designs may be more costly, require more coordination in research administration, and demand more sophisticated statistical treatment, it can answer a rich set of research questions that cannot be answered by other research designs (e.g., depicting and predicting the change trajectories of psychological constructs). It can also improve our answers to research questions by helping establishing time sequence and by ruling out certain alternative explanations (e.g., reversed causality). Further, longitudinal design is necessary to generalize research findings across time (Shadish et al., 2002). As such, we call for more use of longitudinal designs in organizational science research to advance the scientific knowledge of this field.

Emergent Trends

In the prior section, we discussed some quasi-experimental research designs that are useful for uncovering causality in the field. In this section, we will discuss some recent trends in the research literature that require new ways to think about causality and research. We will start our discussion with the increasing application of dynamical systems frameworks to social science phenomena.

Dynamical Systems

It is becoming increasingly common for researchers to conceptualize psychological, organizational, and broader social science phenomena in terms of self-organizing, dynamic systems (e.g., DeShon, Chapter 4 of this handbook; Hanges et al., 2000; Lord et al., 2003; Hanges et al., 2002; Vallacher & Nowak, 1994; Vancouver, Weinhardt, & Schmidt, 2010). A dynamic system is a collection of elements whose behavior, at the system level, evolves over time (Byrne, 1998; DeShon, Chapter 4 of this handbook). This change of behavior can result from environmental pressure (Marion, 1999) or it could result from the system itself, as the result of multiple feedback loops either amplifying or minimizing fluctuations among elements within the system (DeShon, Chapter 4 of this handbook). In terms of the two types of causal models discussed earlier, dynamical systems clearly fit in the reciprocal causal model category (see Figure 3.2).

While simple dynamic systems can be developed with only a few variables and perhaps one or two feedback loops (see Figure 3.2A), social science researchers have been increasingly interested in the potential of complex adaptive systems for explaining social science phenomena. Complex adaptive systems—a set of special cases of dynamic systems—are composed of multiple, richly interconnected elements that interact and influence one another over time through various feedback loops (Levy, 1992; Hanges et al., 2002). The nervous system, social groups, organizations, and societal cultural systems are all examples of complex adaptive systems. All of these examples are composed of multiple elements (e.g., neurons, people) that are richly interconnected (e.g., neurons are connected by a rich interconnected network that communicate using electrical impulses and neurochemicals, whereas people are increasingly interconnected and can communicate through face-to-face communications, e-mails, social media, phone, written letters, etc.). These elements influence one another and learn from their interactions. This learning can be seen in that over time the entire system starts to self-organize. That is, the interactions among the elements tend to become more hierarchically organized over time (Morel & Ramanujam, 1999). This self-organization result in emergent behavior (e.g., organizational human capital, leadership, team learning and development of team mental-models, culture) that is observed at the holistic, system level of analysis (Bell, Kozlowski, & Blawath, Chapter 26 of this handbook; Hanges, Dorfman, Shteynberg, & Bates, 2006; Hanges et al., 2000; Ployhart, Chapter 8 of this handbook; Ployhart & Moliterno, 2011; Vallacher & Nowak, 1994).

It is critical to note that emergent behaviors cannot be traced back to behavior or characteristics of specific, individual elements (e.g., neurons, people) in a system. Rather, emergent behavior is a result of the interactions *among* the elements within the system. This idea was captured by systems theorist Buckminster Fuller and his colleagues when they wrote, "I don't know what I am. I know that I am not a category. I am not a thing—a noun. I seem to be a verb, an evolutionary process" (Fuller, Agel, & Fiore, 1970). It was also reflected by Norbert Wiener, the father of cybernetics, in his classic 1954 book:

It is the pattern maintained by this homeostasis which is the touchstone of our personal identity. Our tissues change as we live: the food we eat and the air we breathe become flesh of our flesh and bone of our bone, and the momentary elements of our flesh and bone pass out of our body with our excreta. We are but whirlpools in a river of everflowing water. We are not stuff that abides, but patterns that perpetuate themselves.
(p. 96)

Thus, as shown by these two quotes, systems theorists have long recognized that emergent behavior is a result of interactions (i.e., a verb) and is not traceable to the individual elements that make up the system (flesh, bones, etc.).[6] What complex adaptive systems bring to the discussion by systems theorists like Fuller and Weiner are techniques that social scientists can use for modeling patterns in behavior that our field was not capable of accomplishing previously (e.g., Hanges, 1987; Hanges, Braverman, & Rentsch, 1991; Hazy, 2007; Nowak, Vallacher, Tesser, & Borkowski, 2000; Vancouver et al., 2010).

With regard to causality and the methods that we have been discussing in this chapter, complex adaptive systems have very tangled feedback loops among the system's elements, and causal influence flows in all directions within the system. Thus, the utility of applying research designs that assume unidirectional causality in an attempt to understand how elements within a complex adaptive system produce emergent behavior is clearly suspect. Aiken and Hanges (2011) recently discussed modifications to research designs needed to study complex adaptive systems. First, as indicated previously, complex dynamic systems change; therefore, it is absolutely necessary to study system behavior phenomena over time. Cross-sectional research designs that have relied on single observations per person or per group overlook the dynamism inherent in complex systems. Researchers investigating such systems will be unable to discover and model emergent properties by using such designs (Aiken & Hanges, 2011; Kozlowski, Chapter 42 of this handbook).

Second, research can also use computational models to study complex adaptive systems. With this methodology, researchers build a computer model of the complex adaptive system as suggested by their verbal theories. The model specifies the elements of the system and the connections, as well as feedback loops among the elements (Figure 3.2B is an example of a specification of elements that could be modeled). The patterns of emergent behavior produced by the computer model are compared to the behavioral patterns of the real system. The computer specification of the theory is supported if there is a match between the predicted pattern and the data. See the work of Vancouver and colleagues (Vancouver, Tamanini, & Yoder, 2010; Scherbaum & Vancouver, 2010; Vancouver et al., 2010), as well as Hazy (2007) and Nowak et al. (2000), for excellent illustrations and discussions of this methodology.

Finally, we wanted to note that qualitative research designs can collect useful information with regard to complex adaptive systems, in addition to quantitative research designs. For example, several researchers have successfully used daily diary research and provided their participants with technology that indicated when to respond to a series of questions throughout the day. Daily diary studies have been conducted to assess a number of issues, including stress and alcohol consumption (Armeli, Carney, Tennen, Affleck, & O'Neil, 2000), affective responses to psychological contract breach (Briner, 2002), and organizational citizenship behaviors (Ilies, Scott, & Judge, 2006).

In summary, we have discussed how dynamic and complex adaptive systems require a change in thinking regarding the utility of unidirectional causal relationships for understanding how system elements influence one another and create emergent behavioral patterns. Perhaps the best we can hope to accomplish at the element level of analysis is to specify functional relationships. Indeed, the computational modeling approach discussed earlier is consistent with this functional perspective because the richly interconnected elements in the computational model result in causal influence flowing in all directions within the system. At the level of the emergent behavior, however, discussions of causation and causal modeling of the relationship among constructs might still have utility. In the next section, we will discuss the interest in person-centered research methods.

Person-Centered Research Methods

In many areas of research in organizational science, we are familiar with using the dimensional approaches (e.g., factor analysis) to understand individual or organizational phenomena and to theorize corresponding constructs and processes. A key characteristic of dimensional approaches is that the focus is on capturing the interrelatedness (often in the form of covariance or latent factor) between or among different variables and using it to infer the underlying processes or causes. This interrelatedness is particularly important for establishing Mill's second condition of causation—a relationship exists

between the hypothesized causal agent and the dependent variable. However, this only represents one way of looking at the data and establishing causal relationships. An equally valid and complimentary way is to consider the interrelatedness between or among different variables as a function of the unobserved heterogeneity of the population (Hagenaars & McCutcheon, 2002; Muthén, 2003; Wang & Hanges, 2011). For example, in some situations, interrelatedness could be explained away by recognizing the unobserved heterogeneity in the population distribution, showing a case of conditional independence between observed variables. More commonly, the interrelatedness between or among different variables may vary, depending on the unobserved heterogeneity. In organizational science research, studying this unobserved heterogeneity (i.e., heterogeneity in multivariate distributions that is unobserved; also known as latent classes or latent mixture) often means indentifying specific configurations or patterns of observed individual and/or environmental variables (e.g., different types of person-environment fit), and thus represents a person-centered approach for exploring and establishing causal relationships. This person-centered approach certainly differs from the variable-centered approach often used in the organizational sciences (e.g., exploring explanations by associating one property with another), but provides a way for us to preserve the worker's integrity as a person (e.g., considering different configurations of characteristics). Therefore, this person-centered approach may be better suited for the recent movement in studying person-centric work psychology (Liu, Zhan, & Wang, 2011; Weiss & Rupp, 2011), as it offers the background for us to better understand the potential differences that we may discover in workers' subjective experiences.

A family of statistical methods, called latent class procedures, has been developed to estimate the unobserved heterogeneity in the person-centered approach. The development of latent class procedures can be traced back to more than 50 years ago (e.g., Gibson, 1959; Goodman & Kruskal, 1959). Over the years, the research interest on these procedures has grown exponentially (Bauer & Curran, 2003). As a result, a series of powerful yet flexible latent class procedures now exist for us to use. These procedures not only include methods that complement the dimensional approaches (e.g., latent class cluster analysis), but also include methods that further incorporate the focus of the dimensional approaches (i.e., the interrelatedness between/

among observed variables) with the focus on identifying latent mixture in the population (e.g., factor mixture analysis, mixed model item response theory, and growth mixture modeling). Consequently, the latent class procedures can be viewed as a more general statistical framework within which the dimensional approaches represent the special cases in which the population is assumed to be homogenous. Although this assumption of homogeneity is often taken for granted by researchers, latent class procedures can provide meaningful ways to test this assumption. Further, latent class procedures can also reveal unobserved moderators for statistical relationships estimated by the dimensional approaches.

With the significant advancement in the latent class procedures, it is important for researchers to recognize how this advancement may serve us for developing better theories and answering novel research questions. It has been pointed out that the concurrent developments of theory and methods have allowed researchers to more accurately and realistically model organizational phenomena and explore underlying processes (Bliese, Chan, & Ployhart, 2007). Accordingly, the recent development of latent class procedures has enabled researchers to integrate multiple theories in explaining work-related psychological processes and to refine methods to more accurately describe and evaluate organizational phenomena. For example, using growth mixture modeling (GMM) technique, Wang (2007) was able to integrate role theory, continuity theory, and the life course perspective to form a resource-based theoretical framework (Wang, Henkens, & van Solinge, 2011) to account for multiple change patterns of retirees' psychological well-being over time. Further, using latent class cluster analysis, Lawrence and Zyphur (2011) developed a model-based approach to more efficiently identify organizational fault lines and evaluate their defining components.

Conclusion

In this chapter, we provided an explicit definition of the causal relationship and identified two general forms of causal relationships discussed in the scientific literature. We also discussed the process by which causal relationships are established—focusing on John Stuart Mill's third criterion, isolation of the hypothesized causal agent. Scientific methods are explicit attempts to isolate the causal agents—to make them exogenous—so that their unique influence on the dependent variable can be identified. The Campbell Causal Model (CCM)

emphasizes research design solutions to isolate hypothesized causal variables. However, the reader should note that while one should strive to reduce as many threats as possible in any given study, it is impossible to develop a study free from any threats to validity. Gelso (2006) describes this problem as the bubble hypothesis:

> [T]he research process is likened to the placement of a sticker on a car windshield, where a bubble appears in the sticker. One may press the bubble in an effort to eliminate it, only to have it appear elsewhere. The bubble cannot be eliminated, unless one tears the sticker off the windshield. (p. 8)

Gelso's bubble hypothesis metaphor reminds us that there is no perfect study. Eliminating one threat may increase the likelihood of another. Thus, for a single study, researchers must decide on the most critical threats and choose a design that eliminates these alternative explanations. However, it is possible to control for all of the most serious threats over a series of carefully designed studies using the CCM approach. Thus, while there may be no perfect single study, there can be a tightly constructed series of studies that eliminate all reasonable alternative explanations.

The Rubin Causal Model (RCM) emphasizes analytic methods for eliminating the biasing effect of non-random assignment of participants to conditions. Consistent with CCM, RCM assumes that the classic randomized experiment yields the best estimate of a causal effect. Both CCM and RCM attempt to satisfy Mill's third, and most difficult, criterion for establishing causation: the isolation of hypothesized causal agents from the influence of other variables. Both approaches are compatible with each other, and it is our hope that organizational scientists will start to use RCM along with CCM to improve the quality of organizational science research in the future.

We finished our chapter by discussing recent trends in research design. In particular, we discussed the use of person-centered, as opposed to variable-centered, research designs, as well as the trend to conceptualize psychological, group, and organizational phenomena as resulting from complex adaptive systems. This last trend has the potential for, once again, changing the way that scientists think about causality and the causal effect. Complex adaptive systems, which are examples of non-recursive causal models, have richly interconnected elements in which behavior at the system level emerges as a result of the interactions among all the elements. The old scientific approach of dissecting a system to find the small subset of elements that cause the system level emergent behavior is a doomed effort.

At the beginning of the previous century, Russell (1913) claimed that the concept of causation was not necessary and that instead we need to focus on the identification of functional relationships. As we discussed earlier, Russell's argument was formally dismissed by Suppes (1970). However, perhaps it is time again to reconsider this argument, although with a slightly revised, multilevel version of it. As we discussed, trying to model unidirectional causal relationships among individual elements in a complex adaptive system does not appear useful. Perhaps at the level of the individual element, Russell's argument holds—the best we can hope for is specification of functional relationships. However, when we focus at the level of the emergent behavior, specifying causal agents—at and above the level of the emergent behavior—might make sense once again.

Notes

1. In this formula, the pressure and volume of a gas is represented by P and V, respectively. T represents the gas temperature on the Kelvin scale (a.k.a. absolute temperature). R is the ideal gas constant or $1.38*10^{-23}$ and n represents the amount of a substance of the gas measured in moles.

2. Schrödinger's Cat refers to a thought experiment used by Erwin Schrödinger to describe the quantum physics concept of superposition. The thought experiment goes something as follows: A living cat is placed into a sealed chamber that contains both a vial of poison gas and a hammer posed to break the vial. Outside the chamber is a small amount of radioactive material and a Geiger counter. The radioactive material decays at a slow rate (e.g., 50% probability that one atom of the material will be released over some pre-specified time period). If an atom is released, the Geiger counter will detect it and activate a mechanism that causes the hammer to break the vial, releasing the gas that kills the cat. The state of the cat is not known unless we open the chamber and see whether the cat is dead or alive. Thus, before opening the chamber, the cat is in a superposition of two opposite states: dead and alive. Only when we open the chamber and observe the cat's condition does the superposition state collapse and the cat takes on one of two possible states: dead or alive. Thus, similar to Schrödinger's cat, before conducting a study, the possibility of measuring the causal effect for an individual exists because the individual is in a superposition of two states: influenced by both the treatment and control groups. However, once an observation takes place, the superposition collapses and the causal effect for an individual cannot be obtained.

3. While this phrase is statistically equivalent to the more frequently used "randomly assigning participants to conditions," we prefer to state that "conditions are randomly assigned to participants," as coined by Rosenbaum (1984). This slight change does not affect the independence of the conditions, but it does guarantee that there will be an equal number of observations per cell in experimental designs. This wording also is a more accurate reflection of how randomized research is actually conducted.

4. Cook and Campbell (1979) defined essentialists as philosophers who hold that the term *causality* should be limited to causal agents that are both necessary and sufficient for an effect to occur. In other words, essentialists limit the use of causality to situations in which an antecedent infallibly creates the effect. Cook and Campbell (1979) reject the essentialist perspective because they believe that causal relationships in the social sciences, at this stage in our development, are fallible (i.e., probabilistic) rather than inevitable. We agree with Cook and Campbell, especially with the current conclusions drawn from complexity science demonstrating that even a completely deterministic system will produce unpredictable behavior.

5. The Rubin Causal Model (RCM) can be conceptualized as a method for mathematically capturing and describing the assignment process in quasi-experiments and incorporating this mathematical description into the statistical analysis of the data from these designs. The difference is that RCM attempts to isolate the manipulation from any alternative variables, whereas in RDD the manipulation is perfectly confounded with at least one alternative variable—the assignment variable.

6. Recognition that phenomena is emergent and has no inherent content can be seen as early as 400 to 500 BCE in the Buddhist teaching on emptiness and dependent co-arising (Macy, 1991).

References

Aiken, J. R., & Hanges, P. J. (2011). Research methodology for studying dynamic multi-team systems: application of complexity science. In S. J. Zaccaro, M.A. Marks, L. DeChurch (Eds.), *Multi-team systems: An organization form for dynamic and complex environments* (pp. 431–458). New York: Routledge Academic.

Antonakis, J., Bendahan, S., Jacquart, P., & Lalive, R. (2010). On making causal claims: A review and recommendations. *The Leadership Quarterly, 21,* 1086–1120.

Argyris, C. (1975). Dangers in applying results from experimental social psychology. *American Psychologist, 30,* 469–485.

Armeli, S., Carney, M. A., Tennen, H., Affleck, G., & O'Neil, T. P. (2000). Stress and alcohol use: A daily process examination of the stressor-vulnerability model. *Journal of Personality and Social Psychology, 78,* 979–994.

Austin, J. T., Boyle, K. A., & Lualhati, J. C. (1998). Statistical conclusion validity for organizational science researchers: A review. *Organizational Research Methods, 1,* 164–208.

Bandura, A. (1982). Self-efficacy mechanism in human agency. *American Psychologist, 37,* 122–147.

Bauer, D. J., & Curran, P. J. (2003). Overextraction of latent trajectory classes: Much ado about nothing? Reply to Rindskopf (2003), Muthen (2003), and Cudeck and Henly (2003). *Psychological Methods, 8,* 384–393.

Beier, M. E., & Kanfer, R. (2010). Motivation in training and development: A phase perspective. In S. W. J. Kozlowski & E. Salas (Eds.), *Learning, training, and development in organizations,* SIOP Frontiers book series (pp. 65–97). New York: Routledge Academic.

Bliese, P. D., Chan, D., & Ployhart, R. E. (2007). Multilevel methods: Future directions in measurement, longitudinal analyses, and nonnormal outcomes. *Organizational Research Methods, 10,* 551–563.

Bliese, P. D., & Hanges, P.J. (2004). Being both too liberal and too conservative: The perils of treating grouped data as though it is independent. *Organizational Research Methods, 7,* 400–417.

Bolger, N., Davis, A., & Rafaeli, E. (2003). Diary methods: Capturing life as it is lived. *Annual Review of Psychology, 54*, 579–616.

Boring, E. G. (1945). The use of operational definitions in science. *Psychological Review, 52,* 243–245.

Brewer, M. B. (2000). Research design and issues of validity. In H. T. Reis and C. M. Judd. (Eds.). *Handbook of research methods in social and personality psychology* (pp. 3–39). Cambridge, UK: Cambridge University Press.

Briner, R. B. (2002). A daily diary study of affective responses to psychological contract breach and exceeded promises. *Journal of Organizational Behavior, 23,* 287–302.

Bunge, M. (2009). *Causality and modern science* (4th Rev. Ed.). New Brunswick, NJ: Transaction Publishers.

Byrne, D. (1998). *Complexity theory and the social sciences: An introduction.* New York: Routledge Press.

Campbell, C.A. (1957) *On selfhood and godhood.* London: George Allen and Unwin

Campbell, J. P. (1986). Labs, fields, and straw issues. In E.A. Locke (Ed.), *Generalizing from laboratory to field settings* (pp. 269–279). Lexington, MA: Heath.

Campbell, D., & Stanley, J. (1963). *Experimental and quasi-experimental designs for research.* Chicago: Rand-McNally.

Carver, R. P. (1978). The case against statistical significance testing. *Harvard Educational Review, 48,* 378–399.

Chan, D. (1998a). Functional relations among constructs in the same content domain at different levels of analysis: A typology of composition models. *Journal of Applied Psychology, 83,* 234–246.

Chan, D. (1998b). The conceptualization and analysis of change over time: An integrative approach incorporating longitudinal mean and covariance structures analysis (LMACS) and multiple indicator latent growth modeling (MLGM). *Organizational Research Methods, 1,* 421–483.

Chan, D. (2001). Latent growth modeling. In F. Drasgow & N. Schmitt (Eds.), *Measuring and analyzing behavior in organizations* (pp. 302–349). San Francisco: Jossey-Bass.

Chan, D., & Schmitt, N. (2000). Interindividual differences in intraindividual changes in proactivity during organizational entry: A latent growth modeling approach to understanding newcomer adaptation. *Journal of Applied Psychology, 85,* 190–210.

Chen, G., Bliese, P. D., & Mathieu, J. E. (2005). Conceptual framework and statistical procedures for delineating and testing multilevel theories of homology. *Organizational Research Methods, 8,* 375–409.

Cochran, W. G., & Cox, G. M. (1950). *Experimental designs.* New York: John Wiley and Sons.

Cohen J. (1962). The statistical power of abnormal-social psychological research: A review, *Journal of Abnormal Psychology, 65,* 145–153.

Cohen, J. (1979). *Statistical power for the behavioral sciences* (Rev. Ed.). New York: Academic Press.

Cohen, J. (1994). The earth is round (p < .05). *American Psychologist, 49,* 997–1003.

Collett, D. (2003). *Modeling survival data in medical research.* Boca Raton, FL: Chapman & Hall/CRC.

Cook, T. D., & Campbell, D. T. (1976). The design and conduct of true experiments and quasi-experiments in field settings. In M. D. Dunnette (Ed.), *Handbook of Industrial and Organizational Psychology* (pp. 223–326) Skokie, IL: Rand McNally.

Cook, T. D., & Campbell, D. T. (1979). *Quasi-experimentation: Design and analysis issues for field settings.* Boston: Houghton Mifflin Company.

Cortina, J. M., & Dunlap, W. P. (1997). On the logic and purpose of significance testing. *Psychological Methods, 2,* 161–172.

Cortina, J. M., & Landis, R. S. (2011). The Earth is not round (p = 00). *Organizational Research Methods, 14,* 332–349.

Cronbach, L. J., & Meehl, P. E. (1955). Construct validity in psychological tests. *Psychological Bulletin, 52,* 281–302.

Csikszentmihalyi, M., & LeFevre, J. (1989). Optimal experience in work and leisure. *Journal of Personality and Social Psychology, 56,* 815–822.

Curran, P. J. (2003). Have multilevel models been structural equation models all along? *Multivariate Behavioral Research, 38,* 529–569.

DeShon, R. P., Kozlowski, S. W. J., Schmidt, A. M., Milner, K. R., & Wiechmann, D. (2004). Multiple goal feedback effects on the regulation of individual and team performance in training. *Journal of Applied Psychology, 89,* 1035–1056.

Dickson, M. W., Resick, C. J., & Goldstein, H. W. (2008). Seeking explanations in people, not in the results of their behavior: Twenty-plus years of the attraction-selection-attrition model. In D. B. Smith (Ed.), *The people make the place: Dynamic linkages between individuals and organizations* (pp. 5–36). New York: Lawrence Erlbaum.

Dienes, Z. (2011). Bayesian versus orthodox statistics: Which side are you on? *Perspectives on Psychological Science, 6,* 274–290.

Dvir, T., Eden, D., Banjo, M. L. (1995). Self-fulfilling prophecy and gender: Can women be Pygmalion and Galatea? *Journal of Applied Psychology, 80,* 253–270.

Edwards, J. R., & Berry, J. W. (2010). The presence of something or the absence of nothing: Increasing theoretical precision. *Management Research Organizational Research Methods, 13,* 668–689.

Elandt-Johnson, R., & Johnson, N. (1999). *Survival models and data analysis.* New York: John Wiley & Sons.

Farman, J. C., B. G. Gardiner, and J. D. Shanklin. (1985). Large losses of total ozone in Antarctica reveal seasonal ClOx/NOx interaction. *Nature* 315: 207–210.

Fisher, R. A. (1935). *The design of experiments.* New York: Hafner.

Frone, M. R. (2008). Are stressors related to employee substance use? The importance of temporal context assessments of alcohol and illicit drug use. *Journal of Applied Psychology, 93,* 199–206.

Fuller, B., Agel, J., & Fiore, Q. (1970). *I seem to be a verb: Environment and man's future.* New York: Bantam Books.

Garst, H., Frese, M., & Molenaar, P. C. M. (2000). The temporal factor of change in stressor-strain relationships: A growth curve model on a longitudinal study in East Germany. *Journal of Applied Psychology, 85,* 417–438.

Gelso, C.J. (2006). On the making of a scientist-practitioner: A theory of research training in professional psychology. *Training and Education in Professional Psychology, S,* 3–16.

Gibson, W. A. (1959). Three multivariate models: Factor analysis, latent structure analysis, and latent profile analysis. *Psychometrika, 24,* 229–252.

Goodman, L. A., & Kruskal, W. H. (1959). Measures of association for cross-classifications. II: Further discussion and references. *Journal of the American Statistical Association, 54,* 123–163.

Grant, A. M. & Wall, T. D. (2009). The neglected science and art of quasi-experimentation: Why-to, when-to, and how-to advice for organizational researchers. *Organizational Research Methods, 12,* 653–686.

Guo., S. & Fraser, M. W. (2010). *Propensity score analysis: Statistical methods and applications.* Thousand Oaks, CA: SAGE Publications.

Hagenaars, J. A. & McCutcheon, A. (2002). *Applied latent class analysis.* Cambridge: Cambridge University Press.

Haney, C., Banks, C., & Zimbardo, P. (1973). Interpersonal dynamics in a simulated prison. *International Journal of Criminology and Penology, 1,* 69–97.

Hanges, P. J. (1987). A catastrophe model of control theory's decision mechanism: The effect of goal difficulty, task difficulty, goal direction, and task direction on goal commitment. Dissertation. University of Akron. Akron, Ohio.

Hanges, P. J., Braverman, E. P. & Rentsch, J. R. (1991). Changes in raters' impressions of subordinates: A catastrophe model. *Journal of Applied Psychology, 76,* 878–888.

Hanges, P. J., Dorfman, P. W., Shteynberg, G., & Bates, A. (2006). Culture and leadership: A connectionist information processing model. In W. H. Mobley & E. Weldon (Eds.), *Advances in global leadership* (Vol. 4, (pp. 7–37).). New York: JAI Press.

Hanges, P. J., Lord, R. G., & Dickson, M. W. (2000). An information processing perspective on leadership and culture: A case for connectionist architecture. *Applied Psychology: An International Review, 49,* 133–161.

Hanges, P. J., Lord, R. G., Godfrey, E. G., & Raver, J. L. (2002). Modeling nonlinear relationships: Neural networks and catastrophe analysis. In S. Rogelberg (Ed.), *Handbook of Research Methods in Industrial and Organizational Psychology* (pp. 431–455). Malden, MA: Blackwell Publishers.

Harrison, D. A., & Klein, K. J. (2007). What's the difference? Diversity constructs as separation, variety, or disparity in organizations. *Academy of Management Review, 32,* 1199–1228.

Hazy, J.K. (2007). Computer models of leadership: Foundations for a new discipline or meaningless diversion? *Leadership Quarterly, 18,* 391–410.

Heckman, J. J. (1974) Shadow prices, market wages, and labor supply. *Econometrica, 42,* 679–694.

Hedges, L. V. & Pigott, T. D. (2004). The power of statistical tests for moderators in meta-analysis. *Psychological Methods, 9,* 426–445.

Highhouse, S. (2009). Designing experiments that generalize. *Organizational Research Methods, 12,* 554–566.

Highhouse, S., & Gillespie, J. Z. (2008). Do samples really matter that much? In C. E. Lance & R. J. Vandenberg (Eds.), *Statistical and methodological myths and urban legends: Doctrine, verity and fable in the organizational and social sciences* (pp. 247–266). New York: Psychology Press.

Hofstede, G. H. (1980). *Culture consequences: International differences in work-related values,* London: Sage Publications.

House, R. J., Hanges, P. J., Javidan, M., Dorfman, P. W., & Gupta, V. (2004). *Leadership, culture, and organizations: The GLOBE study of 62 societies.* Thousand Oaks, CA: Sage Publications.

Ilies, R., Scott, B. A., & Judge, T. A. (2006). The interactive effects of personal traits and experiences states on intraindividual patterns of citizenship behavior. *Academy of Management Journal, 49,* 561–575.

Judge, T. A., Woolf, E. F., & Hurst, C. (2009). Is emotional labor more difficult for some than for others? A multilevel, experience-sampling study. *Personnel Psychology, 62,* 57–88.

Kaplan, D. (2008). An overview of Markov chain methods for the study of stage-sequential developmental processes. *Developmental Psychology, 44,* 457–467.

Katz, D., & Kahn, R. L. (1978). *The social psychology of organizations* (2nd ed.). New York: Wiley.

Kelloway, E. K., Gottlieb, B. H., & Barham, L. (1999). The source, nature, and direction of work and family conflict: A longitudinal investigation. *Journal of Occupational Health Psychology, 4,* 337–346.

Kirk, R. E. (1995). *Experimental design: Procedures for the behavioral sciences* (3rd Ed.). Pacific Grove, CA: Brooks/Cole Publishing.

Kozlowski, S. W. J., & Klein, K. J. (2000). A multilevel approach to theory and research in organizations: Contextual, temporal, and emergent processes. In K. J. Klein & S. W. J. Kozlowski (Eds.), *Multilevel theory, research, and methods in organizations: Foundations, extensions, and new directions* (pp. 3–90). San Francisco: Jossey-Bass.

Kruschke, J. K. (2011a). Bayesian assessment of null values via parameter estimation and model comparison. *Perspectives in Psychological Science, 6,* 299–312.

Kruschke, J. K. (2011b). *Doing Bayesian data analysis: A tutorial with r and bugs.* New York: Academic Press.

Lakatos, I., (1978). *The methodology of scientific research programmes.* Cambridge: Cambridge University Press.

Langeheine, R., & Van de Pol, F. (2002). Latent Markov chains. In J. A. Hagenaars & A. L. McCutcheon (Eds.), *Applied Latent Class Analysis* (pp. 304–341). Cambridge: Cambridge University Press.

Lawrence, B., & Zyphur, M. (2011). Identifying organizational faultlines with latent class cluster analysis. *Organizational Research Methods, 14,* 32–57.

Levy, S. (1992). *Artificial life: The quest for new creation.* New York: Random House.

Liu, S., Wang, M., Zhan, Y., & Shi, J. (2009). Daily work stress and alcohol use: Testing the cross-level moderation effects of neuroticism and job involvement. *Personnel Psychology, 62,* 575–597.

Liu, S., Zhan, Y., & Wang, M. (2011). Person-centric work psychology: Additional insights on its tradition, nature, and research methods. *Industrial and Organizational Psychology: Perspectives on Science and Practice, 4,* 105–108.

Locke, J. ([1690] 1849). *An essay concerning human understanding* (13th Ed.). London: William Tegg & Co. Available at http://books.google.com/ebooks?id=YxwGAAAAQAAJ&printsec= frontcover&output=reader. Accessed June 2011.

Lord, R. G., Hanges, P. J., & Godfrey, E. G. (2003). Integrating neural networks into decision making and motivational theory: Rethinking VIE theory. *Canadian Psychologist, 44,* 21–38.

Lykken, D. T. (1968) Statistical significance in psychological research. *Psychological Bulletin, 70,* 151–159.

Mackie, J. L. (1974). *The cement of the universe.* Oxford: Oxford University Press.

Macy, J. (1991). *Mutual causality in Buddhism and general systems theory: The Dharma of natural systems.* Albany: State University of New York Press.

Marion, R. (1999). *The edge of organization: Chaos and complexity theories of formal social organization.* Newbury Park, CA: Sage.

McGrayne, S. B. (2011). *The theory that would not die: How Bayes' rule cracked the enigma code, hunted down Russian submarines, and emerged triumphant from two centuries of controversy.* New Haven, CT: Yale University Press.

Meehl, P. E. (1967). Theory-testing in psychology and physics: A methodological paradox. *Philosophy of Science, 34,* 103–115.

Meehl, P. E. (1990). Appraising and amending theories: The strategy of Lakatosian defense and two principles that warrant it. *Psychological Inquiry, 1,* 108–141.

Meehl, P. E. (1991). Why summaries of research on a psychological theory are often uninterpretable. In R. Snow & D. E. Wiley (Eds.), *Improving inquiry in the social sciences: A volume in honor of Lee J. Cronbach* (pp. 13–59). Hillsdale, NJ: Lawrence Erlbaum.

Messick, S. (1981). Constructs and their vicisitudes in educational and psychological measurement. *Psychological Bulleint, 89,* 575–588.

Messick, S. (1995). Validity of psychological assessment: Validation of inferences from persons' responses and performances as scientific inquiry into score meaning. *American Psychologist, 50,* 741–749.

Michell, J. (1990). *An introduction to the logic of psychological measurement.* Hillsdale, NJ: Lawrence Erlbaum.

Mill, J. S. (1843). *A System of Logic, Ratiocinative and Inductive* (Vol. 1). London: John W. Parker. Available at http://books.google.com/books?id=y4MEAAAAQAAJ&dq=a%20system%20of%20logic&pg=PR1#v=onepage&q&f=false. Accessed June 2011.

Mone, M. A., Mueller, G. C., & Mauland, W. (1996). The perception and usage of statistical power in applied psychology and management research. *Personnel Psychology, 49,* 103–120.

Morel, B. M., & Ramanujam, R. (1999) Through the looking glass of complexity: Organizations as adaptive and evolving systems, *Organization Science, 10,* 278–293.

Morgan, S. L., & Winship, C. (2007). *Counterfactuals and causal inference: Methods and principles of social research.* Cambridge: Cambridge University Press.

Morita, J. G., Lee, T. W., & Mowday, R. T. (1989). Introducing survival analysis to organizational researchers: A selected application to turnover research. *Journal of Applied Psychology, 74,* 280–292.

Murphy, J. (1990). A most respectable prejudice: Inequality in educational research and policy. *British Journal of Sociology, 41,* 29–54.

Muthén, B. (2003). Statistical and substantive checking in growth mixture modeling. *Psychological Methods, 8,* 369–377.

Muthén, B. (2004). Latent variable analysis: Growth mixture modeling and related techniques for longitudinal data. In D. Kaplan (Ed.), *Handbook of quantitative methodology for the social sciences* (pp. 345–368). Newbury Park, CA: Sage Publications.

Naquin, S. S., & Baldwin, T.T. (2003). Managing transfer before learning begins: The transfer-ready learner. In E. F. Holton III & T. T. Baldwin (Eds.), *Improving learning transfer in organizations* (pp. 80–96). San Francisco: Jossey-Bass.

Nickerson, R. S. (2000). Null hypothesis significance testing: A review of an old and continuing controversy. *Psychological Methods, 5,* 241–301.

Noe, R. A. (1986). Trainee attributes and attitudes: Neglected influences on training effectiveness. *Academy of Management Review, 11,* 736–749.

Nowak, A., & Lowenstein, M. (1994). Dynamical systems: A tool for social psychology? In *Dynamical systems in social psychology* (pp. 17–53). San Diego: Academic Press.

Nowak, A., Vallacher, R., Tesser, A., & Borkowski, W. (2000). Society of self: The emergence of collective properties in self-structure. *Psychological Review, 107,* 39–61.

Ployhart, R. E., & Hakel, M. D. (1998). The substantive nature of performance variability: Predicting interindividual differences in intraindividual performance. *Personnel Psychology, 51,* 859–901.

Ployhart, R. E., & Moliterno, T. P. (2011). Emergence of the human capital resource: A multilevel model. *Academy of Management Review, 36,* 127–150.

Popper, K. R. (1959). *The logic of scientific discovery.* New York: Basic Books.

Reis, H. T., & Gable, S. L. (2000). Event-sampling and other methods for studying everyday experience. In T. H. Reis & M. C. Judd (Eds.), *Handbook of research methods in social and personality psychology* (pp. 190–222). New York: Cambridge University Press.

Rosel, J., & Plewis, I. (2008). Longitudinal data analysis with structural equations. *Methodology, 4,* 37–50.

Rosenbaum, P. (1984) The consequences of adjustment for a concomitant variable that has been affected by the treatment. *Journal of the Royal Statistical Society, Series A, 147,* 656–666.

Rosenthal, R. (1994). Science and ethics in conducting, analyzing, and reporting psychological research. *Psychological Science, 5,* 127–134.

Roy, A. (1951). Some thoughts on the distribution of earnings. *Oxford Economic Papers 3,* 1, 35–46.

Rozeboom, W. W. (1997). Good science is abductive, not hypothetico-deductive. In L. L. Harlow, S. A. Mulaik & J. H. Steiger (Eds.), *What if there were no significance tests?* (pp. 335–392). Mahwah, NJ: Erlbaum.

Rubin, D. (1974). Estimating causal effects of treatments in randomized and nonrandomized studies. *Journal of Educational Psychology, 66,* 688–701.

Rubin, D. (1977). Assignment to treatment group on the basis of a covariate. *Journal of Educational Statistics, 2,* 1–26.

Rubin, D. (1981). The Bayesian bootstrap, *Annals of Statistics 9* 130–134.

Rubin, D. (1990). Formal modes of statistical inference for causal effects. *Journal of Statistical Planning and Inference 25,* 279–292.

Rublin, D. (2010). Reflections stimulated by the comments of Shadish (2010) and West & Thoemmes (2010). *Psychological Methods, 15,* 38–46.

Russell, B. (1913). On the notion of cause. *Proceedings of the Aristotelian Society 13,* 1–26.

Sackett, P. R., & Larson, J. R., Jr. (1990). Research strategies and tactics in industrial and organizational psychology. In M. D. Dunnette & L. M. Hough (Eds.), *Handbook of industrial and organizational psychology* (2nd Ed., Vol. 1, pp. 419–489). Palo Alto, CA: Consulting Psychologists Press.

Scherbaum, C. A., & Vancouver, J. B. (2010). If we produce discrepancies, then how? Testing a computational process model of positive goal revision. *Journal of Applied Social Psychology, 40,* 2201–2231.

Schmidt, F. L. (1996). Statistical significance testing and cumulative knowledge in psychology: Implications for training of researchers. *Psychological Methods, 1,* 115–129.

Schneider, B. (1987). The people make the place. *Personnel Psychology, 40,* 437–453.

Shadish, W. R. (2010) Campbell and Rubin: A primer and comparison of their approaches to causal inference in field settings. *Psychological Methods, 15,* 3–17

Shadish, W. R. (2011). The truth about validity. *New Directions for Evaluation, Special Edition: Advancing Validity in Outcome Evaluation: Theory and Practice, 130,* 107–117.

Shadish, W. R., & Cook, T. D. (2009). The renaissance of field experimentation in evaluating interventions. *Annual Review of Psychology 60,* 607–629.

Shadish, W., Cook, T., & Campbell, D. (2002). *Experimental and quasi-experimental designs for generalized causal inference.* Boston, MA: Houghton Mifflin.

Singer, J. D., & Willett, J. B. (2003). *Applied longitudinal data analysis: Modeling change and event occurrence.* Oxford: Oxford University Press.

Stone-Romero, E. F., & Rosopa, P. J. (2008). The relative validity of inferences about mediation as a function of research design characteristics. *Organizational Research Methods, 11,* 326–352.

Stone-Romero, E. F. & Rosopa, P. J. (2010). Research design options for testing mediation models and their implications for facets of validity. *Journal of Managerial Psychology, 25,* 697–712.

Spencer, S. J., Zanna, M. P., & Fong, G. T. (2005). Establishing a causal chain: Why experiments are often more effective than mediational analyses in examining psychological processes. *Journal of Personality and Social Psychology, 89,* 845–851.

Suppes, P. (1970) *A probabilistic theory of causality.* Amsterdam: North-Holland Publishing.

Thistlethwaite, D. L., & Campbell, D. T. (1960) Regression-discontinuity analysis: An alternative to the ex-post facto experiment. *Journal of Educational Psychology. 51,* 309–317.

Totterdell, P., & Parkinson, B. (1999). Use and effectiveness of self-regulation strategies for improving mood in a group of trainee teachers. *Journal of Occupational Health Psychology, 4,* 219–232.

Trougakos, J. P., Beal, D. J., Green, S. G., & Weiss, H. M. (2008). Making the break count: An episodic examination of recovery activities, emotional experiences, and positive affective displays. *Academy of Management Journal, 51,* 131–146.

Vallacher, R. R., & Nowak, A. (1994). *Dynamical systems in social psychology.* New York: Academic Press.

Vancouver, J. B., Tamanini, K. B., & Yoder, R. J. (2010). Using dynamic computational models to reconnect theory and research: Socialization by the proactive newcomer as example. *Journal of Management, 36,* 764–793.

Vancouver, J. B., Weinhardt, J. M., & Schmidt, A. M. (2010). A formal, computational theory of multiple-goal pursuit: Integrating goal-choice and goal-striving processes. *Journal of Applied Psychology, 95,* 985–1008.

von Bertalanffy, L. (1950). An outline of general system theory. *British Journal for the Philosophy of Science 1,* 139–164.

von Bertalanffy, L. (1956). General system theory. *General Systems, 1,* 1–10.

von Bertalanffy, L. (1968). *General system theory: Foundations, development, applications.* New York: George Braziller.

Wang, M. (2007). Profiling retirees in the retirement transition and adjustment process: Examining the longitudinal change patterns of retirees' psychological well-being. *Journal of Applied Psychology, 92,* 455–474.

Wang, M., & Bodner, T. E. (2007). Growth mixture modeling: Identifying and predicting unobserved subpopulations with longitudinal data. *Organizational Research Methods, 10,* 635–656.

Wang, M., & Chan, D. (2011). Mixture latent Markov modeling: Identifying and predicting unobserved heterogeneity in longitudinal qualitative status change. *Organizational Research Methods, 14,* 411–431.

Wang, M., & Hanges, P. (2011). Latent class procedures: Applications to organizational research. *Organizational Research Methods, 14,* 24–31.

Wang, M., Henkens, K., & van Solinge, H. (2011). Retirement adjustment: A review of theoretical and empirical advancements. *American Psychologist, 66,* 204–213.

Wang, M., Liao, H., Zhan, Y., & Shi, J. (2011). Daily customer mistreatment and employee sabotage against customers: Examining emotion and resource perspectives. *Academy of Management Journal, 54,* 312–334.

Wang, M., Liu, S., Zhan, Y., & Shi, J. (2010). Daily work-family conflict and alcohol use: Testing the cross-level moderation effects of peer drinking norms and social support. *Journal of Applied Psychology, 95,* 377–386.

Wang, M., & Takeuchi, R. (2007). The role of goal orientation during expatriation: A cross-sectional and longitudinal investigation. *Journal of Applied Psychology, 92,* 1437–1445.

Wang, M., Zhan, Y., McCune, E., & Truxillo, D. (2011). Understanding newcomers' adaptability and work-related outcomes: Testing the mediating roles of perceived P–E fit variables. *Personnel Psychology, 64,* 163–189.

Weiner, N. (1954). *The human use of humans: Cybernetics and society.* Boston: Houghton Mifflin.

Weiss, H. M., & Rupp, D. E. (2011). Experiencing work: An essay on a person-centric work psychology. *Industrial and Organizational Psychology: Perspectives on Science and Practice, 4,* 83–97.

West, S. G., Biesanz, J. C., & Pitts, S. C. (2000). Causal inference and generalization in field settings: Experimental and quasi-experimental designs. In H. T. Reis and C. M. Judd (Eds.), *Handbook of research methods in social and personality psychology* (pp. 40–84). Cambridge: Cambridge University Press.

West, S. G., & Thoemmes, F. (2010). Campbell's and Rubin's perspectives on causal inference. *Psychological Methods, 15,* 18–37.

Wheeler, L., & Nezlek, J. (1977). Sex differences in social participation. *Journal of Personality and Social Psychology, 35,* 742–754.

Wheeler, L., & Reis, H. T. (1991). Self-recording of everyday life events: Origins, types, and uses. *Journal of Personality, 59,* 339–354.

Willett, J. B., & Sayer, A. G. (1994). Using covariance structure analysis to detect correlates and predictors of individual change over time. *Psychological Bulletin, 116,* 363–381.

Multivariate Dynamics in Organizational Science

Richard P. DeShon

Abstract

Theories in organizational science place increased emphasis on dynamic relations among multiple theoretically relevant variables. Variants of the hierarchical linear model provide the primary approach used to evaluate dynamic processes in organizational science. This model is well suited to the analysis of univariate outcomes with recursive relations. However, many theories in organizational science posit cycles of influence among multiple variables. The analysis of multivariate, non-recursive data structures requires a new analytic approach. The vector autoregressive model is presented as a useful approach for the analysis of longitudinal data that may possess dynamic cycles of influence among multiple variables. The implementation and applicability of this data analytic approach to the modeling and evaluation of organizational science theories is demonstrated using multiple examples.

Key Words: Dynamics, multivariate, longitudinal, hierarchical linear model, vector autoregressive model

Multivariate Dynamics in Organizational Science

Multivariate statistical analysis is a term that describes a large set of algorithms used to identify patterns of dependence existing between variables that comprise a joint probability distribution. Regression, factor analysis, and principal component analysis remain popular but other, once common analyses, such as multivariate analysis of variance and discriminant analysis, appear to have largely fallen out of favor. Structural equation modeling (SEM) now dominates the analysis of cross-sectional, multivariate data, and random coefficient or multilevel modeling currently dominates the analysis of longitudinal, multivariate data. Numerous, excellent reviews of these methods exist (e.g., Collins, 2006; MacCallum & Austin, 2000; McArdle & Nesselroade, 2003; Raudenbush, 2001; Rosen, 1991) and there is no need for yet another presentation of the models and their use. The important topic of multivariate dynamics, however,

has not received a systematic treatment in either the organizational sciences or general psychology literature. This chapter seeks to fill this gap by providing a systematic overview of linear multivariate dynamics and the analysis of stationary dynamic systems.

Recent research efforts, in virtually all subdisciplines of psychological science, place increasing emphasis on modelng the dynamics of important psychological variables such as self-regulatory processes (Louro, Pieter, & Zeelenberg, 2007), depression (Hankin, Fraley, & Abela, 2005), workplace emotions (Bono, Foldes, Vinson, & Muros, 2007), workplace stress (Fuller et al., 2003), and organizational performance (Short, Ketchen, Bennett, & duToit, 2006). In fact, research interest in dynamic processes is increasing exponentially. A topic search for the terms *dynamic* and *dynamics* in Thomsons's Web of Science, social science database yielded over 81,996 hits over the period covered from 1956 to 2009. An examination the frequency of the topic by year indicates that interest in dynamic process is growing exponentially. Prior to 1990, the topic of dynamics occurred at a rate of approximately 100 to 600 per year, growing slowly but steadily over the 34-year span from 1956 to 1990. In the 1990s, dynamics was an increasingly popular article topic, yielding a steady increase of hits from 621 in 1990 to over 3,031 in 1999. This rate continued to increase from 3,132 in 2000 to 7,299 in 2009. Clearly, something is going on here, and it appears that the coming decade is likely to be characterized by the study of individual, team, and organizational dynamics.

Interestingly, as the focus on dynamic processes increased, so too did the length and complexity of longitudinal data structures. This is not surprising, since modeling dynamic processes often requires the observation of the process or system over many time periods within the focal unit of analysis (e.g., individuals, teams, groups, organizations). It was not long ago that a researchers proudly presented longitudinal research consisting of two or three waves of data. Now, that same data structure would engender a litany of inferential limitations in a discussion section of a research article. In contrast, the increasingly common use of experience sampling methods frequently yields observation windows that contain 30 or more time periods for each sampled unit. Naturally, research attention is also directed at examining the static and time-varying variables thought to be associated with the dynamic trajectories in a focal variable. The result is a multivariate, longitudinal data structure that typically has many observations over time on a relatively small sample. Walls and Schafer (2006) refer to these increasingly common data structures as intensive longitudinal data.

It is useful to begin by presenting the distinguishing features of a dynamic process and the capability of current SEM and hierarchical linear model (HLM) approaches to modeling the resulting data structures. Consider the bivariate time series data presented in panel A of Figure 4.1. Observations for the two series are recorded at the same 50 occasions and, given the research foci in organizational science, would commonly represent two variables within a single unit (e.g., the sharedness of a team's mental models and the team's performance level), or responses to a single variable provided by multiple units (e.g., two employees' ratings of safety climate, dyadic ratings of coworker satisfaction, return on investments (ROIs) for two organizations). Two critical issues are immediately apparent in the graph of the two time series. First, there appears to be a positive trend in both series, making the notion of growth curves salient. Second, the series appear to move together over time, with the most pronounced co-movement occurring between occasions 10 and 30. Further, the co-movement between the series appears to have a lagged relationship so that the upward and downward movements in each series occur at slightly different occasions. Early in the series, the movement in the dashed line appears to slightly trail the movement in the solid line; later, movement in the solid line appears to trail the movement in the dashed line. This interesting pattern of co-movement suggests that there may be a relationship between the series.

To explore the notion of co-movement, panel B in Figure 4.1 presents the cross-correlation between the two series. In this approach, the observations

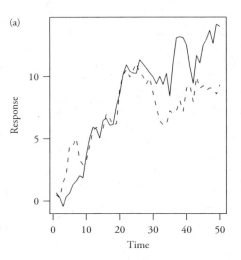
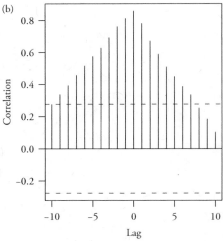

Figure 4.1 Multivariate Trajectories (A) and Cross Correlations (B)

of one series are correlated with the observations of another series for a wide range of positive and negative lags to identify possible leading and trailing indicators of change. For these series, the simultaneous correlation between the series (lag 0) is surprisingly large at 0.86. The remaining correlations represent the relationships when one of the series is shifted forward and backward in time through a sequential set of lags. The correlation is strongest at a lag of zero but remains substantial and statistically significant out to at least ±5 lags (0.58, 0.45).

It is clear that the series are contemporaneously correlated and that they demonstrate substantial correlation for both positive and negative lags. However, interpreting the meaning underlying this commonly observed empirical result is the researcher's challenge. What model should be used to capture the interesting features present in the multivariate time series data represented in Figure 4.1 and how should the adequacy of the selected model be evaluated?

Figure 4.2 presents a series of increasingly complex bivariate relationships that evolve over time and are possible data-generating mechanisms underlying the time series data represented in Figure 4.1. Panel A in Figure 4.2 represents a simple correlational model in which the concurrent observations in each series are simply correlated using the standard Pearson product moment correlation coefficient. Although not immediately obvious, this simple correlational representation is essentially the same as latent growth curve approaches that attempt to model the correlation of trends among multiple time series across multiple dynamic systems such as individuals (e.g., Hertzog, Linderberger, Ghisletta, & vonOertzen, 2006).

Panel B in Figure 4.2 represents a slightly more complicated model in which variation in one time series (X) is treated as causally related to contemporaneous variation in another time series (Y). In this model, current values on both variables are unrelated to future values. This time-varying covariate relationship is, by far, the most common model used in current investigations of multivariate dynamics using multilevel models, latent growth curves, or even traditional repeated measures analysis. The prevalence of this model is somewhat surprising, given the importance of temporal ordering in the philosophy of causation.

Panel C in Figure 4.2 modifies the time-varying covariate model by introducing a relationship between current values of the dependent variable (Y) and immediately subsequent values of the

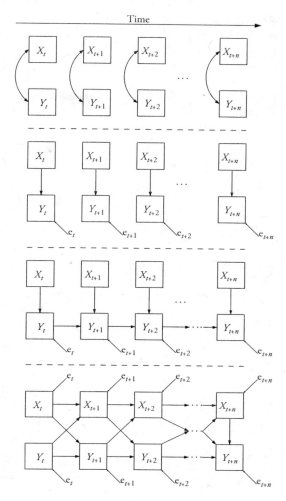

Figure 4.2 Bivariate Dynamic Models

dependent variable. This autoregressive structure is consistent with the notion that prior values of a variable are often good predictors of future values of a variable, such as performance. Although lagged values of a dependent variable are rarely incorporated into psychological models, both random coefficient and structural equation models are capable of representing this data-generating mechanism by incorporating one or more lagged values of the dependent variables as additional predictor variables (X) in the model.

The final panel in Figure 4.2, Panel D, adds two important components to the representation of bivariate time series relations. Here, current values on each variable relate, in a possibly strong manner, to future values of each value. This autoregressive relationship is probably best thought of in terms of stability rather than causality. In other words, from one day to the next, individuals, teams, and organizations remain highly self-similar. For instance, an individual's current body weight (or conscientiousness) is strongly related to the individual's immediately subsequent body weight. Of course, there is a physiological causal process underlying weight maintenance that is responsible for the self-similarity, but current weight does not cause, in the traditional sense of the term, future weight. The cross-variable relations, on the other hand, are causal. Current values of X influence future values of Y ($X_t \rightarrow Y_{t+1}$) and current values of Y influence future values of X ($Y_t \rightarrow X_{t+1}$), that, in turn, influence future values of Y ($Y_t \rightarrow X_{t+1} \rightarrow Y_{t+2}$). The cross-variable influence results in a cyclical, reciprocal, or mutual influence relationship in which the notion of independent and dependent variables loses its meaning. Multilevel modeling techniques are ill-equipped to model this structure. It is possible to model this simple structure using structural equation models (e.g., du Toit & Browne, 2007) but the implementation is not simple, and models of more complex processes become prohibitively difficult to specify.

A final, important feature present in Figure 4.1 requires attention before discussing models designed to represent multivariate dynamic cycles and reciprocal relations. Although not widely recognized among organizational scientists, the positive trends present in both variables represented in Figure 4.1 present substantial modeling and inferential difficulties. The problem of spurious correlation among times series has been known since Yule (1926) first highlighted it and computed, as an example, a correlation of 0.95 between the annual mortality rate and the annual ratio of marriages in the Church of England to all marriages over the period of 1866–1911. From a computational perspective, the reason for the strong observed correlation is simply due to the fact that both series increase over time such that high scores on one series co-occur with high scores on the other series. Stated another way, the observed correlation is due to the common dependence of the series on a function of time. From an inferential perspective, however, the appropriate interpretation of this correlation is entirely unclear.

Yule (1926)—and many others since—highlighted that time is not a causal factor in the growth observed in the time series data. Instead, one or more underlying processes are responsible for the growth trends, and these processes need not be related to observe a strong correlation between multivariate times series. Even worse, the underlying process responsible for the apparent growth trends in the time series data

may be due to observing an inadequate window of time samples or even due to entirely random processes. Although beyond the scope of the current presentation, the two highly correlated time series (r = 0.86) presented in Figure 4.1 are actually two instantiations of a simple random walk. These random walks are stochastically independent and, therefore, no substantively meaningful interpretation can be attached to the large observed correlation between the series. The difficulty of modeling and interpreting trends in time series data continues and, as Phillips (2005) points out, the only thing that is clear is that we have not yet figured out how to adequately model trends over time. In this vein, the common modeling approach to this problem in psychology and the organizational sciences of including a linear time variable in the model certainly does not reduce inferential ambiguity and likely accentuates it. The issue of trends in time series data receives more attention in a later section once the additional tools present in the study of linear dynamic systems are discussed.

Linear Dynamic Systems

New ways of thinking about multivariate dynamics and new methods are required to capitalize upon the wealth of information present in intensive longitudinal data and the depth of theory addressing the dynamics of psychological processes. Linear dynamic systems provide a promising approach to model the increased complexity of our data and theory. In this section, the basic deterministic mathematics of linear, dynamic systems are presented. This approach is then generalized by incorporating error and focusing attention on stochastic processes. Finally, methods for estimating the model parameters are described and an example is presented.

The dynamic models literature is massive, ranging across virtually all scientific disciplines from physics and engineering to biology, economics, and social sciences. The current presentation addresses only a small, but highly important, segment of this literature, limited to linear systems with Gaussian errors. Formally, a deterministic dynamical system can be defined as a tuple (X, m, T), where X is a separable metric space, m is a probability measure on the Borel σ-algebra of X, and $T : X \nsubseteq X$ is a continuous measure preserving transformation. If, in addition, X is a linear topological vector space and T a continuous linear transformation, then the dynamical system is linear (Flytzanis, 1976).

Less formally, a linear dynamic system is a system that evolves over time through the iterated application of an underlying rule governing the transition of the system from a given state at time t to a state at time $t+1$. The transition rule describes the change of the system state in terms of prior system states and may also include external inputs. External inputs are possible but not necessary to the functioning of a dynamical system. In other words, a set of initial states may be specified, and then the system can evolve over time according to the transition rule with no further input. The progression of states over time forms a trajectory of the system in its phase space (the set of all possible states of the system). Even very simple rules that govern the state transitions over time can result in highly complex system behavior.

The transition rule governing the evolution of current states into future states can treat time as either a discrete variable represented by the integers (e.g., 1, 2, 3, 4,...) or a continuous variable represented by the real numbers. The mathematics of the former are described by difference equations, and the mathematics of the latter are described by differential equations. One perspective on the conceptualization of dynamics is that if a model is not representable in terms of difference or differential equations, then the model is not a truly dynamic model (Boulding, 1955). The discrete representation of time is most consistent with both the conceptualization of events and the common measurement processes in the organizational sciences. Therefore, the focus here is on the discrete representation of time that increments by a constant unit (e.g., second, minutes, months, years) and the underlying difference equations that govern the evolution of system trajectories.

Numerous, equivalent representations of linear dynamic systems exist (cf. Caines, 1988; Hannan & Deistler, 1988). The state space representation has two distinct advantages for the purposes of this presentation. First, it is most similar to existing simultaneous equation models commonly used in psychological research, making it a relatively smooth transition for an individual already familiar with the matrix approach to SEM. Second, the state space representation of linear dynamic systems is intimately connected to the dominant parameter estimation methods. For these reasons, the state space representation is adopted and used exclusively throughout this presentation.

A linear dynamic system is represented in state space form as:

$$y_{t+1} = Ay_t + b, \quad t = 1, 2, 3, \ldots, T \quad (1)$$

where $\mathbf{y}_{t+1}$ is a K-dimensional column vector of future states determined by pre-multiplying the K-dimensional vector of current states, $\mathbf{y}_t$, by the $K \times K$ transition weight matrix, $\mathbf{A}$, and $\mathbf{b}$ is a K-dimensional column vector of time invariant additive terms, commonly referred to as the forcing or driving term. For those who do not speak linear algebra as a second language, it is helpful to represent the transition matrix, the forcing terms, and the time dependent state vectors in Equation 1 in expanded matrix form as:

$$
\begin{bmatrix} y_{1_{t+1}} \\ y_{2_{t+1}} \\ y_{3_{t+1}} \\ \vdots \\ y_{n_{t+1}} \end{bmatrix}
=
\begin{bmatrix} a_{11} & a_{12} & a_{13} & \cdots & a_{1n} \\ a_{21} & a_{22} & a_{23} & \cdots & a_{2n} \\ a_{31} & a_{32} & a_{33} & \cdots & a_{3n} \\ \vdots & \vdots & \vdots & \ddots & \vdots \\ a_{n1} & a_{n2} & a_{n3} & \cdots & a_{nn} \end{bmatrix}
\begin{bmatrix} y_{1t} \\ y_{2t} \\ y_{3t} \\ \vdots \\ y_{nt} \end{bmatrix}
+
\begin{bmatrix} b_1 \\ b_2 \\ b_3 \\ \vdots \\ b_n \end{bmatrix},
$$
$$t = 1, 2, 3, \ldots, T$$

$$(2)$$

In the mathematics literature, Equation 1 is referred to as an autonomous, first order, K-dimensional difference equation. In the statistics literature, Equation 1 is typically referred to as a deterministic, vector autoregressive process. The transition matrix, $\mathbf{A}$, is responsible for most of the interesting trajectory dynamics and, as such, is typically the focus of dynamic analysis. However, as will be shown below, the constant values in the vector of forcing terms, $\mathbf{b}$, substantially impact the trajectories. Finally, it is important to understand that Equations 1 and 2 describe an abstract system. To specify or identify a particular set of system trajectories, resulting from Equation 1, it is necessary to provide a K-dimensional column vector of initial conditions ($\mathbf{y}_0$) to start the recursion.

The system states (y_t) are completely general and are constrained only by the researcher's imagination and knowledge of the system. Possible states useful for representing intraperson system dynamics might be self-regulatory systems (e.g., goals, effort, self-efficacy, and performance), affective systems (positive and negative affect in response to events), and personality systems (agreeableness, conscientiousness, extraversion, neurotocism, and openness). Researchers interested in group or team dynamics might focus on the manifestation of a single variable (e.g., efficacy, perceptions of cohesion, or fear) as it evolves over time in each member of a team or group. Generalizations to represent multiple variables that interact dynamically across multiple actors or team members are straightforward and will become apparent as the model is developed.

The state trajectories of any system that may be represented by Equation 1 are completely determined by the vector of initial conditions ($\mathbf{y}_0$), the forcing term constants, and the pattern of weights (a_{ij}) in the transition matrix ($\mathbf{A}$). When modeling dynamic systems, primary attention is focused on the weights in the transition matrix. The weights on the principal diagonal of the transition matrix reflect the self-similarity of each state over time, whereas the off-diagonal weights capture the dynamics of the state interactions. So, for example, a researcher may be interested in understanding the dynamics of cohesion perceptions within a team. The diagonal weights reflect the self-similarity of each team member's cohesion perceptions over time, and the off-diagonal weights reflect the relative influence of other team members' cohesion perceptions on a given team member's cohesion perceptions. Unlike correlation or covariance matrices, the transition matrix need not be symmetric. This means that cohesion perception held by team member 2 may have a substantial impact on the cohesion perception of team member 4 ($a_{24} > 0$) but the cohesion perception of team member 4 may have no impact on the cohesion perception of team member 2 ($a_{42} = 0$).

As discussed in detail in the following section, the transition coefficients in stationary linear systems must be less than 1.0 in absolute value. A transition coefficient greater than 1.0 results in an explosive system that is unlikely to maintain coherence over a long period of time, and a transition coefficient of exactly 1.0 results in a special form of non-stationary trajectory evolution termed a *random walk*. Values near 1.0 on the diagonal indicate that a particular team member's current cohesion perception is much like immediately prior cohesion perceptions. Values near −1.0 on the diagonal indicates that a particular team member's current cohesion perception oscillates back and forth between lower and higher levels of perceived cohesion. Similar effects happen with off-diagonal coefficients such that large positive coefficients result in the fluctuations in one time series having a greater impact on the fluctuations in another time series. Also, negative off-diagonal coefficients set up negative feedback processes between one or both of the time series such that one time series may oscillate in response to changes in another time series, or both series may oscillate with respect to fluctuations in the other time series. Examples of these trajectory patterns are presented in the following section. The vast majority of mathematical work in the area of linear dynamic systems addresses the solution of the multidimensional difference equations contained in Equation 1 and the characterization of system equilibria and stability. Each of these two central concepts are introduced next.

State Trajectory Characterization

A solution to the linear dynamic system in Equation 1 is a trajectory of the state variables, $\mathbf{y}$, that satisfies the linear relationship at each time point. The solution relates the state variables at any time point, t, to the vector of initial conditions, $\mathbf{y}_0$, the coefficients in the transition matrix, $\mathbf{A}$, and the vector of forcing terms, $\mathbf{b}$. The general solution to the first order difference equation underlying the linear dynamic model is well known (e.g., Galor, 2007; Luenberger, 1979) and may be represented as:

$$y_t = \mathbf{A}^t y_0 + \sum_{i=0}^{t-1} \mathbf{A}^i \mathbf{b} \qquad (3)$$

In words, the current states for each variable in the system at time t is an additive function of the weighted starting points and the sum, across all the prior time points, of the exponentiated transition matrix and the vector of forcing terms. The apparent simplicity of Equation 3 belies the complexity of the resulting state trajectories that may, depending upon the weights in the transition matrix, either evolve monotonically or demonstrate oscillatory behavior and, in the long run, may converge to a steady state, diverge to ± infinity, or evolve into periodic cycles.

A sample of possible trajectories consistent with the linear dynamic system represented in Equations 1–3 are presented in the four panels of Figure 4.3. Panel A represents the trajectories resulting from the following dynamic system:

$$\begin{bmatrix} y_{1_{t+1}} \\ y_{2_{t+1}} \\ y_{3_{t+1}} \end{bmatrix} = \begin{bmatrix} 0.8 & 0 & 0 \\ 0 & 0.7 & 0 \\ 0 & 0 & 0.65 \end{bmatrix} \begin{bmatrix} y_{1_t} \\ y_{2_t} \\ y_{3_t} \end{bmatrix} + \begin{bmatrix} 0.5 \\ 3.0 \\ 1.5 \end{bmatrix}, \qquad (4)$$
$$t = 1, 2, 3, \ldots, 75$$

with starting values, $\mathbf{y}_0$, of $[18.0, 30.0, -10.0]'$. This is one of the simplest linear dynamic systems possible. Again, the off-diagonal entries in the transition matrix represent the influence of one state on other systems' states, and the pattern of influence need not be symmetric. In this case, all off-diagonal entries are zero and, therefore, the present values of any given state do not influence the future values of the other states. The diagonal values represent the notion of self-similarity over time such that smaller coefficients result in less self-similarity over time. Examination of the trajectories in panel A of Figure 4.3 highlights that over time each state moves quickly from its starting point to a unique level where it remains. Comparing the trajectories of the 1st and 3rd state variables highlights that state 3 moves to its unique level more quickly (i.e., less self-similar) than state 1. Other than moving to a unique level and doing so at different rates from different starting points, the trajectories in panel A are highly similar.

Panel B in Figure 4.3 is obtained by simply switching the first coefficient in the transition matrix in the system presented above from 0.80 to -0.80. All other values in the system remain the same, including the starting points. As can be seen in the figure, the effect of switching the coefficient for state 1 from a positive to a negative value is

dramatic, and the trajectory enters into an oscillating pattern consistent with states that are subject to a control mechanism or negative feedback loops. Oscillating trajectories such as this should be highly interesting to individuals who research regulatory process at the individual, group, or organizational levels of analysis. Interestingly, the state 1 trajectory also converges to a different unique level from that obtained by state 1 in Panel A of Figure 4.3.

Panel C in Figure 4.3 incorporates non-zero off-diagonal values of 0.11 into the transition matrix presented above, thereby allowing the current value of a given state to influence the future values of the other states. The pattern of influence represented in this transition matrix is mutual, symmetric, and cyclic, meaning that the current value of a present state influences future values of both the given state and the other states in the system, and that the prior values of the other states influenced the present value of the given state. This is a trivariate version of the relationship depicted in the last panel of Figure 4.2 and

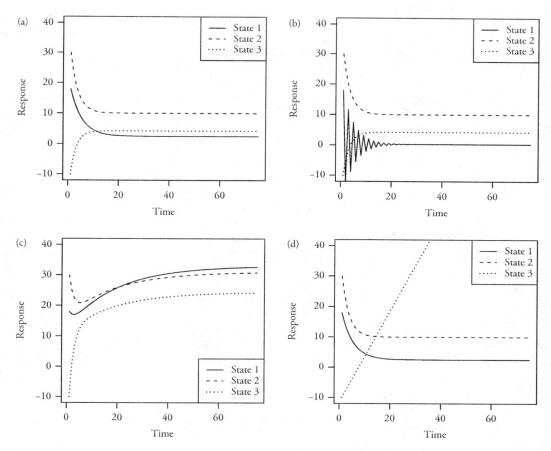

Figure 4.3 Illustrative System State Trajectories

in network or graph theory would be referred to as a complete directed graph having bidirectional edges and loops. The impact of incorporating the reciprocal relations into the dynamic model in Equation 4 may be clearly seen by comparing panels A and C in Figure 4.3. In panel A, State 1 converged to a level lower than the other states, but in panel C state 1 converges to a level higher than the other states. As happened in panel A, the trajectories in panel C demonstrate rapid short-run dynamics. However, unlike the trajectories in panel A, those in panel C do not quickly settle into a particular level but continue to evolve slowly toward what appears to be a stable level in the long run. Finally, the levels at which the trajectories converge are strongly impacted by the levels at which the other series converge, as can be most easily seen by comparing state 3 across panels A and C. In panel A, state 3 converges to a level close to 5.0, but in Panel C it is drawn upward toward the other two trajectories and appears to converge to a level close to 25.0. This demonstrates that even small cross-state coefficients in the transition matrix can have a substantial impact on the state dynamics and the eventual system convergence levels obtained in the long run.

Finally, panel D in Figure 4.3 highlights a critically important issue that occurs in dynamic modeling. The trajectories in panel A and D are identical in all ways, with a single exception. The self-similarity coefficient for state 3 is changed from 0.65 to 1.0. The result is explosive, exponential growth in the trajectory for state 3. If the coefficient were changed to -1.0, then state 3 would demonstrate increasingly large swings in oscillatory behavior indicating, for instance, catastrophic failure of a control system. Neither case appears consistent with normal functioning of either individuals, teams, or organizations as unregulated growth or decline in a process is rarely, if ever, seen, unless the system experiences unsustainable evolution resulting in catastrophic failure. On the other hand, it is possible that the death throes of an organization or the dissolution of a team results in highly unstable and unsustainable trajectories. This issue deserves more attention but, for now, the focus will remain on processes that evolve over time in a stable or non-explosive manner.

System Equilibria and Stability

With the exception of the single, explosive trajectory, the states represented in Figure 4.3 all converge to a set of levels and then remain in these states. This long-run behavior is a highly desirable characteristic of linear dynamic systems that, for example, makes it possible to forecast or predict future states using

knowledge of the coefficients in the dynamic system. If a system of states converge to a set of levels, then the corresponding levels, $\bar{y}$, are referred to as the *steady state equilibrium* of the K-dimensional system. Once the states evolve into the steady state equilibrium, the system will remain in this state indefinitely unless external perturbations or disturbances push one or more of the states from their respective equilibria points. Further, the equilibrium is stable if, once one or more of the system states are perturbed, the system returns to the original equilibrium states. Bandura's bobo doll (Bandura, Ross, & Ross, 1961) is an excellent example of a oscillating dynamic system that returns again and again to the same equilibrium after receiving strong perturbations via children's hands and feet. A linear dynamic system will converge to a stable equilibrium whenever the absolute value of all eigenvalues of the transition matrix, **A**, are less then 1.0. Further, the steady states that the system will achieve in the long run may be computed using the simple formula:

$$\bar{y} = [I - A]^{-1}b \qquad (5)$$

where **I** is the K-dimensional identity matrix.

The dynamic systems presented above algebraically and represented visually in Figure 4.3 can be used to exemplify the determination of whether the system will converge to a stable equilibrium and, if so, how to compute the vector of states associated with the equilibrium. The eigenvalues associated with the transition matrix for the system depicted in panel A of Figure 4.3 and Equation 4 are 0.8, 0.7, 0.65. Since the absolute value of each eigenvalue is less than 1.0, this system is stable and the states will converge to a steady state equilibrium. Similarly, the eigenvalues for the system represented in panel B of Figure 3 are -0.8, 0.7, 0.65 and, therefore, converge to a stable equilibrium. The eigenvalues for the interrelated states in the dynamic systems depicted in panel C are 0.95, 0.64, 0.56, and this system also reaches a stable equilibrium. In contrast, the eigenvalues associated with panel D in Figure 4.3, where one of the states demonstrates explosive growth, are 0.8, 0.7, 1.0, and it is clear that this system does not meet the condition for a stable equilibrium.

The vector of states associated with the stable equilibrium for the three stable systems represented in Figure 4.3 may be computed using Equation 5. For the system in panel A, the steady states are 2.5, 10.0, 4.29 for states 1 through 3, respectively. For the system in panel B, the steady states are 0.28, 10.0, 4.29. Finally, for the system in panel C, the steady states are 33.02, 31.06, 24.43. There is no set of steady states for the system in Panel D.

Higher Order Dynamics

The linear dynamic system presented in Equation 1 is deceptively simple. This apparent simplicity is misleading as the system can be easily expanded to incorporate substantially more complex linear dynamics. A natural expansion of the model is to consider systems in which the current states may depend upon the immediately prior states as well as more time-distal states (i.e., higher order difference equations). The first-order model presented above assumes that the impact of the entire history of the system on the current states occurs through the immediately preceding states. Individuals and organizations have impressive memory systems and often use more than the knowledge of current states when setting future state goals and developing plans for achieving the state goals. Higher order systems may also arise when the frequency of dynamics differs across variables in the dynamic system. For instance, it is often argued that affective processes within an individual operate and update more quickly than controlled cognitive processes. If so, then models of human motivation that incorporate both affective and cognitive variables may need to incorporate longer lags so that recent affective trajectories can impact current and future cognitive evaluations (e.g., Hsee & Abelson, 1991). Finally, higher order systems are capable of yielding far more complex cyclic behavior than the standard, first-order model and, from the perspective of empirical modeling, this complexity may be needed to adequately represent the cyclic complexity present in the focal phenomena of organizational science.

Higher order dynamic systems may be represented using Equation 1 by simply treating additional lagged state values as unique system states. To be concrete, a single variable system with p lags may be represented as:

$$y_t = a_1\, y_{t-1} + a_2\, y_{t-2} + \ldots + a_p\, y_{t-p} + b_t \quad (6)$$

or, more generally, in matrix form by stacking the lagged states as:

$$
\begin{bmatrix} y_t \\ y_{t-1} \\ \vdots \\ y_{t+1-p} \end{bmatrix}
=
\begin{bmatrix} a_1 & a_2 & \cdots & a_p \\ 1 & 0 & \cdots & 0 \\ \vdots & \ddots & & \vdots \\ 0 & \cdots & 1 & 0 \end{bmatrix}
\begin{bmatrix} y_{t-1} \\ y_{t-2} \\ \vdots \\ y_{t-p} \end{bmatrix}
+
\begin{bmatrix} b_t \\ 0 \\ \vdots \\ 0 \end{bmatrix}
\quad (7)
$$

In matrix form, the first row of the transition matrix, A, contains the vector of coefficients for the p lagged relationships, the entries below the primary diagonal are all 1.0, and all other values in the matrix are 0.0. The elegance of this representation is clear when the system is generalized to p lags of K variables. In this case, the dynamic system may be represented as:

$$y_t = A_1\, y_{t-1} + A_2\, y_{t-2} + , \ldots , + A_p\, y_{t-p} + b_t \quad (8)$$

where y_t and y_{t-i} are K-dimensional column vectors, the A_i are $K \times K$ coefficient matrices for each of the p lags, and b_t is an n-dimensional column vector. As above, this equation may also be represented in stacked, matrix form as:

$$
\begin{bmatrix} y_t \\ y_{t-1} \\ \vdots \\ y_{t+1-p} \end{bmatrix}
=
\begin{bmatrix} A_1 & A_2 & \cdots & A_p \\ I_n & 0_n & \cdots & 0_k \\ \vdots & \ddots & & \vdots \\ 0_n & \cdots & I_n & 0_k \end{bmatrix}
\begin{bmatrix} y_{t-1} \\ y_{t-2} \\ \vdots \\ y_{t-p} \end{bmatrix}
+
\begin{bmatrix} b_t \\ 0 \\ \vdots \\ 0 \end{bmatrix}
\quad (9)
$$

where I_K is a $K \times K$ identity matrix and 0_K is a $K \times K$ matrix of zeros. In this form, it becomes clear that the general transition matrix, A, becomes a partitioned matrix consisting of subtransition matrices that represent the relationships that exist among the K variables at each of the p lags.

Examples

At this point, the basic mathematics needed to understand multivariate dynamics are largely in place. The approach is extremely general, subsuming the entirety of linear random coefficient models and structural equation models as they are currently applied to longitudinal data. Example applications of the model are presented here to illustrate how these models can be used to study phenomena of central importance in the organizational sciences.

Leadership

Although a consensus definition of leadership remains elusive, many, if not most, leadership scholars agree that a key component of leadership is the process of influencing others to achieve goals (i.e., Northouse, 2007; Yukl, 2006). A multivariate dynamic model is uniquely suited to the study of complex patterns of influence that function over time as the process of leadership unfolds. In the following examples, assume that you have one leader and three followers, sorted as {L, F₁, F₂, F₃}. A transition matrix consistent with a strong leader who influences others on a variable and is not, in turn, influenced by his or her followers on the same variable might take the form of:

$$A = \begin{bmatrix} .90 & 0 & 0 & 0 \\ .31 & .60 & 0 & 0 \\ .30 & 0 & .60 & 0 \\ .33 & 0 & 0 & .60 \end{bmatrix} \qquad (10)$$

where the leader is the first person represented. In this case, a leader has three followers, and the leader exerts substantial downward influence on the followers, with little or no corresponding upward influence from the followers on the leader. This transition matrix consists of a single leader and only three followers. In actual use, the transition matrix used to represent leadership dynamics would likely be substantially larger and may incorporate more than a single leader with hierarchically clustered patterns of influence. Leader-member exchange (LMX) theory (e.g., Sparrowe & Liden, 2005) is a popular approach to leadership, positing that specific followers with high-quality relationships with the leader are able to exert substantial upward influence on the leader even as they, in turn, are influenced by the leader. The strong leadership transition matrix just presented can be easily modified to represent patterns of influence consistent with LMX theory. For instance, it may be the case that the third follower is able to reciprocally influence the leader. If so, the transition matrix might look something like the following:

$$A = \begin{bmatrix} .85 & .01 & .01 & .15 \\ .31 & .60 & .01 & .01 \\ .30 & .01 & .60 & .01 \\ .33 & .01 & .01 & .60 \end{bmatrix} \qquad (11)$$

In this case, the third follower has a small, but non-trivial, upward influence on the leader (a_{14} = .15). Many other transition matrices would be consistent with LMX theory and, as long as the absolute value of the largest eigenvalue associated with the transition matrix is less than 1.0, the influence dynamics will be stable. Finally, it should be emphasized that this process is easy to generalize beyond leadership to virtually all known forms of social influence (e.g., team mental models, team

efficacy perceptions, organizational safety climate) and easily encompasses French's dynamic models of social power (French, 1956.

Dynamic Mediation

Mediated relationships are one of the most commonly studied models in the organizational sciences. Unfortunately, these models are frequently described as a process that unfolds over time and yet they are studied using cross-sectional methods. The inferential problems resulting from this disconnect between the conceptualized process and the adopted research strategy are known and are nearly insurmountable (Maxwell & Cole, 2007). Dynamic mediation models do exist (e.g., Pitariu & Ployhart, 2010) but rely upon variants of random coefficient models as their foundation. As such, they suffer the same limitations present in all single equation models, largely centered on difficulties associated with reciprocal relations. In contrast, dynamic mediation models are easy to represent and evaluate in a system of dynamic equations using linear dynamic systems theory.

As an example, Pitariu and Ployhart (2010) examined a longitudinal mediation model where the relationship between team diversity and individual performance was mediated by individual effort expenditures. In their most complex model, individual effort and performance varied over time, but team diversity was conceptualized as a higher level variable that remained static. However, on many important variables, team diversity (e.g., mental models, attraction-selection-attrition models, workload distribution, experience) is expected to change over time, and it makes sense to conceptualize each of these variables as possibly varying over time. Using the dynamic system representation makes it possible to conceptualize many forms of increasingly complex and interesting forms of mediation. The simplest form of mediation is a unidirectional influence chain (i.e., full mediation). In the context of the example, this would mean that team diversity influences effort, and effort, in turn, influences performance. Assuming the variables are ordered as diversity, effort, and performance, then a dynamic transition matrix consistent with full mediation takes the general form of:

$$A = \begin{bmatrix} a_{11} & 0 & 0 \\ a_{21} & a_{22} & 0 \\ 0 & a_{23} & a_{33} \end{bmatrix} \qquad (12)$$

Alternatively, partial mediation takes place, in this example, when the coefficient, a_{31}, is meaningfully different from zero.

When modeling mediated relationships over time, a critically important issue to consider is the lag structure of the data that would be consistent with the temporal ordering implied by the model. The Pitariu and Ployhart (2010) approach to dynamic mediation implies simultaneous or contemporaneous causation. This is inconsistent with the dominant philosophy of causation, in which temporal ordering is a key component of a causal relation. The transition matrix above allows lagged relations and, as such, is more consistent with the implied temporal ordering of a mediated relationship. However, this transition matrix specifies that effort at time, t, is a function of team diversity at time, $t - 1$. This is as it should be. Unfortunately, the transition matrix also specifies that effort at time, $t - 1$, influences performance at the same time, $t - 1$. If the timing of measurement could be aligned with the timing of the dynamic mediated relationship under study, then a higher order model incorporating a second lag (e.g., Equation 8) is needed to adequately represent the dynamics implied by a dynamic mediation model.

Loosely Coupled Systems

As Orton and Weick (1990) boasted, the notion of a loosely coupled system is loosely defined and underspecified. This may be a reasonable perspective if the concept of loosely coupled systems is meant to serve as a thought experiment or a heuristic for organizational dynamics. This perspective is not desirable if the notion of a loosely coupled system is meant to be researched and understood. Glassman (1973) represented the degree of coupling between two systems with respect to the interdependent activity of the variables that the two systems share. According to Weick (1976), systems are loosely coupled when the elements in the systems are responsive to each other but retain evidence of separateness and identity. Although not clearly specified, dynamic processes are fundamental to the conceptualization of loosely coupled systems, These verbal representations of loose coupling can be translated into a simple, yet specific, mathematical representation using linear dynamic systems theory.

Loose coupling between systems can take many forms, such as: an asymmetric boundary spanning individual who influences one or more members in another system without being influenced by that system's members; or symmetric boundary spanning, where a member of one system influences one or more members in another system and is, in turn, influenced by the members of the other system and transmits this influence back to the members in his or her system. It is also easy to conceive of loosely coupled systems where multiple members in each system weakly influence each other in either symmetric or asymmetric ways. For the moment, assume that two organizational systems are loosely coupled with respect to a single variable, say the value of work-life balance, via an asymmetric boundary spanning individual in the first system who weakly influences all members in the second system. For didactic reasons only, further assume that each system consists of three (3) substantially equivalent individuals with respect to the value placed on work-life balance and the influence of a particular individual's value of work-life balance on the other system members' values of work-life balance. A transition matrix consistent with this system representation is:

$$A = \begin{bmatrix} .5 & .2 & .2 & 0 & 0 & 0 \\ .2 & .5 & .2 & 0 & 0 & 0 \\ .2 & .2 & .5 & 0 & 0 & 0 \\ .1 & 0 & 0 & .5 & .2 & .2 \\ .1 & 0 & 0 & .2 & .5 & .2 \\ .1 & 0 & 0 & .2 & .2 & .5 \end{bmatrix} \quad (13)$$

This system may easily be expanded to incorporate multiple dimensions of loose coupling across the systems by simply associating two or more states with each individual or unit. Astute readers will recognize that a loosely coupled system is a specific instance of a multilevel system, and this approach provides a vehicle for studying multilevel system dynamics.

Motivational Feedback Systems

In most, if not all, variants of psychological control theory (e.g., Carver & Scheier, 1998; Lord & Levy, 1994; Powers, 1973), perceived discrepancies between a current state and a goal state induce efforts to reduce the perceived discrepancy. The dynamics contained in this simple verbal description are represented graphically in Figure 4.4. The solid line connections (i.e., edges) in this figure represent single lag relations and so there is no need to provide a time subscript on the variables (i.e., nodes).

The curved arrow originating at a node and pointing to the same node represents an autoregressive, self-similarity effect for each variable. As an aside, additional line types (e.g., dashed, dotted) could be used to represent higher order lagged relations for more complex models. This figure highlights that a perceived discrepancy at the current time point, t, is positively related to effort expenditures in the immediately subsequent time point, $t + 1$. Further, effort at time t is negatively related to perceived discrepancies in the subsequent time point, $t + 1$. The result is a discrepancy-effort cycle with a negative feedback loop very much like a highly simplified version of thermostatic control of heat that occurs in a house. Assuming that the first state represents perceived discrepancies and that the second represents effort expenditures, a transition matrix consistent with this dynamic motivational process is:

$$A = \begin{bmatrix} a_{11} & a_{12} \\ -a_{21} & a_{22} \end{bmatrix} \qquad (14)$$

As shown above in Figure 4.3, whenever all the eigenvalues of the transition matrix are less than 1.0 in absolute value, the negative weight between effort and perceived discrepancies results in oscillatory system behavior, with decreasing amplitude over time as the system moves toward a stable equilibrium. The cycling of the system sets up a lead lag structure in the time series such that large perceived discrepancies precede large increases in effort that, in turn, precede smaller perceived discrepancies. Although simple, this example highlights the key features likely to be present in more complex motivational processes that include affect, goal setting, self-efficacy, and state variants of goal orientation (e.g., DeShon & Gillespie, 2005).

Stochastic Linear Dynamic Systems

The systems commonly encountered in the organizational sciences are internally complex and

fundamentally open to interactions with the environment in which the system exists. In terms of the state representation presented here, this means that any particular state is potentially determined by a multitude of dynamically coupled causes that are located both within the system and external to the system. While, in theory, it may be possible to represent the system using a massively complex deterministic model, in practice it is impossible to record and model each event that influences a particular state over time. Instead, a set of focal variables is selected for modeling, and the remaining unmeasured influences are treated as a combined source of error. Feasible modeling of system dynamics, then, shifts the focus from deterministic dynamics to stochastic dynamics.

Stochastic processes comprise a mature and a highly general domain of probability theory. Formal definitions of stochastic processes are now so general that they no longer convey the underlying notions that led to the development of the field. For current purposes, a stochastic process is the evolution of a trajectory, subject to random disturbances that occur at each point in time (Basu, 2003). The disturbances or perturbations are treated as random realizations from a distribution of possible values. Typically, the disturbances are assumed to be realizations of a normal distribution, and this is the only disturbance distribution considered here. Just as in traditional cross-sectional regression analysis, the value of a disturbance at a given time point is assumed to be a composite of all the unassessed variables and events that impact the state.

The notion of dynamic criteria provides an excellent example of a stochastic process that is important in the organizational sciences. The concept of dynamic criteria refers to the observed variability of individual work performance over time and the resulting decreased ability to predict (i.e., forecast) individual differences in work performance at increasingly distal, future time points (Barrett, Alexander, & Doverspike, 1992; Deadrick & Madigan, 1990). The observed performance dynamics results in the well-known simplex pattern of decreasing correlations over time such that performance instances that are close in time are more highly correlated than performance instances that occur further apart in time (Humphreys, 1960). It is now understood that dynamic criteria and the existence of the simplex correlational structure simply represent the functioning of a stochastic autoregressive process (Jöreskog, 1970; Rogosa & Willett, 1985). In general, an individual is more similar to

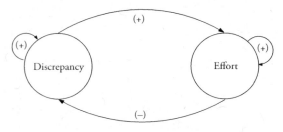

Figure 4.4 Graphic Representation of Self-Regulatory Dynamics

him- or herself at proximal time points than distal time points.

Figure 4.5 presents two possible performance trajectories that reflect from the same underlying autoregressive process, with the exception that one is deterministic and the other is stochastic. In both cases, the data were generated using the same autoregressive function with a difference in the value of a single parameter and an initial value of 4.0 ($SE_0 = 4.0$). The data-generating mechanism underlying both trajectories is $SE_t = .3 + .9SE_{t-1} + e_t$, where e_t is a random value sampled from normal distribution with a mean of zero. The smooth trajectory was generated with the variance of the errors set to zero, yielding, in effect, a deterministic process. The highly variable series was generated by setting the error variance to 0.0625 ($\sigma_e = .25$), yielding a stochastic, dynamic process. The smooth trajectory in Figure 4.5 appears to converge to a stable equilibrium. As discussed above, the stability of the autoregressive process may be determined by examining the absolute value of the transition matrix, A. In this case, the transition matrix contains only a single value, $a_{11} = .9$, The eigenvalue of a scalar equals the scalar itself, and so a stable equilibrium exists since the autoregressive weight is less than 1.0 in absolute value. Consistent with the smooth line in Figure 4.5, the actual equilibrium point is:

$$\frac{b}{1-a} = \frac{0.3}{0.1} = 3.$$

The highly volatile line in Figure 4.5 results from adding a simple stochastic process to the deterministic autoregressive process. The addition of this stochastic process results in added interpretational and statistical complexity. From an interpretation perspective, the volatility makes it difficult to discern the actual dynamics responsible for the trajectory. Despite the existence of a stable underlying performance process, it appears that performance is highly variable or even unstable. It also appears that something important may have happened around day 190, resulting in a large performance drop and a possible discontinuity in the system dynamics. In reality, this is simply the result of a random series of negative events that happened to occur in a sequential that "push" performance down over a period of time. If one has access to information detailing the negative events (i.e., predictor variables), then it may be possible to explain the run of decreased performance. In either case, the underlying dynamics remain constant.

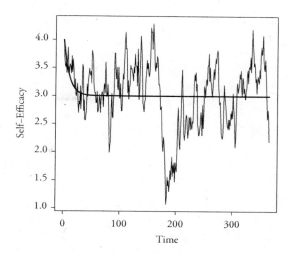

Figure 4.5 Deterministic and Stochastic Versions of an Autoregressive Process

From a statistical perspective, the transition to stochastics requires a fundamental shift in the representation of the system dynamics. In a deterministic system, once the starting point is specified, the resulting trajectory will be exactly identical, no matter how many times the system is examined. In other words, for a given parameterization and set of initial values, there is only a single trajectory in a univariate deterministic system, or a single set of trajectories in a multivariate deterministic system. In a stochastic system, the random shocks or system inputs represented by the error term result in distinct trajectories, and the pattern of random shocks determines the particulars of the system trajectories. Therefore, the same underlying system dynamics can result in an infinite set of possible system trajectories.

As a result, a particular trajectory is conceptualized as a random realization of a stochastic dynamic system, and the inferential focus shifts from characterizing a particular trajectory to characterizing the probability distribution of possible trajectories. Figure 4.6 presents a set of five independent trajectory realizations for the stochastic autoregressive system presented above for 100 time points. To increase the distinctiveness of the trajectories in this graph, the number of time points was reduced from 365 to 100 and the error variance was reduced from .0625 ($\sigma_e = .25$) to .0225 ($\sigma_e = .15$). Other than sharing a common starting point ($SE_0 = 4.0$) and maintaining roughly similar levels of self-efficacy over time, the small stochastic disturbances result in distinct trajectories that are not obviously a result of the same data-generating mechanism.

The right side of the graph in Figure 4.6 presents the marginal distribution of all observations. The error distribution responsible for the stochastics in this linear system is normally distributed and, therefore, so is the marginal distribution. More important, the eigenvalue associated with the transition coefficient is less than 1.0 in absolute value. In a deterministic system, this means that the system converges to a stable equilibrium. In a stochastic system, the corresponding result is that the moments of the marginal distribution associated with the stochastic process are invariant across time. If all moments of the marginal distribution are invariant over time, then the process is referred to as being strictly stationary. Usually it is sufficient to focus on the first two moments of the marginal distribution, and this weaker, but more common, condition is termed *weak* or *covariance stationarity*. The first two moments of the marginal distribution of the univariate autoregressive process described here are:

$$\mu_y = \frac{b}{1-a} = \frac{.3}{.1} = 3.00$$
$$\sigma_y^2 = \frac{\sigma_e^2}{1-a^2} = \frac{.0225}{.19} = 0.12 \qquad (15)$$

and these values are consistent with the empirical distribution presented on the right hand side of Figure 4.6. In brief, stationarity is to a stochastic system what stability is to a deterministic system. When the absolute value of the eigenvalues of the transition matrix are less than 1.0, a deterministic system is stable and a stochastic system is (covariance) stationary.

Despite the added stochastic complexity, the series depicted in Figure 4.6 are more "interesting" and certainly more consistent with the series observed in the organizational sciences. The consistency argument is obvious, but in what way are the series more interesting? A simple, univariate model was used to introduce the functioning of linear stochastic systems. With this knowledge we can now return to the multivariate system domain and more fully address the "interesting" aspects of stochastic series.

Using multivariate time series methods, Chan and Wallis (1978) studied the well-known population dynamics that exist between Canadian muskrat (prey) and mink (predator). This is obviously not an example from organizational science. However, the example is useful to communicate important stochastic principles because knowledge of predator-prey dynamics in the population ecology literature

Figure 4.6 Stochastic Realizations of a Univariate Autoregressive Process

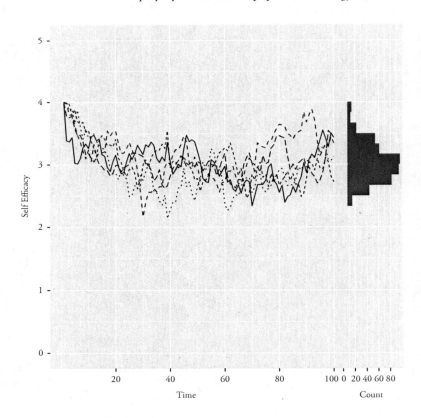

is highly developed, and it represents the stochastic dynamics that can occur in open systems. After detrending and transforming the 25-year population size series—a practice I do not recommend—Chan and Wallis (1978) estimated the bivariate transition matrix and found it to be:

$$A = \begin{bmatrix} 0.79 & -.68 \\ 0.29 & 0.51 \end{bmatrix} \qquad (16)$$

This transition matrix contains a negative relationship ($a_{12} = -0.68$) between mink population size at $t-1$ and muskrat population size at time t and a positive relationship ($a_{21} = 0.29$) between muskrat population size at time $t-1$ and mink population size at t. In essence, this sets up a positive feedback loop between the current muskrat population size and the mink population size the following year and a negative feedback loop between the current mink population size and the muskrat population size the following year. This is sensible because an abundance of muskrats can support a larger mink population, but a large mink population should result in a scarcity of muskrats. The deterministic system is stable and the stochastic system is stationary, as indicated by the eigenvalues of the transition matrix (0.65+0.42i and 0.65−0.42i). The existence of the negative sign in the transition matrix yielded

eigenvalues that are complex numbers, but the absolute value (i.e., modulus) of these eigenvalues is less than 1.0 (0.774 and 0.774).

Using the Chan and Wallis (1978) transition matrix, Figure 4.7 presents an abstracted representation of the muskrat-mink population dynamics for deterministic series (Panel A) and stochastic series (Panel B). The differences between the deterministic and stochastic versions of the same underlying dynamic process nicely illustrate the "interesting" aspect of the stochastic system relative to the deterministic system. Both the deterministic and stochastic multivariate time series are based on the same dynamic model. However, the linkage between the series is not obvious in the deterministic graph, where the trajectories quickly flatline at the system equilibrium. In contrast, the stochastic variant of the dynamic system shows a clear lead-lag structure that is consistent with the notion of dynamic cycles. As can be seen in Panel B of Figure 4.7, both series begin with declining population numbers. However, as the mink series continues to decrease, the muskrat series rebounds and starts a sharp increase in muskrat numbers. The mink series, lagging two to three years behind the muskrat series, then starts to increase in response to the muskrat munificence. Both series continue to increase until the mink numbers become too large, and then the muskrat numbers begin to decrease, followed soon

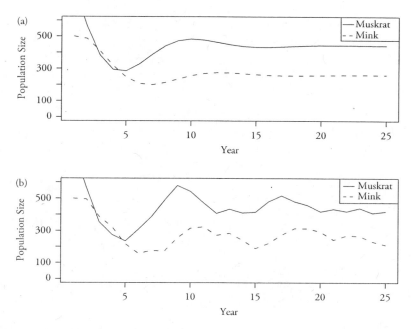

Figure 4.7 Deterministic and Stochastic Predator-Prey Dynamics for Muskrat and Mink

by decreasing numbers of mink. This basic pattern continues as long as the underlying population dynamics remain constant.

The stochastic version of the muskrat-mink population dynamics also highlights that the action is in the error term, and this is why errors are often referred to as innovations in the time series literature. The interesting dynamics in Figure 4.7 are the result of unmeasured and unmodeled events that influence one or both series directly and then have lagged dynamic effects as the event influences other series through the dynamics specified in the transition matrix. In essence, the transition matrix determines the system dynamics but the dynamics only shine through when the system is perturbed, the perturbations percolate through the system, and the system again and again counters the perturbations by moving back toward the mean of the stationary distribution.

Parameter Estimation and Model Interpretation

To this point, the presentation has relied upon known data-generating mechanisms to demonstrate interesting features of dynamic models. When working with dynamic models in practice, however, it is rare to have knowledge of the actual data-generating mechanism. A rich literature exists detailing various statistical approaches to the estimation of linear dynamic system parameters, the evaluation of model fit, and forecasting methods. These methods vary fundamentally with respect to the assumed or required knowledge about the underlying data-generating mechanism. The simplest place to enter into this literature is, without question, the multivariate or vector autoregressive model (VAR). The basic VAR model is deceptively simple and remarkably powerful. It requires little a priori knowledge about the underlying data-generating mechanism. As detailed below, the cost of this flexibility is that VAR models are often highly parameterized and suffer from all the standard problems associated with highly parameterized models in general (i.e., large confidence intervals and poor cross-validation).

The general form of a VAR may be represented as:

$$y_t = \mathbf{v} + \sum_{i=1}^{p} \mathbf{A}_i y_{t-i} + \varepsilon_t \qquad (17)$$

where K is the number of response variables being studied, p is the memory span (i.e., lag length) of the system under study, $\mathbf{v}$ is a $K \times 1$ vector of constant y-intercepts, $\mathbf{y}_t$ is a $K \times 1$ vector of response variables, $\mathbf{A}_i$ is a $K \times K$ matrix of transition coefficients for the ith lag, ε_t is a $K \times 1$ vector of errors (aka innovations), and $\mathbf{Y}_t$ is a $K_p \times 1$ vector of stacked response vectors yielding $(\mathbf{y}_t \cdots \mathbf{y}_{t-p-1})'$. After accounting for the serial dependence present in the data by including the lagged response variables in the model, the errors in ε are assumed to be serially independent and distributed $N[0, \Sigma]$. For reasons discussed later, the cross-equation errors at any time point cannot reasonably be treated as independent and so Σ is unstructured instead of diagonal. This is clearly a stochastic version of the general linear dynamic model presented in Equations 8 and 9.

In a standard vector autoregressive model, prior values of all response variables are used to predict current values of each response variable. To communicate a VAR model, then, only the order of the VAR (i.e., number of lags) needs to be specified. So, for instance, a VAR(2) with three response variables implies the following model:

$$y_t = \mathbf{v} + \mathbf{A}_1 y_{t-1} + \mathbf{A}_2 y_{t-2} + \varepsilon_t \qquad (18)$$

or, in expanded form:

$$
\begin{aligned}
y_{1_t} &= \mathbf{v}_1 + A_{1,11}\, y_{1_{t-1}} + A_{1,12}\, y_{2_{t-1}} + A_{1,13}\, y_{3_{t-1}} \\
&\quad + A_{2,11}\, y_{1_{t-2}} + A_{2,12}\, y_{2_{t-2}} + A_{2,13}\, y_{3_{t-2}} + \varepsilon_1 \\
y_{2_t} &= \mathbf{v}_2 + A_{1,21}\, y_{1_{t-1}} + A_{1,22}\, y_{2_{t-1}} + A_{1,23}\, y_{3_{t-1}} \\
&\quad + A_{2,21}\, y_{1_{t-2}} + A_{2,22}\, y_{2_{t-2}} + A_{2,23}\, y_{3_{t-2}} + \varepsilon_2 \\
y_{3_t} &= \mathbf{v}_3 + A_{1,31}\, y_{1_{t-1}} + A_{1,32}\, y_{2_{t-1}} + A_{1,33}\, y_{3_{t-1}} \\
&\quad + A_{2,31}\, y_{1_{t-2}} + A_{2,32}\, y_{2_{t-2}} + A_{2,33}\, y_{3_{t-2}} + \varepsilon_3
\end{aligned}
\qquad (19)
$$

With the model in hand, it is possible to describe the general process of conducting and interpreting a VAR analysis. The first step in any VAR analysis of a system is to carefully select the variables for inclusion in the analysis. Using theory and prior empirical results as a guideline, a limited set of variables believed to have strong dynamic interdependencies should be selected. If the data are archival, then you do the best with what you have available. If the data are going to be collected in the future, then a few issues are critical to the success of the analysis. First, the timing of measurement should be aligned with the anticipated cycles that exist in the system. For instance, affective reactions will likely need to be measured at a much higher frequency over a unit of time than organizational ROI. The number of repeated observations also places an upper limit on the information that you can extract from the data when studying a dynamic system. It is possible to conduct VAR analyses on short time series or intensive longitudinal data with only 5 to 10 observation periods. However, depending upon the amount of error in the system, 20 to 30 repeated observations are desirable (e.g., event sampling research) and 100 repeated observations would not be excessive. Once the variables have been selected and that data collected, a VAR analysis goes through a fairly routine set of steps, including the evaluation of stationarity, lag-length evaluation, parameter estimation, model fit evaluation, model interpretation, and, possibly, system forecasting. In the following, a running example investigating the relationship between self-efficacy and performance is used to illustrate each of these steps.

SELF-EFFICACY AND PERFORMANCE EXAMPLE

Self-efficacy and performance are thought to have positive reciprocal effects on one another such that high levels of performance boost subsequent self-efficacy, and current self-efficacy is thought to positively impact subsequent performance (Bandura, 1997). Many positive outcomes are attributed to this positive self-efficacy cycle. Recent longitudinal work, however, suggests that the robust, positive correlation between self-efficacy and performance found when using cross-sectional methods may not represent the functioning of the process within a person over time. In fact, recent work suggests that the relationship between self-efficacy and performance may be negligible or even negative (e.g., Schmidt & DeShon, 2010; Vancouver, Thompson, & Williams, 2001). This longitudinal work is based on standard random coefficient models, and different results may arise using more flexible models that allow for richer dynamics.

The data for this example are a single participant's self-efficacy ratings and performance scores over 50 time points. Participants in this data collection were asked to perform a temporary worker–hiring task in which the underlying performance model was governed by a four-arm bandit process (Puterman, 1994). Participants made 50 blocks of 50 employment decisions (2,500 decision trials) in which they chose to employ a worker from one of four temporary employment agencies. If the temporary employee was successful, they gained one point, and if the temporary employee was not, they gained zero points. Each company had a unique probability of success that remained static

throughout the experiment such that the same employment agency was the optimal choice across all 2,500 trials. Performance is the number of successful hires made in each block of trials. Before each block of trials, participants rated their self-efficacy for performing well on the subsequent trial by indicating how confident they were in reaching 10 different performance levels. Self-efficacy was then calculated by averaging across all these ratings, a method consistent with Vancouver et al. (2001) and Bandura (1997).

All analyses performed in this example were conducted using the free and powerful set of time series routines found in R, and the code used to perform the described analyses is presented in the Appendix. Figure 4.8 provides a graphic depiction of the self-efficacy and performance trajectories. The scaling of both variables is largely arbitrary, and the fact that self-efficacy ratings are larger than performance scores is not meaningful. Both series appear to be stationary over time with constant means and variances. There is a relatively large swing in the self-efficacy ratings that occurs around block 23, but it is not so large to be of concern. The co-movement of the series is of central importance. Looking at the trajectories, it appears that changes in performance lead to changes in self-efficacy. There is no obvious response of performance to changes in self efficacy. Visual inspection of the co-movements between trajectories is useful as a guide, but discerning underlying dynamic processes typically requires statistical analysis. The first step in moving forward, then, is to evaluate the stationarity of the series to determine whether a VAR analysis is appropriate.

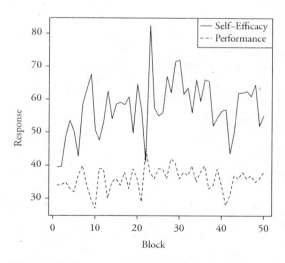

Figure 4.8 Performance and Self-efficacy Trajectories

STATIONARITY EVALUATION

The VAR model is primarily applicable to time series that are weakly (i.e., covariance) stationary or series that can be rendered covariance stationary by incorporating a determinist time trend. In practice, the model is often fit to non-stationary time series that have been differenced to remove stochastic trends. Alternative analyses exist to model non-stationary series directly, and fitting VAR(p) models to differences series is not a recommended practice (Harvey, 1989). Since stationarity is a precondition of performing a VAR(p) analysis, the evaluation of stationarity typically occurs immediately after data acquisition and cleaning. Numerous tests for time series stationarity exist, but the augmented Dickey-Fuller (ADF; Dickey & Fuller, 1979; Said & Dickey, 1984) test is, by far, the most commonly used. The ADF test is applied to each series separately by fitting the model:

$$\Delta Y_t = \alpha + \gamma Y_{t-1} + \sum_{i=1}^{p} \delta_p \Delta Y_{t-p} + \varepsilon_t \quad (20)$$

where Y_t is the time series, Δ is the difference operator such that $\Delta Y_t = Y_t - Y_{t-1}$, α is constant, $\gamma = 0$ is the null hypothesis of non-stationarity, p is the lag order of the autoregressive process, δ_p are the structural autoregressive effects, and ε_t is the error term. If the null hypothesis, $\gamma = 0$, is rejected, then the series is distinguishable from a non-stationary series. Because the ADF test includes lagged values of the response variable, the number of lags to include in the evaluation must be determined in some way. Including too few lags results in bias and inaccurate tests, and including too many lags decreases the power of the test. The lag structure of a time series is investigated by looking at the autocorrelation and partial autocorrelation functions, and it is common to select the lags using the Akaike information criterion (AIC) to select the best-fitting model. R includes the ADF in its set of analytical techniques as well as the autocorrelation and partial autocorrelation functions.

With respect to the self-efficacy and performance time series in the example, the ADF model allowing for the possibility of a deterministic trend was fit to the two time series. In both cases, the AIC indicated that only single lag was needed in the ADF test. The significance test on the γ parameter estimate is not distributed as a standard t-test and, therefore, the t-test is compared to critical values provided by Dickey and Fuller (1979). For the performance time series, $\gamma = -1.09$ with a *t*-test of -5.44. This value is larger than the critical value ($\alpha = .05$) of -3.50 and so the null hypothesis of non-stationarity is rejected. For the self-efficacy time series, $\gamma = -0.88$ with a *t*-test of -4.67. This value is larger than the critical value ($\alpha = .05$) of -3.50 and so the null hypothesis of non-stationarity is also rejected. Based on these results, it is reasonable to conclude that both series are stationary and the VAR(p) analysis can continue. If the data turned out to be non-stationary, then more advanced co-integration or structural model techniques are needed to model the linkages among the time series.

The ADF test is not a powerful test, and it is not uncommon to be unable to reject the non-stationarity hypothesis for series that are truly stationary. More powerful, but less well evaluated, methods now exist that attempt to overcome the power limitations of the ADF test. The most popular alternative among these newer tests is the ADF-GLS procedure developed by Elliott, Rothenberg, and Stock (1996). Since the ADF test rejected the null hypothesis of non-stationarity for both time series these more powerful alternatives are not needed.

LAG LENGTH EVALUATION

When the underlying data-generating mechanism is not known, it is difficult to specify the correct order for the VAR analysis. It is possible for a system to have a long memory such that states of one variable extending back through time over many periods influence current states on either the same variable or another variable. For instance, recurring sources of friction in social systems (e.g., dyads or teams) may function as long memory phenomena in which disagreements that occurred many time periods in the past can influence present disagreements and current reactions to the disagreements. Alternatively, it is possible that the impact of a variable's state on the future state of either the same variable or a different variable occurs after a number time periods have passed. So, for instance, if the state of one variable changes more quickly than the state of another variable, then time will pass before the slower changing variable impacts the changes in the faster changing variable. An example of this sort of dynamic process might occur in performance feedback systems where formal feedback is provided at a far less frequent rate than the actual dynamics that occur in daily, weekly, or even monthly performance. If performance updates on a monthly cycle and formal performance feedback is updated biannually, then there may be a six-month lag between feedback and performance.

Lag length selection is a tight wire balancing act. If too few lags are used, then important relationships will not be modeled and the resulting parameter estimates will be biased to an unknown extent. If too many lags are included, then an overabundance of parameters are estimated and the standard errors become large, thereby reducing power. The standard approach to this problem is to fit a large number of VAR models with the lag length (p) ranging from one to a large number. The maximum p varies with the expected dynamics of the process and the length of the time series included in the analysis. For long time series (e.g., $T > 30$), there is a maximum lag length of 10. The VAR lag length is then identified by choosing the value of p that minimizes one of many fit functions. The Akaike information criterion (AIC) is the most commonly used fit index, but the Schwarz-Bayesian (BIC) and the Hannan-Quinn (HQ) fit indices are often used for this purpose.

Table 4.1 presents the AIC, SB, and HQ fit indices for VAR analyses fit with lags (p) of one through five. Lags greater than five continued the clear trend of decreasing fit and are not presented. The minimum value for each fit index is in boldface font and, fortunately, all three indices agree that a single lag provides the best-fitting model. In the case of disagreements among the indices, the AIC is usually relied upon. Lutkepohl (2005) provides an in-depth treatment of the performance of the various lag-selection indices.

PARAMETER ESTIMATION

A highly attractive feature of the VAR model is the ease of estimating the unknown parameters. As Zellner (1962) demonstrated, the parameters in the simultaneous equation VAR model may be estimated using ordinary least squares (OLS) regression applied to each equation separately, with no loss of

efficiency relative to more complex generalized least squares methods. The OLS estimation of the system equation-by-equation is statistically consistent and asymptotically efficient. In fact, the equation-by-equation OLS estimation is also equivalent to the conditional maximum likelihood estimator (MLE; Hamilton, 1994). This means that it is possible to perform a VAR(p) analysis using any software that will perform OLS regression (e.g., Microsoft Excel) by simply forming new variables that are lags of the response variables and including the same set of lagged variables as predictors in each of the regression equations for the focal response variables. The maximum likelihood estimator of the error covariance, $\hat{\Sigma}$, is then computed by outputting the residuals from each regression equation into a $T \times K$ matrix, $\hat{e}$, and then computing, $\hat{\Sigma} = \frac{1}{T}\hat{e}'\hat{e}$. Of course, many software packages include special routines that make the analysis even simpler to implement, such as the VAR package in R (Pfaff, 2008).

Using R to perform a VAR(1) analysis of the self-efficacy data resulted in the following estimates:

$$SE_t = -17.36 \ (8.06) + 0.18 \ (.08) \ SE_{t-1} + 1.80 \ (.19) \ P_{t-1}$$
$$t = -2.16 \qquad t = 2.26 \qquad t = 9.48$$
$$P_t = 34.06 \ (6.19) + -0.03 \ (.06) \ SE_{t-1} + 0.11 \ (.15) \ P_{t-1}$$
$$t = 5.50 \qquad t = -0.54 \qquad t = 0.72$$

$$(21)$$

The estimated coefficients are presented in the first row of each equation, the standard errors for each parameter estimate are presented in parentheses directly below the corresponding coefficient, and the t-test for each coefficient is presented immediately below the standard errors. The degrees of freedom for each test are $(1, 46)$ and so values larger than 2.04 are statistically significant. The coefficients in the model are interpreted, just as in a cross-sectional regression such that the constant represents the y-intercept when time equals zero and the remaining coefficients are interpreted as partial slopes. To maintain consistency with the presentation above, the transition matrix for this model is

$$A = \begin{bmatrix} 0.18 & 1.8 \\ -.03 & 0.11 \end{bmatrix} \qquad (22)$$

with the vector of constants $v = [-17.36, 34.06]'$. The eigenvalues of the transition matrix are all less than 1.0 in absolute value and so the VAR(1) process is stationary.

Table 4.1 Fit Indices for Self-Efficacy VAR for $p \le 10$.

p	AIC	SB	HQ
1	**5.75**	**5.99**	**5.84**
2	5.77	6.17	5.92
3	5.85	6.41	6.06
4	6.00	6.72	6.27
5	6.13	7.01	6.46

Note: AIC = Akaike information criterion; SB = Schwarz-Bayesian criterion; HQ = Hannan-Quinn criterion

Interestingly, prior values of self-efficacy and performance are related to the current level of self-efficacy. In contrast, immediately prior values of self-efficacy and performance do not appear to be related to current performance for this individual performing this task. This within-person analysis of a single participant's data does not support the theorized relationship between self-efficacy and performance.

MODEL FIT EVALUATION

Before concluding that the data do not support the theoretical predictions of Bandura's (1997) self-efficacy theory and are inconsistent with the existing cross-sectional results on the correlation between self-efficacy and performance, it is important to evaluate the fit of the model. An advantage to using one of the developed VAR analysis software packages is that the log-likelihood of the data, given the model, is output by default. As in other maximum likelihood estimation procedures (e.g., SEM or HLM) the log-likelihood from two nested models can be compared using a chi-square statistic to evaluate whether a less constrained model fits better than a more constrained model. Only a single model was performed above, and so there is no need to use this test to evaluate the self-efficacy VAR analysis. If the lag-order statistics yielded more ambiguous results, then two or more models might be fit and compared using the log-likelihood chi-square.

Another way to evaluate the fit of the model is to examine whether the model assumptions are violated. It is assumed that the residuals from the VAR analysis are normally distributed and serially independent. The Jarque-Bera statistic (Jarque & Bera, 1987) provides a simultaneous test of the skewness and kurtosis of either the univariate residuals equation-by-equation or the multivariate residuals across all equations simultaneously. The null hypothesis for this statistic is that the residuals are normally distributed. For the bivaraite VAR(1) presented above, the Jarque-Bera $\chi^2_{(2)} = 0.18$, $p > .05$. The kurtosis and skewness of the univarite residuals can also be evaluated. Consistent with the multivariate evaluation, none of the univariate tests indicated a problem with the distribution of the residuals. A multivariate Portmanteau χ^2 provides an evaluation of the serial correlation remaining in the errors after fitting the VAR(p) model. Again, the null hypothesis is that there is no serial correlation. For the bivariate VAR(1) presented above, the adjusted (for small samples) Portmanteau $\chi^2_{36} = 35.36$, $p > .05$ indicated that there is no evidence of serial correlation.

Finally, the structure of the error covariance matrix provides useful information regarding possible model misspecification. Inference is least ambiguous when the errors are uncorrelated (diagonal structure). There are two primary reasons to find moderate to large correlations in the error structure. First, an unmodeled variable may be influencing or perturbing more than one response variable at the same time. This implies that the model is misspecified, resulting in the well-known problem with specification bias. Second, the VAR model is based on the implicit assumption that there is a temporal ordering to the influences between the variables in the system, and simultaneous cause-effect relations are not modeled. This is consistent with the philosophy of causation but may not be consistent with the relationships present in the data. If the measurement frequency is not aligned with the frequency of change in a discrete time system, then potentially important dynamics occur between measurement occasions, and it will appear as if there are concurrent relations in the data. Because these concurrent covariances are not captured in the VAR model, they appear in the structure of the error covariance matrix and result in a phenomenon known as simultaneity bias. Both of these possible sources of bias make inference somewhat ambiguous since the parameter estimates are biased to an unknown, and possibly unknowable, extent. For the VAR(1) analysis presented above, the variance-covariance matrix of the errors of the self-efficacy and performance equations, respectively, are:

$$\hat{\Sigma} = \begin{bmatrix} 22.83 & -1.19 \\ -1.19 & 13.47 \end{bmatrix} \quad (23)$$

The correlation between the residuals is easier to interpret, and for these data it is $-.07$. This small correlation lends further weight to the good fit of the VAR model and supports the inferences provided above.

MODEL INTERPRETATION

The apparent dynamics in the self-efficacy data are relatively simple. There are only two response variables, the error covariance is small, and only a single lag is needed to account for the serial dependence in the response process. Understanding the dynamics of more complex models is more challenging because perturbations or innovations percolate through the system across multiple lags, and so there may be a delay in the impact of a perturbation of one equation onto a different equation and the impact of a perturbation on one or more of the response variables may persist across many lags. Further, seemly small, non-significant relations may end up having non-trivial effects as the perturbations compound over lags. A number of interpretational aids have been developed to improve the understanding of complex system dynamics. In economics, researchers almost always ignore the estimated coefficients to the point of not even reporting them and move directly to the interpretational aids discussed here. The three most common interpretational aids are Granger causality evaluation, impulse response analysis, and forecast error variance decomposition. The first two of these interpretational aids are presented next.

GRANGER CAUSALITY

Finding little utility for empirical research in philosophical treatments of causality, Granger (1969) adapted Wiener's (1956) definition of causality to provide an operational definition of causality that can be evaluated via statistical analysis. Not surprisingly, this approach sparked substantial debate leading Granger (1980) to clarify and expand his operationalization of Wiener's theory of causality. To begin, let Ω_t be the entire universe of knowledge up to and including time, t. Let $\Omega_t - X_t$ be the entire universe of knowledge excluding only knowledge of the single variable, X, up to and including time t. Assuming that Y_{t+1} is a random variable, it can be represented as $Prob(Y_{t+1} \in A)$. Then X_t Granger-causes Y_{t+1} if:

$$Prob\,(Y_{t+1} \in A \setminus \Omega_t) \neq Prob$$
$$(Y_{t+1} \in A \setminus \Omega_t - X_t) \quad for\ some\ A \tag{24}$$

Since, in practice, the entire set of knowledge relevant to the prediction of Y at time t is never known, Granger-causality reduces to whether knowledge of a trajectory, X, up to and including time t is useful for predicting the value of another series, Y, at time $t + 1$.

The evaluation of Granger-causality is most straightforward in a bivariate VAR(p). In this case, Granger-causality simply implies that all the coefficients relating the p lags of one series to another series are equal to zero. Applying the Granger-causality tests to the self-efficacy and performance series suggests that performance Granger-causes self-efficacy ($F_{(1,92)} = 89.86$, $p < .05$) but that self-efficacy does not Granger-cause performance ($F_{(1,92)} = 0.28$, ns). So, knowledge of the current performance level is useful to the prediction of future

self-efficacy but current values of self-efficacy do not aid in the prediction of future performance.

Careful readers will notice that the Granger-causality tests are within rounding error of the t-tests provided in the VAR(1) results presented above. This relationship will not hold for $p \geq 2$. Readers interested in an example of evaluating Granger-causality with $p = 4$ may find entertaining Thurman and Fisher's (1988) evaluation of the age-old question of "Which came first, the chicken or the egg?" Finally, evaluating Granger-causality between three or more series is substantially more complex because of the numerous possible pathways that one series, X, may aid in the prediction of another series, Y, via indirect pathways through another series, Z (i.e., mediation).

IMPULSE RESPONSE ANALYSIS

An interesting and often useful way to evaluate the relationships among a set of times series is to introduce a perturbation into one of the series and observe the impact of the perturbation on the other series. This is particularly useful in high dimensional systems (i.e., $K > 2$) with multiple lags (i.e., $p > 1$), where discerning the patterns of influence is particularly challenging. In a sense, this is an empirical analog of a multivariate, interrupted time series design in which an event occurs at a specified time point, directed at changing the level of one of the series (e.g., teen smoking and anti-smoking advertising campaigns).

There are two questions that must be dealt with in this approach. First, how large a perturbation should one introduce into the system? Even a trivial relationship between system states can appear important if a large enough perturbation is introduced into the system. The standard is to use an impulse (i.e., perturbation) equal to either one unit or one standard deviation on the focal trajectory. Given the difference in scales that often exists in organizational data, the one standard deviation impulse will generally be the most useful approach in the organizational sciences.

The second question is more challenging, and it is useful to draw a loose analogy with a familiar concept in the organizational sciences. The relative importance of predictors in a regression model is a commonly desired inference (e.g., Johnson & LeBreton, 2004). This inference is reasonably easy to evaluate when the predictors in a regression equation are uncorrelated. However, when the predictors are correlated, it is very difficult to reasonably allocate importance across a set of partly redundant predictors. The same phenomenon occurs in VAR(p) models when the disturbances impacting the series are correlated. Examining the impact of a perturbing a state on the other system states is straightforward when the state perturbations (AKA disturbances or innovations) are uncorrelated over time. As is the case for relative importance inferences, when the errors across the series are correlated over time, the interpretation of impulse responses becomes murky. Lutkepohl (2005) provides an excellent account of the reasons for the murky inference.

The most commonly adopted approach for computing impulse response functions when errors are correlated is to transform the VAR(p) by orthogonalizing the error covariance matrix using a Choleski decomposition. This transformation decreases the ambiguity associated with the correlated errors by imposing a recursive structure on the instantaneous or contemporaneous relationships among the system states. The order of the variables entered into the VAR(p) analysis determines the recursive structure (i.e., chain of influence) of the instantaneous effects such that state 1 is not caused by any other states, state 2 is caused only by state 1, state 3 is caused directly by state 2 and indirectly by state 1 via the linkage to state 2, and so forth. Different orders imply different mappings on this causal chain and may result in different impulse response functions, depending upon the magnitude of the error correlations. If large error correlations exist, one should either rely upon strong theory to justify the specific model or great care should be taken when using the model to support inference.

With respect to the self-efficacy and performance VAR(p), the errors are not correlated to any

large extent, making the interpretation of impulse responses an easy task. Figure 4.9 provides a graphic depiction of the orthogonalized response of each state to a one standard deviation perturbation of the other state along with 95% bootstrapped confidence intervals. Panel A shows the response of the performance state to a perturbation of the self-efficacy state. Consistent with the results presented above, there is a hardly noticeable response to this perturbation, and the lower confidence interval always contains zero. In contrast, Panel B shows that self-efficacy shows a sharp response to a one standard deviation impulse applied to the performance state and that the impact of the perturbation persists at least for two, and probably three, lags.

EXTENSIONS OF THE VECTOR AUTOREGRESSIVE MODEL

The VAR model is at least 30 years old, and the research effort directed at it is intense and unrelenting. Lutkepohl (2005) is the standard reference for VAR models, and the fact that he devoted 764 pages to its description conveys, in part, the maturity and the complexity of the approach. The current presentation only scratches the surface of the strengths and limitations of the VAR(p) approach. Three extensions to the current approach do merit attention here.

First, it is easy to add predictors to the VAR(p) model yielding the VARX(p,s) model:

$$y_t = v + \sum_{i=1}^{p} A_i y_{t-i} + \sum_{i=0}^{s} \Phi_i X_{t-i} + \varepsilon_t \quad (25)$$

where s is the number of desired lags for the predictor variables, M is the number of included

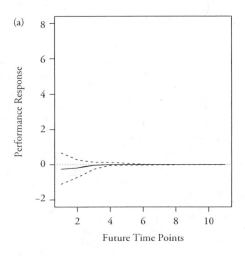

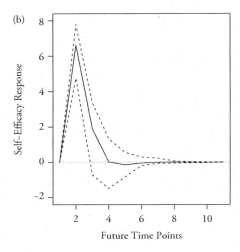

Figure 4.9 Impulse Responses for the Self-efficacy and Performance Trajectories

predictors, ϕ_i is a $K \times M$ matrix of coefficients for the predictors at lag s, $\mathbf{x}_{t-i}$ is a $M \times 1$ vector of predictors at time $t - i$ including the intercept terms, time trends, seasonal dummies, and any additional external variables thought to relate to the system dynamics, and the remaining terms are defined as above. Notice that, unlike the response variables, the predictor variables are allowed to have an immediate effect on the states at time t (i.e., $s = 0$). As long as each equation has the same set of lagged response variables and (possibly lagged) predictors, then OLS estimation of the parameters equation-by-equation remains efficient.

Second, the simplicity of using OLS regression is a desirable feature of the VAR(p) and VAR(p,s) models. However, the cost of using OLS is that each equation must have the same set of predictors, even if it is known or believed that particular predictors should not be in all equations. Large standard errors result from keeping predictors in the model that have no relation with the response variable. To limit the negative impact of keeping an overabundant number of predictors in each equation, it is possible to add linear equality constraints to the model, forcing specific coefficients to be equal to other coefficients or equal to a particular value such as zero. The benefit of using constraints in a VAR model become readily apparent when, for instance, one state has a long memory requiring many lags to model, but the other variables in the system are short-memory processes. The cost of using constrained estimation in a VAR or VARX model is that OLS is no longer efficient and GLS (generalized least squares) or SUR (seemingly unrelated regressions; Zellner, 1962) must be used to maintain efficient estimation.

The third issue dealing with single-subject estimation versus panel estimation requires far more attention than can reasonably be devoted here. Only a single participant's data contributed to the self-efficacy and performance example provided above. It is possible to estimate VAR(p) models for multiple units using panel VAR techniques (e.g., Canova & Ciccarelli, 2009) but, at this nascent stage of dynamic models in organizational science, it is likely premature to use these methods. So, how should dynamic models be estimated when multiple units provide multivariate time series data? At this time, the most reasonable path forward is to estimate the models separately for each unit, taking care to evaluate the appropriate number of lags for each analysis and check the model fit information to evaluate the adequacy of the fitted

model. Once the models are fit for each unit, the pattern of dynamics across units can be examined. In the unlikely case that the same VAR(p) model with reasonably similar parameter estimates fits well for all units, then the parameters can be averaged. This yields a pooled-mean estimator similar to, but less efficient than, the fixed effect estimates in a random coefficient model and provides information on the variability of the effects across units. If averaging is used, it is important to remember that relatively small differences in the transition matrix coefficients can yield qualitatively different dynamic patterns, and this is particularly so when coefficients vary about the zero point across units. The more likely case to observe is that the pattern of coefficients after estimating the models separately for each unit indicates distinct clusters of dynamic processes. In this case, it may be reasonable to average the coefficients across relatively homogenous units within each cluster and interpret the result. If neither of these cases is obtained, then interesting and almost certainly important information exists detailing the heterogeneity of dynamics across units. Explaining the reasons for the obtained heterogeneity is where the art in science comes into play.

Conclusion

The study of stochastic, linear dynamic systems has great promise for improving knowledge and theory in the organizational sciences. It is an exciting time to be involved in organizational research. I am optimistic that organizational scholars will add VAR methods to their analytic tool box and will begin to move out of the recursive models domain (e.g., SEM and random-coefficient models) and into the exploration of dynamic cycles, reciprocal relations, feedback loops, and the ebb and flow of processes over time. The focus here on linear systems may, at first, appear to be limiting. Chaos, catastrophe theory, and logistic maps are certainly appealing, but it seems prudent to avoid the sirens' call to chaos until the limits of linear systems theory have been identified and clear, non-linear functions exist for estimation. Even if non-linear systems are identified in organizational science, linear approximations of non-linear dynamic systems are often easier to understand and use, and they generally perform very well (e.g., Tomas-Rodriguez & Banks, 2003).

While I am optimistic about the future use of VAR methods in organizational research, the VAR model is only an entry into this fascinating literature, and it has many limitations. The VAR model has received intense scrutiny and use over the past 30 years in empirical economics. Despite the widespread popularity of this model in economics, many econometricians now believe that the knowledge gains attributable to this approach are, at best, meager. It is increasingly common for econometricians to use Zellner's modification of the VAR acronym and refer to the method as a "very awful regression." Population ecologists, on the other hand, seem to have faired better and are more favorably disposed toward the model in general. In either case, it is important to remember that inferring causation using observational data and fancy analyses is not a likely path to successful inference. At its root, a VAR(p) is a regression model and, as such, it shares the same set of well-known limitations with respect to causal inference. The potential reciprocal relations present in a VAR model also impose identification problems with respect to simultaneous causation, rendering the VAR model even less able to support strong causal inference. On the other hand, coupling a VARX(p) model with carefully timed measurements and experimental or quasi-experimental methods could provide a vehicle for powerful inference.

Author's Note

R. P. DeShon gratefully acknowledges the National Aeronautics and Space Administration (NASA, NNX09AK47G, S. W. J. Kozlowski, PI; R. P. DeShon, N. Schmitt, & S. Biswas, Co-Is) for support that, in part, assisted the composition of this chapter. Any opinions, findings, and conclusions or recommendations expressed are those of the author and do not necessarily reflect the views of NASA. Direct correspondence concerning this manuscript to: Richard P. DeShon, 306 Psychology Building, Michigan State University, East Lansing, MI 48824.

References

Bandura, A. (1997). *Self-efficacy: The exercise of control*. New York: W. H. Freeman.

Bandura, A., Ross, D., & Ross, S. A. (1961). Transmission of aggression through imitation of aggressive models. *Journal of Abnormal and Social Psychology, 63*, 575–582.

Barrett, G. V., Alexander, R. A., & Doverspike, D. (1992). The implications for personnel selection of apparent declines in predictive validities over time: A critique of Hulin, Henry, and Noon. *Personnel Psychology, 45*, 601–617.

Basu, A. K. (2003). *Introduction to stochastic process*. Oxford: Alpha Science International.

Bono, J. E., Foldes, H. J., Vinson, G., & Muros, J. P. (2007). Workplace emotions: The role of supervision and leadership. *Journal of Applied Psychology, 92*, 1357–1367.

Boulding, K. E. (1955). In defense of statics. *The Quarterly Journal of Economics, 69*, 485–502.

Caines, P. E. (1988). *Linear stochastic systems*. New York: John Wiley and Sons.

Canova, F, & Ciccarelli, M. (2009). Estimating multi-country var models. *International Economic Review, 50*, 929–961.

Carver, C. S., & Scheier, M. (1998). *On the self-regulation of behavior*. New York: Cambridge University Press.

Chan, W. Y. T., & Wallis, K. F. (1978). Multiple time series modeling: Another look at the mink-muskrat interaction. *Applied Statistics, 27*, 168–175.

Collins, L. M. (2006). Analysis of longitudinal data: The integration of theoretical model, temporal design, and statistical model. *Annual Review of Psychology, 57*, 505–528.

DeShon, R. P., & Gillespie, J. Z. (2005). A motivated action theory account of goal orientation. *Journal of Applied Psychology, 90*, 1096–1127.

Deadrick, D. L., & Madigan, R. M. (1990). Dynamic criteria revisited: A longitudinal study of performance stability and predictive validity. *Personnel Psychology, 43*, 717–744.

Dickey, D. A., & Fuller, W. A. (1979). Distribution for the estimators for autoregressive time series with a unit root. *Journal of the American Statistical Association, 44*, 427–431.

du Toit, S. H. C., & Browne, M. W. (2007). Structural equation modeling of multivariate time series. *Multivariate Behavioral Research, 42*, 67–101.

Elliott, G, Rothenberg, T. J., & Stock, J. H. (1996). Efficient tests for an autoregressive unit root. *Econometrica, 64*, 813–836.

Flytzanis, E. (1976). Linear dynamical systems. *Proceedings of the American Mathematical Society, 55*, 367–370.

French, J. R. P. (1956). A formal theory of social power. *Psychological Review, 63*, 181–194.

Fuller, J. A., Stanton, J. M., Fisher, G. G., Spitzmueller, C, Russell, S. S., & Smith, P. C. (2003). A lengthy look at the daily grind: Time series analysis of job stress and satisfaction. *Journal of Applied Psychology, 88*, 1019–1033.

Galor, O. (2007). *Discrete dynamical systems*. Berlin: Springer.

Glassman, R. B. (1973). Persistence and loose coupling in living systems. *Behavioral Science, 18*, 83–98.

Granger, C. W. J. (1969). Investigating causal relations by econometric models and cross-spectral methods. *Econometrica, 37*, 424–438.

Granger, C. W. J. (1980). Testing for causality: A personal viewpoint. *Journal of Economic Dynamics and Control, 2*, 329–352.

Hamilton, J. D. (1994). *Time series analysis*. Princeton, NJ: Princeton University Press.

Hankin, B. L., Fraley, R. C., & Abela, J. R. Z. (2005). Daily depression and cognitions about stress: Evidence for a trait like depressogenic cognitive style and the prediction of depressive symptoms in a prospective daily diary study. *Journal of Personality and Social Psychology, 88*, 673–685.

Hannan, E. J., & Deistler, M. (1988). *The statistical theory of linear systems*. New York: John Wiley & Sons.

Harvey, A. C. (1989). *Forecasting, structural time series models, and the kalman filter*. Cambridge, UK: Cambridge University Press.

Hertzog, C, Linderberger, U, Ghisletta, P, & vonOertzen, T. (2006). On the power of multivariate latent growth curve models to detect correlated change. *Psychological Methods, 11*, 244–252.

Hsee, C. K., & Abelson, R. P. (1991). The velocity relation: Satisfaction as a function of the first derivative of outcome over time. *Journal of Personality and Social Psychology, 60,* 341–347.

Humphreys, L. G. (1960). Investigations of the simplex. *Psychometrika, 25,* 313–323.

Jarque, C. M., & Bera, A. K. (1987). A test for normality of observations and regression residuals. *International Statistical Review, 55,* 163–172.

Johnson, J., & LeBreton, J. M. (2004). History and use of relative importance indices in organizational research. *Organizational Research Methods, 7,* 238–257.

Jöreskog, K. G. (1970). Estimation and testing of simplex models. *British Journal of Mathematical and Statistical Psychology, 23,* 121–145.

Lord, R. G., & Levy, P. E. (1994). Control theory: Moving from cognition to action. *Applied Psychology: An International Review, 43,* 335–367.

Louro, M. J., Pieters, R., & Zeelenberg, M. (2007). Dynamics of multiple-goal pursuit. *Journal of Personality and Social Psychology, 93,* 174–193.

Luenberger, D. G. (1979). *Introduction to dynamic systems: Theory, models, and applications.* New York: John Wiley and Sons.

Lutkepohl, H. (2005). *New introduction to multiple time series analysis.* Berlin: Springer-Verlag.

MacCallum, R. C., & Austin, J. T. (2000). Applications of structural equation modeling in psychological research. *Annual Review of Psychology, 51,* 201–226.

Maxwell, S. E., & Cole, D. A. (2007). Bias in cross-sectional analyses of longitudinal mediation. *Psychological Methods, 12,* 23–44.

McArdle, J. J., & Nesselroade, J. R. (2003). Growth curve analysis in contemporary research. In J. A. Schinka, W. F. Velicer & I. B. Weiner (Eds.), *Handbook of psychology: Research methods in psychology* (Vol. 2, pp. 447–480). Hoboken, NJ: Wiley.

Northouse, P. G. (2007). *Leadership: Theory and practice* (4th ed.). Thousand Oaks, CA: Sage.

Orton, J. D., & Weick, K. E. (1990). Loosely coupled systems: A reconceptualization. *Academy of Management Review, 15,* 203–223.

Pfaff, B. (2008). VAR, svar and svec models: Implementation within r package VARs. *Journal of Statistical Software, 27,* 1–32.

Phillips, P. C. B. (2005). Challenges of trending time series econometrics. *Mathematics and Computers in Simulation, 68,* 401–416.

Pitariu, A. H., & Ployhart, R. E. (2010). Explaining change: Theorizing and testing dynamic mediated longitudinal relationships. *Journal of Management, 36,* 405–429.

Powers, W. T. (1973). *Behavior: The control of perception.* Chicago: Aldine de Gruyter.

Puterman, M. L. (1994). *Markov decision processes: Discrete stochastic dynamic programming.* Hoboken, NJ: John Wiley & Sons.

Raudenbush, S. W. (2001). Comparing personal trajectories and drawing causal inferences from longitudinal data. *Annual Review of Psychology, 52,* 501–525.

Rogosa, D., & Willett, J. B. (1985). Satisfying a simplex structure is simpler than it should be. *Journal of Educational Statistics, 10,* 99–107.

Rosen, D. von. (1991). The growth curve model: A review. *Communications in Statistics: Theory and Methods, 20,* 2791–2822.

Said, S. E., & Dickey, D. A. (1984). Testing for unit roots in autoregressive-moving average models of unknown order. *Biometrika, 71,* 599–607.

Schmidt, A. M., & DeShon, R. P. (2010). The moderating effects of performance ambiguity on the relationship between self-efficacy and performance. *Journal of Applied Psychology, 95,* 572–581.

Short, J. C., Ketchen, D. J., Bennett, N, & duToit, M. (2006). An examination of firm and industry effects on performance using hierarchical linear modeling. *Organizational Research Methods, 9,* 259–284.

Sparrowe, R. T., & Liden, R. C. (2005). Two routes to influence: Integrating leader-member exchange and network perspectives. *Administrative Science Quarterly, 50,* 505–535.

Thurman, W. N., & Fisher, M. E. (1988). Chickens, eggs, and causality, or which came first? *American Journal of Agricultural Economics, 70,* 237–238.

Tomas-Rodriguez, M., & Banks, S. P. (2003). Linear approximations to nonlinear dynamical systems with applications to stability and spectral theory. *IMA Journal of Mathematical Control and Information, 20,* 89–103.

Vancouver, J. B., Thompson, C. M., & Williams, A. A. (2001). The changing signs in the relationships among self-efficacy, personal goals, and performance. *Journal of Applied Psychology, 86,* 605–620.

Walls, T. A., & Schafer, J. L. (2006). *Models for intensive longitudinal data.* New York: Oxford University Press.

Weick, K. E. (1976). Educational organizations as loosely coupled systems. *Administrative Science Quarterly, 21,* 1–19.

Wiener, N. (1956). The theory of prediction. In E. F. Beckenbach (Ed.), *Modern mathematics for engineers* (Vol. 1, pp. 165–190). New York: McGraw-Hill.

Yukl, G. (2006). *Leadership in organizations* (6th ed.). Upper Saddle River, NJ: Pearson-Prentice Hall.

Yule, G. U. (1926). Why do we sometimes get nonsense correlations between time-series? A study in sampling and the nature of time series. *Journal of the Royal Statistical Society, Series A, 89,* 1–69.

Zellner, A. (1962). An efficient method of estimating seemingly unrelated regressions and tests for aggregation bias. *Journal of the American Statistical Association, 57*(e), 348–368.

Appendix

R code used to examine self-efficacy and performance dynamics

LOAD VAR SOFTWARE PACKAGE AND READ IN DATA
```
library(vars)
df <- as.ts(read.csv('Sub524.csv'))
```

PLOT THE TWO SERIES ON THE SAME GRAPH
```
plot(df, plot.type='single', ylab='Response', xlab='Block', lty=1:2)
legend("topright", c("Self-Efficacy","Performance"), cex=0.8, lty=1:2)
```

ADF TESTS OF NON-STATIONARITY
```
perf.adf <- ur.df(df$perf, type='trend', selectlags='AIC') summary(perf.adf)
se.adf <- ur.df(df$se, type='trend', selectlags='AIC') summary(se.adf)
```

SELECT VAR LAG LENGTH
```
VARselect(df, lag.max=5, type='const')
```

ESTIMATE THE VAR(1) MODEL
```
M1 <- VAR(df, p=1)
summary(M1)
```

MODEL FIT EVALUATIONS
```
normality.test(M1, multivariate.only=TRUE)
serial.test(M1, lags.pt=10, type='PT.adjusted')
```

GRANGER CAUSALITY EVALUATION
```
causality(M1, cause='SE')
causality(M1, cause='Performance')
```

IMPULSE RESPONSE FUNCTIONS AND GRAPHS
```
plot(irf(M1, impulse='SE', response='Performance'), main='(A)', sub="Future Time Points", ylim=c(-2,8))
plot(irf(M1, impulse='Performance', response='SE'), main='(B)', sub="Future Time Points", ylim=c(-2,8))
```

Individual Differences: Challenging Our Assumptions

Ann Marie Ryan *and* Paul R. Sackett

Abstract

Organizational psychologists often make assumptions regarding the variability and stability of individual differences (e.g., ability, personality, interests). In this chapter, we discuss the evidence regarding interindividual variability in individual differences in workplace contexts, intraindividual stability in individual differences across adult working years, and intraindividual variability across attributes (e.g., variability across a profile of ability or personality characteristics). We highlight the ways in which mistaken assumptions may affect conclusions regarding the predictive and explanatory power of individual differences, and we provide suggestions for research to enhance understanding of the variability and stability of commonly assessed individual differences.

Key Words: Individual differences, intraindividual stability, intraindividual variability, range restriction, interindividual variability

Individuals vary in ways that enable us to describe, predict, and understand their behavior and attitudes. Ackerman and Humphreys (1990) distinguished three varieties of individual differences: interindividual differences (differences between individuals), intraindividual differences in a given characteristic over time (e.g., trait stability), and intraindividual differences between attributes (e.g., profiles). They noted that examination of these individual differences is fundamental to many areas of organizational psychology: selection focuses on interindividual differences; training focuses on intraindividual differences over time; and classification, coaching and development of employees relates to intraindividual differences across attributes. In this chapter, we build upon their discussion of individual differences to point to progress and needed research.

We deliberately avoid a summary review of types of individual differences typically studied by organizational psychologists and their usefulness in predicting and understanding behavior—much has been written already to summarize this research. Our focus instead is on challenging the assumptions underlying approaches to research on individual differences in organizational settings. In this chapter, we argue that when researchers examine the role of individual differences such as abilities, personality traits, or interests in organizational psychology, they make assumptions regarding the variability and stability of those differences in the work context that are not always viable. Specifically, organizational psychology researchers often assume that there is interindividual variability in differences in a work setting when assessing the usefulness of those differences for prediction or for explanation, without questioning that assumption. Second, researchers assume that the differences examined are relatively stable over time and situations within individuals, without any evidence regarding the tenability of that assumption. Third, assumptions that are made regarding covariability, or lack thereof, of individual differences in specific contexts also should be examined. Our aim in this chapter is to call the reader's attention to these assumptions and to push researchers and practitioners to question them each time that conclusions are made about the predictive or explanatory value of individual differences in a domain of study. That is, before generic statements are made that "characteristic X" would or would not be useful in selection, should be considered or can be ignored in training program design, contributes or does not contribute to leader or team effectiveness, or detracts from or contributes to the usefulness of workplace motivational interventions, responsible organizational psychologists should address the viability of these assumptions in the particular context under study.

In this chapter, we will review literature on whether there is support for assumptions of interindividual variability, intraindividual stability over time, intraindividual stability over situations, and intraindividual differences across characteristics. We will discuss the ways that these assumptions are typically addressed in organizational psychology, and we conclude with a research agenda regarding what we see as critical areas for advancing our understanding of the role of individual differences in the workplace.

Assumptions of Interindividual Variability

A fundamental assumption of differential psychology is that there is sufficient variability across people in a given individual difference variable to be of potential interest in predicting and understanding behavior. That is, the traditional focus of differential psychology is differences among persons (Nesselroade, 2002). One concern in research on individual differences in the workplace is that we do not always investigate or clearly specify the extent of variability of an attribute with respect to a population of interest. That is, we can point to examples in which researchers and practitioners have assumed greater between-individual variability than is present, as well as cases in which erroneous assumptions with regard to range restriction led to mistaken conclusions about the explanatory power of an individual difference.

As a primary example, there has been considerable debate over time in the extensiveness of range restriction in selected applicant and incumbent samples on individual differences relative to the general population (for a recent debate example, see Schmidt, Le, Oh, & Shaffer, 2007; Schmitt, 2007). The general question is: To what extent are those working or applying to work at an organization less variable in a particular individual difference than the general working population? The answer to this question affects our conclusions regarding the value of individual differences in explaining behavior and attitudes at work. As another example of the importance of careful consideration of range restriction, typical effect sizes found for dichotomous moderators are quite small (Aguinis, Beaty, Boik, & Pierce, 2005). While most individual differences are continuous variables, some have suggested that range restriction is the reason that there is often a failure to find strong effects for hypothesized moderators (Schneider, 2001). Knowing the extent of range restriction operating in a given context has consequences for interpreting the accuracy of effect sizes for individual difference moderators.

We want to emphasize that there are two major reasons that the people who join an organization may be more homogeneous than the workforce as a whole. The first is decisions by individuals, such as whether to enter a given occupation or to apply for a given job; the second is decisions by organizations, such as the imposition of test cutoffs that must be exceeded as a prerequisite to organizational entry. Both restrict the range of individuals found within a given organization. We return to this distinction after discussing three streams of research, which are pertinent to the question of how much interindividual variability exists in the workplace, on key individual difference constructs: the gravitational hypothesis, the attraction-selection-attrition (ASA) model, and range restriction corrections in selection contexts.

First, there is research showing that there is some gravitation toward certain jobs of individuals with certain interests and skills, and therefore less variability in those aspects among jobholders than in the general population (Furnham, 2001). Wilk, Desmarais, and Sackett (1995) found support for this hypothesis in that those whose cognitive ability was greater than the cognitive complexity of their current job tended to move into jobs with higher cognitive requirements, while those whose ability was lower than the cognitive complexity of their current job tended to move to jobs requiring less cognitive ability over a five-year period. They also found that longer tenure groups were more homogenous in cognitive ability than those with less experience, although differences were small. Wilk and Sackett (1996) extended this work with a longitudinal study.

With regard to gravitation and interests, there is considerable research to suggest that interests affect occupational choice. Indeed, Holland's (1997) popular vocational model (RIASEC) is based on the existence of mean differences in interests across occupations. However, the amount of resulting restriction in levels of interest within occupational groupings is less well documented. Further, Laing, Swaney, and Prediger (1984) noted that across many studies, expressed choice is a better predictor of occupation than measured interests, presumably because one's choice of career is based on factors beyond interests, such as abilities, job availability, and social influences. This suggests that variability in interests within occupation may still be substantial. Finally, Deng, Armstrong, and Rounds (2007) noted that the restriction in the occupations that were used to develop Holland's (1997) model (e.g., less variability in prestige than is present in the U.S. workforce) may have led to a limited view of the structure of interests. Studies of the role of interests in the workplace may be less informative if there is restriction in the occupations included. In sum, research on gravitation suggests that there is less interindividual variability in ability and interests within occupations relative to the general working population.

Second, Schneider's (1987) ASA theory suggests that over time, homogeneity in personality characteristics occurs in organizations because of the attraction of people possessing certain characteristics, the selection of people possessing those characteristics, and the attrition of those who do not fit. Several studies have found evidence of organizational mean differences in the personality characteristics of managers (Schaubroeck, Ganster, & Jones, 1998; Schneider, Smith, Taylor, & Fleenor, 1998). Schneider, Goldstein, and Smith (1995) summarized evidence of personality homogeneity in organizations and concluded that indirect research on person-environment fit (e.g., Judge & Bretz, 1992), lab studies of paper organizations (e.g., Turban & Keon, 1993), and a few field studies (e.g., Jordan, Herriott, & Chalmers, 1991) suggested support for the ASA model, although the extent of variability reduction is unclear.

Further, when looking at how a construct manifests itself at different levels (such as personality at the individual and organizational unit level), one needs to clarify what type of emergence leads to the higher level variable (Kozlowski & Klein, 2000). Ployhart, Weekley, and Baughman (2006) clarified that the ASA model of personality emergence suggests a *consensus model*, or similarity within units, as represented by the mean level of personality of a unit. That is, personality of a unit is defined as the mean level of a characteristic in that unit. This has been the focus of previous ASA research (Jordan et al., 1991; Schaubroeck et al., 1998; Schneider et al., 1998). However, there are other aspects of personality clustering that should be considered. Ployhart et al. (2006) note that one can also look at a *compilation model* and examine the variance in a unit rather than or in addition to looking at consensus. They suggest that this conceptualization of homogeneity would be more meaningful in understanding the positive and negative consequences of homogeneity over time than the examination of mean differences, as is typically undertaken. Also, Ployhart et al. (2006) found that these ASA processes operate in a hierarchical manner such that effects are stronger at the job than the organizational level. Indeed, Satterwhite, Fleenor, Braddy, Feldman, and Hoopes (2009) found incumbents to be more similar within occupations than within organizations. Similarly, Schaubroeck et al. (1998) noted the importance of distinguishing levels, as their findings suggested that attraction and selection effects at the occupational level may compensate or may be in opposition to effects at the organizational level.

In sum then, there is some research evidence, albeit primarily indirect, to suggest mean differences in personality levels across organizations, and this is often taken as evidence of less personality variability within organizations than in the general working population. However, the variance in personality of units is typically not explicitly examined, the size of effects is unclear, and careful attention has not been given to effects at different levels (i.e., restriction at organizational and occupational levels).

The need to consider levels at which restriction occurs can also be seen in work on individual differences and teams. While range restriction of individual differences at the team level has not been a focus of research, the variability and level of individual differences in groups has been linked to group effectiveness. For example, teams with higher levels of cognitive ability adapt to unforeseen change better (LePine, 2003, 2005), learn more (Ellis et al., 2003), and perform better (LePine, Hollenbeck, Ilgen, & Hedlund, 1997). A meta-analysis found that teams with higher levels of and less variability in agreeableness and conscientiousness perform better (Peeters, Van Tuijl, Rutte, & Reymen, 2006). For example, Barrick, Stewart, Neubert, and Mount (1998) found that the score of the team member lowest on conscientiousness and agreeableness was related to team performance. Thus, there is research to suggest that restrictions in individual difference variability are related to team effectiveness; whether teams that are more variable become poorer performers and are thus less likely to continue to exist (i.e., poor performing teams disband, are reconstituted, etc.) is unclear.

The third research stream that sheds light on how much interindividual variability there is in the workplace is on range restriction corrections when estimating the validity of various individual difference measures in selection contexts. Sackett and Yang (2000) noted that because range restriction can result in major differences between population and restricted sample correlations, it is imperative that attention be paid to the appropriate use of corrections. For example, Schmidt, Oh, and Le (2006) demonstrated that correcting for direct range restriction when indirect restriction is occurring (i.e., on another individual difference) has led to underestimates of relationships in many areas.

While this research clearly demonstrates that one would be remiss to ignore range restriction, other research shows that intuitive assumptions regarding the *levels* of range restriction typically occurring due to self-selection may be off base. For example, Sackett and Ostgaard (1994) noted that while many believe applicant pools for particular jobs are less variable in ability than the workforce as a whole due to the gravitation hypothesis and ASA processes, differences between occupation-specific applicant pools and national samples are not particularly large. They found that standard deviations for ability tests were 3% smaller for occupation-specific pools than national norms and 10% smaller for jobs of greater complexity. These findings suggest that assumptions regarding less interindividual variability in cognitive ability among applicants than among the population as a whole are correct but should be tempered.

Similar concerns have been raised regarding whether the level of range restriction that occurs for personality measures is less than the level that traditionally has been assumed to occur when comparing applicant-specific pools versus population norms (e.g., Anderson & Ones, 2003). While Ones and Viswesvaran (2003) did find that job-specific applicant pools were less variable than population norms would suggest (from 2–9% less, depending on the dimension examined), they also concluded that job applicant pools are not drastically homogeneous.

Sackett and Ostgaard (1994) did note that there may be situations that do have greater range restriction, a point illustrated by Kuncel and Klieger (2007), who found school-specific applicant standard deviations to be 23% smaller than population estimates in a law school admissions context where scores and acceptance rates are known by individuals prior to application. Hence, our understanding of likely levels of interindividual variability needs to be informed by frameworks of what factors lead to range restriction and assessment of their operation in specific contexts.

Returning to our earlier point about reductions in interindividual variability due to both self-selection and organizational selection, we offer the general proposition that while self-selection clearly does take place (e.g., gravitational processes), the evidence reviewed above shows that the reduction in variance on individual difference measures due to these processes is relatively modest. In contrast, organizational selection has the potential to reduce variance far more substantially. An organization with a large applicant pool and a very favorable selection ratio could screen in, say, the top 1% on some individual difference measure, thus effectively reducing variance on that characteristic to near zero. We are not persuaded that self-selection processes reduce variability on individual difference variables of interest to an extent that negates the value of using individual difference variables in selection systems.

In addition, while organizational selection on variables correlated with individual differences does reduce variance on the individual difference measure, we believe that it is common to overestimate the degree of this reduction. For example, it is not uncommon to hear assertions that since a college degree is a requirement for job, that requirement restricts the range of cognitive ability to such an extent that there is no value in attempting to further screen using ability. Berry, Gruys, and Sackett (2006) document a correlation of .63 between cognitive ability and educational attainment in a nationally representative sample: using the formula for the standard error of estimate in using educational attainment to estimate ability, we find that in z-score terms an ability SD of 1.0 in an unscreened sample would be reduced to .78 in a sample screened on educational attainment. Substantial ability variance clearly remains.

In sum, the study of individual differences in the workplace assumes that individuals differ. Entry into the workplace leads to restrictions in this variability. The research reviewed above indicates that there is reduced interindividual variability at several levels in occupations, in specific jobs, in organizations, and possibly in work groups relative to the general population in abilities and personality characteristics due to self-selection. However, it is also clear that these reductions in variability may not be large (Sackett & Ostgaard, 1994; Ones & Viswesvaran, 2003). Further, restrictions due to organizational selection processes could, in theory, be much more substantial, depending on selection ratios, tools used, and so on. Hence, correcting for range restriction in estimating the validity of individual difference predictors is essential. Many studies involving individual differences are not focused on the validity of predictors, take place outside selection contexts, and draw samples from a single organization or single job category. It is important that the effects of range restriction on the conclusions of these studies also be considered—in some cases, restrictions in interindividual variability may be negligible, but in others they may be quite substantial. Thus, assumptions regarding interindividual variability in individual differences should be tested rather than taken for granted.

Assumptions of Intraindividual Stability Over Time

A second assumption underlying individual difference research in the workplace is that there is some stability within people over time and across situations in their standing on the variable of interest. There are two kinds of differences that have received attention in assessing this assumption: *intraindividual change*, or *trait changes* over time due to processes such as maturation and learning (i.e., changing intraindividual mean), and *intraindividual variability, or state variation*, which relates to rapid and reversible changes around the intraindividual mean (Hamaker, Nesselroade, & Molenaar, 2006). We discuss the first in this section and the latter in the next.

While there has been considerable investigation of stability of individual differences from childhood to adulthood (Roberts & DelVecchio, 2000; Roberts, Walton, & Viechtbauer, 2006), organizational psychologists are interested in stability over the prototypical working years (i.e., 16–65) and across prototypical work situations (i.e., not family or leisure settings). A historical interest in intraindividual change over time (e.g., Cattell, 1963) has been supplemented in recent decades by advancements in longitudinal modeling techniques, such as latent growth curve modeling and time series analyses, that allow for examining this stability (see Nesselroade, 2002, for an overview).

Investigation of individual difference stability over time can take several forms (Lockenhoff

et al., 2008). First, and most common, is examining rank-order consistency (test-retest reliability estimates). Second, changes in group mean levels over time can be examined. Third, some researchers have looked at ipsative stability or the consistency of an individual's trait profile over time. Fourth, measurement invariance over time may be examined. Finally, some researchers have created indices to examine individual-level stability (e.g., when there is no change at the group level but individuals are moving in different directions).

What do we know about the stability over time of individual differences? With regard to *abilities*, Ackerman and Humphreys (1990) summarized findings on training and learning and noted that while there is evidence of plasticity in lower order abilities (e.g., short term memory capacity, reading), there is also evidence of limitations in intraindividual changes in task performance that can be gained from training. During early working years, one might expect some changes in cognitive abilities; fluid intelligence appears to peak at about age 22 and crystallized intelligence at about age 36 (McArdle, Ferrer-Caja, Hamagami, & Woodcock, 2002). After that, research suggests relative stability in cognitive abilities until declines in some abilities in later adulthood (i.e., over 65; Caskie, Schaie, & Willis, 1999; Finkel, Reynolds, McArdle, Gatz, & Pedersen, 2003). However, domain-specific knowledge can increase into late adulthood (see Reeve & Hakel, 2000, for a review). Also, research suggests increasing dispersion or within-person variability across cognitive tasks with advancing age (Hilborn, Strauss, Hultsch, & Hunter, 2009).

In sum, while cognitive abilities are relatively stable across one's working years, there should not be an assumption of no change over time. Increases in early adulthood and declines in later adulthood should be factored into our theories regarding cognitive ability and performance, as well as into our estimates of effects of various training and development interventions that presume a certain consistency in levels of cognitive ability.

With regard to *personality*, Blonigen, Carlson, Hicks, Krueger, and Iacono (2008) summarized and replicated the research that suggests there is moderate to strong rank-order stability from late adolescence across the lifespan for almost all personality traits (e.g., Donnellan, Conger, & Burzette, 2007; Roberts, Caspi, & Moffitt, 2001). There are also different individual-level change patterns such that those who are most mature in late adolescence show less change than those who are less well-adjusted

(Donnellan et al., 2007; Roberts et al., 2001). However, Roberts and Mroczek (2008) recently noted that there has been a reevaluation of statements regarding the level of stability of personality in adulthood, with researchers now concluding that personality continues to change throughout adulthood. In particular, individuals tend to increase in agreeableness, emotional stability, and conscientiousness from young adulthood to middle age, and show declines in openness in old age, with most change occurring between the ages of 20 and 40 (Roberts & Mroczek, 2008). Further, Jackson et al. (2009) showed that while studies suggest conscientiousness increases a full standard deviation from young adulthood through old age, these changes are not uniform across facets of conscientiousness (e.g., orderliness does not change, industriousness increases from young to middle adulthood only). They also demonstrated that self-reports of personality reflect changes in young adulthood that are not reflected in observer evaluations of personality until older age (i.e., people report that they have changed before others notice that they have changed).

Thus, for most working adults, we can expect that their standing on personality traits is likely to be stable, but there will be movement toward what is generally described as social maturity (Wood & Roberts, 2006). Further, some evidence exists that work experiences are associated with changes in personality (Roberts, 1997; Roberts, Caspi, & Moffitt, 2003) such that those experiencing more success and satisfaction in careers increase more in emotional stability and conscientiousness in young adulthood.

What are the implications of research on personality stability over time for understanding behavior and attitudes in the workplace? For one, we should investigate how early socialization and success experiences at work may lead toward positive changes in personality. For example, Jackson et al., (2009) suggest that increasing expectations in work and family roles in early adulthood lead one to realize that being impulsive and unreliable has costs in career and family roles. For those assessing personality in certain work contexts that involve large numbers of young adults (e.g., service jobs, campus recruitment studies), a consideration of both normative and individual changes may need to be better factored into our conclusions. We should consider what intraindividual stability findings mean for working across generational cohorts and how to foster the social maturity of young workers through appropriate developmental workplace experiences. Findings that work experiences influence personality trait levels suggest a shift from thinking of individual differences solely as predictors of work behavior, but also as outcomes of work experiences.

With regard to *interests*, Low, Yoon, Roberts, and Rounds (2005) noted that the widely held assumptions are that interests become stable between ages 25 and 30 and change very little thereafter. Supporting these assumptions, they found vocational interests to be highly stable past the college years, exhibiting even greater stability than personality from early adolescence until age 40. Hence, the assumption of intraindividual stability in interests over the working years is probably a safe one.

Before leaving our discussion of intraindividual stability, we would like to note how erroneous assumptions affect our interpretation of environment versus person changes. For example, researchers have examined and interpreted simplex patterns found in examining correlations of predictors with performance over time (Deadrick & Madigan, 1990; Farrell & McDaniel, 2001; Hulin, Henry, & Noon, 1990); that is, correlations decline as a function of temporal distance. The interpretation of these patterns is often that the job or the criterion is changing, but such findings can be reflective of changes in interindividual standing on individual differences due to intraindividual changes (Ackerman & Humphreys, 1990). One should provide evidence to back assumptions of personal stability, rather than assuming that change of relationships over time is a result only of a changing environment.

Also, Roberts and colleagues (Roberts & Caspi, 2003) have discussed how the environment relates to trait continuity. They note that there is an iterative process of greater fit as individuals select environments to fit their identity *and* change environments to suit one's preference (e.g., job crafting; Wrzesniewski & Dutton, 2001). Thus, processes such as gravitation and ASA do not just affect interindividual variability in organizations; they also affect intraindividual stability (i.e., you don't need to change if the environment fits).

We also should note that beliefs regarding the stability and malleability of individual differences are themselves an individual difference. Dweck (1999) has established that some people implicitly hold entity theories, and see characteristics as relatively fixed traits, whereas others endorse an incremental theory and see characteristics as malleable through effort and education. Whether self-theories regarding malleability of personal attributes actually influence one's level of intraindividual stability is an interesting question, and there is some evidence to suggest this to be true (Dweck, 2008). Further, given that there is evidence that individuals can be taught to hold a more malleable theory and that reinforcement can also create such beliefs (Blackwell, Trzesniewski & Dweck, 2007; Mueller & Dweck, 1998), organizational psychologists should further consider how changing worker beliefs about the stability of individual differences may change their behavior at work. Interestingly, in terms of typical characteristics examined by organizational psychologists, Maurer and Lippstreu (2008) found that the general working population tended to believe that it is possible to change almost any knowledge, skill, or ability with effort (although experts were much less optimistic). They noted the downside to these optimistic beliefs regarding malleability (e.g., individuals' pursuit of positions for which they are not qualified, on the assumption that they can develop qualities; support of workplace training with little evidence of effectiveness). Hence, individual beliefs regarding the stability of individual differences are as important to consider as actual levels of stability.

Assumptions of Intraindividual Stability Across Situations

Fleeson and Leicht (2006) summarize research that suggests that in the area of intraindividual personality differences, one typically finds that there is large within-person variability across situations (see also Mischel, 2004). The last decade has seen a strong interest in theories of intraindividual personality coherence (Shoda, Mischel, & Wright, 1994), or a focus on predicting intraindividual variability across situations (i.e., when a person shows conscientious behavior and when they do not). Fleeson's work on density distributions (Fleeson, 2001; Fleeson & Leicht, 2006; Fleeson, Malanos, & Achille, 2002) shows that intraindividual variability is a stable individual difference (see also Baird, Le, & Lucas, 2006).

For some specific individual differences, there has been considerable work investigating the situational contingencies that may explain variability within individuals. As one example, Crocker and Wolfe (2001) reviewed the large body of evidence regarding contingencies of self-esteem (i.e., what situational factors lead an individual to hold a more positive or negative view of self-worth; see also Kernis, 2005). They argued that behavior is more influenced by fluctuations in self-esteem than by one's typical level of trait self-esteem, so understanding how contingencies are acquired and how they change is critical to really understanding the

effects of self-esteem. This argument can be extrapolated to many other individual differences of interest to organizational psychologists—understanding situational contingencies is a critical step in understanding the importance of individual differences at work.

We discuss two streams of workplace research that focus on this issue of cross-situational variability in manifestations of individual differences: research on frame-of-reference (FOR) effects in selection testing and research on situational moderators of individual difference to performance links.

With regard to the former, researchers and practitioners have examined how the contextualization of personality measures (i.e., to refer to work contexts) affects their psychometric properties and hence value in selection (Hunthausen, Truxillo, Bauer, & Hammer, 2003; Lievens, De Corte, & Schollaert, 2008; Robie, Schmit, Ryan, & Zickar, 2000; Schmit, Ryan, Stierwalt, & Powell, 1995). Lievens et al. (2008) noted that the contextualization of items results in reducing within-person inconsistency, not that use of a frame of reference reduces between-person variability. They advocate that using a frame of reference that is conceptually relevant to the criterion is key to increasing validity. While studies to date on FOR effects in testing mirror social psychology findings on personality variability across roles (e.g., work and family; Donahue & Harary, 1998; Wood & Roberts, 2006), variability across types of work settings has not been explored. That is, the research on FOR effects has not yet taken the next step of contextualizing personality assessments according to key psychological features of workplace situations (e.g., high v. low autonomy, cooperative v. competitive). Such measurement approaches would be premised on the work of Fleeson and others that shows individual differences in intraindividual variability across situations can be reliably assessed.

Second, researchers have considered how the situation moderates the link of individual differences to performance. The most well-established relation is that job complexity moderates the relationship of cognitive ability to performance (Hunter & Hunter, 1984). In terms of personality, Barrick and Mount (1993) found that trait-performance relationships are strongest in situations that provide high worker autonomy (see also Gellatly & Irving, 2001). Stewart and Barrick (2004) suggest that the cooperative or competitive nature of situations would be a potential key psychological feature of situations. Mount, Barrick, and Stewart (1998) found that whether situations were dyadic or involved groups and teamwork affected the relationship of personality traits to performance. Thus, while there has been study of situational features in relation to individual differences, the focus has largely been on how those affect the role of interindividual differences in the workplace, rather than on intraindividual differences across situations. Once again, the next evolution for assessment of personality as a predictor of workplace behavior is to build in consideration of situation.

The challenge suggested by both of these research areas is to determine key psychological features of work situations to examine. Research from a social-cognitive theory perspective (Shoda & Mischel, 1993; Shoda et al., 1994) has worked on identifying shared psychological features of situations to determine patterns of individual behavior. Hattrup and Jackson (1996) suggested considering information, task, and physical and social attributes of situations as starting points for conceptualization. Some of the situational features examined as moderators in the research noted above (autonomy, interdependence) may be important here as well.

Assumptions Regarding Intraindividual Differences

One last assumption regarding individual differences that we wish to note is the level of covariances among them and whether that is important in a given context. Schneider (1996) suggests that researchers seldom focus on profiles of attributes and tend to study one dimension at a time, rather than looking at configurations of individual differences. We can point to some solid research streams on the interrelationships of individual differences with an interindividual focus. For example, researchers have investigated the relationships of cognitive ability and personality, suggesting near zero correlations for conscientiousness and cognitive ability (Schmitt, Rogers, Chan, Sheppard, & Jennings, 1997), negative relations of ability to neuroticism, and positive relations of extraversion to abilities (Ackerman & Heggestad, 1997). Research has focused on how interest types relate to personality traits (e.g., Barrick, Mount, & Gupta, 2003; Mount, Barrick, Scullen, & Rounds, 2005) and to cognitive ability (Ackerman & Heggestad, 1997) and their incremental validity in predicting work-related outcomes (e.g., deFruyt & Mervielde, 1999).

However, Schneider's (1996) point is that we need to consider interactive effects and profiles of differences. For example, researchers have looked at the interactive effects of conscientiousness and

cognitive ability (Mount, Barrick, & Strauss, 1999) and of conscientiousness and agreeableness (Witt, Burke, Barrick, & Mount, 2002). Ackerman and Heggestad (1997) found several trait complexes (i.e., combinations of ability, personality, and interest characteristics) emerging from their meta-analysis and suggest that greater consideration of individual differences in tandem occur.

Assumptions regarding interindividual variability have sometimes led to erroneous conclusions regarding intraindividual variability across traits and abilities. For example, Berry, Sackett, and Landers (2007) demonstrated that more accurate considerations of range restriction led to different conclusions regarding the magnitude of relationships between interview scores and cognitive ability test scores. While interviews may measure many different things, one can extrapolate from their work that our conclusions about the intercorrelations of traits are affected by whether we are making correct assumptions about interindividual variability. Further, faulty assumptions regarding covariance levels for traits and abilities can lead to erroneous conclusions regarding the predictive value of individual differences. Sackett, Lievens, Berry, and Landers (2007) demonstrated that when examining intercorrelations of individual differences, indirect range restriction can be important and that underestimates of intercorrelations can lead to overestimates of relations to outcomes.

Understanding how individual differences covary should not be limited to just the individual level. Examining the configuration of traits in an organization can be important from an ASA perspective. Schaubroeck et al. (1998) argue that organizations may become more homogeneous on certain traits through ASA processes while remaining diverse on others. That is, the configurations at the organizational level may change.

Further, Hamaker et al. (2006) noted that relationships between variables may differ at the intraindividual and interindividual level. That is, the way in which states covary within a person may not be the same as the way in which traits covary in the population. They note that relationships can have local homogeneity or identical relationships at both these levels, or they can differ between the intraindividual and interindividual level, exhibiting local heterogeneity. Testing these assumptions is important in order to ensure that inappropriate inferences are not made.

Table 5.1 provides a summary of the issues we have raised regarding assumptions of the stability

Table 5.1 Challenging Our Assumptions

Issue	Conclusion	Recommendations
Is there sufficient interindividual variability on an individual difference variable that it will be useful for prediction and understanding of behavior?	In some cases, researchers and practitioners assume greater interindividual variability than is present; in others, they assume greater range restriction than is present.	Test assumptions of interindividual variability in all settings. Consider possible range restriction effects at multiple levels (job, occupation, team, organization). Correct for range restriction when appropriate/feasible. State conclusions and temper findings in light of possible range restriction.
Is there intraindividual change over time in the individual difference variable that might affect conclusions?	Organizational psychology researchers often assume complete stability in individual differences in adulthood but that is not necessarily the case.	Investigate intraindividual change over time in individual differences of interest. Consider environmental influences on individual difference stability. Appropriately note how age of a sample might relate to any range restriction/changes in individual differences of interest. Evaluate study findings and state conclusions in light of known research on changes in individual differences during working years.
Is there intraindividual variability (state changes) in the individual difference variable that may affect conclusions?	Organizational psychology researchers often treat intraindividual variability in individual differences as error rather than as predictable and useful information.	Investigate situational contingencies that explain intraindividual variability in individual differences. Evaluate study findings and state conclusions with appropriate consideration of potential situational contingencies.
Are there patterns of intraindividual differences of importance to the research question?	Investigation of interactive effects of individual differences is often not considered.	Investigate individual difference interactions, trait complexes, and profiles. Measure rather than assume levels of individual difference covariation in specific settings/studies.

and variability of individual differences, our conclusions regarding the state of organizational psychology literature with regard to these assumptions, and our recommendations for researchers and practitioners regarding better consideration of these assumptions.

Other Critiques of the Individual Difference Tradition in Organizational Psychology

Consideration of individual differences has been part of I/O psychology from its inception, as one can point to the work of Hugo Munsterberg, Louis Thurstone, Walter Bingham, and the U.S. Army in considering individual differences in the selection of employees in the early 1900s (Zickar & Gibby, 2007). Early leadership research focused on individual differences as predictors of leader emergence and effectiveness (Stogdill, 1948). Indeed, differential

psychology, which holds as its premise that individual variation is not error but a focal point of study, is considered a core influence on the development of I/O psychology (Zickar & Gibby, 2007). In 1996, Murphy edited a volume that summarized decades of workplace research in four individual difference domains: cognitive ability, personality, values and interests, and affect. Despite this long-standing role for individual differences, the field has been self-critical regarding their treatment, and we would be remiss if we did not acknowledge these concerns as well: amount and nature of focus on taxonomies of individual differences, minimization of environmental effects, and focus on individual level and ignorance of higher level constructs.

Lack of Taxonomies

One criticism is that there is a lack of careful attention to the taxonomic structure of individual difference variables and the confounding of constructs into heterogeneous categories (Hough, 2001; Hough & Schneider, 1996; Smith & Schneider, 2004). There has been a focus on general categories (e.g., conscientiousness) and a tendency to consider distinct facets (e.g., achievement orientation, order) as interchangeable. While this criticism has largely been directed toward personality-related research, the dismissal of the role of specific abilities in the workplace has also been noted (Mount, Oh, & Burns, 2008). It is interesting to note the difference in the pattern of findings in the ability domain versus the personality domain. In the ability domain, the issue tends to be framed in terms of the increment in criterion-related validity of specific abilities over general cognitive ability, with a general finding of quite small increments. In the personality domain, recent work has shifted focus from the broad dimension level to the facet level, with clear evidence that facets are not interchangeable. Dudley, Orvis, Lebiecki, and Cortina (2006) illustrate this in the domain of conscientiousness. While overall conscientiousness measures typically reflect some combination of the subfacets of achievement, dependability, order, and cautiousness, these authors show that the power of conscientiousness for predicting job performance and other criteria is driven largely by two of these four facets, namely, achievement and dependability. This illustrates the continuing tension between the parsimony offered by the use of broad measures and the value of understanding the role of various subfacets of broad individual differences. Clearly, an inference that the validity findings obtained using broad conscientiousness measures can be generalized to measures of single facets is misguided, and consideration should be given to the appropriateness of the specificity level for the question at hand.

With this caution in mind, there are disadvantages in placing too strong a focus on the taxonomic structure of individual differences. While a description of basic tendencies is certainly useful for developing theories of individual differences, it is insufficient by itself. Cervone (2005) noted that a classification construct (such as a "Big Five" personality trait) describes but does not necessarily explain. For organizational psychology, a focus on the predictive capacity of individual differences sometimes leads to a lack of sufficient attention to theory-building to explain why those relationships occur (Hattrup & Jackson, 1996). Indeed, one of Mischel's (1973) original critiques of personality psychology was that simply describing a taxonomy

of between-person differences does not allow for an understanding of behavior because it does not connect those individual differences to the basic cognitive and affective processes underlying behavior. In thinking about workplace behavior, the challenge is the same—how do those oft-studied individual differences that we examine in predicting behavior at work enable us to explain behavior at work? That said, we also do not want to devalue the clear applied usefulness of information about predictive relationships, even if we lack clear understanding of the conceptual basis for these empirical relationships. Understanding individual behavior in organization and applied prediction are two distinct issues, and it would be a mistake to discount consistent evidence of predictive relationships just because a clear understanding of the conceptual underpinnings of these relationships is not yet fully developed.

De-emphasis of Environmental Factors

Schneider (2001) notes that the focus on individual differences leads to seeing environmental variables as moderators of person-outcome relations, but that an interaction goes both ways in that the individual differences moderate the relation between environmental attributes and outcomes. For example, cognitive ability and personality characteristics predict performance, but those relationships are enhanced by job autonomy (Barrick & Mount, 1993; Morgeson, Delaney-Klinger, & Hemingway, 2005). Whereas the typical recommendations for enhancing performance from an individual difference perspective are to select for high levels of those characteristics, one could also take the levels of individual differences in a population as a given and focus instead on designing jobs with the best levels of autonomy for that population. Thus, the question is whether the adopters of an individual difference perspective focus too narrowly in drawing implications and making suggestions for practice.

Inattention to Higher Level Constructs

Another point raised by Schneider (2001) is that an individual difference focus may lead to a tendency to focus on individual level outcomes (e.g., performance, satisfaction). Yet, environmental and higher level outcomes may also be affected by individual differences in terms of aggregates of those characteristics. Our sense is that there has been a substantial shift in our field's research emphasis, with a long tradition of studying outcomes at the individual level now augmented by a substantial body of work that shifts the unit of analysis to higher levels. Also, a growing trend is the use of individual difference variables as the bases for new constructs at higher levels of analyses, such as attempts to create group-level indices of ability or personality (e.g., Barrick et al., 1998; LePine, 2003, 2005; Mohammed & Angell, 2003), raising intriguing issues about alternate ways of characterizing aggregates (e.g., groups) in terms of individual differences. Alternatives include the mean level of the variable in the group, the variance within the group, the highest level found in the group, and the lowest level found in the group, among others. Theoretical and empirical work is emerging to examine the conditions under which each is appropriate. As these new variables exist at the aggregate level, they are not, of course, individual difference variables per se. Nonetheless, they are composed of individual difference variables and are, we believe, appropriately included in discussions of the role of individual differences in organizational settings.

Research Directions

While we can think of a multitude of research questions on specific individual difference variables and their role in theories of workplace behavior and work attitudes, there are several "big picture" issues that we see as important directions for further research.

First, as noted throughout the chapter, there is a need for better estimates of interindividual variability and intraindividual stability over time and situations for key individual difference variables. This research needs to be conducted at multiple levels of analysis (e.g., for interindividual variability at the job, work group, organizational, and occupational levels) and cumulative effects across levels need to be better understood. It needs to inform our understanding of covariances among individual differences at different levels as well. Accomplishing this calls for: (a) large-scale, longitudinal efforts whereby individual difference measures are collected pre-employment and at multiple intervals throughout an individual's working life; (b) multi-organizational data collections to examine individual difference variability within occupations, organizations, and other levels of aggregation; and (c) within-individual, over time examinations of intraindividual stability, such as event sampling studies. All of these are high-investment research efforts requiring considerable collaborative relationships and funding resources, which may explain why they are not undertaken. However, we can visualize the rich contributions to knowledge that might come from such undertakings, and encourage their pursuit.

Second, a better understanding of key psychological features of situations is needed. While Fleeson (2007) has looked at the task orientation, friendliness, and anonymity of a situation as key to intraindividual variability patterns, research specifically focused on features most relevant to the workplace is needed. For example, Ten Berge and De Raad (1999) reviewed nine different taxonomies of situations that could be considered in determining such features/dimensions (e.g., autonomous, rewarding, ambiguous, competitive). Recent efforts to examine intraindividual variability hold much promise. For example, Huang and Ryan (2011) have used experience-sampling methodology to examine the moment-to-moment influence of situational characteristics on personality states (i.e., situational contingencies) during social interactions in customer service employees over 10 days at work. At the within-individual level, state conscientiousness was associated with the immediacy of the task, whereas state extraversion, agreeableness, conscientiousness, and openness were associated with the friendliness of the other party in the interaction. Similar efforts can increase our understanding of what contingencies exist, how they are acquired, and how they might be changed, leading to better utility of individual difference measures in prediction of workplace behavior, as well as in explanation of worker attitudes and behaviors.

Third, attention to time is needed. Over a decade ago, Hattrup and Jackson (1996) noted that individual difference theorizing needed to adopt a dynamic perspective, recognizing that persons influence and are influenced by situations, and that experience with situations can influence perceptions of them. A true understanding of intraindividual stability and processes of homogenization, such as gravitation and ASA, requires longitudinal data and dynamic models. Addressing these types of research questions will require that organizational psychologists be trained in methodological tools more common to developmental psychology. Such methods are becoming more common in the organizational psychology literature (e.g., Lang & Bliese, 2009, present an application of discontinuous growth modeling techniques).

Fourth, the study of group differences in individual differences should continue. A long-standing area of focus for organizational psychology with regard to interindividual differences has been on demographic group differences in individual differences (e.g., research on ethnic differences in abilities, Roth, Bevier, Bobko, Switzer, & Tyler,

2001; research in gender differences in abilities and personality, Hough, Oswald, & Ployhart, 2001). Much of this research has derived from practical goals related to reducing subgroup differences on selection tools; however, better theory as to why interindividual differences occur has been a grappling point for psychology in general (e.g., debate on reasons for black/white score gaps, Sackett, Schmitt, Ellingson, & Kabin, 2001; debate on reasons for male/female differences in math performance, Halpern et al., 2007). Further, Roth, Van Iddekinge, Huffcutt, Eidson, and Bobko (2002) demonstrated that our field has adopted some inaccurate estimates regarding the size of subgroup differences on certain predictors because of a lack of appropriate consideration of the sources and size of range restriction—another example of how a lack of close examination of assumptions is problematic. In addition, Schneider (1996) suggested that we study individual differences concurrently with the way they are grouped, but not just in the traditional categories of differential psychology (i.e., demographics). He suggests looking at interindividual differences with subgroups formed by organizational characteristics such as mechanistic versus organic organizational design, size, and so on.

Fifth, a long-standing focus in psychology is on aptitude-treatment interactions (ATIs), which more generally refer to any individual difference that predisposes individuals to be more ready for an intervention and hence to benefit more from it. While early conclusions were that ATIs are fairly elusive, the potential to take advantage of them (should reliable ATIs be identified) increases as our ability to customize training and other interventions increases due to technological advances. For example, one can customize learner environments in online training to match regulatory focus or learning style (DeRouin, Fritzsche, & Salas, 2005), or one can target recruitment materials toward different groups of individuals to enhance attraction (Avery & McKay, 2006). Snow (1991) notes that one can manipulate conditions of situations to capitalize on strengths and compensate for weaknesses (e.g., training might be designed to compensate for likely anxiety effects or to capitalize on achievement motivation). Hence, as customization currently is increasing in practice, we need to heighten our scrutiny of the assumptions regarding individual differences that underlie these practices.

Finally, as we noted earlier, development of composition and compilation models that enable us to better understand how individual differences play a role in higher level outcomes is needed (Ployhart

et al., 2006). For example, Stewart, Fulmer, and Barrick (2005) examined both composition and compilation processes to understand how personality traits of team members affect team outcomes. To date, studies of work group composition in terms of personality and ability (e.g., Barrick et al., 1998) tend to be more comparisons of the effectiveness of groups varying in composition rather than of examining processes whereby a group evolves to a certain composition. Multilevel conceptualizations of the role of individual differences in work behavior and attitudes may lead to greater understanding of the importance of individual differences in the workplace.

Final Thoughts

Much has been made of how changes in the workplace—such as globalization, changing technology, shift from manufacturing to a service and information focus, and focus on team-based work structures—have influenced the focus of our field (Howard, 1995). As we conclude this chapter, we want to note how these changes in the workplace should make us more rather than less concerned about individual differences. That is, some in our field decry a focus on selection and other areas heavily based on individual difference considerations because of rapidly changing environments. However, the changing nature of the workplace and the requirements regarding adaptability (Zaccaro & Banks, 2004) suggest that now, more than ever, we need to increase our understanding of the stability and malleability of individual differences. Further, we have echoed a point of others that individuals may revise their jobs to fit their person, values, and interest (Kohn & Schooler, 1982). The changing nature of the workplace suggests that it is important to consider both how the individual adapts the environment as well as how the environment changes the individual.

This does not mean that there is not a danger in unwarranted focus on individual differences. Ackerman and Humphreys (1990) pointed out that gathering information about individual differences that are irrelevant or of marginal diagnosticity can have negative effects on decision quality, as needless attention is paid to such information. In both research and practice today, the capacity to easily collect more information, fueled by technological advances, may be leading us too often to devote resources to tracking individual differences with little theoretical or practical value in a context simply because it is easy to do so.

Fleeson and Leicht (2006) note that those coming from an individual difference perspective tend to focus on differences between people, whereas those with a situation perspective tend to focus on explaining the processes of perceiving, interpreting, and adapting to situations. As we noted at the beginning of the chapter, the individual difference approach in our field has been criticized because of this lack of a focus on process. We hope that this chapter elucidates the many ways in which individual difference researchers are moving toward providing explanations by focusing on intraindividual as well as interindividual differences.

References

Ackerman, P. L., & Heggestad, E. D. (1997). Intelligence, personality and interests: Evidence for overlapping traits. *Psychological Bulletin, 121,* 219–245.

Ackerman, P. L., & Humphreys, L. G. (1990). Individual differences theory in industrial and organizational psychology. In M. D. Dunnette & L. M. Hough (Eds.), *Handbook of industrial and organizational psychology* (pp. 223–282). Palo Alto, CA: Consulting Psychologists Press.

Aguinis, H., Beaty, J. C., Boik, R. J., & Pierce, C. A. (2005). Effect size and power in assessing moderating effects of categorical variables using multiple regression: A 30-year review. *Journal of Applied Psychology, 90*(1), 94–107.

Anderson, N., & Ones, D. S. (2003). The construct validity of three entry level personality inventories used in the UK: Cautionary findings from a multiple-inventory investigation. *European Journal of Personality, 17,* S39-S66.

Avery, D. R., & McKay, P. F. (2006). Target practice: An organizational impression management approach to attracting minority and female job applicants. *Personnel Psychology, 59*(1), 157–187.

Baird, B. M., Le, K., & Lucas, R. E. (2006). On the nature of intraindividual personality variability: Reliability, validity, and associations with well-being. *Journal of Personality and Social Psychology, 90,* 512–527.

Barrick, M. R., & Mount, M. K. (1993). Autonomy as a moderator of the relationships between the Big Five personality dimensions and job performance. *Journal of Applied Psychology, 78,* 111–118.

Barrick, M. R., Mount, M. K., & Gupta, R. (2003). Meta-analysis of the relationship between the five-factor model of personality and Holland's occupational types. *Personnel Psychology, 58,* 45–74.

Barrick, M. R., Stewart, G. L., Neubert, M. J., & Mount, M. K. (1998). Relating member ability and personality to work-team processes and team effectiveness. *Journal of Applied Psychology, 83,* 377–391.

Berry, C. M., Gruys, M. L., & Sackett, P. R. (2006). Educational attainment as a proxy for cognitive ability in selection: Effects on levels of cognitive ability and adverse impact. *Journal of Applied Psychology, 91,* 696–705.

Berry, C. W., Sackett, P. R., & Landers, R. N. (2007). Revisiting interview-cognitive ability relationships: Attending to specific range restriction mechanisms in meta-analysis. *Personnel Psychology, 60,* 837–874.

Blackwell, O. L., Trzesniewski, K., & Dweck, C. S. (2007). Implicit theories of intelligence predict achievement across an adolescent transition: A longitudinal study and an intervention. *Child Development, 78,* 246–263.

Blonigen, D. M., Carlson, M. D., Hicks, B. M., Krueger, R. F., & Iacono, W. G. (2008). Stability and change in personality traits from late adolescence to early adulthood: A longitudinal twin study. *Journal of Personality, 76,* 229–266.

Caskie, G. I., Schaie, K. W., & Willis, S. L. (1999). Individual differences in the rate of change in cognitive abilities during adulthood. *Gerontologist, 39,* 398.

Cattell, R. B. (1963). The interaction of hereditary and environmental influences. *British Journal of Statistical Psychology, 16,* 191–210.

Cervone, D. (2005). Personality architecture: Within-person structures and processes. *Annual Review of Psychology, 56,* 423–452.

Crocker, J., & Wolfe, C. T. (2001). Contingencies of self-worth. *Psychological Review, 108,* 593–623.

Deadrick, D. L., & Madigan, R. M. (1990). Dynamic criteria revisited: A longitudinal study of performance stability and predictive validity. *Personnel Psychology, 43,* 717–744.

deFruyt, F., & Mervielde, I. (1999). RIASEC types and big five traits as predictors of employment status and nature of employment. *Personnel Psychology, 52,* 701–727.

Deng, C., Armstrong, P. I., & Rounds, J. (2007). The fit of Holland's RIASEC model to U.S. occupations. *Journal of Vocational Behavior, 71,* 1–22.

DeRouin, R. E., Fritzsche, B. A., & Salas, E. (2005). Learner control and workplace e-learning: Design, person, and organizational issues. In J. J. Martocchio (Ed.), *Research in personnel and human resources management* (Vol. 24, pp. 181–214). Greenwich, CT JAI Press.

Donahue, E. M., & Harary, K. (1998). The patterned inconsistency of traits: Mapping the differential effects of social roles on self-perceptions of the Big Five. *Personality and Social Psychology Bulletin, 24,* 610.

Donnellan, M. B., Conger, R. D., & Burzette, R. G. (2007). Personality development from late adolescence to young adulthood: Differential stability, normative maturity, and evidence for the maturity-stability hypothesis. *Journal of Personality, 75,* 237–263.

Dudley, N. M., Orvis, K. A., Lebiecki, J. E., & Cortina, J. M. (2006). A meta-analytic investigation of conscientiousness in the prediction of job performance: Examining the intercorrelations and the incremental validity of narrow traits. *Journal of Applied Psychology, 91,* 40–57.

Dweck, C. S. (1999). *Self-theories: Their role in motivation, personality and development.* Philadelphia: Taylor and Francis/Psychology Press.

Dweck, C. S. (2008). Can personality be changed? The role of beliefs in personality and change. *Current Directions in Psychological Science, 17,* 391–394.

Ellis, A. P. J., Hollenbeck, J. R., Ilgen, D. R., Porter, C. O. L. H., West, B. J., & Moon, H. (2003). Team learning: Collectively connecting the dots. *Journal of Applied Psychology, 88*(5), 821–835.

Farrell, J. N., & McDaniel, M. A. (2001). The stability of validity coefficients over time: Ackerman's (1988) model and the General Aptitude Test Battery. *Journal of Applied Psychology, 86,* 60–79.

Finkel, D., Reynolds, C. A., McArdle, J. J., Gatz, M., & Pedersen, N. L. (2003). Latent growth curve analyses of accelerating decline in cognitive abilities in late adulthood. *Developmental Psychology, 39*(3), 535–550.

Fleeson, W. (2001). Toward a structure- and process-integrated view of personality: Traits as density distributions of states. *Journal of Personality and Social Psychology, 80*, 1011–1027.

Fleeson, W. (2007). Situation-based contingencies underlying trait-content manifestation in behavior. *Journal of Personality, 75*, 825–862.

Fleeson, W., & Leicht, C. (2006). On delineating and integrating the study of variability and stability in personality psychology: Interpersonal trust as illustration. *Journal of Research in Personality, 40*, 5–20.

Fleeson, W., Malanos, A. B., & Achille, N. M. (2002). An intraindividual process approach to the relationship between extraversion and positive affect: Is acting extraverted as "good" as being extraverted? *Journal of Personality and Social Psychology, 83*, 1409–1422.

Furnham, A. (2001). Personality and individual differences in the workplace: Person-organization-outcome fit. In B. W. Roberts & R. Hogan (Eds.), *Personality psychology in the workplace* (pp. 223–252). Washington, DC: American Psychological Association.

Gellatly, I. R., & Irving, P. G. (2001). Personality, autonomy, and contextual performance of managers. *Human Performance, 14*, 231–245.

Halpern, D. F., Benbow, C. P., Geary, D. C., Gur, R. C., Hyde, J. S., & Gernsbache, M. A. (2007). The science of sex differences in science and mathematics. *Psychological Science in the Public Interest, 8*(1), 1–51.

Hamaker, E. L., Nesselroade, J. R., & Molenaar, P. C. M. (2006). The integrated trait-state model. *Journal of Research in Personality, 41*, 295–315.

Hattrup, K., & Jackson, S. E. (1996). Learning about individual differences by taking situations seriously. In K. R. Murphy (Ed.), *Individual differences and behavior in organizations* (pp. 507–547). San Francisco: Jossey-Bass.

Hilborn, J. V., Strauss, E., Hultsch, D. F., & Hunter, M. A. (2009). Intraindividual variability across cognitive domains: Investigation of dispersion levels and performance profiles in older adults. *Journal of Clinical and Experimental Neuropsychology, 31*, 412–424.

Holland, J. L. (1997). *Making vocational choices: A theory of vocational personalities and work environments* (3rd ed.). Odessa, FL: Psychological Assessment Resources, Inc.

Hough, L. M. (2001). IOwes its advances to personality. In B. W. Roberts & R. Hogan (Eds.), *Personality psychology in the workplace* (pp. 19–44). Washington, DC: American Psychological Association.

Hough, L. M., Oswald, F. L., & Ployhart, R. E. (2001). Determinants, detection and amelioration of adverse impact in personnel selection procedures: Issues, evidence and lessons learned. *International Journal of Selection and Assessment, 9*(1–2), 152–194.

Hough, L. M., & Schneider, R. J. (1996). Personality traits, taxonomies, and applications in organizations. In K. R. Murphy (Ed.), *Individual differences and behavior in organizations* (pp. 31–88). San Francisco: Jossey-Bass.

Howard, A. (Ed.). (1995). *The changing nature of work.* San Francisco: Jossey-Bass.

Huang, J. L., & Ryan, A. M. (2011). Beyond personality traits: A study of personality states and situational contingencies in customer service jobs. *Personnel Psychology, 64*(2), 451–488.

Hulin, C. L., Henry, R. A., & Noon, S. L. (1990). Adding a dimension: Time as a factor in the generalizability of predictive relationships. *Psychological Bulletin, 107*, 328–340.

Hunter, J. E., & Hunter, R. F. (1984). Validity and utility of alternative predictors of job performance. *Psychological Bulletin, 96*, 72–98.

Hunthausen, J. M., Truxillo, D. M., Bauer, T. N., & Hammer, L. B. (2003). A field study of frame-of-reference effects on personality test validity. *Journal of Applied Psychology, 88*(3), 545–551.

Jackson, J. J., Bogg, T., Walton, K. E., Wood, D., Harms, P. D., Lodi-Smith, J., Edmonds, G. W., & Roberts, B. W. (2009). Not all conscientiousness scales change alike: A multimethod, multi-sample study of age differences in the facets of conscientiousness. *Journal of Personality and Social Psychology, 96*, 446–459.

Jordan, M., Herriott, P., & Chalmers, C. (1991). Testing Schneider's ASA theory. *Applied Psychology: An International Review, 40*, 47–54.

Judge, T. A., & Bretz, R. D. (1992). Effects of work values on job choice decisions. *Journal of Applied Psychology, 77*, 261–271.

Kernis, M. H. (2005). Measuring self-esteem in context: The importance of stability of self-esteem in psychological functioning. *Journal of Personality, 73*, 1569–1605.

Kohn, M. L., & Schooler, C. (1982). Job conditions and personality: A longitudinal assessment of their reciprocal effects. *American Journal of Sociology, 87*, 1257–1286.

Kozlowski, S. W. J., & Klein, K. J. (2000). A multilevel approach to theory and research in organizations: Contextual, temporal, and emergent processes. In K. J. Klein & S. W. J. Kozlowski (Eds.), *Multilevel theory, research, and methods in organizations* (pp. 3–90). San Francisco: Jossey-Bass.

Kuncel, N. R., & Klieger, D. M. (2007). Application patterns when applicants know the odds: Implications for selection research and practice. *Journal of Applied Psychology, 92*, 586–593.

Laing, J., Swaney, K., & Prediger, D. J. (1984). Integrating vocational interest inventory results and expressed choices. *Journal of Vocational Behavior, 25*(3), 304–315.

Lang, J. W. B., & Bliese, P. D. (2009). General mental ability and two types of adaptation to unforeseen change: Applying discontinuous growth models to the task-change paradigm. *Journal of Applied Psychology, 94*, 411–428.

LePine, J. A. (2003). Team adaptation and postchange performance: Effects of team composition in terms of members' cognitive ability and personality. *Journal of Applied Psychology, 88*(1), 27–39.

LePine, J. A. (2005). Adaptation of teams in response to unforeseen change: Effects of goal difficulty and team composition in terms of cognitive ability and goal orientation. *Journal of Applied Psychology, 90*(6), 1153–1167.

LePine, J. A., Hollenbeck, J. R., Ilgen, D. R., & Hedlund, J. (1997). Effects of individual differences on the performance of hierarchical decision-making teams: Much more than g. *Journal of Applied Psychology, 82*(5), 803–811.

Lievens, F., De Corte, W., & Schollaert, E. (2008). A closer look at the frame-of-reference effect in personality scale scores and validity. *Journal of Applied Psychology, 93*(2), 268–279.

Lockenhoff, C. E., Terracciano, A., Bienvenu, O. J., Patriciu, N. S., Nestadt, G., McCrae, R. R., et al. (2008). Ethnicity, education, and the temporal stability of personality traits in the East Baltimore Epidemiologic Catchment Area study. *Journal of Research in Personality, 42*, 577–598.

Low, K. S. D., Yoon, M., Roberts, B. W., & Rounds, J. (2005). The stability of vocational interests from early adolescence to middle adulthood: A quantitative review of longitudinal studies. *Psychological Bulletin, 131*, 713–737.

Maurer, T. J., & Lippstreu, M. (2008). Expert vs. general working sample differences in KSAO 'improvability' ratings and relationships with measures relevant to occupational and organizational psychology. *Journal of Occupational and Organizational Psychology, 81*, 813–829.

McArdle, J. J., Ferrer-Caja, E., Hamagami, F., & Woodcock, R. W. (2002). Comparative longitudinal structural analyses of the growth and decline of multiple intellectual abilities over the life span. *Developmental Psychology, 38*(1), 115–142.

Mischel, W. (1973). Toward a cognitive social learning reconceptualization of personality. *Psychological Review, 80*, 252–283.

Mischel, W. (2004). Toward an integrative science of the person. *Annual Review of Psychology, 55*, 1–22.

Mohammed, S., & Angell, L. C. (2003). Personality heterogeneity in teams: Which differences make a difference for team performance? *Small Group Research, 34*(6), 651–677.

Morgeson, F. P., Delaney-Klinger, K., & Hemingway, M. A. (2005). The importance of job autonomy, cognitive ability, and job-related skill for predicting role breadth and job performance. *Journal of Applied Psychology, 90*(2), 399–406.

Mount, M. K., Barrick, M. R., Scullen, S. M., & Rounds, J. (2005). Higher-order dimensions of the big five personality traits and the big six vocational interest types. *Personnel Psychology, 58*, 447–478.

Mount, M. K., Barrick, M. R., & Stewart, G. L. (1998). Five-factor model of personality and performance in jobs involving interpersonal interactions. *Human Performance, 11*, 145–165.

Mount, M. K., Barrick, M. R., & Strauss, J. (1999). The joint relationship of conscientiousness and ability with performance: Test of the interaction hypothesis. *Journal of Management, 25*, 707–721.

Mount, M. K., Oh, I., & Burns, M. (2008). Incremental validity of perceptual speed and accuracy over general mental ability. *Personnel Psychology, 61*(1), 113–139.

Mueller, C. M., & Dweck, C. S. (1998). Intelligence praise can undermine motivation and performance. *Journal of Personality and Social Psychology, 75*, 33–52.

Murphy, K. R. (1996). Individual differences and behavior in organizations: Much more than g. In K. R. Murphy (Ed.), *Individual differences and behavior in organizations* (pp. 3–30). San Francisco: Jossey-Bass.

Nesselroade, J. R. (2002). Elaborating the differential in differential psychology. *Multivariate Behavioral Research, 37*, 543–561.

Ones, D. S., & Viswesvaran, C. (2003). Job-specific applicant pools and national norms for personality scales: Implications for range-restriction corrections in validation research. *Journal of Applied Psychology, 88*, 570–577.

Peeters, M. A. G., Van Tuijl, H. F. J. M., Rutte, C. G., & Reymen, I. M. M. J. (2006). Personality and team performance: A meta-analysis. *European Journal of Personality, 20*(5), 377–396.

Ployhart, R. E., Weekley, J. A., & Baughman, K. (2006). The structure and function of human capital emergence: A multilevel examination of the attraction-selection-attrition model. *Academy of Management Journal, 49*, 661–678.

Reeve, C. L., & Hakel, M. D. (2000). Toward an understanding of adult intellectual development: Investigating within-individual convergence of interest and knowledge profiles. *Journal of Applied Psychology, 85*, 897–908.

Roberts, B. W. (1997). Plaster or plasticity: Are work experiences associated with personality change in women? *Journal of Personality, 65*, 205–232.

Roberts. B. W., & Caspi. A. (2003). The cumulative continuity model of personality development: Striking a balance between continuity and change in personality traits across the life course. In R. M. Staudinger & U. Lindenberger (Eds.), *Understanding human development: Lifespan psychology in exchange with other disciplines* (pp. 183–214). Dordrecht, the Netherlands: Kluwer Academic.

Roberts, B. W., Caspi, A., & Moffitt, T. E. (2001). The kids are alright: Growth and stability in personality development from adolescence to adulthood. *Journal of Personality and Social Psychology, 81*, 670–683.

Roberts, B. W., Caspi, A., & Moffitt, T. E. (2003). Work experiences and personality development in young adulthood. *Journal of Personality and Social Psychology, 84*, 582–593.

Roberts, B. W., & DelVecchio, W. F. (2000). The rank-order consistency of personality from childhood to old age: A quantitative review of longitudinal studies. *Psychological Bulletin, 126*, 3–25.

Roberts, B. W., & Mroczek, D. (2008). Personality trait change in adulthood. *Current Directions in Psychological Science, 17*, 31–35.

Roberts, B. W., Walton, I., & Viechtbauer, W. (2006). Patterns of mean-level change in personality traits across the life course: A meta-analysis of longitudinal studies. *Psychological Bulletin, 132*, 1–25.

Robie, C., Schmit, M. J., Ryan, A. M., & Zickar, M. J. (2000). Effects of item context specificity on the measurement equivalence of a personality inventory. *Organizational Research Methods, 3*, 348–365.

Roth, P. L., Bevier, C. A., Bobko, P., Switzer, F. S., III., & Tyler, P. (2001). Ethnic group differences in cognitive ability in employment and educational settings: A meta-analysis. *Personnel Psychology, 54*(2), 297–330.

Roth, P. L., Van Iddekinge, C. H., Huffcutt, A. I., Eidson, C. E., & Bobko, P. (2002). Corrections for range restriction in structured interview ethnic group differences: The values may be larger than researchers thought. *Journal of Applied Psychology, 87*, 369–376.

Sackett, P. R., Lievens, F., Berry, C. M., & Landers, R. N. (2007). A cautionary note on the effects of range restriction on predictor intercorrelations. *Journal of Applied Psychology, 92*, 538–544.

Sackett, P. R., & Ostgaard, D. J. (1994). Job-specific applicant pools and national norms for cognitive ability tests: Implications for range restriction corrections in validation research. *Journal of Applied Psychology, 79*, 680–684.

Sackett, P. R., Schmitt, N., Ellingson, J. E., & Kabin, M. B. (2001). High-stakes testing in employment, credentialing, and higher education: Prospects in a post-affirmative-action world. *American Psychologist, 56*(4), 302–318.

Sackett, P. R., & Yang, H. (2000). Correction for range restriction: An expanded typology. *Journal of Applied Psychology, 85*, 112–118.

Satterwhite, R. C., Fleenor, J. W., Braddy, P. W., Feldman, J., & Hoopes, L. (2009). A case for homogeneity of personality at the occupational level. *International Journal of Selection and Assessment, 17*, 154–164.

Schaubroeck, J., Ganster, D. C., & Jones, J. R. (1998). Organization and occupation influences in the attraction-selection-attrition process. *Journal of Applied Psychology, 83*, 869–891.

Schmidt, F. L., Le, H., Oh, I., & Shaffer, J. (2007). General mental ability, job performance, and red herrings: Responses to Osterman, Hauser, and Schmitt. *Academy of Management Perspectives, 21,* 64–76.

Schmidt, F. L., Oh, I., & Le, H. (2006). Increasing the accuracy of corrections for range restriction: Implications for selection procedure validities and other research results. *Personnel Psychology, 59,* 281–305.

Schmit, M. J., Ryan, A. M., Stierwalt, S. L., & Powell, A. B. (1995). Frame-of-reference effects on personality scale scores and criterion-related validity. *Journal of Applied Psychology, 80,* 607–620.

Schmitt, N. (2007). The value of personnel selection: Reflections on some remarkable claims. *Academy of Management Perspectives, 21,* 19–23.

Schmitt, N., Rogers, W., Chan, D., Sheppard, L., & Jennings, D. (1997). Adverse impact and predictive efficiency of various predictor combinations. *Journal of Applied Psychology, 82,* 719–730.

Schneider, B. (1996). When individual differences aren't. In K. R. Murphy (Ed.), *Individual differences and behavior in organizations* (pp. 548–572). San Francisco: Jossey-Bass.

Schneider, B. (1987). The people make the place. *Personnel Psychology, 40,* 437–453.

Schneider, B. (2001). Fits about fit. *Applied Psychology: An International Review, 50,* 141–152.

Schneider, B., Goldstein, H. W., & Smith, D. B. (1995). The ASA framework: An update. *Personnel Psychology, 48,* 747–775.

Schneider, B., Smith, D. B., Taylor, S., & Fleenor, J. (1998). Personality and organizations: A test of the homogeneity of personality hypothesis. *Journal of Applied Psychology, 83,* 462–470.

Shoda, Y., & Mischel, W. (1993). Cognitive social approach to dispositional influences: What if the perceiver is a cognitive social theorist? *Personality and Social Psychology Bulletin, 19,* 574–585.

Shoda, Y., Mischel, W., & Wright, J. C. (1994). Intraindividual stability in the organization and patterning of behavior: Incorporating psychological situations into the idiographic analysis of personality. *Journal of Personality and Social Psychology, 67,* 674–687.

Smith, D. B., & Schneider, B. (2004). Where we've been and where we're going: Some conclusions regarding personality and organizations. In B. Schneider & D. B. Smith (Eds.), *Personality and organizations* (pp. 387–404). Mahwah, NJ: Lawrence Erlbaum.

Snow, R. E. (1991). Aptitude-treatment interaction as a framework for research on individual differences in psychotherapy. *Journal of Consulting and Clinical Psychology, 59,* 205–216.

Stewart, G. L., & Barrick, M. R. (2004). Four lessons learned from the person-situation debate: A review and research agenda. In B. Schneider & D. B. Smith (Eds.), *Personality and organizations* (pp. 61–86). Mahwah, NJ: Lawrence Erlbaum.

Stewart, G. L., Fulmer, I. S., & Barrick, M. R. (2005). An exploration of member roles as a multilevel linking mechanism for individual traits and team outcomes. *Personnel Psychology, 58,* 343–365.

Stogdill, R. M. (1948). Personal factors associated with leadership: A survey of literature. *Journal of Personality, 25,* 35–71.

Ten Barge, M. A., & De Raad, B. (1999). Taxonomies of situations from a trait psychological perspective: A review. *European Journal of Personality, 13,* 337–360.

Turban, D. B., & Keon, T. L. (1993). Organizational attractiveness: An interactionist perspective. *Journal of Applied Psychology, 78,* 184–193.

Wilk, S. L., Desmarais, L. B., & Sackett, P. R. (1995). Gravitation to jobs commensurate with ability: Longitudinal and cross-sectional tests. *Journal of Applied Psychology, 80,* 79–85.

Wilk, S. L., & Sackett, P. R. (1996). Longitudinal analysis of ability-job complexity fit and job change. *Personnel Psychology, 49,* 937–968.

Witt, L. A., Burke, L. A., Barrick, M. R., & Mount, M. K. (2002). The interactive effects of conscientiousness and agreeableness on job performance. *Journal of Applied Psychology, 87,* 164–169.

Wood, D., & Roberts B. W. (2006). Cross-sectional and longitudinal tests of the Personality and Role Identity Structural Model (PRISM). *Journal of Personality, 74,* 779–810.

Wrzesniewski, A., & Dutton, J. E. (2001). Crafting a job: Revisioning employees as active crafters of their work. *Academy of Management Review, 26*(2), 179–201.

Zaccaro, S. J., & Banks, D. (2004). Leader visioning and adaptability: Bridging the gap between research and practice on developing the ability to manage change. *Human Resource Management, 43,* 367–380.

Zickar, M. J., & Gibby, R. E. (2007). Four persistent themes throughout the history of I-O psychology in the United States. In L. L. Koppes (Ed.), *Historical perspectives in industrial and organizational psychology* (pp. 61–80). Mahwah, NJ: Lawrence Erlbaum.

Behavior, Performance, and Effectiveness in the Twenty-first Century

John P. Campbell

Abstract

Sometime during the 1980s, industrial and organizational (I/O) psychology stopped merely complaining about the "criterion problem" and began thinking about occupational or work role performance as a construct that could be substantively modeled. Subsequently, there has been considerable theory and research dealing with the substantive latent structure of performance, performance dynamics, and performance measurement issues. This chapter reviews these developments and argues that, despite differences in terminology and points of emphasis, there is virtually complete convergence concerning the principal components of job performance. The convergent picture is described, along with its implication for theory and research in I/O psychology. Finally, and somewhat unexpectedly, it is argued that at a particular level of generality/specificity the substantive structure of individual work performance is invariant, regardless of occupation, organizational level, situational context, or performance dynamics.

Key Words: Models of work performance, leadership performance, management performance, performance adaptability, performance dynamics.

In spite of its title, this chapter is not meant to be a retrospective of *Managerial Behavior, Performance, and Effectiveness* (Campbell, Dunnette, Lawler, & Weick, 1970). The objectives, slightly paraphrased, of the project on which the book was based were to: (a) survey and summarize all published *and* unpublished literature (broadly defined) pertaining to the identification, development, support, and assessment of managerial effectiveness; (b) develop a framework/model for managerial effectiveness and its determinants that would serve to organize the available information in a meaningful way, identify the critical variables, and review both the strengths and the weaknesses of the research record; and (c) compare the prescriptions for the identification, development, and nurturance of managerial talent with prevailing human resources (HR) practices.

Could this same approach be used again? In a word, no. Thankfully, there has been a virtual explosion in the scope and complexity of the *independent* variable landscape, and the models/theories used to represent particular parts of it. Consequently, the Campbell et al. (1970) modus operandi won't work and its function must be replaced by handbooks such as this one; and even very large handbooks must struggle to represent the landscape.

The objective of this chapter is to revisit the dependent variable side and to consider again the implications of the distinctions among behavior, performance, and effectiveness for research and practice. Much has happened since 1970, and the degree to which there is a consensus on how behavior, performance, and effectiveness should be represented (i.e., modeled) and assessed will be reviewed in some detail. But first the context.

The Context of I/O Psychology

The context of industrial and organizational (I/O) psychology is multifaceted, and this complexity is both a strength and a source of some conflict. However, when building theory, conducting research, developing applications, or practicing what we know how to do, it is important to recognize the assumptions that we are making about the context in which we are working. The way in which the context is framed can have a significant influence on how questions are asked, how data are interpreted, and how applications are designed. It is particularly important when talking about "performance" and "effectiveness," words which sometimes take on Rorschach like properties.

The contextual issues that deserve attention are at least the following.

1. Should the substantive domain of I/O psychology be defined broadly or narrowly? If what concerns us is behavior in organizations, should it be individual behavior, group (e.g., team) behavior, or the "behavior" of some larger unit? Are the organizations of interest limited to those that employ adults, or can they be educational, social, or volunteer organizations? Can there be "organizations" of N = 1 (as in the self-employed plumber)? The perspective taken here is that of the individual and/or the team within an organization when the organization is construed as broadly as possible.

2. Toward what goals should the work of I/O psychology be directed? Should it be the goals of the organization, be it profit or nonprofit, public or private? That is, should the managements' goals be our goals? Or should it be toward the goals of the individual, as in achieving overall well-being, career success, job satisfaction, or employment itself? Or should our goal simply be the advancement of the science of behavior in organizations, with no thought of application? All are legitimate. However, choices among such goals are value judgments, and they have a lot to do with how the resources of I/O psychology are invested.

3. When conducting research, must all research questions be overtly "theory driven," or can specific questions, in the context of discovery (Reichenbach, 1938), be every bit as legitimate, so long as answering the questions advances the field, even if they are not overtly derived from theory? The position here is that theory should be a facilitator, not a constraint.

The Dependent Variable

As one learns when first studying the scientific method in middle school, the dependent variable (DV) is the variable of *real* interest. It is the property that we want to predict, change, or explain. It is not a means to an end—it is the end. The dependent variable must be valued for its own sake. In contrast, independent variables (IV) have no extrinsic or intrinsic value, except as they are able to account for variance in the dependent variable. For example, the measurement of general mental ability, personality, priming effects, or cognitive expectancies have no value, except as they are able to account for variance in one or more important dependent variables. However, it is also true that today's dependent variables could be tomorrow's independent variable. We could value college GPA as an end in itself, or we could exploit college GPA as a predictor of occupational performance. A counter argument is that college GPA is *never* an end in itself; its only value is in what it can predict.

The above paragraph may sound sophomoric, but the IV/DV distinction is frequently lost in the literature, and the potential impact of a particular kind of research, be it goal setting or competency modeling, is not perfectly clear. However, it does beg the question of just what our dependent variables are, anyway. Answering the question depends on some value judgments, and these have to do with basic versus applied research, science versus practice, and the individual versus institutional (i.e., organizational) point of view.

For purposes of this chapter, the most important of these value judgments is the individual versus organizational distinction, which Cronbach and Gleser (1965) viewed as being of fundamental importance when modeling the utility of personnel decision making. Simply put, what dependent variables studied by I/O psychology are important for the goals of the organization and its management, and which are important for the goals of the individual? Consider the following lists.

From the organization point of view

- Individual performance in a work role
- Voluntary turnover
- Team performance
- Team viability
- Organizational unit effectiveness
- Productivity (in the economist's sense) of:
  - Individuals
  - Teams
  - Organizational units

From the individual point of view

- Career/occupational achievement
- Satisfaction with the outcomes of working (which could include satisfaction with performance achievement)

- Fair treatment
- Overall health and well-being

These two lists carry at least the following assumptions and/or qualifications.

1. Organizations are not concerned about job satisfaction or subjective well-being as dependent variables, but only as independent variables that have implications for performance, productivity, effectiveness, or turnover.

2. Information pertaining to the determinants of performance may be used in a selection system, to benefit the organization; or in a career guidance system to benefit the individual (e.g., using ability, personality, and interest assessment to plan educational or job search activities.) Similarly, training programs that produce higher skill levels can enhance individual performance for the benefit of the organization or enhance career options for individuals.

3. Fair and equitable treatment of individual employees *may* be an important dependent variable for the organization if it is incorporated as a goal in the organization's ethical code or in a policy statement of corporate social responsibility for which the management is then held responsible.

For the most part, I/O psychology does not operate from the individual point of view, even though a number of its early pioneers did, such as Donald Paterson or Walter van Dyke Bingham (cf., Koppes, Thayer, Vinchur, & Salas, 2007). At some point, vocational psychology (i.e., the individual point of view) became part of counseling psychology (Campbell, 2007; Meyer, 2007). The concern in this chapter is individual performance, and primarily from the organizational point of view, broadly interpreted.

Individual Performance

From the organizational point of view, individual performance in the work setting is our dominant dependent variable. As many have noted, in spite of its criticality, there was almost no treatment of performance as a construct in its own right before the mid- to late 1980s. There was simply the "criterion problem" (Austin & Villanova, 1992; Campbell, 1991a), and investigators searched for specific measures that might be judged as "good" measures of performance, perhaps defined as an indicator of an individual's overall contribution to the organization. Virtually all the theory and research attention was on the independent variables (e.g., individual abilities, skills, and motivation).

Much has changed in the last 25 years. There is now a bona fide theory and research literature on performance as a construct; and an integrated description of current views follows in the next section. However, the influence of this literature on I/O psychology research has been depressingly small. When investigating the influence of various domains of independent variables on performance, researchers do not generally locate the measures of performance within a broader *substantive* picture. Perhaps the prime offenders are meta-analyses that average correlations between well-known predictor variables and a multitude of unspecified "criterion" measures that are lumped in a category labeled as "performance measures." It is difficult to know what the meta-analytically estimated mean correlation represents under these circumstances. Consider the current chapter as an attempt to "try again."

A Definition of Performance

There seem to have been no major disagreements with Campbell et al. (1970) specifications for behavior, performance, and effectiveness, although there have been extensive elaborations. That is, individuals enter the work setting and they do things. Some, hopefully a lot, of the things they do are directed toward the achievement of organizational goals. These actions must be at least potentially observable. For example, sometimes it takes a great deal of covert thinking before the individual does something. Performance is the action, not the thinking that preceded the action. This has nothing to do with the cognitive psychology versus behaviorism debate. That debate focuses on what controls the actions; some say it's our reinforcement histories, some say it's our cognitions. However, someone must identify those actions that are relevant to the organization's goals and those which are not. For those that are (i.e., performance), the level of proficiency with which the individual performs them must be scaled. Both the judgment of relevance and the judgment of level of proficiency depend on a specification of the important *substantive* goals of the organization, not content-free goals such as "make a profit."

Nothing in this definition requires that a set of performance actions be circumscribed by the term *job* or that they remain "static" over a significant length of time. Neither does it require that the goals of an organization remain fixed, or that a particular management cadre is responsible for determining the organization's goals (a.k.a. "vision"). Neither does it say that actions, or goals, must be described at a certain level of specificity. However, for performance assessment to take place, the major operative goals of the organization, within some meaningful time frame, must be known; and the methods by which individual actions are judged to be goal relevant, and scaled in terms of what represents high and low proficiency, must be legitimized. Consequently, it is not a violation of this definition of performance for individual organization members to decide themselves what actions are most relevant for what they think the goals of the organization are, or should be. That is, they can be quite active (Frese, 2008), or proactive (Griffen, Neal, & Parker, 2007) in this regard. However, these goal choices, and decisions about what actions best serve them, must be legitimized by the stakeholders empowered to do so by the organization's charter. Otherwise, there is no organization. Perhaps the indictment of "conventional" job analysis (e.g., see Pearlman & Sanchez, 2010) should be that it does not validly reflect current and future goals and does not consider the most relevant set of actions that could serve those goals, when it uses "job analysts" to make important judgments about a job's performance requirements, because job analysts are not sufficiently knowledgeable about the organization's goals.

The distinction between performance, as defined above, and effectiveness (a.k.a. organizational outcomes, the bottom line, organizational goal achievement) is that effectiveness is not solely determined by the performance of a particular individual, even if that individual is one of the organization's critical "leaders." For example, effectiveness indicators, judged to be valid measures of a unit's effectiveness, such as sales volume, number of windows installed in new housing, number of on-time arrivals along a bus route, dollar value of research grants, or standardized test scores of middle school students, are not solely a function of the individual performance of the salesperson, carpenter, bus driver, researcher, or public schoolteacher. If these indicators represent the goals of the organization, then individual performance should certainly be related to them (if not, the specifications for individual performance are wrong and need changing, or conversely, the organization is pursuing the wrong goals). However, by definition, effectiveness indicators have other determinants as well, for which the individual should not be held responsible. If the variability in an effectiveness indicator is *totally* under the control of the individual, then it *is* a measure of performance.

Similar definitions apply to team performance, but team performance is not a simple aggregation of the individual performance of team members.

Virtually by definition, team performance requires some form of collective *interdependent* actions on the part of the team members (Kozlowski & Ilgen, 2006). However, the analogous distinction between team performance and team effectiveness is a real one, if variance in measures of team effectiveness is determined by sources (e.g., resource availability) not under the control of the team itself (see Mathieu, Maynard, Rapp, & Gilson, 2008).

Modeling Performance

Since the mid-1980s, there have been several efforts to specify the "dimensionality" of performance, in the context of the latent structure of the actions required by a particular occupation, job, position, or work role (see Borman & Brush, 1993; Borman & Motowidlo, 1993; Campbell, McCloy, Oppler, & Sager, 1993; Griffen et al., 2007; Murphy, 1989a; Organ, 1988; Yukl, Gordon, & Taber, 2002). These have become known as performance models, and they seem to offer differing specifications for what constitutes the nature of performance as a construct. However, the argument here is that there is virtually total correspondence. To support this assertion, a brief synopsis of each is presented first, followed by a discussion of why they might seem different, but aren't. All of this leads to assembling a composite picture of performance dimensionality that *could* be used for identifying appropriate dependent variables for specific research or HR management purposes, *and* to code research results for archival storage (i.e., to be used in meta-analyses).

Some Issues

Proceeding along this path raises some important issues. First, proposing models of performance seems quite normative. That is, they seem to stipulate that performance in any job or work role of the moment is composed of the same set of components, or dimensions. How can that be, if performance is characterized as a set of actions relevant for a particular organization's goals? Doesn't that make the substantive content of performance unique to a particular time and place? The only legitimate answer must be that at a particular level of specificity/generality, research has shown that particular sets of actions (e.g., refraining from substance abuse, showing consideration for coworkers, setting goals with subordinates) contribute to goal accomplishment in virtually any organization. The story is not quite the same for what is called the "technical performance" factor in each of the models, but more about that later.

A second issue arises because there are really two different kinds of performance models in the literature. The first kind specifies performance as a set of *substantive* content factors (e.g., flying an airplane, delegating responsibilities to subordinates), and the second focuses on sets of cognitive/behavioral processes, such as "active" performance (Frese, 2008), or performance "adaptability" (Pulakos, Arad, Donovan, & Plamondon, 2000). Although not always perfectly clear, there are major distinctions to be made between these two kinds of models. It is argued below that they are complementary and not competing renditions.

A third issue is whether or not the models are, or should be, hierarchical in nature (i.e., performance components are identified at more than one level of specificity. That is, can major factors be decomposed into subfactors; and if they are, are the different levels fully nested? The argument below is that yes, they are hierarchical; and they are fully nested, even after different models are aggregated into a composite.

As might be anticipated, the aggregation process will start with brief discussion of the individual models, Campbell et al. (1993) first.

The Campbell et al. Model

This model posits eight major substantive factors at the highest level of generality that seems useful. That is, each factor describes a specifiable content domain of goal-relevant actions such that aggregating them into a smaller number of higher order factors would tend toward adding apples and oranges. The eight factors are briefly characterized in Table 6.1.

The argument for eight factors was not made solely on the basis of the observed or forecasted intercorrelation matrix of scores on measures of the factors, although the available data indicate the "corrected" (for attenuation and method variance) estimates of the factor intercorrelations to be considerably less than 1.0 (Campbell & Knapp, 2001; Sager, 1990; Visweswaran, Schmidt, & Ones, 2005). It is also based on the judged appropriateness of describing each of the eight factors as a *construct*. There is a distinction to be made between composite scores that are simply aggregations of scores on different constructs and scores that do represent a definable construct. And, as Podsakoff, MacKenzie, Podsakoff, & Lee (2003) point out, they require different latent models. By this same reasoning, while a criterion intercorrelation matrix will usually yield a general factor, due to common determinants (e.g., GMA) or method variance, the notion of overall performance has no substantive meaning as a construct.

Performance is not one thing. If it is, no one as yet has been able to provide a substantive description of what it is without simply appealing to the aggregation of scores across different factors. Now, this does not rule out the possibility that individual "raters" might base their "overall" performance assessments on their personal combination of several latent factors, or primarily on the basis of one factor, and not tell anybody, or even be aware of what they were doing when they made such a rating.

The identification of the factors in Table 6.1 came from two primary sources. The first was simply the extant literature, as it existed in the late 1980s. For example, the much maligned two factors of leadership and supervisory behavior, consideration and initiating structure, are very robust and appeared in study after study (Bass, 1990). Also, there is a frequently appearing structure for the functions of management (Borman & Brush, 1993; Yukl, 2010), and both leadership and management functions are ascribed to peers in certain kinds of work teams such that it is possible to make a distinction between peer leadership and supervisory leadership, when the subfactors within each are similar (Hiller, Day, & Vance, 2006).

The second major influence was the work on modeling individual performance conducted as part of Project A (Campbell & Knapp, 2001). In Project A, two cohorts of 10,000 army enlisted personnel separated by three years and distributed over a wide range of skilled, but entry-level, jobs were assessed on multiple indicators of individual performance. Each cohort was assessed after approximately three years on their first job (Military Occupational Specialty; MOS in army parlance), and then a second time approximately four years later, after reenlisting and beginning to take on leadership/supervisory responsibilities. The multiple performance indicators were reduced, via subject matter expert (SME) judgment and a series of correlational analyses, to a set of 24 basic performance scores, varying in both content and method, which were then subjected to a series of confirmatory factor analyses. That is, alternative substantive factor models of the latent structure of the 24 scores were proposed and evaluated for best fit in each of the two cohorts at each of the two points in time. The conceptual generation of alternative models was done independently for each of the four performance data sets. The clear winners were a five-factor model of entry-level performance and a six-factor model of leader/supervisory performance (see Campbell & Knapp, 2001, for details). Within organizational level, the best-fitting models in each

Table 6.1 A Taxonomy of Higher Order Performance Components

1. Job-specific technical task proficiency
The first factor reflects the degree to which the individual performs the core substantive or technical tasks that are central to his or her job. They are the job-specific performance behaviors that distinguish the substantive content of one job from another. Constructing custom kitchens, doing word processing, designing computer architecture, driving a bus through Chicago traffic, and directing air traffic are examples.

2. Non-job-specific technical task proficiency
This factor reflects the situation that in virtually every organization, but perhaps not all, individuals are required to perform tasks that are not specific to their particular job. For example, in research universities the faculty must teach classes, advise students, make admission decisions, and serve on committees. All faculty must do these things, in addition to practicing chemistry, psychology, economics, or electrical engineering.

3. Written and oral communication task proficiency
Many jobs in the workforce require the individual to make formal oral or written presentations to audiences that may vary from one to tens of thousands. For those jobs, the proficiency with which one can write or speak, independent of the correctness of the subject matter, is a critical component of performance.

4. Demonstrating effort
The fourth factor refers to the consistency of an individual's effort day by day, the frequency with which people will expend extra time when required, and the willingness to keep working under adverse conditions. It is a reflection of the degree to which individuals commit themselves to all job tasks, work at a high level of intensity, and keep working when it is cold, wet, or late.

5. Maintaining personal discipline (counterproductive work behavior)
The fifth component is characterized by the degree to which negative behavior, such as alcohol and substance abuse at work, law or rules infractions, and excessive absenteeism, is avoided.

6. Facilitating peer and team performance
Factor 6 is defined as the degree to which the individual supports his or her peers, helps them with job problems, and acts as a de facto trainer. It also encompasses how well an individual facilitates group functioning by being a good model, keeping the group goal directed, and reinforcing participation by the other group members. Obviously, if the individual works alone, this component will have little importance.

7. Supervision/leadership
Proficiency in the supervisory component includes all the behaviors directed at influencing the performance of subordinates through face-to-face interpersonal interaction and influence. Supervisors set goals for subordinates, they teach them more effective methods, they model the appropriate behaviors, and they reward, punish, or are supportive in appropriate ways. The distinction between this factor and the preceding one is a distinction between peer leadership and supervisory leadership.

8. Management/administration
This factor is intended to include the major elements in management that are distinct from direct supervision. It includes the performance behaviors directed at articulating goals for the unit or enterprise, organizing people and resources to work on them, monitoring progress, helping to solve problems or overcome crises that stand in the way of goal accomplishment, controlling expenditures, obtaining additional resources, and representing the unit in dealings with other units, with other organizations, or with the public.

of the two cohorts were identical. Further, when the model identified in one cohort was subjected to confirmatory analysis in the other, the fit was also identical. The lawfulness of these data had an influence on the specifications for the Campbell et al. (1993) model. All but one of the Project A factors, Military Presence and Bearing, which was unique to the army, appear in some form in Table 6.1.

In retrospect, the distinction between factor one and factor two, which was also generated by the Project A data, is a bit too military-centric. That is, there is a large category of technical performance actions (e.g., first aid) that every uniformed individual must be able to do, in addition to the technical side of his or her specialty. This dichotomy may not appear in many occupations, although it certainly does in education (i.e., research versus teaching). Also, the use of the word "task" as if it were synonymous with the technical components of performance was ill-advised. Task is simply a unit of description, and could be used as the unit of description in any of the factors.

The "demonstrating effort" factor, depending on how it is framed, also might be problematic. Effort underlies performance on all factors and in that sense is a determinant of individual differences in performance, not an independent performance action. However, this factor was intended to represent observable actions that are independent of performance on the other factors, such as putting in more time, and continuing under different kinds of adverse conditions (e.g., extensive traveling). Defined in this way, the factor repeatedly emerged from critical incident data collections in Project A; and, as detailed below, it also appears in various forms as an Organizational Citizenship factor (Organ, 1988) and as a Contextual Performance factor in the Borman and Motowidlo (1997) model.

Again, Table 6.1 represents a substantive content model. It does not preclude performance dynamics. Such dynamics must surely occur. It does not preclude changes in the sample of behaviors or actions comprising each factor, or changes in the level of difficulty of the performance requirements. It only requires that the required actions in each factor be sampled from the same construct *domain*.

Viewed from this model, individual differences in performance itself are a function of two sets of determinants: (1) direct, and (2) indirect.

1. The direct determinants are *current* job-related knowledge and skill, and three volitional choices (euphemistically referred to as "motivation") corresponding to the traditional (a) choice to perform, or choice to expend effort, (b) the amplitude or level of effort to which the individual commits, and (c) the persistence, over time, of that level of effort expenditure. The direct determinants operate in real time, or "on the job," so to speak. The knowledge and skill versus volitional choice distinction is similar to the resource level versus resource allocation distinction discussed by Beal, Weiss, Barros, and MacDermid (2005). Variance in performance can also be accounted for by their interactions. For example, being highly knowledgeable about a particular job requirement could increase the probability of choosing to do it and investing effort in it.

2. Indirect determinants are all the things that produce individual differences in the direct determinants (e.g., IQ, personality, training, goal setting, reward preferences, self efficacy, etc.). They can influence performance only by influencing the direct determinants. That is, the direct determinants totally mediate the effects of the indirect determinants. The available path model studies support this assertion (Borman, White, & Dorsey, 1995; Borman, White, Pulakos, & Oppler, 1991; Hunter, 1983; Lance & Bennett, 2000; Schmidt & Hunter, 1992).

The model also distinguishes determinants of individual differences in performance from influences on the mean of performance, for a specific sample of individuals. For example, one of the most important influences on the performance mean these days, at least in the *opinion* of many people, is technology. Technology only becomes a determinant of individual differences in performance if we assess the individual differences in how well people have learned to use the technology. Then it becomes part of factor one. The same would be true for any intervention, constraint, or situational factor that is intended to influence the mean.

Individual differences in performance can also be a function of the interactions among individual determinants, or between individual differences and features of the intervention, constraint, or situation. For example, while a particular constraint (time limits) could lower the mean, higher ability people could compensate more effectively.

The above specifications are presented in the context of the variance *among* individuals. It also can portray the substantive content and the determinants to performance differences across time *within* individuals. The relative importance of skill level versus choice behavior may be different for the variance between versus the variance within, although changes in skill level could occur quickly for an individual.

Core, Contextual, Pro-social, and Organizational Citizenship Performance

Since 1990, considerable conceptual and research activity has been focused on the Borman and Motowidlo (1993, 1997) distinction of core technical versus contextual performance and on categories of performance behaviors referred to as Organizational Citizenship (Organ, 1988; Smith, Organ, & Near, 1983). Both are examples of substantive models of performance; and, in terms of the behaviors that make up their content, there is considerable, if not complete, overlap. Probably the most comprehensive discussions of the similarities and differences are in the papers comprising a special issue of the *Human Resource Management Review* (Spring, 2000) and in a comprehensive review of research on organizational citizenship behavior (OCB) by Podsakoff, MacKenzie, Paine, and Bachrach (2000), which summarizes research on the dimensionality of OCB, the determinants of individual differences in performance on OCB dimensions, and the relationship of the OCB dimensions to indicators of unit/organizational effectiveness.

Technical Core and Contextual Performance

As described by Borman and Motowidlo (1997), individual performance is comprised of two major factors.

1. *Core technical task performance* is defined as... "activities that contribute to the organization's technical core either directly by implementing a part of its technological process, or indirectly by providing it with needed materials or services. Examples of task performance dimensions for a sales job might include, Product Knowledge, Closing the Sale, and Organization and Time Management. For a firefighter job, Performing Rescue Operations, Conducting Salvage Operations, and Applying Ventilation Procedures are good examples of task dimensions" (pp. 99–100).

This definition is not without its ambiguities. Is a technical core synonymous with a product or service? Is there more than one? Are there nontechnical cores (e.g., providing a particular community service)? Also, for the sales example, do product knowledge and time management constitute performance itself or are they determinants of individual differences in performance?

These ambiguities notwithstanding, the Borman and Motowidlo (1997) core technical performance factor is very similar to the substantive technical factor that appears in other models.

2. *Contextual performance* consists of activities that "contribute to organizational effectiveness in ways that shape the organizational, social, and psychological context that serves as a catalyst for task activities and processes. Contextual activities include volunteering to carry out task activities that are not formally part of the job and helping and cooperating with others in the organization to get tasks accomplished" (p. 100). As noted by Organ (1997), this definition contains language with considerable surplus meaning (i.e., *shape* the organizational, social, and psychological *contexts* that *serve* as *catalysts* for task activities and processes). Their 1997 taxonomy of contextual

performance subfactors helps reduce much of the ambiguity. The five subfactors described there are as follows.

1) Persisting with enthusiasm and extra effort as necessary to complete ones task activities successfully.

2) Volunteering to carry out activities that are not formally part of ones job.

3) Helping and cooperating with others, including coworkers, customers (in some jobs).

4) Following organizational rules and procedures.

5) Endorsing, supporting, and defending organizational objectives.

The five-factor taxonomy is also intended to subsume the performance factors discussed by Smith et al. (1983) and Organ (1988, 1997) under the rubric of organizational citizenship behavior (OCB), which refers to performance behaviors that are relevant for the organization's goals but are not required by the prevailing job description. The original OCB measure (Smith et al., 1983) contained 16 items, which yielded two factors when used in a hypothetical rating task. The first factor, labeled altruism, contained items dealing with helping others, which may in fact be voluntary in most organizations. The second factor, labeled compliance, contained items (e.g., punctuality, not taking too many breaks, giving advance notice of absences) which *are* requirements in most job settings. Organ (1988) subsequently added the factors labeled: Civic Virtue (responsible involvement in the governance of the organization); Organizational Courtesy (showing respect for others); and Sportsmanship (tolerating less than desirable organizational conditions for the good of the enterprise). The compliance factor was subsequently relabeled as Conscientiousness. Podsakoff and his colleagues (e.g., Podsakoff & MacKenzie, 1994) developed scales to assess the five OCB dimensions and they have been used in considerable empirical research, meta-analyses of which have been reported by Hoffman, Blair, Meriac, and Woehr (2007), LePine, Erez, and Johnson (2002), Organ and Ryan (1995), Podsakoff and MacKenzie (1997), and Podsakoff et al. (2000). Given the method variance that must be accounted for when ratings are the principal measurement method, the pattern of results is familiar. The relatively high intercorrelations among factor scores yield both a general factor as well as evidence for distinctiveness among the dimensions.

Conway (1999) found similar results for the factors commonly subsumed under contextual performance, as well as some evidence for the distinctiveness of the two higher order factors, Task vs. Contextual performance as conceptualized by Borman and Motowidlo (1997). However, as Hoffman et al. (2007) point out, the assessment of contextual performance has not been as consistently grounded in the same set of measures as it has for OCB.

As seems so often to be the case in I/O psychology, investigators must put their own stamp on things, and the number of variations in the OCB dimensions has grown. In their review of the OCB literature, Podsakoff et al. (2000) counted "almost 30" different variables describing OCB. Because many of the variations in substantive content seemed small, or investigators simply used different words for the same thing, Podsakoff et al. (2000) identified seven common themes or dimensions that seemed to represent all the individual scales that had been used.

1. *Helping behavior*, which seems to combine the dimensions of altruism and courtesy and is directed at coworkers, subordinates, supervisors/managers, or clients/customers.

2. *Sportsmanship*, generally as defined by Organ (1988).

3. *Organizational loyalty*, that part of Civic Virtue related to identifying with the organizations goals and management, and promoting and defending the organization to outsiders.

4. *Organizational compliance*, with regard to organizational policies, regulations, norms, and work rules.

5. *Individual initiative*, or going well beyond minimal requirements for adherence to rules and policies, taking on additional tasks and responsibilities, and commitments of time and resources.

6. *Civic virtue*, participating actively in organizational governance, administration, and policy making—from reading one's mail, to attending nonrequired meetings, to offering views on policies and problems.

7. *Self-development*, which refers to voluntary behaviors intended to improve one's own knowledge, skill, and performance capabilities. As noted by Podsakoff et al. (2000), given the common distinction between performance and its determinants, this dimension is better described as a determinant of performance and not performance itself. Consequently, it falls outside the definition of OCB.

Whether the content and dimensional structure of contextual performance and organizational citizenship behavior/performance are the same or different is discussed at some length by Motowidlo (2000) and Organ (1997), and the conclusions seemed to be there are no substantive differences between the content of contextual performance and citizenship performance, with the possible exception of civic virtue. However, even though the idea for a dimension labeled "civic virtue" came from political philosophy applied to organizational behavior (Graham, 2000), the content of the dimensions could just as well have come from the participation in decision-making literature (Vroom & Jago, 1988). Consequently, civic virtue might just as well be viewed as individual participation in certain management functions. Whether participation is "granted" by higher management or seized by the participants themselves, and whether the goals being served are the organization's or the individual's, are different issues.

As noted by Organ, cited in Motowidlo (2000), perhaps the only difference between contextual and citizenship performance is that the former is "cold, gray, and bloodless" compared to the latter. That is, to paraphrase, the OCB labels have more emotional and exciting connotations. The synthesis of all existing models found later in this chapter will seem even colder, but then its origins are in the far North.

Pro-social Behavior

Pro-social behavior as a category of performance actions was introduced to the I/O psychology literature by Brief and Motowidlo (1986), where it was defined as behavior directed toward individuals, groups, or organizations with whom the individual interacts, and which is intended to promote the welfare of the individual, group, or organization to whom it is directed. The *functional* subcategories of pro-social *organizational* behavior are things like: providing service or products to consumers, helping customers with personal matters, suggesting organizational improvements, putting forth extra effort, volunteering for additional assignments, staying with the organization during hard times, and representing the organization favorably to outsiders. As is frequently pointed out, many of these kinds of actions were described by Katz and Kahn (1978) as extra-role (i.e., not prescribed by the management) behaviors that in fact contribute to the effectiveness of the unit or organization. Brief and Motowidlo (1986) did not make this distinction. Pro-social behaviors could be either; and, as described later in this chapter, can be sorted into existing dimensions identified in subsequent performance models.

The phenomenon of pro-social behavior has been a much bigger topic in social psychology for many decades (e.g., see Batson & Shaw, 1991; Cialdini & Kendrick, 1976; Darley & Latané, 1968; Eisenberg & Miller, 1987; Penner, Dovidio, Piliavin, & Schroeder, 2005), where it is generally specified as "actions that are defined by some significant segment of society and/or one's social group as generally beneficial to other people" (Penner et al., 2005, p. 22).

In the social psychology literature, the general issues have been: (a) whether pro-social behavior is altruistic or egoistic (i.e., does the giver expect some sort of return or reward, or benefit?); (b) what are the origins and determinants of pro-social behavior, including genetic predispositions (e.g., Rushton, 1991; Trivers, 1971); (c) is "empathy" a requirement for pro-social behavior; and (d) is there a pro-social personality? Issues b, c, and d are concerned with the determinants of pro-social performance, not the nature of pro-social performance itself; and issue a remains unsettled. That is, identifying performance actions that are motivated by altruism is experimentally difficult.

Modeling Leadership and Management Performance

The literature on leadership is of course voluminous (e.g., Bass, 1990; Yukl, 2010). Virtually since the beginning of written history there have been theories/models of what leadership performance is, what determines individual differences in leadership performance, and what effects leadership performance has on subordinate, group, and organizational effectiveness. A part of this literature is concerned with describing the substantive content of leader performance. It is also true that the substantive specifications for leader performance are almost always embedded within a model or theory of leadership dynamics, although not all models are perfectly clear about what they mean by leader performance itself. It is certainly not the intent here to attempt a review of leadership theory. Bass (1990) and Yukl (2010), and the *Yearly Review of Leadership* issues of the *Leadership Quarterly* do that quite thoroughly. However, over the last 60 to 70 years, a succession of leadership theories have incorporated specifications for the actions (behaviors) that comprise leader performance. A brief list is as follows. The somewhat disdainful criticisms of this literature are discussed later. Be advised that ambiguities concerning the identity of the dependent variable and the confusion of performance with both its determinants and its outcomes (i.e., effectiveness) seem rampant throughout the leadership literature.

Beginning soon after World War II, a series of "behavioral" leadership models attempted to describe what high-performing leaders do. The results of the Ohio State studies (Fleishman, 1983) and research at the University of Michigan's Survey Research Center, the Research Center for Group Dynamics (Cartwright & Zander, 1960), and the Institute for Social Research (Likert, 1961) converged on a four factor description, which was summarized in the classic paper by Bowers and Seashore (1966), both of whom were at Michigan. The four factors are given below. The equivalent titles from the Ohio State studies are shown in parentheses.

1. Support (Consideration)
Behavior that enhances someone else's feeling of personal worth and importance and shows mutual trust and respect.

2. Interaction facilitation (Sensitivity)
Behavior that encourages members of the group to develop close, mutually satisfying relationships and shows awareness of potential conflict and stressors.

3. Goal emphasis (Production emphasis)
Behavior that stimulates an enthusiasm for meeting the group's goal or achieving excellent performance.

4. Work facilitation (Initiating structure)
Behavior that helps achieve goal attainment by such activities as scheduling, coordinating, planning, providing ways to get the job done, and by providing resources such as tools, materials, and technical knowledge. Note that the factor does not refer to being unilaterally directive and "telling people what to do."

From the 1960s to the present, these basic factors occur again and again in leadership theory and research. Sometimes only two of the factors are emphasized (i.e., consideration and structure) and sometimes more fine-grained subfactors are used, as in the Leader Behavior Description Questionnaire (LBDQ-12; Stogdill, Goode, & Day, 1962) or the Managerial Behavior Survey (Yukl & Nemeroff, 1979; Yukl, Wall, & Lepsinger, 1990). Virtually all the "contingency" models of leadership, such as Fiedler's (1967) LPC (Least Preferred Coworker) and Path-Goal theory (House, 1971; House & Mitchell, 1974), incorporate the same factors. For example, leaders acting in a high LPC environment, rely on consideration and participation, while leaders acting in a low LPC environment rely on being structured and directive. The House and Mitchell (1974) version of the Path-Goal model uses four factors that are virtually identical to the four factors described by Bowers and Seashore (1966). What is characteristic of the contingency models is that the effectiveness of high scorers on particular performance dimensions is influenced by (i.e., contingent upon) certain characteristics of the situation, including the characteristics of the followers. However, the research support for major interactive effects in this regard, after various artifacts are accounted for, is very sketchy (Yukl, 2010). For example, the initial LPC contingency effects did not cross-validate well (Graen, Alvares, Orris, & Martella, 1970).

The models discussed so far essentially deal with leadership as a one-on-one process. Another group of models frame leadership influence in the group context. That is, the concern is how leadership performance influences work group effectiveness. Certainly this was the orientation early on at the University of Michigan Institute for Group Dynamics (e.g., Bales, 1958; Cartwright & Zander, 1960), when the collective concerns of both leaders and group members in high-performance groups were with behaviors directed at achieving the group's goals and behaviors directed at group maintenance (i.e., keeping people involved, interested, feeling rewarded, and committed), which are the group-centered analogues to structure and consideration at the individual level. Blake and Mouton (1964, 1983) incorporated these same two dimensions in a model of group leadership known as the Managerial Grid. The two dimensions were labeled "Production Centered" and "Employee Centered" and the Grid stipulated that it was most advantageous for a leader/manager to be proficient in both.

The group and one-on-one perspectives are essentially merged in Leader-Member-Exchange (LMX) theory (Graen & Uhl-Bien, 1995) which emphasizes that the influence process is reciprocal. That is, a leader develops a distinct relationship with each of his or her subordinates because of a mutual influence process that moves through several stages to a relatively stable psychological contract that essentially specifies who will do what for whom under what circumstances. The nature of the contract (i.e., the quality of LMX) can vary widely across leader-member pairs, as a function of the performance capabilities and reward preference of each and the success of mutual influence attempts based on, in so many words, high consideration, mutually satisfying initiating structure, agreement on important goals, and sensitivity to sources of conflict and stress in the LMX relationship.

Currently, the leadership literature seems dominated by leader performance and effectiveness descriptions incorporated in the concepts of charismatic leadership and transformational leadership (Hunt, 1999). Charismatic behavior has been characterized by Conger and Kanungo (1998), House (1977), Shamir, House, and Arthur (1993), Weber (1947), and Yukl, 1999, 2010) as: articulating important and "visionary" goals for the organization, communicating the vision in a very expressive and positive emotional way, showing a willingness to take risks to accomplish the goals, communicating high expectations for followers, expressing optimism and confidence in followers, and empowering followers to participate in decision making associated with achieving the visionary goals.

The specifications for transformational leadership performance were first articulated by the historian J. M. Burns (1978) after studying the careers of widely recognized national leaders. Transformational leadership was brought into the I/O psychology mainstream by Bass (1985) and his colleagues (Bass, Avolio, Jung, & Berson, 2003). In general, transformational leadership performance is seen as less emotional and less hero-centered than charismatic leadership, but no less visionary, and focused on future goals of great importance. The measurement of transformational and transactional leadership has been facilitated by the development of the Multifactor Leadership Questionnaire (Bass & Avolio, 1990). The scales pertaining to transformational leadership performance include individualized consideration, intellectual stimulation, inspirational motivation, and idealized influence, although the item assignments to factors are not without ambiguity (Hinkin & Schriesheim, 2008). Some of the items also assess the follower's reactions to the leader (i.e., without reference to things the leaders did), which makes them assessment of effectiveness outcomes, rather than leader performance actions. Given these ambiguities, the item content for the first three scales bears a striking resemblance to consideration, structure, and production emphasis from the Ohio State studies and to the support, work facilitation, and goal emphasis factors from the Bowers and Seashore (1966) synthesis. As part of the MLQ description, the high-performing transformational leader also communicates confidence, enthusiasm, and the importance of collective interests regarding the goals to be accomplished. Consequently, Idealized Influence might also be referred to as "modeling" the attitudes and behaviors desired from others.

From this brief examination of current and past attempts to specify the behaviors and actions that comprise leadership performance, one major conclusion stands out. There is simply an amazing degree of consistency across models and theories stretching from 1950 to the present, in terms of the basic dimensions that constitute the latent structure of leader performance when performance is defined as this chapter defines it. The literature is not helter-skelter; it converges. Further, as will be subsequently discussed, the same latent structure seems to be applicable to any organizational level, and to peer leadership as well. It deserves to be part of any comprehensive model of individual performance.

Leadership Performance versus Management Performance

The relationship between leadership and management is a traditional issue in the literature. Are they the same thing? Are they mutually exclusive? Do they overlap? Is one part of the other? It is possible to find proponents for each of the above alternatives, but the core of the issue is whether there are a set of functions, or performance dimensions, that can be called "leadership" and a relatively distinct set of other functions or dimensions that can be called "management." Whether or not the two sets of functions can be found in the same work role, or performed by the same person, or whether they are always part of the same role, is another issue. This chapter is concerned with the first issue, not the second.

To some degree, there has been a separate literature devoted to identifying the performance dimensions comprising management that parallels the leadership literature. For example, there have been intensive case studies of a small number of managers (e.g., Kotter, 1996; Mahoney, Jerdee, & Carroll, 1963; Mintzberg, 1973), several critical incident data collections intended to identify categories of management performance (see Borman & Brush, 1993), and several research programs that developed questionnaire assessments of management performance behavior (e.g., Hemphill, 1959; Mahoney, Jerdee, & Carroll, 1965; Page & Tornow, 1987; Wilson, O'Hare, & Shipper, 1990; Yukl & Nemeroff, 1979; Yukl et al., 1990).

There is also a parallel literature on management theory (see Carroll & Gillen, 1987, for a review) which provides specifications for critical management functions such as planning, coordinating resources, negotiating, monitoring and evaluating, and staffing. Prescriptions for the formal functions of management go back to Weber (1947), Fayol (1949), Urwich (1952), and others, and can be found in virtually any management textbook.

Within I/O psychology there have been two major efforts to provide a composite picture of management performance dimensions, and they each used a very different approach. However, comparing where they ended up and how they relate to the leadership performance models previously discussed is instructive.

Borman and Brush (1993) analyzed the results from 7 published and 19 unpublished critical incident studies of management performance by first aggregating the distinct dimensions indentified in each study, the total of which was 187, and then asking an SME sample of 30 I/O psychologists to sort the 187 dimensions into homogeneous categories. The resulting matrix of similarities was factor analyzed, and an 18-factor solution seemed the most appropriate. A brief description of the 18 factors is shown in Table 6.2.

Yukl et al. (2002) developed a composite set of 12 leadership-management performance dimensions by reviewing all available measures of management-leadership performance, from the Ohio State Leader Behavior Description Questionnaire to his own Managerial Practice Survey (Yukl et al., 1990) to the Bass and Avolio (1990) Multi-Factor Leadership Questionnaire (MLQ), and categorizing the dimensions from each into the twelve factors shown in Table 6.3.

Looking at the results of the Borman & Brush (1993) and Yukl et al. (2002) efforts suggests the following:

1. There is a great deal of overlap, but some dimensions found in one were not identified in the other.
2. Both sets contain dimensions that some call leadership and some might call management (e.g., planning and organizing).
3. Some dimensions seem to be neither (e.g., technical proficiency, persistence in reaching goals).
4. Some dimensions seem reminiscent of contextual or OCB factors (representing the organization, organizational commitment).

Resolving these issues, or at least making them clearer, requires a more explicit specification of leadership versus management.

The position taken here is that leadership and management each involve a distinct set of functions to carry out, or roles to perform. That is, each has its own set of performance dimensions, which can be differentiated, to a degree that is useful for selection, training and development, job design, and performance assessment purposes. Most often,

Table 6.2 Dimensions of Management Performance (from Borman & Brush, 1993)

1.	Planning and organizing: formulating short- and long-term goals and objectives, forecasting possible problems for the unit/organization, and developing strategies for addressing these problems.
2.	Guiding, directing, and motivating subordinates and providing feedback: providing guidance and direction to subordinates.
3.	Training, coaching, and developing subordinates: identifying training needs and assisting subordinates in improving their job skills.
4.	Communicating effectively and keeping others informed, both orally and in written form.
5.	Representing the organization to customers and the public: contributing professional expertise in response to community needs, including those of stockholders and government agencies.
6.	Technical proficiency: keeping up to date technically, solving technical problems, providing technical advice to others in the organization.
7.	Administration and paperwork: performing day-to-day administrative tasks such as reviewing reports, approving routine requests, and administering policies, as appropriate.
8.	Maintaining good working relationships: developing and maintaining smooth and effective working relationships with superiors, peers, and subordinates.
9.	Coordinating subordinates and other resources to get the job done: properly utilizing personnel and other resources to increase until and organizational effectiveness.
10.	Decision making/problem solving: making sound and timely decisions, and developing effective solutions to organizational problems.
11.	Staffing: maintaining staff and workforce; recruiting, interviewing, selecting, transferring, and promoting: maintaining an effective career development system.
12.	Persisting to reach goals: persisting with extra effort to attain objectives and overcoming obstacles to get the job done.
13.	Handling crises and stress: recognizing and responding effectively to crises and stress, addressing conflict appropriately.
14.	Organizational commitment: working effectively with policies, procedures, rules: carrying out orders and directives.
15.	Monitoring and controlling resources: controlling cost and personnel resources and monitoring and overseeing utilization of funds.
16.	Delegating: assigning subordinates duties and responsibilities in line with their interests and abilities as well as the needs of the organization.
17.	Selling/influencing: persuading others in the organization to accept good ideas, presenting own positions clearly and decisively.
18.	Collecting and interpreting data: knowing what data are relevant to address a problem or issue; properly interpreting numerical data and other information.

these two sets of functions are, to some degree, the responsibility of one individual, who usually carries the title of supervisor, manager, or executive (Yukl & Lepsinger, 2005). However, individuals with other job, occupation,. or work role titles can perform these functions as well, and the composition of a particular work role can change dramatically,

as regards management and leadership functions, when the goals of the organization or unit change. That is, there is nothing that is particularly static about these two sets of responsibilities.

For present purposes, the overall distinction between these two sets of performance dimensions is that leadership involves direct interpersonal

Table 6.3 Yukl's 12 Factors

Clarifying roles: assigning tasks and explaining responsibilities, objectives, and expectations.	

Clarifying roles: assigning tasks and explaining responsibilities, objectives, and expectations.

Monitoring operations: monitoring progress and evaluating individual and unit performance.

Short-term planning: determining how to use personnel and resources to accomplish a task efficiently.

Consulting: checking with people before making decisions that affect them, encouraging participation in decision-making, and using the ideas and suggestions of others.

Supporting: showing consideration, sympathy, and support when someone is anxious, and providing encouragement when there is a difficult task.

Recognizing: providing praise and recognition for effective performance, special contributions, and performance improvements.

Developing: providing coaching, advice, and opportunities for skill development.

Empowering: allowing substantial responsibility and discretion, and trusting people to solve problems and make decisions without getting prior approval.

Envisioning change: presenting an appealing description of desirable outcomes that can be achieved by the unit with great enthusiasm and conviction.

Taking risks for change: taking personal risks and making sacrifices to encourage and promote desirable change in the organization.

Encouraging innovative thinking: challenging people to question their assumptions about the work and consider better ways to do it.

External monitoring: analyzing information about events, trends, and changes in the external environment to identify threats and opportunities for the organizational unit.

influence. That is, actions taken in the name of leadership attempt to influence the behavior of other people such that their performance is enhanced, both individually and collectively. Individual performance can be enhanced by other processes as well (e.g., online training), but direct interpersonal influence is, by definition, the domain of "leadership." This definition was not handed down from some higher authority. It simply seems to be very useful.

As distinct from leadership, management involves activities that best use (i.e., manage) the organization's resources to achieve its goals. They involve cognitive and communicative processes that influence others, but they do not rely, again by definition, on interpersonal influence. For example, developing a budget is a management function that will have important effects on others. However, selling it to other individuals may take interpersonal influence (i.e., leadership).

Again, there is no one best way to define leadership and management. The above is simply one that seems to be useful for developing a comprehensive substantive model of individual performance at work.

A Synthesized Taxonomy

Given the above working definition of leadership and management, and based on the accumulated research summarized above that attempts to specify the latent structure of leadership and management performance, a proposed synthesis is presented in Table 6.4. Given that the world of work can never be carved up quite so neatly, a set of caveats and conditionals follows.

Table 6.4 is intended to be a distillation of all previous taxonomic, or taxonomic-appearing, research on the substantive performance content of leadership and management. There are 14 factors, written at a fairly high level of generality. Both higher order and more specific subfactors can be found in the literature (see Yukl, 2010). The level of generality/specificity was chosen because 60 years of theory and research seem to converge on it. Using fewer higher order factors would seem to cover up some useful distinctions. Using more specific factors would be both possible and useful for specific research or application purposes, such as determining training needs or investigating particular kinds of performance dynamics.

Table 6.4 A Proposed Set of Basic Factors Comprising Leadership and Management Performance

Leadership Performance Factors

1. *Consideration, support, person-centered*: providing recognition and encouragement, being supportive when under stress, giving constructive feedback, helping others with difficult tasks, building networks with and among others.

2. *Initiating structure, guiding, directing*: providing task assignments, explaining work methods, clarifying work roles, providing tools, critical knowledge, and technical support.

3. *Goal emphasis:* encouraging enthusiasm and commitment for the group/organization goals, emphasizing the important missions to be accomplished.

4. *Empowerment, facilitation*: delegating authority and responsibilities to others, encouraging participation, allowing discretion in decision making.

5. *Training, coaching*: one-on-one coaching and instruction regarding how to accomplish job tasks, how to interact with other people, and how to deal with obstacles and constraints.

6. *Serving as a model*: models appropriate behavior regarding interacting with others, acting unselfishly, working under adverse conditions, reacting to crisis or stress, working to achieve goals, showing confidence and enthusiasm, and exhibiting principled and ethical behavior.

Management Performance Factors

1. *Goal setting, planning, organizing, and budgeting*: formulating operative goals; determining how to use personnel and resources (financial, technical, logistical) to accomplish goals; anticipating potential problems; estimating costs.

2. *Coordination*: actively coordinating the work of two or more units, or the work of several work groups within a unit; scheduling operations; includes negotiating and cooperating with other units.

3. *Monitoring unit effectiveness*: evaluating progress and effectiveness of units against goals; monitoring costs and resource consumption.

4. *External representation*: representing the organization to those not in the organization (e.g., customers, clients, government agencies, nongovernmental organizations, the "public"); maintaining a positive organizational image; serving the community; answering questions and complaints from outside the organization.

5. *Staffing*: Procuring and providing for the development of human resources; not one-on-one coaching, training, or guidance; but providing the human resources the organization or unit needs.

6. *Decision making, problem solving, and strategic innovation*: making sound and timely decisions about major goals and strategies; includes gathering information from both inside and outside the organization, staying connected to important information sources, and forecasting future trends and formulating goals (innovative or potentially profitable) to take advantage of them.

7. *Administration*: performing day-to-day administrative tasks, keeping accurate records, documenting actions. analyzing routine information, and making information available in a timely manner.

8. *Commitment and compliance*: compliance with the policies, procedures, rules, and regulations of the organization; full commitment to orders and directives, together with loyal constructive criticism of organizational policies and actions.

Again, no jobs, occupations, or work roles would comprise only leadership factors, or only management factors. Many positions might incorporate substantially all of them, but some would not. The 14 factors are meant to represent leadership and management wherever they might occur. It is intended that the same factors could be used to describe executive, management, supervisory, and peer leadership and management, although the criticality or relative emphasis of the factors might change significantly across different levels.

Although to a certain extent this separation of leadership and management performance content is forced, they do come from different research streams, and the differential emphasis on direct interpersonal influence seems meaningful. Two factors that are not in Table 6.4 but which do appear in the management literature are *communication* performance and performance in the appropriate *technical* specialty. These two factors appear as separate dimensions in most performance models and they have no particular link to leadership and management. Consequently, they are omitted from Table 6.4, but are included in the general model to be discussed subsequently.

It is noteworthy that virtually all of the performance dimensions discussed under the headings of contextual performance and organizational citizenship behavior (OCB) also appear as major dimensions in the leadership/management literature. For example, helping and cooperating with others, organizational courtesy, and altruism have specifications that are very similar to the leader consideration factor. The external representation factor in the management taxonomy is very similar to the contextual factor of endorsing, supporting, and defending organizational objectives and to the civic virtue factor of OCB. Both the contextual performance taxonomy and the OCB taxonomy have factors reflecting compliance with organizational policies, regulations, work rules, and norms. Theory and research dealing with management performance also produced such a factor. A study by Conway (1999) also supports the convergence between leadership and OCB.

The considerable overlap between the content of contextual/OCB and leadership/management performance lends credence to the previous assertion that peer leadership and peer management performance can be described with the same factors as supervisor/manager/executive leadership and management performance. Whether such dimensions are in-role or extra-role is a separate issue (e.g., see Vey & Campbell, 2004).

In the Campbell et al. (1993) model, effort appears as a separate factor, even though performance on every substantive factor is in part a function of effort. This seems to confuse performance and its determinants. Again, Campbell et al. (1993) tried to avoid this conundrum by defining effort in observable substantive terms, such as working extra hours or working under extreme conditions of weather or risk, which would contribute independently to the organization's goals. Specifying the "content" of effort in terms of such observables serves to make effort at least somewhat independent of the other substantive factors. It is noteworthy that contextual performance and OCB, as well as the management performance literature (see Table 6.4) include a factor labeled "persistence," or "extra effort," or "individual initiative," defined much as Campbell et al. (1993) defined effort. Consequently, this factor does not appear in Table 6.4 because it is not specific to a leadership or management role, regardless of the organizational level at which the role is located. It appears later as part of the overall model of individual performance.

The Negative Reaction Potential

Asserting that six decades of theory and research have produced a virtual consensus regarding the latent structure of leadership and management performance, when performance is defined as it is in this chapter, will probably not sit well with the current community of leadership scholars and researchers in organizational behavior, as represented by their publications in the *Journal of Applied Psychology*, the *American Academy of Management Journal/Review*, and the *Leadership Quarterly*. Such an assertion will be labeled as naïve, simpleminded, and mired in static, out-of-date overly positivist leadership models that focus on one-on-one leader/follower relationships at only one organizational level (e.g., see Drath et al., 2008). Making a big deal of such a latent structure could be seen as committing serious errors because it does not take into account multilevel effects, the myriad interactions with the complex features of the context in which leadership takes place, and the dynamic complexity of organizational functioning in the twenty-first century (Uhl-Bien, Marion, & McKelvey, 2007). Further, some make the argument that there has been a genuine paradigm shift in leadership theory that has revitalized that field, and markedly reduced the usefulness of Table 6.4. To be specific, the argument is that introduction of transformational leadership theory, and the reformulation of charismatic leadership, speak to issues that excite scholars, researchers, and practitioners (Hunt, 1999). Table 6.4 does not.

The message here is not to worry. Asserting that Table 6.4 is a consensus about the latent structure of leadership and management performance is really not incompatible with any recent major developments in leadership theory, unexciting as that might seem. For example, it is not incompatible with any of the chapters in the Society of I/O Psychology Frontiers Series volume on organizational leadership edited by Zaccaro and Klimoski (2001). One reason is that leadership is an area where the independent and dependent variable *do* get confused and the distinctions among behavior, performance, and effectiveness are anything but consistent. Also, new labels are frequently invented for the same phenomenon, and "theory" sometimes becomes an end in itself rather than a means to an end. Theories and models are not the dependent variable, and our goal is not to "prove" whether a theory is right or wrong (Campbell, 1991b). The function of theory is to identify critical research questions (or hypotheses if you prefer) that, if answered (or tested), would advance our knowledge of: (a) the assessment of leadership performance; (b) the prediction and development of leadership performance; (c) the relationship of leadership performance to peer, team, unit, and organizational effectiveness; (d) the processes by which leaders (or leadership) influence other people and thereby achieve desired outcomes; and (e) the optimal allocation of leadership resources across the organization.

Again, the assertion that there is a consensus regarding the latent structure of leadership performance is not incompatible with any previous or current theory/model of leadership, and the assertion is not guilty of most of the charges leveled against it. The following is a list of perceived shortcomings that are misdirected.

1. Leadership theory itself, in scientific psychology, is frequently seen as representing a historical progression from one competing model to the next, in which the newest model supplants those that came before, as if they were competing explanations for the same thing, so out with the old and in with the new. In the beginning there were "trait" models (see Mann, 1965; Stogdill, 1948) that were found wanting and were supplanted by the "behavior" models developed at Michigan and Ohio State. However, "trait" models and "behavioral" models don't address the same issues. The traits in question were predictors or *determinants* of leader performance, and most of the research focused on predicting who would "emerge" as the nominated leader in (initially) leaderless, small groups. As discussed previously, the Michigan and Ohio State studies focused on specifying the substantive content of leader *performance*. Consequently, in the beginning there was an immediate confusion between performance itself and its determinants, some of which could be, and are, traits. They are not competing explanations of "leadership."

Similarly, the subsequent contingency models (Fiedler, 1967; Hersey & Blanchard, 1977; House, 1971; House & Mitchell, 1974) did not reject the consensus latent structure of leadership performance. Instead, they attempted to specify the properties of the context that would moderate the effects of different dimensions of leader performance on the behavior of subordinates (an outcome). This does not invalidate the consensus latent structure model. It makes its identification even more critical. Leader Member Exchange (LMX; Graen & Uhl-Bien, 1995) goes further and says that the influence process is reciprocal and says that the initial performance of the "other" will in turn influence what the leader does subsequently. A high-performing leader will emphasize the

most appropriate performance actions as LMX continues. That is, the latent structure of leader performance has the same meaning, but the dimensions that are emphasized with each subordinate, or peer, are unique to that person, and also vary as a function of the developmental stage in the LMX process. High-performing leaders optimize this differential emphasis to achieve the highest quality LMX that is possible, given the characteristics of the other individual and the context in which exchange is occurring.

The consensus latent structure is also not contradicted by the charismatic (Conger & Kanungo, 1987) or transformational (Bass, 1985) leadership models. They are compatible with their historical predecessors and do not represent a paradigm shift in the Kuhnian (1963) sense, as asserted by Hunt (1999). The differences are really a matter of degree, even if it is a fairly large degree. That is, the specifications for leader performance incorporated in the charismatic and transformational models cover most of the latent factors listed in Table 6.4, but they emphasize the high end of the performance distribution, or "exceptional" leadership, in Bass's terms (1985). Conversely, Bass's notion of laissez-faire leadership really represents the low scorers on certain leadership dimensions. Because it does focus on exceptionally high performance, the transformational model resonates with people who are worried about the increased intensity and dynamics of the global economy, and there is nothing wrong with that, but it is not really a paradigm shift regarding the latent structure of leadership performance, when performance is defined as it is in this chapter.

Something called the complexity theory of leadership is also a recent development (Marion & Uhl-Bien, 2001; Uhl-Bien et al., 2007). It addresses leadership in the kinds of modern organizations referred to as complex adaptive systems (CAS). The principal point is that for such systems (i.e., organizations) to be effective, leadership must be distributed throughout the system via teams, groups, and networks, which can be both formal or informal, such that the system can react quickly and effectively to changing conditions without having to rely on a cumbersome central chain of command to provide leadership resources. This notion is not incompatible with previous work on leadership functions in high-performance teams (Goodman, Devadas, & Griffith-Hughson, 1988; Weick &

Roberts, 1993). Nothing in the consensus model says that these leadership capabilities cannot distribute themselves across the organization to meet the dynamics and complexities of the twenty-first century organizations. However, what the consensus model does say is that the content of the leadership *and* management capabilities being distributed are described by the consensus latent structure. The current literature on complexity leadership does seem to focus more on management functions than leadership functions, as they are distinguished in Table 6.4.

2. Some (e.g., Zaccaro, Rittman, & Marks, 2001), seem to argue that the Table 6.4 specifications of leadership and management performance are much less useful than a *functional* specification of leadership (McGrath, 1962) that directs the leadership focus to getting done whatever needs to be done to accomplish group, unit, or organizational goals (Kozlowski & Ilgen, 2006). However, discussions of leadership functionality seem to confuse performance and effectiveness by virtually equating functional leadership with leadership effectiveness, or the achievement of valued outcomes. Consequently, there is no fundamental incompatibility between Table 6.4 and a functional view of leadership. The form of the relationship between leadership performance and functional leadership (i.e., leadership effectiveness) is as discussed earlier in this chapter.

3. By implication (e.g., Day & Harrison, 2007), Table 6.4 is viewed as not being able to describe leadership performance at multiple organizational levels. However, the argument here has been just the opposite. The latent structure described in Table 6.4 is applicable at any organizational level, although the relative emphasis across the performance dimensions may vary, and the actions with each dimension that are the most critical may vary. For example, the nature of the training and coaching role would be different for supervisors versus executives, but there would still be such a role.

4. Team leadership in the modern era is seen by some (e.g., Day, Gronn, & Salas, 2006) as qualitatively different from the leadership role in more traditional settings. Consequently, one should not look to Table 6.4 for specifications of leadership performance in team settings. However, what is different about leadership in teams is not that the latent structure of leadership performance is different, but that the team members also take on leadership and management responsibilities,

and leadership is often shared across levels (Burke et al., 2006; Day et al., 2006; Hiller et al., 2006). When performance is defined as it is in this chapter, the available data support the assertion that the dimensions shown in Table 6.4 describe the major leadership and management components of team member *and* team leader performance.

5. Leadership at different organizational levels is not to be confused with "level effects," which refer to the unit of analysis. Table 6.4 refers to the performance of individuals. Could it also describe the performance of a team, a unit, or an organization? That is, for example, could research focus on the independent effects of individual *team member* consideration/support, goal emphasis, and problem solving, and on the same "actions" as provided by the group, as a group? The group or organizational effect is often referred to as the management/leadership climate or culture, but there is no consensus about the latent structure of leadership/management climate that rivals that of Table 6.4. The dimensions described in Table 6.4 are individual performance dimensions, not climate dimensions; although leadership climate may interact with leadership performance.

6. The latent structure portrayed in Table 6.4 does *not* preclude a multitude of context effects (e.g., Mumford, Antes, Caughron, & Friedrich, 2008; Osborn, Hunt, & Jauch, 2002) that govern how leadership performance will influence outcomes. Contextualizing leadership/management does not remove the need for a latent structure of performance, defined in the way this chapter defines it. It is simply the case that performance, contextual effects, the interaction of performance and context, and leader performance outcomes (i.e., effectiveness) should not be confused.

7. Modeling leadership as a political process *does* have implications for Table 6.4 (e.g., see Ammeter, Douglas, Gardner, Hochwarter, & Ferris, 2002). Invoking a political model implies that there are genuine conflicts among constituencies over goals and the distribution of resources. Table 6.4 implies that high performance on certain critical dimensions can resolve such conflicts in the best interests of achieving the organizational goals. If leadership and management performance, as characterized by Table 6.4, fails to resolve the conflict, then a political process could ensue that would to some degree call for different performance actions on the part of leadership and management within the competing factions. The use of power, political influence, and manipulative

social influence tactics to carry the day does stand in contrast to Table 6.4, and we probably have all been in organizations where it happens.

8. The leadership dimensions in Table 6.4 are sometimes referred to as "styles" (e.g., Schriesheim, Wu, & Scandura, 2009). Lord & Hall (2005) are particularly dismissive when they refer to them as mere styles that can be learned in a short time. They then go on to talk at length about the development of leadership "skills" (i.e., performance determinants), which in their view, is a long and complex process of developing expertise. Again, Table 6.4 is meant to be a portrayal of the principal things leaders *do*. For example, production emphasis is not a style. It is a set of performance actions required by a leadership role, although its specific content may vary, depending on organizational level, and so on. There is no implication that being a high performer on this dimension is easy and can be learned in a few days. Acquired skills, which may take a long time to develop, are important determinants of performance on this factor, and also on other factors. Performance has multiple determinants.

The overall moral here regarding theory and research in management and leadership is that both modernists and postmodernists (Esade & McKelvey, 2010) should not make negative comparisons between the new and the old until it is perfectly clear that they are talking about the same thing. Very often, they are not.

Team Member Performance

The literature on work team functioning has grown considerably over the past 25 years (e.g., Ilgen, Hollenbeck, Johnson, & Jundt, 2005; Kozlowski & Ilgen, 2006). One reason for the expansion is that an increasing amount of an individual's work is performed in a team context, where a team is defined as a group of individuals with somewhat different roles and responsibilities, but who must work interdependently, and who are chartered to accomplish a set of *team* goals or objectives. The team goals usually, but not necessarily, flow from the team's role in accomplishing the goals of a larger organizational system (i.e., there may be no larger system). There are many varieties of such work teams (e.g., see Guzzo & Dickson, 1996), ranging from advisory groups, to specific project groups, to ongoing production or service teams, to so-called action teams that spend most of their time preparing for the occasion when they must address their chartered goals

in a very intense context (e.g., firefighting units or sports teams). Work teams may exist over long periods of time, or over relatively short periods of time; however, their defining characterizations are a common goal, or set of goals, and the need for coordinated or integrated effort. Consequently, they are to be distinguished from the traditional hierarchical work group in that the team members assume some level of leadership and management responsibilities (Goodman et al., 1988).

Considerable research and theory have been directed at the determinants of work team success, such as the abilities, personality, and motivation of the team members; the teamwork processes that are used to accomplish objectives; the quality of team leadership; the nature of the goals to be pursued; and a variety of situational and context efforts, such as technology, the organizational climate/culture, group norms, group cohesion, team efficacy, team member diversity, and so on (Guzzo & Shea, 1992; Hackman, 1992; Salas, Stagl, & Burke, 2004).

Somewhat strangely, relatively little attention has been devoted to individual performance *as a team member*. That is, what must team members *do* to meet the performance requirements of being on a particular team at a particular time and place within a particular structure with a certain set of objectives? In other words, how should individual performance as a team member be modeled, or can it be? There have been only a few efforts in that direction. Stevens and Campion (1994) developed specifications for individual teamwork "skills" by synthesizing what literature was available. Podsakoff, Ahearne, and MacKenzie (1997) used an OCB framework to describe team member performance. Olson (2000) used a critical incident strategy to identify individual teamwork performance factors, and Hiller et al. (2006) proposed and tested a four-factor model that included: (a) planning and organizing, (b) problem solving, (c) support and consideration, and (d) development and mentoring. All of these efforts made the assumption that at some level of generality the dimensions of individual teamwork performance could be specified such that they would not be situationally specific.

The study by Olson (2000) is helpful because it is based both on a review of the previous literature, which yielded a set of seven dimensions, and on a relatively extensive critical incident data collection that produced a revised taxonomy. Several hundred (650) critical incidents were collected from four high-performance work teams. Two were project teams in engineering firms, and two were advisory/

planning teams in medical centers (total N = 93). Each individual was asked to describe examples they had observed of both "effective" and "ineffective" performance *as a team member*. A random sample of 200 incidents was sorted into categories by 20 SMEs. These sorts were both (a) retranslated by another sample of SMEs, and (b) subjected to a principal component analysis of the 200 x 200 agreement matrix. The process was then replicated using another random sample of incidents. The final set of dimension specifications is shown in Table 6.5.

The critical incidents were unprimed in the sense that no a priori structure was provided to the incident writers. However, what emerged was something very similar to the specifications that emerged from the leadership/management literature. Members of high-performance work teams do in fact see their roles as having leadership and management responsibilities, in addition to their technical performance

responsibilities. Also, they are very much aware of the coordination, work load distribution, and problem-solving components of their teamwork role. Overall, their inductively derived specifications are quite consistent with the previous teamwork literature, with the subsequent research by Hiller et al. (2006), with the previous 60 years of research on leadership and management as portrayed in Table 6.4, and with the previous 25 years of research on job performance modeling, including the research on contextual performance and organizational citizenship.

While the focus of this chapter is on individual performance, including individual performance as a team member, the above literature is also consistent with the findings of Marks, Mathieu, and Zaccaro (2001) and LePine, Piccolo, Jackson, Mathieu, and Saul (2008), who focused on the team itself as the unit of analysis. Their dimensions of what they call

---

Table 6.5 A Taxonomy of Components of Individual Performance as a Team Member (from Olson, 2000)

1. *Fulfilling team-related task responsibilities*. Takes ownership for and completes assigned tasks according to committed timelines. Does not pass work off to others or take shortcuts that compromise quality.

2. *Peer leadership: Initiating structure*. Helps to define goals and organize and prioritize tasks. Generates plans and strategies for task completion, identifies resources needed to meet team goals, and shares resources or guides team members to resources to help them complete their tasks.

3. *Peer leadership: Consideration*. Provides social support and empathy, offers verbal encouragement, and acts respectfully toward other team members, especially when tasks or situations are difficult or demanding. Facilitates cohesion and effective working relationships between team members by acting honestly, communicating openly, and helping to manage or resolve conflicts. Does not embarrass team members in front of others, act impatiently, or blame others.

4. *Training team members/Sharing task information*. Shares information with team members, provides task explanations and demonstrations, answers questions, and gives timely and constructive feedback to team members. Does not withhold information about team-related tasks.

5. *Team member helping/Backup relief*. Fills in or covers for team members who are overwhelmed or absent. Rearranges own schedule and demonstrates flexibility to help other team members. Puts in extra time and effort to help team members without being asked and without complaining. Does not engage in off-task activities when other team members could use help.

6. *Monitoring performance*. Observes and is knowledgeable about the performance of other team members. Pays attention to what individual team members are doing. Evaluates progress of self and others and recognizes when team members may need help.

7. *Monitoring team effectiveness*. Pays attention to the team's situation, including relevant conditions, procedures, policies, resources, systems, equipment, technology, and level of team accomplishment. Notices and identifies ream-relevant problems and obstacles.

8. *Individual contributions to problem solving*. Helps in identifying alternative solutions, strategies, or options for dealing with problems, obstacles, or decisions. Helps in evaluating courses of action, and takes preventive measures to avoid future problems.

9. *Individual contributions to workload distribution/coordination*. Contributes to and encourages discussion of work distribution, workload balance, potential workload problems, and the sequencing of team member activities. Coordinates own task activities with other team members. Does not make unnecessary request or overload other team members.

---

team *processes* map very well onto the dimensions in Table 6.5, as well as the broader taxonomy represented in Table 6.4. Useful research questions would revolve around the relationships between individual assessments of performance as a team member and assessment of the performance of the "team" on the same dimensions.

Models of Performance Revisited

Given this brief synopsis of approaches to modeling individual work role performance, is there a useful synthesis? The simple answer here is an emphatic "yes." Further, there is so much commonality across the various models that very little "synthesis" or "integration" is actually needed. Many of the differences noted in the literature (without naming names) seem to be straw people.

The following properties of the synthesized description should be kept in mind.

a. The model is composed of *dimensions* of *performance*, when performance is *defined as it is in this chapter*. That is, each dimension is intended to circumscribe a domain, or universe, of actions/behaviors, each of which belongs in that particular domain, and not some other one. There are most likely identifiable subdomains, or subfactors, within each. However, each dimension should not be characterized as a small finite list of specific behaviors. To do so is to set up a straw person. Each major dimension constitutes a domain of behavior. Measurement must necessarily sample from each domain, and for various purposes, the samples could be nonrandom, as in assessing theft behavior at various organizational levels.

Again, the actions that comprise a particular factor cannot be divorced from a consideration of unit or organization goals. The content of a dimension must be goal relevant, in either a positive or negative way, and scalable in terms of the level of performance exhibited by an individual.

b. The composite model, as well as the individual models on which it is based, is intended to identify the *substantive* content of performance. It does *not* address how performance proficiency develops, or how individual differences in performance interact with parameters of the "situation" to influence particular outcomes. These are research questions to be addressed, but they should be addressed using a meaningful substantive specification for the main effects, in this case, individual performance.

c. The model is intended to be taxonomic and hierarchical, and there are most certainly multiple levels in the hierarchy, only some of which are currently specified.

d. The model is intended to be applicable to any occupation, job, or work role, however briefly occupied. That is, accusations of being anachronistically tied to "jobs" reflect a straw person.

e. At any given time, a particular work role is composed of more than one dimension of performance, but not necessarily all of them, at a particular level in the hierarchy. However, there may be universals (e.g., technical performance, counterproductive work behavior), and there may be more management or leadership requirements in many work roles than would be expected by the conventional wisdom.

f. The model does not address issues of adaptability or performance dynamics. More about these issues later, but to accuse it of being a "static" picture is to invoke another straw person. Both the performance requirements of the work role and the performance capabilities of the individual can readily change. *However*, all such changes should be described in terms of the content of the model.

Given these perspectives, an extended discussion of the composite picture of the dimension of work performance follows.

A Composite Model of Individual Work Performance Dimensions

This composite is intended to be based on all work in I/O psychology, and related fields, as of the current date. Consequently, it reflects empirical factor analytic work, job analyses, case studies, conceptual frameworks that seem to have stood the test of time, and performance measurement efforts. Orthogonality is not asserted or implied, but content distinctions among dimensions that have different implications for selection, training, and organizational outcomes certainly are. While scores on the different dimensions may be added together for a specific measurement purpose, it is not possible to provide a *substantive* specification for a "general" factor. Whether there can be dimensions as general as contextual performance or citizenship behavior will be addressed later.

The Basic Factors

The basic substantive factors of individual performance in a work role stated at the highest feasible level of generality seem to be the following. (They are *not* synonymous with Campbell et al., 1993).

Factor 1: technical performance. All models acknowledge that virtually all jobs or work roles have technical components. Such requirements can vary by substantive area (driving a vehicle vs. analyzing data) and by level of complexity or difficulty within area (driving a taxi vs. driving a jetliner; tabulating sales frequencies vs. modeling institutional investment strategies). By definition, such performance content does not involve interpersonal influence relative to subordinates, superiors, or coworkers, or general management functions, but it could involve persuasion of customers or clients to make choices beneficial to the organization. Consequently, persuasion and negotiation qualify as technical content for some jobs or roles. Technical performance is not to be confused with "task" performance. A task is simply one possible unit of description that could be used for any performance dimension.

The subfactors for this dimension are obviously numerous, and the domain could be parsed into large or narrow slices. In days of old, the Dictionary of Occupational Titles (DOT) contained technical task descriptions for 13,000+ "jobs." Currently, the U.S. Department of Labor uses occupational classifications at varying levels of technical specificity. The Occupational Information Network (O*NET; Peterson, Mumford, Borman, Jeanneret, & Fleishman, 1999) is based on the Department of Labor's Standard Occupational Classification (SOC) structure, which currently uses 821 occupations for describing the distinctions of technical task content across the entire labor force; the 821 occupations are further aggregated into three higher order levels consisting of 449, 96, and 23 occupational clusters, respectively. Interestingly, the managers of O*NET have divided some of the SOCs into narrower slices to better suit user purposes and have also added "new and emerging" occupations such that O*NET 14.0 collected data on 965 occupations. The number will grow in the future (National Research Council, 2010). Potentially at least, an occupational classification based on technical task content could be used to archive I/O psychology research data on individual performance.

Factor 2: communication. The Campbell et al. (1993) model is the only one that isolated communication as a separate dimension. More typically, it is part of the technical factor or appears as a facet of management (Yukl et al., 2002). It remains in this composite picture because it does "seem" to be part of many occupations, ranging from teaching, to research, to the arts, to sales, to customer service, to management. Again, it refers to the proficiency with which one conveys information that is clear, understandable, and well organized. It is independent of subject matter expertise. The two major subfactors would be oral and written communication.

Factor 3: initiative, persistence, and effort. This factor emerged from the contextual performance and management performance literatures, as well as the OCB literature, where it was referred to as individual initiative. To make this factor conform to the definition of performance used in this chapter, it must be composed of substantive observable actions. Consequently, it is typically specified in terms of extra hours, voluntarily taking on additional tasks, working under extreme or adverse conditions, and so on.

Factor 4: counterproductive work behavior. As it has come to be called, counterproductive work behavior (CWB) refers to a category of individual actions or behaviors that have negative implications for accomplishment of the organization's goals. While such counterproductive actions as theft on the job, absenteeism, and freeloading have been studied as single phenomena, the first study to include such variables as specifications for a latent dimension of performance was Project A (Campbell, 1991a), where it was termed *personal discipline*. It was derived from archival and ratings data and included a wide variety of rule infractions and disciplinary actions. The factor appeared in the covariance analyses of the performance indicators in all four of the Project A data sets. The dimension had no positive end, just varying degrees of a lack of personal discipline.

The current literature does not speak with one voice regarding the meaning of CWB, but the specifications generally circumscribe actions that are intentional, that violate or deviate from prescribed norms, and which have a negative effect on the individual's contribution to the goals of the unit or organization. Descriptions of this domain are provided by Gruys and Sackett (2003) and Robinson and Bennett (1995). There seems to be general agreement that there are two major subfactors (e.g., see Bennett & Robinson. 2000; Berry, Ones, & Sackett, 2007; Dalal, 2005) distinguished by the deviant behaviors directed at the organization (theft, sabotage, falsifying information, malingering) and behavior directed at individuals, including the self (e.g., physical attacks, verbal abuse, sexual harassment, drug and alcohol abuse). Although not yet fully substantiated by research, it seems reasonable to also expect an approach/avoidance, or moving toward versus moving away distinction for both organizational deviance and individual deviance. That is, the CWBs dealing with organizational deviance seems to divide between aggressively destroying or misusing resources versus avoiding or withdrawing from the responsibilities of the work role. Similarly, CWBs directed at individuals seem to divide between aggressive actions that are directed at other people and destructive actions directed at the self, such as alcohol and drug abuse, and neglect of safety precautions. The approach-avoidance distinction is a recurring one in the study of motivation (Elliot & Thrash, 2002; Gable, Reis, & Elliot, 2003) and of personality (Watson & Clark, 1993), including a major two-factor model of psychopathology (Markon, Krueger, & Watson, 2005). It is also suggested in a study of counterproductive work behavior by Marcus, Schuler, Quell, and Humpfner (2002). Consequently, CWBs that reflect aggressive actions should be predicted by different factors from CWBs that represent withdrawal.

A major issue in the CWB literature is whether its principal subfactors are simply the extreme negative end of other performance factors, or whether they are independent constructs. For example, do withdrawal actions constitute the negative end of the Initiative, Persistence, Effort factor, and do the deviant behaviors directed at individuals constitute the negative end of the peer leadership factors, or do they constitute a different construct? The general question is whether two variables constitute one bipolar variable or two independent variables (i.e., an individual could be high or low on both, and individual differences on each item variable are predicted by different things). This is a classic issue in psychological measurement and "more research is needed"; however, the evidence currently available (Berry et al., 2007; Dalal, 2005; Kelloway, Loughlin, Barling, & Nault, 2002; Miles, Borman, Spector, & Fox, 2002; Ones & Viswesvaran, 2003; Spector, Bauer, & Fox, 2010), suggest that CWBs are not simply the negative side of other performance components. Low scores on other performance dimensions could result from a lack of knowledge or skill, but low scores on CWB reflect intentional deviance and are dispositional in origin.

One area of research and theory that has not been incorporated in the CWB discussion thus far pertains to the definition and assessment of business ethics (e.g., Henle, Giacolone, & Jurkiewicz, 2005). To the extent that unethical behavior is judged to be counterproductive for the organizations goals,

the ethics literature is relevant for modeling job performance.

Factor 5: supervisory, manager, executive (i.e., hierarchical) leadership. This factor refers to leadership in a hierarchical relationship and the substantive content is most parsimoniously described by the six leadership factors in Table 6.4. Again, the parsimony results from the remarkable convergence of the literature from the Ohio State and Michigan studies through the contingency theories of Fielder, House, Vroom, and Yetton to the current emphasis on being charismatic and transformational, leading the team, and operating in highly complex and dynamic environments. Depending on the particular research stream, or the leadership model under consideration, the emphasis may be on leader performance, as defined in this chapter, or it may be on the outcomes of leader actions (i.e., effectiveness), or on the determinants (predictors) of leadership performance, or on the contextual influences on leader performance or effectiveness. However, when describing or assessing leadership *performance*, the specifications are always in terms of one or more of these six factors. The relative emphasis may be different, and different models may hypothesize different paths from leader performance to leader effectiveness, which for some people may be the interesting part, but the literature's characterization of leader performance itself seems always within the boundaries of these six subfactors.

Similarly, the six subfactors circumscribe hierarchical leadership performance at all organizational levels. However, the relative emphasis may change at higher organizational levels, and the specific actions with each subfactor may also receive differential emphasis. For example, at the supervisory level, consideration/support and training/coaching may be more important than at the executive level; while goal emphasis becomes dominant at the higher executive levels to the point that it becomes transformational when skillfully done.

Factor 6: management performance (hierarchical). Within a hierarchical organization, this factor includes those actions that deal with obtaining, preserving, and allocating the organization's resources to best achieve its goals. The major subfactors of management performance are also given in Table 6.4. As it was for the components of leadership, there may be considerably different emphases on the management performance subfactors across work roles. For example, there may be no Staffing requirement, or the External Representation factor may dominate everything (think BP CEO performance during the

Gulf oil spill). Situational changes may change the emphasis on different subfactors, or specific managers may emphasize different factors, as a way of designing their own job. The model does not imply that the management performance requirements of a particular position or work role are static and cannot change. The relative emphasis most likely will change as a function of the type of organization, the organizational level, changes in the situational context, changes in organization goals, and so on. However, these six subfactors are intended to provide the general specifications for the performance domain labeled "management."

Factor 7: peer/team member leadership performance. The content of this factor is parallel to the actions that comprise hierarchical leadership (factor 5 above). That is, the subfactors are: providing consideration and support; providing structure, guidance, and direction (to one's peers); emphasizing goals; facilitating the participation of others in decision making and problem solving; training and coaching others; and serving as a model. The defining characteristic is that these actions are in the context of peer or team member interrelationships; and the peer/team relationships in question can be at any organizational level (e.g., production teams vs. management teams). That is, the team may comprise non-supervisory roles or a management team of unit managers. Again, at different organizational levels the peer leadership performance requirements may differ in terms of the relative importance of the subfactors. For example, depending on a number of context factors, the importance of goal emphasis may increase and the importance of teaching and coaching may decrease at higher organizational levels. However, the overall domain of peer leadership and support is intended to be described by the six leadership subfactors in Table 6.4.

Factor 8: team member/peer management performance. A defining characteristic of the high-performance work team (Goodman et al., 1988) is that team members perform many of the management functions shown in Table 6.4. For example, the team member performance factors in the Olson (2000) taxonomy that are not accounted for by the technical performance factors or the peer leadership factor concern such management functions as planning and problem solving, determining within-team coordination requirements and workload balance, and monitoring team performance. In addition, the contextual performance and OCB literatures both strongly indicate that representing the unit or organization to external stakeholders

and exhibiting commitment and compliance to the policies and procedures of the organization are critical performance factors at any organizational level. Consequently, to a greater extent than most researchers realize or acknowledge, there are important elements of management performance in the peer or team context as well as in the hierarchical (i.e., management/subordinate) setting.

Summary

As stated at the outset, these eight factors are intended to be an integrative synthesis of what the literature has suggested are the principal dimensions of performance in a work role. They are meant to encompass all previous work on individual performance modeling, team member performance, and leadership and management. Even though the different streams of literature may use somewhat different words for essentially the same performance actions, there is great consistency across the different sources.

It must be kept in mind that these eight factors address the substantive content of individual work performance when performance is defined as it is in this chapter. The model does not speak to the determinants of individual differences in performance on these factors, or to the contextual factors that might influence the group mean on a particular factor, or to the effect of performance differences on various outcome measures. It also does not speak to the dynamics of performance or to the processes by which individual performance affects other variables or outcomes. Other chapters in this handbook take up these issues in some detail. However, substantive models such as this one do have some important implications for these other issues, one of which is performance dynamics.

Performance Dynamics

When attempting to summarize I/O psychology's collective efforts to model work performance, it is important to distinguish between substantive and nonsubstantive properties of individual performance. So far, this chapter has centered on a substantive model of performance content, about which there is virtually a consensus.

There is a parallel universe that addresses the parameters of performance dynamics, including the concepts of active, proactive, and adaptive performance. These two areas of inquiry, the latent structure of work performance content and the nature of performance dynamics, are not in competition. They address different issues, but each has important implications for the other.

Again, excellent discussions of performance dynamics appear elsewhere (e.g., Sonnentag & Frese, chapter 17 of this handbook), and they are not repeated here. However, the major parameters of performance dynamics are summarized below for purposes of illustrating their juxtaposition with the latent structure of performance content.

No one seriously argues that individual work performance does not change over time, and there are many reasons that such changes could occur. Obviously, the performance requirements for an individual could change. That is, the substantive content of a work role could change over time (perhaps a short time), with the result that specific individuals will make lesser contributions to the organization's goals unless they change as well. However, there are at least three ways in which performance requirements could change: (a) the substantive content of the requirements; (b) the level of performance expected; or (c) the conditions under which a particular level of performance is expected; or some combination of these. Change is complicated. If the changes in performance requirements were the same for each person, but the within-person changes in performance varied by individual, then the rank ordering of people in a sample would also change over time. If the changes in performance requirements are not identical across people and there are interactive effects between individuals and the nature of the work role content changes, then changes in the rank ordering of people over time results from multiple sources. Given the current and future nature of employment, it is reasonable to expect that such things will happen, and are happening.

Much of I/O psychology research and practice deals with planned interventions designed to enhance the individual knowledge, skill, and motivational determinants of performance, such as training and development, goal setting, feedback, rewards of various kinds, better supervision, and so on. Such interventions, with performance requirements held constant, could increase the group mean, or have differential effects across people, or both. The performance changes produced can be sizable (e.g., Carlson, 1997; Katzell & Guzzo,1983; Locke & Latham, 2002).

Interventions designed to enhance individual performance determinants can also be implemented by the individual's own processes of self-management and regulation (Kanfer, Chen, & Pritchard, 2008; Lord, Diefendorff, Schmidt, & Hall, 2010). That is, as a result of an individual's self-monitoring and self-evaluation of his or her own performance

against goals, additional training can be sought (perhaps from coworkers), different performance goals can be self-set, feedback can be sought, and self-efficacy could change. The effectiveness of these self-regulation processes could vary widely across people. In addition, if they have the latitude to do so, individuals could conduct their own job redesign (i.e., change the substantive content of their work role) to better utilize their knowledge and skills and increase the effort they are willing to spend. Academics are fond of doing that.

As noted by Sonnentag and Frese (chapter 17 of this handbook), individual performance can also change simply as a function of the passage of time. Of course, time is a surrogate for such things as: practice and experience, the aging process, or changes in emotional states (Beal et al., 2005).

It is most likely the case that for any given individual over any given period of time, many of these sources of performance change can be operating simultaneously. Performance dynamics are complex, and attempts to model the complexity have taken many forms. For example, there could be characteristic growth curves for occupations (e.g., Murphy, 1989b), differential growth curves across individuals (Hofmann, Jacobs, & Gerras, 1992; Ployhart & Hakel, 1998; Stewart & Nandkeolyar, 2006; Zyphur, Chaturvedi, & Arvey, 2008), both linear and nonlinear components for growth curves (Deadrick, Bennett, & Russell, 1997; Reb & Cropanzano, 2007; Sturman, 2003), and cyclical changes resulting from a number of self-regulatory mechanisms (Lord et al., 2010). Empirical demonstrations of each of these have been established.

Active, Proactive, and Adaptive Performance

Perceptions that organizations face increasing amounts of uncertainty and that the substantive performance requirements of jobs and work roles are becoming more fluid and dynamic have produced increased interest in modeling performance capabilities that can deal with this increase in change and uncertainty. Frese (2008) uses the term *active performance* to describe individual capabilities for going beyond the organization's prescribed requirements and taking additional actions that will better result in achieving valued outcomes. Active performance means taking the initiative, hopefully in a useful way, in responding to the organization's goals. Griffen et al. (2007) use a very similar term, *proactive performance*, to describe "the extent to which the individual takes self-directed actions to anticipate or initiate change in the work system or work role" (p. 329).

The concepts of "active" or "proactive" performance are quite similar to the older, and broader, notion of performance adaptability. The concept of adaptability has taken on many meanings in the literature (Ployhart & Bliese, 2006), but was given a big boost in I/O psychology by Hesketh and Neal (1999) and by the widely cited study by Pulakos et al. (2000) that used a critical incident methodology to identify eight dimensions of adaptive performance. In its broadest sense, adaptability refers to being able to deal effectively with some combination of: changes in organization goals; changes in individual performance requirements; or changes in the performance environment, which have been either already identified or are anticipated. This would include using knowledge and skill learned in training to deal with performance requirements in the work role that were not incorporated in the training objectives. Kozlowski, Gully, Nason, and Smith (1999) refer to this as *adaptive transfer*.

Adaptability can be viewed either as a characteristic of performance itself (i.e., a category of performance actions), as do Hesketh and Neal (1999), or as a property of the individual (i.e., a determinant of performance). Ployhart and Bliese (2006) present a thorough discussion of this issue and argue that it is more useful to model (i.e., identify the characteristics of) the adaptive individual than it is to propose adaptability as a distinct content dimension of performance. One reason is that the general definition of adaptability is not content domain specific, and it has been difficult to provide specifications for adaptability as a performance dimension. The best attempt is represented by the Pulakos et al. (2000) factors shown in Table 6.6. The factors were obtained by mining a large database of critical incidents of performance, and using systematic SME judgments to identify and categorize incidents reflective of adaptation.

However, the interpretation of the factors as representing adaptability is not straightforward. To take the eight factors in order, factor one (handling emergencies) could also be viewed as a subfactor of the technical performance dimension for certain jobs or work roles (e.g., medic, police officer, military personnel). Factors two (handling stress), three (solving problems), four (dealing with unpredictable situations), and five (learning tasks and procedures) are essentially domain general and could be viewed as general *skills* (i.e., performance determinants) that would support domain-specific performance when performance requirements changed. Factor six (interpersonal adaptability) seems to be part of the peer leadership factor discussed previously, and is consequently a domain-specific performance factor. Factor seven (cultural adaptability) is also a domain-specific performance subfactor that could be classified in the peer leadership dimension. Finally, factor eight (physical adaptability) can be viewed as a subfactor of the "initiative, effort" dimension in the revised model.

In general, the Pulakos et al. (2000) taxonomy illustrates the difficulty of trying to treat components of adaptability as domain-specific dimensions of performance. Some of them fit, others seem not to. Ployhart and Bliese (2006) chose to treat the eight factors as a set of variables that *predicts* adaptive responses to changes in substantive performance requirements.

Domain-Specific Dynamics

In sum, it can be taken as a given that work role performance requirements change over time, sometimes over very short periods of time, as the result of factors such as changes in organization/work goals, increased competition, organization and work redesign, technological advances, personnel changes, changes in the organization's environment (e.g., increased government regulations), and so on. If performance requirements change, can individuals change (i.e., adapt) to meet them, and at what level of proficiency? Also, can individuals change (i.e., adapt) in *anticipation* of changes in performance requirements? Many interventions (e.g., training, goal setting, reward systems) have been developed to help individuals adapt to changing performance requirements. Individuals can also actively engage in their own self-management to develop additional knowledge and skill and to regulate the direction and intensity of their effort. If the freedom to do so exists, they can even proactively change their own performance responsibilities, or at least their relative emphases, so as to better utilize their own knowledge and skill or to better accomplish unit goals. Even if performance requirements remain relatively constant, individual performance can change over time as the result of practice, feedback, increasing experience, cognitive and physical changes resulting from aging, or even fluctuation in affect or subjective well-being.

These known dynamics of performance have resulted in an increasing body of research dealing with such issues as: (a) what individual differences predict or explain adaptability; (b) the extent to which performance correlates with performance

Table 6.6 Eight Dimensions of Adaptive Performance (adapted from Pukalos et al., 2000)

Title	Definition
1. Handling emergencies or crisis situations	Reacting appropriately in life-threatening, dangerous, or emergency situations; maintaining emotional control and objectivity while keeping focus on the situation and taking action.
2. Handling work stress	Remaining composed when faced with difficult circumstances or a highly demanding workload or schedule; not overreacting to unexpected news or situations; managing frustration well by directing effort to constructive solutions rather than blaming others; acting as a calming and settling influence to whom others look for guidance.
3. Solving problems creatively	Employing unique types of analyses and generating new, innovative ideas in complex areas; integrating seemingly unrelated information and developing creative solutions; entertaining wide-ranging possibilities others may miss; developing innovative methods of obtaining or using resources.
4. Dealing with uncertain and unpredictable work situations	Taking effective action when necessary; readily and easily changing gears in response to unpredictable or unexpected events and circumstances; effectively adjusting plans, goals, actions, or priorities to deal with changing situations.
5. Learning work tasks, technologies, and procedures	Demonstrating enthusiasm for learning new approaches and technologies; doing what is necessary to keep knowledge and skills current; quickly and proficiently learning new methods or how to perform previously unlearned tasks; anticipating changes in work demands; taking action to improve work performance deficiencies.
6. Demonstrating interpersonal adaptability	Being flexible and open-minded when dealing with others; listening to and considering others' viewpoints and opinions and altering own opinion when it is appropriate to do so; being open and accepting of negative or developmental feedback regarding work; working well and developing effective relationships with highly diverse personalities.
7. Demonstrating cultural adaptability	Taking action to learn about and understand the climate, orientation, needs, and values of other groups, organizations, or cultures; integrating well into and being comfortable with different values, customs, and cultures; willingly adjusting behavior or appearance as necessary to show respect for others' values and customs.
8. Demonstrating physically oriented adaptability	Adjusting to challenging environmental states such as extreme heat, humidity, cold, or dirtiness; frequently pushing self physically to complete strenuous or demanding tasks, adjusting weight and muscular strength or becoming proficient in performing physical tasks as necessary for the job.

over time (i.e., a between-individuals effect); and (c) the patterns of intraindividual change across time, given relatively constant performance requirements. Consequently, one might ask what implications performance dynamics and individual adaptability have for substantive models of individual work performance. This is not the right question. A more appropriate question is what implications substantive models of performance have for studying performance dynamics and individual adaptability.

As noted by Ployhart and Bliese (2006), virtually all of the research and conversation dealing with performance dynamics and adaptation is in the context of technical task performance (i.e., dimension one in the composite model, or with reference to "overall" performance [unspecified]). However, the message in this chapter is that the latent structure of individual work performance is multidimensional, and the eight factors discussed previously represent a consensus developed over several decades. In terms of investigating such things as (a) the determinants of adaptive performance, (b) the correlation of performance with performance over time (and the reasons that it increases or decreases), (c) characteristic performance growth curves for occupations, (d) intraindividual growth curves, or (e) the nature of performance changes over time, the research should be *domain specific*. That is, the dynamics of technical performance and the dynamics of peer leadership, or management performance, may not be the same. For example, for a particular occupation or work role, do peer leadership and technical performance exhibit similar growth curves over time? What predicts adaptation to changes in technical performance requirements (dimension one) versus adaptation to changes in requirements for initiative and persistence (dimension three). To date, only one study of performance dynamics (Iles, Scott, & Judge, 2006) has moved outside the context of performance on the technical factor (i.e., dimension one).

Implications for Measurement

The realities of performance criterion measurement are always complex and scary, but in contrast to the state of affairs in 1970, thorough reviews of criterion measurement issues, from a number of perspectives, are now available (e.g., see Bennett, Lance, & Woehr, 2006; Farr & Tippins, 2010; Scott & Reynolds, 2010). However, it is not the intent here to summarize the current state of criterion measurement research and practice, but only to note the critical implications of the substantive latent structure of performance, and its dynamic features, for performance measurement methods.

In general, there are three principal purposes for performance assessment.

1. For research purposes only, whether it is in a controlled situation (e.g., a training or laboratory environment) or in the naturally occurring work situation.
2. For developmental feedback, where the goal is to improve performance, not evaluate it, and the complexities and dynamics of feedback itself become relevant.
3. For operational administrative decision making where there is something "riding on it" for both the assessee and the assessors, and the goals of both assessor and assessee must be considered.

For any one of these three measurement purposes, both the substantive latent structure of performance and the dynamic properties of individual performance have implications for performance assessment. There are two overarching considerations. First, while virtually any estimated matrix of intercorrelations among multiple performance measures will yield a general factor, the substantive meaning of the general factor cannot be specified, except by aggregation of the substantive factors that load on it. Consequently, measurement must always focus on the substantive latent factors. Asking raters to rate overall performance is no solution. Although ratings of overall performance do show non-zero reliabilities and exhibit correlations with other variables, it is the rater who must first aggregate performance on the latent factors, in one way or another (e.g., Rotundo & Sackett, 2002), and in ways that we may not like.

Second, performance on each of the substantive latent factors certainly may change over time, as the result of changes in the person, changes in the performance requirements, changes in the environmental conditions, or because of the interactions among them. Performance assessment must accommodate these potential dynamics. How it accommodates them is in part a function of how well they can be anticipated. It is also a function of the measurement purpose. For example, the assessment of occupational training achievement is intended to assess performance at a particular point in time (e.g., at the end of the course). In contrast, the assessment of transfer may be with reference to a particular date by which transfer should occur, if it is going to occur. Ignoring a host of other problems, such as those described by Murphy and Cleveland (1995), performance appraisal for compensation purposes could be intended to sum past performance on each factor over a particular period (e.g., six months or one year). In contrast, performance assessment for promotion purposes must try to anticipate both changes in performance requirements that will occur and the intraindividual growth curves on the latent factors, such that the individual with the highest probability of excelling on the future performance requirements should be promoted. This is a complex set of considerations, even before the assessment goals and motives of the assessors and assessees are considered.

Performance Outcomes and Performance Effectiveness

This chapter has repeatedly made a distinction between performance, specified in terms of individual actions, and the outcomes of performance (i.e., effectiveness). This is not a distinction between "behavior" and "nonbehavior" or a distinction between "subjective" and "objective" measurement. It is a distinction between what an individual should do (i.e., what actions he or she should take), and do well, to optimize the individual's contribution to the goals of the organization, and subsequent assessments of the bottom line, or the organizationally relevant outcomes that are produced, at least in part, by individual performance. Again, *performance* measures and *effectiveness* measures could be either "subjective" or "objective." By definition, individual differences in a performance measure are the result of what individuals *do*, plus the inevitable measurement error and contamination error. Variation in indicators of effectiveness is a function of measurement error, contamination error, *and* individual performance (hopefully), as well as additional sources of variation that might not be regarded as contamination. For example, team effectiveness depends on the performance of the team members (including the leader, if there is one) and on the availability of various kinds of team resources as a function of budget constraints—similarly, this also applies to such things as per unit costs, sales, return on investment (ROI), and so on. If it can be demonstrated that variation in an indicator is solely a function of the individual's actions plus measurement error then, by definition, it is a measure of performance. The influence of contamination errors detract from the construct validity of the measure as an indicator of individual performance. As assessments of performance, both subjective and objective measures can be contaminated with systematic sources of variation that are unwanted.

As already noted, work roles are (or should be) designed to contribute to organizational goal attainment (i.e., effectiveness). Consequently, if individual performance is multidimensional, then a particular indicator of effectiveness is most likely a function of more than one performance dimension. Differential effects across dimensions are expected and should be investigated.

Performance Ratings (i.e., Subjective Measures)

As a method of performance measurement, "ratings" of one person by another have generated a substantial literature (e.g., Lance, Baxter, & Mahan, 2006), which will not be reviewed here. Only the main points will be summarized to provide a fuller context for discussing the implications of performance models for performance assessment.

There is no doubt that performance ratings are contaminated, are not highly reliable, and assess varying degrees of valid systematic variance as a function of rater type, rater characteristics (within type), rater training, rating method, rating format (within method), and ratee characteristics unrelated to their performance, as well as a host of interactions

among the various sources of variation. As a function of the measurement objective (i.e., for research, development, or operational appraisal), the goals of the rater and ratee also influence ratings (Murphy & Cleveland, 1995), and goal effects are more pronounced when operational appraisal is the measurement purpose. For example, for both good reasons and bad, the rater(s) may not want to rate anyone as a low performer. This obviously disturbs the rank ordering of the ratees on "true" performance and compromises performance measurement for research purposes.

In spite of the frequency and complexity of unwanted sources or variation, research also suggests the following conclusions.

1. If reasonably well-constructed and implemented, ratings do reflect actual differences in individual performance (e.g., Conway, & Huffcutt, 1997), as well as the influence of measurement error and contamination error.

2. Although reliabilities (i.e., inter-rater agreement) are not high, they are sufficient to yield a consistent and meaningful pattern of correlations with predictor variables used in personnel selection (LeBreton, Burgess, Kaiser, Atchley, & James, 2003; Schmidt & Hunter, 1998). Meta-analytic estimates of single rater reliability for a single performance dimension range from .35 to .50. Using the mean of several raters and/or composite scores obtained from several individual dimensions will yield commensurably higher estimates. It is also true that the reliability estimates may be partially a function of systematic differences across ratees that are unrelated to performance, such as interpersonal liking (Conway, 1998).

3. Differences across rater types (e.g., supervisor, peer, subordinate), holding ratees constant, may be due to a variety of sources, one of which is that different rater types see different parts of a ratee's performance, in addition to those aspects of an individual's performance that are observed by all raters (e.g., see Lance, Teachout, & Donnelly, 1992). That is, all differences across rater types should not be assumed to be error.

4. Individual rating scales, when carefully developed to assess well-specified factors, do yield meaningful factor structures, in spite of a general factor due to common determinants and/or common method variance (Hoffman, Lance, Bynum, & Gentry, 2010; Viswesvaran et al., 2005).

5. There are various forms of rater training designed to improve rating accuracy, most often

defined as the correspondence between the rater's judgment and a "true score" rating provided by experts or between a rater's assessment of a videotaped model and the model's scripted performance levels. The major kinds of rater training are:

a) *Rater error training* designed to reduce some combination of halo, leniency, and central tendency.

b) *Performance dimension training* intended to better explain to the rater the meaning and specifications for the performance dimensions to be rated.

c) *Frame-of-reference training* which, in addition to familiarizing raters with the meaning of the dimensions to be rated, also attempt to calibrate the specifications for what constitutes different levels of performance on the dimension.

d) *Behavioral observation training* deals with trying to improve the ways in which the potential rater observes, collects, and stores information on performance actions relevant for particular performance dimensions. Such training should lead to better recall of relevant information when the time for the actual rating comes.

Based on meta-analyses of the extant research literatures (Woehr & Huffcutt, 1994), a reasonable conclusion is that each of the rater training methods produces gains in accuracy and reductions in the classic rating errors. Using two or more of the four methods in the same rater training program produces significant incremental gain, compared to using just one method.

6. When performance rating is viewed through the lens of the person-perception literature, some additional complications occur.

a) Specific negative information about a ratee has a disproportionate weight on summary ratings. Raters sometimes use themselves as an anchor against which ratees are compared, and there is most likely a recency effect (e.g., McIntyre & James, 1995).

b) Raters may have very strong personal or implicit theories about the latent structure of performance for a particular work role (Borman, 1987), which may or may not correspond to the content of the dimensions to be rated that are specified by the organization. If the implicit models are strongly held, or even operate without conscientious awareness, then it would be difficult for rater training to succeed in getting raters to use the prescribed dimensions/scales, and so on. We need to know a lot more about the dimensions

that the raters are *really* using when the ratees are assessed, even when measurement is for research purposes only. Do raters still use their implicit model? Do they still formulate rating goals (Murphy & Cleveland, 1995) that do not correspond to the researchers' goals?

In sum, the rating process is a complex activity about which much is known, and about which much more needs to be known, and there are at least three major implications of substantive and dynamic properties of performance modeling for assessments of performance via ratings.

1. The content of rating scales should reflect the latent structure of performance. The specific scales may be more general or more specific, but they should be locatable in the eight-factor structure described previously, even if highly specific technical, leadership, or team member responsibilities are selected as the dependent variable in an experiment. Ratings of "quality" or "productivity" do not meet this specification.

2. The time frame over which the rater is asked to aggregate information about a ratee should be made explicit, and should correspond to the measurement purpose.

3. Finally, while research on rater training has produced valuable results, we need to know much more about the latent structure and measurement goals that the rater actually uses. There is really a dearth of research on the implicit, or personal, theories of performance held by raters in the work setting. Such research is needed both for the research context, and for the operational context, where distortions of the measurement goal could be quite deliberate.

Subjective versus Objective Measures

The need for, and the advantages of, objective measures of performance have been argued for a long time, most recently by Pulakos (2008) and Pulakos and O'Leary (2010). However, the distinctions between the two are not always perfectly clear (Muckler & Seven, 1992). For example, the choice of which objective indicators to use is inherently a subjective one, and the estimated degree of construct validity possessed by an objective indicator for a specific purpose is also a subjective judgment. Also, as noted previously, an objective indicator could be used either as an indicator of individual performance itself or as an indicator of the outcomes of performance, which by definition have legitimate determinants of variance that are not under the individual's control. When used as a measure of individual performance, the indicator cannot (i.e., should not) be contaminated by significant sources of variance over which the individual has no control. What has now become a classic example is the measurement of teacher performance by assessing student gains in standardized achievement test scores. Many things that cannot be controlled by the teacher (e.g., the student actually having parents at home) affect such scores.

There is a modest literature comparing subjective and objective indicators. The most frequently cited is a meta-analysis by Bommer, Johnson, Rich, Podsakoff, & MacKenzie (1995), who reported an overall corrected correlation of .39 between subjective and objective measures. When the objective measure was "sales," it was slightly higher, .41. Generally, in these studies, the objective and subjective measures were not designed to assess the same performance factors. However, in a small number of instances, when both measures were intended to measure individual performance on the same performance dimension, the corrected correlation was .71, which indicates a much higher degree of correspondence, but still leaves room for significant contamination.

A previous meta-analysis by Heneman (1986) had explicitly examined the relationship between supervisory ratings and measures of results. Depending on the rating format, the corrected mean correlations ranged from .19 to .60. The lowest correlation was for ratings of "overall" performance. One way to look at these findings is that direct (but still contaminated) measures of performance (i.e., the ratings) have reasonably high correlations with bottom line results, which is as it should be.

Pulakos and O'Leary (2010) have tried to finesse the potential contamination of objective measures by proposing wider use of assessments of performance achievement against specific objectives, in the Locke and Latham (2002) way. Implicit in the setting of such objectives are provisions for choosing objectives that are indeed a function of the individual's actions. Consequently, the contamination frequently experienced when objective metrics are chosen off the shelf is, in theory, controlled at the outset. The "results" measures that Pulakos and O'Leary describe are very close to what this chapter means by performance. The definition of performance used here does not stipulate that ratings are the only permissible assessment method.

The implications of a multidimensional substantive latent structure and the dynamic characteristics of performance described elsewhere in this handbook are the same for objective or goal achievement measures as they are for subjective (rating) measures. That is, the substantive content of the indicators must be a valid representation (in the construct validity sense) of a specified performance dimension, and the specified context for measurement must correspond to a time frame that is appropriate for the measurement purpose and consistent with what is known about the dynamics of that particular performance dimension.

Conclusion

The chapter has belabored the point that, at a particular level of specificity, there is a virtual consensus about the latent variables that comprise individual performance at work. Going only a small step further, it is strongly suggested that this latent structure is invariant across work roles, organizational levels, organizational structures, organizational contexts, and so on, and so on. This is *not* an argument that the importance or utility of individual differences on each latent variable is the same across work roles, organizational levels, and situations. For example, not all jobs would have a significant management component (although this number may be larger than we think), and communication, as specified there, might be a critical component of only a small percentage of jobs.

The assertion of invariance is also not an argument that individuals won't adapt their performance behavior to changing contexts or situations. It is, rather, that such adaptations or differential emphases across situations are best described within the consensus latent structure framework.

Also, asserting that the latent structure of performance is invariant across levels of work roles is not synonymous with saying that the actions comprising high and low performance on the dimension are invariant. However, it comes close. When is technical performance expertise not good? When is expert communication not good? When is a lack of CWB not good? When are extra effort and initiative not good? When is it not good to be highly competent on the components of leadership and management, *even if* the relative utility of the subfactors varies across situations? The only possible exceptions are with regard to the influence of culture. For some of the leadership subfactors, the same actions may have different effects on peers or subordinates as a function of cultural values. However, even here, the numbers of such cultural interactions may be relatively small (den Hartog, House, Hanges, & Ruiz-Quintanilla, 1999; Gibson & McDaniel, 2010).

This chapter has also harped on the distinctions among the determinants of performance, performance itself, and the outcomes, or effectiveness, of performance. They are often confused, to the detriment of knowledge accumulation in I/O psychology. For example, what is a "competency?" What is adaptability? What is charisma? An inability to locate these concepts in an agreed-upon latent structure does produce déjà vu all over again.

There is a consensus. We know what performance is, and how to distinguish it from its determinants and its outcomes. More of our research and practice should be referenced to this consensus.

References

Ammeter, A. P., Douglas, C., Gardner, W. L., Hochwarter, W. A., & Ferris, G. R. (2002). Toward a political theory of leadership. *Leadership Quarterly, 13*, 751–796.

Austin, J. T., & Villanova, P. (1992). The criterion problem 1917–1992. *Journal of Applied Psychology, 77*, 836–874.

Bales, R. F. (1958). Task roles and social roles in problem solving groups. In E. E. Maccoby, T. M. Newcomb, & E. L. Hartley (Eds.), *Readings in social psychology* (pp 437–447). New York: Holt.

Bass, B. M. (1985). *Leadership and performance beyond expectations.* New York: Free Press.

Bass, B. M. (1990). *Handbook of leadership: A survey of theory and research.* New York: Free Press.

Bass, B. M., & Avolio, B. J. (1990). *Multifactor leadership questionnaire.* Palo Alto, CA: Consulting Psychologists Press.

Bass, B. M., Avolio, B. J., Jung, D. I., & Berson, Y. (2003). Predicting unit performance by assessing transformational and transactional leadership. *Journal of Applied Psychology, 88*, 207–218.

Batson, C. D., & Shaw, L. L. (1991). Encouraging words concerning the evidence for altruism. *Psychological Inquiry, 2*, 159–168.

Beal, D. J., Weiss, H. M., Barros, E., & MacDermid, S. M. (2005). An episodic process model of affective influences on performance. *Journal of Applied Psychology, 90*, 1054–1068.

Bennett, W., Lance, C. E., & Woehr, D. J. (2006). *Performance measurement: Current perspectives and future challenges.* Mahwah, NJ: Erlbaum.

Bennett, R. J., & Robinson, S. L. (2000). Development of a measure of workplace deviance. *Journal of Applied Psychology, 85*, 349–360.

Berry, C. M., Ones, D. S., & Sackett, P. R. (2007). Interpersonal deviance, organizational deviance, and their common correlates: A review and meta-analysis. *Journal of Applied Psychology, 92*, 410–424.

Blake, R. R., & Mouton, J. S. (1964). *The managerial grid.* Houston: Gulf Publishing.

Blake, R. R., & Mouton, J. S. (1983). Management by grid principles or situationalism: Which? *Group and Organization Studies, 7*, 207–210.

Bommer, W. H., Johnson, J., Rich, G. A., Podsakoff, P. M., & MacKenzie, S. B. (1995). On the interchangeability of objective and subjective measures of employee performance: A meta-analysis. *Personnel Psychology, 48*, 587–605.

Borman, W. C. (1987). Personal constructs, performance schemata, and "folk theories" of subordinate effectiveness:

Explorations in an Army officer sample. *Organizational Behavior and Human Decision Processes, 40*, 307–322.

Borman, W. C., & Brush, D. H. (1993). More progress toward a taxonomy of managerial performance requirements. *Human Performance, 6*, 1–21.

Borman, W. C., & Motowidlo, S. J. (1993). Expanding the criterion domain to include elements of contextual performance. In N. Schmitt & W. C. Borman (Eds.), *Personnel selection in organizations* (pp. 71–98). San Francisco: Jossey-Bass.

Borman, W. C., & Motowidlo, S. J. (1997). Task performance and contextual performance: The meaning for personnel selection research. *Human Performance, 10*, 99–109.

Borman, W. C., White, L. A., & Dorsey, D. W. (1995). Effects of ratee task performance and interpersonal factors on supervisor and peer performance ratings. *Journal of Applied Psychology, 80*, 168–177.

Borman, W. C., White, L. A., Pulakos, E. D., & Oppler, S. H. (1991). Models of supervisory job performance ratings. *Journal of Applied Psychology, 76*, 863–872.

Bowers, D. G., & Seashore, S. E. (1966). Predicting organizational effectiveness with a four-factor theory or leadership. *Administrative Science Quarterly, 11*, 238–263.

Brief, A. P., & Motowidlo, S. J. (1986). Prosocial organizational behaviors. *Academy of Management Review, 11*, 710–725.

Burke, C. S., Stagl, K. C., Klein, C., Goodwin, G. F., Salas, E., & Halpin, S. M. (2006). What type of leadership behaviors are functional in teams? A meta-analysis. *Leadership Quarterly, 17*, 288–307.

Burns, J. M. (1978). *Leadership.* New York: Harper & Row.

Campbell, J. P. (1991a). Modeling the performance prediction problem in Industrial and Organizational Psychology. In M. D. Dunnette (Ed.), *Handbook of industrial and organizational psychology* (Rev. ed., pp. 687–732). Palo Alto, CA: Consulting Psychologists Press.

Campbell, J. P. (1991b). The role of theory in industrial and organizational psychology. In M. D. Dunnette (Ed.), *Handbook of industrial and organizational psychology* (Rev. ed., pp. 38–74). Palo Alto, CA: Consulting Psychologists Press.

Campbell, J. P. (2007). Profiting from history. In L. L. Koppes, P. W. Thayer, A. J. Vinchur, & E. Salas (Eds.), *Historical perspectives in industrial and organizational psychology* (pp. 441–460). Mahway, NJ: Erlbaum.

Campbell, J. P., Dunnette, M. D., Lawler, K. E., & Weick, K. E. (1970). *Managerial behavior, performance, and effectiveness.* New York: McGraw-Hill.

Campbell, J. P., & Knapp, D. (2001). *Exploring the limits of personnel selection and classification.* Hillsdale, NJ: Erlbaum.

Campbell, J. P., McCloy, R. A., Oppler, S. H., & Sager, C. E. (1993). A theory of performance. In N. Schmitt & W. C. Borman (Eds.), *Frontiers in industrial/organizational psychology: Personnel selection and classification* (pp. 35–71). San Francisco: Jossey-Bass.

Carlson, K. D. (1997). *Impact of instructional strategy on training effectiveness.* Ph.D. dissertation, University of Iowa, Iowa City, IA.

Carroll, S. J., Jr., & Gillen, D. J. (1987). Are the classical management functions useful in describing managerial work? *Academy of Management Review, 12*, 38–51.

Cartwright, D., & Zander, A. (1960). *Group dynamics research and theory.* Evanston, IL: Row, Peterson.

Cialdini, R. B., & Kendrick, D. T. (1976). Altruism as hedonism: A social development perspective on the relationship of negative mood state and helping. *Journal of Personality and Social Psychology, 34,* 907–914.

Conger, J. A., & Kanungo, R. N. (1987). Toward a behavioral theory of charismatic leadership in organizational settings. *Academy of Management Journal, 26,* 637–647.

Conger, J. A., & Kanungo, R. N. (1998). *Charismatic leadership in organizations.* Thousand Oaks, CA: Sage Publications.

Conway, J. M. (1998). Understanding method variance in multitrait-multirater performance appraisal matrices: Examples using general impressions and interpersonal affect as measured method factors. *Human Performance, 11*(1), 29–55.

Conway, J. M. (1999). Distinguishing contextual performance from task performance for managerial jobs. *Journal of Applied Psychology, 84,* 3–13.

Conway, J. M., & Huffcutt, A. L. (1997). Psychometric properties of multisource performance ratings: A meta-analysis of subordinate, supervisor, peer, and self-ratings. *Human Performance, 10,* 331–360.

Cronbach, L. J., & Gleser, G. C. (1965). *Psychological tests and personnel decisions* (2nd ed.). Urbana: University of Illinois Press.

Dalal, R. S. (2005). A meta-analysis of the relationship between organizational citizenship behavior and counterproductive work behavior. *Journal of Applied Psychology Special Section: Theoretical Models and Conceptual Analyses – Second Installment, 90,* 1241–1255.

Darley, J. M., & Latané, B. (1968). Bystander intervention in emergencies: Diffusion of responsibility. *Journal of Personality and Social Psychology, 8,* 377–383.

Day, D. V., Gronn, P., & Salas, E. (2006). Leadership in team-based organizations: On the threshold of a new era. *Leadership Quarterly, 17,* 211–216.

Day, D. V., & Harrison, M. M. (2007). A multilevel, identity-based approach to leadership. *Human Resource Management Review, 17,* 360–373.

Deadrick, D. L., Bennett, N., & Russell, C. J. (1997). Using hierarchical linear modeling to examine dynamic performance criteria over time. *Journal of Management, 23,* 745–757.

den Hartog, D. N., House, R. J., Hanges, P. J., & Ruiz-Quintanilla, S. A. (1999). Culture specific and cross-culturally generalizable implicit leadership theories: Are attributes of charismatic/transformational leadership universally endorsed? *Leadership Quarterly, 10,* 219–256.

Drath, W. H., McCauley, C. D., Paulus, C. J., Van Velsor, E., O'Connor, P. M. G., & McGuire, J. B. (2008). Direction, alignment, commitment: Toward a more integrative ontology of leadership. *Leadership Quarterly, 19,* 635–653.

Eisenberg, N., & Miller, P. A. (1987). The relation of empathy to prosocial and related behaviors. *Psychological Bulletin, 101,* 91–119.

Elliot, A. J., & Thrash, T. M. (2002). Approach-avoidance motivation in personality: Approach and avoidance temperaments and goals. *Journal of Personality and Social Psychology, 82,* 804–818.

Esade, M. B., & McKelvey, B. (2010). Integrating modernist and postmodernist perspectives on organizations: A complexity science bridge. *Academy of Management Review, 35,* 415–433.

Farr, J. L., & Tippins, N. T. (2010). *Handbook of employee selection.* New York: Routledge.

Fayol, H. (1949). *General and industrial management.* London: Pitman.

Fiedler, F. E. (1967). *A theory of leadership effectiveness.* New York: Academic Press.

Fleishman, E. A. (1983). The description of supervisory behavior. *Personnel Psychology, 26,* 1–6.

Frese, M. (2008). The word is out: We need an active performance concept for modern workplaces. Commentary on focal article by Macey & Schneider: The meaning of employee engagement. *Industrial and Organizational Psychology: Perspectives on Science and Practice, 1,* 67–69.

Gable, S. L., Reis, H. T., & Elliot A. J. (2003). Evidence for bivariate systems: An empirical test of appetition and aversion across domains. *Journal of Research in Personality, 37,* 349–372.

Gibson, C. B., & McDaniel, D. M. (2010). Moving beyond conventional wisdom: Advancements in cross-cultural theories of leadership, conflict, and teams. *Perspectives on Psychological Science, 5,* 450–462.

Goodman, P. S., Devadas, R., & Griffith-Hughson, T. L. (1988). Groups and productivity: Analyzing the effectiveness of self-management teams. In J. P. Campbell, R. J. Campbell & Associates (Eds.), *Productivity in organizations: New perspectives from industrial and organizational psychology* (pp. 295–327). San Francisco: Jossey-Bass.

Graen, G., Alvares, J. M., Orris, J. B., & Martella, J. A. (1970). Contingency model of leadership effectiveness: Antecedent and evidential results. *Psychological Bulletin, 74,* 285–296.

Graen, G. B., & Uhl-Bien, M. (1995). Relationship-based approach to leadership: Development of leader-member exchange (LMX) theory of leadership over 25 years: Applying a multi-level multi-domain perspective. *Leadership Quarterly, 6,* 219–247.

Graham, J. W. (2000). Promoting civic virtue organizational citizenship behavior: Contemporary questions rooted in classical quandaries from political philosophy. *Human Resource Management Review, 10,* 61–77.

Griffen, M. S., Neal, A., & Parker, S. K. (2007). A new model of work role performance: Positive behavior in uncertain and interdependent contexts. *Academy of Management Journal, 30,* 327–347.

Gruys, M. L., & Sackett, P. R. (2003). Investigating the dimensionality of counterproductive work behavior. *International Journal of Selection and Assessment, 11,* 30–42.

Guzzo, R. A., & Dickson, M. W. (1996). Teams in organizations: Recent research on performance and effectiveness. *Annual Review of Psychology, 47,* 307–338.

Guzzo, R. A., & Shea, G. P. (1992). Group performance and intergroup relations in organizations. In M. D. Dunnette & L. M. Hough (Eds.), *Handbook of industrial and organizational psychology* (Vol. 3, pp. 269–313). Palo Alto, CA: Consulting Psychologists Press.

Hackman, J. R. (1992). Group influences on individuals in organizations. In M. D. Dunnette & L. M. Hough (Eds.), *Handbook of industrial and organizational psychology* (Vol. 3, pp. 199–267). Palo Alto, CA: Consulting Psychologists Press.

Hemphill, J. K. (1959). Job descriptions for executives. *Harvard Business Review, 37* (September–October), 55–67.

Heneman, R. L. (1986). The relationship between supervisory ratings and results-oriented measures of performance: A meta-analysis. *Personnel Psychology, 39,* 811–826.

Henle, C. A., Giacolone, R. A., & Jurkiewicz. C. L. (2005). The role of ethical ideology in workplace deviance. *Journal of Business Ethics, 56,* 219–230.

Hersey, P., & Blanchard, K. H. (1977). *The management of organizational behavior* (3rd ed.). Englewood Cliffs, NJ: Prentice Hall.

Hesketh, B., & Neal, A. (1999). Technology and performance. In D. R. Ilgen & E. D. Pulakos (Eds.), *The changing nature of performance: Implications for staffing, motivation, and development* (pp. 21–55). San Francisco: Jossey-Bass.

Hiller, N. J., Day, D. V., & Vance, R. J. (2006). Collective enactment of leadership roles and team effectiveness: A field study. *Leadership Quarterly, 17*, 387–397.

Hinkin, T. R., & Schriesheim, C. A. (2008). A theoretical and empirical examination of the transactional and non-leadership dimensions of the Multifactor Leadership Questionnaire (MLQ). *Leadership Quarterly, 19*, 501–513.

Hoffman, B. J., Blair, C. A., Meriac, J. P., & Woehr, D. J. (2007). Expanding the criterion domain? A quantitative review of the OCB literature. *Journal of Applied Psychology, 92*, 555–566.

Hoffman, B., Lance, C. E., Bynum, B., & Gentry, W. A. (2010). Rater source effects are alive and well after all. *Personnel Psychology, 63*, 119–151.

Hofmann, D. A., Jacobs, R., & Gerras, S. J. (1992). Mapping individual performance over time. *Journal of Applied Psychology, 77*, 185–195.

House, R. J. (1971). A path-goal theory of leader effectiveness. *Administrative Science Quarterly, 16*, 321–338.

House, R. J. (1977). A 1976 theory of charismatic leadership. In J. G. Hunt & L. L. Larson (Eds.), *Leadership: The cutting edge* (pp. 189–207). Carbondale: Southern Illinois University Press.

House, R. J., & Mitchell, T. R. (1974). Path-goal theory of leadership. *Contemporary Business, 3*, 81–98.

Hunt, J. G. (1999). Transformational/charismatic leadership's transformation of the field: An historical essay. *Leadership Quarterly, 10*, 129–144.

Hunter, J. E. (1983). A causal analysis of cognitive ability, job knowledge, job performance, and supervisor ratings. In F. Landy, S. Zedeck, & J. Cleveland (Eds.), *Performance measurement and theory* (pp. 257–266). Hillsdale, NJ: Erlbaum.

Iles, R., Scott, B. A., & Judge, T. A. (2006). The interactive effects of personal traits and experienced states on intraindividual patterns of citizenship behavior. *Academy of Management Journal, 49*, 561–575.

Ilgen, D. R., Hollenbeck, J. R., Johnson, M., & Jundt, D. (2005). Teams in organizations: From input-process-output models to IMOI models. *Annual Review of Psychology, 56*, 517–543.

Kanfer, R., Chen, G., & Pritchard, R. (Eds.). (2008). *Work motivation: Past present and future*. New York: Taylor and Francis Group.

Katz, D., & Kahn, R. L. (1978). *The social psychology of organizations* (2nd ed.). New York: John Wiley & Sons.

Katzell, R. A., & Guzzo, R. A. (1983). Psychological approaches to productivity improvement. *American Psychologist, 38*, 468–472.

Kelloway, E. K., Loughlin, C., Barling, J., & Nault, A. (2002). Self-reported counterproductive behaviors and organizational citizenship behaviors: Separate but related constructs. *International Journal of Selection and Assessment, 10*, 143–151.

Koppes, L. L, Thayer, P. W., Vinchur, A. J., & Salas, E. (Eds.). (2007). *Historical perspectives in industrial and organizational psychology*. Mahwah, NJ: Erlbaum.

Kotter, J. P. (1996). *Leading change*. Boston, MA: Harvard Business School Press.

Kozlowski, S. W. J., Gully, S. M., Nason, E. R., & Smith, E. M. (1999). Developing adaptive teams: A theory of compilation and performance across levels and time. In D. R. Ilgen & E.

D. Pulakos (Eds.), *The changing nature of work performance: Implications for staffing, personnel actions, and development* (pp. 240–292). San Francisco: Jossey-Bass.

Kozlowski, S. W. J., & Ilgen, D. R. (2006). Enhancing the effectiveness of work groups and teams. *Psychological Science in the Public Interest, 7*, 77–124.

Kuhn, A. (1963). *The study of society: A unified approach*. Homewood, IL: Irwin.

Lance, C. E., Baxter, D., & Mahan, R. P. (2006). Evaluation of alternative perspectives on source: Effects in multisource performance measures. In W. Bennett, C. E. Lance, & C. Woehr (Eds.), *Performance measurement: Current perspectives and future challenges* (pp. 49–76). Mahwah, NJ: Erlbaum.

Lance, C. E., & Bennett, W. (2000). Replication and extension of models of supervisory job performance ratings. *Human Performance, 13*, 139–158.

Lance, C. E., Teachout, M. S., & Donnelly, T. M. (1992). Specification of the criterion construct space: An application of hierarchical confirmatory factor analysis. *Journal of Applied Psychology, 77*, 437–452.

LeBreton, J. M., Burgess, J. R. D., Kaiser, R. B., Atchley, E. K., & James, L. R. (2003). The restriction of variance hypothesis and interrater reliability and agreement: Are ratings from multiple sources really dissimilar? *Organizational Research Methods, 6*(1), 80–128.

LePine, J. A., Erez, A., & Johnson, D. E. (2002). The nature and dimensionality of organizational citizenship behavior: A critical review and meta-analysis. *Journal of Applied Psychology, 87*, 52–65.

LePine, J. A., Piccolo, R. F., Jackson, C. L., Mathieu, J. E., & Saul, J. R. (2008). A meta-analysis of teamwork processes: Tests of a multidimensional model and relationships with team effectiveness criteria. *Personnel Psychology, 61*, 273–307.

Likert, R. (1961). *New patterns of management*. New York: McGraw-Hill.

Locke, E. A., & Latham, G. P. (2002). Building a practically useful theory of goal setting and task motivation: A 35-year odyssey. *American Psychologist, 57*, 705–717.

Lord, R. G., Diefendorff, J. M., Schmidt, A. M., & Hall, R. J. (2010). Self-regulation at work. *Annual Review of Psychology, 61*, 543–568.

Lord, R. G., & Hall, R. J. (2005). Identity, deep structure and the development of leadership skill. *Leadership Quarterly, 16*, 591–615.

Mahoney, T. A., Jerdee, T. H., & Carroll, S. J., Jr. (1963). *Development of managerial performance: A research approach*. Cincinnati, OH: South-Western.

Mahoney, T. A., Jerdee, T. H., & Carroll, S. J., Jr. (1965). The jobs of management. *Industrial Relations, 4*, 97–110.

Mann, F. C. (1965). Toward an understanding of the leadership role in formal organizations. In R. Dubin, G. C. Homans, F. C. Mann, & D. C. Miller (Eds.), *Leadership and productivity* (pp. 68–103). San Francisco: Chandler.

Marcus, B., Schuler, H., Quell, P., & Humpfner, G. (2002). Measuring counterproductivity: Development and initial validation of a German self-report questionnaire. *International Journal of Selection and Assessment, 10*, 18–35.

Marion, R., & Uhl-Bien, M. (2001). Leadership in complex organizations. *Leadership quarterly, 12*, 389–418.

Markon, K. E., Krueger, R. F., & Watson, D. (2005). Delineating the structure of normal and abnormal personality: An integrative hierarchical approach. *Journal of Personality and Social Psychology, 88*, 139–157.

Marks, M. A., Mathieu, J. E., & Zaccaro, S. J. (2001). A temporally based framework and taxonomy of team processes. *Academy of Management Review, 26*, 356–376.

Mathieu, J., Maynard, M. T., Rapp, T., & Gilson, L. (2008). Team effectiveness 1997–2007: A review of recent advancements and a glimpse into the future. *Journal of Management, 34*, 410–476.

McGrath, J. E. (1962). *Leadership behavior: Requirements for leadership training*. Prepared for U.S. Civil Service Commission Office of Career Development, Washington, DC.

McIntyre, M. D., & James, L. R. (1995). The inconsistency with which raters weight and combine information across targets. *Human Performance, 8*, 95–111.

Meyer, H. H. (2007). Influence of formal and informal organizations on the development of I-O psychology. In L. L. Koppes, P. W. Thayer, A. J. Vinchur, & E. Salas (Eds.), *Historical perspectives in industrial and organizational psychology* (pp.139–168). Mahwah, NJ: Erlbaum.

Miles, D. E., Borman, W. C., Spector, P. E., & Fox, S. (2002). Building an integrative model of extra role work behaviors: A comparison of counterproductive work behavior with organizational citizenship behavior. *International Journal of Selection and Assessment, 10*, 51–57.

Mintzberg, H. (1973). *The nature of managerial work*. New York: Harper & Row.

Motowidlo, S. J. (2000). Some basic issues related to contextual performance and organizational citizenship behavior in human resource management. *Human Resource Management Review, 10*, 115–126.

Muckler, F. A., & Seven, S. A. (1992). Selecting performance measures: "Objective" versus "subjective" measurement. *Human Factors, 34*, 441–455.

Mumford, M. D., Antes, A. L., Caughron, J. J., & Friedrich, T. L. (2008). Charismatic, ideological, and pragmatic leadership: Multi-level influences on emergence and performance. *Leadership Quarterly, 19*, 144–160.

Murphy, K. R. (1989a). Dimensions of job performance. In R. Dillon & J. Pellingrino (Eds.), *Testing: Applied and theoretical perspectives* (pp. 218–247). New York: Praeger.

Murphy, K. R. (1989b). Is the relationship between cognitive ability and job performance stable over time? *Human Performance, 2*, 183–200.

Murphy, K. R., & Cleveland, J. N. (1995). *Understanding performance appraisal: Social organizational and goal based perspectives*. Thousand Oaks, CA: Sage.

National Research Council (2010). *A database for a changing economy: Review of the Occupational Information Network (O*NET)*. Washington, DC: The National Academies Press.

Olson, A. M. (2000). *A theory and taxonomy of individual team member performance*. Ph.D. dissertation. Minneapolis: University of Minnesota.

Ones, D. S., & Viswesvaran, C. (2003). Personality and counterproductive work behaviors. In M. Koslowsky, S. Stashevsky, & A. Sagie (Eds.), *Misbehavior and dysfunctional attitudes in organizations* (pp. 211–249). Hampshire, UK: Palgrave MacMillan.

Organ, D. W. (1988). *Organizational citizenship behavior: The good soldier syndrome*. Lexington: Lexington Books.

Organ, D. W. (1997). Organizational citizenship behavior: It's construct clean-up time. *Human Performance, 10*, 85–97.

Organ, D. W., & Ryan, K. (1995). A meta-analytic review of attitudinal and dispositional predictors of organizational citizenship behavior. *Personnel Psychology, 48*, 775–802.

Osborn, R. N., Hunt, J. G., & Jauch, L. R. (2002). Toward a contextual theory of leadership. *Leadership Quarterly, 13*, 797–837.

Page, R., & Tornow, W. W. (1987, April). *Managerial job analysis: Are we farther along?* Paper presented at the Second annual Conference of the Society for Industrial and Organizational Psychology, Atlanta.

Pearlman, K., & Sanchez, J. I. (2010) Work analysis. In J. Farr & N. Tippins (Eds.), *Handbook of employee selection* (pp. 73–98). New York: Routledge.

Penner, L. A., Dovidio, J. F., Piliavin, J. A., & Schroeder, D. A. (2005). Prosocial behavior: multilevel perspectives. *Annual Review of Psychology, 56*, 365–392.

Peterson, N. G., Mumford, M. D., Borman, W. C., Jeanneret, P. R., & Fleishman, E. A. (1999). *An occupational information system for the 21st century: The development of O*NET*. Washington, DC: American Psychological Association.

Ployhart, R. E., & Bliese, P. D. (2006). Individual Adaptability (I-ADAPT) Theory: Conceptualizing the antecedents, consequences, and measurement of individual differences in adaptability. In E. Salas (Ed.), *Advances in human performance and cognitive engineering research* (Vol. 6, pp. 3–39). Oxford: Emerald Group Publishing Limited.

Ployhart, R. E., & Hakel, M. D. (1998). The substantive nature of performance variability: Predicting interindividual differences in intraindividual performance. *Personnel Psychology, 51*, 859–901.

Podsakoff, P. M., Ahearne, M., & MacKenzie, S. B. (1997). Organizational citizenship behavior and the quantity and quality of work group performance. *Journal of Applied Psychology, 82*, 262–270.

Podsakoff, P. M., & MacKenzie, S. B. (1994). Organizational citizenship behaviors and sales unit effectiveness. *Journal of Marketing Research, 3*, 351–363.

Podsakoff, P. M., & MacKenzie, S. B. (1997). Impact of organizational citizenship behavior on organizational performance: A review and suggestions for future research. *Human Performance, 10*, 133–151.

Podsakoff, P. M., MacKenzie, S. B., Paine, J. B., & Bachrach, D. G. (2000). Organizational citizenship behaviors: A critical review of the theoretical and empirical literature and suggestions for future research. *Journal of Management, 26*, 513–563.

Podsakoff, P. M., MacKenzie, S. B., Podsakoff, N. P., & Lee, J. Y. (2003). The mismeasure of man(agement) and its implications for leadership research. *Leadership Quarterly, 14*, 615–656.

Pulakos, E. D. (2008). *Performance management: How you can achieve important business results*. Oxford, England: Blackwell.

Pulakos, E. D., Arad, S., Donovan, M. S., & Plamondon, K. E. (2000). Adaptability in the workplace: Development of a taxonomy of adaptive performance. *Journal of Applied Psychology, 8*, 612–624.

Pulakos, E. D., & O'Leary, R. S. (2010). Defining and measuring results of workplace behavior. In J. Farr & N. Tippins (Eds.), *Handbook of employee selection* (pp. 513–529). New York: Routledge.

Reb, J., & Cropanzano, R. (2007). Evaluating dynamic performance: The influence of salient gestalt characteristics on performance ratings. *Journal of Applied Psychology, 92*, 490–499.

Reichenbach, H. (1938). *Experience and prediction*. Chicago: University of Chicago Press.

Robinson, S. L., & Bennett, R. J. (1995). A typology of deviant workplace behaviors: A multidimensional scaling study. *Academy of Management Journal, 38*, 555–572.

Rotundo, M., & Sackett, P. R. (2002). The relative importance of task, citizenship, and counterproductive performance to global ratings of job performance: A policy-capturing approach. *Journal of Applied Psychology, 87*, 66–80.

Rushton, J. P. (1991). Is altruism innate? *Psychological Inquiry, 2*, 141–143.

Sager, C. E. (1990). *A component model of halo: Peer and supervisory ratings of job performance.* Ph.D. Dissertation. Minneapolis: University of Minnesota.

Salas, E., Stagl, K. C., & Burke, C. S. (2004). 25 years of team effectiveness in organizations: Research themes and emerging needs. *International Review of Industrial and Organizational Psychology, 19*, 47–91.

Schmidt, F. L., & Hunter, J. E. (1992). Development of a causal model of processes determining job performance. *Current Directions in Psychological Science, 1*, 89–92.

Schmidt, F. L., & Hunter, J. E. (1998). The validity and utility of selection methods in personnel psychology: Practical and theoretical implications of 85 years of research. *Psychological Bulletin, 124*, 262–274.

Schriesheim, C. A., Wu, J. B., & Scandura, T. A. (2009). A meso measure? Examination of the levels of analysis of the Multifactor Leadership Questionnaire (MLQ). *Leadership Quarterly, 20*(4), 604–616.

Scott, J. C., & Reynolds, D. H. (Eds.). (2010). Handbook workplace assessment: Evidence based practices for selecting and developing organizational talent. San Francisco: Jossey-Bass.

Shamir, B., House, R. J., & Arthur, M. B. (1993). The motivational effects of charismatic leadership: A self-concept theory. *Organization Science, 4*, 1–7.

Smith, C. A., Organ, D. W., & Near, J. P. (1983). Organizational citizenship behavior: Its nature and antecedents. *Journal of Applied Psychology, 68*, 653–663.

Spector, P. E., Bauer, J. A., & Fox, S. (2010). Measurement artifacts in the assessment of counterproductive work behavior and organizational citizenship behavior: Do we know what we think we know? *Journal of Applied Psychology, 95*, 781–790.

Stevens, M. J., & Campion, M. A. (1994). The knowledge, skill, and ability requirements for teamwork: Implications for human resource management. *Journal of Management, 20*, 503–530.

Stewart, G. L., & Nandkeolyar, A. K. (2006). Adaptation and intraindividual variation in sales outcomes: Exploring the interactive effects of personality and environmental opportunity. *Personnel Psychology, 59*, 307–332.

Stogdill, R. M. (1948). Personal factors associated with leadership: A survey of the literature. *Journal of Psychology, 25*, 35–71.

Stogdill, R. M., Goode, O. S., & Day, D. R. (1962). New leader behavior description subscales. *Journal of Psychology, 54*, 259–269.

Sturman, M. C. (2003). Searching for the inverted u-shaped relationship between time and performance: Meta-analyses of the experience/performance, tenure/performance, and age/performance relationships. *Journal of Management, 29*, 609–640.

Trivers, R. L. (1971). The evolution of reciprocal altruism. *The Quarterly Review of Biology, 46*, 35–57. .

Uhl-Bien, M., Marion, R., & McKelvey, B. (2007). Complexity leadership theory: Shifting leadership from the industrial age to the knowledge era. *Leadership Quarterly, 18*, 298–318.

Urwich, L. F. (1952). *Notes on the theory of organization.* New York: American Management Association.

Vey, M. A., & Campbell, J. P. (2004). In-role versus extra-role organizational citizenship behaviors. *Human Performance, 17*, 119–135.

Viswesvaran, C., Schmidt, F. L., & Ones, D. S. (2005). Is there a general factor in ratings of job performance? A meta-analytic framework for disentangling substantive and error influences. *Journal of Applied Psychology, 90*, 108–131.

Vroom, V. H., & Jago, A. G. (1988). *The new leadership: Managing participation in organizations.* Englewood Cliffs, NJ: Prentice Hall.

Watson, D., & Clark, L. A. (1993). Behavioral disinhibition versus constraint: A dispositional perspective. In D. M. Wegner & J. W. Pennebaker (Eds.), *Handbook of mental control* (pp. 506–527). New York: Prentice Hall.

Weber, M. (1947). *The theory of social and economic organization.* New York: Free Press.

Weick, K. E., & Roberts, K. H. (1993). Collective mind in organizations: Heedful interrelating on flight decks. *Administrative Science Quarterly, 38*, 357–381.

Wilson, C. L., O'Hare, D., & Shipper, F. (1990). Task cycle theory: The processes of influence. In K. E. Clark & M. B. Clark (Eds.), *Measures of leadership* (pp. 185–204). West Orange, NJ: Leadership Library of America.

Woehr, D. J., & Huffcutt., A. I. (1994). Rater training for performance appraisal: A quantitative review. *Journal of Occupational and Organizational Psychology, 67*, 189–205.

Yukl, G. A. (1999). An evaluation of conceptual weaknesses in transformational and charismatic leadership theories. *Leadership Quarterly, 10*, 285–305.

Yukl, G. A. (2010). *Leadership in organizations* (7th ed.). Upper Saddle River, NJ: Prentice Hall.

Yukl, G. A., Gordon, A., & Taber, T. (2002). A hierarchical taxonomy of leadership behavior: Integrating a half century of behavior research. *Journal of Leadership and Organizational Studies, 9*, 15–32.

Yukl, G. A., & Lepsinger, R. (2005). Why integrating the leading and managing roles is essential for organizational effectiveness. *Organizational Dynamics, 34*, 361–375.

Yukl, G. A., & Nemeroff, W. (1979). Identification and measurement of specific categories of leadership behavior: A progress report. In J. G. Hunt & L. L. Larson (Eds.), *Crosscurrents in leadership* (pp. 164–200). Carbondale: Southern Illinois University Press.

Yukl, G. A., Wall, S., & Lepsinger, R. (1990). Preliminary report on validation of the managerial practices survey. In K. E. Clark & M. B. Clark (Eds.), *Measures of leadership* (pp. 223–238). West Orange, NJ; Leadership Library of America.

Zaccaro, S. J., & Klimoski, R. J. (Eds.). (2001). *The nature of organizational leadership: Understanding the performance imperatives confronting today's leaders.* San Francisco: Jossey-Bass.

Zaccaro, S. J., Rittman, A. L., & Marks, M. A. (2001). Team leadership. *Leadership Quarterly, 12*, 451–483.

Zyphur, M. J., Chaturvedi, S., & Arvey, R. (2008). Job performance over time is a function of latent trajectories and previous performance. *Journal of Applied Psychology, 93*, 217–224.

PART 3

Aligning Person and Job Characteristics

Recruitment and Competitive Advantage: A Brand Equity Perspective

Kang Yang Trevor Yu *and* Daniel M. Cable

Abstract

Leaders care about applicant reactions to their recruitment and hiring processes due to the profound effect on the organization's future composition and sustained competitive advantage. In addition to causing applicants to select into or out of the organization, recruitment experiences presocialize job seekers about what to expect from the organization (i.e., culture and values) and the job (i.e., required skills and abilities). In this chapter we take a strategic look at recruitment by applying a resource-based view. We argue that firms can use applicant reactions to recruitment and hiring processes to create and sustain competencies that are valuable, rare, and hard to imitate. Recruitment facilitates applicant self-selection because it communicates to them the unique attributes that characterize successful employees in the firm. Drawing upon ideas from person-environment fit, organizational image, and job design, our chapter covers the process and benefits of using the recruitment process to differentially attract a workforce that delivers a consistent and unique product to customers. In this way, recruitment can be a key component of the value creation process that drives a firm's competitive advantage.

Key Words: recruitment, strategic human resource management, employer brand equity, person-environment fit, organizational image, presocialization, employer reputation

Organizational leaders are acutely aware of the importance of managing human talent in today's knowledge-driven economy, wherein organizational success is largely dependent on the contributions of employees. This chapter focuses on the attraction and retention of talent as a business strategy through which organizations can build a sustained competitive advantage. A marked growth in interest in recruitment and applicant reactions has resulted in an impressive amount of research in these areas during the last three decades. Building on several past reviews of these topics (Barber, 1998; Breaugh & Starke, 2000; Chapman, Uggerslev, Carroll, Piasentin, & Jones, 2005; Rynes & Cable, 2003), our chapter begins with a discussion of how research on recruitment and applicant reactions has developed and evolved to its current state. We then devote particular attention to research that has occurred since the last comprehensive review by Rynes and Cable (2003). Next, we present a resource-based strategic view of recruitment, which links recruitment, applicant reactions, and retention to overall organizational success. Our model is derived from a brand equity perspective whereby the beliefs that job seekers develop about organizations during the recruitment process play a crucial role in determining organizational attraction, and ultimately the ability of employees to contribute to organizational competitive advantage. In other words, we explain how organizations can capitalize on their image and reputations to build a talent force that is valuable, rare, and hard to imitate (Barney, 1986).

Pre- to Mid-1980s Recruitment Research

Recruitment refers to the "practices and activities carried on by the organization with the primary purpose of identifying and attracting potential employees" (Barber, 1998; p. 5). For the most part, pre-1980s recruitment research adopted a rational information-processing paradigm, which focused on the systematic evaluation of job information and how the different sources of such information (i.e., recruitment sources) influenced job choice and post-hire outcomes (Schwab, Rynes, & Aldag, 1987). Some key findings from this era are that informal job sources (e.g., friends and personal acquaintances) tend to contribute more to a successful job search compared to other sources, such as direct application to companies, newspaper advertisements, and employment agencies (Rosenfeld, 1975). Informal sources were also linked to more favorable post-hire outcomes like job satisfaction and turnover (Schwab, 1982).

Studies before 1980 also investigated the nature of the job information that is evaluated by job seekers. Specifically, job attributes such as job security, type of work, pay, benefits, and working hours featured prominently in such investigations (e.g., Feldman & Arnold, 1978; Jurgensen, 1978; Zedeck, 1977). However, research in which participants rank the importance of job attributes to their job choice decisions, and policy-capturing studies in which people evaluate multi-attribute job alternatives have produced inconsistent results when it comes to determining the relative importance of job attributes (Schwab et al., 1987).

Research into the process by which job information is evaluated also was less than conclusive. Two major perspectives have dominated thinking on this process. The most widely used models of job choice assumed that multiple job alternatives are simultaneously evaluated against each other to determine a most preferred option (e.g., Schwab et al., 1987; Vroom, 1964). In contrast, models of sequential job search assumed that job alternatives are evaluated sequentially as information on them is encountered (e.g., Lippman & McCall, 1976). Unfortunately, concerns about methodological limitations and confounds mean that decades of empirical research cannot furnish a definitive answer about the relative superiority of the simultaneous or sequential perspectives (Schwab et al., 1987).

Mid-1980s to Early 1990s Recruitment Research

The growing popularity of recruitment research in the organizational sciences during the mid-1980s signaled the need for a more systematic approach to the entire recruitment process. To this end, Rynes's (1991) differentiation of recruitment variables, processes, and the outcomes that they influence (e.g., pre- versus post-hire) proved to be a useful starting point for recruitment theory developed during this period.

As noted by Rynes (1991), research on recruitment variables was characterized by a focus on three main topics: (a) recruiter characteristics, (b) recruitment sources, and (c) recruitment policies and procedures. And, three categories of recruiter characteristics were investigated: (a) recruiter demographics (e.g., race, sex, and age), (b) functional area, and (c) personality/behavioral traits. The impact of recruiter demographics seems limited to impressions of the recruiters, with only small effects on actual job choice (Rynes, 1991; Taylor & Bergmann, 1987). Research into functional areas of recruiters has compared the effects of line versus personnel recruiters (Harris & Fink, 1987; Taylor & Bergmann, 1987), and the effects of job incumbents versus organizational recruiters on job seeker impressions (Fisher, Ilgen, & Hoyer, 1979). Findings from these studies indicate that job seekers interviewed by personnel recruiters seemed to be less attracted to jobs (Taylor & Bergmann, 1987), while job incumbents were more trusted than professional recruiters, who were also associated with the lowest probabilities of accepting a job (Fisher et al., 1979). Research on recruiter personality and behavioral traits reveals that the two main factors of perceived recruiter affect (e.g., warmth, personableness, empathy, etc.) and the ability to provide information related to the job vacancy account for the most variance in job seeker outcomes (Harris & Fink, 1987; Liden & Parsons, 1986; Powell, 1984; Rynes, 1991; Rynes & Miller, 1983). In her summary of the effects of recruiter characteristics, Rynes (1991) states that recruiters have a limited impact on actual job choices because the small effect sizes associated with such characteristics become even smaller when: (a) outcome variables move away from intentions and get closer to job choice, (b) vacancy factors are controlled for, and (c) applicants progress to later stages of the recruitment process (p. 413).

Research on recruitment sources has mainly focused on how different sources of learning about a job opening affect post-hire outcomes such as turnover, absenteeism, and job attitudes. Such research has suggested that people recruited via employee referrals have more desirable outcomes compared to others recruited through newspaper advertisements, employment agencies, or direct application (e.g., Breaugh & Mann, 1984; Decker & Cornelius, 1979; Latham & Leddy, 1987). Two explanations have been proposed to account for the differential impact of recruitment sources on posthire outcomes. The realistic information hypothesis suggests that certain sources give job seekers better preparation for early work experiences, which in turn leads to positive outcomes such as reduced turnover and better job performance and attitudes (Breaugh & Mann, 1984; Rynes, 1991). In contrast, the self-selection hypothesis argues that recruitment source differences attract different types of individuals to an organization. In other words, job seekers self-select into certain jobs and organizations based on the fit between their individual attributes and those of the job and organizational environment (Rynes, 1991; Taylor & Schmidt, 1983). Attempts to compare the relative efficacy of these two explanations yielded mixed results, sometimes favoring the realistic information hypothesis (Breaugh & Mann, 1984), other times lending support to a self-selection explanation (Taylor & Schmidt, 1983).

The majority of research on administrative policies and practices has been devoted to investigating the impact of realism in recruitment messages on post-hire outcomes (Rynes, 1991). Built on the assumed relationship between realism and turnover, research on realistic job previews (RJPs) are based on the idea that people are more likely to stay with organizations when recruited using realistic messages. The logic behind the linkage is that realistic messages lead to met expectations between pre-hire expectancies and post-hire job experiences, allow new hires to anticipate and cope with problems encountered early on the job, and cause people to develop a stronger sense of commitment to employers that provide them with the information required to make informed job choices (Breaugh, 1983; Premack & Wanous, 1985; Rynes, 1991). Some meta-analyses have found evidence for the usefulness of RJPs in reducing turnover (McEvoy & Cascio, 1985; Reilly, Brown, Blood, & Malatesta, 1981), while others report rather small effect sizes that reduce to nonsignificance once sampling and measurement error are accounted for (Premack & Wanous, 1985).

Early to Late 1990s Recruitment Research

Research in the 1990s continued to add to our knowledge in the three established areas of recruiter characteristics, recruitment sources, and recruitment policies and procedures. Research on recruiter characteristics shed more light on the effects of training and focus (e.g., recruitment versus selection focused) on the impressions of job seekers. For instance, trained recruiters were perceived to be more effective (Connerley, 1997), professional, and prepared (Stevens & Campion, 1998) by applicants. Furthermore, recruiters who focused on recruitment activities both created more positive impressions (Turban & Dougherty, 1992) and allowed applicants to learn more information about the organization compared to recruiters who focused on selection activities. Additional research also established a link between perceptions of recruiter characteristics and judgments of organizational attributes (Goltz & Giannantonio, 1995; Turban & Dougherty, 1992). Recruiters and organizational representatives were also responsible for applicant perceptions of whether they were a good or bad fit for a particular organization, even after job and organizational attributes were taken into account (Rynes, Bretz, & Gerhart, 1991).

Subsequent research on recruitment sources has yielded support for both the self-selection hypothesis and the realistic information hypotheses, where certain sources attracted different groups of applicants and also transmitted more realistic information about the jobs (Blau, 1990; Griffeth, Hom, Fink, & Cohen, 1997; Werbel & Landau, 1996; Williams, Labig, & Stone, 1993). Further meta-analyses on recruitment practices revealed only a small effect of RJPs on applicant withdrawal, and similar weak relationships to other post-hire outcomes such as turnover, job satisfaction, organizational commitment, and job performance (Phillips, 1998).

Some investigations during this era extended past research regarding the effects of vacancy characteristics on job seeker perceptions and behavior. For example, Barber and Roehling (1993) showed that salary, benefits, and location were important factors considered by job applicants when deciding whether or not to apply to companies. Cable and Judge (1994) looked beyond pay level and showed that job seekers generally preferred individual to team-based pay, fixed to variable pay, and flexible to fixed benefits. Williams and Dreher (1992) found that pay level is linked to applicant attraction, but not the time taken to fill vacancies or applicant pool size. More recently, Trank, Rynes, and Bretz (2002) highlighted the importance of pay practices and other work attributes like job flexibility and fast-track promotion systems in attracting high-ability applicants.

In the decade that followed Rynes's (1991) review, a stream of research investigated the phenomenon of signaling, or how applicants form beliefs about unknown job and organizational attributes based on the observable or known attributes. For instance, Rynes, Bretz, and Gerhart (1991) observed that job seekers tended to form impressions of organizational inefficiency in response to delays in the recruitment process. The number of women and minorities met during site visits also influenced perceptions of hiring organizations' attitudes to toward diversity. In another study, Barber & Roehling (1993) found that applicants used job title and industry information to infer characteristics about the amount of challenge and responsibility that a job offered. In addition, salary served as an indicator of the number of work hours, while firm size and benefits signaled the level of job security. Cable and Judge's (1994) study suggested that job applicants use elements of pay systems other than pay level (e.g., individual versus team-based pay, fixed versus variable pay) to make inferences about organizational culture, such that they try to match their own personalities to certain pay systems. Other studies have investigated how initial beliefs and impressions of job seekers influence subsequent job search behavior. For example, Stevens (1997) showed that job applicants with more positive initial beliefs about hiring organizations tended to employ more impression management techniques and ask more questions that elicited more positive information about the organization.

Other research during this era focused on how job seekers' information-seeking behaviors vary along the job search process. Such research supports the view that job seekers seem to first engage in an expansive search for possible employers and then proceed to a narrower and more intensive job search, during which more detailed and credible information was sought (Barber, Daly, Giannantonio, & Phillips, 1994; Blau, 1994). It has also been observed that applicant post-interview intentions were actually good predictors of subsequent decisions to accept second interviews and even job offers (Judge & Cable, 1997; Powell & Goulet, 1996). Certain studies have also highlighted the social nature of the recruitment process in which employment outcomes are influenced by social referrals, and such referrals can be influenced by race and gender (Leicht & Marx, 1997). Job seekers' social networks also seem to contribute to job choice decisions over and above the established factors of individual preferences and academic qualification (Barber et al., 1994; Kilduff, 1990).

Research on recruitment processes during this period focused on how organizations, jobs, and various aspects of the recruitment process are evaluated by different types of job seekers. For example, higher quality applicants (those with more experience and academic achievement) tend to be more critical in their evaluation of their negative experiences during the recruitment process (e.g., recruitment delays and unprofessional recruiters; Bretz & Judge, 1998; Connerley & Rynes, 1997; Rynes et al., 1991). Likewise, personality traits seem to be related to preferences for certain types of pay systems; for example, high self-efficacy has been linked to preferences for individualized pay (Cable & Judge, 1994).

The recruitment literature's focus on the interaction between individual differences and the recruitment environment was part of a surge in interest in the area of person-organization (P-O) fit. Based on interactionist concepts, where individual attributes such as values and beliefs interact with organizational attributes to influence behavior and attitudes, P-O fit became a prevalent framework to study the development of job-related choices and attitudes during the recruitment process (Kristof, 1996). Findings from recruitment research in this area generally indicate that individuals are more interested in joining firms with values similar to their own (Cable & Judge, 1996; Judge & Bretz, 1992; Judge & Cable, 1997; Turban & Keon, 1993). In fact, research suggested that P-O fit is more influential than many aspects of the job (e.g., pay and location) when it comes to job choice (Cable & Judge, 1996). Not surprisingly, job seekers' organizational culture preferences were linked to Big Five personality traits (i.e. neuroticism, extraversion, openness to experience, agreeableness, and conscientiousness). Congruence between these preferences and hiring organizations' perceived cultures affects organizational attraction (Judge & Cable, 1997). This stream of recruitment research added an organizational culture focus to the literature, which prior to the 1990s seldom differentiated between job and organizational attributes (Rynes, 1991; Schwab et al., 1987). One exception to this was Tom (1971), who called attention to the role of organizational personality and images in determining job seekers' preferred employers.

So far, we have reviewed some of the key findings and trends across three decades of recruitment research. In the sections below, we focus on some of the more recent trends in the recruitment research literature.

Increasing Focus on Organizational Attributes

The prevalence of P-O fit studies in the 1990s coincided with increasing interest in the role that organizational characteristics play in recruitment processes. Schneider's theoretical work on organizational attraction, selection, and attrition advocated a focus on personality measures to study differences across entire organizations, and the role that these differences play in attracting unique types of people during the recruitment process (Schneider, 1987). Noticing that several P-O fit studies also detected significant large effects for organizational attributes such as values and culture on job seeker outcomes, Rynes and Cable (2003) highlighted the need for more research on organizational factors and the ways in which they impact recruitment.

Some research has revealed that differences in organizational characteristics were related to differences in recruitment practices. For example, firms with older workers, more challenging jobs, and a greater emphasis on short-term staffing strategies were more likely to adopt recruiting practices targeted at attracting more experienced hires, while smaller organizations adopted less formal and bureaucratic recruitment practices compared to larger firms (Rynes, Orlitzky, & Bretz, 1997). Another study by Barber, Wesson, Roberson, and Taylor (1999) found that smaller firms were less likely to use full-time recruiters, less likely to provide recruiter training, and more likely to use advertising, internal referrals, and external agencies to attract college applicants (as opposed to campus placement services) than their larger counterparts. Such firms were also less likely to begin recruitment well before the intended hire date, to give their applicants more time to make choices, and to accommodate flexibility in start dates (Barber et al., 1999).

It was during this period of increased focus on organizational attributes that more and more attention was devoted to investigating the role that corporate image and reputation can play in perceptions of organizational attractiveness and the propensity to apply for jobs (Gatewood, Gowan, & Lautenschlager, 1993; Turban & Greening, 1997). This increased focus on image and reputation heralded a brand equity perspective to recruitment, which has become one of the main approaches to the study of recruitment processes in the new millennium.

In the next section, we review research conducted from the brand equity perspective for two reasons. First, this research has not been the focus in past reviews of recruitment research due to the fact that most studies applying brand equity ideas have been published only recently, in the last decade or so. Second, the brand equity perspective serves as a key component within our proposed resource-based model of recruitment, in which we argue that employers can enjoy the benefits of sustained competitive advantage and organizational success via the effective utilization of brand equity to attract valuable and unique employees.

Employer Brand Equity: Image and Reputation in Recruitment Research
Precursors to Brand Equity Research

We start our in-depth review of the recruitment brand equity literature with several studies conducted prior to the year 2000, which were among the earliest to spark interest in the role of organizational images and reputations in the recruitment process. While these studies make no explicit reference to "brand equity," they nonetheless established links between recruitment activities, image and reputation, and job seeker outcomes. These links formed the basis for the subsequent development of the brand equity view of recruitment (Cable & Turban, 2001).

The beginnings of research into image and reputation in recruitment can be traced back to early work by Belt and Paolillo (1982), who highlighted the importance of organizational image in job seeker decision making. In fact, the researchers found that corporate image was actually more predictive of the likelihood of job seekers responding to recruitment advertisements compared to specific information about job demands. In other words, an employer with a poor image would be enough to deter job seekers from responding to a recruitment advertisement, regardless of the actual content of the advertisement. In another early study conducted on this topic, Harris and Fink (1987) found that recruiter characteristics such as personableness and informativeness influenced perceptions of job attributes, which included company reputation. Perceived recruiter personableness and informativeness were also linked to recruitment outcomes such as regard for company and expectation of a job offer, and intentions to accept a job offer (Harris & Fink, 1987).

Additional recruitment research highlighted the influential role that corporate image and reputation can play in perceptions of organizational attractiveness and the propensity to apply for jobs. Gatewood and colleagues (1993) found that organizational image (i.e., the image associated with the name of an organization) was influenced by a job seeker's experience with company advertisements, products, and even studying the organization in class, while recruitment image (i.e., the image associated with an organization's recruitment message) was influenced by information presented in recruitment ads and by other job seekers who worked with the company. Both an organization's overall image and recruitment image were positively related to job applicant intentions to pursue employment with it. Similarly, Turban and Greening (1997) found that organizational reputation, or perceptions of how a firm is seen in the eyes of the public, was influenced by third-party ratings of a firm's corporate social performance (i.e., an organization's responsibilities to multiple stakeholders such as employees and its community). For example, independent ratings of the quality of community relations, employee relations, treatment of the environment, quality of products and services, and treatment of women and minorities of 168 companies were all significantly related to organizational reputation. These results highlight the influential role that an organization's non-economic–related policies and practices may play in shaping its reputation among job seekers. In addition, firm reputation was also related to its perceived attractiveness as an employer (Turban & Greening, 1997).

In another study linking recruitment activities to image and job seeker outcomes, Turban, Forret, and Hendrickson (1998) found that perceptions of recruiter behaviors, such as personableness, informing, and selling during employment interviews, influenced organizational attraction via job seekers' beliefs about job attributes (e.g., challenging work) and organizational attributes (e.g., work environment). According to the researchers, these findings support signaling theory, in which recruiter behaviors act as signals for unknown job and organizational attributes among job seekers (Rynes, 1991). Interestingly, Turban et al. (1998), also found a negative relationship between reputation and attraction, and speculated that this finding could be due either to unmet expectations (after interviews for firms with positive reputations), or bolstering (where candidates lowered their attractiveness ratings when they felt there was little chance of getting a job at a reputable employer).

In summary, the research studies reviewed above called attention to the important roles that employer image and reputation play in influencing individual reactions during the recruitment process.

However, there was no consensus among studies regarding what employer image and reputation were. More importantly, the absence of an overall guiding framework to account for the antecedents to image and reputation and the ways in which they influence recruitment outcomes, was also conspicuous. The next section describes a framework that was designed to address these gaps in our understanding.

Brand Equity Theory

Brand equity theory is a conceptual framework borrowed from the marketing literature that has been used to understand the impact of organizational image and reputation in the context of recruitment (Cable & Turban, 2001). In the recruitment context, employer brands refer to beliefs or knowledge about potential employers. Brand equity theory is thus built on the premise that organizations manage their images so that job seekers develop certain types of beliefs about them (Allen, Mahto, & Otondo, 2007; Cable & Turban, 2001; Collins & Stevens, 2002). According to this perspective, there are several important components of employer brands. First, *familiarity* with the organization refers to the level of awareness that a job seeker has of the employer (Cable & Turban, 2001; Keller, 1993). Familiarity is a prerequisite for job seekers to obtain and recall information related to the other two dimensions of an employer brand: image and reputation.

Next, employer *image* itself is a multifaceted construct that can refer to both the content of the beliefs held by job seekers about the attributes of an employing organization (Cable & Turban, 2001) and the attitudes held toward an employer (Barber, 1998; Collins & Stevens, 2002; Gatewood et al., 1993; Rynes, 1991). Cable and Turban (2001) further propose that there are three categories of employer image: (a) employer information refers to knowledge to do with the attributes of the organization; such attributes may range from the objective (e.g., company policies, size, structure, and procedures) to the subjective (e.g., values, culture, and social awareness); (b) job information refers to knowledge about the characteristics of a particular job that an organization is offering; examples of such job attributes include type of work performed, job requirements, pay level, and promotion opportunities; (c) people information refers to the type of individuals who currently work at the employing organization and are thus potential coworkers of job seekers.

The third dimension of employer brand is employer *reputation*, which refers to a job seeker's beliefs about the public's affective evaluation of an organization as an employer. Therefore, brand equity theory distinguishes image from reputation in two ways: (a) unlike image, reputation consists of an evaluative component; and (b) reputation is a job seeker's beliefs about how an employer is evaluated by others, whereas image comprises an individual's own beliefs (Cable & Turban, 2001).

Our review of recruitment research from a brand equity perspective has three parts: First, we cover research exploring the antecedents of employer brands. Next, we review research investigating how different recruitment sources transmit organizational and job information that influences brand equity. Third, we review research linking the three components of employer brands (familiarity, image, and reputation) to recruitment individual-level outcomes. Finally, a review of research that links brand equity to organizational-level outcomes rounds off this section.

Factors Influencing Employer Brands

The first set of studies that we review explores the antecedents to employer brands. Knowing the factors that influence employer brands is important because employers need to know what tools they have at their disposal when managing their brands to benefit from brand equity. For instance, findings from a series of studies conducted by Cable and Graham (2000) suggested that employer reputation is highly dependent on the industry in which employers operate. Results gathered from three separate studies using different methodologies of verbal protocol analysis, policy capturing, and field data all pointed toward industry as being particularly salient in the minds of job seekers when they were making reputation judgments. In line with earlier the findings of Gatewood and colleagues (1993), organizational familiarity also had a significant positive relationship with reputation ratings. In addition, results from the policy capturing and field studies also indicate that company profitability played an influential role in perceptions of reputation, in which profitability was actually the best predictor of reputation in the field study. In explaining these findings, the researchers suggest that a job seeker's reputation perceptions may be based on organizational attributes that are public and relevant to an individual's personal identity. Hence, job seekers would be inclined to associate their identities with firms operating in industries that produce respectable

or prestigious products and services. Likewise, an employer's profitability may also be attractive to job seeker identity because it gives them the chance to "bask in the reflective glory" of the company's financial performance (Cialdini et al., 1976)

Other research has also called attention to the awareness of an employer's products and services as important influences of employer brand equity. For instance, findings from Cable, Aiman-Smith, Mulvey, and Edwards (2000) suggest that an employer's products may be an effective tool via which it can manage job seeker beliefs about its company culture. This study investigated how different types of information sources influenced the accuracy of beliefs that job applicants developed about a hiring company. Data gathered from applicants indicated that information about organizational culture that was gathered through product (e.g., the company's advertisements for its products) and company (e.g., videos and brochures that the company sent to campus recruiting offices) sources led to inaccurate beliefs of the prospective employer's culture. For instance, applicants who relied on product and company information sources developed beliefs that overestimated the extent to which the company had a culture of risk taking, whereas applicants who did not rely on such sources developed more accurate beliefs. These findings suggest that it is possible for hiring organizations to manage their image during the recruitment process through company and product information sources. Rather surprisingly, applicants who relied on other sources that would typically be less susceptible to image management such as social networks (i.e., word of mouth) and prior work experience (e.g., internships) did not develop more accurate beliefs about the company's culture.

A more recent study by Collins (2007) also found that product awareness was related to all three facets of employer brands (i.e., familiarity, image, and reputation). In addition, the effects of certain recruitment practices (e.g., recruitment advertisements, sponsorships, and employee endorsements) were also dependent on the level of awareness that job seekers had about employers' products and services. Specifically, low-information recruitment practices such as general recruitment advertisements and sponsorships influenced employer familiarity and reputation more when product awareness was low. In contrast, high-information recruitment practices like detailed recruitment advertisements and word-of-mouth endorsements influenced employer reputation and image more when product awareness was high. Collins (2007) argued that these results were observed because product awareness provided motivation for job seekers to process detailed information from these high-information sources, which resulted in a stronger positive influence on reputation and image.

In all, the above studies show that employer brands and their respective components can be influenced by both recruitment activities and also by factors that have nothing to do with the recruitment process. Studies in the next section expand on this section by asking how characteristics of different recruitment sources influence the transmission of job and organizational information that is ultimately used to form perceptions of employer brands.

Factors Influencing the Delivery of Organization and Job Information

Researchers have investigated the specific characteristics of recruitment and non-recruitment sources that influence the communication of job and organization information used to develop employer brands. Such research has focused on the properties of various media used to communicate job and organization information.

Utilizing media richness theory, Allen, Scotter, and Otondo (2004) illustrate the importance of media characteristics such as media richness and credibility in determining job seeker reactions to recruitment messages. Results from their study indicated that the type of recruitment media matters because of differing abilities to facilitate the communication of different amounts of information, two-way communication, personal focus, social presence, and symbolism in recruitment messages. This study also highlighted the importance of understanding the role of job seeker perceptions when it comes to evaluating the richness qualities of recruitment media. For instance, while face-to-face recruitment was rated highest in two-way communication, it was also rated low on other richness properties such as social presence. Text, which is usually not considered a rich medium, actually scored higher than audio and face-to-face mediums in certain cases. Even more significantly, the above-mentioned features of recruitment media were positively related to outcomes of the communication process such as perceived credibility and satisfaction, which in turn predicted affective (e.g., attraction) and cognitive job seeker outcomes (e.g., intentions to pursue employment).

Cable and Yu (2006) also used utilized media richness theory to examine how the media richness and credibility of different recruitment sources affect image alignment, or the correspondence between job seeker beliefs about employer image and employers' intended projected images. MBA job seekers in this study perceived career fairs as more media rich (i.e., higher in the ability to permit timely feedback, convey multiple language cues such as words and facial expression, and tailor messages according to the needs of the target) compared to company web sites and electronic bulletin boards (e.g., vault. com). Company web sites were also perceived to be more media rich than vault.com. Electronic bulletin boards were seen as the least credible recruitment medium, possibly because job seekers assume that negative information posted on these sites about a company's culture are from disgruntled employees posting false information to harm their companies. Results also revealed that media richness and credibility affected the way in which recruitment media brought job seeker beliefs in line with an employer's intended projected image. Specifically, results suggested that in most dimensions of image that were examined, richness and credibility positively influenced job seeker beliefs of company image, regardless of whether they initially over- or underestimated the particular image dimension (e.g., powerful, achievement-oriented, stimulating). Consistent with Cable et al. (2000), these results imply that a fair amount of impression management occurs during recruitment, where companies attempt to create the most positive beliefs about their image among job seekers.

The increasing popularity of online recruitment has spawned other research focused on studying the phenomenon of web-based recruitment. As seen in Cable and Yu's (2006) study, researchers have devoted special attention to the unique opportunities that the Internet provides recruiting organizations when it comes to communicating recruitment information and attracting future employees. For instance, Dineen, Ash, and Noe (2002) not only highlighted the importance of credibility of the recruitment medium in the context of web recruitment, but also called attention to the potential of customized feedback to attract job seekers. Their experiment manipulated the amount of feedback that participants received about person-organization (P-O) fit with a prospective employer. Results revealed that people were more attracted to the company when more P-O fit feedback was provided. Objective P-O fit—or fit between actual individual preferences of organizational culture and third-party ratings of a particular employer's culture—also was a significant predictor of organizational attraction. Most notably, the level of fit feedback was more predictive of attraction when perceived agreement with that feedback was high compared to when agreement was low. Conversely, objective P-O fit was a stronger influence on attraction when agreement with feedback was low compared to when agreement was high. These results suggest that P-O fit feedback is discounted when it is perceived to be not credible, which also causes individuals to rely on more objective information, such as objective P-O fit, when rating their attraction toward employers (Van Hoye & Lievens, 2005).

A more recent web-based recruitment study by Dineen, Juan, Ash, and DelVecchio (2007) calls attention to the importance of aesthetic features of web sites, as well as the amount of customized information regarding P-O fit. Specifically, information recall was facilitated when customized fit information was presented together with good aesthetic properties (i.e., job postings featured colors, pictures, multiple fonts, and a patterned background). Customized information also had a stronger effect on viewing time when web site aesthetics were good compared to when they were bad (i.e., plain black text on a white background). Moreover, results indicated that pleasing aesthetics and customized fit information were more likely to encourage individuals with poor fit to self-select out, rather than encouraging those with good fit to self-select in. These results highlight the practical usefulness of aesthetics and customization when it comes to web-based recruitment. Namely, employers may manipulate these factors to "weed out" poorly fitting individuals from the recruitment process.

Overall, research in this area has highlighted the importance of media richness and credibility as properties of recruitment media that influence the effectiveness in which recruitment messages are communicated. Hence, organizations seeking to influence image and reputation beliefs associated with their employment brand would be well-served by paying close attention to the characteristics of recruitment media that facilitate change in job seeker beliefs. In the next section, we illustrate the equity accrued to employer brands by reviewing research linking image, reputation, and familiarity to job seeker outcomes.

Employer Brand Equity and Individual Recruitment Outcomes

In this section, we review research showing how employer image, reputation, and familiarity can impact job seeker outcomes in a variety of ways. Our review thus contains two types of research: one that has detected direct relationships between these three components of employer brands and job seeker attitudes and behaviors, and another that has analyzed the interactive effects of image, reputation, and familiarity on individuals during recruitment.

Image and Job Seeker Outcomes

Some research on employer images indicates that job seekers use these images to differentiate between various potential employers. For instance, Highhouse, Zickar, Thorsteinson, Stierwalt, and Slaughter (1999) suggested that job seekers can distinguish between images of companies within the same industry (e.g., fast food) on the basis of different employment images associated with the different employers. These researchers employed a forced-choice inductive methodology to identify critical dimensions that members of two job applicant pools (e.g., high school students and retirees) used to distinguish among company employment images. Consequently, they found evidence that differences across such dimensions were linked to perceptions of a company's attractiveness as an employer.

Lievens and Highhouse (2003) further argue that it is the symbolic value of employer images that plays a decisive role in attracting certain job seekers to certain companies. Specifically, they argued that in addition to instrumental attributes that are based on objective and factual information such as pay, bonuses, benefits, and flexible working hours, job seekers also use symbolic attributes that describe jobs and organizations in terms of subjective and intangible attributes (e.g., innovativeness and prestige) to describe prospective employers. Their study highlighted the importance of trait inferences of innovativeness and competence in the assessment of a firm's attractiveness as an employer. Firm innovativeness was characterized by traits such as daring, trendy, exciting, cool, spirited, and young, while competence was described by traits like secure, intelligent, and reliable. This study on applicant pools targeted by the banking industry revealed that instrumental job and organizational attributes may be of interest to job seekers because information on such attributes is used to calculate the potential utility of accepting a job with a particular employer. However, the researchers explain that symbolic attributes and the meanings that are associated with prospective employers also served to attract applicants to certain employers because such attributes allow applicants to express parts of their self-concept and personality. In fact, findings from this study even suggest that it might be easier for job seekers to differentiate among hiring organizations on the basis of trait inferences as compared to traditional job and organizational attributes. Therefore, it seems that job seekers rely on organizational image in the form of both instrumental and symbolic attributes to differentiate between prospective employers (Lievens, 2007).

The symbolic nature of employer images was further evidenced in a series of studies by Slaughter, Mohr, Zickar, and Highhouse (2004) that conceptualized image in terms of unique personalities. According to Slaughter et al. (2004), organizations have different personalities, whereby they can be differentiated across dimensions identified as Boy Scout, Innovativeness, Dominance, Thrift, and Style. They also argue that these dimensions that are used to distinguish organizational-level personality appear to be distinct from those that exist in individual personality (i.e., the Big Five). The utility of organizational personality measures was also demonstrated when it was linked to organizational attractiveness, reputation, and intentions to pursue employment among prospective job applicants, even after familiarity with the company was accounted for.

While the three studies reviewed so far in this section have established relationships between organizational image and job seeker outcomes, a study by Collins and Stevens (2002) goes a step further by providing evidence that image mediates the impact of recruitment activities on job seekers. Specifically, they found that activities typically carried out early in the recruitment process, such as publicity, sponsorships, word-of-mouth endorsements, and advertising, influenced job-related intentions and decisions through job seeker beliefs associated with the employer's brand image. This study highlighted the importance of two components of an employer's brand: general attitudes toward the company and perceptions of job attributes. Strong relationships were observed between word-of-mouth endorsements and both dimensions of employer brand image, prompting the researchers to suggest that capitalizing on such endorsements might provide a "highly effective and economical method for increasing applicant pools." Interestingly, results also suggested that companies stand to gain most when the above recruitment practices are employed in conjunction with one another. For instance, employer brand image was far stronger when publicity was used together with sponsorship, word-of-mouth, and advertising compared to when publicity or sponsorship was employed alone.

Overall, these studies illustrate the significant effect that employer images can have on job seeker attitudes and behavior. Considering that image can act as a key link between recruitment practices and job seeker outcomes, we move on to explore the exact processes that underlie the positive impact of employer image.

Why Image Matters: An Interactionist Perspective

Research that has sought to explain *why* employer images impact job seeker behavior has typically focused on how job seekers self-select in or out of the recruitment process based on how well they fit with particular images of employers. Job seekers are more likely to react favorably to the employer when fit exists between person and employer characteristics because they are more likely to feel comfortable and competent (Cable & Judge, 1996; Chatman, 1989). Likewise, it has also been argued that person-environment fit fulfills a variety of needs, such as for belonging and self-actualization, which in turn produces positive attitudes and behavior toward an employer (Cable & Edwards, 2004; Edwards & Shipp, 2007). Therefore, the research reviewed in this section shows how image interacts with individual characteristics to attract certain job seekers to certain employers.

In support of this interactionist perspective, Turban and Keon (1993) found that individual differences moderated the effects of certain organizational characteristics on job seeker attraction. Participants in their experiment with low self-esteem (SE) were more attracted to decentralized and larger companies than their high self-esteem counterparts. Presumably, people lower in SE had less confidence in their ability and thus preferred to share decision-making responsibilities with other organizational members. Participants with a high need for achievement (nAch) were more attracted to organizations that offered rewards based on performance in place of seniority. This relationship was expected because high-nAch individuals prefer to have more control over the outcomes of their performance.

As reviewed above, Cable and Judge (1994) provide further evidence that other personality-type individual differences moderate the impact of compensation systems on the attractiveness of certain pay policies. For instance, job seekers with an internal locus of control experienced more attraction to organizations with flexible benefits compared to those with an external locus of control, while those who valued individualism were more attracted to individual-based pay schemes than collectivists. Job seekers with high self-efficacy also preferred organizations offering more individualized and skill-based pay. Last but not least, risk-adverse job seekers were more attracted to organizations offering non-contingent pay packages compared to those with a higher appetite for risk.

Evidence for the moderating role of individual differences on the relationships between organizational image and firm attraction has also been detected in Asian-based settings by Turban and colleagues (2001). In a study conducted in the People's Republic of China, individuals who were more risk averse and had a lower need for pay were more attracted to state-owned rather than foreign-owned firms. Based on the argument that type of firm ownership in China serves as a signal for working conditions offered to employees, the authors suggest that risk-averse individuals preferred state-owned enterprises because these firms are commonly believed to provide more job security and less variable compensation than foreign companies. Similarly, individuals with a higher need for pay were more attracted to foreign firms because they pay significantly more than their state-owned counterparts.

Several studies have also identified the moderating effect of work values on the relationship between organizational image and job seeker attitudes. For instance, Judge and Bretz (1992) found that beliefs about the values that are espoused by an organization interacted with individual preferences of the same values to influence job choice decisions. In other words, individuals were more likely to opt for jobs at organizations whose values (e.g., concern for others, fairness, and achievement) matched that of their own (Cable & Judge, 1996; Dineen et al., 2002; Judge & Cable, 1997).

Additional research has also highlighted how various human resource policies contribute to perceptions of organizational image (Avery & McKay, 2006; McKay & Avery, 2006). In line with interactionist and P-O fit ideas, the impact of such perceptions of policies on job seekers also depends on certain individual differences. For instance, individuals with high role conflict are more attracted to organizations that offer flexible work schedules compared to those that did not offer such arrangements. This relationship could occur because flextime arrangements reduce costs associated with

making role transitions by having flexible temporal boundaries, making them attractive to people with high levels of role conflict. In contrast, individuals with low role conflict were more attracted to organizations that offered telecommuting compared to those that did not. It appears that those experiencing less role conflict are attracted to telecommuting because they can minimize the costs associated with transitioning between roles (Rau & Hyland, 2002).

In addition, older workers looking for work after retirement are attracted to human resource policies such as scheduling flexibility and equal employment opportunity (Rau & Adams, 2005). Research has also investigated individual differences that moderate the impact of diversity-related policies. For example, African Americans are only more attracted to recruitment advertisements that portray racial diversity when the advertisements extend to supervisory positions, while such advertisements had no effects on Caucasian respondents. However, blacks with higher other-group orientations (i.e., those who enjoy interacting with members of other racial or ethnic groups) seemed to prefer organizations whose ads portrayed no diversity over those that portrayed a restricted amount of diversity. Apparently, such individuals perceive non-diverse organizations as offering the best opportunity to interact with members of other groups (Avery, 2003).

In all, there is a good deal of evidence supporting the view that fit between image beliefs and individual attributes are related to various pre-entry outcomes (Kristof-Brown et al., 2005). In a brand equity context, employer images interact with various individual differences to attract certain types of job seekers. Hence, these attracted job seekers self-select to stay within the recruitment process and try to join the firm. From employer image, we proceed to discuss how and why employer reputation influences recruitment outcomes.

Why Reputation Matters: Maintaining a Positive Social Identity

Unlike employer image, which deals with an individual's own beliefs about employer attributes, employer reputation focuses on individual perceptions of how *other* people feel about the employer. As such, the motivations underlying the relationship between reputation and job seeker outcomes are also different from the interactionist person-environment fit processes that occur with employer image. Employers occupy an important part of people's self-concepts. Hence, a person's self-concept is influenced by the characteristics that others may infer about them based on where they work (Dutton & Dukerich, 1991; Dutton, Dukerich, & Harquail, 1994). Therefore, job seekers are attracted to reputable employers because membership in these organizations facilitates social approval and the development of a socially desirable identity (Ashforth & Mael, 1989; Cable & Turban, 2001).

Studies on corporate social responsibility have highlighted the motivation of having a positive social identity in reactions to company reputations among job seekers. For example, studies by Turban and Greening show that firm corporate social performance was positively related to employer attractiveness because job seekers expect to enjoy more positive self-concepts from being hired by companies that are known for more socially responsible actions (Greening & Turban, 2000; Turban & Greening, 1997).

Similar findings were observed by Cable and Turban (2003), who found that corporate reputation and corporate familiarity contributed job seeker perceptions of employer reputation. More importantly, employer reputation in turn influenced the pride that individuals expected from organizational membership. In fact, job seekers were actually willing to make sacrifices in terms of lower wages to join firms with more positive reputations. Therefore, it appears that the attainment of positive social identities underlies the positive impact of reputations on job seeker attitudes and behavior.

More recently, Highhouse and colleagues (2007) found that job seeker social identity concerns moderated the effect of symbolic inferences about a company's reputation on organizational attraction. These researchers identified two main social identity-related concerns of job seekers: *social adjustment* refers to the desire of job seekers to impress others through their affiliation with a high-status organization, while *value expression* is the desire to express to others an association with socially desirable values through one's affiliation with highly respected employers. Findings supported the authors' hypotheses that a social adjustment consciousness was predictive of job seeker attraction to organizations with impressive reputations (i.e., prestigious), whereas a value expression consciousness was mostly related to attraction to organizations with respected reputations (i.e., honorable). Thus, social identity concerns of job seekers accounted for the relationship between company reputation and attraction.

In all, the studies reviewed in this section indicate that reputation impacts job seeker outcomes because individuals see job choice as a way to enhance their social identities. In the next section, we discuss how the last component of employer brands—familiarity—influences job seeker outcomes.

Familiarity as an Anchor for Image and Reputation

Unlike employer image and reputation, familiarity does not influence job seeker outcomes directly. Instead, familiarity acts as an anchor upon which employers can build their image and reputation to influence job seeker behavior. Cable and Turban (2001) argued that familiarity should have a positive impact on image and the content of beliefs associated with an employer because it acts as a template upon which job seekers can collect and store job and organizational information. Moreover, familiarity also can signal the legitimacy of a firm as an employer, which also affects the content of employer images.

In a study examining relationships among different dimensions of employer brand, results from Brooks and colleagues (2003) suggest that the relationship between employer familiarity and beliefs about the employer (i.e., image) may be more complex than typically assumed (Brooks, Highhouse, Russell, & Mohr). Namely, most perspectives on organizational image and reputation assume that familiarity is a positive determinant of image and organizational attraction (Cable & Turban, 2001; Turban, 2001; Turban, Lau, Ngo, Chow, & Si, 2001). In contrast, Brooks and colleagues provide evidence that familiar employers can actually influence image and attraction both positively and negatively. They argue that this relationship occurs because familiarity provides a larger pool of *both* positive and negative information from which job seekers draw when forming image beliefs and judgments of attraction. Therefore, the direction of relationship between familiarity and both image and attraction depends on the judgment context and the degree to which it requires the retrieval of positive or negative information. For instance, participants in this particular study ranked more familiar companies higher up on *both* lists of most *admirable* companies and most *contemptible* companies compared to less familiar companies.

Evidence for a positive influence of familiarity on job seekers was found by Turban (2001) in a study of the recruitment activities of a large petrochemical corporation at various college campuses across the United States. This study obtained evidence for a significant effect of organizational familiarity on firm attraction, where people more familiar with the firm were also more attracted to it. Also consistent with a brand equity perspective, beliefs about the potential job and organization (i.e., organizational image) mediated the effects of recruitment activities on organizational attraction. In addition, reputation also played a significant role in predicting attraction to the firm, where the impressions of the firm's image as an employer according to university personnel were also related to levels of attraction of potential applicants.

Lievens, Van Hoye, and Schreurs (2005) also found considerable evidence for the utility of all three aspects of employer brand: familiarity, image, and reputation. Conducted in the context of the Belgian Armed Forces, familiarity significantly predicted attraction to the army as an employer. Similarly, image beliefs about certain aspects of the job and organization, such as the amount of social activities and task diversity, also influenced attraction toward the organization. The researchers also found that employer reputation in the form of trait inferences (i.e., whether the organization was associated with excitement, cheerfulness, and prestige) was also linked to attraction. Though it is debatable whether this latter conceptualization of organizational reputation is valid since it essentially deals with job seeker beliefs about the hiring organization and not their beliefs about what the public thinks about the organization (Cable & Turban, 2001), these results nonetheless highlight the importance of familiarity and existing beliefs of organizations to organizational attraction. Further relative importance analysis revealed that trait inferences of the Armed Forces were actually the most important of the three predictors of organizational attraction. Most pertinently, image and trait inferences also had stronger effects on attraction when familiarity was high, prompting the researchers to argue that familiarity with the employer "serves as an anchor to which other associations can be attached" (Lievens et al., 2005; p. 565).

Further support for the role of familiarity in brand equity theory has also been obtained in the context of web-based recruitment. Allen et al. (2007) observed that organization image significantly predicted job seekers' attitudes toward hiring organizations, which in turn influenced intentions to pursue employment with each particular employer. These relationships were observed after participants in this study were exposed to job and organizational information via the web sites of actual Fortune 500 organizations. However, organizational familiarity

was not directly related to applicant attitudes and attraction. Referring to this latter finding, the authors went on to suggest that familiarity with an organization alone may not be enough to positively influence organizational attraction.

Another recent study by Collins (2007) highlights the role of familiarity in the form of product awareness in the recruitment context and the development of employer brand equity. Awareness of an employer's products and services played an important role in the development of various dimensions of the employer brand. Specifically, product awareness, or the extent to which job seekers were familiar with an employer's products or services, moderated the relationships between recruiting practices and different aspects of employer brand. For example, low-information recruitment practices such as general recruitment advertisements and sponsorships were positively related to application outcomes through employer familiarity and reputation, when product awareness was low. According to Collins (2007), this relationship occurred because low-information recruitment practices and product awareness acted as substitutes to influence initial familiarity with the employer and also to create positive beliefs about employer reputation. Likewise, high-information recruitment practices such as detailed recruitment advertisements and employee endorsements are related to job seeker outcomes through employer reputation and image, when product awareness was high. This finding could be due to product awareness giving rise to initial employer familiarity and interest in the employer, which is needed to motivate potential applicants to seek out and process the large amounts of information delivered by these recruitment practices. Furthermore, the familiarity created by product awareness also could serve as a memory anchor on which potential applicants can store beliefs relating to employer image. Therefore, the effectiveness of high-information recruitment practices seems to be contingent on a good amount of initial employer familiarity, which may arise from awareness of the employer's products (Collins, 2007).

Results from recent meta-analyses concluded that organizational image is strongly related to recruitment outcomes including job pursuit intentions, job-organization attraction, and acceptance intentions (Chapman et al., 2005). The research reviewed in these past sections on employer brand equity suggests that, in addition to image, employer reputation and familiarity also play a role in determining job seeker outcomes. Our review has so far highlighted that these three different components of employer brands influence job seekers via different processes. Image interacts with individual characteristics to determine job seeker fit with the hiring organization, whereas reputation evokes concerns to manage one's social identity by being associated with a particular employer. Last but not least, familiarity acts as an anchor to image and reputation by moderating their effects on job seeker outcomes. We now shift our level of analysis by proceeding to discuss research that has linked employer brands to organizational-level recruiting outcomes.

Brand Equity and Organizational-Level Outcomes

All the research reviewed so far has focused on relationships involving employer brand equity and individual job seeker attitudes and behavior. Some research has begun to ask whether employer brands actually benefit hiring organizations as a whole. For instance, Turban and Cable (2003) found that employer reputation predicted the quantity and quality of applicants that firms can attract across two studies. Employers with more positive reputations as rated by publications such as *Businessweek* and *Fortune* attracted larger applicant pools, as evidenced in not only applications submitted but also the number of information sessions attended, and the number of credits willing to be spent to interview with such firms. Firms with positive reputations were also able to attract applicants with higher grade point averages. Furthermore, employers with higher reputations interviewed applicants with higher grade point averages, competencies in foreign languages and extracurricular activities, and overall ratings.

Collins and Han (2004) provide further evidence that early recruitment practices, corporate advertising, and firm reputation are all directly linked to applicant pool quantity and quality. Additionally, corporate advertising was found to have the most direct impact on applicant pool quality and quantity. In line with the brand equity perspective, the authors argue that corporate advertising influences organizational recruitment outcomes through increasing the familiarity of the organization as an employer and also by constructing a positive image of the organization. Furthermore, different types of recruitment practices also interacted with corporate advertising levels and firm reputation. For instance, low-involvement recruitment practices like general recruitment ads and sponsorships were more effective for employers who had low levels of

corporate advertising and reputation because these practices influence applicant pool quantity and quality by creating initial awareness and signaling the availability of job openings. In contrast, such practices do not affect organizational recruitment outcomes when firms have already high levels of corporate advertising and reputation. On the other hand, high-involvement recruitment practices like detailed recruitment ads and employee endorsements (i.e., word of mouth) were most effective when employers had already high levels of corporate advertising and reputation because they influence recruitment outcomes by furnishing job seekers with detailed information about the employer and its job openings. Conversely, without a significant amount of preexisting awareness and beliefs about the firm, such practices did not lead to improvements in applicant pool quality and quantity.

In summary, when combined with the earlier research reviewed that focused on individual recruitment outcomes, these findings support a new focus for recruitment research where organizations manage their employer brand equity to market themselves to job seekers. Next, we build on these recent advances in brand equity recruitment research by proposing an expanded model that uses brand equity to link individual recruitment outcomes to an organization's competitive advantage. Consistent with recommendations from previous reviews (Rynes, 1991; Rynes & Cable, 2003), the brand equity approach accounts for both individual and organizational (e.g., image, reputation, and familiarity) factors that influence job seeker attitudes and behavior. Moreover, given the lack of understanding of how recruitment messages are linked to job seeker outcomes (Breaugh & Billings, 1988; Breaugh & Starke, 2000), the brand equity approach allows us to understand how recruitment messages are conveyed in the form of perceptions of organizational image and reputation. Finally, our proposed model provides a comprehensive linkage from recruitment practices to post-hire outcomes that incorporates crucial mediating processes such as image formation and self-selection, leading to a more complete understanding of the entire recruitment process.

A Resource-Based View of Recruitment

To be considered a sustained competitive advantage, an organization's workforce must create something valuable in the eyes of the firm's customers that is rare or unique relative to competitors, and that is hard for competitors to imitate (Barney, 1986). We argue that brand equity can be instrumental to building a competitive advantage for organizations by attracting human capital that is valuable, rare, and hard to imitate. Specifically, the research reviewed above suggests that employers can gain a competitive advantage through their employer brand equity by: (a) attracting a larger and higher quality applicant pool to select from, and (b) attracting certain types of job seekers who deliver the unique behaviors and outputs that customers enjoy.

By explicitly linking recruitment to competitive advantage, a resource-based view on recruitment complements and builds on traditional recruitment research that has largely focused on predicting pre- and post-hire job seeker attitudes and behaviors (Breaugh & Starke, 2000; Rynes & Cable, 2003). This idea is consistent with arguments that human resources research needs to expand its focus from individual-level recruitment and selection research to multilevel research demonstrating the impact of these practices at the business unit or organizational level (Van Der Heijde & Van Der Heijden, 2006; Ployhart, 2006). Following research in strategic human resource management that has demonstrated a link between successful HR systems and organizational performance (Batt, 2002; Collins & Clark, 2003; Collins & Smith, 2006), a successful recruitment policy hinges on its ability to complement or

even drive a firm's business strategy and competitive advantage (Bowen & Ostroff, 2004; Breaugh & Starke, 2000; Ulrich, 1998).

Our model illustrated in Figure 7.1 emphasizes the importance of human capital as a valuable resource for organizations by positioning organizational competitive advantage as a possible outcome of the entire recruitment process. This focus on organizational success and competitive advantage links recruitment with recent research emphasizing employee-based competencies (e.g., top management team social networks) as mediators of the relationship between HR practices and firm performance (Collins & Clark, 2003; also see Hitt, Bierman, Shimizu, & Kochhar, 2001). Our focus also highlights the notion that firms can market positive organizational climates of trust and cooperation (in our case, with job seekers) to improve their performance and competitiveness (Collins & Smith, 2006).

In the following sections of this chapter, we first highlight the important considerations that firms have to make when recruiting for competitive advantage. We apply brand equity concepts to show how firms can achieve valuable, rare, and hard-to-imitate workforce deliverables through recruitment. Finally, we explain how employer brands can be used to reinforce an organizational culture that is a competitive advantage and drives organizational success.

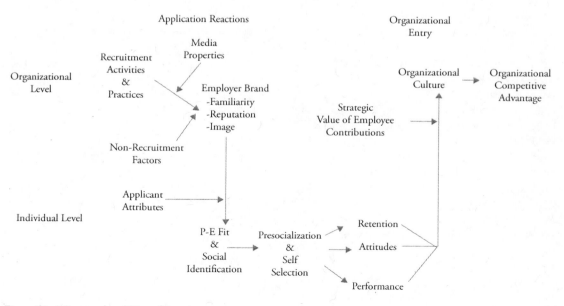

Figure 7.1 A Resource-based View of Recruitment.

Who Do We Want to Attract? Competitive Advantage and Strategic Value of Employee Contributions

In order to understand how a firm can develop a competitive advantage through recruitment, it is necessary to understand the type of workforce that can create the specific outcomes the organization needs in order to surpass its competition. A firm's recruitment strategy therefore starts with determining the valuable, rare, and hard-to-imitate workforce characteristics that drive a firm's key performance indicators that are closely tied to its strategy (Bowen, Ledford, & Nathan, 1991; Cable, 2007). These characteristics usually take the form of specific knowledge, values, abilities, and personalities possessed by job seekers that make them uniquely willing and able to execute the firm's strategy. For instance, Harley Davidson might prefer employees in many functions to be bikers and Harley owners because that may lead to customer-focused innovations and may contribute to brand loyalty and street credibility among its customers. Similarly, Southwest Airlines may target fun-loving people who are interdependent on others at work, because its competitive advantage depends on employees having flexible role definitions and having a good time with colleagues and customers alike.

Second, employers must consider the strategic value of the various jobs that comprise the organization because some jobs are more critical than other jobs to differentiating an organization from competitors and developing a competitive advantage (Boudreau & Ramstad, 2005). For instance, truck drivers in a shipping company might differentiate the company in the eyes of its customers by developing and maintaining relationships with customers' plant managers. In contrast, the accountants employed by the same wood-shipping company hold jobs that are of less strategic importance to the company—even though they are essential to the basic operations necessary to run the company. In other words, according to the company's strategy, truck drivers help the company differentiate and win, while the accountants keep the organization from losing (Cable, 2007).

Having determined the unique attributes of the job seekers they want to attract, firms are now positioned to achieve their organizational goals through the recruitment and retention of the right individuals that comprise the valuable, rare, and hard-to-imitate workforce. As shown in our model (see Figure 7.1), this multilevel process starts with organizational recruitment activities and practices (e.g.,

use of recruitment sources, type of recruitment information communicated), which combine with non-recruitment factors (e.g., employer's products and services, financial performance, corporate social responsibility) to influence individual job seeker perceptions of an employer brand. The employer brand creates equity for the organization through individual-level processes of person-environment fit and social identification such that more of the necessary types of applicants are attracted to the organization, and are presocialized to accept the necessary requirements of the organization. Thus, by attracting and retaining the right talent, presocialization and self-selection processes allow organizations to retain employees with the right attitudes, and who are capable of creating differentiated products and services that customers want but that competitors cannot duplicate. These latter processes translate employee contributions to an organizational competitive advantage. We now discuss the key relationships of this model in more detail.

Positive Impact of Employer Brands on Individual Attitudes and Behavior

Our next discussion describes how employer brands bring about desirable individual outcomes upon organizational entry through the processes of presocialization and self-selection. As illustrated in Figure 7.1, these relationships constitute the first step of our multilevel processes model in which employer brand at the organizational level impacts individual attitudes and behavior pre- and post-organizational entry.

Employer Brands Create Equity Through Positive Job Attitudes

Employer brands presocialize job seekers to develop certain beliefs about jobs and organizational environments. Job seekers then self-select into certain jobs based on a comparison between such beliefs and whether they have the knowledge, skills, and abilities (KSAs) to perform the job, and whether the organizational culture is congruent with their own personal values (Cable & Judge, 1996; Judge & Cable, 1997). In addition to getting the knowledge, values, and skills needed to execute their competitive strategy, organizations also get more positive workforce attitudes (e.g., job satisfaction, organizational commitment) when job seekers self-select based on person-job (P-J) fit and person-organization (P-O) fit (Kristof-Brown et al., 2005). For instance, the relationship between pre-hire fit and post-hire employment quality was demonstrated by Saks and Ashforth (2002), who found that perceptions of P-O and P-J fit that job seekers developed during their job search process predicted job attitudes (e.g., job satisfaction, turnover intentions) and organizational attitudes (e.g., organizational commitment and organizational identification) after joining their organizations.

There are several reasons for this positive link between P-O and P-J fit and job attitudes. As described by Edwards and Cable (2009), P-O fit gives rise to positive work attitudes because it improves communication among and attraction between coworkers, it implies that employees can better predict organizational activities, and it makes employees more likely to view their organization as trustworthy. Moreover, P-J fit leads to positive work attitudes due to the sense of accomplishment and self-actualization that comes with being able to meet the demands and challenges of one's job (Edwards & Shipp, 2007; Feather, 1991; Harrison, 1978).

From a resource-based view of recruitment, positive work attitudes can lead to employee behaviors that help develop a competitive advantage, such as information sharing among coworkers, and more innovation and proactivity on the job (e.g., Harrison, Newman, & Roth, 2006). Moreover, recent qualitative and quantitative reviews have emphasized a significant link between job satisfaction and job performance (Judge, Thoresen, Bono, & Patton, 2001). The benefits of positive job attitudes to the larger organization are highlighted by the finding that overall job satisfaction is also related to firm-level performance in the form of return on assets (ROA) and market performance (e.g., earnings per share; Schneider, Hanges, Smith, & Salvaggio, 2003).

Employer Brands Create Equity Through Reduced Turnover

Employers also gain value from their employer brands when they attract job seekers who are likely to stay with the firm for longer periods of time. In other words, when job seekers use employer brands to self-select based on P-O fit (i.e., value congruence) and P-J fit, the firm develops a more committed workforce where turnover is less likely (Bowen, Ledford & Nathan, 1991; Schneider, 1987). Employee fit with corporate culture and job demands are key factors in determining how embedded employees are in their jobs, where organizations with more embedded employees are less likely to experience voluntary turnover (Mitchell, Holtom, & Lee, 2001; Mitchell, Holtom, Lee, Sablynski, &

Erez, 2001). In her study on the selection and socialization of new recruits in accounting firms, Chatman (1991) found that recruits adjust to their new jobs more quickly when they have matching values (i.e., P-O fit) upon joining the organization (also see Cable & Judge, 1996).

The observed relationship between self-selection and retention can also be explained through met expectations theory—assuming that that the employer brand is accurate. In other words, pre-hire job and organizational beliefs make up the expectations that job seekers have about their new jobs. When these job seekers become new hires, these expectations are compared to their actual job and organizational experiences. Dissatisfaction arises when there is a discrepancy between initial pre-hire expectations and post-hire experiences, which leads to turnover (Porter & Steers, 1973; Wanous, Poland, Premack, & Davis, 1992).

Employer Brands Create Equity Through Job Performance

In addition to improving employee retention, organizations' recruitment brands can also help bring about the needed job behaviors and performance that are the source of a firm's competitive advantage. By allowing employers to attract job seekers with the critical KSAs that meet specific, unique job demands, employer brands position employees to become important contributors to a firm's competitive advantage (Dawis & Lofquist, 1984; Muchinsky & Monahan, 1987). Likewise, when employees have values that are similar to their coworkers, they are more likely to be able to communicate and cooperate better with them (Day & Bedeian, 1995; Edwards and Cable, 2009; Jehn, Northcraft, & Neale, 1999). These processes facilitate the learning of task-based information and skills, as well as improving the predictability and efficiency of on-the-job behaviors (Motowidlo, 2003).

Individuals with values that are congruent with their company cultures are also more likely to engage in more extra-role and citizenship behaviors because people prefer to help others who are similar to themselves (Edwards & Shipp, 2007). In fact, similarity of employee and organizational values has been linked specifically to organizational citizenship behaviors (Cable & DeRue, 2002). Furthermore, in-role and extra-role performance increases when employee preferences are matched by the design and structure of their jobs. For instance, the degree to which employers match employee preferences for certain work arrangements (e.g., full-time or part-time status, schedule, shift, and number of hours) is positively linked to in-role and extra-role performance (Holtom, Lee, & Tidd, 2002).

Finally, employment brands influence the type of expectations that job seekers carry into the company as new hires. To the extent that an employer brand is accurate, the expectations of new hires are more likely to be in line with the actual job and organizational environment. As such, these individuals are more likely to have their psychological contracts fulfilled by their employers, which is in turn linked to organizational citizenship behavior and improved job performance (Turnley, Bolino, Lester, & Bloodgood, 2003; Zhao, Wayne, Glibkowski, & Bravo, 2007).

In summary, the positive impact of employer brands on individual attitudes (e.g., job satisfaction and organizational commitment) and behavior (e.g., retention and job performance) highlights how employer brands can create and sustain a valuable workforce. As discussed next, another way in which employer brands can bring about organizational success is via their impact on organizational culture.

Employer Brands Create Equity by Reinforcing Organizational Culture

Recent research has called attention to the economic benefits of having a noticeable culture. Rindova, Pollock, and Hayward (2006) argue that a well-managed culture can create an image of celebrity for organizations, which can in turn increase the number of economic opportunities available to the firm. For instance, positive perceptions of an organization's culture can increase customers' trust in the organization's ability to deliver quality products and services. As such, a well-regarded culture allows certain organizations to charge a premium price for their services (Rindova, Williamson, Petkova, & Sever, 2005).

Employer brands can play a key role in the helping organizations build and reinforce a culture that supports a competitive advantage. When managed strategically via a firm's recruitment activities, employer brands attract new employees who have characteristics and values that support valuable, unique, and hard-to-imitate cultures (Bowen et al., 1991; Cable & Turban, 2001). In addition to the above benefits that culture has for transactions with external stakeholders, it also affects how organizations function internally. Namely, organizational culture can create a competitive advantage because it defines which stakeholders are most important

to winning, and influences how firms interact with these key stakeholders through its effect on the decisions and behavior of its members (Barney, 1986). Because organizational cultures are idiosyncratic social phenomena made up of unique combinations of values, assumptions, and experiences of organizational members (Barley, 1983; Schein, 1990), they enable firms to operate in customer-pleasing ways that cannot be easily imitated by competitors (Barney, 1986; Cable, 2007).

Discussion

The goals of this chapter have been twofold. First, we reviewed recruitment research with a focus on the research that has been conducted since Rynes and Cable's (2003) last comprehensive review. In particular, we approached our review through the lens of employer brand equity, an area in which recruitment research has recently flourished. We then developed a model that linked past recruitment research with the notion of a sustained competitive advantage. Specifically, we argued that recruitment activities and practices combine non-recruitment factors (e.g., product awareness) to affect employer brands (i.e., employer image, reputation, and familiarity). Our model suggests that employer brands can be used to attract people with the unique work capabilities (i.e., KSAs) and the unique personal qualities (i.e., values, goals, and personalities) that execute a firm's business strategy and lead to a competitive advantage. Drawing from the resource-based view of the firm, which treats human capital as a valuable resource for organizational success (Barney, 1986), our model conceptualizes recruitment and employer brand as means to create organizational cultures that are valuable, rare, and hard to imitate. Specifically, employer brands create equity because they presocialize job seekers such that those who fit core competency demands are more likely to self-select into the firm.

Methodological Issues

Though there has been significant progress in recruitment research throughout the last decade, several methodological concerns remain. These concerns hamper our ability to understand the recruitment process as a dynamic multilevel process involving both individuals and employers. Perhaps most important, there is a distinct lack of research on organizational-level phenomena in recruitment. Despite calls for more research to supplement recruitment research's traditional focus on individual experience, we still know very little about how organizations manage—and are affected by—their recruitment strategies (Barber, 1998; Breaugh & Starke, 2000; Rynes & Cable, 2003). Thus, researchers in this area should work to study recruitment issues across populations of organizations, with the specific intent of linking recruitment strategy and practices to organization-level outcomes. Ideally, such organizational-level research would employ longitudinal or experimental designs that facilitate the interpretation of cause and effect (Dineen et al., 2007; Highhouse et al., 2007).

There is also a related need to use research methods capable of examining cross-level issues in recruitment. Recruitment is a process whereby individuals are constantly interacting with and reacting to the attributes and practices of employers. As such, research should focus on understanding the relative effects of individual (e.g., personality and values) and organizational (e.g., strategy and practices) factors, and how they interact with each other to influence job seeker behavior. Methods of analyses such as random coefficient modeling or hierarchical linear modeling are suited to the analysis of these multilevel relationships (Bliese, 2002; Kozlowski & Klein, 2000; Raudenbush & Bryk, 2002;).

Much existing research on brand equity and organizational image has used established personality and values instruments such as the Big Five and Organizational Culture Profile (OCP) to assess perceptions of employers. The use of such measures introduces demand characteristics that may obscure important dimensions of firms' brand images that might be relevant for particular organizations, vocations, or industries. Therefore, there is a need for more descriptive research based on inductive theory building that is capable of accounting for the uniqueness and idiosyncrasies of specific groups of job seekers and employers (Rynes & Cable, 2003).

Finally, little effort has been devoted to understanding recruitment among experienced job seekers and professionals. Despite the fact that companies are constantly recruiting both experienced and inexperienced workers (Barber, 1998), the majority of recruitment research has focused on first-time job seekers (e.g., students) and hypothetical applicants (Chapman et al., 2005). Similarly, the field needs more research documenting how individuals go through different phrases of the recruitment process, from early recruitment where contact with an employer is first established, to latter points where interactions between job seekers and employers become more frequent (i.e., the interview and job offer stages; Breaugh & Starke, 2000).

Future Research

Looking forward, we see several fruitful areas for research from a resource-based view of recruitment. First, research examining the specific link between recruitment and organizational-level outcomes is sorely lacking. Previous research has observed significant relationships between human resource practices (i.e., work-family policies, skill requirements, employee involvement, and pay incentives) and firm performance (Batt, 2002; Batt & Valcour, 2003; Collins & Clark, 2003; Collins & Smith, 2006; Huselid, 1995), but to our knowledge no research has specifically examined whether and how recruitment gives rise to organizational performance.

Second, recruitment research should also expand its focus on applicant pre-entry reactions to include a wider range of experiences and beliefs. Traditional research in this area has viewed applicant reactions during the pre-hire phrase of recruitment as strictly the attitudes (i.e., attraction) and behaviors (i.e., application behaviors and job choice) that job seekers develop in response to recruitment activities and practices (Rynes, 1991). We argue that reactions to the recruitment process must focus not only on job seekers' attraction but what specific beliefs they hold about employers (image, reputation, and familiarity), how these beliefs are affected by non-recruitment factors (e.g., products and services, other human resource policies), and how these beliefs interact with individual differences (e.g., values and KSAs) to influence pre- and post-hire outcomes.

Third, given that some jobs are more central to the employer's competitive advantage than others, consideration should also be made for the possibility of differential investments in recruitment activities depending on the strategic leverage of the job. The most pivotal roles may demand more attention and resources because they target individuals with unique skill sets and personal qualities that support the firm's competitive advantage. Such recruitment activities should naturally prove to be more time-consuming and expensive since they select from a smaller, more differentiated applicant pool. In contrast, jobs that are concerned with the basic operations necessary to run a company without adding to a firm's competitive advantage draw from a more generic applicant pool, and thus should require fewer resources to target, presocialize, and select potential hires. Research is needed both to study the extent to which companies differentiate their recruitment investments for different types of jobs, and how such strategies impact firm performance.

Next, more research is needed to investigate specific relationships between recruitment activities and the process of presocialization. Although some recruitment research has examined how beliefs about employer image and reputation are affected by recruitment activities (Cable & Yu, 2006; Collins, 2007), we still know little about how expectations change during this presocialization process. This gap in our understanding is glaring because most conceptualizations of the socialization process involve a change in attributes of the individual (Bauer, Morrison, & Callister, 1998; Van Maanen & Schein, 1979).

Finally, more research is needed that examines how person-job (P-J) and person-organization (P-O) fit evolves during various stages of the recruitment process. While research has established that both P-J and P-O fit are important predictors of pre- and post-hire outcomes (Cable & Judge, 1996; Judge & Cable, 1997; Saks & Ashforth, 2002), little is known about how P-J and P-O fit perceptions evolve during the recruitment process. Indeed, it is reasonable to assume that these two forms of fit could be subject to constant change if job seekers are continuously learning more about the job and organization from different sources of recruitment. For instance, individuals could react to their experiences during the recruitment process by adjusting either or both of their perceptions of their own individual attributes (e.g., KSAs, values, goals) and of employer brand (e.g., image and reputation). Understanding how fit develops and evolves, and learning when fit is most malleable, could help employers strategically orient their recruitment activities to have a greater effect on employer brand and ultimately on competitive advantage.

References

Allen, D. G., Mahto, R. V., & Otondo, R. F. (2007). Web-based recruitment: Effects of information, organizational brand, and attitudes toward a web site on applicant attraction. *Journal of Applied Psychology, 92,* 1696–1708.

Allen, D. G., Scotter, J. R. V., & Otondo, R. F. (2004). Recruitment communication media: Impact on prehire outcomes. *Personnel Psychology, 57,* 143–171.

Ashforth, B. E., & Mael, F. (1989). Social identity theory and the organization. *Academy of Management Review, 14*(1), 20–39.

Avery, D. R. (2003). Reactions to diversity in recruitment advertising: Are differences black and white? *Journal of Applied Psychology, 88*(4), 672–679.

Avery, D. R., & McKay, P. F. (2006). Target practice: An organizational impression management approach to attracting minority and female job applicants. *Personnel Psychology, 59*(1), 157–187.

Barber, A. E. (1998). *Recruitment employees.* Thousand Oaks, CA: Sage Publications.

Barber, A. E., Daly, C. L., Giannantonio, C. M., & Phillips, J. M. (1994). Job search activities: An examination of changes over time. *Personnel Psychology, 47,* 739–766.

Barber, A. E., & Roehling, M. V. (1993). Job postings and the decision to interview: A verbal protocol analysis. *Journal of Applied Psychology, 78,* 845–856.

Barber, A. E., Wesson, M. J., Roberson, O. M., & Taylor, M. S. (1999). A tale of two job markets: Organizational size and its effects on hiring practices and job search behavior. *Personnel Psychology, 52,* 841–867.

Barley, S. R. (1983). Semiotics and the study of occupational and organizational cultures. *Administrative Science Quarterly, 28,* 393–413.

Barney, J. B. (1986). Organizational culture: Can it be a source of sustained competitive advantage? *Academy of Management Review, 11,* 656–665.

Batt, R. (2002). Managing customer services: Human resource practices, quit rates, and sales growth. *Academy of Management Journal, 45*(3), 587–597.

Batt, R., & Valcour, P. M. (2003). Human resources practices as predictors of work-family outcomes and employee turnover. *Industrial Relations, 42*(2), 189–220.

Bauer, T. N., Morrison, E. W., & Callister, R. R. (1998). Organizational socialization: A review and directions for future research. In G. R. Ferris (Ed.), *Research in personnel and human resources management* (Vol. 16, pp. 149–214). Greenwich, CT: JAI Press.

Belt, J. A., & Paolillo, J. G. P. (1982). The influence of corporate image and specificity of candidate qualifications on response to recruitment advertisement. *Journal of Management, 8,* 105–112.

Blau, G. (1990). Exploring the mediating mechanisms affecting the relationship of recruitment source to employee performance. *Journal of Vocational Behavior, 37,* 303–320.

Blau, G. (1994). Testing a two-dimensional measure of job search behavior. *Organizational Behavior and Human Decision Processes, 59,* 288–312.

Bliese, P. D. (2002). Multilevel random coefficient modeling in organizational research: Examples using SAS and S-PLUS. In F. Drasgow & N. Schmitt (Eds.), *Measuring and analyzing behavior in organizations: Advances in measurement and data analysis* (pp. 401–445). San Francisco: Jossey-Bass.

Boudreau, J., & Ramstad, P. M. (2005). Where's your pivotal talent? *Harvard Business Review, 83,* 23–24.

Bowen, D. E., Ledford, G. E., Jr., & Nathan, B. R. (1991). Hiring for the organization, not the job. *Academy of Management Executive, 5*(4), 35–51.

Bowen, D. E., & Ostroff, C. (2004). Understanding HRM-firm performance linkages: The role of the 'strength' of the HRM system. *Academy of Management Review, 29*(2), 203–221.

Breaugh, J. A. (1983). Realistic job previews: A critical appraisal and future research directions. *Academy of Management Review, 8*(4), 612–619.

Breaugh, J. A., & Billings, R. S. (1988). The realistic job preview: Five key elements and their importance for research and practice. *Journal of Business and Psychology, 2*(4), 291–305.

Breaugh, J. A., & Mann, R. B. (1984). Recruiting source effects: A test of two alternative explanations. *Journal of Occupational Psychology, 57,* 261–267.

Breaugh, J. A., & Starke, M. (2000). Research on employee recruitment: So many studies, so many remaining questions. *Journal of Management, 26*, 405–434.

Bretz, R. D., & Judge, T. A. (1998). Realistic job previews: A test of the adverse self-selection hypothesis. *Journal of Applied Psychology, 83*, 330–337.

Brooks, M. E., Highhouse, S., Russell, S. S., & Mohr, D. C. (2003). Familiarity, ambivalence, and firm reputation: Is corporate fame a double-edged sword? *Journal of Applied Psychology, 88*(5), 904.

Cable, D. M. (2007). *Change to strange*. Philadelphia: Wharton School Publishing.

Cable, D. M., Aiman-Smith, L., Mulvey, P. W., & Edwards, J. R. (2000). The sources and accuracy of job applicants' beliefs about organizational culture. *Academy of Management Journal, 43*, 1076–1085.

Cable, D. M., & DeRue, D. S. (2002). The convergent and discriminant validity of subjective fit perceptions. *Journal of Applied Psychology, 87*(5), 875–884.

Cable, D. M., & Edwards, J. R. (2004). Complementary and supplementary fit: A theoretical and empirical integration. *Journal of Applied Psychology, 89*, 822–834.

Cable, D. M., & Graham, M. E. (2000). The determinants of job seekers' reputation perceptions. *Journal of Organizational Behavior, 21*, 929–947.

Cable, D. M., & Judge, T. A. (1994). Pay preference and job search decisions: A person-organization fit perspective. *Personnel Psychology, 47*, 317.

Cable, D. M., & Judge, T. A. (1996). Person-organization fit, job choice decisions, and organizational entry. *Organizational Behavior and Human Decision Processes, 67*, 294–311.

Cable, D. M., & Turban, D. (2001). Recruitment image equity: Establishing the dimensions, sources and value of job seekers' employer knowledge during recruitment. In G. R. Ferris (Ed.), *Research in personnel and human resources management* (Vol. 20, pp. 115–163). Greenwich, CT: JAI Press.

Cable, D. M., & Turban, D. B. (2003). The value of organizational reputation in the recruitment context: A brand-equity perspective. *Journal of Applied Social Psychology, 33*(11), 2244–2266.

Cable, D. M., & Yu, K. Y. T. (2006). Managing job seekers' organizational image beliefs: The role of media richness and media credibility. *Journal of Applied Psychology, 91*, 828–840.

Chapman, D. S., Uggerslev, K. L., Carroll, S. A., Piasentin, K. A., & Jones, D. A. (2005). Applicant attraction to organizations and job choice: A meta-analytic review of the correlates of recruiting outcomes. *Journal of Applied Psychology, 90*, 928–944.

Chatman, J. A. (1989). Improving interactional organizational research: A model of person-organization fit. *Academy of Management Review, 14*, 333–349.

Chatman, J. A. (1991). Matching people and organizations: Selection and socialization in public accounting firms. *Administrative Science Quarterly, 36*(3), 459–484.

Cialdini, R. B., Borden, R. J., Thorne, A., Walker, M. R., Freeman, S., & Sloan, L. R. (1976). Basking in reflected glory: Three (football) field studies. *Journal of Personality and Social Psychology, 34*, 366–375.

Collins, C. J. (2007). The interactive effects of recruitment practices and product awareness on job seekers' employer knowledge and application behaviors. *Journal of Applied Psychology, 92*, 180–190.

Collins, C. J., & Clark, K. D. (2003). Strategic human resource practices, top management team social networks, and firm performance: The role of human resource practices in creating organizational competitive advantage. *Academy of Management Journal, 46*(6), 740–751.

Collins, C. J., & Han, J. (2004). Exploring applicant pool quantity and quality: The effects of early recruitment practice strategies, corporate advertising, and firm reputation. *Personnel Psychology, 57*(3), 685–717.

Collins, C. J., & Smith, K. G. (2006). Knowledge exchange and combination: The role of human resource practices in the performance of high-technology firms. *Academy of Management Journal, 49*(3), 544–560.

Collins, C. J., & Stevens, C. K. (2002). The relationship between early recruitment-related activities and the application decisions of new labor-market entrants: A brand equity approach to recruitment. *Journal of Applied Psychology, 87*, 1121–1133.

Connerley, M. L. (1997). The influence of training on perceptions of recruiters' interpersonal skills and effectiveness. *Journal of Occupational & Organizational Psychology, 70*, 259–272.

Connerley, M. L., & Rynes, S. L. (1997). The influence of recruiter characteristics and organizational recruitment support on perceived recruiter effectiveness: Views from applicants and recruiters. *Human Relations, 50*, 1563–1586.

Dawis, R. V., & Lofquist, L. H. (1984). *A psychological theory of work adjustment*. Minneapolis: University of Minnesota Press.

Day, D. V., & Bedeian, A. G. (1995). Personality similarity and work-related outcomes among African-American nursing personnel: A test of the supplementary model of person-environment congruence. *Journal of Vocational Behavior, 46*(1), 55–70.

Decker, P. J., & Cornelius, E. T. (1979). A note on recruiting sources and job survival rates. *Journal of Applied Psychology, 64*, 463–464.

Dineen, B. R., Ash, S. R., & Noe, R. A. (2002). A web of applicant attraction: Person-organization fit in the context of web-based recruitment. *Journal of Applied Psychology, 87*, 723–734.

Dineen, B. R., Juan, L., Ash, S. R., & DelVecchio, D. (2007). Aesthetic properties and message customization: Navigating the dark side of web recruitment. *Journal of Applied Psychology, 92*, 356–372.

Dutton, J. E., & Dukerich, J. M. (1991). Keeping an eye on the mirror: Image and identity in organizational adaptation. *Academy of Management Journal, 34*(3), 517–554.

Dutton, J. E., Dukerich, J. M., & Harquail, C. V. (1994). Organizational images and member identification. *Administrative Science Quarterly, 39*(2), 239.

Edwards, J. R., & Cable, D. M. (2009). The value of value congruence. *Journal of Applied Psychology, 94*(3), 654–677.

Edwards, J. R., & Shipp, A. J. (2007). The relationship between person-environment fit and outcomes: An integrative theoretical framework. In C. Ostroff & T. A. Judge (Eds.), *Perspectives on organizational fit* (pp. 209–258). New York: Erlbaum.

Feather, N. T. (1991). Human values, global self-esteem, and belief in a just world. *Journal of Personality, 59*(1), 83–107.

Feldman, D. C., & Arnold, H. J. (1978). Position choice: Comparing the importance of organizational and job factors. *Journal of Applied Psychology, 63*, 706–710.

Fisher, C. D., Ilgen, D. R., & Hoyer, W. D. (1979). Source credibility, information favorability, and job offer acceptance. *Academy of Management Journal, 22*, 94–103.

Gatewood, R. D., Gowan, M. A., & Lautenschlager, G. J. (1993). Corporate image, recruitment image and initial job choice decisions. *Academy of Management Journal, 36*, 414–427.

Goltz, S. M., & Giannantonio, C. M. (1995). Recruiter friendliness and attraction to the job: The mediating role of inferences about the organization. *Journal of Vocational Behavior, 46*, 109–118.

Greening, D. W., & Turban, D. B. (2000). Corporate social performance as a competitive advantage in attracting a quality workforce. *Business & Society, 39*(3), 254.

Griffeth, R. W., Hom, P. W., Fink, L. S., & Cohen, D. J. (1997). Comparative tests of multivariate models of recruiting sources effects. *Journal of Management, 23*, 19.

Harris, M. M., & Fink, L. S. (1987). A field study of applicant reactions to employment opportunities: Does the recruiter make a difference? *Personnel Psychology, 40*, 765.

Harrison, R. V. (1978). Person-environment fit and job stress. In C. L. Cooper & R. Payne (Eds.), *Stress at work* (pp. 175–205). New York: Wiley.

Harrison, D. A., Newman, D. A., & Roth, P. L. (2006). How important are job attitudes? Meta-analytic comparisons of integrative behavioral outcomes and time sequences. *Academy of Management Journal, 49*(2), 305–325.

Highhouse, S., Thornbury, E. E., & Little, I. S. (2007). Social-identity functions of attraction to organizations. *Organizational Behavior and Human Decision Processes, 103*(1), 134–146.

Highhouse, S., Zickar, M. J., Thorsteinson, T. J., Stierwalt, S. L., & Slaughter, J. E. (1999). Assessing company employment image: An example in the fast food industry. *Personnel Psychology, 52*, 151–172.

Hitt, M. A., Bierman, L., Shimizu, K., & Kochhar, R. (2001). Direct and moderating effects of human capital on strategy and performance in professional service firms: A resource-based perspective. *Academy of Management Journal, 44*(1), 13–28.

Holtom, B. C., Lee, T. W., & Tidd, S. T. (2002). The relationship between work status congruence and work-related attitudes and behaviors. *Journal of Applied Psychology, 87*(5), 903–915.

Huselid, M. A. (1995). The impact of human resource management practices on turnover, productivity, and corporate financial performance. *Academy of Management Journal, 38*(3), 635–672.

Jehn, K. A., Northcraft, G. B., & Neale, M. A. (1999). Why differences make a difference: A field study of diversity, conflict, and performance in workgroups. *Administrative Science Quarterly, 44*(4), 741–763.

Judge, T. A., & Bretz, R. D. (1992). Effects of work values on job choice decisions. *Journal of Applied Psychology, 77*(3), 261–272.

Judge, T. A., & Cable, D. M. (1997). Applicant personality, organizational culture, and organization attraction. *Personnel Psychology, 50*, 359–394.

Judge, T. A., Thoresen, C. J., Bono, J. E., & Patton, G. K. (2001). The job satisfaction-job performance relationship: A qualitative and quantitative review. *Psychological Bulletin, 127*(3), 376–407.

Jurgensen, C. E. (1978). Job preferences (What makes a job good or bad?). *Journal of Applied Psychology, 63*, 267–276.

Keller, K. L. (1993). Conceptualizing, measuring, managing customer-based brand equity. *Journal of Marketing, 57*(1), 1–22.

Kilduff, M. (1990). The interpersonal structure of decision making: A social comparison approach to organizational choice. *Organizational Behavior and Human Decision Processes, 47*, 270–288.

Kozlowski, S. W. J., & Klein, K. J. (2000). A multilevel approach to theory and research in organizations: Contextual, temporal, and emergent processes. In K. J. Klein & S. W. J. Kozlowski (Eds.), *Multilevel theory, research, and methods in organizations: Foundations, extensions, and new directions* (pp. 3–90). San Francisco: Jossey-Bass.

Kristof, A. L. (1996). Person-organization fit: An integrative review of its conceptualizations, measurement, and implications. *Personnel Psychology, 49*, 1–49.

Kristof-Brown, A. L., Zimmerman, R. D., & Johnson, E. C. (2005). Consequences of individuals' fit at work: A meta-analysis of person-job, person-organization, person-group, and person-supervisor fit. *Personnel Psychology, 58*(2), 281–342.

Latham, V. M., & Leddy, P. M. (1987). Source of recruitment and employee attitudes: An analysis of job involvement, organizational commitment, and job satisfaction. *Journal of Business and Psychology, 1*, 230–235.

Leicht, K. T., & Marx, J. (1997). The consequences of informal job finding for men and women. *Academy of Management Journal, 40*, 967–987.

Liden, R. C., & Parsons, C. K. (1986). A field study of job applicant interview perceptions, alternative opportunities, and demographic characteristics. *Personnel Psychology, 39*, 109–122.

Lievens, F. (2007). Employer branding in the Belgian Army: The importance of instrumental and symbolic beliefs for potential applicants, actual applicants, and military employees. *Human Resource Management, 46*, 51–69.

Lievens, F., & Highhouse, S. (2003). The relation of instrumental and symbolic attributes to a company's attractiveness as an employer. *Personnel Psychology, 56*, 75–102.

Lievens, F., Van Hoye, G., & Schreurs, B. (2005). Examining the relationship between employer knowledge dimensions and organizational attractiveness: An application in a military context. *Journal of Occupational and Organizational Psychology, 78*(4), 553–572.

Lippman, S. A., & McCall, J. J. (1976). The economics of job search: A survey. *Economic Inquiry, 14*, 155.

McEvoy, G. M., & Cascio, W. F. (1985). Strategies for reducing employee turnover: A meta-analysis. *Journal of Applied Psychology, 70*, 342–353.

McKay, P. F., & Avery, D. R. (2006). What has race got to do with it? Unraveling the role of racioethnicity in job seeker's reactions to site visits. *Personnel Psychology, 59*(2), 395–429.

Mitchell, T. R., Holtom, B. C., & Lee, T. W. (2001). How to keep your best employees: Developing an effective retention policy. *Academy of Management Executive, 15*(4), 96–109.

Mitchell, T. R., Holtom, B. C., Lee, T. W., Sablynski, C. J., & Erez, M. (2001). Why people stay: Using job embeddedness to predict voluntary turnover. *Academy of Management Journal, 44*(6), 1102–1121.

Motowidlo, S. J. (2003). Job performance. In D. R. Ilgen & W. C. Borman (Eds.), *Handbook of psychology: Industrial and organizational psychology* (Vol. 12, pp. 39–53). New York: John Wiley & Sons.

Muchinsky, P. M., & Monahan, C. J. (1987). What is person-environment congruence? Supplementary versus complementary models of fit. *Journal of Vocational Behavior, 31*(3), 268–277.

Phillips, J. M. (1998). Effects of realistic job previews on multiple organizational outcomes: A meta-analysis. *Academy of Management Journal, 41*, 673–690.

Ployhart, R. E. (2006). Staffing in the 21st century: New challenges and strategic opportunities. *Journal of Management, 32*(6), 868–897.

Porter, L. W., & Steers, R. M. (1973). Organizational, work, and personal factors in employee turnover and absenteeism. *Psychological Bulletin, 80*(2), 151–176.

Powell, G. N. (1984). Effects of job attributes and recruiting practices on applicant decisions: A comparison. *Personnel Psychology, 37*, 721–732.

Powell, G. N., & Goulet, L. R. (1996). Recruiters' and applicants' reactions to campus interviews and employment decisions. *Academy of Management Journal, 39*, 1619–1640.

Premack, S. L., & Wanous, J. P. (1985). A meta-analysis of realistic job preview experiments. *Journal of Applied Psychology, 70*, 706–719.

Rau, B. L., & Adams, G. A. (2005). Attracting retirees to apply: Desired organizational characteristics of bridge employment. *Journal of Organizational Behavior, 26*(6), 649–660.

Rau, B. L., & Hyland, M. M. (2002). Role conflict and flexible work arrangements: The effects on applicant attraction. *Personnel Psychology, 55*(1), 111–136.

Raudenbush, S. W., & Bryk, A. S. (2002). *Hierarchical linear models: Applications and data analysis methods* (2nd ed.). Thousand Oaks, CA: Sage Publications.

Reilly, R. R., Brown, B., Blood, M. R., & Malatesta, C. Z. (1981). The effects of realistic previews: A study and discussion of the literature. *Personnel Psychology, 34*, 823–834.

Rindova, V. P., Pollock, T. G., & Hayward, M. L. A. (2006). Celebrity firms: The social construction of market popularity. *Academy of Management Review, 31*, 50–71.

Rindova, V. P., Williamson, I. O., Petkova, A. P., & Sever, J. M. (2005). Being good or being known: An empirical examination of the dimensions, antecedents, and consequences of organizational reputation. *Academy of Management Journal, 48*(6), 1033–1049.

Rosenfeld, C. (1975). Jobseeking methods used by American workers. *Monthly Labor Review, 98*, 39.

Rynes, S. L. (1991). Recruitment, job choice, and post-hire consequences: A call for new research directions. In M. D. Dunnette & L. M. Hough (Eds.), *Handbook of industrial and organizational psychology* (Vol. 2, pp. 399–444). Palo Alto, CA: Consulting Psychologists Press.

Rynes, S. L., Bretz, R. D., & Gerhart, B. (1991). The importance of recruitment in job choice: A different way of looking. *Personnel Psychology, 44*, 487–521.

Rynes, S. L., & Cable, D. M. (2003). Recruitment research in the twenty-first century. In W. C. Borman & D. R. Ilgen (Eds.), *Handbook of psychology: Industrial and organizational psychology* (Vol. 12, pp. 55–76). New York: John Wiley & Sons.

Rynes, S. L., & Miller, H. E. (1983). Recruiter and job influences on candidates for employment. *Journal of Applied Psychology, 68*, 147–154.

Rynes, S. L., Orlitzky, M. O., & Bretz, R. D., Jr. (1997). Experienced hiring versus college recruiting: Practices and emerging trends. *Personnel Psychology, 50*, 309–339.

Saks, A. M., & Ashforth, B. E. (2002). Is job search related to employment quality? It all depends on the fit. *Journal of Applied Psychology, 87*(4), 646–654.

Schneider, B. (1987). The people make the place. *Personnel Psychology, 40*, 437–453.

Schneider, B., Hanges, P. J., Smith, D. B., & Salvaggio, A. N. (2003). Which comes first: Employee attitudes or organizational financial and market performance? *Journal of Applied Psychology, 88*(5), 836–851.

Schein, E. H. (1990). Organizational culture. *American Psychologist, 45*, 109–119.

Schwab, D. P. (1982). Recruiting and organizational participation. In K. M. Rowland & G. R. Ferris (Eds.), *Personnel management* (pp. 103–128). Boston: Allyn & Bacon.

Schwab, D. P., Rynes, S. L., & Aldag, R. J. (1987). Theories and research on job search and choice. In K. M. Rowland & G. R. Ferris (Eds.), *Research in personnel and human resources management* (Vol. 5, pp. 126–166). Greenwich, CT: JAI Press.

Slaughter, J. E., Mohr, D. C., Zickar, M. J., & Highhouse, S. (2004). Personality trait inferences about organizations: Development of a measure and assessment of construct validity. *Journal of Applied Psychology, 89*, 85–103.

Stevens, C. K. (1997). Effects of preinterview beliefs on applicants' reactions to campus interviews. *Academy of Management Journal, 40*, 947–966.

Stevens, C. K., & Campion, M. A. (1998). Antecedents of interview interactions, interviewers' ratings, and applicants' reactions. *Personnel Psychology, 51*, 55–85.

Taylor, M. S., & Bergmann, T. J. (1987). Organizational recruitment activities and applicants' reactions at different stages of the recruitment process. *Personnel Psychology, 40*, 261–285.

Taylor, M. S., & Schmidt, D. W. (1983). A process-oriented investigation of recruitment source effectiveness. *Personnel Psychology, 36*, 343–354.

Tom, V. R. (1971). The role of personality and organizational images in the recruiting process. *Organizational Behavior and Human Performance, 6*, 573–592.

Trank, C. Q., Rynes, S. L., & Bretz, R. D. (2002). Attracting applicants in the war for talent: Differences in work preferences among high achievers. *Journal of Business and Psychology, 16*, 331–345.

Turban, D. B. (2001). Organizational attractiveness as an employer on college campuses: An examination of the applicant population. *Journal of Vocational Behavior, 58*(2), 293–312.

Turban, D. B., & Cable, D. M. (2003). Firm reputation and applicant pool characteristics. *Journal of Organizational Behavior, 24*(6), 733–751.

Turban, D. B., & Dougherty, T. W. (1992). Influences of campus recruiting on applicant attraction to firms. *Academy of Management Journal, 35*, 739–765.

Turban, D. B., Forret, M. L., & Hendrickson, C. L. (1998). Applicant attraction to firms: Influences of organization reputation, job and organizational attributes, and recruiter behaviors. *Journal of Vocational Behavior, 52*, 24–44.

Turban, D. B., & Greening, D. W. (1997). Corporate social performance and organizational attractiveness to prospective employees. *Academy of Management Journal, 40*, 658–672.

Turban, D. B., & Keon, T. L. (1993). Organizational attractiveness: An interactionist perspective. *Journal of Applied Psychology, 78*(2), 184–193.

Turban, D. B., Lau, C.-M., Ngo, H.-Y., Chow, I. H. S., & Si, S. X. (2001). Organizational attractiveness of firms in the People's Republic of China: A person-organization fit perspective. *Journal of Applied Psychology, 86*(2), 194–206.

Turnley, W. H., Bolino, M. C., Lester, S. W., & Bloodgood, J. M. (2003). The impact of psychological contract fulfillment on the performance of in-role and organizational citizenship behaviors. *Journal of Management, 29*(2), 187–206.

Ulrich, D. (1998). A new mandate for human resources. *Harvard Business Review, 76*(1), 124.

Van Der Heijde, C. M., & Van Der Heijden, B. I. J. M. (2006). A competence-based and multidimensional operationalization and measurement of employability. *Human Resource Management, 45*(3), 449–476.

Van Hoye, G., & Lievens, F. (2005). Recruitment-related information sources and organizational attractiveness: Can something be done about negative publicity? *International Journal of Selection and Assessment, 13*, 179–187.

Van Maanen, J., & Schein, E. H. (1979). Toward a theory of organizational socialization. In B. M. Staw (Ed.), *Research in organizational behavior* (pp. 209–264). Greenwich, CT: JAI Press.

Vroom, V. H. (1964). *Work and motivation.* Oxford: Wiley.

Wanous, J. P., Poland, T. D., Premack, S. L., & Davis, K. S. (1992). The effects of met expectations on newcomer attitudes and behaviors: A review and meta-analysis. *Journal of Applied Psychology, 77*(3), 288–297.

Werbel, J. D., & Landau, J. (1996). The effectiveness of different recruitment sources: A mediating variable analysis. *Journal of Applied Social Psychology, 26*, 1337–1350.

Williams, C. R., Labig, C. E., & Stone, T. H. (1993). Recruitment sources and posthire outcomes for job applicants and new hires: A test of two hypotheses. *Journal of Applied Psychology, 78*, 163–172.

Williams, M. L., & Dreher, G. F. (1992). Compensation system attributes and applicant pool characteristics. *Academy of Management Journal, 35*, 571–595.

Zedeck, S. (1977). An information processing model and approach to the study of motivation. *Organizational Behavior & Human Performance, 18*, 47–77.

Zhao, H., Wayne, S. J., Glibkowski, B. C., & Bravo, J. (2007). The impact of psychological contract breach on work-related outcomes: A meta-analysis. *Personnel Psychology, 60*(3), 647–680.

Personnel Selection: Ensuring Sustainable Organizational Effectiveness Through the Acquisition of Human Capital

Robert E. Ployhart

Abstract

In this chapter I propose a vision for the field of personnel selection: *ensuring sustainable organizational effectiveness through the acquisition of human capital*. This vision is used to organize and review historical approaches to selection, critique contemporary approaches, and identify future research needs. It is argued that while there is a rich history of research on personnel selection practices and techniques, this research falls short of achieving the vision. Rather, scholars will need to take a broader, and frequently more contextualized, orientation if they are to show the organizational benefits of selection procedures.

Key Words: Personnel selection, staffing, talent acquisition, assessment, hiring

Visions are powerful ways to stimulate and enact change. Think, for example, of "We will put a man on the moon in 10 years" by John F. Kennedy, "I have a dream" by Martin Luther King, or "Don't be evil" by Google. Visions present an illustration of what should be and what is possible if resources and energy are focused on the vision. Vision statements need not be true today, but instead represent an idealized outcome that will hopefully become true if members work collaboratively toward the vision. In a sense, vision statements are what we want the world to be.

I suggest that the vision of personnel selection should be *ensuring sustainable organizational effectiveness through the acquisition of human capital*. It would be hard to argue for anything else. Selection is fundamentally about acquiring human capital through rigorous assessment methods. Human capital is defined as the aggregate of individual knowledge, skills, abilities, and other characteristics (KSAOs). If selection does not enhance organizational effectiveness in a sustainable manner, then why should we do it? Yet, as innocent as this vision appears, there is still a long way to go before we make it a reality. Research on personnel selection has been productive over the last 100 years, and as a profession we know a great deal about how to best identify KSAO requirements for jobs, develop methods to assess those KSAOs, and combine the scores from the assessments into appropriate hiring decisions. But this by itself does not ensure that selection creates *sustainable organizational effectiveness*. Rather, fulfilling this vision will require a broader perspective than the individual-level research that has so dominated the selection profession since its inception.

This chapter has three purposes. First, it will briefly review the historical antecedents of personnel selection, giving a particular emphasis to contrasting changes in private industry with personnel selection research and practice. Second, it will provide a critical review of current selection research and practice. Included in this review is a process and framework for thinking about predictor constructs and methods. Finally, the chapter concludes with a look toward the future and identifies several directions for future research.

Scope of the Chapter

The scope of this chapter is on personnel selection, that is, the processes, methods, and strategies used to make appropriate hiring decisions. This chapter is not about recruitment (i.e., attracting people to become and remain applicants), nor is it about criteria and job performance. However, please recognize that selection is dependent on both recruitment and criteria. Selection is most important when there are many good candidates from which to choose. There are a variety of recruiting practices and policies that need to be considered, which are discussed in Yu and Cable (chapter 7 of this handbook). The choice of selection KSAOs and methods is dependent on the nature of performance criteria (Wallace, 1965). This chapter will discuss criteria, but for a full treatment of criterion issues please see Campbell (chapter 6 of this handbook).

Various inferences of validity are used to support a relationship between KSAOs and criteria, but this chapter is not going to discuss the concept of validity in great detail. Modern interpretations of validity (e.g., Messick, 1995) treat all inferences of validity as supporting *construct validity* (whether the assessment measures the intended KSAO; whether scores are appropriate for their intended purpose). This chapter's use of validity is consistent with this interpretation, but it will frequently be necessary to discuss different types of validity evidence. These types include *criterion-related* (correlations between measures of KSAOs and criteria) and *content* (judgment of the overlap between a KSAO or predictor method and a criterion). Key features of construct validity also include *convergent* validity (strong correlations between measures of similar KSAOs) and *discriminant* validity (weak correlations between measures of dissimilar KSAOs).

Finally, this chapter will generally avoid discussing legal issues and implications. This is intentional, even though the legal and political environments obviously have a substantial impact on what is considered acceptable selection practice. Laws and regulations vary dramatically across countries and cultures (Myors et al., 2008). Most published selection research has been conducted in the United States, but discussing these laws makes the present chapter unnecessarily country specific. Therefore, this chapter will generally avoid consideration of legal issues, but it will consider factors that lead to legal issues (e.g., demographic subgroup test score differences).

The Past: Steadfast Selection in an Ever-Changing World

Personnel selection is considered by many to be one of the great success stories of industrial and organizational (I/O) psychology. Schmidt and Hunter (1998), summarizing 85 years of research, show some pretty impressive relationships between selection predictors (e.g., cognitive ability, conscientiousness, interviews) and job performance. They also show some pretty impressive *estimates* regarding the financial impact of using these predictors (vs. not using them). One should recognize, however, that this research only partially speaks to the vision of selection proposed above because it ignores the consideration of sustainable organizational effectiveness. Understanding why requires a brief discussion of the changing world of work and the history of selection.

The practice of personnel selection has existed at least since 700 A.D. in China (see Ployhart, Schneider, & Schmitt, 2006). They implemented what were essentially civil service exams to determine who would gain access to desirable government positions. Surprisingly, these exams lasted until the early 1900s. By some reports, the Chinese civil service exams were adapted for use throughout Asia. Around the same time that the Chinese civil service exams were being eliminated, the scientific study of selection in Western countries evolved from the educational testing of Binet and Simon. Their purpose was to use tests of mental ability to identify children who would not perform well in the public school system; these tests evolved into tests of general mental ability. Binet and Simon's functional approach to testing became widely used during World War I by many countries. After the war, these principles and tests were then applied to industry in numerous forms. World War II further solidified the functional value of selection via the application of tests to assign recruits to positions (a process known as *classification*). After World War II, testing and selection were firmly ingrained in civil and private sectors.

Major accomplishments in the period after World War II included advancements in the conceptualization and measurement of KSAOs to include a variety of cognitive and non-cognitive constructs. For example, much of the research on the latent structure of cognitive ability and personality was conducted in the two decades after World War II. In the mid 1960s, there was a call by McNemar (1964) to start showing how individual differences such as intelligence contributed to real world outcomes (a term he called "social usefulness"). A decade later, research by Schmidt, Hunter, and colleagues led to validity generalization and meta-analysis. The importance of this contribution cannot be overstated because it has had a profound effect on personnel selection research and practice. For example, much of the research that will be reviewed in the next section is based on meta-analyses. Prior to validity generalization, it was believed that criterion-related validity was situation-specific, and hence a new validation study would need to be conducted in every context (even if the job was the same). Validity generalization ended the situational-specificity hypothesis to the point that professional guidelines such as the SIOP Principles (2003) now explicitly recognize the role of meta-analysis as a validation strategy. An edited book by Murphy (2002) provides an excellent review of validity generalization.

The major contribution of the 1980s was to advance the conceptualization and measurement of job performance, and address a number of fundamental selection issues (e.g., estimating cross-validity; comparing predictive versus concurrent designs). In the 1990s, selection researchers welcomed the "reemergence" of personality, yet grappled with the validity-diversity dilemma, a dilemma that results from many of the most valid predictors having large racio-ethnic subgroup differences. Research on that dilemma continues into the twenty-first century, as does research on the performance domain (e.g., counterproductive work behaviors) and new types of predictor methods and constructs. Thus far, much of the work in the 2000s has followed in this tradition.

In contrast, the world of work has hardly remained constant in the 100 or so years of scientific selection research. Near the end of the 1800s, the economies in many developed countries began to shift from an agricultural economy to an industrial economy. The hallmark of the industrial economy was the "interchangeability" of employees performing manual, repetitive tasks. While many believe that the assembly line was started by Henry Ford, he, in fact, got the idea from the slaughterhouses in Chicago. The purpose of the assembly line was to ensure consistent production in the most efficient manner possible. The job rarely changed and was performed in terms of relatively isolated tasks. The role of personnel selection was to ensure that the people working the line had the necessary KSAOs; these KSAOs were based on discrete tasks that did not change very much. Further, since the job was primarily one of "additive inputs," the economic value of selection was based on the idea that individual performance could be decomposed into more discrete elements and summed to produce a unit-level estimate of value.

Let's fast forward to modern times, to what many call the "knowledge economy," which is largely an extension of the information economy. In the knowledge economy, the key "products" are ideas and information; hence the critical resource that firms use to compete with each other is human capital (although the overall importance of human capital relative to other forms of capital is variable, as illustrated in the current economic situation). The term *human capital* has its origins in economics (Becker, 1964) but has come to be known as the aggregate KSAOs of a firm's workforce. The term *knowledge worker* has its roots in Drucker (1966) and refers to employees whose primary contribution is based on ideas and information. The shift toward knowledge work is profound because, unlike other forms of capital, human capital cannot be owned by a firm. Employees can choose to withhold effort, switch jobs, or steal ideas and sell them to competitors. Jobs are more fluid because work is increasingly being performed in project teams, which form to complete a project and then disband when the project is finished. Finally, globalization and technological changes such as the Internet have made the world "flat" so that human capital need not be in the same geographic area. Obvious examples include the offshoring of customer service, engineering, and accounting jobs to India. A flat world contributes to greater exposure to people from diverse cultures and languages.

Just as the developed economies have come to recognize the importance of human capital, incredible societal changes have evolved to frequently make human capital in scarce supply. These include an aging workforce, a more diverse workforce, and a global economy. Popularized by the "War for Talent" studies conducted by McKinsey, many firms now realize that talent (a term to reference desired human capital) is critical for their strategic success. For example, a broad sample of almost 7,000 managers found that approximately 90% of them believed recruiting and selection were increasingly difficult challenges affecting their business (Axelrod, Handfield-Jones, & Welsh, 2001). Although the McKinsey research is not without some sizable limitations, the fact remains that many organizational leaders recognize that talent acquisition is critical to their survival. For example, a special report in *The Economist* (2006) highlighted the global challenges of finding qualified talent to meet the needs of the new economy.

Thus, the modern world is characterized by work that is knowledge-based, dynamic, often uses project teams, and is frequently global in scope. Of course, there are still plenty of jobs that are similar to those in the older industrial age, and many jobs are still primarily hands-on and physical in nature. But the jobs that drive the developed and developing economies are increasingly knowledge-based. Given such incredible change, one would think personnel selection practices have changed as well. Interestingly, this is not so. True, personnel selection practices and processes have evolved through programmatic research, and technology has affected the way in which personnel selection is implemented (e.g., web-based testing), but by and large the basic model for selection is still one of the industrial age, which matches individuals to jobs devoid of context. Although it is doubtful that the intention of validity generalization research is to eliminate a concern for context, this may be what has happened. Selection is still a profession of treating tasks as though they are relatively static and unrelated to other employees, linking individual KSAOs to those tasks isolated from the broader context, and estimating value based on an additive model (see Cascio & Aguinis, 2008a; Ployhart & Schneider, 2002).

Some evidence of this is found in a recent review of research published in the last 45 years at *Journal of Applied Psychology* and *Personnel Psychology*. Cascio and Aguinis (2008b) found that topics on personnel selection were consistently within the top five in both journals. However, the topics studied within personnel selection tended to be somewhat peripheral to those reflecting important human capital trends. Indeed, as they so eloquently noted:

> On the basis of our review, if we extrapolate past emphases in published research to the next 10 years, we are confronted with one compelling conclusion, namely, that I-O psychology will not be out front influencing the debate on issues that are (or will be) of broad organizational and societal appeal. (p. 1074)

The field of personnel selection has held steadfast despite a whirlwind of change. This is not as bad as it sounds because, at least in terms of practices designed to maximize individual job performance, the field of personnel selection is at a high level of sophistication. The next section will review the research on these practices. However, in terms of achieving the vision set out at the start of this chapter, personnel selection research must take a broader

perspective, and this perspective will be discussed in the third and final section.

The Present: We Shall Be Known by Our Models and Methods

This section provides a focused yet critical review of contemporary selection research and practice. The field of personnel selection combines diverse theory and research from a variety of disciplines, including individual differences, differential psychology, psychometrics, and statistics. As such, there is no "theory" of personnel selection, but rather various frameworks that are used to organize the way we research and practice selection (e.g., Aguinis & Smith, 2007; Binning & Barrett, 1989; Heneman & Judge, 2006; chapter 7 in Ployhart et al., 2006; Schmitt, Cortina, Ingerick, & Wiechmann, 2003). Given such diversity of perspectives, it is important to develop an understanding of the basic process of selection and to compare and contrast various predictor methods. Therefore, a general framework of the personnel selection process is first presented, followed by a framework to compare and contrast measures of KSAOs.

The Personnel Selection Model

Of Robert Guion's many contributions to the field of selection, one of the most profound is the recognition that the process of personnel selection is really one of hypothesis testing. That is, we make a hypothesis that a given predictor is related to job performance, and then collect the data to test that hypothesis. A less sophisticated way to think about selection is one of making a bet. That is, we bet on a *future* event (i.e., effective job performance) based on limited information we have *today* (i.e., scores on predictors). Such predictions are a tough business, but we make better predictions if we carefully collect and thoroughly attend to the relevant pieces of information. This process is facilitated by using a model of personnel selection specifying how we should collect the relevant information.

Figure 8.1 shows the basic personnel selection model and is adapted from Binning and Barrett (1989). The boxes represent indicators that we can measure; they are manifest scores that can be observed (e.g., test performance, interview scores). Circles represent unobservable latent constructs that cannot be directly observed or measured but are instead inferred through scores on manifest measures. The distinction between manifest variables and latent constructs is important because the boxes represent measures of KSAOs that are affected

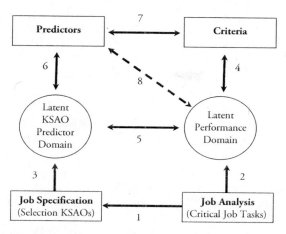

Figure 8.1 The Personnel Selection Framework. The dashed line represents the key interest in selection.

to some degree by unreliability, contamination, and deficiency. The latent constructs are "free" from such imperfections and represent our theory of what the KSAO predictor and performance domains should represent. For example, we may measure cognitive ability based on a written test, but the test is fallible because it has various sources of measurement error that make it an imperfect indicator of "true" cognitive ability. The arrows represent the many *inferences* or hypotheses that occur in the selection process; one-headed arrows represent a specific causal direction, and two-headed arrows represent a covariance or recursive relationship.

The most important hypothesis or bet that we make in selection is that scores on manifest predictors are indicators of latent performance on the job (inference 8 in Figure 8.1). This is because we base hiring decisions on fallible predictor scores, with the expectation that doing so will be related to "true" or latent job performance. This is a far from perfect bet, but the better we collect the relevant information, the more accurate our bet. The better we are able to support inferences 1–7, the more accurate inference 8 becomes. Thus, one can see that hiring decisions are ultimately derived from multiple inferences that should be based on sound reasoning, judgment, and, if at all possible, empirical support.

Notice in Figure 8.1 that there is a specific causal direction to developing and supporting inference 8. This process starts with a job analysis. Speaking broadly, *job analysis* is a systematic, purposeful process designed to comprehensively identify the important tasks and KSAOs required for effective performance on the job. Job analysis follows a specific causal sequence, such that we first identify

the critical tasks and then identify the essential KSAOs necessary to perform these tasks (inference 1). Identification of essential KSAOs is frequently called *job specification* (Harvey & Wilson, 2000); the distinction highlights the fact that the choice of KSAOs and predictors is inherently determined by the job. The essential KSAOs are often called *selection KSAOs* to recognize that they will be used as a basis for hiring.

There are many ways to collect job analysis and job specification information, such as meetings with subject matter experts (SMEs), surveys, observation, and reviews of manuals and standard operating procedures. Historically, there were many different job analysis techniques, such as functional job analysis (Fine & Wiley, 1974), the Position Analysis Questionnaire (PAQ), and critical incident techniques (Flanagan, 1954). The common feature across these alternatives is to identify the critical tasks and KSAOs. Of the many tasks performed on a job, not all are essential. Hence, after compiling a list of all job tasks, job analysis methods often ask SMEs to rate how frequent, difficult, or critical the task is for the job. These and other approaches are comprehensively detailed in Gatewood and Feild (1998) and Brannick, Levine, and Morgeson (2007). However, in today's world it is more common to use a combination of approaches as relevant, such as SME interviews, observation, and surveys. But private firms are often resistant to devote the considerable money and resources needed to conduct a comprehensive job analysis. In such situations, firms may instead choose to use the U.S. Federal Government's Occupational Information Network (referred to as O*NET). The O*NET system covers nearly every occupation in the United States. It provides a holistic perspective on work and provides information on six major content areas for each job: worker characteristics, worker requirements, experience requirements, occupational requirements, occupation-specific requirements (tasks more specific to the job), and occupation characteristics (labor and economic factors affecting the occupation). This information is also linked to a variety of state databases. O*NET is freely available on the internet (http://online.onetcenter.org/). Regardless of which approach is used, what is most important is that the job analysis is comprehensive and has identified the most essential tasks and KSAOs needed to perform the job.

After identifying the critical tasks and selection KSAOs, the next steps involve defining the latent performance domain (inference 2) and the latent predictor domain (inference 3). Because these domains are latent, inference 5 cannot be tested, but must be inferred through inference 1. Defining the latent performance domain determines the types of criteria that will be measured (inference 4). These criteria may include job performance behaviors, but also many other types of criteria such as turnover, absenteeism, and safety (see Campbell, chapter 6 of this handbook, for a comprehensive treatment of job performance). Likewise, defining the latent predictor domain determines the types of KSAO constructs and predictor measures that will be used for the basis of making selection decisions (inference 6; see Ryan and Sackett, chapter 5 of this handbook). Inference 7 represents the empirical correlation (i.e., criterion-related validity) of the predictor scores with the criterion scores. Thus, as one can see, appropriate support for inferences 1–7 is necessary to adequately support inference 8 (Binning & Barrett, 1989).

Before leaving Figure 8.1, it is important to recognize that each inference is often based on considerable human judgment. In recent years, it has become appreciated that a host of perceptual, cognitive, and social factors can influence this judgment and ultimately the results and accuracy of job analyses. Morgeson and Campion (1997) present a comprehensive review of factors likely to influence job analysis results (e.g., conformity pressures, impression management). Empirical research has found that job analysis information is frequently affected by these factors (e.g., Morgeson, Delaney-Klinger, Mayfield, Ferrara, & Campion, 2004), as well as organizational context (Dierdorff & Morgeson, 2007). However, the major source of variance in job analysis ratings appears to be due to idiosyncratic differences among the raters (Van Iddekinge, Putka, Raymark, & Eidson, 2005). These findings do not negate the importance of job analysis, but rather raise awareness of the fact that jobs are perceived and in many ways socially constructed (Ilgen & Hollenbeck, 1991).

To provide empirical support for the inferences (hypotheses) shown in Figure 8.1, there are a variety of methodological issues that must be considered. These methodological issues represent the intersection between statistics and psychometrics with personnel selection processes and practices. Importantly, these methodological and statistical issues directly impact the types and nature of support for the inferences shown in Figure 8.1. Hence, questions about the appropriateness of these issues directly relate to questions about the appropriateness

of the conclusions and generalizations we make from selection research. Summaries of methodological and statistical issues are presented in chapter 3 (by Hanges and Wang), and chapter 4 (by DeShon) of this handbook, as well as Johnson and Oswald (2010) and Van Iddekinge and Ployhart (2008). Here only a concise summary is provided.

While the key inference in personnel selection is that of inference 8 in Figure 8.1, one of the best ways we can substantiate this inference is through empirically supporting inference 7 via a correlation coefficient (i.e., criterion-related validity). There are a variety of factors (sometimes called statistical or measurement artifacts) that can distort (usually downward) the size of the correlation coefficient and hence support for inference 7 (and by extension, inference 8).

Measurement error represents one of the most pervasive artifacts because every manifest variable contains multiple sources of variance. The extent to which these various sources of variance are unwanted contributes to the error variance of the measure. As alluded to in Figure 8.1 by inferences 5 and 6, measures of predictors and criteria are imperfect representations of the latent underlying "true score." Measurement error is one of the causes of these imperfections. *Measurement error* contributes to the unreliability of the measure, and the lower the reliability, the lower the criterion-related validity (i.e., the size of the correlation). For example, error variance may stem from the wording of test questions or transient error. As a result, a considerable amount of research has sought to examine what sources of error variance may be present in predictors and criteria, and how to best correct the observed correlations to obtain estimates of the construct relationships. That is, research has sought to take the observed (also known as an *uncorrected*) correlation from inference 7 and, through various corrections, obtain an *estimate* (via a *corrected* correlation) of inference 5. Schmidt and Hunter (1996) provide an excellent overview of different sources of error in psychological measurement. By realizing there are multiple sources of error, the difficulty then comes in trying to understand whether to correct all forms of error variance, and the sequence by which to correct them. This is a complex issue beyond the scope of the present chapter, but interested readers are referred to DeShon (2002), Murphy and DeShon (2000), Schmidt, Le, and Ilies (2003), and Schmidt, Viswesvaran, and Ones (2000). What is important to realize is that different assumptions about what comprises error variance will influence the magnitude of the enhancement to the observed validity coefficient; the more sources of variance treated as error, the larger the correction to the correlation coefficient.

Range restriction represents a second artifact affecting the size of the correlation coefficient used to support inference 7. Correlations are attenuated to the extent that one or both variables lack variance. Range restriction occurs when the variance in the predictor, criterion, or both, is reduced relative to what it would be in the larger population. For example, suppose that we look at the correlation between interview ratings and supervisory ratings of job performance. Unfortunately, the supervisors refuse to make distinctions between employees and rate *all* employees a 10 on a 10-point scale. There will be zero variance in the criterion, and hence the correlation will be zero. However, in reality, if supervisors had been willing to make appropriate distinctions, the correlation coefficient may have been .20. Thus, as with measurement error, range restriction lowers the magnitude of the correlation coefficient, and as with measurement error, there are a variety of corrections that can be used to provide better estimates of inference 5 via extension of inference 7. Sackett and Yang (2000) identified 11 different scenarios that affect the magnitude of indirect and direct range restriction, and the appropriate formulae needed to correct correlations in these situations. Further work on using range restriction corrections in practice is offered by Hunter, Schmidt, and Le (2006), Sackett, Laczo, and Arvey (2002), Sackett, Lievens, Berry, and Landers (2007), and Schmidt, Oh, and Le (2006).

Should statistical artifact corrections be used and, if so, which corrections should be used? These simple questions evoke some dramatic responses from I/O psychologists. At the risk of oversimplification, there are two camps; one camp advocates the use of corrections to enhance the size of the correlation coefficient, and the other camp either espouses a conservative approach to the use of corrections or ignores them entirely. This "divide" can be found in numerous places, for example, from the debate over whether to correct rating criteria for interrater unreliability (measurement error discussed above), to the debate over whether personality criterion-related validities are large (discussed below). The crux of the debate is that there is no empirical way to support inference 5, hence the issue is whether the observed (uncorrected) correlation supporting inference 7 provides a reasonable estimate of inference 5. Therefore, any support for inference 5 by

extension of inference 7 must be evaluated in terms of whether the correction procedures are appropriate. This is where opinions differ, and an excellent exchange on this issue is provided by Le, Oh, Shaffer, and Schmidt (2007), Schmidt, Le, Oh, and Shaffer (2007), and Schmitt (2007).

CREATING PREDICTOR COMPOSITES

Most selection systems will use multiple predictor constructs and methods, such as resumes, interviews, and possibly some form of cognitive, knowledge, or personality tests. When multiple predictors comprise a selection battery, it becomes necessary to combine the scores in some fashion to produce a final hiring decision. This task becomes more complicated when the system is one involving multiple hurdles or cutoffs, such that only applicants who score above a threshold at one stage move on to subsequent stages of the process. Gatewood and Feild (1998) offer an excellent description of different selection system combination strategies. There are multiple ways to estimate predictor importance, including relative importance (i.e., the contribution of each predictor to the overall regression model), incremental validity, and relative weight/dominance analysis. A variety of issues that should be considered when evaluating predictor importance are reviewed by Johnson and Oswald (2010) and Van Iddekinge and Ployhart (2008). One should also recognize that different ways of combining predictors can influence the overall subgroup difference and adverse impact of the selection system (Sackett & Ellingson, 1997; Sackett & Roth, 1996).

VALIDATION METHODOLOGICAL ISSUES

The two basic criterion-related validation designs include predictive (predictor scores from *applicants* are correlated with their *later* performance scores collected as incumbents on the job) and concurrent (current *incumbent* employees complete the predictors, and their scores are correlated with their performance on the job). A variety of KSAOs may differ between these two contexts, including test-taking motivation, knowledge of the job and organization, and experience. As such, the validation design can influence the magnitude of the correlation observed to support inference 7 in Figure 8.1. The size of the criterion-related validity for non-cognitive constructs and predictors is usually larger in concurrent contexts (Van Iddekinge & Ployhart, 2008). Likewise, a predictor administered to job incumbents may be responded to differently by applicants and hence offer clouded support for construct validity (inference 6 in Figure 8.1). A good example is personality testing; as discussed below, administering a self-report personality inventory to applicants produces very high mean scores and reduced variance, hence support for inference 6 and thus 7 becomes diminished in predictive validation studies. Similarly, range restriction can occur in different ways and by different amounts in concurrent and predictive studies (Sackett & Yang, 2000).

A new issue that has become important in recent years is the retesting of applicants. Many civil service organizations, and even some private firms, allow rejected applicants to reapply for the job after a specified period of time has elapsed. In general, cognitive test scores tend to increase with repeated testing (Hauserknecht, Halpert, Di Paolo, & Moriarty Gerrard, 2007) whereas personality test scores do not (Ellingson, Sackett, & Connelly, 2007; Hogan, Barrett, & Hogan, 2007). Criterion-related validity tends to be a bit higher for the initial test score for cognitive tests (Hauserknecht, Trevor, & Farr, 2002).

A Framework for Comparing Predictors

Ployhart et al. (2006) define a predictor as follows:

> Any manifest measure whose scores represent individual differences on latent knowledge, skills, abilities, or other characteristics linked to effective criterion performance, and which is used (at least in part) as the basis for selection or promotion. (p. 366)

Predictors are the "indicators" that we use to gauge whether an applicant is likely to perform well on the job (i.e., inference 8 in Figure 8.1). As a result, selection scholars spend enormous energy seeking to better understand and improve predictors. This research has produced many different types of predictor constructs and KSAOs. *Predictor constructs* are measures of homogenous KSAOs and include cognitive, knowledge, personality, values/needs/interests, and physical domains. *Predictor methods* assess multiple constructs simultaneously (i.e., are multidimensional) and include experience and biographical data (biodata), interviews, situational judgment tests, assessment centers, and work samples. Thus, there are many choices in predictors of job performance, even for the same type of performance and job. As a result, selection experts often must make choices about which predictor measures to use for a given KSAO (i.e., inference 6 in Figure 8.1). Following Aguinis and Smith (2007), Heneman and Judge (2006), and Ployhart

et el. (2006), this section uses a framework that consists of multiple dimensions to compare and contrast predictors: criterion-related validity, fakability, subgroup differences, economic return, and user acceptability.

Criterion-related validity represents the degree to which scores on the predictor are related to scores on the criterion (inference 7 in Figure 8.1). Criterion-related validity is where "the rubber meets the road;" it is the *empirical* evidence to support inferences that scores on the predictor are related to latent job performance (Binning & Barrett, 1989). While criterion-related validity studies are frequently not feasible in practice (e.g., need for a large sample size), criterion-related validity is traditionally one of the most important indices of a predictor's value and one of the key drivers of economic utility (at least as estimated in classic utility models). According to Ployhart et al. (2006), uncorrected criterion-related validity estimates of .10, .20, and .30 represent small, medium, and large validities.

Fakability concerns whether predictor scores are affected by intentional response distortion. Given that most applicants want to score high enough to receive a job offer, it is possible that applicants will intentionally provide more favorable reports of self-reported past behavior, accomplishments, personality, and work ethic and values, than they might if there were no consequences for their test scores. Hence, in high-stakes testing environments where the outcome is important, one must be critical of whether the scores truly reflect the latent underlying KSAOs or impression management. Indeed, nearly every study comparing high-stakes (e.g., applicants) to low-stakes (e.g., job incumbents) testing situations finds higher scores on personality (and related self-report measures) in high-stakes contexts (Smith & Robie, 2004). It appears the criterion-related validity can be cut in half as a result of response distortion (Hough, 1998). Although there is some disagreement about whether faking affects the validity or practical usefulness of non-cognitive measures, it is a very important concern for practitioners because inflated test scores reduce the distinctions between applicants.

Subgroup differences indicate how much of a mean difference in predictor scores exists between subsamples within an overall sample. Normally, the subgroups are those representing protected groups through employment regulations; common examples include race, ethnicity, sex, and age. When there are mean differences between subgroups, and organizations hire the top-scoring applicants first, the consequence is that members from the higher scoring subgroup will be hired more frequently than those from the lower scoring subgroup. The larger the subgroup difference, the more likely it is that higher scoring subgroup members will be hired. For example, physical ability tests have large differences between men and women, so in a selection process with even a moderate selection ration (e.g., hire 30% of the applicant pool), men could be hired to the near total exclusion of women. Subgroup differences are usually expressed in terms of standardized mean differences (denoted as d values), so any score differences are conveniently expressed in standard deviation units. Please note that subgroup differences on predictor scores do not mean that the predictor is biased or discriminatory against the lower scoring group. Two groups may have a sizable mean difference, but if the test predicts equally well for both groups, there is no differential prediction (Cleary, 1968; Schmidt, 1988). Hence, subgroup differences are not (by themselves) proof of discrimination.

Economic return indicates whether the value provided by a predictor or selection system outweighs the costs of development and/or implementation. Every predictor has an associated cost that includes development or purchase, administration, and scoring. Among personnel selection scholars, utility analysis is often used as a means to convey economic return. There are numerous models of utility analysis (see Boudreau & Ramstad, 2003), but they share some common features in that they attempt to show how much financial improvement will occur from implementing a selection system with a given amount of validity, selection ratio, and related factors. Reports of some studies show these financial improvements to be quite large (Schmidt, Hunter, McKenzie, & Muldrow, 1979). However, many practitioners are not persuaded by utility estimates, particularly when they do not have HR or I/O backgrounds (e.g., Latham & Whyte, 1994). This is likely due to the fact that utility analysis is complex, based on many assumptions, and ultimately an estimate of a unit-level consequence of individual-level selection (Schneider, Smith, & Sipe, 2000). There are many other selection metrics that practitioners attend to, including job performance, retention, time-to-hire, cost-per-hire, and productivity-per-employee. Different firms have different metrics, but whatever metrics are used, economic return is paramount in practice.

User acceptability refers to whether the various stakeholders who are affected by the selection process believe (or at least accept) the results. It is sometimes called face validity, but face validity is more narrow in that it is defined as whether people that believe the predictor measures what it claims to measure. User acceptability is a broader term because even though a predictor may be face valid, it still may not be acceptable because of other factors (e.g., cost, appearance, subgroup differences). Note that user acceptability is an inclusive term that includes managers, HR personnel, and the applicants (Kehoe, Mol, & Anderson, 2009). Each of these stakeholders defines acceptability differently. Line managers want a short, quick, and accurate system. HR personnel want a cost-effective, legally defensible, and sustainable system. Applicants want a short, quick, and fair system and, although they may often say that they want it to be accurate, in reality they likely want it to be one in which they do well. These are frequently different and competing perspectives, and it is a tension that must be balanced. For example, managers will sometimes choose a less valid system over a more valid selection for many reasons, including cost, unacceptable negative effects on diversity, or political battles between HR and management. At least in the United States, there is no law that requires a private firm to use a valid selection system unless it is discriminatory against a protected subgroup (Pyburn, Ployhart, & Kravitz, 2008), so manager beliefs have a strong influence on what gets implemented.

In the next sections, the criterion-related validity, fakability, subgroup differences, economic return, and user acceptability framework is used to help critically compare and contrast research on predictor KSAO constructs and methods. Table 8.1 provides an overview and summary.

Predictor KSAO Constructs

There are five major domains of predictor constructs: cognitive, knowledge, personality, values/needs//interests, and physical abilities. These represent the broad spectrum of individual differences of most relevance to personnel selection. Ryan and Sackett in chapter 5 of this handbook discusses these individual differences in more detail, so here the literature is summarized more specifically to personnel selection practices.

Cognitive

There has been extensive research that seeks to understand the latent structure of cognitive ability (also known as general mental ability, or g), and several different models exist (see Drasgow, 2003). However, most share in common a hierarchical

Table 8.1. Framework for Comparing Predictor Constructs and Methods (adapted from Ployhart et al., 2006)

Predictors	Criterion-Related Validity	Fakability	Subgroup Differences (Race/Gender)	Economic Return	User Acceptability
			Dimension		
Effect Sizes	*Correlation* .10 = Low .20 = Moderate .30 = High	N/A	*d* value .20 = Small .50 = Moderate .80 = Large	N/A	N/A
Predictor Constructs					
Cognitive					
Cognitive Ability	High	Low	Large/Small	High	Moderate
Job Knowledge	High	Low	Moderate/Small	High	Favorable
Non-cognitive					
Personality	Low	High	Small/Small	Moderate	Unfavorable
Values/Needs/ Interests	Low	Moderate to High	Small/Small	Low	Unfavorable
Physical					
Psychomotor & Physical Ability	High	Low	Small/Large	Moderate	Moderate
Predictor Methods					
Experience & Biodata	Moderate	Moderate	Small/Small	Low to Moderate	Moderate to Unfavorable
Interview-Structured	High	Moderate	Small/Small	Moderate	Moderate
Interview-Unstructured	Low	Moderate to High	Small/Small	Low	Moderate
Situational Judgment	Moderate	Moderate	Moderate/Small	High	Favorable
Assessment Centers	High	Low to Moderate	Small to Moderate/Small	Moderate	Favorable
Work Samples	High	Low	Small to Large /Unknown	Moderate	Favorable

Note: Estimates for validity and subgroup differences are based on uncorrected values.

structure, such that specific abilities (e.g., verbal, numerical, and reasoning ability) are subsumed within general cognitive ability (operationalized as the first factor when conducting a factor analysis on the more specific abilities). Carroll's (1993) hierarchical model is perhaps the most comprehensive, which posits that general cognitive ability subsumes eight more specific abilities (e.g., fluid intelligence, crystallized intelligence, general memory and learning), which in turn subsume even more specific abilities (e.g., speed of reasoning, reading comprehension, memory span). Several studies have demonstrated that the specific abilities do not predict broad criteria better than general cognitive ability (Ree, Earles, & Teachout, 1994). Hence, because general cognitive ability is more predictive and more efficient than administering a longer battery of specific abilities, most personnel selection practitioners use general cognitive ability.

Cognitive ability represents one of the most important individual differences in employment contexts because it is one of the strongest predictors of performance across most jobs (Schmidt & Hunter, 1998). Further, as the cognitive demands of the job increase, generally so does the criterion-related validity of cognitive ability (Hunter & Hunter, 1984). Given the increased prevalence of knowledge work, the importance of cognitive ability may become even greater as the modern economy evolves. Cognitive ability tests have no concerns about faking because the answers are either correct or incorrect. Cognitive ability also tends to produce at least moderate acceptance from users and high economic return because measures of general ability are relatively inexpensive and easy to administer.

However, general cognitive ability also manifests some of the largest racio-ethnic subgroup differences of any predictor construct or method. Relative to whites, blacks score *up to* a full standard deviation lower and Hispanics score from half to over three-quarters of a standard deviation lower (Asians score about one-fifth of a standard deviation higher than whites; see Roth, Bevier, Bobko, Switzer, & Tyler, 2001). These differences are large enough that, under typical selection ratios, the hiring rate of blacks and oftentimes Hispanics will be considerably lower than that of whites (Sackett & Wilk, 1994). Sex differences tend to be small for general cognitive ability. Racio-ethnic and sex differences are more variable for specific abilities, and in some cases sex differences can be quite a bit larger (Hough, Oswald, & Ployhart, 2001). For example, men score higher than women on quantitative abilities, while women score higher than men on verbal abilities.

The fact that cognitive ability produces high criterion-related validity but also large racio-ethnic subgroup differences puts practitioners in what has been called the validity-diversity dilemma (Pyburn et al., 2008). Because of the negative effect that cognitive ability will have on the hiring rates of many racio-ethnic minority candidates, there has been enormous effort devoted to trying to understand and reduce racio-ethnic subgroup differences (see Sackett, Schmitt, Ellingson, & Kabin, 2001). This is critical because organizational decision makers frequently shy away from using (or fully weighting) cognitive ability tests due to their negative effects on diversity (Pyburn et al., 2008); this also explains why the user acceptance of cognitive ability is only moderate. The size and pervasiveness of racio-ethnic subgroup differences make them extremely difficult to eliminate, so the goal has been to find strategies and approaches for reducing them. Ployhart and Holtz (2008) identified 16 different strategies that have been offered to reduce racio-ethnic and sex subgroup differences and found that the only strategy that would meaningfully reduce subgroup differences and not substantially reduce criterion-related validity was to supplement a cognitive predictor with non-cognitive predictors that have smaller subgroup differences (see Bobko, Roth, & Potosky, 1999; Sackett & Ellingson, 1997; Sackett & Roth, 1996). One thing that is important to realize is that even though cognitive ability tests produce large racio-ethnic subgroup differences, they are not biased toward any minority candidates because the criterion-related validity is not moderated by racio-ethnic group membership (Schmidt, 1988). Excellent reviews and debates of the cognitive ability–testing literature can be found in Drasgow (2003) and a special issue of *Human Performance* (2002).

Knowledge

Whereas cognitive ability is generic to different work situations, knowledge is domain specific because it is acquired through experience or education. Examples include knowledge of accounting, finance, human resources, and selection practices. Knowledge may be broadly construed into two main types: *declarative* is knowledge of facts and principles, while *procedural* is knowledge of processes and how to apply facts and principles to a given problem. Knowledge is not fixed or constant but accumulates over time (Kanfer & Ackerman, 2004). Those with more experience and greater cognitive ability will be more likely to acquire knowledge; thus knowledge partially mediates the relationship between cognitive ability and performance (Hunter, 1983). Knowledge may be generic to a specific occupation, or specific to a particular firm, although in selection we are most typically interested in occupation or job-specific knowledge (as opposed to firm-specific knowledge).

Job knowledge predictors tend to have high criterion-related validity (Schmidt & Hunter, 1998), rivaling that of general cognitive ability (but of course being job or domain specific). A benefit of knowledge tests being domain specific is that they are clearly face valid and have favorable user acceptability. Because they are easy to administer and relatively simple to develop, they also offer high economic return. On the other hand, knowledge tests have moderate racio-ethnic subgroup differences (whites score about half a standard deviation higher; Roth, Huffcutt, & Bobko, 2003). Sex differences are small, although they may be larger if the knowledge overlaps with abilities that manifest sex subgroup differences (e.g., verbal ability and a knowledge test of English). It is also possible that knowledge tests may suffer from faking, but this is not much of an issue because knowledge tests have right/wrong answers.

Personality

Most selection research conducted over the last 20 years has been based on minor variations of the Five Factor Model (FFM). The FFM is composed of the following traits: emotional stability (sometimes known as neuroticism), extraversion, openness to experience, agreeableness, and conscientiousness. As with cognitive ability, the FFM is hierarchical in that these five traits are the broadest and subsume various more specific traits within them (e.g., conscientiousness subsumes dutifulness, achievement, and dependability). Although other structures of personality exist, the FFM has dominated selection research and practice.

Personality testing within selection contexts has traveled a bumpy road (for a historical review, see Schneider, 2007). Early summaries of criterion-related validity reached rather pessimistic conclusions about their usefulness (Ghiselli, 1966; Guion & Gottier, 1965). Meta-analyses conducted 25 years later found highly similar uncorrected criterion-related validities, but reached the opposite conclusion and led to a "rebirth" of personality testing (Barrick & Mount, 1991). Schmitt (2004) noted that for the most part, uncorrected personality criterion-related validities have not changed much over time and tend to be moderate to low. For example, conscientiousness has the largest criterion-related validity of the FFM constructs, but this uncorrected estimate is only .13 (Barrick & Mount, 1991). It is apparent that personality testing now sees widespread use in practice because even though the validities are low, they are not zero and hence contribute to the prediction of performance in modest ways. But many have come to question whether, given such validities, personality tests should be used. An exchange of opinions on this topic may be found in Morgeson et al. (2007a, 2007b), Ones, Dilchert, Viswesvaran, and Judge (2007), and Tett and Christiansen (2007).

Further compounding the frustrations with personality testing is the likelihood of applicants faking their responses to increase the probability of scoring well. Unlike cognitive ability and job knowledge, personality tests do not have correct answers, and it is relatively easy to misrepresent oneself on most self-report measures. As with personality test validity, there is not strong consensus over whether faking is a problem. Some argue that faking will not negate the criterion-related validity of personality tests (Hough & Furnham, 2003; Ones & Viswesvaran, 1998; Ones, Viswesvaran, & Reiss, 1996), even though the validity may be reduced by up to half (Hough, 1998). It is nearly ubiquitous that personality tests administered to applicants will have higher mean scores than when the same tests are completed by incumbents (Smith & Robie, 2004). This by itself may not affect validity too much, but it will often affect one's ability to distinguish between candidates because of tie scores due to ceiling effects. Hence, user acceptability of personality tests tends to be mixed because applicants and organizational decisions makers often believe that the scores are rendered incomprehensible due to faking. Faking and low validities also lead to personality tests having low economic return.

Given such a discouraging review, one might wonder why personality testing has had a rebirth in practice. The reason likely has to do with the fact that personality constructs have relatively small racio-ethnic and sex subgroup differences (although the differences are larger for facets relative to FFM constructs; Foldes, Duehr, & Ones, 2008). Hence, including personality along with a cognitive ability test will generally enhance validity and (to a degree) reduce racio-ethnic subgroup differences (Sackett & Roth, 1996). It is also important to realize that there are strategies that can be implemented to increase the criterion-related validity of personality tests. In particular, the use of personality composites developed to maximally predict performance for certain occupations (e.g., managerial jobs, customer service; Hough & Schneider, 1996) or tailoring the personality items to specific contexts (Lievens, DeCorte, & Schollaert, 2008) can manifest validities larger than the FFM constructs. Similarly, linking specific traits to narrow criteria can increase validity (Dudley, Orvis, Lebiecki, & Cortina, 2006). New approaches to personality measurement have also been proposed to help reduce faking and enhance validity (e.g., James, 1998). In commonsense terms, it is hard to believe that personality does not affect job performance; the challenge for I/O psychologists is how to better measure it. For more information on personality at work, please see edited books by Barrick and Ryan (2003) and Schneider and Smith (2004), as well as reviews by Hough and Furnham (2003) and Hough and Oswald (2008).

Values, Needs, and Interests

A person's values or needs represent his or her latent styles, preferences, or desires (Dawis & Lofquist, 1984). As such, they direct attention and motivation without the individual often being aware of them. Interests represent a person's preferences for certain types of work. Holland's RIASEC model (1997) has been the most influential and is part of the O*NET system. The RIASEC model suggests that people choose occupations that match their values, needs, and interests. The six dimensions in the RIASEC model include *realistic* (conforming), *investigative* (analytic), *artistic* (open), *social* (gregarious), *enterprising* (ambitious), and *conventional* (obedient). Together, values, needs, and interests influence the environments that individuals will prefer to enter, and the satisfaction that they will derive from different environments. For example, a person with a high need for achievement might be more attracted to firms that require and reward achievement than firms that emphasize equality among employees.

Values, needs, and interests have rather relatively low criterion-related validity for job performance criteria. Rather, values, needs, and interests can have a strong influence on the perceived fit that one has with a job and organization. *Perceived fit* is a person's perception of whether his/her KSAOs, values, needs, or interests match the work environment. There are different kinds of fit, including a perceived match between the person's values and those of the job (person-job fit) and organization (person-organization) fit), as well as whether the person's KSAOs match those required and rewarded by the job (needs-supplies; Cable & DeRue, 2002). Perceived fit, in turn, is predictive of job/firm attraction, the satisfaction one derives from a job, and retention (Cable & Parsons, 2001; Kristof-Brown, Zimmerman, & Johnson, 2005). However, a recent meta-analysis found that fit was a rather weak predictor of job performance (Arthur, Bell, Villado, & Doverspike, 2006). Like personality tests, measures of values, needs, and interests are moderately to highly fakable and show low economic return. Values, needs, and interests are often perceived negatively by applicants, but value measures are often desired by employers who wish to determine whether an applicant will fit within the organization (particularly for entry-level managerial jobs in which the candidate will be groomed for higher level positions). These measures have small racio-ethnic and sex subgroup differences. Although this summary does not offer much empirical enthusiasm for using measures of values, needs, and interests as a basis for hiring decisions, the relationships that these constructs have with job choice and retention make them important parts of the broader staffing context. For a broad review of the fit literature, see Edwards (2008) and an edited book by Ostroff and Judge (2007).

Psychomotor and Physical Abilities

Whereas most jobs in the older economy were based on physical ability, most jobs in the modern economy are based on mental ability. This might explain why there has not been much new research on physical ability testing in I/O psychology over the last 20 years (the other explanation is that this research has shifted to other disciplines, such as human factors). In the I/O literature, most research has focused on two main types. The first type is psychomotor abilities that include sensory abilities (e.g., vision) and dexterity. The second type is physical abilities that include muscular strength, cardiovascular endurance, and movement quality (Hogan, 1991).

Physical abilities have high criterion-related validity and low fakability (no wonder; it would be impossible to fake a good bench press!). Economic return is moderate (because of the cost of testing; it must be hands-on). Both applicants and organizational decision makers tend to find these tests at least moderately acceptable. On the other hand, the sex subgroup differences can be large, ranging from one standard deviation (for muscular endurance) to over two standard deviations (for muscular power) favoring males (Ployhart & Holtz, 2008).

Predictor Methods

There are five major types of predictor methods: experience and biographical data (biodata), interviews, situational judgment tests, assessment centers, and work samples. As a caveat to the review that follows, one should realize that, by definition, predictor methods can assess multiple constructs. Therefore, even though the criterion-related validity, fakability, subgroup differences, economic return, and user acceptability of predictor methods are discussed, one should realize that these findings average across different KSAO constructs. The conclusions presented below may differ depending on the specific construct being assessed (Arthur & Villado, 2008). In general, predictor methods that assess or are more strongly related to cognitive ability will show higher criterion-related validity and larger racio-ethnic subgroup differences. This latter finding has been recognized as far back as Spearman (1927), who noted that the stronger the cognitive loading of an assessment, the larger the black-white subgroup difference. Please keep this caveat in mind when reviewing the following summary.

Experience and Biographical Data (Biodata)

Predictors based on experience rely on the adage that "the best predictor of future behavior is past behavior" (Wernimont & Campbell, 1968). Experience is a broad, multidimensional construct that often serves as a proxy for knowledge. There are many different kinds of experience, such as experience with an occupation, a job within a firm, or employment within a given firm. For example, a person might have 15 years of experience at the same firm, but 10 years of experience as a software designer and five years as a manager. Experience may range from generic to firm-specific, although this distinction has had much more attention in economics (e.g., Becker, 1964) than it has had in I/O psychology. Experience may further be assessed by amount, time, or type (Quiñones, Ford, & Teachout, 1995; Tesluk & Jacobs, 1998). Biographical data (biodata) is a more structured way to assess experience. With biodata, one usually starts by identifying the kinds of developmental experiences and/or constructs that are necessary for success on the job. Items are then written to measure these experiences and/or constructs. The end result is a measurement instrument that is structured to assess specific types of experience relevant to a specific job. Mael (1991) and Russell (1994) are useful sources for how to generate biodata items.

Experience and biodata-based predictors have moderate validity, with biodata having better uncorrected criterion-related validity than simpler measures of experience. Both tend to have small racio-ethnic and sex subgroup differences, although the more the items represent cognitively oriented variables, such as educational degrees or academic achievements, the more likely it is that there may be racio-ethnic differences (Berry, Gruys, & Sackett, 2006). Experience and biodata forms may be fakable; however, faking can be reduced through the use of warnings, using verifiable items, and asking participants to elaborate on their answers (e.g., if the question asks how many languages a person speaks, require the applicant to elaborate and list the languages; Schmitt, Oswald, Kim, Gillespie, Ramsay, & Yoo, 2003). Experience and biodata vary in terms of their acceptability; most people believe that experience is related to job performance but the nature of biodata forms sometimes leads to less acceptance. Experience and biodata offer low to moderate economic return, depending on how strongly related they are to job performance. An edited book on biodata by Stokes, Mumford, and Owens (1994) provides considerably more detail.

Interviews

Interviews are one of the most frequently used selection methods (Ulrich & Trumbo, 1965) and have been the focus of research for decades (for a recent review, see Posthuma, Morgeson, & Campion, 2002; see also an edited book by Eder & Harris, 1999). Interviews have different purposes; for example, there are screening interviews used to make hiring decisions, and recruiting or informational interviews, which serve as recruiting tools (for present purposes, we will focus primarily on screening interviews). Interviews are considered a predictor method because there are multiple ways to structure interviews and to ask the questions, and thus there are multiple constructs that can be assessed. *Interview structure* refers to how the interview is developed, administered, and scored in order to enhance construct validity and efficiency. Campion, Palmer, and Campion (1997) identified 15 different elements of structure, which include basing the interview on a job analysis, asking the same questions of all applicants, minimizing the use of extraneous information, making detailed notes, and training the interviewers. A related aspect of structure is whether the interview is conducted by a single person or a panel composed of multiple interviewers. In terms of *interview questions*, there are three broad types, which include behavior (asking about past behavior), situational (asking about future behavior or hypothetical situations), or job knowledge (asking about how to perform specific job tasks). Finally, as one might imagine, different questions may be asked to measure different *constructs*. A meta-analysis by Huffcutt, Conway, Roth, and Stone (2001) found that the most common constructs assessed by interviews were personality and social skills. Other commonly assessed constructs included cognitive ability, knowledge and skill, interests and preferences, fit, and physical abilities and attributes.

In general, the more structured the interview, the higher the criterion-related validity and reliability (Cortina, Goldstein, Payne, Davison, & Gilliland, 2000). There is some evidence that behavioral interviews have higher validity than situational interviews (Huffcutt, Weekley, Wiesner, Degroot, & Jones, 2001). It appears that one of the main reasons that unstructured interviews have lower validity is because they have less reliability; but using at least four independent interviewers for each applicant can help offset this limitation (Schmidt & Zimmerman, 2004). Interviews tend to receive moderate acceptance from applicants and managers, and they have moderate economic return. They also show relatively small racio-ethnic and sex subgroup differences, with the differences being smaller for structured interviews. The content and structure of an interview can influence the prevalence of applicant impression management (McFarland, Ryan, & Kriska, 2003), and unstructured interviews are more fakable than unstructured interviews.

Situational Judgment Tests (SJT)

Situational judgment tests (SJTs) are sometimes considered "low-fidelity simulations" because they present applicants with a brief work-related situation, and then ask how they should or would respond to the situation (Motowidlo, Dunnette, & Carter, 1990). The situations are usually derived from the critical incident technique and represent real situations that are fairly common, but difficult and challenging to address. The situations will not have a clearly correct answer, so they create variability in test-taker responses. In terms of responses, SJTs usually present four to six behavioral options that indicate what a person should or would do. Like interviews, SJTs are considered predictor methods because they can be used to measure a variety of constructs. However, SJTs do not measure constructs in a homogenous manner, and it is unclear whether an SJT can be developed to do so (Schmitt & Chan, 2006). SJTs tend to most commonly measure some composite of cognitive ability, personality, experience, and knowledge (McDaniel, Morgeson, Finnegan, Braverman, & Campion, 2001; McDaniel & Nguyen, 2001). The construct validity of SJTs is in part affected by the wording of instructions. When the instructions ask what you "should do," the SJT is more strongly related to cognitive ability; when the instructions ask what you "would do," the SJT is more strongly related to personality (McDaniel, Hartman, Whetzel, & Grubb, 2007).

The criterion-related validity of SJTs is moderate and, although related to cognitive ability and personality, still shows incremental validity over these other predictors (e.g., Clevenger, Pereira, Wiechmann, Schmitt, & Harvey, 2001). SJTs tend to be viewed favorably by applicants and managers because they are face valid and are tied to specific parts of the job (see Bauer & Truxillo, 2006). They offer reasonably high economic return because they can be administered in an efficient manner and have moderate validity. Sex subgroup differences are small, but racio-ethnic subgroup differences tend to be small to moderate (see Ployhart & Holtz, 2008). Racio-ethnic differences are largely due to the reading requirements and cognitive loading of an SJT; the more the SJT requires reading ability, the larger the subgroup difference. Some research has found that faking may reduce the criterion-related validity of SJTs (Peeters & Lievens, 2005), although considerably more needs to be learned to understand faking effects with SJTs. An edited book by Weekley and Ployhart (2006) offers more detailed information about SJTs.

Assessment Centers

Assessment centers are predictor methods that present candidates with different *exercises* designed to assess a variety of KSAOs. Assessment centers are not known by any particular exercise, but rather a collection of exercises. The most commonly used exercises include role plays, leaderless group discussions, in-basket exercises that stress setting priorities and delegation, business games and simulations, and mock presentations (Spychalski, Quiñones, Gaugler, & Pohley, 1997). Most assessment centers use an average of four to five exercises (Woehr & Arthur, 2003). These exercises measure of variety of different KSAO *dimensions*, with the average being 10 to 11. The most common dimensions include social skills, communication, motivation, persuasion and influence, organization and planning, and problem solving (Arthur, Day, McNelly, & Edens, 2003). In most assessment centers, trained raters will observe or grade the applicant's performance on the dimensions.

Assessment centers have high criterion-related validity because they usually require one to actually perform the behavior (instead of a self-report of the behavior), and they measure a variety of different KSAO dimensions linked to performance on the job. Likewise, they are difficult to fake because they involve the actual performance of the target behaviors. Sex subgroup differences are small, but racio-ethnic subgroup differences are small to moderate, depending on the construct and exercise. As the relationship between the exercise and cognitive ability increases, so does the racio-ethnic subgroup difference (Goldstein, Yusko, Braverman, Smith, & Chung, 1998; Goldstein, Yusko, & Nicolopoulos, 2001). Economic return is moderate because of the cost to develop and administer the assessment center. Both applicants and managers tend to perceive assessment centers favorably, although the administrative costs can sometimes make them less favorable to managers.

Most of the empirical data provide good support for the use of assessment centers. However, their biggest limitation is that they often show little construct validity (an issue shared with SJTs). Specifically, it is nearly always the case that assessment centers manifest exercise factors and not dimension (construct) factors (Klimoski & Brickner, 1987; Lance, Lambert, Gewin, Lievens, & Conway, 2004). The reason for this finding appears to be due to the nature of applicants themselves: construct validity is only likely to be found when candidates manifest high consistency across exercises *and* high differentiation across dimensions (Lievens, 2002). This seems rather unlikely in practice. Research continues to explore and debate the construct validity of assessment centers (see Lance, 2008).

Work Samples

As their name implies, work samples are assessments that are based on actual samples of behavior and tasks performed on the job. Common examples include flight simulators for pilots, welding tests for welders, and, in many ways, a doctoral dissertation for Ph.D. students. Like SJTs and assessment centers, work samples are predictor methods that can measure a variety of KSAO constructs. Much of their popularity is owed to an article by Wernimont and Campbell (1968) that argued for prediction using "samples" of behavior. That is, they suggested that, in contrast to self-report measures that offer "signs" of an applicant's potential, it is more productive to evaluate actual samples of behavior. In general, the higher the psychological and physical fidelity of a predictor, the greater its validity.

Because there is such a high physical and psychological overlap between the job and the assessment, work samples have high criterion-related validity. Further, because they represent actual job behaviors and tasks, they have high acceptance from applicants and organizational decision makers. It is nearly impossible to fake work samples because applicants

need to actually perform the relevant behaviors. Economic return on work samples is only moderate because of the costs to develop and administer them. The size of subgroup differences is larger than most prior research had indicated, however. Roth, Bobko, McFarland, and Buster (2008) found that racio-ethnic subgroup differences range from small to large, depending on the nature of the constructs assessed. These latter findings raise some concern over whether work samples are an effective means to address the diversity-validity dilemma. It is difficult to report the sex subgroup difference; some studies report small differences and others report larger differences, so at this point it is not appropriate to make even a general speculation.

Measurement Methods

Thus far we have considered predictor constructs and methods, but it is important to realize that even predictor constructs are always assessed by a particular measurement method (Arthur & Villado, 2008). For example, we speak of cognitive ability tests as though they are always measured using paper-and-pencil formats, but in practice they may be assessed by a variety of methods including other paper formats, the Internet, and even interviews. Hence, it bears repeating that every predictor is associated with a measurement method. If one collapses across constructs, measurement methods will differ in their reliability, cost, customization, user acceptability, and sources of contamination and deficiency. Ployhart et al. (2006) review these issues in some detail, but to summarize, the major types of assessment methods include paper-and-pencil (written) assessments, Internet/computerized assessments, oral/aural assessments (e.g., phone interviews or video-based testing), and rating/judgment assessments. There is little research that focuses on comparing methods of assessment, but that which has been conducted finds (not surprisingly) that methods are important. For example, Chan and Schmitt (1997) found that video-based assessments of SJTs had smaller black-white subgroup differences than written SJTs (due to lower reading requirements). Currently unknown is an understanding of the *ideal* measurement method for different selection goals, purposes, and constructs.

View From the Top of the Mountain: Does Anybody Know We Are Here?

This concise review illustrates that personnel selection is a vibrant area of research. More direct evidence is provided by Cascio and Aguinis (2008b), who find that topics in personnel selection rank in the top five most-published articles in the *Journal of Applied Psychology* and *Personnel Psychology* over the last several decades. Personnel selection practices have become highly refined, and the technology underlying the personnel selection process is sophisticated. As a profession, selection scholars sit atop a mountain of achievement and understanding. Yet it is lonely at the top. There have been concerns raised over whether personnel selection as a profession of scientists and practitioners is having an impact on, quite bluntly, the real world. These concerns come from several perspectives and sources. Rynes, Brown, and Colbert (2002) surveyed actual managers and found that the HR area of selection showed the largest discrepancies between research findings versus manager beliefs. Cascio and Aguinis (2008a, 2008b) argued that continued emphasis on the usual personnel selection topics is somewhat disconnected from broader industry trends and emphasis on human capital, and that personnel selection must become more contextualized if it is to become more relevant. Ployhart (2006) noted that personnel selection is missing a golden opportunity to demonstrate its strategic value, and that continued focus on research disconnected from practical concerns in private industry limits the relevance of our science. Highhouse (2008) suggested that we need to understand the beliefs, judgments, and decision making processes of managers who must approve and live with selection systems. Finally, Anderson (2005) discussed the very different worlds in which academics and practitioners live and work.

What is at issue here is not whether we have selection processes and practices that improve hiring decisions. On this point, there is an abundance of evidence to suggest that we do (Schmidt & Hunter, 1998, and the research reviewed above). Instead, what is at issue is whether these practices are implemented to the extent that they should be. Highhouse (2008) is almost certainly correct that manager beliefs have a huge influence on the types of selection practices that are implemented. But one could also legitimately argue that personnel selection has not done much to show its value to firm-level outcomes—that is, show its value to *the business* (Ployhart, 2006; Schneider et al., 2000). Utility analysis represents an attempt to show the value of personnel selection practices, and while there are many sophisticated utility analysis methods and models (see Boudreau & Ramstad, 2003; Cascio 2000), it has not had much *widespread* impact on conveying the importance of our research

to those outside academia. Indeed, if it had, why are useful selection practices not more frequently implemented?

There is no point in quibbling over the value of utility analysis; it has a particular purpose and is valuable as a tool for understanding the costs and economic return of HR practices. But continued focus on utility analysis, ways to increase validity through statistical corrections, or the search for the "ultimate predictor" are unlikely to increase the use of valid selection practices in private industry. Addressing this issue will require a fairly radical extension of how we define personnel selection research and practice. It will involve broadening Figure 8.1 to include other criteria and processes that extend beyond the individual level, and it will require becoming familiar with the strategic management literature. We cannot achieve the vision of "Ensuring Sustainable Organizational Effectiveness Through the Acquisition of Human Capital" if we continue our current trajectory.

The Future: Research to Ensure Sustainable Organizational Effectiveness Through the Acquisition of Human Capital

If one adopts the vision of personnel selection proposed above, then it is clear that selection scholars and practitioners have a lot of work to do because we do not know much about the "ensuring sustainable organizational effectiveness" part of the vision—the very part which is likely of most interest to organizational decision makers. In the subsections that follow, I propose five missions through which selection research should be conducted to achieve this vision.

Mission #1: Show the Business-Unit Impact of Personnel Selection

There is only limited theory and empirical data suggesting that personnel selection actually improves business-unit effectiveness. Utility analysis is an attempt to estimate a cross-level relationship between individual level staffing and unit effectiveness, but it is only an estimate and is often based on questionable assumptions (Schneider et al., 2000). The search for more direct empirical evidence is discouraging. One of the most highly cited studies that is used to support the organizational-level impact of selection, Terpstra and Rozell (1993), surveyed managers and had them self-report *both* the type of selection practices they used and their opinion of their firm's effectiveness. Such common-source, common-method research would never be published today, but it remains an article highly cited as "proof" that selection matters. More compelling evidence is offered by scholars conducting research in the area of strategic human resource management (SHRM). These studies have found that business units using valid selection systems performed better than those that did not (Hatch & Dyer, 2004; Huselid, 1995; Koch & McGrath, 1996; MacDuffie, 1995). Manager self-reports are usually the way in which selection system variables are measured. These studies are helpful in that they show that use of selection practices contribute to unit effectiveness, but they are limited in that they rely on manager self-reports, and they do not actually show how selection relates to unit effectiveness (see Becker & Huselid, 2006, who discuss this issue more generally with HR).

Schneider et al. (2000) made the point that selection researchers need to start demonstrating how the selection of individuals contributes to better functioning organizations. Subsequent multilevel theory has provided direction for how to conceptualize and link individual- and business-unit level theory and research on human capital and selection (Ployhart & Schneider, 2002, 2005). Ployhart (2004, 2006) proposed a multilevel model of selection that ties individual KSAOs to unit-level human capital and unit effectiveness. Figure 8.2 is adapted from Ployhart and Weekley (2010) and provides a simple overview of this model. First, notice that the business unit's strategy influences the types of selection practices used (there is more on strategy in the next section; see also Snow and Snell, chapter 30 of this handbook). The types of selection practices used (e.g., cognitive ability tests, interviews) will impact the types of KSAOs acquired and retained. Systematic selection on job-related KSAOs contributes to the formation of unit-level human capital constructs; this process is known as *human capital emergence*. When unit-level human capital is related to unit effectiveness (because it is consistent with the firm's strategic direction), human capital contributes to sustained competitive advantage and hence offers *human capital advantage*. Notice that this approach is quite different from the usual selection approach that is contained entirely within the individual level of analysis (see Ployhart, 2004; 2006).

There is some empirical research that supports key relationships in Figure 8.2. First, research finds that KSAOs are in fact nested within business units and hence emerge to form unit-level human capital (Ployhart, Weekley, & Baughman, 2006; Schaubroeck, Ganster, & Jones, 1998; Schneider,

Smith, Taylor, & Fleenor, 1998). Second, research has found evidence for human capital advantage. Van Iddekinge et al. (2009) found that units that had a greater percentage of employees who passed a validated selection test had greater customer service performance, retention, and financial success. Ployhart, Weekley, and Ramsey (2009) found that individual differences in service orientation not only created unit-level service orientation (human capital), but that this human capital also had a positive effect on the unit's financial effectiveness. While this unit-level relationship helps to support the *unit-level financial impact* of personnel selection, it also highlighted some important differences between micro and macro human capital. In particular, the relationship at the unit level was nonlinear over time and heterogeneous across units, suggesting that the stable relationships found at the individual level may not be so stable at the unit level. DeNisi, Hitt, and Jackson (2003) asked, "...if hiring 'better' people results in higher productivity, how exactly does the selection of individuals translate into improved organizational performance?" (p. 12). One answer is through human capital emergence and human capital advantage (see Figure 8.2).

Future research needs to expand our understanding of how selection on individual differences contributes to better functioning organizations. We need to move beyond the individual level and utility analysis to understand how selection impacts higher level criteria. The field of SHRM has grown rapidly and arguably had an important impact because its key dependent variables are firm or business unit-level outcomes that organizational decision makers care about (Gerhart, 2005). As an applied science, selection researchers and practitioners should care about them too.

Mission #2: Match Selection to the Firm's Strategy

The field of strategic management focuses on explaining between-firm differences in effectiveness (see Snow and Snell, chapter 30 of this handbook, for considerably more detail about strategic human resource management). It addresses the very lofty goal of how to compete against other firms. Given that personnel selection should contribute to this lofty goal, one would hope that there is some consideration of selection as a part of a firm's strategy. Yet there is almost no reference to the strategic management literature in selection scholarship, with the possible exception of SHRM scholarship. The firm's strategy should drive most operational decisions,

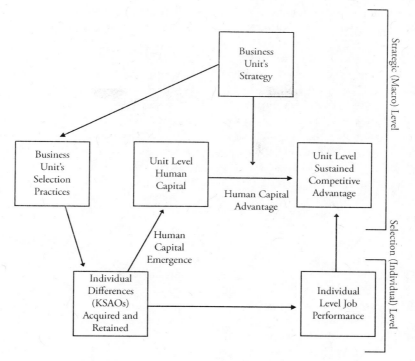

Figure 8.2 A Multilevel Framework for Personnel Selection (adapted from Ployhart & Weekley, 2010).

including choice of HR practices (Wright, Dunford, & Snell, 2001). To the extent that HR practices offer value to the firm's strategy, the practices are more likely to be implemented and supported. It therefore seems that researchers might seek to better connect the ties between firm strategy and selection.

Ployhart and Weekley (2010) discuss this issue in some detail, and Figure 8.2 highlights the link between strategy and selection on a superficial level. As the figure shows, the firm's strategy not only determines the nature of HR practices that will be used but also moderates the relationship between unit-level human capital and unit effectiveness. That is a critically important point because, unlike individual-level validity generalization research, at the unit level one would expect the effect of human capital on effectiveness to be context specific (Barney, 1991). For example, service orientation human capital may be critical for a firm whose competitive advantage is based on customer service (e.g., Neiman Marcus), but much less so for a firm whose competitive advantage is based on efficiency (e.g., Wal-Mart). Note that in both companies, a service orientation predictor would likely have similar levels of criterion-related validity for individual job performance. Thus, because organizational

decision makers seek to support the firm's strategy, research should examine how personnel selection can support strategy and reinforce strategy.

Mission #3: Demonstrate the Sustainability of Personnel Selection Processes and Practices

There are two ways in which one may conceptualize selection system sustainability. On the one hand, Kehoe et al. (2009) refer to sustainability as a selection system that is consistent with the firm's governance, strategy, culture, and stakeholder preferences. They note that, even though a selection system may have great sophistication and technical rigor, it may not be sustainable because it is not supported or is inconsistent with the firm's vision and mission. Consistent with this thinking, recent approaches have started to look at selection processes in a more integrated manner (Aguinis & Smith, 2007).

The other major way to view sustainability is from a competitive/economic perspective. Sustainable competitive advantage refers to a situation in which a firm generates above-average returns relative to competitors over a reasonable period of time (Armstrong & Shimizu, 2007). Sustainable competitive advantage clearly implies a longitudinal perspective, and that the resources that create the competitive advantage are not depleted to the point of being useless. Yet selection research is dominated by an emphasis on practices usually conducted cross-sectionally at the individual level. For example, Cascio and Aguinis (2008a) remind us that determinations of whether criterion-related validity is "significant" are often made to a comparison standard of zero validity (i.e., the correlation coefficient is zero). The standard is only that the selection system works better than random hiring; it says nothing about sustainability. As another example, a selection system that attracts and hires the most qualified candidates, who then leave the firm after a few weeks, is not a sustainable system. There may be validity for the predictors, but this by itself does not guarantee sustainability of the system.

A useful means for understanding sustainability is provided by the resource-based view of the firm (RBV; Barney, 1991; Peteraf, 1993). Simply described, the RBV posits that between-firm differences occur because of differences in the firm's resource endowments. Resources may include such forms of capital as physical, financial, and human. Firms differ in their effectiveness because there are between-firm differences in their resources, just as individuals perform differently because there are individual differences in their KSAOs. And as at the individual level, not all firm-level resources contribute to sustained competitive advantage. Resources must be valuable, rare, inimitable, and non-substitutable if they are to provide a basis for sustained competitive advantage. Valuable and rare resources may contribute to competitive advantage in the short term or parity with other competitors (Barney & Wright, 1998). However, to provide sustained competitive advantage, the resource cannot be easily copied by competitors (inimitable), and it cannot be substituted with other resources.

When viewed from the RBV, it becomes apparent that valid personnel selection will not always contribute to *sustained* competitive advantage (see Ployhart & Weekley, 2010). First, if the selection process is not consistently applied, human capital emergence cannot occur. Second, if the human capital is not consistent with the firm's strategy, human capital advantage will be lessened or nonexistent. Third, the value of human capital is context- and firm-specific (Barney, 1991). Here is, of course, where the importance of training is recognized. By converting the "raw materials" of cognitive ability and personality into specific forms of knowledge and skill, the context-specific KSAOs become important drivers of competitive advantage. Unfortunately, there is only limited research that links selection and training (for an exemplary article that conducts such an integration, see Van Iddekinge et al., 2009). Fourth, only human capital can provide the basis for sustainable competitive advantage (Barney & Wright, 1998). Selection practices like interviews or personality tests can be easily copied by competitors and hence cannot provide sustained competitive advantage. To become sustainable, a critical mass of human capital must be developed because it cannot be easily or quickly duplicated. Obviously, empirical research is needed to test these claims, and doing so will require selection researchers to expand their perspective to take a much more explicit consideration of context (Cascio & Aguinis, 2008a; Schneider et al., 2000). One critical change will be a shift from focusing on selection predictors to an understanding of the human capital that is created from these practices.

Mission #4: Show the Value of Selection on High-Impact Jobs to High-Impact Managers

Most empirical personnel selection research has focused on large-scale hiring of entry-level (or more generally, lower level) employees. These jobs are viewed as important, but not necessarily valuable or unique (Lepak & Snell, 1999). Instead, jobs that are valuable and unique are those that "drive the business." Key managerial roles, top management teams, and obviously line directors, presidents, and CEOs are illustrative of jobs that are both valuable and unique. These are considered "A" jobs and should require a different set of selection practices than lower level "B" or "C" jobs. For example, Lepak and Snell (1999) predict that those in jobs with high value and uniqueness should be developed internally, so HR practices should emphasize commitment to the firm and selection processes should focus on aptitude (e.g., basic ability and personality) instead of current knowledge and skill. Differences in HR configurations across employees differing in their value and uniqueness (Lepak & Snell, 2002) help support these predictions.

Future selection research should expand beyond the large-scale studies to also consider situations where there are fewer numbers of jobs, but the jobs are more important. For example, how does one best staff a top management team? Recent research has started to examine psychological variables and processes that may impact top management team effectiveness (Barrick, Bradley, Kristof-Brown, &

Colbert, 2007; Colbert, Kristof-Brown, Bradley, & Barrick, 2008). This work follows in the tradition of an "upper echelons" perspective (Hambrick & Mason, 1984) and provides a compelling means to unite micro and macro perspectives. For many key roles, there will likely be highly intensive selection processes based on relatively few candidates. In this situation, the literature on individual assessment is relevant (see an edited book by Jeanneret & Silzer, 1998).

Switching gears slightly, it is also important that selection research take a broader view of its stakeholders and understand the managers who make the final decisions on selection system processes and own their implementation (Highhouse, 2008). Much of the personnel selection literature reads as though the end "customer" of the research is either an I/O practitioner, HR specialist, or an applicant. In many, if not most, organizational contexts, I/O psychologists will be interacting directly with HR or line managers who may have little to no background in selection. Hence, we need to understand their beliefs, preferences, and constraints. Ployhart (2006) stated: "If organizational decision makers are perhaps the ultimate consumers of our science, how is it that we have little understanding of what our customers want, need, or are willing to use?" (p. 891). It is rare that validity would be the primary consideration for deciding whether to implement a selection system (at least in private industry); so validity must also be balanced against cost, potential for adverse impact, the firm's strategy, internal politics, and acceptability among those who must implement the system. Kehoe et al. (2009) provide a comprehensive treatment of these complex issues.

Mission #5: Connect to Private Industry

Selection as a profession is very applied in its orientation. That does not mean that selection research published in top journals is tightly connected to the current realities facing firms in private industry (Cascio & Aguinis, 2008b). First, there are many pressing issues facing private firms that have received scant attention from the scientific community. A good example is technology; firms struggle with understanding how to best implement web-based testing and selection, and yet there are few empirical studies and lots of fundamental questions that need answers (see Reynolds & Dickter, 2010; Tippins et al., 2006). Second, many research-based findings and best practices do not frequently consider whether they can be applied in private industry. For example, many selection best practices are so complex, detailed, time-consuming, or burdensome that they are likely to never be used as intended.

Note the emphasis on private firms. Much of the knowledge of selection practices has focused on, and been acquired from, civil service organizations (e.g., state police and firefighter departments). There is nothing wrong with this data, but it must be realized that civil service organizations and private firms differ from each other in many profound ways. For example, ensuring demographic representation may be part of a civil service organization's charter, but there is no such charter among private firms (Pyburn et al., 2008). Consequently, research and debates surrounding the appropriateness of banding have occurred (see Aguinis, 2004), but I have never seen or heard of an application of banding in private industry. This is not to say that we should abandon civil service firms or become slaves to the fickle fashion and frequent foolishness of private industry. Rather, it means that selection research must continue to conduct rigorous scientific research with a clear understanding of how the research applies to private firms *and* civil service firms. To illustrate this need, consider that many private firms struggle with talent issues surrounding globalization. There is some research that speaks to how selection practices may be affected by cultural differences (Myors et al., 2008; Ryan, McFarland, Baron, & Page, 1999), but there is little systematic research examining how global firms should attract, select, and retain talent from multiple cultures and countries. These are the issues that keep HR and line managers up at night, and as a science, selection is less relevant if it does not consider them.

Selection Is Dead: Long Live Selection!

The vision of personnel selection should be to *ensure sustainable organizational effectiveness through the acquisition of human capital*. Achieving this vision will require selection researchers and practitioners to build from nearly 100 years of research on the *acquisition of human capital* to also *ensure sustainable organizational effectiveness*. Doing so does nothing to devalue or abandon the rigorous and sophisticated scholarship that has been the tradition for the last century. On the contrary, doing so only increases the chances that professionally developed selection predictors and practices will be employed to achieve sustained competitive advantage.

Author Note

I thank Doug Hawks for his assistance in compiling the references and gathering articles.

References

Aguinis, H. (2004). *Test score banding in human resource selection: Legal, technical, and societal issues*. Westport, CT: Quorum Books.

Aguinis, H., & Smith, M. A. (2007). Understanding the impact of test validity and bias on selection errors and adverse impact in human resource selection. *Personnel Psychology, 60*, 165–199.

Anderson, N. R. (2005). Relationships between practice and research in personnel selection: Does the left hand know what the right is doing? In A. Evers, N. R. Anderson, & O. Smit-Voskuyl (Eds.), *The Blackwell handbook of personnel selection* (1–24). Oxford: Blackwell.

Armstrong, C. E., & Shimizu, K. (2007). A review of approaches to empirical research on the resource-based view of the firm. *Journal of Management, 33*, 959–986.

Arthur, W., Jr., Bell, S. T., Villado, A. J., & Doverspike, D. (2006). The use of person-organization fit in employment decision making: An assessment of its criterion-related validity. *Journal of Applied Psychology, 91*, 786–801.

Arthur, W., Jr., Day, E. A., McNelly, T. L., & Edens, P. S. (2003). A meta-analysis of the criterion-related validity of assessment center dimensions. *Personnel Psychology, 56*, 125–153.

Arthur, W., & Villado, A. J. (2008). The importance of distinguishing between constructs and methods when comparing predictors in personnel selection research and practice. *Journal of Applied Psychology, 93*, 435–442.

Axelrod, E. L., Handfield-Jones, H., & Welsh, T. A. (2001). War for talent, Part 2. *The McKinsey Quarterly, 2*, 9–12.

Barney, J. B. (1991). Firm resources and sustained competitive advantage. *Journal of Management, 17*, 99–120.

Barney, J. B., & Wright, P. W. (1998). On becoming a strategic partner: The role of human resources in gaining competitive advantage. *Human Resource Management, 37*, 31–46.

Barrick, M. R., Bradley, B. H., Kristof-Brown, A. L., & Colbert, A. E. (2007). The moderating role of top management team interdependence: Implications for real teams and working groups. *Academy of Management Journal, 50*, 544–557.

Barrick, M. R., & Mount, M. K. (1991). The Big Five personality dimensions and job performance: A meta-analysis. *Personnel Psychology, 44*, 1–26.

Barrick, M. R., & Ryan, A. M. (2003). *Personality and work: Reconsidering the role of personality in organizations*. San Francisco: Jossey-Bass.

Bauer, T. N., & Truxillo, D. M. (2006). Applicant reaction to situational judgment tests: Research and related practical issues. In J. A. Weekley & R. E. Ployhart (Eds.), *Situational judgment tests: Theory, measurement and application* (pp. 233–252). Mahwah, NJ: Erlbaum.

Becker, B. E., & Huselid, M. A. (2006). Strategic human resource management: Where do we go from here? *Journal of Management, 32*, 898–925.

Becker, G. S. (1964). *Human capital: A theoretical and empirical analysis with special reference to education*. New York: National Bureau of Economic Research.

Berry C., Gruys, M., & Sackett, P. R. (2006). Educational attainment as a proxy for cognitive ability in selection: Effects on levels of cognitive ability and adverse impact. *Journal of Applied Psychology, 91*, 696–705.

Binning, J. F., & Barrett, G. V. (1989). Validity of personnel decisions: A conceptual analysis of the inferential and evidential bases. *Journal of Applied Psychology, 74*, 478–494.

Bobko, P., Roth, P. L., & Potosky, D. (1999). Derivation and implications of a meta-analysis matrix incorporating cognitive ability, alternative predictors, and job performance. *Personnel Psychology, 52*, 561–589.

Boudreau, J. W., & Ramstad, P. M. (2003). Strategic industrial and organizational psychology and the role of utility analysis models. In W. C. Borman, D. R. Ilgen, & R. J. Klimoski (Eds.), *Handbook of psychology* (Vol. 12, pp. 193–224). Hoboken, NJ: Wiley.

Brannick, M. T., Levine, E. L., & Morgeson, F. P. (2007). *Job and work analysis: Methods, research, and applications for human resource management* (2nd ed.). Thousand Oaks, CA: Sage.

Cable, D. M., & DeRue, D. S. (2002). The convergent and discriminant validity of subjective fit perceptions. *Journal of Applied Psychology, 87*, 875–884.

Cable, D. M., & Parsons, C. K. (2001). Socialization tactics and person-organization fit. *Personnel Psychology, 54*, 1–24.

Campion, M. A., Palmer, D. K., & Campion, J. E. (1997). A review of structure in the selection interview. *Personnel Psychology, 50*, 655–702.

Carroll, J. B. (1993). *Human cognitive abilities*. New York: Cambridge University Press.

Cascio, W. F. (2000). Costing human resources: The financial impact of behavior in organizations. Cincinnati, OH: Southwestern.

Cascio, W. F., & Aguinis, H. (2008a). Staffing twenty-first-century organizations. *Academy of Management Annals, 2*, 133–165.

Cascio, W. F., & Aguinis, H. (2008b). Research in industrial and organizational psychology from 1963 to 2007: Changes, choices, and trends. *Journal of Applied Psychology, 93*, 1062–1081.

Chan, D., & Schmitt, N. (1997). Video-based versus paper-and-pencil method of assessment in situational judgment tests: Subgroup differences in test performance and face validity perceptions. *Journal of Applied Psychology, 82*, 143–159

Cleary, T. A. (1968). Test bias: Prediction of grades of Negro and white students in integrated colleges. *Journal of Educational Measurement, 5*, 115–124.

Clevenger, J., Pereira, G. M., Wiechmann, D., Schmitt, N., & Harvey, V. S. (2001). Incremental validity of situational judgment tests. *Journal of Applied Psychology, 86*, 410–417.

Colbert, A. E., Kristof-Brown, A. L., Bradley, B. H., & Barrick, M. R. (2008). CEO transformational leadership: The role of goal importance congruence in top management teams. *Academy of Management Journal, 51*, 51–96.

Cortina, J. M., Goldstein, N. B., Payne, S. C., Davison, H. K., & Gilliland, S. W. (2000). The incremental validity of interview scores over and above cognitive ability and conscientiousness scores. *Personnel Psychology, 53*, 325–351.

Dawis, R. V., & Lofquist, L. H. (1984). *A psychological theory of work adjustment*. Minneapolis: University of Minnesota Press.

DeShon, R. P. (2002). A generalizability theory perspective on measurement error corrections in validity generalization. In K. R. Murphy (Ed.), *Validity generalization: A critical review* (pp. 365–402). Mahwah, NJ: Erlbaum.

DeNisi, A. S., Hitt, M. A., & Jackson, S. E. (2003). The knowledge-based approach to sustainable competitive advantage. In S. E. Jackson, M. A. Hitt, & A. S. DeNisi (Eds.), *Managing knowledge for sustained competitive advantage* (pp. 3–33). San Francisco: Jossey-Bass.

Dierdorff, E. C., & Morgeson, F. P. (2007). Consensus in work role requirements: The influence of discrete occupational context on role expectations. *Journal of Applied Psychology, 92*, 1228–1241.

Dudley, N. M., Orvis, K. A., Lebiecki, J. A., & Cortina, J. M. (2006). A meta-analytic investigation of conscientiousness in the prediction of job performance: Examining the intercorrelations and the incremental validity of narrow traits. *Journal of Applied Psychology, 91,* 40–57.

Drasgow, F. (2003). Intelligence in the workplace. In W. C. Borman, D. R. Ilgen, & R. J. Klimoski (Eds.), *Handbook of psychology: Industrial and organizational psychology* (Vol. 12, pp. 107–130). Hoboken, NJ: Wiley.

Drucker, P. (1966). *The effective executive.* New York: Harper & Row.

Eder, R. W., & Harris, M. M. (Eds.). (1999). *The employment interview handbook.* Thousand Oaks, CA: Sage.

The Search for Talent, *The Economist.* (October 7, 2006). 381 (8498), 11.

Edwards, J. R. (2008). Person-environment fit in organizations: An assessment of theoretical progress. *The Academy of Management Annals, 2,* 167–260.

Ellingson, J. E., Sackett, P. R., & Connelly, B. S. (2007). Personality assessment across selection and development contexts: Insights into response distortion. *Journal of Applied Psychology, 92,* 386–395.

Fine, S. A., & Wiley, W. W. (1974). An introduction to functional job analysis. In F. A. Fleishman & A. R. Bass (Eds.), *Studies in personnel and industrial psychology* (3rd ed., pp. 6–13). Homewood, IL: Irwin.

Flanagan, J. C. (1954). The critical incident technique. *Psychological Bulletin, 51,* 327–355.

Foldes, H. J., Duehr, E. E., & Ones, D. S. (2008). Group differences in personality: Meta-analyses comparing five U.S. racial groups. *Personnel Psychology, 61,* 579–616.

Gatewood, R. D., & Feild, H. S. (1998). *Human resource selection.* Fort Worth, TX: The Dryden Press/Harcourt Brace.

Gerhart, B. (2005). Human resources and business performance: Findings, unanswered questions, and an alternative approach. *Management Revue, 16,* 174–185.

Ghiselli, E. E. (1966). *The validity of occupational aptitude tests.* New York: Wiley.

Goldstein, H. W., Yusko, K. P., Braverman, E. P., Smith, D. B., & Chung, B. (1998). The role of cognitive ability in the subgroup differences and incremental validity of assessment center exercises. *Personnel Psychology, 51,* 357–374.

Goldstein, H. W., Yusko, K. P., & Nicolopoulos, V. (2001). Exploring black-white subgroup differences of managerial competencies. *Personnel Psychology, 54,* 783–807.

Guion, R. M., & Gottier, R. F. (1965). Validity of personality measures in personnel selection. *Personnel Psychology, 18,* 49–65.

Hambrick, D. C., & Mason, P. A. (1984). Upper echelons: The organization as a reflection of its top managers. *Academy of Management Review, 9,* 193.

Harvey, R. J., & Wilson, M. A. (2000). Yes Virginia, there *is* an objective reality in job analysis. *Journal of Organizational Behavior, 21,* 829–854.

Hatch, N. W., & Dyer, J. H. (2004). Human capital and learning as a source of sustainable competitive advantage. *Strategic Management Journal, 25,* 1155–1178.

Hausknecht, J. P., Halpert, J. A., Di Paolo, N. T., & Moriarty Gerrard, M. O. (2007). Retesting in selection: A meta-analysis of coaching and practice effects for tests of cognitive ability. *Journal of Applied Psychology, 92,* 373–385.

Hausknecht, J. P., Trevor, C. O., & Farr, J. L. (2002). Retaking ability tests in a selection setting: Implications for practice effects, training performance, and turnover. *Journal of Applied Psychology, 87,* 243–254.

Heneman, H. G., & Judge, T. A. (2006). *Staffing organizations* (5th ed.). New York: Irwin/McGraw-Hill.

Highhouse, S. (2008). Stubborn reliance on intuition and subjectivity in employee selection. *Industrial and Organizational Psychology, 3,* 333–342.

Hogan, J. (1991). Physical abilities. In M. D. Dunnette & L. M. Hough (Eds.), *Handbook of industrial and organizational psychology* (2nd ed., Vol. 2, pp. 753–831). Palo Alto, CA: Consulting Psychologists Press.

Hogan, J., Barrett, P., & Hogan, R. (2007). Personality measurement, faking, and employment selection. *Journal of Applied Psychology, 92,* 1270–1285.

Holland, J. L. (1997). Making vocational choices: A theory of vocational personalities and work environments (3rd ed.). Odessa, FL: PAR

Hough, L. M. (1998). Personality at work: Issues and evidence. In M. Hakel (Ed.), *Beyond multiple choice: Evaluating alternatives to traditional testing for selection* (pp. 131–166). Mahwah, NJ: Erlbaum.

Hough, L. M., & Furnham, A. (2003). Use of personality variables in work settings. In W. C. Borman, D. R. Ilgen, & R. J. Klimoski (Eds.), *Handbook of psychology: Industrial and organizational psychology* (Vol. 12, pp. 131–169). Hoboken, NJ: Wiley.

Hough, L. M. & Oswald, F. L. (2008). Personality testing and industrial-organizational psychology: Reflections, progress, and prospects. *Industrial and Organizational Psychology, 3,* 272–290.

Hough, L. M., Oswald, F. L., & Ployhart, R. E. (2001). Determinants, detection, and amelioration of adverse impact in personnel selection procedures: Issues, evidence, and lessons learned. *International Journal of Selection and Assessment, 9,* 152–194.

Hough, L. M., & Schneider, R. J. (1996). Personality traits, taxonomies, and applications in organizations. In K. R. Murphy (Ed.), *Individual differences and behavior in organizations* (pp. 3–30). San Francisco: Jossey-Bass.

Huffcutt, A. I., Conway, J. M., Roth, P. L., & Stone, N. J. (2001). Identification and meta-analytic assessment of psychological constructs measured in employment interviews. *Journal of Applied Psychology, 86,* 897–913.

Huffcutt, A. I., Weekley, J. A., Wiesner, W. H., Degroot, T. G., & Jones, C. (2001). Comparison of situational and behavior description interview questions for higher-level positions. *Personnel Psychology, 54*(3), 619–644.

Hunter, J. E. (1983). A causal analysis of cognitive ability, job knowledge, job performance, and supervisory ratings. In F. Landy, S. Zedeck, & J. Cleveland (Eds.), *Performance measurement and theory* (pp. 257–266). Hillsdale, NJ: Erlbaum.

Hunter, J. E., & Hunter, R. F. (1984). Validity and utility of alternative predictors of job performance. *Psychological Bulletin, 96,* 72–95.

Hunter, J. E., Schmidt, F. L., & Le, H. (2006). Implications for direct and indirect range restriction for meta-analysis methods and findings. *Journal of Applied Psychology, 91,* 594–612.

Huselid, M. A. (1995). The impact of human resource management practices on turnover, productivity, and corporate financial performance. *Academy of Management Journal, 38,* 635–672.

Ilgen, D. R., & Hollenbeck, J. R. (1991). The structure of work: Job design and roles. In M. D. Dunnette & L. M. Hough

(Eds.), *Handbook of industrial and organizational psychology*, (Vol. 2, pp. 165–207). Palo Alto, CA: Consulting Psychologists Press.

James, L. R. (1998). Measurement of personality via conditional reasoning. *Organizational Research Methods, 1*, 131–163.

Jeanneret, R. P., & Silzer, R. (1998). *Individual assessment: Predicting behavior in organizational settings.* San Francisco: Jossey-Bass.

Johnson, J. W., & Oswald, F. L. (2010). Test administration and the use of test scores. In J. L. Farr & N. T. Tippins (Eds.), *Handbook of employee selection* (pp. 151–170). New York: Taylor & Francis.

Kanfer, R., & Ackerman, P. L. (2004). Aging, adult development, and work motivation. *Academy of Management Review, 29*, 440–458.

Kehoe, J., Mol S., & Anderson, N. R. (2010). Managing sustainable selection programs. In J. L. Farr & N. T. Tippins (Eds.). *Handbook of employee selection* (pp. 213–234). New York: Taylor & Francis.

Klimoski, R. J., & Brickner, M. (1987). Why do assessment centers work? The puzzle of assessment center validity. *Personnel Psychology, 40*, 243–260.

Koch, M. J., & McGrath, R. G. (1996). Improving labor productivity: Human resource management policies do matter. *Strategic Management Journal, 17*, 335–354.

Kristof-Brown, A. L., Zimmerman, R. D., & Johnson, E. C. (2005). Consequences of individuals' fit at work: A meta-analysis of person-job, person-organization, person-group, and person-supervisor fit. *Personnel Psychology, 58*, 281–342.

Lance, C. E. (2008). Why assessment centers do not work and the way they are supposed to. *Industrial and Organizational Psychology, 1*, 84–97.

Lance, C. E., Lambert, T. A., Gewin, A. G., Lievens, F., & Conway, J. M. (2004). Revised estimates of dimension and exercise variance components in assessment center postexercise dimension ratings. *Journal of Applied Psychology, 89*, 377–385.

Latham, G. P., & Whyte, G. (1994). The futility of utility analysis. *Personnel Psychology, 47*, 31–47.

Le, H., Oh, I., Shaffer, J., & Schmidt, F. (2007). Implications of methodological advances for the practice of personnel selection: How practitioners benefit from meta-analysis. *Academy of Management Perspectives, 21*, 6–15.

Lepak, D. P., & Snell, S. A. (1999). The human resource architecture: Toward a theory of human capital allocation and development. *Academy of Management Review, 24*, 31–48.

Lepak, D. P., & Snell, S. A. (2002). Examining the human resource architecture: The relationships among human capital, employment, and human resource configurations. *Journal of Management, 28*, 517–543.

Lievens, F. (2002). Trying to understand the different pieces of the construct validity puzzle of assessment centers: An examination of assessor and assessee effects. *Journal of Applied Psychology, 87*, 675–686.

Lievens, F., DeCorte, W., & Schollaert, E. (2008). A closer look at the frame-of-reference effect in personality scale scores and validity. *Journal of Applied Psychology, 93*, 268–279.

MacDuffie, J. P. (1995). Human-resource bundles and manufacturing performance: Organizational logic and flexible production systems in the world auto industry. *Industrial & Labor Relations Review, 48*, 197–221.

Mael, F. A. (1991). A conceptual rationale for the domain and attributes of biodata items. *Personnel Psychology, 44*, 763–792.

McDaniel, M. A., Hartman, N. S., Whetzel, D. L., & Grubb, W. L. (2007). Situational judgment tests, response instructions, and validity: A meta-analysis. *Personnel Psychology, 60*(1), 63–91.

McDaniel, M. A., Morgeson, F. P., Finnegan, E. B., Campion, M. A., & Braverman, E. P. (2001). Use of situational judgment tests to predict job performance: A clarification of the literature. *Journal of Applied Psychology, 86*(4), 730–740.

McDaniel, M. A., & Nguyen, N. T. (2001). Situational judgment tests: A review of practice and constructs assessed. *International Journal of Selection and Assessment, 9*(1–2), 103–113.

McFarland, L. A., Ryan, A. M., & Kriska, S. D. (2003). Impression management use and effectiveness across assessment methods. *Journal of Management, 29*, 641–661.

McNemar, Q. (1964). Lost: Our intelligence. Why? *American Psychologist, 19*, 871–882.

Messick, S. (1995). Validity of psychological assessment: Validation of inferences from persons' responses and performances as scientific inquiry into score meaning. *American Psychologist, 50*, 741–749.

Morgeson, F. P., & Campion, M. A. (1997). Social and cognitive sources of potential inaccuracy in job analysis. *Journal of Applied Psychology, 82*, 627–655.

Morgeson, F. P., Campion, M. A., Dipboye, R. L., Hollenbeck, J. R., Murphy, K., & Schmitt, N. (2007a). Reconsidering the use of personality tests in personnel selection contexts. *Personnel Psychology, 60*, 683–729.

Morgeson, F. P., Campion, M. A., Dipboye, R. L., Hollenbeck, J. R., Murphy, K., & Schmitt, N. (2007b). Are we getting fooled again? Coming to terms with limitations in the use of personality tests in personnel selection. *Personnel Psychology, 60*, 1029–1049.

Morgeson, F. P., Delaney-Klinger, K., Mayfield, M. S., Ferrara, P., & Campion, M. A. (2004). Self-presentation processes in job analysis: A field experiment investigating inflation in abilities, tasks, and competencies. *Journal of Applied Psychology, 89*, 674–686.

Motowidlo, S. J., Dunnette, M. D., & Carter, G. W. (1990). An alternative selection procedure: The low-fidelity simulation. *Journal of Applied Psychology, 75*, 649–647.

Murphy, K. R., & DeShon, R. P. (2000). Interrater correlations do not estimate the reliability of job performance ratings. *Personnel Psychology, 53*, 873–900.

Murphy, R. R. (2002). *Validity generalization: A critical review.* Mahwah, NJ: Erlbaum.

Myors, B., Lievens, F., et al. (2008). International perspectives on the legal environment for selection. *Industrial and Organizational Psychology: Perspectives on Science and Practice, 1*, 206–246.

Ones, D. S., & Viswesvaran, C. (1998). The effects of social desirability and faking on personality and integrity assessment for personnel selection. *Human Performance, 11*, 245–269.

Ones, D. S., Dilchert, S., Viswesvaran, C, & Judge, T. A. (2007). In support of personality assessment in organizational settings. *Personnel Psychology, 60*, 995–1027.

Ones, D. S., Viswesvaran, C., & Reiss, A. D. (1996). Role of social desirability in personality testing for personnel selection: The red herring. *Journal of Applied Psychology, 81*, 660–679.

Ostroff, C., & Judge, T. A. (2007). *Perspectives on organizational fit.* Mahwah, NJ: Erlbaum.

Peeters, H., & Lievens, F. (2005). Situational judgment tests and their predictiveness of college students' success: The influence of faking. *Educational and Psychological Measurement, 65,* 70–89.

Peteraf, M. A. (1993). The cornerstones of competitive advantage: A resource-based view. *Strategic Management Journal, 14,* 179–191.

Ployhart, R. E. (2004). Organizational staffing: A multilevel review, synthesis, and model. In J. J. Martocchio (Eds.), *Research in personnel and human resource management* (Vol. 23, pp. 121–176). Oxford: Elsevier.

Ployhart, R. E. (2006). Staffing in the 21st century: New challenges and strategic opportunities. *Journal of Management, 32,* 868–897.

Ployhart, R. E., & Holtz, B. C. (2008). The diversity-validity dilemma: Strategies for reducing racioethnic and sex subgroup differences and adverse impact in selection. *Personnel Psychology, 61,* 153–172.

Ployhart, R. E., & Schneider, B. (2002). A multilevel perspective on personnel selection: Implications for selection system design, assessment, and construct validation. In F. J. Dansereau & F. Yammarino (Eds.), *Research in multi-level issues,* Volume 1: *The many faces of multi-level issues* (pp. 95–140). Oxford: Elsevier.

Ployhart, R. E., & Schneider, B. (2005). Multilevel selection and prediction: Theories, methods, and models. In A. Evers, O. Smit-Voskuyl, & N. Anderson (Eds.), *Handbook of personnel selection* (pp. 495–516). Oxford: Blackwell.

Ployhart, R. E., Schneider, B., & Schmitt, N. (2006). *Staffing organizations: Contemporary practice and theory* (3rd ed.). Mahwah, NJ: Erlbaum.

Ployhart, R. E., & Weekley, J. A. (2010). Strategy, selection, and sustained competitive advantage. In J. Farr & N. Tippins (Eds.) *Handbook of employee selection.* Mahwah, NJ: Erlbaum.

Ployhart, R. E., Weekley, J. A., & Baughman, K. (2006). The structure and function of human capital emergence: A multilevel examination of the ASA model. *Academy of Management Journal, 49,* 661–677.

Ployhart, R. E., Weekley, J. A., & Ramsey, J. (2009). The consequences of human resource stocks and flows: A longitudinal examination of unit service orientation and unit effectiveness. *Academy of Management Journal.*

Posthuma, R. A., Morgeson, F. P., & Campion, M. A. (2002). Beyond employment interview validity: A comprehensive narrative review of recent research and trends over time. *Personnel Psychology, 55,* 1–81.

Pyburn, K., Ployhart, R. E., & Kravitz, D. A. (2008). The diversity-validity dilemma: Overview and legal context. *Personnel Psychology, 61,* 143–151.

Quiñones, M. A., Ford, J. K., & Teachout, M. S. (1995). The relationship between work experience and job performance: A conceptual and meta-analytic review. *Personnel Psychology, 48,* 887–910.

Ree, M. J., Earles, J. A., & Teachout, M. S. (1994). Predicting job performance: Not much more than g. *Journal of Applied Psychology, 79,* 518–524.

Reynolds, D. H., & Dickter, D. N. (2010). Technology and employee selection. In J. Farr & N. Tippins, (Eds.), *The handbook of employee selection* (2010). Mahwah, NJ: Erlbaum.

Roth, P. L., Bevier, C. A., Bobko, P., Switzer, F. S., III, & Tyler, P. (2001). Ethnic group differences in cognitive ability in employment and educational settings: A meta-analysis. *Personnel Psychology, 54,* 297–330.

Roth, P. L., Bobko, P., McFarland, L. A., & Buster, M. (2008). Work sample tests in personnel selection: A meta-analysis

of black-white differences in overall and exercise scores. *Personnel Psychology, 61,* 637–662.

Roth, P. L., Huffcutt, A. I., & Bobko, P. (2003). Ethnic group differences in measures of job performance: A new meta-analysis. *Journal of Applied Psychology, 88,* 694–706.

Russell, C. J. (1994). Generation procedures for biodata items: A point of departure. In G. S. Stokes, M. D. Mumford, & W. A. Owens (Eds.), *Biodata handbook: Theory, research, and use of biographical information in selection and performance prediction* (pp. 17–38). Palo Alto, CA: Consulting Psychologists Press.

Ryan, A. M., McFarland, L. A., Baron, H., & Page, R. (1999). An international look at selection practices: Nation and culture as explanations for variability in practice. *Personnel Psychology, 52,* 359–391.

Rynes, S. L., Brown, K. G., & Colbert, A. E. (2002). Seven misconceptions about human resource practices: Research findings versus practitioner beliefs. *Academy of Management Executive, 16,* 92–103.

Sackett, P. R., & Ellingson, J. E. (1997). The effects of forming multi-predictor composites on group differences and adverse impact. *Personnel Psychology, 50,* 707–721.

Sackett, P. R., Laczo, R. M., & Arvey, R. D. (2002). The effects of range restriction on estimates of criterion interrater reliability: Implications for validation research. *Personnel Psychology, 55,* 807–825.

Sackett, P. R., Lievens, F., Berry, C. M., & Landers, R. N. (2007). A cautionary note on the effects of range restriction on predictor intercorrelations. *Journal of Applied Psychology, 92,* 538–544.

Sackett, P. R., & Roth, L. (1996). Multi-stage selection strategies: A Monte Carlo investigation of effects on performance and minority hiring. *Personnel Psychology, 49,* 549–572.

Sackett, P. R., Schmitt, N., Ellingson, J. E., & Kabin, M. B. (2001). High-stakes testing in employment, credentialing, and higher education: Prospects in a post-affirmative action world. *American Psychologist, 56,* 302–318.

Sackett, P. R., & Wilk, S. L. (1994). Within-group norming and other forms of score adjustment in preemployment testing. *American Psychologist, 49,* 929–954.

Sackett, P. R., & Yang, H. (2000). Correction for range restriction: An expanded typology. *Journal of Applied Psychology, 85,* 112–118.

Schaubroeck, J., Ganster, D. C., & Jones, J. R. (1998). Organization and occupation influences in the attraction-selection-attrition process. *Journal of Applied Psychology, 83,* 869–891.

Schmidt, F. L. (1988). The problem of group differences in ability test scores in employment selection. *Journal of Vocational Behavior, 33,* 272–292.

Schmidt, F. L., & Hunter, J. E. (1996). Measurement error in psychological research: Lessons from 26 research scenarios. *Psychological Methods, 1,* 199–223.

Schmidt, F. L., & Hunter, J. E. (1998). The validity and utility of selection methods in personnel psychology: Practical and theoretical implications of 85 years of research findings. *Psychological Bulletin, 124,* 262–274.

Schmidt, F. L., Hunter, J. E., McKenzie, R., & Muldrow, T. (1979). Impact of valid selection procedures on workforce productivity. *Journal of Applied Psychology, 64,* 609–626.

Schmidt, F. L., Le, H., & Ilies, R. (2003). Beyond alpha: An empirical examination of the effects of different sources of measurement error on reliability estimates for measures of individual-differences constructs. *Psychological Methods, 8,* 206–224.

Schmidt, F., Le, H., Oh, I., & Shaffer, J. (2007). General mental ability, job performance, and red herrings: Responses to Osterman, Hauser, and Schmitt. *Academy of Management Perspectives, 21,* 64–76.

Schmidt, F. L., Oh, I. S., & Le, H. (2006). Increasing the accuracy of corrections for range restriction: Implications for selection procedure validities and other research results. *Personnel Psychology, 59,* 281–305.

Schmidt, F. L., Viswesvaran, C., & Ones, D. S. (2000). Reliability is not validity and validity is not reliability. *Personnel Psychology, 53,* 901–912.

Schmidt, F. L., & Zimmerman, R. D. (2004). A counterintuitive hypothesis about employment interview validity and some supporting evidence. *Journal of Applied Psychology, 89*(3), 553–561.

Schmitt, N. (2004). Beyond the Big Five: Increases in understanding and practical utility. *Human Performance, 17,* 347–357.

Schmitt, N. (2007). The value of personnel selection: Reflections on some remarkable claims. *Academy of Management Perspectives, 21,* 19–23.

Schmitt, N., & Chan, D. (2006). Situational judgment tests: Method or construct? In J. A. Weekley & R. E. Ployhart (Eds.), *Situational judgment tests: Theory, measurement, and application* (pp. 135–155). Mahwah, NJ: Erlbaum.

Schmitt, N., Cortina, J. M., Ingerick, M. J., & Wiechmann, D. (2003). Personnel selection and employee performance. In W. C. Borman, D. R. Ilgen, & R. J. Klimoski (Eds.), *Handbook of psychology,* Volume 12: *Industrial and organizational psychology* (pp. 77–105). Hoboken, NJ: Wiley.

Schmitt, N., Oswald, F. L., Kim, B. H., Gillespie, M. A., Ramsay, L. J., & Yoo, T. Y. (2003). Impact of elaboration on socially desirable responding and the validity of biodata measures. *Journal of Applied Psychology, 88,* 979–988.

Schneider, B. (2007). Evolution of the study and practice of personality at work. *Human Resource Management, 46,* 583–610.

Schneider, B., & Smith, D. B. (2004). *Personality and organizations.* Mahwah, NJ: Erlbaum.

Schneider, B., Smith, D. B., & Sipe, W. P. (2000). Personnel selection psychology: Multilevel considerations. In K. J. Klein & S. W. J. Kozlowski (Eds.), *Multilevel theory, research, and methods in organizations: Foundations, extensions, and new directions* (pp. 91–120). San Francisco: Jossey-Bass.

Schneider, B., Smith, D. B., Taylor, S., & Fleenor, J. (1998). Personality and organizations: A test of the homogeneity of personality hypothesis. *Journal of Applied Psychology, 83,* 462–470.

Smith, D. B., & Robie, C. (2004). The implications of impression management for personality research in organizations. In B. Schneider & D. B. Smith (Eds.), *Personality and organizations* (pp. 111–138). Mahwah, NJ: Erlbaum.

Society for Industrial and Organizational Psychology, I. (2003). *Principles for the validation and use of personnel selection procedures* (4th ed.). Bowling Green, OH: Author.

Spearman, C. (1927). *The abilities of man.* New York: Macmillan.

Spychalski, A. C., Quiñones M. A., Gaugler, B. B., & Pohley, K. (1997). A survey of assessment center practices in organizations in the United States. *Personnel Psychology, 50,* 71–90.

Stokes, G. S., Mumford, M. D., & Owens, W. A. (Eds.). (1994). *Biodata handbook: Theory, research, and use of biographical information in selection and performance appraisal.* Palo Alto, CA: Consulting Psychologists Press.

Terpstra, D. E., & Rozell, E. J. (1993). The relationship of staffing practices to organizational level measures of performance. *Personnel Psychology, 46,* 27–48.

Tesluk, P. E., & Jacobs, R. R. (1998). Toward an integrative model of work experience. *Personnel Psychology, 51,* 321–355.

Tett, R. P., & Christiansen, N. D. (2007). Personality tests at the crossroads: A response to Morgeson, Campion, Dipboye, Hollenbeck, Murphy, and Schmitt. *Personnel Psychology, 60,* 967–993.

Tippins, N. T., Beaty, J., Drasgow, F., Gibson, W. M., Pearlman, K., Segall, D. O., & Shepherd, W. (2006). Unproctored internet testing in employment settings. *Personnel Psychology, 59,* 189–225.

Ulrich, L., & Trumbo, D. (1965). The selection interview since 1949. *Psychological Bulletin, 63,* 100–116.

Van Iddekinge, C. H., Ferris, G. R., Perrewe, P. L., Perryman, A. Z., Blass, F. R., & Heetderks, T. D. (2009). Effects of selection and training on unit-level performance over time: A latent growth modeling approach. *Journal of Applied Psychology, 94,* 829–843.

Van Iddekinge, C. H., & Ployhart, R. E. (2008). Developments in the criterion-related validation of selection procedures: A critical review and recommendations for practice. *Personnel Psychology, 61,* 871–925.

Van Iddekinge, C. H., Putka, D. J., Raymark, P. H., & Eidson, C. E., Jr. (2005). Modeling error variance in job specification ratings: The influence of rater, job, and organization-level factors. *Journal of Applied Psychology, 90,* 323–334.

Wallace, S. R. (1965). Criteria for what? *American Psychologist, 20,* 411–417.

Weekley, J. A., & Ployhart, R. E. (Eds.). (2006). *Situational judgment tests: Theory, measurement and application.* Mahwah, NJ: Erlbaum.

Wernimont, P. R., & Campbell, J. P. (1968). Signs, samples, and criteria. *Journal of Applied Psychology, 52,* 372–376.

Woehr, D. J., & Arthur, W., Jr. (2003). The construct-related validity of assessment center ratings: A review and meta-analysis of the role of methodological factors. *Journal of Management, 29,* 231–258.

Wright, P. M., Dunford, B. D., & Snell, S. A. (2001). Human resources and the resource based view of the firm. *Journal of Management, 27,* 701–721.

Work Design: Creating Jobs and Roles That Promote Individual Effectiveness

John Cordery *and* Sharon K. Parker

Abstract

In this chapter, our objective is to review existing knowledge relating to the psychological impact of work design (task, job, and work role characteristics) on individuals, and to set a clear, specific agenda for future research. Our starting point is an analysis of emergent trends in the characteristic nature of tasks and work roles within major contemporary and developing forms of work and occupation. This is necessary, as recent decades have witnessed dramatic shifts in how work is typically organized and performed within most occupations and industries, reflecting broader societal, environmental, technological, and economic changes. Following this analysis, we review key historical perspectives on work design before presenting an integrative theoretical model for considering the effects of work design on people. The chapter then moves to a consideration of the primary psychological processes and states, linking three broad categories of work design characteristics (task-related, relational, and contextual characteristics) to individual effectiveness outcomes. Our concern here is to update and expand theory relating to the effects of work design, integrating major recent bodies of research and theory, such as those dealing with motivational states and goal striving, self-determination, regulatory focus, work engagement, and social identity. The chapter concludes with a comprehensive research agenda for the years to come.

Key Words: Job design, work design, effectiveness, organizational behavior, work roles, motivation, performance, well-being, work attitudes, work redesign

Introduction

"...if one wanted to crush and destroy a man entirely,...all one would have to do would be to make him do work that was completely and utterly devoid of usefulness and meaning."
(Dostoyevsky, 1985, p. 43)

"If you don't let people grow and develop and make more decisions, it's a waste of human life—a waste of human potential. If you don't use your knowledge and skill, it's a waste of life."
(process worker, quoted in Zuboff, 1989, p. 414)

Work is the activity that occupies most of the waking lives of billions of people around the world,

providing the means to many significant material, social, and psychological ends. It has been described as "a search for daily meaning as well as daily bread, for recognition as well as cash, for astonishment rather than torpor, in short for a sort of life rather than a Monday to Friday sort of dying. Perhaps immortality too is part of the quest" (Terkel, 1972, p. xi). On a social level, the collective act of working is what creates and sustains whole communities, and shapes cultures; it is hardly surprising that statistics on the availability of employment are one of the universal yardsticks by which we assess the viability of individuals and societies.

Activities engaged in at work thus exert a powerful influence on how people think, feel, behave, and relate to one another—both in the moment of their enactment and beyond. For some, work activities are a source of positive, energizing, and fulfilling experiences:

> "The project I'm working on includes the restoration of a historical building, reconstruction of a demolished historic room, and an addition of a new building to an old one. That's a lot of complexity, and difficult as far as projects go. It's also the one that gets me excited about coming into the office." (architectural draftsperson, quoted in Kahn, 1990, p. 704)

> "I tried everything that I knew to do... in order to compound the resin and nothing worked. Then I tried something that had not been done before, to my knowledge, and it is working wonderfully at this moment. Ain't science wonderful?.|.|. God, I love it when a plan comes together." (chemical company employee, quoted in Amabile, Barsade, Mueller, & Staw, 2005, p. 387)

For others, the work they do is experienced as negative, enervating, and stressful:

> "I suffer from mental fatigue; your brain gets overloaded. Although taking enquiries is not necessarily a difficult job, it is when you get all these culminating factors coming through, mostly the repetitiveness, call after call, and you get annoyed about something and you just think 'no'!... As a home insurance advisor I use the same script, so you do the same thing every day, repeating the same things, asking the same questions, getting the same answers back." (call center operator, quoted in Taylor & Bain, 1999, p, 109)

> "...he coughed and was irritated by the tube (the interviewee was extubating a 10-year-old boy after incision of a peritonsillar abscess)...I misjudged the situation, I thought he was in a lighter state...so I extubated him. And the airway was completely obstructed. He developed laryngospasm; I had pulled the tube out at the wrong moment. It was impossible to ventilate. His pulse rate increased and so did mine. His pulse rate slowed down, mine went on increasing. Then I felt as if someone was sitting on my back with claws penetrating my skin, I was losing control...and finally, in this darkness of blood and cyanosis, I managed to get a tube down...it was awful, it was traumatic...." (anesthetist, cited in Larson, Rosenquist, & Holmström, 2007)

After a rather lean period of research and theorizing, at the end of which some commentators suggested that we probably now knew all we needed to know about the topic (Ambrose & Kulik, 1999), interest in psychological aspects of work design has revived considerably in recent times (Fried, Levi, & Laurence, 2008; Grant, Fried, & Juillerat, 2011; Humphrey, Nahrgang, & Morgeson, 2007; Morgeson & Campion, 2003; Morgeson & Humphrey, 2008; Parker & Ohly, 2008; Parker, Wall, & Cordery, 2001). The reasons for this resurgence lie in the fact that the landscape of work, jobs and roles has undergone dramatic change over recent decades.

Several key features have come to characterize this dynamic landscape (Morgeson & Humphrey, 2008; National Academy of Sciences, 1999). In the first place, rapid advances in digital technology continue to result in the emergence of entirely new forms and patterns of work (and the disappearance of others), transforming the characteristic content of tasks, jobs, and roles performed by workers in all industries. Many people now work in production and service environments, where performance is almost entirely mediated via digital technology, as in call centers and virtual teams (Holman, 2005; Kirkman, Gibson, & Kim, chapter 25 of this handbook; Majchrzak, Malhotra, Stamps, & Lipnack, 2004). Across all industries, the types of tasks and activities that make up jobs and occupations continue to evolve as a function of technological advances. In industries traditionally characterized by manual and mechanical forms of work, for example, simple manual, mechanical tasks are continually supplanted by more cognitively complex activities, incorporating analytical, problem-solving, and decision-making tasks. This in turn has blurred traditional distinctions between managerial and non-managerial work. In addition, digital technologies have also enabled work activities to transcend barriers of time and location, and have further eroded the boundaries between work and non-work activity (Ashforth, Kreiner, & Fugate, 2000; Bailey & Kurland, 2002; Olson-Buchanan & Boswell, 2006).

Second, increasing global competition has also affected transformations in the type of work that people perform. Many forms of low- and semi-skilled manufacturing and services work continue to be relocated to developing economies in order to reduce labor costs. Nearly three-quarters of the world's 3 billion workers are now located in developing economies (Ghose, Majid, & Ernst, 2008). In the United Kingdom and in the United States, for example, more than 75% of the civilian labor force is now employed in the services sector, while this sector employs only 50% of all workers in

China and the Philippines and less than one-third in countries in South Asia and Sub-Saharan Africa (International Labour Organization, 2008). The shift toward service and knowledge work within developed economies has meant that, among other things, interpersonal interactions have become an increasing part of jobs and work roles, reflecting increasing teamwork and customer interactions. Within developed economies in particular, competitive pressures have also encouraged firms to energetically pursue goals of greater efficiencies in the use of physical, human, and financial resources, through technological automation, work redesign, and organizational restructuring. Organizational restructuring (interacting with the changes to demographics, markets, and technologies) has resulted in leaner, flatter organizations, has increased the use of teams and other collaborative structures (e.g., organizational communities of practice; Wenger, McDermott, & Snyder, 2002), and has changed the nature and flexibility of employment contracts, such as through portfolio work (Cohen & Mallon, 1999; Fraser & Gold, 2001) and individually negotiated employment arrangements (i-deals; Rousseau, 2005; Rousseau, Hornung, & Kim, 2009).

Third—and often omitted in discussions of work design—there have been noticeable changes in the demographic characteristics of the workforce within many industries and national economies. Generational changes in workforce characteristics are leading people to question traditional notions of what makes workers thrive in work contexts and are requiring commensurate shifts in how work is structured and organized (Cartwright & Holmes, 2006; Egri, 2004; Hewlett, Sherbin, & Sumberg, 2009). Commentators have noted that workplaces these days are likely to be more diverse with respect to the experience and backgrounds of people performing the work, and that:

> [j]obs are shaped by the interactive effect of (1) managerial and engineering choices with respect to work design and technology and (2) the knowledge, skills, abilities and outlooks that individuals bring to the job. The increased variation in demographics that we are witnessing within any one occupation suggests the prospect of broader variation in job content. (National Academy of Sciences, 1999, p. 266)

Changes to the nature of work brought about by these three sets of forces over recent decades have raised concerns regarding how work and jobs impact on people, highlighting gaps in our understanding of such effects, and requiring academics and practitioners to investigate novel approaches to the design of work. In this context, fresh theorizing about the psychological salience of work-related activities has begun to emerge, and it is this that is the focus of this review.

Job, Role, and Work Design

Historically, the term *job design* within industrial and organizational (I/O) psychology has been used to denote research and practice relating to the content, structure, and organization of tasks and activities that are performed by an individual on a day-to-day basis in order to generate work products (Brannick, Levine, & Morgeson, 2007; Grant et al., 2011; Morgeson & Humphrey, 2008). As the field has developed, however, it has broadened its focus to incorporate the design of both jobs *and* associated roles, the latter being sets of recurrent behaviors expected of a person occupying a particular position (Polzer, 2005). As Morgeson & Humphrey (2008) point out, this expanded focus on both job and role design has become necessary in order to adequately describe and assess the impact of the sorts of changes to technology, work, and patterns of working described earlier, and it offers at least three advantages. First, it recognizes that the characteristic content and pattern of work, as it affects workers, emerges not solely from the immediate somewhat-fixed demands of the task environment, but also from the dynamic physical, social, and organizational context within which work is performed. For example, a worker may experience variety in his or her work that arises both as a consequence of the discrete activities that he or she has to perform while creating or transforming work products on a day-to-day basis; but he or she may also experience variety by virtue of normative position rotation practices or as a consequence of positional interdependencies that exist within the team to which she or he belongs. Second, it acknowledges the fact that most jobs can be seen as comprising both prescribed and predetermined tasks and activities, typically those things that need to be done in order to create or transform work products, and discretionary and/or emergent components (Ilgen & Hollenbeck, 1991). Incorporating the notion of role injects a flexible, dynamic element, such that the design of work can be seen as something that emerges and evolves over time and which may result in situation- or individual-specific outcomes. Finally, it recognizes that, in most work settings, matching a person to a job is a decision that involves considering not just his or her capacity to perform particular tasks, but also to occupy particular roles.

Thus, for the purposes of this review, we adopt *work design* as an overarching term to describe the content, structure, and organization of tasks, activities, and roles that are performed by individuals and groups in work settings. In the next section, we explore the historical development of work design theory and practices as they impact on individual functioning in work settings.

Historical Perspectives on Work Design and Individual Effectiveness

In pre-industrialized societies, work activity was typically indistinguishable, in terms of its timing and location, from the ordinary everyday activities of individuals and communities (Barley & Kunda, 2001). Following the Industrial Revolution, however, work became increasingly carried out as a separate, more distal, production activity—performed at fixed times during the week, in designated locations such as factories and offices, and under the direction of people who were socially disconnected from the worker. As this occurred, so principles for the effective organization of these segregated work activities began to be developed. Among the earliest work design principle to find favor was that of the "division of labor," referring to the process of dividing a complex work process into sets of simpler subtasks and requiring individual workers to specialize in the performance of one of those sets of activities. The eighteenth-century economist Adam Smith was one of the first to describe the potential productivity advantages associated with the division of labor, though he also acknowledged that the high level of repetition that this might involve could have deleterious psychological effects on workers:

> The man whose whole life is spent in performing a few simple operations, of which the effects are perhaps always the same, or very nearly the same, has no occasion to exert his understanding or to exercise his invention in finding out expedients for removing difficulties which never occur. He naturally loses, therefore, the habit of such exertion, and generally becomes as stupid and ignorant as it is possible for a human creature to become. The torpor of his mind renders him not only incapable of relishing or bearing a part in any rational conversation, but of conceiving any generous, noble, or tender sentiment, and consequently of forming any just judgment concerning many even of the ordinary duties of private life.
> (Smith, 1776)

In the early part of the twentieth century, industrial engineers such as Frank Gilbreth and Frederick Taylor (Gilbreth, 1911; Locke, 1982; Taylor, 1911) gave further impetus to the development of what was fast becoming the dominant paradigm for work design in industrial settings—job specialization and simplification. In a treatise entitled "The Principles of Scientific Management," Taylor (1911) argued the benefits of further job specialization, into those involving the execution of simple, specialized physical tasks (to be performed by workers) and those involving more complex "scientific" tasks, such as planning, scheduling, and the exercise of initiative (to be carried out by professional managers).

> Thus all of the planning which under the old system was done by the workman, as a result of his personal experience, must of necessity under the new system be done by the management in accordance with the laws of the science. (Taylor, 1947; quoted in Vroom and Deci, 1970, pp. 297, 300)

The overwhelming efficiency benefits to be derived from designing work as sets of highly specialized, simplified, and standardized tasks and activities have proven to be such that this approach to work design remains a dominant approach to this day, both in manufacturing and service settings (Campion, Mumford, Morgeson, & Nahrgang, 2005; Cordery & Parker, 2007; Morgeson & Campion, 2002). The benefits derived from this approach arise from factors such as the reduced time spent switching between tasks, increased potential for automation of subtasks, greater ease in selecting and training employees, the development of concentrated expertise, and increased quantity of output.

When Taylor's "scientific management" approach to work design was first introduced in the Midvale Steel plant in the late 1880s, however, it was notable that workers reportedly resorted to sabotaging the operation of their machines in an attempt to reduce the strain that the new system was placing them under—until they were fined heavily for doing so (Taylor, 1911). Subsequently, evidence slowly began to accumulate of heightened mental and physical fatigue, boredom, dissatisfaction, and absenteeism arising in a range of industrial settings where work was designed in this manner (Fraser, 1947; Walker & Guest, 1952). Researchers also observed that these attitudes and behaviors were not solely influenced by the design of the tasks per se, but also seemed to be powerfully affected by the opportunity for, and nature of, social interactions embedded in different work designs (Mayo, 1949; Roethlisberger & Dickson, 1939).

Man's desire to be continuously associated in work with his fellows is a strong, if not the strongest, human characteristic. Any disregard of it by management or any ill-advised attempt to defeat this human impulse leads instantly to some form of defeat for management itself. (Mayo, 1949, p. 99)

Reflecting growing concerns regarding the human impact of traditional mechanistic work designs, the latter half of the twentieth century saw the development of several influential streams of theorizing in respect of the social and psychological consequences of work design. The first of these developed from the work of human relations researchers based at the Tavistock Institute in the United Kingdom, and has come to be known as socio-technical systems theory (STS; Pasmore, 1988). STS developed as a set of broad principles for designing effective organizations (e.g., Cherns, 1976; Clegg, 2000), where effectiveness is defined as the extent to which the functioning of both human and technological subsystems are mutually reinforcing—a process referred to as "joint optimization" (Trist, 1981). Early work by STS researchers demonstrated that technological systems whose operation required high levels of task specialization were frequently disruptive of important and necessary social relationships, both within and outside work, as well as denying workers the opportunity to engage in activities they found meaningful and satisfying (e.g., Rice, 1958; Trist & Bamforth, 1951). Importantly, they also demonstrated, though practical interventions, how industrial work might be effectively designed around groups or teams of workers in order to achieve balance between the socio-psychological needs of workers on the one hand, and requirements for effective and efficient operation of technology and equipment on the other.

The signature approach to work design pioneered by STS researchers involved the use of autonomous work groups to control and execute work tasks. Sometimes called semi-autonomous work groups (and, more recently, self-managing work teams), these were work groups whose task boundary encompasses the production of a relatively whole unit of work, and whose members are able to exercise considerable collective discretion with respect to how and when tasks are performed. This approach to work design differed from the dominant "mechanistic" paradigm in several key ways. First, though it still allowed for a degree of individual job specialization, it also afforded members the possibility of learning a range of related jobs within the group and rotating between them (thereby avoiding some of the problems associated with boredom and repetition under more traditional work designs). Second, it "de-specialized" some of the planning and decision-making tasks and roles that traditional "mechanistic" work designs assign to administrative and managerial personnel, reintegrating them into workers' jobs as a shared role responsibility, distributed across all members of the group. Autonomous work group members were thus provided with increased opportunities to participate directly in decisions that directly affected their work and themselves, an aspect lacking in traditional work designs. Third, the autonomous work group provided increased opportunities for social contract and interaction, both between members as they assumed responsibility for coordinating and controlling work activities within the group and also with people outside the boundaries of the group (e.g., suppliers, managers, members of other work units, and customers).

From a productivity point of view, autonomous work groups were seen as offsetting any losses in productive efficiency arising as a result of losses in job specialization and simplification by virtue of improved control over key variances (any significant deviation from the ideal operating state of a production system), through increased motivation and satisfaction, through the more flexible allocation of labor, as well as through workers (a) developing greater knowledge of overall system functioning, and (b) having the license to take rapid action in order to control key variances (Cordery, 1996). The empirical evidence on the effectiveness of autonomous work groups is equivocal, however. On the one hand, in many situations their introduction appears to redress many of the problems of low morale and negative work attitudes that arise within more traditional work designs (Cordery, Mueller, & Smith, 1991; Wall, Kemp, Jackson, & Clegg, 1986). However, they have also been found to be associated with higher rates of turnover and absenteeism and coercive, negative employee behaviors (Barker, 1993; Levy, 2001). This has led to suggestions that their effectiveness depends on the context in which they are introduced (Cordery, Morrison, Wright, & Wall, 2009; Pearce & Ravlin, 1987; Wright & Cordery, 1999), as well as the care with which they are designed and implemented (Kirkman & Rosen, 2000; Wageman, 1997).

A second major stream of work design research to develop in the latter half of the twentieth century was generated by researchers interested in what motivated individual employees at work. McGregor

(1960) argued that many of the ways in which work was organized were based on assumptions regarding human nature that were patently wrong. He called this set of assumptions "Theory X," which hold that people are inherently lazy, are primarily motivated by economic rewards, dislike expending effort, prefer to be told what to do, and will avoid responsibility at all costs. Rather, McGregor (1960) argued that most people have the potential to derive considerable satisfaction from working, and willingly exercise effort, self-control, and self-direction at work in pursuit of goals that matter to them. He termed this perspective "Theory Y," and suggested that it was dangerous to create work systems that did not provide workers with such opportunities:

> People, deprived of opportunities to satisfy at work the needs which are now important to them, behave exactly as we might predict—with indolence, passivity, unwillingness to accept responsibility, resistance to change, willingness to follow the demagogue, unreasonable demands for economic benefits. (McGregor, 1960, p. 42)

The motivator-hygiene theory developed by Herzberg & colleagues (Herzberg, 1968; Herzberg, Mausner, & Snyderman, 1959) was the first to make an explicit link between job design and employee motivation and satisfaction. This theory proposed that satisfaction at work is caused by the presence of "motivators," such as recognition, the work itself,

and responsibility, while dissatisfaction is caused by "hygiene factors" such as supervision, work conditions, salary, status, and job security. Herzberg (1968) argued that jobs could be "enriched" to produce higher levels of employee motivation and satisfaction by enhancing the motivational factors. Central to the notion of enrichment was the practice of vertical job loading (Herzberg, 1968); strategies for vertical job loading included: removing supervisory controls, increasing an individual's accountability for his or her own work, giving a person a complete, "natural" unit of work, granting increased freedom to employees in their jobs, providing regular performance reports directly to employees, adding new and more complex tasks, and assigning individuals to specialized "expert" tasks.

Though motivator-hygiene theory helped to identify the potential for work redesign to improve work motivation and satisfaction, as a work design theory it suffers from several limitations. First, it is not clear how some of the motivators (e.g., achievement, recognition) relate to measurable intrinsic properties of jobs and roles, and this makes it difficult to use the theory to guide the redesign of existing jobs. Second, the theory assumes, incorrectly, that all employees react similarly to motivators and to jobs that have been vertically loaded (Hackman & Oldham, 1976; Hulin, 1971). Empirically, subsequent research has provided disconfirming evidence for the two-factor theory (e.g., Wall & Stephenson,

Figure 9.1 The Job Characteristics Model of Motivation

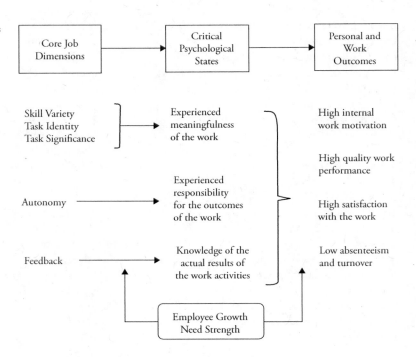

1970), showing that the distinction between motivational and hygiene factors was largely a methodological artifact.

The next step in the articulation of a "motivational" approach to work design is marked by the development of the Job Characteristics Model (JCM; Hackman & Lawler, 1971; Hackman & Oldham, 1975; Hackman & Oldham, 1976; Oldham & Hackman, 2005). Drawing on an earlier idea by Turner & Lawrence (1965), the JCM (see Figure 9.1) identified five "core" properties of individual work content (autonomy, skill variety, task identity, task significance, and feedback) as important for generating the following positive outcomes: internal work motivation, performance quality, work satisfaction (particularly satisfaction with opportunities for growth and development), low absenteeism, and low rates of turnover.

The mechanisms whereby these five job attributes engender positive outcomes within individuals were described in terms of three "critical psychological states." Autonomy, the degree to which an individual is able to choose how and when to carry out the work, engenders a sense of personal responsibility for outcomes of work. Skill variety was defined as the extent to which work entails a variety of actions that require the exercise of a number of different skills and abilities. Task significance is the extent to which the work activities performed by the individual have a substantial impact on the lives of others, while task identity refers to the degree to which the job entails completing a "whole" piece of work from start to finish. Collectively, these three job characteristics are held to contribute to the experience of psychological meaningfulness—the extent to which a person cares about the work in which they are engaged. Finally, feedback that arises directly from the performance of the work itself affects the extent to which a person experiences knowledge of results, or comprehension of how well he or she is performing the job. According to the JCM, carrying out work that engenders these three "critical psychological states" results in "positive affect" that rewards effort expenditure. This potentially creates a situation in which performance becomes its own reward, a virtuous "self-perpetuating cycle of positive work motivation powered by self-generated rewards, that is predicted to continue until one or more of the three psychological states is no longer present, or until the individual no longer values the internal rewards that derive from good performance" (Hackman & Oldham, 1976, p. 256).

Several other aspects of the JCM are worth noting. First, the model suggests that the core job characteristics have a combined effect on all the predicted outcomes. Hackman and Oldham (1975) developed the Job Diagnostic Survey to measure the key components of the model (including employee perceptions of job characteristics), and it was proposed (Hackman & Oldham, 1976) that the overall motivational potential of a job could be scored as the multiplicative product of autonomy, feedback, and the average of skill variety, task identity, and task significance (Autonomy x Feedback x [Skill variety + Task Identity + Task Significance]/3). Thus, while a job could theoretically continue to be motivating with a low score on one or other of the three "meaningfulness"-related dimensions, it could not do so if scores on either autonomy or feedback approached zero.

Second, the JCM accommodates the notion that the effects of work design (and redesign), at least as far as the core job dimensions contained in this model are concerned, will vary across individuals. The idea that some people are more suited to simple, routine, and non-responsible jobs, on grounds of ability, was argued at length by Taylor (1911). However, it has also frequently been argued that some people simply prefer this type of work (Hulin & Blood, 1968). The original JCM holds that the relationships between job characteristics, psychological states, and behavioral work outcomes will be stronger for individuals who are stronger in "growth need strength," a dispositional variable reflecting the strength of desire for the satisfaction of higher order needs, such as the need for achievement, accomplishment, and self-actualization (Hackman & Lawler, 1971; Warr, 2007). In later iterations, two further categories of moderator were added, namely: (a) knowledge, skills, and abilities, and (b) satisfaction with the work context (Oldham, Hackman, & Pearce, 1976).

The JCM offered a number of clear advantages to those seeking to understand (and redress) some of the psychological disadvantages associated with high levels of work specialization and simplification. First, it identified specific guidance for those who wish to redesign work to achieve improved motivational outcomes. Second, it was able to accommodate suggestions that enriched jobs are not for all. Finally, the core motivational premise of the model appeared to hold true. A number of meta-analyses have been conducted which support the view that core job characteristics generate favorable attitudinal and behavioral outcomes, mediated by at least some of the three critical psychological states (Fried, 1991; Humphrey et al., 2007; Johns, Xie, & Fang, 1992). The JCM has not been without its critics, however. In the main, these criticisms have been related to the quality of empirical research used in developing and testing the model (e.g., Grant et al., 2011; Parker & Wall, 1998; Roberts & Glick, 1981) and not the theory itself. However, the model has also been criticized for its narrow focus, in terms of the job characteristics identified, the mediating mechanisms, and the behavioral outcomes predicted (Parker & Wall, 1998).

One attempt to overcome aspects of the "breadth" criticism was the interdisciplinary perspective on work design developed by Campion and colleagues (Campion, 1988; Campion & McClelland, 1993; Campion et al., 2005; Campion & Thayer, 1985; Campion & Thayer, 1987). Campion and colleagues suggested that four different perspectives on work design (mechanistic, motivational, perceptual-motor, and biological) can be identified, both in practice and in the scholarly literature. What differentiated the perspectives was that each sought to achieve different outcomes. The four approaches are summarized in Table 9.1.

The interdisciplinary model suggests that pursuing one or other of these approaches to work design involves making trade-offs in terms of the benefits sought. For example, pursuing work simplification (mechanistic approach) achieves efficiency outcomes that are typically traded off against lower levels of worker motivation and satisfaction. The motivational approach can lead to high levels of motivation and job satisfaction, but can also involve higher training costs and higher levels of mental strain. Until relatively recently, it was assumed that the two most common work design approaches, mechanistic and motivational, were mutually exclusive. However, Morgeson and Campion (2002) were able to demonstrate that this is in fact not the case. Earlier, Wong and Campion (1991) had made the distinction between task-level characteristics and job-level characteristics (about which the JCM is ambivalent). Subsequently, Edwards, Scully, and Brtek (1999, 2000) had shown that each of the four approaches to job design is multidimensional, with mechanistic work designs being high on a work simplification dimension (related to efficiency) and low on a skill use dimension (related to satisfaction), and the reverse applying for motivational work designs. Morgeson and Campion (2002) demonstrated that it might be possible to avoid this inherent trade-off if these different work design approaches were applied to task clusters within a single job. For example, incorporating a range of similar task clusters within a single job can narrow the range of tasks performed by that individual, thereby improving efficiency, but it may also enable the development and exercise of greater depths of skill and expertise, and may also generate enhanced task identity and task significance. At the team level, a similar type of mutual compatibility can be observed when individuals

Table 9.1 The Interdisciplinary Approach to Work Design

Model	Disciplinary Foundations	Typical Approach	Typical Benefits	Possible Trade-offs
Mechanistic	Industrial engineering	Specialization and simplification.	Greater efficiency. Ease of staffing. Reduced training costs.	Lower motivation. Job dissatisfaction. Increased absence.
Motivational	Organizational Psychology	Job enrichment and empowerment	Enhanced motivation. Reduced turnover. Increased satisfaction. Reduced absence.	Increased training costs. Role overload. Increased errors. Higher stress.
Perceptual/Motor	Human factors Experimental Psychology	Match demands of job to cognitive capabilities	Fewer mistakes. Reduced fatigue. Lower accident rate. Less role overload.	Boredom. Job dissatisfaction.
Biological	Biomechanics Work Physiology	Minimising sources of physical strain and environmental stress	Better physical health. Less stress. Fewer injuries.	Cost of equipment. Lack of stimulation.

Adapted from Campion, Mumford, Morgeson, & Nahrgang (2005, p. 369)

specialize in some aspects of task performance, but share overall responsibility for others.

The interdisciplinary approach to work design has been influential in encouraging researchers and practitioners to consider that the design of work needs to achieve more than simply just motivation or just efficiency. Different aspects of work design can engage many different psychological processes and facilitate many different types of psychological outcomes. Importantly, it has highlighted the need to consider the cost-benefits associated with different work design approaches, and to explore ways in which the goals of several different work design paradigms can be achieved.

Recent Perspectives

Recent theoretical developments in work design have sought to extend and adapt the range of job/role characteristics considered in response to the changing nature of work and to recognize the role of contextual factors in work design. Regarding the former, it has long been argued that frameworks such as the JCM encompassed too narrow a range of job characteristics to be able to offer a meaningful analysis of emerging forms of work (Parker & Wall, 1998). Responding to this, Parker, Wall, and Cordery (2001) offered an elaborated work design framework, in which an expanded list of work characteristics (and their antecedents), mediating mechanisms, contingency variables, and outcomes was identified as a guide to frame future research. This framework can be distinguished from those specified by earlier theorists in several significant ways. First, it draws together disparate ideas regarding additional psychologically salient work characteristics, over and beyond the five specified within the JCM. These included factors such as cognitive and emotional demands, social contact, and opportunities for skill acquisition. Second, it recognizes that some work characteristics are experienced at the team, as opposed to individual, level. Third, it acknowledged the fact that work characteristics may interact (e.g., task interdependence and autonomy) in their psychological effects. Fourth, it identified four types of mediating mechanisms whereby work design can affect individual, group, and organizational outcomes: motivation, quick response, learning and development, and social interaction (discussed below). Finally, this model recognized research showing that work design can have effects beyond those identified in the JCM, affecting, for example, safety, innovation, and knowledge transfer.

The role of organizational factors in the emergence and maintenance of different forms of work design, such as those identified by Campion and colleagues, was addressed by Cordery and Parker (2007). Drawing on frameworks developed by Harvard-based researchers in the area of human resource management (e.g., Beer, Spector, Lawrence, Mills, & Walton, 1985; Walton, 1985) and earlier work highlighting the role of the organizational context in affecting work design (e.g., Oldham & Hackman, 1980), they proposed a systems approach to work design, where work characteristics are seen as embedded within an interacting system of work organization. They suggested that different work design configurations, or *archetypes,* emerge, and are sustained, as a result of the complex interplay between four organizational subsystems. These are the (1) content of the work (i.e., work characteristics), (2) technology, (3) people, and (4) leadership and management. They identified three common work design archetypes: mechanistic, motivational, and concertive. The latter has work designed around teams, rather than individuals, in order to best manage the variability associated with the technology, and is supported by practices such as coaching-oriented leadership, team-based pay, training in self-managing skills, shared feedback systems, and team-level work descriptions. The apparent popularity of concertive team-based work systems over recent decades has been well documented (Lawler, Mohrman, & Ledford, 1995; Staw & Epstein 2000).

This systems-oriented framework makes a number of contributions. First, it suggests how changes to work design come about. For example, the degree of autonomy that someone experiences in his or her job/role may be a function of the variations in the type of leadership practices that are exerted locally, as well as choices made by different types of people selected into that role. Second, it recognizes that much of the work in contemporary organizations is designed around collectives or teams. Third, it helps explain why work redesign is such a difficult proposition, since attempts to alter the parameters of one element of the system inevitably are constrained by the other elements. Fourth, it recognizes the role played by broader economic and social context in determining the sorts of choices that are made regarding work design. For example, the choice of a mechanistic over a motivational approach to work design may be made based on strategic goals being pursued by the firm. Finally, this perspective provides an important link into the strategic human resource management and high-performance work systems literatures, which tend to consider groups of interrelated factors as important for generating outcomes, rather than focusing on one system (work design) alone (Snow & Snell, chapter 30 of this handbook).

Following this, Morgeson & colleagues have recently provided an empirically based formulation of an expanded work design theory. They began by developing an instrument, the Work Design Questionnaire, to measure an expanded list of work design characteristics (Morgeson & Humphrey, 2006) and to address some of the psychometric deficiencies of the MJDQ (see Edwards et al., 1999). Using the classification developed by Morgeson and Campion (2003), they classified work design characteristics as being motivational, social, or contextual, and developed items to measure key facets of each. Humphrey et al. (2007) further validated this expanded three-category framework using meta-analysis. Interestingly, they found that the inclusion of these additional work design features increased the prediction of a range of outcomes. So, while motivational work design characteristics were strongly predictive of performance, job satisfaction, and organizational commitment, including social and work context characteristics increased both the range and extent of prediction. However, though the expanded range of work design features is useful, the model only specifies the three critical psychological states from the JCM and is silent with respect to mediating processes/states for social and work context characteristics. The theoretical extension also does not address the issue of moderators.

Seeking to address the failure of theories of work design to come to terms with the shift from manufacturing to service work in developed economies, Grant (2007) argued that existing models of work design had neglected the role of the social environment in shaping motivational properties of work. He developed the Job Impact Framework, which proposes that the "relational" architecture of a job has the potential to generate valuable motivational, cognitive, and behavioral outcomes. The two relational work characteristics he identified are: (a) impact on beneficiaries (conceptually similar to task significance), and (b) contact with beneficiaries. Grant (2007) proposes that these two work design characteristics influence a person's motivation to make a pro-social difference—"the desire to positively affect the beneficiaries of one's work" (p. 3)—and that this can lead to an increase in motivated performance, especially helping behaviors, as well as affecting a person's sense of identity (sense of competence, self-determination and social worth). Empirical support for expanding the range of work design theory to include these two relational work design characteristics exists in the form of a series of recent studies conducted by Grant and colleagues (Grant, 2008a, 2008b; Grant et al., 2007), and in the results of an earlier study by Parker and Axtell (2001) in which contact with beneficiaries was demonstrated to improve perspective-taking among job incumbents. A useful recent summary of evidence relating to relational inputs to work design is provided in Grant and Parker (2009).

In the next section, we seek to summarize all of these disparate theoretical frameworks regarding the impact of work design on individual effectiveness within jobs and roles. We do so with the assistance of an overarching heuristic framework that describes key categories of work design inputs, mediating psychological processes, and moderating variables that relate to an individual's effectiveness within his job and/or role.

An Overarching Framework for Work Design

In Figure 9.2 we provide a model that serves as a heuristic to summarize the relationships that are of primary concern within contemporary work design theory (for other similar integrative approaches, see

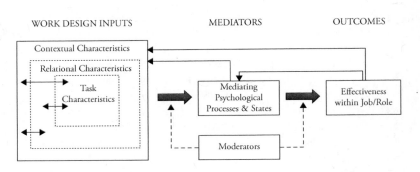

Figure 9.2 A Framework for Considering the Impact of Work Design on Individual Job/Role Effectiveness

Grant et al., 2011; Morgeson & Humphrey, 2008; and Parker & Ohly, 2008). The model seeks to summarize work design inputs arising from tasks and relational and contextual aspects of work that influence individual effectiveness within a given job or role. It is important to note that our work design framework is specified at the individual level, as opposed to the group or organizational level. In other words, we are concerned about describing how an individual's experience of working (which may be in a team context) influences her behavior, attitudes, cognitions, and well-being. We do this in order to distinguish it from models of work group effectiveness (e.g., Mathieu, Maynard, Rapp, & Gilson, 2008), and from models of human resource management that are specified at the organizational level (e.g., Beer et al., 1985; Pfeffer, 1994; Youndt, Snell, Dean, & Lepak, 1996), and also to avoid the conceptual difficulties that inevitably arise when seeking to describe group- and organizational-level outcomes in terms of individual-level processes (Kozlowski & Klein, 2000).

Individual Effectiveness

As indicated above, we are concerned with work design outputs at the individual level, as they relate to the effectiveness of the individual employee within jobs and roles. Thus, we do not consider more distal organizational outcomes such as organizational or team performance (cf. Morgeson & Humphrey, 2008). This is not because these relationships do not exist, but rather, because we see them as either second-order outcomes that flow from work design's impact on the capacity of individuals to be effective in work settings, or as outcomes of processes that arise at either the level of the work unit or the organization. The categorization of individual job/role effectiveness outcomes that we use is derived from Humphrey et al.'s (2007) meta-analytic study and classifies potential work design outcomes as: (a) behavioral, (b) attitudinal, (c) cognitive, and (d) health and well-being related.

Behavioral Outcomes

Historically, one of the most important sets of criteria for evaluating the impact of work design on people has been how they act or behave as a consequence of different work design configurations. It is, naturally, expected that work design will impact on individual performance in the job or role, and so the quantity, efficiency, and quality of individual work outputs and the productivity of workers are typically considered as important outcome variables. Evidence is somewhat mixed. Reviews typically conclude that more consistent effects of work design have been obtained for attitudinal outcomes, such as job satisfaction, than for job performance (e.g., Fried & Ferris, 1987). However, methodological issues pervade many of the studies covered by these reviews. There are a handful of studies with rigorous research designs that suggest performance benefits of work redesign (e.g., Griffin, 1991; Jackson & Wall, 1991; Kelly, 1992; Leach, Wall, & Jackson, 2003). Moreover, the effect of work design on broader performance concepts, such as citizenship, have rarely been considered (Parker & Turner, 2002).

Models such as the JCM and the interdisciplinary perspective also predict that work design influences employee withdrawal behaviors, including absenteeism and voluntary employee turnover, and the empirical evidence has generally supported such predictions (Campion, 1988; Fried & Ferris, 1987; Humphrey et al., 2007; Pousette & Hanse, 2002). Similarly, aspects of work design have been found to influence intentions to withdraw, including intention to quit and retirement intentions (Krausz, Sagie, & Biderman, 2000; Mitchell, Holtom, Lee, Sablynski, & Erez, 2001; Sibbald, Bojke, & Gravelle, 2003). For example, jobs that provide greater opportunities to form linkages with other employees and to exert control over what one does in one's work have been found to lessen the likelihood that an employee will form an intention to leave her or his current job.

In addition, researchers have recently begun to argue that work design predicts, and can be used to promote, an extended range of individual behaviors (Parker et al., 2001). For example, evidence exists to show that work design affects such outcomes as creativity and innovation (Axtell, Holman, Unsworth, Wall, & Waterson, 2000; Harrison, Neff, Schwall, & Zhao, 2006; Ohly, Sonnentag, & Pluntke, 2006; Shalley, Zhou, & Oldham, 2004), proactivity (Parker, Williams, & Turner, 2006), citizenship (Chiu & Chen, 2005; Pearce & Gregersen, 1991; Piccolo & Colquitt, 2006), adaptivity (Griffin, Neal, & Parker, 2007), voice (Tangirala & Ramanujam, 2008), and helping (Axtell, Parker, Holman, & Totterdell, 2007; Grant, 2007; Grant et al., 2007). Hambrick, Finkelstein, and Mooney (2005) have also argued that work design characteristics (job demands) affect the type of strategic choices made by senior executives. They suggested that those facing higher demands were more likely to make extreme decisions, to imitate other firms, and to vacillate in their decisions than those facing low or moderate demands.

As already noted, there are often perceived to be trade-offs in the type of behavioral outcomes between different work design configurations, for example between productivity and efficiency outcomes on the one hand and performance quality, creativity, innovation, safety, and citizenship on the other (Campion et al., 2005; Cordery & Parker, 2007). However, the degree to which these outcomes must necessarily be traded off is a matter for debate. For example, it may be argued that providing employees with increased control, variety, and discretion not only motivates greater proactivity and innovation, but also makes it more likely that employees will be able to identify potentials for increased efficiencies and will be motivated to implement them (viz. Pfeffer, 1994).

Attitudinal Outcomes

A considerable body of evidence exists to support the assertion that the characteristic content of work design helps shape work attitudes, principally job satisfaction (Dorman & Zapf, 2001; Loher, Noe, Moeller, & Fitzgerald, 1985), job involvement (Brown, 1996; Mathieu & Zajac, 1990), affective empathy (Axtell et al., 2007; Parker & Axtell, 2001), and organizational commitment (Fedor, Caldwell, & Herold, 2006; Meyer, Stanley, Herscovitch, & Topolnytsky, 2002). Task-related and social work design characteristics appear to be more influential than work context–related work design characteristics in shaping work attitudes, and satisfaction with growth opportunities and job involvement appear to be most strongly impacted by motivational work design characteristics (Humphrey et al., 2007).

Cognitive Outcomes

Much of the emphasis within work design theory and research has been devoted to assessing behavioral and attitudinal outcomes. However, research has also demonstrated that work design influences the way that people think: their cognitive performance, the type of knowledge they possess, and how they perceive themselves and others at work. Echoing the comments of Adam Smith (1776) quoted earlier on some of the risks associated with simple, repetitive work, there is growing evidence that work design exerts significant long-term impacts on intellectual functioning (Avolio & Waldman, 1990; Kohn & Schooler, 1982; Schooler, Mulatu, & Oates, 2004). For example, Potter, Helms, and Plassman (2008)

recently found that people who had been in intellectually demanding jobs tended to demonstrate better cognitive performance during retirement, even when differences in education and intelligence were controlled.

The type of work performed can also influence the job-related knowledge that people possess. One of the rationales that is frequently given for providing work designs that are high in variety, feedback, and autonomy is that they increase the range of situations encountered by workers who, through processes of active learning (Bell & Kozlowski, 2008), develop greater understanding of how, say, a production system operates or what clients typically seek in a service arrangement. In jobs that provide for higher autonomy and feedback, workers are also able to experience a greater sense of "cause and effect" between their actions and work outcomes, all of which adds to their knowledge and skill. The knowledge, both tacit and explicit, that is developed as a consequence of empowered or motivational work designs (Parker & Axtell, 2001; Wall, Cordery & Clegg, 2002) mediates effective performance, but can also be seen as an increase in human capital for the employee—something she can take with her to other jobs. For example, individuals working in team settings may, over time, develop interpersonal and self-management knowledge and capabilities as a consequence of the heightened task interdependence and work role autonomy that they experience in those settings (Morgeson, Reider, & Campion, 2005; Stevens & Campion, 1994, 1999).

Other cognitive outcomes of work design relate to an individual's self-definition (Parker, Wall, & Jackson, 1997) and, in particular, the various identities that they develop in the context of the work they do, such as occupational, career, relational (Ashforth, Harrison, & Corley, 2008). Lower order forms of identification (e.g., work, subunit, team) may arise as proximal outcomes of work design characteristics, such as task identity and interdependence, but ultimately impact on higher order identifications (e.g., career, occupational). For example:

> Because organizations tend to be structured around occupational specialties, organization members are largely known by their occupations and come to situate themselves in terms of their occupations (Trice, 1993; Van Maanen & Barley, 1984).

> Pipefitters for Exxon likely will have a much different perspective of the workplace and their role within

it than will PR managers, and they likely will be regarded by others in much different ways.... Thus, job titles serve as prominent identity badges. (Ashforth & Kreiner, 1999, p. 417)

Other research has suggested that organizational and other forms of identification may be directly affected by the nature of work design, for example as a consequence of dispersion, isolation, and independence produced by "virtual" work (Conner, 2003; Wegge, van Dick, Fisher, Wecking, & Moltzen, 2006; Wiesenfeld, Raghuram, & Garud, 2001) and as a consequence of working in teams (Van der Vegt & Bunderson, 2005). Grant (2007) has proposed that the relational architecture of a job (the extent to which a work involves contact with and has impact on others) also shapes a person's identity, expressed in terms of a set of beliefs regarding one's competence, self-determination, and social worth. In other words, as the earlier quotation from Terkel (1972) suggested, the nature of the work that we perform shapes our sense of who we are, what purpose we serve, and what value we represent to society at large.

Work design can also influence how people perceive those with whom they interact in the course of their work. Parker and Axtell (2001) proposed that one of the consequences of people working in jobs/roles where there was high autonomy and heightened interaction with end-users of the product of that work (in this case, suppliers) was that they were more likely to develop positive attributions regarding those suppliers. This cognitive outcome arises out of the process of "perspective taking," an intellectual process that is influenced by the content of the work, and which also has affective empathy outcomes.

Health and Well-being Outcomes

A considerable body of evidence has built up over the years to suggest that work design impacts on the psychological and physiological well-being of workers (Parker, Turner, & Griffin, 2003; Theorell & Karasek, 1996; Warr, 1987). For example, job autonomy can reduce anxiety because it allows individuals to better manage the demands they face, and it can lower depression because individuals experience a sense of self-determination. Indeed, many countries now have national surveillance systems designed to identify psychosocial risk factors within the workforce; systems frequently include survey-based measures of work design characteristics (Dollard, Skinner, Tuckey, & Bailey, 2007). Well-being outcomes that have been specifically linked to work design include stress, anxiety, and

depression (LaMontagne, Keegel, Vallance, Ostry, & Wolfe, 2008; Leach, Wall, Rogelberg, & Jackson, 2005; Melchior et al., 2007; Paterniti, Niedhammer, Lang, & Consoli, 2002), emotional fatigue and burnout (Barnes & Van Dyne, 2009; Hakanen, Schaufeli, & Ahola, 2008; Schaufeli & Bakker, 2004; Xie & Johns, 1995), suicide risk (Agerbo, Gunnell, Bondea, Mortensen, & Nordentoft, 2007; Reichenberg & MacCabe, 2007), expatriate adjustment (Takeuchi, Shay, & Li, 2008), as well as a range of somatic health symptoms (Schaubroeck, Walumbwa, Ganster, & Kepes, 2007; Shaw & Gupta, 2004; Warren, Carayon, & Hoonakker, 2008), including weight gain (Block, He, Zaslavsky, Ding, & Ayanian, 2009), sleep quality (Knudsen, Ducharme, & Roman, 2007), and the risk of coronary heart disease (Aboa-Eboule et al., 2007).

There is also evidence that work design characteristics such as job autonomy/control, role clarity, and workload affect individual employee safety (Barling, Kelloway, & Iverson, 2003; Parker, Axtell, & Turner, 2001; Zacharatos, Barling, & Iverson, 2005). The degree to which people are able to experience balance between their involvement in work and non-work activities is also affected by job and role characteristics (Ahuja, Chudòba, Kacmar, McKnight, & George, 2007; Aryee et al., 2005; Cartwright & Holmes, 2006; Valcour, 2007).

Work Design Inputs

Much of the initial appeal of the JCM as a work design theory to both researchers and practitioners lay in its identification of a set of objective, manipulable job design parameters (autonomy, task identity, etc.). However, researchers now recognize the need for a broader specification of the parameters affecting contemporary job and role design, and thus the characteristic content and organization of work activity can be seen as a function of design choices relating to three categories of input (Morgeson & Humphrey, 2008). First, there are properties of work that arise directly from the characteristics of tasks, activities, and duties that are routinely performed by the individual incumbent in producing work outputs (*task characteristics*). Second, work design is shaped by the characteristics of interpersonal interactions and relationships that are embedded in assigned tasks and roles, particularly in service settings (Grant et al., 2011). Though some have termed these as *social characteristics* (Humphrey et al., 2007; Morgeson & Humphrey, 2008), we prefer to describe these work design characteristics as *relational characteristics*, reflecting the fact that they are properties of tasks and roles that emerge out of social interactions (e.g., interdependence, collective autonomy), rather than being properties of the social context in their own right (e.g., group consensus, team climate). Finally, the characteristic experience of work content is also determined by properties of the broader organizational environment (*contextual characteristics*) within which work is performed. In this category of work design inputs are included such factors as the physical arrangements for working, organizational supports, managerial and supervisory behavior, and resource availability. Again, these are defined as variables that directly generate work characteristics, or which exert a cross-level influence on relational and task characteristics, rather than as variables that moderate the impact of work design properties on individual effectiveness at work or generate effectiveness outcomes in their own right.

In the sections that follow, we describe in detail the nature of task, relational, and contextual characteristics that have been identified as affecting the behavioral, attitudinal, cognitive, and health and well-being outcomes identified earlier.

Task Characteristics

Task characteristics are those that arise from the task/activity environment, and have traditionally been the primary focus of psychological research into the effects of work design. As the nature of work has changed, the types of task characteristics that have been identified as influencing individual effectiveness at work have also changed. We begin with those properties of jobs and roles that have been most commonly identified and studied, before moving on to more recently identified properties of emerging jobs and roles.

Perhaps the most recognized and studied of all task-level work design characteristics, *autonomy* is a multifaceted property of a job/role, denoting the amount of discretion or control that a person is afforded (Hackman & Oldham, 1975). Individual autonomy is generally regarded as one of the most potent work design characteristics when it comes to promoting individual effectiveness within a job/role. Meta-analytic studies have shown autonomy to be positively related to most of the effectiveness indicators (Humphrey et al., 2007), and this task attribute (and its interaction with job demands and support) plays a central role in theories of work stress and burnout/engagement (Schaufeli & Bakker, 2004; Spector, 1986) and in theories of motivated behavior (e.g., Self-determination Theory; Gagne & Deci, 2005). Three distinct facets of autonomy have been identified in

the literature (Breaugh, 1985; Jackson, Wall, Martin, & Davids, 1993; Morgeson & Humphrey, 2006). They are *work scheduling autonomy, work methods autonomy,* and *decision-making autonomy*. Each refers to a different location of autonomy within job/role performance, implying different points of potential intervention, though these aspects are rarely separated in empirical research.

While increasing individual autonomy is generally held to be a good thing, it has sometimes been argued that the relationship between autonomy and certain outcomes is non-linear, or that it may depend on the context within which that autonomy is exercised. For example, Tangirala and Ramanujam (2008) report a U-shaped relationship between employee perceptions of personal control (of which autonomy is a component) at work and employee voice behavior (expression of work-related opinions, concerns, and ideas). De Jonge and Schaufeli (1998) found that the relationship between autonomy and emotional exhaustion followed an inverted U-shape, though they suggest that this may reflect the influence of "hidden" moderators such as need for autonomy, and a more recent study has in fact demonstrated that the relationship between autonomy and well-being is generally positive and linear (Rydstedt, Ferrie, & Head, 2006). There is also very little empirical support for the view, derived from activation theory, that the relationship between autonomy and performance follows an inverted U-shape (Edwards, Guppy, & Cockerton, 2007). Langfred (2004) found that increasing individual autonomy within an MBA team context generally had negative effects on the performance of the team when trust was also high and hence team members were reluctant to monitor each other.

Feedback from the job has been defined as "the extent to which a job imparts information about an individual's performance" (Humphrey et al., 2007, p. 1333). From a work design perspective, this refers to feedback that is obtained directly by a worker from the performance of the job, rather than feedback interventions that arise as a consequence of performance appraisal mechanisms or goal-setting interventions (Parker & Wall, 1998). Job-related feedback has been found to correlate strongly with reduced stress and anxiety, lower role conflict and ambiguity, and more positive work attitudes; however, it appears to be less strongly related to behavioral outcomes such as absenteeism, turnover, and performance. (Humphrey et al., 2007; Millette & Gagne, 2008). The latter finding is somewhat surprising, given the established importance of performance feedback in research into goal setting, self-regulatory processes, and performance (e.g., Ilies & Judge, 2005; Kluger & DeNisi, 1996).

Skill variety has been defined as "the degree to which a job requires a variety of different activities in carrying out the work, which involve the use of a number of different skills and talents of the employee" (Hackman & Oldham, 1975, p. 161). However, Humphrey et al. (2007) have argued that it is necessary to distinguish between a job's inherent requirement to use a variety of skills (skill variety) and engaging in a variety of tasks or activities, which they term *task variety*. Task variety is a characteristic of "enlarged" jobs (Campion & McClelland, 1991; Herzberg, 1968), and serves to lessen the worker's engagement in repetitive actions. This, in turn, potentially affords the incumbents greater motivation and satisfaction, and reduces exposure to mechanical strain (Moller, Mathaiessen, Franzon, & Kihlberg, 2004), but at the cost of increasing the likelihood of work overload (Humphrey et al., 2007). Skill variety has been found to be associated with positive psychological benefits in terms of increased employee motivation, engagement, and job satisfaction, but has not shown a strong relationship to behavioral outcomes (Humphrey et al., 2007). A lack of skill variety has, however, been linked with a number of well-being outcomes, including burnout and depression (Karasek & Theorell, 1990; Parker, 2003).

Specialization results from "the division of the total production process into a series of technologically separate operations" (Jones, 1984, p. 685). According to Morgeson and Humphrey (2008), specialization refers to the *depth* of knowledge and skill involved in job tasks, whereas skill and task variety refers to the breadth or range of activities performed and skills utilized. Specialization, defined thus, has not been studied much by work design researchers, who have generally treated it as analogous to task variety or autonomy. However, in research on human development and aging, professional specialization is treated as a key component in the "getting of wisdom," which in turn is seen as a primary goal of successful adult and leadership development (Baltes & Smith, 1990; Staudinger, Smith, & Baltes, 1992; Sternberg, 2003). Wisdom is defined as having "expert knowledge of what is important and how things work" (Helson & Srivastava, 2002, p. 1431). For these reasons, Morgeson and Humphrey (2008) suggest that professional specialization may be one mechanism whereby the efficiency/satisfaction trade-off so frequently observed in work design

can be avoided. Specialization by site and stage of work may also help overcome some of the negative implications of functional specialization (Hoffer Gittell, Weinberg, Bennett, & Miller, 2008).

Task significance refers to the degree to which performing the job or role has a positive impact on the lives or work of other people, whether inside or outside the organization (Hackman & Oldham, 1975; Morgeson & Humphrey, 2008). Grant (2008b) recently furnished evidence that researchers may have underestimated the importance of this characteristic, particularly as it impacts on job performance. In a series of three field experiments, Grant (2008b) demonstrated that experimental manipulations designed to increase task significance (other task characteristics remaining constant) resulted in markedly improved performance for fund-raisers and lifeguards.

Task identity is the degree to which a job involves completing a "whole," identifiable piece of work, such as producing an identifiable product or meeting all the needs of a given client in a service relationship. Clearly, this is one characteristic that is adversely affected by some types of specialization and the division of labor. Combining tasks to form a "natural unit of work" to be performed by a worker is a motivational work redesign strategy that is advocated within both the job enrichment/ job characteristics and socio-technical systems perspectives on work design (Hackman & Oldham, 1980; Herzberg, 1968), even though, in isolation, empirical research indicates that it is only modestly related to attitudinal, behavioral, and well-being work design outcomes (Humphrey et al., 2007). As we discuss later, this may be because task identity requires the presence of other work design characteristics in order to activate key psychological processes and states.

Job complexity has often been used, along with job scope and job challenge, to refer to either additive or multiplicative combinations of job characteristics (e.g., high autonomy, high skill, and task variety; Schaubroeck et al., 2007; Xie & Johns, 1995). However, it is increasingly argued that job complexity should be treated as a design characteristic in its own right (Morgeson & Humphrey, 2006), referring to "the extent to which a job is multifaceted and difficult to perform" (Humphrey et al., 2007, p. 1335). Wood (1986) classifies the elements of complexity associated with tasks as: (a) component, (b) coordinative, and (c) dynamic. Component complexity denotes the number of different task elements that exist; coordinative complexity refers to the interconnectedness (interdependence) of tasks within the one job; and dynamic complexity arises when tasks and activities change over time. Interestingly, given that increasing complexity may be seen as the reverse of what happens in mechanistic approaches to work design, meta-analysis indicates that it is positively related to performance ratings, in addition to showing more predictable positive associations with job satisfaction, job involvement, and role overload (Humphrey et al., 2007). Job complexity has been demonstrated to have a sustained impact on cognitive performance over time (Potter, Plassman, Helms, Foster, & Edwards, 2006). Recently, Elsbach and Hargadon (2006) have pointed out that many jobs involve switching between complex and simple work tasks (see also Madjar & Shalley, 2008). They suggest that the occasional performance of simple, readily mastered tasks of low cognitive difficulty ("mindless work") may in fact have beneficial outcomes, freeing up cognitive processing capacity and thereby enabling people to think more creatively.

One of the most obvious ways in which work has been altered by technological developments in the past two decades is in the extent to which core tasks and activities involve the processing of information, or *information-processing demands*. Reflecting this, two forms of information-processing demands have been of particular interest in the work design field: problem-solving demands arise when a job requires incumbents to generate new ideas, deal with non-routine problems, and correct errors; attentional demands are those which require a person to exercise a high level of vigilance or monitoring in the course of work (Jackson, Wall, Martin, & Davids, 1993; Wall, Jackson & Mullarkey, 1995). Despite the growth of so-called knowledge work within all industry sectors, and the fact that the concept of job demands plays a central role in theories of occupational stress and coping (Janssen, Peeters, de Jonge, Houkes, & Tummers, 2004; Karasek & Theorell, 1990; Schaufeli & Bakker, 2004), relatively little research has specifically focused specifically on cognitive demands (Morgeson & Humphrey, 2008), as distinct from other types of job demand (e.g., physical and emotional demands; Hockey, 2000).

Grant et al. (2011) have suggested that an important property of work design relates to the *time horizon* within which work is performed. Cycle time is one of the indicators traditionally used to assess repetitiveness of task activities (Turner & Lawrence, 1965), and time pressure is another temporal property of jobs that has been linked (negatively)

to employee creativity, stress, and well-being (Elsbach & Hargadon, 2006; Mauno, Kinnunen, & Ruokolainen, 2007).

Though sometimes treated as a feature of the work context (Humphrey et al., 2007), there are *physical demands* that arise at the task/activity level. These include such things as the physical actions required for task performance and the degree to which the tasks involve carrying or manipulating heavy loads (Edwards et al., 2000). Research has shown that physically uncomfortable tasks and either lifting/carrying or pushing/pulling heavy loads increase the likelihood of long-term sickness absence (Lund, Labriola, Christensen, Bultmann, & Villadsen, 2006).

For some job holders, the consequences of failure or making a mistake in the execution of a task or role can be severe, and this will inevitably shape their approach and reactions to their work (Brannick et al., 2007; Zhao & Olivera, 2006). It has been suggested that high *error consequences* will reduce the degree to which a person is willing to accept accountability and/or exercise autonomy or skill variety in a work role (Morgeson & Humphrey, 2008). Cost responsibility, or the financial costs associated with errors, has also been shown to interact with attentional demand to cause strain (Martin & Wall, 1989).

Relational Characteristics

In the research that preceded the development of the Job Characteristics Model, consideration was given to the inclusion of two aspects of social interactions as determinants of intrinsic work motivation, work attitudes, and behavior: "dealing with others" and "friendship opportunities" (Hackman & Lawler, 1971). However, it was concluded that that these "two interpersonal dimensions do not relate very consistently or strongly either to employee affective responses to the job, or to their actual work performance" (Hackman & Lawler, 1971, p. 274). One potential explanation for this is lies in the restricted range of 13 jobs that were studied (all from a single telephone company); however, the net effect of this was that these characteristics were omitted from the JCM, and relational characteristics then pretty well disappeared from job characteristics–based work design theory and research for the next 40 years (Grant et al., 2011). These days, however, the social networks, processes and relationships that are embedded in tasks and roles are being increasingly recognized as key parameters of effective work design.

Interdependence can be observed at the within-job level (see *job complexity*); however, it is most often considered as a work design characteristic that arises at the between-job level. In this respect, interdependence describes the extent to which the tasks and activities of the job/role incumbent are dependent on the work outputs of other people (received interdependence), and the extent to which the work performed by other people is affected by the work outputs of the job/role incumbent (initiated interdependence) (Kiggundu, 1981, 1983). The degree of interdependence of this type is often classified as pooled (low), sequential (moderate, unidirectional), or reciprocal (high, multidirectional) (Thompson, 1967). Meta-analysis suggests that overall interdependence encourages learning and skill development, is positively correlated with intrinsic work motivation, job satisfaction, and organizational commitment, and negatively correlated with turnover intentions (Humphrey et al., 2007). The latter finding may reflect the fact that interdependence may help foster job embeddedness by forging links to coworkers (Mitchell et al., 2001).

People working in jobs/roles that are embedded within team structures are generally required to participate in collective decision making with other group or team members, as a consequence of increased opportunities for self-management that is afforded the team (Campion, Medsker, & Higgs, 1993; Stewart, 2006). This requirement for *participative decision making* for individuals can arise even within groups whose members have quite low (e.g., pooled) task interdependence, and it injects a social dimension into the work. Participation in decision making, as distinguished from job autonomy, has been found to have modest positive impacts on individual performance and satisfaction (Batt & Appelbaum, 1995; Wagner, 1994).

Feedback from others/agents is "the degree to which the employee receives clear information about his or her performance from supervisors or from coworkers" (Hackman & Oldham, 1975, p. 162), as distinguished from feedback that arises from the job itself (Morgeson & Humphrey, 2008). The opportunity afforded by the job to receive feedback from these sources plays an important part in clarifying role expectations, facilitating self-regulation, and, depending on the nature of that feedback, it can enhance job performance (Kluger & DeNisi, 1996). This type of feedback has also been found to be positively associated with job satisfaction, and negatively associated with turnover intentions (Humphrey et al., 2007).

Impact on others may be defined as "the degree to which a job provides opportunities for employees

to affect the lives of beneficiaries" (Grant, 2007, p. 397), where beneficiaries may be people or groups within or outside the organization. These benefits may relate to the physical, psychological, and material well-being of others. Grant (2007) has suggested that the potency of this work design attribute, as it affects employee motivation and helping behaviors, depends not just on the magnitude and frequency of the perceived impact of one's actions on others, but also on the scope and focus of that impact. For example, a human resource manager responsible for determining remuneration policy within a large organization has the potential to affect the material well-being of many employees (scope). The focus of the impact can also vary, from a focus on preventing harm to others (e.g., safety inspector) to one of promoting positive gains (e.g., training officer). There is also the possibility that the impact on others may involve tasks that harm some people in the interest of achieving a greater good (Molinsky & Margolis, 2005). For example, some procedures performed by health professionals may involve inflicting pain and discomfort in order to deliver long-term health benefits for people. Policing and prison officer work may involve tasks that are seen as having a negative impact on the well-being of offenders, but which have a positive benefit for members of a broader community. Margolis & Molinsky (2008) have found that the emotional demands created by performing such "necessary evils" can have complex effects on employees' psychological engagement/disengagement and the potential for stress and burnout.

Interpersonal interaction is a further important relational characteristic. Even when work has the potential to have a major impact on the well-being of others, its performance may involve relatively little direct contact with beneficiaries. According to Grant (2007), frequency of contact with the beneficiaries of the work influences the extent to which a worker is less able to develop accurate knowledge regarding the impact of their actions. This, in turn, will affect a worker's motivation, affective commitment and performance in the role. In the context of service jobs, level of contact with people outside the organization is also associated with reported job satisfaction (Humphrey et al., 2007), and also with a greater need to expend effort in regulating displays of emotion (Morris & Feldman, 1996).

Social support is the "extent to which a job provides opportunities for getting assistance and advice from either supervisors or coworkers" (Humphrey et al., 2007, p. 1336). The availability of such support within one's work role has been found to reduce fatigue and to increase intrinsic work motivation (Van Yperen & Hagedoorn, 2003) and is associated with higher job satisfaction, lower anxiety, less absenteeism, reduced intentions to quit, and less role ambiguity and conflict (Humphrey et al., 2007). Though it has been argued that social support also acts to buffer the negative impact of job demands on psychological well-being, the empirical evidence for this is not conclusive (Sanne, Mykletun, Dahl, Moen, & Tell, 2005; Van der Doef & Mayes, 1999).

Situational accountability refers to the requirement, as a part of one's job, to justify and/or explain one's thoughts, emotions, and behaviors to other people (Grant & Ashford, 2008; Lerner & Tetlock, 1999). Research suggests that such increased accountability increases the likelihood that a person will engage in proactive behaviors and will be motivated to produce higher levels of performance, but that it can also result in higher levels of stress, and an increased likelihood that the employee will engage in selfish and politically motivated behaviors (Hochwarter et al., 2007).

Emotion display rules are "the standards for the appropriate expression of emotions on the job" (Diefendorff, Croyle, & Gosserand, 2005). It has been argued that a role that incorporates the requirement to hide high levels of emotion experienced during work, or to act contrary to felt emotions, may predispose a person to emotional exhaustion and burnout, though this may depend on the particular display strategy chosen (Grandey, 2003; Wharton, 2009). For example, Brotheridge & Grandey (2002) found that "deep acting" in order to prevent breach of emotional display rules was associated with positive feelings of personal accomplishment, while the relationship was negative for "surface acting."

Contextual Characteristics

Features of the broader environment within which tasks are performed can also be seen as manipulable and psychologically salient elements of work design (Grant et al., 2011; Morgeson & Humphrey, 2006; Morgeson & Humphrey, 2008; Stone & Guetal, 1985). Physical inputs to work design include the physical work conditions (e.g., lighting, heat, noise, physical hazards, etc.), and physical layout (e.g., space, density). Though these characteristics have been given relatively less attention by mainstream work design theorists, meta-analytic results provided by Humphrey et al. (2007) demonstrated that a range of physical job characteristics accounted for significant additional variance in stress (16%) and satisfaction (4%) outcomes, even when task and relational characteristics had been controlled for in the analyses.

The physical design of the workplace has been the factor given most attention by work design researchers to date, with spatial density emerging as a key variable affecting a person's ability to regulate interactions (e.g., interruptions) with others, and affecting a wide range of cognitive, affective, and behavioral outcomes, including lateness, satisfaction, creativity, and goal achievement (see May, Oldham & Rathert, 2005; Oldham, Cummings, & Zhou, 1995; Shalley et al., 2004; Zhou, Oldham, & Cummings, 1998).

Yet another category of important contextual work design inputs arises from the technical and organizational environment that surrounds the worker and which shapes and constrains the roles they occupy (Cordery & Parker, 2007; Morgeson & Humphrey, 2008; Parker, Wall, & Cordery, 2001). As with physical design, the influence of such elements on behavioral, cognitive, affective, and well-being outcomes is sometimes mediated via more proximal task and role characteristics. For example, close, direct supervision will constrain levels of autonomy experienced by individuals (Cordery & Wall, 1985; Griffin, 1981; Yeh, 2007), while higher quality leader-follower relationships can result in followers being provided with more "enriched" work opportunities (Graen & Uhl-Bien, 1995; Lapierre, Hackett, & Taggar, 2006). Transformational leadership has also been found to affect follower perceptions of their job characteristics (Piccolo & Colquitt, 2006). Characteristics of the broader technical system are also influential in work design. For example, the complexity of technical systems influences the degree of predictability associated with tasks and activities (uncertainty), thereby affecting task-level characteristics such as information processing demands and task interdependence (Wall et al., 2002; Wright & Cordery, 1999). Human resource management policies and practices regarding selection and training could be expected, via their influence on worker capabilities and preferences, to influence the extent to which work roles may be created to accommodate increased autonomy, participation, skill variety, and professional specialization (Judge, Bono, & Locke, 2000; Morgeson & Humphrey, 2008), while widespread information sharing is certain to influence the availability of job feedback (Pfeffer & Veiga, 1999). Likewise, the introduction of new organizational practices have been shown to affect behaviors and attitudes through impinging on task characteristics. For example, evidence shows how task characteristics are affected by lean production (Jackson & Mullarkey, 2000), just-in-time management (Jackson & Martin, 1996), performance monitoring (Carayon, 1994), temporary employment contracts (Parker, Griffin, Sprigg, & Wall, 2002), and team working (Kirkman & Rosen, 1999; Sprigg, Jackson, & Parker, 2000). Finally, structural properties of the organization, such as size, formalization, and centralization have been found to influence task-level work design characteristics, such as the degree of control (Briscoe, 2007; Oldham & Hackman, 1981).

Reflecting the trend in the nature of work and working arrangements noted at the beginning of this chapter, interest has also been growing in *virtuality* as a contextual influence on work design. Virtual work is that which is electronically mediated and where those performing the work are not physically located with interdependent others in a primary workplace (Morgeson & Humphrey, 2008). A recent study of telecommuting arrangements found that this form of virtual working had beneficial effects on the degree of autonomy experienced by individual workers but negatively affected relationships with coworkers (Gajendran & Harrison, 2007). Telework has also been found to reduce exhaustion, increase organizational commitment, and weaken turnover intentions (Golden, 2006).

Mediators

One area in which work design research and theory has not been particularly strong is identifying the precise mechanisms whereby work design influences employee outcomes. We know that work redesign works, but we cannot really be confident in saying precisely why it works (Mitchell, 1997). In part, this is because such a plethora of different cognitive, motivational, affective, and behavioral mechanisms have been suggested. Broadly speaking, these mechanisms fall into two categories: *psychological states*, which are manifested as proximal psychological reactions to work design inputs and which influence more distal effectiveness outcomes; and mediating *processes*, which are the means whereby work design inputs get translated into cognitive and behavioral activities that determine effectiveness within a job or role.[1]

Psychological States

The JCM identified three "critical psychological states" as arising from perceptions of work design,

and being associated with positive individual work outcomes. They were knowledge of results, experienced meaningfulness of the work, and experienced responsibility for outcomes. *Knowledge of results* is the "degree to which the employee knows and understands, on a continuous basis, how effectively he or she is performing the job" (Hackman & Oldham, 1975, p.162). This is affected by job/role characteristics (e.g., task significance, task identity), relational characteristics such as task interdependence, interaction outside the organization, and contact with beneficiaries, and also by work context characteristics such as virtuality of the work.

Experienced meaningfulness of the work is the "degree to which the employee experiences the job as one which is generally meaningful, valuable, and worthwhile" (Hackman & Oldham, 1975, p. 162). Wrzesniewski, Dutton, and Debebe (2003) identified two types of meaning that develop as a consequence of the occupancy of particular jobs and roles—an understanding of the content (tasks, activities, and their characteristics) of the jobs and roles, and the interpreted value of that content. According to this perspective, tasks, activities, and roles can be viewed differently, depending on employees' own values and the social context within which they are executed. According to Wrzesniewski et al. (2003), employees also develop a sense of self-meaning as a consequence of performing tasks and roles, including an understanding of the content of the self (e.g., how expert am I at what I do) and an evaluation (positive and negative) of the self at work. Self-evaluations are characteristics that one imputes to the self while at work, and these may include perceptions of social worth (Grant et al., 2007), since "it is through interpersonal episodes at work that employees come to know the content of who they are" (Wrzesniewski et al., 2003, p. 113).

Experienced responsibility for work outcomes is defined as the "degree to which the employee feels personally accountable and responsible for the results of the work he or she does" (Hackman & Oldham, 1975, p. 162). In the JCM, this state is principally associated with the experience of autonomy, though Humphrey et al. (2007) found that this state was the principal mediator between word design characteristics and outcomes. Recently, Pierce, Jussila, & Cummings (2009) have proposed that experienced responsibility for outcomes is best viewed as a component of an overall state of *psychological ownership*, "that state where an individual feels as though the target of ownership or a piece of that target is 'theirs'" (Pierce, Kostova, & Dirks,

2003, p. 86), a state which has both cognitive and affective components and which is produced in reaction to all the core job characteristics in the JCM, not just autonomy. According to Parker et al. (2006), *flexible role orientation* is a specific psychological state that derives from an overarching sense of psychological ownership. It refers to "how an individual defines their work role, such as how broadly they perceive their role; what types of tasks, goals, and problems they see as relevant to their role; and how they believe they should approach those tasks, goals, and problems to be effective" (Parker, 2007, p. 406). Job autonomy has emerged as a primary situational antecedent of flexible role orientation (Parker, Williams, & Turner, 2006), and the behavioral consequences include proactive work behaviors and overall job performance (Axtell et al., 2000; Parker, 2007; Parker et al., 2006).

Work design is commonly associated with motivation to perform (Mitchell, 1997), and a number of motivational states have been identified as key mediators of work design effects. *Intrinsic motivation* is "the desire to expend effort based on interest in and enjoyment and enjoyment of the work itself" (Grant, 2008a). According to Ryan & Deci (2000), the propensity for intrinsic motivation is an innate human tendency that may be elicited and sustained, or suppressed and diminished by situational conditions that provide for self-determination, autonomy, and the development and expression of competence. Intrinsic motivation has been found to predict positive outcomes such as performance and psychological well-being (Burton, Lydon, D'Alessandro, & Koestner, 2006; Deci & Ryan, 1985). A number of different types of intrinsic motivation have been proposed within the literature, for example the state of "flow," a subjective experience of deep involvement and absorption in a task activity that is experienced as highly rewarding in and of itself (Csikszentimihalyi, 2000; Keller & Bless, 2008). Similar to "flow," *job engagement* has been identified as "a positive, work-related state of mind that is characterized by vigor, dedication, and absorption" (Schaufeli & Bakker, 2004, p. 295) that arises when a person experiences certain job "resources," such as autonomy and social support (Schaufeli & Bakker, 2004). Engagement has been found to predict absence frequency, health, and turnover intentions (Schaufeli & Bakker, 2004; Schaufeli, Bakker, & Van Rhenen, 2009).

Closely related to the concept of intrinsic motivation is *psychological empowerment*, which has been described as a "motivational state manifested in four cognitions: meaning, competence, self-determination, and impact" (Spreitzer, 1995, p. 1444). Individual psychological empowerment has been found to correlate with features of the job and organizational context, including task characteristics, information sharing, and the use of teams, and to mediate the relationship between these inputs and job satisfaction, organizational commitment, and performance (Liden, Wayne, & Sparrowe, 2000; Seibert, Silver, & Randolph, 2004). One of the cognitions that comprise psychological empowerment—competence—refers to self-efficacy beliefs. Various efficacy beliefs have been investigated as mediators of work design inputs-outcomes relationships, including *role breadth self-efficacy*, or individuals' confidence in their ability to take on more proactive, integrative, and interpersonal tasks (Parker, 1998)—and self-management efficacy (Burr & Cordery, 2001).

Grant (2008a) makes a distinction between intrinsic motivation and *pro-social motivation*, the latter being viewed as a type of internalized extrinsic motivation in which the decision to expend effort is driven, not by personal enjoyment of the work itself, but by goals such as promoting self-esteem and fulfilling personal values (Ryan & Deci, 2000). Grant's (2008a) study suggests that the two motivational states are distinct, but interact in their effect on outcomes. In studies of firefighters and fundraising callers, he found that high levels of intrinsic motivation were associated with a positive impact of pro-social motivation on performance and productivity, while low intrinsic motivation resulted in either no impact or a negative impact of pro-social motivation. He concluded that forcing oneself to complete a task in the absence of any enjoyment of that task can have deleterious effects, no matter how much one identifies with the goal (in this case benefiting others).

Parker & Ohly (2008) have proposed that *regulatory focus and goal orientations* are perceptual-cognitive motivational states that arise as a result of features of work designs. Work designs that are characterized by low autonomy will result in workers experiencing a sense of being externally controlled, resulting in the development of a "prevention focus," whereas employees in autonomous work roles will experience feelings of internal control, resulting in a "promotion focus." These two regulatory foci have been found to predict different types of behavioral outcomes at work (Chen, Thomas, & Wallace, 2005), with a promotion focus likely resulting in higher levels of performance and creativity than a prevention focus (Friedman & Foerster, 2005; Meyer, Becker, & Vandenberghe, 2004).

Work design may also shape the sorts of goals that an individual is oriented to pursue. The three types of goal orientation most commonly identified in the literature are *learning, prove performance*, and *avoid performance* (Payne, Youngcourt, & Beaubien, 2007). A learning orientation reflects a desire to develop knowledge/skills and master a task; a prove performance orientation reflects a desire to demonstrate competence relative to others; and an avoid performance orientation reflects a desire to avoid the demonstration of incompetence relative to others. People with a learning orientation tend to be focused on the development of personal competence and mastery, will tend to actively engage with situations that are likely to provide a challenge to their existing proficiency, and are willing to see errors as an opportunity to learn. Research has shown that a learning orientation promotes a more positive, adaptive pattern of self-regulation (e.g., self-efficacy, cognitive focus, positive affect) than either of the performance orientations, leading to better training performance and transfer (Bell & Kozlowski, 2008; Brett & VandeWalle, 1999; Kozlowski & Bell, 2006; Payne et al., 2007; VandeWalle, Brown, Cron, & Slocum, 1999). Those with a performance orientation, on the other hand, are concerned with demonstrating their ability relative to others, and will tend to engage with situations in which they are able to demonstrate what they are already good at and avoid situations that may highlight areas of performance weakness (Kozlowski & Bell, 2006; Latham, 2006). The approach performance orientation has positive and negative elements. It is associated with an external focus which can be maladaptive for some processes and outcomes (interest, anxiety; Elliot, Shell, Bouas Henry, & Maier, 2005). In general, however, approach performance orientation is expected to be adaptive because it is associated with approach-oriented processes (effort, persistence). Recent research at the between-person level has shown positive links between performance-approach orientation and performance (Urdan, 2004). The avoid performance orientation is viewed as maladaptive, because it is linked with avoid-oriented processes (withdrawal of effort, distraction; Elliot et al., 2005). Parker and Ohly (2008) propose that "enriched" jobs can lead to increased self-efficacy beliefs, which in turn foster learning orientations (Payne et al., 2007). Jobs that are high on accountability, on the other hand, may promote one or other of the performance orientations.

Perceptual states that have been identified as causative in work design's impact on stress and well-being include *role overload, role ambiguity*, and *role conflict* (Humphrey et al., 2007). Role conflict is "the experience of contradictory, incompatible, or competing role expectations" (Riordan, 2005, p. 356), whereas role ambiguity arises as "uncertainty about the expectations, behaviors, and consequences associated with a particular role" (Polzer, 2005, p. 356). Role conflict is a particular feature of jobs that have multiple reporting relationships (e.g., in matrix structures), where people are members of multiple project teams, or where interdependence is high (Daniels, 2006). Role ambiguity is a common consequence of work designs where tasks are performed in a dynamic and uncertain environmental context. Both role conflict and role ambiguity have been found to be less within work designs characterized by increased autonomy and feedback from the job, and high social support (Humphrey et al., 2007). Role overload occurs when someone experiences too many role demands given the time available to meet them (Hecht, 2001). Some researchers have argued that role overload is increasingly a part of the modern work environment, caused by ever-expanding role expectations on the part of employers (Bolino & Turnley, 2005; Organ & Ryan, 1995), interdependence and responsibility for others (Dierdorff & Ellington, 2008), and resulting in increased stress and work-family conflict (Ahuja et al., 2007; Dierdorff & Ellington, 2008).

Another state-like variable that potentially mediates between social work design characteristics and individual effectiveness outcomes is *interpersonal trust* (Dirks & Ferrin, 2001; Langfred, 2007). Trust can also arise as a consequence of task-level work design characteristics. Perrone, Zaheer, and McEvily (2003) found that trust, defined in terms of a person's expectations that someone could be depended on to fulfill obligations, behave in a predictable manner, and act fairly when the possibility existed to do otherwise, varied as a function of role autonomy. Purchasing managers given autonomy in their role interpreted this as a sign of others' trust in themselves and reciprocated by engaging in discretionary behaviors toward suppliers that signaled their trustworthiness (e.g., being more responsive, and upholding commitments).

The impact of emotion display rules on attitudinal and well-being outcomes such as job satisfaction, stress, and emotional exhaustion has been attributed to the creation of a state of *emotional dissonance*, in which a person experiences a discrepancy between the emotions they feel and those that the role requires them to show (Wharton, 2009; Zapf & Holz, 2006).

Finally, Elsbach and Hargadon (2006) have proposed that the periodic performance of "mindless" work potentially engages beneficial psychological states that are important in fostering creativity and which do not necessarily arise when someone is engaged in complex, intellectually demanding activities. These states are *cognitive capacity* (the absence of task-related cognitive load), *psychological safety* (the feeling that one can be oneself without fear of negative consequences), and *positive affect* (enjoyment, positive emotion).

Processes

By far the bulk of research into mediators of work design outcomes is concerned with the cognitive, attitudinal, and motivational states that work design engenders and which intervene between work design and more distal outcomes such as job satisfaction, organizational commitment, performance, and health. Far less attention has been devoted to the way in which work design influences what people do in order to become more effective in their job or role; that is, the cognitive, behavioral, and social activities that they engage in as a consequence of the opportunities and constraints afforded them by work design. Broadly speaking, we classify these mediating processes as involving *planning*, *action*, and/or *interaction*. Planning processes are those that involve activities such as goal setting, evaluating progress, and developing performance strategies. Action processes are those that involve coordinating and executing tasks, and monitoring and adjusting performance; interactional processes are those that involve coordinating activities with other people. While not all processes identified by work design researchers fit neatly into one or other of these categories, it nevertheless is a useful way of thinking about work design's impact on how people enact their tasks and roles.

An important set of work design-related processes that span the planning/action dimensions has been labeled *proactivity* (Grant & Ashford, 2008; Grant & Parker, 2009), defined as "the extent to which individuals engage in self-starting, future-oriented behavior to change their individual work situations, their individual work roles, or themselves" (Griffin, Neal, & Parker, 2007, p. 332). According to Grant & Ashford (2008, p. 9), proactivity is a "process that can be applied to any set of actions through anticipating, planning, and striving to have

an impact" and it is facilitated by work designs that emphasize autonomy, uncertainty (ambiguity), and accountability. In practice, proactivity at work may take many different forms, including actions taken by an individual to modify tasks, roles, relationships, the context within which work is performed, the job as a whole, and even changes to personal attributes such as competencies in order to achieve better person-job fit (Grant & Parker, 2009).

Most research into proactivity as a work design–related process has focused on how individuals respond to the opportunities afforded by work design to modify the content of their job or role (e.g., Parker et al., 2006). Role innovation, role adjustment, taking charge, personal initiative, task revision, and job crafting are some of the terms that have been used to describe proactive behaviors that are observed among people working in work designs that provide requisite levels of autonomy, complexity, and variability (Clegg & Spencer, 2007; Frese, Garst, & Fay, 2007; Sluss, van Dick, & Thompson, 2011). For example, job crafting (Wrzesniewski & Dutton, 2001) can be an attempt to align work content with evaluative information received from others regarding the value of that work. They provide the example of a hospital cleaner who experiences positive interactions and evaluative praise for his contributions from patients, who then would be motivated to go out of his way to increase the extent to which his daily tasks involve interacting with and cleaning up after patients. By contrast, cues given to hospital cleaners by doctors and nurses suggesting that the job/role has little worth might be expected to affect the degree to which cleaners engaged in similar tasks in respect to doctors and nurses. Berg, Wrzesniewski, and Dutton (2010) found that higher rank employees tended to view job crafting as a response to their own expectations of how they should spend their time, whereas lower rank employees used it in response to prescribed role requirements and others' expectations of them. Clegg and Spencer (2007) have proposed that these proactive role innovation/adjustment behaviors potentially form part of a virtuous, dynamic spiral in which good performance creates trust, which motivates role adjustments (e.g., increased autonomy), creating more intrinsically motivating work, which in turn promotes performance improvements.

ADAPTIVE RESPONDING

Socio-technical systems theorists have long argued that increasing autonomy for people actively involved in transforming work products results in more timely and effective decisions being made about what to do when deviations from optimal system functioning are encountered (Cherns, 1976; Clegg, 2000), and this view has received empirical support within the work design literature. For example, Wall et al. (1992) found that the provision of increased operator control over the management of faults associated with the operation of a robotics line in a manufacturing plant led to an almost instantaneous improvement in the amount of machine downtime (similar effects have been observed when autonomy is increased for teams; Cordery et al., 2009). This improvement was seen as evidence that decisions were being made more rapidly and that previously under-utilized skills and knowledge were now being applied to solving problems. Increased autonomy, accountability, and complexity in work designs create the need and opportunity for workers to utilize more fully their existing knowledge and skills and to make timely decisions about what actions to take when problems arise in the course of their work (Wall, Cordery, & Clegg, 2002).

GOAL GENERATION AND GOAL STRIVING

Work design also plays a role in shaping a range of psychological processes that individuals use as they select, prioritize, and accomplish goals, processes that are fueled in part by the proximal motivational states we identified earlier (Chen & Kanfer, 2006; Parker & Ohly, 2008). Goal generation involves planning processes (deciding which goal to pursue and how to best to pursue it), whereas goal striving refers to action processes—the "cognitive and affective activities that support behaviors leading to goal attainment" (Chen & Kanfer, 2006, p. 229), for example keeping concentration on the task in hand, monitoring one's behavior and its consequences, evaluating progress to goal attainment, and managing self-evaluations (Parker & Ohly, 2008). In addition to (via its influence on motivational states) influencing the difficulty, temporal horizon, and complexity of goals selected, work design potentially affects goal generation and goal striving via some non-motivational pathways. For example, by enhancing available knowledge skills and abilities, and also by the development of habits and routines (Parker & Ohly, 2008).

ACTIVE LEARNING

The design of an individual's job or role potentially provides an enabling context for new skills and knowledge to be developed via processes of experiential learning. Work designs that require people to regularly interact with others (e.g., through their membership on teams or in communities of practice), to gather and process information, to analyze and solve problems, and to act autonomously engage individual learning competencies that result in additional skill and knowledge being accumulated (Bell & Kozlowski, 2008; Edmondson, Dillon, & Roloff, 2007; Frese & Zapf, 1994; Sims, 1983). Work designs that involve simple and predictable tasks may also result in people learning habitual, automatic ways of responding (Wood & Neal, 2007).

RELATIONAL COORDINATION

Work designs that are characterized by relational characteristics require people to integrate their own activities with interdependent others (Grant & Parker, 2009). In part, social characteristics of the work design, such as interdependence, generate such accommodative behavior, though the degree to which this occurs is influenced by moderating variables, such as the supervisory span of control, coaching, and feedback, as well as the quality of interpersonal relationships (Hoffer Gittell, 2001; Hoffer Gittell et al., 2008). It may also be affected by the level and type of task interdependence that exist. Very high levels of interdependence may make effective communication and coordination with others difficult (MacDuffie, 2007).

PERSPECTIVE TAKING

Contact with others and autonomy have been linked to processes whereby jobholders empathize with those with whom they interact and develop positive attributions regarding their behavior (Parker & Axtell, 2001). Adopting the perspective of others has been found to facilitate a range of cooperative and helping behaviors, including improved customer service (Axtell et al., 2007).

Moderators

A number of individual differences have been found to moderate the strength of relationships between work design inputs and individual effectiveness outcomes (Morgeson & Humphrey, 2008).

Higher Order Needs

Growth need strength (GNS) is an individual difference variable that reflects the overall strength of a person's desire to satisfy higher order needs (growth, development, feelings of accomplishment; Alderfer, 1969; Maslow, 1954) on the job (Hackman & Lawler, 1971). People who are high on GNS "want to learn new things, stretch themselves, and strive to do better in their jobs" (Shalley, Gilson, & Blum, 2009), and therefore find complex, challenging, and "enriched" jobs more satisfying and enjoyable (Bottger & Chew, 1986; Saavedra & Kwun, 2000; Spector, 1985). *Need for achievement* (McClelland, 1961, 1987) has also been studied in the context of work design, and found to moderate the impact of work design on intrinsic motivation: people with a stronger need for achievement typically demonstrate greater intrinsic interest in, and react more positively to, work that is more challenging and skilful than those who have a low need for achievement (Eisenberger, Jones, Stinglhamber, Shanock, & Randall, 2005). It has also been argued that placing people with a high need for achievement in low autonomy, simple, repetitive work increases the risk that they will suffer stress and emotional exhaustion as a consequence of continually striving to achieve something in a job that offers few opportunities to do so (Morgeson & Humphrey, 2008). Though less studied, it has also been predicted that *need for affiliation* (a person's desire for social contact and feelings of belonging) will determine how people react to relational work design characteristics, such as interdependence, and virtual working (Morgeson & Humphrey, 2008; Wiesenfeld et al., 2001).

Personality

A number of dispositional variables have been found to affect employee reactions to work design. For example, high levels of *dispositional affect* appear to reduce the importance of work design characteristics as a source of satisfaction (Staw & Cohen-Charash, 2005). Internal *locus of control* has been shown to facilitate the development of better strategies for dealing with stress in demanding and insecure jobs (Parkes, 1994), while an intervention designed to increase task significance was found to have a stronger impact on performance when *conscientiousness* was low (Grant, 2008b). A good deal of recent interest has centered on the influence of *proactive personality* on behavior in organizations (Fuller & Marler, 2009), defined as a "disposition toward making anticipatory change" (Morgeson & Humphrey, 2008, p. 57). Proactive individuals have been shown to respond with lower strain to jobs that are high on job demands and autonomy (Parker & Sprigg, 1999), likely because they engage in a range of proactive behaviors that, in turn, generate higher levels of performance and satisfaction (Fuller & Marler, 2009). Finally, *propensity to trust others* has been linked to individual preferences for working in contexts characterized by heightened interdependence (Kiffin-Petersen & Cordery, 2003; Morgeson & Humphrey, 2008).

Knowledge, Skills, and Abilities

To be able to perform well in work that is characterized by complexity, high interdependence, skill variety, and autonomy, it would seem axiomatic that workers possess the requisite knowledge, skills, and abilities. Though a limited amount of research has been carried out into such moderators, *cognitive ability* (Morgeson, Delaney-Klinger, & Hemingway, 2005), *teamwork knowledge*, and *social skills* (Morgeson et al., 2005) have been found to be important predictors of the degree to which work design influences individual performance.

Values and Attitudes

Grant (2008b) found that *pro-social values* (the degree to which someone regards protecting and promoting the welfare of others as an important goal in life) had the potential to enhance the impact of increased task significance on the performance of fund-raising callers. A similar construct, *other orientation*, has been found to moderate affective reactions to job attributes such as autonomy (Meglino & Korsgaard, 2007), weakening the impact of "enriched" job attributes on job satisfaction. National *cultural values* such as power-distance and individualism have been found to attenuate relationships between work design characteristics such as autonomy and interdependence and positive work outcomes (Robert, Probst, Martocchio, Drasgow, & Lawler, 2000; Roe, Zinovieva, Dienes, & Ten Horn, 2000). An individual's *dissatisfaction with work context* (coworkers, supervisors, job security, and pay) has also been identified as a set of attitudes that potentially weakens the impact of work design on intrinsic motivation (Oldham et al., 1976).

Summary

In sum, our organizing framework (Figure 9.2) builds on and expands the five job characteristics and the relatively narrow set of mediators, moderators, and outcomes proposed in the dominant job characteristics model. We suggest that good quality work design influences cognitive, affective, behavioral, and health and well-being outcomes, both in the short term, such as individuals' feelings of enthusiasm, and in the long term, such as intellectual development. Building on the recognition that work design is as much about roles as tasks, the framework identifies not only task attributes as key defining inputs, but also relational and contextual inputs. This perspective provides a more rounded way of understanding jobs that better encapsulates the challenges of today's workplaces. The framework then suggests that these work design elements affect outcomes, by influencing individuals' psychological states (not only the critical psychological states from the JCM, but also self-efficacy, pro-social motivation, and others) and/or by influencing planning, action, and interaction processes (such as goal generation, adaptive responding, or perspective taking). Finally, in our framework, the moderators depict that the influence of the work design inputs on individual outcomes depends to some extent on the individuals themselves—such as what type of person the individual is, what he or she values, and what he or she knows or can do. The key variables and relationships we have identified in our discussion of this framework are summarized in Table 9.2.

Our framework incorporates prior recommendations that have been put forward by scholars in the field, such as the need for greater specification of mechanisms (Morgeson & Humphrey, 2006; Parker & Ohly, 2008) and the importance of a stronger relational and perspective on work design because of the increased interdependence and uncertainty of work, respectively (Grant & Parker, 2009). There are, of course, many other important ways forward, and it is these that we turn to in the next section.

Conclusions: Where Is Work Design Headed?

A number of priorities for research have emerged in the course of conducting this review, and these are identified below.

Expanding on the Role of Context

One theme consistently identified in reviews of the field is the need to focus more attention on the broader environmental, social, and organizational

Table 9.2 Summary of Work Design Inputs, Mediators, Moderators, and Effectiveness Outcomes Identified by Researchers

INPUTS	MEDIATORS	EFFECTIVENESS OUTCOMES
Task characteristics Autonomy, Feedback from job, Skill variety, Task variety, Task significance, Task identity, Job complexity, Specialization, Information processing, Temporal horizon, Physical demands, Error consequences.	**Psychological states** Knowledge of results, Experienced meaningfulness of work, Experienced responsibility for work outcomes, Intrinsic motivation, Job engagement, Psychological empowerment, Role breadth self-efficacy, Self-management efficacy, Pro-social motivation, Regulatory focus, Goal orientation, Role overload, Role ambiguity, Role conflict, Interpersonal trust, Emotional dissonance, Cognitive capacity, Psychological safety, Positive affect.	**Behavioral** Performance (quantity, efficiency, quality), Withdrawal behavior (absenteeism, turnover), Creativity and innovation, Citizenship behavior, Proactive behavior, Voice, Helping behavior, Strategic decision making.
Relational characteristics Interdependence, Participative decision-making, Feedback from others/agents, Impact on others, Interpersonal interaction, Social support, Situational accountability, Emotion display rules.		**Attitudinal** Job satisfaction, Job involvement, Affective empathy, Organizational Commitment. **Cognitive** Cognitive performance, Knowledge and skill, Self-definition, Positive other-attributions.
Contextual characteristics Physical workplace features, Leadership, Technological complexity, Ergonomics, Human resource management policies and practices, Organization structure and design, Virtuality.	**Psychological processes** Proactivity, Adaptive responding, Goal generation, Goal striving, Active learning, Relational coordination, Perspective taking.	**Health and well-being** Stress, Anxiety, Depression, Emotional fatigue, burnout, Suicide risk, Work adjustment, Somatic health symptoms, Safety, Work-life balance.
	MODERATORS Growth need strength, Need for achievement, Need for affiliation, Dispositional affect, Locus of control, Conscientiousness, Proactive personality, Propensity to trust, Cognitive ability, Teamwork knowledge, Social skills, Pro-social values, Other orientation, Cultural values, Context satisfaction.	

context within which work designs exist. In addition to acting as a source of work design characteristics, context has the potential to restrict the range of the input variables in our model and to affect the base rate on these variables (Johns, 2006). Context may also influence the relative strength, salience, and direction of mediational mechanisms in our framework. For example, it has been suggested that we do not pay sufficient heed to the manner in which national culture affects how work is designed, enacted, and experienced—an especially significant issue given globalization (Grant et al., 2011). Humphrey et al. (2007) have also pointed out that there is limited knowledge of the extent to which different types of work performed in different types of industries and occupations affect the nature of relationships between work design inputs and outcomes. For example, albeit with some exceptions (e.g., Elsbach & Hargadon, 2006), work design issues for knowledge workers and professionals have been neglected (Parker & Ohly, 2008). In a similar vein, scholars have advocated extending the boundary of work design. To some extent, this has already occurred with greater focus on the home-work interface reflecting the blurring of boundaries between work and home (Allen, chapter 34 of this handbook; Rousseau, 1977). But the boundaries are changing in other ways. For example, Cordery (2006) advocated applying work design principles to both employee and non-employee roles, for example where customers are expected to "co-produce" work outputs. Likewise, instead of focusing on the boundary of a specific job, Fried, Grant, Levi, Hadani, and Slowik (2007) have proposed looking at work design from the perspective of a longer term career.

Examining Interactional and Configurational Effects

It is apparent from our guiding framework that the overall design of work may vary on many dimensions, both within and across the task, relational, and contextual categories of input. Furthermore, it is known that many individual input variables, such as autonomy, task significance, feedback, interdependence, interpersonal interaction, and physical workplace features, are themselves multidimensional constructs (Grant, 2007; Grant et al., 2011; Kluger & DeNisi, 1996; May et al., 2005; Morgeson & Humphrey, 2006). However, most research in the field has tended to ignore the multidimensionality of work design, for example by studying single input variables and/or by assuming

that work design variables exert their effects independently of each other (Morgeson & Humphrey, 2008). To date, research into interactions between work design inputs has been largely confined to examining the interactive effects of job demands, job control (autonomy), and social support on stress and well-being (e.g., Bakker, Demerouti, & Euwema, 2005). However, limited research into other input interactions (e.g., Grant et al., 2007) suggests that this is likely to be an important area for future investigation.

Likewise, more research is needed into the nature and impact of different configurations of work design inputs (Morgeson & Humphrey, 2008). Historically, a limited number of "pure" work design configurations have been identified (e.g., Campion et al., 2005; Cordery & Parker, 2007), though it seems likely that the changing environment for work (by emphasizing different work design characteristics) is raising awareness of other work design configurations (e.g., relational work designs in service settings; Grant, 2007) that have different psychological implications. Research is also needed into "mixed" work design configurations, for example where different design attributes apply at the task, activity, and role levels (e.g., Morgeson & Campion, 2002).

Mapping Specific Mediational Pathways

Our primary intention in this review has been to identify and describe work design inputs, mediating states/processes, and outcomes. In doing so, we have adopted a largely taxonomic approach. However, it has certainly not been our intention to imply that every input influences every mediational state or process that we have described, and hence all effectiveness criteria. There is considerable scope to refine and extend existing knowledge of how the various elements in our framework are linked. In future research, it is clearly going to be important to develop more fine-grained theoretical specifications linking the three levels of inputs to individual outcomes via specific motivational, cognitive, affective, and interactional pathways. There is also a need to increase our understanding of how individual work design inputs influence group processes and outcomes. Parker and Ohly (2008) advocated considering how job designs affect organizing-oriented outcomes, such as the development of swift trust, collaboration, group mental models, and group norms. Similarly, Morgeson and Humphrey (2008) recommended the need for a greater understanding between job and team design—a point that is pursued in Harrison and Humphrey (2010). At the same time, scholars have advocated the need to look in more depth at temporal processes, such as investigating when work characteristics have their effects and how long those effects last. Another recommendation (Vough & Parker, 2008) for getting underneath the surface of work design is to look more closely at meaning as a mechanism, with topics like the "meaning of work" and work engagement (e.g., Kahn, 1990) having evolved in parallel with work design theory, yet with little cross-dialogue. Other researchers have called for additional mediating mechanisms to be investigated, for example decision-making processes (Grant et al., 2011). Finally, though research has sometimes shown relationships between work design inputs and outcomes to be curvilinear (e.g., Xie & Johns, 1995), little is known about the degree to which different levels on work design input variables may engage different mediational processes (Humphrey et al., 2007), thereby generating non-linear relationships between work design and psychological outcomes.

Improving Research Methodologies

One aspect that many reviewers of the field have consistently agreed on over the years is that there is considerable scope for improvement in the approaches that have been used to formulate and test work design theory (Humphrey et al., 2007; Parker & Wall, 1998; Roberts & Glick, 1981). Recent work on developing and validating more comprehensive measurement tools for use in work design research (e.g., Morgeson & Humphrey, 2006) has helped considerably when it comes to providing reliable and valid instruments for testing an expanded theory of work design such as we have presented here. However, eliminating (or at least discounting) common-source bias as a source of contamination in studies linking work design measures to individual effectiveness outcomes remains a particular problem and priority for research being conducted in this area (Humphrey et al., 2007), and there continues to be a dearth of longitudinal and quasi-experimental field studies of work design (Grant et al., 2011).

Investigating Emergent Elements of Work Designs

Over and above these recommendations for future research directions, a recurring theme has been the call by scholars to adapt work design theory and research in light of the constantly changing nature of work. While there have been big strides

made in addressing this concern over recent years (viz. Grant, 2007; Parker, Wall, & Cordery, 2001), there continue to be calls for work design theory and research to address new, emergent aspects of tasks and roles. For example, Grant et al. (2011) have suggested that a fourth category of work design input variable, temporal characteristics, may need to be added in order to reflect aspects of the time horizons (e.g., cycle times, time pressure) that increasingly characterize the performance and enactment of tasks and roles.

Next, we elaborate this theme to consider some of the radical changes occurring in the world of work, and some illustrative implications for work design theory and practice. However, somewhat paradoxically, we recognize that many jobs are in fact not changing much at all. We therefore then shift the focus to how we might influence the practice of work design. Bringing these ideas together, if we are better able to influence and shape how jobs are designed, then we as scholars might be better equipped—not just to evaluate and understand what happens in the world of future work—but to more actively shape it.

Transformation in the Workplace

Although some commentators dispute the depth and spread of the organizational transformation occurring in the world of work, there is no doubt that some organizations are indeed changing, especially those at the leading edge in new technology sectors (Morris, 2004).

A trend that cannot be disputed in Western economies is that work is becoming increasingly distributed. Facilitated by advances in technology as well as other forces, people increasingly need to work collaboratively, even though they: work in different places (e.g., increasing real estate prices, dual careers, and ease of communications mean that employees will work in cheaper offices away from the main site); work at different times (because of flexible working, different time zones); work in different legal entities (joint ventures, alliances, outsourcing, networks, supply-chain partnerships, and other cross-organizational relationships means that people often have the same end goal but different legal entities), and work on different contracts (e.g., "staff" can be self-employed, temporary staff, contractors, customers, partners). All of these trends give rise to significant work design challenges, some of which scholars and practitioners have barely considered.

For example, how does supervision and control operate if the employer is not at the workplace, if there is more than one employer present, or if the employee is on loan/seconded/outsourced to another employer? Consider the case of a city council that outsourced their operation of housing benefits (Rubery, Earnshaw, Marchington, Lee Cooke, & Vincent, 2000). For legal reasons, the council was required to authorize payments processed by the outsourcer. This meant that those employees who now worked for the outsourcer (who had previously worked for the council) had to have their work checked by council employees. They were no longer able to authorize their own work, but needed it to be signed off by a second employer. There was a need for the employer to control the outsourced tasks; yet, at the same time, the employer needed to cultivate the cooperation of employees on both sides. This scenario illustrates how control issues in organizations will likely become more complex, and how trust between the parties and other relational processes might significantly influence the enacted work designs.

As another example, it is projected that individuals will increasingly work on a project or temporary basis for virtual organizations, calling into question how individuals' social and collective needs will be met. One possibility is that "guilds" will develop for professional societies, alumni associations, and temporary agencies, with the sole purpose of fostering the well-being and success of members (Laubacher & Malone, 1997). Guilds might also become responsible for providing insurance, learning opportunities, a sense of community, and other services. Thus, the relational elements of jobs that we have discussed in this article, such as social support and opportunities for growth, as well as other task characteristics (e.g., opportunities for learning), might themselves become distributed across organizations. This echoes our earlier suggestion to consider not just "jobs" but broader "work roles."

On the "supply" side, as we described earlier, work forces are becoming more diverse. Harrison and Humphrey (2010) identified a range of ways that diversity might influence team work design. For example, teams might distribute tasks that vary in desirability based on status and stereotypes, which could deepen fault lines, inhibit skill development, and impair team performance. Work designs that involve "one or two step" rotation might prevent such consequences. A further "supply" issue is that there will also be slower labor force growth in many Western economies. A consequence will be the need to enhance participation in the labor force from, for example, the elderly, women, and people with disabilities. This gives rise to intriguing work design

questions. For example, because their government anticipates labor shortages in the future, a project has been initiated in the Netherlands to design effective jobs for employees with special needs, such as developmental disabilities or mental health disorders. The work designs need to meet the special needs of individuals, as well as the needs of organizations for competitiveness and flexibility, while also taking into account task interdependencies with regular coworkers. We know little about what types of work designs are best at meeting this range of criteria, or the best processes for designing them.

The above examples are not intended to be exhaustive. Rather, they illustrate the varied ways that work and organizations are changing, and therefore how we need to develop proactively our theories to reflect these changes. Importantly, however, we advocate that research and theory should also *inform and shape* these developments; it is to this issue of applying knowledge that we now turn.

Continuity in the Workplace
Somewhat paradoxically, as well as recognizing that work is indeed changing, it is important to recognize that work—at least its quality—is also not changing. Many sociologists suggest that the grand claims of radical workplace transformation are overstated, or at least limited only to a subset of organizations (e.g., Neumark, 2002). Certainly, evidence from national surveys of work design practice suggest that, despite decades of research showing the importance of work enrichment, there are still many impoverished work designs. For example, the United Kingdom's ESRC's Future of Work survey (Taylor, 2002, p. 8) conducted in 2000 noted that, in relation to the quality of work life, "the most striking conclusion in assessing the new data is the degree of continuity as much as any drastic change in today's workplaces." Indeed, one of the key changes they reported is how work is becoming less satisfying and more stressful. Likewise, in excess of one-third of U.S. workers report that their jobs are "often" or "always" stressful (Murphy & Sauter, 2003). Moreover, poor quality job designs are dominant in many developing countries. For example, Gamble, Morris, and Wilkinson (2004) report that mass production and Taylorist job designs are alive and well in the newly industrializing economies. The bottom line is that there are still many jobs with simplified work designs that would be well-served by a dose of good "old fashioned" job enrichment.

If there are still many poorly designed jobs, the question that arises is how to influence this practice.

Obviously, such a question can be tackled from a broader institutional and policy perspective. Policies that are relevant to work design include, for example, those concerned with health and safety (e.g., the UK health and safety guidance for work stress focuses extensively on work design), with the labor market conditions (e.g., structures for union representation, flexibility of contracts, etc.), and with economic performance and innovation. Adopting a cross-national, and more sociological, perspective is important in understanding the role of policy—it is clear that some countries have better quality work designs than others. For example, in an investigation of different types of market economies, Gallie (2007) cites clear evidence of higher task autonomy, skill variety, and opportunities for self-development in Scandinavian countries (Denmark, Finland, and Sweden) relative to countries such as Germany and the United Kingdom. The difference is partly attributable to the Scandinavian countries having complex and diversified product market strategies (therefore requiring more skilled employees), but also to other factors, such as the representation systems by which employees influence work conditions. The superiority of work design in Scandinavian countries relative to others is thus consistent with the policy importance that these countries attach to quality of work programs.

But it is not just about influencing what governments do: it is also about influencing the practices of businesses and other organizations and stakeholders (McIlroy, Marginson, & Regalia, 2004). For example, it is possible to influence how managers manage; how unions organize; how chief executives, consultants, and others design or redesign organizations; and how engineers design technology (e.g., building in more or less latitude for employee control or social interaction). Unfortunately, influencing practice is not easy, as has been frequently lamented in articles on evidence-based management. In the case of management, for example, we need to take active steps to encourage managers to make better use of existing evidence, such as changing how we educate professional managers and establishing collaborative networks among managers, educators, and researchers (Rousseau, 2006).

Endeavors to influence practice and policy will be helped by work design scholars developing and disseminating understanding about the process of design and redesign. The latter includes considering how other work systems and structures (e.g., technology, human resource practices, etc.) relate to, and augment or constrain, work design (Cordery

& Parker, 2007; Morgeson & Humphrey, 2006). Exactly how key stakeholders design jobs also needs more attention (Morgeson & Humphrey, 2008). For example, Campion and Stevens (1991) showed that management college students' natural propensity is to design jobs along Tayloristic principles (e.g., by grouping similar tasks together), although it is also possible to train them to adopt more motivationally oriented approaches. The best strategies for work redesign should also be investigated. It might be, for example, that a combination of top-down-style work redesigns (e.g., structural empowerment initiatives), as well as training individuals to actively change their own jobs from the bottom up (such as by job crafting, role innovation, or negotiating i-deals), is the most powerful way to achieve sustained job redesigns. We need more attention to the "how" of work design and redesign.

In the future, therefore, we recommend that work design scholars not only seek to understand and assess the effects of new forms of work organization, but that they proactively seek to influence them. Regarding the quest for understanding, given the current healthy state of work design research (e.g., see Grant, Fried, Parker, & Frese, 2010), we are optimistic that many of these avenues will be pursued. Regarding the quest for influence, a more concerted effort is needed by work design scholars to influence policy and practice, in part by giving greater attention to the process of work design and redesign, and in part by promoting evidence-based management. As we have argued, just because research has well established the positive consequences of work enrichment, this does not mean that practitioners have embraced this thinking. The same will be true of our more advanced insights into new work design issues if we do not find better ways to influence practice.

Note

1. This distinction between states and processes is similar to that made in recent conceptualizations of the determinants of team effectiveness (Marks, Mathieu, & Zaccaro, 2001; Mathieu, Maynard, Rapp, & Gilson, 2008).

References

Aboa-Eboule, C., Brisson, C., Maunsell, E., Masse, B., Bourbonnais, R., Vezina, M., Milot, A., Theroux, P., & Dagenais, G. R. (2007). Job strain and risk of acute recurrent coronary heart disease events. *Journal of the American Medical Association, 298*, 1652–1660.

Agerbo, E., Gunnell, D., Bondea, J. P., Mortensen, P. B., & Nordentoft, M. (2007). Suicide and occupation: The impact of socio-economic, demographic and psychiatric differences. *Psychological Medicine, 37*, 1131–1140.

Ahuja, M. K., Chudoba, K. M., Kacmar, C. J., McKnight, D. H., & George, J. (2007). IT road warriors: Balancing work-family conflict, job autonomy, and work overload to mitigate turnover intentions. *MIS Quarterly, 31*, 1–17.

Alderfer, C. P. (1969). An empirical test of a new theory of human needs. *Organizational Behavior and Human Performance, 4*, 142–175.

Amabile, T. M., Barsade, S. G., Mueller, J. S., & Staw, B. M. (2005). Affect and creativity at work. *Administrative Science Quarterly, 50*, 367–403.

Ambrose, M. L., & Kulik, C. T. (1999). Old friends, new faces: Motivation in the 1990s. *Journal of Management, 25*, 231–292.

Aryee, S., Srinivas, E. S., & Tan, H. W. (2005). Rhythms of life: Antecedents and outcomes of work-family balance in employed parents. *Journal of Applied Psychology, 90*, 132–146.

Ashforth, B. E., Harrison, S. H., & Corley, K. G. (2008). Identification in organizations: An examination of four fundamental questions. *Journal of Management, 34*, 325–374.

Ashforth, B. E., & Kreiner, G. E. (1999). 'How can you do it?': Dirty work and the challenge of constructing a positive identity. *Academy of Management Review, 24*, 413–434.

Ashforth, B. E., Kreiner, G. E., & Fugate, M. (2000). All in a day's work: Boundaries and micro role transitions. *Academy of Management Review, 25*, 472–491.

Avolio, B. J., & Waldman, D. A. (1990). An examination of age and cognitive test performance across job complexity and occupational types. *Journal of Applied Psychology, 75*, 43–50.

Axtell, C. M., Holman, D. J., Unsworth, K. L., Wall, T. D., & Waterson, P. E. (2000). Shopfloor innovation: Facilitating the suggestion and implementation of ideas. *Journal of Occupational & Organizational Psychology, 73*, 265–385.

Axtell, C. M., Parker, S. K., Holman, D. J., & Totterdell, P. (2007). Enhancing customer service: Perspective taking in a call centre. *European Journal of Work & Organizational Psychology, 16*, 141–168.

Bailey, D. E., & Kurland, N. B. (2002). A review of telework research: Findings, new directions, and lessons for the study of modern work. *Journal of Organizational Behavior, 23*, 383–400.

Bakker, A. B., Demerouti, E., & Euwema, M. C. (2005). Job resources buffer the impact of job demands on burnout. *Journal of Occupational Health Psychology, 10*, 170–180.

Baltes, P. B., & Smith, J. (1990). Toward a psychology of wisdom and its ontogenesis. In R. J. Sternberg (Ed.), *Wisdom: Its nature, origins, and development* (pp 87–120). Cambridge: Cambridge University Press.

Barker, J. R. (1993). Tightening the iron cage: Concertive control in self-managing teams. *Administrative Science Quarterly, 38*, 408–437.

Barley, S. R., & Kunda, G. (2001). Bringing work back in. *Organization Science, 12*, 76–95.

Barling, J., Kelloway, E. K., & Iverson, R. D. (2003). High-quality work, job satisfaction, and occupational injuries. *Journal of Applied Psychology, 88*, 276–283.

Barnes, C. M., & Van Dyne, L. (2009). 'I'm tired': Differential effects of physical and emotional fatigue on workload management strategies. *Human Relations, 62*, 59–92.

Batt, R., & Appelbaum, E. (1995). Worker participation in diverse settings: Does the form affect the outcome, and if so, who benefits? *British Journal of Industrial Relations, 33*, 353–378.

Beer, M., Spector, B., Lawrence, P. R., Mills, D. Q., & Walton, R. E. (1985). *Human resource management: A general manager's perspective*. New York: Free Press.

Bell, B. S., & Kozlowski, S. W. J. (2008). Active learning: Effects of core training design elements on self-regulatory processes, learning and adaptability. *Journal of Applied Psychology, 93*, 296–316.

Berg, J. M., Wrzesniewski, A., & Dutton, J. E. (2010). Perceiving and responding to challenges in job crafting at different ranks. *Journal of Organizational Behavior, 31*, 158–186.

Block, J. P., He, Y., Zaslavsky, A. M., Ding, L., & Ayanian, J. Z. (2009). Psychosocial stress and change in weight among US adults. *American Journal of Epidemiology, 170*, 181–192.

Bolino, M. C., & Turnley, W. H. (2005). The personal costs of citizenship behavior: The relationship between individual initiative and role overload, job stress, and work-family conflict. *Journal of Applied Psychology, 90*, 740–748.

Bottger, P. C., & Chew, I. K. (1986). The job characteristics model and growth satisfaction: Main effects of assimilation of work experience and context satisfaction. *Human Relations, 39*, 575–594.

Brannick, M. T., Levine, E. L., & Morgeson, F. P. (2007). *Job analysis: Methods, research, and applications for human resource management* (2nd ed.). Thousand Oaks, CA: Sage.

Breaugh, J. A. (1985). The measurement of work autonomy. *Human Relations, 38*, 551–570.

Brett, J. F., & VandeWalle, D. (1999). Goal orientation and goal content as predictors of performance in a training program. *Journal of Applied Psychology, 84*, 863–873.

Briscoe, F. (2007). From iron cage to iron shield? How bureaucracy enables temporal flexibility for professional service workers. *Organization Science, 18*, 297–314.

Brotheridge, C., & Grandey, A. A. (2002). Emotional labor and burnout: Comparing two perspectives of "people work." *Journal of Vocational Behavior, 60*, 17–39.

Brown, S. P. (1996). A meta-analysis and review of organizational research on job involvement. *Psychological Bulletin, 120*, 235–255.

Burr, R., & Cordery, J. L. (2001). Self-management efficacy as a mediator of the relation between job design and employee motivation. *Human Performance, 14*, 27–44.

Burton, K. D., Lydon, J. E., D'Allessandro, D. U., & Koestner, R. (2006). The differential effects of intrinsic and identified motivation and well-being and performance: Prospective, experimental, and implicit approaches to self-determination theory. *Journal of Personality and Social Psychology, 91*, 750–762.

Campion, M. A. (1988). Interdisciplinary approaches to job design: A constructive replication with extensions. *Journal of Applied Psychology, 73*, 467–481.

Campion, M. A., & McClelland, C. L. (1991). Interdisciplinary examination of the costs and benefits of enlarged jobs: A job design quasi-experiment. *Journal of Applied Psychology, 76*, 186–198.

Campion, M. A., & McClelland, C. L. (1993). Follow-up and extension of the interdisciplinary costs and benefits of enlarged jobs. *Journal of Applied Psychology, 78*, 339–351.

Campion, M. A., Medsker, G. J., & Higgs, A. C. (1993). Relations between work group characteristics and effectiveness: Implications for designing effective work groups. *Personnel Psychology, 46*, 823–850.

Campion, M. A., Mumford, T. V., Morgeson, F. P., & Nahrgang, J. D. (2005). Work redesign: Eight obstacles and opportunities. *Human Resource Management, 44*, 367–390.

Campion, M. A., & Stevens, M. J. (1991). Neglected questions in job design: How people design jobs, task-job predictability, and influence of training. *Journal of Business and Psychology, 6,* 169–191.

Campion, M. A., & Thayer, P. W. (1985). Development and field evaluation of an interdisciplinary measure of job design. *Journal of Applied Psychology, 70,* 29–43.

Campion, M. A., & Thayer, P. W. (1987). Job design: Approaches, outcomes, and trade-offs. *Organizational Dynamics, 15,* 66–79.

Carayon, P. (1994). Effects of electronic performance monitoring on job design and worker stress: Results of two studies. *International Journal of Human-Computer Interaction, 6,* 177–190.

Cartwright, S., & Holmes, N. (2006). The meaning of work: The challenge of regaining employee engagement and reducing cynicism. *Human Resource Management Review, 16,* 199–208.

Chen, G., & Kanfer, R. (2006). Toward a system theory of motivated behavior in work teams. *Research in organizational behavior, 27,* 223–267.

Chen, G., Thomas, B., & Wallace, J. (2005). A multilevel examination of the relationships among training outcomes, mediating regulatory processes, and adaptive performance. *Journal of Applied Psychology, 90,* 827–841.

Cherns, A. B. (1976). The principles of socio-technical systems design. *Human Relations, 29,* 783–792.

Chiu, S., & Chen, H. (2005). Relationship between job characteristics and organizational citizenship behavior: The mediational role of job satisfaction. *Social Behavior and Personality, 33,* 523–539.

Clegg, C. W. (2000). Sociotechnical principles for system design. *Applied Ergonomics, 21,* 463–477.

Clegg, C. W., & Spencer, C. (2007). A circular and dynamic model of the process of job design. *Journal of Occupational and Organizational Psychology, 80,* 321–339.

Cohen, L., & Mallon, M. (1999). The transition from organisational employment to portfolio working: Perceptions of 'boundarylessness'. *Work, Employment and Society, 13,* 329–352.

Conner, D. S. (2003). Social comparison in virtual work environments: An examination of contemporary referent selection. *Journal of Occupational and Organizational Psychology, 76,* 133–147.

Cordery, J. (1996). Autonomous work groups and quality circles. In M. West (Ed.), *Handbook of work group psychology* (pp. 225–248). Chichester, UK: Wiley.

Cordery, J. L. (2006, May). *One more time: How do you motivate…customers? Applying work design principles to co-production arrangements in service organizations.* Paper presented at the 21st Annual Conference of the Society for Industrial and Organizational Psychology, Dallas, TX.

Cordery, J. L., Morrison, D. L., Wright, B. M., & Wall, T. D. (2009). The impact of autonomy and task uncertainty on team performance: A longitudinal field study. *Journal of Organizational Behavior, 30,* 5, 1–19.

Cordery, J. L., Mueller, W. S., & Smith, L. M. (1991). Attitudinal and behavioral effects of autonomous group working: A longitudinal field study. *Academy of Management Journal, 43,* 464–476.

Cordery, J. L., & Parker, S. K. (2007). Work organisation. In P. Boxall, J. Purcell, & P. Wright (Eds.), *Oxford handbook of human resource management* (pp. 187–209). Oxford: Oxford University Press.

Cordery, J. L., & Wall, T. D. (1985). Work design and supervisory practices: A model. *Human Relations, 38,* 425–441.

Csikszentimihalyi, M. (2000). Happiness, flow and economic equality. *American Psychologist, 55*(10), 1163–1164.

Daniels, K. (2006). Rethinking job characteristics in work stress research. *Human Relations, 59,* 267–290.

Deci, E. L., & Ryan, R. M. (1985). *Intrinsic motivation and self-determination in human behavior.* New York: Plenum.

De Jonge, J., & Schaufeli, W. (1998). Job characteristics and employee well-being: A test of Warr's vitamin model in health care workers using structural equation modelling. *Journal of Organizational Behavior, 19,* 387–407.

Diefendorff, J. M., Croyle, M. H., & Gosserand, R. H. (2005). The dimensionality and antecedents of emotional labor strategies. *Journal of Vocational Behavior, 66,* 339–357.

Dierdorff, E. C., & Ellington, J. K. (2008). It's the nature of work: Examining behavior-based sources of work-family conflict across occupations. *Journal of Applied Psychology, 93,* 883–892.

Dirks, K. T., & Ferrin, D. L. (2001). The role of trust in organizational settings. *Organization Science, 12,* 450–467.

Dollard, M., Skinner, N., Tuckey, M. R., & Bailey, T. (2007). National surveillance of psychosocial risk factors in the workplace: An international overview. *Work & Stress, 21,* 1–29.

Dorman, C., & Zapf, D. (2001). Job satisfaction: A meta-analysis of stabilities. *Journal of Organizational Psychology, 22,* 483–504.

Dostoyevsky, F. (1985). *The house of the dead.* Harmondsworth: Penguin.

Edmondson, A. C., Dillon, J. R., & Roloff, K. S. (2007). Three perspectives on team learning: Outcome improvement, task mastery, and group process. In A. Brief & J. Walsh (Eds.), *The Academy of Management annals* (Vol. 1, pp. 269–314).

Edwards, J. A., Guppy, A., & Cockerton, T. (2007). A longitudinal study exploring the relationships between occupational stressors, non-work stressors, and work performance. *Work & Stress, 21,* 99–116.

Edwards, J. R., Scully, J. A., & Brtek, M. D. (1999). The measurement of work: Hierarchical representation of the Multimethod Job Design Questionnaire. *Personnel Psychology, 52,* 305–334.

Edwards, J. R., Scully, J. A., & Brtek, M.D. (2000). The nature and outcomes of work: A replication and extension of interdisciplinary work design research. *Journal of Applied Psychology, 85,* 860–868.

Egri, C. (2004). Generation cohorts and personal values: A comparison of China and the United States. *Organization Science, 15,* 210–220.

Eisenberger, R., Jones, J. J., Stinglhamber, F., Shanock, L., & Randall, A. Y. (2005). Flow experiences at work: For high achievers alone? *Journal of Organizational Behavior, 26,* 755–775.

Elliot, A., Shell, M., Bouas Henry, K., & Maier, M. (2005). Achievement goals, performance contingencies, and performance attainment: An experimental test. *Journal of Educational Psychology, 97*(4), 630–640.

Elsbach, K. D., & Hargadon, A. B. (2006). Enhancing creativity through "mindless" work: A framework of workday design. *Organization Science, 17,* 470–483.

Fedor, D. B., Caldwell, S., & Herold, D. M. (2006). The effects of organizational changes on employee commitment: A multilevel investigation. *Personnel Psychology, 59,* 1–29.

Fraser, J., & Gold, M. (2001). 'Portfolio workers': Autonomy and control amongst freelance translators. *Work, Employment and Society, 15*, 679–697.

Fraser, R. (1947). *The incidence of neurosis among factory workers* (Industrial Health Research Board, Rep. No. 90). London: HMSO.

Frese, M., Garst, H., & Fay, D. (2007). Making things happen: Reciprocal relationships between work characteristics and personal initiative in a four-wave longitudinal structural equation model. *Journal of Applied Psychology, 92*, 1084–1102.

Frese, M., & Zapf, D. (1994). Action as the core of work psychology: A German approach. In H. C. Triandis, M. D. Dunnette & L. M. Hough (Eds.), *Handbook of industrial and organizational psychology* (Vol. 1, pp. 271–340). Palo Alto, CA: Consulting Psychologists Press.

Fried, Y., & Ferris, G. R. (1987). The validity of the job characteristics model: A review and meta-analysis. *Personnel Psychology, 40*, 287–322.

Fried, Y. (1991). Meta-analytic comparison of the Job Diagnostic Survey and Job Characteristics Inventory as correlates of work satisfaction and performance. *Journal of Applied Psychology, 76*, 690–697.

Fried, Y., Grant, A. M., Levi, A. S., Hadani, M., & Slowik, L. H. (2007). Job design in temporal context: A career dynamics perspective. *Journal of Organizational Behavior, 28*, 911–927.

Fried, Y., Levi, A. S., & Laurence, G. (2008). Motivation and job design in the new world of work. In C. Cooper & C. Cartwright (Eds.), *The Oxford handbook of personnel psychology* (pp. 586–611). Oxford: Oxford University Press.

Friedman, R. S., & Foerster, J. (2005). Effects of motivational cues on perceptual asymmetry: Implications for creativity and analytical problem solving. *Journal of Personality and Social Psychology, 88*, 263–275.

Fuller, B., & Marler, L. E. (in press). Change driven by nature: A meta-analytic review of the proactive personality literature. *Journal of Vocational Behavior*. Accessed November 16, 2009 at doi:10.1016/j.jvb.2009.05.008.

Gagne, M., & Deci, E. L. (2005). Self-determination theory and work motivation. *Journal of Organizational Behavior, 26*, 331–362.

Gajendran, R. S., & Harrison, D. A. (2007). The good, the bad, and the unknown about telecommuting: Meta-analysis of psychological mediators and individual consequences. *Journal of Applied Psychology, 92*, 1524–1541.

Gallie, D. (2007). Production regimes and the quality of employment in Europe. *Annual Review of Sociology, 33*, 85–104.

Gamble, J., Morris, J., & Wilkinson, B. (2004). Mass production is alive and well: The future of work and organization in East Asia. *International Journal of Human Resource Management, 15*, 397–409.

Ghose, A. K., Majid, N., & Ernst, C. (2008). *The global employment challenge*. Geneva: ILO.

Gilbreth, F. B. (1911). *Motion study*. London: Constable and Company

Golden, T. D. (2006). Avoiding depletion in virtual work: Telework and the intervening impact of work exhaustion on commitment and turnover intentions. *Journal of Vocational Behavior, 69*, 176–187.

Graen, G. B., & Uhl-Bien, M. (1995). Relationship-based approach to leadership: Development of leader–member exchange (LMX) theory of leadership over 25 years: Applying a multi-level multi-domain perspective. *Leadership Quarterly, 6*, 219–247.

Grandey, A. A. (2003). When "the show must go on": Surface acting and deep acting as determinants of emotional exhaustion and peer-rated service delivery. *Academy of Management Journal, 46*, 86–96.

Grant, A. M. (2007). Relational job design and the motivation to make a prosocial difference. *Academy of Management Review, 32*, 393–417.

Grant, A. M. (2008a). Does intrinsic motivation fuel the prosocial fire? Motivational synergy in predicting persistence, performance, and productivity. *Journal of Applied Psychology, 93*, 48–58.

Grant, A. M. (2008b). The significance of task significance: Job performance effects, relational mechanisms, and boundary conditions. *Journal of Applied Psychology, 93*, 108–124.

Grant, A. M., & Ashford, S. J. (2008). The dynamics of proactivity at work. *Research in Organizational Behavior, 28*, 3–34.

Grant, A. M., Campbell, E. M., Chen, G., Cottone, K., Lapedis, D., & Lee, K. (2007). Impact and the art of motivation maintenance: The effects of contact with beneficiaries on persistence behavior. *Organizational Behavior and Human Decision Processes, 103*, 53–67.

Grant, A. M., Fried, Y., & Juillerat, T. (2011). Work matters: Job design in classic and contemporary perspectives. In S. Zedeck (Ed.), *APA handbook of industrial and organizational psychology*. Washington, DC: American Psychological Association.

Grant, A. M., Fried, Y., Parker, S. K., & Frese, M. (2010). Putting job design in context: Introduction to the special issue. *Journal of Organizational Behavior, 31*(2), 145–157.

Grant, A. M., & Parker, S. K. (2009). Redesigning work design theories: The rise of relational and proactive perspectives. *Academy of Management Annals, 3*, 311–375.

Griffin, M. A., Neal, A., & Parker, S. K. (2007). A new model of work role performance: Positive behavior in uncertain and interdependent contexts. *Academy of Management Journal, 50*, 327–347.

Griffin, R. W. (1981). Supervisory behavior as a source of perceived task scope. *Journal of Occupational Psychology, 54*, 175–182.

Griffin, R. W. (1991). Effects of work redesign on employee perceptions, attitudes and behaviours: A long-term investigation. *Academy of Management Journal, 34*, 425–435.

Hackman, J. R., & Lawler, E. E., III. (1971). Employee reactions to job characteristics. *Journal of Applied Psychology, 55*, 259–286.

Hackman, J. R., & Oldham, G. R. (1975). Development of the Job Diagnostic Survey. *Journal of Applied Psychology, 60*, 159–170.

Hackman, J. R., & Oldham, G. R. (1976). Motivation through the design of work: Test of a theory. *Organisational Behaviour and Human Performance, 15*, 250–279.

Hackman, J. R., & Oldham, G. R. (1980). *Work redesign*. Reading, MA: Addison-Wesley.

Hakanen, J. J., Schaufeli, W. B., & Ahola, K. (2008). The job demands-resources model: A three-year cross-lagged study of burnout, depression, commitment, and work engagement. *Work & Stress, 22*, 224–241.

Hambrick, D. C., Finkelstein, S., & Mooney, A. C. (2005). Executive job demands: New insights for explaining strategic decisions and leader behaviors. *Academy of Management Review, 30*, 472–481.

Harrison, D. A., & Humphrey, S. E. (2010). Designing for diversity or diversity for design? Tasks, interdependence, and within-unit differences at work. Forthcoming in the *Journal of Organizational Behavior, 31*, 328–337.

Harrison, M. M., Neff, N. L., Schwall, A. R., & Zhao, X. (2006, April). *A meta-analytic investigation of individual creativity and innovation.* Paper presented at the 21st Annual Conference of the Society for Industrial and Organizational Psychology, Dallas, TX.

Hecht, L. M. (2001). Role conflict and role overload: Different concepts, different consequences. *Sociological Inquiry, 71*, 111–121.

Helson, R., & Srivastava, S. (2002). Creative and wise people: Similarities, differences, and how they develop. *Personality and Social Psychology Bulletin, 28*, 1430–1440.

Herzberg, F. (1968). One more time: How do you motivate employees? *Harvard Business Review, 46*, 53–63.

Herzberg, F., Mausner, B., & Snyderman, B. B. (1959). *The motivation to work.* New York: Wiley.

Hewlett, S. A., Sherbin, L., & Sumberg, K. (2009). How Gen Y and boomers will reshape your agenda. *Harvard Business Review, 87*, 71–76.

Hochwarter, W. A., Ferris, G. R., Gavin, M. B., Perrewe, P. L., Hall, A. T., & Fink, D. (2007). Political skill as neutralizer of felt accountability-job tension effects on job performance ratings: A longitudinal investigation. *Organizational Behavior and Human Decision Processes, 102*, 226–239.

Hockey, G. R. J. (2000). Work environments and performance. In N. Chmiel (Ed.), *Introduction to work and organizational psychology* (pp. 206–230). Oxford: Blackwell.

Hoffer Gittell, J. (2001). Supervisory span, relational coordination, and flight departure performance: A reassessment of postbureaucracy theory. *Organization Science, 12*, 468–483.

Hoffer Gittell, J., Weinberg, D. B., Bennett, A. L., & Miller, J. A. (2008). Is the doctor in? A relational approach to job design and the coordination of work. *Human Resource Management, 47*, 729–755.

Holman, D. J. (2005). Call centres. In D. Holman, T. D. Wall, C. W. Clegg, P. Sparrow, & A. Howard (Eds.), *The essentials of the new workplace: A guide to the human impact of modern working practices* (Rev. ed., pp. 111–132). Chichester, UK: Wiley.

Hulin, C. L. (1971). Individual differences and job enrichment: The case against general treatments. In J. R. Maker (Ed.), *New perspectives in job enrichment* (pp. 159–191). New York: Van Nostrand Reinhold.

Hulin, C. L., & Blood, M. R. (1968). Job enlargement, individual differences and worker responses. *Psychological Bulletin, 69*, 41–55.

Humphrey, S. E., Nahrgang, J. D., & Morgeson, F. P. (2007). Integrating motivational, social, and contextual work design features: A meta-analytic summary and theoretical extension of the work design literature. *Journal of Applied Psychology, 92*, 1332–1356.

Ilgen, D. R., & Hollenbeck, J. R. (1991). The structure of work: Job design and roles. In M. D. Dunnette & L. M. Hough (Eds.), *Handbook of industrial and organizational psychology* (Vol. 2, pp. 165–208). Palo Alto, CA: Consulting Psychologists Press.

Ilies, R., & Judge, T. A. (2005). Goal regulation across time: The effects of feedback and affect. *Journal of Applied Psychology, 90*, 453–467.

International Labour Organization. (2008). *Global employment trends: January 2008.* Geneva: ILO.

Jackson, P. R., & Martin, R. (1996). Impact of just-in-time on job content, employee attitudes, and well-being: A longitudinal analysis. *Ergonomics, 39*, 1–16.

Jackson, P. R., & Mullarkey, S. (2000). Lean production teams and health in garment manufacture. *Journal of Occupational Health Psychology, 5*, 231–245.

Jackson, P. R., & Wall, T. D. (1991). How does operator control enhance performance of advanced manufacturing technology? *Ergonomics, 34*, 1301–1311.

Jackson, P. R., Wall, T. D., Martin, R., & Davids, K. (1993). New measures of job control, cognitive demand, and production responsibility. *Journal of Applied Psychology, 78*, 753–762.

Janssen, P. M., Peeters, M. C. W., de Jonge, J., Houkes, I., & Tummers, G. E. (2004). Specific relationships between job demands, job resources and psychological outcomes and the mediating role of negative work-home interference. *Journal of Vocational Behavior, 65*, 411–429.

Johns, G. (2006). The essential impact of context on organizational behavior. *Academy of Management Review, 31*, 386–408.

Johns, G., Xie, J. L., & Fang, Y. (1992). Mediating and moderating effects in job design. *Journal of Management, 18*, 657–676.

Jones, G. R. (1984). Task visibility, free riding, and shirking: Explaining the effect of structure and technology in employee behavior. *Academy of Management Review, 9*, 684–695.

Judge, T. A., Bono, J. E., & Locke, E. A. (2000). Personality and job satisfaction: The mediating role of job characteristics. *Journal of Applied Psychology, 85*, 237–249.

Kahn, W. A. (1990). Psychological conditions of personal engagement and disengagement at work. *Academy of Management Journal, 33*, 692–724.

Karasek, R. A., & Theorell, T. (1990). *Healthy work.* New York: Basic Books.

Keller, J., & Bless, H. (2008). Flow and regulatory capability: An experimental approach to the flow model of intrinsic motivation. *Personality and Social Psychology Bulletin, 34*, 196–209.

Kelly, J. E. (1992). Does job re-design theory explain job re-design outcomes? *Human Relations, 45*, 753–774.

Kiffin-Petersen, S. A., & Cordery, J. L. (2003). Trust, individualism and job characteristics as predictors of employee preference for teamwork. *International Journal of Human Resource Management, 14*, 93–116.

Kiggundu, M. N. (1981). Task interdependence and the theory of job design. *Academy of Management Review, 6*, 499–508.

Kiggundu, M. N. (1983). Task interdependence and job design: Test of a theory. *Organizational Behavior and Human Performance, 31*, 145–172.

Kirkman, B. L., & Rosen, B. (1999). Beyond self-management: Antecedents and consequences of team empowerment. *Academy of Management Journal, 42*, 58–75.

Kirkman, B. L., & Rosen, B. (2000). Powering up teams. *Organizational Dynamics, 28*, 48–66.

Kluger, A. N., & DeNisi, A. (1996). Effects of feedback intervention on performance: A historical review, a meta-analysis, and a preliminary feedback intervention theory. *Psychological Bulletin, 119*, 254–284.

Knudsen, H., Ducharme, L. J., & Roman, P. M. (2007). Job stress and poor sleep quality: Data from an American sample of full-time workers. *Social Science Medicine, 64*, 1997–2007

Kohn, M. L., & Schooler, C. (1982). Job conditions and personality: A longitudinal assessment of their reciprocal effects. *American Journal of Sociology, 87*, 1257–1286.

Kozlowski, S. W. J., & Bell, B. S. (2006). Disentangling achievement orientation and goal setting: Effects on self-regulatory processes. *Journal of Applied Psychology, 91*(4), 900–916.

Kozlowski, S. W. J., & Klein, K. J. (2000). A multilevel approach to theory and research in organizations: Contextual, temporal, and emergent processes. In K. L. Klein & S. W. J. Kozlowski (Eds.), *Multilevel theory, research, and methods in organizations: Foundations, extensions, and new directions* (pp. 3–90). San Francisco: Jossey-Bass.

Krausz, M., Sagie, A., & Biderman, Y. (2000). Actual and preferred work schedules and scheduling control as determinants of job-related attitudes. *Journal of Vocational Behavior, 56*, 1–11.

LaMontagne, A. D., Keegel, T., Vallance, D., Ostry, A., & Wolfe, R. (2008). Job strain–attributable depression in a sample of working Australians: Assessing the contribution to health inequalities. *BMC Public Health, 8*, 181–190.

Langfred, C. W. (2004). Too much of a good thing? Negative effects of high trust and individual autonomy in self-managing teams. *Academy of Management Journal, 47*, 385–399.

Langfred, C. W. (2007). The downside of self-management: A longitudinal study of the effects of conflict on trust, autonomy, and task interdependence in self-managing teams. *Academy of Management Journal, 50*, 885–900.

Lapierre, L. M., Hackett, R. D., & Taggar, S. (2006). A test of the links between family interference with work, job enrichment and leader-member exchange. *Applied Psychology: An International Review, 55*, 489–511.

Larson, J., Rosenquist, U., & Holmström, I. (2007). Enjoying work or burdened by it? How anaesthetists experience and handle difficulties at work. *British Journal of Anaesthesia, 99*, 493–499.

Latham, G. P. (2006). *Work motivation: History, theory, research, and practice*. Thousand Oaks, CA: Sage.

Laubacher, R. J., & Malone, T. W. (1997). Flexible work arrangements and 21st century workers' guilds, MIT Initiative on "Inventing the Organizations of the 21st Century," Working Paper No. 004.

Lawler, E. E., III., Mohrman, S. A., & Ledford, G. E. (1995). *Creating high performance organizations: Practices and results of employee involvement*. San Francisco: Jossey-Bass.

Leach, D. J., Wall, T. D., & Jackson, P. R. (2003). The effect of empowerment on job knowledge: An empirical test involving operators of complex technology. *Journal of Occupational and Organizational Psychology, 76*, 27–52.

Leach, D. J., Wall, T. D., Rogelberg, S. G., & Jackson, P. R. (2005). Team autonomy, performance, and member job strain: Uncovering the teamwork KSA link. *Applied Psychology: An International Review, 54*, 1–24.

Lerner, J. S., & Tetlock, P. E. (1999). Accounting for the effects of accountability. *Psychological Bulletin, 125*, 255–275.

Levy, P. F. (2001). The Nut Island effect: When good teams go wrong. *Harvard Business Review, 79*, 51–59.

Liden, R. C., Wayne, S. J., & Sparrowe, R. T. (2000). An examination of the mediating role of psychological empowerment on the relations between the job, interpersonal relationships, and work outcomes. *Journal of Applied Psychology, 85*, 407–416.

Locke, E. A. (1982), The ideas of Frederick W. Taylor: An evaluation. *Academy of Management Review, 7*, 14–24.

Loher, B. T., Noe, R. A., Moeller, N. L., & Fitzgerald, M. P. (1985). A meta-analysis of the relation of job characteristics to job satisfaction. *Journal of Applied Psychology, 70*, 280–289.

Lund, T., Labriola, M., Christensen, K. B., Bultmann, U., & Villadsen, E. (2006). Physical work environment risk factors for long term sickness absence: Prospective findings among a cohort of 5357 employees in Denmark. *British Medical Journal, 332*, 449–452.

MacDuffie, J. P. (2007). HRM and distributed work: Managing people across distances. *Academy of Management Annals, 1*, 549–615.

Madjar, N., & Shalley, C. E. (2008). Multiple tasks' and multiple goals' effects on creativity: Forced incubation or just a distraction? *Journal of Management, 34*, 786–805.

Majchrzak, A., Malhotra, A., Stamps, J., & Lipnack, J. (2004). Can absence make a team grow stronger? *Harvard Business Review, 82*, 131–137.

Margolis, J. D., & Molinsky, A. L. (2008). Navigating the bind of necessary evils: Psychological engagement and the production of interpersonally sensitive behavior. *Academy of Management Journal, 51*, 847–872.

Marks, M. A., Mathieu, J. E., & Zaccaro, S. J. (2001). A temporally based framework and taxonomy of team processes. *Academy of Management Review, 26*, 356–376.

Martin, R., & Wall, T. D. (1989). Attentional demand and cost responsibility as stressors in shopfloor jobs. *Academy of Management Journal, 32*, 69–86.

Maslow, A. H. (1954). *Motivation and personality*. New York: Harper.

Mathieu, J. E., Maynard, T., Rapp, T., & Gilson, L. (2008). Team effectiveness 1997–2007: A review of recent advancements and a glimpse into the future. *Journal of Management, 34*, 410–476.

Mathieu, J. E., & Zajac, D. M. (1990). A review and meta-analysis of the antecedents, correlates, and consequences of organizational commitment. *Psychological Bulletin, 108*(2), 171–194.

Mauno, S., Kinnunen, U., & Ruokolainen, M. (2007). Job demands and resources as antecedents of work engagement: A longitudinal study. *Journal of Vocational Behavior, 70*, 149–171.

May, D. R., Oldham, G. R., & Rathert, C. (2005). Employee affective and behavioral reactions to the spatial density of physical work environments. *Human Resource Management, 44*, 21–33.

Mayo, E. (1949). *The social problems of an industrial civilization*. London: Routledge & Kegan Paul.

McClelland, D. C. (1961). *The achieving society*. Princeton, NJ: Van Nostrand.

McClelland, D. C. (1987). *Human motivation*. Cambridge: Cambridge University Press.

McGregor, D. (1960). *The human side of the enterprise*. New York: McGraw-Hill.

McIlroy, R., Marginson, P., & Regalia, I. (2004). Regulating external and internal forms of flexibility at local level: Five European regions compared. *International Journal of Human Resource Management, 15*, 295–313.

Meglino, B. M., & Korsgaard, M. A. (2007). The role of other orientation in reactions to job characteristics. *Journal of Management, 33*, 57–83.

Melchior, M, Caspi, A., Milne, B. J., Danese, A., Poulton, R., & Moffitt, T. E. (2007). Work stress precipitates depression and anxiety in young, working women and men. *Psychological Medicine, 37*, 1119–1129.

Meyer, J. P., Becker, T. E., & Vandenberghe, C. (2004). Employee commitment and motivation: A conceptual analysis and integrative model. *Journal of Applied Psychology,* *89,* 991–1007.

Meyer, J. P., Stanley, D. J., Herscovitch, L., & Topolnytsky, L. (2002). Affective, continuance, and normative commitment to the organization: A meta-analysis of antecedents, correlates, and consequences. *Journal of Vocational Behavior, 61,* 20–52.

Millette, V., & Gagne, M. (2008). Designing volunteer's tasks to maximize motivation, satisfaction and performance: The impact of job characteristics on volunteer engagement. *Motivation and Emotion, 32,* 11–22.

Mitchell, T. R. (1997). Matching motivational strategies with organisational contexts. *Research in Organisational Behavior, 19,* 57–149.

Mitchell, T. R., Holtom, B. C., Lee, T. W., Sablynski, C. J., & Erez, M. (2001). Why people stay: Using job embeddedness to predict voluntary turnover. *Academy of Management Journal, 44*(6), 1102–1121.

Molinsky, A., & Margolis, J. (2005). Necessary evils and interpersonal sensitivity in organizations. *Academy of Management Review, 30,* 245–268.

Moller, T., Mathaiessen, S. E., Franzon, H., & Kihlberg, S. (2004). Job enlargement and mechanical exposure variability in cyclic assembly work. *Ergonomics, 47,* 19–40.

Morgeson, F. P., & Campion, M. A. (2002). Minimizing tradeoffs when redesigning work: Evidence from a longitudinal quasi-experiment. *Personnel Psychology, 55,* 589–612.

Morgeson, F. P., & Campion, M. A. (2003). Work design. In W. C. Borman, D. R. Ilgen, & R. J. Klimoski (Eds.), *Handbook of psychology,* Volume 12: *Industrial and organizational psychology* (pp. 423–452). New York: John Wiley.

Morgeson, F. P., Delaney-Klinger, K., & Hemingway, M. A. (2005). The importance of job autonomy, cognitive ability, and job-related skill for predicting role breadth and job performance. *Journal of Applied Psychology, 90,* 399–406.

Morgeson, F. P., & Humphrey, S. E. (2006). The work design questionnaire (WDQ): Developing and validating a comprehensive measure for assessing job design and the nature of work. *Journal of Applied Psychology, 91,* 1321–1339.

Morgeson, F. P., & Humphrey, S. E. (2008). Job and team design: Toward a more integrative conceptualization of work design. In J. J. Martocchio (Ed.), *Research in personnel and human resource management* (Vol. 27, pp. 39–92). Bradford, United Kingdom: Emerald Group Publishing Limited.

Morgeson, F. P., Reider, M. H., & Campion, M. A. (2005). Selecting individuals in team settings: The importance of social skills, personality characteristics, and teamwork knowledge. *Personnel Psychology, 58,* 583–611.

Morris, J. (2004). The future of work: organizational and international perspectives. *The International Journal of Human Resource Management, 15,* 263–275.

Morris, J. A., & Feldman, D. C. (1996). The dimensions, antecedents, and consequences of emotional labor. *Academy of Management Review, 21,* 906–1010.

Murphy, L. R., & Sauter, S. L. (2003). The USA perspective: Current issues and trends in the management of work stress. *Australian Psychologist, 38,* 151–157.

National Academy of Sciences. (1999). *The changing nature of work: Implications for occupational analysis.* Washington, DC: National Academy Press.

Neumark, D., (2002). Drawing the line: Comment by David Neumark. *Industrial and Labour Relations Review, 54,* 716–723.

Ohly, S., Sonnentag, S., & Pluntke, F. (2006). Routinization, work characteristics and their relationships with creative and proactive behaviors. *Journal of Organizational Behavior, 27,* 257–279.

Oldham, G. R., Cummings, A., & Zhou, J. (1995). The spatial configuration of organizations: A review of the literature and some new research directions. In G. Ferris (Ed.), *Research in personnel and human resources management* (Vol. 13, pp. 1–37). Greenwich, CT: JAI Press.

Oldham, G. R., & Hackman, J. R. (1980). Work design in the organizational context. In B. M. Staw & L. L. Cummings (Eds.), *Research in organizational behavior* (Vol. 2, pp. 247–278). Greenwich, CT: JAI Press.

Oldham, G. R., & Hackman, J. R. (1981). Relationships between organizational structure and employee reactions: Comparing alternative frameworks. *Administrative Science Quarterly, 26,* 66–83.

Oldham, G. R., & Hackman, J. R. (2005). How job characteristics theory happened. In K. G. Smith & M. A. Hitt (Eds.), *The Oxford handbook of management theory: The process of theory development* (pp. 151–170). Oxford: Oxford University Press.

Oldham, G. R., Hackman, J. R., & Pearce, J. L. (1976). Conditions under which employees respond positively to enriched work. *Journal of Applied Psychology, 61,* 395–403.

Olson-Buchanan, J. B., & Boswell, W. (2006). Blurring boundaries: Correlates of integration and segmentation between work and non-work. *Journal of Vocational Behavior, 68,* 432–445.

Organ, D. W., & Ryan, K. (1995). A meta-analytic review of attitudinal and dispositional predictors of organizational citizenship behavior. *Personnel Psychology, 48,* 775–802.

Parker, S. K. (1998). Role breadth self-efficacy: Relationship with work enrichment and other practices. *Journal of Applied Psychology, 83,* 835–852.

Parker, S. K. (2003). Longitudinal effects of lean production on employee outcomes and the mediating role of work characteristics. *Journal of Applied Psychology, 88,* 620–634.

Parker, S. K. (2007). 'That is my job': How employees' role orientation affects their job performance. *Human Relations, 60,* 403–434.

Parker, S. K., & Axtell, C. M. (2001). Seeing another viewpoint: Antecedents and outcomes of employee perspective taking. *Academy of Management Journal, 44,* 1085–1101.

Parker, S. K., Axtell, C. M., & Turner, N. (2001). Designing a safer workplace: Importance of job autonomy, communication quality, and supportive supervisors. *Journal of Occupational Health Psychology, 6,* 211–228.

Parker, S. K., Griffin, M. A., Sprigg C. A., & Wall, T. D. (2002). Effect of temporary contracts on perceived work characteristics and job strain: A longitudinal study. *Personnel Psychology, 55* (3), 689–719.

Parker, S. K., & Ohly, S. (2008). Designing motivating work. In R. Kanfer, G. Chen, & R. Pritchard (Eds.), *Work motivation: Past, present and future* (pp. 233–284). New York: Taylor & Francis.

Parker, S. K., & Sprigg, C. A. (1999). Minimizing strain and maximizing learning: The role of job demands, job control, and proactive personality. *Journal of Applied Psychology, 84,* 925–939.

Parker, S. K., & Turner, N. (2002) Work design and individual job performance: Research findings and an agenda for future inquiry. In S. Sonnentag (Ed.), *Psychological management* of individual performance: A handbook in the psychology of management in organizations (pp. 69–94). Chichester, UK: Wiley.

Parker, S. K., Turner, N., & Griffin, M. A., (2003). Designing healthy work. In D. A. Hofmann & L. E. Tetrick (Eds.), *Health and safety in organizations: A multi-level perspective* (pp. 91–130). San Francisco: Jossey-Bass.

Parker, S. K., & Wall, T. D. (1998). *Job and work design: Organizing work to promote wellbeing and effectiveness.* London: Sage.

Parker, S. K., Wall, T. D., & Cordery, J. L. (2001). Future work design research and practice: An elaborated work characteristics model. *Journal of Occupational & Organizational Psychology, 73,* 414–440.

Parker, S. K., Wall, T. D., & Jackson, P. R. (1997). 'That's not my job': Developing flexible employee work orientations. *Academy of Management Journal, 40,* 899–929.

Parker, S. K., Williams, H. M., & Turner, N. (2006). Modeling the antecedents of proactive behavior at work. *Journal of Applied Psychology, 91,* 636–652.

Parkes, K. R. (1994). Personality and coping as moderators of work stress processes: Models, methods and measures. *Work and Stress, 8,* 110–129.

Pasmore, W. A. (1988). *Designing effective organizations: The sociotechnical systems perspective.* New York: Wiley.

Paterniti, S., Niedhammer, I., Lang, T., & Consoli, S.M. (2002). Psychosocial factors at work, personality traits and depressive symptoms. *British Journal of Psychiatry, 181,* 111–117.

Payne, S. C., Youngcourt, S. S., & Beaubien, J. M. (2007). A meta-analytic examination of the goal-orientation nomological net. *Journal of Applied Psychology, 92,* 128–150.

Pearce, J. A., & Ravlin, E. C. (1987). The design and activation of self-regulating work groups. *Human Relations, 40,* 751–782.

Pearce, J., & Gregersen, H. B. (1991). Task interdependence and extrarole behavior: A test of the mediating effects of felt responsibility. *Journal of Applied Psychology, 76,* 838–844.

Perrone, V., Zaheer, A., & McEvily, B. (2003). Free to be trusted? Organizational constraints on trust in boundary spanners. *Organization Science, 14,* 422–439.

Pfeffer, J. (1994). *Competitive advantage through people: Unleashing the power of the workforce.* Boston: Harvard Business School Press.

Pfeffer, J., & Veiga, J. F. (1999). Putting people first for organizational success. *Academy of Management Executive, 13,* 37–48.

Piccolo, R. F., & Colquitt, J. A. (2006). Transformational leadership and job behaviors: The mediating role of core job characteristics. *Academy of Management Journal, 49,* 327–340.

Pierce, J. L., Jussila, I., & Cummings, A. (2009). Psychological ownership within the job design context: Revision of the job characteristics model. *Journal of Organizational Behavior, 30,* 477–496.

Pierce, J. L., Kostova, T., & Dirks, K. T. (2003). The state of psychological ownership: Integrating and extending a century of research. *Review of General Psychology, 7,* 84–107.

Polzer, J. T. (2005). Role ambiguity. In N. Nicholson, P. Audia, & M. Pillutla (Eds.), *Blackwell encyclopedia of management: Organizational behavior* (2nd ed., p. 356). Cambridge, MA: Blackwell.

Potter, G. G., Helms, M. J., & Plassman, B. L. (2008). Associations of job demands and intelligence with cognitive performance among men in late life. *Neurology, 70,* 1803–1808.

Potter, G. G., Plassman, B. L., Helms, M. J., Foster, S. M., & Edwards, N. W. (2006). Occupational characteristics and cognitive performance among elderly male twins. *Neurology, 67,* 1377–1382.

Pousette, A., & Hanse, J. J. (2002). Job characteristics as predictors of ill-health and sickness absenteeism in different occupational types: A multigroup structural modelling approach. *Work and Stress, 16,* 229–250.

Reichenberg, A., & MacCabe, J. H. (2007). Feeling the pressure: Work stress and mental health. *Psychological Medicine, 37,* 1073–1074.

Rice, A. K. (1958). *Productivity and social organisation: The Ahmedabad experiment.* London: Tavistock Publications.

Riordan, C. (2005). Role conflict. In N. Nicholson, P. Audia, & M. Pillutla (Eds.), *Blackwell encyclopedia of management: Organizational behavior* (2nd ed., p. 356). Cambridge, MA: Blackwell.

Robert, C., Probst, T. M., Martocchio, J. J., Drasgow, F., & Lawler, J. J. (2000). Empowerment and continuous improvement in the United States, Mexico, Poland, and India: Predicting fit on the basis of the dimension of power distance and individualism. *Journal of Applied Psychology, 85,* 643–658.

Roberts, K. H., & Glick, W. (1981). The job characteristics approach to task design: A critical review. *Journal of Applied Psychology, 66,* 193–217.

Roe, R. A., Zinovieva, I. L., Dienes, E., & Ten Horn, L. A. (2000). A comparison of work motivation in Bulgaria, Hungary, and the Netherlands: Test of a model. *Applied Psychology: An International Review, 49,* 658–687.

Roethlisberger, F. J., & Dickson, W. J. (1939). *Management and the worker.* Boston: Harvard University Press.

Rousseau, D. M. (1977). Technological differences in job characteristics, employee satisfaction, and motivation: A synthesis of job design research and sociotechnical systems theory. *Organizational Behavior & Human Performance, 19,* 18–42.

Rousseau, D. M. (2005). *I-deals: Idiosyncratic deals employees bargain for themselves.* New York: Sharpe.

Rousseau, D. M., (2006). Is there such a thing as evidence-based management? *Academy of Management Review, 31,* 256–269.

Rousseau, D. M., Hornung, S., & Kim, T. G. (2009). Idiosyncratic deals: Testing propositions on timing, content and the employment relationship. *Journal of Vocational Behavior, 74,* 338–348.

Rubery, J., Earnshaw, J., Marchington, M., Lee Cooke, F., & Vincent, S. (2000). Changing organisational forms and the employment relationship. ESRC Future of Work Programme, Working Paper No. 14. ISSN 1469–1531.

Ryan, A. M., & Deci, E. L. (2000). Self-determination theory and the facilitation of intrinsic motivation, social development, and well-being. *American Psychologist, 55,* 68–78.

Rydstedt, L. W., Ferrie, J., & Head, J. (2006). Is there support for curvilinear relationships between psychosocial work characteristics and mental well-being? Cross-sectional and long-term data from the Whitehall II study. *Work & Stress, 20,* 6–20.

Saavedra, R., & Kwun, S. K. (2000). Affective states in job characteristics theory. *Journal of Organizational Behavior, 21,* 131–146.

Sanne, B., Mykletun, A., Dahl, A. A., Moen, B., & Tell, G. E. (2005). Testing the job demand-control-support model with anxiety and depression as outcomes: The Hordaland health study. *Occupational Medicine, 55,* 463–473.

Schaubroeck, J., Walumbwa, F. O., Ganster, D. C., & Kepes, S. (2007). Destructive leadership traits and the neutralizing influence of an "enriched" job. *The Leadership Quarterly, 18,* 236–251.

Schaufeli, W. B., & Bakker, A. B. (2004). Job demands, job resources and their relationship with burnout and engagement: A multi-sample study. *Journal of Organizational Behavior, 25,* 295–313.

Schaufeli, W. B., Bakker, A. B., & Van Rhenen, W. (2009). How changes in job demands and resources predict burnout, work engagement, and sickness absenteeism. *Journal of Organizational Behavior, 30,* 893–917.

Schooler, C., Mulatu, M. S., & Oates, G. (2004). Occupational self-direction, intellectual functioning, and self-directed orientation in older workers: Findings and implications for individuals and societies. *American Journal of Sociology, 110,* 161–197.

Seibert, S. E., Silver, S. R., & Randolph, W. A. (2004). Taking empowerment to the next level: A multiple-level model of empowerment, performance and satisfaction. *Academy of Management Journal, 47,* 332–349.

Shalley, C. E., Gilson, L. L., & Blum, T. C. (2009). Interactive effects of growth need strength, work context, and job complexity on self-reported creative performance. *Academy of Management Journal, 52,* 489–505.

Shalley, C. E., Zhou, J., & Oldham, G. R. (2004). The effects of personal and contextual characteristics on creativity: Where should we go from here? *Journal of Management, 30,* 933–958.

Shaw, J. D., & Gupta, N. (2004). Job complexity, performance, and well-being: When does supplies-values matter? *Personnel Psychology, 57,* 847–879.

Sibbald, B., Bojke, C., & Gravelle, H. (2003). National survey of job satisfaction and retirement intentions among general practitioners in England. *British Medical Journal, 326,* 22–26.

Sims, R. R. (1983). Kolb's experiential learning theory: A framework for assessing person-job interaction. *Academy of Management Review, 8,* 501–508.

Sluss, D. M., van Dick, R., & Thompson, B. (2011). Role theory in organizations: A relational perspective. In S. Zedeck (Ed.), *Handbook of I/O Psychology.* Washington, DC: American Psychological Society.

Smith, A. (1776). *An inquiry into the nature and causes of the wealth of nations.* (Book 5, Part 3, Article II). Retrieved November 16, 2009, from http://www.adamsmith.org/smith/won/won-b5-c1-article-2-ss3.html).

Spector, P. E. (1985). Higher-order need strength as a moderator of the job scope-employee outcome relationship: A meta-analysis. *Journal of Occupational Psychology, 58,* 119–127.

Spector, P. E. (1986). Perceived control by employees: A meta-analysis of studies concerning autonomy and participation at work. *Human Relations, 39,* 1005–1016.

Spreitzer, G. M. (1995). Individual empowerment in the workplace: Dimensions, measurement, validation. *Academy of Management Journal, 38,* 1442–1465.

Sprigg, C. A., Jackson, P. R., & Parker, S. K. (2000). Production team-working: The importance of interdependence for employee strain and satisfaction. *Human Relations, 53,* 1519–1543.

Staudinger, U. M., Smith, J., & Baltes, P. B. (1992). Wisdom-related knowledge in a life review task: Age differences and the role of professional specialization. *Psychology and Aging, 7,* 271–281.

Staw, B. M., & Cohen-Charash, Y. (2005). The dispositional approach to job satisfaction: More than a mirage, but not yet an oasis. *Journal of Organizational Behavior, 26,* 59–78.

Staw, B. M., & Epstein, L. D. (2000). What bandwagons bring: Effects of popular management techniques on corporate performance, reputation, and CEO pay. *Administrative Science Quarterly, 45,* 523–556.

Sternberg, R. G. (2003). WICS: A model of leadership in organizations. *Academy of Management Learning and Education, 2,* 386–401.

Stevens, M. J., & Campion, M. A. (1994). The knowledge, skill, and ability requirements for teamwork: Implications for human resource management. *Journal of Management, 20,* 503–550.

Stevens, M. J., & Campion, M. A. (1999). Staffing work teams: Development and validation of a selection test for teamwork settings. *Journal of Management, 25,* 207–228.

Stewart, G. L. (2006). A meta-analytic review of relationships between team design features and team performance. *Journal of Management, 32,* 29–54.

Stone, E. F., & Guetal, H. G. (1985). An empirical derivation of the dimensions along which characteristics of jobs are perceived. *Academy of Management Journal, 28,* 376–396.

Takeuchi, R., Shay, J. P., & Li, J. (2008). When does decision autonomy increase expatriate managers' adjustment? An empirical test. *Academy of Management Journal, 51,* 45–60.

Tangirala, S., & Ramanujam, R. (2008). Exploring non-linearity in employee voice: The effects of personal control and organizational identification. *Academy of Management Journal, 51,* 1189–1203.

Taylor, F. W. (1911). *The principles of scientific management.* New York: W. W. Norton.

Taylor, F. W. (1947). The principles of scientific management. In V. H. Vroom, & E. L. Deci (Eds.), *Management and motivation* (pp. 295–301). Harmondsworth, UK: Penguin.

Taylor, P., & Bain, P. (1999). 'An assembly line in the head': Work and employee relations in the call centre. *Industrial Relations Journal, 30,* 101–117.

Taylor, R. (2002). *Britain's world of work: Myths and realities.* Swindon, UK: Economic and Social Research Council.

Terkel, S. (1972). *Working.* New York: Pantheon.

Theorell, T., & Karasek, R. A. (1996). Current issues relating to psychosocial job strain and cardiovascular disease research. *Journal of Occupational Health Psychology, 1,* 9–26.

Thompson, J. (1967). *Organizations in action.* New York: McGraw-Hill.

Trice, H. M. 1993. *Occupational subcultures in the workplace.* Ithaca, NY: ILR Press.

Trist, E. L. (1981). The sociotechnical perspective. In A. H. Van de Ven & W. F. Joyce (Eds.), *Perspectives on organization design and behavior* (pp. 19–75). New York: Wiley.

Trist, E. L., & Bamforth, K. M. (1951). Some social and psychological consequences of the longwall method of coal-getting. *Human Relations, 4,* 3–38.

Turner, A. N., & Lawrence, P. R. (1965). *Industrial jobs and the worker.* Cambridge, MA: Harvard University Press.

Urdan, T. (2004). Predictors of academic self-handicapping and achievement: Examining achievement goals, classroom goal structures, and culture. *Journal of Educational Psychology, 96,* 251–264.

Valcour, M. (2007). Work-based resources as moderators of the relationship between work hours and satisfaction with work-family balance. *Journal of Applied Psychology, 92,* 1512–1523.

VandeWalle, D., Brown, S. P., Cron, W. L., & Slocum, J. W. (1999). The influence of goal orientation and self-regulation tactics on sales performance: A longitudinal field test. *Journal of Applied Psychology, 84,* 249–259.

Van der Doef, M., & Mayes, S. (1999). The job demand-control (-support) model and psychological well-being: A review of 20 years of empirical research. *Work & Stress, 13,* 87–114.

Van der Vegt, G. S., & Bunderson, J. S. (2005). Learning and performance in multidisciplinary teams: The importance of collective team identification. *Academy of Management Journal, 48,* 532–547.

Van Maanen, J., & Barley, S. R. (1984). Occupational communities: Culture and control in organizations. In B. M. Staw & L. L. Cummings (Eds.), *Research in organizational behavior* (Vol. 6, pp. 287–365). Greenwich, CT: JAI Press.

Van Yperen, N. W., & Hagedoorn, M. (2003). Do high job demands increase intrinsic motivation or fatigue or both? The role of job control and job social support. *Academy of Management Journal, 46,* 339–348.

Vough, H. C., & Parker, S. (2008). Work design: Still going strong. In J. Barling & C. L. Cooper (Eds.), *Handbook of organizational behavior.* Los Angeles: Sage.

Vroom, V. H., & Deci, E. L. (Eds.). (1970). *Management and motivation.* Harmondsworth, UK: Penguin.

Wageman, R. (1997). Critical success factors for creating superb self-managing teams. *Organizational Dynamics, 26,* 37–49.

Wagner, J. A. (1994). Participation's effect on performance and satisfaction: A reconsideration of research evidence. *Academy of Management Review, 19,* 312–331.

Walker, C. R., & Guest, R. H. (1952). *The man on the assembly line.* Cambridge, MA: Harvard University Press.

Wall, T. D., Cordery, J. L., & Clegg, C. W. (2002). Empowerment, performance and operational uncertainty: A theoretical integration. *Applied Psychology: An International Review, 51,* 146–149.

Wall, T. D., Jackson, P. R., & Davids, K. (1992). Operator work design and robotic system performance: A serendipitous field study. *Journal of Applied Psychology, 77,* 353–362.

Wall, T. D., Jackson, P. R., & Mullarkey, S. (1995). Further evidence on some new measures of job control, cognitive demand and production responsibility. *Journal of Organizational Behavior, 16,* 31–455.

Wall, T. D., Kemp, N. J., Jackson, P. R., & Clegg, C. W. (1986). Outcomes of autonomous workgroups: A long-term field experiment. *Academy of Management Journal, 29,* 280–304.

Wall, T. D., & Stephenson, G. M. (1970). Herzberg's two-factor theory of job attitudes: A critical evaluation and some fresh evidence. *Industrial Relations Journal, 1,* 41–65.

Walton, R. E. (1985). From control to commitment. *Harvard Business Review, 63,* 77–84.

Warr, P. B. (1987). *Work, unemployment, and mental health.* Oxford: Oxford University Press.

Warr, P. B. (2007). *Work, happiness, and unhappiness.* Mahwah, NJ: Erlbaum.

Warren, J. R., Carayon, P., & Hoonakker, P. (2008). Changes in health between ages 54 and 65: The role of job characteristics and socioeconomic status. *Research on Aging, 30,* 672–700.

Wegge, J., van Dick, R., Fisher, G. K., Wecking, C., & Moltzen, K. (2006). Work motivation, organizational identification, and well-being in call centre work. *Work & Stress, 20,* 60–83.

Wenger, E., McDermott, R., & Snyder, W. M. (2002), *A guide to managing knowledge: Cultivating communities of practice.* Cambridge, MA: Harvard Business School Press.

Wharton, A. S. (2009). The sociology of emotional labor. *Annual Review of Sociology, 35,* 147–165.

Wiesenfeld, B. M., Raghuram, S., & Garud, R. (2001). Organizational identification among virtual workers: The role of need for affiliation and perceived work-based social support. *Journal of Management, 27,* 213–229.

Wong, C., & Campion, M. A. (1991). Development and test of a task level model of motivational job design. *Journal of Applied Psychology, 76,* 825–837.

Wood, R. E. (1986). Task complexity: Definition of the construct. *Organizational Behaviour and Human Decision Processes, 37,* 60.

Wood, W., & Neal, D. T. (2007). A new look at habits and the habit-goal interface. *Psychological Review, 114,* 843–863.

Wright, B. M., & Cordery, J. L. (1999). Production uncertainty as a contextual moderator of employee reactions to job design. *Journal of Applied Psychology, 84,* 456–463.

Wrzesniewski, A., & Dutton, J. E. (2001). Crafting a job: Revisioning employees as active crafters of their work. *Academy of Management Review, 26,* 179–201.

Wrzesniewski, A., Dutton, J. E., & Debebe, G. (2003). Interpersonal sensemaking and the meaning of work. *Research in Organizational Behavior, 25,* 93–135.

Xie, J. L., & Johns, G. (1995). Job scope and stress: Can job scope be too high? *Academy of Management Journal, 38,* 1288–1309.

Yeh, Q. (2007). The link between managerial style and the job characteristics of R&D professionals. *R&D Management, 26,* 127–140.

Youndt, M. A., Snell, S. A., Dean, J. W., & Lepak, D. P. (1996). Human resource management, manufacturing strategy, and firm performance. *Academy of Management Journal, 39,* 836–866.

Zacharatos, A., Barling, J., & Iverson, R. D. (2005). High-performance work systems and occupational safety. *Journal of Applied Psychology, 90,* 77–93.

Zapf, D., & Holz, M. (2006). On the positive and negative effects of emotion work in organizations. *European Journal of Work and Organizational Psychology, 15,* 1–28.

Zhao, B., & Olivera, F. (2006). Error reporting in organizations. *Academy of Management Review, 31,* 1012–1030.

Zhou, J., Oldham, G. R., & Cummings, A. (1998). Employee reactions to the physical work environment: The role of childhood residential attributes. *Journal of Applied Social Psychology, 28,* 2213–2238.

Zuboff, S. (1989). *In the age of the smart machine.* Oxford: Heinemann.

Performance Management

James W. Smither

Abstract

This chapter focuses on the continuous process of performance management rather than the discrete event of performance appraisal. The chapter begins by defining job performance and then reviews research concerning each of the core elements of performance management, including goal setting, feedback, developing employees (including coaching), evaluating performance, and rewarding performance. Several topics are reviewed that are of special interest to performance management: contextual performance, counterproductive work behavior, team performance, the role of technology, cross-cultural issues, and perceptions of fairness. The chapter concludes by presenting directions for future research.

Key Words: Performance management, performance appraisal, performance evaluation, goal setting, feedback, coaching, employee development, pay for performance

Latham and his colleagues (Latham, Almost, Mann, & Moore, 2005; Latham & Mann, 2006) recently noted that there has been a paradigm shift from thinking of performance appraisal as a discrete event to a continuous process of performance management in which coaching is inherent in the process. This paradigm shift follows the recognition that performance appraisal research became too interested in measurement issues and not interested enough in examining how performance can be enhanced (DeNisi & Pritchard, 2006). Because of this paradigm shift, Latham and Mann (2006) state that their review "may be the last review of the literature where performance appraisal is in the title" (p. 296). This chapter is the first to appear in a handbook of industrial and organizational psychology in which the focus is on performance management rather than performance appraisal.

Several definitions of performance management have been offered, and most share common elements. Aguinis (2009; Aguinis & Pierce, 2008) defines performance management as "a continuous process of identifying, measuring, and developing the performance of individuals and teams and aligning performance with the strategic goals of the organization." Cascio (2006) states that performance management involves defining performance (e.g., setting goals and assessing progress toward goals), facilitating performance (e.g., providing adequate resources, staffing effectively, removing roadblocks to successful performance), and encouraging performance (providing timely and fair rewards for successful performance). Den Hartog, Boselie, and Paauwe (2004) state that performance management involves defining, measuring, and stimulating employee performance, with the goal of improving the organization's performance. Hedge and Borman (2008) state that performance management is more than an annual performance review meeting between a supervisor and employee and that performance management includes ongoing coaching, feedback, and support from the supervisor. Finally,

Heslin, Carson, and VandeWalle (2009) state simply, "Performance management involves all the initiatives whereby managers strive to guide and motivate high performance by employees." In sum, the key elements of performance, at a minimum, include goal setting, feedback, employee development (and coaching), performance evaluation, and rewarding performance.

Aguinis (2009) argues that effective performance management systems offer many potential advantages. These include: greater clarity about organizational goals as well as the behaviors and results required for successful employee performance; enhancing employees' understanding of their strengths and weaknesses (and hence valuable developmental activities); increasing employees' motivation, competence, and self-esteem; better distinguishing between good and poor performers and thereby increasing the fairness of administrative decisions (such as pay increases, promotions, and terminations); protecting the organization from lawsuits; and facilitating organizational change. At the same time, Aguinis (2009) notes that ineffective performance management systems have the potential to waste time and money, damage relationships, decrease motivation and job satisfaction, increase employee turnover, create perceptions of unfairness, and thereby increase risks of litigation.

This chapter begins by defining job performance. Research concerning each of the core elements of performance management is then reviewed: goal setting, feedback, developing employees (including coaching), evaluating performance, and rewarding performance. Next, several topics are reviewed that are of special interest to performance management: contextual performance, counterproductive work behavior, team performance, the role of technology, cross-cultural issues, and perceptions of fairness. Finally, directions for future research are presented.

Defining Job Performance

There is no universally accepted definition of "job performance." Most authors argue that job performance is best defined by employee behaviors. For example, Campbell, McCloy, Oppler, and Sager (1993) stated that performance is:

> something that people actually do and can be observed. By definition, it includes only those actions or behaviors that are relevant to the organization's goals and that can be scaled (measured) in terms of each person's proficiency (e.g., level of contribution). Performance is what the organization hires one to

do, and do well. Performance is not the consequence or result of action, it is the action itself. Performance consists of goal-relevant actions that are under the control of the individual, regardless of whether they are cognitive, motor, psychomotor, or interpersonal. (pp. 40–41)

Other authors have also emphasized that job performance should be conceptualized as behaviors under the control of the employee that are related to organizational goals (Murphy & Cleveland, 1991; Rotundo & Sackett, 2002).

In contrast, Bernardin, Hagan, Kane, and Villanova (1998) define performance as the record of outcomes produced on a specified job function, activity, or behavior during a specified time period. Their definition makes clear that performance is something separate and distinct from the person who produced it or that person's characteristics (e.g., traits). They do, however, include in their definition of a "performance outcome" how frequently a performer exhibits a behavior related to some aspect of value such as quantity, quality, timeliness, cost effectiveness, interpersonal impact, and need for supervision. For example, the record of outcomes for the behavior "seeks input from knowledgeable parties before making a decision" would be the frequency of this behavior relative to all possible occasions when the employee had an opportunity to seek such input before making a decision. Finally, they argue that the definitions of outcomes should be derived from important critical internal and external customers.

Motowidlo (2003, p. 39) defined job performance as "the total expected value to the organization of the discrete behavioral episodes that an individual carries out over a standard period of time." He also draws a distinction between behavior (what people do), performance (expected organizational value of what people do), and results (states or conditions that are changed by what people do in ways that contribute to or detract from organizational effectiveness).

Both broad and more differentiated models of job performance can play a useful role in understanding and predicting job performance (Bartram, 2005). Borman & Motowidlo (1993) introduced the important distinction between task performance and contextual performance (or organizational citizenship behaviors; Podsakoff, Ahearne, & MacKenzie, 1997). Contextual performance (organizational citizenship behavior) includes personal support (e.g., helping and cooperating with coworkers), organizational support (e.g., following organizational policies, presenting a favorable view of the organization to others), and conscientious initiative (e.g., showing initiative and displaying extra effort to complete work; Borman, Buck, et al., 2001). The distinction between task performance and contextual performance is supported by research showing that ability is a better predictor of task performance than is personality, whereas personality is a better predictor of contextual performance than is ability (Borman, Penner, Allen, & Motowidlo, 2001).

Several models of performance further disaggregate the criterion domain. For example, Campbell et al. (1993) presented an eight-factor model of work performance: job-specific task proficiency, non-job-specific task proficiency, written and oral communication, demonstrating effort, maintaining personal discipline, facilitating team and peer performance, supervision and leadership, and management and administration. Bartram (2005), defining competencies as sets of behaviors that are instrumental in the delivery of desired results or outcomes, proposed eight broad performance competencies: leading and deciding, supporting and cooperating, interacting and presenting, analyzing and interpreting, creating and conceptualizing, organizing and executing, adapting and coping, and enterprising and performing. Analyzing multisource feedback ratings, Scullen, Mount, and Judge (2003) created a performance model with four factors: technical skills, administrative skills, human skills, and citizenship behaviors.

The importance of including counterproductive behaviors (e.g., antisocial behavior, incivility, sabotaging equipment, stealing from the company, blaming or gossiping about coworkers, deviant behaviors, withholding effort) in a taxonomy of work behaviors has also been noted by several authors (Motowidlo, 2003; Robinson & Bennett, 1995; Rotundo & Sackett, 2002; Sackett, 2002).

Recently, the importance of adaptive performance (i.e., adapting to complex, novel, turbulent, or unpredictable work environments), both for teams and individuals, has been recognized as an important aspect of job performance (Chen, Thomas, & Wallace, 2005; Ford, Smith, Weissbein, Gully, & Salas, 1998; Kozlowski et al., 2001; Marks, Zaccaro, & Mathieu, 2000). Pulakos, Arad, Donovan, and Plamondon (2000) developed a taxonomy of adaptive performance that includes eight dimensions: handling emergencies or crisis situations; handling work stress; solving problems creatively; dealing with uncertain and unpredictable work situations; learning work tasks, technologies, and procedures; demonstrating interpersonal adaptability; demonstrating cultural adaptability; and demonstrating physically oriented adaptability.

Other authors have drawn attention to the importance of acknowledging that performance changes over time (Reb & Cropanzano, 2007; Schmitt, Cortina, Ingerick, & Wiechmann, 2003) and that, in addition to mean performance over time, performance trends (e.g., flat, linear-improving, linear-deteriorating, U-shaped, ∩-shaped) influence performance ratings. Ployhart and Hakel (1998) found that there were individual differences in intraindividual performance variability over time and that these differences could be predicted moderately well by biodata.

In the applied context of performance management, both employee behaviors and the outcomes or results of those behaviors are important. Also, performance management is concerned with task performance, contextual performance, counterproductive work behavior, adaptive performance, and changes in performance over time.

The Role of Goals in Performance Management

A central premise of performance management systems is that individual (and team) goals need to be closely aligned with higher level organizational goals. For example, Schiemann (2009) describes how Continental Airlines selected on-time performance to be an organization-wide goal, in part because so many different roles (e.g., logistics, pilots, flight attendants, gate agents, maintenance, baggage handlers) can affect on-time performance. On-time performance thereby served as a unifying goal for different functional groups across the organization.

At the individual level, goal setting is also an important element of effective performance management (Heslin et al., 2009; Latham & Mann, 2006). Perhaps the most central tenet of goal-setting theory, illustrated in hundreds of studies, is that specific, difficult goals lead to higher performance than "do your best" goals (Locke & Latham, 1990). Moreover, specific, difficult goals have positive effects not only for individuals and teams but also for organizations (Baum, Locke, & Smith, 2001; Rodgers & Hunter, 1991). Research indicates that the benefits of goals occur because goals focus employees' attention on a specific objective (rather than other activities), lead to higher levels of effort to attain those objectives, enhance persistence in the face of setbacks and obstacles, and stimulate employees to develop new approaches and strategies when faced with complex tasks (Heslin et al., 2009; Latham, 2004; Locke & Latham, 2002).

Self-efficacy (i.e., the employee's belief that he or she can attain the goal) also plays a central role in goal-setting research. Social cognitive theory (Bandura, 1986) argues that self-efficacy, goal setting, anticipated outcomes, and reinforcements work together to help people attain their goals. Self-efficacy influences choices about what behaviors to undertake, the amount of effort to put forth, and how much one should persist when faced with obstacles. High self-efficacy leads to higher levels of effort and persistence, which in turn lead to higher performance, which in turn enhances self-efficacy. Self-efficacy can be enhanced by providing the employee with mastery experiences (e.g., by breaking down complex tasks into smaller, easier steps that gradually become more challenging), enabling the employee to observe a role model (who is perceived as similar to the employee on a number of attributes) successfully perform the task, and providing verbal encouragement that the employee has the ability to learn and perform the task successfully (Heslin et al., 2009).

A meta-analysis by Klein and colleagues (Klein, Wesson, Hollenbeck, & Alge, 1999) found that goal commitment is important if goals are to affect performance, and this is especially true when goals are difficult. Goal commitment can be strengthened in several ways (Heslin et al., 2009; Locke & Latham, 2002), including having people make a public commitment to the goal (Cialdini, 2001), increasing self-efficacy, and increasing the attractiveness of outcomes associated with goal attainment (e.g., by communicating a compelling vision, providing monetary incentives, or changing employees' perceptions concerning the consequences of attaining or not attaining the goal; Latham, 2001).

One concern is that setbacks or failures experienced during the pursuit of goals might lower self-efficacy. This is less likely to occur when people have an implicit belief that ability is malleable (and can therefore be developed over time with persistent effort) rather than fixed (Wood & Bandura, 1989). The implicit belief that ability is fixed has been labeled an entity theory of ability, whereas the implicit belief that ability is malleable has been labeled an incremental theory of ability (Dweck, 1986; and more recently referred to as a growth mind-set, Dweck, 2006). Research indicates that the belief that ability is malleable can be enhanced

by telling people that their skills can be developed via practice (Wood & Bandura, 1989) and by praising effort (rather than ability) following successful performance (Mueller & Dweck, 1998).

Meta-analysis (Wood, Mento, & Locke, 1987) shows that the benefits of difficult goals on performance are diminished when task complexity is high (e.g., when the task involves many acts and information cues that are interrelated and change over time; referred to by Wood, 1986, as component complexity, coordinative complexity, and dynamic complexity). Moreover, assigning challenging distal goals during the early stages of skill acquisition on a complex task can lead to decrements in performance (Kanfer & Ackerman, 1989). However, proximal (i.e., short-term, intermediate) goals can be helpful (when coupled with distal goals) during the early stages of skills acquisition on complex tasks (Latham & Seijts, 1999). Feedback related to proximal goals can provide (a) markers of progress (thereby increasing self-efficacy) and (b) information that can help people change strategies when it appears that their current task strategies are suboptimal (Latham & Seijts, 1999). Providing learning goals during the early stages of skills acquisition on complex tasks can also be helpful because such goals direct attention to learning the task rather than worrying about a distal performance outcome (Noel & Latham, 2006; Winters & Latham, 1996).

The stress that can accompany a difficult goal can be perceived as either a challenge (e.g., the situation provides an opportunity for self-growth, and coping strategies are available to deal with the demands of the situation) or a threat (e.g., where failure seems likely and coping strategies are not available). Drach-Zahavy and Erez (2002) showed that, when the situation was perceived as a threat, a difficult goal on a complex task lowered performance; when the situation was perceived as a challenge, the same difficult goal on the same complex task increased performance. This is consistent with the finding that persistence and performance are higher when goals are framed positively (e.g., emphasizing the consequences of attaining the goal) rather than negatively (e.g., emphasizing the consequences of not attaining the goal; Roney, Higgins, & Shah, 1995).

Goal setting also plays an important role in team performance (O'Leary-Kelly, Martocchio, & Frink, 1994). Heslin et al. (2009) note that it is important for individual goals to be aligned with team goals (and for team goals to be aligned with organizational goals). A meta-analysis by Gully, Incalcaterra, Joshi, and Beaubien (2002) found that team efficacy (the team's perceptions about whether it is capable of successfully performing a specific task) was more strongly related to team performance when task, goal, and outcome interdependence were high. That is, when the team context encourages cooperation among members, team efficacy is more strongly related to performance than when it does not. Team efficacy also affects the difficulty of team-set goals (Durham, Knight, & Locke, 1997). Participation in setting team goals also yields more consistently positive effects than assigned team goals (O'Leary-Kelly et al., 1994).

A recent meta-analysis (Payne, Youngcourt, & Beaubien, 2007) examined antecedents, proximal consequences, and distal consequences of three dimensions of goal orientation (GO): learning (approaching the task with the goal of learning for its own sake); prove performance (the desire to prove, and gain favorable judgments about, one's competence); and avoid performance (the desire to avoid disproving, and avoid negative judgments about, one's competence). In terms of antecedents, although unrelated to cognitive ability, learning GO had a small positive relationship with having an incremental view of intelligence (believing that intelligence is malleable rather than fixed). It was positively associated with need for achievement, conscientiousness, extraversion, openness to experience, agreeableness, emotional stability, self-esteem, and general self-efficacy. The proximal consequences of learning GO included higher levels of task-specific self-efficacy, self-set goals, effective learning strategies, and feedback seeking, along with lower levels of state anxiety. The distal consequences of learning GO included higher levels of learning, academic performance, and job performance. Using a meta-correlation matrix, the authors found that learning GO predicted job performance above and beyond cognitive ability and personality. In contrast, avoid performance GO generally had negative relationships with the antecedents and consequences listed above, while prove performance GO was generally unrelated to the antecedents and consequences.

A meta-analysis by Rodgers and Hunter (1991) found that the widely used performance management approach called management by objectives (MBO), which combines goal setting, participation in decision making, and objective feedback, was associated with productivity gains in 68 out of 70 studies. Also, when top management's commitment to MBO was high, the average gain in productivity was 56% versus only 6% when commitment from top management was low.

Organizational Goal Setting

One trend related to organizational goal setting is the use of balanced scorecards. Kaplan and Norton's (1992, 1996) balanced scorecard framework is based on the premise that focusing only on financial goals and measures is insufficient because such measures are lag indicators (i.e., they describe merely the outcomes of leaders' past actions) and can promote behavior that sacrifices long-term value for short-term performance. Balanced scorecards select a limited number of critical measures within each of four perspectives (financial, customer, internal processes, learning and innovation). Recently, the balanced scorecard concept has been extended to include strategy maps (Kaplan & Norton, 2004), which show the cause-and-effect relationships among the multiple measures on a balanced scorecard, including leads, lags, and feedback loops. Because balanced scorecards measure performance drivers as well as outcomes, they provide indicators of future performance as well as an assessment of historical results. Balanced scorecards are also based on the premise that firms with different strategies require different measures. The mere use of financial and non-financial goals and measures does not constitute a balanced scorecard. Instead, effective balanced scorecards are closely linked to the organization's strategy so that people can understand the strategy by looking only at the scorecard and its strategy map (Kaplan & Norton, 2001, 2004). Across all four perspectives, there are usually only 15 to 20 measures. Balanced scorecards can heighten awareness of the potential trade-offs among various goals and thereby help ensure that the organization does not optimize one goal (e.g., profit) at the expense of another (e.g., customer satisfaction; Schiemann, 2009).

Examples of financial measures include economic value added, return on capital employed, operating profit, cash flow, return on assets, project profitability, sales backlog, return on equity, and earnings per share. Examples of customer measures include customer retention, customer satisfaction (e.g., from surveys), on-time delivery, share of key accounts' purchases, market share, brand image, and the firm's share in the most profitable segments. Examples of measures of internal business processes include quality, speed to market, rework, safety indices, complaint resolution time, cycle time, yield, and unit cost. Examples of learning and innovation measures include employee skill development, rate of improvement in key operational measures, number and quality of employee suggestions, development time for the next generation of products, percent of sales from new products, employee turnover, and employee satisfaction (from surveys). In an experiment with MBA students, Ritchie-Dunham (2003) found that, contrasted with a financial scorecard, a balanced scorecard positively affected decision makers' mental models of how elements of a simulated firm dynamically interrelate, which led to improved performance.

In sum, balanced scorecards can provide an overarching framework that drives and aligns organizational, department, team, and individual goal setting. For example, in some organizations, each employee and each team explicitly link their goals to specific elements in the organization's balanced scorecard.

The Role of Feedback in Performance Management

Feedback plays a vital role in performance management in that, without feedback, the effect of goals on performance is diminished (Erez, 1977; Locke & Latham, 1990; Neubert, 1998). Alvero, Bucklin, and Austin (2001) note that performance feedback has been defined in several ways (e.g., information given to people about the quantity or quality of their past performance, information about performance that allows the person to adjust his or her performance) and that feedback can serve several functions (as an antecedent, reinforcer, or punisher). Moreover, feedback can serve both an informational purpose and a motivational purpose (Ilgen, Fisher, & Taylor, 1979). For example, information contained in feedback can help recipients learn and develop more effective task strategies. At the same time, the evaluative nature of feedback can have an incentive (or disincentive) effect.

In their review of performance feedback in organizational settings, Alvero et al. (2001) found that feedback yielded desired and consistent effects in 58% of the 64 applications they reviewed, mixed effects (i.e., desired effects in some, but not all, of the participants, settings, and/or behaviors analyzed) in 41% of the applications, and no effects in only 1% of the applications. In a widely cited meta-analysis, Kluger and DeNisi (1996) found that feedback interventions, on average, improved performance ($d = .41$); however, in about one-third of the studies examined, feedback had a negative effect on performance. There was also large variability among effect sizes and this variability could not be explained by feedback sign (i.e., positive vs. negative feedback), thereby suggesting that positive feedback leads to performance improvement for some people (or in some situations), whereas negative feedback leads to performance improvement for other people (or in other situations). Feedback can point to a gap between one's goals and current performance without necessarily leading to efforts to improve performance because, as Kluger and DeNisi (1996) noted, a goal-feedback gap can be reduced by (a) increasing effort, (b) abandoning the goal, (c) changing (or lowering) the goal, or (d) rejecting the feedback message.

Reactions and Responses to Feedback

Despite the importance of feedback, it is often noted that employees are sometimes reluctant to receive and act on feedback (Cleveland, Lim, & Murphy, 2007). Receiving feedback that one is "satisfactory" can be disappointing and can lead to a stable drop in organizational commitment (Pearce & Porter, 1986). Moreover, feedback is often associated with affective reactions that, in turn, can affect work performance (Kluger, Lewinsohn, & Aiello, 1996). Feedback that is discouraging or that threatens the recipient's self-esteem decreases the effectiveness of feedback interventions (Kluger & DeNisi, 1996). Comer (2007) found that receiving negative feedback directly from the task itself was more intrinsically motivating and led to less negative emotion than receiving negative feedback from interpersonal sources.

Kinicki, Prussia, Wu, and McKee-Ryan (2004) found that a set of cognitive variables completely mediated the relationship between an employee's receipt of and response to feedback. Specifically, a feedback-rich environment and perceiving the supervisor as credible (e.g., trustworthy and competent) led to perceptions that the feedback was accurate, which in turn affected the desire and intent to respond to the feedback, which in turn affected performance one year later.

Swann and Schroeder (1995) proposed that responses to feedback can proceed in three phases, with each consecutive phase requiring more cognitive resources. During the first phase, when people receive feedback they initially classify it as favorable or unfavorable, and there is a tendency to embrace positive feedback (i.e., consistent with a positivity or self-enhancement striving). If sufficient motivation and cognitive resources are available, people proceed to the second phase, in which they compare the feedback to their beliefs about who they actually are (i.e., the actual self) and react favorably to feedback that is consistent with their self-views (consistent with a self-verification striving). If their self-view is uncertain, they will compare the feedback to various possible selves (e.g., ideal self or ought self). If sufficient motivation and cognitive resources remain available, people proceed to the third phase, in which they analyze the feedback more carefully (a cost-benefit analysis). For example, at this phase people might consider whether and how the feedback might be used to improve their performance. This depth of processing model suggests that feedback recipients need to be encouraged to reflect on and analyze feedback (and be provided with the time and resources to do so), thereby creating the possibility that they might use the feedback for self-improvement.

Self-evaluations (Atwater, 1998; Fletcher, 1986) can shape reactions to feedback. For example, Korsgaard (1996) found that individuals who appraised themselves favorably were more likely to agree with positive (rather than negative) feedback from others. For individuals who appraised themselves unfavorably, agreement was unrelated to the favorableness of feedback. At the same time, receiving favorable feedback had a larger, positive effect on the subsequent performance of individuals who had appraised themselves unfavorably.

Feedback reactions can also be shaped by the recipient's personality and attitudes. For example, Lam, Yik, and Schaubroeck (2002) examined responses to performance appraisal feedback. They found that, for employees with low negative affectivity but not for employees with high negative affectivity, attitudes of higher rated performers improved one month after receiving a favorable appraisal and that these improved attitudes persisted six months after the performance appraisal. The attitudes of lower rated employees did not change over time. Renn (2003) proposed that high goal commitment (relative to low goal commitment) leads to more effective acquisition, processing, and use of feedback, which in turn leads to higher performance. In a study with rehabilitation counselors, he found that the amount of task feedback had a positive relationship with work performance for counselors with high goal commitment but had a negative relationship with performance for those counselors with low goal commitment.

Regulatory Focus and Reactions to Feedback

Higgins (1997; Brockner & Higgins, 2001) has distinguished between a promotion regulatory focus, which orients the person toward attaining positive outcomes, versus a prevention regulatory focus, which orients the person toward minimizing negative outcomes. Promotion focus concerns striving for ideals (presumably set by the self), whereas prevention focus concerns being motivated by oughts (often expectations established by others). Higgins (1997) has argued that regulatory focus, in part, develops as a consequence of nurturance-oriented parenting (which instills a promotion focus in children) or security-oriented parenting (which instills a prevention focus). In this sense, regulatory focus can be thought of as a dispositional variable. However, Higgins (1997) and others also acknowledge that regulatory focus can be situationally induced (e.g., Thorsteinson & Highhouse, 2003; Van-Dijk & Kluger, 2004) and that the effects of regulatory focus are comparable, regardless of whether it varies as a function of persons (i.e., a dispositional variable) or situations (Higgins, 1997). Indeed, research has shown that situational features can make one or the other regulatory focus more accessible (at least temporarily) and thereby influence the goals that people set and their persistence and achievement (Roney et al., 1995).

It appears that self-regulatory focus can influence a person's emotional reactions and subsequent responses to positive versus negative feedback. That is, a promotion-oriented regulatory focus (i.e., on gains) might lead one to respond more positively to positive feedback than would a prevention-oriented regulatory focus (i.e., on losses). Higgins, Shah, and Friedman (1997) experimentally manipulated regulatory focus and found that a promotion focus (relative to a prevention focus) led to a stronger increase in cheerfulness after success feedback, whereas a prevention focus (relative to a promotion focus) led to a stronger increase in agitation after failure feedback. Similar results were obtained by Idson, Liberman, and Higgins (2000). Van-Dijk and Kluger (2004) suggested that task motivation (and hence effort and performance) will increase when a person's self-regulatory focus is congruent with the sign of feedback. Idson and Higgins (2000) found that chronic self-regulatory focus and feedback sign interacted to predict task performance such that people with a promotion focus improved their performance more after positive feedback and people with a prevention focus improved their performance more after negative feedback.

Delivering Feedback

Larson (1986) found that supervisors give feedback less often about poor performance than good performance, although when given, feedback about poor performance was more specific than feedback about good performance. When the supervisor's rewards were dependent on employee performance, supervisors provided feedback more often when the employee showed a pattern of gradually worsening performance.

Kluger and DeNisi (1996) state that feedback interventions affect performance by changing the recipient's locus of attention and hence the allocation of cognitive resources. They found that feedback that directs the recipient's attention to the task is more effective than feedback that directs the recipient's attention to the self and away from the task (e.g., supervisor-delivered or verbal feedback versus computer-delivered feedback, feedback designed to discourage the recipient or that threatens the recipient's self-esteem). The review by Alvero et al. (2001) found that feedback was more consistently effective when delivered via graphs with written or verbal feedback than when delivered via verbal feedback, written feedback, or graphs alone. Also, feedback was more consistently effective when delivered at the group level than when delivered at the individual level.

Viswesvaran (2001) summarized the conditions for appraisal feedback to have a positive effect as including a balanced review (both positive and negative) of the employee's performance, discussing no more than two limitations in one meeting, a participative style that allows the employee to state his or her views, and good ongoing communication between the supervisor and employee outside the appraisal meeting. Ilgen and Davis (2000) have argued that the most important issue when providing negative feedback is to strike a balance so that it becomes possible for the recipient to accept responsibility for performance that did not meet expectations, while at the same time not lowering the recipient's self-concept. Finally, the Alvero et al. (2001) review found that the feedback was more consistently effective when it was used in combination with other procedures (e.g., antecedents such as training, job aids, or supervisory prompts; goal setting; and/or behavioral consequences such as praise, monetary incentives, or time off work for desired behavior).

Several cautions about delivering feedback are noteworthy. For example, one tenet of performance management is the importance of providing ongoing, informal feedback to employees. But providing (versus not providing) informal feedback affects subsequent ratings of the employee. Larson and Skolnik (1985) found that giving informal feedback about good (or poor) interpersonal performance subsequently led to more positive (or negative) ratings of interpersonal performance (relative to ratings obtained when informal feedback had not been provided), although this effect was not observed for task performance. Also, providing more specific feedback (i.e., feedback that guides recipients to correct responses by helping them identify behaviors that are appropriate or inappropriate for successful performance) is not always beneficial. More specific feedback appears beneficial for performance during practice but can discourage exploration during practice, so that its advantages do not endure over time or transfer to performance when the task is more complex and very specific feedback is no longer available (Goodman & Wood, 2004; Goodman, Wood, & Hendrickx, 2004). Finally, by directing attention to the self rather than the task, praise can detract from, rather than enhance, performance on a cognitively demanding task (Kluger & DeNisi, 1996).

Feedback Seeking

Employees are not merely passive recipients of feedback; they also actively seek feedback (Ashford, Blatt, & VandeWalle, 2003; Ashford & Cummings, 1983) by using inquiry (directly asking for feedback from others) or monitoring (observing the environment for indications of how one is viewed by others and how one is performing). Employees can seek feedback to satisfy one or more of three motives. One motive is instrumental (i.e., feedback can help employees regulate their behavior and attain their goals). For example, as the perceived diagnostic value of feedback increases, employees seek it more frequently, especially in uncertain situations (e.g., when the employee is new to a job or when role ambiguity is high). The instrumental value of feedback is also affected by the employee's goal orientation (learning orientation is associated with more feedback seeking) and the source of feedback (feedback is sought more often from one's supervisor and credible sources). Managers might be especially likely to seek feedback because feedback is often less available to them (e.g., employees are less likely to offer negative feedback to managers at high levels in the organization), and the nature of their work is often more ambiguous than the work of others. A second motive for feedback seeking is ego-based (i.e., to protect or enhance one's ego), and this can lead employees to avoid, distort, or discount feedback, especially if they have a performance goal orientation. Consistent with this motive, individuals with high self-confidence are more likely (and employees with low performance expectations are less likely) to seek feedback. The third motive is image-based (i.e., to protect or enhance the impressions that others hold about the employee). For example, an employee might seek feedback from the supervisor shortly after an instance of good performance (even if the feedback has no instrumental value) to make the performance salient to the supervisor and elicit the supervisor's praise. In contrast, when employees think that seeking feedback will make them look bad, they are less likely to use inquiry as a method of seeking feedback (even if the feedback has instrumental value). Lam, Huang, and Snape (2007) found that employee feedback seeking was positively related to the quality of the leader-member exchange and to an objective measure of work performance, but only when supervisors interpreted the employee's feedback seeking as reflecting the employee's desire to enhance performance rather being driven by impression management motives.

Moss, Valenzi, and Taggart (2003) noted that the feedback management strategies of poor performers have received relatively little research attention. Rather than seeking feedback, poor performers might engage in feedback-avoiding behavior (e.g., by avoiding interactions with the supervisor). They might also engage in feedback-mitigating behavior (e.g., by offering excuses, apologizing, or telling the supervisor about the problem before the supervisor becomes angry) to reduce the harshness of feedback they expect to receive. Moss et al. (2003) developed a 17-item scale to measure feedback-seeking, feedback-mitigating, and feedback-avoiding behaviors.

The feedback environment can also affect the frequency and nature of feedback seeking. For example, feedback seeking is more likely in a supportive environment (Williams, Miller, Steelman, & Levy, 1999). Whitaker, Dahling, and Levy (2007), using the feedback environment scale (Steelman, Levy, & Snell, 2004) found that employees who perceived a supportive feedback environment (one where workplace characteristics encourage the use of active inquiry) had increased feedback seeking, higher role clarity, and higher ratings of performance. Of course, whether feedback seeking is viewed as a sign of insecurity is likely to be affected by the organization's culture (which can therefore make feedback seeking more or less likely; London & Smither, 2002).

The outcomes of feedback seeking are noteworthy. For example, Renn and Fedor (2001) found that feedback-seeking behavior increased goal setting, which in turn improved performance. Evidence has also indicated that seeking more negative feedback is associated with higher effectiveness ratings from coworkers (Ashford & Tsui, 1991, Edwards, 1995). Ashford and Northcraft (1992) found that feedback seeking generally enhanced rather than diminished one's image, except for poor performers. Moreover, Ashford et al. (2003) note that poor performers are disadvantaged because they both receive and seek less feedback.

Feedback in Team Settings

In many team settings, members have both individual and team goals. They need to direct effort to attaining individual goals and responsibilities but also need to coordinate and work cooperatively with other team members. In such settings, one practical issue is whether feedback should focus on individual performance, team performance, or both. DeShon, Kozlowski, Schmidt, Milner, and Wiechmann (2004) found that feedback (about individual performance, team performance, or both) affected the way that team members allocated their resources, such that team members who received feedback that was focused only on individual performance focused their attention and effort on individual performance (and hence had the highest level of individual performance), whereas team members who received feedback focused only on team performance focused their attention and effort on team performance (and hence had the highest team performance). It is noteworthy that team members who received both individual and team-level feedback were not able to make optimal use of the feedback (i.e., the highest levels of individual and team performance occurred when team members received feedback focused on only individual or team performance, respectively).

The Productivity Measurement and Enhancement System

Pritchard, Harrell, DiazGranados, and Guzman (2008) recently meta-analyzed 83 field studies of the Productivity Measurement and Enhancement System (ProMES), an intervention aimed at enhancing the productivity of work units within organizations through performance measurement and feedback. The implementation of ProMES begins with forming a design team that establishes objectives, quantitative indicators of output, and contingencies (a graphic utility function that relates the amount of each indicator to its value for the organization). The system is then implemented by collecting data on the indicators and distributing a printed feedback to each unit employee after each performance period. A feedback meeting is also held after each performance period to review the feedback report and identify ways of making improvements. The Pritchard et al. (2008) meta-analysis found that ProMES results in large improvements in productivity in many different types of settings (e.g., type of organization, type of work and worker, country) and that these effects are sustained over time (in some cases, years). However, ProMES was somewhat less effective in highly interdependent units, perhaps because feedback focused on outputs (such as those provided in ProMES) rather than processes is less effective for highly interdependent units.

Multisource Feedback

Multisource feedback refers to collecting performance evaluations from more than one source. A variant of multisource feedback, called 360-degree feedback, collects feedback from key constituents who represent the full circle of relevant viewpoints: supervisor(s), peers, direct reports, and, in some cases, customers. Self-ratings are sometimes also collected. The intent is to help feedback recipients understand how they are viewed by others (and, when necessary, help the recipient develop more realistic self-views; e.g., Atwater, Roush, & Fischthal, 1995) and for the recipient to use the feedback to set developmental goals and guide behavior change. A policy-capturing study by Greguras, Ford, and Brutus (2003) found that multisource feedback recipients attended to all rater sources (peers, direct reports, and supervisors), but for certain dimensions they attended to some rater sources more than others.

A review of research on multisource feedback (Smither, London, & Reilly, 2005) found evidence for the concurrent validity of multisource ratings in that they are positively related to assessment center performance, annual appraisals, objective performance data, and the satisfaction and retention of subordinates. Also, raters in different roles (e.g., supervisors, peers, direct reports) appear to share a common conceptualization of managerial performance dimensions. Smither, London, and Reilly (2005) then conducted a meta-analysis of 24 longitudinal studies and found that improvement in direct report ($d = .15$), peer ($d = .05$), and supervisor ratings ($d = .15$) over time is generally small. Moderator analyses found that improvement was greater when feedback was used only for developmental purposes (rather than for administrative purposes). Specifically, across rater sources (excluding self-ratings), the average effect size in the developmental purpose studies was .25 (versus .08 in the administrative purpose studies). They also found that a large percentage of variance in effect sizes was not explained by sampling error, even after accounting for the effects of moderator variables, thereby indicating that other factors likely affect the extent of behavior change associated with multisource feedback. They presented a theoretical framework and reviewed empirical evidence, suggesting that performance improvement is more likely for some feedback recipients than others. Specifically, improvement is most likely to occur when feedback indicates that change is necessary, recipients have a positive feedback orientation, perceive a need to change their behavior, react positively to the feedback, believe change is feasible, set appropriate goals to regulate their behavior, and take actions that lead to skill and performance improvement.

In a study examining reactions to and behavior change after receiving multisource feedback, Atwater and Brett (2005) found that leaders who expressed more motivation and had more positive emotions immediately after receiving multisource feedback subsequently improved in terms of direct report ratings (one year later), while those who expressed negative emotions showed a decline in direct report ratings. These findings are important because they demonstrate that immediate reactions to feedback are not merely transitory mood states without relevance to subsequent behavior.

Several studies have examined the relationship between dispositional variables and reactions to and behavior change after receiving multisource feedback. Smither, London, and Richmond (2005) found that feedback recipients' emotional stability was positively related to a psychologist's ratings (completed immediately after the leader received multisource feedback) of the recipient's motivation to use the results from multisource feedback. They also found that recipients' extraversion was positively related to requesting additional feedback and conscientiousness was positively related to subsequently participating in developmental activities. Dominick, Reilly, and Byrne (2004) found that conscientiousness and openness to experience were positively related to performance improvement (i.e., enhanced effectiveness as a team member) after receiving peer feedback from classmates (where ratings were collected from different peers over a two-semester period). Heslin and Latham (2004) found that recipients with high self-efficacy and a learning goal orientation subsequently improved more than other managers. Atwater, Waldman, Atwater, and

Cartier (2000) found that feedback recipients who were low in organizational cynicism subsequently improved their performance more than others. However, Walker et al. (2006) described three studies that found no evidence that personality (neuroticism, extraversion, openness to experience, agreeableness, and conscientiousness) was related to improvement in multisource ratings over time.

Feedback recipients who receive unfavorable feedback or who initially overrate themselves tend to improve more than others (Atwater et al., 1995; Johnson & Ferstl, 1999; Smither et al., 1995; Walker & Smither, 1999). In each of these studies, the improvement of feedback recipients who initially overrated themselves or who initially received unfavorable feedback was greater than what would be expected on the basis of statistical regression to the mean.

Not surprisingly, performance improvement is likely only for feedback recipients who take appropriate action. For example, Smither, London, Flautt, Vargas, and Kucine (2003) found that managers who worked with an executive coach were more likely than other managers to set specific (rather than vague) goals, to solicit ideas for improvement from their supervisors, and to improve in terms of subsequent direct report and supervisor ratings. However, the differences between managers who worked with a coach and those who did not were small in magnitude (albeit statistically significant). In a five-year study of upward feedback, Walker & Smither (1999) found that: (a) managers who met with direct reports to discuss their upward feedback improved more than other managers, and (b) managers improved more in years when they discussed the previous year's feedback with direct reports than in years when they did not discuss the previous year's feedback with direct reports. Smither et al. (2004) also found that sharing multisource feedback and asking for suggestions from raters was positively related to improvement over time. Hazucha, Hezlett, and Schneider (1993) found that managers who participated in training programs and other development activities (e.g., receiving coaching and feedback, reviewing progress quarterly) after receiving multisource feedback were more likely to improve than other managers.

Developing Employees

Although employee development can occur through formal training and education, in the context of performance management more emphasis is usually placed on development through ongoing coaching (usually from supervisors) and other less formal approaches to development, such as mentoring, task force assignments, and learning from challenging work (Zaleska & de Menezes, 2007). London and Smither (1999a) presented a model of career-related continuous learning, an individual-level process characterized by a self-initiated, discretionary, planned, and proactive pattern of formal or informal activities that are sustained over time for the purpose of applying or transporting knowledge for career development. Their model identifies characteristics of the environment (e.g., value migration, deregulation, technology change), employee (e.g., self-efficacy, openness to experience, learning orientation, proactivity), and organization (e.g., learning resources and climate) that shape pre-learning, learning, and the application of learning. London and Smither (1999b) have also noted the importance of self-development, which involves employees seeking and using feedback, setting development goals, engaging in developmental activities, and tracking progress on their own. They argue that organizations can encourage self-development by providing employees with a clear understanding of organizational goals and the implications of those for employee performance and learning, holding both managers and employees accountable for continuous learning, providing task- and behavior-focused feedback, and rewarding learning.

Next, this section briefly reviews research about formal training. Then, because of its importance in the context of performance management, research about coaching (including executive coaching) is reviewed.

Formal Training

The value of formal organizational training has been widely documented. A comprehensive meta-analysis of the impact of organizational training (Arthur, Bennett, Edens, & Bell, 2003) found medium to large effect sizes for reaction ($d = .60$), learning ($d = .63$), behavior ($d = .62$), and results ($d = .62$) criteria as well as positive effects for enhancing cognitive, psychomotor, and interpersonal skills. Meta-analyses have demonstrated the positive effects of training for management skills (Burke, & Day, 1986; Collins & Holton, 2004), team performance (Salas, Nichols, & Driskell, 2007), and expatriate performance and adjustment (Deshpande, Joseph, & Viswesvaran, 1994; Morris & Robie, 2001). The economic utility (positive return on investment) of corporate training has also been demonstrated (Morrow, Jarrett, & Rupinski, 1997). Despite the widespread positive effects usually associated with formal training, some confidence intervals from meta-analyses include zero, indicating that not all training is effective.

Meta-analyses have demonstrated the efficacy of specific training methods such as overlearning (Driskell, Willis, & Copper, 1992), web-based instruction (Sitzmann, Kraiger, Stewart, & Wisher, 2006), audiovisual, equipment simulators, lecture, discussion, programmed instruction (Arthur et al., 2003), and behavior modeling (Taylor, Russ-Eft, & Chan, 2005). Meta-analysis has also shown that some training methods can be especially valuable for certain learners. For example, Callahan, Kiker, and Cross (2003) found that small group size and self-paced training, where learners can progress at their own pace, are especially helpful for older learners.

Error management training (EMT, Frese et al., 1991) encourages learners to make errors during training and to view errors as opportunities to learn what does not work (e.g., errors are a natural part of the learning process; the more errors you make, the more you learn). EMT facilitates learning (Heimbeck, Frese, Sonnentag, & Keith, 2003), in part by reducing the learner's anxiety and in part by increasing the learner's use of planning and monitoring (Keith & Frese, 2005). A meta-analysis by Keith and Frese (2008) found that, relative to error avoidant training or exploratory training without error encouragement, EMT was more effective ($d = 0.44$) for post-training transfer performance (but not for within-training performance). It was especially effective for performance on adaptive tasks (i.e., novel problems that require the development of new solutions) relative to analogical tasks (that are similar or analogous to the training task). Both active exploration (where participants are not guided to correct solutions but work independently to find solutions on their own) and error encouragement contribute to the effectiveness of EMT. Also, there is evidence that an organizational error management culture (which consists of norms and common practices that involve communicating about errors, sharing error knowledge, helping in error situations, and quickly detecting and handling errors) is positively related to organizational goal achievement and indicators of firm economic performance (van Dyck, Frese, Baer, & Sonnentag, 2005).

Bell and Kozlowski (2008) recently found that active learning interventions (such as error encouragement framing and exploratory learning) influence the nature, quality, and focus of self-regulatory activity. Compared with alternative, more traditional interventions (such as error avoidance framing or proceduralized instruction), these active learning interventions led to better adaptive transfer (although they do not necessarily lead to better performance during training).

Self-management training has also been shown to increase performance (as well as self-efficacy; Frayne & Geringer, 2000) and decrease absenteeism (Frayne & Latham, 1987; Latham & Frayne, 1989). It involves: (a) identifying the behaviors to modify, (b) establishing goals for those behaviors, (c) maintaining a record of progress toward goal attainment, (d) establishing self-rewards and self-punishments for performance relative to goals, (e) identifying high-risk situations that might frustrate goal attainment, and (f) preparing a written contract with oneself that lists goals, plans, contingencies, and so on.

On-the-Job Coaching

The shift in emphasis from performance appraisal (a discrete event) to performance management (a continuous process) has focused attention on the important role of coaching in employee performance and development (Latham et al., 2005). Over 60 years ago, Lewis referred to coaching as "really just good supervision" (1947, p. 316). And being an effective coach continues to be viewed as an essential feature of effective management (Hamlin, Ellinger, & Beattie, 2006). Employees believe that behaviors associated with effective coaching include communicating clear performance expectations, providing regular feedback, observing employee performance, developing self-improvement plans, and building a warm relationship (Graham, Wedman, & Garvin-Kester, 1993). Gittell (2001) found that narrow spans of control create the opportunity for supervisors to provide more coaching and feedback. Supervisors with narrow spans of control also had more opportunity to work side by side with their group members, which in turn reduced the informational and social distance between the supervisor and the group and led to shared goals. Shared goals made the group more receptive to coaching and feedback from the supervisor and reduced the need for supervisory monitoring.

There is some evidence that coaching skills can be developed. For example, a program designed to enhance managers' coaching skills had a positive effect on five of eight target behaviors (Graham et al., 1993). But managers are unlikely to provide coaching if they believe that employee performance cannot be improved. Heslin and colleagues (Heslin,

Latham, & VandeWalle, 2005) examined managers' implicit person theories and found that managers who held incremental beliefs (i.e., ability is malleable and can therefore be developed with effort) were more likely than managers who held entity beliefs (i.e., ability is fixed, innate, and unalterable) to recognize both improvements and declines in employee performance. In a separate study, these authors used a 90-minute workshop based on self-persuasion techniques (Aronson, 1999) to help participants who initially held entity beliefs to acquire incremental beliefs and to sustain those beliefs over a six-week period. This change led to greater acknowledgment of improvement in employee performance than was exhibited by entity theorists in a placebo control group. They also found that inducing incremental beliefs increased entity theorist managers' willingness to coach a poor performing employee, as well as the quantity and quality of their performance improvement suggestions (Heslin & VandeWalle, 2008; Heslin, VandeWalle, & Latham, 2006).

A number of studies have found evidence supporting the value of coaching. For example, a survey by Ellinger, Ellinger, and Keller (2003) found that supervisory coaching behaviors (e.g., providing and asking for feedback, helping employees think through issues by asking questions rather than providing solutions, setting expectations, providing resources) were positively related to employee job satisfaction and performance. Edmondson (1999) found that coaching by the team leader was positively related to the team's psychological safety, which in turn was positively related to its learning behavior. Cannon and Edmondson (2001) found that coaching on the part of the manager can help a group overcome the interpersonal and organizational barriers to discussing errors, problems, and conflict. Konczak, Stelly, and Trusty (2000) found that coaching for innovative performance (e.g., encouraging employees to try out new ideas even if there is a chance that they might not succeed) was positively associated with employee job satisfaction and organizational commitment. Bennett (1987) found that the addition of on-site coaching to other training elements (theory, demonstration, practice, and feedback) increased the utilization of newly learned skills and strategies in classroom instruction. Rappe and Zwick (2007), in a quasi-experiment, showed that a combination of leadership workshops and individual coaching by an internal consultant had positive effects on self-reported leadership competencies of first-line managers. Acosta-Amad and Brethower (1992)

found that a combination of on-the-job coaching, training, and feedback improved the note-writing performance of staff members in a psychiatric hospital. In a quasi-experimental study, Gyllensten and Palmer (2005) found that recipients perceived coaching (provided by an internal coach with the goal of reducing anxiety and stress) to be effective, but pre-post differences in anxiety and stress among those who were coached did not differ significantly from those who were not coached. Scandura (1992) found that career coaching by mentors was positively related to managers' promotion rate.

More recent theoretical and empirical work suggests that coaching is likely to be effective in some settings but not in others. For example, Hackman and Wageman's (2005) theory of team coaching proposes that coaching interventions that focus on team effort, strategy, and knowledge and skill will facilitate team effectiveness more than interventions that focus on members' interpersonal relationships. Also, they suggest that timing is important in determining the optimal type of coaching such that motivational coaching will be most helpful at the beginning of a performance period, consultative coaching will be most helpful at the midpoint of a performance period, and educational coaching (i.e., helping the team capture what can be learned from the collective work just completed) will be most helpful after performance activities have been completed.

In a study of external leadership of self-managing teams, Morgeson (2005) found that supportive coaching (reinforcing the team for its self-management behaviors and thereby fostering a sense of competence and independence in the team without becoming directly involved in the team's task work) was positively related to perceptions of leader effectiveness; however, active coaching (i.e., becoming directly involved in helping the team perform its work) and leader sense making (i.e., the leader interpreting events for the team) were negatively related to satisfaction with leadership but positively related to perceptions of leader effectiveness when disruptive events occur.

Wageman (2001) found that positive coaching (e.g., providing informal rewards and other cues that the group as a whole is responsible for managing itself; teaching the group to use a problem-solving process; facilitating problem-solving discussions) was positively related to team self-management and the quality of team process, but not to team performance. Negative coaching (e.g., intervening in the task, dealing directly with a team's customer without involving the team, identifying the team's problems) was negatively related to team self-management and member satisfaction, but not to team performance. She also found that effective coaching helps well-designed teams more than poorly designed teams, and that ineffective coaching hurts poorly designed teams more than well-designed teams.

Executive Coaching

Executive coaching has been defined as a short- to medium-term relationship between an executive and a consultant, with the purpose of improving the executive's work effectiveness (Feldman & Lankau, 2005). Hall, Otazo, and Hollenbeck (1999) state that executive coaching is "a practical, goal-focused form of personal one-to-one learning for busy executives. It may be used to improve performance, to improve or develop executive behaviors, to work through organizational issues, to enhance a career, or to prevent derailment." Executive coaching can take a number of different forms. Some executives use coaching to learn specific skills, others to improve performance on the job or to prepare for advancement in business or professional life, and still others to support broader purposes, such as an executive's agenda for major organizational change (Witherspoon & White, 1996). Feldman and Lankau (2005) note that executive coaches differ from advisers (who share their business or technical expertise), career counselors (who help match executives to jobs in the external labor market), mentors (usually more experienced employees who help protégés), and therapists (who help employees with emotional or behavioral problems), and that, because coaching is unregulated, anyone can describe himself or herself as an executive coach.

Generally, executive coaching includes several stages, such as establishing the coaching relationship, data gathering (about the executive and the organization), feedback (presenting the executive with the results of the data gathered from interviews, psychological assessments, multisource feedback, etc.), goal setting, periodic coaching sessions, and evaluation (to determine progress toward the goals of coaching; Feldman & Lankau, 2005; Smither & Reilly, 2001).

Latham (2007) has argued that the practice of coaching needs to be explicitly linked to well-established psychological frameworks (e.g., implicit person theory, goal setting, socio-cognitive theories) to create an evidence-based approach to coaching. To date, psychologists have approached executive coaching from a variety of conceptual frameworks, including social psychology, positive psychology, rational-emotive therapy, cognitive-behavior therapy, emotional intelligence, psychoanalysis, family therapy, hypnosis, person-centered, systems-oriented, psychodynamic, multimodal therapy, and even eye movement desensitization and reprocessing (e.g., Biswas-Diener & Dean, 2007; Feldman & Lankau, 2005; Peltier, 2001; Smither & Reilly, 2001).

Coaching clients want coaches to have graduate training in psychology; experience in (or an understanding of) business; listening skills, and an established reputation (Wasylyshyn, 2003). In a survey of 428 executive coaches, Bono, Purvanova, Towler, and Peterson (2009) compared the practices (e.g., approaches to coaching, use of assessment tools) of psychologist and non-psychologist coaches, as well as the practices of coaches from various psychological disciplines (e.g., counseling, clinical, and industrial/organizational). They found: (a) the differences between psychologist and non-psychologists were generally small ($d = .26$), and (b) as many differences between psychologists of differing disciplines as between psychologist and non-psychologist coaches. It is possible that psychological training is valuable in some circumstances but not in others. For example, Kilburg (2004) suggests that psychological interventions might be especially relevant when a manager continues to under-perform despite being motivated to do better, or when a manager lacks sufficient knowledge or skills to cope with a challenging situation or problem, or when the manager's interpersonal relationships limit his or her ability to perform the job or advance in the organization.

Although human resource professionals who sponsor executive coaching have positive perceptions of its benefits (Dagley, 2006), the vast majority of articles about executive coaching rely on case studies or vignettes as illustrations or sources of evidence, and only a small number of empirical studies have examined the impact of executive coaching (Feldman & Lankau, 2005). Of these, many have relied on self-reports and surveys of coaching recipients to evaluate the impact of coaching. These studies have found that coaching recipients perceive coaching as valuable and believe that they benefited from it (e.g., progress toward goals, sustained behavior change; Evers, Brouwers, & Tomic, 2006; Feggetter, 2007; Hall, Otazo, & Hollenbeck, 1999; Hollenbeck & McCall, 1999; Kombarakaran, Yang, Baker, & Fernandes, 2008; Wasylyshyn, 2003; Wasylyshyn, Gronsky, & Haas, 2006). McGovern et al. (2001) examined the impact of executive coaching on 100 executives from 56 organizations. Coaching programs generally ranged from 6 to 12 months in duration. Based on interviews, they found that 86% of participants and 74% of stakeholders (immediate supervisors or HR representatives) indicated that they were very satisfied or extremely satisfied with the coaching process. Participants estimated that the return on coaching was nearly 5.7 times the investment in coaching. However, these results relied on executives' estimates of impact, as contrasted with input from other stakeholders.

A small number of studies have relied on somewhat more objective indicators (relative to self-reports). Olivero, Bane, and Kopelman (1997) examined the effects of executive coaching in a public sector agency where managers participated in a three-day management development program and then worked with an internal executive coach for eight weeks. The authors found that both the management development program and coaching increased productivity, with executive coaching resulting in a significantly greater gain compared to the management development program alone. Luthans and Peterson (2003) found that a combination of 360-degree feedback and coaching (focused on enhanced self-awareness and behavioral management) was associated with improvements in coworkers' ratings of the feedback recipients (managers) and improvements in job satisfaction, organizational commitment, and turnover intentions for the managers and their employees. However, there was no control group, and the design of the study also did not allow the authors to disentangle the effects of coaching from those of the 360-degree feedback. Smither et al. (2003) used a quasi-experimental design that examined 1,361 managers who received multisource feedback; 404 of those managers worked with an executive coach to review their feedback and set goals. One year later, managers who worked with an executive coach were more likely than other managers to have: (a) set specific (rather than vague) goals ($d = .16$), (b) solicited ideas for improvement from their supervisors ($d = .36$), and (c) improved more in terms of direct report and supervisor ratings ($d = .17$). Although executive coaching had a statistically significant and positive effect, the effects sizes were quite small. Bowles, Cunningham, De La Rosa, and Picano (2007) found that middle (but not executive-level) managers who volunteered to receive eight hours of formal training followed by, on average, six to seven hours of coaching outperformed (e.g., achievement of quotas) managers who

had not received the training and coaching. Because the participants were volunteers and the coaching was combined with formal training, the impact of coaching on performance remains uncertain. Bowles and Picano (2006) found that managers who more frequently applied coaching advice (delivered by an external coach via telephone conference calls) reported more work satisfaction, but coaching was not related to productivity. Kampa-Kokesch (2001) compared ratings of transformational and transactional leadership of executives in the early versus late stages of coaching and found only one significant difference (which was related to a transactional leadership scale). Support from an external (to the team) coach has been shown to predict the emergence of shared leadership in teams (whereby leadership is distributed among team members rather than focused on a single designated leader; Carson, Tesluk, & Marrone, 2007). Sue-Chan and Latham (2004) found that MBA students coached by an external coach showed more teamwork behavior and higher grades than those coached by peers, and that an external coach was perceived as being more credible than peer coaches. In sum, the limited research indicates that sponsors and recipients have favorable reactions to coaching, and some positive benefits have been found. However, due to limitations in the design of most studies, it is difficult to make firm conclusions about the impact of executive coaching on performance.

Evaluating Performance

Most performance evaluation or appraisal processes ask the supervisor to rate the effectiveness of the employee on several dimensions of performance and to provide a rating of overall performance (although sometimes rankings, rather than ratings, are used). These ratings are often linked to administrative decisions such as salary increases, promotions, or terminations. However, evidence indicates that employees who perceive the use of performance appraisal to be developmental are more satisfied with the appraisal and the supervisor, even after accounting for the effects of justice perceptions and the appraisal rating (Boswell & Boudreau, 2000).

Research on performance appraisal has been flourishing for nearly a century. Because objective measures of performance are not available for many (if not most) jobs, subjective (e.g., supervisor) ratings play a central role in evaluating employee performance. Even when objective measures are available, research has repeatedly shown that ratings of performance are only modestly related to objective measures of performance (Bommer, Johnson, Rich, Podsakoff, & MacKenzie, 1995; Cascio & Valenzi, 1978; Heneman, 1986; Kirchner, 1960; Seashore, Indik, & Georgopoulos, 1960). Although this likely reflects limitations associated with ratings, it also likely reflects problems with objective measures such as criterion deficiency and contamination. Wexley and Klimoski (1984) suggested that there is no "true" job performance. Instead, ratings and objective measures (e.g., productivity) are different indicators that tap different aspects of performance.

Thorndike's classic paper on rating errors (1920) led to a long-standing focus on how to reduce such errors, under the assumption that less rating error would lead to more rating accuracy. Much attention was centered on developing rating formats that might reduce rating errors. Numerous formats were developed, including forced choice (Sisson, 1948), critical incidents (Flanagan, 1954), behaviorally anchored rating scales (Smith & Kendall, 1963), mixed standard scales (Blanz & Ghiselli, 1972), behavioral observation scales (Latham, Fay, & Saari, 1979; Latham & Wexley, 1977), and performance distribution assessment (Kane, 1986). At the same time, rater training programs focused on reducing rater errors such as halo and first impressions (Latham, Wexley, & Pursell, 1975).

An influential review by Landy and Farr (1980) noted that rating formats or scales had little if any effect on reducing rating errors or increasing agreement among raters. (Although it should be noted that rating format can have other effects. For example, raters generally prefer behavioral observation scales relative to behavioral expectation scales or trait scales; and behavioral observation scales, relative to graphic rating scales, yield higher levels of goal clarity, acceptance, and commitment; Tziner & Kopelman, 1988; Wiersma, van den Berg, & Latham, 1995). Landy and Farr (1980) suggested that it made more sense to view the rater (rather than the rating scale) as the "instrument" and that research should therefore focus on the rater. This led to cognitive approaches to (or models of) performance appraisal (see DeNisi, 1996, for a summary). Papers by DeCotiis and Petit (1978), Feldman (1981), Ilgen and Feldman (1983), and DeNisi, Cafferty, and Meglino (1984) all focused on raters' cognitive processes (rather than rating formats). These models borrowed heavily from research on person perception and social cognition that was taking place in social psychology. Moreover, these models looked at how raters recognize, attend to, and observe employee behavior (or other information

related to employee performance); represent, organize, and store this information in memory; retrieve the information from memory; and integrate the information to form a judgment about or evaluation of the employee. This research illustrated the important role that categories and schemas play in automatic processing (where little cognitive energy is expended) and showed that controlled processing (which requires more deliberate cognitive effort) occurs only when information is acquired about an employee that is quite inconsistent with the category or schema to which the employee has already been assigned by the rater. It also showed how categories and schemas shape subsequent information processing (e.g., what raters attend to and recall) and ratings of performance.

More recently, conceptual models have emphasized the important role of context and goals in appraisals (Murphy & Cleveland, 1991; Murphy & Cleveland, 1995). Contextual factors include proximal variables that directly affect the rater, such as the nature of the relationship between the supervisor and employee (e.g., close and informal versus distant and formal), the nature of the job, time constraints on the rater, and the consequences of ratings. They also include distal variables that influence the rater less directly, such as the organization's culture and values.

There are numerous examples of contextual effects on ratings. For example, a meta-analysis by Jawahar and Williams (1997) found that the purpose of the appraisal influences leniency in ratings such that appraisals obtained for administrative purposes (e.g., to influence pay raises or promotions) were about one-third of a standard deviation higher than those obtained for employee development or research purposes, especially when the ratings were made by practicing managers in real-world settings. Trust in the appraisal process (whether a rater believes that others in the organization will provide fair and accurate appraisals) also affects leniency in ratings (Bernardin & Orban, 1990). Raters high in agreeableness provide more lenient ratings when they expect to have a face-to-face meeting with the employee, but this effect is attenuated when using a behavior checklist rather than a graphic rating scale (Yun, Donahue, Dudley, & McFarland, 2005). Similarly, raters accountable to others with authority or higher status provide more accurate ratings compared with raters who are accountable to a lower status audience and raters who do not have to justify their ratings (Mero, Guidice, & Brownlee, 2007). In a lab experiment, Shore, Adams, and Tashchian

(1998) showed that self-appraisals can influence the supervisor's appraisal of the employee such that supervisors' ratings are higher when they receive a favorable (rather than unfavorable) self-appraisal from the employee.

Prior impressions of the ratee or receiving indirect information (e.g., from others) about the ratee's performance also influence evaluations (Buda, Reilly, & Smither, 1991; Smither, Reilly, & Buda, 1988; Reilly, Smither, Warech, & Reilly, 1998). For example, individual raters who were told that a group had been judged to be very good (before observing the group) subsequently recalled more effective behaviors (including behaviors that had not occurred) and fewer ineffective behaviors than raters who were told that the (same) group had been judged to be very poor (Martell & Leavitt, 2002). That is, knowledge of the target's performance serves as a cue that leads raters to recall cue-consistent attributes (effective or ineffective behaviors) as having occurred (even if they had not). However, Salvemini, Reilly, and Smither (1993) showed that motivating raters (by offering an incentive to be accurate) eliminated this bias, and Martell and Leavitt (2002) demonstrated that this bias can be eliminated when ratings are completed by a group (rather than by individuals).

Moreover, the rater's goal need not necessarily be to provide an accurate rating of the employee's performance. For example, Murphy and Cleveland (1991, 1995) note that judgments (the rater's private view) and ratings (the rater's public statement) are not identical. Because ratings do not necessarily reflect the rater's judgments, a supervisor (or other raters) might hold an accurate view of an employee's performance but deliberately provide an inaccurate rating. For example, a supervisor might provide a rating that is more favorable than the supervisor's judgment of the employee, perhaps to avoid an unpleasant or difficult conversation or to help the employee obtain a higher salary increase. Ratings (as contrasted with judgments) are especially likely to be shaped by political considerations (Longnecker, Gioia, & Sims, 1987). For example, because a poor rating might damage the supervisor's relationship with an employee, the supervisor might provide an inaccurate (more favorable) rating and thereby create a climate in which the two can work together more comfortably. Or a supervisor might provide a poor rating (that is lower than the supervisor's judgment of the employee's performance) to teach a disruptive or uncooperative employee a lesson. A scale to measure perceptions of the extent to which performance appraisals are affected by organizational politics has been developed by Tziner, Latham, Price, and Haccoun (1996).

Harris (1994) noted that much of the research concerning performance appraisal had focused on the rater's ability to provide accurate ratings (e.g., by providing raters with training and behaviorally focused rating formats), but little attention had been directed to the rater's motivation in the appraisal process. He argued that there are three determinants of rater motivation: rewards (e.g., whether providing accurate ratings or feedback to employees will be rewarded by the organization or will indirectly affect the rater's rewards by leading to improved employee performance); negative consequences (e.g., whether ratings or feedback might demoralize the employee or damage the manager-employee relationship); and impression management (e.g., adhering to organizational norms or wanting to give favorable ratings so that the manager is perceived by others as having an effective work group). Harris (1994) argued that several situational factors will enhance rater motivation. These include accountability (having to justify one's ratings to others), interdependence (when the rater's outcomes and rewards are highly dependent on the employee's performance), trust in the appraisal system (believing that others will provide fair, rather than lenient, ratings of their employees), and ease of use (appraisal forms that are not too difficult or time-consuming to complete). Harris (1994) also emphasized that rater motivation can affect all stages of the performance appraisal process, including observing employee performance, storing the observed information in long-term memory, retrieving complete information, integrating this information, rating the employee, and providing feedback. Moreover, motivated raters are more likely to use deliberate or controlled information-processing strategies rather than quick, heuristic-based, or automatic information-processing strategies at each of these stages.

Problems with the concept of rater errors (although long noted by some) have become more widely acknowledged. For example, covariance among different performance dimensions and a small intra-employee standard deviation of ratings across dimensions were often viewed as indicators of halo error. Similarly, when favorable ratings were given to several employees, this was viewed as an indicator of leniency error. Of course, in some instances, employees might perform effectively (or ineffectively) across several dimensions (or a group of employees might all be especially effective performers). In such instances, rater "errors" might actually be associated with more accurate ratings (Cooper, 1981a, 1981b). Several studies in which true scores were known (e.g., by using expert ratings of videotaped performance) found paradoxically positive correlations between error (halo) and accuracy (e.g., Borman, 1977, 1979). Hence, research attention turned away from rater errors and toward enhancing rater accuracy. This was accompanied by a shift in rater training to increase accuracy rather than reduce errors (Bernardin & Buckley, 1981; Bernardin & Pence, 1980; Hauenstein, 1998). Such training (often referred to as frame of reference training) generally involves familiarizing raters with the definitions and behavioral indicators of each performance dimension, providing opportunities to complete practice ratings (using either written vignettes or videos to present the performance examples), and delivering feedback concerning the accuracy of the practice ratings (by comparing them with target ratings that represent the organization's estimate of the effectiveness levels demonstrated in the performance examples). A cumulative research review by Woehr and Huffcutt (1994) showed that frame of reference training is an effective approach to increase rating accuracy.

Viswesvaran (2001) reviewed criteria that can be considered to determine the quality of performance appraisals. These include discriminability across individuals, practicality, acceptability (e.g., to users), reliability, comprehensiveness (i.e., the absence of criterion deficiency), and construct validity (i.e., job-relatedness and the absence of criterion contamination). Despite the importance of reliability, the inter-rater reliability of performance ratings is notoriously low. A meta-analysis by Viswesvaran, Ones, and Schmidt (1996) found that the inter-rater reliability of supervisor ratings of overall job performance was .52 (for peer ratings it was .42). Rothstein (1990) found that inter-rater reliability is positively related to the opportunity to observe the ratee (especially over the first 12 months); however, the asymptotic value of reliability was only .55. It is important to note that different raters often observe the employee on different occasions and in different settings; therefore lack of agreement between raters does not necessarily indicate that either or both raters are in error.

Murphy and Cleveland (1995) have questioned whether the benefits of performance appraisal outweigh the costs. And, despite decades of research, Murphy (2008) argues that the relationship between job performance and ratings of job performance remains weak or uncertain. He states that some models of performance ratings assume that the difference between job performance and ratings is simply obscured by measurement error and that the variance in ratings can be partitioned into true score and error variance (with the corresponding recommendation that, when examining the correlates of ratings, problems with ratings can be remedied by correcting for attenuation due to unreliability). But Murphy (2008) argues that it is unreasonable to assume that, after random measurement error is removed from ratings, the portion that is left is simply job performance. Instead, he states that differences between job performance and ratings are not "inexplicable, idiosyncratic errors on the part of raters, but rather are the result of a combination of systematic and random factors in the environment in which ratings are obtained" (p. 155; many of these factors are described above). Ultimately, Murphy (2008) concludes that organizations need to create an environment in which "raters have: (a) incentives, tools and opportunities to observe and recall ratees' job performance, (b) incentives to provide ratings that faithfully reflect the rater's evaluation of each ratee's performance, and (c) protection against the negative consequences of giving honest ratings" (p. 157). There is no easy practical solution to the problems associated with ratings. One approach used by many organizations is to require supervisors to share, discuss, and justify their ratings of employees with others (e.g., the supervisor's manager or a panel of peers). This approach might help calibrate ratings made by different supervisors and lessen unjustifiable leniency in ratings but, as Murphy notes, it also make raters more vulnerable to social influence effects (e.g., norms about rating distributions) that might actually reduce the accuracy of ratings in some instances.

Forced Distributions

During the past several years, perhaps no other aspect of performance management has garnered as much attention in the popular press as the use of forced distributions or rankings (Dominick, 2009). In absolute rating systems (such as behaviorally anchored rating scales and behavioral observation scales), raters make judgments about the extent to which each employee displays a variety of job-related behaviors; all employees are evaluated relative to the same behaviors (standards), and it is therefore possible that all employees could receive the same rating. In contrast, relative rating systems, which include forced ranking or distribution systems, require raters to evaluate employees relative to one another, determining which employees are best, next best, and so on. One approach to forced distributions uses an approximate normal distribution to slot employees into a bell-curve shaped distribution (e.g., 10% in the top category, 15% in the next category, 50% in the middle category, 15% in the next category, and 10% in the bottom category). More commonly, most employees are placed into one of the top three categories of a five-point rating scale (e.g., 10% in the top category, 20% in the next category, 60% in the middle category, and the remaining 10% in the bottom two categories).

Advocates argue that forced distribution systems reduce or eliminate artificially inflated ratings (Taylor & Wherry, 1951), thereby enabling organizations to identify and adequately reward top performers while also holding poor performers accountable. They also argue that forced distributions are fair to poor performers because the system lets such employees know where they stand so they have an opportunity to do something about it (perhaps by moving to other organizations or jobs where they can succeed). Critics argue that forced distributions are as susceptible to favoritism, manipulation, and organizational politics as any other rating process and that they are unreasonable when the number of employees in the rating group is small. Concerns have also been raised about the effects of forced distribution systems on perceived fairness and employee morale (McBriarty, 1988), as well as legal compliance (Dominick, 2009). Several features of forced distribution systems appear especially related to the controversy concerning their use. These include the consequences of being rated in the lowest categories (e.g., will such employees be terminated?), the difference in rewards received by employees in different categories, and the number of employees in the rating group.

Two meta-analyses indicate that relative rating formats (which include forced distributions) appear to offer advantages compared to absolute rating formats. Heneman (1986) found that the correlation between supervisory ratings and results-oriented measures of performance was higher for relative rating formats than for absolute rating formats. Nathan and Alexander (1988) found that validity coefficients for clerical ability tests were higher when supervisory rankings rather than supervisory ratings were used as criteria.

In a policy-capturing study, Blume, Baldwin, and Rubin (2007) found that more favorable reactions to forced distribution rating systems were associated with the absence of severe consequences for poorly ranked employees, having a reasonably large rating (comparison) group, and a process that ensured that employees receive frequent feedback. In two studies examining reactions to forced distribution rating systems, Schleicher, Bull, and Green (2007) found that such systems were less likely to be perceived as fair and more likely to be seen as difficult when there were administrative consequences (e.g., termination, compensation, and so on) and when there was little variability in performance among those being ranked. They also found that a forced distribution system was perceived as less fair than an absolute rating format. Finally, it has been argued that forced distribution systems are better suited to some organizational cultures (e.g., highly results-oriented cultures, where success does not depend heavily on teamwork) than others (Guralnik, Rozmarin, & So, 2004).

One recurring concern raised about forced distribution ratings systems is their potential to create competition rather than collaboration among employees (Guralnik, Rozmarin, & So, 2004; Hymowitz, 2001, McBriarty, 1988). Supporting this concern, Garcia and colleagues (Garcia & Tor, 2007; Garcia, Tor, & Gonzalez, 2006) have shown that rivals near the top of a distribution were less likely to cooperate when doing so had the potential to advance the other person's standing.

In a survey of human resource professionals, Lawler (2003) found that, compared to those not using forced distributions, those using forced distributions judged their systems as better able to differentiate between levels of performance (e.g., to identify and reward top talent, identify and manage out poor performers), but also judged their systems as less effective at developing talent and less effective overall.

Rewarding Performance

Performance management systems seek to link rewards (e.g., money, recognition) to performance. Indeed, from a practical perspective, performance evaluations are often conducted, at least in part, because they serve as the basis for decisions about compensation. Yet a recent review by Rynes, Gerhart, and Parks (2005) notes that relatively little psychological research has examined the consequences of linking pay to performance (although such research has occurred more often in other disciplines, such as management, economics, and finance). They argue that three motivation theories have had the perhaps unintended effect of diminishing research interest in the linkage between performance evaluation and pay for performance. For example, Maslow's hierarchy of needs theory (1943) acknowledged the importance of lower level physiological and safety needs (which presumably can be satisfied by money) but emphasized the importance of higher order needs such as love, esteem, and self-actualization (which presumably could be better met through engagement in meaningful work than by money). Herzberg's motivation-hygiene theory (Herzberg, Mausner, Peterson, & Capwell, 1957) viewed satisfaction and dissatisfaction as two distinct constructs and suggested that money was more likely to play a role in creating or reducing dissatisfaction than in increasing satisfaction. Deci and Ryan's cognitive evaluation theory (1985) has been interpreted by some (albeit inaccurately) to mean that any emphasis on external rewards (such as pay) will inevitably diminish intrinsic interest in the work itself. Collectively, these three theories can be seen as indicating that money plays only a small or perhaps negative role in motivation. Rynes et al. (2005) show that the small role of money as a motivator in Maslow's (1943) and Herzberg's (1957) theories is not supported by empirical evidence. They also note that evidence from Deci and Ryan's (1985) theory is based almost entirely on research with children and college students in laboratory settings rather than with adults in real-world work settings.

Types of Pay-for-Performance Plans

Heneman and Gresham (1998) note that pay-for-performance plans can focus on individual performance (e.g., merit pay, skill-based pay, piece rates, sales commissions, employee suggestion systems), team performance (e.g., team incentives, team recognition), or organizational performance (e.g., gain sharing, profit sharing, stock ownership).

At the individual level, merit pay plans involve linking pay increases to subjective (usually the supervisor's) ratings of the employee's performance in the previous time period. Merit plans can also reward behaviors related to effective teamwork (e.g., collaboration, communication, conflict resolution) to encourage cooperation and limit competition among team members. In skill-based pay, increases in compensation are based on mastery (usually defined via certification by supervisors, trainers, or peers) of carefully defined skill sets. Skill-based pay makes sense when its higher costs (for training and compensation) are outweighed by the advantages of a more flexible workforce (Heneman & Gresham, 1998). Employee suggestion systems provide rewards to individual employees for suggestions that

lead to cost savings or that enhance revenues. One potential downside of individual-level pay for performance is that employees might see little value in cooperating with coworkers (which can create problems when cooperation would benefit the group or organization as a whole).

At the team level, team incentives can be used in situations where (a) the team produces an identifiable output, and (b) it is difficult or impossible to measure the contribution of individual team members. Usually the incentive is divided equally among team members. Team recognition plans provide monetary or non-monetary rewards to teams that identify more efficient methods to produce a product or deliver a service. One downside to pay for performance at the team level is what has been referred to as social loafing or free riding, in which some employees limit their efforts when they believe that their individual contributions cannot or will not be assessed and others on the team will work very hard to ensure the team's success (Albanese & Van Fleet, 1985; Cooper, Dyck, & Frohlich, 1992; Heneman & von Hippel, 1995; Kidwell & Bennett, 1993; Shepperd, 1993). When individual contributions to team success can be assessed, then team rewards can be distributed proportional to those contributions. Consistent with what would be expected based on social loafing or free rider research, the size of the group moderates the effectiveness of group pay plans, with a larger impact occurring in smaller firms (Rynes et al., 2005).

At the facility or organization level, gain-sharing plans provide rewards for cost (or time) savings or revenue enhancement. Heneman and Gresham (1998) note that an attractive feature of gain-sharing plans is that they pay for themselves because rewards are not distributed until costs are reduced or revenue is enhanced. Gain-sharing plans generally use joint committees of employees and managers who solicit, screen, and help implement suggestions from employees. The cost savings or increased revenues are split between employees (with each employee receiving an equal amount) and management (who can reinvest the money). Sometimes, each employee receiving the same amount (reward) can create resentment among employees who think that their contributions were greater than the contributions of other employees.

Profit-sharing plans are based on the financial performance of the entire organization (e.g., as measured by a predetermined metric such as net income, return on assets, economic value added, earnings per share, etc.) and can provide employees with the associated reward soon after the amount of profit has been determined or can defer payment until the employee retires (or a combination of both). Stock ownership and stock options can also link pay to organizational performance. One issue associated with all organization-level pay-for-performance plans has been referred to as the "line of sight" problem, in which employees see little connection between their performance and the performance of the organization as a whole (Heneman & Gresham, 1998). This is especially likely to be a problem when poor organizational performance and hence low plan payouts are perceived as being due to factors beyond employees' control, such as poor decisions made by executives (Rynes et al., 2005).

Heneman and Gresham (1998) also argue that pay-for-performance plans should be matched to business objectives. For example, skill-based pay plans would be a good fit for employee development objectives, individual plans (e.g., piece rate) and gain-sharing plans would be a good fit for productivity (e.g., revenue enhancement or cost reduction) objectives, team recognition and team incentives would be a good fit for teamwork objectives, and profit sharing would be a good fit for profit objectives.

Many organizations link pay to performance at multiple levels (e.g., merit pay, team incentives or recognition, and profit sharing) in an attempt to retain the advantages of each approach while minimizing its potential negative consequences (Rynes et al., 2005). Unfortunately, little research exists concerning the consequences of combining several approaches (for exceptions, see Wageman, 1995, and Crown & Rosse, 1995).

Research on Pay for Performance

In a survey of Fortune 500 companies, Lawler (2003) found that respondents thought that performance management systems are more effective when there is a strong connection between appraisals and rewards (salary increases, bonuses, stock awards). Research generally supports this belief. However, exempt employees tend to be more supportive of performance-based pay than non-exempt employees, who are more supportive of pay based on seniority and cost of living (Heneman, 1992).

Generally, individual-level plans (e.g., piece rate, sales commissions) have larger effects on productivity than unit-level plans (such as gain sharing), which in turn have a greater impact than corporate-wide

plans such as profit sharing (Heneman & Gresham, 1998; Rynes et al., 2005). In an early meta-analysis, Locke and colleagues (Locke, Feren, McCaleb, Shaw, & Denny, 1980) concluded that individual pay incentives increased performance by an average of 30%, and had a greater impact than goal setting, job enrichment, or employee participation. A meta-analysis by Judiesch (1995) concluded that the increase in output due to individual incentive compensation systems is on average 33 percent. A meta-analysis by Guzzo, Jette, and Katzell (1985) also found that financial incentives had a positive effect on performance ($d = .57$). Finally, a meta-analysis by Jenkins, Mitra, Gupta, and Shaw (1998) found the correlation between financial incentives and performance quantity was .34, with field experiments (.48) yielding effects twice as large as those found in lab experiments (.24); however, financial incentives were not related to performance quality.

Unfortunately, very little research exists concerning the impact of merit pay (the most popular method of linking pay to performance) on subsequent behavior and performance, although there is a good deal of research on attitudinal reactions to merit pay (Heneman & Gresham, 1998; Heneman & Werner, 2005; Rynes et al. 2005). A detailed research review by Heneman and Werner (2005) found that merit pay was usually but not always associated with positive employee attitudes (e.g., satisfaction with pay, the job, or the employer), but its relationship to improved performance has been inconsistent and sometimes disappointing (sometimes a positive but sometimes no effect on performance). Also, there is little evidence about the effects of skill-based pay on productivity.

Rochat (1998) studied gain sharing in 37 organizations and concluded that such plans were markedly successful. She identified several correlates associated with gain-sharing success. For example, a non-union environment, more frequent payout periods, less complex and better communicated plans, and less use of a consultant in plan design were associated with more effective plans. The success of gain sharing (e.g., lower production costs) has also been shown to be, in part, related to the cumulative number of implemented employee suggestions (Arthur & Huntley, 2005).

Early research found that firms with a higher percentage of managers eligible for stock options had higher returns on assets than firms with a lower percentage of managers eligible (Gerhart & Milkovich, 1990). More recently, there has been debate about the consequences of stock options, in part driven by examples in which executives have manipulated stock prices for personal gain (Rynes et al. 2005) and in part driven by recent research that has shown that stock options sometimes have negative consequences. For example, Sanders and Hambrick (2007) found that the more a CEO is paid in stock options, the more extreme the subsequent performance of the CEO's firm and the more likely that the extreme performance will be a big loss rather than a big gain. O'Connor, Priem, Coombs, and Gilley (2006) found that increasing CEO stock options led to less fraudulent financial reporting when CEO duality (i.e., the CEO also serves as the chair of the firm's board of directors) and board stock options were either simultaneously present or simultaneously absent, but led to more fraudulent financial reporting when either CEO duality or board stock options was present while the other was absent.

Prior to June 2005, there was no requirement that stock options granted to employees had to be recognized as an expense on the firm's income statement, although their cost was disclosed in footnotes to financial statements. Stock options are likely to be less attractive to many firms since 2005, when the Financial Accounting Standards Board began to require that companies treat employee stock option compensation as an expense on corporate income statements (thereby making the cost of such options more transparent).

One question of practical importance is how strong the link should be between performance and pay. Although stronger links should enhance employee motivation and performance, they might also have unintended side effects, such as employees focusing only on criteria that are rewarded (e.g., attending only to quantity when quantity, but not quality, is rewarded) or manipulating (or gaming) the system (e.g., by artificially inflating results measures) to receive short-term plan payouts at the expense of the organization's long-term well-being (Rynes et al. 2005).

Despite the potential benefits of pay for performance, Beer and Cannon (2004) have described case studies in which managers thought that: (a) the costs of pay-for-performance programs exceeded their benefits, and (b) alternatives such as effective leadership, clear goals, coaching, and training were a better investment.

In sum, research indicates that pay for performance can have very positive effects on performance, although problems can occur when such programs are poorly implemented (see reviews by Heneman & Gresham, 1998; Rynes et al., 2005). However, much of the research about pay for performance is based on studies in which an objective performance measure was available. This raises the question of whether pay for performance is useful in the many settings where no objective measure of performance is available and hence performance is assessed via ratings (which suffer from poor inter-rater reliability).

In addition to their effects on performance, Rynes et al. (2005) note that pay-for-performance plans can potentially create sorting effects that lead different types of people to apply to and stay with the organization. For example, individuals with high ability (Trank, Rynes, & Bretz, 2002; Trevor, Gerhart, & Boudreau, 1997), self-efficacy (Cable & Judge, 1994), and need for achievement (Bretz, Ash, & Dreher, 1989) appear to be more attracted to organizations where pay is closely linked to individual performance.

Behavioral Management Programs

A recent meta-analysis (Stajkovic & Luthans, 2003) found that behavioral management programs (sometimes referred to as organizational behavior modification), which are based on the premise that behaviors that enhance performance must be contingently reinforced, led to a 16% increase in performance ($d = .47$) and that the greatest effect was obtained when three reinforcers—money, feedback, and social recognition—were used in combination (45% increase in performance) rather than separately. Earlier, Stajkovic and Luthans (1997) found that the effect of behavioral management programs was much greater in manufacturing than in service organizations.

Do External Rewards Diminish Intrinsic Motivation?

Deci and Ryan's cognitive evaluation theory (CET) states that psychological needs for autonomy and competence underlie intrinsic motivation; hence the effects of a reward on intrinsic motivation depend on how it affects the recipient's perceived self-determination and perceived competence. That is, it is not the reward per se but rather the reward's meaning to the recipient that determines its effect on intrinsic motivation. CET proposes that rewards that enhance perceived self-determination or perceived competence will increase intrinsic motivation, whereas rewards that diminish perceived self-determination or perceived competence will decrease intrinsic motivation (Deci, Koestner, &

Ryan, 1999). A meta-analysis by Deci et al. (1999) examined the effects of tangible rewards and verbal rewards (positive feedback) on intrinsic motivation in experiments with children and college students (with activities ranging from word games to construction puzzles and rewards ranging from dollar bills to marshmallows). Verbal rewards (positive feedback) enhanced intrinsic motivation (for college students) presumably because they affirmed the recipient's competence; however, tangible rewards lowered intrinsic motivation. It is noteworthy that verbal rewards enhanced intrinsic motivation when the feedback was perceived as informational but lowered intrinsic motivation when the feedback was perceived as controlling (e.g., "you performed well, just as you *should*"). Feedback can be delivered in an informational (rather than a controlling) style by praising good performance without trying to use rewards to try to strengthen or control the behavior, providing the recipient with choice about how to do the task, emphasizing the interesting or challenging aspects of the task, and avoiding the use of an authoritarian or pressuring style (Deci et al., 1999).

In sum, according to CET, the effect of rewards on intrinsic motivation depends on the meaning of the reward to the recipient. Also, research on CET has been conducted almost exclusively with children and college students in laboratory settings; there is no evidence that workplace rewards lower the intrinsic motivation of employees.

Special Topics in Performance Management
Managing Contextual Performance

Tippins and Coverdale (2009) argue that performance management programs should incorporate expectations concerning contextual performance and evaluate such performance. This makes sense because the outcomes of contextual performance can include unit or team performance, customer satisfaction, productivity, revenue, and profits (Koys, 2001; Podsakoff, et al., 1997; Podsakoff & MacKenzie, 1994; Podsakoff, MacKenzie, Paine, & Bachrach, 2000; Sobel Lojeski, Reilly, & Dominick, 2007; Walz & Niehoff, 2000).

Contextual performance refers to behaviors such as helping coworkers, voluntarily performing extra-role activities, persevering to complete assignments, defending the organization to others, and following the organization's policies even when it is inconvenient to do so. There are several distinctions between task performance and contextual performance. Task performance contributes directly to the mechanisms by which an organization produces goods and services, whereas contextual performance supports the organization's social and psychological environment. Behaviors associated with task performance are usually prescribed (e.g., listed in the job description), whereas behaviors related to contextual performance are generally discretionary (Borman & Motowidlo, 1993; Motowidlo & Van Scotter, 1994). The knowledge, skills, and abilities required for effective task performance usually vary depending on the job, whereas contextual performance is related to attributes (such as personality and motivation) that are common across all jobs. A very closely related concept is organizational citizenship behavior (OCB), defined by Organ (1988) as "individual behavior that in the aggregate aids organizational effectiveness, but is neither a requirement of the individual's job nor directly rewarded by the formal system." OCB has been viewed as including three factors: helping behaviors, civic virtue, and sportsmanship (Podsakoff & MacKenzie, 1994). Borman et al. (2001) have described three factors associated with contextual performance: interpersonal support, organizational support, and conscientiousness initiative. Finally, behaviors related to contextual performance can be viewed as essential for effective teamwork (LePine, Hanson, Borman, and Motowidlo, 2000) and hence formally recognized as job requirements.

Reilly and Aronson (2009) have reviewed antecedents of contextual performance, which include personality (agreeableness and conscientiousness; Hurtz & Donovan, 2000) national culture (low power distance, Paine & Organ, 2000; high collectivism, Lam, Hui, & Law, 1999), organizational culture (e.g., norms and expectations regarding appropriate and inappropriate behaviors), leadership (high-quality exchange relationships, supportive leader behavior, and leader fairness; Pillai, Schruesheum & Williams, 1999; Podsakoff, MacKenzie & Bommer, 1996; Schnake, Cochran, & Dumler, 1995; Uhl-Bein & Maslyn, 2003), quality of feedback (Findley, Giles, & Mossholder, 2000; Norris-Watts & Levy, 2004), and mentoring (Donaldson, Ensher, & Grant-Vallone, 2000). Contextual performance is also related to job satisfaction (Organ & Ryan, 1995) perhaps because satisfied employees reciprocate by engaging in contextual performance (e.g., helping coworkers), while dissatisfied employees withhold contextual performance. Organ and Ryan's (1995) meta-analysis found a small positive relationship between contextual performance and organizational commitment.

Contextual performance also explains unique variance in overall ratings of individual performance beyond that explained by task performance (MacKenzie, Podsakoff, & Fetter, 1993; Motowidlo & Van Scotter, 1994; Van Scotter & Motowidlo, 1996), perhaps because supervisors reward employees for contextual performance by providing more favorable ratings (MacKenzie et al., 1993). The effect of contextual performance on overall ratings of performance appears to be especially strong in team-based cultures and among peers (Lievens, Conway, & De Corte, 2008). Contextual performance also appears to influence formal and informal rewards above and beyond task performance (Kiker & Motowidlo, 1999; Van Scotter, Motowidlo, & Cross, 2000). However, Reilly and Aronson (2009) note that all employees do not have an equal opportunity to display contextual performance (e.g., those who work in collaborative settings have more opportunity than those who do not), thereby creating the possibility that some employees would be unable to earn rewards associated with high levels of contextual performance.

Dealing with Counterproductive Work Behavior

Spector and Fox (2005, pp. 151–152) defined counterproductive work behavior (CWB) as "volitional acts that harm or intend to harm organizations and their stakeholders (e.g., clients, coworkers, customers, and supervisors)." Managers appear to place as much weight on counterproductive behaviors as on task performance when evaluating employees (Rotundo & Sackett, 2002). Five dimensions of CWB have been identified (Spector, Fox, Penney, Bruursema, Goh, & Kessler, 2006): (1) abuse against others (e.g., incivility, workplace violence, sexual harassment); (2) production deviance such as poor performance; (3) sabotage (damaging or destroying the organization's property); (4) theft (potentially ranging from minor offenses such as taking office supplies home to embezzlement); and (5) withdrawal (e.g., absenteeism, lateness). Each of these dimensions of CWB has negative consequences for the organization. For example, employees who experience incivility, workplace violence, or sexual harassment report negative outcomes such as psychological distress, reduced self-esteem, lower job satisfaction and organizational commitment, and increased intentions to quit (Cortina, Magley, Williams, & Langhout, 2001; Fitzgerald, Drasgow,

Hulin, Gelfand, & Magley, 1997; Glomb, Munson, Hulin, Bergman, & Drasgow, 1999; Schneider, Swan, & Fitzgerald, 1997; Willness, Steel, & Lee, 2007). Tepper, Henle, Lambert, Giacalone, and Duffy (2008) found that abusive supervision affects commitment to the organization, which in turn affects counterproductive work behaviors, and that this effect is stronger when coworkers approve of organization deviance or engage in more counterproductive work behaviors.

Dealing effectively with CWB requires accurately diagnosing the cause of the problem. Employees are more likely to attribute their performance problems to external causes than are observers (Ilgen & Davis, 2000). Attributing poor performance or behavior to internal causes (the employee's lack of effort or ability) is especially likely when the employee has a history of poor performance (Mitchell & Wood, 1980). A review by Atwater and Elkins (2009) indicates that the causes of CWB can include drug and alcohol abuse; family problems (such as divorce, ill parents, ill children); financial problems; the employee's personality (e.g., trait anger); interpersonal conflict in the workplace; abusive supervision or toxic leadership (Goldman, 2006); coworkers who are disruptive, uncivil, or bullies; feelings of injustice (either distributive, procedural, or interactional); job dissatisfaction; situational constraints (inadequate resources or training); and organizational climate (e.g., concerning ethics or sexual harassment).

Research indicates that managers typically have a preference for handling performance problems in ways that do not require bold or and complicated confrontation (Morris, Gaveras, Baker, & Coursey, 1990), perhaps by helping the employee correct the undesirable behavior without making an issue out of the problem, identifying adjustments in work arrangements that might reduce or eliminate the problem (e.g., changing an employee's work schedule who has difficulty arriving on time due to problems at home), or restating performance expectations in a group setting. Unfortunately, it is not uncommon to delay (or entirely avoid) giving feedback to poor performers or to distort such feedback to make it appear less negative (Bond & Anderson, 1987; Larson, 1986). Recognizing positive aspects of an employee's performance can sometimes mitigate negative reactions to negative feedback (Lizzio, Wilson, Gilchrist, & Gallois, 2003).

Research shows that managers typically consider a number of factors when considering punishment. These include the employees' work history (Butterfield, Trevino, & Ball, 1996), the severity of the offense (Liden et al., 1999; Rosen & Jerdee, 1974), the effect on the employee's family (Butterfield et al., 1996), and the extent to which the manager likes the employee (Fandt, Labig, & Urich, 1990). The manager's attributions concerning the cause of the performance problem also play a role such that more serious sanctions are associated with internal (rather than external) causes (Liden et al., 1999). Of course, punishment can have negative effects on recipients (Atwater & Elkins, 2009), such as embarrassment, anger, loss of respect for the manager, and bad feelings about the organization. Consistent with social learning theory, punishment, when it is perceived as appropriate, can have positive consequences on observers (Atwater & Elkins, 2009), such as enhanced motivation, satisfaction, and performance, and the absence of punishment when it was deserved can increase observers' feelings of inequity (O'Reilly & Puffer, 1989). A recent meta-analysis (Podsakoff, Bommer, Podsakoff, & MacKenzie, 2006) found that the relationship between punishment and employee performance was more positive when punishment was contingent (on negative behavior) as opposed to non-contingent (the recipient does not understand what led to the punishment).

Finally, there are a number of legal issues associated with employee discipline and termination (Atwater & Elkins, 2009), such as employment at will (including statutory exceptions such as the National Labor Relations Act, the Fair Labor Standards Act, Title VII of the Civil Rights Act, the Age Discrimination in Employment Act, the Americans with Disabilities Act, and others, and common law exceptions such as implied contract, covenant of good faith and fair dealing, and public policy), collective bargain contracts, and negligent retention.

Managing Team Performance

Kozlowski and Ilgen (2006) presented a comprehensive review of research related to enhancing the effectiveness of work teams. Effective teams perform well (as judged by relevant others), have satisfied members, and are viable (i.e., members are willing to remain in the team). Kozlowski and Ilgen (2006) reviewed the (a) cognitive, (b) interpersonal, motivational, and affective, and (c) behavioral processes that influence team effectiveness. Important team cognitive processes include team climate, team mental models (e.g., shared knowledge structures or information), transactive memory (i.e., members' understanding of the unique knowledge held by individual team members or "who knows what"), and team learning (i.e., team members acquiring knowledge and skills through experience and interaction). Interpersonal, motivational, and affective processes include team cohesion, team efficacy (i.e., a shared belief in the team's ability to attain a given level of performance on a specific task) and potency (i.e., a shared belief in the team's ability to be effective across multiple tasks and contexts), team affect (i.e., the mean and dispersion of affect across team members), and team conflict. Behavioral processes include coordination of effort and actions (while reducing social loafing), team member competencies (see Cannon-Bowers & Salas, 1997; Cannon-Bowers, Tannenbaum, Salas, & Volpe, 1995; Fleishman & Zaccaro, 1992; Stevens & Campion, 1994, 1999), and team regulation (e.g., the ability of the team to self-regulate and adapt to shifting circumstances and demands).

Kozlowski, Watola, Jensen, Kim, and Botero (2009) have developed a prescriptive meta-theory of team leadership that shows how the role and focus of team leaders needs to evolve as the team progresses through several phases over time. For example, during the first phase (team formation), the leader adopts the role of mentor and focuses on helping members identify with the team and commit to its mission, values, and goals. During the second phase (task and role development), the leader adopts the role of instructor and focuses on helping members develop individual task mastery that will lead to effective team performance in later phases. During the third phase (team development), the leader adopts the role of coach and focuses on teamwork capability by promoting coordination and trust among team members. During the fourth phase (team improvement), the leader adopts the role of facilitator and focuses on adaptive capability (i.e., the ability to rapidly respond to novel and changing task demands). Within each of these phases, there is a distinct cycle of preparation, action, and reflection.

Salas, Weaver, Rosen, and Smith-Jentsch (2009) describe four capacities that should play an important role in team performance management: adaptive capacity (the ability of the team to maintain focus on its environment so that it can adjust and align its efforts to that environment and thereby maximize its performance); leadership capacity (the ability of the team leader and members to set direction for the team and guide the team's activities in that direction); management capacity (the ability of the team to use its resources effectively and efficiently); and technical capacity (the ability to effectively and efficiently deliver products and services to customers). Salas et al. (2009) also describe several research-based approaches to build each of these capacities.

Building adaptive capacity requires developing flexible and adaptive team members (who can engage in mutual performance monitoring and back-up behavior in an atmosphere of mutual trust) who have a large repertoire of possible task strategies (allowing them to switch to a more effective strategy based on situational demands). Simulation-based training can allow teams to practice different task strategies in environments that replicate the real world but without the risks associated with failure (Salas, Priest, Wilson, & Burke, 2006). It is also important that teams have an awareness of their external environment as well as the internal workings of the team. Such awareness could be developed via team cue recognition training (Salas, Cannon-Bowers, Fiore, & Stout, 2001) and perceptual contrast training (Wilson, Burke, Priest, & Salas, 2005). Training in team communication skills can also help ensure that important changes detected by one team member are quickly and accurately communicated to the rest of the team (Smith-Jentsch, Zeisig, Acton, & McPherson, 1998). Also, guided error training can help teams determine when the routine response is not the correct response and how to deal with novel situations (Lorenzet, Salas, & Tannenbaum, 2005). Adaptive capacity requires teams that can learn from their past performance; this requires a team learning orientation (Bunderson & Sutcliffe, 2003) and psychological safety (Edmondson, 1999).

To build leadership capacity, Salas et al. (2009) argue that the team's leader or its members need to create a shared vision (defined in measurable terms) that is aligned with the vision of the broader organization. The team also must manage external expectations (e.g., via feedback seeking and ambassadorship) and have malleable individual and team goals that can be revised to reflect unforeseen changes in the team's external environment. Team members also need to offer positive reinforcement to the team as a whole for its accomplishments (as well as support when mistakes are made); however, because of the interdependent nature of work in most teams, caution should be exercised about using individual incentives that might undermine cooperation.

To build management capacity, Salas et al. (2009) state that it is important to develop measures that are diagnostic of performance (to understand "why" outcomes occurred), to gather performance data from multiple sources, to measure typical (rather than maximal) team performance continuously (so that real-time feedback can be provided), and to include teamwork (e.g., collaboration) as well as taskwork competencies in performance evaluations.

Finally, Salas et al. (2009) note that technical capacity requires that team members are competent at their individual tasks (taskwork) and at managing the interdependencies between their own work and that of other team members (teamwork). Teams must be able to leverage all of the expertise and experience on the team by ensuring that all members feel comfortable contributing, the team has accurate transactive memory (i.e., members know who knows what on the team), and each team member's input is weighted by the person's expertise rather than the person's formal status (Hollenbeck et al., 1995). It is also important that shared mental models are developed (via cross-training or interpositional knowledge training; Cooke et al., 2007). It is desirable for team leaders to facilitate after-event reviews not only of team failures but also of team successes because debriefing successes as well as failures can lead to greater improvement (and yield richer mental models) than debriefing only failures (Ellis & Davidi, 2005).

Technology in Performance Management

Krauss and Snyder (2009) note growing interest in using technology to support performance management and describe a variety of ways in which technology can facilitate the effectiveness of performance management. For example, goals can be made accessible to all employees, and employees can easily update their goals over time. Employees can enter information about current projects into the system (along with the contact information for the project's stakeholders) and, when a project is completed, the system can automatically solicit feedback from those stakeholders (and make the feedback available to the employee, the manager, and designated stakeholders). Technology can help the employee and manager to create, store, and revise a performance plan in a shared electronic workspace (especially when the employee and manager are not co-located). An online database of training and development opportunities can be linked to the plan. Sample career paths (and associated competencies) can be available in the system and can be used by employees to construct their own potential career paths and share the information with mentors or coaches. Performance data stored in the system can be used to identify and track high-potential employees, determine appropriate developmental opportunities, and help create mentoring relationships (Stone, Stone-Romero & Lukaszewski, 2003).

Technology can also support completing formal appraisals, for example by generating an initial draft narrative to be included in an employee's feedback report and reviewing final appraisal narratives for discriminatory language or other statements that might raise legal concerns (Cardy & Miller, 2003). Automated performance management systems enable easier data entry and data extraction than paper-based systems, and can provide tools that summarize and compare performance across employees. Automated performance management systems can be integrated with other human resource information systems (e.g., compensation and payroll).

Despite the potential advantages of technology-supported performance management, a number of challenges exist (Krauss & Snyder, 2009), such as information overload (Eppler & Mengis, 2004; Klausegger, Sinkovics, & Zou, 2007), time required to input data, frustration associated with inadequate user interfaces (Lazar, Jones, & Shneiderman, 2006), and the requirement that users have a reasonable level of technology literacy (Marler, Liang, & Dulebohn, 2006).

One well-established research stream related to technology and performance management concerns electronic performance monitoring (EPM). EPM can involve the surveillance, measurement, and recording of employee activities of employees using electronic means (Bates & Holton, 1995; Stanton, 2000). EPM often captures performance indicators such as productivity, accuracy, speed, and errors. EPM offers the opportunity to continuously monitor performance (even of physically distant employees) using objective measures, but it has been questioned by some who perceive it as an invasion of privacy that can be related to increased stress and health complaints and lower quality work relationships (Bates & Holton, 1995; Hawk, 1994). Using EPM only for job-related activities leads to greater acceptance of EPM, reduced perceptions of invasion of privacy, and enhanced perceptions of procedural justice perceptions (Alge, 2001; Grant & Higgins, 1991; McNall & Roch, 2007). Employees also report more favorable responses to EPM when they are given discretion as to when they are monitored or what types of tasks are monitored (Aiello & Svec, 1993; Amick & Smith, 1992). Also, more positive attitudes occur when employees are offered an opportunity to participate in the development

of, or voice their opinions about, an EPM system (Alge, 2001; Westin, 1992). EPM can also be used to send an automatic notice to managers when there are changes in performance status, thereby enabling managers to provide immediate coaching and feedback. EPMs designed for employee development rather than prevention of undesirable behavior are also viewed more positively (Amick & Smith, 1992; Chalykoff & Kochan, 1989; Wells, Moorman, & Werner, 2007). Finally, EPM might cause a decline in performance and satisfaction among those still learning the task or assigned difficult performance standards (Aiello & Kolb, 1995; Stanton, 2000).

Performance Management Across Cultures

Day and Greguras (2009) note that a major obstacle to effective performance management in multinational companies is understanding and coping with the role of national culture. Culture shapes expectations about what is appropriate behavior.

Cross-cultural implementation of a performance management system can be fraught with challenges (Eggebeen, 2002), such as subtle differences in the interpretation of competencies used to evaluate performance, the willingness of managers to directly communicate negative feedback, and the willingness of employees to provide feedback to their managers (and the receptivity of managers to such feedback).

Project GLOBE (House, Hanges, Javidan, Dorfman, & Gupta, 2004) gathered data from over 60 countries and 17,000 managers who represented over 950 organizations. Building on earlier cross-cultural research (Hofstede, 2001; Schwartz, 1994; Triandis, 1994), Project GLOBE identified eight cultural dimensions (or practices) whose implications for performance management have been described by Day and Greguras (2009). In high *individualism* cultures (Germany, Italy, Argentina) individual goals and achievement are important and employees are likely to change companies often, whereas in low individualism cultures (i.e., high collectivism cultures, e.g., Japan, Singapore, Sweden) group goals, harmony, and achievement are likely to be valued and long-term employment with the same company is more common. Nisbett and colleagues (Nisbett, Peng, Choi, & Norenzayan, 2001) note that Easterners (generally high collectivism cultures) are more likely to take context into consideration (leading to more external attributions for performance), whereas Westerners (generally high individualism cultures) tend to focus primarily on the person or object (rather than its context) and hence fail to acknowledge the role of contextual factors (leading to more internal attributions for performance; Chiang & Birtch, 2007). Research has also shown that employees from high collectivism cultures rate themselves more modestly than do employees from high individualism cultures (Kurman, 2002). In high *power distance* cultures (e.g., Morocco, El Salvador) people accept unequal distribution of power in organizations and hence show considerable deference to those in authority, whereas in low power distance cultures (e.g., Israel, Netherlands) power and information are more widely shared across organization levels and hence employees would be expected to be more comfortable with involvement in goal setting and providing upward feedback (Peretz & Fried, 2008). In high *humane orientation* cultures (e.g., Ireland, Philippines) fairness, generosity, support, and the well-being of others are especially important, whereas in low humane orientation cultures (e.g., Spain, Hungary) greater emphasis is placed on self-interest, self-enjoyment, and material possessions. When interacting with their employees, managers from high humane orientation cultures might be expected to display more support, concern, and tolerance for errors (and contextual performance in general is likely to be more valued in high humane orientation cultures). In high *uncertainty avoidance* cultures (e.g., Singapore, Denmark) employees tend to prefer order and formal procedures (e.g., clear documentation as part of the performance management process) and are likely to show less tolerance for rule violations and more resistance to change, whereas in low uncertainty avoidance cultures (e.g., Greece, Bolivia) employees tend to prefer more informal interactions (and perhaps less formal feedback), trust verbal agreements made with others, and display more tolerance for rule violations and less resistance to change. High *performance orientation* cultures (e.g., Switzerland, Hong Kong) value initiative and results and reward high performance, whereas low performance orientation cultures (e.g., Greece, Venezuela) are more likely to value and reward seniority and loyalty. High *future orientation* cultures (Singapore, Netherlands) tend to delay gratification, have longer strategic horizons, and value intrinsic motivation and long-term success (and are therefore likely to set long-term goals and emphasize employee development and succession planning), whereas low future orientation cultures (e.g., Russia, Argentina) place a greater emphasis on immediate rewards and extrinsic

motivation (and are therefore likely to emphasize short-term goals). Cultures with high *gender egalitarianism* (e.g., Denmark, Sweden) place little or no emphasis on an employee's sex in determining roles (and hence will likely provide equal opportunities for men and women in career development), whereas cultures with low gender egalitarianism (e.g., Kuwait, India) are more likely to place males in powerful roles. Where gender egalitarianism is low, female managers might face resentment (especially when conveying negative feedback); where gender egalitarianism is high, male managers who condescend to female employees are likely to be viewed unfavorably. Finally, high *assertiveness* cultures (e.g., Germany, Nigeria) value direct and blunt communication, whereas low assertiveness cultures (e.g., Japan, New Zealand) value modesty and face saving (and hence view assertive communication as inappropriate). Thus, negative feedback is likely to be communicated more directly and clearly in high assertiveness cultures.

Of course, within any country, there can be wide variations in cultural practices, hence Day and Greguras (2009) emphasize that there is a risk in taking the generalizations associated with these cultural dimensions too far. Moreover, the strength of the organization's culture relative to national culture is an important consideration. In a strong organizational culture with broad acceptance concerning its core values, norms, and desired behaviors, organizational culture can trump national culture (Day & Greguras, 2009).

Perceptions of Fairness in Performance Management

Several dimensions of fairness (justice) perceptions have been identified. Procedural justice (Leventhal, 1980) refers to whether procedures are viewed as ethical, applied consistently, free from error and bias, and include opportunities for employees to appeal, grieve, and voice their opinions. Distributive justice refers to whether outcomes are perceived as being fair. For example, employees will form expectations (e.g., by comparing themselves with coworkers) regarding the performance evaluation and associated rewards they will receive. If the actual evaluation or reward fails to meet those expectations, the outcome will be perceived as unfair. Interactional justice is often viewed as having two components: informational and interpersonal (Bies & Moag, 1986; Colquitt, 2001). Informational justice refers to whether decision makers are perceived as truthful and as providing an adequate explanation for an outcome, while interpersonal justice refers to whether employees believe they have been treated with respect and dignity. Procedural justice and interactional justice are especially important when performance evaluations are negative (Brockner & Wiesenfeld, 1996; Folger & Cropenzano, 1998).

Gilliland and Langdon (1998) also note that perceptions of appraisal fairness are related to trust in supervisor, organizational commitment, and intentions to stay with the organization. Also, some research has found small relationships between fair procedures (e.g., opportunity to participate in the appraisal process) and changes in performance (Nathan, Mohrman, & Milliman, 1991).

Gilliland and Langdon (1998) offered recommendations to enhance the perceived fairness performance appraisals. These include: (1) having employees provide input into the appraisal process (e.g., via discussion with the manager prior to the appraisal being completed or by completing self-evaluations); (2) ensuring that consistent standards are applied when evaluating different employees; (3) minimizing supervisor biases during the appraisal process (e.g., by having ratings reviewed by the rater's peers or by higher-level management; (4) ensuring that raters are familiar with the employee's work (e.g., by keeping a log concerning the employee's work or soliciting input from coworkers); (5) ensuring that appraisal ratings and feedback are job-related; (6) communicating performance expectations prior to the appraisal process; (7) avoiding surprises (especially unexpected negative evaluations) by providing ongoing feedback throughout the evaluation period; (8) ensuring that appraisal feedback is provided in an atmosphere of respect and courtesy, characterized by a two-way conversation that adopts a cooperative, problem-solving style rather than a tell-and-sell approach (Wexley, Singh, & Yukl, 1973); (9) allowing employees to challenge or appeal their evaluation; and (10) basing administrative decisions (decisions about compensation, promotions, etc.) on ratings.

The level of employee participation in appraisal review meetings appears to be influenced more by which manager conducts the review than by the circumstances of the specific review (Greller, 1998). Meta-analysis results (Cawley, Keeping, & Levy, 1998) show that there is a strong relationship between employee participation in the performance appraisal process and employee reactions (e.g., satisfaction, acceptance, motivation) and, albeit counterintuitive, that value-expressive participation (i.e., for the sake of having one's voice heard) generally had a stronger relationship with employee reactions than did instrumental participation (i.e., to influence the end result).

Directions for Research
Research Concerning Specific Elements of Performance Management

Taken individually, there is a well-developed research literature concerning several key elements of performance management, especially goal setting, feedback, performance evaluation, and some aspects of pay-for-performance. However, two key elements of performance management deserve attention in future research: coaching and merit pay.

COACHING

One promising trend that is likely to encourage additional research can be seen in recent efforts to develop and validate scales to assess coaching behaviors and skills (Arnold, Arad, Rhoades, & Drasgow, 2000; Grant & Cavanagh, 2007; McLean, Yang, Kuo, Tolbert, & Larkin, 2005; Peterson & Little, 2005). Of course, it will be important to establish that coaching is conceptually and empirically distinct from aspects of leadership that have already been described in well-established leadership models. For example, to what extent does coaching overlap with directive leadership behaviors, as described in path-goal theory (House, 1971)? Coaching also appears to be an element of (or perhaps identical to) the individualized consideration component of transformational leadership (Bass, Avolio, Jung, & Berson, 2003). For example, Bass (1997) describes individualized consideration as including behaviors such as listening attentively, furthering the development of others, advising, teaching, and coaching. And the individualized consideration scale of the Multifactor Leadership Questionnaire includes items such as "helps others develop their strengths" (Leslie & Fleenor, 1998) and "spends time teaching and coaching" (Mind Garden, 2008). Research that compares coaching scales to other well-established measures of leadership can help establish the nomological net of the coaching construct. Ultimately, it will be important for researchers to determine whether coaching can explain variance in important outcomes beyond that explained by other models of leadership.

Bennett (2006) identified six themes for future coaching research: the coach (e.g., characteristics and competencies of effective coaches), the client (e.g., characteristics of clients who benefit from coaching), the coach/client relationship (e.g., criteria for matching coaches and clients), the process of coaching (e.g., models of coaching, the effectiveness of coaching in-person versus over the phone), the results of coaching (e.g., sustainability of results, return on investment), and theories related to the practice and teaching of coaching (the evidence-based, theoretical foundations to guide coaching). Research is also needed to examine the extent to which coaching practices need to be shaped by organizational context (e.g., organizational cultures, small and medium vs. large enterprises), national culture (e.g., Noer, Leupold, & Valle, 2007; Peterson, 2007), and recipient characteristics (personality, experience, ability, organizational level).

With regard to executive coaching, there is a great need for research about whether and when executive coaching results in behavior change. As Feldman and Lankau (2005) note, research also needs to examine whether executive coaching has a tangible effect on organizational outcomes (rather than merely the behavior of the coaching recipient). They also note the importance of determining whether executive coaching can, under some conditions, result in negative outcomes. Research needs to move beyond self-reports of the people being coached (who generally report high levels of satisfaction with executive coaching) and beyond short-term executive coaching interventions (e.g., with only three or four meetings), such as those examined by Smither et al. (2003). We need studies that examine the relative effectiveness of executive coaching compared to other developmental interventions (e.g., formal training, multisource feedback, etc.), as well as how executive coaching might interact with (complement or detract from) such interventions (Feldman & Lankau, 2005). It will also be important for future research to examine factors that mediate and moderate the impact of coaching. Asking "Is executive coaching effective?" is probably too broad a question. Because coaches use a variety of approaches and pursue a range of goals, it will be more productive for research to examine which coaching approaches are most effective and whether certain configurations of coaching approaches, goals, and clients yield different outcomes from others (e.g., is approach X effective when applied to certain goals and types of clients but not to other goals and clients?). That is, it is possible (perhaps likely) that executive coaching will be effective in some situations but not others. It will also be helpful to learn whether coaching provided by other organizational members (e.g., human resource

managers, organization development specialists, or the employee's supervisor) might be equally, more, or less effective than coaching provided by external executive coaches. One challenge is that there are no universally accepted criteria for what constitutes a successful outcome in executive coaching, in part due to the range of activities undertaken by coaches (MacKie, 2007). Finally, another area for future research is identifying competencies (knowledge, skills, abilities, personality, education, work experience, and so on) that distinguish effective coaches from less effective coaches. Note that this approach differs from merely asking coaches what competencies are important. Instead, it first requires identifying more effective and less effective coaches and then assessing the competencies that distinguish the two groups. Similarly, qualitative research is needed to determine what more (vs. less) successful coaches actually do. Such research would require in-depth interviews with coaches, the managers they work with, and perhaps their organizational sponsors.

MERIT PAY

Given the widespread use of merit pay, the absence of well-designed research concerning its consequences reflects a major gap in our understanding of performance management systems. There is a desperate need for research on the impact of merit pay plans on subsequent performance (at both the individual and unit level). Rynes et al. (2005) note that such research would ideally occur in multiple units of the same organization and, in addition to measures of employee performance and satisfaction, would incorporate the indirect effects of merit pay plans on promotions and the quality of employees attracted and retained. Research is also needed to understand the causal processes (e.g., employee-level or team-level attitudes and behaviors) that mediate the relationship between various pay-for-performance plans and employee, team, and organizational performance.

OTHER ASPECTS OF PERFORMANCE MANAGEMENT

Aguinis and Pierce (2008) have offered directions for research about other aspects of performance management. One area concerns the effects of the supervisor's power and influence. For example, will employees more readily accept and act on feedback provided by a supervisor who is perceived as powerful (i.e., who has the ability to influence financial rewards and other outcomes) than a supervisor who is perceived as less powerful? Another area concerns the effects of group dynamics and close interpersonal relationships. For example, how can performance management practices best cope with situations in which the parties involved have a close interpersonal relationship and thus a potential conflict of interest? Another area of interest concerns communication. For example, what organizational-level communication practices (e.g., descriptions of the system's goals and the processes involved in implementing the system) are likely to lead to more effective systems?

Another area worthy of research attention is adaptive performance (i.e., adapting to complex, novel, turbulent, or unpredictable work environments). For example, Kozlowski et al. (2001) found that self-efficacy and knowledge structure coherence predicted adaptive performance (i.e., generalization to a more difficult and complex version of a task) after controlling for prior training performance and declarative knowledge. Other research (Edmondson, Bohmer, & Pisano, 2001) has found that teams that adapt successfully to innovative technology go through a qualitatively different learning process from teams that do not adapt successfully. This process involves enrollment to motivate the team, preparatory practice sessions and early trials to create psychological safety and encourage new behaviors, and promoting shared meaning and process improvement through reflective practices. Still, we know relatively little about how to manage adaptive performance. Research is needed to better understand how to set goals in such environments and how to coach individuals and teams to perform effectively as they adapt to such changes.

Performance management research will also need to consider multiple levels of analysis (den Hartog et al., 2004; DeNisi, 2000). For example, performance at each level (individual, team, organizational) affects and is affected by performance at other levels (DeNisi, 2000).

Research Concerning Performance Management Systems as a Whole

Performance management is not merely a collection of individual practices (goal setting, feedback, coaching, and so on). Instead, these practices are presumed to be mutually interdependent and reinforcing. That is, the impact of a well-designed and implemented performance management system should be greater than the sum of its parts. Although Schiemann (2009) notes that many organizations do not formally evaluate the impact of their performance management systems (including how effectively the system was implemented), approaches to do so have been described by several authors (Harper & Vilkinas, 2005; Silverman & Muller, 2009; Spangenberg & Theron, 1997). Indeed, perhaps the most important agenda for future research is examining the impact of performance management systems (as a whole) rather than merely studying one or two of their elements in isolation. It appears that more acceptable performance management systems can increase trust for top management (Mayer & Davis, 1999) yet we know almost nothing about the impact of performance management systems (as a whole) on organizational performance.

High performance work practices (HPWPs, e.g., use of selection tests, incentive compensation, training, performance appraisal, promotion from within) purportedly enhance organizational performance by increasing the level of employees' knowledge and skills and by empowering and motivating employees to use their knowledge and skills to benefit the organization. A number of studies have shown that HPWPs are linked to organization-level productivity and performance (Collins & Smith, 2006; Guest, Michie, Conway, & Sheehan, 2003; Guthrie, 2001; Huselid, 1995; Huselid, Jackson, & Schuler, 1997; Ichniowski, Shaw, & Prennushi, 1997; Wright, Gardner, Moynihan, & Allen, 2005; Youndt & Snell, 2004; Youndt, Snell, Dean, & Lepak, 1996; Zatzick & Iverson, 2006), although not all studies find such a relationship (Capelli & Neumark, 2001). A meta-analysis by Combs, Yongmei, Hall, and Ketchen (2006) found that HPWPs are related to organizational performance ($r = .20$) and that the relationship is stronger for systems of HPWPs than for individual HPWPs. Unfortunately, the design of many of these studies makes the direction of causality difficult to establish. In a recent study designed to help establish causal direction, Birdi et al. (2008) studied the effects of operational management and human resource practices on organizational productivity in 308 companies over 22 years. They found positive effects from empowerment and extensive training (that were enhanced by the adoption of teamwork), but found no direct effect of operational management practices (integrated manufacturing and lean production) on organizational productivity. There was also a time lag before the effects of a management practice translated into changes in organizational productivity. For empowerment, effects were observed one to four years after its introduction, whereas for teamwork, effects were observed six to nine years after implementation. Although some of these studies examined the impact of performance appraisal (e.g., behavior-based vs. results-based), none examined the impact of performance management systems as a whole.

Future research needs to examine the impact of performance management systems using the framework of strategic human resource management (den Hartog et al., 2004). The resource-based view of the firm suggests that human resource practices can help create a sustained competitive advantage to the extent that they help develop knowledge that becomes embedded in the firm's culture and that is specific to the company. Such knowledge, which is developed within the company rather than being imported from outside the company, is context-specific, and hence not easily imitated by other firms (Barney, Wright, Ketchen, 2001; Wright, Dunford, & Snell, 2001). To the extent that performance management systems link the knowledge, skills, and competencies that are enhanced via employee development and coaching to organization-specific goals, they hold the potential to enhance the firm's competitive advantage (Lado & Wilson, 1994).

Research also needs to consider universalistic, contingency, and configuration predictions concerning the impact of performance management practices (Delery & Doty, 1996). The universalistic perspective argues that there are some best practices in human resource management that are always better than others and that all organizations should adopt these best practices. The contingency perspective argues that organizations adopting a particular strategy require human resource practices that differ from those required by organizations with different strategies. The configurational perspective focuses on bundles or ideal typologies of human resource practices that are equally effective to the extent that there is both horizontal (i.e., internally consistent configurations of human resource practices) and vertical (congruence of human resource practices with firm strategy) fit. Much of the literature related to performance management has implicitly assumed a universalistic approach. For example, it is generally assumed that: (a) specific and difficult individual and team goals should be aligned with organizational goals; (b) employees should receive feedback and support for employee development; and (c) individual and team performance should be linked to rewards. But Schiemann (2009) interviewed several leading firms about their performance management systems and concluded that they "appear to uniquely tailor the performance management system to their strategy, culture and management style." For example, to the extent that organizations emphasize internal staffing and have low employee turnover, performance management systems (with their emphasis on feedback and employee development) are likely to play a more important role in shaping organizational success than in organizations that rely on external staffing (where top talent is carefully selected from the external marketplace) and perhaps have higher rates of employee turnover. Also, the core elements of performance management (as described above) might play a greater role in the success of firms with a defender strategy (Miles & Snow, 1978), whereas the ability to manage adaptive performance might play a greater role in the success of firms with a prospector strategy (with its constant search for new products and markets). Birdi et al.'s (2008) finding that the impact of extensive training varied across companies (from substantial positive effects to weak negative effects) and Youndt et al.'s (1996) finding that human resource systems have a greater impact when they are aligned with manufacturing strategy also point to the potential value of adopting a contingency framework in theorizing about the impact of performance management systems.

It will be especially important for future research to examine not only the presence of performance management elements and systems but also the quality of their implementation. Moreover, the quality with which performance management systems are implemented is likely to explain unique variance in the impact of performance management on organizational performance.

Performance Management in the Future

Tippins and Coverdale (2009) have described workplace trends and their implications for performance management in the future. Each of these trends points to a direction for future research. For example, the increase in geographically dispersed teams (sometimes in different countries and time zones) raises questions such as how to address the fact that the opportunity to directly observe performance is no longer feasible (which is likely to pose a greater problem in service work than production work) and how to address changes in how and when managers interact with employees. The increasing use of outsourcing can further exacerbate such challenges in that "team members" who are vital to organizational success can literally work for another company. Although technology (videoconferencing, instant messaging, e-mail) offers some potential solutions to communication in geographically dispersed teams, we need to know more about the consequences of using these technologies in place of face-to-face interactions (e.g., how does the absence of nonverbal cues influence the effectiveness of feedback delivered electronically?). Changes in worker characteristics, including predicted declines in the number of qualified workers and changing employee expectations, also have potential implications for performance management. How should performance management processes be designed to deal with unskilled or undereducated workers who often lack basic literacy and numeracy skills? How can performance management processes be modified to deal effectively with employees who are predicted to increasingly expect opportunities for personal growth and development, rapid career progression (which will be especially difficult as organizations tend to become flatter), and work-family balance (and how can rewards be tailored to match the values of such employees)?

Finally, performance management research might be shaped by emerging theory and research from other areas of psychology such as cognitive, social, and neuroscience. For example, Smith, Jostmann, Galinsky, and van Dijk (2008) recently found that powerlessness impairs executive-function tasks such as updating, inhibiting, and planning, and that this impairment is driven by goal neglect, thereby suggesting that empowering employees might reduce costly organizational errors. Worthy, Maddox, and Markman (2007) recently showed that regulatory fit, which increases exploration of alternative response strategies even when exploration is suboptimal, can enhance performance on some tasks but harm performance on other tasks. Finally, examining event-related potentials (ERPs), Mangels, Butterfield, Lamb, Good, and Dweck (2006) found that implicit beliefs (i.e., entity vs. incremental theorists) can influence learning success through top-down biasing of attention and conceptual processing toward goal-congruent information. In sum, research from other areas of psychology can help industrial and organizational psychologists ensure that their hypotheses are well-grounded in the basic building blocks of human learning and behavior.

References

Acosta-Amad, S., & Brethower, D. M. (1992). Training for impact: Improving the quality of staff's performance. *Performance Improvement Quarterly, 5*, 2–12.

Aguinis, H. (2009). *Performance management* (2nd ed.). Upper Saddle River, NJ: Pearson Prentice Hall.

Aguinis, H., & Pierce, C. A. (2008). Enhancing the relevance of organizational behavior by embracing performance management research. *Journal of Organizational Behavior, 29*, 139–145.

Aiello, J. R., & Kolb, K. J. (1995). Electronic performance monitoring and social context: Impact on productivity and stress. *Journal of Applied Psychology, 80*, 339–353.

Aiello, J. R., & Svec, C. M. (1993). Computer monitoring of work performance: Extending the social facilitation framework to electronic presence. *Journal of Applied Social Psychology, 53*, 537–548.

Albanese, R., & Van Fleet, D. D. (1985). Rational behavior in groups: The free-riding tendency. *Academy of Management Review, 10*, 244–255.

Alge, B. J. (2001). Effects of computer surveillance on perceptions of privacy and procedural justice. *Journal of Applied Psychology, 86*, 797–804.

Alvero, A. M., Bucklin, B. R., & Austin, J. (2001). An objective review of the effectiveness and essential characteristics of performance feedback in organizational settings. *Journal of Organizational Behavior Management, 21*, 3–29.

Amick, B. C., & Smith, M. J. (1992). Stress, computer-based work monitoring and measurement systems: A conceptual overview. *Applied Ergonomics, 23*, 6–16.

Arnold, J. A., Arad, S., Rhoades, J. A., & Drasgow, F. (2000). The Empowering Leadership Questionnaire: The construction and validation of a new scale for measuring leader behaviors. *Journal of Organizational Behavior, 21*, 249–269.

Aronson, E. (1999). The power of self-persuasion. *American Psychologist, 54*, 873–890.

Arthur, J. B., & Huntley, C. L. (2005). Ramping up the organizational learning curve: Assessing the impact of deliberate learning on organizational performance under gainsharing. *Academy of Management Journal, 48*, 1159–1170.

Arthur, W., Jr., Bennett, W., Jr., Edens, P. S., & Bell, S. T. (2003). Effectiveness of training in organizations: A meta-analysis of design and evaluation features. *Journal of Applied Psychology, 88*, 234–245.

Ashford, S. J., Blatt, R., & VandeWalle, D. (2003). Reflections on the looking glass: A review of research on feedback-seeking behavior in organizations. *Journal of Management, 29*, 773–799.

Ashford, S. J., & Cummings, L. L. (1983). Feedback as an individual resource: Personal strategies of creating information. *Organizational Behavior and Human Performance, 32*, 370–398.

Ashford, S. J., & Northcraft, G. B. (1992). Conveying more (or less) than we realize: The role of impression-management in feedback seeking. *Organizational Behavior and Human Decision Processes, 53*, 310–334.

Ashford, S. J., & Tsui, A. S. (1991). Self-regulation for managerial effectiveness: The role of active feedback seeking. *Academy of Management Journal, 34*, 251–280.

Atwater, L. E. (1998). The advantages and pitfalls of self-assessment in organizations. In J. W. Smither (Ed.), *Performance appraisal: State-of-the-art in practice.* San Francisco: Jossey-Bass.

Atwater, L. E., & Brett, J. F. (2005). Antecedents and consequences of reactions to developmental 360° feedback. *Journal of Vocational Behavior, 66*, 532–548.

Atwater, L., & Elkins, T. (2009). Diagnosing, understanding, and dealing with counterproductive work behavior. In J. W. Smither & M. London (Eds.), *Performance management: Putting research into practice.* San Francisco: Jossey-Bass.

Atwater, L. E., Roush, P., & Fischthal, A. (1995). The influence of upward feedback on self- and follower raters of leadership. *Personnel Psychology, 48*, 34–60.

Atwater, L. E., Waldman, D. A., Atwater, D., & Cartier, P. (2000). An upward feedback field experiment: Supervisors' cynicism, reactions, and commitment to subordinates. *Personnel Psychology, 53*, 275–297.

Bandura, A. (1986). *Social foundations of thought and action.* Englewood Cliffs, NJ: Prentice Hall.

Barney, J., Wright, M., & Ketchen, D. J., Jr. (2001). The resource-based view of the firm: Ten years after 1991. *Journal of Management, 27*, 625–641.

Bartram, D. (2005). The Great Eight competencies A criterion-centric approach to validation. *Journal of Applied Psychology, 90*, 1185–1203.

Bass, B. M. (1997). Does the transactional-transformational leadership paradigm transcend organizational and national boundaries? *American Psychologist, 52*, 130–139.

Bass, B. M., Avolio, B. J., Jung, D. I., & Berson, Y. (2003). Predicting unit performance by assessing transformational and transactional leadership. *Journal of Applied Psychology, 88*, 207–218.

Bates, R. A., & Holton, B. F., III. (1995). Computerized performance monitoring: A review of human resource issues. *Human Resource Management Review, 5*, 267–288.

Baum, J. R., Locke, E., & Smith, K. (2001). A multi-dimensional model of venture growth. *Academy of Management Journal, 44*, 292–303.

Beer, M., & Cannon, M. D. (2004). Promise and peril in implementing pay-for-performance. *Human Resource Management, 43*, 3–48.

Bell, B. S., & Kozlowski, S. W. J. (2008). Active learning: Effects of core training design elements on self-regulatory processes, learning, and adaptability. *Journal of Applied Psychology, 93*, 296–316.

Bennett, B. B. (1987). *The effectiveness of staff development training practices: A meta-analysis (coaching).* Ph.D. dissertation, University of Oregon. Retrieved September 11, 2008, from Dissertations & Theses: A&I database. (Publication No. AAT 8721226).

Bennett, J. L. (2006). An agenda for coaching-related research: A challenge for researchers. *Consulting Psychology Journal: Practice and Research, 58*, 240–249.

Bernardin, H. J., & Buckley, M. R. (1981). Strategies in rater training. *Academy of Management Review, 6*, 205–212.

Bernardin, H. J., Hagan, C. M, Kane, J. S., & Villanova, P. (1998). Effective performance management: Precision in measurement with a focus on customers and situational constraints. In J. W. Smither (Ed.), *Performance appraisal: State-of-the-art in practice* (pp. 537–547). San Francisco: Jossey-Bass.

Bernardin, H. J., & Orban, J. A. (1990). Leniency effect as a function of rating format, purpose for appraisal, and rater individual differences. *Journal of Business and Psychology, 5*, 197–211.

Bernardin, H. J., & Pence, E. C. (1980). Effects of rater error training: Creating new response sets and decreasing accuracy. *Journal of Applied Psychology, 65*, 60–66.

Bies, R. J., & Moag, J. F. (1986). Interactional justice: Communication criteria of fairness. In R. J. Lewicki, B. H. Sheppard, & M. H. Bazerman (Eds.), *Research on negotiations in organizations* (Vol. 1, pp. 43–55). Greenwich, CT: JAI Press.

Birdi, K., Clegg, C., Patterson, M., Robinson, A., Stride, C. B., Wall, T. D., & Wood, S. J. (2008). The impact of human resources and operational management practices on company productivity: A longitudinal study. *Personnel Psychology, 61*, 467–501.

Biswas-Diener, R., & Dean, B. (2007). *Positive psychology coaching: Putting the science of happiness to work for your clients.* Hoboken, NJ: John Wiley & Sons.

Blanz, F., & Ghiselli, E. E. (1972). The mixed standard scale: A new rating system. *Personnel Psychology, 25*, 185–199.

Blume, B. D., Baldwin, T. T., & Rubin, R. S. (2007, April). *All forced distribution systems are not created equal.* Paper presented at the 22nd Annual Conference of the Society for Industrial and Organizational Psychology. New York.

Bommer, W. H., Johnson, J., Rich, G. A., Podsakoff, P. M., & MacKenzie, S. B. (1995). On the interchangeability of objective and subjective measures of employee performance: A meta-analysis. *Personnel Psychology, 48*, 587–605.

Bond, C. F., & Anderson, E. L. (1987). The reluctance to transmit bad news: Private discomfort or public display? *Journal of Experimental Social Psychology, 23*, 176–187.

Bono, J. E., Purvanova, R. K., Towler, A. J., & Peterson, D. B. (2009). A survey of executive coaching practices. *Personnel Psychology, 62*, 361–404.

Borman, W. C. (1977). Consistency of rating accuracy and rating errors in the judgment of human performance. *Organizational Behavior and Human Performance, 20*, 238–252.

Borman, W. C. (1979). Format and training effects on rating accuracy and rater errors. *Journal of Applied Psychology, 64*, 410–421.

Borman, W. C., Buck, D. E., Hanson, M. A., Motowidlo, S. J., Stark, S., & Drasgow, F. (2001). An examination of the comparative reliability, validity, and accuracy of performance ratings made using computerized adaptive rating scales. *Journal of Applied Psychology, 86*, 965–973.

Borman, W. C., & Motowidlo, S. J. (1993). Expanding the criterion domain to include elements of contextual performance. In N. Schmitt & W. C. Borman (Eds.), *Personnel selections in organizations.* San Francisco: Jossey-Bass.

Borman, W. C., Penner, L. A., Allen, T. D., & Motowidlo, S. (2001). Personality predictors of citizenship performance. *International Journal of Selection and Assessment, 9*, 52–69.

Boswell, W. R., & Boudreau, J. W. (2000). Employee satisfaction with performance appraisals and appraisers: The role of perceived appraisal use. *Human Resource Development Quarterly, 11*, 283–299.

Bowles, S., Cunningham, C. J. L., De La Rosa, G. M., & Picano, J. (2007). Coaching leaders in middle and executive management: Goals, performance, buy-in. *Leadership & Organization Development Journal, 28*, 388–408.

Bowles, S. V., & Picano, J. J. (2006). Dimensions of coaching related to productivity and quality of life. *Consulting Psychology Journal: Practice and Research, 58*, 232–239.

Bretz, R. D., Ash, R. A., & Dreher, G. F. (1989). Do people make the place? An examination of the attraction-selection-attrition hypothesis. *Personnel Psychology, 42*, 561–581.

Brockner, J., & Higgins, E. T. (2001). Regulatory focus theory: Implications for the study of emotions at work. *Organizational Behavior and Human Decision Processes, 86*, 35–66.

Brockner, J., & Wiesenfeld, B. M. (1996). An integrative framework for explaining reactions to decisions: Interactive effects of outcomes and procedures. *Psychological Bulletin, 120*, 189–208.

Buda, R., Reilly, R. R., & Smither, J. W. (1991). The influence of indirect knowledge of prior performance on evaluations of present performance: The generalizability of assimilation effects. *Journal of Psychology and the Behavioral Sciences, 6*, 89–99.

Bunderson, J. S., & Sutcliffe, K. M. (2003). Management team learning orientation and business unit performance. *Journal of Applied Psychology, 88*(3), 552–560.

Burke, M. J., & Day, R. R. (1986). A cumulative study of the effectiveness of managerial training. *Journal of Applied Psychology, 71*, 232–245.

Butterfield, K. D., Trevino, L. K., & Ball, G. A. (1996). Punishment from the manager's perspective: A grounded investigation and inductive model. *Academy of Management Journal, 39*, 1479–1512.

Cable, D. M., & Judge, T. A. (1994). Pay preferences and job search decisions: A person-organization fit perspective. *Personnel Psychology, 47*, 317–348.

Callahan, J. S., Kiker, D. S., & Cross, T. (2003). Does method matter? A meta-analysis of the effects of training method on older learner training performance. *Journal of Management, 29*, 663–680.

Campbell, J. P., McCloy, R. A., Oppler, S. H., & Sager, C. E. (1993). A theory of performance. In N. Schmitt & W. C. Borman (Eds.), *Personnel selection in organizations* (pp. 35–70). San Francisco: Jossey-Bass.

Cannon, M. D., & Edmondson, A. C. (2001). Confronting failure: Antecedents and consequences of shared beliefs about failure in organizational work groups. *Journal of Organizational Behavior, 22*, 161–177.

Cannon-Bowers, J. A., & Salas, E. (1997). Teamwork competencies: The interaction of team member knowledge, skills, and attitudes. In H. F. O'Neil, Jr. (Ed.), *Workforce readiness: Competencies and assessment* (pp. 151–174). Mahwah, NJ: Erlbaum.

Cannon-Bowers, J. A., Tannenbaum, S. I., Salas, E., & Volpe, C. E. (1995). Defining team competencies and establishing team training requirements. In R. Guzzo & E. Salas (Eds.), *Team effectiveness and decision making in organizations* (pp. 333–380). San Francisco: Jossey-Bass.

Capelli, P., & Neumark, D. (2001). Do "high-performance" work practices improve establishment-level outcomes? *Industrial and Labor Relations Review, 54*, 737–775.

Cardy, R. L., & Miller, J. S. (2003). Technology: Implications for HRM. In E. Salas & D. Stone (Eds.), *Advances in human performance and cognitive engineering research* (Vol. 3, pp. 99–118). Oxford: Elsevier Science.

Carson, J. B., Tesluk, P. E., & Marrone, J. A. (2007). Shared leadership in teams: An investigation of antecedent conditions and performance. *Academy of Management Journal, 50*, 1217–1234.

Cascio, W. F. (2006). Global performance management systems. In G. K. Stahl & I. Björkman (Eds.), *Handbook of research in international human resource management* (pp. 176–196). Northampton, MA: Edward Elgar Publishing.

Cascio, W. F., & Valenzi, E. R. (1978). Relations among criteria of police performance. *Journal of Applied Psychology, 63*, 22–28.

Cawley, B. D., Keeping, L. M., & Levy, P. E. (1998). Participation in the performance appraisal process and employee reactions: A meta-analytic review of field investigations. *Journal of Applied Psychology, 83*, 615–633

Chalykoff, J., & Kochan, T. A. (1989). Computer-aided monitoring: Its influence on employee job satisfaction and turnover. *Personnel Psychology, 42*, 807–834.

Chen, G., Thomas, B., & Wallace, J. C. (2005). A multilevel examination of the relationships among training outcomes, mediating regulatory processes, and adaptive performance. *Journal of Applied Psychology, 90*, 827–841.

Chiang, F. F. T., & Birtch, T. A. (2007). Examining the perceived causes of successful employee performance: An East-West comparison. *International Journal of Human Resource Management, 18*, 232–248.

Cialdini, R. B. (2001). *Influence: Science and practice*. Needham Heights, MA: Allyn & Bacon.

Cleveland, J. N., Lim, A. S., & Murphy, K. R. (2007). Feedback phobia? Why employees do not want to give or receive performance feedback. In J. Langan-Fox, C. L. Cooper, & R. J. Klimoski (Eds.), *Research companion to the dysfunctional workplace: Management challenges and symptoms* (pp. 168–186). Northampton, MA: Edward Elgar Publishing.

Collins, C. J., & Smith, K. G. (2006). Knowledge exchange and combination: The role of human resource practices in the performance of high-technology teams. *Academy of Management Journal, 49*, 544–560.

Collins, D. B., & Holton, E. F., III. (2004). The effectiveness of managerial leadership development programs: A meta-analysis of studies from 1982 to 2001. *Human Resource Development Quarterly, 15*, 217–248.

Colquitt, J. A. (2001). On the dimensionality of organizational justice: A construct validation of a measure. *Journal of Applied Psychology, 86*, 386–400.

Combs, J., Yongmei, L., Hall, A., & Ketchen, D. (2006). How much do high performance work practices matter? A meta-analysis of their effects on organizational performance. *Personnel Psychology, 59*, 501–528.

Comer, C. L. (2007). Benefits of the task for the delivery of negative feedback. *Dissertation Abstracts International: Section B: The Sciences and Engineering 68*(4-B), 2694.

Cooke, N. J., Cannon-Bowers, J. A., Kiekel, P. A., Rivera, K., Stout, R. J., & Salas, E. (2007). Improving teams' interpositional knowledge through cross training. *Human Factors and Ergonomics Society Annual Meeting Proceedings, 2*, 390–393.

Cooper, C. L., Dyck, B., & Frohlich, N. (1992). Improving the effectiveness of gainsharing: The role of fairness and participation. *Administrative Science Quarterly, 37*, 471–490.

Cooper, W. H. (1981a). Ubiquitous halo. *Psychological Bulletin, 90*, 218–244.

Cooper, W. H. (1981b). Conceptual similarity as a source of illusory halo in job performance ratings. *Journal of Applied Psychology, 66*, 302–307.

Cortina, L. M., Magley, V. J., Williams, J. H., & Langhout, R. D. (2001). Incivility in the workplace: Incidence and impact. *Journal of Occupational Health Psychology, 6*, 64–80.

Crown, D. F., & Rosse, J. G. (1995). Yours, mine, and ours: Facilitating group productivity through the integration of individual and group goals. *Organizational Behavior and Human Decision Processes, 64*, 138–150.

Dagley, G. (2006). Human resources professionals' perceptions of executive coaching: Efficacy, benefits and return on investment. *International Coaching Psychology Review, 1*(2), 34–44.

Day, D. V., & Greguras, G. J. (2009). Performance management in multinational companies. In J. W. Smither & M. London (Eds.), *Performance management: Putting research into practice* (pp. 271–296). San Francisco: Jossey-Bass.

Deci, E. L., Koestner, R., & Ryan, R. M. (1999). A meta-analytic review of experiments examining the effects of extrinsic rewards on intrinsic motivation. *Psychological Bulletin, 125*, 627–668.

Deci, E. L., & Ryan, R. M. (1985). *Intrinsic motivation and self-determination in human behavior.* New York: Plenum.

DeCotiis, T. A., & Petit, A. (1978). The performance appraisal process: A model and some testable hypotheses. *Academy of Management Review, 21,* 635–646.

Delery, J. E., & Doty, D. H. (1996). Modes of theorizing in strategic human resource management: Tests of universalistic, contingency, and configurational performance predictions. *Academy of Management Journal, 39,* 802–835.

den Hartog, D. N., Boselie, P., & Paauwe, J. (2004). Performance management: A model and research agenda. *Applied Psychology: An International Review, 53,* 556–569.

DeNisi, A. S. (1996). *Cognitive approach to performance appraisal: A program of research.* New York: Routledge.

DeNisi, A. S. (2000). Performance appraisal and performance management: A multilevel analysis. In K. J. Klein & S. W. J. Kozlowski (Eds.), *Multilevel theory, research, and methods in organizations: Foundations, extensions, and new directions* (pp. 121–156). San Francisco: Jossey-Bass.

DeNisi, A. S., Cafferty, T. P., Meglino, B. M. (1984). A cognitive view of the performance appraisal process: A model and research propositions. *Organizational Behavior and Human Performance, 33,* 360–396.

DeNisi, A. S., & Pritchard, R. D. (2006). Performance appraisal, performance management and improving individual performance: A motivational framework. *Management and Organization Review, 2,* 253–277.

DeShon, R. P., Kozlowski, S. W. J., Schmidt, A. M., Milner, K. R., & Wiechmann, D. (2004). Multiple-goal, multilevel model of feedback effects on the regulation of individual and team performance. *Journal of Applied Psychology, 89,* 1035–1056.

Deshpande, S. P., Joseph, J., & Viswesvaran, C. (1994). Does use of student samples affect results of studies in cross-cultural training? A meta-analysis. *Psychological Reports, 74,* 779–785.

Dominick, P. G. (2009). Forced rankings: Pros, cons, and practices. In J. W. Smither & M. London (Eds.), *Performance management: Putting research into practice* (pp. 411–444). San Francisco: Jossey-Bass.

Dominick, P. G., Reilly, R. R, & Byrne, J. C. (2004, April). *Individual differences and peer feedback: Personality's impact on behavior change.* Paper presented at the 19th Annual Conference of the Society for Industrial and Organizational Psychology. Chicago.

Donaldson, S. I., Ensher, E. A., & Grant-Vallone, E. J. (2000). Longitudinal examination of mentoring relationships on organizational commitment and citizenship behavior. *Journal of Career Development, 26,* 233–349.

Drach-Zahavy, A., & Erez, M. (2002). Challenge versus threat effects on the goal-performance relationship. *Organizational Behavior and Human Decision Processes, 88,* 667–682.

Driskell, J. E., Willis, R. P., & Copper, C. (1992). Effect of overlearning on retention. *Journal of Applied Psychology, 77,* 615–622.

Durham, C. C., Knight, D., & Locke, E. A. (1997). Effects of leader role, team-set goal difficulty, efficacy, and tactics on team effectiveness. *Organizational Behavior and Human Decision Processes, 72*(2), 203–231.

Dweck, C. S. (1986). Motivational processes affecting learning. *American Psychologist, 41,* 1040–1048.

Dweck, C. S. (2006). *Mindset: The new psychology of success.* New York: Random House.

Edmondson, A. (1999). Psychological safety and learning behavior in work teams. *Administrative Science Quarterly, 44,* 350–383.

Edmondson, A. C., Bohmer, R. M., & Pisano, G. P. (2001). Disrupted routines: Team learning and new technology implementation in hospitals. *Administrative Science Quarterly, 46,* 685–716.

Edwards, J. R. (1995). Alternatives to difference scores as dependent variables in the study of congruence in organizational research. *Organizational Behavior and Human Decision Processes, 64,* 307–324.

Eggebeen, S. L. (2002). Going global: Additional considerations inherent in cross-cultural implementation. In J. W. Hedge & E. D. Pulakos (Eds.), *Implementing organizational interventions: Steps, processes, and best practices* (pp. 270–296). San Francisco: Jossey-Bass.

Ellinger, A. D., Ellinger, A. E., & Keller, S. B. (2003). Supervisory coaching behavior, employee satisfaction, and warehouse employee performance: A dyadic perspective in the distribution industry. *Human Resource Development Quarterly, 14,* 435–458.

Ellis, S., & Davidi, I. (2005). After-event reviews: Drawing lessons from successful and failed experience. *Journal of Applied Psychology, 90,* 857–871.

Eppler, M., & Mengis, J. (2004). The concept of information overload: A review of literature from organization science, accounting, marketing, MIS, and related disciplines. *The Information Society, 20,* 325–344.

Erez, M. (1977). Feedback: A necessary condition for the goal setting-performance relationship. *Journal of Applied Psychology, 62,* 624–627.

Evers, W. J. G., Brouwers, A., & Tomic, W. (2006). A quasi-experimental study on management coaching effectiveness. *Consulting Psychology Journal: Practice and Research, 58,* 174–182.

Fandt, P. M., Labig, C. E., & Urich, A. L. (1990). Evidence and the liking bias: Effects on managers' disciplinary actions. *Employee Responsibilities and Rights Journal, 3,* 253–265.

Feggetter, A. J. W. (2007). A preliminary evaluation of executive coaching: Does executive coaching work for candidates on a high potential development scheme? *International Coaching Psychology Review, 2,* 129–142.

Feldman, D. C., & Lankau, M. J. (2005). Executive coaching: A review and agenda for future research. *Journal of Management, 31,* 829–848.

Feldman, J. M. (1981). Beyond attribution theory: Cognitive processes in performance appraisal. *Journal of Applied Psychology, 66,* 127–148.

Findley, H. M., Giles, W. F., & Mossholder, K. W. (2000). Performance appraisal process and systems facets: Relationships with contextual performance. *Journal of Applied Psychology, 85,* 634–640.

Fitzgerald, L. F., Drasgow, F., Hulin, C. L., Gelfand, M. J., & Magley, V. J. (1997). Antecedents and consequences of sexual harassment in organizations: A test of an integrated model. *Journal of Applied Psychology, 82,* 578–589.

Flanagan, J. C. (1954). The critical incident technique. *Psychological Bulletin, 51,* 327–358.

Fleishman, E. A., & Zaccaro, S. J. (1992). Toward a taxonomy of team performance functions. In R. W. Swezey & E. Salas (Eds.), *Teams: Their training and performance* (pp. 31–56). Westport, CT: Ablex Publishing.

Fletcher, C. (1986). The effects of performance review in appraisal: Evidence and implications. *Journal of Management Development, 5,* 3–12.

Folger, R., & Cropenzano, R. (1998). *Organizational justice and human resource management.* Thousand Oaks, CA: Sage Publications.

Ford, J. K., Smith, E. M., Weissbein, D. A., Gully, S. M., & Salas, E. (1998). Relationships of goal orientation, metacognitive activity, and practice strategies with learning outcomes and transfer. *Journal of Applied Psychology, 83,* 218–233.

Frayne, C. A., & Geringer, J. M. (2000). Self-management training for improving job performance: A field experiment involving salespeople. *Journal of Applied Psychology, 85,* 361–372.

Frayne, C. A., & Latham, G. P. (1987). Application of social learning theory to employee self-management of attendance. *Journal of Applied Psychology, 72,* 387–392.

Frese, M., Brodbeck, F. C., Heinbokel, T., Mooser, C., Schleiffenbaum, E., & Thiemann, P. (1991). Errors in training computer skills: On the positive function of errors. *Human-Computer Interaction, 6,* 77–93.

Garcia, S. M., & Tor, A. (2007). Rankings, standards and competition: Task vs. scale comparisons. *Organizational Behavior and Human Decision Processes, 102,* 95–108.

Garcia, S. M., Tor, A., & Gonzalez, R. D. (2006). Ranks & rivals: A theory of competition. *Personality & Social Psychology Bulletin, 32,* 970–982.

Gerhart, B., & Milkovich G. T. (1990). Organizational differences in managerial compensation and financial performance. *Academy of Management Journal, 33,* 663–691.

Gilliland, S. W., & Langdon, J. C. (1998). Creating performance management systems that promote perceptions of fairness. In J. W. Smither (Ed.), *Performance appraisal: State-of-the-art in practice* (pp. 209–243). San Francisco: Jossey-Bass.

Gittell, J. H. (2001). Supervisory span, relational coordination, and flight departure performance: A reassessment of postbureaucracy theory. *Organization Science, 12,* 468–483.

Glomb, T. M., Munson, L. J., Hulin, C. L., Bergman, M. E., & Drasgow, F. (1999). Structural equation models of sexual harassment: Longitudinal explorations and cross-sectional generalizations. *Journal of Applied Psychology, 84,* 14–28.

Goldman, A. (2006). High toxicity leadership: Borderline personality disorder and the dysfunctional organization. *Journal of Managerial Psychology, 21,* 733–746.

Goodman, J. S., & Wood, R. E. (2004). Feedback specificity, learning opportunities, and learning. *Journal of Applied Psychology, 89,* 809–821.

Goodman, J. S., Wood, R. E., & Hendrickx, M. (2004). Feedback specificity, exploration, and learning. *Journal of Applied Psychology, 89,* 248–262.

Graham, S., Wedman, J. F., & Garvin-Kester, B. (1993). Manager coaching skills: Development and application. *Performance Improvement Quarterly, 6,* 2–13.

Grant, A. M., & Cavanagh, M. J. (2007). The Goal-Focused Coaching Skills Questionnaire: Preliminary findings. *Social Behavior and Personality, 35,* 751–760.

Grant, R. A., & Higgins, C. A. (1991). The impact of computerized performance monitoring on service work: Testing a causal model. *Information Systems Research, 2,* 116–142.

Greguras, G. J., Ford, J. M., & Brutus, S. (2003). Manager attention to multisource feedback. *Journal of Management Development, 22,* 345–361.

Greller, M. M. (1998). Participation in the performance appraisal review: Inflexible manager behavior and variable worker needs. *Human Relations, 51,* 1061–1083.

Guest, D. E., Michie, J., Conway, N., & Sheehan, M. (2003). Human resource management and corporate performance in the UK. *British Journal of Industrial Relations, 41,* 291.

Gully, S. M., Incalcaterra, K. A., Joshi, A., & Beaubien, J. M. (2002). A meta-analysis of team-efficacy, potency, and performance: Interdependence and level of analysis as moderators of observed relationships. *Journal of Applied Psychology, 87*(5), 819–832.

Guralnik, O., Rozmarin, E., & So, A. (2004). Forced distribution: Is it right for you? *Human Resource Development Quarterly, 15*(3), 339–345.

Guthrie, J. P. (2001). High-involvement work practices, turnover, and productivity: Evidence from New Zealand. *Academy of Management Journal, 44,* 180–190.

Guzzo, R. A., Jette, R. D., & Katzell, R. A. (1985). The effects of psychologically based intervention programs on worker productivity: A meta-analysis. *Personnel Psychology, 38,* 275–291.

Gyllensten, K., & Palmer, S. (2005). Can coaching reduce workplace stress? A quasi-experimental study. *International Journal of Evidence Based Coaching and Mentoring, 3,* 75–85.

Hackman, J. R., & Wageman, R. (2005). A theory of team coaching. *Academy of Management Review, 30,* 269–287.

Hall, D. T., Otazo, K. L., & Hollenbeck, G. P. (1999). Behind closed doors: What really happens in executive coaching. *Organizational Dynamics, 27*(3), 39–53.

Hamlin, R. G., Ellinger, A. D., & Beattie, R. S. (2006). Coaching at the heart of managerial effectiveness: A cross-cultural study of managerial behaviours. *Human Resource Development International, 9,* 305–331.

Harper, S., & Vilkinas, T. (2005). Determining the impact of an organisation's performance management system. *Asia Pacific Journal of Human Resources, 43,* 76–97.

Harris, M. M. (1994). Rater motivation in the performance appraisal context: A theoretical framework. *Journal of Management, 20,* 737–756.

Hauenstein, N. M. A. (1998). Training raters to increase the accuracy of appraisals and the usefulness of feedback. In J. W. Smither (Ed.), *Performance appraisal: State of the art in practice* (pp. 404–442). San Francisco: Jossey-Bass.

Hawk, S. R. (1994). The effects of computerized performance monitoring: An ethical perspective. *Journal of Business Ethics, 13,* 949–957.

Hazucha, J. F., Hezlett, S. A., & Schneider, R. J. (1993). The impact of multisource feedback on management skills development. *Human Resource Management, 32,* 325–351.

Hedge, J. W., & Borman, W. C. (2008). Career and performance management with consultants. In J. W. Hedge & W. C. Borman (Eds.), *The I/O consultant: Advice and insights for building a successful career.* Washington, DC: American Psychological Association.

Heimbeck, D., Frese, M., Sonnentag, S., & Keith, N. (2003). Integrating errors into the training process: The function of error management instructions and the role of goal orientation. *Personnel Psychology, 56,* 333–361.

Heneman, R. L. (1986). The relationship between supervisory ratings and results-oriented measures of performance: A meta-analysis. *Personnel Psychology, 39,* 811–826.

Heneman, R. L. (1992). *Merit pay: Linking pay increases to performance ratings.* Reading, MA: Addison-Wesley.

Heneman, R. L., & Gresham, M. T. (1998). Performance-based pay plans. In J. W. Smither (Ed.), *Performance appraisal: State-of-the-art in practice* (pp. 496–536). San Francisco: Jossey-Bass.

Heneman, R. L., & von Hippel, C. (1995). Balancing group and individual rewards: Rewarding individual contributions to the team. *Compensation and Benefits Review, 27*(4), 63–68.

Heneman, R. L., & Werner, J. M. (2005). *Merit pay: Linking pay to performance in a changing world*. Greenwich, CT: Information Age Publishing.

Herzberg, F., Mausner, B., Peterson, R. O., & Capwell, D. F. (1957). *Job attitudes: Review of research and opinion*. Pittsburgh, PA: Psychological Service of Pittsburgh.

Heslin, P., Carson, J. B., & VandeWalle, D. (2009). Practical applications of goal setting theory to performance management. In J. W. Smither & M. London (Eds.), *Performance management: Putting research into practice* (pp. 89–114). San Francisco: Jossey-Bass.

Heslin, P. A., & Latham, G. P. (2004). The effect of upward feedback on managerial behavior. *Applied Psychology: An International Review, 53*, 23–37.

Heslin, P. A., Latham, G. P., & VandeWalle, D. M. (2005). The effect of implicit person theory on performance appraisals. *Journal of Applied Psychology, 90*, 842–856.

Heslin, P. A., & VandeWalle, D. M. (2008). Managers' implicit assumptions about personnel. *Current Directions in Psychological Science, 17*, 219–223.

Heslin, P. A., VandeWalle, D. M., & Latham, G. P. (2006). Keen to help? Managers' implicit person theories and their subsequent employee coaching. *Personnel Psychology, 59*, 871–902.

Higgins, E. T. (1997). Beyond pleasure and pain. *American Psychologist, 52*, 1280–1300.

Higgins, E. T., Shah, J., & Friedman, R. (1997). Emotional responses to goal attainment: Strength of regulatory focus as moderator. *Journal of Personality and Social Psychology, 72*, 515–525.

Hofstede, G. (2001). *Culture's consequences: Comparing values, behaviors, institutions, and organizations across nations* (2nd ed.). Thousand Oaks, CA: Sage.

Hollenbeck, G. P., & McCall, M. W. (1999). Leadership development: Contemporary practices. In A. I. Kraut & A. K. Korman (Eds.), *Evolving practices in human resource management* (pp. 172–200). San Francisco: Jossey-Bass.

Hollenbeck, J. R., Ilgen, D. R., Sego, D. J., Hudlund, J., Major, D. A., & Phillips, J. (1995). Multilevel theory of team decision making: Decision performance in teams incorporating distributed expertise. *Journal of Applied Psychology, 80*, 292–316.

House, R. J. (1971). A path-goal theory of leader effectiveness. *Administrative Science Quarterly, 16*, 321–338.

House, R. J., Hanges, P. J., Javidan, M., Dorfman, P. W., & Gupta, V. (Eds.). (2004). *Culture, leadership, and organizations: The GLOBE study of 62 societies*. Thousand Oaks, CA: Sage.

Hurtz, G. M., & Donovan, J. J. (2000). Personality and job performance: The Big Five revisited. *Journal of Applied Psychology, 85*, 869–879.

Huselid, M. A. (1995). The impact of human resource management practices on turnover, productivity and corporate financial performance. *Academy of Management Journal, 38*, 635–672.

Huselid, M. A., Jackson, S., & Schuler, R. (1997). Technical and strategic human resource management effectiveness as determinants of firm performance. *Academy of Management Journal, 40*(1), 171–188.

Hymowitz, C. (2001). In the lead: Ranking systems gain popularity but have many staffers riled. *Wall Street Journal*, B1, May 15.

Ichniowski, C., Shaw, K., & Prennushi, G. (1997). The effects of human resource management practices on productivity: A study of steel finishing lines. *The American Economic Review, 87*, 291–313.

Idson, L. C., & Higgins, E. T. (2000). How current feedback and chronic effectiveness influence motivation: Everything to gain version everything to lose. *European Journal of Social Psychology, 30*, 583–592.

Idson, L. C., Liberman, N., & Higgins, E. T. (2000). Distinguishing gains from nonlosses and losses from nongains: A regulatory focus perspective on hedonic intensity. *Journal of Experimental Social Psychology, 36*, 252–274.

Ilgen, D. R., & Davis, C. A. (2000). Bearing bad news: Reactions to negative performance feedback. *Applied Psychology: An International Review, 49*, 550–565.

Ilgen, D. R., & Feldman, J. M. (1983). Performance appraisal: A process focus. *Research in Organizational Behavior, 5*, 141–197.

Ilgen, D. R., Fisher, C. D., & Taylor, M. S. (1979). Consequences of individual feedback on behavior in organizations. *Journal of Applied Psychology, 64*, 349–371.

Jawahar, I. M., & Williams, C. R. (1997). Where all the children are above average: The performance appraisal purpose effect. *Personnel Psychology, 50*, 905–925.

Jenkins, D. G., Mitra, A., Gupta, N., & Shaw J. D. (1998). Are financial incentives related to performance? A meta-analytic review of empirical research. *Journal of Applied Psychology, 83*, 777–787.

Johnson, J. W., & Ferstl, K. L. (1999). The effects of interrater and self-other agreement on performance improvement following upward feedback. *Personnel Psychology, 52*, 271–303.

Judiesch, M. K. (1995). The effects of incentive compensation systems on productivity, individual differences in output variability and selection utility. *Dissertation Abstracts International Section A: Humanities and Social Sciences 55*(12-A), 3914.

Kampa-Kokesch, S. (2001). Executive coaching as an individually tailored consultation intervention: Does it increase leadership? Unpublished Ph.D. dissertation, Western Michigan University.

Kane, J. S. (1986). Performance distribution assessment. In R. A. Berk (Ed.), *Performance assessment: Methods and applications* (pp. 237–274). Baltimore: Johns Hopkins University Press.

Kanfer, R., & Ackerman, P. L. (1989) Motivation and cognitive abilities: An integrative/aptitude-treatment interaction approach to skill acquisition. *Journal of Applied Psychology, 74*, 657–690.

Kaplan, R. S., & Norton, D. P. (1992). The balanced scorecard: Measures that drive performance. *Harvard Business Review, 70*, 71–80.

Kaplan, R. S., & Norton, D. P (1996). *The balanced scorecard: Translating strategy into action*. Boston: Harvard Business School Press.

Kaplan, R. S., & Norton, D. P. (2001). Transforming the balanced scorecard from performance measurement to strategic management: Part I. *Accounting Horizons, 15*, 87–104.

Kaplan, R. S., & Norton, D. P. (2004). Strategy maps. *Strategic Finance, 85*, 26–35.

Keith, N., & Frese, M. (2005). Self-regulation in error management training: Emotion control and metacognition as mediators of performance effects. *Journal of Applied Psychology, 90,* 677–691.

Keith, N., & Frese, M. (2008). Effectiveness of error management training: A meta-analysis. *Journal of Applied Psychology, 93,* 59–69.

Kidwell, R. E., & Bennett, N. (1993). Employee propensity to withhold effort: A conceptual model to intersect three avenues of research. *Academy of Management Review, 18,* 429–456.

Kiker, D. S, & Motowidlo, S. J. (1999). Main and interaction effects of task and contextual performance on supervisory rewards decisions. *Journal of Applied Psychology, 84,* 602–609.

Kilburg, R. R. (2004). When shadows fall: Using psychodynamic approaches in executive coaching. *Consulting Psychology Journal: Practice and Research, 56,* 246–268.

Kinicki, A. J., Prussia, G. E., Wu, B., & McKee-Ryan, F. M. (2004). A covariance structure analysis of employees' response to performance feedback. *Journal of Applied Psychology, 89,* 1057–1069.

Kirchner, W. K. (1960). Predicting ratings of sales success with objective performance information. *Journal of Applied Psychology, 44,* 398–403.

Klausegger, C., Sinkovics, R. R., & Zou, H. (2007). Information overload: A cross-national investigation of influence factors and effects. *Marketing Intelligence & Planning, 25,* 691–718.

Klein, H. J., Wesson, M. J., Hollenbeck, J. R., & Alge, B. J. (1999). Goal commitment and the goal-setting process: Conceptual clarification and empirical synthesis. *Journal of Applied Psychology, 84,* 885–896.

Kluger, A. N., & DeNisi, A. (1996). Effects of feedback intervention on performance: A historical review, a meta-analysis, and a preliminary feedback intervention theory. *Psychological Bulletin, 119,* 254–284.

Kluger, A. N., Lewinsohn, S., & Aiello, J. R. (1996). The influence of feedback on mood: Linear effects on pleasantness and curvilinear effects on arousal. *Organizational Behavior and Human Decision Processes, 60,* 276–299.

Kombarakaran, F. A., Yang, J. A., Baker, M. N., & Fernandes, P. B. (2008). Executive coaching: It works! *Consulting Psychology Journal: Practice and Research, 60,* 78–90.

Konczak, L. J., Stelly, D. J., & Trusty, M. L. (2000). Defining and measuring empowering leader behaviors: Development of an upward feedback instrument. *Educational and Psychological Measurement, 60,* 301–313.

Korsgaard, M. A. (1996). The impact of self-appraisals on reactions to feedback from others: The role of self-enhancement and self-consistency concerns. *Journal of Organizational Behavior, 17,* 301–311.

Koys, D. J. (2001). The effects of employee satisfaction, organizational citizenship behavior, and turnover on organizational effectiveness: A unit-level, longitudinal study. *Personnel Psychology, 54,* 101–115.

Kozlowski, S. W. J., Gully, S. M., Brown, K. G., Salas, E., Smith, E. M., & Nason, E. R. (2001). Effects of training goals and goal orientation traits on multidimensional training outcomes and performance adaptability. *Organizational Behavior and Human Decision Processes, 85,* 1–31.

Kozlowski, S. W. J., & Ilgen, D. R. (2006). Enhancing the effectiveness of work groups and teams. *Psychological Science in the Public Interest, 7,* 77–124.

Kozlowski, S. W. J., Watola, D. J., Jensen, J. M., Kim, B. H., & Botero, I. C. (2009). Developing adaptive teams: A theory of dynamic team leadership. In E. Salas, G. F. Goodwin, & C. S. Burke (Eds.), *Team effectiveness in complex organizations: Cross-disciplinary perspectives and approaches* (pp. 113–156). New York: Routledge Academic.

Krauss, A. D, & Snyder, L. A. (2009). Technology and performance management. In J. W. Smither & M. London (Eds.), *Performance management: Putting research into practice* (pp. 445–490). San Francisco: Jossey-Bass.

Kurman, J. (2002). Measured cross-cultural differences in self enhancement and the sensitivity of the self-enhancement measure to the modesty response. *Cross-Cultural Research, 36,* 73–95.

Lado, A. A., & Wilson, M. C. (1994). Human resource systems and sustained competitive advantage: A competency-based perspective. *The Academy of Management Review, 19,* 699–728.

Lam, W., Huang, X., & Snape, E. (2007). Feedback-seeking behavior and leader-member exchange: Do supervisor-attributed motives matter? *Academy of Management Journal, 50,* 348–363.

Lam, S. K., Hui, C., & Law, K. S. (1999). Organizational citizenship behavior: Comparing perspectives of supervisors and subordinates across four international samples. *Journal of Applied Psychology, 84,* 594–601.

Lam, S. S. K., Yik, M. S. M., & Schaubroeck, J. (2002). Responses to formal performance appraisal feedback: The role of negative affectivity. *Journal of Applied Psychology, 87,* 192–201.

Landy, F. J., & Farr, J. L. (1980). Performance rating. *Psychological Bulletin, 87,* 72–107.

Larson, J. R. (1986). Supervisors' performance feedback to subordinates: The impact of subordinate performance valence and outcome dependence. *Organizational Behavior and Human Decision Processes, 37,* 391–408.

Larson, J. R., & Skolnik, Y. (1985). The effect of giving informal performance feedback on subsequent formal memory-based performance evaluations. *Journal of Applied Social Psychology, 15,* 428–442.

Latham, G. P. (2001). The importance of understanding and changing employee outcome expectancies for gaining commitment to an organizational goal. *Personnel Psychology, 54,* 707–716.

Latham, G. P. (2004). The motivation benefits of goal setting. *Academy of Management Executive, 18,* 126–129.

Latham, G. P. (2007). Theory and research on coaching practices. *Australian Psychologist, 42,* 268–270.

Latham, G. P., Almost, J., Mann, S., & Moore, C. (2005). New developments in performance management. *Organizational Dynamics, 34,* 77–87.

Latham, G. P., Fay, C. H., & Saari, L. M. (1979). The development of behavioral observation scales for appraising the performance of foremen. *Personnel Psychology, 32,* 299–311.

Latham, G. P., & Frayne, C. A. (1989). Self-management training for increasing job attendance: A follow-up and a replication. *Journal of Applied Psychology, 74,* 411–416.

Latham, G. P., & Mann, S. (2006). Advances in the science of performance appraisal: Implications for practice. In G. P Hodgkinson & J. K. Ford (Eds.), *International review of industrial and organizational psychology* (Vol. 21, pp. 295–337). Hoboken, NJ: Wiley.

Latham, G. P., & Seijts, G. H. (1999). The effects of proximal and distal goals on performance on a moderately complex task. *Journal of Organizational Behavior, 20*, 421–429.

Latham, G. P., & Wexley, K. N. (1977). Behavioral observation scales for performance appraisal purposes. *Personnel Psychology, 30*, 255–268.

Latham, G. P., Wexley, K. N., & Pursell, E. D. (1975). Training managers to minimize rating errors in the observation of behavior. *Journal of Applied Psychology, 60*, 550–555.

Lawler, E. E. (2003). Reward practices and performance management system effectiveness. *Organizational Dynamics, 32*, 396–404.

Lazar, J., Jones, A., & Shneiderman, B. (2006). Workplace user frustration with computers: An exploratory investigation of the causes and severity. *Behaviour & Information Technology, 25*, 239–251.

LePine, J. A., Hanson, M. A., Borman, W. C., & Motowidlo, S. J. (2000). Contextual performance and teamwork. Implications for teamwork. *Research in personnel and human resources management, 19*, 53–90.

Leslie, J. B., & Fleenor, J. W. (1998). *Feedback to managers: A review and comparison of multi-rater instruments for management development.* Greensboro, NC: Center for Creative Leadership.

Leventhal, G. S. (1980). What should be done with equity theory? New approaches to the study of fairness in social relationship. In K. J. Gergen, M. S. Greenberg, and R. H. Willis (Eds.), *Social exchange: Advances in theory and research* (pp. 27–55). New York: Plenum.

Lewis, P. B. (1947). Supervisory training methods. *Personnel Journal, 25*, 316–322.

Liden, R. C., Wayne, S. J., Judge, T. A., Sparrowe, R. T., Kraimer, M. L., & Franz, T. M. (1999). Management of poor performance: A comparison of manager, group member, and group disciplinary decisions. *Journal of Applied Psychology, 84*, 835–850

Lievens, F., Conway, J. M., & De Corte, W. (2008). The relative importance of task, citizenship and counterproductive performance to job performance ratings: Do rater sources and team-based culture matter? *Journal of Occupational and Organizational Psychology, 81*, 11–27.

Lizzio, A., Wilson, K. L., Gilchrist, J., & Gallois, C. (2003). The role of gender in the construction and evaluation of feedback effectiveness. *Management Communication Quarterly, 16*, 341–379.

Locke, E. A., Feren, D. B., McCaleb, V. M., Shaw, K. N., & Denny, A. T. (1980). The relative effectiveness of four ways of motivating employee performance. In K. D. Duncan, M. M. Gruenberg, & D. Wallis (Eds.), *Changes in working life,* (pp. 363–388). New York: John Wiley & Sons.

Locke, E. A., & Latham, G. P. (1990). *A theory of goal setting and task performance.* Englewood Cliffs, NJ: Prentice Hall.

Locke, E. A., & Latham, G. P. (2002). Building a practically useful theory of goal setting and task motivation: A 35-year odyssey. *American Psychologist, 57*, 705–717.

London, M., & Smither, J. W. (1999a). Career-related continuous learning: Defining the construct and mapping the process. *Research in Personnel and Human Resources Management, 17*, 81–121.

London, M., & Smither, J. W. (1999b). Empowered self-development and continuous learning. *Human Resource Management, 38*, 3–16.

London, M., & Smither, J. W. (2002). Feedback orientation, feedback culture, and the longitudinal performance management process. *Human Resource Management Review, 12*, 81–100.

Longnecker, C. O., Gioia, D. A., & Sims, H. P. (1987). Behind the mask: The politics of employee appraisal. *Academy of Management Executive, 1*, 183–193.

Lorenzet, S. J., Salas, E., & Tannenbaum, S. I. (2005). Benefiting from mistakes: The impact of guided errors on learning, performance, and self-efficacy. *Human Resource Development Quarterly, 16*, 301–322.

Luthans, F., & Peterson, S. J. (2003). 360 degree feedback with systematic coaching: Empirical analysis suggests a winning combination. *Human Resource Management, 42*, 243–256.

MacKenzie, S. B., Podsakoff, P. M., & Fetter, R. (1993). The impact of organizational citizenship behavior on the evaluations of salesperson performance. *Journal of Marketing, 57*, 70–80.

MacKie, D. (2007). Evaluating the effectiveness of executive coaching: Where are we now and where do we need to be? *Australian Psychologist, 42*, 310–318.

Mangels, J. A., Butterfield, B., Lamb, J., Good, C., & Dweck, C. S. (2006). Why do beliefs about intelligence influence learning success? A social cognitive neuroscience model. *Social Cognitive and Affective Neuroscience, 1*, 75–86.

Marks, M. A., Zaccaro, S. J., & Mathieu, J. E. (2000). Performance implications of leader briefings and team-interaction training for team adaptation to novel environments. *Journal of Applied Psychology, 85*, 971–986.

Marler, J. H., Liang, X., & Dulebohn, J. H. (2006). Training and effective employee information technology use. *Journal of Management, 32*, 721–743.

Martell, R. F., & Leavitt, K. N. (2002). Reducing the performance-cue bias in work behavior ratings: Can groups help? *Journal of Applied Psychology, 87*, 1032–1041.

Maslow, A. H. (1943). A theory of human motivation. *Psychological Review, 50*, 370–396.

Mayer, R. C., & Davis, J. H. (1999). The effect of the performance appraisal system on trust for management: A quasi-experimental field study. *Journal of Applied Psychology, 84*, 123–136.

McBriarty, M. A. (1988). Performance appraisal: Some unintended consequences. *Public Personnel Management. 17*, 421–434.

McGovern J., Lindemann, M., Vergara, M., Murphy, S., Barker, L., & Warrenfeltz, R. (2001). Maximizing the impact of executive coaching: Behavioral change, organizational outcomes, and return on investment. *The Manchester Review, 6*, 1–9.

McLean, G. N., Yang, B., Kuo, M.-H. C., Tolbert, A. S., & Larkin, C. (2005). Development and initial validation of an instrument measuring managerial coaching skill. *Human Resource Development Quarterly, 16*, 157–178.

McNall, L. A., & Roch, S. G. (2007). Effects of electronic monitoring types on perceptions of procedural justice, interpersonal justice, and privacy. *Journal of Applied Social Psychology, 37*, 658–682.

Mero, N. P., Guidice, R. M., & Brownlee, A. L. (2007). Accountability in a performance appraisal context: The effect of audience and form of accounting on rater response and behavior. *Journal of Management, 33*, 223–252.

Miles, R. E., & Snow, C. C. (1978). *Organizational strategy, structure, and process.* New York: McGraw-Hill.

Mind Garden. (2008). Available at http://www.mindgarden.com/products/mlq.htm (retrieved September 12, 2008).

Mitchell, T. R., & Wood, R. E. (1980). Supervisor's responses to subordinate poor performance: A test of an attributional model. *Organizational Behavior & Human Performance, 25*, 123–138.

Morgeson, F. P. (2005). The external leadership of self-managing teams: Intervening in the context of novel and disruptive events. *Journal of Applied Psychology, 90*, 497–508.

Morris, G. H., Gaveras, S. C., Baker, W. L., & Coursey, M. L. (1990). Aligning actions at work: How managers confront problems of employee performance. *Management Communication Quarterly, 3*, 303–333.

Morris, M. A., & Robie, C. (2001). A meta-analysis of the effects of cross-cultural training on expatriate performance and adjustment. *International Journal of Training and Development, 5*, 112–125.

Morrow, C. C., Jarrett, M. Q., & Rupinski, M. T. (1997). An investigation of the effect and economic utility of corporate-wide training. *Personnel Psychology, 50*, 91–119.

Moss, S. E., Valenzi, E. R., & Taggart, W. (2003). Are you hiding from your boss? The development of a taxonomy and instrument to assess the feedback management behaviors of good and bad performers. *Journal of Management, 29*, 487–510.

Motowidlo, S. J. (2003). Job performance. In W. C. Borman, D. R. Ilgen, & R. J. Klimoski (Eds.), *Handbook of psychology*, Volume 12, *Industrial and organizational psychology* (pp. 39–53). Hoboken, NJ: Wiley.

Motowidlo, S. J., & Van Scotter, J. R. (1994). Evidence that task performance should be distinguished from contextual performance. *Journal of Applied Psychology, 79*, 475–480.

Mueller, C. M., & Dweck, C. S. (1998). Praise for intelligence can undermine children's motivation and performance. *Journal of Personality & Social Psychology, 75*, 33–52.

Murphy, K. R. (2008). Explaining the weak relationship between job performance and ratings of job performance. *Industrial and Organizational Psychology: Perspectives on Science and Practice, 1*, 148–160.

Murphy, K. R., & Cleveland, J. N. (1991). *Performance appraisal: An organizational perspective*. Boston, MA: Allyn & Bacon.

Murphy, K. R., & Cleveland, J. N. (1995). *Understanding performance appraisal: Social, organizational, and goal-based perspectives*. Thousand Oaks: CA: Sage

Nathan, B. R., & Alexander, R. A. (1988). A comparison of criteria for test validation: A meta-analytic investigation. *Personnel Psychology, 41*, 517–535.

Nathan, B. R., Mohrman, A. M., Jr., & Milliman, J. (1991). Interpersonal relations as a context for the effects of appraisal interviews on performance and satisfaction: A longitudinal study. *Academy of Management Journal, 34*, 352–369.

Neubert, M. J. (1998). The value of feedback and goal setting over goal setting alone and potential moderators of this effect: A meta-analysis. *Human Performance, 11*, 321–335.

Nisbett, R. E., Peng, K., Choi, I., & Norenzayan, A. (2001). Culture and systems of thought: Holistic versus analytic cognition. *Psychological Review, 108*, 291–310.

Noel, T., & Latham, G. P. (2006). The importance of learning goals versus outcome goals for entrepreneurs. *International Journal of Entrepreneurship and Innovation, 7*, 213–220.

Noer, D. M., Leupold, C. R., & Valle, M. (2007). An analysis of Saudi Arabian and U.S. managerial coaching behaviors. *Journal of Managerial Issues, 19*, 271–287.

Norris-Watts, C., & Levy, P. E. (2004). The mediating role of affective commitment in the relation of the feedback environment to work outcomes. *Journal of Vocational Behavior, 65*, 351–365.

O'Connor, J. P., Jr, Priem, R. L., Coombs, J. E., & Gilley, K. M. (2006). Do CEO stock options prevent or promote fraudulent financial reporting? *Academy of Management Journal, 49*, 483–500.

O'Leary-Kelly, A. M., Martocchio, J. J., & Frink, D. D. (1994). A review of the influence of group goals on group performance. *Academy of Management Journal, 37*(5), 1285–1301.

Olivero, G., Bane, K. D., & Kopelman, R. E. (1997). Executive coaching as a transfer of training tool: Effects on productivity in a public agency. *Public Personnel Management, 26*, 461–469.

O'Reilly, C. A., & Puffer, S. M. (1989). The impact of rewards and punishments in a social context: A laboratory and field experiment. *Journal of Occupational Psychology, 62*, 41–53

Organ, D. W. (1988). *Organizational citizenship behavior: The good soldier syndrome*. Lexington, MA: Lexington Books:

Organ, D. W., & Ryan, K. (1995). A meta-analytic review of attitudinal and dispositional predictors of organizational citizenship behavior. *Personnel Psychology, 48*, 775–802.

Paine, J. B., & Organ, D. W. (2000). The cultural matrix of organizational citizenship behavior: Some preliminary conceptual and empirical observations. *Human Resources Management Review, 10*, 45–59.

Payne, S. C., Youngcourt, S. S., & Beaubien, J. M. (2007). A meta-analytic examination of the goal orientation nomological net. *Journal of Applied Psychology, 92*, 128–150.

Pearce, J. L., & Porter, L. W. (1986). Employee responses to formal performance appraisal feedback. *Journal of Applied Psychology, 71*, 211–218.

Peltier, B. (2001). *The psychology of executive coaching: Theory and application*. New York: Routledge.

Peretz, H., & Fried, Y. (2008, August). *National values, performance appraisal and organizational performance: A study across 21 countries*. Paper presented at the Annual Meeting of the Academy of Management, Anaheim, CA.

Peterson, D. B. (2007). Executive coaching in a cross-cultural context. *Consulting Psychology Journal: Practice and Research, 59*, 261–271.

Peterson, D. B., & Little, B. (2005). Invited reaction: Development and initial validation of an instrument measuring managerial coaching skill. *Human Resource Development Quarterly, 16*, 179–184.

Pillai, R., Schruesheum, C. A., & Williams, E. S. (1999). Fairness perceptions and trust as mediators for transformational and transactional leadership: A two sample study. *Journal of Management, 25*, 897–933.

Ployhart, R. E., & Hakel, M. D. (1998). The substantive nature of performance variability: Predicting interindividual differences in intraindividual performance. *Personnel Psychology, 51*, 859–901.

Podsakoff, P. M., Ahearne, M., & MacKenzie, S. B. (1997). Organizational citizenship behavior and the quantity and quality of work group performance. *Journal of Applied Psychology, 82*, 262–270.

Podsakoff, P. M., Bommer, W. H., Podsakoff, N. P., & MacKenzie, S. B. (2006). Relationships between leader reward and punishment behavior and subordinate attitudes, perceptions, and behaviors: A meta-analytic review of existing and new research. *Organizational Behavior and Human Decision Processes, 99*, 113–142.

Podsakoff, P. M., & MacKenzie, S. B. (1994). Organizational citizenship behavior and sales unit effectiveness. *Journal of Marketing Research, 31*, 351–336.

Podsakoff, P. M., MacKenzie, S. B., & Bommer, W. H. (1996). A meta-analysis on the relationship between Kerr and Jermier's substitute for leadership and employee job attitudes, role perceptions, and performance. *Journal of Applied Psychology, 81*, 380–399.

Podsakoff, P. M., MacKenzie, S. B., Paine, J. B., & Bachrach, D. G. (2000). Organizational citizenship behaviors: A critical review of the theoretical and empirical literature and suggestions for future research. *Journal of Management, 26*, 513–563.

Pritchard, R. D., Harrell, M. M., DiazGranados, D., & Guzman, M. J. (2008). The productivity measurement and enhancement system: A meta-analysis. *Journal of Applied Psychology, 93*, 540–567.

Pulakos, E. D., Arad, S., Donovan, M. A., & Plamondon, K. E. (2000). Adaptability in the workplace: Development of a taxonomy of adaptive performance. *Journal of Applied Psychology, 85*, 612–624.

Rappe, C., & Zwick, T. (2007). Developing leadership competence of production unit managers. *Journal of Management Development, 26*, 312–330.

Reb, J., & Cropanzano, R. (2007). Evaluating dynamic performance: The influence of salient gestalt characteristics on performance ratings. *Journal of Applied Psychology, 92*, 490–492.

Reilly, R. R., & Aronson, Z. H. (2009). Managing contextual performance. In J. W. Smither & M. London (Eds.), *Performance management: Putting research into practice* (pp. 297–328). San Francisco: Jossey-Bass.

Reilly, S. P., Smither, J. W., Warech, M. A., & Reilly, R. R. (1998). The influence of indirect knowledge of previous performance on ratings of present performance: The effects of job familiarity and rater training. *Journal of Business and Psychology, 12*, 421–435.

Renn, R. W. (2003). Moderation by goal commitment of the feedback-performance relationship: Theoretical explanation and preliminary study. *Human Resource Management Review, 13*, 561–580.

Renn, R. W., & Fedor, D. B. (2001). Development and field test of a feedback seeking, self-efficacy, and goal setting model of work performance. *Journal of Management, 27*, 563–583.

Ritchie-Dunham, J. L. (2003). Balanced scorecards, mental models, and organizational performance: A simulation experiment. *Dissertation Abstracts International Section A: Humanities & Social Sciences 64*, 987.

Robinson, S. L., & Bennett, R. J. (1995). A typology of deviant workplace behaviors: A multidimensional scaling study. *Academy of Management Journal, 38*, 555–572.

Rochat, K. D. (1998). Gainsharing plan effectiveness and its correlates. *Dissertation Abstracts International: Section B: The Sciences and Engineering 59*(6-B), 3106.

Rodgers, R., & Hunter, J. E. (1991). Impact of management by objectives on organizational productivity. *Journal of Applied Psychology, 76*, 322–336.

Roney, C. J. R., Higgins, E. T., & Shah, J. (1995). Goals and framing: How outcome focus influences motivation and emotion. *Personality and Social Psychology Bulletin, 21*, 1151–1160.

Rosen, B., & Jerdee, T. H. (1974). Factors influencing disciplinary judgments. *Journal of Applied Psychology, 59*, 327–331.

Rothstein, H. R. (1990). Interrater reliability of job performance ratings: Growth to asymptote level with increasing opportunity to observe. *Journal of Applied Psychology, 75*, 322–327.

Rotundo, M., & Sackett, P. R. (2002). The relative importance of task, citizenship, and counterproductive performance to global ratings of job performance: A policy-capturing approach. *Journal of Applied Psychology, 87*, 66–80.

Rynes, S. L., Gerhart, B., & Parks, L. (2005). Performance evaluation and pay for performance. *Annual Review of Psychology, 56*, 571–600.

Sackett, P. R. (2002). The structure of counterproductive work behaviors: Dimensionality and relationships with facets of job performance. *International Journal of Selection and Assessment, 10*, 5–11.

Salas, E., Cannon-Bowers, J. A., Fiore, S. M., & Stout, R. J. (2001). Cue-recognition training to enhance team situation awareness. In M. McNeese, E. Salas, & M. Endsley (Eds.), *New trends in collaborative activities: Understanding system dynamics in complex environments* (pp. 169–190). Santa Monica, CA: Human Factors and Ergonomics Society.

Salas, E., Nichols, D. R., & Driskell, J. E. (2007). Testing three team training strategies in intact teams: A meta-analysis. *Small Group Research, 38*, 471–488.

Salas, E., Priest, H. A., Wilson, K. A., & Burke, C. S. (2006). Scenario-based training: Improving military mission performance and adaptability. In A. B. Adler, C. A. Castro & T. W. Britt (Eds.), *Military life: The psychology of serving in peace and combat* (Vol. 2, *Operational stress*, pp. 32–53). Westport, CT: Praeger Security International.

Salas, E., Weaver, S. J., Rosen, M. A., & Smith-Jentsch, K. A. (2009). Managing team performance in complex settings: Research-based best practices. In J. W. Smither & M. London (Eds.), *Performance management: Putting research into practice* (pp. 197–232). San Francisco: Jossey-Bass.

Salvemini, N. J., Reilly, R. R., & Smither, J. W. (1993). The influence of rater motivation on assimilation effects and accuracy in performance ratings. *Organizational Behavior and Human Decision Processes, 55*, 41–60.

Sanders, W. M. G., & Hambrick, D. C. (2007). Swinging for the fences: The effects of CEO stock options on company risk taking and performance. *Academy of Management Journal, 50*, 1055–1078.

Scandura, T. A. (1992). Mentorship and career mobility: An empirical investigation. *Journal of Organizational Behavior, 13*, 169–174.

Schiemann, W. A. (2009). Aligning performance management with organizational strategy, values, and goals. In J. W. Smither & M. London (Eds.), *Performance management: Putting research into practice* (pp. 45–88). San Francisco: Jossey-Bass.

Schleicher, D. J. Bull, R. A., & Green, S. G. (2007, April). *Rater reactions to forced distribution rating systems.* Paper presented at the 22nd Annual Conference of the Society for Industrial and Organizational Psychology. New York.

Schmitt, N., Cortina, J. M., Ingerick, M. J., & Wiechmann, D. (2003). Personnel selection and employee performance. In W. C. Borman, D. R. Ilgen, & R. J. Klimoski (Eds.), *Handbook of psychology,* Volume 12, *Industrial and organizational psychology* (pp. 77–105). Hoboken, NJ: Wiley.

Schnake, M., Cochran, D. M., & Dumler, M. P. (1995). Encouraging organizational citizenship behavior: The effects of job satisfaction, perceived equity, and leadership. *Journal of Managerial Issues, 7*, 209–221.

Schneider, K. T., Swan, S., & Fitzgerald, L. F. (1997). Job-related and psychological effects of sexual harassment in the workplace: Empirical evidence from two organizations. *Journal of Applied Psychology, 82*, 401–415.

Schwartz, S. H. (1994). Beyond individualism-collectivism: New cultural dimensions of values. In N. N. Ashkanasy, C. Wilderon, & M. F. Peterson (Eds), *The handbook of organizational culture and climate* (pp. 417–436). Newbury Park, CA: Sage.

Scullen, S. E., Mount, M. K., & Judge, T. A. (2003). Evidence of the construct validity of developmental ratings of managerial performance. *Journal of Applied Psychology, 88*, 50–66.

Seashore, S. E., Indik, B. P., & Georgopoulos, B. S. (1960). Relationships among criteria of job performance. *Journal of Applied Psychology, 44*, 195–202.

Shepperd, J. A. (1993). Productivity loss in performance groups: A motivation analysis. *Psychological Bulletin, 113*, 67–81.

Shore, T. H., Adams, J. S., & Tashchian, A. (1998). Effects of self-appraisal information, appraisal purpose, and feedback target on performance appraisal ratings. *Journal of Business and Psychology, 12*, 283–298.

Silverman, S. B., & Muller, W. M. (2009). Assessing performance management programs and policies. In J. W. Smither & M. London (Eds.), *Performance management: Putting research into practice* (pp. 527–554). San Francisco: Jossey-Bass.

Sisson, E. D. (1948). Forced choice: The new Army rating. *Personnel Psychology, 1*, 365–381.

Sitzmann, T., Kraiger, K., Stewart, D., & Wisher, R. (2006). The comparative effectiveness of web-based and classroom instruction: A meta-analysis. *Personnel Psychology, 59*, 623–664.

Smith, P. C., & Kendall, L. M. (1963). Retranslation of expectations: An approach to the construction of unambiguous anchors for rating scales. *Journal of Applied Psychology, 47*, 149–155.

Smith, P. K., Jostmann, N. B., Galinsky, A. D., & van Dijk, W. W. (2008). Lacking power impairs executive functions. *Psychological Science, 19*, 441–447.

Smither, J. W., London, M., Flautt, R., Vargas, Y., & Kucine, I. (2003). Can working with an executive coach improve multisource feedback ratings over time? A quasi-experimental field study. *Personnel Psychology, 56*, 23–44.

Smither, J. W., London, M., Flautt, R., Vargas, Y., & Kucine, I. (2004). Does discussing multisource feedback with raters enhance performance improvement? *Journal of Management Development, 23*(5), 456–468.

Smither, J. W., London, M., & Reilly, R. (2005). Does performance improve following multisource feedback? A theoretical model, meta-analysis, and review of empirical findings. *Personnel Psychology, 58*, 33–66.

Smither, J. W., London, M., & Richmond, K. R. (2005). The relationship between leaders' personality and their reactions to and use of multisource feedback: A longitudinal study. *Group and Organization Management, 30*, 181–210.

Smither, J. W., London, M., Vassilopoulos, N. L., Reilly, R. R., Millsap, R. E., & Slavering, N. (1995). An examination of the effects of an upward feedback program over time. *Personnel Psychology, 48*, 1–34.

Smither, J. W., & Reilly, S. P. (2001). Coaching in organizations: A social psychological perspective. In M. London (Ed.), *How people evaluate others in organizations: Person perception and interpersonal judgment in I/O psychology* (pp. 221–252). Mahwah, NJ: Erlbaum.

Smither, J. W., Reilly, R. R., & Buda, R. (1988). The effect of prior performance information on ratings of present performance: Contrast versus assimilation revisited. *Journal of Applied Psychology, 73*, 487–496.

Smith-Jentsch, K. A., Zeisig, R. L., Acton, B., & McPherson, J. A. (1998). Team dimensional training: A strategy for guided team self-correction. In J. A. Cannon-Bowers & E. Salas (Eds.), *Making decisions under stress: Implications for individual and team training* (pp. 271–297). Washington, DC: American Psychological Association.

Sober Lojeski, K., Reilly, R. R., & Dominick, P. (2007, January). Multitasking and innovation in virtual teams. *Proceedings of the 39th Annual Hawaii International Conference on System Sciences.* Honolulu, HI.

Spangenberg, H. H., & Theron, C. C. (1997). Developing a performance management questionnaire. *South African Journal of Psychology, 27*, 143–150.

Spector, P. E., & Fox, S. (2005). The stressor-emotion model of counterproductive work behavior. In S. Fox & P. E. Spector (Eds.), *Counterproductive work behavior: Investigations of actors and targets* (pp. 151–174). Washington, DC: American Psychological Association.

Spector, P. E., Fox, S., Penney, L. M., Bruursema, K., Goh, A., & Kessler, S. (2006). The dimensionality of counterproductivity: Are all counterproductive behaviors created equal? *Journal of Vocational Behavior, 68*, 446–460.

Stajkovic, A. D., & Luthans, F. (1997). A meta-analysis of the effects of organizational behavior modification on task performance, 1975–95. *Academy of Management Journal, 56*, 155–194.

Stajkovic, A. D., & Luthans, F. (2003). Behavioral management and task performance in organizations: Conceptual background, meta-analysis, and test of alternative models. *Personnel Psychology, 56*, 155–194.

Stanton, J. M. (2000). Reactions to employee performance monitoring: Framework, review, and research directions. *Human Performance, 13*, 85–113.

Steelman, L., Levy, P., & Snell, A. F. (2004). The feedback environment scale (FES): Construct definition, measurement, and validation. *Education and Psychological Measurement, 64*, 165–184.

Stevens, M. J., & Campion, M. A. (1994). The knowledge, skill, and ability requirements for teamwork: Implications for human resource management. *Journal of Management, 20*, 503–530.

Stevens, M. J., & Campion, M. A. (1999). Staffing work teams: Development and validation of a selection test for teamwork settings. *Journal of Management, 25*, 207–228.

Stone, D. L., Stone-Romero, E. F., & Lukaszewski, K. (2003). The functional and dysfunctional consequences of human resource information technology for organizations and their employees. In E. Salas & D. Stone (Eds.), *Advances in human performance and cognitive engineering research* (Vol. 3, pp. 37–68). Oxford: Elsevier Science.

Sue-Chan, C., & Latham, G. P. (2004). The relative effectiveness of external, peer, and self-coaches. *Applied Psychology: An International Review, 53*, 260–278.

Swann, W. B., & Schroeder, D. G. (1995). The search for beauty and truth: A framework for understanding reactions to evaluations. *Personality and Social Psychology Bulletin, 21*, 1307–1318.

Taylor, E. K., & Wherry, R. J. (1951). A study of leniency in two rating systems. *Personnel Psychology. 4*, 39–47.

Taylor, P. J., Russ-Eft, D. F., & Chan, D. W. L. (2005). A meta-analytic review of behavior modeling training. *Journal of Applied Psychology, 90*, 692–709.

Tepper, B. J., Henle, C. A., Lambert, L. S., Giacalone, R. A., & Duffy, M. K. (2008). Abusive supervision and subordinates' organization deviance. *Journal of Applied Psychology, 93*, 721–732.

Thorndike, E. (1920). A constant error in psychological ratings. *Journal of Applied Psychology, 4*, 25–29.

Thorsteinson, T. J., & Highhouse, S. (2003). Effects of goal framing in job advertisements on organizational attractiveness. *Journal of Applied Social Psychology, 33*, 2393–2412.

Tippins, N. T., & Coverdale, S. H. (2009). Performance management of the future. In J. W. Smither & M. London (Eds.), *Performance management: Putting research into practice* (pp. 555–584). San Francisco: Jossey-Bass.

Trank, C. Q., Rynes, S. L., & Bretz, R. D., Jr. (2002). Attracting applicants in the war for talent: Differences in work preferences among high achievers. *Journal of Business and Psychology, 16*, 331–345.

Trevor, C. O., Gerhart, B., & Boudreau, J. W. (1997). Voluntary turnover and job performance: Curvilinearity and the moderating influences of salary growth and promotions. *Journal of Applied Psychology, 82*, 44–61.

Triandis, H. C. (1994). *Culture and social behavior*. New York: McGraw-Hill.

Tziner, A., & Kopelman, R. (1988). Effects of rating format on goal-setting dimensions: A field experiment. *Journal of Applied Psychology, 73*, 323–326.

Tziner, A., Latham, G. P., Price, B. S., & Haccoun, R. (1996). Development and validation of a questionnaire for measuring perceived political considerations in performance appraisal. *Journal of Organizational Behavior, 17*, 179–190.

Uhl-Bein, M., & Maslyn, J.M. (2003). Reciprocity in manager-subordinate relationship: Components, configurations and outcomes. *Journal of Management, 29*, 511–532.

Van Scotter, J. R., & Motowidlo, S. J. (1996). Interpersonal facilitation and job dedication as separate facets of contextual performance. *Journal of Applied Psychology, 81*, 525–531.

Van Scotter, J. R., Motowidlo, S. J., & Cross, T. C. (2000). Effects of task and contextual performance on systematic rewards. *Journal of Applied Psychology, 85*, 526–535.

Van-Dijk, D., & Kluger, A. N. (2004). Feedback sign effect on motivation: Is it moderated by regulatory focus? *Applied Psychology: An International Review, 53*, 113–135.

van Dyck, C., Frese, M., Baer, M., & Sonnentag, S. (2005). Organizational error management culture and its impact on performance: A two-study replication. *Journal of Applied Psychology, 90*, 1228–1240.

Visweswaran, C. (2001). Assessment of individual job performance: A review of the past century and a look ahead. In N. Anderson, D. Ones, H. K. Sinangil, & C. Visweswaran (Eds.), *Handbook of industrial, work, and organizational psychology*, Volume 1, *Personnel psychology* (pp. 110–126). Thousand Oaks, CA: Sage.

Visweswaran, C., Ones, D. S., & Schmidt, F. L. (1996). Comparative analysis of the reliability of job performance ratings. *Journal of Applied Psychology, 81*, 557–574.

Wageman, R. (1995). Interdependence and group effectiveness. *Administrative Science Quarterly, 40*, 145–180.

Wageman, R. (2001). How leaders foster self-managing team effectiveness: Design choices versus hands-on coaching. *Organization Science, 12*, 559–577.

Walker, A. G., Atwater, L. E., Dominick, P. G., Brett, J. F., Smither, J. W., & Reilly, R. R. (2006, May). *The role of personality in multisource feedback performance improvement over time*. Paper presented in a symposium titled "The Four "Rs" of 360° Feedback: Second Generation Research on Determinants of Its Effectiveness" (Chair: Bryan C. Hayes) at the Twenty-First Annual Conference of the Society for Industrial and Organizational Psychology, Dallas.

Walker, A. G., & Smither, J. W. (1999). A five-year study of upward feedback: What managers do with their results matters. *Personnel Psychology, 52*, 393–423.

Walz, S. M., & Niehoff, B. P. (2000). Organizational citizenship behaviors: Their relationship to organizational effectiveness. *Journal of Hospitality and Tourism Research, 24*, 301–319.

Wasylyshyn, K. M. (2003). Executive coaching: An outcome study. *Consulting Psychology Journal: Practice and Research, 55*, 94–106.

Wasylyshyn, K. M., Gronsky, B., & Haas, J. W. (2006). Tigers, stripes, and behavior change: Survey results of a commissioned coaching program. *Consulting Psychology Journal: Practice and Research, 58*, 65–81.

Wells, D. L., Moorman, R. H., & Werner, J. M. (2007). The impact of the perceived purpose of electronic performance monitoring on an array of attitudinal variables. *Human Resource Development Quarterly, 18*, 121–138.

Westin, A. F. (1992). Two key factors that belong in a macroeconomic analysis of electronic monitoring: Employee perceptions of fairness and the climate of organizational trust or distrust. *Applied Ergonomics, 23*, 35–42.

Wexley, K. N., & Klimoski, R. J. (1984). Performance appraisal: An update. In K. Rowland & G. Ferris (Eds.), *Research in personnel and human resources management* (Vol. 2, pp. 35–79). Greenwich, CT: JAI Press.

Wexley, K. N., Singh, J. P., & Yukl, G. A. (1973). Subordinate personality as a moderator of the effects of participation in three types of appraisal interviews. *Journal of Applied Psychology, 58*, 54–59.

Whitaker, B. G., Dahling, J. J., & Levy, P. (2007). The development of a feedback environment and role clarity model of job performance. *Journal of Management, 33*, 570–591.

Wiersma, U. J., van den Berg, P. T., & Latham, G. P. (1995). Dutch reactions to behavioral observation, behavioral expectation, and trait scales. *Group & Organization Management, 20*, 297–309.

Williams, J. R., Miller, C. E., Steelman, L. A., & Levy, P. E. (1999). Increasing feedback seeking in public contexts: It takes two (or more) to tango. *Journal of Applied Psychology, 84*, 969–976.

Willness, C. R., Steel, P., & Lee, K. (2007). A meta-analysis of the antecedents and consequences of workplace sexual harassment. *Personnel Psychology, 60*, 127–162.

Wilson, K. A., Burke, C. S., Priest, H. A., & Salas, E. (2005). Promoting health care safety through training high reliability teams. *Quality and Safety in Healthcare, 14*, 303–309.

Winters, D., & Latham, G. (1996). The effect of learning versus outcome goals on a simple versus a complex task. *Group and Organization Management, 21*, 236–250.

Witherspoon, R., & White, R. P. (1996). Executive coaching: A continuum of roles. *Consulting Psychology Journal: Practice & Research, 48*, 124–133.

Woehr, D. J., & Huffcutt, A. I. (1994). Rater training for performance appraisal: A quantitative review. *Journal of Occupational and Organizational Psychology, 67*, 189–205.

Wood, R. E. (1986). Task complexity: Definition of the construct. *Organizational Behavior and Human Decision Processes, 37*, 60–82.

Wood, R. E., & Bandura, A. (1989). Impact of conceptions of ability on self-regulatory mechanisms and complex decision making. *Journal of Personality and Social Psychology, 56*, 407–415.

Wood, R. E., Mento, A. J., & Locke, E. A. (1987). Task complexity as a moderator of goal effects: A meta-analysis. *Journal of Applied Psychology, 72*, 416–425.

Worthy, D. A., Maddox, W. T., & Markman, A. B. (2007). Regulatory fit effects in a choice task. *Psychonomic Bulletin and Review, 14*(6), 1125–1132.

Wright, P. M., Dunford, B. B., & Snell, S. A. (2001). Human resources and the resource based view of the firm. *Journal of Management, 27*, 701–721.

Wright, P. M., Gardner, T. M., Moynihan, L. M., & Allen, M. R. (2005). The relationship between HR practices and firm performance: Examining causal order. *Personnel Psychology, 58*(2), 409–446.

Youndt, M. A., & Snell, S. A. (2004). Human resource configurations, intellectual capital, and organizational performance. *Journal of Managerial Issues, 16*, 337–360.

Youndt, M. A, Snell, S. A, Dean, J. W., & Lepak, D. P. (1996). Human resource management, manufacturing strategy, and firm performance. *Academy of Management Journal, 39*, 836–866.

Yun, G. J., Donahue, L. M., Dudley, N. M., & McFarland, L. A. (2005). Rater personality, rating format, and social context: Implications for performance appraisal ratings. *International Journal of Selection and Assessment, 13*, 97–107.

Zaleska, K. J., & de Menezes, L. M. (2007). Human resources development practices and their association with employee attitudes: Between traditional and new careers. *Human Relations, 60*, 987–1017.

Zatzick, C. D., & Iverson, R. D. (2006). High involvement management and workforce reduction: Competitive advantage or disadvantage? *Academy of Management Journal, 49*, 999–1015.

Learning, Training, and Development in Organizations

Eduardo Salas, Sallie J. Weaver, *and* Marissa L. Shuffler

Abstract

A 2008 Bureau of Labor Statistics report indicates that the youngest of the baby boom generation (i.e., individuals born between 1957 and 1964) held an average of 10.8 different jobs between the ages of 18 and 42. To remain viable, today's workforce must continually develop new knowledge, skills, and attitudes in order to adapt to changing technological and environmental demands. Training is the classic mechanism for such skill enhancement. This chapter provides an overview of training and other developmental activities from the organizational science perspective, including mentoring and coaching. Several classic models of training are reviewed, and an overarching organizational framework delineating the key variables of the training process is presented. Several suggestions for furthering our understanding of training and other forms of development are also offered.

Key Words: Organizational learning, training, training design, training delivery, organizational development, organizational change

Dramatic changes have shaped a new organizational landscape in the last decade. Rapid technological evolution and integration, loss of stability in the employment contract between employers and employees, rapidly flattening hierarchies and omnipresent restructuring, as well as increasing organizational diversity have greatly impacted the way that organizations think about learning, training, and career development (Higgins & Kram, 2001). Globalization has also pushed organizations and the employees comprising them to be flexible and adaptable at an unparalleled speed. These changes have led to unprecedented emphasis on the vital role of continuous learning and employee development in organizational success. Furthermore, employees with cultural, technological, and interpersonal skills, who are also adaptable and flexible, have become a commodity (Manpower, 2008). Therefore, organizations recognize, now more than ever, the role that

continuous learning and development play in competitive advantage.

The American Society for Training and Development's (ASTD) 2008 "State of the Industry" report, for example, demonstrated that the average dollar amount spent on employee learning and development increased to $1,103 in 2007, a 6 percent increase from 2006 (ASTD, 2008). Additionally, winners of ASTD's BEST award, those organizations demonstrating enterprise-wide success as a result of employee learning and development, spent an average of $1,451 per employee in 2007. Such spending increases indicate organizational recognition of training and development as a competitive advantage in today's globalized economy. Organizations making investments in their human capital through properly designed training and development systems reap the rewards of a skilled and prepared workforce—including optimized productivity, better service quality, fewer errors, and improved safety, as well as higher morale, job satisfaction, commitment, and teamwork. For example, an analysis of ASTD's training database confirmed that firms which spent more than average on employee learning and development have total stockholder returns (change in stock price plus any dividends issued in a given year) nearly 86% higher compared to firms spending less than average (Bassi, Ludwig, McMurrer, & Buren, 2002). Training has also been linked with employee creativity and innovation (Bauernschuster, Falck, & Heblich, 2008); vital components of organizational competitive advantage (Aghion, Bloom, Blundell, Griffith, & Howitt, 2005). Conversely, an underdeveloped workforce can negatively impact organizational outcomes, raising costs due to legal fees (e.g., Goldman, 2000) and errors (e.g., Beaman, Waldmann, & Krueger, 2005), as well as negatively impacting leadership succession and impeding the development of intellectual capital (e.g., Mayo, 2000).

While the specific purpose and content of organizational training and development initiatives vary widely (e.g., error reduction and safety improvement, team training, leadership development, product quality, innovation, decision making, etc.), the overarching goal is to create the highest quality workforce possible in order to produce goods and services valuable to customers. To ensure high quality and effectiveness, however, the science of training and learning must form the foundation for the design, development, implementation, and evaluation of such initiatives as noted in previous reviews (see Aguinis & Kraiger, 2009; Kraiger, 2003; Salas & Cannon-Bowers, 2001; Tannenbaum & Yukl, 1992). Efforts dedicated to understanding how, when, and why training is effective have broadened our understanding of workplace learning and development. No longer is training a place to which employees are "sent" for the day, nor is it a particular curriculum or particular strategy (Salas & Cannon-Bowers, 2000). The increase in our scientific understanding of training developed over the past several decades has fed a growing evidence base of characteristics, processes, and other factors underlying training effectiveness.

The purpose of the current chapter is to provide an overview of the science of training (Salas & Cannon-Bowers, 2001; Tannenbaum & Yukl, 1992) and to present several open questions to help guide further scientific development. To this end, we first define training, provide an overview of several models of training, and present the framework through which this chapter will be organized. Our purpose is not to present a new framework or

model of training, however. We utilize an updated version of the model of training effectiveness originally proposed by Tannenbaum and colleagues (1993; Cannon-Bowers, Salas, Tannenbaum, & Mathieu, 1995) to provide structure to the review and synthesis of the existent literature. Found in Figure 11.1, each component of this model will be discussed in greater detail in subsequent sections. It should be noted that each component of the model is annotated with a number linking it to relevant in-text discussion. Throughout these sections, relevant research questions will also be posed, with the hope of continuing to further the science and our understanding.

In addition to covering factors relevant to training planning, design, implementation, and transfer, we will also discuss several learning and development methodologies above and beyond traditional training, such as e-learning, coaching, and mentoring. We will then look at training through the lens of organizational change, specifically defining and discussing the notion of learning organizations and the role of training and development in organizational change initiatives and culture change. In closing, we draw conclusions regarding the current state of training in the organizational literature. We offer open questions and suggestions designed to feed future research and knowledge development, thus helping scientists and practitioners to continue to generate and apply scientifically derived principles, methodologies, and tools to optimize organizational learning, training, and development.

Definitions: Learning, Training, and Development

The concepts of learning, training, and development are integrally intertwined. Though there are many definitions of learning available in the literature, they traditionally center upon learning as a relatively permanent change in behavior as a result of experience or practice (e.g., Atkinson, Atkinson, Smith, Bem, & Nolen-Hoeksema, 1996; Myers, 2004). A separate school of thought, however, contradicts this notion that learning must result in behavior change. Huber (1991) summarizes this perspective in his stipulation that "an entity learns, if, through its processing of information, the *range of its potential behaviors* is changed" (p. 89).

Supporting this more recent conceptualization, available evidence suggests that a fraction of knowledge, skills, and abilities (KSAs) learned in training actually transfer to the work environment. That is, trainees can declaratively demonstrate increases in

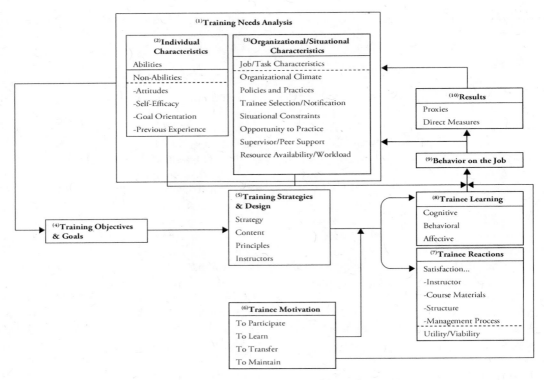

Figure 11.1 Organizational Framework for the Chapter, Founded upon the Model of Training Effectiveness Developed by Cannon-Bowers, Salas, Tannenbaum, and Mathieu (1995)

their knowledge (i.e., tell you, for example, what the correct strategy for handling interpersonal conflict is); however, they have a much harder time translating this knowledge into behavior on the job (i.e., they may not use this strategy in the heat of the moment, when actually dealing with interpersonal conflict). For example, meta-analyses of various training strategies continually demonstrate larger effect sizes for learning outcomes compared to behavioral outcomes (e.g., Arthur, Bennett, Edens, & Bell, 2003; Salas, DiazGranados, et al., 2008; Salas, Nichols, & Driskell, 2007; Sitzmann, Kraiger, Stewart, & Wisher, 2006). Furthermore, Alliger and colleagues (1997) found low weighted correlations between .08 and .18 between learning and behavior on the job in their meta-analysis of the relationship among various training evaluation outcomes. Such results underscore the importance of the systems view of training suggested by Goldstein (1993; Goldstein & Ford, 2002), which argues that training alone does not ensure behavior change because it does not occur in a vacuum. Learning therefore is a process that continues outside the classroom. As Ruark (2009) notes, "Knowledge continues to expand and alter as we...make new discoveries, test what we think we know, and learn more about the situational contexts in which current knowledge is applied" (p. 53). Trainees must actually take the knowledge, skills, and abilities learned in training and mold them into their own "working" versions in order to apply them on the job. Therefore, some KSAs may not be transferred to the actual working environment, especially if this environment is non-supportive and is racked with barriers, as discussed in greater detail in later sections of this chapter. Additionally, as indicated by Aguinis and Kraiger (2009) the effects of training and development initiatives today reach far beyond the individual and even beyond the organization itself, further expanding the range of this systems viewpoint.

The definition of learning has also been expanded in an attempt to parse apart learning outcomes from learning processes (see Huber, 1991; Kraiger, Ford, & Salas, 1993; Lachman, 1997) and the role of the learner in the learning process has become a more central focus (Bell & Kozlowski, 2008; Simpson & Bourner, 2007). Organizationally speaking, learning can occur through multiple vehicles including training and other developmental interactions such as coaching and mentoring. Specifically, training is defined as:

> ...the systematic acquisition of knowledge (i.e., what we *need to know*), skills (i.e., what we *need to do*), and attitudes (i.e., what we need to *feel*) (KSAs) that together lead to improved performance in a particular environment. (Salas, Wilson, Priest, & Guthrie, 2006, p. 473)

From an organizational perspective, the aim of training may be to achieve cognitive, behavioral, and/or attitudinal change through concrete understanding and practical application of job-relevant competencies. Instructional strategies must be aligned with the specific needs of the organization, its employees, and other key stakeholders to achieve this aim (Aguinis & Kraiger, 2009; Brown & Gerhardt, 2006; Salas & Cannon-Bowers, 2001). Furthermore, training is not simply a location where people go, a particular curriculum that is "applied," or a single day event (Salas & Cannon-Bowers, 2000). Additionally, training is not synonymous with the simulation or other technology utilized as the delivery vehicle. Effective training allows trainees to learn, practice, and receive constructive feedback, while also preparing them to encounter and overcome barriers to applying their training on the job. This means that while technology can form the basis for effective training, it must be supplemented with theoretically sound instructional strategies (e.g., diagnostic performance measurement and feedback) in order to enhance performance.

In addition to training, learning in organizations can occur through other developmentally focused mechanisms. The term *developmental interaction* has been utilized to describe interactions between two or more people with the goal of personal or professional development (D'Abate, Eddy, & Tannenbaum, 2003). These interactions tend to be long-term focused and can include a wide range of KSAs. Our goal is not to detail all of the interactions that fall under this broad umbrella; however, we discuss several, such as mentoring and coaching, in later sections of this chapter. For a detailed treatment of these constructs, we refer readers to D'Abate et al. (2003), as well as Eby (chapter 19 of this handbook), Allen, Eby, Poteet, Lentz, and Lima (2004), and Passmore and Gibbes (2007).

Since Campbell's (1971) review and indictment of the literature related to training and organizational learning as "volumous, non-empirical, non-theoretical, poorly written, and dull" (p. 565), the scientific and theoretical literature on organizational

training and learning has exploded. The good news is that more comprehensive, thorough frameworks and models have evolved, furthering our understanding of the design, delivery, and outcomes of organizational training endeavors (Salas & Cannon-Bowers, 2001). In the subsequent section, we provide a review of several models that have helped to increase our understanding of the mechanisms of learning, training, and development in organizations.

The Science of Learning, Training, and Development
A Foundation in the Science of Learning

Conceptualizing training and development begins with a foundation in theories of learning and instructional design. Classic models of learning, such as the three-phase model proposed by Fitts and Posner (1967), conceptualize learning as a sequential progression of skill acquisition and refinement. This model postulates that skill development begins with a cognitive phase, in which the learner identifies the key components of the skill and forms a mental conceptualization of the skill in action. In the cognitive phase, the learner knows all of the pieces necessary for the skill, but cannot put them together. In the subsequent acquisition phase, the learner links the components together, leveraging practice and feedback to learn the most effective and efficient combination. Unlike the acquisition phase, in which the learner must actively think about linking the skill components together, the final autonomous phase is reached when the learner is able to perform the skill automatically, with little conscious attention. Fitts and Posner's (1967) work has been extremely influential in work on procedural skill acquisition and the impact of practice on skill acquisition.

The foundational work of Knowles and colleagues (Knowles, 1973, 1984; Knowles et al., 2005) on adult learning recognized five significant factors impacting adult learning, differentiating adults' learning styles from those of children. Knowles (1984) first assumption was that adults are autonomous and self-directed, meaning that learning experiences must actively involve them in the learning process, thus changing the role of trainers and teachers toward facilitation. Second, adults come into the learning environment with a reservoir of knowledge and experience. Knowles (1984) argued that successful adult education makes connections between new material and these previous experiences. Empirical work on training has demonstrated the effectiveness of this strategy. For example, in a sample of pilots, Smith-Jentsch, Jentsch, Payne, and Salas (1996) found that negative pre-training experiences related to training content were linearly related to performance in a post-training simulation session. Knowles's (1984) third assumption is related to readiness to learn—specifically, that adults' readiness to learn is related to the developmental tasks of their social roles. This means that adults are goal-oriented, often knowing what they want to attain from the learning experience. Fourth, adult orientation to learning is problem focused versus subject focused; that is, adults focus on the relevancy and immediacy with which they can apply the knowledge, skills, or attitudes targeted in the learning experience. Finally, adult motivation to learn is assumed to be mainly internally driven. This perspective changed the lens through which learning was viewed in models of training and development, opening the black box of "learning" in such models to uncover some of the key mechanisms and assumptions.

Other models (e.g., Jarvis, 1987; Kolb, 1984; Kolb, Boyatzis, & Mainemalis, 2001; Mezirow, 1978, 1981, 2000) also emphasize the impact of experience in the adult learning process. Mezirow (2000), for example, frames learning as a process of transforming the learner's frames of references (e.g., mind-sets, meaning perspectives). The specific steps in this transformative process are outlined in Table 11.1. Additionally, the theory differentiates between instrumental learning (i.e., task-oriented learning) and communicative learning (i.e., socially oriented learning) and outlines four specific ways in which learning occurs: expansion of existing meaning; creation of new meanings that complement existing frames of reference; transformation

Table 11.1 The 10-step Transformative Learning Process Outlined by Mezirow (2000)

Process for Transformative Learning

Experience a disorienting dilemma.
Undergo self examination.
Conduct a deep assessment of personal role assumptions and alienation created by new roles.
Share and analyze personal discontent and similar experiences with others.
Explore options for new ways of acting.
Build competence and self-confidence in new roles.
Plan a course of action.
Acquire knowledge and skills for action.
Try new roles and assess feedback.
Reintegrate into society with a new perspective.

of point of view; and transformation of point of reference. Transformation of point of reference refers to changes in "other"-related perspectives; point of view transformation refers to changes in deeper level, usually more "self"-focused perspectives. Critical to Mezirow's (2000) theory are the concepts of reflection, critique, and analysis of one's cognitive and affective assumptions, and his conceptualization of discourse—specialized use of dialogue with the intent of examining supporting/non-supporting evidence and arguments in order to examine alternative perspectives. While criticisms of Mezirow's (2000) theory posit that it has an overly individualized focus (e.g., Clark & Wilson, 1991), such theories of adult learning helped to formulate practical instructional strategies and have helped drive models of training and training transfer.

More focused theories have integrated learning theory with the instructional design perspective. Elaborating on the idea of the phase learning–based model is Anderson's (1996) ACT* model, which builds on the work of Fitts and Posner (1967) to view learning as a series of stages in which different types of learning are important during each stage. The ACT* model emphasizes three phases of learning: the declarative phase, which focuses on gaining factual knowledge about a task, with the emphasis being memory; the knowledge compilation phase, which focuses on actually knowing how to do a task; and, lastly, procedural knowledge, or actual acquisition of the skill. Evidence has been found to support this model, particularly in relation to goal-setting interventions (Kanfer & Ackerman, 1989).

Self-regulated learning has also been emphasized within the broader context of informal social learning and has been closely identified with the notion of intrinsically motivated learning (Kozlowski, Gully, et al., 2001; Schunk & Zimmerman, 2008). Specifically related to learning, self-regulation theory posits that effective learners engage in meta-cognitive processes such as goal setting, self-monitoring, and strategy to master these self-imposed learning objectives (Lajoie, 2008). Couched in the early work on meta-cognition (e.g., Flavell, 1976), empirical investigations suggest that the goal-setting and monitoring components of self-regulation may account for much of its effectiveness (Azevedo, 2005; Kozlowski, Gully, et al., 2001). Additionally, training or other developmental techniques can focus on optimizing self-regulation skills themselves in order to facilitate acquisition of other KSAs at a later point. In this sense, self-regulation can be conceptualized as a meta-competency, a broad, overarching competency area that facilitates the acquisition and implementation of other, more specific competencies (Brown, 1993).

Together, these foundational theories underscore that effective, valid training is heavily frontloaded; that is, several key factors are important to consider before training has even been developed and conceptualized. In the next section we provide an overview of these factors and processes and suggest potential areas for future research.

Theoretical Underpinnings of Training: Modeling Training Transfer

The goal of training and development endeavors is to change behavior on the job; therefore, most models of training effectiveness focus on factors related to training transfer. Models of training transfer tend to focus on three main categories of variables: (a) individual difference factors and relevant pre-training experience, which impact the degree of learning achieved; (b) activities and instructional strategies that occur during training; and (c) environmental factors that impact transfer of training to the actual job environment. However, the models vary in scope from narrow to broad conceptualizations of training and the factors that impact transfer.

Goldstein's (1986) instructional systems design (ISD) model of training, for example, narrowly focuses on the steps within the training process, their outcomes, and the recursive relationship in which training outcomes feed back into needs analysis. The ISD model focuses on the training program itself, the actual instructional process, and validity of the program (see Figure 11.2). Specifically, the model begins with a training needs analysis (discussed in greater detail in subsequent sections), which underlies the development of instructional objectives and design decisions. Specific criteria are then developed to evaluate training outcomes. Most importantly, Goldstein's (1986) model highlights several components of training-related validity through which evaluation can occur, including training validity (i.e., do trainees gain knowledge/skills during training?), transfer validity (i.e., are the KSAs learned in training translated on the job into enhanced performance?), intraorganizational validity (i.e., does training produce similar results with new training classes over time?), and interorganizational validity

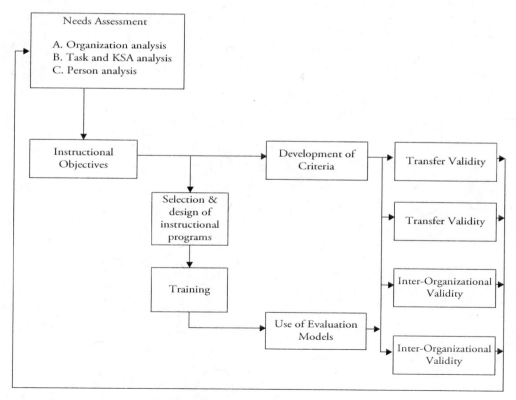

Figure 11.2 Goldstein's (1986) Instructional Systems Design Model of Training

(i.e., will a training program validated in one organization be successful in another?).

Incorporating a broader focus, Baldwin and Ford's (1988) classic model considers factors beyond training design that impact transfer. Utilizing an input-process-output framework to stipulate the inputs and outputs of training, this model focused heavily on three classes of training inputs (see Figure 11.3): individual characteristics, training design, and the work environment. The model stipulates that all three impact the training outcomes of learning and retention, while individual and environmental factors also directly impact training transfer.

Further developing this model, Thayer and Teachout (1995; see Figure 11.4) stipulated seven pre-training variables, supported by the literature, which indirectly influence transfer through the learning process. Specifically, these variables include: (a) reactions to previous training, (b) previous knowledge and skills, (c) pre-training self-efficacy, (d) ability, (e) locus of control, (f) job involvement, and (g) career/job attitudes. Self-efficacy, for example, is discussed as both an antecedent and outcome of training; that is, pre-training levels of self-efficacy can enhance (or hinder) learning, and learning, in turn, affects post-training self-efficacy. The main contribution of this model, however, was its consideration of specific transfer-enhancing training activities and the integration of the notion that organizational climate impacts transfer. For example, Thayer and Teachout (1995) suggest several in-training strategies supported by the training, adult learning, and cognitions literatures to enhance learning and transfer including: using distributed practice high in cognitive fidelity (Brannick, Prince, & Salas, 2005), over-learning (Rohrer, Taylor, Pasher, Wixted, & Cepeda, 2004), goal setting (Locke &Latham, 2002), relapse prevention (Burke & Baldwin, 1999), and self-monitoring cues (Gist, Bavetta, & Stevens, 1990; Gist, Stevens, & Bavetta, 1991). Additionally, their model integrates the conceptualization of transfer climate developed by Rouiller and Goldstein (1993)—breaking down organizational climate for transfer into cues related to trained behavior (e.g., goal cues, social cues) and consequences for using trained behaviors on the job (e.g., reinforcement, punishment).

Kozlowski and Salas (1997) expanded to a multilevel perspective in their model of training implementation and transfer (see Figure 11.5). Though the overall focus of this model narrows generally to the training process itself, similar to Goldstein's (1986) ISD theory, it significantly broadens our understanding of the process by unpacking the multilevel factors impacting training transfer. By considering relevant factors at the individual, team, and organizational levels, this model embodies the systems view of training. In addition to this multilevel theme, the model has two additional focal themes: content and congruence. In terms of

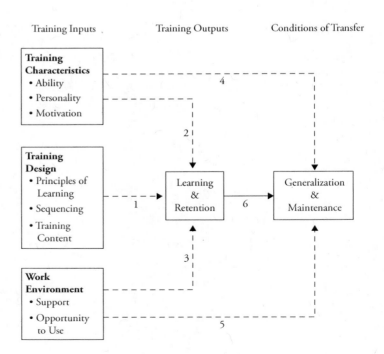

Figure 11.3 Model of Training Developed by Baldwin and Ford (1988)

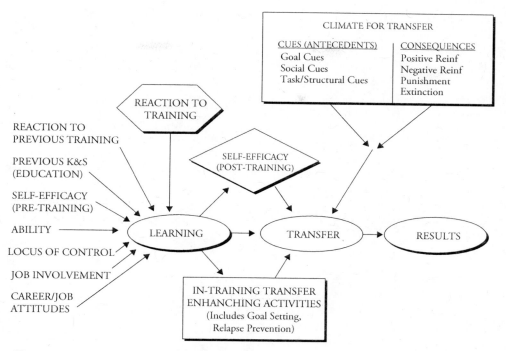

Figure 11.4 Model of Training Transfer Developed by Thayer and Teachout (1995)

content, Kozlowski and Salas (1997) differentiate between techno-structural factors (e.g., individual KSAs, task interdependence, organizational goals/ resources) and enabling processes (e.g., individual social/interpersonal skills, team coordination, organizational culture/climate). Finally, the key to the model lies in the theme of congruence. Kozlowski and colleagues (Kozlowski & Salas, 1997; Kozlowski et al., 2000) argue that alignment of the critical factors and processes among all three levels is vital for training effectiveness. It is through alignment both within and between levels that trained knowledge, skills, and attitudes can permeate to the actual work environment. Overall, this model and corresponding propositions embodied the shift in the scientific conceptualization of training by addressing the reciprocal interplay of variables at various levels and the impact of congruence between these factors.

More recent work has also focused on adaptive transfer, that is, when trainees utilize the KSAs learned in training to solve a completely novel problem or apply the skills learned in training to a completely novel situation or task (Ivancic & Hesketh, 2000). For example, Kozlowski and colleagues (1999; Bell & Kozlowski, 2008; Kozlowski, Toney, et al., 2001) present a model for integrated-embedded training systems designed to enhance

adaptability. Their model,focuses on training components and strategies that facilitate self-regulation and, ergo, retention and adaptation. A detailed review of the adaptive training and transfer literature can be found in Bell and Kozlowski (2009).

While our intention is not to present a new model of training, a revised version of the comprehensive model of training originally proposed Tannenbaum and colleagues (1993; Cannon-Bowers et al., 1995) is used as an organizational framework for the remainder of this chapter (see Figure 11.1). This model integrates the multilevel perspective and a unique process-oriented, longitudinal approach in the consideration of those factors important before, during, and after training. Additionally, it integrates Kirkpatrick's (1976) framework for training evaluation (discussed in greater detail later in this chapter) and explicitly includes trainee attitudes, motivation, and expectations. The comprehensive nature of this model lays a foundation for the discussion of the science of training; therefore, we utilize it as a basis for the organizational framework for this chapter.

We begin with those factors and processes relevant to the planning, design, and development of training, followed by a discussion of instructional strategies and other considerations relevant during training itself. Finally, we cover training evaluation

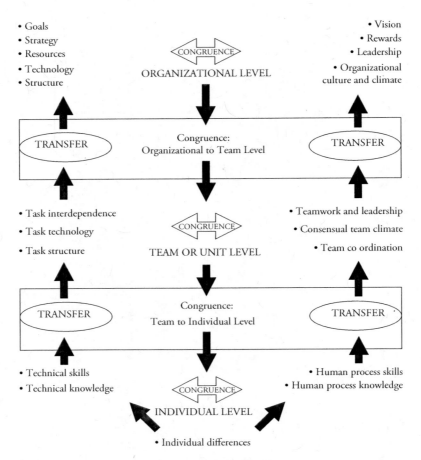

Figure 11.5 Multilevel Model of Training Transfer by Kozlowski and Salas (1997)

and the feedback loops that exist among evaluation outcomes and initial design factors. Each box in the model is annotated with a number linking it to relevant in-text discussion.

Training Antecedents: Training Needs Analysis and Consideration of Multilevel Factors

To develop training that addresses important organizational objectives in a strategic and effective manner, the science of training has demonstrated training needs analysis as a vital first step in the training process. In this section we begin with a discussion of the components of training needs analysis, followed by a deeper examination of the state of science regarding individual, team, and organizational antecedents. Numbers appearing next to headings in subsequent sections map back to the chapter framework presented in Figure 11.1.

Training Needs Analysis[1]

A thorough needs analysis includes the answers to three key questions: (a) what training is needed, (b) where training is needed, and (c) who needs to be trained (Goldstein & Ford, 2002). In providing this essential targeting information, the needs analysis process is considered the indispensable starting point for training program development. Nearly all models of training and instructional design include needs analyses in their first step (e.g., Cannon-Bowers et al., 1995; Dick & Carey, 1996; Molenda, Pershing, & Reigeluth, 1996).

The purpose of the needs analysis process is to (a) specify specific learning objectives, (b) provide vital insight regarding how training should be designed and delivered, and (c) develop training effectiveness criteria (Salas, Wilson, et al., 2006). To achieve these goals, need analysis is comprised of three subanalyses: organizational analysis, job/task analysis, and person analysis. The components and steps of each are discussed next.

ORGANIZATIONAL ANALYSIS

Organizational analysis is the first step in conducting a training needs analysis. The goal of this system-wide analysis is to determine the state of environmental conditions and the availability of resources that may impact training delivery and transfer of trained skills into the real job setting (Goldstein, 1993). Even the most well-designed and implemented training programs may fail due to organizational barriers and constraints; however, organizational analysis allows such factors to be identified and potentially amended prior to training. Such analyses must include explicit consideration of organizational goals, norms, culture and climate, policies, resources available, potential barriers and constraints, and support for training transfer and their level of congruence with training objectives (Salas & Cannon-Bowers, 2001). Cannon-Bowers and colleagues (1995) also note that organizational factors, such as culture, history, and policies, can have an indirect impact on training effectiveness by influencing trainee expectations and motivation.

Organizational analysis is intimately related to training transfer. Models of training transfer, such as those discussed previously, provide a framework for conducting such analysis, as they focus on factors generally exterior to the training program itself that may exert significant impact on the trainees' abilities to implement and utilize trained skills in their daily working environment. These models tend to emphasize the role of organizational culture and climate in transfer; ergo, detailed analyses of these factors are a vital first step in organizational analysis. For example, Rouiller and Goldstein (1993) proposed and tested a conceptual framework for measuring transfer climate, breaking the construct down into two types of workplace cues and eight distinct dimensions. *Situation cues* relate to the salience of opportunities to utilize trained skills on the job and were proposed to include four dimensions: goal cues, social cues, task cues, and self-control cues. *Consequence cues*, meanwhile, relate to the ramifications and feedback that trainees receive when utilizing trained competencies on the job. Again, this cue is also conceptualized by four dimensions: positive feedback, negative feedback, no feedback, and punishment.

Overall organizational analysis involves thinking about and examining those pre-, during-, and post-training factors that will enhance or inhibit the attainment of training objectives and on-the-job use of trained competencies. Analyzing these factors in the beginning ensures that the strongest foundation possible is laid to support training success.

JOB/TASK ANALYSIS

Analysis of the job and the actual tasks involved in the job comprise the second step in training needs analysis. The purpose of this second step is to determine and define the characteristics of the tasks being trained in order to formulate clear, comprehensive training objectives. It is vital to note that the end product of a job analysis results is a description of the job itself, not any individual worker filling the job at any particular time (Goldstein, 1991). While we provide a general overview in this section, comprehensive treatments of job/task analysis and its methodologies can be found in both Goldstein (1991) and Brannick and Levine (2002).

Generally, a job analysis comprises three main steps. The first entails clarifying the job description itself. This involves gathering information regarding the relevant work functions of the job and necessary resources. While behaviorally based methods of task analysis (e.g., observation of on-the-job behaviors) offer a means to determine overt job-relevant behavioral tasks, cognitive task analysis (CTA) has been developed as a means to establish understanding of the cognitive-processing requirements and the required implicit knowledge of a given job (Hoffman & Militello, 2008; Schraagen, Chipman, & Shalin, 2000). Various methods are included under the umbrella of CTA, including structure interviews with both job experts and non-experts, critical incident and critical decision techniques, and concept mapping (Crandall, Klein, & Hoffman, 2006; Roth, 2008). A practically based "how-to" overview of CTA can be found in Crandall and colleagues (2006).

Another resource for developing task statements and determining underlying competencies and skills is the O*NET online occupational network database (www.online.onetcenter.org) developed by the U.S. Department of Labor. Each occupational listing in the O*NET database is accompanied by a list of tasks and work activities, technologies utilized, relevant KSAs, related work styles and interests, and wage/employment trends compiled from the U.S. Bureau of Labor statistics. Specifically, the descriptions in O*NET are organized around the O*NET Content Model (National Center for O*NET Development, n.d.) which includes six major categories of information about each occupation: (a) worker characteristics (e.g., occupational interests, work style), (b) worker requirements (e.g., KSAs), (c) experience requirements (e.g., training, licensing), (d) occupation-specific information (e.g., tasks, tools/technology), (e) workforce characteristics (e.g., labor market, occupational outlook), and (f) occupational requirements (e.g., work activities, organizational context).

The job description, as well as interviews with incumbents, supervisors, and information gathered from other sources is then used to specify in detail the actual tasks comprising the job and the conditions under which these tasks are completed. Specific statements are generated to describe the details of each task. Though there are several variants on the "rules" of writing task statements (e.g., Fine & Cronshaw, 1999; Prien, Goldstein, & Macey, 1987; U.S. Department of Labor, 1972), the literature tends to agree that they should be formulated in present tense, should be very short, should utilize functional verbs, and should describe, at the least, the "who, what, and why" of each task. For example, Fine and Cronshaw (1999) describe the structure of task statements in terms of answers to the specific set of questions presented in Table 11.2.

Once task statements are developed, they are organized into clusters, as defined by subject matter experts (SMEs), and/or using statistical techniques such as factor analysis of SME responses to ratings of the task statements on various dimensions, such as the dimensions of criticality, frequency, difficulty, and so on, suggested by Gael (1983). The final phase of job analysis is to determine the competencies (knowledge, skills, and abilities) associated with each cluster and task. Defining the necessary KSAs and linking them with tasks can be the most difficult step of job analysis; however,

Table 11.2 Fine and Cronshaw's (1999) List of Questions Suggested for Writing and Formatting Task Statements

Question
Who? (subject)
Performs what action? (action verb)
To whom or what? (verb object)
Upon what instructions or sources of information? (phrase)
Using what tools, equipment, or work aids? (phrase)
To produce/achieve what output? (in order to…)

Adapted from Fine & Cronshaw (1999, p. 50).

in the context of training, it is also the most vital step. Not only does this drive the formulation of training objectives, but during this step trainers can also determine if they will utilize actual job tasks for training purposes or need to rely on simulation or other proxies during training (Goldstein, 1991).

PERSON ANALYSIS

The purpose of the final stage of a training needs analysis, the person analysis, is to determine who needs to be trained and what kind of training and instruction these specific individuals need (Goldstein, 1991; Tannenbaum & Yukl, 1992). Person analysis ensures that the right people receive the right training, targeting the KSAs they need.

The end product of this needs analysis process should be a set of clearly defined, yet concise, training objectives (i.e., what are the goals of training?), learning objectives (i.e., desired cognitive, affective, and behavioral outcomes), and enabling objectives (i.e., what must be done to enable transfer and skill use on the job?). Most importantly, this set of objectives should also be defined so that they are clearly measurable.

Now that the process of training needs analysis has been described, we delve deeper into the potential content areas to be considered during such analysis. In terms of our organizational framework, this includes discussion of individual trainee characteristics, organizational characteristics, trainee motivation, and expectations.

Individual Trainee Characteristics[2]

Characteristics of individual trainees must be considered during both pre-training planning and post-training, as they exert significant impact on learning and behavioral outcomes. Cognitive ability, self-efficacy, goal orientation, locus of control, organizational commitment, expectations, and motivation have all been conceptualized as important factors influencing training effectiveness. These factors form the foundation of learning, upon which an effective training design and transfer environment must be overlaid in order to facilitate the learning and application of new job skills.

COGNITIVE ABILITY

The effects of cognitive ability, known as g or general ability, have been studied in regard to training through the lens of knowledge acquisition. Early meta-analytic work by Hunter (1983) demonstrated that cognitive ability exerts causal influence on both objective work sample performance and supervisory rated job performance via its impact on job knowledge acquisition. This notion has been supported in other models and subsequent empirical validation tests (e.g., Borman, 1991; Schmidt, Hunter, & Outerbridge, 1986). These results have been extended by investigating the impact of g on training performance. Specific to training, cognitive ability has been found to influence job knowledge attainment, especially knowledge attained during the early stages of training. For example, Ree, Carretta, and Teachout (1995) conducted path analysis using longitudinal data from military pilots completing a 53-week aviation training course. Their results showed that cognitive ability was most strongly related to job knowledge.

In addition to traditional conceptualizations of cognitive ability, Salas and Cannon-Bowers (2001) argue that training developers and researchers should also consider the impact of factors such as practical intelligence, tacit knowledge, and adaptability on both traditional training and newer forms of training, such as simulations-based training, computer-based training, and on-the job training. For example, cognitive flexibility (Cañas, Quesada, Antoli, & Fajardo, 2003), defined as the ability to adapt cognitive processes and strategies in response to environmental or situational changes, may be an important predictor to consider, especially in training programs focused on problem solving, decision making, and creativity. Cognitively flexible individuals are able to actively break away from entrenched ways of thinking and redefine problems, enabling them to learn and create new ideas in complex and ill-structured environments (Spiro & Jehng, 1990). The validity of cognitive ability and related concepts as predictors of training transfer, however, will vary depending on the nature of the job itself. Many jobs require competencies beyond such abilities, such as psychomotor demands and motivational issues.

ATTITUDES

The attitudes that an individual holds regarding his or her organization and the training itself can impact motivation, approach, and involvement in training. Attitudes play a role both as training antecedents and outcomes of training. Two attitudes that have been examined include job involvement and organizational commitment.

Job involvement is defined as the degree to which one's job is "central to the individual and their identity" (Blau, 1985, p. 34). Theoretically, individuals who value their job as part of their personal character and sense of self should value the outcomes related to participation in training and use of trained KSAs (Colquitt, LePine, & Noe, 2000; Mathieu & Martineau, 1997; Mathieu, Tannenbaum, & Salas, 1992). Empirically, the literature has demonstrated mixed results. Clark (1990) found that job involvement impacts training outcomes through its effects on pre-training motivation, and earlier work by Noe and Schmitt (1986) also found a significant relationship between job involvement and pre-training motivation ($r = .25$). The path analysis conducted by Noe and Schmitt (1986), however, did not support the link between job involvement and pre-training motivation when the hypothesized model was tested. Meta-analytic findings have also not demonstrated that same support for this link as found in such singular samples. For example, while Colquitt et al. (2000) found a significant relationship between motivation to learn and job involvement (corrected $r = .20$), path analysis results did not support job involvement as a predictor of motivation to learn (beta = .06). Additionally, their results did not indicate any significant relationships between job involvement and learning outcomes.

Another relevant attitude to consider is organizational commitment. Cannon-Bowers and colleagues (1995) suggest that organization commitment may be related to training performance because committed individuals may: (a) be more likely to perceive that training is beneficial, (b) be willing to put forth greater effort to solidify their success in training, and (c) have a stronger desire to perform well in training in order to solidify their position within the organization itself. Organizational commitment has shown significant relationships with motivation to learn during training ($r = .53$; Tannenbaum, Mathieu, Salas, & Cannon-Bowers, 1991) and also to be positively related to training generalization (Tesluk, Farr, Mathieu, & Vance, 1995).

SELF-EFFICACY

Self-efficacy (SE), or beliefs in one's own abilities (Bandura, 1977; Chen, Gully, & Eden, 2001), is another individual characteristic that has been found to be intimately related to learning and performance. A topic of extensive empirical investigation throughout the last decade, the literature generally supports a positive relationship between self-efficacy, whether developed before or during training, learning, and performance (e.g., Gist, Stevens, & Bavetta, 1991; Mathieu, Martineau, & Tannenbaum, 1993; Stajkovic & Luthans, 1998; Tracey, Hinkin, Tannenbaum, & Mathieu, 2001). Specifically, self-efficacy has been shown to be positively related to trainee reactions, including their perceptions of training utility (Guthrie & Schwoerer, 1994; Mathieu et al., 1992), and motivation (Quiñones, 1995; Switzer, Nagy, & Mullins, 2005; Tannenbaum et al., 1991)

Furthermore, Gist and Mitchell (1992) suggest that that efficacy perceptions are malleable and that specific strategies related to training can positively impact SE. Early work by Mathieu and colleagues (1993) found support for this notion by measuring self-efficacy at multiple times throughout the course of an eight-week long training course. Specifically, the results of their structural equation model indicated that pre-training SE level predicted mid-course SE, which, in turn, predicted both trainee performance ($\beta = .37$) and reactions to training ($\beta = .2$). In this sense, self-efficacy came to be viewed as both an input and output of the training process. Moreover, meta-analytic results by Colquitt et al. (2000) found significant relationships between pre-training SE and motivation to learn (corrected $r = .42$), skill acquisition (corrected $r = .32$), and transfer (corrected $r = .47$). However, others have argued for SE as a product of training compared to an important antecedent. For example, Heggestad and Kanfer (2005) found that when past performance during training was considered SE only accounted for 2 percent of the variance in current training performance, thus lending some support to the view of SE as an output, rather than a strong predictor of training performance.

GOAL ORIENTATION

The construct of goal orientation (GO) was developed as a means for accounting for individual differences in the cognitive, affective, and behavioral reactions of individuals in achievement settings, such as training. Though various conceptualizations of goal orientation exist, the definition espoused by Dweck (1986; Dweck & Leggett, 1988) describes it as "individual differences in goal preferences in achievement situations." These early models described two major classes of goal orientations: (a) learning/mastery goal orientation, and (b) performance goal orientation. The former describes a motivation to develop competence and skill mastery; the latter describes a motivation to demonstrate competence in hopes of gaining praise and avoiding negative judgments. Vandewalle (1997) later parsed performance goal orientation into two sub-components, prove performance goal orientation and avoid performance goal orientation, resulting in a tri-dimensional model. Specifically, prove orientations are driven by a desire to prove one's competence and gain favorable judgments about it. Conversely, avoid orientations are driven to avoid the disproving of competence, in order to avoid negative judgments. Importantly, these orientations are not viewed as orthogonal (i.e., mutually exclusive) and are generally thought to be a product of both individual and situational factors. Additionally, meta-analytic results by Day, Yeo, and Radosevich (2003) supported this three-factor model, demonstrating that this model explained 7 percent more variance in academic performance then the traditional two-factor model.

Most recently, a four-factor model has also been suggested by Elliot and McGregor (2001), which breaks down learning goal orientation into mastery approach goal orientation and mastery avoid orientation. From a mastery approach orientation, competence is defined in absolute/interpersonal terms and is positively valenced. While mastery avoid orientation still defines competence in terms of absolute/interpersonal terms, competence is negatively valenced and more salient. Elliot and McGregor (2001) give the example of perfectionists who strive to make no mistakes.

While much of the study of the effects of GO in achievement situations has focused on the primary and secondary educational settings, research has implicated GO in organizational training transfer. For example, Chiaburu and Marinova (2005) investigated the relationship with skill transfer in a sample of 186 U.S. employees. Structural equation modeling analysis indicated that mastery approach orientation was significantly related to skill transfer to the job environment through the mechanism of pre-training motivation. Experimental results also support these findings. Kozlowski, Gully, et al. (2001) manipulated state goal orientation, inducing either a learning or performance goal orientation. Their results indicated that learning orientation was significantly related to post-training self-efficacy which, in turn, was related to adaptive post-training performance. Meta-analytic results (e.g., Payne, Youngcourt, & Beaubien, 2007) have supported generally positive relationships between learning GO and important outcomes such as feedback seeking, learning strategies, actual learning, and performance. Conversely, avoid performance

GO has been negatively related, and relationships with prove GO have been mixed. Additionally, trait GO, conceptualized as a more longitudinally stable individual difference, has demonstrated less strong effects compared to experimentally induced state GO. From a training perspective, such results suggest that inducing a trainee learning orientation may increase learning outcomes.

PREVIOUS EXPERIENCE

Theories of learning underscore that adults enter training—and any other learning/development experience—not as blank slates, but rather as banks of previous experiences. This previous experience is important to consider, as it has been found to impact training transfer, though results have been mixed. In general, studies that operationalized experience in terms of tenure find little to no relationship between experience and training outcomes (e.g., Gordon, Cofer, & McCullough, 1986); rather, the type of experience seems to matter. Specifically, negative pre-training experiences related to training objectives have been shown to impact training outcomes. Smith-Jentsch and colleagues (1996), for example, examined the impact of previous negative experiences in a sample of pilots undergoing assertiveness training. Negative events were coded into three categories directly related to training objectives regarding the use of assertiveness in the cockpit: (a) life-threatening events, (b) events involving flying with a captain using unsafe procedures, and (c) events in which the trainee felt pressured to take flight despite mechanical or environmental concerns. Their results demonstrated a linear relationship between the number of negative events experiences pre-training and performance in a behavioral exercise carried out one week after training. Though mediational analysis was not possible, it is suggested that these effects may be mediated by trainee motivation; that is, trainees with more negative pre-training experiences may be more motivated to attend and learn from training and, ergo, achieve greater transfer and outcomes. In support of this hypothesis, Holt and Crocker (2000) found that negative experiences moderated the impact of achievement motivation on exam performance in a sample of trainees participating in computer-use training, though the effect size was small in both models tested ($\triangle R^2 = .009$, $p < .10$ and $\triangle R^2 = .012$, $p < .05$).

Organizational Characteristics [3]

The pre-training organizational environment also indirectly affects training outcomes by impacting trainee expectations about training, motivation, and individual trainee characteristics. In addition to shaping several of the individual characteristics mentioned above (e.g., self-efficacy), organizational characteristics embody the environment into which newly acquired KSAs will need to be applied. Thus, they can moderate the transfer of learned skills on the job. The next section summarizes several of these relevant factors.

ORGANIZATIONAL CULTURE/CLIMATE

Organizational culture pervades every aspect of organizational operations—from how employees interact with one another, as well as with clients and customers, to the task strategies used to accomplish the work itself. Though there is no single uniformly accepted definition of organizational culture (e.g., Cooper, 2000; Denison, 1996; Guldenmund, 1998; Schein, 1990), the definition presented by Uttal (1983) captures the fundamental nature of the domain:

> ... shared values (what is important) and
> beliefs (how things work) that interact with
> a company's people, organizational structures
> and control systems to produce behavioral
> norms (the way we do things around here).
> (p. 68)

Specifically, culture has been conceptualized as employee behavior, attitudes, cognitions, interactions, norms, and values. Culture facilitates shared understanding of situations among organization members, making coordination and cooperation possible (Alvesson, 2002). Additionally, there are multiple aspects of an organization's culture (Guion, 1973). Furthermore, culture has been argued to impact all organizational outcomes, including training and development outcomes.

Similarly, organizational climate is defined as employee perceptions of organizational culture (Choudhry, Fang, & Mohamed, 2007). In the strict sense, the literature has dictated that using questionnaires to measure employee perceptions of culture falls under the category of climate because it lacks the ability to measure all aspects of culture, such as actual behavior, rules, and norms (Cooper, 2000).

As noted by Tannenbaum and colleagues (1993), trainees look for cues in the organizational culture regarding the degree to which training is important and valued, whether training/development is considered a punishment or reward, and whether others who are successful in the organization have attended similar training/development opportunities. In addition to peers, supervisors and leadership play key roles in the formation and transmission of culture (Burke, 1997). The literature has repeatedly demonstrated the impact of supervisory support both pre- and post-training on training outcomes. Trainees with supportive supervisors report putting more effort toward transferring KSAs that they had learned to the workplace (Cohen, 1990; Huczynski & Lewis, 1980). Additionally, such support has been linked with pre-training motivation (Facteau, Dobbins, Russell, Ladd, & Kudisch, 1995) and post-training simulation performance (Smith-Jentsch, Salas, & Brannick, 2001).

Post-training transfer climate has been found to have a strong impact upon the degree to which employee training is transferred to the job (Kraiger, 2003). Transfer climate has been found to influence trainees' ability to generalize skills acquired in training, post-training self-efficacy, and motivation to transfer (Cheng & Hampson, 2008; Rouiller & Goldstein, 1993; Tracey et al., 1995; Tziner, Haccoun, & Kadish, 1991; Xiao, 1996). Other studies have found connections between social, peer, subordinate, and supervisor support and transfer, such that the level of support predicts training transfer (Burke & Baldwin, 1999; Facteau et al., 1995; Seyler, Holton, Bates, Burnett, & Carvalho, 1998). Overall, these results imply a strong connection between the post-training environment, particularly in terms of climate, and training transfer. Organizations must therefore be aware of this fact throughout the training process and must ensure that the environment provides opportunities to apply skills and knowledge developed through training on the job.

POLICIES AND PROCEDURES

Organizational policies and procedures are two factors central to organizational culture and climate. Formal organizational policies are broad requirements set forth by management embodying expectations for various aspects of organizational membership, including job performance, dress, and on-the-job behavior (Degani & Wiener, 1997). Procedures establish the means through which employees are to adhere to the policies. For example, to adhere to regulatory guidelines, accredited U.S. hospitals have a policy requiring their surgical teams to complete a time-out—a brief review of the patient, procedure, and site of the upcoming surgical procedure—to help ensure that the correct procedure will be performed on the correct body part of the correct patient. To achieve this, many have adopted pre-surgical procedures involving a checklist listing each element to be discussed. Even

if a well-designed training program was utilized to teach employees about the policy and provide them with opportunities to practice using the checklist, issues arise when informal social elements of the organizational culture or other organizational goals run counter to either component, as has been underscored in the literature on workplace safety (e.g., Hofmann & Stetzer, 1996; Mullen, 2004). For example, subjective social norms, time pressures, or competing goals, may subversively encourage employees to deviate from formal policies or procedures. Formal policies and procedures can also be incomplete or it may be unclear when certain formal procedures are appropriate. Additionally, if employees perceive that leaders place total emphasis on organizational goals related to productivity or efficiency, they may perceive training to be related to skills less important for desirable workplace outcomes, such as promotion. Therefore, motivation to attend, learn, and transfer trained KSAs may suffer when organizational policies and procedures do not explicitly demonstrate the value of training or reinforce the use of newly learned material on the job.

TRAINEE SELECTION/NOTIFICATION

The methods in which trainees are selected and notified of training have also been found to be important factors in training effectiveness. Focal issues include voluntary participation, how training is framed, and the information that trainees receive prior to training. These issues are summarized by Quiñones and Ehrenstein (1997), who assert that trainee motivation to learn is affected by the degree to which decisions to participate in training are perceived as being fair, whether trainees have control over the decision to participate in training, and whether training is framed positively. Traditional motivational theories emphasizing the role of controllability (e.g., Pritchard & Ashwood, 2008) support the link between trainee control over their decision to participate in training and motivation to learn. Additionally, empirical work has demonstrated that trainees given a choice regarding participation report higher motivation and pre-training self-efficacy, more positive reactions to training, and demonstrate a higher degree of learning (e.g., Baldwin & Magjuka, 1997; Baldwin, Magjuka, & Loher, 1991; Hicks & Klimoski, 1987; Mathieu et al., 1993)

The way in which training is framed is another important factor. As indicated by Baldwin and Ford (1988), training can be portrayed as "punishment for past sins" (p. 119) or as an opportunity for advancing one's career. The *opportunity* frame has been found to be positively related to trainee efficacy and learning outcomes, and negatively related to anxiety (Martocchio, 1992). Drawing from the literature on social justice (e.g., Gamliel & Peer, 2006), framing may also impact trainee perceptions of justice in training selection and may, in turn, potentially affect pre-training motivation.

Tied to the way in which training is framed, the amount and type of information provided to employees also has been suggested as a key pre-training factor. Existing evidence suggests that simply providing positive information about training is not enough. Realistic previews of training that, include information regarding the difficulty, rigor, and time commitment to the program, have been more consistently linked with trainee motivation to learn (Hicks & Klimoski, 1987; Martocchio, 1992; Russ-Eft, 2002; Webster & Martocchio, 1995).

SITUATIONAL CONSTRAINTS

Several situational constraints have also been argued to impact training effectiveness, including resource availability (e.g., necessary equipment, supplies, and information), workload, and opportunities to use newly learned KSAs. Goldstein (1993) emphasized that trainee perceptions of the work environment and availability of resources impact motivation to learn and the degree to which trainees are actively able to transfer new competencies. Mathieu and colleagues (1992) also found that trainee perceptions of situational constraints in the transfer environment have negatively impacted motivation to learn. Without the tools, equipment, or resources necessary to utilize new competencies on the job, transfer and generalization become impossible.

In addition to physical and informational resources, learning and transfer also require time and energy. Therefore, an individual's (or team's) workload can help or hinder motivation to learn and transfer (Russ-Eft, 2002). Several studies have found negative relationships between workload, stress, and on-the-job skill use (Decker & Nathan, 1985). Rooney (1985), for example, examined training transfer in a sample of social caseworkers. Results implicated high caseload volume and time constraints in the failure of certain components of training to transfer into the actual work environment.

Related to the impact of workload, opportunities to use trained competencies on the job play a key role in training transfer and effectiveness (Tannenbaum & Yukl, 1992). In a study of computer skills training, Pentland (1989) found that long-term retention was related to the degree to

which trainees applied new skills immediately after training. Similar conclusions have been drawn by Seyler and colleagues (1998) and Clarke (2002). Ford, Quiñones, Sego, and Sorra (1992) found that supervisor support for training played a significant role in the provision of opportunities to perform trained competencies in a military sample. In essence, such opportunities provide vital practice needed to retain and generalize newly learned skills (Ghodsian, Bjork, & Benjamin, 1997; Schmidt & Bjork, 1992). Additionally, opportunities to apply training in varied situations lead to the generation of usable knowledge structures (i.e., mental models), which enhance performance (Satish & Streufert, 2002; Shih & Alessi, 1994).

Trainee Motivation and Expectations [6]

Individual characteristics and organizational characteristics shape trainee expectations prior to training. These pre-formed "first impressions" can exert a strong influence on training motivation. Furthermore, the degree to which these expectations are met (or unmet) has been argued as a key factor in training transfer (Feldman, 1989; Hicks & Klimoski, 1987; ; Hoiberg & Berry, 1978; Holton, 1996; Tannenbaum et al., 1991). Holton (1996) coined the term *intervention fulfillment* to describe the degree to which trainee expectations about training are met. Tannenbaum and colleagues (1991) took a unique perspective on the fulfillment of trainee expectations. They conceptualized fulfillment in a way that accounted for individual differences in valence (desirability) of various training experiences, giving the example that all trainees may expect the training to be rigorous; however, some may desire such a challenge, whereas others may not. Their results indicated that fulfillment of training expectations was related to attitudes targeted during military recruit socialization training (e.g., organizational commitment, self-efficacy) and training motivation.

MOTIVATION TO LEARN

Training motivation is defined in terms of the intensity, direction, and persistence of effort that trainees apply to learning activities before, during, and after training (Kanfer, 1991; Salas & Cannon-Bowers, 2000). As discussed in the previous section, trainee motivation to attend and learn from training is directly impacted by both individual characteristics (e.g., self-efficacy, cognitive ability, personality) and organizational factors (e.g., organizational culture/climate, feedback). Meta-analytic results by

Colquitt et al. (2000) also support training motivation as a multifaceted construct impacted by these factors. Furthermore, Latham (1989) stipulates that motivation should be considered as both an input and output of training.

In most models of training, motivation is the key mechanism through which these factors impact training outcomes, as well as the driver of training effectiveness. This theoretical foundation is supported empirically by results demonstrating that motivation is related to learning during training, completion of the training program, retention of KSAs after training, and trainee willingness to transfer skills to the actual workplace (e.g., Martocchio, 1992; Mathieu et al., 1992; Quiñones, 1995).

Transfer occurs over an extended period of time; therefore maintenance of motivation to transfer and maintenance of trained skills is important for training effectiveness. Empirical evidence shows that training motivation decreases over time (Tannenbaum et al., 1991). It has been argued, however, that a critical period for transfer occurs immediately following training (e.g., Baldwin & Ford, 1988). As pointed out by Marx (1982), this period is when errors in use of new KSAs may occur; therefore opportunities to practice with feedback and reinforcement by management during this time play vital roles in prolonged skill use. Axtell, Maitlis, and Yearta (1997) found motivation to transfer related to trainee ratings of transfer at both one month and one year after a training course. In recognition that motivation wanes over time, methods have been developed to enhance post-training motivation and to prolong transfer. These are discussed in greater detail in the later section on maintenance interventions.

During Training: Instructional Strategies and Design [5]

The information yielded in training needs analysis plays a vital role in training and learning for organizations, but the process does not simply stop at this point. Moving from training antecedents into training design, there are many elements that are key to the successful development of instructional systems. In the following section, we review training content, strategies, and principles that may impact training design and learning in organizations, as modeled in Figure 11.1. Furthermore, we will highlight both individual and organizational characteristics that may impact training design. Finally, we will address future needs that must be addressed to ensure the development of successful instructional strategies and design.

Training Content: Developing Training Objectives and Determining Targeted Competencies

The development of training objectives ends the needs assessment phase and moves into the training design phase of work instructional systems. Training objectives are defined as precise statements which detail a desired behavioral expectation that is conducted to a particular performance standard under certain conditions (Goldstein & Ford, 2002). These objectives reflect training needs and a standard of performance that makes it clear when and how learning can be demonstrated. According to Noe (2008), training objectives have three components: (a) a statement of what the employee is expected to do, (b) a statement of the acceptable quality or level of performance, and (c) a statement of the conditions under which the trainee is expected to perform the desired outcome.

Training objectives are the result of identifying tasks and their necessary KSAs, identified during needs analysis (Goldstein & Ford, 2002). Given a particular task that requires a specific set of KSAs, objectives should identify the behaviors required in order to successfully accomplish this task. Furthermore, the objective should identify any necessary resources needed to complete the specific behaviors. Training objectives should also identify any conditions under which the behavior is expected to occur, including conditions of the physical work setting, mental stresses, or equipment failures (Noe, 2002). Additionally, objectives may also identify ineffective behaviors that do not lead to successful task completion.

Within a training program, there are typically different types of objectives (Noe, 2002). These objectives include program objectives, which are broad statements that summarize the general purpose of the training. Course (or lesson) objectives are a second type of objective identified, and are related to the goals of a specific course or lesson within a program of training. Once these objectives are developed, they must be assigned a sequence in the instructional design such that prerequisite knowledge is acquired before more complex information is introduced (Gagne, Briggs, & Wager, 1992). No matter what type of objective is developed, it should provide a clear understanding as to what is expected of trainees at the end of training. Objectives should not simply aid in informing training design, but should also be utilized to measure training outcomes (Noe, 2002). Measures of performance should be designed around the objects of a training program, as will be discussed further in this chapter.

Instructional Strategies and Principles

With the development and sequencing of learning objectives, instructional design development begins (Goldstein & Ford, 2002). Given that the goal of training is to ensure that trainees are learning material and are transferring it back to the workplace, understanding the learning process plays an important role in determining appropriate instructional strategies (Salas & Cannon-Bowers, 2001). According to Salas and Cannon-Bowers (1997), instructional strategies are tools, methods, and content, combined to create an instructional approach. Selecting the appropriate instructional strategy based upon clearly defined learning objectives is key to the success of any training program, as inappropriate strategies will prevent the effective transfer of training to practice. For example, common mismatches include objectives that require trainees to demonstrate specific behaviors matched with instructional strategies that do not provide adequate opportunity to practice targeted behaviors. Evolving conceptualizations of instructional design directly incorporate learning theory, such as active learning approaches (e.g., Bell & Kozlowski, 2008, 2009; Kozlowski, Toney, et al., 2001). In this section, we will highlight several strategies commonly used in training design development. We will then present instructional principles that should be considered when utilizing these strategies.

TYPES OF STRATEGIES

First, it is necessary to present the different types of strategies used in training design. The most common strategies utilized in training today tend to fall into three categories: information-based, demonstration-based, and practice-based strategies (Salas & Cannon-Bowers, 1997). While the goal of each of these strategies is to successfully present learning objectives, each takes a slightly different approach in the methods utilized to present the information.

Information-based strategies are grounded in providing information to trainees, primarily through methods such as lectures, presentations, or web-based instruction. These are the most widely used methods for training, as they are easy to implement and are cost effective, particularly when large numbers of individuals need training. However, these methods do not allow for individuals to interact with the material being presented, as they are a passive means of learning.

In order to promote more interactivity with the training material, two additional strategies are often used. First, demonstration-based strategies are focused primarily on providing opportunities for trainees to observe required behaviors and actions. These methods are often used when complex information is to be learned, as they allow for multiple learning objectives to be embedded in one demonstration. However, trainees are simply observers and are unable to actually interact with practicing the task itself.

The final instructional strategy, practice, engages learners in active use of targeted knowledge, skills, or attitudes during learning sessions. Practice alone, as will be discussed later in this chapter, is not sufficient in itself for learning, but with the appropriate structuring can be a very useful tool. Practice utilizes cueing, coaching, and feedback in order to support the development, transfer, and generalization of targeted KSAs. Practice can involve role playing, behavioral modeling, computer-based simulation, and guided practice (Salas et al., 2006). Although practice can be a beneficial instructional strategy, it is often misused and is not well understood (Salas & Cannon-Bowers, 1997). Therefore, it is important that with this strategy—as well as all of the others—training designers carefully consider the principles of effective information sharing, demonstration, and deliberate practice.

INSTRUCTIONAL PRINCIPLES FOR TRAINING DESIGN

Each of the aforementioned strategies can be useful in a variety of training designs. However, without applying sound instructional principles during the implementation of these strategies, none will be successful. There are numerous instructional principles that can be applied to instructional design, including providing feedback, using cognitive and behavioral modeling, allowing for meaningful practice, and breaking down complex objectives into manageable pieces. While models of adult learning were discussed in previous sections, the following section highlights several basic learning principles such as these that are critical to the success of training design.

Learning is not a one-time event, but instead occurs and evolves over time, so the proceduralization of knowledge should be a key aspect of any instructional design. Essentially, an effective training design will promote the proceduralization of knowledge, which will in turn lead to expertise (Ford & Kraiger, 1995). This expertise can only be developed, however, by training systems that have a strong theoretical foundation. Although training design may take a variety of formats, depending on the knowledge acquired through the needs assessment and the type of information that is to be taught, if it does not incorporate basic learning principles, it can lead to poor learning outcomes (Campbell, 1988; Salas & Cannon-Bowers, 2001). The following section discusses in further detail current learning and cognition theories and how they can be successfully incorporated into training design to maximize knowledge acquisition as well as ensure successful transfer.

Gagne et al. (1992) emphasize a set of categories of learning outcomes that organize human performance into intellectual skills, cognitive strategies, verbal information, attitudes, and motor skills. Intellectual skills focus primarily upon procedural knowledge, while cognitive strategies involve a type of strategic knowledge that requires problem-solving practice. Gagne and colleagues (1992) theorized that tasks and behaviors should be categorized into one of these outcomes in order to match them to the appropriate learning conditions. Therefore, it is important that learning outcomes are taken into consideration not only for training design, but also in analyzing the needs of an organization (Goldstein & Ford, 2002).

Adult learning is another concept that must be taken into consideration during training, particularly in training design. Realizing that adult learning is different from adolescent learning is a critical step in designing an effective training program, as there are basic assumptions about adult learners that must be considered. As noted in the earlier section on models of adult learning, adults tend to want to know why they are learning something, need to be self-directed, bring more experience, enter with a problem-centered approach to learning, and are motivated to learn for both extrinsic and intrinsic reasons (London & Mone, 1999). Understanding how adults learn can affect the entire instructional system, as it will impact how they perceive the suggestion for training, the actual training design itself, and how well the information transfers to the workplace. Clearly, learning processes play a large role in instructional systems, whether it involves taking learning principles into account during needs assessment or utilizing appropriate learning outcomes in the evaluation of a training design.

Cognition must also be a consideration in instructional design, as training is a behavioral/cognitive/affective event (Kraiger et al., 1993). Training should tie cognitive events to design principles in order to enforce the acquisition of expertise. One of the primary considerations related to cognition is the idea of expertise versus novice understanding of a task (Salas & Cannon-Bowers, 2001). Experts have an automaticity of knowledge that is not present in a novice, which allows them to establish effective mental models of information. Gitomer (1988) studied the development of mental models in experts and novices, and found expert mental models much more developed and organized than those of novices, allowing experts to complete tasks in a more efficient manner.

Smith and colleagues note the importance of building adaptive expertise as environments constantly change (Smith, Ford, & Kozlowski, 1997). Developing expertise is therefore an essential cognitive process that must be considered in instructional systems, particularly training design. Another implication would be during the development of KSA-task clusters in the needs assessment process. Ford and Kraiger (1995) argue that KSA-task clusters do not get at the depth of knowledge that experts tend to have, especially in relation to mental models. They present cognitive task analysis as an alternative that can target not only surface skills and tasks, but a deeper understanding of how tasks are accomplished. By developing this deeper understanding, a better training program can be developed, which should ensure more successful transfer via more precise learning objectives.

Individual and Organizational Characteristics Influencing Training Design

There are several areas within training design in which organizational and individual characteristics variables must be considered. As previously discussed, individual characteristics such as attitudes, abilities, and self-efficacy can influence training motivation and expectations about training. Furthermore, organizational factors such as organizational climate and opportunities to practice have been linked to successful training outcomes. Therefore, it is important that organizations consider both types of factors when developing training design. In the following section, we will discuss areas in which organizational and individual characteristics come into play during training design. These include determining whether training should be individual or team based, allowing opportunities for practice, and providing feedback.

TEAMS VERSUS INDIVIDUALS

An important facet of training that must be considered in training design is whether individuals will be trained by themselves or with team members.

Training teams has become a major issue in recent years, as there has been an increase in the use of teams in organizations (Salas & Cannon-Bowers, 2001). Team training involves the development of instructional strategies that can be utilized to influence team processes (Salas, Cannon-Bowers, & Smith-Jentsch, 2006). Team training has two primary facets: training team members together to complete a task, or training team members separately to work interdependently (Salas & Cannon-Bowers, 2001). Which method to utilize depends on the nature of the task and the longevity of the team. Organizations must therefore carefully analyze this information during training design in order to ensure that the most beneficial method of training is selected.

Several factors have been identified as critical to effectively determining whether to train as individuals or to train teams. Most importantly, training should be viewed from an organizational systems perspective, as this enables organizations to see training as more than just an individual-level intervention, but instead as a means to invoke organizational change at multiple levels (Kozlowski & Salas, 1997; Kozlowski, Toney, et al., 2001). According to Kozlowski and Salas (1997), there are three dimensions that factor into decisions regarding where training should be targeted: levels, content, and congruence.

First, there is a need for organizations to identify the level of analysis required to achieve training-induced change, as this aids in driving what the focal unit of training will be and how this unit can be targeted in order to ensure the upward transfer of training. Furthermore, identifying the focal content provides further information regarding where to target training, as it operationalizes the constructs of interest for a given training situation. Finally, congruence involves ensuring contextual consistency across levels and content areas. By considering each of these three facets, organizations can weigh the organizational factors and processes that impact training success and transfer. In doing so, the most appropriate level of analysis for targeting training can be successfully identified to ensure maximal gain from such training interventions.

If conducted correctly, team training can lead to highly successful teams that are better prepared than individuals to tackle highly integrated and interdependent tasks. Leadership can also play a role in team training, as effective leaders can help teams develop by selecting which issues need more focus (Kozlowski, Gully, Salas, & Cannon-Bowers, 1996). While team training can be a great advantage for interdependent tasks, it can be very time

and resource consuming, particularly training in teams. Also, since the focus is both task and team development, team training can be very challenging (Goldstein & Ford, 2002).

PRACTICE OPPORTUNITIES

Practice is an important element in the training process, as it allows trainees an opportunity to utilize the skills they have learned in an environment that is safe for mistakes and errors (Ericsson & Charness, 1994; Goldstein & Ford, 2002). Practice involves reducing errors in enactment of the targeted training ability by having the trainee repeat the task. There are two primary ways to approach practice: massed and spaced. Massed practice involves practicing with few intervals within practice sessions, whereas spaced practice involves spreading out training with rest intervals (Goldstein & Ford, 2002).

In general, practice is necessary for successful training transfer and heightened performance. In a multilevel analysis, Yeo and Neal (2004) found that the relationship between effort and performance was heightened by practice. Differing effects have been found for spaced and massed practice, with certain variables affecting the relationship of practice and performance (Goldstein & Ford, 2002). According to DeCecco (1968), spaced practice appears to be more effective for motor skill tasks. Donovan and Radosevich (1999) found in their meta-analysis that the nature of the task, the intertrial time period, and the interaction of task and time moderated the relationship between practice conditions and performance, although massed practice was generally found to be less effective that spaced practice. The primary drawback to practice is the amount of time needed to effectively practice tasks to expertise, especially if spaced practice is involved. Organizations that want to encourage successful training transfer to on-the-job behaviors must therefore allow time for practice. Furthermore, the organization's climate must promote an acceptance of practice and a culture of learning if transfer is to occur. The implications of organizational culture and climate on training will be discussed later in the chapter.

FEEDBACK

Incorporating feedback into training design is also a crucial step to promote successful training transfer (Kluger & DeNisi, 1996; Yeo & Neal, 2004). Feedback has numerous functions, including the evaluation of performance and practice, as well as cuing what a trainee is doing correctly or incorrectly. Another function of feedback is the type of information provided, whether it is process or outcome. Process feedback provides information about how successfully processes to accomplish a task were performed, and provides a trainee with direct information about where changes can be made, building better mental models and promoting a more successful reception of feedback. Outcome feedback focuses solely on the performance outcomes, whether or not they were successful. This type of feedback can be less useful, as it does not tell the trainee what specific changes need to be made.

Feedback is a focal point of training design considerations, as it was one of the first variables found to support learning (Goldstein & Ford, 2002). Numerous studies have been conducted in order to better understand how feedback impacts performance and learning, with varying results. Feedback has been recognized by some as essential for organizational effectiveness; without it, anxiety, inaccurate self-evaluations, and a diversion of effort toward feedback-gathering activities will occur (Taylor, Fisher, & Ilgen, 1984). Other research has illustrated links between feedback and employees' job motivation, satisfaction, absenteeism, and turnover (Fried & Ferris, 1987).

However, the connections between feedback and performance outcomes are not always positive. Kluger and DeNisi (1996) noted that while feedback has often been viewed as beneficial to performance, studies to determine its impacts have in fact found contradictory and often negative effects. Their meta-analysis revealed that while feedback interventions improved performance on average, over a third of interventions actually led to decreases in performance. The resulting feedback intervention theory (FIT) was proposed in order to account for these differences. This theory explains the differences in feedback interventions as a result of changes in the locus of attention among three levels of control: task learning, task motivation, and meta-tasks (including self-related). As the focus of attention moves up the hierarchy and closer to the self, feedback interventions decrease in effectiveness.

While not all interventions are successful, some methods of providing feedback have been found to be more beneficial than others. In particular, feedback from multiple sources has been found to be especially useful in terms of enhancing performance, as noted by Smither and colleagues (2005) in their meta-analysis. Their results found that multisource feedback was linked to leadership effectiveness and performance. Additionally, their findings revealed that improvement is most likely to occur when

feedback indicates that change is necessary, recipients have a positive feedback orientation, identify a need to alter their behavior, believe change is possible, set appropriate goals, and take actions leading to skill and performance improvement.

One of the primary limitations of feedback is the fact that individual differences can play a large role in giving and receiving feedback. Some people take cuing feedback very negatively and see it as an overall evaluation of performance. Therefore, it is critical that feedback is provided in an effective manner that is most applicable to the individuals being trained. Salas and colleagues (2002) provide several guidelines for the successful delivery of feedback. These include providing feedback in a timely manner so that knowledge can be adjusted before incorrect behaviors become habitual. Additionally, giving both types of feedback (both process and outcome) that is clear, concise, and constructive will allow a more comprehensive understanding of correct and incorrect behaviors. Salas and colleagues also recommend that feedback be based on training objectives, as well as being linked to specific skill performance. These recommendations are designed to ensure that feedback is focused on the task and not the person, as this type of feedback is most optimal in reducing the potentially negative views of feedback.

Continuing to Build the Science of Training Strategies and Design

While many advances in the way in which we develop instructional programs have paved the way for present training design practices, it is important to look to the future in regard to advances in training strategies and design. With the advance of technology, training design strategies have begun to incorporate more advanced methods of training, including e-learning, distance learning, and simulation-based training (Salas, Wilson, et al., 2006). These environments provide intensely rich environments in which trainees cannot actively take all of it in or process all information during the training. Debriefings and reviews may need to be incorporated into these types of training so that trainees have an opportunity to reflect and receive feedback in order to promote retention and transfer of training. Therefore, further research is needed to understand successful strategies that can aid in the regulation of feedback and information following training sessions.

Another relevant issue that must be considered in the development of training design pertains to the interaction of team and individual training. As previously discussed, training can be received either at the individual level or at the team level, with differential advantages to each strategy. Aguinis and Kraiger (2009) suggest that at times, instruction at one level may be beneficial to the other. For example, individuals receiving training on how to work in multicultural environments may find that these skills impact team-level performance. Future research is needed to more fully understand how instructional programs can be designed to facilitate this type of cross-transfer, particularly for skills that expand beyond just the individual level and into organizational and societal outcomes.

After Training: Transfer, Generalization, and Evaluation

If training is successful, learning does not simply cease at the completion of training. Instead, it is transferred over and utilized on the job. However, the success or failure of training transfer is highly dependent upon both organizational and individual factors. Furthermore, once training is completed, an evaluation is necessary in order to determine exactly why success or failure occurred, and to make necessary changes for future training designs. In this section, we will discuss elements of both training evaluation and transfer to the job environment, including training results, trainee learning, and trainee reactions. Relevant to each topic, we will synthesize the current literature and best practices.

Training Transfer

A training program is only as good as its ability to promote transfer of training into on-the-job performance (Machin, 2002). Certainly, the billions of dollars spent on formal training programs must be justified with some type of return on investment for organizations (Baldwin & Ford, 1988). Unfortunately, some reports indicate that as little as 10% of what is learned in training actually gets applied on the job (Fitzpatrick, 2001). Saks and Belcourt (2006) acknowledge that there has historically been a lack of application of what we know about transfer to the improvement of training design. It is therefore critical that we not simply address what impacts training transfer, but also how transfer can be improved. In the following sections, we will define what is meant by transfer, as well as highlight aspects of the post-training environment, job aids, and re-training that can be utilized to positively impact the transfer of training.

The Mechanisms of Transfer

If training is not transferred successfully to the job, it will be perceived as a waste of time and resources by both organizations and individuals alike (Machin, 2002). Training transfer is defined as "the effective and continuing application, by trainees on their jobs, of the knowledge and skills gained in training—both on and off the job" (Broad & Newstrom, 1992, p. 6). Transfer refers to both the generalization of learning materials to the job as well as the continuous maintaining of trained skills over time (Baldwin & Ford, 1988). Transfer is traditionally assessed using the comparison of a control group to an experimental group that has received training (Goldstein & Ford, 2002). If the experimental group's performance after training is significantly higher than that of the control group, positive transfer is said to have occurred. However, if the control group performs higher than the experimental group, negative transfer has occurred. Finally, when no difference occurs between the two groups, zero transfer has been recorded.

While this method provides for a relatively accurate understanding of the level of transfer, it is not always possible to conduct such testing in real world settings. Control groups are not always possible, and even if they are available, outside variables can have an influence on training transfer. Because of this, researchers have begun to focus upon the transfer process in terms of what it is influenced by and methods in which it can be improved (Cheng & Hampson, 2008).

Numerous models of the transfer of training have been developed in order to explain exactly how information is transferred from training programs into practice, many of which were sparked by Baldwin and Ford's (1988) review of the transfer literature.

This review provided a critique of existing transfer research, pointing out the idea that training transfer is learning extended outside training. They also proposed that training transfer failures were the result of not just poor training design but also individual and organizational characteristics. Baldwin and Ford (1988) additionally highlighted future research needs, including the need to test training design operationalizations that have been posited to have a relationship with transfer, as well as the need to develop a research framework that addresses the effects of trainee characteristics on transfer.

Based on this review, several new models of transfer emerged, including those by Broad and Newstrom (1992), Foxon (1993, 1994), Thayer and Teachout (1995), Kozlowski and Salas (1997), and

Machin (2002). Cheng and Hampson (2008) provide a comprehensive review of these models and others designed to assess transfer. Their review found that while these models do provide insight into the transfer process, there is a great deal of unexpected and inconsistent findings that prevent an adequate understanding of transfer. Some of these inconsistencies include Colquitt and colleagues' (2000) meta-analysis of training motivation models, in which many proposed relationships were significant but in the opposite direction of that hypothesized (e.g., locus of control and age were negatively related to post-training self-efficacy, whereas conscientiousness negatively impacted skill acquisition). Further, Cheng and Hampson's (2008) review found counterintuitive results for variables such as transfer climate, social support, and opportunity to transfer. Based on these findings, they propose that planned behavior theory may be a more effective perspective upon which to assess training transfer. This theory provides a focus upon the trainee's intentions to transfer behavior, and is hypothesized to reduce some of the inconsistencies found in prior models of training transfer.

Research on training transfer continues to grow and explore new issues. Hurtz and Williams (2009) have utilized the theory of planned behavior to explain the factors that influence ongoing participation in development activities for employees. In their empirical study across four organizations, they found that while attitudinal and motivational antecedents such as personal control and higher levels of voluntariness were negatively associated with participation, intentions to participate and the availability of high-quality opportunities were the strongest predictors of higher participation rates. Even more recently, Kozlowski and colleagues (2009) have brought the multilevel nature of organizations to the forefront when considering transfer of training. Expanding upon previous work addressing the need to emphasize organizations as multilevel systems when developing training (Kozlowski & Salas, 1997), Kozlowski and colleagues address transfer as being both horizontal and vertical (Kozlowski et al., 2000). While traditional training literature has focused primarily upon horizontal training transfer, in which skills are transferred from a training setting to the workplace, vertical training is focused upon accounting for the fact that training can be transferred upward within an organization. This underexplored facet of training effectiveness merits future attention, as it challenges organizations to think of transfer as not simply something that impacts an individual or team. Instead, organizations must consider the multilevel impacts of training, and account for transfer as a way to enhance individual, team, and organizational learning as a system. Certainly, there is much still to be uncovered in terms of our understanding of the transfer of training.

Training Evaluation

As previously mentioned, the most critical aspect of any instructional system is whether or not the information presented is transferred to the workplace (Goldstein & Ford, 2002). In order to determine if training is effective and if transfer has occurred, numerous methods of evaluation have been developed, with some being more effective than others (Arthur et al., 2003). While some methods tend to reach only surface information, such as "smile" sheets (Brown, 2005), other methods look at training transfer in a more rigorous manner that parallels experimental design (Goldstein & Ford, 2002). In the following section, we will highlight the differences between evaluation and effectiveness, examine classic and more recent methods of evaluation, and discuss design issues and barriers that may negatively impact training evaluation.

DISTINCTION BETWEEN TRAINING EVALUATION AND EFFECTIVENESS

Although training evaluation and effectiveness are often considered to be one and the same, they are in fact two different concepts. According to Alvarez, Salas, and Garofano (2004), training effectiveness is the theoretical approach utilized to understand learning outcomes, whereas training evaluation is focused upon the methodologies designed to measure such outcomes. Training evaluation can be viewed as serving three purposes: decision making, feedback, and marketing (Kraiger, 2002). Evaluations provide information regarding the usefulness and appropriateness of a program, as well as identifying the strengths and weaknesses of the program so that improvements can be made (Noe, 2002). Furthermore, evaluation results can be utilized in marketing in order to sell the program to potential trainees or other organizations (Kraiger, 2002). As such, training evaluation can be seen as primarily focused upon the learning outcomes and how their measurement can be used to benefit the organization, providing more of a microview for the results of training (Alvarez et al., 2004). Kirkpatrick's (1976) classic typology of training evaluation, described in further detail below, is perhaps the most common evaluation technique and provides an example as to how evaluations have this more microlevel focus on the measurement of reactions to training, learning, behaviors, and results.

In contrast to evaluation of training, Alvarez and colleagues (2004) propose that training effectiveness is centered upon the factors that can influence training outcomes at different stages of the training process. These factors can be individual, training, or organizational characteristics, and can either enhance or detract from learning outcomes. Individual characteristics include facets of the trainee brought to the situation, such as personality traits or attitudes. Training characteristics involve factors of the training program itself, such as practice and feedback. Organizational characteristics refer to the context upon which training is designed, and include factors such as organizational climate and policies. These characteristics play an important role in understanding training effectiveness, as they contribute to our understanding of what affects the success of a training program, and how this success can change, depending upon variability in these characteristics. This broader, more macroview of training results also benefits the organization, but does so by focusing on why outcomes occurred the way they did, thus providing information regarding how training can be improved.

Several models have been developed in order to address the variables involved in determining training effectiveness, primarily focusing upon the relationship between learning and transfer (Salas, Burgess, & Cannon-Bowers, 1995). Baldwin and Ford's (1988) model of training effectiveness proposed that individual and organizational characteristics have a direct relationship with both learning and transfer performance. They further suggest that individual and organizational characteristics as well as training characteristics impact transfer indirectly through learning. An extension by Holton and Baldwin (2003) of this model provided more detail regarding the specific characteristics that impact learning and transfer, particularly ability, motivation, individual differences, prior experience with the transfer system, learner and organizational interventions, and training content and design.

Alvarez and colleagues (2004) present a model of training evaluation and effectiveness, described in more detail in the following sections, integrating aspects of all of these models, as well as common models of training evaluation, in order to provide a more comprehensive perspective. While training evaluation and effectiveness do have similarities, it is important to highlight the fact that these are indeed two separate constructs, for which each should receive attention in order to maximize the benefits of training.

KIRKPATRICK'S CLASSIC TYPOLOGY

As previously mentioned, Kirkpatrick's (1976) typology is the most often cited method of training evaluation. Kirkpatrick identified four levels of training criteria that increase in complexity: reaction data, learning, behavior, and results. This typology resulted from a series of articles published by Kirkpatrick (1959a, 1959b, 1960a, 1960b) that were originally designed to be primarily general guidelines for practitioners. However, these guidelines met a need in organizations for some type of training evaluation criteria and were quickly accepted by the industrial/organizational psychology field (Alliger & Janak, 1989; Cascio, 1987).

TRAINEE REACTIONS [7]

In the first level of the model, reactions of trainees to the training program are assessed in order to ensure that trainees are in fact motivated and interested in what they are learning (Kirkpatrick, 1976). Reactions are essentially measures of the trainee's feelings about the training program and are typically collected via self-report measures (Klein, Sims, & Salas, 2006). Reaction measures can include measures related to the instructor, course materials, structure, and management of the program, as well as trainee opinions on the usability and viability of the training content. While most training evaluations tap trainee reactions, valid evaluation goes beyond the collection of reactionary data.

TRAINEE LEARNING [8]

The second level of the model centers on learning, in which acquired knowledge, skill improvement, and changed attitudes are measured in order to assess learning. Learning is typically the most commonly assessed factor for organizations (Klein, Sims, & Salas, 2006). Kraiger et al. (1993) stipulate a three-dimensional framework for classifying learning outcomes: cognitive outcomes (i.e., changes in verbal knowledge, knowledge organization, or cognitive strategies), skill-based outcomes (i.e., proceduralization and automaticity), and affective outcomes (i.e., changes in attitudes and/or motivation). It is important to capture those learning outcomes targeted by training objectives in order to evaluate training in a valid manner.

BEHAVIOR ON THE JOB [9]

The third level measures behavior by assessing the transfer of training. This level is designed to address the increases in KSAs that a trainee achieves from a training program that are actually carried over to the job. An important aspect of this level is that changes in behavior are actually reflective of training transfer and not other factors.

RESULTS[10]

Finally, the fourth level of Kirkpatrick's (1976) model measures the results of training, related primarily to tangible outcomes such as the number of sales, productivity, profits, and employee turnover. This level is focused upon the gains that the organization receives due to individual training.

The first and second levels of Kirkpatrick's (1976) model are internal criteria collected immediately following training, before trainees return to their jobs, whereas the third and fourth levels are external criteria measured after the trainee returns to the job (Noe, 2002). Although many changes have occurred in training design over the past four decades, Kirkpatrick's (1976) model of training evaluation has remained relatively constant in terms of its use as an evaluation method. However, research is beginning to recognize that new models of evaluation should be implemented, as Kirkpatrick's (1976) model is not necessarily the most effective.

BEYOND KIRKPATRICK'S TYPOLOGY

While Kirkpatrick's (1976) typology of training evaluation remains the standard practice, researchers have begun to move beyond Kirkpatrick's (1976) typology in order to address some of the limitations of the approach. Kraiger (2003) summarized several criticisms that have been posed in the last decade. First, Kirkpatrick's (1976) approach can be viewed as atheoretical and based primarily in a behavioral perspective that does not address cognitive-based theories of learning that have since emerged. Second, this approach to evaluation is relatively simplistic and therefore unable to capture the multidimensionality of constructs such as trainee reactions and learning. Third, assumptions regarding the positive relationships between training outcomes identified by Kirkpatrick (1976) have not been empirically supported. For example, Alliger and colleagues (1997) found in their meta-analysis of studies utilizing Kirkpatrick's (1976) model that utility-type reaction measures had a stronger relationship with learning and transfer than affective-type reaction measures. Finally, according to Kraiger (2003), Kirkpatrick's (1976) approach does not necessarily account for the purpose of evaluations; instead of simply moving from one step of the evaluation process to another, evaluations should be centered around the intended purpose of the data collection.

These concerns for Kirkpatrick's (1976) model have driven research in training evaluation to begin to look past Kirkpatrick (1976) to other models that are more successful in their ability to capture the evaluation of training effectively. Goldsmith and Kraiger's (1996) method of structural assessment of a learner's domain-specific knowledge and skills has been employed with success in several domains (Kraiger et al., 1993; Stout, Salas, & Fowlkes, 1997). Kraiger (2002) has provided an updated taxonomy based on the work of Jonassen and Tessmer (1996–1997), which links training purposes to outcomes and provides measures for each of five outcomes. This connection of training purposes to suggested learning measures is relatively straightforward, yet it is also comprehensive in its approach.

Kraiger et al. (1993) take Kirkpatrick's (1976) levels a step further by exploring the outcomes (skill-based, cognitive, affective) that must be evaluated after training. This model takes a multidimensional approach to training evaluation that can be utilized in more completely assessing and learning outcomes. They argue that this method gets at a deeper level of training evaluation that matches outcomes to what is being learned. Ford, Kraiger, and Merritt (2009) have provided an update of the Kraiger et al. (1993) model of training evaluation, reviewing the literature on evaluation since 1993 that incorporated the Kraiger et al (1993) model, and identifying new evaluation methodologies since that time as well. Their review produced the addition of two cognitive outcomes (mental models and meta-cognition) and two affective outcomes (goal orientation and attitude strengths) as facets that should be considered in the evaluation process.

To provide a more holistic understanding of evaluation and effectiveness, Alvarez et al. (2004) developed an integrated model of training evaluation and effectiveness that incorporates four prior evaluation models. This incorporation of models found 10 training effectiveness variables that consistently influenced training outcomes. Furthermore, it identified cognitive learning, training performance, and transfer performance as the evaluation measures most related to post-training attitudes. While this model is an excellent start to better understanding the training evaluation process, this type of integration of research must continue in order to further the advancement of training evaluation processes.

Evaluation Design Issues and Barriers

Although advancements in training evaluation methods have aided in reducing the barriers to adequate evaluations, issues still exist that must be addressed. Salas and Cannon-Bowers (2001) note that while evaluation is necessary, it is also a labor intensive, costly, and often political process. Furthermore, evaluation faces the important challenge of determining whether or not observed changes in behavior are actually the result of training, or if other factors are playing a role (Klein et al., 2006). Fortunately, researchers have begun to recognize these issues and have worked to develop methods that can be used in order to overcome these barriers.

Goldstein and Ford (2002) identify several issues that could result in barriers to effective evaluation. First, threats to internal validity, or variables other than the instructional system that can impact outcomes, can be problematic in determining whether or not improvements in performance are actually the result of training. These threats including history, or specific events occurring during training that can provide alternate explanations for performance. Pre- and post-testing issues can also be problematic, as improved performance may simply be a result of the sensitization to the material presented in the pre-test. Changes in measurement instruments are another potential barrier, as they may capture information differently or inaccurately.

There are also several barriers recognized by Goldstein and Ford (2002) as being directly related to the participants within a training program. Methods used to select participants for training may impact their transfer and subsequent performance; specifically, if random or matched selection is not used in selecting comparison groups, training evaluation may not be accurate. Further, participants may be selected using extreme scores so that they are very high or very low in terms of abilities before entering training. Finally, attrition of participants from training can impact the ability to effectively evaluate a design, particularly if matching was used to select control groups.

Goldstein and Ford (2002) also acknowledge intervention threats that may impact evaluation, including compensatory equalization of treatment, compensatory rivalry between respondents receiving less desirable treatments, and resentful demoralization of respondents receiving less desirable treatments. External validity is also problematic, as there may be reactive effects in terms of pre-testing, the group actually receiving training, and the experimental setting.

Given these barriers to effective evaluation designs, researchers must employ the design that is the most practical and feasible given the training content, as

well as the design that minimizes the potential validity threats (Klein et al., 2006). For example, although a formal experimental design is often viewed as the best method for evaluating training, Sackett and Mullen (1993) propose other alternatives, such as post-testing only and having no control group, that are driven by the purpose of the evaluation. As collecting the data necessary to perform Level 3 and 4 evaluations recommended by Kirkpatrick (1976), simpler strategies such as Haccoun and Hamtiaux's (1994) internal referencing strategy can be utilized to more easily assess training transfer. This strategy, based on the idea that training-relevant content should show more change after training than training-irrelevant content, has been empirically shown to mirror results similar to those in more complex experimental designs. Certainly, reaching beyond traditional methods of evaluation design may aid in overcoming many of the design issues and barriers common to training evaluation.

Beyond Training: Alternative Forms of Learning and Development

In addressing the increasingly complex learning and development needs demanded by today's global economy, organizations have reached beyond traditional training. Development and learning now also take the form of computer-based and e-learning, simulation, mentoring, coaching, expertise, and various combinations (e.g., online mentoring).

E-learning, Simulations, and Gaming

As technology has increased in prevalence, its incorporation into training has become inevitable. While traditional methods such as classroom-based training and lectures are still prevalent, technologically advanced methods such as web-based e-learning, simulations, and games have become prominent supplements to these more traditional strategies. E-learning allows for instruction to be conducted from any location and at any time, which can be very advantageous for organizations needing to train a large number of individuals on a variety of topics (Mayer, 2009; Salas & Cannon-Bowers, 1997). Simulation-based training (SBT) is another new technology that can be leveraged to enhance learning and development. According to Salas, Wildman, & Piccolo (2009), SBT is any practice environment that is synthetically created to impart knowledge, attitudes, concepts, skills, or rules. Such training simulations and games are becoming increasingly popular, as they utilize both demonstration-based and practice-based strategies that can emulate realistic environments and situations without the risks and costs of putting trainees into the real environments unprepared (Cannon-Bowers & Bowers, 2009; Tannenbaum & Yukl, 1992). While the use of such strategies have become dominant in the past several decades, further research is needed in order to clarify when they are most effective and how they can best be utilized by organizations (see Cannon-Bowers & Bowers, 2009, for a more in-depth review).

Mentoring

Mentors have typically been defined as individuals with more advanced organizational knowledge and experience who advise, guide, and support more junior individuals, known as protégés (Allen et al., 2004; Kram, 1985). Specifically, the mentoring process has been conceptualized by Kram (1985) in terms of two categories of support: (a) career support (e.g., sponsorship, coaching, etc.), and (b) psychosocial support (e.g., enhancing the protégé's sense of personal identity and competence). Meta-analytic and empirical evidence suggests mentoring as a successful means for increasing both objective protégé outcomes (e.g., compensation, promotion) and subjective outcomes (e.g., career satisfaction, job satisfaction, self-efficacy) (Allen et al., 2004; Smith-Jentsch, Scielzo, Yarbrough, & Rosopa, 2008; Tonidandel, Avery, & Phillips, 2007). However, the relationship between mentoring and learning outcomes remains unclear. More detailed treatment of the role of mentoring can be found by Eby (chapter 19 of this handbook).

Coaching

Executive coaching is another alternative to more traditional formulations of training that has exploded in recent years as a means for employee development, especially for middle and upper level managers (Conference Board, 2008). While there is no singularly agreed upon definition of executive coaching, the various conceptualizations found in the still developing literature (e.g., Garman, Whiston, Zlatoper, 2000; Kampa-Kokesch & Anderson, 2001; Kilburg, 1996; Stern, 2004) share several commonalities summarized by Gregory and colleagues (2000): coaching is a one-on-one, collaborative relationship focused on optimizing performance through the collection of data, goal setting, and feedback. With roots in both the counseling and management perspectives, coaching shares features with other forms of development, such as mentoring. In an effort to provide construct clarity,

D'Abate et al. (2003) compared and contrasted coaching, mentoring, and 11 other related terms utilized in the literature across a broad range of categories, including participant demographics, interaction characteristics, organizational distance, and so forth. Compared to mentors, executive coaches are, by definition, individuals external to the organization. Unlike mentors, it is not vital for coaches to have expertise in the industry/arena in which the coachee works, as coaches tend to focus more on developing broader skill sets related to communication and leadership. A comprehensive overview of the coaching literature is available from Feldman and Lankau (2005), and Joo (2005) offers a conceptual framework of coaching.

Expertise

In order to achieve global, long-term competitiveness, organizations must orient themselves to develop more than just high performers; they must strive to develop and maintain expertise. Experts hold a deep, conceptual understanding of their domain based on high levels of detailed domain-specific knowledge, which they combine with skilled memory, thus allowing them to develop and leverage complex domain knowledge structures (Charness & Tuffiash, 2008). These advanced knowledge structures (e.g., mental models) allow experts to recognize cues and patterns quickly and effectively in order to make inferences, make decisions, and take action (Hoffman, 2007). In addition to simply holding greater domain-relevant knowledge and engaging in meaningful pattern recognition, experts also engage in meta-cognitive processes and self-regulation (Feltovich, Prietula, & Ericsson, 2006).

The traditional expertise literature suggests that expertise is a product of deliberate practice over a prolonged period of time. Specifically, Dreyfus and Dreyfus (1986) specify a five-stage model of expertise development. In the first stage, novices focus on applying explicit, context-free rules to clearly defined situations. By gaining experience applying these rules in a wide variety of real-world situations, the novice moves on to the second stage, advanced beginner. Advanced beginners start to recognize and encode situational factors and thus use reason and logic in order to apply more complex rules. By engaging in a wide range of experiences and situations, the advanced beginner is able to broaden his or her cue library and domain knowledge and thus progresses into the third stage of expertise, competence. The competent stage of expertise is characterized by an ability to manage complex situational cues in reference to relevant goals. Once individuals start to combine cues into patterns and cognitively represent situations as complex wholes (versus simply sums of their parts), then they have achieved the fourth stage of expertise, proficient performer. By building complex mental models, proficient performers are able to rapidly identify relevant cues in order to gain situational understanding. However, they must still allocate cognitive resources to active reasoning regarding the most appropriate course of action. Individuals finally achieve the last stage, expertise, when they are able to efficiently and relatively effortlessly assess the situation *and* engage in rapid decision making based upon the pattern of cues they have observed.

More recent conceptualizations have further built upon this developmental framework, suggesting a differentiation between expertise and adaptive expertise (Hatano & Inagaki, 1986, 1992). While traditional experts "do what normally works" (Dreyfus & Dreyfus, 1986, p. 31), adaptive experts focus on innovation, inventing new approaches, procedures, and decisions based on their expert knowledge. From this perspective, adaptive expertise has been conceptualized in terms of both efficiency and innovation, meaning that these experts are able to rapidly retrieve situationally relevant KSAs, reorganize or revise their mental models, and suspend heuristically based reactions that go beyond functionally fixed behavior (Schwartz, Bransford, & Sears, 2005).

So what can organizations do to develop and maintain expertise? Salas and Rosen (2009) draw from the scientific literature on training and development, adult learning, cognition, and expertise to provide 17 principles for developing expertise in organizations. These principles are organized according to four main mechanisms of development (see Table 41.5 in Salas, Rosen, & DiazGranados, chapter 41 of this handbook, for a complete description of the mechanisms and principles). The first mechanism of development is *deliberate and guided practice*. Expertise is developed by engaging in repetitive performance of similar tasks that incorporate minor variations and that build on preexisting knowledge (Ericsson, Krampe, & Tesch-Römer, 1993). Additionally, this performance must be followed by immediate constructive feedback, and the individual must be motivated to expend the effort necessary to engage in the practice activities. Thus, the second mechanism of expertise development is *motivation to learn*. This motivation to learn drives the desire to engage in deliberate practice and continual learning.

Specifically, motivation to learn has been linked with individual self-efficacy (Zimmerman, 2006), goal orientation (Seijts & Latham, 2005), valence of the task, and ultimate learning outcomes.

Related to motivation is the third mechanism of development, as described by Salas and Rosen (2009), long-term goals. Expertise takes time to develop; therefore, individuals must maintain learning goals over a prolonged period of time. These individuals must have a long-term desire to make small strides toward their ultimate goal. These small strides toward improvement are related to the final mechanism of development, *feedback seeking*. In order to self-regulate, self-correct, and continually improve performance, individuals must proactively seek feedback on their own performance. They must actively seek to determine the root causes of performance errors and learn how to mitigate and manage performance better in the future.

While expertise has a long history in the cognitive and human factors psychology traditions, practical implications on how to develop expertise in organizational settings remains a blossoming area.

Learning, Training, Development, and Organizational Change

Globalization, technology, and the contraction of the skilled workforce pool have led to an unprecedented need for organizational adaptability and flexibility through the mechanism of continuous learning. The concept of the "learning organization" (Gephart, Marsick, Van Buren, & Spiro, 1996; Jones & Hendry, 1994; Kozlowski et al., 2009; Senge, 2006) has been developed within recent literature and practice as framework for understanding how organizations and individuals successfully transform in light of dynamic internal and external pressures. The notion of organizational learning has been conceptualized as both an organizational process and outcome, with multilevel impact (Kozlowski et al., 2009). Rooted in early notions of organizational action-learning, learning organizations have been defined as those which foster the continuous development of organizational competence through a non-threatening, empowering culture that focuses on collective learning, fosters the ability of the workforce to expand their KSAs to reach their desired results, and nurtures new patterns of thinking (Senge, 2006; USACE Learning Organization Doctrine, 2003), however, a singularly agreed upon definition is lacking in the literature. In essence, this definition of learning organizations defines them in terms of their culture—that is, the degree to which learning is valued and incorporated into organizational norms, symbols, artifacts, and rituals. Most importantly, organizational learning goes beyond the notion of individual-level learning to encompass group and team learning, noting that combining information from multiple sources leads to both new information and new understanding (Huber, 1991). Additionally, it emphasizes that learning occurs outside traditional training and development initiatives in the form of experiential, experimental, vicarious, and on-the-job learning (Huber, 1991; Jones & Hendry, 1994).

The learning organization perspective emphasizes that learning and development are the gateways to organizational adaptability and change. Though these notions date back to early organizational science, and a great deal has been written from a practical perspective, much empirical works remains to be done. For example, it is not yet clear which dimensions of an organizational learning culture are most predictive of workforce learning and organizational performance: Marsick and Watkins's (2003) learning organization model integrated over a decade of literature and case studies in order to specify the dimensions of learning culture and, in turn, develop a diagnostic questionnaire with practical implications for guiding change. However, empirical reports utilizing such measurement tools to actively assess culture and the impact of attempts to affect it are scare in current scientific literature. Additionally, like a tree with many roots, the learning organization concept has grown out of a multidisciplinary perspective. Maintaining this perspective in empirical investigations by incorporating views from the educational, sociological, anthropological, and broader organizational science communities will ensure that we are fully tapping into the power of learning as an engine for organizational adaptability and competitive advantage.

Conclusions and the Road Ahead

Overall, a well-developed science of training has arisen in the last several decades. We have comprehensive models underlying our understanding of factors impacting training transfer and effectiveness, processes for identifying who, what, and where training and development is needed, training strategies mapped to models of learning, and methodologies for evaluating these efforts. Table 11.3 (adapted from Salas & Stagl, 2009) provides a practically based summary of the science of training in terms of principles and guidelines based upon the reviewed literature and the authors'

personal experiences facilitating learning in various organizations. Specifically, it addresses training in terms of four broad phases: determining training needs through need analysis, developing training content, implementation, and evaluation. The table demonstrates that our current understanding of the training process is characterized by both breadth and depth; however, open questions remain on the road ahead. Table 11.4 provides a summary of the future research needs, which are further discussed below.

Despite models of transfer and multilevel evaluation frameworks, we still lack a clear indication of the extent to which learned material is actually transferred back into the work environment. While the estimates that only 10–20% of material learned in training actually transfer are common, and estimates of training impact on performance found in popular outlets are even lower (e.g., Broad & Newstrom, 2001; Cross, 2006), they are not supported by the little existing evidence. For example, in a survey of 150 training and development professionals, Saks and Belcourt (2006) concluded that approximately 38% of training initially fails to transfer. As noted earlier, meta-analytic results of various training strategies also demonstrate a greater impact on learning outcomes compared to behavioral and performance outcomes (e.g., Arther et al., 2002) and learning outcomes have demonstrated minimal relationships with behavioral and transfer criteria (Alliger et al., 1997). To move forward, we must make concerted efforts to establish our true impact, that is, to clarify the linkages between learning, transfer, and performance. This includes consideration of how trainees adapt what is learned in training during transfer and generalization (e.g., Bell & Kozlowski, 2009). Without a clear conceptualization of how trainees apply trained KSAs on the job and adapt them to work within the actual work environment, our models and understanding of the training process remain incomplete.

Along similar lines, we must further develop our understanding of new and informalized forms of training and learning, such as simulation-based training, on-the-job training, and just-in-time training. Our science up to this point is vastly skewed and is based, for the most part, on traditional forms of training. The current reality is that, in many aspects, practice is moving faster than our scientific understanding in this arena. For example, several hospitals have begun to explore just-in-time simulation training, allowing residents to practice a procedure via simulation immediately before walking into the operating room to perform the same

Table 11.3 Summary of Training Phases, Principles, and Guidelines

TRAINING PHASE	GUIDING PRINCIPLE	TRAINING GUIDELINES
Analyze Training Needs	Conduct Due Diligence	Describe an organization's mission, strategy, structure, context and desired outcomes
		Articulate the benefits for individuals, teams and higher-level units (division, organization, society)
		Link solutions to specific organizational outcomes (performance, effectiveness, profitability)
		Consider the impact on organizational performance-related factors (satisfaction, reputation, social capital)
		Frame cross-level effects of contextual factors on motivation, learning, and transfer
		Specify how individual results emerge to impact unit- or organization-level outcomes (vertical transfer)
		Conduct a stakeholder analysis to identify and understand parties advocating for and against training
		Estimate the expected net present value of proposed training solutions
	Define Performance Requirements	Leverage established theories of performance and taxonomies of processes to guide criteria specification
		Disaggregate dependent variables to illuminate the specific aspects of performance targeted by training
		Use task inventories, cognitive task analysis, and critical incident interviews to nuance key factors
		Conduct probed protocol analysis to elicit the stimuli, goals, and actions of experts in natural situations
		Map the trajectory of change from novice to expert performance
		Describe the relative importance of taskwork and teamwork processes during performance episodes
	Define Cognitive and Affective States	Frame individual-level cognitive (mental models, situation awareness) and affective (self-efficacy) states
		Describe the types of mental models (equipment, task, team) targeted for development
		Use event-based knowledge-elicitation techniques with subject matter experts to describe shared states
		Model the compositional or compilational emergence of cognitive and affective states
		Determine the relative importance of sharedness and accuracy of cognitive and affective states
	Define KSA Attributes	Specify the direct determinants of the processes and emergent states comprising effective performance

(continued)

Table 11.3 (continued)

TRAINING PHASE	GUIDING PRINCIPLE	TRAINING GUIDELINES
		Leverage knowledge and skill inventories, skill repositories, and performance records
		Describe the declarative, procedural, and strategic knowledge applied to enact performance processes
		Describe the attitudes that can be changed as a result of the learning process
		Identify short-, mid-, and long-term competency requirements given alternative performance requirements
	Delineate Learning Objectives	Translate training needs into training objectives, learning objectives, and enabling objectives
		Contextualize task statements by describing appropriate performance standards
		Delineate behavior-, cognitive-, and affective-based learning objectives
		Ensure learning objectives are clear, concise, and link to measurable learning outcomes
Develop Training Content	Design Learning Architecture	Develop an intelligent scenario management system that allows instructors and users to author content
		Design a dashboard interface that can be used to control training content, sequence, and pace
		Program systems to provide tailored training features based on aptitude-treatment interactions
		Design the capacity to manipulate action tempo and compress the arrival time of events
		Design the capacity to vary the predictability and difficulty of contexts, tasks, events, and situations
		Program intelligent tutors to dynamically monitor, assess, diagnose, intervene, and remediate performance
		Create the capacity to compile performance records and for an on-demand lesson learned repository
	Forge Instructional Experiences	Develop an instructional management plan, instructor guides, and scripts
		Map the branching paths learners can take and forecast where trainees are likely to encounter difficulties
		Construct a chronological timeline of training events
		Craft instructional content that has psychological fidelity as well as physical fidelity

(continued)

Table 11.3 (continued)

TRAINING PHASE	GUIDING PRINCIPLE	TRAINING GUIDELINES
		Include opportunities for trainees to discover knowledge and relationships for themselves
		Develop lectures, exercises, games, reading lists, and illustrative case studies
		Leverage role plays, motion pictures, closed-circuit television, and interactive multimedia to display models
		Increase stimulus variability by manipulating the character and competence of models
		Ramp practice difficulty by including multiple levels and increasingly incongruent environments
		Incorporate routine obstacles, emergency situations, and crisis events trainees must navigate
	Develop Assessment Tools	Develop tools to assess multiple dimensions of trainee learning and performance
		Construct multiple-choice and situational judgment tests to assess knowledge and skill
		Develop concept maps, card sorts, and pair-wise comparison ratings to illuminate knowledge structures
		Assess the fragmentation, structure, and accessibility of knowledge chunks
		Triangulate measurement by leveraging multiple elicitation and representation techniques
		Create tools to dynamically capture trainee key strokes, communication, and perceptual movements
Implement Training	Set the Stage for Learning	Provide trainers with frame of reference and rater error training if ratings are used to evaluate trainees
		Measure and take steps to increase motivation to learn
		Prepare trainees to engage in meta-cognitive and self-regulatory processes
		Provide advanced organizers of learning points
		Prompt trainees to explore, experiment, and actively construct explanations in their training environment
		Frame errors as a natural part of training that contribute to learning
		Ask trainees to reflect over the informative aspects of errors when they occur
	Deliver Blended Solution	Use information presentation techniques such as reading assignments, lectures, and discussions
		Prompt learners to generate knowledge and skills that are targeted for acquisition

(continued)

Table 11.3 (continued)

TRAINING PHASE	GUIDING PRINCIPLE	TRAINING GUIDELINES
		Require trainees to integrate and associate various facts and actions into coherent mental models
		Pose difficult and structured reflection questions after case studies
		Ask trainees to integrate information and discern common themes provided in contrasting cases
		Explore the lessons learned from case studies of effective and ineffective performance
		Guide trainees through deliberate practice by asking them to repeat similar tasks with gradual modifications
		Encourage trainees to persist in practice to the point of overlearning/automaticity
	Support Transfer and Maintenance	Conduct training debriefings organized around key events and learning objectives
		Guide self-correction by keeping the debriefing discussion focused and modeling effective feedback skills
		Reserve instructor input for times when trainees cannot generate input or when clarifications are required
		Indentify lessons learned and areas for continued improvement to guide self-development efforts
		Prompt trainees to set proximal and distal goals for applying new capabilities
		Indentify and implement solutions to accelerate the cycle time required to realize training benefits
		Schedule shorter booster sessions after the main training initiative is complete
Evaluate Training	Execute Evaluation Plan	Determine the purposes, needs, and sophistication of the consumers of training evaluation findings
		Identify an appropriate experimental, quasi-experimental, or passive-observational training design
		Consider alternatives when rigorous experimental designs are not feasible in a given setting
		Review controls for factors that affected the inferences drawn from training evaluation
		Compile subjective evaluations and objective indices of multiple training criteria
		Ensure consistency between the level of focal variables, contextual factors, design, aggregation, and analysis
		Consider the relative efficacy of various approaches to measuring longitudinal change

(continued)

Table 11.3 (continued)

TRAINING PHASE	GUIDING PRINCIPLE	TRAINING GUIDELINES
	Gauge Trainee Learning	Measure the extent to which trainees' expectations were fulfilled as proximal indicators of reactions and learning
		Differentiate between affective and utility reactions
		Assess learning in terms of affective, behavioral, and cognitive outcomes
		Measure short-term retention immediately after training and long-term retention
		Gauge transfer by examining generalization to the job context and maintenance of learning over time
		Plot a maintenance curve and determine reasons for any decrements in maintenance over time
		Consider the interactions of work characteristics and time on the application of skills in the workplace
	Gauge Team Learning	Model unit-level outcomes as the mean of individual-level change when vertical transfer is compositional
		Evaluate both individual-level and unit-level outcomes when vertical transfer is compilation-based
		Use longitudinal designs when evaluating vertical transfer based on compilation emergence models
		Use techniques applicable to analyzing nonlinear configural relationships when emergence is compilational
	Gauge Organizational Impact	Estimate the cross-level relationships of improved individual performance on organizational performance
		Determine whether the costs of training were recouped
		Estimate the return on investment from training
		Estimate the utility or economic impact of a training solution over time
	Disseminate Training Results	Provide trainees with a copy of training evaluation reports
		Ensure the information collected from the transfer context is available to other designated parties
		Ensure designated parties have a clear understanding of the implications of evaluation findings
		Implement solution process changes suggested by the findings of formative evaluations
		Implement changes in the talent management system suggested by summative evaluations

Adapted from Salas & Stagl (2009) with permission.

Table 11.4 Summary of Future Research Areas for Learning, Training, and Development in Organizations

Future Research Needs for Learning, Training, and Development in Organizations

Clarify the linkages between learning, transfer, and performance.
Consider how trainees adapt what is learned in training during transfer and generalization.
Further develop our understanding of new and informalized forms of training and learning, such as simulation-based training, on-the-job training, and just-in-time training.
Establish a better understanding of the active role the learner plays in training outcomes.
Incorporate multilevel perspectives and the factor of time into training design, delivery, and evaluation.
Add a component to the traditional conceptualization of training needs analysis which consciously and deeply analyses the interdependencies of the job/task.
Consider the impact of individual characteristics such as tacit knowledge, practical intelligence, and adaptability.
Utilize a focus that combines both practitioner needs and scientifically sound methods.
Develop a better understanding of technology's impact on training evaluation methods.
Identify moderators that may impact training transfer.

procedure. Similarly, incoming Harvard medical students have been equipped with iPods loaded with vast amounts of training materials, which they can reference at the touch of a button. Most recently, Salas et al. (2009) have provided researchers and practitioners with some initial guidelines regarding the design, development, delivery, and evaluation of simulation-based training; yet more of this type of guidance is needed for organizations to successfully implement such systems. Future research should take a long-term perspective, looking over the horizon, anticipating and exploring what is to come so that such new developments have a base of scientific evidence from which to draw.

We also need better understanding of the active role that the learner plays in training outcomes—how they actively change and manipulate KSAs learned in training during generalization and transfer. An undercurrent of the learner as the passive receiver of learning pervades traditional models of training effectiveness and evaluation. Models of adaptive learning, however, have begun to explore what learners do with information learned in training, how they manipulate it and integrate it into their daily routines in order to achieve transfer and generalization. To gain a full understanding of these processes, we must also incorporate multilevel perspectives and the factor of time.

Continuing to Build the Science of Training Antecedents

While a great deal has been learned about the impact of need analysis and those antecedents impacting training outcomes, the changing nature of work raises some important areas for future consideration. First, the growing complexity of jobs and tasks suggests the need to add a component to

the traditional conceptualization of training needs analysis, which consciously and deeply analyzes the interdependencies of the job/task. While such elements may be implicitly covered in traditional descriptions of needs analysis, creating an explicit category of subanalyses focused on this aspect of the job/task and analyzing its impact would further our understanding and help refine field application. Traditional network analysis (Newman, Barabasi, & Watts, 2006) and social network analysis (Wasserman & Faust, 1994) may offer more comprehensive methods for understanding jobs, enabling more thorough mapping of relevant competencies. Additionally, the ever increasing rate at which jobs are changing as technology emerges suggests that combining both strategic and traditional forms of job analysis may provide a more comprehensive needs analysis—allowing organizations to stay ahead of the curve by training skills relevant to the very near future.

Second, as noted earlier, future research should consider the impact of individual characteristics such as tacit knowledge, practical intelligence, and adaptability. Additionally, developing our understanding of the role that shared knowledge (e.g., shared mental models) plays in training development and transfer is vital, considering the impact on interdependent work and teams (Mathieu, Heffner, Goodwin, Salas, & Cannon-Bowers, 2000)). We must move beyond more traditional conceptualizations of ability and knowledge to understand how these factors relate to training and transfer.

Continuing to Build the Science of Training Transfer, Generalization, and Evaluation

Certainly, we still have much to learn regarding training transfer and evaluation. Undoubtedly, methods that can reduce training evaluation cost and increase training transfer need to be explored. Unfortunately, much of what practitioners need in terms of effective evaluation methods have not always been addressed through previous research. Utilizing a focus that combines both practitioner needs and scientifically sound methods will be the most effective means of continuing to build our understanding of training transfer and evaluation. Organizations may also benefit from a clearer understanding of how to assess which evaluation methods are most practical for their needs.

Further, just as technology impacts training design, it is also an important factor in the evaluation of training strategies. Most traditional models of evaluation focus on traditional classroom training, yet it is not clear if these methods are equally as useful for new, more technologically advanced methods of training design. It is very possible that current evaluation methods may need development in order to best assess these new strategies. Rosen and colleagues (2008) have begun to tackle this issue through their development of a measurement tool to assess the effects of simulation-based training in emergency medicine. However, further work is needed in this area to more clearly understand technology's impact on training evaluation methods.

Another issue in need of future research is the identification of moderators that may impact training transfer. With low rates of transfer occurring in many organizations, it is important to understand what factors could be impeding the retention and application of training knowledge. Although some factors have been identified, such as supervisor support and transfer climate, it is very likely that other moderators exist that affect training transfer. Additional research is needed to more fully understand the current moderators that we are aware of, as well as moderators that are yet to be uncovered.

We offer these thoughts as suggestions to feed future research. Exploring such ideas will further our conceptual and theoretical understanding of the organizational learning and development process. Considering that organizational knowledge is a now a competitive advantage in today's globalized economy, it is highly worthwhile to continue building our scientific, evidence-based understanding of workplace learning and development.

Acknowledgments

This work was supported by NASA Grant NNX09AK48G to Eduardo Salas, Principal Investigator; and Kimberly Smith-Jentsch and Stephen M. Fiore, Co-Principal Investigators, of the University of Central Florida.

References

Aghion, P., Bloom, N., Blundell, R., Griffith, R., & Howitt, P. (2005). Competition and innovation: An inverted-U relationship. *Quarterly Journal of Economics, 120*, 701–728.

Aguinis, H., & Kraiger, K. (2009). Benefits of training and development for individuals and teams, organizations, and society. *Annual Review of Psychology, 60*(45), 451–474.

Allen, T. D., Eby, L. T., Poteet, M. L., Lentz, E., & Lima, L. (2004). Career benefits associated with mentoring for protégés: A meta-analysis. *Journal of Applied Psychology, 89*(1), 127–136.

Alliger, G. M., & Janak, E. A. (1989). Kirkpatrick's levels of training criteria: Thirty years later. *Personnel Psychology, 42*(2), 331.

Alliger, G. M., Tannenbaum, S. I., Bennett, W., Traver, H., & Shotland, A. (1997). A meta-analysis of the relations among training criteria. *Personnel Psychology, 50*, 341–358.

Alvarez, K., Salas, E., & Garofano, C. M. (2004). An integrated model of training evaluation and effectiveness. *Human Resource Development Review, 3*(4), 385–416.

Alvesson, M. (2002). *Understanding organizational culture.* London: Sage.

Anderson, J. R. (1996). ACT: A simple theory of complex cognition. *American Psychologist, 51*, 355–365.

Arthur, W. A., Bennett, W., Edens, P. S., & Bell, S. T. (2003). Effectiveness of training in organizations: A meta-analysis of design and evaluation features. *Journal of Applied Psychology, 88*, 234–245.

American Society for Training & Development. (2008). ATSD 2007 State of the Industry Report Executive Summary. Retrieved November 2, 2008 from: http://www.astd.org/content/research/stateOfIndustry.htm.

Atkinson, R. L., Atkinson, R. C., Smith, E. E., Bem, D. J., & Nolen-Hoeksema, S. (1996). *Hilgard's introduction to psychology* (8th ed.). New York: Harcourt Brace Jovanovich.

Axtell, C. M., Maitlis, S., & Yearta, S. K. (1997). Predicting immediate and long-term transfer of training. *Personnel Review, 26*, 201–213.

Azevedo, R. (2005). Using hypermedia as a meta-cognitive tool for enhancing student learning? The role of self-regulated learning. *Educational Psychologist, 40*(4), 199–209.

Baldwin, T. T., & Ford, J. K. (1988). Transfer of training: A review and directions for future research. *Personnel Psychology, 41*(1), 63–105.

Baldwin, T. T., & Magjuka, R. J. (1997). Training as an organizational episode: Pretraining influences on trainee motivation. In J. K. Ford, S. W. J. Kozlowski, K. Kraiger, E. Salas, & M. Teachout (Eds.), *Improving training effectiveness in work organizations* (pp. 99–127). Mahwah, NJ: Erlbaum.

Baldwin, T. T., Magjuka, R. J., & Loher, B. T. (1991). The perils of participation: Effects of choice on trainee motivation and learning. *Personnel Psychology, 44*, 51–65.

Bandura, A. (1977). Self-efficacy: Toward a unifying theory of behavioral change. *Psychological Review, 84*, 191–215.

Bassi, L., Ludwig, J., McMurrer, D., & Buren, M. V. (2002). Profiting from learning: Firm level effects of training investments and market implications. *Singapore Management Review, 24*(3), 61–76.

Bauernschuster, S., Falck, O., & Heblich, S. (2008). The impact of continuous training on a firm's innovation. *CESifo Working Paper Series*, No. 2258. Retrieved November 2, 2008 from http://www.cesifo.de/pls/guestci/download/CESifo%20

Working%20Papers%202008/CESifo%20Working%20
Papers%20March%202008/cesifo1_wp2258.pdf.

Beaman, I., Waldmann, E., & Krueger, P. (2005). The impact of training in financial modeling principles on the incidence of spreadsheet errors. *Accounting Education, 14*(2), 199–212.

Bell, B. S., & Kozlowski, S. W. (2008). Active learning: Effects of core training design elements on self-regulatory processes, learning, and adaptability. *Journal of Applied Psychology, 93*(2), 296–316.

Bell, B. S., & Kozlowski, S. W. J. (2009). Toward a theory of learner-centered training design: An integrative framework of active learning. In S. W. J. Kozlowski & E. Salas (Eds.), *Learning, training, and development in organizations* (pp. 263–302). New York: Routledge

Blau, G. J. (1985). A multiple study investigation of the dimensionality of job involvement. *Journal of Vocational Behavior, 27*, 19–36.

Borman, W. C. (1991). Job behavior, performance, and effectiveness. In M. D. Dunnette & L. M. Hough (Eds.), *Handbook of industrial and organizational psychology* (2nd ed., Vol. 2, pp. 271–326). Palo Alto, CA: Consulting Psychologists Press.

Brannick, M. T., & Levine, E. L. (2002). *Job analysis: Methods, research and applications for human resource management in the new millennium*. Thousand Oaks, CA: Sage.

Brannick, M. T., Prince, C., & Salas, E. (2005). Can PC-based systems enhance teamwork in the cockpit? *International Journal of Aviation Psychology, 15*, 173–187.

Broad, M., & Newstrom, J. (1992). *Transfer of training*. Cambridge, MA: Perseus.

Broad, M. L., & Newstrom, J. W. (2001). *Transfer of training: Action packed strategies to ensure payoff from training investments*. Cambridge, MA: Perseus Publishing.

Brown, K. G. (2005). An examination of the structure and nomological network of trainee reactions: A closer look at "smile sheets." *Journal of Applied Psychology, 90*(5), 991–1001.

Brown, K. G., & Gerhardt, M. W. (2006). Formative evaluation: An integrative practice model and case study. *Personnel Psychology, 55*(4), 951–983.

Brown, R. B. (1993). Meta-competence: A recipe for reframing the competence debate. *Personnel Review, 22*(6), 25–36.

Burke, R. J. (1997). Culture's consequences: Organisational values, family-friendliness and a level playing field. *Women in Management Review, 12*(6), 222–227.

Burke, L. A., & Baldwin, T. T. (1999). Workforce training transfer: A study of the effect of relapse prevention training and transfer climate. *Human Resource Management, 38*(3), 227–242.

Campbell, J. P. (1971). Personnel training and development. *Annual Review of Psychology, 22*, 565–602.

Campbell, J. P. (1988). Training design for performance improvement. In J. P. Campbell, & R. J. Campbell (Eds.), *Productivity in organizations*. San Francisco: Jossey-Bass.

Cañas, J. J., Quesada, J. F., Antolí, A., & Fajardo, I. (2003). Cognitive flexibility and adaptability to environmental changes in dynamic complex problem-solving tasks. *Ergonomics, 46*(5), 482–501.

Cannon-Bowers, J. A., & Bowers, C. (2009). Synthetic learning environments: On developing a science of simulation, games and virtual worlds for training. In S. Kozlowski & E. Salas (Eds.), *Learning, training, and development in organizations* (pp. 229–262). New York: Routledge

Cannon-Bowers, J. A., Salas, E., Tannenbaum, S. I., & Mathieu, J. E. (1995). Toward theoretically based principles of training

effectiveness: A model and initial empirical investigation. *Military Psychology, 7*(3), 141–164.

Cascio, W. F. (1987). *Costing human resources: The financial impact of behavior in organizations* (2nd ed.). Boston, MA: Kent.

Charness, N., & Tuffiash, M. (2008). The role of expertise research and human factors in capturing, explaining, and producing superior performance. *Human Factors, 50*, 427–432.

Chen, G., Gully, S. M., & Eden, D. (2001). Validation of a new general self-efficacy scale. *Organizational Research Methods, 4*, 62–83.

Cheng, E. W. L., & Hampson, I. (2008). Transfer of training: A review and new insights. *International Journal of Management Reviews, 10*(4), 327–341.

Chiaburu, D. S., & Marinova, S. V. (2005). What predicts skill transfer? Exploratory study of goal orientation, training self-efficacy and organizational supports. *International Journal of Training and Development, 9*, 110–123.

Choudhry, R. M., Fang, D., & Mohamed, S. (2007). The nature of safety culture: A survey of the state-of-the art. *Safety Science, 45*, 993–1012.

Clark, C. S. (1990). Social processes in work groups: A model of the effect of involvement, credibility, and goal linkage to training success. Unpublished Ph.D. dissertation. Knoxville: University of Tennessee, Department of Management.

Clark, M. C., & Wilson, A. L. (1991). Context and rationality in Mezirow's theory of transformational learning. *Adult Education Quarterly, 41*(2), 75–91.

Clarke, N. (2002). Job/work environment factors influencing training transfer within a human service agency: Some indicative support for Baldwin and Ford's transfer climate construct. *International Journal of Training and Development, 63*, 146–162.

Cohen, D. J. (1990). What motivates trainees. *Training Development Journal, 44*, 91–93.

Colquitt, J. A., LePine, J. A., & Noe, R. A. (2000), Toward an integrative theory of training motivation: A meta-analytic path analysis of 20 years of research. *Journal of Applied Psychology, 85*(3), 679–707.

Conference Board. (2008). *2008 executive coaching fee survey*. Retrieved November 1, 2008 from: http://www.chicago-coachfederation.org/userfiles/Conference_Board_2008_Coaching_Fee_Study.pdf.

Cooper, M. D. (2000). Towards a model of safety culture. *Safety Science, 36*, 111–136.

Crandall, B., Klein, G., & Hoffman, R. R. (2006). *Working minds: A practitioner's guide to cognitive task analysis*. Cambridge, MA: Bradford Books/MIT Press.

Cross, J. (2006, March). The low-hanging fruit is tasty. *Chief Learning Officer Magazine*. Retrieved November 1, 2008 from: http://www.clomedia.com/columnists/2006/March/1314/index.php?pt=a&aid=1314&start=3066&page=2.

D'Abate, C. P., Eddy, E. R., & Tannenbaum, S. I. (2003). What's in a name? A literature-based approach to understanding mentoring, coaching, and other constructs that describe developmental interactions. *Human Resource Development Review, 2*, 360–384.

Day, E., Yeo, S., & Radosevich, D. J. (2003, April). *Comparing two- and three-factor models of goal orientation: A meta-analysis*. Paper presented at the annual meetings of the Society for Industrial and Organizational Psychology, Orlando, FL.

DeCecco, J. P. (1968). *The psychology of learning and instruction: Educational psychology*. Englewood Cliffs, NJ: Prentice Hall.

Decker, P. J., & Nathan, B. R. (1985). *Behavior modeling training: Principles and applications.* New York: Prager.

Degani, A., & Wiener, E. L. (1997). Philosophy, policies, procedures and practices: The four P's of flight deck operations. In N. Johnston, N. McDonald, & R. Fuller (Eds.), *Aviation psychology in practice* (pp. 44–67). Hampshire, UK: Avebuy.

Denison, D. R. (1996). What is the different between organizational culture and organizational climate? A native's point of view on a decade of paradigm wars. *Academy of Management Review, 21*(3), 619–654.

Dweck, C. S. (1986). Motivational processes affecting learning. *American Psychologist, 41*(10), 1040–1048.

Dweck, C. S., & Leggett, E. L. (1988). A social cognitive approach to motivation and personality. *Psychological Review, 95*, 256–273.

Dick, W., & Carey, L. (1996). *The systematic design of instruction* (4th ed.). New York: Longman.

Donovan, J. J., & Radosevich, D. J. (1999). A meta-analytic review of the distribution of practice effect: Now you see it, now you don't. *Journal of Applied Psychology, 84*(5), 795–805.

Dreyfus, H. L., & Dreyfus, S. E. (1986). *Mind over machine: The power of human intuition and expertise in the era of the computer.* New York: Free Press.

Elliott, A. J., & McGregor, H. A. (2001). A 2x2 achievement goal framework. *Journal of Personality and Social Psychology, 80*(3), 501–519.

Ericsson, K. A., Krampe, R. T., & Tesch-Römer, C. (1993). The role of deliberate practice in the acquisition of expert performance. *Psychological Review, 100*(3), 363–406.

Ericsson, K. A., & Charness, N. (1994). Expert performance: Its structure and acquisition. *American Psychologist, 49*, 725–747.

Facteau, J. D., Dobbins, G. H., Russell, J. E. A., Ladd, R. T., & Kudisch, J. D. (1995). The influence of general perceptions of training environment on pretraining motivation and perceived training transfer. *Journal of Management, 21*, 1–25.

Feldman, D. C. (1989). Socialization, resocialization, and training: Reframing the research agenda. In I. L. Goldstein (Eds.), *Training and development in organizations* (pp. 377–416). Washington, DC: American Psychological Association.

Feldman, D. C., & Lankau, M. J. (2005). Executive coaching: A review and agenda for future research. *Journal of Management, 31*, 839–848.

Feltovich, P. J., Prietula, M. J., & Ericsson, K. A. (2006). Studies of expertise from psychological perspectives. In K. A. Ericsson, N. Charness, P. J. Feltovich, & R. R. Hoffman (Eds.), *Cambridge handbook of expertise and expert performance* (pp. 41–67). New York: Cambridge University Press.

Fine, S. A., & Cronshaw, S. F. (1999). *Functional job analysis: A foundation for human resources management* (Vol. 2, pp. 1019–1035). New York: John Wiley.

Fitts, P. M., & Posner, M. I. (1967). *Learning and skilled performance in human performance.* Belmont CA: Brock-Cole.

Fitzpatrick, R. (2001). The strange case of the transfer of training estimate. *The Industrial-Organzational Psychologist, 39*(2), 1819.

Flavell, J. H. (1976). Metacognitive aspects of problem-solving. In L.B. Resnick (Ed.), *The nature of intelligence* (pp. 231–235). Hillsdale, NJ: Erlbaum.

Ford, J. K., & Kraiger, K. (1995). The application of cognitive constructs and principles to the instructional systems model of training: Implications for needs assessment, design, and transfer. In C. L. Cooper & I. T. Robertson (Eds.), *International review of industrial and organizational psychology* (pp. 1–48). Chichester, UK: John Wiley.

Ford, J. K., Kraiger, K., & Merritt, S. M. (2009). An updated review of the multidimensionality of training outcomes: New directions for training evaluation research. In S. W. J. Kozlowski & E. Salas (Eds.), *Learning, training, and development in organizations* (pp. 135–168). New York: Routledge.

Ford, J. K., & Noe, R. A. (1987). Self-assessed training needs: The effects of attitudes toward training, managerial level and function. *Personnel Psychology, 40*, 39–53.

Ford, J. K., Quiñones, M. A., Sego, D. J., & Sorra, J. S. (1992). Factors affecting the opportunity to perform trained tasks on the job. *Personnel Psychology, 45*, 511–527.

Foxon, M. J. (1993). A process approach to the transfer of training. Part 1: The impact of motivation and supervisor support on transfer maintenance. *The Australian Journal of Educational Technology, 9*(2), 130–143.

Foxon, M. J. (1994). A process approach to the transfer of training. Part 2: Using action planning to facilitate the transfer of training. *The Australian Journal of Educational Technology, 10*(1), 1–18.

Fried, Y., & Ferris, G. R. (1987). The validity of the job characteristics model: A review and meta-analysis. *Personnel Psychology, 40*, 287–322.

Gael, S. (1983). *Job analysis: A guide to assessing work activities.* San Francisco: Jossey-Bass.

Gagne, R. M., Briggs, L. J., & Wager, W. W. (1992). *Principles of instructional design* (4th ed.). Fort Worth, TX: Harcourt Brace Jovanovich.

Gamliel, E., & Peer, E. (2006). Positive versus negative framing affects justice judgments. *Social Justice Research, 19*, 307–322.

Garman, A. N., Whiston, D. L., & Zlatoper, K. W. (2000). Media perceptions of executive coaching and the formal preparation of coaches. *Consulting Psychology Journal: Practice and Research, 52*, 201–205.

Gephart, M., Marsick, V., Van Buren, M., & Spiro, M. (1996). Learning organizations come alive. *Training and Development, 50*(12), 35–45.

Ghodsian, D., Bjork, R., & Benjamin, A. (1997). Evaluating training during training: Obstacles and opportunities. In M. A. Quiñones & A. Ehrenstein (Eds.), *Training for a rapidly changing workplace: Applications of psychological research* (pp. 63–88). Washington, DC: American Psychological Association.

Gist, M. E., Bavetta, A. G., & Stevens, C. A. (1990). Transfer training method: Its influence on skill generalization, skill repetition, and performance level. *Personnel Psychology, 43*(3), 501–523.

Gist, M. E., & Mitchell, T. R. (1992). Self-efficacy: A theoretical analysis of its determinants and malleability. *Academy of Management Review, 17*, 183–211.

Gist, M. E., Stevens, C. A., & Bavetta, A. G. (1991). Effects of self-efficacy and post-training intervention on the acquisition and maintenance of complex interpersonal skills. *Personnel Psychology, 44*(4), 837–861.

Gitomer, D. H. (1988). Individual differences in technical trouble shooting. *Human Performance, 1*, 111–131.

Goldman. D. (2000). Legal landmines to avoid in employment training. Retrieved November 2, 2008 from: http://www.hr.com.

Goldsmith, T. E., & Kraiger, K. (1996). Applications of structural knowledge assessment to training and evaluation.

In J. K. Ford, S. W. J. Kozlowski, K. Kraiger, E. Salas, & M. Teachout (Eds.), *Improving training effectiveness in work organizations* (pp. 73–97). Mahwah, NJ: Erlbaum.

Goldstein, I. L. (1986). *Training in organizations: Needs assessment, development, and evaluation.* Pacific Grove, CA: Brooks/Cole.

Goldstein, I. L. (1991). Training in work organizations. In M. D. Dunnette & L. M. Hough (Eds.), *Handbook of industrial organization psychology* (Vol. 2, pp. 507–621). Palo Alto, CA: Consulting Psychology Press.

Goldstein, I. L. (1993). *Training in organizations: Needs assessment, development and evaluation* (3rd ed.). Monterey, CA: Brooks/Cole.

Goldstein, I. L., & Ford, J. K. (2002). *Training in organizations: Needs assessment, development, and evaluation* (4th ed.). Belmont, CA: Wadsworth.

Gordon, M. E., Cofer, J. l., & McCullough, P. M. (1986). Relationships among seniority, past performance, interjob similarity, and trainability. *Journal of Applied Psychology, 71,* 518–521.

Gregory, J. B., Levy, P. E., & Jeffers, M. (2000). Development of a model of the feedback process within executive coaching. *Consulting Psychology Journal: Practice and Research, 60*(1), 42–56.

Guion, R. (1973). A note on organizational climate. *Organizational Behavior and Human Performance, 9,* 120–125.

Guldenmund, F. W. (1998). *The nature of safety culture: A review of theory and research.* Paper presented at the 24th International Congress of Applied Psychology, Safety culture Symposium, San Francisco, CA.

Guthrie, J. P., & Schwoerer, C. E. (1994). Individual and contextual influences on self-assessed training needs. *Journal of Organizational Behavior, 15*(5), 405–422.

Haccoun, R. R., & Hamtiaux, T. (1994). Optimizing knowledge tests for inferring learning acquisition levels in single group training evaluation designs: The internal referencing strategy. *Personnel Psychology, 47*(3), 593–604.

Hatano, G., & Inagaki, K. (1986). Two courses of expertise. In H. Stevenson, H. Azuma, & K. Hakuta (Eds.), *Child development and education in Japan* (pp. 262–272). New York: Freeman.

Hatano, G., & Inagaki, K. (1992). Desituating cognition through the construction of conceptual knowledge. In P. Light & G. Butterworth (Eds.), *Context and cognition* (pp.115–133). Hempel Hempstead, UK: Harvester Wheatsheaf.

Heggestad, E. D., & Kanfer, R. (2005). The predictive validity of self-efficacy in training performance: Little more than past performance. *Journal of Experimental Psychology: Applied, 11,* 84–97.

Hicks, W. D., & Klimoski, R. J. (1987). Entry into training programs and its effects on training outcomes: A field experiment. *Academy of Management Journal, 30,* 542–552.

Higgins, M. C., & Kram, K. E. (2001). Reconceptualizing mentoring at work: A developmental network perspective. *Academy of Management Review, 26,* 264–288.

Hoffman, R. R. (Ed.). (2007). *Expertise out of context: Proceedings of the sixth international conference on naturalistic decision making.* New York: Erlbaum.

Hoffman, R. R., & Militello, L. G. (2008). *Perspectives on cognitive task analysis: Historical origins and modern communities of practice.* Boca Raton, FL: CRC Press/Taylor & Francis.

Hofmann, D. A., & Stetzer, A. (1996). A cross-level investigation of factors influencing unsafe behaviors and accidents. *Personnel Psychology, 49,* 307–339.

Hoiberg, A., & Berry, N. H. (1978). Expectations and perceptions of Navy life. *Organizational Behavior and Human Decision Processes, 21*(2), 130–145.

Holt, D. T., & Crocker, M. (2000). Prior negative experiences: Their impact on computer training outcomes. *Computers and Education, 35*(4), 295–308.

Holton, E. F. (1996). The flawed four level evaluation model. *Human Resource Development Quarterly, 7*(1), 5–21.

Holton, E. F., III., & Baldwin, T. T. (2003). Making transfer happen: An action perspective on learning transfer systems. In E. F. Holton, III. & T. T. Baldwin (Eds.), *Improving learning transfer in organizations* (pp. 3–15). San Francisco: Jossey-Bass.

Huber, G. P. (1991). Organizational leaning: The contributing processes and literatures. *Organization Science, 2*(1), 88–115.

Huczynski, A. A., & Lewis, J. W. (1980). An empirical study into the learning transfer process in management training. *The Journal of Management Studies, 17*(2), 227–240.

Hunter, J. (1983). A causal analysis of cognitive ability, job knowledge, job performance and supervisory ratings. In E. Landy, S. Zedeck, & J. Cleveland (Eds.), *Performance measurement and theory* (pp. 257–266). Hillsdale, NJ: Erlbaum.

Hurtz, G. M., & Williams, K. J. (2009). Attitudinal and motivational antecedents of participation in voluntary employment development activities. *Journal of Applied Psychology, 94*(3), 635–653.

Ivancic, K., & Hesketh, B. (2000). Learning from error in a driving simulation: Effects on driving skill and self-confidence. *Ergonomics, 43,* 1966–1984.

Jarvis, P. (1987). *Adult learning in the social context.* London: Croom-Helm.

Jonassen, D., & Tessmer, M. (1996/1997). An outcomes-based taxonomy for instructional systems design, evaluation, and research. *Training Research Journal, 2,* 11–46.

Jones, A. M., & Hendry, C. (1994). The learning organization: Adult learning and organizational transformation. *British Journal of Management, 5*(2), 153–162.

Joo, B. K. (2005). Executive coaching: A conceptual framework from an integrative review of research and practice. *Human Resource Development Review, 4,* 462–488.

Kampa-Kokesch, S., & Anderson, M. Z. (2001). Executive coaching: A comprehensive review of the literature. *Consulting Psychology Journal: Practice and Research, 53,* 205–228.

Kanfer, R. (1991). Motivational theory and industrial and organizational psychology. In M. D. Dunnettee & L. M. Hough (Eds.), *Handbook of industrial and organizational psychology* (2nd ed., pp. 75–170). Palo Alto, CA: Consulting Psychologists Press.

Kanfer, R., & Ackerman, P. L. (1989). Motivation and cognitive abilities: An integrative/aptitude treatment interaction approach to skill acquisition. *Journal of Applied Psychology, 74*(4), 657–690.

Kilburg, R. R. (1996). Toward a conceptual understanding and definition of executive coaching. *Consulting Psychology Journal: Practice and Research, 48,* 134–144.

Kirkpatrick, D. L. (1959a). Techniques for evaluating training programs. *Journal for the American Society of Training Directors, 13*(11), 3–9.

Kirkpatrick, D. L. (1959b). Techniques for evaluating training programs: Part 2 - Learning. *Journal for the American Society of Training Directors, 13*(12), 21–26.

Kirkpatrick, D. L. (1960a). Techniques for evaluating training programs: Part 3 - Behavior. *Journal for the American Society of Training Directors, 14*(1), 13–18.

Kirkpatrick, D. L. (1960b). Techniques for evaluating training programs: Part 4 - Results. *Journal for the American Society of Training Directors, 14*(1), 28–32.

Kirkpatrick, D. L. (1976). Evaluation of training. In R. L. Craig (Ed.), *Training and development handbook: A guide to human resource development* (2nd ed., pp. 1–26). New York: McGraw-Hill.

Klein, C., Sims, D. E., & Salas, E. (2006). Training evaluation. In W. Karwowski (Ed.), *International encyclopedia of ergonomics and human factors* (Vol. 2, pp. 2441–2446). London: Taylor & Francis.

Kluger, A. N., & DeNisi, A. (1996). The effects of feedback interventions on performance: A historical review, a meta-analysis, and a preliminary feedback intervention theory. *Psychological Bulletin, 119*(2), 254–284.

Knowles, M. S. (1973). *The adult learner: A neglected species.* Houston, TX: Gulf Publishing.

Knowles, M. S. (1984). *Andragogy in action: Applying modern principles of adult learning.* San Francisco: Jossey-Bass

Knowles, M. S., Swanson, R. A., & Holton, E. F., III. (2005). *The adult learner: The definitive classic in adult education and human resource development* (6th ed.). London: Elsevier.

Kolb, D. A. (1984). *Experiential learning: Experience as the source of learning and development.* Upper Saddle River, NJ: Prentice-Hall.

Kolb, D. A., Boyatzis, R. E., & Mainemalis, C. (2001). Experiential learning theory: Previous research and new directions. In R. J. Sternburg & L. F. Zhang (Eds.), *Perspectives on thinking, learning, and cognitive styles* (pp. 227–248). Philadelphia: Taylor & Francis, Inc.

Kozlowski, S. W. J., Brown, K. G., Weissbein, D., Salas, E., & Cannon-Bowers, J. A. (2000). A multilevel approach to training effectiveness: Enhancing horizontal and vertical transfer. In K. J. Klein & S. W. J. Kozlowski (Eds.), *Multilevel theory, research and methods in organizations: Foundations, extensions, and new directions* (pp. 157–210). San Francisco: Jossey-Bass.

Kozlowski, S. W. J., Chao, G. T., & Jensen, J. M. (2009). Building an infrastructure for organizational learning: A multilevel approach. In S. W. J. Kozlowski & E. Salas (Eds.), *Learning, training, and development in organizations* (pp. 363–404). New York: Routledge.

Kozlowski, S. W. J., Gully, S. M., Brown, K. G., Salas, E., Smith, E. A., & Nason, E. R. (2001). Effects of training goals and goal orientation traits on multi-dimensional training outcomes and performance adaptability. *Organizational Behavior and Human Decision Processes, 85*, 1–31.

Kozlowski, S. W. J., Gully, S. M., Nason, E. R., & Smith, E. M. (1999). Developing adaptive teams: A theory of compilation and performance across levels and time. In D. R. Ilgen, & E. D. Pulakos (Eds.), *The changing nature of performance: Implications for staffing, motivation, and performance* (pp. 240–292). San Franscico: Jossey-Bass.

Kozlowski, S. W. J., Gully, S. M., Salas, E., & Cannon-Bowers, J. A. (1996). Team leadership and development: Theory, principles, and guidelines for training leaders and teams. In M. Beyerlein, S. Beyerlein, & D. Johnson (Eds.), *Advances in interdisciplinary studies of work teams: Team leadership* (Vol. 3, pp. 253–292). Greenwich, CT: JAI Press.

Kozlowski, S. W. J., & Salas, E. (1997). A multilevel organizational systems approach for the implementation and transfer of training. In. J. K. Ford (Ed.), *Improving training effectiveness in work organizations* (pp. 247–287). Mahwah, NJ: Erlbaum.

Kozlowski, S. W., J., Toney, R. J., Mullins, M. E., Weissbein, D. A., Brown, K. G., & Bell, B. S. (2001). Developing adaptability: A theory for the design of integrated-embedded training systems. In E. Salas (Ed.), *Advances in human performance and cognitive engineering research* (Vol. 1, pp 59–123). Amsterdam: JAI/Elsevier Science.

Kraiger, K. (2002). Decision-based evaluation. In K. Kraiger (Ed.), *Creating, implementing, and maintaining effective training and development: State-of-the-art lessons for practice* (pp. 331–375). San Francisco: Jossey-Bass.

Kraiger, K. (2003). Perspectives on training and development. In W. C. Borman, D. R. Ilgen, & R. J. Klimoski (Eds.), *Handbook of psychology:* Volume 12, *Industrial and organizational psychology* (pp. 171–192). Hoboken, NJ: Wiley.

Kraiger, K., Ford, J. K., & Salas, E. (1993). Application of cognitive, skill-based, and affective theories of learning outcomes to new methods of training evaluation. *Journal of Applied Psychology, 78*(2), 311–328.

Kram, K. E. (1985). *Mentoring at work: Developmental relationships in organizational life.* Glenview, IL: Scott, Foresman.

Lachman, S. J. (1997). Learning is a process: Toward an improved definition of learning. *The Journal of Psychology, 131*(5), 477–480.

Lajoie, S. P. (2008). Metacognition, self-regulation, and self-regulated learning: A rose by any other name? *Educational Psychology Review, 20*(4), 469–475.

Latham, G. E. (1989). Behavioral approaches to the training and learning process. In I. L. Goldstein (Ed.), *Training and development in organizations* (pp. 256–295). San Francisco: Jossey-Bass.

Locke, E. A., & Latham, G. P. (2002). Building a practically useful theory of goal setting and task motivation: A 35 year odyssey. *American Psychologist, 57*(9), 705–717.

London, M., & Mone, E. M. (1999). Continuous learning. In D. R. Ilgen & E. D. Pulakos (Eds.), *The changing nature of performance* (pp. 119–153). San Francisco: Jossey-Bass.

Machin, M. A. (2002). Planning, managing, and optimizing transfer of training. In K. Kraiger (Ed.), *Creating, implementing, and managing effective training and development* (pp. 263–301). San Francisco: Jossey-Bass.

Manpower. (2008). Talent shortage survey: 2008 global results. Retrieved November 6, 2008 from: http://files.shareholder. com/downloads/MAN/292351486x0x189693/9adcf817-96cf-4bb3-ac68-038e79d5facf/Talent%20Shortage%20 Survey%20Results_2008_FINAL.pdf.

Marsick, V. J., & Watkins, K. E. (2003). Demonstrating the value of an organization's learning culture: The dimensions of the learning organization questionnaire. *Advances in Developing Human Resources, 5*(2), 132–151.

Martocchio, J. J. (1992). Microcomputer usage as an opportunity: The influence of context in employee training. *Personnel Psychology, 45*, 529–552.

Marx, R. D. (1982). Relapse prevention for managerial training: A model for maintenance of behavior change. *Academy of Management Review, 7*, 433–441.

Mathieu, J. E., Heffner, T. S., Goodwin, G. F., Salas, E., & Cannon-Bowers, J. A. (2000). The influence of shared mental models on team performance and processes. *Journal of Applied Psychology, 85*(2), 273–283.

Mathieu, J. E., & Martineau, J. W. (1997). Individual and situational influences in training motivation. In J. K. Ford & Associates (Eds.), *Improving training effectiveness in work organizations* (pp. 193–222). Mahwah, NJ: Erlbaum.

Mathieu, J. E., Martineau, J. W., & Tannenbaum, S. I. (1993). Individual and situational influences on the development of self-efficacy: Implications for training effectiveness. *Personnel Psychology, 46*, 125–147.

Mathieu, J. E., Tannenbaum, S. I., & Salas, E. (1992). Influences of individual and situational characteristics on measures of training effectiveness. *Academy of Management Journal, 35*(4), 828–847.

Mayer, R. E. (2009). Research-based solutions to three problems in web-based training. In S. W. J. Kozlowski & E. Salas (Eds.), *Learning, training, and development in organizations* (pp. 203–228). New York: Routledge

Mayo, A. (2000). The role of employee development in the growth of intellectual capital. *Personnel Review, 29*(4), 521–533.

Mezirow, J. (1978). Perspective transformation. *Adult Education, 28*, 100–110.

Mezirow, J. (1981). A critical theory of adult learning and education. *Adult Education Quarterly, 32*(3), 3–24.

Mezirow, J. A. (Ed.). (2000). *Learning as transformation.* San Francisco: Jossey-Bass.

Molenda, M., Pershing, J. A., & Reigeluth, C. M. (1996). Designing instructional systems. In R. L. Craig (Ed.), *The ASTD training and development handbook* (4th ed., pp. 266–293). New York: McGraw-Hill.

Mullen, J. (2004). Investigating factors that influence individual safety behavior at work. *Journal of Safety Research, 35*, 275–285.

Myers, D. G. (2004). *Psychology* (7th ed.). New York: Worth.

National Center for O*NET Development. (n.d.). The O*NET content model: Detailed outline with descriptives. Retrieved March 9, 2009 from: http://www.onetcenter.org/dl_files/ContentModel_DetailedDesc.pdf.

Newman, M., Barabasi, A. L., & Watts, D. J. (Eds.). (2006). *The structure and dynamics of networks.* Princeton, NJ: Princeton University Press.

Noe, R. A. (2002). *Employee training and development* (3rd ed.). Boston, MA: Irwin-McGraw.

Noe, R. A. (2008). *Employee training and development* (4th ed.). Boston, MA: Irwin-McGraw.

Noe, R. A., & Schmitt, N. (1986). The influence of trainee attitudes on training effectiveness: Test of a model. *Personnel Psychology, 39*, 497–523.

Passmore, J., & Gibbes, C. (2007). The state of executive coaching research: What does the current literature tell us and what's next for coaching research? *International Coaching Psychology Review, 2*(2), 116–128.

Payne, S. C., Youngcourt, S. S., & Beaubein, J. M. (2007). A meta-analytic examination of the goal orientation nomological net. *Journal of Applied Psychology, 92*(1), 128–150.

Pentland, B. T. (1989). *The learning curve and the forgetting curve: The importance of time and timing in the implementation of technological innovations.* Paper presented at the 49th annual meeting of the Academy of Management, Washington, DC.

Prien, E. P., Goldstein, I. L., & Macey, W. M. (1987). Multidomain job analysis: Procedures and applications. *Training and Development Journal, 41*, 68–72.

Pritchard, R. D., & Ashwood, E. L. (2008). *Managing motivation: A manager's guide to diagnosing and improving motivation.* New York: Routledge, Taylor & Francis Group.

Quiñones, M.A. (1995). Pretraining context effects: Training assignment as feedback. *Journal of Applied Psychology, 80*, 226–238.

Quiñones, M. A., & Ehrenstein, A. (1997). Psychological perspectives on training in organizations. In M. A. Quiñones & A. Ehrenstein (Eds.), *Training for a rapidly changing workplace: Applications of psychological research* (pp. 1–9). Washington, DC: American Psychological Association.

Ree, M., J., Carretta, T. R., & Teachout, M. S. (1995). Role of ability and prior job knowledge in complex training performance. *Journal of Applied Psychology, 80*(6), 721–730.

Rohrer, D., Taylor, K., Pasher, H., Wixted, J. T., & Cepeda, N. J. (2004). The effect of overlearning on long-term retention. *Applied Cognitive Psychology, 19*, 361–374.

Rooney, R. H. (1985). Does in-service training make a difference? Results of a pilot study of task centered dissemination in a public social service setting. *Journal of Social Services Research, 8*, 33–50.

Rosen, M. A., Salas, E., Lyons, R., & Fiore, S. M. (2008). Expertise and naturalistic decision making in organizations: Mechanisms of effective decision making. In G. P. Hodgkinson & W. H. Starbuck (Eds.), *The Oxford handbook of organizational decision making: Psychological and management perspectives* (pp. 211–230). Oxford: Oxford University Press.

Roth, E. M. (2008). Uncovering the requirements of cognitive work. *Human Factors, 50*(3), 475–480.

Rouiller, J. Z., & Goldstein, I. L. (1993). The relationship between organizational transfer climate and positive transfer of training, *Human Resource Development Quarterly, 4*, 377–390.

Ruark, B. E. (2009, August). The ABCDEs of learning and development's next paradigm. *Training + Development*, 51–55.

Russ-Eft, D. (2002). A typology of training design and work environment factors affecting workplace learning and transfer. *Human Resource Development Review, 1*, 45–65.

Sackett, P. R., & Mullen, E. J. (1993). Beyond formal experimental design: Towards an expanded view of the training evaluation process. *Personnel Psychology, 46*, 613–627.

Saks, A. M., & Belcourt, M. (2006). An investigation of training activities and transfer of training in organizations. *Human Resource Management, 45*(4), 629–648.

Salas, E., Burgess, K. A., & Cannon-Bowers, J. A. (1995). Training effectiveness techniques. In J. Weiner (Ed.), *Research techniques in human engineering* (pp. 439–471). Englewood, NJ: Princeton & Hall.

Salas, E., & Cannon-Bowers, J. A. (1997). Methods, tools, and strategies for team training. In M. A. Quiñones & A. Ehrenstein (Eds.), *Training for a rapidly changing workplace: Applications of psychological research* (pp. 249–280). Washington, DC: American Psychological Association.

Salas, E., & Cannon-Bowers, J. A. (2000). Designing training systems systematically. In E. A. Locke (Ed.), *The Blackwell handbook of principles of organizational behavior* (pp. 43–59). Malden, MA: Blackwell.

Salas, E., & Cannon-Bowers, J. A. (2001). The science of training: A decade of progress. *Annual Review of Psychology, 52*, 471–499.

Salas, E., Cannon-Bowers, J. A., & Smith-Jentsch, K. A. (2006). Principles and strategies for team training. In W. Karwowski (Ed.), *International encyclopedia of ergonomics and human factors* (Vol. 2, pp. 2245–2248). London: Taylor Francis.

Salas, E., DiazGranados, D., Klein, C., Burke, C. S., Stagl, K. C., Goodwin, G. F., & Halpin, S. M. (2008). Does team training improve team performance? A meta-analysis. *Human Factors, 50*(6), 903–933.

Salas E., Nichols, D. R., & Driskell, J. E. (2007). Testing three team training strategies in intact teams: A meta-analysis. *Small Group Research, 38*(4), 471–488.

Salas, E., & Rosen, M. (2009). Experts at work: Principles for developing expertise in organizations. In S. W. J. Kozlowski & E. Salas (Eds.), *Learning, training, and development in organizations* (pp. 99–134). New York: Routledge.

Salas, E., Burke, C. S., & Cannon-Bowers, J. A. (2002). What we know about designing and delivering team training: Tips and guidelines. In K. Kraiger (Ed.), *Creating, implementing, and managing effective training and development: State-of-the-art lessons for practice* (pp. 234–259). San Francisco: Jossey-Bass.

Sales, E., & Stagl, K. C. (2009). Design training systematically: Infuse the science of training: In E. A. Locke (Ed.), *The Blackwell handbook of principles of organizational behavior* (2nd ed.). Oxford: Blackwell.

Salas, E., Wildman, J. L., & Piccolo, R. F. (2009). Using simulation-based training to enhance management education. *Academy of Management Learning & Education, 8*(4), 559–573.

Salas, E., Wilson, K. A., Priest, H. A., & Guthrie, J. W. (2006). Design, delivery, and evaluation of training systems. In G. Salvendy, *Handbook of human factors and ergonomics* (3rd ed., pp. 472–512). New York: Wiley & Sons.

Satish, U., & Streufert, S. (2002). Value of a cognitive simulation in medicine: Towards optimizing decision making and performance of healthcare personnel. *Quality and Safety in Healthcare, 11*, 163–167.

Schein, E. (1990). Organizational culture. *American Psychologist, 45*, 109–119.

Schmidt, F. L., Hunter, J. E., & Outerbridge, A. N. (1986). Impact of job experience and ability on job knowledge, work sample performance, and supervisory ratings of job performance. *Journal of Applied Psychology, 71*, 432–439.

Schmidt, R. A., & Bjork, R. A. (1992). New conceptualizations of practice: Common principles in three paradigms suggest new concepts for training. *Psychological Science, 3*, 207–217.

Schraagen, J. M., Chipman, S. F., & Shalin, V. L. (Eds.). (2000). *Cognitive task analysis.* Mahwah, NJ: Erlbaum.

Schunk, D. H., & Zimmerman, B. J. (Eds.). (2008). *Motivation and self-regulated learning: Theory, research, & applications.* Philadelphia, PA: Routledge

Schwartz, D. L., Bransford, J. D., & Sears, D. L. (2005). Efficiency and innovation in transfer. In J. Mestre (Ed.), *Transfer of learning from a modern multidisciplinary perspective* (pp. 1–51). Scottsdale, AZ: Information Age Publishing.

Seijts, G. H., & Latham, G. P. (2005). Learning versus performance goals: When should each be used? *Academy of Management Executive, 19*, 124–131.

Senge, P. M. (2006). *The fifth discipline: The art and practice of the learning organization.* New York: Random House.

Seyler, D. L., Holton, E. F., III., Bates, R. A., Burnett, M. F., & Carvalho, M. A. (1998). Factors affecting motivation to transfer training. *International Journal of Training and Development, 2*, 2–16.

Shih, Y., & Alessi, S. M. (1994). Mental models and transfer of learning in computer programming. *Journal of Research on Computing in Education, 26*, 154–175.

Simpson, P., & Bourner, T. (2007). What action learning is not in the twenty-first century. *Action Learning: Research and Perspectives, 4*(2), 173–187.

Sitzmann, T., Kraiger, K., Stewart, D., & Wisher, R. (2006). The comparative effectiveness of Web-based and classroom instruction: A meta-analysis. *Personnel Psychology, 59*, 623–664.

Smith, E. M., Ford, J. K., & Kozlowski, S. W. J. (1997). Building adaptive expertise: Implications for training design. In M. A. Quiñones & A. Ehrenstein (Eds.), *Training for a rapidly changing workplace: Applications of psychological research* (pp. 89–118). Washington, DC: APA Books.

Smither, J. W., London, M., & Reilly, R. R. (2005). Does performance improve following multisource feedback? A theoretical model, meta-analysis, and review of empirical findings. *Personnel Psychology, 58*(1), 33.

Smith-Jentsch, K. A., Jentsch, F. G., Payne, S. C., & Salas, E. (1996). Can pre-training experiences explain differences in learning? *Journal of Applied Psychology, 81*(1), 110–116.

Smith-Jentsch, K. A., Salas, E., & Brannick, M. T. (2001). To transfer or not to transfer? Investigating the combined effects of trainee characteristics, team leader support, and team climate. *Journal of Applied Psychology, 86*, 279–292.

Smith-Jentsch, K. A., Scielzo, S. A., Yarbrough, C. S., & Rosopa, P. J. (2008). A comparison of face-to-face and online mentoring: Interactions with mentor gender. *Journal of Vocational Behavior, 72*(2), 193–206.

Spiro, R. J., & Jehng, J. (1990). Cognitive flexibility and hypertext: Theory and technology for the non-linear and multidimensional traversal of complex subject matter. In D. Nix & R. Spiro (Eds.), *Cognition, education, and multimedia* (pp. 163–205). Hillsdale, NJ: Erlbaum.

Stajkovic, A. D., & Luthans, F. (1998). Self-efficacy and work-related performance: A meta-analysis. *Psychological Bulletin, 124*(2), 240–261.

Stern, L. R. (2004). Executive coaching: A working definition. *Consulting Psychology Journal: Practice and Research, 56*, 154–162.

Stout, R. I., Salas, E., & Fowlkes, J. (1997). Enhancing teamwork in complex environments through team training. *Group Dynamics: Theory Research and Practice, 1*, 169–182.

Switzer, K. C., Nagy, M. S., & Mullins, M. E. (2005). The influence of training reputation, managerial support, and self-efficacy on pre-training motivation and perceived training transfer. *Applied H.R.M. Research, 10*(1), 21–34.

Tannenbaum, S. I., & Yukl, G. (1992). Training and development in work organizations. *Annual Review of Psychology, 43*, 399–441.

Tannenbaum, S. I., Cannon-Bowers, J. A., Salas, E., & Mathieu, J. E. (1993). *Factors that influence training effectiveness: A conceptual model and longitudinal analysis* (Tech. Rep. No. 93–011). Orlando, FL: Naval Training Systems Center.

Tannenbaum, S. I., Mathieu, J. E., Salas, E., & Cannon-Bowers, J. A. (1991). Meeting trainees' expectations: The influence of training fulfillment on the development of commitment, self-efficacy, and motivation. *Journal of Applied Psychology, 76*, 759–769.

Taylor, M. S., Fisher, C. D., & Ilgen, D. R. (1984). Individuals' reactions to performance feedback in organizations: A control theory perspective. In K. M. Rowland & G. R. Ferris (Eds.), *Research in personnel and human resource management* (Vol. 2, pp. 231–272). Greenwich, CT: JAI Press.

Tesluk, P. E., Farr, J. L., Mathieu, J. E., & Vance, R. J. (1995). Generalization of employee involvement training to the job setting: Individual and situational effects. *Personnel Psychology, 48*, 607–632.

Thayer, P. W., & Teachout, M. S. (1995). *A climate for transfer model.* (Rep No. ALM-TP-1995–0035). Brooks Air Force Base, TX: Air Force Material Command.

Tonidandel, S., Avery, D. R., & Phillips, M. G.. (2007). Maximizing returns on mentoring: factors affecting subsequent protégé performance. *Journal of Organizational Behavior, 28,* 89–110.

Tracey, J. B., Hinkin, T. R., Tannenbaum, S. I., & Mathieu, J. E. (2001). The influence of individual characteristics and the work environment on varying levels of training outcomes. *Human Resource Development Quarterly, 12*(1), 5–23.

Tracey, J. B., Tannenbaum, S. I., & Kavanagh, M. J. (1995). Applying trained skills on the job: The importance of work environment. *Journal of Applied Psychology, 80,* 239–252.

Tziner, A., Haccoun, R. R., & Kadish, A. (1991). Personal and situational characteristics influencing the effectiveness of transfer of training improvement strategies. *Journal of Occupational Psychology, 64,* 167–177.

U.S. Department of Labor. (1972). *Handbook for analyzing jobs.* Washington, DC: Government Printing Office.

USACE Learning Organization Doctrine (2003, November). Retrieved November 6, 2008 from: http://www.hq.usace.army.mil/cepa/learning/learningdoctrine.pdf.

Uttal, B. (1983, October). The corporate culture vultures. *Fortune Magazine, 108*(8), 66–72.

Vandewalle, D. (1997). Development and validation of a work domain goal orientation instrument. *Educational and Psychological Measurement, 57,* 995–1015.

Wasserman, S., & Faust, K. (1994). *Social network analysis: Methods and applications.* Cambridge, UK: Cambridge University Press.

Webster, J., & Martocchio, J. J. (1995). The differential effects of software training previews on training outcomes. *Journal of Management, 21,* 757–787.

Xiao, J. (1996). The relationship between organizational factors and the transfer of training in the electronics industry in Shenzhen, China. *Human Resource Development Quarterly, 7,* 55–73.

Yeo, G. B., & Neal, A. (2004). A multilevel analysis of effort, practice, and performance: Effects of ability, conscientiousness, and goal orientation. *Journal of Applied Psychology, 89*(2), 231–247.

Zimmerman, B. J. (2006). Development and adaptation of expertise: The role of self-regulatory processes and beliefs. In K. A. Ericsson, N. Charness, P. Feltovich, & R. Hoffman (Eds.), *Cambridge handbook of expertise and expert performance* (pp. 705–722). Cambridge, UK: Cambridge University Press.

Person-Environment Fit in Organizational Settings

Cheri Ostroff

Abstract

The purpose of this chapter is to review and synthesize research on the fit, congruence, and alignment between individuals and their organizational environment. Theoretical foundations and conceptualizations of person–environment (PE) fit are reviewed, highlighting areas of ambiguity and controversy. The framework of fit addresses different fit perspectives (similarity, fulfillment, and compilation), fit to different hierarchical levels (person-individual, person-job, person-group, and person-organization fit), and different modes of defining the environment (person-based versus situational-based). Distinctions are drawn between objective and subjective fit, and a set of organizational and individual differences variables are hypothesized to increase the convergence between the two. Further, misfit is defined, and moderators of the relationship between fit, misfit, and individual outcomes are suggested. Finally, the notion that individuals simultaneously desire to fit in terms of being similar to others and being distinctive from others is addressed as a means to further future research on the PE fit in organizations.

Key Words: Person-environment fit, person-organization fit, misfit, levels of analysis

Over the past two decades, the fields of organizational psychology and organizational behavior have witnessed a burgeoning interest in the concept of person-environment (PE) fit. Fit has become a dominant and core area of study (Schneider, 2001). At the most basic level, PE fit entails the relationship between individuals and the environments in which they find themselves. The study of how and why characteristics of people and their work environment are congruent, match, or are aligned is deemed important because a good fit or the appropriate alignment is purported to be related to outcomes such as satisfaction, performance, adjustment, turnover, superior group dynamics, deviance, creativity, and innovation.

The basic concept of fit is not new and can be traced back to Plato, who emphasized the importance of assigning people to jobs that are congruent with their temperaments and abilities (Kaplan,

1950). Since the 1900s, the notion of fit, also termed congruence, has pervaded theory and research across many social science and organizational domains. For example, Parsons (1909) introduced fit by focusing on matching attributes of individuals to those of different vocations. Subsequently, researchers in vocational behavior developed comprehensive theories and supporting research explicating the importance of a match between vocational personalities (e.g., artistic, realistic) and commensurate dimensions of the work environment (e.g., Holland, 1997). The theory of work adjustment, first introduced in 1964 (Dawis & Lofquist, 1964; 1984), proposed that fit is a dynamic process whereby person and environment constantly adjust to one another, with adjustment indicated by satisfaction on the part of the individual and satisfactoriness of the individual on the part of the work environment. In educational psychology, Stern (1970) applied

Murray's (1938) need-press model to the study of PE fit in high schools and universities showing discrepancies between aggregate student needs and environmental press or demands, while Pervin (Pervin, 1967; Pervin & Rubin, 1967) showed that student dropout was related to a mismatch between students' needs for autonomy and the autonomy contained in the university environment. Further, Pervin (1987, 1989) drew largely on the personality literature in his theory of goals whereby a person searches for opportunities in the environment to satisfy his or her multiple goals while rewards offered in the environment influence the hierarchy of a person's goals.

In organizational research, the concept of fit has influenced nearly every content domain of interest and is a cornerstone of the field (Saks & Ashforth, 1997). For example, the implicit premise of selection and assessment has long been the identification of individuals whose skills, abilities, and attributes fit those required by the job and organization (Breaugh, 1992; Edwards, 1991). Many studies have examined fit between individuals' values and the cultural values of the organization, and the impact of this value congruence on organizational attraction, intentions to hire, attitudes, performance, turnover, stress, and career success (Kristof-Brown, Zimmerman & Johnson, 2005). In the area of leadership, similarity in personality between supervisors' and employees' personalities has been related to satisfaction (Glomb & Welsh, 2005) and leader-follower similarity on gender role congruity has been proposed to lead to attempts to align values, attitudes, and personality (Atwater & Dionne, 2007). Congruence between individual and group or organizational goals has been related to individual attitudes (Kristof-Brown & Stevens, 2001; Vancouver & Schmitt, 1991) and group outcomes (Vancouver, Millsap, & Peters, 1994). Multisource feedback research implicitly or explicitly uses a fit perspective in the correspondence or agreement between self and other ratings of behavior as it relates to performance (e.g., Atwater, Ostroff, Yammarino, & Fleenor, 1998). Fit concepts have also been applied to understanding work-family conflict (Kreiner, 2006; Kreiner, Hollensbe, & Sheep, 2009), volunteerism (Van Vianen, Nijstad, & Voskuijl (2008), perceptions of age similarity (Avery, McKay, & Wilson, 2007), diversity and demography (e.g., Ellis & Tsui, 2007; Sacco & Schmitt, 2005; Van Vianen, de Pater, Kristof-Brown, & Johnson, 2004), and personalities among group members (e.g., Kristof-Brown, Barrick, & Stevens, 2005; Liao, Joshi, & Chuang, 2004).

The construct of PE fit is pervasive, intuitively appealing, and spans many different domains. According to the Merriam-Webster dictionary, fit is defined as: (a) to be suitable for, (b) to harmonize with, (c) to be in agreement or accord with, and (d) to conform or to suit something. Definitions of PE fit in organizational psychology vary but reflect similar components in that individuals whose characteristics are similar to or aligned with those of the environment are deemed to be suitable to, harmonize with, or to be in accordance with the environment. In everyday life, people often use the term fit to describe why they join or leave organizations, and recruiters and organizational decision makers often use the term fit to describe why they select, promote, or seek to retain particular employees. We often hear phrases such as "I think this job is a good fit for me," or "I left my job because it wasn't a good fit for me," when discussing job and organizational choices. When considering hiring an employee, an interviewer might state, "This candidate is a good fit to our department." Yet what does fit encompass? When people speak of fit, are they referring to how their skills and abilities fit the job requirements? Is the reference to having one's needs fulfilled? Is it in reference to fitting in with the people with whom one works? Is it in reference to fitting with the goals and values of the group or the organization? Is fit a good thing for individuals and groups?

As intuitively appealing as the notion of fit is, the simplicity of its definition is deceptive. The conceptual definition and construct space of fit has been fraught with ambiguity (Edwards, 2008; Judge, 2007; Schneider, 2001). The study of person-environment fit is complex because PE fit, by definition, involves multiple levels of analysis as both personal attributes and situational or environmental attributes must be taken into consideration. Further, because organizations have multiple hierarchical levels, fit can be conceived of in terms of fit to other individuals or supervisors, to the job, the group, or the organization as whole. Organizations are multifaceted entities, thus the study of fit can also center on a multitude of different topics such as abilities, goals, values, needs and rewards, personalities, climate, and culture, to name a few. To add to the complexity, fit has also been conceptualized and operationalized by assessing the person and environment separately, or by assessing fit as a single variable representing a cognitive-perceptual construct that exists within a person. Finally, notions of fit can be based on similarity or based on alignment of complementary attributes.

Recently, several papers have provided extensive and comprehensive reviews of PE fit in organizations (cf., Kristof-Brown & Guay, 2010, for a comprehensive review of fit concepts and research; Kristof-Brown et al., 2005, for a meta-analytic review; and Edwards, 2008, for a review of fit theories). Therefore, rather than provide another comprehensive review of the current state of the area, the focus in this chapter is to provide a broad overview of the theoretical foundations of fit, conceptualizations of fit concepts, and levels of analysis issues in fit theories, with particular emphasis on highlighting areas of debate and ambiguity. A model integrating past conceptualizations and new directions for research is then developed. Issues of actual and subjective fit and the relationship between them, the differentiation between fit and misfit and their relationships to outcomes, and examination of multiple aspects of fit simultaneously are discussed.

Theoretical Foundations of PE Fit

Edwards (2008) provides a very thorough and comprehensive review of the multitude of theoretical models of fit as well as an insightful analysis of their utility. Thus, only a brief overview is presented here, focusing on distinctions among three basic categories of theories—fulfillment (or discrepancy) theories, similarity theories, and complementary models of fit.

Fulfillment, Similarity, and Compilation

The foundation of PE fit theories in organizational research stems from both Murray's (1938) need-press model and interactionism (e.g., Endler & Magnusson, 1976; Lewin, 1951; Mischel, 1973). Need-press theories focus on the discrepancy between individuals' needs and equivalent characteristics in the environment producing need satisfaction in the case of congruence and need frustration in the case of a discrepancy. Following this tradition, additional models began appearing, such as needs-supply theory focusing on discrepancies between individuals' needs or values and the ability of the environment to supply attributes to meet this need or value in relation to satisfaction (e.g., Locke, 1976) and psychological stress and strain (French, Caplan, & Harrison, 1982). Ability-demand theories were proposed, focusing on discrepancies between the abilities of the person and the demands of the job or organization in the study of personnel selection and job performance (Edwards, 1991) and stress (French et al., 1982; McGrath, 1976). A common theme across these various theories is the notion of fulfillment. Individuals' needs or values

are fulfilled, or individuals' abilities meet or fulfill the environmental job demands.

Interactionism focuses on the interplay between characteristics of the person and situational factors, mostly widely recognized in Lewin's (1951) field theory that behavior is a function of both person and environment, or B = f(P,E). PE fit theories of congruence are extrapolated from the interactionist perspective to specify how person and environment should interact, namely in the form of a match or congruence. Schneider's attraction-selection-attrition model (Schneider, 1983; Schneider & Reichers, 1983; Schneider, 1987a, 1987b) used the interactionist perspective as a basis to propose that: individuals are attracted to organizations whose culture, goals, and values are similar to their personalities, goals, and values; individuals are selected by organizations when their characteristics match those of the organization; and people leave organizations when a mismatch occurs. During the late 1980s and 1990s, the term person-organization fit became common and was defined as the similarity or congruence between the characteristics of people and the corresponding characteristics of the environment (Chatman, 1989). A broader approach was taken in terms of exploring similarity in values, similarity in goals, and similarity between personality and climate and the relationship between the degree of similarity or congruence and work attitudes, performance, and turnover (Kristof, 1996).

Fulfillment (or discrepancy) models have as a theoretical basis a difference between the attributes that an individual brings to the organization (e.g., abilities or needs) and the extent to which the organization demands that attribute from the individual or supplies it to the individual. Similarity-based theories of congruence focus on the degree to which the individual and environmental attributes are similar or match. While discrepancy models of fit (e.g., needs-supplies and abilities-demands) and congruence or similarity models of fit (e.g., attraction-selection-attrition (ASA) and person-organization congruence) stem from different traditions, they have a core in common—examining the degree to which the characteristics of the person and the characteristics of the situation are close to one another or fit together. At the same time, there are two fundamental differences between discrepancy- and similarity-based models of fit: (a) the underlying psychological mechanisms presumed to operate, and (b) the treatment of mismatches.

The theoretical difference between fulfillment and similarity-based models of fit might be coarsely described as "getting what one wants" versus "being in accord." Fulfillment theories focus predominantly on an underlying premise of need or value fulfillment. For the individual, fit represents getting what one desires, values, or needs from the work context as in need-supply theories, or in reducing the discrepancy between what an individual values (P) and what he or she perceives to be present in the work environment (E) as in Locke's satisfaction theory (Locke, 1976). Further, larger discrepancies between P and E are likely to create feelings of frustration, deprivation, and an inability to achieve valued goals, leading to strain. The fulfillment of needs is purported to result in more positive affective, emotional, and attitudinal responses and better adjustment to the work environment. Likewise, ability-demand theories can be viewed as a form of fulfillment, namely the extent to which the individual's abilities fulfill the demands of the work context. Further, discrepancies in the form of skill demands compared to skills available to the individual are likely to produce frustration and inability to meet one's needs or goals, and discrepancies when employee abilities do not fulfill role demands are likely to produce organizational strain (French et al., 1982; Harrison, 1985).

Similarity-based models of congruence rest on different underlying psychological mechanisms and processes to explain why PE fit is important for understanding individuals' behaviors and responses at work and are based largely on the notion of being in accordance with the environment. Similarity-attraction, social categorization, and social identity theories predominate in similarity models of fit. According to the similarity-attraction paradigm (Byrne, 1971) and the principle of homophily (Lazarsfeld & Merton, 1954), individuals are attracted to others based on similarity, and, therefore, tend to choose to interact with and make connections with similar others. This is consistent with social categorization and identification theories (Tajfel & Turner, 1985) such that a greater degree of similarity in social categories, representing background, attitudes, and lifestyles, leads to a feeling of common identity and a tendency to identify with the referent others. Similarity is viewed as satisfying and reinforcing to the individual (Dawis & Lofquist, 1984; Pervin, 1968).

Further, similarity or congruence with the environment can enhance self-identity (O'Reilly, Chatman, & Caldwell, 1991), consistent with the more recent notion of self-verification which posits that individuals will seek out areas of similarity with others in order to verify their own identity (Swann, Polzer, Seyle, & Ko, 2004). In these models, similarity between P and E is believed to provide psychological comfort or a psychological safety zone (Byrne & Nelson, 1965; Cable & Edwards, 2004), affective and cognitive consistency (Yu, 2009), and lessen the cognitive demands needed to understand the situation (e.g., Kalliath, Bluedorn, & Strube, 1999). Similarity is also purported to enhance the ability to navigate and understand the organization through enhanced communication (Erdogan & Bauer, 2005), predictability in understanding organizational events (Meglino, Ravlin, & Adkins, 1989), and positive interpersonal relationships with others (O'Reilly et al., 1991; Van Vianen, 2000). In terms of how similarity-based fit happens, Schneider's ASA model explicates how the cycle of attraction, selection, and attrition produces similarity and homogeneity over time.

The treatment of incongruity or mismatches differs between fulfillment and similarity models of fit. In general, in similarity theories, matches or congruence along similar dimensions of P and E are purported to represent fit, and mismatches represent misfit. In fulfillment theories, differences between P and E may not necessarily represent a mismatch or be detrimental for behavior and responses of individuals. For example, excess or having more in the environment of what one values or needs (P < E) may still fulfill needs and represent fit, and hence excess may be positively related to attitudes and behaviors. Excess abilities relative to job demands might also represent a type of fit by allowing for efficiency and low strain and work. Deficiency such as receiving less from the environment than what one values or needs (E > P) may lead to feelings of frustration and the inability to meet goals (Caplan, 1983; French et al., 1982). Thus, in general, similarity models of fit presume that a greater degree of similarity between P and E represents a greater degree of fit, whereas fulfillment models focus to a larger extent on discrepancies and allow for discrepancies between P and E, in terms of excess or deficiency, to also represent a degree of fit. Taken together, similarity models point to the need to conceptualize about the match between the P and E factors, while fulfillment models point to the need to conceptualize about differences between P and E factors.

A final theoretical perspective in fit rests on the notion of complementary P and E attributes representing fit. As discussed in more detail below, while some researchers (e.g., Cable & Edwards, 2004; Kristof, 1996) argue that need-supply and ability-demand theories represent complementary fit, the perspective here is to reserve this term to refer to a complementary compilation of attributes that differ but support and reinforce one other. In compilation, the combination of related but distinct characteristics at the lower level, in this case, individual, combine to yield a higher level property (Kozlowski & Klein, 2000). This is distinct from mismatch or incongruence in that the attributes across individuals do not vary randomly but have a distinct pattern. Little theoretical attention has been devoted to the concept of compilation in complementary views of fit; however, some theories do exist. For example, individuals may be attracted to others who have attributes complementary to their own (Pervin, 1968). Similarly, the principal of complementarity in interpersonal interactions has been used to explain how supervisory control invites a complementary and more submissive response from subordinates (Glomb & Welsh, 2005). Complementary but not identical fit to others in the group, whereby individuals' skills and attributes complement those of others in the group, is likely to motivate individuals to work harder and to develop good interpersonal relationships with others (Werbel & Johnson, 2001). Further, individuals are likely to derive a sense of self-worth (Brief & Aldag, 1981), feel a sense of accomplishment, and value the prestige they receive from their peers when they contribute to the group (Ferris & Mitchell, 1987). In compilation, fit is defined by adding a complementary attribute to the group or environmental situation.

The Construct of PE Fit

Not surprisingly, given the multitude of theories, definitions of fit have varied over the years prompting some researchers to call for greater precision in explicating the definition and construct space of PE fit (e.g., Edwards, 2008; Kristof, 1996; Schneider, 2001). While definitions vary, researchers tend to agree on two aspects of PE fit.

First, both person and environment attributes must be considered jointly (Kristof-Brown & Guay, 2010). Harrison (2007) provides a broad definition that fit is based on the compatibility of one or more attributes of the person (P) and a similar set of attributes of the environment (E), where fit is the intersection of these two attributes or sets of attributes. While many definitions suggest a positive connotation (i.e., fit is something that leads to more positive outcomes), more recent definitions (e.g., Harrison, 2007) divorce the definition of fit

itself from its outcomes, making no assumption in the definition about whether fit yields positive or negative outcomes. The demarcation of fit as a construct in and of itself without reference to outcomes in its definition is an important advance in clarifying the boundaries of fit.

Second, the construct of PE, while stemming from the interactionist tradition, represents more than a simple interaction between two variables—in this case, between person and environment attributes (Kristof-Brown & Guay, 2010; Ostroff & Schulte, 2007). The interactionist perspective emphasizes that neither personal nor situational attributes are the primary determinants of behavior and responses; rather, it is the combination of the two that influences responses (Endler & Magnusson, 1976; Schneider, 1983). In the interactionist approach, any two variables can interact with one another, and the interaction may take different forms such as moderation, mediation, additive components, or reciprocity (Terborg, 1981). Fit implies a specific type of interaction such that person and environment variables not only jointly influence outcomes but do so through some form of matching or alignment (Ostroff & Schulte, 2007). Thus, in developing hypotheses about the relationship between fit and behaviors and responses, the theoretical foundation should specify what combination of the two variables (e.g., $P = E$, $P > E$, $P < E$) is expected to relate to different levels of the outcome of interest. Areas where researchers have tended to disagree concern the requirement of commensurate dimensions and the need for strict content equivalence, the notion of similarity versus compatibility or compilation, and whether direct perceptual assessments of fit fall under the rubric of PE fit.

Commensurate versus Non-commensurate Dimensions in the Fit Construct

Since the 1980s, many fit researchers (Caplan, 1987; Edwards, 2008; Edwards, Caplan & Harrison, 1998; Harrison, 2007) have argued that the P and E components need to be conceptualized and defined with the same or commensurate dimensions entailing the same content (e.g., individual need for autonomy and autonomy provided in the environment). In this case, the substance of the construct is the same, but it is delivered or exists within different entities, the person and the environment (Harrison, 2007). Some have argued that the use of commensurate dimensions is one of the key factors that differentiates fit from a simple interactional approach (e.g., Edwards, 1991; Harrison, 2007). The primary rationale behind using commensurate dimensions is that it ensures that the P and E factors are directly and conceptually relevant to one another and further, that their degree of closeness or fit can be determined (Edwards et al., 1998).

Other researchers (e.g., Judge, 2007; Kristof-Brown & Guay, 2010; Ostroff & Schulte, 2007; Schneider, 2001) have argued that, depending on the topic and research dimensions, exactly commensurate dimensions may not be necessary. Schneider's (2001) concern with the overemphasis on the requirement of commensurate dimensions was founded on the concern that it could lead to the need to anthropomorphize organizations. To illustrate, using a fit perspective, Judge and Cable (1997) predicted that certain personality types (e.g., extroverts) would be differentially attracted to different types of organizational cultures. Their underlying rationale rested on assumptions that individuals seek out cultures that are congruent with personality, such as extroverts fitting with team-oriented cultures. Similarly, Anderson, Spataro, and Flynn (2008), using a PE fit framework, showed that extraverts attained more influence in a team-based and service-oriented organization, whereas conscientious individuals possessed more influence in organizations that focused on technical support and individual expertise. In these cases, the requirement of commensurate dimensions would have forced researchers to anthropomorphize the organization through conceptualizing and assessing extroversion as an organizational attribute. Aronoff and Wilson (1985) provided a comprehensive theoretical treatment of congruence between individuals' traits and personalities and features of the group environment. Although the P and E attributes were not exactly commensurate, congruence was specified by proposing the levels of the personality attribute (e.g., moderate affiliation) that were congruent with the level of the group attribute (e.g., high task complexity).

Researchers (e.g., Ostroff, 2007; Schneider 2001) who consider non-commensurate dimensions appropriate in fit studies provide some guidelines for developing fit theories. Fit can be conceptualized with non-commensurate dimensions provided that the point of congruence or alignment (e.g., high values of P when linked to moderate values of E represent fit) is theorized and specified. Further, when dimensions are non-commensurate, there should be some underlying basis for similarity in content or meaning. For example, individuals' value for high power distance (P) and a strong organizational hierarchy (E) have conceptual overlap in that power distance implies respect for differences in hierarchical levels.

The approach taken here is the broader one. Related, but not identical P and E factors can be used as the basis for specifying how and where the two form congruence or alignment, or what Kristof-Brown and her colleagues (Kristof-Brown & Guay, 2010) term general compatibility fit.

Fit Perspectives

In 1987, Muchinsky and Monahan proposed a distinction between supplementary and complementary fit that has been widely adopted, with some deviations. Supplementary fit occurs when the "person fits into some environment because he or she supplements, embellishes or possesses some characteristics which are similar to other individuals in this environment" (p. 269). Supplementary fit has since been taken to refer to a degree of similarity or closeness between person and environmental attributes, whether it be similarity to other people in the environment, as originally suggested by Muchinsky and Monahan (1987), or whether it be similarity between an individual's characteristics (e.g., values) and the environment more generally (e.g., organizational cultural values). This view of supplementary fit has been generally accepted in the literature; however, some ambiguity with respect to complementary fit exists.

Complementary fit was originally defined to mean that "characteristics of the individual serve to 'make whole' or complement the characteristics of the environment" (Muchinsky & Monahan, 1987, p. 271). As such, complementary fit was first based on the organization's perspective by filling a gap in the organization that is necessary for achieving organizational objectives. Yet, Muchinsky and Monahan (1987) provided a caveat in that, at times, selection procedures may result in hiring individuals with similar skill sets as opposed to complementing the array of skills possessed across incumbents. Since that time, the definition of complementary fit has been expanded to include fit from the individual's perspective. For example, ability-demand fit whereby individuals' abilities fit with the requirements of the job, as well as needs-supply fit whereby the environment fulfills a need for the individual, are often considered forms of complementary fit (Cable & Edwards, 2004; Kristof-Brown & Guay, 2010). From the individual's perspective, complementary fit has been taken to mean "making whole" for an individual through psychological need fulfillment such that an individual's need or desired amount of some attribute is fulfilled when it is supplied through the environment (Cable & Edwards, 2004).

One source of confusion stems from the fact that very similar attributes are assessed in studies but from a different point of reference. For example, congruence between individual and organizational values has been taken to represent supplementary fit when individuals are asked to report their own values and individuals' values are compared to organizationally espoused values (e.g., Ostroff, Shin, & Kinicki, 2005). Yet, a complementary view of fit is proposed when individuals are asked to report their desired amount of some value and their desired amount is compared to the degree to which it is supplied by the organization (e.g., Van Vianen 2000). Ability-demand fit is also often considered as a form of complementary fit. However, ability-demand fit is sometimes construed as the extent to which an individual's abilities match the requirements of the job, which is closer in definition to supplementary fit in that abilities (P) and requirements (E) are similar. When ability-demand is construed as an individual fulfilling the unique job requirement needs of the organization, it is closer to the definition of complementary fit of Muchinsky and Monahan (1987).

In an effort to reconcile some of the ambiguities surrounding the requirement of commensurate dimensions and the notions of supplementary and complementary fit, Kristof-Brown and Guay (2010) proposed a continuum of forms of fit. On one end of the continuum is a narrow definition of fit, termed exact correspondence, whereby fit exists when there is an exact match between P and E on commensurate dimensions (e.g., a high rating of P and the same high rating of E reflects fit) and misfit occurs when there is mismatch in either direction (i.e., P > E or P < E). This form of fit is consistent with the supplementary view of congruence. In commensurate compatibility, P and E dimensions must be commensurate, but exact match is not required. Rather, fit can occur at different points, and a discrepancy between P and E could be the basis of fit. This form of fit appears to rely more on ability-demand and need-supply theories and provides a wider range of compatibility between P and E variables. For example, excess, or when the environment provides more than the individual needs, might represent fit. On the other end of the continuum is what Kristof-Brown and Guay (2010) term general compatibility. Here, non-commensurate but conceptually related P and E factors are compared to one another. To illustrate this notion, they provide an example from Turban and Keon (1993) in which high need for achievement individuals were hypothesized to fit better in organizations with a pay-for-performance policy. While Kristof-Brown and Guay's (2010) continuum provides some additional clarity and highlights well the different ways in which fit has been conceptualized, it does not fully address theories of fit from supplementary and complementary notions of fit.

In contrast, Ostroff and Schulte (2007) argued that ability-demand and needs-supply views should be divorced from the definition of complementary fit. For example, as noted in Muchinsky and Monahan's (1987) original article, achieving fit in terms of selecting an individual whose skill set fits the organization's requirement may mean selecting someone whose skills are similar to others. Likewise, when an individual's need matches what the environment offers, the two components can be viewed as similar, albeit fulfilling psychological needs. To avoid these potential problems, Ostroff and Schulte (2007) urged researchers to use theories such as need-supply, need fulfillment, and similarity to explain how and why fit operates in a particular domain and context. Further, they proposed that Muchinsky and Monahan's (1987) original definitions be retained, allowing for a continuum to exist between pure supplementary fit (based on similarity to people) and pure complementary fit (based on alignment of complementing attributes to "make whole" the environment). As such, the concepts of composition and compilation from the levels of analysis literature (Kozlowski & Klein, 2000) were used to provide additional parsimony demarcating the range of ways in which people can fit to environments.

Composition and compilation can be used to help define different aspects of E, and when in combination with P, allow for viewing of range of different forms of supplementary and complementary fit. In composition models, lower level elements combine or coalesce to reflect the higher order property of the same or similar content (Chan, 1998; Kozlowski & Klein, 2000). For example, agreement among employees on organizational values is taken to represent the espoused values of the organization. The P characteristic (individual values) can then be compared to the E characteristic (espoused organizational values) that has the same content or meaning as the individual P characteristic. Composition models can be used to explain pure supplementary fit as defined by Muchinsky and Monahan (1987) such as the extent to which the individual's attribute is similar to the aggregate attribute of others in the environment, as well as more relaxed notions of supplementary fit such as the degree to which an individual's goals are congruent or consistent with the goals of the group. Likewise, needs-supply views of fit can also be compositional in nature in the comparison of an individual's need for structure to the degree of structure of the group.

At the other end of the continuum are compilation models. Compilation refers to a particular configuration or profile or combination of lower level characteristics, such that the different characteristics (e.g., different personalities or different skills) combine in such a way as to complement one another. The compilation model can be viewed somewhat analogously to pure complementary fit as originally defined by Muchinsky and Monahan (1987), or to what Harrison (2007) refers to as interlocking fit as it focuses on the necessity of an array of different attributes with pieces fitting together or interlocking to "make whole."

The differing perspectives pertaining to the need for commensurate dimensions and regarding supplementary and complementary fit highlight a source of ambiguity in the fit literature. The perspective taken here is that a broad-based view of fit encompasses the full range of perspectives of fit, from fit in the form of similarity between the attributes of an individual and the attributes of other people, to compositional forms of either fit based on similarity (or exact match) or congruence based on general correspondence between P and E (or general compatibility or needs-supply), to fit in the form of complementary attributes (or compilation). That said, compilation is a substantively different conceptualization of fit from the modes of fit that are based on compositional notions which compare P to some similar or conceptually linked E, and should be treated as such.

Clearly, there is some debate and ambiguity about how fit is conceptualized and the precise definitions of some of the terminology used in the fit literature. When fit is framed as fulfillment versus similarity, the two can be distinguished. Cable and Edwards (2004) showed that both types of fit independently related to individuals' satisfaction, intention to stay, and identification with the organization suggesting that these two fit perspectives operate simultaneously and can have independent effects on individual-level outcomes. Yet, confusion often arises when researchers strongly couple theoretical models of fit with theoretical approaches to the study of fit in terms of supplementary and

complementary approaches (e.g., value congruence as supplementary and needs-supply as complementary) as well as from broadening the domain of fit from the original approaches and definitions.

At the risk of adding more terminology to the mix, given the confusion and controversy that has surfaced over the terms complementary and supplementary, a simpler approach might be to study of fit from one of three overarching perspectives based on the three different theoretical bases: fit as *similarity*, fit as *fulfillment*, and fit as *compilation*. Fit as similarity and fit as fulfillment are based on compositional levels of analysis models, whereby elements from the lower level P are compared to elements similar in content or meaning to the higher level E. Different theoretical models (e.g., needs-supply, similarity-attraction) can be used as appropriate for either of these two types of fit. Fit as compilation is distinct and is based on the configural or profile approach in the levels of analysis literature, and assumes complementarities between the lower level P elements, with PE fit occurring when an individual provides a complementary attribute.

Fit as Comparative Construct of P and E versus Fit as a Within-Person Construct

In addition to the fit perspectives of similarity, fulfillment, and compilation, some questions have arisen about where the source of fit resides. By definition, PE fit encompasses two levels of analysis and two distinct components, the person and the environment. Early studies of fit tended to rely on separate assessments of these two components, with fit derived through their comparison. More recently, fit has been construed as a single construct residing within the individual, representing an individual's general perception of the degree of fit.

FIT APPROACHES: OBJECTIVE AND SUBJECTIVE FIT

When separate assessments of the P and E constructs have been conceptualized and operationalized, the term indirect fit has often been used (Kristof-Brown & Guay, 2010; Kristof-Brown et al., 2005). Indirect fit can take multiple forms, depending on whether P and E are conceptualized and measured as objective or separate from the individual or whether P and E are based on the subjective interpretations of the individual (Edwards, 2008; Harrison, 1978). The objective P can be attributes such as goals, needs, personality, and skills that an individual possesses, and the objective E is the technical, physical, and higher order social environment in the organization. The subjective P is an individual's perception of his or her own attributes, while subjective E is an individual's perception of the environmental attribute (Yu, 2009). With this as a basis, theoretically four combinations of P and E could be studied as objective or indirect fit: (a) objective P and objective E, (b) subjective P and objective E, (c) objective P and subjective E, and (d) subjective P and subjective E.

Several important distinctions should be noted among these forms of indirect fit. First, while some researchers argue that PE fit is an individual-level construct because it resides in individuals (e.g., Kristof-Brown & Guay, 2010), the definition of fit is cross-level in nature as it entails a comparison of a higher level E variable to an individual-level P variable. However, some conceptualizations of fit are based at the individual level of analysis. The first two combinations (objective P and objective E, and subjective P and objective E) represent fit as a cross-level construct because the E factor is conceptualized and assessed at a higher level of analysis (e.g., job, group, organization) than the P factor which is an individual-level construct. That is, E resides outside the individual at a different level of analysis and is assessed independently from the focal individual thereby necessitating a cross-level conceptualization of fit. The latter two combinations (objective P and subjective E, and subjective P and subjective E) assess fit from the individual level of analysis as both the P and E factors are conceptualized and assessed as residing in the individual.

Second, distinctions have been drawn between objective fit (objective P and E) and subjective fit (subjective P and E). The distinction is theoretically important in that objective fit represents the degree to which the individually actually fits the environment and subjective fit represents how the individual perceives both the self and the environment (Edwards, 2008; French et al., 1982; Yu, 2009). In reality, outside the selection arena where skills and abilities of individuals are assessed independently from the individual's own perception, few if any studies, in organizational psychology have assessed objective fit or measured both P and E components independent of the target individual. Rather, most studies of actual fit assess E independently from P, with P derived from assessments by the target individual. Thus, what is often treated as objective fit is typically operationalized as cross-level fit through comparing objective E to subjective P, with the assumption that the individual is the best source of

his or her own goals, personalities, needs, or other social attributes.

Third, objective fit, or fit as a cross-level construct, is theoretically different from subjective fit. Subjective fit has its roots in personality and social psychological theories of person-situation interactions, namely that it is individuals' perceptions and interpretations of the environment, rather than the actual or objective situation, that drive responses (Endler & Magnusson, 1976; Mischel, 1973). In terms of E, individuals are believed to store mental representations about work environment attributes that they have developed by interacting with the environment through social influence processes and through vicarious learning (James, Hater, Gent, & Bruni, 1978; James, James, & Ashe, 1990). Similarly, individuals construct an internal representation of the self. Thus, subjective P and E can be taken to portray an "as is" assessment and descriptive reporting of person or environment attributes using subjective scales. As such, subjective fit captures fit with the perceived environment rather than the degree of experienced fit (Edwards, Cable, Williamson, Lambert, & Shipp, 2006).

Whether P and E are assessed objectively or subjectively, the premise in both approaches is that fit inherently contains two distinct components, P and E, and as such should be assessed as conceptualized and assessed as two distinct factors. In combination, the congruence or alignment of P with E yields various means of fit (Ostroff & Schulte, 2007). In the case of objective or cross-level fit, the assumption is that there is some objective reality about the environment and the person that can be compared to one another. In the case of subjective fit, the assumption is that individuals form a cognitively based description of themselves and the environment, and can report their descriptions of both P and E so that the two can then be compared to determine the level of fit between them.

DIRECT FIT

In more recent years, a third and different approach to the conceptualization and study of fit has proliferated (cf., Cable & DeRue, 2002; Cable & Judge, 1997; Edwards et al., 2006; Lauver & Kristof-Brown, 2001; Saks & Ashforth, 2002). In direct fit (sometimes termed perceived fit), rather than conceptualizing and examining the attributes of P and E and how they combine to form fit, individuals report the degree to which they feel or perceive that they fit in the situation. Thus, direct fit is an individual's subjective judgment of the extent to which he or she fits (Judge & Cable, 1997) and represents a holistic interpretation of fit (Kristof, 1996). The assumption is that individuals cognitively evaluate and weigh the P and E factors that are important to them, and when their attributes fit the environmental factors, they perceive a greater degree of fit. Thus, PE fit becomes a single construct that resides within the person, as opposed to two constructs, one of which resides in the person and one of which resides in the environment.

To the extent that direct fit is a cognitive appraisal of the P and E factors and how close the two are to one another, the expectation would be that subjective fit (when P and E are reported separately by individuals and then combined analytically to represent fit) and direct fit (when individuals report their own perception of fit) should be closely related. However, relationships between cross-level, subjective, and direct fit tend to be fairly low (cf., Edwards et al., 2006; Judge & Cable, 1997; Van Vuuren, Veldkamp, De Jong, & Seydel, 2007).

Several reasons may account for the low convergence between subjective and direct assessments of fit. First, assessments and conceptualizations of PE fit often do not explicitly account for the notion that fit to some aspects of the environment may be perceived as differentially important to different individuals (Jansen & Kristof-Brown, 2006; Kristof-Brown & Guay, 2010; Resick, Baltes, & Shantz, 2007). Direct fit may reflect differential weighting that is not consistent with the approach taken when individuals are asked to report the P and E variables separately and the two are compared. Some research (e.g., Edwards et al., 2006; Hecht & Allen, 2005), however, has not supported implicit differential weighting or importance as the explanation.

A second reason for the low convergence between subjective and direct fit is that the individuals may expand or contract the range of P and E attributes upon which they focus. This is particularly relevant when global assessments of the extent of fit are employed. When participants are not explicitly primed (e.g., through survey questions) to focus on a specific and narrow aspect of themselves and the environment, individuals tend to consider myriad conceptualizations in their descriptions of what fit represents to them (Rynes, Bretz, & Gerhart, 1991). This makes comparability across perceivers problematic in studies. Further, direct perceptions of fit likely contain a wider array of P and E characteristics than separate subjective assessments of P and E. However, even when very specific aspects of the P and E factors have been assessed, subjective and direct perceptions of fit showed low convergence (Edwards et al., 2006).

A third and compelling reason to explain low convergence between subjective and direct fit is due to individuals' inability to divorce affect from cognition in their responses. When fit is conceptualized as an overarching subjective judgment or feeling of the degree of fit to the environment (Cable & Judge, 1997), the definition begins to resemble an affective state analogous to other affective constructs such as job satisfaction. When individuals are asked "How well do you feel you fit in the organization?" or "How well do your skills fit your job?," an affective response process is likely to be activated because both the construct definition as a feeling of fit and the assessments are affect-laden with "liking" and "feeling." Indeed, particularly high correlations between direct fit and other affective outcomes have been observed (Arthur, Bell, Villado, & Doverspike, 2006; Kristof-Brown et al., 2005; Verquer, Beehr, & Wagner, 2003).

A revealing study by Edwards and his colleagues (Edwards et al., 2006) showed that subjective and perceived fit are not interchangeable. In particular, the researchers examined subjective fit as assessed by a comparison of separate P and E components (what the authors referred to as atomistic) and two types of direct perceptions of fit, perceptions of discrepancy (which the authors referred to as molecular) and perceptions of overall fit or similarity (which the authors referred to as molar). Subjective fit showed some relationships to perceived discrepancies and weak relationships to overall perceived fit or similarity. Taken together, the results suggest that individuals do not systematically combine perceptions of the P and E components in forming judgments about discrepancies or fit, and the authors concluded that direct measures of perceived fit reflect an affective response to the environment much like satisfaction, as opposed to either a cognitive description of the degree of fit or a cognitive comparison of the P and E factors.

Thus, two critical questions can be raised about direct fit approaches. The first is whether direct fit should be considered under the broad rubric of PE fit. Harrison (2007) argues that perceived fit is not equivalent to PE fit and should be treated as a distinct construct, but acknowledged that direct fit has utility if the focus of one's study is on individuals' implicit theories or phenomenologies of fit similar to that of Cable and Edwards (2004). My perspective is that direct overarching perceptions of fit should be construed as an outcome of the PE fit process. The origins of PE fit reside in conceptualizations of both the person and the environment and the degree to which the two converge or align in some way. Direct fit, as an overarching perception, alters PE fit to a single within-person construct; hence, direct perceptions of fit likely tap into very different psychological phenomena (Judge, & Cable, 1997; Meglino & Ravlin, 1998) and are also more ambiguous as to the sources that individuals are using to determine their degree of fit.

A second important question is the extent to which these direct overarching perceptions of fit can be distinguished from other affective responses such as job satisfaction. A similar question was raised many years ago in the climate literature, and subsequent research showed that perceptions of climate as a description of the E was different from satisfaction as an affective response (e.g., Payne, Fineman, & Wall, 1976; Schneider & Snyder, 1975) leading to refinements in item construction to remove feelings from the measures. Additional research is needed to show that direct fit is a separate construct from other affective responses and represents a distinct conceptualization of fit as a within-person construct. As Edwards and his colleagues noted, "If perceived PE fit does not represent the match between the perceived person and environment, then what does it represent?" (Edwards et al., 2006, p. 823).

Relationships Between Objective fit, Subjective Fit, and Outcomes

French and his colleagues (French, Rogers, & Cobb, 1974; French et al., 1982) incorporated both objective and subjective P and E components in their model of fit in relation to stress and strain. Objective reality is purported to influence subjective perceptions. The degree of overlap between the objective and subjective person (P) represents accuracy in self-perception or self-awareness, while the degree of overlap between the objective and subjective environment (E) represents contact with reality or an accurate perception of the work context. In accordance with interactionist theories (e.g., Endler & Magnusson, 1976), subjective fit is purported to be more proximal to outcomes because perceptions drive responses. In support of this contention, recent meta-analytic results revealed that subjective fit has stronger relationships to attitudinal outcomes than does objective fit, although results for turnover and tenure are less clear (Arthur et al., 2006; Kristof-Brown et al., 2005; Verquer et al., 2003).

Figure 12.1 depicts the relationships between objective and subjective P and E components, actual and subjective fit, and outcomes. The figure represents a heuristic model for locating different views of the P and E components, different views of the combination between them, and their relationship to individual-level outcomes. Objective fit is purported to influence subjective fit which in turn influences individual-level

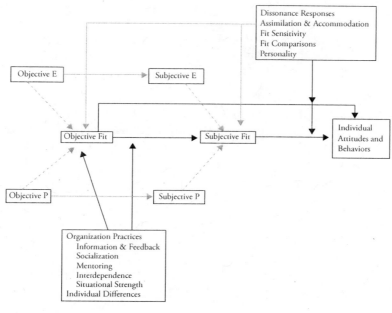

Figure 12.1 Relationships Between Objective Fit, Subjective Fit, and Outcomes.

attitudinal and behavioral outcomes. Objective fit is expected to have direct effects on outcomes, beyond subjective fit, because: (a) individuals may be inaccurate in appraising P or E, hence, subjective fit may not capture the totally of objective fit (Ravlin & Ritchie, 2006); and (b) the group or context has influences on individuals beyond their own perceptions and attributes (Blau, 1960; Salancik & Pfeffer, 1978).

As can be seen in Figure 12.1, organizational practices, such as providing clear information and signals about the work context, socialization, mentoring, and work design that allows for interaction and interdependence, are expected to influence both fit and the relationship between actual and subjective fit by enhancing accuracy in the perception of the P and E components. Likewise, individual differences in cognitive processes, background, and experience are also deemed to influence accuracy of perceptions and to influence the relationship between actual and subjective fit. Relationships between fit and outcomes may also be moderated by a number of processes, in particular through efforts to reduce dissonance experienced when P and E are inconsistent, attempts to change the P components (assimilation) or change the E components (accommodation) to achieve fit, the degree to which individuals are differentially sensitive to fit, and the relative comparison of the salience of different types of fit.

It is important to note that this model serves as a general heuristic and does not include all possible linkages and variables. The purpose is to highlight those relationships that are most critical for integrating various representations of fit. Before explicating the linkages in the model, additional depth about the various subtypes, modes, and approaches to conceptualizing objective and subjective fit is provided.

Subtypes and Modes of Fit

In addition to the different perspectives of fit outlined above—similarity, fulfillment, as well as actual and subjective fit—the construct space of PE can be further subdivided based on levels of analysis, mode for defining E, and level of specificity. A number of sources explain these subdivisions of the construct space of PE fit (e.g., Edwards & Shipp, 2007; Kristof-Brown & Guay, 2010). A summary of the primary means for understanding the multitude of types and modes of fit is presented in the following sections.

Fit to and at Levels

As alluded to above, attention to levels of analysis issues is important in the study of PE fit. An important distinction has been drawn between fit "to" a level of analysis and fit "at" a level of analysis (Ostroff & Schulte, 2007). "Fit to" a level refers to the hierarchical level of analysis of the E component (e.g., group, organization) to which the P component is compared. "Fit at" a level refers to focal level of analysis for the outcome variable of interest.

Contemporary fit theory holds that individuals can fit *to* different hierarchical levels in the organization. Typically, four hierarchical levels are demarcated—an individual (e.g., supervisor or peer), the job, the group or unit, and the organization as a whole. The subdivision of E into different levels of analysis produces different types of PE fit. An individual's attributes (P) could be compared to those of the supervisor, peer, or another individual (PI fit), aspects of the job (PJ fit), aspects of the workgroup (PG fit), or aspects of the organizational contexts (PO fit). Research on PE fit has examined all four subtypes of fit to a level. Further, these four subtypes of fit can be crossed with the different perspectives of similarity, fulfillment, and compilation. For example, in a study of values, an individual's values could be compared to the values espoused by the supervisor (PI similarity fit) or the values of the organization (PO similarity fit). Alternately, an individual's desire for certain values could be compared to the values supplied in the environment, such as a desire for integrity supplies relative to the integrity values in the group (PG fulfillment fit). Values could also be examined from a complementarity perspective such that an individual's values complement those of others in the workgroup (PG compilation fit). The top portion of Table 12.1 illustrates these subtypes of fit to a level by perspective.

Fit *at* a level focuses on the level of analysis at which the theory or research study is conceptualized in reference to the level of the outcome variable (Ostroff & Schulte, 2007). By and large, the criteria of interest in most PE studies to date have been at the individual level of analysis, examining relationships between some index of PE fit and individual-level consequences such as attitudes, adjustment, stress, turnover, or performance. As noted earlier, PE fit can be indexed from a cross-level perspective (e.g., objective E and P) and related to individual outcomes, or from a completely individual level of analysis with individual's own subjective perceptions of P and E linked to individual outcomes. In both cases, the level of analysis of the outcome is at the individual level.

However, PE fit can also be conceptualized and studied at higher levels of analysis (Schneider,

Table 12.1 Illustrative Examples of the Range of PE Fit Across Types, Perspective, and Modes Fit to a Level by Fit Perspective

Fit "to" a Level	Fit Perspective		
	Similarity	Fulfillment	Compilation
Dyadic (supervisor or individual)	Similarity between individual P personal attribute and supervisor E personal attribute (e.g., Colbert et al., 2008)	Individual P desired need or value is met by supervisor E sanctioned situational attribute	Individual P personal attribute is different from but complements supervisor E personal attribute (e.g., Glomb & Welsh, 2005)
Job	Similarity between individual P personal attribute and those of E in job category (e.g., Caldwell & O'Reilly, 1990)	Individual P need or value is met by attribute of job E (e.g., Edwards et al., 2006) or individual P fulfills requirements demanded by job role E (e.g., Cable & Judge, 1997)	Individual P attribute is different from but complements attributes of those in job category E (e.g., Werbel & Gilliland, 1999)
Group	Similarity between individual P personal attribute and the personal attributes of other group members E (e.g., Kristof-Brown & Stevens, 2001)	Individual desired needs or values are met by the group E (e.g., Shaw et al., 2000) or individual abilities fulfill ability needs of the group E, (e.g., Hollenbeck et al., 2002)	Individual P attribute is different from but complements the attributes of others in the group E (e.g., DeRue & Hollenbeck, 2007; Kozlowski et al., 2000)
Organization	Similarity between individual P personal attributes and commensurate dimensions in the organization E (e.g., Chatman, 1991)	Individual desire or value is met by organization E (e.g., O'Reilly et al., 1991)	Individual P attribute is different from but complements the attributes of others in the organization E (e.g., Schneider et al., 2000)

FIT BY MODE of E (Person or Situation): Illustrative Examples

PP Mode by Similarity Perspective by Fit to Supervisor	Similarity between personal attribute (e.g., value) P and supervisor's personal attribute (e.g., value) E (e.g., Ashkanasy & O'Connor, 1997
PP Mode by Similarity Perspective by Fit to Group	Similarity between personal attribute P and collective personal attributes of the group E (e.g., Jansen & Kristof-Brown, 2005; Liao et al., 2004)
Table PS Mode by Fulfillment Perspective by Fit to Supervisor	Personal attribute (e.g., obligation) P is met by a corresponding situational attribute (e.g., obligation provided) S provided by the supervisor (e.g., Dabos & Rousseau, 2004)
PS Mode by Fulfillment Perspective by Fit to Job or Organization	Desired amounts of an attribute P are met by the amount in the job or organization E (Cable & Edwards, 2004; Edwards, 1991)
PP Mode by Compilation Perspective by Fit to Group	Individual's attributes P complement attributes of others in the group E (e.g., Klimoski & Jones, 1995)

Goldstein, & Smith, 1995; Schneider, Kristof-Brown, Goldstein, & Smith 1997). Few studies have examined collective fit as a comparison of collective or aggregate P and E characteristics (Ostroff, 1993a); however, a number of studies have examined the degree of similarity of among group members on some attribute and the relationship between similarity among members and group outcomes (e.g., Barrick, Stewart, Neubert, & Mount, 1998; Sacco & Schmitt, 2005; Taggar & Neubert, 2004). Ostroff and Schulte (2007) provide a comprehensive conceptual treatment and develop a framework for understanding how fit emerges at higher levels of analysis and interested readers are referred to that source. For the purposes here, the focus is limited to fit at the individual level of analysis.

Modes of Conceptualizing E in PE Fit: Personal Attributes versus Fit to Situational Attributes

Numerous variables have been considered on the P side in PE fit conceptualizations and research (Kristof, 1996). P variables can be roughly divided into three broad categories: (a) knowledge, skills, and abilities (KSAs) and related attributes such as experience; (b) personality and person-centered attributes such as traits, needs or preferences, values, goals, interests; and (c) demographic and background characteristics such as race, gender and education. On the E side, an analogous set of characteristics ensues including: (a) collective skills and abilities, and skill and ability requirements; (b) collective personality, contextual features, climate, cultural values, and goals; and (c) demographic and background composition.

While there is little ambiguity in terms of individual P, there are different views of how the E in PE fit should be conceptualized. In particular, the E can be based on the personal characteristics of those comprising the environment representing the interpersonal environment, or E can be based on a higher-order contextual or situational construct representing a higher-order sociocultural or social-psychological environment (Pervin, 1968; Van Vianen, 2000; Wapner & Demick, 2000).

The rationale for describing E based on the personal attributes of those in the environment is largely driven by Schneider's ASA model (1987a, 1987b). In support of this notion, personality and values have been shown to be more similar within organizations than across organizations and industries, suggesting the viability of defining the environment through the personal characteristics of individuals (Giberson, Resick, & Dickson, 2005; Schneider, Smith, Taylor, & Fleenor, 1998). The E in PE fit can be characterized by the aggregate or collective attributes of people because homogeneity in personal attributes such as values, goals, and personality purportedly results over time as people gravitate to, are selected by, and remain in environments composed of people with attributes similar to their own. A number of authors support the view that the E in PE fit can be based on the collective personal attributes of those who inhabit the environment (cf., Hogan & Roberts, 2000; Holland, 1997; Muchinsky & Monahan, 1987; Schneider, 1987a)

and is typically referred to as person-person, or PP, fit. Theoretically, the mechanisms underlying person-person fit are based largely on similarity-attraction notions (Byrne & Nelson, 1965) because similarity is reinforcing and reciprocally rewarding (Pervin, 1968). In addition, person-person fit can enhance self-identity (Swann et al., 2004) and feelings of self-worth (Brief & Aldag, 1981), and can reduce ambiguity and uncertainty (Kalliath et al., 1999).

In contrast, the E in PE fit can be conceptualized as a situational characteristic that exists independently from the individuals within the environment (Chatman, 1989). The organizational situation is divided into two broad domains, the social and the structural-technical context (Katz & Kahn, 1978; Ostroff & Schulte, 2007). Organizations have long been viewed as social systems in which people create social structures through complex patterns of behaviors (Katz & Kahn, 1978). The organizational environment can be described from a social-psychological basis that constitutes higher-order socially interactive constructs, or the social context (Ferris, Hochwarter, Buckley, Harrell-Cook, & Frink, 1999). Higher-order indicates that social structures exist in organizations that cannot be reduced to an aggregation of the perceptions of the individuals currently comprising the environment and are likely to be fundamental and enduring, independent of the occupants in the organization (Chatman, 1989). Roles, norms, values, climate, and culture are illustrative of the social structures that emerge over time in organizations.

It is important to note that the social structures in the organizational environment reside in the cognitions, behaviors, or attributes of individuals. Through processes such as interaction, exchange, sense-making and communications, the individual-level elements converge and emerge into a higher-order social structure (Kozlowski & Klein, 2000). Hence, assessment of the social structures in the situational environment will typically be based on reports of the social situational variable (e.g., values, goals) and when consensus across people is demonstrated, the aggregate across respondents is taken to represent the higher order social-psychological situational variable (cf., Chatman, 1991; Erdogan, Kraimer, & Liden, 2004; Ostroff, 1993b; Vancouver & Schmitt, 1991). When the environment is viewed as a social situational variable, an individual-level attribute is compared to a homologous social situational characteristic, and this social situation is emergent through the convergence of perceptions, values, behaviors, or goals of individuals within the environment.

A second domain of the organizational situation is the structural-technical environment. PE fit in this arena is viewed as a comparison between individuals' attributes and those of the structural and technical components of the situation. The structural domain of the organization is based largely on the technical and production subsystems in the organization with an emphasis on task accomplishment as well as maintenance subsystems with formal procedures and processes geared toward institutionalizing aspects of behavior in the interest of task accomplishment (Katz & Kahn, 1978). Structural aspects of the environment include task requirements, work structures, reward systems, and job characteristics. In conceptualizing fit to the structural domain of the situation, E is not an emergent construct based on convergence among individuals' views, cognitions, or behaviors, as in fit to the social situation. Rather, the E components in the structural domain are based on formal systems, procedures, and objective aspects of the situation (Ostroff & Schulte, 2007).

The underlying mechanisms for both person-social and person-structure fit reside in both similarity perspectives and fulfillment perspectives. The situational element in the environment affords opportunities for individuals to gratify their needs or desires (e.g., Cable & Edwards, 2004; Pervin, 1992), reduces psychological stress and strain (e.g., Shaw & Gupta, 2004), allows people to utilize their skills and abilities effectively (e.g., Edwards, 1991), provides a sense of identity or self-worth due to operating in an environment that is conducive to their attributes (e.g., Brief & Aldag, 1981), or affords comfort and psychological safety through similarity to the context (e.g., Dawis & Lofquist, 1984).

In sum, the modes of defining the E in PE fit can be based on the personal attributes of others in the environment (PP mode) or based on the social or structural situation (PS fit). These modes of fit can be crossed with the various types of fit (PI, PJ, PG, PO) as well as with the differing perspectives of fit (similarity, fulfillment, compilation). The bottom portion of Table 12.1 provides a few illustrative examples of the crossing of types, modes, and perspectives of fit.

Level of Specificity: Global, Domain, and Specific

Edwards & Shipp (2007) further distinguished fit conceptualizations based on the content breadth of the P and E dimensions, ranging from general to specific. The global level refers to a broad array of P and E variables across different content domains.

The domain level is more specific than the global level and encompasses a general content area but does not distinguish specific dimensions within the broad area. At a more refined level, the facet level focuses on specific dimensions of P and E. For example, studies at the global level might assess individual preferences and environmental attributes across a wide range of social and structural aspects such as social relationships, diversity, learning goals, autonomy, and task complexity. An overall index of the degree of fit may be created, such as through profile comparisons (e.g., Chatman, 1991; Gustafson & Mumford, 1995), without attention to specific differences between the different domains. At the domain level, the focus is narrowed to a particular content domain such as values, goals, or job complexity, but different dimensions within that content domain are not specified. At the facet level, specific dimensions are examined separately. For example, in studying value congruence, some researchers have operated at the domain level (e.g., Meglino et al., 1989) while others examine different dimensions of values at the facet level (e.g., Ostroff et al., 2005).

This distinction with respect to level of specificity has implications for relationships between PE fit and outcomes. Meta-analytic results have shown that broader and general attitudes are better predictors of broad-based outcomes while more specific attitudes are better suited for more narrow and specific outcomes (Harrison, Newman, & Roth, 2006). The same is likely to be true in the PE fit area, with global or domain approaches best suited for more general outcomes such as overall satisfaction, commitment, or general performance, while facet approaches may be more important for specific outcomes such as facet satisfaction or task performance. Additional work in this regard is warranted.

Summary

The construct space of PE fit in organizational settings is far reaching. Fit can be examined across a wide range of different content areas encompassing nearly all aspects of organizational life. Further, P and E factors can be combined in a number of ways. As discussed above, fit can be viewed from an objective or subjective approach which can be crossed with: (1) the level of analysis to which the person is compared (PI, PJ, PG, PO), (2) different perspectives (similarity, fulfillment, compilation), (3) the mode for defining the environment (PP or PS), and (4) the level of specificity of the content domain (global, domain, facet). Given the multitude of ways that PE fit can be conceptualized and examined, it is no wonder that some researchers have noted that the study of PE fit is challenging, complex, and often presents seemingly intractable problems (e.g., Judge, 2007; Kristof-Brown et al., 2005; Schneider, Smith, & Goldstein, 2000).

A summary of the key questions and means for classifying PE fit research is contained in Table 12.2. Given the complexity of PE fit, researchers are encouraged to attend to the key identifying features of fit research and to specify the levels of analysis, subtype, mode, and perspective of fit in their work.

Having provided an overview of the different means of considering PE fit and some of the ambiguities and controversies that exist in the area of research, I now return to Figure 12.1 to explicate the linkages between objective fit, subjective fit, and outcomes. Only general processes will be explicated, although the general notions presented are expected to be relevant to the array of types and modes of fit.

Relationships Between Objective and Subjective Fit

As indicated earlier, and following French et al. (1974), objective E and P combine to create objective fit, and subjective E and P combine to create subjective fit (see Figure 12.1). Subjective fit is expected to be more strongly related to outcomes than objective fit because it is perceptions of, rather than the actual reality, that purportedly drive responses (e.g., Mischel, 1977), and the two have different relationships to outcomes (Ravlin & Ritchie, 2006). Two additional reasons can be proposed for why objective and subjective fit have different relationships to individual outcomes.

First, the objective reality may have influences on individuals that bypass their perceptual filters due to the cognitive processing and schemas that people use to interpret reality (Schulte, Ostroff, & Kinicki, 2006). Sociologists have long supported group effects theory, arguing that individuals are guided by their own attributes but also act in accordance with the group (e.g., Blau, 1960). Similarly, the complexity of the work environment is believed to require people to rely on social cues in addition to their own perceptions in order to make sense of the situation Salancik & Pfeffer, 1978), and the cognitive representation of the organizational experience is not only determined by individual patterns of thinking and understanding but also by influential relationships and organizational norms (Gioia, Thomas, Clark, & Chittipeddi, 1994).

Second, perceptions of the self and/or environment may be inaccurate (French et al., 1974).

Determining the accuracy of perception can be difficult. Accuracy in self-assessments may be more readily derived for certain attributes such as skills, abilities, and background, because valid objective measures can be used. However, for other attributes such as personality or leadership attributes, determining the degree of accuracy is more difficult. For these types of attributes, accuracy is often viewed as a form of consistency between how individuals observe and evaluate themselves and how others perceive and evaluate them with respect to that characteristic. In these cases, accuracy is usually viewed as a form of self-awareness. In either case, however, self-assessments are often inaccurate (Ashford, 1989). A similar problem exists in determining the accuracy of perceptions about the environment. For structural elements of the situation (e.g., job requirement or complexity), objective indicators may be available which can then be compared to individuals' perceptions in order to assess perceptual accuracy of the environment. However, for the social context of the environment, such as culture or climate, the reality of the situation is often based on aggregated perceptions of others (provided consensus in perceptions). In these cases, accuracy of E is often based on the degree to which an individual's perception is consistent with the situational reality as defined through collective perceptions of others.

Both environment and person accuracy have been shown to be related to outcomes. For example, multisource feedback studies rest on the notion of self-awareness, and the degree of self-other agreement has been related to individuals' outcomes (e.g., Ostroff, Atwater, & Feinberg, 2004). Studies have also begun to assess perceptual accuracy by comparing an individual's own perceptions of the environment (e.g., values, climate) with collective perceptions of cultural values or unit climate and have shown that consistency is related to outcomes (e.g., McKay, Avery, & Morris, 2009; Ostroff et al., 2005). Given that these types of accuracy are themselves related to outcomes, it is important to understand the factors that may influence convergence between objective and subjective E and objective and subjective P because PE fit combines these elements. Further, higher convergence or greater accuracy should also allow for more similar relationships to be observed between objective and subjective fit and outcomes.

Influences on Fit and Accuracy of Perceptions

The extent of inaccuracies in either perceptions of the environment or perceptions of the self will

Table 12.2 Key Questions and Means for Classifying Fit Theory and Research

Key Question	Definition	General Examples
Fit "to" which level of analysis?	Level of analysis of E component (e.g., supervisor, group, organization)	Combined with P creates fit subtypes such as person-supervisor (PI), person-job (PJ), person-group (PG), or person-organization (PO) fit
Fit "at" which level of analysis?	Level of analysis at which study as a whole is conducted (e.g., individual, group, organization level)	PE fit is related to individuals' performance in an individual-level study Aggregated P and E are related or to group effectiveness in a group-level study
Mode of E in PE fit (collective attributes or situational context)?	E is based on the collective or aggregated personal attributes of those in the environment E is based on a situational context characteristic • Social domain based on higher-order social structures and systems • Structural-Technical domain based on technical, production and maintenance systems	Combined with P creates person-person (PP) fit with E based on attributes such as collective personality or collective values of members Combined with P creates person-situation fit with E based on the context, such as culture or climate (social domain), or job requirement, reward system (structural-technical) domain
Fit perspective (similarity, fulfillment, compilation)?	Similarity or accord between the characteristics of P and E In fulfillment, E fulfills P or P fulfills E Compilation is based on configurations or profiles	P and E are similar such the values of the individual are similar to the cultural values espoused in the organization P such as individuals' desires are met by the characteristics in the E Attributes such as individuals' personality or skills differ but mesh in a complementary way
Level of specificity (global, domain, facet)?	Global encompasses a range of different P and E variables Domain focuses on a specific content area but dimensions within are not distinguished Facet entails specific dimensions of P and E	Multitude of different P and E attributes assessed such as goals, values, and job characteristics and a single overall index of fit is created P and E assessed in reference to a particular content domain such as goals and an overall index of fit is created P and E assessed for one or more specific dimensions such as different types of goals and the index of fit is examined for each dimension separately
Objective or subjective P and E?	P and/or E are assessed objectively independently of individual P and/or E are based on subjective assessments from the focal P	Objective E such as job requirements assessed through job analysis compared to objective P of skills assessed through tests Perceptions of job requirements compared to individuals' perceptions of own skills
Commensurate or non-commensurate dimensions?	With commensurate, P and E components are defined with same dimensions, entailing same content, and ensuring that P and E are conceptually relevant to one another With non-commensurate, P and E components are distinct but conceptually related and the point of congruence or alignment is specified	P is represented as value placed on teamwork and E is teamwork as an espoused cultural value in the environment; fit is similarity between the two P is represented as affiliation personality and E is represented by task interdependence; fit is specified as moderate affiliation combined with high task interdependence

decrease the overlap between objective and subjective fit. A number of organizational practices and individual difference variables have been proposed to influence the degree of fit. As depicted in Figure 12.1, it is also expected that many of these same variables will influence the degree of overlap between objective and subjective fit by increasing the convergence or accuracy between objective and subjective E and objective and subjective P.

INFORMATION, TRAINING, AND FEEDBACK

As explained by Cable and Yu (2007), the extent to which individuals receive information about the organizational context is likely to influence their degree of fit because it better allows them to self-select into environments to which they fit. Likewise, from the organization's perspective, a greater degree of information about individuals allows for selecting and placing individuals into environments for which they fit best. In addition, the degree to which individuals accurately perceive the reality of the organizational environment is expected to be related to the information that they receive. The amount of information, the richness of the information, and the credibility and expertise of the information source have strong influences on perceptions and beliefs. Without sufficient and rich information, individuals will be less likely to carefully consider information about the environment producing less accurate perceptions of E and a lower relationship between objective and subjective fit.

Theoretically, training should also enhance fit, particularly PJ fit (Chatman, 1991; Ostroff, Shin, & Feinberg, 2002; Werbel & Gilliland, 1999). Little research, however, has explicitly tested this proposition. An exception is Chatman (1991) who found that time spent in formal training throughout the first year on the job was not related to greater PO or PJ fit. It may be that training increases fit only when PJ fit is poor to begin with (Ostroff et al., 2002). Alternately, it is likely that the impact of training on fit depends on the skill level of the job. For jobs with major technical requirements (e.g., engineering, nursing), training prior to organizational entry is critical, while for semi-skilled labor occupations, only broad-based or general skills may be important, and training for specific skills can increase PJ fit while on the job (Werbel & Gilliland, 1999). Training is also likely to influence the convergence between objective and subjective fit. Feedback on skills obtained during training will likely increase self-awareness of both technical and interpersonal competencies as well as provide richer information about the job and situational context, increasing the accuracy of both P and E perceptions.

Other sources of feedback may also enhance self-awareness and accuracy of self-perceptions. Feedback from peers, supervisors, and subordinates, as in multisource feedback programs, provides information that is not otherwise readily available (Ashford, 1993).

SOCIALIZATION

Socialization tactics have long been deemed to help create and enhance fit (e.g., Cable & Parsons, 2001; Chatman, 1991; Cooper-Thomas, Van Vianen, & Anderson, 2004; Kim, Cable, & Kim, 2005; Kristof, 1996; Ostroff & Rothausen, 1997; Rynes et al., 1991). The goal of socialization is to facilitate learning about the task, job, role, group, values, people, politics, and goals of the organization (Chao, O'Leary-Kelly, Wolf, Klein, & Gardner, 1994). Socialization enhances sense-making by providing employees with a framework for responding to their work environment and provides a means for coordinating with other employees (Jones, 1986; Van Maanen & Schein, 1979). The socialization process should be fundamental for enhancing fit because it provides information about the context and helps individuals find ways to align their attributes with those of the environment. Some evidence indicates that fit is greater after engaging in socialization because individuals change to be more similar to their organization (e.g., Chatman, 1991) or because perceptions of the environment change over time (Harms, Roberts, & Winter, 2006). The degree to which fit is enhanced over time is also dependent on the type of socialization tactics used, with more encompassing and intensive tactics related to greater fit (Cable & Parsons, 2001). The information provided about the environment with intensive socialization tactics should increase the accuracy of E perceptions directly and also may indirectly influence the accuracy of P perceptions as individuals learn about themselves and their reactions in the new environment. Hence, socialization should increase convergence between objective and subjective fit.

MENTORING

Mentoring can be another means to help individuals achieve PE fit, but little research has explicitly addressed the role of mentoring in fit. Chatman (1991) found that the number of hours spent with a mentor during the first year on the job was found to be related to PO fit in terms of value congruence. Mentors are likely to be important in fit because they help protégés develop technical, interpersonal, and political skills that enable them to navigate the organization more effectively (Kram & Hall, 1989). Mentors provide both career-enhancing support, such as the transmission of knowledge and social capital, as well as psychosocial support relevant to work and professional development. Through interactions with a mentor, protégés may use mentors' perceptions about values and the social context as reference points for themselves. Further, because the career-enhancing function of a mentor are heavily weighted toward a focus on role and organizational issues (Kram, 1985), mentors may be particularly useful for enhancing protégés' PG and PO fit rather than their PJ fit.

The psychosocial support provided by mentors may also help increase individuals' self-accuracy through the feedback and learning that they receive about themselves. Further, individuals with mentors have been shown to learn more about the organizational culture, values, politics, and organizational system than non-mentored individuals (Ostroff & Kozlowski, 1993). The greater amount of information should be particularly useful for enhancing the accuracy of subjective E perceptions about the broad social context of the organization. Taken together, this suggests that mentors can help increase convergence between objective and subjective fit, particularly PO fit, through the information provided about the self and the organization.

INTERDEPENDENCE

The degree to which the work design and social context promotes interdependencies and interactions among individuals should influence PE fit. Interactions with others facilitates sense-making and situational identification (Louis, 1990). Social interactions can lead to greater integration. Further, a greater reliance on the values of others as points of reference for themselves is likely to enhance PO fit over time (Chatman, 1991). When individuals are required to work in groups to a great extent, they come to appreciate the importance of having goals, values, and styles that are consistent with those of their group members (e.g., Kristof-Brown, & Stevens, 2001; Jehn, Northcraft, & Neale, 1999) and rely on the group to provide a sense of physical and emotional support. Hence, they are motivated to change in the direction of achieving PG fit (Yu, 2009).

Further, overlapping perceptions or schemas can be facilitated through social exchange and transactions among employees so that they come to agree on the aspects of the environment to attend to as well as how to interpret these aspects and respond

to them appropriately (Weick, 1995; Wicker, 1992). Employees construct the meaning of organizational events from repeated social interactions, and it is these interactions that are likely to result in conformity (Ashforth, 1985). Informal interaction groups have been shown to attach similar meanings to the organizational context (Fink & Chen, 1995; Rentsch, 1990). Greater interdependence and interactions should promote greater accuracy in perceptions of the environment and should be particularly important for accuracy of perceptions of the social context such as climate or culture. Further, interactions often prompt a social comparison process (Wood, 1989) whereby individuals may compare themselves to others, and in doing so, may increase their self-awareness and the accuracy of their self-perceptions, ultimately enhancing the overlap between objective and subjective fit.

SITUATIONAL STRENGTH

Strong situations should produce greater fit. The environment or situation entails the meaning of situations for the individual *and* the behavior potential of situations for the individual (Endler & Magnusson, 1976). When the situation is strong, individual deviations are not appropriate. As Mischel described:

> Psychological "situations" and "treatments" are powerful to the degree that they lead all persons to construe the particular events the same way, induce *uniform* expectancies regarding the most appropriate response pattern, provide adequate incentives for the performance of that response pattern, and instill the skills necessary for its satisfactory construction and execution. Conversely, situations and treatments are weak to the degree that they are not uniformly encoded, do not generate uniform expectancies concerning the desired behavior, do not offer sufficient incentives for its performance, or fail to provide the learning conditions for successful construction of the behavior.

(*Mischel*, 1973, p. 276; emphasis contained in the original)

Thus, fit, particularly similarity-based fit, is induced in strong situations because individuals will construe the environment in the same way and will behave similarly. Over time, reinforcements in the environment constrain individual behavior to be consistent with the organization (Holland, 1985).

INDIVIDUAL DIFFERENCES

Only recently has attention turned to individual differences that might influence fit or the importance of fit. In particular, prior experience has been deemed an important consideration (e.g., Carr, Pearson, Vest, & Boyar, 2006; Kristof-Brown, Jansen, & Colbert, 2002; Shipp & Jansen, 2011; Shipp, Edwards, & Lambert, 2009; Yu, 2009). A greater degree of experience in organizations can influence anticipatory fit with the organization (Carr et al., 2006) as well as the importance of different types of fit such as PO versus PJ fit (Kristof-Brown et al., 2002). Yu (2009) speculates that greater experience motivates individuals to change E, rather than P, in order to achieve fit. Experience may also influence the accuracy of subjective P and E perceptions. For example, experience was related to lower self-other agreement or self-awareness (Ostroff et al., 2004) but may also increase the ability to accurately assess the environment (Shipp & Jansen, 2011). Exploration into the role of other individual differences as both influences on fit and moderators of the convergence between objective and subjective fit is needed. For example, self-efficacy and growth satisfaction may be important for the degree to which fit changes over time (DeRue & Morgeson, 2007). Differences in the ability to cognitively process information, personality traits such as agreeableness, and work versus life relevance may relate to fit in interesting ways.

Fit, Misfit, and Relationships to Outcomes

While the notion of misfit is an inherent component of PE fit theory and research, it has received relatively little explicit attention in the literature (Judge, 2007; Kristof-Brown & Guay, 2010; Talbot, Billsberry, & Marsh, 2007). In general, researchers tend to conceptualize and treat misfit as lack of fit. In studies of value congruence and goal congruence, misfit has been assumed to be represented by low convergence between the individual and the higher-order social-psychological environment of values or goals (e.g., Chatman, 1991; Kim et al., 2005; Kristof-Brown & Stevens, 2001; Schneider, 1983; Schneider et al., 2000). Misfit has also been construed as dissimilarity between the focal individual and others in the environment (e.g., Avery et al., 2007; Sacco & Schmitt, 2005; Tsui, Egan, & O'Reilly, 1992). Billsberry and his colleagues (Billsberry, van Meurs, Coldwell, & Marsh, 2006) provided an explicit definition of misfit as occurring when compatibility is detrimental to an individual and organization. Despite ample rhetoric about misfit, a systematic approach to misfit's conceptualization and operationalization has not been undertaken.

Misfit

A key premise in defining PE fit and misfit is that it is a construct in and of itself, divorced from outcomes (Harrison, 2007). That is, fit can be related to various organizational outcomes, but inclusion of outcomes in the definition is erroneous for delineating PE fit as a construct. As an independent construct, PE fit may have either positive or negative relationships to outcomes. While many theoretical rationales about PE fit purport that a greater degree of fit will result in more positive outcomes, particularly for individuals (Edwards & Shipp, 2007; Kristof-Brown et al., 2005; Ostroff & Schulte, 2007), relationships are not always hypothesized to be positive (e.g., Schneider et al., 2000). Just as fit should not be defined in terms of its relationship to outcomes, the definition of misfit should not be conceived of in relationship to outcomes (i.e., misfit should not be defined as a state that produces negative outcomes).

Difficulties arise in developing a generic definition of misfit, in part, because what constitutes misfit depends on the perspective adopted (similarity, fulfillment, compilation). At a basic level, misfit can be said to occur when the attribute under investigation is different for P and E, and the largest amount of misfit occurs when P and E are as different as possible (Harrison, 2007). Using this definition, congruence or similarity between P and E constitute fit, and deviations between P and E represent misfit. This definition generally applies when a similarity-based perspective is the foundation for the fit construct as congruence is typically taken to represent fit. However, as Harrison (2007) notes, the application of this definition to fulfillment and compilation perspectives becomes more difficult.

From a theoretical stance, in similarity-based perspectives, fit is represented by congruence or match, and all else (divergence between P and E and complements between P and E) is assumed to be misfit. However, when fulfillment-based perspectives are used, fit can take different forms. P = E and P > E may be deemed fit, and all else assumed misfit (i.e., P < E and complementary P and E attributes); P = E and P < E may be deemed to represent fit and all else assumed misfit; or P = E may be deemed to represent fit and all else misfit. With a compilation perspective, fit occurs with a lack of similarity, but P and E represent a complementarity. In compilation, misfit would be represented by dissimilarities in P and E that do not complement one another. Using Harrison's (2007) definition of misfit, a researcher who hypothesizes that fit is represented when rewards meet or exceed demands, and further that fit and excess relate to higher levels of individual outcomes, would need to state that both fit (P = E) and misfit (in the form of P > E) or excess is related to more positive outcomes. In a compilation model, a researcher would need to explicate that misfit in the form of a complementary is of interest.

Thus, rather than viewing misfit from a singular perspective, a broader approach is proposed here by examining misfit from multiple perspectives. What is deemed misfit from a similarity approach (P and E are not congruent) may represent a complementarity from a compilation perspective and a different form of fit. For example, consider the attribute of age. From a similarity perspective, it might be hypothesized that greater similarity (fit) will be related to more engagement due to social identity, self-categorization, and the ability to develop stronger friendships (Avery et al., 2007). Yet, the age difference might represent a complementarity type of fit as opposed to misfit. From a compilation perspective, it might be hypothesized that an employee in a group of older employees represents a complement such that experienced, older employees share organization-specific skills learned over time with the young employee, and the young employee shares general skills and new approaches with the older employees. In the first case, from a similarity perspective, the difference between the young employee and the older coworkers would be considered misfit. In the second case, with a compilation perspective, that same difference would represent fit through a complement, and similarity and other complements (e.g., middle-aged and older workers) are considered misfit. As another example, from a skill standpoint, consider a nuclear engineer in a unit on a naval ship whose skills are needed to "make whole" the unit. This would represent complementary fit (Muchinsky & Monahan, 1987) or compilation fit (Ostroff & Schulte, 2007). From a similarity standpoint, this would represent misfit because similarity-attraction, self-categorization, and self identity could not operate as the individual does not have similar others (other nuclear engineers) with which to identify. In other words, lack of similarity may not necessarily represent misfit; it may represent a different form of fit through complementary attributes. These examples suggest that the definition and conceptualization of misfit remain ambiguous, and the issue of misfit is in need of further development in several ways.

First, misfit could be conceptualized and studied itself, using a broader perspective that allows for multiple types of misfit simultaneously. A tentative global definition of misfit is offered here. Broadly, misfit can be conceptualized as lack of similarity, lack of fulfillment, *and* lack of complementarity. In other words, fit can be construed as either congruence or as complementary attributes. Overall misfit occurs when an individual is not similar to E, does not have one's needs, values, or abilities fulfilled by the environment, and does not complement E or others in E. Overall misfit is a difference between the person and environment whereby the difference reflects an incompatibility across all three theoretical perspectives of fit. Using a broader perspective opens up avenues for future research to address how misfit such as lack of similarity may (or may not) represent compilation fit.

Second, at a more specific level, the conceptualization and definition of misfit depends on the fit perspective adopted. Researchers should carefully consider the meaning of misfit given the theoretical foundation used in developing fit conceptualizations and rationales, acknowledging that what is assumed to be misfit in a particular study with a particular perspective may represent different forms of fit from another perspective. Misfit from a similarity perspective implies lack of similarity or a divergence between P and E. Misfit from a fulfillment perspective is likely more complex and will depend on the degree to which excess or deficiency can also represent fit. From a compilation perspective, misfit refers to attributes that do not complement E or other individuals in the environment.

A third and critical issue is that the underlying assumption in much of the fit literature has been that fit and misfit are opposite ends of a continuum, yet this assumption has not been explored. An alternative is that fit and misfit are different, but related, constructs. That is, fit may range from a high to low degree of fit, and then a tipping point occurs whereby one moves into misfit as a repelling force. For example, consider fit in the area of teamwork. A high degree of similarity-based fit might include similar goals with respect to cooperation, teamwork, and interdependence. Low fit would be a situation in which the team was high on those goals and an individual was low on those same goals, or vice versa. Misfit, however, may not simply be represented by a high team–low individual goal, but would include individual goals and attributes that actively resist teamwork, oppose cooperating with others in a team, or actively disrupting team processes. As another example, a high degree of fit on the organizational cultural value of integrity could be represented by similar levels of integrity for both the organizational and individual values. A low degree of fit might be represented by a high organizational value for integrity with the individual indicating a low value for integrity. Yet, misfit would be represented by a high organizational value on integrity and an individual who deems cheating, embezzling funds, taking credit for others' work, and the like as acceptable. That is, a low individual value of integrity coupled with a high organizational value may be low fit, not misfit, because it does not represent a repelling force against the value. Similar issues may be present with respect to fulfillment-based fit. The extent to which a need or desire is not fulfilled may represent low fit; misfit would be a situation in which the need or desire is opposed or thwarted in the context. Additional research is needed to determine if fit and misfit are a continuum or separate constructs, whether there is a tipping point from fit to low fit to misfit, and the extent to which the opposing or repelling forces represent misfit.

Relationships Between Fit, Misfit, and Individual Outcomes

A great deal of research, summarized in meta-analytic studies, has been devoted to understanding relationships between PE fit and individual outcomes such as satisfaction, attitudes, adjustment, and turnover (Arthur et al., 2006; Assouline & Meir, 1987; Hoffman & Woehr, 2006; Kristof-Brown et al., 2005; Verquer et al., 2003; Yang, Levine, Smith, Ispas, & Rossi, 2008). The preponderance of theory and empirical research indicates that a greater degree of fit is related to more positive individual-level outcomes, and fit has been studied in relation to a wide array of individual outcome variables. In general, results of meta-analyses reveal that PO, PJ, and PG fit have strong relationships to attitudinal outcomes such as satisfaction, organizational attraction, and commitment; PJ and PG fit show modest relationships while PO fit shows weak relationships to performance; PO fit has low relationships to turnover; and subjective fit is more strongly related to outcomes than objective or indirect-actual fit (Kristof-Brown & Guay, 2010). The underlying assumption, although not directly tested, in this body of work assumes that fit leads to feelings of comfort or ease in dealing with the context, feelings of self-worth, self-identity, need fulfillment, or positive reactions, which in turn lead to positive attitudes, the desire to contribute, and the desire to remain in the situation.

Recently, Edwards and Cable (Cable & Edwards, 2004; Edwards & Cable, 2009) proposed that the relationship between PE fit, specifically value

congruence, and outcomes operates through several mechanisms. Direct effects of value congruence on outcomes were found to be stronger than those mediated through need fulfillment, suggesting that need fulfillment only partially and weakly explains relationships between fit and outcomes (Cable & Edwards, 2004). However, the relationship between value congruence and outcomes of satisfaction, identification, and intention to stay in the organization were explained through the degree of trust that individuals place in the organization, increased communication and information exchange, and the development of positive feelings of friendship or liking for others in the organization (Edwards & Cable, 2009). Their latter findings suggest that PE fit may not only operate on individuals' needs and sense of self but also makes navigating organizational life easier through communications and relationships with others.

The focus of most theory and research begins with fit or congruence and explicates the consequences of fit. Implicit in this perspective is that either low fit or misfit does not produce these positive reactions on the part of individuals and hence leads to lower or negative outcomes. Yet, the process through which misfit leads to less positive outcomes or turnover has not been well explicated (Kristof-Brown & Guay, 2010). It is likely that misfit produces a set of psychological processes and coping mechanisms that differ from those of fit.

Scant theory and research have explicitly investigated misfit (cf., Billsberry et al., 2006; Sacco & Schmitt, 2005; Talbot et al., 2007; Wheeler, Coleman-Gallagher, Brouer, & Sablynski, 2007; Yu, 2009). It is important to more explicitly address misfit because its consequences may be more salient and may show stronger relationships to outcomes than those of fit. Individuals make attributions to explain why they behave in certain ways and look to cues such as consensus among others, distinctiveness, and consistency of signals or events (Kelley, 1973). Consistency in messages has been shown to have a greater effect on attributions than consensus or distinctiveness (McArthur, 1972). Misfit can be viewed as a form of inconsistency in that the messages individuals receive about the environment and about themselves may be inconsistent. Several reactions to misfit and moderators of the relationship between mis(fit) and outcomes are proposed below to stimulate future theory and research (see Figure 12.1).

DISSONANCE RESPONSES

A number of theories point to the notion that individuals strive for consistency in social situations and organizational life (e.g., Cialdini, 2001; Kelley, 1973; Lecky, 1945; Lidz, 1973; Satir, 1988; Siehl, 1985) as a means to protect their self-concept and self-knowledge (Epstein, 1979; Steele & Spencer, 1992). This motive for consistency leads people to seek information that is consistent with what they believe about themselves and to avoid or reject information that presents inconsistencies. Self-verification theory indicates that individuals feel more secure when they believe that others see them as they see themselves, hence they actively seek self-verifying feedback to protect their self-views (Swann, Stein-Seroussi, & Giesler, 1992). Similarly, in accordance with social comparison theory, people compare their attributes with others and draw inferences about themselves (Helgeson & Mickelson, 1995; Wood, 1989). Applying these notions to PE fit suggests that people are likely to strive for a similar type of consistency, in this case between themselves (P) and the environment (E), and when the two differ, individuals' self-views may threatened.

One response may to be avoid or reject the incongruent information presented by a difference between P and E. Rejection of incongruent information may lead individuals to selectively perceive or adjust their perceptions of the self and the environment, thereby enhancing subjective fit and promoting more positive individual responses. However, even with altered perceptions, the degree of objective misfit may still have some impact on the degree to which the individual is able to function effectively in the work situation.

A second response is that inconsistencies between P and E may lead to strong feelings of cognitive dissonance (Festinger, 1957). The inconsistency between P and E may be seen as a form of double-bind communication (Bateson, Jackson, Haley, & Weakland, 1956) whereby the two messages from P (information about the self) and E (information about the environment) are related to each other, dealing with the same content area, but they are incongruent or contradictory. The lack of consistency in double-bind communication can lead to intense cognitive dissonance (Siehl, 1985). Dissonance theory proposes that individuals have a strong motivational drive to reduce the dissonance by changing their cognitions or behaviors (Festinger, 1957) or by developing other coping mechanisms to enhance well-being (Edwards, 1992).

ALTERING P AND E: ASSIMILATION AND ACCOMMODATION

To reduce experienced dissonance from misfit, individuals may attempt either to change themselves to fit the environment or to change the environment to be one in which they will fit better. Theories of fit have traditionally emphasized the dynamic nature of fit (e.g., French et al., 1974; Holland, 1997; Shipp & Jansen, 2011). Adjustment is seen as a continuous and dynamic process whereby individuals seek to achieve and maintain congruence with the work environment (Dawis & Lofquist, 1984) and may result in changes in both P and E over time (Holland, 1976, 1997). Although extant models of fit indicate that individuals are motivated to resolve misfit by changing the objective or subjective person or environment (e.g., French et al., 1974), lesser attention has been devoted to explicating the mechanisms underlying the process of adjustments in P and E (Yu, 2009).

Role transition theory (Nicholson, 1987; Nicholson & West, 1988) is informative as it addresses both personal and environmental change processes that occur when individuals take on new organizational roles. Assimilation or personal change entails a change in the individual in response to the environment. Individual assimilation and change may range from minor adjustments in the self such as changing daily routines and habits, to major adjustments in self-image and self-identity. The desire for a sense of identity and belonging in the work setting makes individuals amenable to personal change (Ashforth, 2001).

Accommodation or role innovation entails adjustments in the environment whereby individuals mold their work role to fit themselves (Nicholson & West, 1988). Adjustments to E can be in the form of minor initiatives such as changing the work schedule, or intensive changes such as changing organizational goals. Changing the environment allows individual to express their valued personal identities, impute meaning and purpose into their role, and accommodate their preferred means of operating and behaving. That is, to role innovate is to "personalize and individualize the way a role is enacted to suit's one's judgment and idiosyncrasies" (Ashforth, 2001, p. 195).

Interestingly, assimilation (personal change) and accommodation (role innovation) tend to be weakly correlated (Ashforth & Saks, 1995), suggesting that changing the self does not mean that changes in the environment are unnecessary in order to achieve adjustment and fit (Nicholson & West, 1988). Changes in both P and E may occur simultaneously or may occur sequentially, such as the individual changing to assimilate but then later desiring to change E to better accommodate their changed self-identity (Ashforth, 2001).

Recently, Yu (2009) proposed an affective-consistency perspective to explain changes in both subjective and objective P and E components. According to this perspective, affect at work acts as a cause of PE fit because individuals need to feel consistent with their experienced affect, and affect biases people to think congruently about the self and environment. Experienced affect may precede perceptions about the self and the environment. Individuals will distort or adjust their perceptions of subjective P and E in order to achieve subjective fit so that consistency exists between PE fit and feelings about the work. Thus, for example, an individual who experiences positive affect when misfit exists will be motivated to change his or her cognitions or behaviors to achieve PE in order to be consistent with his or her experienced affective state.

Much PE fit theory and research points to the notion that fit or congruence will lead to better adjustment, better performance, and more positive attitudes (Kristof-Brown et al., 2005). Likewise, theory and research on the ASA process indicates that individuals who do not fit will eventually leave the organization (Arthur et al., 2006; De Cooman et al., 2009; Kristof-Brown et al., 2005; Schneider, 1983; Schneider et al., 2000). However, misfit may not necessarily lead to more negative outcomes over time. Taken together, role transition theory and affective consistency theory suggest that relationships between misfit and outcomes may depend on the degree of assimilation, accommodation, and perceptual distortion.

As suggested by the feedback loops in Figure 12.1, perceptual distortion in response to dissonance will increase subjective fit through altering perceptions of P and/or E toward fit. Assimilation and accommodation will increase objective fit through changes in the objective P and/or E toward congruence. Further, objective fit is likely to have independent direct relationships to outcomes that are not mediated through subjective fit. One reason for this is perceptual distortion of the subjective P and E components. For example, individuals may distort their views of P and or E toward congruence; however, they may still experience a lack of objective fit. Further, at a given point in time, individuals who do not fit may remain in the organization as they attempt to assimilate (change P) or accommodate (change E) in order to try to achieve fit. The feedback loops in Figure 12.1 imply that, over time, changes in P and/or E may occur, thereby producing a greater degree of PE fit over time.

FIT SENSITIVITY

Individuals are likely to be differentially sensitive to fit and misfit. Equity theory purports that individuals react differently to equity and inequity in the workplace (Adams, 1965). Individuals have been shown to have different tolerances for and reactions to perceived equity and inequity, such that some individuals have great tolerance for inequity (benevolents), others attempt to quickly resolve any inequity (sensitives), and still others expect to receive greater relative benefits than others (entitleds) (Bing & Burroughs, 2001). A similar process is likely with regard to PE fit and misfit. Some individuals are likely to be more sensitive to misfit than others, and the greater sensitivity will lead to different responses. Individuals with a low tolerance for misfit may feel a greater degree of dissonance and may react more strongly to misfit, either in the form of more negative attitudes or in the form of behavioral responses such as turnover. Individuals with a greater sensitivity to misfit may attempt to change either P or E quickly, as noted above, in order to resolve the dissonance associated with misfit. Likewise, individuals who feel entitled to have a desirable workplace and a strong degree of fit are likely to have the least degree of tolerance for misfit and will likely have more negative reactions to situations in which they misfit.

Sensitivity to fit and misfit may also be culturally dependent (Aumann & Ostroff, 2006; Kim et al., 2005; Robert, Probst, Martocchio, Drasgow, & Lawler, 2000). For example, in highly collectivistic cultures, there is less emphasis on individual differences. As a result, the notion of individual fit may be less relevant because the concept of an individual "fitting" to an organization in order to be happy may not be part of the system of work-related values in these societies. In addition, in collectivist cultures, sensitivity to fit may only be relevant for some types of fit, such as PG group. Similarly, in societal contexts that are economically underdeveloped or that rely heavily on agriculture, human resources systems and practices may be of lesser importance (Gelfand, Erez, & Aycan, 2007) and individuals may thus be less sensitive to PE fit in their work context. Investigation into fit sensitivity, as well as the continued expansion of fit research to other countries, may provide important insights about the relationship between fit and outcomes.

COMPARATIVE FIT

The relationship between fit and outcomes may also be dependent on a comparison to other types of fit or in a comparison to other individuals. Similar to propositions advanced in need theory (Alderfer, 1972), when one type of fit is frustrated or lacking, the relevance and importance of other types of fit may become activated. For example, PO fit may become more important when PJ fit is low (Resick et al., 2007). Likewise, once a need is satisfied, other needs may become more important (Maslow, 1943). Experiencing strong PO and PJ fit, but weak PG fit, may increase the salience of PG fit, thereby motivating individuals to change groups (Ostroff et al., 2002). Low fit or misfit may also allow an individual to fulfill other motives, reducing the salience of that particular type of fit (French et al., 1974). For example, excess ability in PJ fit may allow an individual the time and resources to concentrate on his or her degree of fit to the workgroup. Relatively few studies have examined multiple types of fit simultaneously (cf., Dineen & Noe, 2009; Kristof-Brown et al., 2002; Meir & Melamed, 1986; Resick et al., 2007). Nevertheless, results from these studies suggest that different types of fit may be differentially relevant for some people, depending on their background, personal attributes, or circumstances. Thus, in studies in which only a single type of fit is examined, relationships to outcomes may be attenuated or heightened, depending on the degree to which that type of fit under investigation relative to other types of fit, has been activated.

Individuals may also engage in a social comparison process in forming their reactions to PE fit or misfit. According to social comparison (e.g., Wood, 1989), individuals compare their attributes with others to draw inferences about themselves. The conclusions drawn ultimately depend on the person(s) to whom individuals compare themselves. Individuals make upward comparisons, comparing themselves to those better off than themselves (Collins, 1996), and downward comparisons, comparing themselves to those who are slightly worse off or disadvantaged (Wills, 1981). Relationships between fit or misfit and outcomes may depend, in part, on this comparison process. Individuals may look to cues in others to discern the extent to which others fit in the environment. Upward comparisons to individuals with a stronger degree of fit will likely lead to lower individual outcomes or may enhance reactions to misfit. Downward comparisons to individuals with low fit or who misfit will likely enhance the relationship between fit and individual outcomes.

PERSONALITY

Dissonance-prompted responses may also be related to the personality of individuals. For example, individuals high in self-monitoring are more aware of their surroundings and the behavior of others (Snyder, 1974). Because of this, those higher in self-monitoring may have a greater awareness of their degree of fit or misfit and hence have stronger attitudinal or behavioral reactions to fit or misfit. Alternately, because those high in self-monitoring use cues from the environment and social context to monitor and adapt their own behaviors and reactions accordingly (Snyder, 1974), they may also be more likely to assimilate and change P toward fit. Additional personality constructs are also worthy of exploration, such as need for closure (Kruglanski, Webster, & Klem, 1993), because it relates to the ability to accept ambiguity and change opinions and perceptions.

In summary, there are a host of underexplored variables that may moderate or influence relationships between PE fit, misfit, and outcomes, either directly or through changes over time in the P or E components. Additional research is needed to explore the extent to which misfit may result in positive or beneficial outcomes for individuals. For example, poor PJ fit may prompt learning and development (Kristof-Brown & Guay, 2010) while PJ misfit may prompt changing job areas (Ostroff et al., 2002). Low PG fit may motivate individuals to develop stronger interpersonal skills. Exploration of misfit and relationships between misfit and outcomes is an area ripe for future theory and research.

Multiple Fits

Relatively little theory and research has addressed relationships and integrations across the different types, modes, and approaches to fit. Jansen and Kristof-Brown (2006) focused on different types of fit—PI, PJ, PG, PO, and person-vocation fit—proposing that: (a) overall fit is an amalgamation across all types of fit, and (b) different types of fit may be more or less relevant at different stages from pre-hire to post-hire. Ostroff and Schulte (2007) provided an integration of different types of fit—PI, PJ, PG, and PO—with different modes and perspectives, using a levels of analysis perspective to elucidate the different levels and means for evaluating E as well as different conceptualizations of fit at higher levels of analysis. Yu (2009) proposed that work and organizational experience influence the degree to which individuals will attempt to change different types of fit. For example, more work experience was proposed to motivate changes in PJ fit; working in more organizations was proposed to enhance attempts to change PO fit; and working in more groups was proposed to motivate changes in PG fit relative to other types of fit.

A growing body of research has begun to empirically examine the relationships between different types of fit and their relative importance in relation to outcomes. For example, PO fit in the area of value congruence was relatively more important than PJ fit for understanding attitudes, citizenship behaviors, and turnover, while PJ fit in terms of fulfillment was related to job and career satisfaction (Cable & DeRue, 2002; Lauver & Kristof-Brown, 2001). PO fit was found to explain additional variance in attitudes beyond that explained by PJ fit (O'Reilly et al., 1991). In terms of modes of fit, PP fit has been shown to be less important for attitudes and turnover intentions than person-situation (PS) fit, and further, the relative importance of PI, PG, and PO fit was shown to differ depending on the dimension investigated (e.g., Ostroff et al., 2005; Van Vianen, 2000). Different types of fit may also accumulate and their combination is likely to be more explanatory for understanding work-related responses (Meir & Melamed, 1986). As an illustration, Kristof-Brown et al. (2002) found a three-way interaction between PJ, PG, and PO fit indicating that higher fit across all three types was related to higher satisfaction for individuals with more organizational experience.

With respect to simultaneous consideration of fit perspectives, again little work has addressed their relationship. Cable and Edwards (2004) attempted to distinguish between fulfillment and similarity perspectives in subjective fit. They proposed that an individual's values can be framed through need fulfillment, whereby fit is based on the desired amount of the organizational attribute relative to the amount contained in the environment. In contrast, value congruence is founded on the notion that individuals are more comfortable working in environments where the things that are important to them are also important in the environment, with fit based on the degree to which the person and the organization possess the values of interest. While there was some degree of overlap between the two, both fulfillment and similarity were independently related to satisfaction, identification with the organization, and intention to stay, supporting the notion that both of these fit perspectives can operate simultaneously in influencing individual outcomes.

While some attention has been devoted to explaining how multiple types of fit (e.g., PI, PJ, PG, PO) as well as the similarity and fulfillment perspectives might be integrated and operate simultaneously and independently, much less attention

has been devoted to the simultaneous operation of similarity and compilation. Optimal distinctiveness theory (Brewer, 1991) focuses on the notion that individuals have a simultaneous need for both similarity to others and being distinct from, but complementing, others, suggesting that it is important for researchers to adopt more complex views of fit.

Similarity and Distinctiveness

A potential paradox in PE fit resides in the similarity versus compilation perspectives, with the former suggesting that similarity is desirable, and the latter suggesting that a complementary difference in attributes is desirable. Schneider and his colleagues (1995, 1997, 2000) addressed this potential paradox across levels of analysis, purporting that similarity-based fit may be good for individuals, but similarity among individuals drives homogeneity across organizational members and social structures which may ultimately be bad for the long-term survival of and ability of the organization to adapt when change is needed. Schneider's solution to this paradox was that top managers should possess diverse attributes and competencies because they are responsible for decision making while similarity-based fit is more important for lower level employees. A dual model of achieving similarity and compilation was proposed (Schneider et al., 2000) whereby employees should exhibit similarity-based fit on core values and goals, but at the same time have some degree of complementary fit or differences in attributes, such as problem-solving to fit the organizational needs. Similar notions have been proposed to illustrate how both similarity and complementary differences together coalesce and compile to form a consistent and effective pattern for the organization (Ostroff & Schulte, 2007).

By and large, the rhetoric devoted to a simultaneous consideration of similarity and compilation has been largely descriptive in nature, proposing some ways in which both forms of fit might operate together. However, the mechanisms explaining how and why it occurs in individuals have not been delineated. Optimal distinctiveness theory is useful in this regard. The theory proposes that, in group settings, people have two opposing needs and motives, assimilation and differentiation, and these competing needs govern their self-concept and social identification (Brewer, 1991, 2007). The need for assimilation represents a desire for belonging and inclusion while differentiation represents a need to be distinctive from others.

Individuals seek assimilation in groups to avoid feelings of isolation or to mitigate against stigmatization that may result from being highly individuated. Further, individuals are attracted to others and tend to interact and make connections based on similarity (Byrne, 1971; Lazarsfeld & Merton, 1954). In associating strongly with some group, the sense of self shifts toward being a prototype or representative exemplar of the social category and away from the perception of the self as a unique person (Turner, Hogg, Oakes, Reicher, & Wetherell, 1987). Thus, social categorization and social identification with the group involve a type of depersonalization in which one's sense of self is defined through group membership and satisfies needs for assimilation. However, strong inclusion in a group activates the need for differentiation and motivates individuals to distinguish themselves from others. The need for differentiation can be satisfied in one of two ways: (a) by creating exclusive and distinctive identities or subgroups within the larger group, or (b) by comparing the group in which the person is a member to another, very different, group to enhance feelings of being different and distinct (Pickett & Brewer, 2001).

As a group becomes more inclusive, assimilation needs are satisfied but the need for differentiation becomes activated. When individuation increases and inclusiveness decreases, the need for differentiation becomes lower and the need for assimilation becomes activated. The activation of assimilation needs motivates individuals to seek to identities with an inclusive group and leads to responses such as increasing the number of similar others or enhancing intragroup similarity (Pickett & Brewer, 2001; Simon et al., 1997). The arousal of differentiation needs motivates individuals to seek to identify with a smaller, more exclusive group and may prompt actions such as decreasing the number of similar others within the group or increasing in-group and out-group distinctions with another group (Pickett, Silver, & Brewer, 2002; Simon et al., 1997). The degree of intragroup similarity, clarity of group boundaries, and the degree of intergroup similarity can influence the group's ability to satisfy optimal distinctiveness needs of its members (Pickett et al., 2002). The competing assimilation and differentiation drives ensure that one need is not consistently sacrificed to the other need, and together they provide the capacity for social identification. Both needs can be satisfied simultaneously through similarity to an inclusive group coupled with intragroup or intergroup distinctiveness from others (Brewer, 2007).

Optimal distinctiveness theory has several implications for PE fit. First, at a general level, it points to the need to consider both similarity and compilation simultaneously. Individuals need to fit with their environment in ways that promote similarity, but at the same time, they also need to be individuated in some way, suggesting that having different but complementary attributes is also important. Too much similarity-based fit may frustrate individuals' needs to be distinctive from others and will motivate individuals to find ways to distinguish themselves. Reactions might be positive such as developing new skills or competencies that would add to the group or the organization in a different way, or could be negative such as engaging in disruption or deviance as a means to individuation.

Second, optimal distinctiveness theory implies that a great deal of homogeneity or a great deal of heterogeneity in work environments is detrimental. Too much homogeneity frustrates differentiation needs, while too much heterogeneity frustrates assimilation needs. This is related to the notion that there is an optimal level of variance in organizations such that too little or too much person similarity fit will produce long-term negative consequences (Ostroff & Schulte, 2007).

Third, relationships to outcomes may change over time, depending on the degree of activation of assimilation or differentiation needs. For example, over time, a high degree of similarity-based fit might result across group members through the ASA process and other practices such as socialization. In turn, the high degree of similarity-based fit across all members may then create less positive reactions for focal individuals due to frustration of differentiation needs. This implies that it is not only the extent to which the individual fits, but also that the degree of similarity-based fit of other group members may have additional influences on outcomes. Similarly, if an individual has a high degree of similarity-based fit across all types of fit (PI, PJ, PG, PO) and multiple content domains, he or she may begin to experience a sense of depersonalization, thereby lowering attitudes and responses to the work situation. Thus, a high degree of multiple fits simultaneously for an individual, without some means of differentiation, could ultimately be detrimental to reactions at work.

Finally, optimal distinctiveness theory can be used to explain why groups or units within a single organization may have cultures, climates, and social structures that differ from another. When individuals in a group are similar to one another, or when individuals converge on perceptions, cognitions, attitudes, and attributes, a high degree of similarity-based fit across individuals in the group is likely to have occurred. Yet, if similarity also occurred across all groups in the organizations, distinctiveness needs may not be met. Hence, groups within an organization may have a high degree of similarity-based fit within the group, but the E (e.g., culture, climate, goals) to which individuals fit differs between groups to satisfy distinctiveness needs.

Taken together, the discussion above implies that multiple types and modes of fit need to be considered simultaneously in order to understand their relative importance as well as combinatory effects as they relate to outcomes. A number of suggestions have been proffered in the literature pertaining to multiple fits simultaneously (e.g., Edwards et al., 2006; Wheeler, Buckley, Halbesleben, Brouer, & Ferris, 2005). Yet, research is lacking about when and why one type of fit may be more salient or relevant than other types of fit (Jansen & Kristof-Brown, 2006), the extent to which fit to one level or in one domain may spill over to other types of fit (Kristof-Brown & Guay, 2010), the extent to which fit to and at higher levels of analysis constrains fit a lower levels of analysis due to bond strength (Ostroff & Schulte, 2007), or the extent to which fit across multiple areas, through prototype matching, occurs (Wheeler et al., 2005). Further, investigations of the extent to which individuals can fit through similarity and fulfillment but also remain distinctive through providing complementary attributes in compilation are warranted. Idiographic analyses that take into account the pattern of configuration across types of fit and different content areas may be a useful approach (Ostroff & Schulte, 2007).

Conclusion

In the past 25 years, the amount of theory and research devoted to person-environment fit in organizational settings has grown exponentially. As evidence mounted that fit between characteristics of individuals and those of their organizational environment was important for understanding individuals' responses and behavior in organizations, research blossomed from examination of how people fit to their jobs to how people fit to all aspects of their organizational environment, including their leaders, peers, the workgroup, and the organization as a whole. Similarly, the array of content areas about which people can fit has expanded, including preferences, values, personality, goals, knowledge, skills, working styles, and cognitive styles, as has the

range of hypothesized outcomes of fit, including attitudes, organizational attractiveness, adjustment, performance, citizenship behavior turnover, innovation, stress, and well-being.

In many ways, much has been learned about the role of PE fit in organizations as evidenced by recent comprehensive reviews of the area (e.g., Edwards, 2008; Kristof-Brown & Guay, 2010; Kristof-Brown et al., 2005; Verquer et al., 2003; Yang et al., 2008). The accumulated evidence shows that fit is a pervasive aspect of organizational life that is important for understanding how individuals respond in their organizational environment. At the same time, theory and research has tended to be fragmented despite the almost ubiquitous use of fit across domains in organizational research. On the one hand, this fragmentation makes sense because the potential construct space of PE fit is extensive (Edwards & Shipp, 2007), and researchers have tended to tackle small chunks at a time for study. The result, however, is that we have some depth of understanding and knowledge about each type, perspective, and mode of fit, but little understanding about the extent to which different types of fit overlap or how they can be integrated. The recent studies examining multiple fits simultaneously (e.g., Ostroff et al., 2005; Kristof-Brown et al., 2002) and the studies examining how different approaches to fit are related to one another (e.g., Cable & Edwards, 2004; Edwards et al., 2006) have been illuminating, particularly in showing that different views of PE fit are not interchangeable. Further attempts at understanding the relationships between the different types, modes, and perspectives of fit will provide some much needed parsimony to the area. Table 12.3 highlights the major issues discussed in this chapter that are in need of further theory, research, and development.

In this chapter, some general propositions were developed pertaining to the relationship between objective and subjective fit and the mechanisms that may enhance their overlap. In addition, suggestions were offered for the study of fit versus misfit and the factors that may influence their relationship to individual outcomes. Additional attempts to understand the interplay of different types of fit across levels of analysis represent another important area for study.

The primary focus in this chapter was on the effect of fit on individuals in organizations, and the preponderance of research and theory has been directed at the individual level. However, a number of researchers have explicated the relevance of fit

Table 12.3 Suggested Areas for Future Development in PE Fit Research

Topic Area	Potential Future Research Questions
Direct Fit	• Is direct fit part of PE fit or an outcome of PE fit? • Can direct fit be clearly distinguished from other affective responses? • Can direct fit assessments be designed to represent a cognitive comparison of P and E as opposed to meshing both cognitive and affective processes? • How are P and E weighted in direct fit?
Level of Specificity	• Are relationships stronger when the level of specificity between fit measures and outcome measures are similar? • For example, are global assessments of fit more strongly related to broad-based outcomes than to specific outcomes? Are specific dimensions of fit more strongly related to narrowly defined outcomes than to broad-based outcomes?
Misfit	• Are fit and misfit two distinct constructs, or do they fall along a continuum? • Is there a tipping point moving from fit to low fit to misfit? • Can overall misfit as lack of similarity, lack of fulfillment, and lack of complementarity be identified, or does misfit need to be defined separately, depending on the perspective? • Is misfit more salient to individuals than fit? Are relationships between misfit and outcomes stronger than those for fit? • What psychological and cognitive mechanisms explain reactions to misfit and the relationship to outcomes? • When confronted with misfit, under what conditions will individuals attempt to alter P (assimilation), alter E (accommodation), alter perceptions, or remove themselves from the misfit situation?
Mediators and Process	• What psychological and cognitive mechanisms explain the relationship between fit and outcomes? • Do different mechanisms operate for different fit perspectives? • Are the assumed mechanisms of similarity-attraction, self-identity, trust, communication and friendships the key mediating processes in similarity-based perspectives of fit? • Are the assumed mechanisms of need fulfillment, lesser cognitive demands, and ease of dealing with the environment the key mediating processes in fulfillment-based perspectives of it? • Are feelings of self-worth, engagement, or feelings of making a unique contribution the key mediating processes in compilation perspectives?
Balancing Similarity and Individuation	• How can similarity-based fit and compilation-based fit be balanced so that people feel psychological safety from similarity and yet maintain a degree of individuality? • Do reactions to fit change over time as the degree of similarity fit and compilation fit changes?
Sensitivity to Fit and Misfit	• Do individuals differ in the importance of or their degree of sensitivity to fit? • Are some individuals more tolerant of misfit than others? • To what degree does societal culture play a role in sensitivity to fit and misfit?
Comparative Fit	• Are some subtypes (e.g., PI, PG, PJ, PO) or some modes of fit (e.g., PP, PS) or some domains of fit (e.g., values, goals) more important than others? • Are there contextual (e.g., societal culture) or individual difference variables (e.g., personality) that influence which types of fit are more or less important? • Does fit (or low fit) to one subtype or fit in one domain then raise the salience of fitting to other subtypes or domains of fit?
Fit at Higher levels of Analysis	• Is collective fit (similarity- or fulfillment-based) related to positive or negative group and organizational outcomes such as collective attitudes and performance? • Can similarity and compilation be effectively balanced so as to provide sufficient similarity for individuals to enhance individual outcomes and sufficient differences and complementarities to enhance organizational effectiveness?

for understanding higher level aspects of organizational functioning such as group or team effectiveness and organizational performance (e.g., Ostroff & Schulte, 2007; Schneider et al., 2000). Exciting avenues of research open up when one considers how fit across individuals may influence the functioning and effectiveness of groups or organizations. The levels of analysis literature clearly indicates that relationships found at the individual level of analysis may not necessarily apply to higher levels such as the group or organizational level. Are elements that are good for individuals in terms of their fit bad for organizations over time? Are different modes of fit (e.g., compilation of complementary attributes rather than similarity) more important at higher levels of analysis? Can similarity and compilation be balanced in such a way as to maximize positive outcomes across levels of analysis?

Moreover, the extant theory on PE fit suggests that it is not a static process but one that can change and evolve over time as both the person and environment change in response to one another (e.g., Dawis & Lofquist, 1984; Holland, 1985; Ostroff & Schulte, 2007; Shipp & Jansen, 2011; Shipp et al., 2009; Yu, 2009). While the dynamic nature of fit has long been acknowledged, empirical investigations that focus on both P and E changes over time are sparse. Most likely, the ways in which the person and environment change in response to one another will depend on the temporal stage and type of movement into and out of organizations. For example, the process may differ based on why the environment changes for the individual: moving from pre- to post-hire (Jansen & Kristof-Brown, 2006), moving to a different organization or changing groups within an organization (Ostroff et al., 2004), or staying in the same environment but a number of new members join the group or organization changes. All of these would be revealing areas for investigation.

Clearly, there is much more work to be done in the area of PE fit. Many ambiguities remain, making it a challenging area for research. The complexity of organizations as a system, coupled with the pervasive nature of PE to all areas of the system, makes such work challenging and exciting.

References

Adams, J. S. (1965). Inequity in social exchange. *Advances in Experimental Social Psychology, 62,* 335–343.

Alderfer, C. P. (1972). *Existence, relatedness, and growth: Human needs in organizational settings.* New York: Free Press.

Anderson, C., Spataro, S. E., & Flynn, F. J. (2008). Personality and organizational culture as determinants of influence. *Journal of Applied Psychology, 93,* 702–710.

Aronoff, J., & Wilson, J. P. (1985). *Personality in the social process.* Hillsdale, NJ: Lawrence Erlbaum.

Arthur, W., Jr., Bell, S. T., Villado, A. J., & Doverspike, D. (2006). The use of person-organization fit in employment decision making: An assessment of its criterion-related validity. *Journal of Applied Psychology, 91,* 786–801.

Ashford, S. J. (1989). Self-assessments in organizations: A literature review and integrative model. In L. L. Cummings & B. M. Staw (Eds.), *Research in organizational behavior* (pp. 133–174). Greenwich, CT: JAI Press.

Ashford, S. J. (1993). The feedback environment: An exploratory study of cue use. *Journal of Organizational Behavior, 14,* 201–224.

Ashforth, B. E. (1985). Climate formation: Issues and extensions. *Academy of Management Review, 10,* 837–847.

Ashforth, B. E. (2001). *Role transitions in organizational life: An identity-based perspective.* Mahwah, NJ: Lawrence Erlbaum.

Ashforth, B. E., & Saks, A. M. (1995). Work-role transitions: A longitudinal examination of the Nicholson model. *Journal of Occupational and Organizational Psychology, 68,* 157–175.

Ashkanasy, N. M., & O'Connor, C. (1997). Value congruence in leader-member exchange. *The Journal of Social Psychology, 137,* 647–662.

Assouline, M., & Meir, E. I. (1987). Meta-analysis of the relationship between congruence and well-being measures. *Journal of Vocational Behavior, 31,* 319–332.

Atwater, L., & Dionne, S. (2007). A process model of leader-follower fit. In C. Ostroff & T. A. Judge (Eds.), *Perspectives on organizational fit* (pp. 183–208). New York: Lawrence Erlbaum Associates.

Atwater, L. E., Ostroff, C., Yammarino, F. J., & Fleenor, J. W. (1998). Self-other agreement: Does it really matter? *Personnel Psychology, 51,* 577–598.

Aumann, K. A., & Ostroff, C. (2006). Multilevel fit: An integrative framework for understanding HRM practices in cross-cultural contexts. *Research in MultiLevel Issues, 5,* 13–79.

Avery, D. R., McKay, P. F., & Wilson, D. C. (2007). Engaging an aging workforce: The relationship between perceived age similarity, satisfaction with coworkers, and employee engagement. *Journal of Applied Psychology, 92,* 1542–1556.

Barrick, M. R., Stewart, G. L., Neubert, M. J., & Mount, M. K. (1998). Relating member ability and personality to work-team processes and team effectiveness. *Journal of Applied Psychology, 83,* 377–391.

Bateson, G., Jackson, D. D., Haley, J., & Weakland, J. H. (1956). Toward a theory of schizophrenia. *Behavioral Science, 1,* 251–264.

Billsberry, J., van Meurs, N., Coldwell, D.A., & Marsh, P.J. (2006, August). *Towards an explanatory model of fit.* Presented at the annual meetings of the Academy of Management, Atlanta, GA.

Bing, M. N., & Burroughs, S. M. (2001). The predictive and interactive effects of equity sensitivity on teamwork-oriented organizations. *Journal of Organizational Behavior, 22,* 271–290.

Blau, P. M. (1960). Structural effects. *American Sociological Review, 25,* 173–193.

Breaugh, J. A. (1992). *Recruitment: Science and practice.* Boston: PWS-Kent.

Brewer, M. B. (1991). The social self: On being the same and different at the same time. *Personality and Social Psychology Bulletin, 17,* 475–482.

Brewer, M. B. (2007). The importance of being we: Human nature and intergroup relations. *American Psychologist, 62,* 728–738.

Brief, A. P., & Aldag, R. J. (1981). The "self" in work organizations: A conceptual review. *Academy of Management Review,* 6, 75–88.

Byrne, D. (1971). *The attraction paradigm.* New York: Academic Press.

Byrne, D., & Nelson, D. (1965). Attraction as a linear function of proportion of reinforcements. *Journal of Personality and Social Psychology,* 2, 884–889.

Cable, D. M., & DeRue, D. S. (2002). The convergent and discriminant validity of subjective fit perceptions. *Journal of Applied Psychology,* 87, 875–884.

Cable, D. M., & Edwards, J. R. (2004). Complementary and supplementary fit: A theoretical and empirical integration. *Journal of Applied Psychology,* 89, 822–834.

Cable, D. M., & Judge, T. A. (1997). Interviewers' perceptions of person-organization fit and organizational selection decisions. *Journal of Applied Psychology,* 82, 546–561.

Cable, D. M., & Parsons, C. K. (2001). Socialization tactics and person-organization fit. *Personnel Psychology,* 54, 1–23.

Cable, D. M., & Yu, K. Y. T (2007). The genesis of fit judgments: How selection and adjustment develop the beliefs used to assess fit. In C. Ostroff & T. A. Judge (Eds.), *Perspectives on organizational fit* (pp. 155–181). New York: Erlbaum.

Caldwell, D. F., & O'Reilly, C. A., III. (1990). Measuring person-job fit with a profile-comparison process. *Journal of Applied Psychology,* 75, 648–657.

Caplan, R. D. (1983). Person-environment fit: Past, present, and future. In C. L. Cooper (Ed.), *Stress research* (pp. 35–78). New York: Wiley.

Caplan, R. D. (1987). Person-environment fit theory: Commensurate dimensions, time perspectives, and mechanisms. *Journal of Vocational Behavior, 31,* 248–267.

Carr, J. C., Pearson, A. W., Vest, M. J., & Boyar, S. L. (2006). Prior occupational experience, anticipatory socialization, and employee retention. *Journal of Management, 32,* 343–359.

Chan, D. (1998). Functional relations among constructs in the same content domain at different levels of analysis: A typology of composition models. *Journal of Applied Psychology, 83,* 234–246.

Chao, G. T., O'Leary-Kelly, A. M., Wolf, S., Klein, H. J., & Gardner, P. D. (1994). Organizational socialization: Its content and consequences. *Journal of Applied Psychology, 79,* 730–743.

Chatman, J. A. (1989). Improving interactional organizational research: A model of person-organization fit. *Academy of Management Review, 14,* 333–349.

Chatman, J. A. (1991). Matching people and organizations: Selection and socialization in public accounting firms. *Administrative Science Quarterly, 36*(3), 459–484.

Cialdini, R. B. (2001). *Influence: Science and practice.* Needman Heights, MA: Allyn & Bacon.

Colbert, A. E., Kristof-Brown, A. L., Bradley, B. H., & Barrick, M. R. (2008). CEO transformational leadership: The role of goal importance congruence in top management teams. *Academy of Management Journal, 51,* 81–96.

Collins, R. L. (1996). For better or worse: The impact of upward social comparisons on self-evaluations. *Psychological Bulletin, 119,* 51–69

Cooper-Thomas, H. D., Van Vianen, A., & Anderson, N. (2004). Changes in person-organization fit: The impact of socialization tactics on perceived and actual P-O fit. *European Journal of Work and Organizational Psychology, 13,* 52–78.

Dabos, B. E., & Rousseau, D. M. (2004). Mutuality and reciprocity in the psychological contracts of employees and employers. *Journal of Applied Psychology, 89,* 52–72.

Dawis, R. V., England, G. W., & Lofquist, L. H. (1964). A theory of work adjustment. *Minnesota Studies in Vocational Rehabilitation* (No. XV), 1–27. Minneapolis: University of Minnesota, Industrial Relations Center.

Dawis, R. V., & Lofquist, L. H. (1984). *A psychological theory of work adjustment.* Minneapolis: University of Minnesota Press.

De Cooman, R., De Gieter, S., Pepermans, R., Hermans, S., Du Bois, C., Caers, R., & Jegers, M. (2009). Person-organization fit: Testing socialization and attraction-selection-attrition hypotheses. *Journal of Vocational Behavior, 74,* 102–107.

DeRue, S., & Hollenbeck, J. A. (2007). The search for internal and external fit in teams. In C. Ostroff & T. A. Judge (Eds.), *Perspectives on organizational fit* (pp. 259–285). New York: Erlbaum.

DeRue, D. S., & Morgeson, F. P. (2007). Stability and change in person-team and person-role fit over time: The effects of growth satisfaction, performance, and general self-efficacy. *Journal of Applied Psychology, 92,* 1242–1253.

Dineen, B. R., & Noe, R. A. (2009). Effects of customization on application decisions and applicant pool characteristics in a Web-based recruitment context. *Journal of Applied Psychology, 94,* 224–234.

Edwards, J. R. (1991). Person-job fit: A conceptual integration, literature review, and methodological critique. In C. L. Cooper (Ed.), *International review of industrial and organizational psychology* (Vol. 6, pp. 283–357). Chichester, UK: Wiley.

Edwards, J. R. (1992). A cybernetic theory of stress, coping, and well-being in organizations. *Academy of Management Review, 17,* 238–274.

Edwards, J. R. (2008). Person-environment fit in organizations: An assessment of theoretical progress. In *The Academy of Management Annals* (Vol 2, pp. 167–230). London: Routledge.

Edwards, J. R., & Cable, D. M. (2009). The value of value congruence. *Journal of Applied Psychology, 94,* 654–677.

Edwards, J. R., Cable, D. M., Williamson, I. O., Lambert, L. S., & Shipp, A. J. (2006). The phenomenology of fit: Linking the person and environment to the subjective experience of person-environment fit. *Journal of Applied Psychology, 91,* 802–827.

Edwards, J. R., Caplan, R. D., & Harrison, R. V. (1998). Person-environment fit theory: Conceptual foundations, empirical evidence, and directions for future research. In C. L. Cooper (Ed.), *Theories of organizational stress* (pp. 28–67). Oxford: Oxford University Press.

Edwards, J. R., & Shipp, A. J. (2007). The relationship between person-environment fit and outcomes: An integrative theoretical framework. In C. Ostroff & T. A. Judge (Eds.), *Perspectives on organizational fit* (pp. 209–258). New York: Lawrence Erlbaum Associates.

Ellis, A., & Tsui, A. S. (2007). Survival of the fittest or the least fit? When psychology meets ecology in organizational demography. In C. Ostroff & T. A. Judge (Eds.), *Perspectives on organizational fit* (pp. 287–315). New York: Erlbaum

Endler, N. S., & Magnusson, D. (1976). Personality and person by situation interactions. In N. S. Endler & D. Magnusson (Eds.), *Interactional psychology and personality* (pp. 1–25). New York: Hemisphere.

Epstein, S. (1979). The stability of behavior I: On predicting most of the people much of the time. *Journal of Personality and Social Psychology, 37*, 1097–1126.

Erdogan, B., & Bauer, T. N. (2005). Enhancing career benefits of employee proactive personality: The role of fit with jobs and organizations. *Personnel Psychology, 58*, 859–891.

Erdogan, B., Kraimer, M. L., & Liden, R. C. (2004). Work value congruence and intrinsic career success: The compensatory roles of leader-member exchange and perceived organizational support. *Personnel Psychology, 57*, 305–332.

Ferris, G. R., Hochwarter, W. A., Buckley, M. R., Harrell-Cook, G., & Frink, D. D. (1999). Human resource management: Some new directions. *Journal of Management, 25*, 385–415.

Ferris, G. R., & Mitchell, T. R. (1987). The components of social influence and their importance for human resources research. *Research in Personnel and Human Resource Management, 5*, 103–128.

Festinger, L. (1957). *A theory of cognitive dissonance.* Evanston, IL: Row Peterson.

Fink, E. L., & Chen, S. S. (1995). A galileo analysis of organizational climate. *Human Communication Research, 21*, 494–521.

French, J. R. P., Jr., Caplan, R. D., & Harrison, R. V. (1982). *The mechanisms of job stress and strain.* London: Wiley.

French, J. R. P., Jr., Rogers, W., & Cobb, S. (1974). Adjustment as person-environment fit. In D. A. H. G. V. Coelho & J. E. Adams (Ed.), *Coping and adaptation* (pp. 316–333). New York: Basic Books.

Gelfand, M. J., Erez, M., & Aycan, Z. (2007). Understanding human resource management in cultural context. In M. Gelfand, M. Erez, & Z. Aycan (Eds.), *Cross-cultural organizational behavior.* Thousand Oaks, CA: Sage.

Giberson, T. R., Resick, C. J., & Dickson, M. W. (2005). Embedding leader characteristics: An examination of homogeneity of personality and values in organizations. *Journal of Applied Psychology, 90*, 1002–1010.

Gioia, D. A., Thomas, J. B., Clark, S. M., & Chittipeddi, K. (1994). Symbolism and strategy change in academia: The dynamics of sensemaking and influence. *Organization Science, 5*, 363–383.

Glomb, T. M., & Welsh, E. T. (2005). Can opposites attract?: Personality heterogeneity in supervisor-subordinate dyads as a predictor of subordinate outcomes. *Journal of Applied Psychology, 90*, 749–757.

Gustafson, S. B., & Mumford, M. D. (1995). Personal style and person-environment fit: A pattern approach. *Journal of Vocational Behavior, 46*, 196–206.

Harms, P. D., Roberts, B. W., & Winter, D. (2006). Becoming the Harvard man: Person-environment fit, personality development, and academic success. *Personality and Social Psychology Bulletin, 32*, 851–865.

Harrison, D. A. (2007). Pitching fits in applied psychological research: Making fit methods fit theory. In C. Ostroff & T. A. Judge (Eds.), *Perspectives on organizational fit* (pp. 389–416). New York: Lawrence Erlbaum Associates.

Harrison, D. A., Newman, D. A., & Roth, P. L. (2006). How important are job attitudes? Meta-analytic comparisons of integrative behavioral outcomes and time sequences. *Academy of Management Journal, 49*, 305–325.

Harrison, R. V. (1978). Person-environment fit and job stress. In C. L. Cooper & R. Payne (Eds.), *Stress at work* (pp. 175–205). New York: Wiley.

Harrison, R. V. (1985). The person-environment fit model and the study of stress. In T. A. Beehr & R. S. Bhagat (Eds.), *Human stress and cognition in organizations* (pp. 23–55). New York: Wiley.

Hecht, T. D., & Allen, N. J. (2005). Exploring links between polychronicity and well-being from the perspective of person-job fit: Does it matter if you prefer to only do one thing at a time? *Organizational Behavior and Human Decision Processes, 98*, 155–178.

Helgeson, V. S., & Mickelson, K. D. (1995). Motives for social comparison. *Personality and Social Psychology Bulletin, 21*, 1200–1209.

Hoffman, B. J., & Woehr, D. J. (2006). A quantitative review of the relationship between person-organization fit and behavioral outcomes. *Journal of Vocational Behavior, 68*, 389–399.

Hogan, R., & Roberts, B. W. (2000). A socioanalytic perspective on person-environment interaction. In B. Walsh, K. H. Craik, & R. H. Price (Eds.), *Person-environment psychology: New directions and perspectives* (pp. 1–24). Mahwah, NJ: Erlbaum.

Holland, J. L. (1976). Vocational preferences. In M. D. Dunnette (Ed.), *Handbook of industrial and organizational psychology* (pp. 521–570). New York: Wiley.

Holland, J. L. (1985). *Making vocational choices: A theory of vocational personalities* (2nd ed.). Englewood Cliffs, NJ: Prentice-Hall.

Holland, J. L. (1997). *Making vocational choices: A theory of vocational personalities* (3rd ed.). Lutz, FL: Psychological Assessment Resources.

Hollenbeck, J. R. Moon, H., Ellis, A. P. J., West, B. J., Ilgen, R. R., Sheppard, L., Porter, C. O. L. H., & Wagner, J. A., III. (2002). Structural contingency theory and individual differences: Examination of external and internal person-team fit. *Journal of Applied Psychology, 87*, 599–606.

James, L. R., Hater, J. J., Gent, M. J., & Bruni, J. R. (1978). Psychological climate: Implications from cognitive social learning theory and interactional psychology. *Personnel Psychology, 31*, 781–813.

James, L. R., James, L. A., & Ashe, D. K. (1990). The meaning of organizations: The role of cognition and values. In B. Schneider (Ed.), *Organizational climate and culture* (pp. 40–84). San Francisco: Jossey-Bass.

Jansen, K. J., & Kristof-Brown, A. L. (2005). Marching to the beat of a different drummer: Examining the impact of pacing congruence. *Organizational Behavior and Human Decision Processes, 96*, 93–105.

Jansen, K. J., & Kristof-Brown, A. L. (2006). Toward a multidimensional theory of person-environment fit. *Journal of Managerial Issues, 18*, 193–212.

Jehn, K. A., Northcraft, G. B., & Neale, M. A. (1999). Why differences make a difference: A field study of diversity, conflict, and performance in workgroups. *Administrative Science Quarterly, 44*, 741–763.

Jones, G. R. (1986). Socialization tactics, self-efficacy, and newcomers' adjustments to organizations. *Academy of Management Journal, 29*, 262–279.

Judge, T. A. (2007). The future of person-organization fit research: Comments, observations, and a few suggestions. In C. Ostroff & T. A. Judge (Eds.), *Perspectives on organizational fit* (pp. 417–445). New York: Lawrence Erlbaum Associates.

Judge, T. A., & Cable, D. M. (1997). Applicant personality, organizational culture, and organization attraction. *Personnel Psychology, 50*(2), 359–394.

Kalliath, T. J., Bluedorn, A. C., & Strube, M. J. (1999). A test of value congruence effects. *Journal of Organizational Behavior, 20*(7), 1175–1198.

Kaplan, J. D. (1950). *Dialogues of Plato*. New York: Washington Square Press.

Katz, D., & Kahn, R. L. (1978). *The social psychology of organizations*. New York: Wiley.

Kelley, H. H. (1973). The process of causal attribution. *American Psychologist, 28*(2), 107–128.

Kim, T-Y., Cable, D. M., & Kim, S-P. (2005). Socialization tactics, employee proactivity, and person-organization fit. *Journal of Applied Psychology, 90*, 232–241.

Klimoski, R., & Jones, R. G. (1995). Staffing for effective group decision making: Key issues in matching people and teams. In. R. Guzzo, E. Salas, & Associates (Eds.), *Team effectiveness and decision making in organizations* (pp. 291–332). San Francisco: Jossey-Bass.

Kozlowski, S. W. J., Brown, K. G., Weissbein, D. A., Cannon-Bowers, J. A., & Salas, E. (2000). A multilevel approach to training effectiveness: Enhancing horizontal and vertical transfer. In K. J. Klein & S. W. J. Kozlowski (Eds.), *Multilevel theory, research and methods in organizations* (pp. 157–210). San Francisco: Jossey-Bass.

Kozlowski, S. W. J., & Klein, K. J. (2000). *Multilevel theory, research, and methods in organizations: Foundations, extensions, and new directions*. San Francisco: Jossey-Bass.

Kram, K. E. (1985). *Mentoring at work: Developmental relationships in organizational life*. Glenview, IL: Scott, Foresman.

Kram, K. E., & Hall, D. T. (1989). Mentoring as an antidote to stress during corporate trauma. *Human Resource Management, 28*(4), 493–510.

Kreiner, G. E. (2006). Consequences of work-home segmentation or integration: A person-environment fit perspective. *Journal of Organizational Behavior, 27*, 485–507.

Kreiner, G. E., Hollensbe, E. C., & Sheep, M. L. (2009). Balancing borders and bridges: Negotiating the work-home interface via boundary work tactics. *Academy of Management Journal, 52*, 704–730.

Kristof, A. L. (1996). Person-organization fit: An integrative review of its conceptualizations, measurement, and implications. *Personnel Psychology, 49*(1), 1–49.

Kristof-Brown, A. L., Barrick, M. R., & Stevens, C. K. (2005). When opposites attract: A multi-sample demonstration of complementary person-team fit on extraversion. *Journal of Personality, 73*, 935–957.

Kristof-Brown, A. L., & Guay, R. P. (2010). Person-environment fit. In S. Zedeck, (Ed.), *Handbook of industrial and organizational psychology* (Vol. 3). Washington, DC: American Psychological Association.

Kristof-Brown, A. L., Jansen, K. J., & Colbert, A. E. (2002). A policy-capturing study of the simultaneous effects of fit with jobs, groups, and organizations. *Journal of Applied Psychology, 87*, 985–993.

Kristof-Brown, A., & Stevens, C. K. (2001). Goal congruence in project teams: Does the fit between members' personal mastery and performance goals matter? *Journal of Applied Psychology, 86*, 1083–1095.

Kristof-Brown, A. L., Zimmerman, R. D., & Johnson, E. C. (2005). Consequences of individual's fit at work: A meta-analysis of person-job, person-organization, person-group, and person-supervisor fit. *Personnel Psychology, 58*, 281–342.

Kruglanski, A. W., Webster, D. M., & Klem, A. (1993). Motivated resistance and openness to persuasion in the presence or absence of prior information. *Journal of Personality and Social Psychology, 65*(5), 861–876.

Lauver, K. J., & Kristof-Brown, A. L. (2001). Distinguishing between employees' perceptions of person-job and person-organization fit. *Journal of Vocational Behavior, 59*, 454–470.

Lazarsfeld, P. F., & Merton, R. K. (1954). Friendship as a social process: A substantive and methodological analysis. In M. Berger (Ed.), *Freedom and control in modern society* (pp. 18–66). New York: Van Nostrand.

Lecky, P. (1945). *Self-consistency: A theory of personality*. New York: Island Press.

Lewin, K. A. (1951). *Field theory in social science: Selected theoretical papers*. New York: Harper.

Liao, H., Joshi, A., & Chuang, A. (2004). Sticking out like a sore thumb: Employee dissimilarity and deviance at work. *Personnel Psychology, 57*, 969–1000.

Lidz, T. (1973). *Origin and treatment of schizophrenic disorders*. New York: Basic Books.

Locke, E. A. (1976). The nature and causes of job satisfaction. In M. D. Dunnette (Ed.), *Handbook of industrial and organizational psychology* (pp. 1297–1350). Chicago: Rand McNally.

Louis, M. R. (1990). Acculuration in the workplace: Newcomers as lay ethnographers. In B. Schneider (Ed.), *Organizational culture and climate* (pp. 85–129). San Francisco: Jossey-Bass.

Maslow, A. H. (1943). A theory of human motivation. *Psychological Review, 50*, 370–396.

McArthur, L. A. (1972). The how and what of why: Some determinants and consequences of causal attribution. *Journal of Personality and Social Psychology, 22*, 171–193.

McGrath, J. E. (1976). Stress and behavior in organizations. In M. D. Dunnette (Ed.), *Handbook of industrial and organizational psychology* (pp. 1351–1395). Chicago: Rand McNally.

McKay, P. F., Avery, K. R., & Morris, M. A. (2009). A tale of two climates: Diversity climate from subordinates' and managers' perspectives and their role in store unit sales performance. *Personnel Psychology, 62*, 767–791.

Meglino, B. M., & Ravlin, E. C. (1998). Individual values in organizations: Concepts, controversies, and research. *Journal of Management, 24*, 351–389.

Meglino, B. M., Ravlin, E. C., & Adkins, C. L. (1989). A work values approach to corporate culture: A field test of the value congruence process and its relationship to individual outcomes. *Journal of Applied Psychology, 74*(3), 424–432.

Meir, E. I., & Melamed, S. (1986). The accumulation of person-environment congruence and well-being. *Journal of Occupational Behavior, 7*, 315–323.

Mischel, W. (1973). Toward a cognitive social learning conceptualization of personality. *Psychological Review, 80*, 252–283.

Mischel, W. (1977). The interaction of person and situation. In D. Magnusson & N. S. Endler (Eds.), *Personality at the crossroads: Current issues in interactional psychology* (pp. 333–352). Hillsdale, NJ: Erlbaum.

Muchinsky, P. M., & Monahan, C. J. (1987). What is person-environment congruence? Supplementary versus complementary models of fit. *Journal of Vocational Behavior, 31*, 268–277.

Murray, H. A. (1938). *Explorations in personality*. New York: Oxford University Press.

Nicholson, N. (1987). The transition cycle: A conceptual framework for the analysis of change and human resource management. In K. M. Rowland & G. R. Ferris (Eds.), *Research in personnel and human resource management* (pp. 167–222). Greenwich, CT: JAI Press.

Nicholson, N., & West, M. A. (1988). *Managerial job change: Men and women in transition*. Cambridge: Cambridge University Press.

O'Reilly, C. A., Chatman, J., & Caldwell, D. F. (1991). People and organizational culture: A profile comparison approach to assessing person-organization fit. *Academy of Management Journal, 34,* 487–516.

Ostroff, C. (1993a). Relationships between person-environment congruence and organizational effectiveness. *Group and Organization Management, 18,* 103–122.

Ostroff, C. (1993b). The effects of climate and personal influences on individual behavior and attitudes in organizations. *Organizational Behavior and Human Decision Processes, 56,* 56–90.

Ostroff, C. (2007). Methodological issues in fit research. In C. Ostroff & T. A. Judge (Eds.), *Perspectives on organizational fit* (pp. 352–361). Mahwah, NJ: Erlbaum.

Ostroff, C., Atwater, L. E., & Feinberg, B. (2004). Understanding self-other agreement: A look at rater and ratee characteristics, context, and outcomes. *Personnel Psychology, 57,* 333–375.

Ostroff, C., & Kozlowski, S. W. J. (1993). The role of mentoring in the information gathering process of newcomers during early organizational socialization. *Journal of Vocational Behavior, 42,* 170–183.

Ostroff, C., & Rothausen, T. J. (1997). The moderating effect of tenure in person-environment fit: A field study in educational organizations. *Journal of Occupational and Organizational Psychology, 70,* 173–188.

Ostroff, C., & Schulte, M. (2007). Multiple perspectives of fit in organizations across levels of analysis. In C. Ostroff & T. A. Judge (Eds.), *Perspectives on organizational fit* (pp. 3–69). Mahwah, NJ: Lawrence Erlbaum Associates.

Ostroff, C., Shin, Y., & Feinberg, B. (2002). Skill acquisition and person-occupation fit. In D. Feldman (Ed.), *Work careers: A developmental perspective* (pp. 63–92). San Francisco: Jossey-Bass.

Ostroff, C., Shin, Y., & Kinicki, A. J. (2005). Multiple perspectives of congruence: Relationships between value congruence and employee attitudes. *Journal of Organizational Behavior, 26,* 591–623.

Parsons, F. (1909). *Choosing a vocation*. Boston, MA: HoughtonMifflin.

Payne, R. L., Fineman, S., & Wall, T. D. (1976). Organizational climate and job satisfaction: A conceptual synthesis. *Organizational Behavior and Human Performance, 16,* 45–62.

Pervin, L. A. (1967) A twenty college study of student x college interaction using TAPE. *Journal of Educational Psychology, 58,* 290–302.

Pervin, L. A. (1968). Performance and satisfaction as a function of individual-environment fit. *Psychological Bulletin, 69,* 56–68.

Pervin, L. A. (1987). Person-environment congruence in the light of person-situation controversy. *Journal of Vocational Behavior, 31,* 222–230.

Pervin, L. A. (1989). Persons, situations, interactions: The history of a controversy and a discussion of theoretical models. *Academy of Management Review, 14,* 350–360.

Pervin, L. A. (1992). Transversing the individual-environment landscape: A personal odyssey. In W. B. Walsh, K. H. Craik, & R. H. Price (Eds.), *Person-environment psychology: Models and perspectives* (pp. 71–87). Hillsdale, NJ: Erlbaum.

Pervin, L. A., & Rubin, D. B. (1967). Student dissatisfaction with college and the college dropout: A transactional approach. *Journal of Social Psychology, 72,* 285–295.

Pickett, C. L., & Brewer, M. B. (2001). Assimilation and differentiation needs as motivational determinants of perceived ingroup and outgroup homogeneity. *Journal of Experimental Social Psychology, 37,* 341–348.

Pickett, C. L., Silver, D., & Brewer, M. B. (2002). The impact of assimilation differentiation needs on perceived group importance and judgments of ingroup size. *Personality and Social Psychology Bulletin, 28,* 546–558.

Ravlin, E. C., & Ritchie, C. M. (2006). Perceived and actual organizational fit: Multiple influences on attitudes. *Journal of Managerial Issues, 18,* 175–192.

Rentsch, J. R. (1990). Climate and culture: Interaction and qualitative differences in organizational meanings. *Journal of Applied Psychology, 75,* 668–681.

Resick, C. J., Baltes, B. B., & Shantz, C. W. (2007). Person-organization fit and work-related attitudes and decisions: Examining interactive effects with job fit and conscientiousness. *Journal of Applied Psychology, 92,* 1446–1455.

Robert, C., Probst, T. M., Martocchio, J. J., Drasgow, F., & Lawler, J. J. (2000). Empowerment and continuous improvement in the United States, Mexico, Poland, and India: Predicting fit on the basis of the dimensions of power distance and individualism. *Journal of Applied Psychology, 85,* 643–658.

Rynes, S. L., Bretz, R. D., & Gerhart, B. (1991). The importance of recruitment in job choice: A different way of looking. *Personnel Psychology, 44,* 487–521.

Sacco, J. M., & Schmitt, N. (2005). A dynamic multilevel model of demographic diversity and misfit effects. *Journal of Applied Psychology, 90,* 203–231.

Saks, A. M., & Ashforth, B. E. (1997). A longitudinal investigation of the relationships between job information sources, applicant perceptions of fit, and work outcomes. *Personnel Psychology, 50,* 395–426.

Saks, A. M., & Ashforth, B. E. (2002). Is job search related to employment quality? It all depends on the fit. *Journal of Applied Psychology, 87,* 646–654.

Salancik, G. R., & Pfeffer, J. (1978). A social information processing approach to job attitudes and task design. *Administrative Science Quarterly, 23,* 224–253.

Satir, V. (1988). *The new peoplemaking*. Palo Alto, CA: Science and Behavior Books.

Schneider, B. (1983). Interactional psychology and organizational behavior. *Research in Organizational Behavior, 5,* 1–31.

Schneider, B. (1987a). The people make the place. *Personnel Psychology, 40,* 437–454.

Schneider, B. (1987b). Environment=f(P,B): The road to a radical approach to the person-environment fit. *Journal of Vocational Behavior, 31,* 353–361.

Schneider, B. (2001). Fits about fit. *Applied Psychology: An International Review, 50,* 141–152.

Schneider, B., Goldstein, H. W., & Smith, D. B. (1995). The ASA framework: An update. *Personnel Psychology, 48,* 747–773.

Schneider, B., Kristof-Brown, A. L., Goldstein, H. W., & Smith, D. B. (1997). What is this thing called fit? In N. R. Anderson & P. Herriott (Eds.), *International handbook of selection and appraisal* (pp. 393–412). London: Wiley.

Schneider, B., & Reichers, A. (1983). On the etiology of climates. *Personnel Psychology, 36,* 19–40.

Schneider, B., Smith, D. B., & Goldstein, H. W. (2000). Attraction-selection-attrition: Toward a person-environment psychology of organizations. In. W. B. Walsh, K. H. Craik, & R. H. Price (Eds.), *Person-environment psychology* (pp. 61–86). Mahwah, NJ: Erlbaum.

Schneider, B., Smith, D. B., Taylor, S., & Fleenor, J. (1998). Personality and organizations: A test of the homogeneity of personality hypothesis. *Journal of Applied Psychology, 83*, 462–470.

Schneider, B., & Snyder, M. (1975). Some relationships between job satisfaction and organizational climate. *Journal of Applied Psychology, 60*, 318–328.

Schulte, M., Ostroff, C., & Kinicki, A. J. (2006). Organizational climate systems and psychological climate perceptions: A cross-level study of climate-satisfaction relationships. *Journal of Occupational and Organizational Psychology, 79*(4), 645–671.

Shaw, J. D., Duffy, M. K., Stark, E. M. (2000). Interdependence and preference for group work: Main and congruence effects on the satisfaction and performance of group members. *Journal of Management, 26*, 259–279.

Shaw, J. D., & Gupta, N. (2004). Job complexity, performance, and well-being: When does supplies-values fit matter? *Personnel Psychology, 57*, 847–879.

Shipp, A. J., & Jansen, K. J. (2011). Reinterpreting time in fit theory: Crafting and recrafting narratives of fit in medias res. *Academy of Management Review, 36*, 76–101.

Shipp, A. J., Edwards, J. R., & Lambert, L. S. (2009). Conceptualization and measurement of temporal focus: The subjective experience of the past, present, and future. *Organizational Behavior and Human Decision Processes, 110*(1), 1–22.

Siehl, C. J. (1985). After the founder: An opportunity to manage culture. In P. Frost, L. Moore, M. Louis, C. Lundberg, & J. Martin (Eds.), *Organizational culture*. Beverly Hills, CA: Sage.

Simon, L., Greenberg, J., Arndt, J., Pyszczynski, T., Clement, R., & Solomon, S. (1997). Perceived consensus, uniqueness, and terror management: Compensatory responses to threats to inclusion and distinctiveness following mortality salience. *Personality and Social Psychology Bulletin, 23*, 1055–1065.

Snyder, M. (1974). Self-monitoring of expressive behavior. *Journal of Personality and Social Psychology, 30*, 526–537.

Steele, C. M., & Spencer, S. J. (1992). The primacy of self-integrity. *Psychological Enquiry, 3*, 345–346.

Stern, G. G. (1970). *People in context: Measuring person-environment congruence in education and industry*. New York: Wiley.

Swann, W. B., Jr., Polzer, J. T., Seyle, D. C., & Ko, S. J. (2004). Finding value in diversity: Verification of personal and social self-views in diverse groups. *Academy of Management Review, 29*, 9–27.

Swann, W. B., Jr., Stein-Seroussi, A., & Giesler, R. B. (1992). Why people self-verify. *Journal of Personality and Social Psychology, 62*, 392–401.

Taggar, S., & Neubert, M. (2004). The impact of poor performers on team outcomes: An empirical examination of attribution theory. *Personnel Psychology, 57*, 935–968.

Tajfel, H., & Turner, J. C. (1985). The social identity of intergroup behavior. In S. Worchel & W. Austin (Eds.), *Psychology and intergroup relations* (pp. 7–24). Chicago: Nelson-Hall.

Talbot, D., Billsberry, J., & Marsh, P. J. G. (2007). *An exploratory study into the construction of employee fit and misfit*. Paper presented at the British Academy of Management annual conference, Warwick.

Terborg, J. R. (1981). Interactional psychology and research on human behavior in organizations. *Academy of Management Review, 6*, 569–576.

Tsui, A. S., Egan, T. D., & O'Reilly, C. A., III. (1992). Being different: Relational demography and organizational attachment. *Administrative Science Quarterly, 37*, 549–579.

Turban, D. B., & Keon, T. L. (1993). Organizational attractiveness: An interactionist perspective. *Journal of Applied Psychology, 78*, 184–193.

Turner, J. C., Hogg, M., Oakes, P., Reicher, S., & Wetherell, M. (1987). *Rediscovering the social group: A self-categorization theory*. Oxford: Basil Blackwell.

Vancouver, J. B., Millsap, R. E., & Peters, P. A. (1994). Multilevel analysis of organizational goal congruence. *Journal of Applied Psychology, 79*, 666–679.

Vancouver, J. B., & Schmitt, N. W. (1991). An exploratory examination of person-organization fit: Organizational goal congruence. *Personnel Psychology, 44*, 333–352.

Van Maanen, J., & Schein, E. H. (1979). Towards a theory of organizational socialization. In B. M. Staw (Ed.), *Research in organizational behavior* (pp. 209–264). Greenwich, CT: JAI Press.

Van Vianen, A. E. M. (2000). Person-organization fit: The match between newcomers' and recruiters' preferences for organizational cultures. *Personnel Psychology, 53*, 113–149.

Van Vianen, A. E. M., de Pater, I., Kristof-Brown, A. L., & Johnson, E. (2004). Fitting in: The impact of surface-and deep-level cultural diversity on expatriates' adjustment. *Academy of Management Journal, 47*, 697–709.

Van Vianen, A. E. M., Nijstad, B. A., & Voskuijl, O. F. (2008). A person-environment fit approach to volunteerism: Volunteer personality fit and culture fit as predictor of affective outcomes. *Basic and Applied Social Psychology, 30*, 153–166.

Van Vuuren, M., Veldkamp, B. P., De Jong, M. D. T., & Seydel, E. R. (2007). The congruence of actual and perceived person-organization fit. *International Journal of Human Resource Management, 18*, 1736–1747.

Verquer, M. L., Beehr, T. A., & Wagner, S. H. (2003). A meta-analysis of relations between person-organization fit and work attitudes. *Journal of Vocational Behavior, 63*, 473–489.

Wapner, S., & Demick, J. (2000). Person-in-environment psychology: A holistic, developmental, systems-oriented perspective. In B. Walsh, K. H. Craik, & R. H. Price (Eds.), *Person-environment psychology: New directions and perspectives* (pp. 25–60). Mahwah, NJ: Erlbaum.

Weick, K. E. (1995). *Sensemaking in organizations*. Thousand Oaks, CA: Sage.

Werbel, J. D., & Gilliland, S. W. (1999). Person-environment fit in the selection process. In G. R. Ferris (Ed.), *Research in personnel and human resource management* (Vol. 17, pp. 209–243). Stamford, CT: JAI Press.

Werbel, J. D., & Johnson, D. J. (2001). The use of person-group fit for employment selection: A missing link in person-environment fit. *Human Resource Management, 40*, 227–240.

Wheeler, A. R., Buckley, M. R., Halbesleben, J. R., Brouer, R. L., & Ferris, G. R. (2005). The elusive criterion of fit revisited: Toward an integrative theory of multidimensional fit. In J. J. Martocchio (Ed.), *Research in personnel and human resource management* (Vol. 24). Greenwich, CT: Elsevier.

Wheeler, A. R., Coleman-Gallagher, V., Brouer, R. L., & Sablynski, C. J. (2007). When person-organization (mis)fit and (dis)satisfaction lead to turnover: The moderating role of perceived job mobility. *Journal of Managerial Psychology,* *22,* 203–219.

Wicker, A. W. (1992). Making sense of environments. In W. B. Walsh, K. H. Craik, & R. H. Price (Eds.), *Person-environment psychology* (pp. 157–192). Hillsdale, NJ: Erlbaum.

Wills, T. A. (1981). Downward comparison principles in social psychology. *Psychological Bulletin, 90,* 245–271.

Wood, J. V. (1989). Theory and research concerning social comparisons of personal attributes. *Psychological Bulletin, 106,* 231–248.

Yang, L-Q., Levine, E. L., Smith, M. A., Ispas, D., & Rossi, M. E. (2008). Person-environment fit or person plus environment: A meta-analysis of studies using polynomial regression analysis. *Human Resource Management Review,* *18,* 311–321.

Yu, K. Y. T. (2009). Affective influences in person-environment fit theory: Exploring the role of affect as both cause and outcome of P-E fit. *Journal of Applied Psychology, 94,* 1210–1226.

The Research-Practice Gap in I/O Psychology and Related Fields: Challenges and Potential Solutions

Sara L. Rynes

Abstract

The gap between science and practice in I/O psychology and related fields is large and, some believe, getting larger. Although not everyone views this as a matter for concern, there is growing momentum to take actions to strengthen the interface between science and practice. This chapter examines three underlying sources of the gap: lack of awareness of what the other side knows and cares about; lack of belief or confidence in the knowledge generated or held by the other side; and lack of implementation of knowledge or ideas, even in the face of awareness and belief. Based on this analysis, proposed solutions are offered for each source of the gap, as are directions for future research and practice.

Key Words: Research-practice gap, I/O psychology, knowledge transfer, jury decision making, evidence-based management, persuasion

The more I have tried to be an industrial and organizational (I/O) psychologist, the less I have been able to be of practical value to the organizations with and for whom I have worked. As a "practitioner," I have focused on day-to-day organizational problems and opportunities: starting up new plants, reorganizations, increasing teamwork, selecting and developing managers, improving morale, and so on. The more I have focused on solving these practical organizational problems, the more I have found myself drawn away from the I/O psychology community (*Lapointe*, 1990, p. 7).

Hundreds of thousands of talented researchers are spending their time producing little or nothing of lasting value. Because the usefulness of their research is so low, their social environment pays little attention to their research. Many researchers lose the idealism that brought them to their occupation originally, as they shift their priorities to social goals such as tenure and promotions. Seeing that their activities are benefiting no one, some researchers come to

see themselves as having obligations to no one but themselves, and they engage in egocentric demands (*Starbuck*, 2006, pp. 3–4).

Introduction

It has long been recognized that there is a considerable gap between psychology-based management research findings and management practices in organizations (e.g., Campbell, Daft, & Hulin, 1982; Dunnette & Brown, 1968; Johns, 1993). Although this gap is hardly unique to the field of I/O psychology (and related fields such as human resource management [HR], industrial relations [IR], organizational behavior [OB], or organizational development and change [ODC]), it has grown larger over the years, despite a fair amount of discussion about how to narrow it (e.g., Dunnette, 1990; Lawler, Mohrman, Mohrman, Ledford, & Cummings, 1985; Murphy & Saal, 1990). Indeed, the stubborn persistence of the gap has caused some to wonder whether a closer relationship between research and practice is possible at this point (e.g., Hakel, 1994;

Kieser & Leiner, 2009; Oviatt & Miller, 1989), or even desirable (e.g., Earley, 1999; Hulin, 2001).

Despite the long-standing nature of the gap, broad economic and sociopolitical factors appear to be increasing the potential benefits of stronger academic-practitioner interactions (Rynes, Bartunek, & Daft, 2001). On the practitioner side, intensified global competition has escalated pressures for organizational innovation and efficiency, which in turn have increased managerial search for and receptivity to new ideas. As such, research showing consistently positive relationships between certain management practices and organization-level outcomes should be of greater value to practitioners than ever before. A considerable amount of such research now exists at both the within-organization (Arthur & Huntley, 2005; Katz, Kochan, & Gobeille, 1983; Wagner, Rubin, & Callahan, 1988) and between-organization levels (e.g., Arthur, 1994; Gerhart & Milkovich, 1990; Huselid, 1995; Welbourne & Andrews, 1996) Moreover, many of the practices associated with more positive outcomes represent "win-wins" for both managers and employees (e.g., Fulmer, Gerhart, & Scott, 2006; Katz et al. 1983; Orlitzky, Schmidt, & Rynes, 2003; Welbourne & Andrews, 1996). Although the direction of the causal relationships involved is not always clear (Schneider, Hanges, Smith, & Salvaggio, 2003; Wright & Haggerty, 2005), at least some longitudinal studies have shown that high-involvement or high-investment HR management practices are associated with subsequent organizational performance (e.g., Baum, Locke, & Kirkpatrick, 1998; Huselid, 1995; Welbourne & Andrews, 1996; Van Iddekinge et al., 2009).

There are other reasons for practitioners to develop stronger relationships with academics as well. For example, the Supreme Court's 1993 decision in *Daubert v. Merrell Dow Pharmaceuticals, Inc.* has increased the importance to employers of being able to empirically defend the validity of their employment practices (Faigman & Monahan, 2005). In addition, U.S. public policy has changed in ways that encourage cooperation between business and academia, such as the provision of tax breaks for corporate funding of university research and the development of government programs that require industry-university collaboration as a condition of funding (Cohen, Florida, & Goe, 1994). Finally, Ashford (in Walsh, Tushman, Kimberly, Starbuck, & Ashford, 2007) notes that, although organizations have a variety of other options for seeking knowledge or advice, there is "no other institution in society that is so purely aimed at the pursuit of truth and the production of knowledge than the university" (p. 149).

On the academic side, collaboration with practitioners on problems of mutual interest can provide researchers with access to better data sets (larger samples, higher response rates, better measures, fewer errors) that avoid some of the most persistent methodological problems in I/O and related areas of research (Amabile et al., 2001; Edwards, 2008; Starbuck, 2006). Helping practicing managers to deal with problems can be both intellectually stimulating and intrinsically motivating, and can surface questions of theoretical as well as practical importance (e.g., Campbell et al., 1982; Kelemen & Bansal, 2002; Latham, 2007; Tushman & O'Reilly, 2007; Van de Ven, 2007).

Furthermore, collaboration between academics and practitioners often results in very high-quality research, particularly when both sides have a difficult puzzle that they want to solve (Daft, Griffin, & Yates, 1987; Hodgkinson & Rousseau, 2009). For example, since 2003, all but two of the *Academy of Management Journal's* (*AMJ's*) "best paper" awards have gone to intensive theory-building studies conducted in a small number of organizations (e.g., six TV networks and film studios, eight newspapers, eight medical providers, five accounting firms, and one church). As another example, Starbuck (in Walsh et al., 2007) tells how the Profit Impact of Market Strategy (PIMS) database was created by the Marketing Science Institute, a collaboration between 60 firms and a broad base of academic researchers. According to Starbuck, "Its influence in the field of marketing has been remarkable. During the 1990s, projects that MSI sponsored won every award for outstanding research in marketing, and they comprised 60% of the articles in *Journal of Marketing* and *Journal of Marketing Research*" (p. 146). Additionally, Rynes, McNatt, and Bretz (1999) found that researchers who spent more time on-site in projects with organizations were cited more often than those who spent less time in the organizations they studied. Many of these researchers appeared to employ what Craig Russell (personal communication) calls "guerilla research: solving firms' problems while simultaneously weaving in measures and interventions that advance a research agenda, with the firm's full knowledge and support."

Beyond the potential for individual researchers to create high-quality research through collaboration with practitioners, the universities in which academics are employed are also engaging more directly with private-sector organizations than ever before. To a considerable extent, this is because public funding for universities has been decreasing (both proportionately and in real terms) since the 1970s, leaving universities—especially state universities—increasingly dependent on the private sector for monetary and other resources (e.g., Cohen, Florida, Randazzese, & Walsh, 1998; Slaughter & Leslie, 1997). While collaborations with private-sector organizations provide universities with valuable resources for research and teaching, the corporations and other entities that donate funds expect universities to produce not only basic research and theory-based education, but also applied research and skill-based education in return for their support.

Although research is still undoubtedly more highly rewarded than teaching or service, and basic research more prestigious than applied, the pendulum appears to be swinging at least somewhat in the opposite direction in some universities (Cascio, 2008; Latham, 2007; Walsh et al., 2007). Changes in resource dependence are increasing the value of academics who develop bridges between research, teaching, and practice (Ashford in Walsh et al., 2007). Although this development has been more pronounced in business schools than psychology departments (due in large part to media rankings of business school programs that focus heavily on student evaluations of teaching and the quality of student placements; e.g., Corley & Gioia, 2002), broad trends in the funding of research and higher education suggest that psychology and other social sciences will increasingly be subject to similar pressures (Slaughter & Leslie, 1997). In this regard, it is somewhat worrisome that a number of well-known researchers have remarked on the declining influence of psychology and micro-organizational behavior in both management and public policy research and practice (e.g., Blood, 1994; Cascio & Aguinis, 2008; Ferraro, Pfeffer, & Sutton, 2005; Hakel, 1994; O'Reilly, 1990; Miner, in Schwarz, Clegg, Cummings, Donaldson, & Miner, 2007). Other researchers have shown that psychology-based research is becoming increasingly isolated from research in management and economics, which are increasing rather than decreasing in both research and policy influence (Agarwal & Hoetker, 2007).

Finally, for whatever combination of reasons, I/O and related researchers—as well as professional organizations such as the Society for Industrial and Organizational Psychology (SIOP) and the Society for Human Resource Management (SHRM)—have shown increased interest in attempting to narrow the research-practice gap. For example, we have seen:

• An increase in the number of special forums on this topic in journals such as *AMJ* (e.g., Shapiro, Kirkman, & Courtney, 2007), *Human Resource Management* (*HRM*; Burke,

Drasgow, & Edwards, 2004), *Journal of Occupational and Organizational Psychology* (Gelade, 2006), *Journal of Management Inquiry* (Walsh et al., 2007), *Journal of Organizational Behavior* (Greenberg, 2008), *Journal of Management Studies* (Kieser & Leiner, 2009), and *Academy of Management Learning and Education* (Adler & Harzing, 2009);

• An increase in the number of academic colleges, departments, centers, or even individual professors who provide web synopses or "translations" of research for practitioners (e.g., Cornell's "CAHRS' Top Ten," "Knowledge @ Wharton," or Craig Russell's explanations of the Cleary model of test bias and the Brogden-Cronbach-Gleser model of utility; http://www.ou.edu/russell/whitepapers/);

• Emergence of awards for research with important implications for practice (e.g., SIOP's M. Scott Myers Award for Applied Research in the Workplace and the Academy of Management's OB Division's Outstanding Practitioner-Oriented Publication award) and for researchers who have contributed to practice throughout their careers (e.g., the Academy of Management's [AOM's] Scholar-Practitioner Award and SHRM's $50,000 Michael R. Losey award);

• Ongoing efforts to build an Evidence-Based Management Collaborative database (www.cebma.org/);

• An emerging empirical base documenting the extent and content of science-practice gaps in I/O and related fields (e.g., Cascio & Aguinis, 2008; Deadrick & Gibson, 2007; Rynes, Colbert, & Brown, 2002; Rynes, Giluk, & Brown, 2007; Silzer & Cober, 2008);

• Increased government support for industry-university research collaborations both in North America and Europe (e.g., the UK's Advanced Institute of Management [AIM] research collaborative; see Hodgkinson & Rousseau, 2009).

Although it is unclear whether these developments represent long-term trends or just transitory fads, for the purposes of this chapter I assume that interest in greater collaboration will at least persist, and perhaps escalate. If so, understanding as much as we can about the nature of the current gap and its origins is essential to ensuring future progress in narrowing it.

Scope and Organization

One issue affecting scope concerns disciplinary boundaries. Although the central disciplinary focus of this review is I/O psychology, it also includes evidence from the fields of HR, IR, OB, and ODC. This is because: (a) all these fields involve the management, motivation, and development of employees; and (b) research suggests that it is becoming increasingly difficult to clearly differentiate among them (Ruona & Gibson, 2004).

For example, in a large empirical study of the competencies associated with effective HR managers, Ulrich, Brockbank, Yeung, and Lake (1995) found that the ability to manage change (historically considered an ODC function) was more important to HR managers' evaluated effectiveness than the ability to deliver traditional HR practices and services. Similarly, in a historical review of the areas of HR, ODC, and human resource development (HRD), Ruona and Gibson (2004) found all three fields converging around four trends: (1) the increased centrality of people to organizational success; (2) increased focus on whole systems and integrated solutions; (3) emphasis on strategic alignment and impact; and (4) increased importance of the capacity for change and three major competencies: (a) mastery of technical basics, (b) knowledge of business and strategy, and (c) facilitation of organizational change and agility. Finally, a recent survey of SIOP members revealed that I/O practitioners would like SIOP to promote I/O practice and research to the larger business community and to place more I/O psychology articles in HR and general business publications (Silzer & Cober, 2008). Hence, a somewhat multidisciplinary approach seems most appropriate.

A second issue concerns the types of "practitioners" addressed. For purposes of this study, I define practitioners as "those whose decisions or recommendations in organizational contexts impact organizational stakeholders either directly, or indirectly through their influence on HR systems." This definition is a bit narrower than that used by Gelade (2006, p. 154) and Cascio and Aguinis (2008, p. 1062)—"those who make recommendations about the management or development of people in organizational settings, or who advise those who do"—in that it narrows the definition to having actual impact and accountability, as opposed to simply giving advice (as, for example, academics sometimes do). Despite this narrowed definition, however, the educational and experiential backgrounds of practitioners referred to in this chapter are still quite varied (e.g., sometimes they are doctorate-level I/O psychologists, while other times they are HR managers with a variety of educational degrees).

Because of this wide variation in practitioners, care will be taken to specify (wherever possible) the precise types of practitioners being discussed (e.g., whether survey respondents are I/O psychologists or HR managers).

The chapter is organized around two main themes: (a) the nature and sources of the research-practice gap, and (b) potential solutions for narrowing it. Each of these themes is then subdivided into three sections, each of which pertains to one source or cause of the gap: (a) lack of awareness of issues and knowledge on the other side (e.g., practitioners may not be aware of scientific findings, and researchers may not be aware of practitioner needs and challenges); (b) differences in beliefs (e.g., practitioners may hear of a research finding but reject it; researchers may be aware of an emerging practice but dismiss it out of hand); or (c) failures to implement a practice or to change behavior (e.g., practitioners may know about and believe that an alternative practice would be superior but fail to implement it anyway; researchers may believe that collaborative research ventures would produce more important work but fail to collaborate anyway). I first discuss evidence related to the nature and extent of each of these three components of the gap and then, based on those analyses, offer suggestions designed to ameliorate them.

Nature and Sources of the Gap
Gaps in Awareness
THE PRACTICE SIDE
Nature of the Gap

There is considerable evidence to suggest that the biggest discrepancies between research and practice in I/O psychology, HR, and related fields exist in the area of employee selection. One of the most widely documented and persistent of these gaps involves practitioner preferences for using intuitive methods of selection, particularly unstandardized employment interviews, over standardized predictors and/or mechanical (i.e., empirically derived and consistently weighted) combinations of selection techniques.[1] Highhouse (2008) reviewed multiple studies showing that mechanical or statistical predictions of employee behavior are superior to both intuitive methods (such as the unstructured interview) and combinations of mechanical *plus* intuitive methods (e.g., Dawes, 1971; Dawes, Faust, & Meehl, 1989; Grove, Zald, Lebow, Snitz, & Nelson, 2000). Nevertheless, the unstructured interview has been (and continues to be) the most popular and widely used selection procedure over the past 100 years (Buckley, Norris, & Wiese, 2000). Additionally, written tests continue to be perceived by managers as inferior to interviews for evaluating both personality and intelligence (e.g., Lievens, Highhouse, & DeCorte, 2005).

A second well-documented gap concerns practitioners' tendencies not to believe that general mental ability (GMA) or general intelligence (*g*) is the single best predictor of employee performance (e.g., Schmidt & Hunter, 1998). For example, Rynes et al. (2002) found that, contrary to research evidence (see the original study for details), the vast majority of HR managers in their sample believed that both conscientiousness and values are better predictors of performance than intelligence. In addition, approximately half of the respondents believed that intelligence is a disadvantage for performance on low-skilled jobs, while in reality there is a positive validity coefficient (ρ = .23) for GMA in predicting performance on completely unskilled jobs (this coefficient rises to .58 for high-level managerial and professional jobs; Schmidt & Hunter, 1998). Finally, in a policy-capturing study of résumé-based prescreening decisions by campus recruiters, McKinney, Carlson, Mecham, D'Angelo, and Connerley (2003) found that 42% of recruiters ignored grade point average (a proxy for GMA) in deciding whom to interview, while 15% actually selected *against* applicants with high GPAs.

Another selection-related gap pertains to the usefulness of personality testing for selection purposes. As with GMA, Rynes et al. (2002) found that practitioners' beliefs about personality testing were generally more negative than is warranted by relevant research findings. For example, most HR managers in their study tended to believe that integrity tests are not valid predictors of performance and that such tests are likely to produce adverse impact against minorities. However, meta-analytic results have shown that the estimated mean operational validity of integrity tests for predicting supervisory ratings of job performance is ρ = .41 (Ones, Viswesvaran, & Schmidt, 1993) and that minority groups are not adversely affected by either overt integrity tests or disguised-purpose, personality-oriented measures of integrity (Sackett, Burris, & Callahan, 1989).

One other notable gap concerns the relative effectiveness of employee participation versus goal setting for improving performance. Specifically, most of Rynes et al.'s (2002) respondents believed that participation in decision making is more effective than goal setting for improving performance,

whereas research shows the opposite to be true (e.g., Latham, Erez, & Locke, 1988; Locke, Feren, McCaleb, Shaw, & Denny, 1980). For example, Locke et al.'s (1980) meta-analytic findings (based entirely on field research) showed that goal setting produced a 20% improvement in performance on average, while empowerment produced less than 1% on average, and with very high variability. Given the weak average results for participation and empowerment (see also Argyris, 1998; Highhouse, 2007; Wagner, 1994) and the apparent existence of large moderator effects (Wagner, 2009 versus the strong results for goal setting), this gap is also important.

Sources of the Gap

If all practitioners had advanced degrees in I/O psychology or HR, there might not be much of a problem with lack of awareness of research findings. However, this is far from the current situation. Unlike law or medicine, neither general management nor HR management are true professions (Leicht & Fennell, 2001; Trank & Rynes, 2003), although I/O psychology is a different matter. For example, there are no requirements that managers be exposed to scientific knowledge about management, pass examinations in order to become licensed to practice, or pursue continuing education in order to maintain employment. Even in HR, where a certification exam exists and is advocated by the largest professional association (SHRM), certification is not always used by employers in hiring HR practitioners (Aguinis, Michaelis, & Jones, 2005). As a result, elevating the qualifications of individuals placed in HR positions has been a long-standing challenge (Hammonds, 2005; Rynes, Owen, & Trank, 2008).

Second, even if managers or HR managers pursue formal education in the fields of business or management, they are likely to confront a curriculum that is heavily weighted toward mathematically based courses (e.g., finance, economics, accounting, operations) rather than behavioral ones. For example, Navarro (2008) found that while more than 90% of the top 50 MBA programs require courses in marketing, finance, financial accounting, operations, strategy, managerial economics, and quantitative analysis/statistics, only 56% require courses in OB, 36% in general management, and 28% in HR. Moreover, those schools that are most likely to focus on behavioral topics (often referred to as "soft skills" in program descriptions) often do so via case, discussion, and role-playing pedagogies that do not emphasize research results (e.g., Harvard's case study method; see Ellet, 2007). Moreover, recent research by Stambaugh and Trank (2010) suggests that new research findings—particularly those that deviate from currently dominant paradigms—are not readily integrated into textbooks, while largely discredited theories (e.g., Herzberg's two-factor theory or Maslow's hierarchy of needs) continue to be included. Putting these factors together, it seems likely that fewer than half of graduating MBAs have had much if any exposure to the most important I/O findings—at least presented explicitly as "research" findings meriting special consideration among all the other information and opinions provided in textbooks, cases, and classroom discussions.

Third, once students graduate from MBA (or I/O, IR, or HR programs), they are even less likely to be exposed to research findings. For example, Rynes and colleagues (2002) found that less than 1% of HR practitioners at the manager, director, or VP levels usually read *Journal of Applied Psychology* (*JAP*), *Personnel Psychology* (*PPsych*), or *AMJ*, and most (75%) never read any of the three. Rather, these managers most commonly look to other HR practitioners in their own organizations for help in solving HR problems, and least commonly (of seven possible sources of help) to academics. Another study by Offermann and Spiros (2001) surveyed members of the Academy of Management (66% with Ph.D.s and 29% with master's degrees) who spent either all or part of their time in ODC or team development. Even among this highly educated group, only a minority reported that they read *AMJ* (32.5%) or *JAP* (12.6%) to keep up with recent developments in OD or teams.

Finally, the publications that practitioners do read once they leave undergraduate or graduate school sometimes do little to report on recent research findings. For example, Rynes et al. (2007) examined *HRM*, *HR Magazine*, and *Harvard Business Review* (*HBR*) with respect to three topics revealed by the Rynes et al. (2002) study to exhibit large gaps between research findings and practitioner beliefs: the importance of intelligence to job performance, the relationship between personality characteristics and job performance, and the relative effectiveness of goal setting versus participation in improving performance. The authors examined both: (a) how much coverage each of these topics received in each journal, as well as (b) the accuracy of coverage in *HBR*, *HRM* and *HR Magazine* when evaluated against research findings (i.e., how consistent the information in each periodical was with established research findings).

With respect to the first question, coverage of these three topics was almost nonexistent in the three periodicals. Specifically, as a percentage of total articles published in each outlet, intelligence received 1.2% coverage in *HRM*, 0.4% in *HBR*, and no coverage in *HR Magazine* between 2000 and 2005. Personality received 1.2% coverage in *HRM*, 0.6% in *HBR*, and 0.4% in *HR Magazine* over that same time period. Goal setting received 0.6% coverage in *HRM*, 0.6% in *HBR*, and 0.6% in *HR Magazine*. With respect to the second question (research consistency of coverage), results suggested that *HRM*'s coverage was research consistent, while *HR Magazine*'s and *HBR*'s was mixed. For example, *HBR* published two articles on intelligence during the relevant period. One of these was research-consistent (Menkes, 2005), while the other (called "Deep Smarts") confounded the construct of intelligence with specific job experience (Leonard & Swap, 2004).

In summary, research suggests that practitioners are often unaware of basic research findings, particularly in the areas of selection and performance improvement (e.g., goal setting versus employee participation). Practitioners may be unaware of research findings because: (a) they may not have received formal education in psychology, management, HR management, or related fields; (b) even if they received formal education, they may have received little exposure to research findings; (c) once they graduate and become practitioners, they are not likely to read the research literature; and (d) the periodicals that they are most likely to read do little to disseminate research findings. For any or all of these reasons, there may be many practitioners who rarely think of research findings as a potential aid in solving their problems.

THE ACADEMIC SIDE
Nature of the Gap

Although there have been multiple studies about what practitioners don't know about research findings and what they do or don't read, there do not appear to be analogous studies of academic awareness of practitioner issues or concerns. For example, I was unable to find any studies that have directly asked academic researchers such things as whether *they* read practitioner journals, or whether they have accurate knowledge of the major issues and environmental conditions confronting I/O or HR practitioners. This void may exist for several reasons. For example, researchers may simply not think these issues are important to investigate or, even if they do, they may perceive a lack of interest among other academics—and hence, difficulty in getting such research published.

Nevertheless, researchers have attempted to address the issue of gaps on the academic side at least indirectly, by studying how the content of academic journals differs from the content of publications aimed at practitioners. For example, Deadrick and Gibson (2007) examined the primary content areas of more than 4,300 non-methods-focused articles published in four HR-I/O focused journals (*HRM, HR Magazine, JAP*, and *PPsych*) over a 20-year period (1986–2005). The first two journals were characterized as being primarily aimed at practitioner audiences (although *HRM* is probably more accurately described as a "bridge" publication), and the latter two primarily at academics.

Deadrick and Gibson (2007) found that there was a consistently large gap in coverage between academic and practitioner journals with respect to compensation and benefits issues. Specifically, articles on compensation and benefits comprised 14.3% of the content of practitioner journals, but only 2.0% of academic ones. It should be noted, however, that the compensation articles in practitioner outlets focused mostly on compliance-based factual information (e.g., Fair Labor Standards Act, Family and Medical Leave Act, exempt versus non-exempt status, overtime pay)—topics that are more likely to be illuminated by legal advisers than academic researchers. Other areas of apparently greater interest to practitioners than academics were (in order of gap size): HR department issues (11.5% versus 1.7%), strategic HR (9.5% versus 2.8%), technology (8.0% versus 2.6%), and international or global HR (6.0% versus 2.2%).

In a second study, Cascio and Aguinis (2008) compared the content of articles appearing in *JAP* from 1963 to 2007 (broken into five-year periods) with a compilation of the most important human resource trends (as identified by literature reviews) over those same periods. Based on their analysis, Cascio and Aguinis (2008) concluded that academic I/O research is not meeting practitioners' interest levels in a variety of areas, such as recruitment, HR effectiveness at the organization level, and the implications of changing worker demographics for managers, employees, and their organizations. Extrapolating from past research into the next ten years, they predict that "I/O psychology will not be out front in influencing the debate on issues that are (or will be) of broad organizational and societal appeal. It will not produce a substantial

body of research that will inform HR practitioners, senior managers, or outside stakeholders, such as funding agencies, public-policy makers, or university administrators who control budgets" (p. 1024).

Using a somewhat different methodology, a study by Heath and Sitkin (2001) compared the "actual" coverage of organizational topics (as measured by keyword prevalence in *Journal of Organizational Behavior* [*JOB*], *AMJ, JAP, Organizational Behavior and Human Decision Processes* [*OBHDP*], and *Organization Science* [*OS*]) with "ideal" levels of coverage (as measured by beliefs of the editorial board members of *JOB*).[2] They found that there was *less* research than believed desirable in many areas (norms, communication, organizational change, performance, family, risk, cross-cultural, trust, interdependence, cooperation, and learning), and *more* coverage than desirable in four others (job satisfaction, decision making, organizational citizenship, and goal setting).

In trying to make sense of these results, Heath and Sitkin (2001) concluded that the areas where more research was desired were ones that are "most central to the task of organizing" (p. 54). As a result, they suggested that in order to have greater impact, researchers might think more in terms of studying "organizing" behavior rather than "organizational" behavior:

> Under this definition, researchers would devote relatively more attention to topics that help us understand how groups of people organize and carry out their goals. As we view the results of the survey, a number of topics toward the top of the list fall under (this) definition because they help us understand the task of organizing. For example, if we understood more about *social norms,* we would understand more about how groups of people implicitly coordinate their action when they face a complex environment. We would also understand more about organizing if we understood how organizations can facilitate effective *communication* across divisions and hierarchical levels....
> (*Heath & Sitkin*, 2001, p. 54)

A fourth relevant study was performed by Silzer and Cober (2008). They conducted a recent survey of 1,005 SIOP members with varying interests in practice (61% full-time practitioners, 10% part-time practitioners, 19% occasional practitioners, and 10% non-practitioners). One question they asked respondents was whether science, or practice, was "leading" knowledge in a number of areas. Overall, 17 of 26 topics were identified as mainly practitioner-led, including consulting and advising, employment branding, HR technology, executive/management coaching, strategic planning, succession/workforce planning, talent management, labor relations, HR general practices, compensation, employee relations, employee recruitment, organizational development, litigation, and leadership and management development. On the other hand, researchers were seen as leading in the areas of measurement and statistics, job and work analysis, selection and staffing, cross-cultural issues, and individual assessment and assessment centers. Interestingly, there were few notable differences between full-time practitioners and full-time academics in their perceptions, with two exceptions being in the areas of recruitment and leadership/management development.

While the preceding articles have addressed differences in academic and practitioner coverage in I/O psychology, HR, and OB, Austin and Bartunek (2003) looked at differences between research and practice journals in organization development and change (ODC). They found that research in ODC academic journals focused almost exclusively on *change* processes (*how* organizations change; for an excellent review, see Van de Ven & Poole, 1995), while practitioner journals focused primarily on *implementation* processes (*how to* change organizations). Moreover, they found that the more academically oriented publications showed virtually no awareness of prominent ODC implementation technologies, such as appreciative inquiry (Cooperrider & Srivastva, 1987), large-group interventions (Lindaman & Lippitt, 1980), and learning organizations (e.g., Argyris & Schön, 1978; Senge, 1990). The authors highlighted appreciative inquiry (AI) as an area where the gap was particularly notable: "The academic silence and practitioner enthusiasm about AI illustrates the significance of the practitioner/academic theoretical divide....AI challenges several assumptions of previous research on resistance to change....Academic theorizing about change would benefit from more attention to the questions raised by AI practitioners" (Austin & Bartunek, 2003, p. 323; see also Yaeger, Sorensen, & Bengtsson, 2005).

Finally, Shapiro and colleagues (2007) directly assessed whether a sample of 548 members of the AOM (438 academics, 39 business people, 40 consultants, and 31 unidentified) believe there is a gap: (a) in translation of research findings to practitioners (which they call "lost *in* translation"); and/or (b) even before research is translated (which they call "lost *before* translation"), as when academics ask questions of little interest to practitioners. Results showed that AOM members perceive both types of gaps although, consistent with the predominance of academic respondents, a larger gap was perceived "in" translation ($\overline{X}$ = 3.98 on a five-point scale) than "before" it ($\overline{X}$ = 3.65).

Academic Sources of the Gap

Although the scientist-practitioner model[3] has been an important ideal in the history of both I/O psychology (e.g., Dunnette, 1990; Fleishman, 1990) and business schools (e.g., McGrath, 2007), at present most I/O psychologists and management specialists are either one (e.g., scientist) or the other (practitioner). In the face of limited contact between the two groups, the communities have developed very different assumptions, values, goals, interests, and norms (e.g., Beyer & Trice, 1982; Boehm, 1980; Daft & Lewin, 2008; Kieser & Leiner, 2009; Shrivastava & Mitroff, 1984). These differences have tended to reduce the perceived (and almost certainly the real) relevance of academic research to practitioners.

Boehm (1980) argued that one major source of the gap is the difference between the traditional scientific method (emphasizing theoretical problems, formal hypotheses, statistical controls, isolation of phenomena of interest, and search for facts or the "truth") and the messy reality of organizational settings (with multiple processes, stages, and interactions among them, and emphasis on solving real problems). She goes on to say that "the reaction of behavioral scientists, when faced by the realities of the organizational research environment, has been either to attempt modification of the environment to fit the traditional mode of inquiry or else to opt out of the scientific establishment" (Boehm, 1980, p. 498). The results of this divergence are at least fivefold: (1) the failure of "real world" research to disseminate to academics; (2) the failure of academic research to spread to practice (or unanticipated outcomes when it does); (3) limitation of the types of questions asked by academics (to those that come closest to meeting the academic model); (4) a tendency to overlook the positive features of conducting research in organizational settings (e.g., a more accurate model of the world, valuable cross-fertilization between lab and field studies, emphasis on "what works?" more than "why?"); and (5) a variety of in-group/out-group attitudes, stereotypes, and behaviors (see also Empson, 2007; Gulati, 2007, and Vermeulen, 2007).

In addition to differences in norms, goals, values, and research models, academics and practitioners also have different incentive systems. For example, while practitioners often have *dis*incentives to publish their research (e.g., proprietary data, competitive advantage, and legal vulnerabilities; Boehm, 1980), academics generally have more incentives to publish than they do to teach well or perform various types of service (Mowday, 1997). Gomez-Mejia and Balkin (1992) showed that the largest predictor of academic salaries in management (controlling for a variety of personal characteristics) was the number of top-tier publications, followed by the number of moves from one university to another. Such moves are also facilitated primarily by publication records, which are more visible (and more valued) than service or teaching accomplishments.

Not only are the strongest academic incentives to publish, but also to publish in a relatively narrow set of journals with high "impact factors" or citation rates (see Adler & Harzing, 2009; Judge, Cable, Colbert, & Rynes, 2007, and Starbuck, 2006). Critics argue that the growing importance of metrics such as the number of top-tier publications, number of citations, journal impact factors, and the various academic rankings based upon these measures is distorting research away from its original goals and making it less helpful in solving organizational and social problems. For example, Lawrence (2008), cited in Adler & Harzing (2009) says:

> Measurement of scientific productivity is difficult. The measures used . . . are crude. But these measures are now so universally adopted that they determine most things that matter (to scholars): tenure or unemployment, a postdoctoral grant or none, success or failure. As a result, scientists have been forced to downgrade their primary aim from making discoveries to publishing as many papers as possible—and trying to work them into high impact-factor journals. Consequently, scientific behavior has become distorted and the utility, quality, and objectivity of articles have deteriorated. Changes . . . are urgently needed. (p. 1)

Several characteristics of top-tier journals appear to make their research less accessible and relevant to practitioners than research in "lower tier" ones. One such characteristic is the tendency of top-tier journals to uphold the traditional scientific model more religiously than do other journals (e.g., Boehm, 1980; Daft & Lewin, 1990; Locke, 2007). As a case in point, one of the main reasons for the founding of *OS* in 1990 was to "break out of the normal science straitjacket" (Daft & Lewin, 1990, p. 1). However, 18 years later, Daft and Lewin (2008) concluded that this part of the original mission—to be an immediate source of knowledge for practical managerial applications—"was unrealistic and has not been realized" because "as a journal evolves over time, its focus systematically narrows to reflect the orthodoxies of the community of scholars that emerges around it" (p. 178). In the case of *OS*, the "orthodoxies of the community of scholars" served to widen rather than narrow the research-practice gap. (Of course, *OS* is hardly unique in this regard; see Cascio & Aguinis, 2008).

Another characteristic of top-tier journals that decreases their accessibility and relevance is the growing emphasis on theoretical contribution as a publication requirement (e.g., Colquitt & Zapata-Phelan, 2007; Daft & Lewin, 2008; Sutton & Staw, 1995). Although the benefits of good theory are taken for granted by many academics (although they might disagree about what constitutes "good" theory; e.g., Russell, 2009), a number of prominent researchers believe that the current emphasis on theory has gone too far. For example, Hambrick (2007) argues:

> A blanket insistence on theory, or the requirement of an articulation of theory in everything we write, actually retards our ability to achieve our end, (which is) understanding. Our field's theory fetish, for instance, prevents the reporting of rich detail about interesting phenomena for which no theory yet exists. And it bans the reporting of facts—no matter how important or competently generated—that lack explanation but that, once reported, might stimulate the search for an explanation. (p. 1346)

The growing incentive for academics to publish in top-tier journals is perceived to be a very important, if not the *most* important, reason that research has become inaccessible to practitioners and largely ignored by them (Adler & Harzing, 2009; Shapiro et al., 2007; Starbuck, 2006). However, there is the further problem that even when practitioners (and sometimes academics) become aware of research findings, they do not always believe them. I turn now to this issue.

Gaps in Beliefs

Studies such as Rynes et al. (2002) cannot definitively determine whether research-inconsistent beliefs are a result of (1) lack of awareness or (2) disbelief of research findings. Nevertheless, Rynes et al. inferred that the gaps were probably due to lack of awareness, based on circumstantial evidence regarding the reading habits of HR practitioners and the publishing patterns of the major practitioner and bridge journals in the field (i.e., sparse coverage of research findings related to intelligence, personality, and goal setting by practitioner and bridge journals). Of course, the preceding section further suggests that practitioner lack of awareness is also due to the publishing practices of top-tier academic journals, which often make their articles unwelcoming and uninteresting to practitioners.

However, even if a gap is due to lack of awareness, it cannot automatically be assumed that practitioners would actually change their beliefs after being exposed to relevant research. In this section, I first review the (somewhat limited) research on this topic in three areas—utility analysis, predictors of employee performance (i.e., selection), and jury reactions to expert testimony. I then present some of the most difficult challenges to overcoming practitioners' disbelief, including the vexing problem that researchers often do not agree among themselves on many issues.

PRACTITIONER BELIEFS ABOUT RESEARCH FINDINGS
Utility Analysis

In the 1990s, two studies were conducted by Gary Latham and Glen Whyte to assess how practitioners react to utility analysis, a research-based tool that attempts to convert the effect sizes of various HR interventions into financial terms (e.g., Boudreau, 1983; Schmidt & Hunter, 1983). In their first study, Latham and Whyte (1994) had 143 enrollees in an executive MBA program respond to one of four experimental stimuli. Participants were presented with a scenario about a company that was having trouble hiring high-quality clerical workers. The company had hired a psychologist to investigate the issue, and had recommended implementing systematic selection practices. Participants received one of four "systematic practices" to evaluate:

1. Standard validation: the psychologist creates a test tailored to the organization's clerical jobs, validates it against the performance of the organization's current clerical workers, and then uses the results to modify the company's existing practices;

2. Standard validation plus expectancy chart: the psychologist applies the procedures described in "1" above, but also uses an expectancy chart to show the performance improvements attained by another client who used a similar procedure (the amount of improvement suggested by the expectancy chart was not specified in the article);

3. Standard validation plus utility analysis: the psychologist uses the procedures in "1" above, but also explains utility analysis and gives an estimate of the financial gain achievable ($60,208,786) if her advice is followed;

4. All three: The psychologist uses a combination of standard validation, expectancy chart, and utility analysis/financial projection.

The dependent variable was an eight-item scale addressing such participant reactions as commitment to implementing the psychologist's results, confidence in the psychologist's solution, and ability to justify their decision to others about whether or not to accept the psychologist's advice.

Results showed the most favorable reactions to condition "1" and the least favorable to "3." In other words, adding utility analysis to typical validation procedures produced the *least* convincing scenario. In seeking to explain these results, Latham and Whyte (1994) speculated that their results might have occurred either because "managers are suspicious of behavioral consultants who claim to be able to accurately estimate the dollar value of their recommendations" or because of "the large size of the gain typically estimated by utility analysis, which may strain the psychologist's credibility" (p. 42). They also raise the possibility that managers "(may not actually) want sophisticated and systematically collected information regarding their human resources in order to improve their business decisions" (p. 32), citing Mintzberg's (1975) observation that managers rely much less heavily on rational analysis than utility analysis assumes.

In a second study of 41 executive MBA students, Whyte and Latham (1997) used the same basic scenario "1," but added two different conditions. In condition "2," participants received scenario "1" plus written support of standard validation practices from a hypothetical trusted advisor. In condition "3," participants received both "1" and "2" above, but also a written explanation of utility analysis, an actual utility analysis showing large financial benefits from selection validation, a videotaped presentation from an expert on utility analysis (Steven Cronshaw) explaining the underlying logic and benefits of utility analysis, and a live appearance by Cronshaw to answer managers' questions. Similar to the first study, conditions "1" and "2" produced the most favorable (and nearly identical) reactions, and condition "3" the least favorable (by far). Of the 10 items on the "reactions" scale, the three showing the largest differences were commitment to implementation, ability to justify the decision to others, and importance of financial consequences in their evaluations.

Based on these results, Whyte and Latham (1997) concluded that managers do not perceive utility analysis to be a useful tool for HR decision making, and advised I/O psychologists to "reconsider their assumptions regarding the information managers value when making HR policy decisions" (p. 608). They also noted that their results were consistent with Johns's (1993) contention that the adoption of I/O practices is not strongly influenced by technical merit.

In a somewhat unusual (and amusing) addendum to Whyte and Latham (1997), Cronshaw (1997) gave his own view as to why condition "3" was the least effective. He cited Eagly and Chaiken's (1993) theory of psychological reactance, which suggests that positive attitudes toward an attitudinal object can "boomerang" if people "perceive that their freedom to adopt or keep an attitudinal position is threatened by the coercive pressure of high-pressure persuasion" (Cronshaw, 1997, p. 613). Although Cronshaw may be correct in the assumption that his presence was perceived as coercive, this explanation cannot account for the fact that utility analysis did similarly poorly in Study 1, where there was no videotape and he was not present.

PREDICTORS OF EMPLOYEE PERFORMANCE (I.E., SELECTION)

"Perhaps the greatest technological achievement in I/O psychology over the last 100 years is the development of decision aids (e.g., paper-and-pencil tests, structured interviews, mechanical combination of predictors) that substantially reduce error in the prediction of employee performance. Arguably the greatest failure of I/O psychology has been the inability to convince employers to use them" (*Highhouse*, 2008, p. 333).

Although practitioners' lack of enthusiasm for actuarial prediction methods might be due to lack of awareness, Highhouse (2008) argues that the more likely source is failure to be convinced: "Although one might argue that these data merely reflect a lack of knowledge about effective practice, there is considerable evidence that employers simply

do not believe that the research is relevant to their own situation" (p. 333). In attempting to explain this phenomenon, Highhouse focused on two widespread beliefs that reduce enthusiasm for scientific advances in selection.

The first is the common belief that it is possible to achieve near-perfect precision in hiring decisions. Given this belief, people tend not to view selection as a probabilistic process with a low validity ceiling. Thus, validity coefficients that sound good to researchers (such as .5) fail to impress practitioners, particularly when they hear that this translates to "only" 25% of variance explained. Moreover, those who wish to dispute the importance of GMA, particularly proponents of emotional intelligence (EI), have made heavy use of the "variance explained" construct to discredit GMA testing. For example, in *Working with Emotional Intelligence*, Goleman (2000) contends that "IQ alone explains surprisingly little of achievement at work or in life. When IQ test scores are correlated with how well people perform in their careers, the highest estimate of how much difference IQ accounts for is about 25%. A careful analysis, though, suggests a more accurate figure may be no higher than 10%, and perhaps as low as 4%. This means that IQ alone at best leaves 75% of job success unexplained, and at worst 96%—in other words, it does not predict who succeeds and who fails" (p. 19). What, according to Goleman, accounts for the rest? Emotional intelligence!

The second underlying belief is the notion that one can become an expert at predicting human behavior merely through experience. This belief, which has received support (and widespread readership) in the popular press book *Blink: The Power of Thinking Without Thinking* (Gladwell, 2005), leads to an overreliance on intuition and overconfidence in one's judgments (see also Hakel, 1982; Ayres, 2008). Unfortunately, the finding that actuarial methods outperform clinical ones in a wide variety of settings is well documented (e.g., Grove & Meehl, 1996), as is the fact that adding clinical judgments to actuarial ones does not improve things, or makes them worse (Ayres, 2008; Highhouse, 2008).

In addition to the "actuarial versus clinical" gap discussed by Highhouse (2008) (and evident in other fields such as law and medicine as well; Ayres, 2008), Rynes et al. (2002) surfaced a gap between HR practitioners' beliefs and research findings about the importance of GMA to performance. However, their methodology did not permit them to tell whether practitioners were unaware of, or simply disbelieved, research on the (relative) predictive efficacy of GMA.

To remedy this deficiency, Caprar, Rynes, Bartunek, and Do (2011) studied the question more directly. They designed a study in which participants were exposed to three published essays regarding the merits of GMA, emotional intelligence, and employee-organization fit, respectively, for predicting job applicants' subsequent performance. Texts were abstracted from Schmidt and Hunter (2003) for GMA, Goleman (2000) for emotional intelligence (EI), and Pfeffer (1998) for cultural fit (although author names were not included with the texts). Each participant read and responded to all three texts. Texts were equal in length, and order of presentation was balanced across participants.

Based on copious psychological research that people either avoid or devalue information that is threatening to their self-image (e.g., Steele, 1988; Swann & Read, 1981) or self-interest (Miller, 1999) and that people generally dislike the idea that intelligence is important to success (e.g., Hofstadter, 1964; Pinker, 2002), Caprar et al. (2011) predicted that participants would be least persuaded by the essay on the importance of intelligence. Conversely, because nearly everyone can "fit" somewhere, the essay on fit was predicted to be least threatening and hence, the most persuasive (on average). In addition, the authors predicted that there would be individual differences in reactions to the essays, with individuals scoring highest on proxies for GMA (i.e., college entrance exams and grade point averages) being more likely than other participants to find the GMA essay persuasive, and those scoring higher on a measure of EI being more likely than other respondents to be persuaded by the EI essay. All hypotheses were confirmed, suggesting a general dislike of the idea that intelligence is important to performance, a general belief in the importance of fit, and individual differences in beliefs about GMA and EI consistent with theories of both self-affirmation and self-interest.

JURY DECISION MAKING

Although jury decision making is outside the immediate realm of I/O psychology, it is an interesting area to examine because juries are often expected to incorporate expert testimony into their decision processes. A review of this literature shows several important parallels between jury decision making and selection research. For example, as with selection, some expert witnesses use actuarial methods, while others rely on clinical judgments.

Another similarity is that in law, too, actuarial evidence has been shown to consistently outperform clinical judgments in predicting outcomes such as whether a defendant has actually committed a crime or is likely to become a repeat offender in the future (e.g., Ayres, 2008; Krauss & Sales, 2001; Lieberman, Krauss, Kyger, & Lehoux, 2007; Monahan & Steadman, 1994). A third similarity is that, just as with selection, juries are more likely to be persuaded by clinical opinions than by actuarial or statistical evidence (Bornstein, 2004).

For example, evidence obtained from mock juries shows that jurors: place less weight on general statistics than individuating information (Loftus, 1980); are reluctant to base verdicts on statistical information alone (Niedermeier, Kerr, & Messe, 1999); underutilize expert probabilistic testimony compared to Bayesian norms (Kaye & Koehler, 1991); and perceive experts who present anecdotal evidence as more credible than those who present non-anecdotal evidence (Bornstein, 2004). In addition, the stronger influence of clinical prediction remains, even after the presentation of adversarial procedures (e.g., cross-examination) or contradictory opinions by other experts (Krauss & Sales, 2001). This is particularly troublesome because the Supreme Court and many state courts have assumed that juries will appropriately weight scientific evidence according to its quality and that the adversarial system will expose the weaknesses of inferior scientific testimony.

Unfortunately, such does not appear to be the case. For example, in an analysis of how the tobacco companies prevailed in lawsuits brought by injured smokers for more than 40 years, Givelber and Strickler (2006) deconstructed how lawyers for the tobacco industry discredited actuarial epidemiological evidence. This was accomplished via a three-stage process: (1) downgrading the status of epidemiology by getting plaintiffs' expert witnesses to agree that there were no certification processes for determining who was an epidemiologist; (2) insinuating (despite expert witnesses' resistance) that epidemiology was "really only a matter of statistics"; and (3) getting expert witnesses to admit that there is a difference between a "risk factor" and a "cause." Step #2 was particularly important, according to R. J. Reynolds's lawyers.

Reminiscent of Highhouse's (2008) contention that selection practitioners are disappointed with validity evidence because they believe that prediction can approach perfection, analysts of the *Galbraith v. R. J. Reynolds Tobacco* trial said: "The fact that the jurors came into the trial believing that the epidemiological experts would testify to [the fact that cigarettes cause cancer] worked in Reynolds's favor: the jurors *seemed to expect something more* from the witnesses and be disappointed when they did not hear it" (Givelber & Strickler, 2006, pp. 34–35; emphasis added). The authors concluded that "despite judicial efforts to eliminate 'junk science' from lawsuits, a well-financed defendant may succeed in persuading jurors of the epidemiological equivalent of the proposition that the earth is flat" (p. 33).

In summary, research on juries shows the same (generally erroneous) preference for clinical over actuarial evidence, as does research on selection. Moreover, actuarial evidence appears to be more vulnerable than clinical evidence to adversarial persuasive techniques (Givelber & Strickler, 2006; Krauss & Sales, 2001). Combining the evidence from both selection and jury decision making (as well as medical and judicial decisions; see Ayres, 2008, chapters 4, 5) suggests that there are some fundamental challenges involved in getting practitioners or laypeople to accept probabilistic, large-sample research findings. Indeed, most people seem to prefer to take their evidence from samples of one, or anecdotes. Changing this preference will require a better understanding of what causes it.

UNDERLYING SOURCES OF DISBELIEF
Sources Unique to Each Belief

There are many possible reasons that people may not believe research on each of the preceding topics. For example, in the case of intelligence, research findings are likely to conflict with many people's already established beliefs, such as the cherished notion (at least in the United States) that with hard work, anyone can achieve anything, or that emotional intelligence (Goleman, 1995), intuition (Gladwell, 2005), or luck (Gladwell, 2008) are more important than GMA for attaining success. In addition, many people hold negative stereotypes about intelligent people that are not upheld by large-sample evidence, such as beliefs that they are more likely than others to be deceitful, selfish, lacking in empathy, and devoid of "common" sense (Hofstadter, 1964). Along the same lines, people may believe that integrity tests have adverse impact against minorities because they assume that minorities are less honest than whites.

Alternatively, in the case of utility analysis, it is easy to imagine that many people might find the estimates of financial benefits to HR practices unbelievably large, perhaps reasoning that if such practices were *that* effective, employers would

have figured it out by now. (A version of this same logic was used by economists to explain how there "couldn't be" discrimination in labor markets. The reasoning went that if women, Asians, or African Americans were indeed as capable as white males, then some clever employer would have figured this out, started hiring women and minorities [probably at lower wages, given their limited market opportunities], and put everyone else out of business; see, e.g., Blau, Ferber, & Winkler, 2005.)

Thus, although one might come up with unique explanations of each area where there is a research-practice gap, there are also some common sources that undergird multiple gaps.

Common Sources

One factor that is common to findings regarding utility analysis, the importance of GMA, and the superiority of actuarial over clinical prediction is that the research evidence is likely to be threatening to many (if not most) individuals, at least upon first hearing. For example, one can well imagine that the vast majority of practitioners (and perhaps academics as well) who hear about utility analysis for the first time might become apprehensive about the equations involved and their ability to understand them, let alone their ability to explain them to others. Others may be upset by the idea that human efforts can (or, implicitly, "should") be quantified in terms of economic metrics. Similarly, with respect to peoples' preference for clinical or intuitive decision making, the use of actuarial methods not only takes away control from managers (e.g., Ayres, 2008; Dipboye, 1992), but also threatens their self-image as people of good judgment (Ayres, 2008; Highhouse, 2008).

But perhaps the most threatening of the three research-inconsistent beliefs is the idea that intelligence might have a measurable impact on one's vocational and financial success. Pinker (2002) discusses in considerable detail the numerous reasons that people on both sides of the political spectrum tend to find this research threatening.[4] At heart, Pinker argues that many people reflexively disavow scientific findings about intelligence (and the role of genes in human behavior) for two major reasons: they see them both as *deterministic* (omitting or dramatically reducing the possibility of free choice and personal improvement) and *reductionist* (assessing people as collections of specific traits, rather than as integrated "whole" entities). Others reject the Darwinian notion that humans evolved from "lower" animals, rather than having been given dominion over them by God. According to recent opinion polls by Roper, Gallup, and others, only 15% of Americans say they believe that Darwin's theory of evolution and natural selection is the best explanation for the origins of human life, while 76% admit to believing in creationism, angels, the Devil, and ghosts (Pinker, 2002, p. 2). As such, scientific findings about intelligence (and its partial genetic heritability) appear to threaten some very deeply held personal beliefs that are exceedingly difficult to address in either classrooms or boardrooms.

Conflicting Opinions Within Academia

To this point, I have emphasized differences between large-sample research findings and practitioners' beliefs. However, there are also important differences *within* the academic community on some issues, including the importance of intelligence. For example, Pinker (2002) documents how some of the most vitriolic attacks on scientists who assert the importance of intelligence or genetic inheritance of various traits have come from other academics. Specifically, he traces in considerable detail how the writings of academics such as sociobiologists E. O. Wilson and Richard Dawkins and psychologists Paul Ekman and Richard Herrnstein have been misquoted, distorted, and extended far beyond the original treatises to accuse those who assert the importance of intelligence of providing "excuses" for all sorts of social maladies such as racism, promiscuity, male dominance, amorality, and societal inequality (Pinker, chapter 6).

Somewhat closer to home, Murphy, Cronin, and Tam (2003) found that I/O psychologists, too, have diverse beliefs about the usefulness of intelligence tests in employment contexts, despite the fact that all of them have Ph.D.s. For example, within their sample of 703 I/O psychologists, Murphy et al. (2003) found considerable divergence of opinion on items such as "general cognitive ability is the most important individual difference variable" and "the dollar value of diversity can be measured," even though there was widespread consensus that intelligence tests are both valid and fair.

Academic disagreements exist in other areas of I/O psychology as well. Examples include debates about whether or not the validities of personality tests are high enough to be useful as selection devices (e.g., Morgeson et al., 2007, vs. Ones, Dilchert, Viswesvaran, & Judge, 2007) or whether pay-for-performance is an effective motivator (see Rynes, Gerhart, & Parks, 2005, vs. Pfeffer, 1998); or the "dueling meta-analyses" of Eisenberger and Cameron (1996) and Eisenberger, Pierce, and Cameron (1999) vs. Deci, Koestner, & Ryan, (1999a; 1999b).

Thus, the beliefs discussed in this section appear to reflect values and emotions as well as cognition, and to affect academics as well as practitioners. In light of such evidence, it may be difficult to dispel these misperceptions merely through the provision of "information" via essays, lectures, data charts, and other cognitive approaches.

DISTRUST OF STATISTICS AND THE SCIENTIFIC METHOD

Lack of belief in utility analysis, actuarial selection processes, and empirical evidence in lawsuits may all result in part from a general distrust of statistics, nicely captured by Benjamin Disraeli's quip that there are "lies, damned lies, and statistics" (Best, 2001). A concrete example of the distrust of statistics was mentioned in Givelber and Strickler's (2006) account of the *Galbraith v. R. J. Reynolds* trial. According to R. J. Reynolds's lawyers, "The jurors distrusted statistics; in fact, one juror said that she did not believe conclusions which were based on statistics. All the jurors said that the plaintiffs' charts showing the worst statistics from the Surgeon General's reports were ignored, and one juror...dismissed the charts by describing the information contained in them as mere answers to questionnaires" (Givelber & Strickler, 2006, p. 35).

Although Best (2001) believes that most distrust of statistics stems from lack of numerical literacy, skepticism about large-sample research findings can also be found among practitioners with plenty of statistical education (such as I/O psychologists). Boehm (1980) argues that one reason this happens is that the interconnected, messy world in which practitioners operate causes them to be suspicious of findings obtained in the pristine, highly controlled, and decontextualized environments in which much academic research takes place. In other words, it is not lack of knowledge that causes high-level practitioner skepticism of certain results, but rather the perceived lack of generalizability of the findings. This insight sheds some light on Highhouse's (2008) observation that "there is considerable evidence that employers simply do not believe that the research is relevant to their own situation."

Some interesting examples of skepticism about the scientific method (as well as academics' communication skills and lack of agreement on research implications) came up in "friendly reviews" of earlier versions of this manuscript. In order to take the reader "backstage" to these conversations, I reproduce some of the reviewer comments (and the texts that provoked them) in Table 13.1.

Table 13 1. "Friendly Reviewer" Comments on Earlier Versions of this Manuscript*

Text	Reviewer Reaction
Even if a gap is due to lack of awareness, it cannot automatically be assumed that practitioners would actually change their beliefs after being exposed to relevant research.	Perhaps the reason for this is that practitioners' beliefs are consistent with their experiences. Perhaps the experience of practitioners is different from what a controlled experiment concludes. Researchers assume they are correct yet they don't know the reason that someone believes what they believe. Research may not be real to practitioners or may not represent a real phenomenon to them. For example, many practitioners find structured interviewing to be too confining and would never think of hiring someone without an interview at all. (P)
With respect to practitioners' lack of enthusiasm for actuarial prediction methods, Highhouse (2008) argues that the source is failure to be convinced, rather than lack of awareness. He says, "Although one might argue that these data merely reflect a lack of knowledge about effective practice, there is considerable evidence that employers simply do not believe that the research is relevant to their own situation."	Isn't it possible that this is correct—for practitioners, there is no relevance? (P)
Despite practitioners' preference for clinical prediction, the finding that actuarial methods outperform clinical ones in a wide variety of settings is well documented (e.g., Grove & Meehl, 1994), as is the fact that adding clinical judgments to actuarial ones does not improve things or even makes them worse (Highhouse, 2008).	Yes, well documented by research. You are using (understandably) a research frame to argue a research point and to in some ways discount the practitioner's view. Practitioners don't see it this way. (P)
In summary, research on juries shows the same (generally erroneous) preference for clinical over actuarial evidence as does research on selection.	If this is erroneous, are you saying that jury decisions are generally incorrect? Are you also saying that organizations, operated by practitioners, are generally ineffective? How do we explain the successes that practitioners have who don't regularly apply research findings? (P)
For example, Rynes et al. (2002) found that, contrary to research evidence, the vast majority of HR managers in their sample believed that both conscientiousness and values are better predictors of performance than intelligence.	I don't believe that intelligence is the best predictor, either. (A)
Third, even after decades of cumulated research and hundreds of meta-analyses, researchers in various areas still do not agree on the implications of extant findings (e.g., whether or not the validities of personality tests are high enough to be useful as selection devices [see Morgeson et al., 2007 vs. Ones et al., 2007], or whether pay-for-performance is an effective motivator [see Rynes et al., 2005 vs. Pfeffer, 1998; or the "dueling meta-analyses" of Eisenberger and Cameron, 1996 and Eisenberger et al., 1999 versus Deci et al., 1999a, 1999b]).	Maybe part of the reason that practitioners don't leverage research more effectively is because academics can't agree on anything? I hadn't thought about this before your diatribe regarding selection (a rant worthy of Bill Maher, by the way ☺). If this is an example of an area where we know a lot, and the leading researchers can't agree on what it is that we know, it's no wonder that practitioners don't leverage research effectively. We're consumed with the debate whether the true r between GMA and performance is .39 or .44…and the practitioner world yawns. (P)
I was unable to find any studies that have directly asked academic researchers such things as whether they read practitioner journals, or whether they have accurate knowledge of the major issues and environmental conditions confronting I/O or HR practitioners.	We as academics can be moderate to severe intellectual elitists who abuse practitioners with quantitative clubs, rather than finding ways to explain basic concepts like correlation and regression with minimal pain. (A)

(Continued)

Table 13 1. (continued)

Text	Reviewer Reaction
The quickest and most direct way to make research more accessible to practitioners is to get findings into outlets and venues that are already widely used by those who practice. This requires knowing where different types of practitioners go to get their information ... the most effective ways of reaching I/O practitioners would appear to be the SIOP website and for HR practitioners, *HR Magazine* and the SHRM web site.	I suspect that even if all these things happened, managers would stop looking in these locations and go somewhere else. It is the CONTENT of research articles that is turning them off, not the location in which research articles are published. (A)
During the past three decades, pleas have been escalating to give greater attention to the context in which our research is conducted (e.g., Bamberger, 2008; Johns, 2001; Roberts et al., 1978; Rousseau & Fried, 2001; Porter, 2008).	I agree, though unfortunately, pressure from journal publishers to maximize number of articles published while minimizing individual article pages keeps this stuff out—a detailed explanation of strategic utility using a chicken restaurant franchisor was cut out of one of my articles in *PPsych*. (A)
Although it is difficult to know for sure, it is possible that many students (i.e., future managers or other practitioners) leave college without a solid grasp of research principles due to ineffective teaching of research methods, statistics, and analysis.	What? I suspect we all know this—ask undergraduates how they liked their required stats classes. How many additional statistics electives did they take? How do they like running into applications of the stats they learned in their major? I suspect most HR majors chose it because they "like people" and hope the area will permit them to hide from any additional exposure. (A)
For example, the most frequent recommendation (in "implications for practice" sections of top-tier journal articles) was for practitioners to "become aware" of a certain phenomenon, which doesn't seem very likely to be translated into action	Besides, it smacks of something a condescending scholar would say. (A)
In order to increase implementation of research ideas, perhaps few things would help more than some sort of "help line" or chat room for those who are considering a change but have specific questions or problems with respect to implementation.	Most academics would fail miserably here—it is simply not in their skill set. (A)
Although there are certain reasons and situations that call for separation of science and practice, there are others that would benefit from closer interactions between them.	I can't think of any justifying separation. (A)

* Comments from academics are marked (A), and comments from practitioners are marked (P).

Gaps in Implementation

It has long been noted that research-supported I/O and HR practices often are not put into place in organizations (e.g., Bretz, Milkovich, & Read, 1992; Lawler, Mohrman, & Ledford, 1992; Kersley et al., 2006), even when practitioners know about them and believe that they would improve organizational and employee outcomes (Pfeffer & Sutton, 2000). At the same time, however, HR departments have long been accused of being "faddish," moving rapidly from one new program to another (and not always the best programs; e.g., Abrahamson & Eisenman, 2001). These observations have led a number of researchers to try to understand why some research findings get adopted, while others do not (Sturdy, 2004).

FACTORS INFLUENCING ADOPTION OF NEW PRACTICES

An implicit assumption behind evidence-based management (EBM) and discussions of the academic-practice gap is that practitioners "should" adopt practices supported by large-sample research because these offer, on average, technically superior solutions. However, it has long been known that technical or technological superiority is far from the only variable considered when organizations decide whether or not to adopt a new practice. For example, Rogers (2003), who analyzed the diffusion of many kinds of innovations for over 50 years, argued that, in addition to technical performance, adoption of a new idea also depends on its: (1) perceived advantage relative to the idea or practice it is attempting to supersede; (2) compatibility with existing values, past experiences, and needs of potential adopters; (3) simplicity; (4) trialability (the degree to which the idea can be experimented with on a limited basis); and (5) observability (the degree to which the results of its application are visible).

By treating I/O research findings as "innovations," Johns (1993) extended Rogers's framework to explain the limited adoption of technically superior I/O practices. Johns argued that three broad factors explain why technically superior I/O innovations often fail to be adopted. First, managers tend to see I/O practices as administrative, rather than technical, innovations. As such, proposed new practices are evaluated at least as much in terms of their likely effects on social systems (and personal careers) as on production outcomes. (Note: This might be another reason that some people are concerned about hiring intelligent applicants or using actuarial selection models.) Second, Johns (1993) suggested that administrative innovations are perceived by managers as more uncertain than technological ones (see also Highhouse, 2008; Ledford, Lawler, & Mohrman, 1988), resulting in their being adopted less often (Symon & Clegg, 1991). Moreover, even when they are adopted, uncertain innovations are more likely to be adopted for reasons other than technical soundness (e.g., politics or imitation of other organizations; Ayres, 2008; Abrahamson, 1991; DiMaggio & Powell, 1983; Nutt, 1989). Third, decisions to adopt or abandon administrative innovations are affected by extra-organizational factors such as economic crises, interorganizational relations, government regulations (e.g., equal employment legislation), and employee power.

Another model of why some innovations are adopted over others is Abrahamson's theory of "management fashion" (1991, 1996). Abrahamson argues that management fads and fashions[5] are, to some extent, comparable to aesthetic fashions (e.g., hairstyles, clothing, and home décor), which are driven almost exclusively by sociopsychological forces. However, unlike purely aesthetic matters, management fashions are also driven by technical and environmental changes that create performance gaps and a true need for new solutions. Thus, the management fashions that emerge are a joint result of: (a) sociopsychological persuasion by "fashion purveyors" such as consultants, business professors, or management gurus (i.e., the supply side); and (b) real managerial needs, as determined by economic competition, technological change, and other environmental factors (demand side).[6] Furthermore, Abrahamson proposes that the small number of fashions that are ultimately adopted are ones that are seen as both rational (capable of fixing the problem or reducing the gap) and progressive (improving on earlier techniques and solutions).

If Abrahamson's model is correct, then one would predict that management fads will not "go away," but rather are likely to become even more frequent. This is because the supply of knowledge purveyors and the pace of change (and hence, the emergence of new managerial needs) are both increasing.

Indeed, an empirical study of management fashions from the mid-1950s to the late 1990s suggests exactly that. Specifically, Carson, Lanier, Carson, and Guidry (2000) found that management fashions arose more frequently at the end of the twentieth century than during its middle. In addition, they found a shift from people-centered fashions (e.g., management by objectives, employee assistance programs, sensitivity training, and quality of work life programs) to technically and strategically oriented ones (e.g., total quality management, ISO 9000, benchmarking, and reengineering). Carson et al. (2000) also found that more recent fashions tended to have a shorter "shelf life," a finding which they attributed to the greater difficulty of implementing these later fashions. However, their measures of adoption and shelf life were quite indirect—based on the emergence, peak, and eventual decline of academic and popular publications on each fashion—so it is difficult to know the precise reasons behind the apparently shorter life cycles. For example, shorter cycles could also be due to consultants pushing product obsolescence, reporters focusing on "what's new" rather than what works, or top managers having less persistence or shorter time frames than in the past.

Still other studies have examined the rise and fall of "rational" versus "normative" rhetorics urging managers to adopt new practices (Abrahamson, 1997; Barley & Kunda, 1992). According to Abrahamson, rational rhetorics are reminiscent of scientific management and Theory X in that they assume that "work processes can be formalized and rationalized to optimize labor productivity, as can the reward systems that guarantee recalcitrant employees' adherence to these formal processes" and conceive of employees as "largely averse to both responsibility and work" (p. 496). In contrast, normative rhetorics assume that "employees (can be made) more productive by shaping their thoughts and capitalizing on their emotions" (e.g., human relations and corporate culture approaches; Abrahamson, 1997, p. 496).

At the micro level, there is evidence that the adoption of rational versus normative policies and practices is subject to individual differences in such characteristics as cognitive style, openness to experience, political ideology, and "implicit person" theories (Heslin, Vandewalle, & Latham, 2006; Rogers, 2003; Tetlock, 2000). At a more macro level, these techniques and rhetorics also appear to alternate in "long waves" that correspond with upswings and downswings in the economy (e.g., Barley & Kunda, 1992). For example, Abrahamson (1997) found an upsurge in normative rhetorics just before the end of long macroeconomic upswings (e.g., increase in quality- and culture-related techniques in the early 1970s) and under conditions of high employee turnover, unionization rates, or strikes.

Thus, in general, rhetorics (and presumably, practices) appear to become more normative and employee-centric when workers are more powerful and more rational/technical when they are not (see also Kochan, 2007). At the time of this writing, there have been growing disparities in worker power across occupational categories, with a small number of highly placed executives and technicians having very high market power, but most other workers having less and less. In such an environment, it is perhaps not surprising to find calls for highly differentiated HR practices for employees with different skill and ability levels (e.g., Becker, Huselid, & Beatty, 2009; Lepak & Snell, 1999; Stewart, 1998).

HOW INNOVATIONS DIFFUSE

While the preceding section focused on factors that influence the adoption of new practices, it is also useful to examine the processes by which practices diffuse. Two of the most central findings about innovation diffusion processes are that they are (a) social and (b) non-linear (Rogers, 2003). Specifically, according to Rogers, rates of diffusion follow an S-shaped curve, with only a small number of innovators in the beginning, followed by more rapid acceleration as thought leaders and "early majority" adopters join in, and then approaching an asymptote as fewer and fewer organizations (or individuals) are left to adopt. In contrast, unsuccessful innovations either do not capture many thought leaders or early adopters beyond the original inventors, or else they lose momentum as problems with their adoption become widely known (as with quality circles).

At the individual level of analysis, Rogers (2003) indicates that the following characteristics are (positively) associated with early adopters: education level; social status; empathy; openness to experience; positive attitudes toward science; internal locus of control; high aspiration level; strong (and more cosmopolitan) social networks; exposure to mass media communications; high information seeking; frequent contact with change agents; and demonstrated opinion leadership. These, then, are the types of practitioners that academics are most likely to influence with their research.

At the organization level, the first adopters of a new idea are often those for which the particular innovation is seen to be appropriate for solving some real or perceived problem (e.g., Greenwood & Hinings, 2006; Tolbert & Zucker, 1983). However, as the innovation diffuses, it tends to do so earlier among organizations that are larger, less centralized and formalized, more highly skilled, and that have higher connectedness with other organizations, more organizational slack, and change-oriented leaders (Tolbert & Zucker, 1983). Furthermore, as adoptions spread, they tend to do so "locally" (i.e., through managers seeking evaluations of the innovation from earlier adopters in their same industry or labor market Guest, 2007) and through direct rather than indirect ties (Burt, 2007). One exception to this organizational pattern appears to involve *radical* innovations (i.e., ones that destroy current capabilities), which are more likely to be adopted by smaller, newer organizations that are outside the dominant network and that in recent years have destroyed some major organizations that did not adapt quickly enough (Christensen, 1997; Greenwood & Hinings, 2006; Tushman & Murmann, 1998).

While social networks are important in the later stages of diffusion, at the early stages, mass media may play a larger role. The communication medium that is arguably the most successful in launching management trends is the best-seller book (e.g., Furusten, 1999; Kieser, 1997). Best-selling management books follow a certain well-worn formula: focus on a single factor or idea; contrast the "old" and "new" ideas; create a sense of urgency and inevitability; link the idea to highly treasured values; provide case studies of outstanding success; and stress the idea's universal applicability (Clark & Greatbatch, 2004, pp. 401–402). Thus, for example, we have "a new yardstick" (Goleman, 2000, p. 3) for judging and predicting the success of people (emotional intelligence, or EQ), "not just how smart we are" (the old idea, IQ). Moreover, we need to pay attention to this new yardstick because there is "a coming crisis: rising IQ, dropping EQ" (p. 11). As for universality, anyone can acquire EQ because "our level of emotional intelligence is not fixed genetically, nor does it develop only in early childhood. Unlike IQ, which changes little after our teen years, emotional intelligence seems to be largely learned" (p. 7). Moreover, EQ is on the side of virtue, being readily attainable to all who seek it: "there is an old-fashioned word for this growth in emotional intelligence: maturity" (p. 7). And so on.

But simply writing a best seller is not enough to get managers to implement its ideas. Rather, it is often difficult for managers to put research into practice without an explicit "road map" and/or personal support on the part of the researcher, author, or some other change agent (Argyris, 1985; Mohrman, Gibson, & Mohrman, 2001). Thus, in order to turn book sales into additional sources of revenue, the best-seller book industry has responded to this need in a number of ways—for example, by turning certain authors into "brands" (e.g., Jim Collins, Daniel Goleman, John Kotter, or Tom Peters), promoting their ideas across a variety of media (e.g., video and audio-tapes, CD-ROMs, web sites, and book-affiliated consulting groups), and adapting general messages to specific audiences (e.g., sequentially retargeting Goleman's original 1995 book on emotional intelligence toward managers, educators, and parents, or re-focusing Christensen's original 1997 book on disruptive innovations in technology to other industries such as health care and education).

In addition, Clark and Greatbatch (2004) document how, once a writer becomes a brand, his or her future books may emerge from an editor's idea (rather than the writer's) and may even be written primarily by ghost writers. Furthermore, in the service of higher sales, authors, editors, and publishers sometimes create artificial sales figures (e.g., buying thousands of early copies of books to make them "appear" to be popular). According to Clark and Greatbatch (2004):

> The popularity (of best-sellers) with readers cannot be attributed to "real" sales. The writer of the book and the named author on the cover are not necessarily the same individual. Finally, the data or observations

that underpin the ideas being presented cannot be assumed to exist. Thus, the assumption that the books themselves and the ideas they contain are grounded in terms of the authenticity of a referent point does not necessarily hold. They therefore represent a form of pseudoknowledge. (p. 399)

The distortion of information in best-selling books may even apply to best-selling *text*books, which are generally assumed to be credible purveyors of the knowledge base underlying the disciplines they represent (Stambaugh & Trank, 2010). However, this assumption, too, seems questionable. For example, in an article by several best-selling textbook authors (Cameron, Ireland, Lussier, New, & Robbins, 2003), OB textbook writer Stephen Robbins said, "Publishers are in the business of selling books. They'll sell anything if they think people might want it. They don't care about integrity or quality. Moreover, they firmly believe that *they* create books. They have little respect for authors" (p. 716).

In other words, the world of top-tier academic journals is a universe away from that of the management best seller, with "whole industries" often being brought into existence in order to push a best-selling idea (Abrahamson, 1996; Clark & Greatbatch, 2004; Furusten, 1999). Because such practices are generally anathema to academic researchers under current cultural norms, it is perhaps not surprising that few recent management innovations appear to be coming from academia (Pfeffer & Fong, 2002).

Potential Solutions

To this point, I have argued that research-practice gaps occur for (at least) three basic reasons: lack of awareness, lack of belief, and lack of implementation. Below, I present potential solutions to each of these three components of the gap.[7] For an overview of all solutions, see Table 13.2.

Increasing Awareness

At least four general approaches can be used to increase awareness of research findings: (a) make better use of existing practitioner outlets; (b) create new outlets and formats; (c) investigate topics of greater interest to practitioners; and (d) improve social relations and communication skills between academics and practitioners.

MAKE BETTER USE OF EXISTING OUTLETS

The quickest and most direct way to make research more accessible to practitioners is to get findings into outlets and venues that are already

Table 13.2 Proposed Solutions to the Three Components of the Gap

Objective	Potential Solutions
Increase awareness of research	Make better use of existing outlets Create new outlets and formats Investigate topics of greater interest to practitioners Improve social relations and communication skills between academics and practitioners
Increase believability of findings	Communicate more persuasively and empathetically Coproduce research with practitioners or consultants Improve rewards and recognition for research that benefits practice Increase flexibility of top-tier journals Conduct research on persuasiveness of research findings Continue to strengthen the research base Become more effective teachers of research methods, statistics, and critical thinking
Increase implementation	Present advice in form of principles plus examples Improve "implications for practice" sections in primary research studies Increase applications research and research contextualization Provide specific support for implementation

widely used by those who practice. This requires knowing where different types of practitioners go to get their information. For example, the recent SIOP Practice Survey (Silzer & Cober, 2008) found that among full-time practitioners, the sources most frequently used to gain professional knowledge and skills were web sites and other online sources (approximately 95%), followed by (at roughly 80% each) professional conferences; articles, publications, and books about business management or HR; networks of professional colleagues, and nonresearch publications in I/O psychology (75%). Only 55% indicated that they read research articles to keep informed, despite the fact that most (78%) had doctoral degrees. By way of contrast, Rynes et al. (2002) found that HR managers almost never (< 1%) read research articles, while almost all of them read *HR Magazine,* which has a circulation of more than 250,000.

Thus, the most effective ways of reaching I/O practitioners would appear to be through the SIOP web site and conferences, and through non-research-oriented publications in business management and HR. In contrast, the most effective ways to reach HR practitioners would appear to be through the SHRM web site and *HR Magazine* (Cohen, 2007; Rynes et al., 2002).

This knowledge is now being put to good use. For example, since 2008, *HR Magazine* has been increasing research coverage, adding regular research updates to its "Executive Briefing" section, and soliciting academic opinions in feature articles. In addition, SIOP has collaborated with SHRM to create a "SIOP Science for SHRM" board, one of whose first projects will be to create joint-authored (one academic, one practitioner) summaries of research findings and their implications for distribution to more than a quarter of a million SHRM members. In the longer term, the board is exploring the production not only of written content, but also of alternative formats such as webcasts, DVDs, and educational sessions that carry certification credits. In another innovation, SIOP is planning an annual publication, *Science You Can Use: Managing People Effectively,* which will produce somewhat longer summaries of research findings as well as implications for practice. In addition, the SHRM Foundation has created a downloadable *Practice Guidelines* monograph series on the SHRM web site, providing guidance on such topics as compensation and performance management by researchers such as David Allen, David Day, Rob Heneman, Elaine Pulakos, and Robert Vance. Academic professional associations can also hire public relations consultants to place research findings in the popular press. This can be beneficial in at least three ways: by increasing the general visibility of academic disciplines, by reaching much broader audiences beyond those of specialist professional associations, and by bringing the topics that academics study to public attention (McHenry, 2007). Both SIOP and the AOM employ such publicists, who have received considerable popular press attention for such research as Judge and Hurst's (2007) study of the role of self-evaluations and socioeconomic status on mid-career income levels, Trevor and Nyberg's (2008) study of the role of downsizings on subsequent turnover in organizations, and the role of gender and gender role orientation on earnings (Judge & Livingston, 2008).

Of course, all of the above suggestions share the optimistic assumption that "pushing" research out to practitioners will result in increased uptake of research-based recommendations. However, that will not be the case to the extent that practitioners do not see the relevance of the research to their own situations, regardless of how relevant *researchers* think it is.

A third way of making better use of existing venues for reaching practitioners (or future practitioners) is through evidence-based teaching (EBT). According to Rousseau and McCarthy (2007), EBT encompasses the following four principles: (1) focus on principles where the science is clear; (2) develop decision awareness in professional practice; (3) diagnose underlying factors related to decisions; and (4) contextualize knowledge related to evidence use. Although EBT may be standard practice in psychology classes, it is a minority practice in business schools (see Charlier, Brown, & Rynes, 2011), where many managers (and some HR managers) are educated.

Although I am not aware of any evidence regarding the extent to which EBT is practiced in educating I/O psychologists, there are several factors that work against extensive practice of EBT in business schools. One is that business students tend not to like either theories or empirical research (Rousseau & McCarthy, 2007; Trank & Rynes, 2003). Although this might also be somewhat true of psychology students (although I know of no evidence to indicate that this is so), student preferences have a far stronger impact on what gets taught in business schools than in the social sciences because of the role that student opinion plays in popular press rankings of business schools (e.g., *Business Week* or *Forbes*; Gioia & Corley, 2002). Because student opinions count heavily in business school rankings, curricular and pedagogical choices—as well as grades—tend to move in directions favored by students. These trends detract from business schools' efforts to provide a truly professional education in which abstract knowledge or generalizable principles that can be applied to many different situations are taught (Trank & Rynes, 2003).

Another potential deterrent may be the common use of the case method in business schools. The traditional case method focuses on analysis and discussion of the specific problems and context in each case, with students being encouraged to express their own opinions and instructors often emphasizing that there is "no right answer" (Ellet, 2007). According to Greiner, Bhambri, and Cummings (2003), "the Harvard Business School case method advocated that every company situation was unique and not easily amenable to generalization. The learning emphasis was on inductive reasoning as students were expected to learn through Socratic debate and exchange in sharpening not only their analytical abilities, but also their intuition, judgment, and behavioral skills" (p. 403). Greiner et al. (2003) contend that, in recent years, this traditional case method has increasingly given way to one in which students are encouraged to analyze cases in light of theory (i.e., with "right" and "wrong" answers) or empirically based principles—a trend that they (Greiner et al.) find disturbing but others do not (e.g., Hambrick, 1997; Locke, 2002). In any event, analyzing cases vis à vis theory is not the same as analyzing them in light of empirical evidence (Locke, 2007; Russell, 2009), as some theories that continue to be popular have not held up well to empirical evidence (Davis, 1971; Miner, 1984; Rynes, Gerhart, & Parks, 2005).

Thus, it should not be assumed that research findings occupy a major place in business schools or other management education venues. Nor, as Stambaugh and Trank (2010) illustrate in the case of business strategy textbooks, should it be assumed that new research findings easily make their way into management textbooks, especially if they are inconsistent with the "established wisdom." Unfortunately, there are presently few models for EBT in either management or psychology, although some excellent exceptions can be found in Burke and Rau (2010), Charlier et al. (2011), Latham (2007), Pearce (2006), and Rousseau and McCarthy (2007). One particularly effective method may be to integrate inductive or empirically derived principles (Locke, 2002, 2009) with cases or other experiential teaching methods (such as role playing), although this method, too, would require abandoning the HBS assumption that "every situation is unique" and accepting at least the general applicability of meta-analytic results and empirically derived decision tools such as artificial intelligence. (Examples of the latter have emerged in medicine, such as the Isabel system, which suggests the most likely diagnoses for an individual patient's combination of symptoms, or DynaMed, which carries a "Level of

Evidence" rating that reflects the quality of evidence underlying each study examining treatments for particular diagnoses; Ayers, 2008).

CREATE NEW OUTLETS AND FORMATS

In addition to disseminating research through existing practitioner channels, researchers and/ or practitioners can also attempt to create new outlets that are designed to be appealing to both groups. One such venture is the Collaborative for Evidence-Based Management, which is modeled on the Cochrane Collaboration (www.cochrane. org) in medicine. The CEBMa was established as "a community of practice to make evidence-informed management a reality. Its mission is to close the gap between management research and the ways practitioners make managerial and organizational decisions and educators teach organizational behavior, theory, strategy, and human resource management" (EBM Conference, 2007). Its major long-term goal is to build a web site containing systematic research syntheses on various management and organizational science topics, summarized in ways that are easy to use by both practitioners and educators (Rousseau, Manning, & Denyer, 2008; see www.cebma.org). Systematic research syntheses are based on "comprehensive accumulation, transparent analysis, and reflective interpretation of all empirical studies pertinent to a specific question" (Rousseau et al., p. 479). By making such syntheses available in a single place, the collaborative should make it far easier for practitioners to search for the latest research findings. Similarly, the SHRM (www.SHRM.org), SIOP (www.siop.org), and AOM (www.aomonline. org) web sites provide access to research findings in a variety of formats, including online versions of academic journals in the latter two cases.

Another tactic that has been employed to attract practitioners to research-based ideas is the creation of new journals or media. For example, AOM created the *Academy of Management Executive (AME)*, INFORMS (Institute for Operations Research and Management Sciences) created *Analytics*, and SIOP created *I/O Psychology: Perspectives on Science and Practice*. One valuable feature of the last journal is that it also contains articles by practitioners that inform academics about the state of the art in practice (e.g., Tippins's 2009 article on Internet testing). Such articles are important because they can help academics keep up to date in their teaching, while at the same time making them aware of interesting practical research needs.

However, the success of new journals can be highly variable. For example, AOM recently changed the mission (and name) of *AME (to Academy of Management Perspectives)* because an internal study showed that it was not being used by executives. Similarly, an earlier academic journal designed to focus on a practical area, *Journal of Quality Management*, was discontinued after only a few years due to lack of readership. On the other hand, *Analytics*—whose goal is "to provide readers with a better understanding of how data, modeling and mathematical analysis is [sic] used to drive better business decisions and provide concrete competitive advantage"—garnered 1,800 subscribers in its initial year of publication, two-thirds of whom were not current members of INFORMS. Subscriptions have been increased by surveying new subscribers to learn about their needs, analyzing hits to individual articles or issues on the web site, and asking INFORMS members to forward articles or entire issues of *Analytics* to practitioners they know (Bennett, 2008). To the extent that organizations like SIOP and AOM move forward with new publications or other methods of bridging the gap, they would benefit from similar marketing and evaluation strategies to increase the effectiveness of their efforts.

INVESTIGATE TOPICS OF GREATER INTEREST TO PRACTITIONERS

Although creating new outlets and making better use of existing outlets might help, these steps will not make much difference to practitioners if current research topics do not interest or help them. In fact, given serious time constraints, many practitioners (and academics) only seek information in response to immediate problems. Therefore, if a practitioner enters relevant keywords into Google Search and no academic references pop up, the ability of academics to influence him or her may be lost for a very long time.

For this reason, the gaps mentioned earlier between the content interests of academics and practitioners represent serious impediments to research-based knowledge applications. Combining the findings of Cascio (2008), Cascio and Aguinis (2008), Deadrick and Gibson (2007), Heath and Sitkin (2001), McGrath (2007), Offermann and Spiros, (2001) and Silzer and Cober (2008), the following topics appear to be under-researched relative to practitioner interest: compensation and benefits; role of technology and the Internet in HR management; HR as a functional area; macro and strategic HR; consulting and executive coaching; globalization; workforce planning; diversity and cross-cultural issues; change management; communication; trust;

interdependence; sustainable growth; leading in adversity, and employment branding.

In a perverse sort of self-fulfilling cycle, the fact that relatively little academic research currently exists on most of these topics may make it *less* (rather than more) likely that such research will emerge in the future. Although it might seem a "no-brainer" that topics that are both important in the real world and under-researched by academics should be highly attractive to academic researchers, in reality this is often not the case. This is because current practices in top-tier academic publishing place priority on building upon previous research (e.g., Sackett & Larson, 1990) and, more specifically, building on previous *theory* (e.g., Daft & Lewin, 2008; Hambrick, 2007; Locke, 2007). In this way, the lack of prior research (and/or theory) can become a self-perpetuating condition (although perhaps raising issues in well-regarded bridge journals such as *I/O Psychology* will pave the way for future publications in top-tier academic journals as well).

Thus, barring some major changes in editorial policies and/or academic incentives (to be discussed in greater detail shortly), many researchers will not be willing to devote the time or accept the risk involved in building important new research areas from the ground up. Nevertheless, that is precisely what some of the very best researchers do (see, for example, Eisenhardt's work on technological change and speeding products to market, e.g., Brown & Eisenhardt, 1997 and Eisenhardt & Tabrizi, 1995; or Locke and Latham's excellent research program on goal setting, e.g., Locke & Latham, 1984; Locke, 2007). We need to create incentives for more researchers to make these kinds of investments.

BUILD SOCIAL RELATIONSHIPS BETWEEN ACADEMICS AND PRACTITIONERS

In addition to increasing direct access to research findings, some argue that it is also crucial to work indirectly—that is, by building better social relationships between academics and practitioners. For example, Bartunek (2007) has called for "a relational scholarship of integration" (p. 1328) that is based, at least initially, on social (rather than instrumental) relationships between academics and practitioners. March (2005) made much the same point:

> [The facilitation of cooperation across boundaries is] augmented by appropriate attention to the role of wine, flirtation and play. Among strangers, wine can often usefully antedate talk, play can often usefully antedate work, and meetings of the heart can often usefully antedate meetings of the mind. The grim Puritanism of scholarly work has often been intolerant of such frivolity. As a result, scholarly institutions are often designed incorrectly. Conferences are filled with research papers and commentaries, to the exclusion of bottles of wine and opportunities for casual interaction.... And stories of successful collaboration are filled with rationalizations for it, to the exclusion of records of the vintages consumed. These "irrelevant" facilitators of association provide bases for warm social interactions and thus, ultimately, for scholarly exchange and collaboration. (p. 17)

Once social relationships have been cemented, both the transfer of existing knowledge and the joint creation of new knowledge become easier (Brown & Duguid, 2000; Nonaka & Konno, 1998; Rogers, 2003; Wenger, 1999). Thus, social relationships between academics and practitioners should be pursued alongside more instrumentally oriented ones.

Increasing Belief in Research Findings

The task of increasing belief in research findings is, essentially, one of increasing the credibility and perceived relevance of research to practitioners. This might be accomplished in several ways.

COMMUNICATE MORE PERSUASIVELY AND EMPATHETICALLY

> "The best research is as much at home in *Business Week* or *HBR* as it is in *Administrative Science Quarterly* (*ASQ*) or *AMR*. Of course, the jargon is different. But the fundamental ideas in the best research translate into meaningful implications for both researchers and managers" (*Eisenhardt*, 1998).

According to a recent review by Podsakoff, MacKenzie, Podsakoff, and Bachrach (2008), Kathleen Eisenhardt has been the most influential management scholar among academics (as assessed by citations in 30 journals, including I/O psychology-based journals such as *JAP*, *PPsych*, and *OBHDP*) over the past 25 years. Eisenhardt is known not only for her many outstanding academic publications, but also for the frequency with which she translates her work for practitioner audiences via books (e.g., Brown & Eisenhardt, 1998) and articles in bridge journals such as *HBR*. Her experience shows that it is possible for very high-quality research to be successfully translated, even if it does not happen very often.

Earlier, I indicated that book publishers use templates or "formulae" for creating best-selling books (e.g., Clark & Greatbatch, 2004). Similarly, there are templates for how academic research might be "translated" to make it more relevant, credible, and actionable for practitioners (e.g., Gruber, 2006; Sommer, 2006). To give one example, Kelemen and Bansal (2002) analyzed eight ways (research orientation, focus, attitude, data collection/analysis, data aggregation, referential system, rhetorical devices, criteria of goodness) in which Brown and Eisenhardt translated their 34-page *ASQ* article on change in high-velocity environments (Brown & Eisenhardt, 1997) into an 11-page article for *HBR* (Eisenhardt & Brown, 1998). For example, for *ASQ*, Brown and Eisenhardt's objective was to challenge existing theoretical orthodoxy, while for *HBR* it was to describe how various companies handled change well; for *ASQ*, the authors expressed an attitude of tentativeness toward their findings, while for *HBR*, they encouraged managers to use time-based pacing in high-velocity environments; for *ASQ*, company names were disguised and charts were constructed to show the same variables for all firms, while for *HBR*, firm names were included and only successful practices were discussed; data from all six firms were aggregated for *ASQ*, while for *HBR*, each firm represented a separate anecdote; for *ASQ*, the paper was organized around problem definition, link to prior theory, methods, results, discussion, and conclusion, while the *HBR* article used anecdotes, illustrations, text boxes providing more detail, few references to other research, and call-out quotes.

Kelemen and Bansal (2002) argue that "a great deal of research is simply being 'wasted,' either because academics are not skilled at translating their findings in a language that appeals to practitioners or because there are no institutional incentives to do so" (p. 204). This suggests the need for multiple translation strategies that include, but also go beyond, translations by academic authors. For example, professional organizations such as SIOP or SHRM might employ their own research translators; researchers might coauthor with practitioners or get practitioner comments before submitting research translations; or a small number of senior researchers who are committed to translation (such as Walter Borman, Wayne Cascio, Gary Latham, Edwin Locke, Eduardo Salas, and Scott Tannenbaum) might serve on boards such as SIOP's "Science for SHRM" to make sure that the job gets done (in fact, these things are already happening; Latham, 2009a). After all, it sometimes only takes

a small number of individuals to create a tipping point (Gladwell, 2000).

In addition to using a template such as the one above or other exemplary research translations as models, a second way in which academics can more effectively translate their work is by becoming, in Latham's (2007) words, "bilingual":

> As a consultant to clients, I don't "do research"—I get involved in projects and interventions. Included in the projects and interventions is a "framework" or "strategy" rather than a method or procedure for seeking answers to questions of importance to the clients, not only to me.... Rather than point to the need for a control group, I point to the necessity of being able to show senior management what happened in cases in which we did versus did not implement our proposal.... After analyzing the results, rather than discussing an F-test, let alone structural equation modeling, I show managers one or more graphs that make explicit what happened where we did, versus where we did not, implement our ideas.
> (p. 1029)

A third way in which academics might increase the interest of practitioners is by incorporating emotion, as well as logic, into their communications (Bartunek, 2007). According to Heath, Bell, and Sternberg (2001), ideas that "stick" are "selected and retained in part based on their ability to tap emotions that are common across individuals" (p. 1029). Moreover, arguments that generate *positive* emotions are more likely to inspire serious consideration than those that induce negative ones (Bartunek, 2007), at least in voluntary situations such as practitioners considering whether or not to apply research findings.[8]

If Bartunek's notions are correct, articles that reveal gaps between research findings and practitioner beliefs are more likely to engender defensiveness than motivation to change, unless they are accompanied by empathetic statements as to why such beliefs might seem reasonable, as well as specific implementation steps that provide a sense of positive self-efficacy. As a case in point, the article by Rynes et al. (2002)—which highlighted differences between practitioner beliefs and research findings—did give specific advice, but probably did not do enough to acknowledge that the gaps were understandable and were due, in part, to shortcomings on the academic side. Perhaps it is not too surprising, then, that an executive commenting on the articles said, "As a practitioner, I feel somewhat defensive in commenting upon what is a direct criticism of what we do" (Hansen, 2002, p. 103).

A final way in which academics can make research communications more persuasive is by applying the well-known power of anecdotes or "cases of one" to their own writings. Although anecdotes *alone* constitute very weak forms of evidence (Locke & Latham, 2009; Rousseau et al., 2008), when used in conjunction with large-sample evidence they can make empirical findings more interesting and relevant to practitioners, as well as more useful to academics in their role as teachers.[9] A related tactic would be to introduce selected materials from popular business and news media to show either the importance of a problem or its complexity in practice. Although some academic journals discourage the use of any "popular" citations, I believe that certain uses (such as large-sample descriptive statistics, powerful case examples, or information about the costs of a particular problem) can play an enlightening role and make articles more interesting to both academics and practitioners.

CO-PRODUCE RESEARCH WITH PRACTITIONERS OR CONSULTANTS

Co-production of research with non-academics is likely to enhance the believability of findings for several reasons. First, academics often lack credibility with practitioners, particularly if they do not have significant managerial or consulting experience, because people are more likely to listen to someone who has "walked in their shoes." Thus, co-authored articles (such as the ones in the December 2004 issue of *HRM* or those being planned by the *SIOP Science for SHRM* series) are likely to increase receptivity to research-based ideas.

In addition to boosting credibility, co-production can also result in more novel, creative, and important research insights (e.g., Campbell et al., 1982; Cohen, 2007; Hakel, Sorcher, Beer, & Moses, 1982; Lawler et al., 1985; Rynes et al., 1999; Shapiro et al., 2007; Starbuck, 2006). Unfortunately, however, production and coproduction of published research by practitioners has decreased dramatically in I/O psychology over the past 40 years. For example, between 1963 and 1967, 41.3% of authors in *PPsych* and 31.5% in *JAP* had non-academic affiliations (Cascio & Aguinis, 2008). By 2003–2007, these percentages had fallen to only 14.0% in *PPsych* and 4.7% in *JAP*. This implies that finding practitioner coresearchers is likely to be difficult.

Still, several methods are possible. First, as suggested earlier, professional organizations such as the AOM or SIOP can schedule more sessions at which the sole purpose is for academics and practitioners to network and discuss topics of joint interest (Bartunek, 2007; Cohen, 2007; Shapiro et al., 2007). Second, joint activities can be pursued in the context of executive or evening courses in management or psychology, where students are likely to be full-time employees in some organization or another (Latham, 2007a). Tushman and O'Reilly (2007) suggest that this tactic is likely to prove particularly fruitful in evening or executive programs that are designed for specific (usually large) companies with which the university has a special relationship. Alternatively, researchers might gain access to companies when graduates from full-time programs recommend faculty members as consultants to their new employers (for examples of studies that started this way, see Russell, 2001, or Sutton, 1991). Third, long-term relationships can be developed between colleges and universities, private-sector organizations, and governmental agencies through advisory councils or centers (such as the Center for Effective Organizations [CEO] at the University of Southern California or the Center for Advanced Human Resource Studies [CAHRS] at Cornell). Fourth, individual researchers can offer their technical and analytical skills to consulting firms in return for access to large-sample databases and joint publications in top-tier journals and other venues (e.g., see Harter, Schmidt, & Hayes, 2002, or Schneider, Smith, Taylor, & Fleenor, 1998).

Finally, academics might approach potential coauthors by asking what kinds of problems they are having, right now, in a domain of interest (e.g., recruiting).[10] A conversation might then be built around academic findings that have relevance to those problems, followed by discussions of areas for which neither side currently has good evidence or answers. From that starting point, arrangements might be made for the academic partner to take the lead on writing in consultation with the practitioner, who can provide examples and contextual nuances that improve the paper's relevance, interest, and "stickiness." In the best of cases, this step might be followed up with joint research projects in the "unsolved" areas of the domain.

IMPROVE REWARDS AND RECOGNITION FOR RESEARCH THAT BENEFITS PRACTICE

Another way in which researchers can be enticed to move in different directions is to improve incentives and recognition for applied research or research on topics of interest to practice. One potentially effective method of changing research trajectories is to offer funding for researchers willing to conduct specific types of research. For example, the SHRM Foundation and the Management Education Research Institute (the research arm of the Graduate Management Admissions Council) have both sponsored research projects in areas deemed important to practice and education. In times of declining public funding (particularly in the social sciences), such programs can induce researchers and doctoral students to address areas that might not naturally arise as extensions of the research currently appearing in top-tier journals, which is presently the stimulus for nearly all published research in I/O psychology (Sackett & Larson, 1990). A closely related tactic is to create professional awards for research with clear practical implications (e.g., SIOP's M. Scott Myers Award for Applied Research) or for researchers whose overall body of work benefits practice (e.g., SHRM's Michael R. Losey Human Resource Research Award or the Management Education Research Institute's Fellowship program). The number of such awards has increased noticeably over the past ten years and may well be part of the reason for increased academic attention to bridging the gap.

INCREASE FLEXIBILITY OF TOP-TIER JOURNALS

Although prizes and professional recognition are nice, under the present academic reward system the strongest predictor of academic salaries is the number of publications in top-tier journals. To the extent that top-tier publications continue to dominate academic rewards in the future (and some authors fervently hope that they do not; e.g., Adler & Harzing, 2009), one of the most effective ways of changing academic research would be to increase the range of content and methods found in top-tier journals. Of course, this is much easier said than done, as illustrated by the trajectory of OS over its first 18 years (Daft & Lewin, 2008).

Some researchers believe that one of the most important changes journals could make would be to reduce the increasingly prominent role of theory (versus empirical findings) in determining whether or not an article gets published (e.g., Hambrick, 2007; Starbuck, 2006). Over time, some top-tier journals have moved from merely favoring articles that *use* theory to requiring that articles *contribute to* theory (e.g., Colquitt & Zapata-Phelan, 2007; Sutton & Staw, 1995).[11] Both Hambrick (2007) and Starbuck (2006, pp. 107–113) have argued that imposing rigid standards for theoretical contribution impedes, rather than furthers, scientific progress. Their views are also shared by Locke (2007):

Everyone who publishes in professional journals in the social sciences knows that you are supposed to start your article with a theory, then make deductions from it, then test it, and then revise the theory.... In practice, however, I believe that this policy encourages—in fact demands, premature theorizing and often leads to making up hypotheses after the fact—which is contrary to the intent of the hypothetico-deductive method. (p. 867)

The challenge that confronts journal editors is how to loosen theoretical requirements without lowering standards (or, to be frank, status within the academic community). Hambrick (2007) suggested the following alternative standard:

Does the paper have a high likelihood of stimulating future research that will substantially alter managerial theory and/or practice? This new standard would require papers to be—by all appearances—*important*. (p. 1350; emphasis added)

Locke (2007) offered this recommendation:

Instead of demanding a theory to start with, the introduction to a research paper could summarize what is known about the phenomenon in question and state the purpose of the proposed study: how it will go beyond what is known.... Introductions would be much shorter than they are now, because the author would not need to write pages and pages of justification for hypotheses, so long as it was made clear that something new is being done. Then in the discussion section, the author would do the work of inductive integration—tying together the new findings with what was previously known. This means that much of the material formerly in the introduction, if not discarded, would be moved here.... The author could also identify how far along the field is in developing a theory and what more needs to be done (e.g., identify causal mechanisms, identify moderators). (pp. 886–887)

Placing less emphasis on theory – especially in new areas - would almost certainly increase practitioner interest in our findings, not only because different kinds of questions could be asked, but also because there would be more room for reporting the "rich detail about interesting phenomena" (Hambrick, 2007) that is of interest to practitioners and researchers alike (Bamberger, 2008; Bartunek, Rynes, & Ireland, 2006; Cohen, 2007; Guest, 2007; Rousseau & Fried, 2001). Other types of research that might qualify under such revised standards include first descriptions of new phenomena (Hambrick, 2007) and renewed interest in surveys of current practice (e.g., Bretz et al., 1992; Rynes & Boudreau, 1986; Saari, Johnston, McLaughlin, & Zimmerle, 1988). Although these types of studies are of great interest to practitioners (and, I believe, to many researchers as well), because of the difficulty of publishing them in top-tier outlets, academics have all but abandoned practice surveys to consulting firms that often treat the data as proprietary and/or charge large sums of money for access to their findings. Thus, surveying is perhaps another area in which the strong research skills of academics might be allied with the substantive needs of practitioners to create mutual scientific and practical benefits.[12]

Less emphasis on theory might also result in top journals publishing more articles that "mine" huge databases to spot regularities that have not previously been predicted or detected (Anderson, 2008). Although data mining is pejoratively referred to as "fishing" in most methods classes, the huge amounts of information now available on web sites or in company or consulting databases give us a much better chance than before of revealing patterns that will hold up in subsequent analyses (Ayres, 2008; Baker, 2008). Equally important, the regularities uncovered in this way can provoke speculation about possible causes and, in so doing, may aid future theoretical development and insights about human behavior as well. Still, even in the area of medicine, which is believed to be considerably ahead of management in terms of evidence-based practice, it is very difficult to publish results showing even large practical treatment successes if either the basic science behind the treatment has already been published elsewhere or the underlying reason (i.e., theory) for the effectiveness has not yet been discovered (Begley, 2009b). Among other problems, the fact that such studies are unlikely to show up in top-tier journals decreases the likelihood that medical researchers will learn of the results and start searching for the underlying "whys" of successful practice.

CONDUCT RESEARCH ON PERSUASIVENESS OF RESEARCH FINDINGS

One thing that might be very helpful at this juncture is a stronger research base illuminating what causes practitioners to believe, or not believe, our research. For example, although it is clear that the use of personal anecdotes has been successful in selling the popular ideas of emotional intelligence and the alleged unimportance of *g* (e.g., Goleman,

2000; Gladwell, 2008), it is not clear whether the same strategy would work for selling the *un*popular idea of the *importance* of *g*. If not, such studies would provide additional evidence that the importance of intelligence is a fundamentally aversive idea to most people and, more generally, might begin to illuminate the boundary conditions around effective presentation of research ideas.

In particular, we need much more information about how to successfully present evidence that challenges peoples' prior beliefs, such as those pertaining to the importance of *g* or the greater predictive efficacy of actuarial over clinical decision models. This is a very intractable problem that has been shown to exist even in the hard sciences and medicine (Begley, 2009a), where one would think that disbelief would be less likely to arouse emotional reactions than in the social sciences. For example, Halloun and Hestenes (1985) reported on attempts to change the beliefs of students who had completed a physics class, but who still were not convinced that Newtonian physics was more correct than Aristotelian beliefs about motion. They began by asking the students questions that required them to rely on their theories about motion to predict what would happen in a simple physics experiment. After the students had made their projections, the researchers performed an experiment that demonstrated that their assumptions were wrong. They then asked the students to explain the discrepancies between their ideas and the outcome of the experiment:

> What they heard astonished them; many of the students still refused to give up their mistaken ideas about motion. Instead, they argued that the experiment they had just witnessed did not exactly apply to the law of motion in question; it was a special case, or it didn't quite fit the mistaken theory or law that they held as true.... The students performed all kinds of mental gymnastics to avoid confronting and revising the fundamental underlying principles that guided their understanding of the physical universe. Perhaps most disturbing, some of these students had received high grades in the class.
> (*Bain*, 2004, p. 23)

That these results were obtained with a far less "hot" topic than the importance of intelligence suggests that it is very difficult to change fundamental underlying beliefs in a wide variety of domains. Therefore, getting people to use behavioral science research involves far more than simply making it available and giving people guidelines for how to apply it. Making research findings more believable to a general audience is very important to the success of EBM and EBT, particularly since we already know that many people tune out to large-sample empirical evidence. Perhaps I/O psychology, HR, and management researchers can adopt ideas from social psychological research on persuasion and attitude change (e.g., Goldstein, Martin, & Cialdini, 2008; Petty & Cacioppo, 1986), from behavior decision making's emphasis on framing effects (Kahneman, Slovic, & Tversky, 1982), or from medicine's experience with trying to persuade the general public to avoid unsafe behaviors such as smoking or overeating (e.g., Fishbein & Yzer, 2003; Shen & Dillard, 2007). Learning more about why people accept or reject our research findings—and ways to overcome rejection—should be a very high priority for future research.

CONTINUE TO STRENGTHEN OUR RESEARCH BASE

One of the biggest methodological advances over the past 30 years has been the extensive application of meta-analysis (Hunter & Schmidt, 2004) to important questions in I/O psychology and related fields. By combining the results of multiple quantitative studies and correcting for measurement and sampling errors, meta-analyses have been extremely helpful in revealing reliable relationships that formerly seemed to be situation-specific (e.g., the generality of g as a predictor of performance), while at the same time identifying variables that modify the strength or direction of those relationships (e.g., job complexity).

Nevertheless, despite the advances of meta-analysis, there are still conflicting results in many areas, preventing practitioners who might like to use available research from drawing clear implications. To illustrate the problem, I offer an example from my own research. When Amy Colbert, Ken Brown, and I first initiated the project that eventually led to Rynes et al. (2002), our first step was to identify clear, generalizable findings in the seven areas of HR tested by the HR Certification Institute. All three of us were surprised at just how difficult it was to do this. Eventually, we generated a list of nearly 50 such statements, which we then pre-tested for broad consensus using members of the editorial boards of *JAP* and *PPsych*. This pre-test whittled the list of agreed-upon items to 39, which were then responded to by a practitioner sample. By the time the article went to press a year later, another four items had to be removed due to new findings or new critiques of previous work that threw the validity of earlier findings into question.

In short, when we tried to answer Oprah's trademark question, "What do we know for sure?," it seemed to add up to a rather thin list of findings—and not always about terribly important issues. Similar sentiments have been expressed by other academics who suddenly became managers and tried to apply research findings (e.g., Billsberry, 2008; Pearce, 2004).[13]

Some of the conflicting findings that prevent us from being able to draw strong conclusions continue to stem from methodological shortcomings, such as small sample sizes, low response rates, convenience sampling, self-report data, violations of methodological assumptions, common method variance, and varying levels of range restriction (e.g., Edwards, 2008; Starbuck, 2006). As indicated earlier, one of the most effective solutions to sample size and response rate problems would be increased collaboration between academics and other entities such as government, professional associations, consulting firms, or corporations (e.g., Cascio, 2008; Van de Ven & Johnson, 2006; Wall & Wood, 2005). Another helpful change would be to increase the number of studies employing either crucial experiments (Platt, 1964) or triangulated methods (Jick, 1979; Starbuck, 2006), both of which can help in resolving discrepant findings or revealing how statistical relationships "play out" in field settings (e.g., Edmondson, 1996; Latham et al., 1988; Sutton & Rafaeli, 1988).

However, in addition to methodological shortcomings, other factors (such as clashes of ideologies or selective sampling of prior literature) also lead to lack of consensus in the field (Tranfield, Denyer, & Smart, 2003). This has caused some to argue that we need new forms of research cumulation, in addition to narrative reviews and meta-analyses. For example, the management and medical literatures (particularly in the UK) have been experimenting with various types of *systematic reviews*, such as realist synthesis and meta-ethnography (e.g., Tranfield et al., 2003; Rousseau et al., 2008).

Although a full discussion of these methods is beyond the scope of this chapter, in general these additional forms of synthesis aim to review more comprehensive collections of research than meta-analyses (e.g., both quantitative and qualitative studies of varying levels of evidentiary quality) and to provide highly transparent, detailed information about how all methodological decisions were made. In addition, emphasis is placed more on reviewing evidence from an operational perspective (i.e., "What works?") than is usually the case in meta-analysis and narrative reviews, where the primary goal is often to understand underlying processes more than to improve operational effectiveness. Finally, the emphasis on including studies with very diverse methods in amassing the original sample is designed to ensure that controversial areas and critiques of dominant views are not glossed over. Two potential challenges associated with these types of reviews are: (a) the considerable time and effort required to generate them, and (b) the "translation" of such massive documents into formats likely to encourage implementation.

BECOME MORE EFFECTIVE TEACHERS OF RESEARCH METHODS, STATISTICS, AND CRITICAL THINKING

To this point, my suggestions have focused on how academics might modify their research to make it more relevant and believable to practitioners. However, it is also worth considering whether academics, in their dual role as teachers, might become better at helping students become more informed consumers of research (e.g., Burke & Rau, 2010; Rousseau & McCarthy, 2007; Trank & Rynes, 2003). As Abrahamson and Eisenman (2001) and Highhouse (2008) have noted, one reason that practitioners often are not persuaded by academic research is that they have little understanding of why some types of evidence are stronger than others. Until more practitioners truly understand the power of large samples vis-à-vis anecdotes, case studies, and clinical opinions, academic research will continue to fall mostly on deaf ears.

There is considerable evidence that many people distrust statistics because they do not understand them and, indeed, are quite "afraid" of them (Ayres, 2008; Paulos, 2001). Moreover, this lack of understanding produces a sense of threat that can cause defensive or self-protective reactions when confronted with statistical evidence (Bain, 2004). However, many educational experts believe that widespread math anxiety and statistics phobias are not inevitable, but rather have been created by ineffective textbooks and teaching methods (McDonald, 1987; Tobias, 1995).

Given that most students (at least in the United States) enter college with math phobia, it seems highly likely that many students (i.e., future managers or other practitioners) also leave college without a solid grasp of research methods, statistics, and analysis. And, as is true of lower educational levels, ineffective teaching may again be a large part of the problem. For example, the typical statistics or methods text is filled with equations and problems that have little to do with substantive content areas of interest to students. In addition, much is made of issues that, in practice, are often irrelevant (or worse still, misleading), such as the difference between a sample and a population (since most of our data come from convenience samples rather than random or even representative subsets of identifiable populations) and whether or not a difference is "statistically significant" (since the assumptions underlying such tests are almost never met and the results depend heavily on sample size). Finally, there is an overemphasis on what Bain (2004) calls "chug and plug"—memorizing formulae and plugging numbers into equations, rather than problem solving or applying the material to real-world contexts.

The idea that there might be better ways of helping students learn—and that research on teaching and learning can help us answer such questions—has led to the creation of new journals (such as *Academy of Management Learning and Education* [*AMLE*] and *Decision Sciences Journal of Innovative Education* [*DSJIE*]) that may do much to help us improve the effectiveness of our teaching, particularly in technical areas. For example, Aguinis and Branstetter (2007) recently published an article about an effective, empirically validated way of teaching the concept of the sampling distribution of the mean, while Corner (2002) offered a hands-on way to teach research design.

Another way to improve student learning in statistics might be to use popular press books such as *Super Crunchers* (Ayres, 2008) or *Innumeracy* (Paulos, 2001) in conjunction with more formal statistical texts. These books do not delve into the details of the math behind statistical tools, but rather illuminate a variety of ways in which these tools can (and are) being used to make decisions in many areas of life. As such, they richly contextualize the abstract material found in more formal texts. Although formal evaluative research needs to be conducted, anecdotal reviews of these books suggest that they might go a long way toward contextualizing and motivating the study of statistics:

> [*Super Crunchers*] is really interesting because of how it relates to quantitative tools that can be put to use in amazing ways. I read the book in conjunction with a textbook for a MBA level statistics class. I highly recommend it for anyone as a way of seeing the numerous ways that numbers are put to use, most ways (*sic*) I have never even thought of. (review on Amazon.com)

Another possibility is to think about whether, at educational levels below the Ph.D., the goal should be as much (or more) to produce critical thinkers and informed *consumers* of research (e.g., Abrahamson & Eisenman, 2001; Burke & Rau, 2010), rather than would-be elementary statisticians. Much progress might be made, for example, by teaching students or practitioners how to generate and interpret different types of evidence claims (e.g., Billsberry, 2008; Lehman, Lempert, & Nisbett, 1988), even if they do not learn how to conduct formal research. For example, exercises might involve discussing and critically evaluating the validity and reliability evidence provided by a test vendor, or creating structured interview questions to determine the qualifications of consultants seeking to design an attitude survey.

To the extent that courses also cover the actual conduct of research, students at sub-doctoral levels may benefit more from assignments that ask them to construct an opinion survey or run a focus group than how to test for statistical significance or correct for measurement error (see also Billsberry, 2008). With careful planning, these types of learning goals could be embedded in the context of specific functional-area courses (e.g., employee selection, compensation, or performance management), in addition to (or perhaps in place of) dedicated statistics or analysis courses.

Increasing Implementation of Research Findings

Many of the suggestions made to this point will not only help with accessibility, interest, and believability, but also are likely to improve the chances that more practitioners will actually implement research-consistent practices. For example, as part of the e-mail conversations among members of the SIOP Science for SHRM board, Jeff McHenry offered the following observations:[14]

> I was thinking about how HR policy and practice gets set in a large company, based on my experience (which is limited to N = 2 organizations).
> Typically, there are program managers working in centers of excellence who do external research and benchmarking as they start to think about design principles. What are the types of information that they find useful?
>
> Magazine articles—especially those that include both design principles and case studies
>
> Summaries of research and best practices—white papers are OK, but most tend to like PowerPoint decks better (probably because they're more concise,

the info is more user-friendly, and the slides can be reused by the program managers in presentations they make to their senior management)[15]

> Webinars and podcasts—particularly if the speaker knows his/her facts, is somewhat entertaining, and has lots of good examples/case studies
>
> Conferences—similar speaker attributes.

Thus, previous suggestions to publish in practitioner outlets, to consider alternative formats, to include case studies, to describe processes, and to communicate in more interesting ways may increase use of research findings at the same time that they improve accessibility, interest, and credibility.

Once again, coproduction strategies are likely to be useful for improving the odds of implementation (Amabile et al., 2001; Hakel et al., 1982; Jelinek, Romme & Boland, 2008; Mohrman et al., 2001). Indeed, Amabile et al. (2001) suggest that some types of research are unlikely to be accomplished at all without coproduction. Coproduction ensures, at the very least, that practitioners are interested in a topic and are potentially willing to act on what is discovered. However, both Amabile et al. (2001) and Mohrman et al. (2001) indicate that initial interest is insufficient to ensure action. Rather, moving to actual implementation requires trust between academics and practitioners, attention to group process, true two-way dialogue (rather than the top-down discourse embedded in the "principal investigator" model), and considerable "joint sense-making" regarding the data. Moreover, implementation may not extend far beyond the organizations that are initially involved in the research because of the "not invented here" syndrome. As such, other methods also need to be pursued.

PRESENT ADVICE IN THE FORM OF PRINCIPLES PLUS EXAMPLES

Many academics are profoundly uncomfortable with moving from description to prescription (e.g., Bazerman, 2005; Kelman, 2005; Mohrman et al., 2001). The kind of bold pronouncements offered in some management best sellers make academics cringe, realizing that social and organizational worlds are highly complex and difficult to either change or predict.

Still, if academics hope to increase the extent to which managers and other practitioners act on the basis of evidence rather than hunch or myth, they must be willing to offer suggestions based on the best available evidence. Furthermore, those suggestions must be neither too complex (Locke, 2009), nor too simple (Bartunek, 2007). Thus, academics who wish to encourage evidence-based practice must find a way to simplify complexity enough that practitioners will be encouraged to act, but without promising certainty or making unsupportable claims.

Locke (2009) argues that one good way to do this is by offering "principles." Principles are "general truths on which other truths depend...a principle may be described as a fundamental reached by induction" (Peikoff, 1991 p. 218, quoted in Locke). Among the principles offered in Locke's *Handbook of Principles of Organizational Behavior* (2009) are the following: (1) select on intelligence because it is the single best predictor of differences in individual productivity (particularly for high-skilled and knowledge-based jobs); (2) job satisfaction is an important predictor of life satisfaction, and mental challenge is a key factor in job satisfaction; and (3) setting specific, challenging goals for employees is a very effective motivational technique, but only if certain procedures are followed (Rousseau, 2009.

Attempting to elevate the concept of principles to a higher level of abstraction, Pfeffer and Fong (2005) suggested we use "*first* principles" to build general theories that help people (both practitioners and students) "see the connection among diverse, apparently unrelated, topics," because "there are enormous benefits for memory and understanding from coherent, integrated theoretical structures of thought" (p. 373). As an example, they show how the first principle of "self-enhancement" can be used to explain a wide variety of power and influence-related phenomena, including escalation of commitment, similarity attraction, in-group favoritism, the disinhibiting effects of power, and the persistence of hierarchical structures. They also reference other researchers' attempts to build unified explanations from first principles, such as Lawrence and Nohria's (2002) attempt to explain wide swaths of human behavior in relation to "four innate drives—the drives to acquire, to bond, to learn, and to defend" (p. 5). The main point is that, in addition to explaining particular phenomena or solving particular problems one at a time (i.e., an emphasis on dependent variables), Pfeffer & Fong (2005) believe that we should also look for unifying causes or principles (i.e., independent variables) that are associated with multiple outcomes or effects.

Having said this, however, with respect to increasing implementation of research-supported practices, it is probably more useful to frame articles around particular problems (such as turnover or theft) or specific HR functions (such as recruitment or compensation). This is because practitioners are more likely to search for information using problem- or function-based terms than terms associated with principles (e.g., self-enhancement) or first principles (innate drives). As such, perhaps the most promising use of "first principles" will be in teaching or training venues, where they can be introduced at the beginning of a course or session and then integrated into discussions of multiple applications to problems or functional areas.

IMPROVE "IMPLICATIONS FOR PRACTICE" SECTIONS IN PRIMARY RESEARCH STUDIES

The strongest implications for practice flow from aggregations of many research studies, such as meta-analyses and systemic reviews (Hunter & Schmidt, 2004; Locke, 2009; Rousseau et al., 2008). Still, there is also room for improving the way in which researchers formulate implications for practice in the context of single studies. Although it may not be appropriate to require implications for practice in all articles (since that might introduce further rigidity in publishing practices and cause premature prescription; see Locke, 2007), it would be good to think about how these sections might be made more useful, where appropriate.

At present, implications for practice—where offered—are often both "thin" and quite generic. For example, based on a review of articles in *AMJ* for the year 2006, Bartunek (2007) found that 36% had no implications for practice, even though improving practice is part of *AMJ*'s mission. Of the articles that did contain implications for practice, the most common recommendation (in 38% of the articles) was for practitioners to become "more aware" of some phenomenon (examples included "monitoring" demographics, "understanding" how to make governance decisions, or "being cognizant" that HR practices can be used to build human capital). The other three most common types of recommendations were to provide training (21%), to influence others' interactions in some way (17%), or to either increase or decrease employee heterogeneity (17%). Overall, Bartunek (2007) concluded:

> When considered as a whole, much of the advice given in the 2006 *AMJ* articles is not easy for managers or other practitioners to apply. Recommendations to pay special attention to a phenomenon do not help a manager know what to do in response to it. Moreover, little of the advice includes rationales for intended actions, even though there are extensive conceptual rationales for the studies whose findings lead to the proposed actions.

That is, implications are typically suggested in a decontextualized, distant way. Some of the advice would appear to many readers to be contradictory, and some of it is simply hortatory.

(pp. 1325–1326)

A recent extension of Bartunek's study (Bartunek & Rynes, 2009) to five journals (*AMJ, JAP, JOB, OS,* and *PPsych*) over two different time periods (1992–1993 and 2003–2007) showed that the number of articles containing "implications for practice" has grown over time in all of these journals, although they increased much more in some journals than others (specifically, *PPsych* increased from 34% in 1992–1993 to 79% in 2003–2007; *JAP* increased from 29% to 58%; *AMJ* from 27% to 55%; *JOB* from 40% to 58%, and *OS* from 46% to 47%). In this broader sample of journals, the top four implications for practice were also a bit different. Specifically, although "increasing awareness" and "training" were still the top two recommendations, the next two most common pieces of advice were to change the design or structure of something (e.g., an organization, a workgroup, or a career) and to change selection or hiring procedures. On the less encouraging side, the grade level required to read "implications for practice" sections increased by nearly a full grade (from 16.6 to 17.5) between 1992–1993 and 2003–2007.

Another (less formal) finding by Bartunek and Rynes (2009) was that when they presented the results of this paper in various research seminars, many management academics admitted discomfort and uncertainty about whether, and how, to write good "implications for practice" sections. Especially for those academics who conducted lab studies and/or were not interacting very much with practitioners, there was a reluctance to claim that they had discovered anything that could really be "of use" to practitioners. Some academics who read earlier versions of this chapter also commented that implementation is a weak spot for many academics.

Given these reactions, several actions might be useful. For example, it might be helpful to produce a book or a special journal issue of essays by true "scientist-practitioners" about how they apply research findings in practice (i.e., application exemplars). A good example of this type of essay with respect to performance measurement can be found in Tannenbaum (2006). (A similar effort with respect to how academics use research findings in the classroom can be found in some of the essays in André and Frost's [1997] *Researchers Hooked on Teaching*.)

In addition, journals might encourage authors to include implications for teaching as well as implications for theory and practice (Rynes & Trank, 1997). In her presidential address to the AOM, Rousseau (2006) said:

> (T)he most important reason evidence-based management is still a hope and not a reality is not due to managers themselves or their organizations. Rather, professors like me and the programs in which we teach must accept a large measure of blame. *We typically do not educate managers to know or use scientific evidence.*
>
> (p. 262; emphasis in the original)

Providing academic readers with guidance as to how research findings might be used in their teaching (perhaps including one or two examples of firms that seem to do such things well) would constitute one step toward EBT. Of course, professors with primarily teaching (as opposed to research) interests would still have to *read* research findings for this to have any impact. At present, many apparently do not (Rousseau, 2006), which suggests that academic research often fails to reach professors as well as managers and other practitioners.

Given this situation, a different solution would be to combine popular case and experiential learning methods with texts based explicitly on research principles (e.g., Latham, 2009b; Locke, 2009; Pearce, 2006). In this approach, the review, selection, and integration of research findings would be delegated to textbook authors. However, since there is wide variability in the extent to which textbooks are truly research-based (Stambaugh & Trank, 2010), successful implementation of this strategy will require both that (a) instructors value research findings and (b) have the means to assess the research-based credibility of textbook authors.

INCREASE APPLICATIONS RESEARCH AND RESEARCH CONTEXTUALIZATION

The fact that many researchers seem to be uncomfortable writing implications for practice reflects a deeper problem as well. Specifically, the most common methods employed in many areas of I/O and management research are relatively weak in terms of either internal validity, generalizability, or both. For example, Bartunek and Rynes (2009) found that authors who conduct lab studies are particularly uncertain about how generalizable their results are to the field—a concern that is shared by practitioners (Boehm, 1980). In addition, using the widely researched area of organizational justice as an example, Greenberg (2009) argues that "implications" studies—that is, those that show correlations between justice perceptions and some other variable—are weak sources of true implications because they neither show practitioners how to change perceptions nor convincingly demonstrate that it will matter to organizational outcomes if they do (p. 183).

As such, Greenberg (2009) argues that in order for practitioners to "*do* something" with our research, we need far more "application" or intervention studies in which researchers "introduce organizational practices believed to promote justice and then assess the effectiveness of those practices" (p. 184). Applying this distinction, Bauer et al. (2009) examined 545 justice studies published over the past 15 years and found that implication studies outnumbered applications by a factor of 25 to 1.

Of course, Greenberg (2009) is hardly alone in his call for more applications or intervention studies. Indeed, studies for intervention or "action" research go back more than half a century (e.g., Lewin, 1946; French & Bell, 1973). Many who have pondered the need for such studies grapple with the fact that pure experimental designs are rarely possible in field settings, challenging researchers to find alternative designs that nevertheless reduce various threats to internal validity (e.g., Cook & Campbell, 1979; Sackett & Mullen, 1993). Others place less value on purity of design and more on engaging with organizational participants in a series of steps involving pragmatic experimentation, implementation, and evaluation, followed by further experimentation and implementation based on what is learned in the process (e.g., Cooperrider & Srivastva, 1987; Romme & Endenburg, 2006; Van Aken, 2004).

Even in the absence of intervention studies, I/O and related research would be more appealing to practitioners (and more useful to future researchers) if it were less decontextualized (e.g., Bamberger, 2008; Johns, 2001; Porter, 2008; Roberts, Hulin, & Rousseau, 1978; Rousseau & Fried, 2001). Greater contextualization is likely to improve the prospects for implementation in several ways. First, contextualized studies are usually conducted in real organizational settings, which inherently give them more credibility with practitioners than convenience samples. (Convenience samples require "averaging across" or "controlling for" contextual factors, rather than treating them as potentially important pieces of information). Second, in contextualized studies, authors are more likely to tell what happened, how, why, and whether it worked or not (Gephart, 2004). Given this concrete information, readers can decide whether the context seems relevant to their own setting and, if not, whether the "what or how" might be adapted to fit their own situation (Collins, 2004). In other words, contextualization provides a concrete baseline for practitioner reflection, modification, and, potentially, action (e.g., Czarniawska & Sevon, 2005; Schön, 1995).[16]

Relatedly, the importance of context to practitioner receptivity suggests that in order to increase the odds of implementation, we need to match our research contexts more closely to the current distributions of industries, organizational sizes and structures, and so on. Not surprisingly, practitioners are more likely to notice, read, and act on ideas that are presented in a context that reflects their own working environment (e.g., Guest, 2007). Thus, for example, public sector managers prefer to read articles that are tailored specifically to their unique context (Feldman, 2005; Kelman, 2005), as do managers in health care (e.g., Greenhalgh, 2006) and other fields. Closer to home, Weimer (2006) revealed the same preference among academics in their search for literature on the "practice" of teaching. For example, academics in business schools are far more likely to read *JME* or *AMLE* than general education journals, even though many of the findings from the education discipline have relevance for management and psychology.

Given this well-established preference for context-specific research, a recent study by O'Leary and Almond (2009) suggests that managers in certain sectors of the economy are likely to be "underserved" by recent organizational research. Specifically, based on a sample of 914 field studies published in *AMJ, ASQ, JOB* and *OS,* they found "striking, persistent, and growing discrepancies between the industries that are economically important and the industries that have served as settings for organizational research. For example, education and manufacturing are oversampled in relation to their economic importance, while real estate, construction, wholesale, and retail are undersampled" (p. 1). Management of the public sector also appears to be dramatically undersampled, as are small businesses (e.g., Kelman, 2005; Pettigrew, 2005). More generally, Walsh, Meyer, and Schoonhoven (2006) argue that we have over-studied old organizational forms and under-studied new ones (e.g., global, disaggregated organizations with ever-increasing reach into public and private lives). Thus, situating more research in new-style organizations is likely to enhance practitioner interest in I/O and related research.

PROVIDE SPECIFIC SUPPORT FOR IMPLEMENTATION

Other than coproduction of research, perhaps few things would help more to increase implementation of research ideas than some sort of "help line" or chat room for those who are considering a change but have specific questions or problems with respect to implementation. The popularity of such help lines can be seen at SHRM, where their Knowledge Advisors handled 114,458 inquiries by phone, e-mail, and live chat in 2008 and provided 447,000 Express Request e-mail responses for the most common types of inquiries (D. Cohen, personal communication, March 10, 2009). Another useful site for benchmarking, chats, and interest groups is HRM the Journal (http://www.hrmthejournal.com), which at the time of this writing has more than 1,700 members and 29 active discussion groups.

Although neither academics nor consultants can be expected to provide free advice indefinitely, it might be very helpful if the authors of SIOP's research reports for practice would make themselves available for subsequent questioning for at least some minimal period of time after publication on the SIOP, SHRM, and HRM the Journal web sites.

Future Directions

A wide variety of suggestions for future research and practice have already been offered in the previous sections on "solutions." Here, I highlight some of the areas that I consider to be most important for bridging the academic-practice gap:

• One important area for future research is to find the most effective ways to communicate research findings, particularly when those findings run counter to what people currently practice or believe. Given the well-known tendency for people to filter out non-self-affirming information, it is important for researchers to explore ways of breaking through self-protective defenses. Previous research suggests that this is extremely difficult to do, but because it is so crucial, research that sheds light on this issue would make a very valuable contribution.

• Means need to be found to reward, or at a minimum, not to punish, academic-practitioner boundary spanning. Although it is commonly assumed that interactions with practitioners are likely to reduce academics' research productivity, Podsakoff et al.'s (2008) list of the most-cited management scholars—in combination with autobiographical evidence regarding the origins of their research programs (e.g., Bedeian, 2002)— makes it clear that most researchers with the very highest citation rates regularly engage with practitioners (e.g., Kathleen Eisenhardt, Donald Hambrick, Charles O'Reilly, Jay Barney, Michael Hitt, Jane Dutton, and Frank Schmidt). Based on real or imagined pressures from their universities, many academics may be spending too much time protecting themselves from "intrusions" on their research time while missing out on truly exceptional research opportunities (Campbell et al., 1982). Given that relationship building is very important to successful collaborations, boundary-spanning activities should be given more weight in academic reward systems than is generally the case. Senior faculty need to take the lead in pushing for increased value on boundary-spanning activities and research with practical implications (McGrath, 2007) so that doctoral students and junior faculty—typically the source of innovation in most fields—are not discouraged from engaging with the broader community.

• Doctoral programs need to make better use of Ph.D. students' pre-doctoral program experiences. At present, many students feel that Ph.D. programs try to "stomp out" their previous experiences and interests, rather than incorporating or building on them (e.g., Bartunek et al., 2003; Dutton, 2003; Empson, 2007; Vermeulen, 2007). It is important to honor and encourage the passionate interests and big questions with which many Ph.D. students enter our programs.

• It is crucial to build a research base examining processes and outcomes of various forms of evidence-based teaching. Academics also need to empirically evaluate the effectiveness of attempts to teach basic principles of research methodology or critical thinking skills to on-campus students so that they become better consumers of information after graduation (for an early example, see Lehman, Lempert, & Nisbett, 1988). It would also be valuable to examine the extent to which academic coursework changes students' beliefs, attitudes, or mental models, since much of the behavioral science curriculum is designed to influence these variables (Rynes & Brown, 2011).

• Future research should also examine the role of positive versus traditional (i.e., gap- or deficiency-based) approaches to changing behaviors: Is one more effective than the other in reaching across academic-practice boundaries? Both academics and practitioners are increasingly experimenting with positive approaches to change (such as appreciative inquiry and positive psychology), which use self-affirming techniques designed to reduce defensiveness and resistance to change (Austin & Bartunek, 2003). Assuming that positive approaches are indeed successful in reducing defenses, does this reduced defensiveness translate into more, or less, eventual change? What happens when appreciative inquiry bumps up against traditional management? Evidence on this point would be very helpful, since positive approaches are very common in ODC consulting but have rarely been evaluated in terms of subsequent quantitative outcomes (Yaeger et al., 2005).

• We need more research on how managers make decisions about program adoption or non-adoption. Without a clearer understanding of how I/O, HR, and related practitioners decide which interventions to pursue, there will be much more guesswork than necessary in trying to find effective ways to share information across academic-practice boundaries. Latham (2007) suggests that we "conduct research on the adoption and diffusion of human resource research findings in the workforce"…because…"through myriad laboratory experiments, simulations, and field studies, ways to transfer HRM knowledge to HRM practice are likely to be discovered" (p. 1028). I agree.

Conclusion

Here in my adoptive home state of Iowa (in the midwestern United States), people like to say: "If we build it, they will come."[17] The general idea is that if someone produces a valuable service or product, people will buy it. This is akin to the "push" model of research dissemination, which is the primary strategy that I/O and related academics have been using to try to influence practitioners through their research. At the present point in time, this strategy seems to be meeting with rather limited success (e.g., Cohen, 2007; Guest, 2007; Johns, 1993; Lapointe, 1990; Rynes et al., 2002; Silzer & Cober, 2008). At a very minimum, the present push needs to be combined with a "pull" strategy, studying the issues that interest practitioners (e.g., Cascio & Aguinis, 2008; Deadrick & Gibson, 2007; Rynes et al., 2007) and providing more inputs in the form of problem-solving or decision aids (in addition to the more customary topical reviews).

Perhaps a more useful operating principle for narrowing the gap would be "It takes a village." First, there is an emerging consensus that we need to tackle the gap on multiple fronts—building personal relationships, using multiple outlets and creating new ones as needed, producing various types of translations and forums for sharing (Cohen, 2007; Latham, 2007a; Rousseau, 2006; Rynes, 2007). Given these myriad needs, many individuals need to get involved. Second, a village implies "community"—not two separate communities, but two "blended" communities with at least some overlapping interests. The role of community and relationships in producing trust, sharing ideas, and generating new knowledge and processes should not be underestimated (Bartunek, 2007; Dutton & Dukerich, 2006; March, 2005).

Notes

1. Whether these discrepancies between practitioner perceptions and research findings are due to lack of *awareness* (as opposed to lack of belief, despite awareness) is not entirely clear. However, I reserve discussions of gaps due to differences in *beliefs* for the next section, which reviews research that directly assesses practitioners' beliefs following direct exposure to research findings.

2. One important limitation of this study is that the *JOB* board consists mostly of academics. As such, their notion of the "ideal" research portfolio may diverge considerably from that of practitioners.

3. The scientist-practitioner model is a training model for graduate programs that focuses on creating a foundation for both scientific research and practice. It was developed primarily to train clinical psychologists, but has also been the inspiration behind many I/O psychology programs. Under this model, graduate students are trained to be both scientists (i.e., researchers) and practitioners who apply their knowledge and techniques to solve organizational or client problems (e.g., Dunnette, 1990; Fleishman, 1990; Shapiro, 2002).

4. Interested readers are encouraged to read Pinker's entire book, as its arguments are complex and cannot be adequately explained in this space-limited forum.

5. Abrahamson (1991) defines a "fad" as an imitation or diffusion process that is determined primarily by organizations themselves, in contrast to "fashions," where external organizations (e.g., consultants or government agencies) strongly influence imitation and diffusion. For purposes of this paper, I will use the terms interchangeably.

6. Not everyone agrees with this point. For example, Kieser (1997) and Clark & Greatbatch (2004) suggest that performance "gaps" and management "needs" are so thoroughly "manufactured" that no separate theory (beyond a theory of aesthetic fads and fashions) is needed to explain management fads.

7. Placement of particular "solutions" under one component of the gap rather than another is somewhat subjective, since neither the components of the gap nor their solutions are independent of one another.

8. In authoritarian contexts such as work, receiving negative feedback about one's performance (which, at least in the short run, can produce negative emotions and cognitive defenses) generally produces more subsequent improvement than receiving positive feedback (e.g., Atwater, Roush, & Fischthal, 1995; Johnson & Ferstl, 1999; Rynes et al., 2005). However, many of the incentives to improve performance in the face of negative feedback from supervisors or peers are not operative in the case

of practitioners simply reading research accounts that suggest adopting alternative practices.

9. The "power of one" or anecdotes has also been shown in the context of charitable giving. For example, people give more money to charities that highlight a specific child in need than to appeals emphasizing that millions of children are starving in some region of the world (Singer, 2009).

10. Thanks to Craig Russell and Alison Eyring for these ideas.

11. In the interest of full disclosure, I formerly edited a top-tier journal, *AMJ*, which also included "contribution to theory" as a core requirement for publication. Although our editorial team broadened the range of articles that were considered to contribute to theory (see Rynes, 2005), in retrospect I believe we should have gone even further toward reducing the emphasis on theory, along the lines suggested by Hambrick (2007).

12. However, one possible impediment to this cooperation might be that due to top-tier journals' emphasis on issues such as construct validity and reliability, academic-designed surveys might be longer and more complex than those produced by professional organizations or consulting firms, thus reducing response rates (see, for example, Tannenbaum, 2006).

13. Others are more optimistic about the number of implications we can draw for practice from our research (e.g., Locke, 2009; Miner, 2007; Rousseau, 2009). The difference may be that it is easier to draw some "general principles" (which nevertheless are not always true) than to come up with statements that are either true or false under all known conditions.

14. It would be helpful to have the insights of other practitioners as to how new practices get adopted in their own organizations, perhaps using qualitative methods (e.g., structured interviews to track specific instances of implementation) to obtain greater detail than is currently available.

15. Support for this notion can be seen in a recent study (Haynes et al., 2009) published in the online version of the *New England Journal of Medicine,* which embedded links to Power Point slides to encourage the use of a 19-item checklist that the authors found to reduce surgical deaths by 40%.

16. Two excellent examples of highly contextualized implementation studies in the area of reward systems are Petty, Singleton, & Connell (1992) and Wageman (1995).

17. This is a reference to the 1989 movie, *Field of Dreams,* voted the sixth-best fantasy film of all time. A plot synopsis can be found at http://en.wikipedia.org/wiki/Field_of_Dreams.

References

Abrahamson, E. (1991). Management fads and fashion: The diffusion and rejection of innovations. *Academy of Management Review, 16,* 586–612.

Abrahamson, E. (1996). Management fashion. *Academy of Management Review, 21,* 254–285.

Abrahamson, E. (1997). The emergence and prevalence of employee management rhetorics: The effects of long waves, labor unions, and turnover, 1875 to 1992. *Academy of Management Journal, 40,* 491–533.

Abrahamson, E., & Eisenman, M. (2001). Why management scholars must intervene strategically in the management knowledge market. *Human Relations, 54,* 67–75.

Adler, N. J., & Harzing, A. W. (2009). When knowledge wins: Transcending the sense and nonsense of academic rankings. *Academy of Management Learning and Education, 8,* 72–95.

Agarwal, R., & Hoetker, G. (2007). A Faustian bargain? The growth of management and its relationship with related disciplines. *Academy of Management Journal, 50,* 1304–1322.

Aguinis, H., & Branstetter, S. A. (2007). Teaching the concept of the sampling distribution of the mean. *Journal of Management Education, 31,* 467–483.

Aguinis, H., Michaelis, S. E., & Jones, N. M. (2005). Demand for certified human resources professionals in internet-based job announcements. *International Journal of Selection and Assessment, 13,* 160–171.

Amabile, T. M., Patterson, C., Mueller, J., Wojcik, T., Odomirok, P. W., Marsh, M., & Kramer, S. J. (2001). Academic-practitioner collaboration in management research: A case of cross-profession collaboration. *Academy of Management Journal, 44,* 418–431.

Anderson, C. (June 23, 2008). The end of theory: The data deluge makes the scientific method obsolete. *Wired Magazine: 16.07,* http://www.wired.com/science/discoveries/magazine/16-07/pb_theory.

André, R., & Frost, P. J. (1997). *Researchers hooked on teaching: Noted scholars discuss the synergies of teaching and research.* Thousand Oaks, CA: Sage.

Argyris, C. (1985). Making knowledge more relevant to practice: Maps for action. In E. E. Lawler, III., A. M. Mohrman, S. A. Mohrman, G. E. Ledford, Jr., & T. G. Cummings (Eds.), *Doing research that is useful for theory and practice* (pp. 79–125). San Francisco: Jossey-Bass.

Argyris, C. (1998). Empowerment: The emperor's new clothes. *Harvard Business Review, 76*(3), 98–105.

Argyris, C., & Schön, D. (1978). *Organizational learning: A theory of action perspective.* Reading, MA: Addison-Wesley.

Arthur, J. B. (1994). Effects of human resource systems on manufacturing performance and turnover. *Academy of Management Journal, 37,* 670–687.

Arthur, J. B., & Huntley, C. L. (2005). Ramping up the organizational learning curve: Assessing the impact of deliberate learning on organizational performance under gain sharing. *Academy of Management Journal, 48,* 1159–1170.

Atwater, L., Roush, P., & Fischthal A. (1995). The influence of upward feedback on self and follower ratings of leadership. *Personnel Psychology, 48,* 35–59

Austin, J. R., & Bartunek, J. M. (2003). Theories and practice of organizational development. In W. C. Borman, D. R. Ilgen, & R. J. Klimoski (Eds.), *Handbook of psychology:* Volume 12, *Industrial and organizational psychology* (pp. 309–322). New York: John Wiley & Sons.

Ayres, I. (2008). *Super crunchers: Why thinking-by-numbers is the new way to be smart.* New York: Bantam Books.

Bain, K. (2004). *What the best college teachers do.* Boston: Harvard University Press.

Baker, S. (2008). *The numerati.* New York: Houghton-Mifflin.

Bamberger, P. (2008). Beyond contextualization: Using context theories to narrow the micro-macro gap in management research. *Academy of Management Journal, 51,* 839–846.

Barley, S. R., & Kunda, G. (1992). Design and devotion: Surges of rational and normative ideologies of control in managerial discourse. *Administrative Science Quarterly, 37,* 363–399.

Bartunek, J. M. (2007). Academic-practitioner collaboration need not require joint or relevant research: Toward a relational scholarship of integration. *Academy of Management Journal, 50,* 1323–1333.

Bartunek, J. M., Brown, K. G., Aram, J. D., Rynes, S. L., Trank, C. Q., & Hay, G. W. (2003, September). *Academic-practitioner collaboration in doctoral programs – in theory and in practice*. Presentation to the 12th annual EDA-MBA Annual Meeting, Budapest.

Bartunek, J. M., Rynes, S. L., & Ireland, R. D. (2006). What makes research interesting, and why does it matter? *Academy of Management Journal, 49*, 9–15.

Bartunek, J. M. & Rynes, S. L. (2009). The construction and contributions of "implications for practice": What's in them and what might they offer? *Academy of Management Learning and Education, 9*, 100–117.

Bauer, J., Saboe, K., Cho, E., Yang, L. Johnson, R. E., Erol, H. T., Goncu, A. & Tan, J. A. (2009). How prevalent are the different types of organizational justice research? *Industrial and Organizational Psychology, 2,* 196–198.

Baum, J. R., Locke, E. A., & Kirkpatrick, S. A. (1998). A longitudinal study of the relationship of vision and vision communication to venture growth in entrepreneurial firms. *Journal of Applied Psychology, 83,* 43–54.

Bazerman, M. H. (2005). Conducting influential research: The need for prescriptive implications. *Academy of Management Review, 31*, 25–31.

Becker, B. E., Huselid, M. A., & Beatty, R. W. (2009). *The differentiated workforce: Transforming talent into strategic impact.* Boston: Harvard Business School Publishing.

Bedeian, A. G. (2002). *Management laureates: A collection of autobiographical essays,* Volume 6. Greenwich, CT: JAI Press.

Begley, S. (March 9, 2009a). Why doctors hate science. *Newsweek,* p. 49.

Begley, S. (June 15, 2009b). From bench to bedside: Academia slows the search for cures. *Newsweek,* p. 29.

Bennett, G. (2008). New issue of outreach magazine *Analytics* now available. E-mail posting from INFORMS Director of Marketing, December 3.

Best, J. (2001). *Damned lies and statistics: Untangling numbers from the media, politicians, and activists.* Berkeley, CA: University of California Press.

Beyer, J. M., & Trice, H. M. (1982). The utilization process: A conceptual framework and synthesis of empirical findings. *Administrative Science Quarterly, 27*, 591–622.

Billsberry, J. (2008). *The embedded academic: A management academic discovers management.* Working paper. Milton Keynes, UK: The Open University.

Blau, F. D., Ferber, M. A., & Winkler, A. E. (2005). *The economics of women, men and work* (5th ed.). Upper Saddle River, NJ: Prentice-Hall.

Boehm, V. R. (1980). Research in the "real world": A conceptual model. *Personnel Psychology, 33*, 495–503.

Blood, M. (1994). The role of organizational behavior in the business school curriculum. In J. Greenberg (Ed.), *Organizational behavior: The state of the science* (pp. 207–220). Hillsdale, NJ: Erlbaum.

Bornstein, B. H. (2004). The impact of different types of expert scientific testimony on mock jurors' liability verdicts. *Psychology, Crime, and Law, 10*, 429–446.

Boudreau, J. W. (1983). Effects of employee flows on utility analysis of human resource productivity improvement programs. *Journal of Applied Psychology, 68*, 396–406.

Bretz, R. D., Jr., Milkovich, G. T., & Read, W. (1992). The current state of performance appraisal research and practice: Concerns, directions, and implication. *Journal of Management, 18*, 321–352.

Brown, J. S., & Duguid, P. (2000). *The social life of information.* Boston: Harvard Business School Press.

Brown, S., & Eisenhardt, K. (1997). The art of continuous change: Linking complexity theory and time-paced evolution in relentlessly shifting organizations. *Administrative Science Quarterly, 42*, 1–34.

Brown, S., & Eisenhardt, K. (1998). *Competing on the edge.* Boston, MA: Harvard Business School Press.

Buckley, M. R., Norris, A. C., & Wiese, D. S. (2000). A brief history of the selection interview: May the next 100 years be more fruitful. *Journal of Management History, 6*, 113–126.

Burke, L. A., & Rau, B. (2010). The research-teaching gap in management. *Academy of Management Learning and Education, 9*, 132–143.

Burke, M. J., Drasgow, F., & Edwards, J. E. (2004). Closing science-practice knowledge gaps: Contributions of psychological research to human resource management. *Human Resource Management, 41*, 299–304.

Burt, R. S. (2007). Secondhand brokerage: Evidence on the importance of local structure for managers, bankers and analysts. *Academy of Management Journal, 50,* 119–148.

Cameron, K. S., Ireland, R. D., Lussier, R. N., New, J. R., & Robbins, S. P. (2003). Management textbooks as propaganda. *Journal of Management Education, 27*, 711–743.

Campbell, J. P., Daft, R. L., & Hulin, C.L. (1982). *What to study: Generating and developing research questions.* Beverly Hills: Sage.

Caprar, V. D., Rynes, S. L., Bartunek, J. M., & Do, B. (2011). *Why people believe (or don't believe) our research: The role of self enhancement processes.* Working paper: Sydney, Australia: University of New South Wales.

Carson, P. P., Lanier, P. A., Carson, K. D., & Guidry, B. N. (2000). Clearing a path through the management fashion jungle: Some preliminary trailblazing. *Academy of Management Journal, 43*, 1143–1158.

Cascio, W. F. (2008). To prosper, organizational psychology should bridge application and scholarship. *Journal of Organizational Behavior, 29*, 455–468.

Cascio, W. F., & Aguinis, H. (2008). Research in industrial and organizational psychology 1963–2007: Changes, choices and trends. *Journal of Applied Psychology, 93*, 1062–1081.

Charlier, S. D., Brown, K. G., & Rynes, S. L. (2011). Teaching evidence-based management in MBA programs: What evidence is there? *Academy of Management Learning and Education, 10,* 222–236.

Christensen, C. (1997). *The innovator's dilemma: When new technologies cause great firms to fail.* Boston: Harvard Business Press.

Clark, T., & Greatbatch, D. (2004). Management fashion as image-spectacle: The production of best-selling management books. *Management Communication Quarterly, 17*, 396–424.

Cohen, D. J. (2007). The very separate worlds of academic and practitioner publications in human resource management: Reasons for the divide and concrete solutions for bridging the gap. *Academy of Management Journal, 50*, 1013–1019.

Cohen, W. M., Florida, R., & Goe. W. R. (1994). *University-industry research centers in the United States.* Pittsburgh: Heinz School of Public Policy, Carnegie Mellon University.

Cohen, W. M., Florida, R., Randazzese, L., & Walsh, J. (1998). Industry and the academy: Uneasy partners in the cause of technological advance. In R. G. Noll (Ed.), *Challenges to research universities* (pp. 171–199). Washington, DC: Brookings Institution Press.

Collins, D. (2004). Who put the con in consultancy? Fads, recipes and "vodka margarine." *Human Relations, 57*, 553–571.

Colquitt, J. A., & Zapata-Phelan, C. (2007). Trends in theory building and theory testing: A five-decade study of the *Academy of Management Journal. Academy of Management Journal, 50*, 1281–1303.

Cooperrider, D. L., & Srivastva, S. (1987). Appreciative inquiry in organizational life. In R. W. Woodman & W. A. Pasmore (Eds.), *Research in organizational development* (Vol. 1, pp. 129–169). Greenwich, CT: JAI Press.

Corley, K. G., & Gioia, D. A. (2002). The rankings game: Managing business school reputation. *Corporate Reputation Review, 3*, 319–333.

Corner, P. D. (2002). An integrative model for teaching quantitative research design. *Journal of Management Education, 26*, 671–692.

Cook, T. D., & Campbell, D. T. (1979). *Quasi-experimentation: Design and analysis for field settings.* Chicago: Rand-McNally.

Cronshaw, S. F. (1997). Lo! The stimulus speaks: The insider's view on Whyte and Latham's "the futility of utility analysis." *Personnel Psychology, 50*, 611–615.

Czarniawska, B., & Sevon, G. (Eds.). (2005). *Global ideas: How ideas, objects, and practices travel in the global economy.* Frederiksberg, Denmark: Liber & Copenhagen Business School Press.

Daft, R. L., Griffin, R. W., & Yates, V. (1987). Retrospective accounts of research factors associated with significant and not-so-significant research outcomes. *Academy of Management Journal, 30*, 763–785.

Daft, R. L., & Lewin, A. Y. (1990). Can organization studies begin to break out of the normal science straightjacket? *Organization Science, 1*, 1–9.

Daft, R. L., & Lewin, A. Y. (2008). Rigor and relevance in organization studies: Idea migration and academic journal evolution. *Organization Science, 19*, 177–183.

Davis, M. (1971). That's interesting! Toward a phenomenology of sociology and a sociology of phenomenology. *Philosophy of the Social Sciences, 1*, 309–344.

Dawes, R. M. (1971). A case study of graduate admissions: Application of three principles of human decision making. *American Psychologist, 26*, 180–188.

Dawes, R. M., Faust, D., & Meehl, P. E. (1989). Clinical versus actuarial judgment. *Science, 243*, 1668–1774.

Deadrick, D. L., & Gibson, P. A. (2007). An examination of the research-practice gap in HR: Comparing topics of interest to HR academics and HR professionals. *Human Resource Management Review, 17*, 131–139.

Deci, E. L., Koestner, R., & Ryan, R. M. (1999a). A meta-analytic review of experiments examining the effects of extrinsic rewards on intrinsic motivation. *Psychological Bulletin, 125*, 627–668.

Deci, E. L., Koestner, R., & Ryan, R. M. (1999b). The undermining effect is a reality after all – extrinsic rewards, task interest, and self-determination: Reply to Eisenberger, Pierce, and Cameron (1999) and Lepper, Henderlong, and Gingras (1999). *Psychological Bulletin, 125*, 692–700.

DiMaggio, P., & Powell, W. W. (1983). The iron cage revisited: Institutional isomorphism and collective rationality in organizational fields. *American Sociological Review, 48*, 147–160.

Dipboye, R. (1992). *Selection interviews: Process perspectives.* Cincinnati, OH: South-Western.

Dunnette, M. D. (1990). Blending the science and practice of industrial and organizational psychology: Where are we and where are we going? In M. D. Dunnette & L. M. Hough (Eds.), *Handbook of industrial and organizational psychology* (2nd ed., Vol. 1, pp. 1–27). Palo Alto, CA: Consulting Psychologists Press.

Dunnette, M. D., & Brown, Z. M. (1968). Behavioral science research and the conduct of business. *Academy of Management Journal, 11*, 177–188.

Dutton, J. E. (2003). Breathing life into organizational studies. *Journal of Management Inquiry, 12*, 5–19.

Dutton, J. E., & Dukerich, J. M. (2006). The relational foundation of research: An underappreciated dimension of interesting research. *Academy of Management Journal, 50*, 21–26.

Eagly, A. H., & Chaiken, S. (1993). *The psychology of attitudes.* Orlando, FL: Harcourt Brace.

Earley, P. C. (1999). Creating value from scientific endeavor: Can and should we translate research results for the practitioner? In L. Larwood & U. E. Gattiker (Eds.), *Impact analysis: How research can enter application and make a difference* (pp. 97–104). Mahwah, NJ: Erlbaum.

Edmondson, A. (1996). Learning from mistakes is easier said than done: Group and organizational influences on the detection and correction of human error. *Journal of Applied Behavioral Science, 32*, 5–28.

Edwards, J. (2008). To prosper, organizational psychology should…overcome methodological barriers to progress. *Journal of Organizational Behavior, 29*, 469–491.

Eisenberger, R., & Cameron, J. (1996). Detrimental effects of reward: Reality or myth? *American Psychologist, 51*, 1153–1166.

Eisenberger, R., Pierce, W. D., & Cameron, J. (1999). Effects of reward on intrinsic motivation–negative, neutral and positive: Comment on Deci, Koestner, & Ryan (1999). *Psychological Bulletin, 125*, 677–691.

Eisenhardt, K. M. (1998). *Powerful theory.* Presented at the annual meetings of the Academy of Management, San Diego, CA.

Eisenhardt, K. M., & Brown, S. L. (1998). Time pacing: Competing in markets that won't stand still. *Harvard Business Review, 76*(2), 59–69.

Eisenhardt, K. M., & Tabrizi, B. N. (1995). Accelerating adaptive processes: Product innovation in the global computer industry. *Administrative Science Quarterly, 40*, 84–110.

Ellet, W. (2007). *The case study handbook: How to read, discuss, and write persuasively about cases.* Boston, MA: Harvard Business School Press.

Empson, L. (2007, June). *My affair with the "other": The interpenetration of research and practice.* Paper presented at the third annual Organization Studies workshop, Rithymna, Crete.

Faigman, D. L., & Monahan, J. (2005). Psychological evidence at the dawn of law's scientific age. *Annual Review of Psychology, 56*, 631–659.

Feldman, M. S. (2005). Management and public management. *Academy of Management Journal, 48*, 958–960.

Ferraro, F., Pfeffer, J., & Sutton, R. I. (2005). Economics language and assumptions: How theories can become self-fulfilling. *Academy of Management Review, 30*, 8–24.

Fishbein, M., & Yzer, M. C. (2003). Using theory to design effective health behavior interventions. *Communication Theory, 13*, 164–183.

Fleishman, E. A. (1990). Foreward. In K. R. Murphy & F. E. Saal (Eds.), *Psychology in organizations: Integrating science and practice* (pp. ix-x). Hillsdale, NJ: Lawrence Erlbaum Associates.

French, W. L., & Bell, C. H. (1973). *Organization development: Behavioral science interventions for organization improvement.* Englewood Cliffs, NJ: Prentice-Hall.

Fulmer, I. S., Gerhart, B., & Scott, K. S. (2006). Are the 100 best better? An empirical investigation of the relationship between being a "great place to work" and firm performance. *Personnel Psychology, 56*, 965–993.

Furusten, S. (1999). *Popular management books: How they are made and what they mean for organizations*. London: Routledge.

Gelade, G. A. (2006). But what does it mean in practice? The Journal of Occupational and Organizational Psychology from a practitioner perspective. *Journal of Occupational and Organizational Psychology, 79*, 153–160.

Gephart, R. P. (2004). Qualitative research and the Academy of Management Journal. *Academy of Management Journal, 47*, 454–462.

Gerhart, B., & Milkovich, G. T. (1990). Organizational differences in managerial compensation and financial performance. *Academy of Management Journal, 33*, 663–691.

Gioia, D. A., & Corley, K. G. (2002). Being good versus looking good: Business school rankings and the Circean transformation from substance to image. *Academy of Management Learning and Education, 1*, 107–120.

Givelber, D., & Strickler, L. (2006, January). Junking good science: Undoing *Daubert v Merrill Dow* through cross-examination and argument. *Health Policy and Ethics, 96*(1), 33–37.

Gladwell, M. (2000). *The tipping point*. New York: Little, Brown.

Gladwell, M. (2005). *Blink: The power of thinking without thinking*. New York: Little, Brown.

Gladwell, M. (2008). *Outliers: The story of success*. New York: Little, Brown.

Goldstein, N. J., Martin, S. J., & Cialdini, R. B. (2008). *Yes! 50 scientifically proven ways to be persuasive*. New York: Free Press.

Goleman, D. (1995). *Emotional intelligence: Why it can matter more than IQ*. New York: Bantam Books.

Goleman, D. (2000). *Working with emotional intelligence*. New York: Bantam Books.

Gomez-Mejia, L. R., & Balkin, D. B. (1992). Determinants of pay: An agency theory perspective. *Academy of Management Journal, 35*, 921–955.

Greenberg, J. (2008). Introduction to the special issue: To prosper, organizational psychology should…*Journal of Organizational Behavior, 29*, 435–438.

Greenberg, J. (2009). Everybody talks about organizational justice, but nobody does anything about it. *Industrial and Organizational Psychology, 2*, 181–195.

Greenhalgh, T. (2006). *How to read a paper: The basics of evidence-based medicine* (3rd ed.). Malden, MA: Blackwell.

Greenwood, R., & Hinings, C. R. (2006). Radical organizational change. In S. R. Clegg, C. Hardy, T. B. Lawrence, & W. R. Nord (Eds.), *The Sage handbook of organization studies* (2nd ed., pp. 814–842). London: Sage Publications.

Greiner, L. E., Bhambri, A., & Cummings, T. G. (2003). Searching for a strategy to teach strategy. *Academy of Management Learning and Education, 2*, 402–420.

Grove, W. M., & Meehl, P. E. (1996). Comparative efficiency of informal (subjective, impressionistic) and formal (mechanical, algorithmic) prediction procedures: The clinical-statistical controversy. *Psychology, Public Policy, and Law, 2*, 293–323.

Grove, W. M., Zald, D. H., Lebow, B. S., Snitz, B. E., & Nelson, C. (2000). Clinical versus mechanical prediction. *Psychological Assessment, 12*, 19–30.

Gruber, D. A. (2006). The craft of translation: An interview with Malcolm Gladwell. *Journal of Management Inquiry, 15*, 397–403.

Guest, D. E. (2007). Don't shoot the messenger: A wake-up call for academics. *Academy of Management Journal, 50*, 1020–1026.

Gulati, R. (2007). Tent poles, tribalism, and boundary spanning: The rigor-relevance debate in management research. *Academy of Management Journal, 50*, 775–782.

Hakel, M. D. (1982). Employment interviewing. In K. M. Rowland & G. R. Ferris (Eds.), *Personnel Management* (pp. 129–155). Boston: Allyn & Bacon.

Hakel, M. D. (1994). The past, present, and future of OB applications by consulting academicians. In J. Greenberg (Ed.), *Organizational behavior: The state of the science* (pp. 275–287). Hillsdale, NJ: Erlbaum.

Hakel, M. D., Sorcher, M., Beer, M., & Moses, J. L. (1982). *Making it happen: Designing research with implementation in mind*. Beverly Hills, CA: Sage.

Halloun, I. A., & Hestenes, D. (1985). Common sense concepts about motion. *American Journal of Physics, 53*, 1056–1065.

Hambrick, D. C. (1997). Teaching as leading. In R. Andre & P. Frost (Eds.), *Researchers hooked on teaching* (pp. 242–254). Thousand Oaks, CA: Sage.

Hambrick, D. C. (2007). The field of management's devotion to theory: Too much of a good thing? *Academy of Management Journal, 50*, 1346–1342.

Hammonds, K. H. (2005, August). Why we hate HR. *Fast Company, 97*, 40–47.

Hansen, R. A. (2002). Executive commentary. *Academy of Management Executive, 16*, 103.

Harter, J. K., Schmidt, F. L., & Hayes, T. L. (2002). Business-unit-level relationships between employee satisfaction, employee engagement, and business outcomes: A meta-analysis. *Journal of Applied Psychology, 87*, 268–279.

Haynes, A. B., Weiser, T. G., Berry, W. R., Lipsitz, S. R., Abdel-Hadi, S. B., Dellinger, E. P., Herbosa, T., Sudhir, J., Kibatala, P. L., Lapitan, M. C. M., Merry, A. F., Moorthy, K., Reznick, R.K., Taylor, B., & Gawande, A. A. (2009). A surgical safety checklist to reduce morbidity and mortality in a global population. *The New England Journal of Medicine*, http://content.nejm.org/cgi/content/full/NEJMsa0810119. Last accessed on 25 November, 2011.

Heath, C., Bell, C., & Sternberg, R. (2001). Emotional selection in memes: The case of urban legends. *Journal of Personality and Social Psychology, 81*, 1028–1041.

Heath, C., & Sitkin, S. (2001). Big-B versus Big O: What is *organizational* about organizational behavior? *Journal of Organizational Behavior, 22*, 43–58.

Heslin, P. A., Vandewalle, D., & Latham, G. P. (2006). Keen to help? Managers' implicit person theories and their subsequent employee coaching. *Personnel Psychology, 59*, 871–902.

Highhouse, S. (2007). Applications of organizational psychology: Learning through failure or failure to learn? In L. Koppes (Ed.), *Historical perspectives in industrial and organizational psychology* (pp. 331–352). Mahwah, N J: Lawrence Erlbaum Associates.

Highhouse, S. A. (2008). Stubborn reliance on intuition and subjectivity in employee selection. *Industrial and Organizational Psychology: Perspectives on Science and Practice, 1*, 333–342.

Hodgkinson, G. P., & Rousseau, D. M. (2009). Bridging the rigour-relevance gap in management research: It's already happening! *Journal of Management Studies, 46*, 534–546.

Hofstadter, R. (1964). *Anti-intellectualism in American life*. New York: Alfred A. Knopf.

Hulin, C. L. (2001). Applied psychology and science: Differences between research and practice. *Applied Psychology: An International Review, 50,* 225–234.

Hunter, J. E., & Schmidt, F. L. (2004). *Methods of meta-analysis: Correcting error and bias in research findings.* Thousand Oaks, CA: Sage.

Huselid, M. A. (1995). The impact of human resource practices on turnover, productivity, and corporate financial performance. *Academy of Management Journal, 38,* 635–672.

Jelinek, M., Romme, A. G. L., & Boland, R. J. (2008). Introduction to the special issue of organization studies as a science for design: Creating collaborative artifacts and research. *Organization Studies, 29,* 317–329.

Jick, T. D. (1979). Mixing quantitative and qualitative methods: Triangulation in action. *Administrative Science Quarterly, 24,* 602–611.

Johns, G. (1993). Constraints on the adoption of psychology-based personnel practices: Lessons from organizational innovation. *Personnel Psychology, 46,* 569–592.

Johns, G. (2001). In praise of context. *Journal of Organizational Behavior, 22,* 31–42.

Johnson, J. W., & Ferstl, K. L. (1999). The effects of inter-rater and self-other agreement on performance improvement following upward feedback. *Personnel Psychology, 52,* 271–303.

Judge, T. A., Cable, D. M., Colbert, A. E., & Rynes, S. L. (2007). What causes an article to be cited: Article, author, or journal? *Academy of Management Journal, 50,* 491–506.

Judge, T. A., & Hurst, C. (2007). Capitalizing on one's advantages: Role of core self-evaluations. *Journal of Applied Psychology, 92,* 1212–1227.

Judge, T. A., & Livingston, B. A. (2008). Is the gap more than gender? A longitudinal analysis of gender, gender role orientation, and earnings. *Journal of Applied Psychology, 93,* 994–1012.

Kahneman, D., Slovic, P., & Tversky, A. (1982). *Judgment under uncertainty: Heuristics and biases.* Cambridge: Cambridge University Press.

Katz, H., Kochan, T. A., & Gobeille, K. (1983). Industrial relations performance, economic performance, and the quality of working life. *Industrial and Labor Relations Review, 37,* 3–17.

Kaye, D. H., & Koehler, J. J. (1991). Can jurors understand probabilistic evidence? *Journal of the Royal Statistical Society, 154,* 75–81.

Kelemen, M., & Bansal, P. (2002). The conventions of management research and their relevance to management practice. *British Journal of Management, 13,* 97–108.

Kelman, S. (2005). Public management needs help! *Academy of Management Journal, 48,* 967–969.

Kersley, B., Alpin, C., Forth, J., Bryson, A., Bewley, H., Dix, G., & Oxenbridge, S. (2006). *Inside the workplace: First findings from the 2004 workplace employment relations survey.* London: Routledge.

Kieser, A. (1997). Rhetoric and myth in management fashion. *Organization, 4,* 49–74.

Kieser, A., & Leiner, L. (2009). Why the rigour-relevance gap in management research is unbridgeable. *Journal of Management Studies, 46,* 516–533.

Kochan, T. A. (2007). Social legitimacy of the human resource management profession: A U.S. perspective. In P. F. Boxall, J. Purcell, & P. Wright (Eds.), *Oxford handbook of human resource management* (pp. 599–620). New York: Oxford University Press.

Krauss, D. A., & Sales, B. D. (2001). The effects of clinical and scientific expert testimony on juror decision making in capital sentencing. *Psychology, Public Policy, and Law, 7,* 267–310.

Lapointe, J. B. (1990). Industrial/organizational psychology: A view from the field. In K. R. Murphy & F. E. Saal (Eds.), *Psychology in organizations: Integrating science and practice* (pp. 7–24). Hillsdale, NJ: Erlbaum.

Latham, G. P. (2007a). A speculative perspective on the transfer of behavioral science findings to the workplace: "The times they are a-changin." *Academy of Management Journal, 50,* 1027–1032.

Latham, G. P. (2007b). *Work motivation: History, theory, research and practice.* Thousand Oaks, CA: Sage.

Latham, G. P. (2009a). The joys of serving SIOP as president. *The Industrial-Organizational Psychologist, 47,* 11–16.

Latham, G. P. (2009b). *Becoming the evidence-based manager: Making the science of management work for you.* Boston, MA: Davies-Black.

Latham, G. P., Erez, M., & Locke, E. A. (1988). Resolving scientific disputes by the joint design of crucial experiments by the antagonists: Application to the Erez-Latham dispute regarding participation in goal setting. *Journal of Applied Psychology, 73,* 753–772.

Latham, G. P., & Whyte, G. (1994). The futility of utility analysis. *Personnel Psychology, 47,* 31–46.

Lawler, E. E., III, Mohrman, S. A., & Ledford, G. E., Jr. (1992). *Employee involvement and total quality management: Practices and results in Fortune 1000 companies.* San Francisco: Jossey-Bass.

Lawler, E. E., III, Mohrman, A. M., Mohrman, S. A., Ledford, G. E., Jr., & Cummings, T. G. (Eds.). (1985). *Doing research that is useful for theory and practice.* San Francisco: Jossey-Bass.

Lawrence, P. A. (January 31, 2008). Lost in publication: How measurement harms science. *Ethics in Science and Environmental Politics, 8,* published online, 1–3.

Lawrence, P., & Nohria, N. (2002). *Driven: How human nature shapes our choices.* San Francisco: Jossey-Bass.

Ledford, G. E. Jr., Lawler, E. E., III., & Mohrman, S. A. (1988). The quality circle and its variations. In J. P. Campbell & R. J. Campbell (Eds.), *Productivity in organizations* (pp. 255–294). San Francisco: Jossey-Bass.

Lehman, D. R., Lempert, R. O., & Nisbett, R. E. (1988). The effects of graduate training on reasoning: Formal discipline and thinking about everyday-life events. *American Psychologist, 43,* 431–442.

Leicht, K. T., & Fennell, M. L. (2001). *Professional work: A sociological approach.* Malden, MA: Blackwell.

Leonard, D., & Swap, W. (2004). Deep smarts. *Harvard Business Review, 82*(9), 88–97.

Lepak, D. P., & Snell, S. A. (1999). The human resource architecture: Toward a theory of human capital architecture and development. *Academy of Management Review, 24,* 31–48.

Lewin, K. (1946). Action research and minority problems. *Journal of Social Issues, 2,* 34–46.

Lieberman, J. D., Krauss, D. A., Kyger, M., & Lehoux, M. (2007). Determining dangerousness in sexually violent predator evaluations: Cognitive-experiential self-theory and juror judgments of expert testimony. *Behavioral Sciences and the Law, 25,* 507–526.

Lievens, F., Highhouse, S., & De Corte, W. (2005). The importance of traits and abilities in supervisors' hirability decisions as a function of method of assessment. *Journal of Occupational and Organizational Psychology, 78,* 453–470.

Lindaman, E. B., & Lippitt, R. O. (1980). *Choosing the future you prefer: A goal-setting guide*. Ann Arbor: Human Resource Development Associates.

Locke, E. A. (2002). The epistemological side of teaching management: Teaching through principles. *Academy of Management Learning and Education, 1*, 195–205.

Locke, E. A. (2007). The case for inductive theory building. *Journal of Management, 33*, 867–890.

Locke, E. A. (Ed.). (2009. *Handbook of principles of organizational behavior: Indispensable knowledge for evidence-based management* (2nd ed.). Chichester, UK: John Wiley & Sons.

Locke, E. A., Feren, D. B., McCaleb, V. N., Shaw, K. N., & Denny, A. T. (1980). The relative effectiveness of four methods of motivating employee performance. In K. D. Duncan, M. M. Gruneberg, & D. Wallis (Eds.), *Changes in working life* (pp. 363–388). New York: John Wiley & Sons.

Locke, E. A., & Latham, G. P. (1984). *Goal setting: A motivational technique that works!* Englewood Cliffs, NJ: Prentice-Hall.

Locke, E. A., & Latham, G. P. (2009). Has goal setting gone wild, or have its attackers abandoned good scholarship? *Academy of Management Perspectives, 23*, 17–23.

Loftus, E. F. (1980). Psychological aspects of courtroom testimony. *Annals of the New York Academy of Sciences, 347*, 27–37.

March, J. G. (2005). Parochialism in the evolution of a research community: The case of organization studies. *Management and Organization Review, 1*, 5–22.

McDonald, K. A. (November 4, 1987). Science and mathematics leaders call for radical reform in calculus teaching. *Chronicle of Higher Education*, p. 1.

McGrath, R. G. (2007). No longer a stepchild: How the management field can come into its own. *Academy of Management Journal, 50*, 1365–1378.

McHenry, J. (2007, April). A message from your president. *The Industrial-Organizational Psychologist, 44*(4), 7–11.

McKinney, A. P., Carlson, K. D., Mecham, R. L., III., D'Angelo, N. C., & Connerley, M. L. (2003). Recruiters' use of GPA in initial screening decisions: Higher GPAs don't always make the cut. *Personnel Psychology, 56*, 823–845.

Menkes, J. (2005). Hiring for smarts. *Harvard Business Review, 83*(11), 100–109.

Miller, D. T. (1999). The norm of self interest. *American Psychologist, 54*, 1053–1060.

Miner, J. B. (1984). The validity and usefulness of theories in an emerging organizational science. *Academy of Management Review, 9*, 296–306.

Miner, J. B. (2007). *Organizational behavior 4: From theory to practice*. Armonk, NY: M. E. Sharpe.

Mintzberg, H. (1975). The manager's job: Folklore and fact. *Harvard Business Review, 53*(4), 49–61.

Monahan, J., & Steadman, H. (1994). *Violence and mental disorder: Developments in risk assessment*. Chicago: University of Chicago Press.

Mohrman, S., Gibson, C., & Mohrman, A. M. (2001). Doing research that is useful to practice: A model and empirical exploration. *Academy of Management Journal, 44*, 357–375.

Morgeson, F. P., Campion, M. A., Dipboye, R. L., Hollenbeck, J. R., Murphy, K. R., & Schmitt, N. (2007). Reconsidering the use of personality tests in selection contexts. *Personnel Psychology, 60*, 683–729.

Mowday, R. T. (1997). 1996 presidential address: Reaffirming our scholarly values. *Academy of Management Review, 22*, 335–345.

Murphy, K. R., Cronin, B. E., & Tam, A. P. (2003). Controversy and consensus regarding the use of cognitive ability testing in organizations. *Journal of Applied Psychology, 88*, 660–671.

Murphy, K. R., & Saal, F. E. (1990). *Psychology in organizations: Integrating science and practice*. Hillsdale, NJ: Erlbaum.

Navarro, P. (2008). The MBA core curricula of top-ranked U.S. business schools: A study in failure? *Academy of Management Learning and Education, 7*, 108–123.

Niedermeier, K. E., Kerr, N. L., & Messe, L. A. (1999). Jurors' use of naked statistical evidence: Exploring bases and implications of the Wells effect. *Journal of Personality and Social Psychology, 76*, 533–542.

Nonaka, I., & Konno, N. (1998). The concept of "ba": Building a foundation for knowledge creation. *California Management Review, 40*(3), 40–54.

Nutt, P. C. (1989). *Making tough decisions: Tactics for improving managerial decision making*. San Francisco: Jossey-Bass.

Offermann, L. R., & Spiros, R. K. (2001). The science and practice of team development. *Academy of Management Journal, 44*, 376–392.

O'Leary, M. B., & Almond, B. A. (2009). The industry settings of leading organizational research: The role of economic and non-economic factors. *Journal of Organizational Behavior, 30*, 497–524.

Ones, D. S., Dilchert, S., Viswesvaran, C., & Judge, T. A. (2007). In support of personality assessment in organizational settings. *Personnel Psychology, 60*, 995–1027.

Ones, D. S., Viswesvaran, C., & Schmidt, F. L. (1993). Comprehensive meta-analysis of integrity test validities: Findings and implications for personnel selection and theories of job performance. *Journal of Applied Psychology, 78*, 679–703.

O'Reilly, C. A. (1990). Organizational behavior: where we've been, where we're going. *Annual Review of Psychology, 42*, 427–458.

Orlitzky, M. O., Schmidt, F. L., & Rynes, S. L. (2003). Corporate social and financial performance: A meta-analysis. *Organization Studies, 24*, 403–442.

Oviatt, B. M., & Miller, W. D. (1989). Irrelevance, intransigence, and business professors. *Academy of Management Executive, 3*, 304–312.

Paulos, J. A. (2001). *Innumeracy: Mathematical illiteracy and its consequences*. New York: Hill & Wang.

Pearce, J. L. (2004). What do we know and how do we really know it? *Academy of Management Review, 29*, 175–179.

Pearce, J. L. (2006). *Organizational behavior*. Irvine, CA: Melvin & Leigh.

Peikoff, L. (1991). *Objectivism: The philosophy of Ayn Rand*. New York: Dutton.

Pettigrew, A. M. (2005). The character and significance of management research on the public services. *Academy of Management Journal, 48*, 973–977.

Petty, M. M., Singleton, B., & Connell, D. W. (1992). An experimental evaluation of an organizational incentive plan in the electric utility industry. *Journal of Applied Psychology, 77*, 427–436.

Petty, R. E., & Cacioppo, J. T. (1986). *Communication and persuasion: Central and peripheral routes to attitude change*. New York: Springer.

Pfeffer, J. (1998). *The human equation*. Boston: Harvard Business School Press.

Pfeffer, J., & Fong, C. T. (2002). The end of business schools? Less success than meets the eye. *Academy of Management Learning and Education, 1*, 78–95.

Pfeffer, J., & Fong, C. T. (2005). Building organization theory from first principles: The self-enhancement motive and understanding power and influence. *Organization Science, 16*, 372–388.

Pfeffer, J., & Sutton, R. I. (2000). *The knowing-doing gap: How smart companies turn knowledge into action*. Boston: Harvard Business School Press.

Pinker, S. (2002). *The blank slate: The modern denial of how the mind works*. New York: Viking.

Platt, J. R. (1964). Strong inference. *Science, 146*, 3642.

Podsakoff, P. M., Mackenzie, S. B., Podsakoff, N. P., & Bachrach, D. G. (2008). Scholarly influence in the field of management: A bibliometric analysis of the determinants of university and author impact in the management literature in the past quarter century. *Journal of Management, 34*, 641–720.

Porter, L. W. (2008). Organizational psychology: A look backward, outward, and forward. *Journal of Organizational Behavior, 29*, 519–526.

Roberts, K. H., Hulin, C. L., & Rousseau, D. M. (1978). *Developing an interdisciplinary science of organizations*. San Francisco: Jossey-Bass.

Rogers, E. M. (2003). *The diffusion of innovations*. New York: The Free Press.

Romme, A. G. L. & Endenburg, G. (2006). Construction principles and design rules in the case of circular design. *Organization Science, 17*, 287–297.

Rousseau, D. M. (2007). A sticky, leveraging, and scalable strategy for high-quality connections between organizational practice and science. *Academy of Management Journal, 50*, 1037–1042

Rousseau, D. M. (2009). A second's thoughts: Reflections on my tenure as *JOB* editor. *Journal of Organizational Behavior, 30*, 9–13.

Rousseau, D. M. (2009). Preface: A handbook for developing evidence-based practitioners, pp. xv–xxiv In E. A. Locke (Ed.), *Handbook of principles of organizational behavior: Indispensable knowledge for evidence-based management* (2nd ed.). Chichester, UK: John Wiley & Sons, Ltd.

Rousseau, D. M., & Fried, Y. (2001). Location, location, location: Contextualizing organizational behavior. *Journal of Organizational Behavior, 22*, 1–15.

Rousseau, D. M., Manning, J., & Denyer, D. (2008). Evidence in management and organizational science: Assembling the field's full weight of scientific knowledge through syntheses. *The Academy of Management Annals, 2*, 475–515.

Rousseau, D. M., & McCarthy, S. (2007). Educating managers from an evidence-based perspective. *Academy of Management Learning and Education, 6*, 84–101.

Ruona, W. E. A., & Gibson, S. K. (2004). The making of twenty-first-century HR: An analysis of the convergence of HRM, HRD, and OD. *Human Resource Management, 43*, 49–66.

Russell, C. J. (2001). A longitudinal study of top-level executive performance. *Journal of Applied Psychology, 86*, 560–573.

Russell, C. J. (2009. Establishing the usefulness of strategic management research: On inverted Lewinians and naked strategy scholars. In D. Ketchen & D. Bergh (Eds.), *Research Methods in Strategy and Management* (vol. 5, pp. 55–71). Bingley, UK: Emerald Group Publishing Limited.

Rynes, S. L. (2005). From the editors: Taking stock and looking ahead. *Academy of Management Journal, 48*, 9–15.

Rynes, S. L. (2007). Let's create a tipping point: What academics and practitioners can do, alone and together. *Academy of Management Journal, 50*, 987–1008.

Rynes, S. L., Bartunek, J. M., & Daft, R. L. (2001). Across the great divide: Knowledge creation and transfer between practitioners and academics. *Academy of Management Journal, 44*, 340–356.

Rynes, S. L., & Boudreau, J. B. (1986). College recruiting in large organizations: Practice, evaluation, and research implications. *Personnel Psychology, 39*, 729–757.

Rynes, S. L., & Brown, K. G. (2011). Where are we in the "long march to legitimacy?" Assessing scholarship in management learning and education. *Academy of Management Learning and Education, 10*, 561–582.

Rynes, S. L., Colbert, A. E., & Brown, K. G. (2002). HR professionals' beliefs about effective human resource practices: Correspondence between research and practice. *Human Resources Management, 41*, 149–174.

Rynes, S. L., Gerhart, B., & Parks, L. (2005). Personnel psychology: Performance evaluation and pay for performance. *Annual Review of Psychology, 56*, 571–600.

Rynes, S. L., Giluk, T. L., & Brown, K. G. (2007). The very separate worlds of academic and practitioner periodicals in human resource management: Implications for evidence-based management. *Academy of Management Journal, 50*, 1046–1054.

Rynes, S. L., McNatt, D. B., & Bretz, R. D. (1999). Academic research inside organizations: Inputs, processes, and outcomes. *Personnel Psychology, 52*, 869–898.

Rynes, S. L., Owens, S., & Trank, C. Q. (2008). "Be there or be in HR!" The trials and tribulations of human resource management in business schools. In V.G. Scarpello (Ed.), *The handbook of human resource management education: Promoting an effective and efficient curriculum* (pp. 345–360). Thousand Oaks, CA: Sage.

Rynes, S. L., & Trank, C. Q. (1997). Behavioral science in the business school curriculum: Teaching in a changing institutional environment. *Academy of Management Review, 24*, 808–824.

Saari, L. M., Johnston, T. R., McLaughlin, S. D., & Zimmerle, D. M. (1988). A survey of management training and education practices in United States companies. *Personnel Psychology, 41*, 731–743.

Sackett, P. R., Burris, L. R., & Callahan, C. (1989). Integrity testing for personnel selection: An update. *Personnel Psychology, 42*, 491–529.

Sackett, P. R., & Larson, J. R., Jr., (1990). Research strategies and tactics in industrial and organizational psychology. In: M. D. Dunnette and L. M. Hough (Eds.), *Handbook of industrial and organizational psychology* (Vol. 1, pp. 419–489). Palo Alto, CA: Consulting Psychologists Press.

Sackett, P. R., & Mullen, E. J. (1993). Beyond formal experimental design: Towards an expanded view of the training evaluation process. *Personnel Psychology, 46*, 613–627.

Schmidt, F. L., & Hunter, J. E. (1983). Individual differences in productivity: An empirical test of estimates derived from studies of selection procedure utility. *Journal of Applied Psychology, 68*, 407–414.

Schmidt, F. L., & Hunter, J. E. (1998). The validity and utility of selection methods in personnel psychology: Practical and theoretical implications of 85 years of research findings. *Psychological Bulletin, 124*, 262–274.

Schmidt, F. L., & Hunter, J. E. (2003). Select on intelligence. In E. A. Locke (Ed.), *The Blackwell handbook of principles of organizational behavior* (pp. 3–14). Oxford: Blackwell.

Schneider, B., Hanges, P. J., Smith, D. B., & Salvaggio, A. N. (2003). Which comes first? Employee attitudes or organizational financial and market performance? *Journal of Applied Psychology, 88*, 836–851.

Schneider, B., Smith, D. B., Taylor, S., & Fleenor, J. (1998). Personality and organizations: A test of the homogeneity of personality hypothesis. *Journal of Applied Psychology, 83*, 462–470.

Schön, D. A. (1995). *The reflective practitioner: How professionals think in action.* London: Ashgate Publishing.

Schwarz, G. M., Clegg, S., Cummings, T. G., Donaldson, L., & Miner, J. B. (2007). We see dead people? The state of organization science. *Journal of Management Inquiry, 16*, 300–317.

Senge, P. (1990). *The fifth discipline: The art and practice of the learning organization.* New York: Doubleday/Currency.

Shapiro, D. A. (2002). Renewing the scientist-practitioner model. *The Psychologist, 15*, 232–234.

Shapiro, D. L., Kirkman, B. L., & Courtney, H. G. (2007). Perceived causes and solutions of the translation gap in management. *Academy of Management Journal, 50*, 249–266.

Shen, L, & Dillard, J. P. (2007). The influence of behavioral inhibition/approach systems and message framing on the processing of persuasive health messages. *Communication Research, 34*, 433–467.

Shrivastava, P., & Mitroff, 1.1. 1984. Enhancing organizational research utilization: The role of decision makers' assumptions. *Academy of Management Review, 9*, 18–26.

Silzer, R., & Cober, R. (2008, April). *Practitioner needs survey 2008: Results overview.* Paper presented at the annual meeting of the Society of Industrial and Organizational Psychology, San Francisco, CA.

Singer, P. (2009). *The life you can save.* New York: Random House.

Slaughter, S., & Leslie, L. L. (1997). *Academic capitalism: Politics, policies, and the entrepreneurial university.* Baltimore, MD: Johns Hopkins.

Sommer, R. (2006). Dual dissemination: Writing for colleagues and the public. *American Psychologist, 61*, 955–958.

Stambaugh, J. E. & Trank, C. Q. (2010). Not so simple: Integrating new research into textbooks. *Academy of Management Learning and Education, 9*, 663–681.

Starbuck, W. H. (2006). *The production of knowledge: The challenge of social science research.* Oxford: Oxford University Press.

Steele, C. M. (1988). The psychology of self-affirmation: Sustaining the integrity of the self. In L. Berbowitz (Ed.), *Advances in Experimental Social Psychology* (Vol. 21, pp. 261–302). New York: Academic Press.

Stewart, T. A. (1998). *Intellectual capital: The new wealth of organizations.* New York: Broadway Books.

Sturdy, A. (2004). The adoption of management ideas and practices. *Management Learning, 35*, 155–179.

Sutton, R. I. (1991). Maintaining norms about expressed emotions: The case of bill collectors. *Administrative Science Quarterly, 36*, 245–268.

Sutton, R. I., & Rafaeli, A. (1988). Untangling the relationship between displayed emotions and organizational sales: The case of convenience stores. *Academy of Management Journal, 31*, 461–487.

Sutton, R. I., & Staw, B. M. (1995). What theory is not. *Administrative Science Quarterly, 40*, 371–384.

Swann, W. G., Jr., & Read, S. J. (1981). Self-verification processes: How we sustain our self-conceptions. *Journal of Experimental Social Psychology, 17*, 351–372.

Symon, G., & Clegg, C. W. (1991). Technology-led change: A study of the implementation of CADCAM. *Journal of Occupational Psychology, 64*, 273–290.

Tannenbaum, S.I. (2006). Applied performance measurement: Practical issues and challenges. In W. Bennett, Jr., C. E. Lance, & D. J. Woehr, D. J. (Eds.), *Criterion development and performance measurement: Past issues, current research, and future practice* (pp. 297–318). Mahwah, NJ: LEA Press.

Tetlock, P. E. (2000). Cognitive biases and organizational correctives: Do both disease and cure depend on the politics of the beholder? *Administrative Science Quarterly, 45*, 293–326.

Tippins, N. T. (2009). Internet alternatives to traditional proctored testing: Where are we now? *Industrial and Organizational Psychology: Perspectives on Science and Practice, 2*, 2–13.

Tobias, S. (1995). *Overcoming math anxiety.* New York: W. W. Norton.

Tolbert, P. S., & Zucker, L. G. (1983). Institutional sources of change in the formal structure of organizations: The diffusion of civil service reform, 1880–1935. *Administrative Science Quarterly, 28*, 22–39.

Tranfield, D., Denyer, D. & Smart, P. (2003). Towards a methodology for developing evidence-informed management knowledge by means of systematic review. *British Journal of Management, 14*, 207–222.

Trank, C. Q., & Rynes, S. L. (2003). Who moved our cheese? Reclaiming professionalism in business education. *Academy of Management Learning and Education, 2*, 189–205.

Trevor, C. O., & Nyberg, A. J. (2008). Keeping your headcount when all about you are losing theirs: Downsizing, voluntary turnover rates, and the moderating role of HR Practices, *Academy of Management Journal, 51*, 651–671.

Tushman, M., & Murmann, J. P. (1998). Organizational evolution: a metamorphosis model of convergence and reorientation. *Research in Organizational Behavior, 20*, 231–266.

Tushman, M., & O'Reilly, C., III. (2007). Research and relevance: Implications of Pasteur's quadrant for doctoral programs and faculty development. *Academy of Management Journal, 50*, 769–774.

Ulrich, D., Brockbank, W., Yeung, A. K., & Lake, D. G. (1995). Human resource competencies: An empirical assessment. *Human Resource Management, 34*, 473–495.

Van Aken, J. E. (2004). Management research based on the paradigm of the design sciences: The quest for field-tested and grounded technological rules. *Journal of Management Studies, 41*, 219–246.

Van de Ven, A. H. (2007). *Engaged scholarship: A guide for organizational and social research.* New York: Oxford University Press.

Van de Ven, A. H., & Johnson, P. E. (2006). Knowledge for theory and practice. *Academy of Management Review, 31*, 802–821.

Van de Ven, A. H., & Poole, M. S. (1995). Explaining development and change in organizations. *Academy of Management Review, 20*, 510–540.

Van Iddekinge, C. H., Ferris, G. R., Perrewe, P. L., Perryman, A. A., Blass, F. R., & Heetderks, T. D. (2009). Effects of selection and training on unit-level performance over time: A latent growth modeling approach. *Journal of Applied Psychology, 94*, 829–843.

Vermeulen, F. (2007). "I shall not remain insignificant": Adding a second loop to matter more. *Academy of Management Journal, 50*, 754–761.

Wageman, R. (1995). Interdependence and group effectiveness. *Administrative Science Quarterly, 40,* 145–180.

Wagner, J. A. III. (1994). Participation's effects on performance and satisfaction: A reconsideration of research evidence. *Academy of Management Review, 19,* 312–330.

Wagner, J. A. III. (2009. Use participation to share information and distribute knowledge. In E. A. Locke (Ed.), *Wiley handbook of principles of organizational behavior: Indispensible knowledge for evidence-based management* (2nd ed.).Chicester, UK: John Wiley & Sons.

Wagner, J. A., III., Rubin, P., & Callahan, T. J. (1988). Incentive payment and nonmanagerial productivity: An interrupted time series analysis of magnitude and trend. *Organizational Behavior & Human Decision Processes. 42,* 47–74.

Wall, T. D., & Wood, S. J. (2005). The romance of human resource management and business performance and the case for big science. *Human Relations, 58,* 429–462.

Walsh, J. P., Meyer, A., & Schoonhoven, C. (2006). A future for organization theory: Living in and living with changing organizations. *Organization Science, 17,* 657–671.

Walsh, J. P., Tushman, M. L., Kimberly, J. R., Starbuck, B., & Ashford, S. (2007). On the relationship between research and practice: Debates and reflection. *Journal of Management Inquiry, 16,* 128–154.

Weimer, M. (2006). *Enhancing scholarly work on teaching and learning: Professional literature that makes a difference.* San Francisco: Jossey-Bass/Wiley.

Welbourne, T. M. & Andrews, A.O. (1996). Predicting the performance of initial public offerings: Should human resource management be in the equation? *Academy of Management Journal, 39,* 891–919.

Wenger, E. (1999). *Communities of practice: Learning, meaning, and identity.* Cambridge: Cambridge University Press.

Whyte, G., & Latham, G. P. (1997). The futility of utility analysis revisited: When even an expert fails. *Personnel Psychology, 50,* 601–610.

Wright, P. M., & Haggerty, J. J. (2005). Missing variables in theories of strategic human resource management: Time, cause, and individuals. *Management Revue, 16,* 164–173.

Yaeger, T. F., Sorensen, P. F., Jr., & Bengtsson, U. (2005). Assessment of the state of appreciative inquiry: Past, present, and future. *Research in Organizational Change and Development, 15,* 297–319.

PART 4

Motivation, Job Attitudes and Affect, and Performance

Work Motivation: Theory, Practice, and Future Directions

Ruth Kanfer

Abstract

This chapter focuses on recent scientific advances and use-inspired research on motivation related to adult work. The chapter is divided into four sections. The first section reviews basic motivation constructs and processes, and the issues that delineate the scope and content of the field. The second section reports on research progress and the implications of new conceptualizations for understanding and predicting work behaviors and performance. The third section reviews findings on the major determinants of work motivation, organized into three broad categories: content (person variables), context (situation variables), and change (temporal variables). The fourth and final section identifies current gaps in our knowledge, practical challenges, and promising new research directions.

Key Words: Employee motivation, self-regulation, goals, implicit motives, self-efficacy, self-determination, motivational dynamics, motivational traits, trait-performance relations, work environment

Introduction

Work motivation is arguably one of the most vibrant areas in work and organizational psychology today. Since 1990 there has been astonishing progress on many topics that were largely undeveloped two decades ago (see Kanfer, 1990). The most important change in the field pertains to the way that dissimilar theories and research streams have coalesced around the goal construct to form a complex but viable "big picture" of motivation related to work. As the broad outlines of this picture continue to become clearer, more researchers are developing and testing formulations that integrate different portions of the motivation domain. Organizational scientists have also sought out and incorporated advances in allied fields of psychology, economics, communications, and sociology to help fill in remaining gaps in our understanding of non-conscious processes and the impact of multilevel, multifaceted social contexts on work motivation and behaviors. New research methodologies and analytic methods have been adopted that permit the study of motivation over time and the analysis of motivation as it is embedded in ongoing work relationships, teams, organizations, and the employee life course. Theories developed during the mid-twentieth century (that continued to dominate the scene in the 1980s) have been transformed into formulations that provide a better fit to the scientific questions and organizational concerns salient in the early twenty-first century. Prior questions about the applicability of work motivation findings to real-world problems have been replaced by questions about work motivation driven by real-world problems in specific contexts. New views of the self, affect, and the context in which work motivation operates have also spurred the development of new research programs, many of which have adopted a person-centered perspective. The result of this activity is a field that looks very little like the field in the 1980s. Although our understanding of work motivation remains far from complete, the field is clearly on the move.

Overview

The purpose of this chapter is to review advances and emerging trends in work motivation over the past few decades, and to identify promising topics for future work. Reviews that provide greater detail on earlier developments in the field are available from a number of sources. Historically oriented reviews of the field through the latter part of the twentieth century are provided by Ambrose and Kulik (1999), Campbell and Pritchard (1976), Kanfer (1990, 1992), Kanfer, Chen, and Pritchard (2008), Katzell and Thompson (1990), Latham (2007), Latham and Pinder (2005), Mitchell and Daniels (2003), and Pinder (2008). In addition, a number of reviews organized around specific theoretical perspectives are available, including qualitative reviews and meta-analyses on goal setting (Austin & Klein, 1996; Locke, Shaw, Saari, & Latham, 1981), self-regulation (Lord, Diefendorff, Schmidt, & Hall, 2010), goal orientation (Payne, Youngcourt, & Beaubien, 2007), expectancy-value and decision theories (Klein, Austin, & Cooper, 2008; Mitchell, 1974, 1982), organizational justice (Colquitt, Conlon, Wesson, Porter, & Ng, 2001; Folger & Cropanzano, 1998), self-determination theory (Gagne & Deci, 2005), and work design (Fried & Ferris, 1987; Humphrey, Nahrgang, & Morgeson, 2007; Parker & Ohly, 2008). Reviews are also available on the role of motivation in specific situations and settings, including, for example, in teams (Chen & Gogus, 2008; Chen & Kanfer, 2006; Kozlowski & Ilgen, 2006; Salas, Cooke, & Rosen, 2008), leadership (Zaccaro, Ely, & Nelson, 2008), job search (Kanfer, Wanberg, & Kantrowitz, 2001), workforce aging (Kanfer, 2009; Shultz & Adams, 2007), and in learning and skill training (Beier & Kanfer, 2009; Colquitt, LePine, & Noe, 2000). Erez (2008) provides a review of social-cultural influences on work motivation and Gelfand, Erez, and Aycan (2007) provide a review of work motivation across cultures.

The chapter is organized into four sections. The first section highlights foundational issues and a work motivation definition that delineates the broad scope and content of the field. The second section describes scientific progress on basic motivational processes, and their relationships to outcomes of individual and organizational interest (e.g., behavior, sense of competency, job performance). The third section describes recent findings on major determinants of work motivation, organized into three broad categories: content (person variables), context (situation variables), and change (temporal variables). The fourth section identifies some of the current gaps in our knowledge, and promising new research directions for the study of work motivation over the next few decades.

Foundations for Theory and Research in Work Motivation

In the narrow sense, the study of work motivation examines the psychological processes and mechanisms by which individuals form and commit to work-related goals, formulate plans for goal accomplishment, allocate personal and social resources across a range of possible actions, and regulate thoughts, behaviors, and affect for the purpose of goal attainment. Although there has been a tendency to view work motivation as a cognitive phenomena, modern research makes it clear that motivational processes are not just cognitive; they are supported by and involve biological processes, unconscious perceptions, sensations, affect, and cognitions.

More broadly, the study of work motivation also includes theory and research on the person and situation factors that influence motivation processes, and the pathways by which they do so. Consistent with the Latin root of the word *motivation*, meaning "to move," work motivation researchers and scientists seek to understand the internal and external forces that facilitate or hinder behavior change. Work motivation is also a topic of great practical importance, and includes work on the consequences of motivation for employees and the organizations in which they work. Work motivation research focuses on multiple dimensions of behavior change, including the direction, intensity, and persistence of workplace actions and job performance within the broader, continuing stream of experiences that characterize the person in relation to his or her work (Kanfer, 1990).

Pinder (1998) provides an encompassing definition of work motivation as "a set of energetic forces that originate both within as well as beyond an individual's being, to initiate work-related behavior and to determine its form, direction, intensity, and duration" (p. 11). Consistent with definitions of motivation found in many areas of psychology, definitions of work motivation emphasize the following points:

1. Motivation is not directly observed and must be inferred.

Because motivation cannot be directly assessed, changes in motivation are inferred by associated changes in behavior, learning, or task/job performance. The use of performance measures to index motivation, however, is often problematic since performance is not univocally determined by motivation, but is also determined by employee knowledge and skills and/or the availability (or lack) of external resources (e.g., equipment) necessary for successful performance. The use of performance ratings or scores to index motivation importantly depends on the extent to which changes in motivation are directly reflected in changes in performance.

In general, performance measures to index motivation are appropriate in contexts where task performance is effort-sensitive—that is, changes in effort produce proportional changes in performance. However, when changes in motivation affect performance through effects on cognitions, behavior, or affect, performance indices of motivation are less appropriate. In these situations, the more appropriate criteria are those changes in behavior, cognitions, and/or affect that are the direct consequence of a change in motivation. Thus, researchers often use multiple measures of behavior (e.g., time spent on a task) as well as performance score to index a change in motivation. In the job search literature, for example, motivation may be assessed by time spent on job search activities (persistence), the type of job search activities performed (direction), and self-reports of effort expended on job search (intensity). In studies of motivation during training, motivation is often assessed not just in terms of performance but also in terms of self-report measures that assess the individual's goal commitment and self-efficacy, and/or behavioral measures of attendance, task persistence, and self-regulatory activities.

2. Outcomes of motivation include changes in the initiation, direction, intensity, modulation, or persistence of action.

The type of measure used to assess motivation depends upon the question of interest. When the question is about how motives or contexts "turn on" or instigate work-related behaviors, researchers may use initiation measures. The impact of achievement motives on innovative performance, for example, may be evaluated by assessing the frequency with which an employee asks questions or seeks information. Choice and intention measures are often used to assess the direction of action. Intensity indices capture the proportion of an individual's personal resources allocated to a goal or task. Intensity measures often assess subjective or subjective task effort, energy, time spent on the task, or other personal

resources directed to task performance. Persistence measures represent assessments of the duration of time that an individual allocates personal resources to a particular task or action. As such, persistence integrates direction and the temporal dimension of intensity.

3. Motivation emerges as a consequence of the person-in-context; motivation is not univocally or consistently determined by a single personal attribute or feature of the environment.

As Pinder's (1998) definition indicates, the forces that influence motivation occur both within as well as externally to the individual. That is, although the psychological processes involved in work motivation occur internally, motivation is not a stable characteristic of the person across all situations. Individuals who show high levels of motivation for action in one situation (e.g., reading a novel), may show low levels of motivation for action in another situation (e.g., reading a textbook). The purpose of action and the context in which it occurs must always be taken into account.

Motivation is also not simply a function of the environment. Even in extremely "strong" situations (e.g., the battlefield), individual differences in personal attributes, such as tolerance for ambiguity, contribute to motivation and performance. In the moderate or weak situations that characterize most workplaces, motivation depends on individual propensities and preferences as well as situational affordances and constraints. As Lewin (1938) suggested over a half century ago, "Motivation can only be properly analyzed by taking into account characteristics of the person in the context of dynamic social, physical, and psychological environments that facilitate and constrain person tendencies for action."

4. Motivation is always in flux.

Motivation is a state that changes constantly. Changes in motivation, with associated changes in beliefs, behaviors, and affect, occur over different time cycles (Lord et al., 2010) and are often measured on different timescales, depending on the question of interest (Kanfer et al., 2008). Lord et al. (2010) propose four major cycle levels for motivational phenomena that correspond to the measurement of motivation processes and outcomes on different timescales. Examples of the different cycles, their associated measurement timescales, the dominant motivational foci, and the dominant methods used at different levels are shown in Figure 14.1.

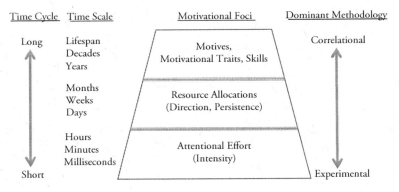

Figure 14.1 Timescales/Orders of Magnitude, Motivation Targets, and Methods in Work Motivation Research

As shown in Figure 14.1, intraindividual cognitive and affective processes involved in motivation are typically fast and are assessed in terms of milliseconds or minutes. Studies at this level of analysis are typically conducted in controlled, laboratory conditions and tend to focus on differences in motivational intensity toward a target. In contrast, studies of work motivation over very long time frames, such as years or decades, capture information about the influence of the broader social and work culture and relatively stable person traits and tendencies on motivation and the trajectories of work behaviors and performance over the life course.

Most work motivation researchers and professionals focus on motivation changes that occur during relatively short timescales (e.g., hours, days, weeks). Analyses at this level capture the impact of proximal personal influences (e.g., work goals) and environmental conditions (e.g., job autonomy) on motivation, behavior, and job performance. Studies at this level are both logistically feasible and practically useful for examining the effects of specific organizational interventions, such as goal setting, on motivation and work performance.

Because motivational processes take place on different cycles or timescales, multilevel models are also needed to examine how factors and processes that operate at one level may influence another level. Changes in the organizational culture over the course of a year, for example, are likely to affect the value that is placed on different aspects of employee performance, which in turn affect the individual's work and task goal choices. Cross-level effects between motivational processes that operate on different timescales may be indirect, such as when changes in organizational culture instigate different motives and promote the adoption of worker goals that facilitate learning and higher

levels of competence. Cross-level effects may also be moderated by short cycle motivation processes, such as when employees who are highly anxious develop a response of adopting performance goals (rather than learning goals) that prompt the use of less effective learning strategies. Multilevel studies of work motivation offer an exciting opportunity for systematizing knowledge about the dynamics of multi-scale motivation processes and their effects on work behavior and job attitudes.

Work motivation is a unique branch of motivational science.

Work motivation is not just a subordinate section of the larger field of motivational science. In other branches of human motivation, such as achievement motivation, research is often organized and accumulated around a single theoretical perspective, and the context for research is often driven by the target theoretical issue. In work motivation, however, research is also driven by the underlying practical concern for how motivation influences organizationally relevant work behaviors, such as job performance. Over the past few decades, changes in the conceptualization of the criterion space have spurred new theories of work motivation. In contrast to previous formulations that focused on motivational influences on technical performance, such as speed and quality of production, the changing nature of work has focused more attention on the relationship between motivation and non-technical or contextual dimensions of job performance, including, for example, the quality of an employee's relationships with coworkers and clients, organizational citizenship behaviors, and adaptability to changes in job demands, organizational structure, and the external marketplace. The shift in the dimensions of performance to be predicted has, in turn, encouraged the development of new perspectives that address motivational effects on these outcomes. On the negative side, there has been a sharp increase in the number of criterion-specific work motivation "mini-theories." On the positive side, the enlarged criterion space has stimulated connections with other fields, such as affective science, personality psychology, and even mental health.

Is there more to work motivation than we can tell?

A final foundational issue pertains to the growing interest in implicit motives and non-conscious processes as they influence work motivation and behavior. The notion of non-conscious influences on motivation is certainly not new to psychology, but has received little research attention in work motivation until recently. Over the past few decades, however, research on implicit motives and non-conscious processes in other areas of psychology has begun to influence mainstream work motivation theory and research (see, e.g., James, 1998; Johnson & Steinman, 2009; Kehr, 2004; Latham, Stajkovic, & Locke, 2010; Lord et al., 2010). The impetus for renewed attention to non-conscious motives and processes stems from advances that show: (a) self-report measures of individual differences in non-ability traits and action preferences do not capture important personal influences on motivation, and (b) not all motivation processes are cognitively mediated. In accord with these advances, recent progress in I/O psychology appears in two areas: (a) the assessment of individual differences in implicit motives, and (b) theory building on the relationship between implicit motives and non-conscious processes and goal selection and pursuit.

IMPLICIT MOTIVES

In contrast to explicit motives, implicit motives are not accessible for conscious self-report. Individual differences in explicit motives, such as extraversion, are typically assessed using self-report measures in which persons report their behavioral tendencies and outcome preferences. Such self-reports are cognitively mediated in that the individual reports what she thinks best describes her. In contrast, implicit motives are not accessible through direct self-report since these motives do not reflect cognitively mediated action tendencies, but rather affectively charged motivators that are activated by intrinsic outcomes associated with action. In contrast to explicit motives, whose impact is typically on cognitively mediated behaviors, implicit

motives are further posited to influence spontaneous, rather than cognitively mediated, behaviors (Michalak, Puschel, Joormann, & Schulte, 2006). Individuals who are high in implicit power motive, for example, would be expected to demonstrate more spontaneous power-oriented behaviors during the performance of tasks that afford the opportunity for acquiring influence over others than individuals low in implicit motive for power.

Modern conceptions of implicit motives build upon arguments made by McClelland (1987) that the low correlation often obtained between direct (self-report) and indirect (projective; e.g., TAT) measures of individual differences in the achievement motive reflected the difference between implicit and explicit motives for achievement, rather than measurement error. McClelland (1987) further proposed three implicit motives: achievement, affiliation, and power, and argued that each of these motives were distinct from explicit motives of the same or similar names. After years of controversy, evidence to support McClelland's (1987) notions regarding differences between implicit and explicit motives related to achievement was provided in a meta-analytic review by Spangler (1992).

Nonetheless, measurement problems continue to thwart progress in the study of implicit motives. Well-founded criticisms of projective and quasi-projective measures, such as the Thematic Apperception Test (TAT), hampered research for decades. In the past 15 years or so, however, new theoretical approaches have been employed to develop measures of non-conscious motives through perceptual and cognitive processing (see e.g., Greenwald, McGhee, & Schwartz, 1998; James & Rentsch, 2004; Schultheiss & Pang, 2007). One of the most promising new methods for assessing implicit motive strength builds upon Conditional Reasoning Theory (CRT; James, 1998). In CRT measures, individuals read a series of constructed scenarios and select a response based on conditional reasoning, rather than based on affective reactions to a stimuli. Initial evidence for the validity of these measures and the basic tenets of CRT are provided by a series of studies by James and his colleagues (Frost, Ko, & James, 2007; James et al., 2005) that show negligible correlations between CRT and explicit measures, and significant predictive validity of CRT measures for achievement, aggressive, and dominant behaviors in organized settings. Further evidence on the validity of these implicit motive measures will significantly speed progress in implicit motivation.

NON-CONSCIOUS PROCESSES

A second, complimentary stream of research focuses on the delineation of a non-conscious motivation *system* and its relationship to explicit goal choice and goal striving. Most evidence for the existence of non-conscious motivational system comes from research findings in cognitive neuroscience and social psychology (see Ferguson, Hassin, & Bargh, 2008). Findings in these areas show the influence of goals on pre-conscious attentional processes in sensory systems, the influence of subliminal priming on non-conscious motivational processing and action, and the impact of non-conscious neurological processes in explicit goal choice and self-regulation (see Bargh, Gollwitzer, & Oettingen, 2010; Ruud & Aarts, 2010). Recent work by Lord and his colleagues (Johnson, Lord, Rosen, & Chang, 2007; Johnson, Tolentino, Rodopman, & Cho, 2010; Lord & Moon, 2006) and others (e.g., Stajkovic, Locke, & Blair, 2006) have extended this work into the organizational domain, and have shown that fast, non-conscious, automatic cognitive processes also affect explicit motivational processes relevant in the work setting (see Diefendorff & Lord, 2008).

Another line of inquiry focuses on the relationship between implicit and explicit motivational processes (e.g., Brunstein & Maier, 2005; Schultheiss & Brunstein, 2001). Lord et al. (2010) have proposed a dynamic model in which non-conscious motives and processes may exert influence at multiple levels in motivational processing, including goal choice as well as self-regulation. Kehr (2004) has proposed that implicit motives interfere with explicit motivation when the implicit motive fails to support explicit goals. According to Kehr (2004), a basic purpose for the instigation of goal striving, or self-regulatory processes, is to prevent contrary implicit motive tendencies from diverting critical resources away from goal accomplishment.

Rapid progress is being made in elucidating the influence of implicit motives and non-conscious processes on explicit motivation and behavior (see Johnson et al., 2010; Ruud & Aarts, 2010). The development of valid and reliable measures of implicit motives remains problematic, but it is clear that new approaches based on cognitive and neuroscience advances are overcoming problems that were for many decades insurmountable. At the same time, work motivation researchers have begun to study how implicit motives and non-conscious processes impact goal choice, self-regulation, and behavior. Continued progress in this area can be expected to cause a sea-change in how work motivation is conceptualized and studied over the next few decades.

Goal Choice and Goal Pursuit

The term *motivation* is often used in work and organizational psychology to encompass all the processes by which individuals formulate and execute established goals. In motivational science, however, a distinction is often made between the processes involved in goal choice and goal commitment, and the processes involved in goal pursuit. Among some researchers, motivation refers to the choice portion of the system, while cognitive, affective, and self-regulatory processes in goal pursuit are regarded as volition. Consistent with the common use of the term motivation, I distinguish the two, related motivational subsystems in terms of goal choice and goal striving (or pursuit) and reserve the term *motivation* to reference both goal choice and goal striving processes.

Over the past few decades, motivational scientists have come to a consensus on the organization of explicit (or conscious) motivation processes. This consensus has been achieved by using goals as the coordinating construct for disparate streams of research on goal choice and goal striving. Although some theories remain better suited to understanding and predicting goal choice and other theories to understanding and predicting goal striving, there has been a sharp rise in the number of studies that simultaneously examine elements of both systems (e.g., Kozlowski & Bell, 2006).

To put recent developments in perspective, I first provide a brief review of late twentieth century progress on goals, goal choice, goal setting, and goal striving. Following this review, I describe recent work on goal orientation and related perspectives.

Goals

Goals are the mental representations of outcome states that an individual seeks to realize. In the workplace, goals may refer to learning outcomes (e.g., learn to install a pipe), performance outcomes (e.g., design a web page), or consequence outcomes (e.g., obtain a registered nursing degree). Goals direct attention and help to organize and sustain the individual's effort and actions for the purpose of goal accomplishment.

Because goals direct behavior toward the accomplishment of desired outcomes, including job performance, work motivation researchers have studied two goal-related issues in depth: goal selection (the goal that an individual adopts) and goal commitment (the extent to which the individual binds him- or herself to goal accomplishment). In these areas, research has focused on a number of related questions, including the role of personal and situational variables on goal adoption (e.g., Barrick, Mount, & Strauss, 1993; see Hollenbeck & Klein, 1987), how individuals allocate attention and effort across multiple goals (DeShon, Kozlowski, Schmidt, Milner, & Wiechmann, 2004; see Mitchell, Harmon, Lee, & Lee, 2008), and how and why individuals revise their goals (Schmidt & DeShon, 2007; Tolli & Schmidt, 2008).

Research in cognitive and personality-social psychology indicates that goals are rarely developed in isolation. Rather, goals are situated in a web of complex, interrelated goal hierarchies. Goals at the top of the hierarchy represent outcomes that occur as a consequence of accomplishing goals at lower levels in the hierarchy. Earning a medical degree, for example, requires accomplishment of lower order goals distributed over time, such as passing different courses required for the degree. Higher level goals are typically distal, complex, and may be ill-defined with respect to the lower order goals required for higher order goal accomplishment. The adoption of a higher order consequence goal, such as attaining a medical degree, sets into motion an integrated stream of cognitive and motivational processes that direct attention and action toward interim or lower order goal accomplishments. Problems encountered in the execution of lower order goals may also redirect attention to the higher order goal, and may contribute to outcome goal revision or abandonment.

Goals are also distinguished in terms of their attributes and/or focus. Goals may be specific or vague, easy or difficult, simple or complex, behavioral, cognitive, or affective, proximal or distal, or adopted for different reasons (e.g., to demonstrate competence or avoid appearing incompetent). Different theories of work motivation, such as Locke's (1976) task goal theory and VandeWalle's (1997) goal orientation formulation, emphasize different aspects of the articulated goal that, in turn, have different implications for motivational processing and performance.

GOAL CHOICE

Cognitive theories of motivation, such as Fishbein and Ajzen's (1975) theory of reasoned action, Triandis's (1980) theory of interpersonal behavior, and Vroom's (1964) expectancy-value formulation (VIE), are frequently used to predict behavior

intentions, goal choice, and motivational force for goal accomplishment, respectively. Although these and related models differ in a number of ways, such as how the criterion is operationalized, the role of affect, and the way that social influences are represented, each model has its roots in the family of expectancy-value models developed first in economics and subsequently adopted in psychology during the mid-1900s.

Expectancy value formulations make several strong assumptions. These models assume that individuals are rational decision makers who choose among perceived courses of action by applying the hedonic principle of maximizing pleasure and minimizing pain. As rational decision makers, an individual's goal choice or behavior intention decision is posited to reflect the outcome of an internal, cognitive analysis regarding the relative costs and benefits associated with different choice options. For example, according to Vroom's (1964) VIE theory, individuals choose among different possible work goals based on their subjective perceptions about: (a) whether the goal can be accomplished with the effort and other personal resources available to the individual (e.g., can I accomplish the performance goal?; expectancy), (b) whether goal accomplishment will bring about the target outcome (e.g., the instrumentality of achieving the performance goal for obtaining a pay raise; instrumentality), and (c) the perceived valence of the performance outcome (e.g., the attractiveness of a pay raise, the unattractiveness of feeling fatigued as a result of sustained mental effort; valence).

The introduction of Vroom's expectancy-value formulation into the I/O literature in the mid-1960s stimulated decades of empirical research on theoretical and methodological aspects of expectancy-value formulations. Excellent reviews of the empirical evidence on the predictive validity of expectancy value theories and methodological issues are provided by Mitchell (1974, 1980) and Sheppard, Hartwick, and Warshaw (1988). Overall, empirical findings on expectancy value formulations indicate that these theories are most effective for predicting choice among mutually incompatible courses of action, such as which of several job offers to accept.

As Mitchell (1974, 1980) indicates, VIE and related models suffer from both conceptual and methodological problems. Some of the biggest problems with theory and research in expectancy-value research pertain to the episodic nature of the theories, the use of between-subject designs to test a within-subject formulation, and the inability of the theories to account for motivation processes that occur in the gap between intention and behavior. Although tests using within-subject designs show improved predictive validity for behavior and task performance, expectancy-value formulations remain more useful for predicting discrete choice than performance streams. An even broader criticism of expectancy-value theories involves the assumption that individuals are rational decision makers. There is substantial evidence in allied fields which shows that individuals do not choose goals after performing a full rational analysis of options or solely on the basis of maximizing positive outcomes. Image theory (Beach & Mitchell, 1987) addresses this and other issues using a match-type model in which individuals are proposed to make decisions based on the compatibility match between images related to goals and strategy with self-concept. Although there has been some empirical support for image theory, this formulation is not often used in work motivation research.

Later expectancy value formulations by Naylor, Pritchard, and Ilgen (1980) and Kanfer and Ackerman (1989) incorporated advances from cognitive psychology. Extending earlier expectancy value models, Naylor et al. (1980) and Kanfer and Ackerman (1989) portrayed personal resources as multidimensional, including not only attentional effort and time, but potentially other personal resources such as social capital. In addition, these formulations conceptualized choice as a personal resource allocation process across a range of activities, including self-regulatory processes and non-task activities. The conceptualization of choice as a continuous resource allocation process that occurs as a function of personal attributes, task demands, and self-regulatory and non-task activities improved the viability of these models for predicting ongoing behavior and skill acquisition (see Kanfer & Ackerman, 1989).

Despite the many criticisms of classic expectancy value formulations, modified formulations remain popular. Social psychological models, such as Ajzen's (1991) theory of planned behavior, that take into explicit account the social context in which behavioral intentions are formed, continue to attract research attention, particularly in the prediction of discrete behaviors, such as attendance and turnover (see Armitage & Conner, 2001; Fishbein & Ajzen, 2010). Resource allocation models also continue to be used in studies investigating multiple goals, goal revision processes, self-regulatory activities, and

performance over time in the context of skill acquisition and teams (see Kanfer, Ackerman, Murtha, Dugdale, & Nelson, 1994; Lam, DeRue, Karam, & Hollenbeck, 2011; Porter, Webb, & Gogus, 2010). Using the Naylor et al. (1980) formulation, Pritchard and his colleagues have also shown the efficacy of resource allocation models in the development of programs to enhance work motivation and performance in organizational settings (see Pritchard, Harrell, DiazGranados, & Guzman, 2008).

GOAL SETTING

As criticisms of expectancy-value formulations in I/O psychology and related fields mounted during the 1970s, work motivation researchers turned their attention to goal setting. Consistent with other cognitive formulations, Locke (1968) proposed that goals served as the immediate regulators of action, and that difficult, specific goals led to higher levels of performance than easy, non-specific goals. Goal setting research findings reviewed by Locke et al. (1981) provided strong empirical support for the beneficial influence of goal setting on task performance, particularly with respect to the setting of difficult and specific goals. Locke et al. (1981) proposed that goals influenced performance by: (a) directing attention and action, (b) mobilizing effort, (c) prolonging goal-directed effort over time, and (d) motivating the individual to develop effective strategies for goal attainment.

Goal-setting theory and research flourished during the late twentieth century, and goal setting rapidly eclipsed expectancy value as the dominant work motivation paradigm in the field. A large number of empirical studies provided general support for each of the four proposed mechanisms by which goals influenced performance, and goal-setting theory quickly expanded to incorporate self-regulation constructs and processes in the explanation of how goals influenced task performance (Locke & Latham, 1990).

As goal-setting theory and research progressed, attention began to focus on potential boundary conditions associated with the beneficial effects of goal setting on performance. The first issue pertained to observed differences between the differential influence of assigned versus self-set goals (see Locke & Schweiger, 1979). In most work settings, employees are assigned task goals. In these instances, the issue is not predicting the direction of action, but rather what factors predict the employee's willingness to adopt the assigned goal and the employee's commitment or intensity of personal resource allocation to the goal. Findings by Latham, Erez, and Locke (1988) showed the criticality of the employee's participation in the goal-setting process, even if only minimally, when supervisors employed a "sell" rather than "tell" procedure, for goal setting to exert a positive effect on performance. The findings on the effects of psychological participation in goal setting, in turn, spurred a new stream of theory and research on goal commitment.

A second condition under which goal setting might be less effective pertains to the complexity of the task. Review findings by Wood, Mento, and Locke (1987) showed that goal setting was more effective in enhancing motivation and performance when used with simple tasks than with complex tasks. Using a complex air traffic simulation task, Kanfer and Ackerman (1989) showed that the impact of performance goal setting on performance might be beneficial or detrimental depending on the attentional demands of the task, the individual's cognitive abilities, and the self-regulatory activities undertaken as a result of goal setting. In accord with predictions, they found that among individuals with lower levels of cognitive abilities, the provision of performance goal assignments during the early (cognitively demanding) phase of skill learning was detrimental to performance, but that goal assignments made later in skill acquisition (when the task was cognitively less demanding) had a beneficial effect on performance.

The differential impact of goal setting on performance as a function of individual differences in cognitive abilities, task demands, and self-regulatory activities focused attention on the characteristics of goals that might divert attentional resources and hinder task performance. Kanfer and Ackerman (1989) argued that performance goals implemented early in training diverted critical attentional resources needed for performance toward the management of negative emotions associated with inability to accomplish the goal. This notion was supported in subsequent studies by Latham and his colleagues (Latham & Brown, 2006; Seijts & Latham, 2005; Winters & Latham, 1996), who showed that the provision of learning goals (that reduced rather than exacerbated concern about performance accomplishment) in complex task performance exerted a greater beneficial effect on performance than performance goals. These findings are also consistent with goal orientation theory and research that shows that the purpose of action (embedded in this paradigm as goal type) exerts a motivational influence on performance through its effects on the direction of resource allocations during action.

GOAL STRIVING

Goal choice sets the stage for action, but when intentions cannot be readily accomplished, individuals activate self-regulatory processes to support goal-directed action. Goal striving refers to the self-regulatory processes and actions by which individuals support goal intentions over time and/or in the face of personal or environmental obstacles to goal accomplishment.

Theory and research on self-regulation processes have their modern origins in the expansion of behavioral models during the 1960s and 1970s (Bandura, 1969, 1973; Kanfer & Phillips, 1969; Mischel, 1968; Mischel & Ebbesen, 1970). Social learning, cognitive-behavioral, and social-cognitive models of action all emphasized the self-regulatory processes by which individuals exercise control over their behavior, affect, and cognitions for purposes of goal attainment. Self-control is a form of self-regulation in which the individual seeks to attain a goal that is not supported by prevailing environmental contingencies, such as when an employee seeks to write a report while coworkers are holding a party, or when an employee's goal for completing a project requires that he or she work late into the night despite growing fatigue. Meta-cognition, defined by Flavell (1979) as the meta-cognitive knowledge and experiences used to manage cognitions, affect, and behavior strategies in goal-directed learning, represents another subset of the broader domain of self-regulation, often studied in educational psychology.

In work and organizational psychology, conscious self-regulation of action is typically not required when goals can be readily accomplished, or involve habitual or highly routinized behaviors, such as typing a letter. However, when goal accomplishment requires planning (studying for a test), coordination of actions (making a presentation), mid-course adjustments in strategy (e.g., winning a race), or resisting environmental presses that run counter to goal accomplishment (working instead of going out with friends), self-regulatory processes facilitate sustained motivation and performance. In the modern workplace, where work often takes place in non-work contexts (e.g., home), involves self-management of emotions in dealing with clients and coworkers, and is directed toward the accomplishment of complex goals over time, effective self-regulation has become an important feature of performance.

Investigation of self-regulatory processes during the mid-twentieth century delineated three key subprocesses: self-monitoring, self-evaluations, and self-reactions. Self-monitoring refers to the individual's attention to the outcomes of one's actions related to the goal. Self-monitoring is necessary for self-evaluation and self-reactions, though what the individual monitors may or may not be relevant for goal attainment. Self-evaluations refer to cognitive processes that determine goal progress. Self-evaluation processes serve both an informational and motivational function, providing information about whether the current action strategy must be adjusted for goal attainment and whether personal resource allocations are sufficient. Self-reactions, the most well-known of which is self-efficacy, pertain to the individual's integrated cognitive-affective judgment of confidence regarding the likelihood of goal attainment.

Broad interest in self-regulation among organizational scientists during the late twentieth century also spurred the development of many research programs on the influence of different self-regulation components, such as self-monitoring and self-efficacy judgments. In 1983, Ashford and Cummings proposed a theory of feedback seeking based on the notion that feedback seeking from others was a primary means by which employees self-monitor their performance. Consistent with self-regulation approaches, Ashford and Cummings (1983) showed that individuals who did not seek feedback from others (for fear of obtaining negative feedback) developed less accurate perceptions of performance than individuals who used active feedback-seeking strategies. From a motivational perspective, the Ashford and Cummings (1983) findings suggest that problems in goal striving may begin early in the self-regulatory sequence if individuals do not accurately monitor their performance.

Interest in self-regulation and goal striving among work motivation researchers also grew in response to findings that showed that goals and behavioral intentions were often only weakly associated with performance, particularly when performance was difficult or occurred over a protracted time period. Early studies on the role of self-regulation in work motivation and performance were conducted by Latham and his colleagues (Frayne & Latham, 1987; Latham & Frayne, 1989) in the context of goal-setting research. Latham and Frayne (1989) examined the effectiveness of self-regulatory training as an adjunct to goal setting in a field study designed to increase attendance among employees with chronic histories of absenteeism. They found that employees who participated in self-regulatory

skills training showed subsequently higher levels of job attendance than employees who did not receive self-management training. Subsequent research by Gist, Bavetta, and Stevens (1990) compared the relative efficacy of goal setting alone and goal setting plus self-management training on the transfer of training in a salary negotiation task. Gist et al. (1990) found that individuals in the goal setting plus self-management training condition showed greater transfer of training and overall performance than individuals in the goal setting–alone condition. The theoretical integration of goal setting and self-regulation formulations during the late 1980s (see Locke & Latham, 1990) led to numerous studies investigating the impact of self-efficacy on goal choice, commitment, and performance.

Most modern motivation theories accord self-efficacy judgments a major causal role in determining work motivation and performance. Self-efficacy judgments, though powerful predictors of action in novel contexts or early skill acquisition, have also been shown to exert weaker causal influence on motivation and performance in the context of skill acquisition (e.g., Heggestad & Kanfer, 2005; Mitchell, Hopper, Daniels, George-Falvy, & James, 1994; see Kanfer, 1993). One recent controversy about the relationship between self-efficacy judgments and performance further suggests that our understanding about the role that self-efficacy plays at different points in the motivation system may be incomplete. In essence, the argument pertains to the relationship between self-efficacy judgments and performance. Although many studies show that self-efficacy judgments are positively related to motivation and performance (see Bandura & Locke, 2003), several studies have been reported that show a negative, rather than positive relationship between self-efficacy and performance (Vancouver, Thompson, Tischner, & Putka, 2002; Vancouver, Thompson, & Williams, 2001; Yeo & Neal, 2006). Vancouver has argued that these findings are consistent with cybernetic models of self-regulation that posit a negative (not positive) relationship between self-efficacy and personal resource allocations when performance meets or exceeds the goal, in much the same way that a thermostat turns off the heater when the desired temperature is reached. Vancouver, More, and Yoder (2008) have recently proposed a multiple goal-process explanation for reconciliation of the discrepant findings. Schmidt and Deshon (2009, 2010) provide strong empirical evidence for explanations that focus on the conditions in which the relationship is examined, including prior task success and task ambiguity. Although the controversy continues, it appears that the discrepancies obtained in the sign of the self-efficacy–performance relationship reflect the influence of important, understudied questions related to the dynamics between task conditions, the purpose of action, and goal revision over time.

Purposive Approaches to Motivation

Over the past 15 years or so, work motivation researchers have concentrated on the motivational and performance consequences of an individual's purpose or reason for goal accomplishment. Whereas prior goal-setting research focused largely on the impact of goal attributes such as difficulty or specificity, purposive approaches focus on the mental orientation that accompanies the formulation and pursuit of difficult, specific goals. In this section, I describe several streams of research in this developing paradigm. First, I describe two conceptualizations that distinguish and connect the explicit goal-choice and goal-striving motivation subsystems: namely, Gollwitzer's (Gollwitzer, 1990; Gollwitzer & Kinney, 1989) mind-set theory and Meyer, Becker, and Vandenberghe's (2004) integrative model of employment commitment and motivation. Next, I discuss theory and research in intrinsic motivation. Finally, I review theory and research on the impact of goal orientation on motivation processes and performance.

PURPOSE AND THE RELATIONSHIP BETWEEN GOAL CHOICE AND GOAL STRIVING

According to Gollwitzer (1990, 2003), goal choice and goal striving involve different mind-sets, or motivational orientations. Individuals engaged in goal choice are proposed to employ a deliberative mind-set that emphasizes seeking accurate, unbiased information and using that information to perform a cognitive appraisal of goal options. Following goal choice, however, Gollwitzer argued there is a useful change in mind-set from deliberative to implemental. He proposed that during the planning and execution phases of goal-directed action (i.e., goal striving) individuals adopt an implementation mind-set, characterized by selective attention to information that supports the desirability of the chosen goal.

Findings from a series of studies by Gollwitzer (Gollwitzer & Kinney, 1989; Taylor & Gollwitzer, 1995) and others (e.g., Armor & Taylor, 2003; Webb & Sheeran, 2008) provide empirical support for the difference between motivational orientations held during goal choice and goal striving. These studies show that individuals who hold a deliberative mind-set are more attentive to negative goal-related information than individuals who hold an implemental mind-set. Further, individuals who hold an implemental mind-set report stronger illusions of control, increased self-efficacy, and more optimistic outcome expectations about goal accomplishment than individuals who hold a deliberative mind-set.

Gollwitzer's mind-set theory underscores the long-standing distinction between goal choice as a decisional process and goal striving as an action process. Mind-set findings also increase the salience of a second long-standing question in motivation science; namely, what connects the two mind-set processes? Heckhausen (1991) suggests that the strength of the goal developed in the choice system is an important variable in determining the initiation and maintenance of goal-striving processes. One way that goal strength has been conceptualized in the work motivation literature is in terms of goal commitment, or the "force that binds an individual to a course of action that is of relevance to a particular target" (Meyer & Herscovitch, 2001).

Mind-set theory emphasizes the differences in mental orientation associated with goal choice and goal pursuit. In I/O psychology, however, theory and research have focused on the factors and processes that bridge the two motivation subsystems and bind the individual to the pursuit of selected goals; namely, goal commitment. The Meyer and Allen (1991) multidimensional conceptualization of commitment compliments mind-set theory by distinguishing among dimensions of commitment and their influence on goal striving. Specifically, Meyer and Allen (1991) proposed three forms of commitment: affective commitment, or the binding of the goal to action as a function of desire; normative commitment, or the steadfastness of goal pursuit out of a sense of obligation to others; and continuance commitment, or the resoluteness of goal persistence as a consequence of perceived costs for not adopting the goal, or goal abandonment (also see Meyer & Allen, 1997). Although different mind-sets may be involved in goal choice and implementation processes, the Meyer and Allen (1991) conceptualization suggests that the motivation for goal commitment may also affect the manner in which decisions are implemented in action. Consistent with this notion, Meyer et al. (2004) have recently proposed an integrative model of commitment and motivation that links different dimensions of commitment to different goal purposes or foci. Although the Meyer et al. (2004) model is relatively new and in need of empirical testing, the proposed linkages between goal purpose and commitment dimension have important implications for practice. For example, in some work settings and collectivist cultures, the formulation of goals-based sense of obligation (e.g., finish assigned work on a team project because others depend on this performance) may yield higher levels of continuance of goal commitment and stronger self-regulatory processes than goals formulated to maximize pleasure and sustained through affective goal commitment (e.g., finish assigned work on a team project because it is interesting and will bring about feelings of competence).

Intrinsic and Extrinsic Motivation

The notion that goals may be adopted for intrinsic and/or extrinsic purposes and, in turn, affect goal pursuit is well-established in psychology, and serves as the foundation for theory and research in intrinsic motivation. Intrinsic motivation refers to psychological processes involved in task performance for the purpose of enjoyment and interest; that is, tasks performed for their own sake. In contrast, extrinsic motivation typically refers to processes involved in task performance for the attainment of outcomes from others or the environment (extrinsic incentives). Theory and research on intrinsic motivation are arguably the most well-known topic in the domain linking purpose and motivation.

Research on intrinsic motivation builds upon theories which assume that all people possess motives for autonomy, competence, and control. Theories of intrinsic motivation hold that individuals are intrinsically motivated when they attribute the cause of their actions to be self-determined, rather than determined by external forces (that do not permit satisfaction of autonomy or control motives). Individuals who attribute their behavior to external causes are said to be extrinsically motivated.

Studies by Deci, Lepper, and their colleagues during the 1970s and 1980s (see Kanfer, 1990) showed that the provision of extrinsic rewards (e.g., money) undermined intrinsic motivation, and was associated with reduced task motivation and task persistence. Early theories (Cognitive Evaluation Theory; Deci, 1975) proposed that the detrimental influence of extrinsic events on intrinsic motivation depended on the extent to which the individual perceived the event as controlling (vs. informational). This explanation subsequently focused research on the conditions under which extrinsic events, such as rewards and feedback, were interpreted as controlling, and their downstream effects on task interest, enjoyment, and behavior.

Over the past decade, Deci and his colleagues have proposed a new formulation; self-determination theory (SDT; Deci & Ryan, 2000, 2002). In contrast to CET, SDT provides a detailed description of how environments support and disrupt expression of the self-determination motive. SDT also proposes that the motive for self-determination may be satisfied in some conditions that include extrinsic rewards or feedback. Specifically, SDT organizes extrinsic and intrinsic motivation conditions along a continuum. At the lowest level on the continuum is a motivation, a condition in which there are no intrinsic or extrinsic prompts or attributions for action. The next level is external regulation, or the classic condition in which individuals perceive that the reason for their behavior is due solely to obtain the external reward. Beyond that, however, SDT proposes another form of extrinsic motivation called introjected regulation. In this form of extrinsic motivation there is some self-determination and autonomy, as the individual performs in order to satisfy self-worth contingencies, such as wanting to look competent to others. A yet more self-determining form of extrinsic motivation occurs in what Deci refers to as identified regulation contexts, in which the individual performs an activity because he or she identifies with its value or meaning. The most self-determining form of extrinsic motivation is posited to occur in integrated regulation, when an individual performs an activity because it has become part of the individual's sense of self. At the top level of the continuum is intrinsic motivation, in which the individual performs the activity for its own sake and enjoyment.

In contrast to previous formulations, the SDT framework is more relevant to the workplace, where extrinsic reward contingencies and feedback are commonplace. Further, the mapping of attributions for action along a single regulation continuum provides a useful framework for systematic investigation of differences in self-regulatory activities as a function regulation level. As a consequence, research using SDT has begun to attract greater attention among work motivation researchers (e.g., Gagne & Deci, 2005; Gagne & Forest, 2008).

Goal Orientation Formulations

Early intrinsic motivation research focused on the effect of perceived extrinsic control on task motivation and behavior, but did not examine how the perceived purpose for performance influenced specific self-regulatory variables or strategies. Intrinsic motivation research also focused on the motivational and performance consequences of the individual's (past-oriented) attributions for the cause of action, rather than the individual's (future-oriented) goals. In the late 1970s and early 1980s, education psychology researchers began to study how the purpose of task performance affects the goals that an individual adopts and the self-regulatory processes that are used to attain the goal.

Nicholls (1984) and Dweck (1986; Dweck & Leggett, 1988) articulated early goal orientation perspectives in the context of understanding why children who adopted a similar goal often showed different patterns of goal striving, learning, and performance (beyond the effects of cognitive abilities). According to Nicholls (1984) and Dweck (1986), children who hold a learning or task goal orientation also maintain a self-referenced conception of ability (i.e., focus on how much had been learned) and tend to view performance improvement and greater task mastery as positive outcomes. In contrast, individuals who hold an ego or performance goal orientation are proposed to regard task performance as a means to an end, and to view performance useful only insofar as it provides a demonstration of one's ability to others. These differences in goal orientation, in turn, affect the quality of goal-striving strategies used to accomplish the goal, persistence following failure or setbacks, and learning and performance.

Similar to early research in intrinsic motivation, the applicability of goal orientation formulations to work settings was not readily apparent, and early interest among work motivation researchers was limited (see Kanfer, 1989). However, with the development of two adult measures of individual differences in goal orientation in the late 1990s (Button, Mathieu, & Zajac, 1996; DeShon & Gillespie, 2005; VandeWalle, 1997), investigations of goal orientation in the work motivation domain grew dramatically. In the development of adult goal orientation measures, Button et al. (1996) and VandeWalle (1997) showed that goal orientation was best understood as a multidimensional construct, and could be fruitfully applied to understanding work motivation in the work setting. Button et al. (1996) developed a two-dimensional adult measure of goal orientation based upon Dweck's formulation; VandeWalle (1997) developed a three-dimensional measure that further distinguished the performance goal dimension into two dimensions—performance goal orientation directed to proving one's competencies and gaining positive judgments from others

(performance-prove), and performance goal orientation directed toward avoiding demonstration of one's lack of ability and negative judgments from others (performance-avoid).

Although goal orientation has been conceptualized as both a trait and a state, the majority of work motivation studies to date have examined the effects of goal orientation states (induced through instructions or context) on motivation and performance. Quantitative and qualitative reviews of the goal orientation research literature are provided by Carr, DeShon, and Dobbins (2001), Day, Yeo, and Radosevich (2003), Payne et al. (2007), Rawsthorne and Elliot (1999), and Utman (1997). In general, these reviews provide support for the facilitative effect of learning goal orientation on goal setting, self-regulatory activities, learning, and performance. In contrast, many, but not all, studies find a significant negative relationship between performance-prove or performance-avoid goal orientation, goal striving, and performance. Findings with respect to the impact of performance-prove goal orientation are inconsistent. Building on these findings, current research has broadened to examine the impact of goal orientation in leadership (e.g., Whitford & Moss, 2009), in training (e.g., Chiaburu & Marinova, 2005; Colquitt & Simmering, 1998; Cox & Beier, 2009), and job search (e.g., Creed, King, Hood, & McKenzie, 2009; Van Hooft & Noordzij, 2009). Recently, some researchers have proposed integrative formulations that place goal orientation processes within broader self-regulation frameworks (DeShon & Gillespie, 2005; Yeo, Loft, Xiao, & Kiewitz, 2009).

Motivational Orientation: Trait Conceptualizations

In contrast to goal orientation at the state level, stable individual differences in goal and motivational orientation at the trait level operate over a longer timescale. Individuals who are high in trait learning goal orientation, for example, are not only more likely to adopt a learning goal orientation to specific tasks, but also to show higher levels of self-regulatory skill in overcoming obstacles to goal attainment. That is, goal and motivation orientation traits can be expected to exert cross-level effects at multiple points in motivational processing. Elliot and McGregor (2001) and Elliot and Thrash (2001) provide summary reviews of findings with respect to the effects of achievement and avoidance motivational orientations on goals and self-regulatory processes.

During the past two decades, interest in trait-level goal and motivational orientation has burgeoned. Different programs of research in neurobiology, personality and social psychology, and motivation provide convergent evidence for two trait orientations and their differential impacts on motivational processing, learning, and performance. Formulations by Elliot and Harackiewicz (1996), Higgins (1998), and Kanfer and Heggestad (1997) posit that individuals who score high on what is variously described as approach motivation (Elliot & Harackiewicz, 1996), promotion regulatory focus (Higgins, 1998), or performance mastery orientation (Kanfer & Heggestad, 1997) engage in more effective learning, meta-cognitive, and self-regulatory activities during goal adoption and goal striving than persons who score high in avoidance motivation (Elliot & Harackiewicz, 1996; Kanfer & Heggestad, 1997), prevention regulatory focus (Higgins, 1998), or performance-avoid goal orientation (VandeWalle, 1997). These motivational orientations are further consistent with evidence from neurobiology theory and research on the existence of two general neurobehavioral systems: a behavioral activation system (BAS) sensitive to rewards and characterized by positive emotion and approach; and a behavioral inhibition system (BIS) sensitive to punishment and characterized by negative emotion and inhibition.

Although the antecedents, mechanisms, and consequences studied in different approaches vary, findings across these research paradigms provide convergent empirical evidence for the positive influence of approach-related goal and motivational orientation on learning and performance. However, findings on the deleterious impact of avoidance-related goal and motivational orientations on learning and performance are less uniform and appear to depend on the nature of the task as well as the motivation and performance outcomes studied. In the organizational domain, Diefendorff & Mehta (2007) found that workplace deviance measures were negatively related to approach motivation traits, but positively related to avoidance motivation traits. Similarly, Heimerdinger and Hinsz (2008) found that avoidance motivation was negatively related to performance in an idea-generation task.

Summary

Work motivation researchers have taken advantage of recent advances in other areas of psychology to develop new theories and to conduct research directed toward understanding the impact of implicit motives and non-conscious processes on explicit goal setting and self-regulation processes. Two issues currently hinder further advances in these areas. First, the development of reliable and valid measures of individual differences in implicit motives is still in the early stages. Second, most research to date has looked at the influence of non-conscious processes on behaviors and motivational mechanisms as they occur in controlled settings using carefully designed tasks. Research is needed to determine whether these findings scale up to affect goal choice and behavior in work settings. Questions about the generalizability of findings to the workplace include, but are not limited to, understanding when non-conscious processes are most likely to affect behavior, the role of non-conscious affect-driven processes in goal commitment and goal shielding, and the extent to which individuals are able to effectively modulate non-conscious tendencies that disrupt progress toward goal attainment (e.g., to control feelings of fatigue in order to complete a project). During the past decade, work motivation researchers have worked on both these issues. Early findings suggest that investigation of implicit motives and non-conscious processes offers great promise in further clarifying the role of personality and affect in work motivation and performance outcomes.

Goals remain the focal point for most work motivation theorizing and research. But the focus of goal-related research has changed. Investigations of how specific attributes of the goal affect self-regulation and performance have declined as work motivation researchers have adopted a more holistic and person-centered view of goals. New person-centered perspectives emphasize the impact of purpose on how information is processed (mind-sets associated with selecting a goal and accomplishing a goal) and the meta-cognitive strategies used in self-regulatory activities in goal pursuit. With the exception of self-efficacy, theory and research on self-regulatory processes that occur during goal pursuit have also shifted. In contrast to earlier research focused on the impact of goal attributes on specific self-regulatory components (such as performance monitoring), recent studies have focused on the relationship between goal orientation and self-regulatory strategies and patterns during goal pursuit.

Work motivation research has also begun to focus on abiding and difficult questions about the impact of goal dynamics on motivational processes and performance. In many instances, the impetus for research on these questions comes from the real-world work setting. In the workplace, individuals are often assigned more than one task, each with unique task demands, goals, and time lines for completion. Understanding how individuals allocate resources and regulate their activities across tasks is likely to yield knowledge that can be used in work design. Another important area in goal dynamics pertains to the personal and situational factors that contribute to goal revision, the resolution of goal conflicts, and goal abandonment. From a practical perspective, research is needed to understand different ways that individuals cope with goal conflicts and the distinct motivational orientation states and self-regulatory patterns associated with goal revision compared to goal abandonment.

Determinants of Motivation: Content, Context, and Change

Organizations and the employees who work in them often turn to work motivation researchers for evidence-based knowledge about the personal and situational characteristics that most influence work motivation and the ways in which this influence occurs. Not surprisingly, a large portion of theory and research in work motivation pertains to the influence of personal attributes and environmental conditions on motivation, learning, and performance. Over the years a multitude of personal characteristics and situational factors have been studied,

alone and in different combinations. Although the development of the five-factor model has helped to organize research on the influence of personality traits on work motivation, there have been few attempts to systematize research on the effects of situation and context on work motivation (see Johns, 2006; Meyer, Dalal, & Hermida, 2010). And neither the five-factor model nor situational frameworks address motivation issues related to time.

Recently, Kanfer et al. (2008) proposed a broad "three C's" meta-heuristic scheme for organizing the relevant determinants of work motivation. A non-exhaustive list of determinants in the content, context, and change categories is provided in Table 14.1.

Content determinants include variables related to interindividual differences, such as knowledge, skills, abilities, personality traits, motives, affective tendencies, interests, and values. Context determinants refer to exogenous (external to the individual) features of the action setting. Context variables may be further organized into features of the immediate work setting (e.g., supervision, work demands), features associated with the broader socio-technical work context (e.g., organizational policies, organizational climate), variables related to the individual's non-work demands and activities (e.g., care-giving demands), and variables related to the broader sociocultural and economic environment (e.g., cultural norms, values, unemployment rate).

Table 14.1 Work Motivation Determinants Organized by Content, Context, and Change Domain

Content (Interindividual) Influences on Work Motivation	
Cognitive abilities	Personality and motivational traits
Knowledge and skills	Affective/implicit and explicit motives
Interests	Values
Beliefs, attitudes	Self-concepts

Context Influences on Work Motivation	
Culture (societal)	Off-job demands and constraints
Organizational and team culture/climate	Organizational practices and policies
Leadership/social relations	Work role and job demands/design

Change-Related Influences on Work Motivation	
Organizational change	Adult development (within-person change)
Team processes	Self-regulatory activities
Work role/job redesign	Job experience/learning

The third C refers to change; that is, factors associated with the temporal dimension. Temporal influences on work motivation may come into play in several ways. In terms of motivational processes per se, time-sensitive factors, such as fatigue, may influence goal pursuit and the willingness to revise one's goal. Alternatively, time-sensitive factors, such as the development of knowledge and skills as a result of job performance, may affect work motivation by altering perceived person-task or person-job fit. Time also plays a role in distinguishing among employees. Changes in cognitive abilities, motives, and interests over the life course can affect work motivation through their impact on self-efficacy, the utility of performance for attaining valued outcomes, and age-related changes in the utility of high levels of cognitive and physical effort (Kanfer, 1987). Figure 14.2 displays a schematic of the "three C's" and their relationship to motivation processes. In the remainder of this section, I describe notable advances in each determinant class.

Content Influences: Personal Attributes and Traits

In 1990, with the exception of research in achievement motivation, there was relatively little systematic research on the influence of personality traits on work motivation and behavior (see Kanfer, 1990). A major reason for this state of affairs was the absence of a conceptually sound structure for organizing the multitude of personality traits that had been studied (see Guion & Gottier, 1965). The introduction of the five-factor model (FFM) of personality structure into I/O psychology in the early 1990s provided a much-needed solution to this problem, and launched a prolific period of research on the impact of personality traits on motivation and performance (see Judge & Ilies, 2002, and Kanfer & Kantrowitz, 2002, for reviews).

Over the past two decades, research on personal determinants of work motivation has also broadened beyond the study of the broad five personality traits. Recent studies have focused on traits not well-specified in the FFM, including affective traits (e.g., negative and positive affectivity), motivational traits (e.g., action orientation), and self-related traits (e.g., core self-evaluations, personal initiative). To further organize the broad array of person attributes currently under investigation in work motivation, I use a modified version of the framework originally proposed by Thorndike in 1947 for the purpose of categorizing different types of personal influences on test performance. The adapted meta-organizing framework for personal attributes is shown in Figure 14.3.

Consistent with the Thorndike scheme, personal attributes are classified on the basis of their permanence (i.e., lasting or temporary) and scope (i.e., general or specific). For present purposes, I classify individual differences in cognitive abilities, knowledge, and skills, and non-ability traits, such as the FFM personality traits, as lasting influences on motivation and action. These personal

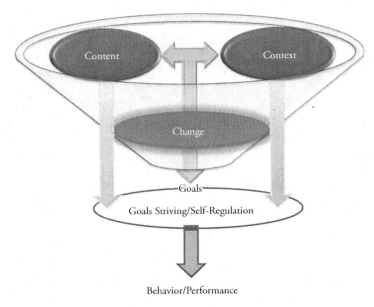

Figure 14.2 A Static Representation of the "Three C's" model of work motivation.

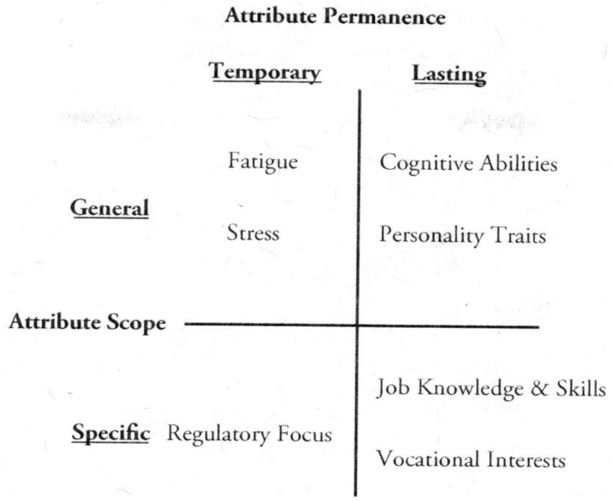

Attribute Permanence

Figure 14.3 An Organizing Framework for Personal Attributes That Influence Work Motivation (Adapted from Thorndike) and Examples of Personal Attributes

characteristics are not posited to vary appreciably across contexts (although their expression may vary across contexts) or time, and are generally viewed as exerting an indirect or distal influence on motivation through their effects on goals. Permanent personal attributes that are also general include most personality traits, such as conscientiousness. Lasting but specific personal attributes, such as job knowledge, exert their influence on motivation in a narrower range of contexts. In contrast to lasting and general personal attributes, lasting but specific personal characteristics, such as interests, are likely to affect motivation through their impact on select variables, such as goal commitment and self-efficacy.

Transient personal attributes refer to personal influences that occur as a consequence of the person-situation interaction. These personal characteristics contribute to motivation by creating what is often referred to as a motivational state. Biologically based personal attributes, such as fatigue and stress, are examples of general (pervasive) but temporary personal attributes that can affect motivation through their impact on resource availability. In contrast, transient and context-specific personal attributes, such as regulatory focus or anger, are likely to influence motivation through their effect on self-regulation processes.

The organization of personal influences on motivation using Thorndike's (1947) classification scheme is generally consistent with findings across disparate research literatures that show an indirect influence of general personal attributes and a direct influence of transient personal attributes on motivational processes. To date, most work motivation research has focused on general and lasting attributes (such as personality traits) and transient and specific personal characteristics (such as anger).

PERSONALITY TRAITS

In contrast to earlier reviews of the relationship between personality traits and performance that did not benefit from an empirically derived organization of the personality trait domain (e.g., Guion & Gottier, 1965), the Barrick and Mount (1991) meta-analysis of personality trait–performance relations using the FFM trait scheme revealed significant relationships between individual differences in conscientiousness and neuroticism and diverse measures of performance. Specifically, conscientiousness showed a positive relationship to performance, while neuroticism showed a negative relationship to performance. Subsequent studies on personality-performance relations (see Hurtz & Donovan, 2000) provide further support for the predictive validities of these broad personality traits on performance.

In an attempt to explain these observed relations, Kanfer (1992) suggested that personality traits influence performance through their effects on motivational processes. Empirical support for this notion was obtained in studies by Barrick et al. (1993) and Barrick, Stewart, and Piotrowski (2002), in which motivational variables were found to mediate the trait-performance relationship, and in a study by Chen, Gully, Whiteman, & Kilcullen (2000), which found that the impact of trait variables on performance was mediated by goals and self-efficacy. Results of a later meta-analysis by Judge and Ilies (2002), investigating the relationship between personality traits and motivational variables (e.g., goal level) further indicated the robustness of the relationship between two personality traits (conscientiousness and neuroticism) and motivation using criterion variables from three different work motivation theories. Although research investigating the influence of the FFM trait dimensions on motivation and performance remains popular, there have also been more studies investigating select traits that are not well-represented in the five-factor structure of personality, such as motivational traits (Kanfer & Heggestad, 1997), core-self-evaluations (Judge, Locke, & Durham, 1997), and personal initiative (Frese & Fay, 2001; Frese, Kring, Soose, & Zempel, 1996).

The Thorndike meta-organizational scheme implies that general and lasting personal attributes (personality and other non-ability traits such as interests) operate in a similar manner to affect work motivation. However, to date, most work motivation research on personality traits has been studied in isolation from studies that examine other important general and lasting personal attributes, such as individual differences in cognitive abilities, vocational interests, or values. Ackerman (1997) and Lubinski (2000) have suggested that an integration of historically disparate streams of research in cognitive abilities, personality, vocational interests, knowledge, and values can improve our understanding and prediction of motivation and performance. These researchers argue that commonalities among general and lasting personal attributes arise as a consequence of the common biological influences and environmental affordances that promote the tandem development of individual differences in cognitive and non-cognitive traits over the life course. In developed countries, for example, individual differences in cognitive abilities are typically assessed prior to entry into elementary school and are used to place students in different learning environments that are considered optimal for the child's aptitudes. These environments directly impact the level and type of intellectual and social challenges the child experiences in the school setting. It is not unreasonable to expect that the interaction of the individual's characteristics and his or her school environment, in turn, influences later work interests, work values, as well as the work opportunities available to the individual during the transition to adult employment.

From a structural perspective, the association of different general and lasting personal characteristics into broad constellations or complexes may be conceptualized hierarchically, with basic dimensions of cognition, temperament, and motives often showing strong associations with the development of select personality traits, vocational interests, and even work values. Research that uses theory-driven integrations of related personal attributes to study their effects on motivation and performance encourages the development of more parsimonious and practically useful approaches to understanding personal influences on motivation and performance.

ORGANIZATIONAL JUSTICE MOTIVES

One complex of general and lasting personal attributes that continues to command attention in the work motivation literature pertains to universal motives for justice. Similar to traits, interests, and values, universal motives for justice reflect outcome preferences that remain relatively stable across situations and the life course, even if the particular conceptualization of justice may be culture-specific. In contrast to personality traits, however, individuals do not appreciably differ in strength for satisfaction of justice motives. Rather, justice motives activate motivational processes as a consequence of the person-situation transaction. In this sense, although justice motives are lasting and general, the influence of the motive on motivation and action occurs only when the individual perceives a threat to motive satisfaction.

Early theories of organizational justice grew out of equity and exchange formulations (e.g., Adams, 1965). According to equity theories, situations that an individual perceives to be unfair or unjust create heightened psychological tension. Motivation arises from the desire to reduce the psychological tension, though the way that individuals accomplish this reduction in tension may be through changes in cognition rather than changes in behavior. Theory and research on organizational justice through the 1980s focused largely on delineating the motivational pathways by which perceptions of procedural injustice or unfairness influenced work behavior (see Greenberg & Cropanzano, 1999).

Over the past two decades, theories of organizational justice have matured, and research has expanded to examine the determinants and consequences of other forms of justice, including interactional justice, relational justice, and informational justice. As with research on procedural justice, research on relational and informational forms of justice has focused primarily on the contextual features that elicit perceptions of injustice and subsequent behavior change. In a comprehensive meta-analysis of justice research findings between 1975 and 1999, Colquitt et al. (2001) found that both distributive and procedural forms of justice were positively related to motivational outcomes, such as job commitment and task performance.

In the past few years, research on the impact of motive violations has declined as attention has shifted to examining impact of personal characteristics on justice perceptions. Studies by Truxillo, Bauer, Campion, and Paronto (2006) and Shi, Lin, Wang, and Wang (2009), for example, examined the relationship between the FFM personality traits and justice perceptions in the context of personnel selection and among incumbent employees, respectively. Both studies found a positive relationship between agreeableness and organizational justice perceptions, and a negative relationship between neuroticism and organizational justice perceptions. From a motivational perspective, these results suggest that violations of justice motives in the workplace may be more salient to individuals high in neuroticism than individuals low in neuroticism. To date, however, there has been little attention to the impact of fairness perceptions on motivational orientation and self-regulatory activities used for goal accomplishment. Studies are also needed to illuminate the relationship between different forms of perceived injustice and associated patterns of motivation and behavior over time.

Summary

Research on the influence of personal characteristics on work motivation has increased dramatically over the past two decades. This increase is due largely to the introduction of the FFM of personality into the organizational domain. Using this scheme, work motivation researchers have been able to accumulate research findings and obtain consistent evidence for the relationship between conscientiousness and neuroticism traits and motivational variables and outcomes. Emerging programs of research on specific variables, such as personal initiative, reflect a further maturation of this portion of the field, as researchers attempt to identify and study the impact of key behavioral tendencies for work motivation. Consistent with recommendations by Ackerman (1996, 1997) and Lubinski (2000), programs of research by Judge and his colleagues on core self-evaluations (e.g., Judge & Bono, 2001; Judge & Hurst, 2007) and Kanfer and Ackerman and their colleagues (e.g., Kanfer, Ackerman, & Heggestad, 1996; Kanfer, Wolf, Kantrowitz, & Ackerman, 2009) have also focused on delineating the relationship between trait complexes, motivation processes, and performance.

Nonetheless, there are still a number of important gaps in our knowledge. Theory and research on the impact of personal attributes in the general but temporary category, including health, stress, and fatigue variables, have received substantial research attention in the occupational health literature, but have yet to be incorporated into mainstream work on motivation. Similarly, there is also surprisingly little research directed toward the influence of individual differences in affect on motivation and performance. Seo, Feldman-Barrett, and Bartunek (2004) proposed an integrative model for the role of affective experience in work motivation, using the concept of "core affective experience" to capture the impact of affective experiences on goal choice and goal commitment. In addition, there has been little attention to identifying the distinct motivational signatures of discrete emotions (Kanfer & Stubblebine, 2008). Research to identify the goal characteristics and self-regulatory strategies that are uniquely associated with different emotions is likely to be helpful to supervisors in the services sector. It may also be, for example, that individual differences in affective tendencies influence not only the experience of an emotion, but also the goals that are formed in response to the emotion and the effectiveness of self-regulatory activities to modulate the emotion. Research to investigate the impact of specific affective person attributes, such as hostility, on emotion and motivation is another area that has potentially important theoretical and practical implications.

Contextual Influences on Motivation

Context refers to the milieu in which work motivation takes place, and may be described in a multitude of ways. At the simplest level, context may be distinguished in terms of function, such as skill acquisition, job search, or teamwork. Although such an organizing scheme is useful for noting the importance of motivation across the range of organizational activities, it does not capture the complex relationships among situational variables or the communalities and distinctions among contextual variables across settings.

Most work motivation theory and research over the past 50 years have focused on the impact of variables active in the immediate performance setting, such as rewards, decision latitude, social interactions, and task variety (see Hackman & Oldham, 1976; Karasek, 1979, 1989). Although research findings in these perspectives often show significant relationships between job demands and work conditions with work motivation, several factors have contributed to a general decline in scientific study of context using these models. First, researchers have identified several conceptual and methodological problems with formulations that focus primarily on job task variables. In addition, the changing nature of work has shifted attention to the question of whether and how other layers of context, such as societal culture, influence work motivation (e.g., see Gelfand et al., 2007).

In a related vein, the introduction of social, information-processing (SIP) approaches by Salancik and Pfeffer (1978) and Lord and Foti (1986) encouraged new ways of thinking about context and its effects on work motivation. Specifically, these researchers argued that individuals actively construct perceptions of the work context based on social cues in the environment. These perceptions are then organized and stored in schemas that, once developed, tend to promote the neglect of information that is inconsistent with the existing schema (Lord & Foti, 1986). Although SIP models have not attracted a great deal of attention among work motivation researchers, the SIP perspective differs from job-based formulations in several important ways for work motivation. First, SIP approaches formally recognize the role of pre-conscious processes that direct attention to particular features of the work environment. Contemporary research in non-conscious motivation processes expand upon this notion. Second, building on advances in cognitive, information-processing psychology through the 1980s, Lord and his colleagues showed how features of work were mentally represented in cognitive schemas, and the impact of schemas for decision making. In modern work motivation research, non-conscious schemas contribute to the development of automaticity, as well to problems in behavior change. Third, SIP approaches refocus attention to the role that interpersonal relations play in perceptions of the workplace and job context. In the modern work motivation theory, the impact of social cues on work motivation has moved to investigation of the influence that an individual's coworker relations, social network, and social capital play in motivational outcomes, such as organizational citizenship behavior (e.g., Bowler & Brass, 2006) and turnover (Randel & Ranft, 2007).

As the physical and psychological context for job performance broadens (e.g., coffee shop meetings; teamwork), organizational researchers have begun to study context influences from a variety of levels, ranging from the impact of features associated with the immediate work environment to the impact of organizational and national cultures on expectations and norms for work behavior. One potentially useful heuristic for thinking about different levels of context is to use the analogy of an onion. Like an onion, people perform work in a context that is multilayered, with each layer influencing other layers. With the individual at the center, variables that capture features of the immediate work setting, such as task demands and social relations, can be represented as the layer that is most proximal to the individual, yet fully embedded in the broader organization, represented as the next layer of the onion. Salient socio-technical features of the organization context that may exert direct or indirect effects on the individual include, for example, the unique culture, climate, and norms of the organization. In turn, organizations are embedded in societies and cultures that may also be distinguished in terms of characteristics such as norms, values, and orientations with respect to social relations and power.

Similar to an onion, changes at any layer may exert direct and lagged impact on other layers and the individual. The introduction of new production technology, such as the desktop computer in the 1980s, for example, can rapidly change the individual's context of work within a work unit and the schedule of intrinsic rewards associated with performance of reconfigured jobs. Perhaps the most important point in using the onion analogy is that changes at different levels of context rarely occur in isolation. Features of the workplace, compensation, the organization, leadership, and societal norms for how and when non-work family and leisure activities should occur often covary in ways that create distinct, complex situation constellations that distinguish occupational families. For example, knowledge work, whether it be directed toward product design, software development, or teaching, is often performed in settings characterized by high levels of decision latitude, task interdependence, non-contingent pay structures, non-hazardous work conditions, and the use of reward structures that reinforce outcomes (e.g., new product development, teamwork) rather than single behaviors (e.g., attendance). Further, these features of work are often associated with the use of a management style and an organizational culture and climate that differ significantly from the style and culture that exists in production work. Even more broadly, organizations that produce knowledge, rather than products, tend to grow best in stable economic mediums and in developed or rapidly developing countries.

Managing the context in which work is performed in order to promote work motivation and positive work attitudes is arguably the principal task of most supervisors and unit leaders. Unfortunately, however, there is currently no theory of situations to guide managers or work motivation researchers in systemizing and aggregating findings about the effects of context on motivation (Johns, 2006). Meyer and his colleagues (Meyer & Dalal, 2009; Meyer, Dalal, & Bonaccio, 2009; Meyer, Dalal, & Hermida, 2010) have recently proposed a formulation that organizes features of the work setting using the psychological concept of "situational strength." Based in part on Mischel's (1968) notion of situational strength, Meyer et al. (2010) define situational strength as "implicit or explicit cues provided by external entities regarding the desirability of potential behaviors" (p. 122). According to Meyer et al. (2010), the overall strength of a work situation is comprised of strength in four dimensions: clarity, consistency, consequences, and constraints. Clarity refers to the extent to which attributes of the workplace and social cues create a clear understanding of work role and job responsibilities. Consistency refers to the extent that workplace attributes and social cues create perceptions of the job as comprising compatible tasks and roles. Constraints refer to the extent to which physical, technical, and social attributes of the job place limits on the influence of an individual's decisions and behaviors. The consequences dimension refers to the extent to which contextual variables affect the significance of action for self, coworkers, the unit, and the organization.

Meyer et al. (2009) provide initial evidence for the feasibility of this framework in an investigation of the moderating role that occupation-level constraints and consequences have on the relationship between conscientiousness and job performance. Concordant with their theory, Meyer et al. (2009) found that the conscientiousness-performance relation was stronger in occupations characterized by low levels of constraint on the consequences and constraint dimensions than those with higher levels on these dimensions. The utility of this approach for organizing the impact of various contextual variables appears promising, but requires further empirical testing. In particular, research to identify the differential impact of situational strength dimensions on self-efficacy and intrinsic motivation is likely to be quite useful for building a conceptual bridge between context and motivation.

Both older and newer approaches to contextual influences on work motivation hold that the impact of exogenous variables on work motivation obtains as a consequence of how features of the environment are perceived and interpreted by the individual. An important next step in this area will be to illuminate the effects of personal attributes, time and variable constellations on the perception and interpretation of work milieu, and subsequent influences on goal choice and goal pursuit. It may well be, for example, that the impact of situational variables on work motivation changes over time as a function of the individual's goals. Among novice emergency medical technicians (EMTs), for example, strong situations that provide detailed guides for what to do and pay attention to while trying to stabilize a patient for hospital transfer are likely to enhance effective resource allocations and performance. Among experienced EMTs, however, strong situations may diminish work motivation (although not job performance) for precisely the same reason; namely, perceived inflexibility in how performance is enacted and reduced opportunity for self-determination. How different layers of context influence situational strength, and the conditions in which strength facilitates or diminishes work motivation, are important questions for future research in this area.

CONTEXT-GROUNDED MOTIVATION RESEARCH

Motivation is always studied in context, but over the past few decades, changes in the nature of work and the workforce have focused attention on the role of motivation in two specific contexts: namely, training and teams. The widespread integration of self-regulation perspectives in training theory and research and the development of more sophisticated models of learning have revitalized motivation research in this context (Bell & Kozlowski, 2002, 2008; Ford, Smith, Weissbein, Gully, & Salas, 1998; Sitzmann, Bell, Kraiger, & Kanar, 2009). In contrast to older models of learning that assume stability in motivation across the course of training, contemporary models propose more dynamic conceptions of motivation during training. Similarly, the extension of self-regulation to the study of team processes has spurred theory and research on the influence of teams and team dynamics on individual motivation and performance in the team context. Recent advances in these situations are highlighted below.

MOTIVATION IN TRAINING AND DEVELOPMENT

There is a long history of theory and research on the role of motivation in job skill training and development (Goldstein, 1993). Prior to the latter part of the twentieth century, however, training and development research focused largely on the impact of training design characteristics (e.g., feedback, modeling) on performance of new job entrants engaged in job-specific skill training, such as typing or operating a printing press. Little attention was paid to individual differences in motivation to learn, perform, and transfer training outcomes or to motivational processes as they unfolded during training (see Noe, 1986).

Over the past four decades, however, there has been a steady increase in the role that motivation plays in training and development. In the current work world, training is no longer constrained to the front end of careers and jobs, but rather is an activity that can be expected to occur with regularity across the career course. In some occupational sectors, such as IT and health care, new technologies are driving major changes in the skill sets required for maintaining a high level of job performance over time. For individuals who are increasingly likely to spend five or more decades in the labor workforce, lifelong learning is becoming a prerequisite for career success and employability. In the research arena, investigations of goal setting and self-regulation in learning and training environments have repeatedly shown the importance of motivational processing in complex skill acquisition (e.g., Kanfer & Ackerman, 1989). Given these trends, it is not at all surprising that theory and research on the role of motivation in contemporary training contexts have burgeoned (Kozlowski & Salas, 2010).

One area of great interest to organizations concerned with continuous learning pertains to understanding of what motivates individuals to enroll in development activities. The decision to participate in skill training represents the first and perhaps most critical step in training, since failure to participate makes the question of motivation during learning and motivation for transfer of training moot. Meta-analytic findings by Colquitt et al. (2000) indicate that individual differences in select traits, such as locus of control, play an important role in motivation for training. Findings by Baldwin, Magjuka, and Loher (1991), Guerrero and Sire (2001), and others (see Mathieu & Martineau, 1997) also indicate that employees who are allowed to decide whether they participate in organizationally sponsored or supported training show higher levels of motivation for training (as reflected in training commitment, allocation of time and effort toward class attendance, time spent in on-task learning) than employees who are not allowed to participate in the enrollment decision. These findings are consistent with motivation

theories that emphasize self-determination and participatory decision making. In terms of voluntary training participation, Hurtz and Williams (2009) found that perceived availability of development activities and high learning goal orientation exerted significant positive effects on training participation.

However, factors that motivate the decision to enroll in training may be quite different from factors that motivate sustained learning over the duration of training (Beier & Kanfer, 2009). A large number of studies in educational and social/personality psychology, as well as in industrial and organizational psychology, have examined self-regulatory processes during learning and skill acquisition (Elliot, 2008; Kanfer & Ackerman, 1989; Zimmerman & Schunk, 2001). Findings from these complementary streams of research indicate the importance of self-efficacy and active self-regulation of emotion and behavior during learning for positive learning outcomes. Many studies also show that performance goal orientation exerts a negative effect on learning outcomes, though the mechanisms by which this negative effect occurs is still not well understood (DeShon & Gillespie, 2005; Payne et al., 2007).

Two current streams of research in training, by Frese and his colleagues and Bell and Kozlowski and their colleagues, highlight the role of motivation in modern training environments. In the early 1990s, Frese and Zapf (1994) suggested that giving trainees the opportunity to make errors and encouraging trainees to learn from their errors during training may improve learning outcomes. In contrast to training approaches that focus on error avoidance, error management training (EMT) assumes that errors are unavoidable in active learning and that total elimination of errors may be difficult to achieve in complex tasks. From a motivational perspective, the EMT–active learning approach is posited to improve learning in part by enhancing task engagement. As Keith and Frese (2005) noted, however, the positive effects of EMT on performance are moderated by the extent to which the task and training environment provide clear, unambiguous feedback. Keith and Frese (2005) examined the motivational influence of EMT compared with error avoidant training approaches using a sample of college students learning to use the PowerPoint 2000 computer program. After an introduction to the program, participants were randomly assigned to one of three conditions: (a) error avoidant training, (b) error management training, or (c) error management plus meta-cognitive instruction. The results provided support for the proposed mediating role of emotion regulation and meta-cognitive activities in the effects of training condition on performance. Consistent with resource allocation theories (e.g., Kanfer & Ackerman, 1989), Keith and Frese (2005) found that the positive effects of the two error management training conditions over the error avoidant condition on performance were fully attributable to their influence on enhancing emotion control and meta-cognitive activities during training. Specifically, trainees in the error management conditions reported higher levels of emotion regulation following errors than trainees in the error avoidant conditions.

Results of a recent meta-analysis of EMT effects on training and transfer task performance by Keith and Frese (2008) provide support for basic tenets of the framework. From a motivational perspective, the positive impact of EMT on adaptive transfer performance appears to occur through two pathways: (a) reduction of disruptive emotional reactions that divert attentional resources away from learning, and (b) more frequent activation of meta-cognitive processes following error detection. However, the findings in EMT research suggest several important boundary conditions on the efficacy of EMT for motivation and enhanced transfer performance, including the provision of training environments that provide clear performance feedback and the impact of training on adaptive transfer performance (versus analogous or near transfer performance). In addition, investigations on the effectiveness of EMT approaches for adaptive transfer performance have been limited to college-educated adult samples for use in software skills and other computer-related skills. Additional research is needed to assess the generalizability of these findings to other workers in different domains.

A second distinct, but related stream of motivation research in the training context by Kozlowski, Bell, and colleagues has examined the impact of different active learning interventions on training performance, as well as skill transfer and adaptation. Bell and Kozlowski (2008) examined three self-regulatory pathways (cognitive, motivational, and emotional) by which different active learning interventions influenced performance. Individuals who adopted a mastery goal orientation to training showed increased levels of self-efficacy, intrinsic motivation, and meta-cognitive ability. Bell and Kozlowski (2008) also showed that error framing interacted with trainees' trait goal orientations to affect state goal orientation during training. However, the effect of error framing was largely to increase state mastery goal orientation among trainees low in trait mastery goal orientation; error framing had no effect on individuals already high in mastery goal orientation. The Bell and Kozlowski (2008) findings shed light on the importance of evaluating the interactive effects of trainee traits and training designs on learning outcomes.

MOTIVATION IN TEAMS

Historically, the bulk of theory and research on individual-level motivation in the team context has focused on the impact of group characteristics (e.g., size) and the downward impact of team-level phenomena, such as team cohesion, on individual team member motivation and behavior. For example, recent findings by Pearsall, Christian, and Ellis (2010) show that reward system characteristics play an important role in motivating team member effort and mitigating team-level social loafing phenomena. Over the past few decades, however, there has been a trend toward the development of theories and research on motivation in the team context that focus on the relationship between individual- and team-level processes Recent theoretical work by Marks, Mathieu, and Zaccaro (2001) and Chen and Kanfer (2006) on motivational processes in team contexts build upon evidence of homology between goal choice and self-regulatory motivational processes at the individual and team level, and advances in multilevel modeling (Chen, Bliese, & Mathieu, 2005; Chen et al., 2002; DeShon et al., 2004). Meta-analytic findings by DeChurch and Mesmer-Magnus (2010) provide empirical support for the influence of proposed motivational states on team performance. Micro-analytic studies by Chen, Kirkman, Kanfer, Allen, and Rosen (2007) and Chen, Kanfer, DeShon, Mathieu, and Kozlowski (2009) provide additional support for the cross-level influence of team efficacy on individual level motivational processes over time.

Change (Temporal) Influences on Motivation

Most work and organizational theories focus on the effects of motivation on behavior or performance at a specific point in time or on average over an aggregated period of time (e.g., a week or month). Nonetheless, motivational scientists have long recognized that motivation occurs *over time*, and that time and time-sensitive factors can also exert important influences on the direction and intensity of resource allocations. Over the past decade, interest in temporal and time-related influences on work motivation has blossomed, with researchers pursuing questions about the influence of time from many different perspectives (e.g., Carstensen, 1992; Fried, Grant, Levi, Hadant, & Slowik, 2007; Kanfer & Ackerman, 2004; Marks et al., 2001; Schmidt, Dolis, & Tolli, 2009; Simons, Vansteenkiste, Lens, & Lacante, 2004; Steel & Konig, 2006; Vancouver et al., 2001).

The first problem that confronts researchers interested in investigating the effects of time on motivation is how to conceptualize and assess the effects of time on motivation separately from the array of changes in other determinants that take place over time. For example, endogenous, biological factors contribute to increasing levels of fatigue as a function of time-on-task. Motivation, however, may mediate the impact of fatigue on performance, and may support a pattern of sustained performance over time (Ackerman, 2011). Investigations to examine the impact of time on goal choice or goal pursuit thus require repeated assessment of proximal internal and external determinants and consequences of motivation, rather than just distal traits and performance trends.

The study of temporal influences on motivation highlights an abiding problem in motivation psychology: namely, the interplay of biological factors, self-related factors, and environmental demands (e.g., task demands) on the pattern of resource allocation observed. Most studies of work motivation focus on the impact of a personal or situational variable (e.g., performance incentives) on the allocation of resources to a specific target task, independent of other tasks and factors. However, as Kanfer and Ackerman (1989) note, the impact of personal and situational factors on motivation for performance of a single task must also take into account task demands and time-linked changes in task demands as a consequence of practice. The provision of difficult, specific goals, for example, may initially increase motivation and facilitate learning. For tasks that can be proceduralized (e.g., driving), however, the demands on attention lessen with practice, and task performance may be sustained by changes in knowledge and skill, rather than continued high levels of resource allocation. That is, motivation may remain constant over time, but the impact of motivation on performance changes as a function of how practice influences task demands. In these instances, high levels of performance after practice may be maintained by knowledge and skill development rather than by high levels of motivation.

In contrast, in jobs and tasks where performance cannot be improved through the development of automaticity through practice, sustained levels of motivation are required to maintain performance. In these situations, performance provides a relatively accurate assessment of motivation change over time, but motivation may be more strongly determined by within-subject factors than by an intervention such as goal setting. In summary, the use of performance measures to assess motivation over time requires consideration of dynamic task demands, self-processes, and competing goal demands.

The influence of time on work motivation processes may be captured at different levels of analysis, and may be assessed directly or indirectly. Repeated measurement of expectancies, goals, goal orientation, self-efficacy, self-evaluative behaviors, the direction of attentional effort, the use of different self-regulatory strategies, and time spent on the task permits direct assessment of changes in motivation over time. Direct methods may be used to assess changes in motivational processes as a function of time on task or to assess changes in motivation across longer timescales, such as during a new employee's probationary period. The influence of time-related variables may also be studied indirectly, using between-subject designs to evaluate how variables such as an employee's future time perspective and chronological age affect goal choice, goal striving, and changes in resource allocation policies over time within and across tasks.

Research on the effects of time on motivational strength for performance of a specific task has waxed and waned over the past 40 years. Atkinson and Birch (1970) proposed a theory of motivational dynamics and task switching in which target task performance was hypothesized to decline over time as a function of the declining value of further performance and the increasing attractiveness of performing an alternative task. Raynor and Entin (1982) proposed an extension of the expectancy-value formulation, taking into account the influence of the length of the subordinate pathway for final outcome goal accomplishment and the relationship among elements in the pathway to the final goal. Neither the Atkinson and Birch (1970) nor the Raynor and Entin (1982) formulations generated much interest in work motivation, although there has been some recent work on the impact of future time perspective. For example, Simons, Dewitte, and Lens (2004) suggest that in the context of student achievement, individual differences in future time perspective influence intrinsic motivation and the self-regulatory strategies used to accomplish task performance.

One currently prominent line of inquiry on the effects of time on motivation involves the temporal depletion and replenishment of personal resources needed for motivational processes. Baumeister's ego depletion theory (Baumeister, Bratslavsky, Muraven, & Tice, 1998; Muraven, Tice, & Baumeister, 1998) posits that the personal resources required for self-regulation and self-control diminish with use. According to ego depletion theory, sustained self-regulation (as is often required to perform a complex task over long periods of time) drains the personal resource pool and diminishes the capacity for and effectiveness of self-regulatory activities. Several studies provide support for the notion that the effectiveness of self-regulation, particularly in the service of emotion regulation, diminishes over time in situations that involve continuous use. Resource depletion has also been shown to occur when individuals must engage in goal choice activities over time, such as might occur among EMTs when responding to a disaster. Baumeister argues that individuals are unlikely to fully deplete their limited resources for goal choice and self-regulation, particularly in situations where they anticipate that self-regulation will be required for future performance. That is, unlike a flashlight battery that will completely discharge if the flashlight is left on, Baumeister et al. (1998) and Hobfoll (1989) argue that individuals attempt to conserve or slow the rate of resource depletion when they perceive future demands for self-regulation prior to any opportunity for resource replenishment (i.e., pacing oneself with respect to resource consumption). Whereas Baumeister's theory emphasizes resource depletion associated with length of use, Hobfoll's conservation of resources theory (1989) emphasizes the impact of job stressors on rate of resource loss and depletion.

Baumeister also argues that resources needed for motivation and self-regulation may be replenished over time through rest and the pursuit of activities that do not require self-regulation. Sonnentag and her colleagues (Sonnentag & Frese, 2003; Sonnentag & Fritz, 2007; Sonnentag & Kruel, 2006) have examined this idea in a series of studies designed to identify the conditions that promote resource recovery following work-related resource depletion. Using experience sampling methodology, Sonnentag investigated work and non-work factors that might influence resource recovery following depletion associated with job performance

(Binnewies, Sonnentag, & Mojza, 2009; Fritz & Sonnentag, 2005, 2006).

A central question for future research in this line of inquiry is to determine what features of work most strongly influence resource depletion and recovery. For example, Hobfoll's (1989) theory suggests that work conditions, such as supervisory support, may buffer the negative impact of resource loss associated with sustained self-regulation, and a study by Tice, Baumeister, Shmueli, and Muraven (2007) suggests that positive affect may also buffer resource depletion. Further research is needed to understand the role of tasks, personal characteristics, and social context on resource depletion and recovery (Bakker, Hakanen, Demerouti, & Xanthopoulou, 2007). For example, in the context of skill acquisition, Kanfer and Ackerman (1989) found that individuals with higher levels of attentional resources (i.e., cognitive abilities) reported fewer resource-consumptive off-task cognitions during skill acquisition than individuals with lower levels of attentional resources. Extending this finding to the workplace suggests that certain forms of supervisory or coworker support or technologies that reduce work load may attenuate resource depletion in demanding tasks. In emergency situations and high-risk teamwork, for example, individuals often demonstrate high levels of sustained motivational intensity over long periods of time. Investigation of how team member interactions operate to slow the pace of resource depletion, thus facilitating sustained task effort for long periods of time, is a promising avenue for future research.

Individuals may also implement their own strategies to reduce or prevent resource depletion associated with job demands. Research in the life span literature suggests two broad strategies, accommodation and transformation, by which individuals may reduce demands on personal resources (e.g., Heckhausen & Schultz, 1995). Accommodation refers to actions an individual may take to alter the environment in ways that better accommodate personal goals, needs, and motives. During the course of performance, for example, anxious individuals who experience resource depletion associated with emotion regulation may revise work goals downward to conserve resources and shield secondary goals related to sense of competence. Similarly, individuals with more available resources and less demand for emotion regulation during job performance may revise work goals upward to sustain task motivation and satisfy secondary goals related to mastery. To date, however, there has been little research on what motivates the use of accommodation strategies in taxing jobs and tasks.

Individuals may also use transformation strategies to reduce resource depletion. Transformation strategies refer to behaviors taken to improve the person-job fit by making self-changes that promote resource conservation. As Heckhausen and Schultz (1995) note, transformation strategies require additional resource allocations and are typically only used when accommodation strategies are not possible or are ineffective. Improving job skills and knowledge is one obvious transformation strategy for resource conservation in the workplace. However, as Heckhausen and Schultz (1995) suggest, the additional resource demands associated with learning and behavior change in order to better meet job demands may make transformation strategies less attractive than accommodation strategies that shape the environment to the person. Although research using Baumeister and Hobfill's resource frameworks have only recently gained the attention of work motivation researchers, these conceptualizations appear quite promising for understanding the costs of sustained emotion regulation in the workplace and the most effective interventions for slowing the rate of depletion and improving resource recovery in the workplace. In particular, it would be quite useful to know the conditions that trigger the use of self-initiated strategies for resource conservation, and the factors that determine the choice to use transformation versus accommodation strategies for resource conservation.

Another interesting approach for understanding motivation over time focuses on a time-linked outcome of considerable importance in the workplace, namely, procrastination. Although there have been several studies investigating the influence of traits (e.g., action control; see Kuhl, 1986) on procrastination, Steel and Konig (2006) have recently proposed a general motivation formulation that specifically addresses resource allocation policies across activities as a function of time and their effects on procrastination. According to Steel and Konig (2006), time influences individual resource allocations across tasks through its effect on the value that individuals attach to events and outcomes that occur in the future. Using temporal discounting theory, Steel and Konig (2006) propose that individuals will discount the value of events and outcomes that occur in the future and will allocate fewer resources to accomplishment of distal outcomes than to accomplishment of proximal goals that have not been discounted. Steel and Konig (2006) describe

a number of interesting implications of Temporal Motivational Theory (TMT) for the development of motivational interventions to mitigate the temporal discounting effect on goal choice and allocations of time across tasks, and for the mitigation of procrastination behavior.

As Dalal and Hulin (2008) note, task goals provide a naturally occurring and useful demarcation for studying motivation processes over time. Analysis of time effects across single goal performance cycles also corresponds well to single-cycle theories of work motivation. However, other units of analysis may shed further light on how time affects resource allocation policies across concurrent task goals. Use of temporal cycles organized around personal attributes, such as Type A tendencies, may also shed light on whether individual differences exert a separate effect on the speed and quality of explicit goal choice processes and the strength of self-regulatory activities over time.

TIME INFLUENCES ON WORK MOTIVATION ASSOCIATED WITH EMPLOYEE AGE

Research in developmental and lifespan psychology documents changes within the person that occur across the life span, including declines in select cognitive processing abilities that contribute to fluid intelligence, increases in declarative knowledge that contributes to crystallized intelligence, changes in motive primacy, and changes in intensity of select personality traits (see Kanfer & Ackerman, 2004, for a review). Intraindividual differences in these abilities and traits occur very slowly, and the impact of age-related differences in motivation is typically studied using cross-sectional samples that compare individuals at different chronological age periods (e.g., young, midlife, old). Findings obtained to date indicate a general downward shift with age in the valence of common extrinsic rewards, such as a promotion or increased pay, and a general upward shift with age in the attractiveness of intrinsic outcomes, such as autonomy (in the form of flexible work scheduling) and competency (in the form of opportunity to utilize skills; Warr, 2008).

Age has also been shown to be negatively related to training speed and learning self-efficacy, most likely as a consequence of the age-related decline in fluid intellectual abilities that influence both these variables. Taken together with the age-related decline in the attractiveness of extrinsic rewards, these findings suggest that older workers (with lower levels of learning self-efficacy) are likely to be less motivated to participate in new skill learning than younger workers. However, findings by Simpson, Greller, & Stroh (2002) indicate that older workers are no less motivated than younger workers for learning opportunities, and were more likely to participate in such opportunities when the criterion for participation extended to non-organizationally sponsored learning opportunities. Studies by Sitzmann and her colleagues (Sitzmann et al., 2009; Sitzmann & Ely, 2010) suggest that the use of prompts to employ self-regulatory strategies during training enhanced learning and reduced attrition over the course of training. These results suggest that motivational declines associated with perceptions of slow progress and poor performance among older workers may be mitigated by the use of instructional designs that assist and promote effective self-regulation strategies.

Transactional Perspectives

The allocation of personal resources to work-related activities is not a single decision, but rather an ongoing process that is influenced by changes in the person, the environment, and the transaction between the person and the environment. In this section, I briefly review recent work on the motivational processes by which person-environment transactions influence performance and attitudes.

MATCH THEORIES OF JOB PERFORMANCE AND WORK ATTITUDES

A central thesis in the person-environment research literature—and a widely held belief among organizational practitioners—is that alignment of employee and organization goals, values, interests, and competencies facilitates work motivation, positive job attitudes and job intentions (e.g., job satisfaction, organizational commitment), and performance. These models do not posit that values, objectives, and competencies needed by the organization and possessed by the individual be identical, only that the individual *perceives* that his or her values, objectives, and competencies are congruent with the demands of the job. As George and Brief (1996) suggested, a high level of perceived congruence between an employee's goals and that of his or her team members may exert a positive impact on performance through its effect on adjusting resource allocation policies, or as Kristof (1996) suggests, by helping persons know "the right thing" to do. Similarly, perceptions of poor alignment or lack of congruence between one's goals and those of other team members is expected to exert a negative

impact on motivational processes and, in turn, work behavior and attitudes.

Perceptions of congruence are contextually sensitive, and research has shown the impact of a wide range of personal and situational variables on different fit perceptions (Kristof, 1996, for a review). Organizational change programs and the way in which they are implemented, for example, may substantially change employee perceptions of fit and congruence at one or more levels, including organizational, work group, and job levels. Employee perceptions of fit may also occur as a function of job tenure and age-related and/or non-work-related change associated with the person, rather than the environment. At hire, employees may perceive job tasks as challenging and report a high level of perceived congruence between the cognitive demands of the job and one's knowledge, skills, and abilities. Over time, however, the perception of abilities-demand fit may weaken as the demands of the job no longer require substantial effort or attention. For these employees, a once challenging job has become boring.

A large research literature exists on the consequences of different forms of fit between an individual and his or her work environment (Kristof, 1996). Surprisingly, however, only a relatively small portion of this research focuses directly on motivational processes. During the 1980s, Dawis and Lofquist (1984) proposed a theory of work adjustment that emphasized the importance of person-environment fit, and described fit in terms of its effects on employee motivation and need satisfaction. Although Dawis and Lofquist (1984) delineated the motivational processes by which perceptions of fit direct and energize work performance, there has been relatively little research to examine the validity of the their proposed pathways between fit and work outcomes. From a different but complementary perspective, French, Caplan, and Van Harrison (1982) highlighted the negative motivational consequences associated with perceptions of poor person-environment (P-E) in terms of higher feelings of job stress, higher levels of negative affect, and more physical health problems (see Edwards, 1996; Shaw & Gupta, 2004).

Greguras and Diefendorff (2009) describe a promising new direction for theory and research on the motivational processes and mechanisms by which perceived congruence may affect performance and attitudes. Noting the communality between need satisfaction models and universal motive theories, Greguras and Diefendorff (2009) proposed that intrinsic motives for autonomy, relatedness, and competence mediate perceived fit-outcome relations. Findings obtained using a sample of managers provide support for the mediating role of individual differences in perceived satisfaction of these motives in different perceived fit-performance and attitude relations. Consistent with SDT, as well as the theory of work adjustment (Dawis & Lofquist, 1984), these findings indicate that perceptions of congruence in different dimensions influence work performance and attitudes through their influence on intrinsic motive satisfaction.

The Greguras and Diefendorff (2009) findings represent part of a growing trend in fit research to investigate the positive, rather than negative, consequences of perceptions of different types of fit on work behavior and performance (Vancouver & Schmitt, 1991).

Consequences of Motivation: The Criterion Problem

Most work motivation research evaluates motivation in terms of the behaviors and performance observed on a single target task. In the modern workplace, however, employees are often assigned multiple tasks, each with a different deadline for completion. In these instances, assessments of motivation require measurement of the individual's resource allocation across tasks, as well as resource allocations within each task. In multiple goal or task situations, the assessment of motivation across tasks typically involves measures of time allocated to each task. To fully evaluate motivation in multiple goal or task environments, however, researchers must also assess the impact of time to total resource allocation across all tasks, and how changes in goals, self-efficacy, and goal pursuit in each component task affect time allocations to other tasks. An excellent example of the complexities and advantages involved in assessing motivation in a multiple goal regulation setting is provided by Schmidt et al. (2009).

Changes in the nature of work also raise the question of what the appropriate indices of work motivation are. Extant models of work motivation are designed to provide prediction of effort and persistence on a single, well-defined task (e.g., painting a room). However, many modern jobs require motivation to accomplish multiple, interdependent tasks (e.g., prepare and launch a new store opening) or ill-defined tasks (e.g., produce a new company slogan). Motivation in these job tasks is likely to involve complex and interrelated resource allocation policies governing the use of time, effort intensity, and

the use of personal capital (e.g., social and technical knowledge) for successful performance. Research is needed to determine the factors that influence effective and ineffective strategies for goal pursuit in multiform and creative task accomplishments. Findings from this line of work are likely to be of substantial practical importance for the early identification of motivational problems, and for the development of effective interventions in these task settings.

Work Motivation Strategies and Practices

Advances in work motivation are closely connected to changes in the nature of work. During most of the twentieth century, motivation theory and practice focused on identifying the fundamental determinants of work motivation, the psychological processes involved in goal choice and goal pursuit, and effective organizational strategies to increase employee effort on the job and to reduce turnover. Expectancy-value theories, goal setting, participative decision-making approaches, job characteristics theories, and equity theory generated research that added new knowledge to predicting motivation for a specific work task.

At the start of the twenty-first century, however, most employees perform multiple work tasks, often concurrently. Over the course of a workweek, a registered nurse may treat a dozen patients, communicate information about each patient to physicians, radiologists, surgeons, and physical therapists, update electronic patient files, counsel patient families, and negotiate schedule and workload with other nurses on the unit. Accomplishment of each task requires allocation of personal resources that vary as a function of task demands, task deadlines, importance, and intrinsic interest in the task. It is no longer feasible or desirable for organizations to monitor and reward the performance of each job task as it occurs. In the twenty-first century job, employees are often tasked with motivating themselves to organize job tasks, to allocate personal resources to different task goals as conditions dictate, and to modify allocation policies when performance progress is not sufficient. In short, job performance in many workplaces today demands self-management. From a resource allocation perspective, the most effective motivational strategy is one in which performance accomplishments are associated with attainment of valued rewards. In short, the most effective strategy is intrinsic motivation, in which tasks are performed for their own sake and performance accomplishments satisfy intrinsic motives for competence, achievement, control, self-determination, and autonomy. Consistent with this notion, purposive theories, such as Dweck's goal orientation theory and Deci's SDT, have rapidly gained popularity.

Purposive theories of motivation emphasize goal pursuit and the use of intrinsic incentives to power self-regulatory activities over time for goal accomplishment. As Steel and Konig's (2006) TMT suggests, extrinsic incentives, such as yearly bonuses, are frequently too far in the future to motivate allocations of time and effort to the accomplishment of immediate subgoals prerequisite for achieving the complex goal outcome at some future date. In training, for example, extrinsic incentives (e.g., promotion or pay raise contingent on final course performance) are not powerful incentives for allocating more time to studying at the beginning of the course. And the provision of extrinsic incentives for attainment of each subgoal is not a realistic option. SDT and purposive theories of motivation address this practical problem by delineating the conditions that promote sustained self-regulation of effort over time using intrinsic incentives, such as a sense of self-determination, communion with others, competence, control, and autonomy.

Accordingly, the problem in modern motivation theory and practice is not whether extrinsic rewards undermine intrinsic motivation, but rather how to use extrinsic rewards to promote and sustain intrinsic task motivation. Although more empirical research is needed on this question, the findings to date suggest that the negative impact of extrinsic rewards on intrinsic motivation may be limited to specific person-situation conditions. In routine jobs, such as cashiering, initial interest in work tasks and performance motivation may be low without the provision of performance-contingent extrinsic bonus payments to stimulate the adoption of difficult goals and goal striving. Over the course of goal pursuit, however, individuals are likely to become more proficient at the job, and goal attainment may yield intrinsic as well as extrinsic rewards. As intrinsic incentives become more salient, extrinsic rewards for performance accomplishment may be phased out, as individuals pursue higher levels of performance for purposes of intrinsic motive satisfaction. Depending on the task, however, intrinsic motivation may wane over time as further allocations of time and effort yield smaller improvements in performance and correspondingly weaker intrinsic rewards. Experienced cashiers, for example, are likely to perform at a high level with less effort due to task proceduralization, making further performance improvement and intrinsic rewards for performance

less likely, unless the individual allocates substantial increases in time and effort. However, the provision of performance-contingent extrinsic rewards again at this point, in the form of social recognition or employee/team competitions among similarly experienced individuals, may stimulate the higher allocations of time and effort necessary for improved performance and heightened feelings of competence and self-determination. In summary, this analysis suggests that the primary purpose of extrinsic rewards in the modern workplace (beyond rewards associated with the employment contract) is to promote and sustain intrinsic work motivation, rather than to directly sustain motivation and performance indefinitely.

Findings in goal setting and goal orientation research provide indirect evidence to support this conceptualization. Numerous studies show that extrinsic rewards exert a positive influence on goal choice, but can also exert a detrimental impact on goal pursuit. Findings in goal orientation further show that individuals who adopt goals for purposes related to the satisfaction of intrinsic motives related to learning, mastery, and accomplishment employ more effective self-regulatory strategies and show higher levels of performance than persons who adopt goals for purposes related to satisfaction of other-oriented, extrinsic motives (to prove one's ability to others, to avoid looking incompetent to others). In some instances, however, when task demands are low or individuals are experienced at the task, the adoption of a performance-prove goal orientation may promote the use of effective self-regulation strategies and higher levels of performance.

To date, researchers have focused on the goal attributes that facilitate intrinsically rewarded forms of goal pursuit and higher levels of performance. However, as reviews by Parker and Ohly (2008) and Fried and Ferris (1987) suggest, intrinsic motivation may also be promoted or diminished by the context of action. For example, using Meyer's notion of situational specificity, work contexts that are high in clarity and consistency are likely to produce environments that are conducive to the development of intrinsic motivation, while environments that are high in constraints and consequences are likely to diminish intrinsic motivation. Similarly, the effectiveness of transformation leaders in enhancing subordinate motivation may be best understood in terms of what these leaders do to create conditions that induce intrinsic motivation among subordinates. Organizing diverse motivational strategies in terms of their impact on facilitating intrinsic forms of motivation is likely to greatly facilitate the translation of research findings into effective managerial practices.

Practical Challenges and Emerging Research Directions

The previous sections highlighted recent progress in work motivation theory and practice. Although theory and research continues in the quest for basic understanding (e.g., Stokes, 1997), practical concerns have spurred research in a number of new directions. In this section, I describe a few current practical challenges, and their implications for research and practice.

Aging and Work Motivation

Over the next three decades, the proportion of the workforce over the age of 65 is predicted to grow to nearly 30%. Organizations are already struggling with how to effectively recruit, manage, motivate, retrain, and retain older workers. Early theory and research on work motivation as a function of adult development suggests that age-related changes in cognitive abilities and non-ability traits, motives, and interests exert an important influence on work motivation and performance. In particular, age-related changes in abilities and skills among individuals who perform jobs that place strong demands on these abilities and skills (e.g., firefighter) are likely to have a direct influence on perceptions of person-job fit, work attitudes, and retirement intentions. Age and job tenure may also exert a negative influence on work motivation among individuals who perform a routine job that does not make demands on age-sensitive abilities and skills, but rather affords few opportunities for skill utilization or intrinsic motive satisfaction. Employee age may also play a negative role in work motivation as a consequence of age-sensitive attitudes and behaviors of coworkers, supervisors, or clients. In these instances, motivation for work may decline sharply as opportunities for satisfaction of affiliation motives and a positive self-concept shrink.

To date, organizations have responded to age-related problems in work motivation using a variety of strategies, including changing the work role, providing age-appropriate incentives for staying on the job, and educating managers about the influence of age on work competencies. However, few applications are evidence-based, and studies of age-related changes in motives, interests, and self-regulation strategies remain sparse (for exceptions, see Kooij, De Lange, Jansen, Kanfer, & Dikkers, 2011;

see Shultz & Adams, 2007, for a review). Future research in this area will require a reconsideration of the achievement construct and longitudinal research designs that permit investigation of how personal and occupational characteristics influence motivation to work and motivation at work.

Motivation in Teams

Teams are ubiquitous in organizations, and new technologies have spurred the increasing use of inter-professional teams and teams of teams, or multiteam systems in the workplace (Marks, DeChurch, Mathieu, Panzer, & Alonso, 2005). Corresponding to this trend, theory and research on team-level processes and motivation surged during the late twentieth century. Nonetheless, there are still a number of practically important questions to be addressed regarding the determinants and consequences of motivational processes in the team context. Marks et al. (2001) suggest that motivational processes play a crucial role in team-level activities to manage interpersonal relationships that support team performance. Despite these advances in team motivation, our understanding of cross-level influences between team-level and team member motivation processes remains incomplete. To date there has been relatively little research examining the relationship between different motivational states and interpersonal management strategies (see Rico, Sanchez-Manzanares, Gil, & Gibson, 2008). We also do not fully understand the key factors that influence the spread of affective states, such as disappointment, across members of the team, or the cross-level effects of affective states on individual- and team-level decision making as they may play out in real-world military, health care, and other work team settings. In a related vein, research to understand the influence of motivational orientations on action processes and interpersonal goal conflicts is another promising direction for future research. Using the adaptive team leadership model proposed by Kozlowski, Watola, Jensen, Kim, and Botero (2009) as an organizing framework for such research may be quite fruitful.

Relational Dynamics and Work Motivation

As jobs move from production to services, relationships with coworkers, supervisors, and clients take on increased importance in ratings of job performance. Findings across a variety of topics suggest that these social relationships are also potentially important determinants of work motivation and behavior. Numerous studies in leadership, for example, have focused on the impact of a leader's relationship with a subordinate on employee work motivation, job attitudes, and performance. Studies of emotion regulation in service jobs, and research on events that trigger strong affective reactions, also suggest that interpersonal conflicts demand additional resource allocations for emotion regulation and restoration of attentional focus to work goals. Interpersonal dynamics are also frequently implicated in the direction of resource allocations, such as toward helping others or engaging in counterproductive behaviors.

Research is needed to understand how coworker dynamics facilitate and dampen work motivation and influence the direction of action. Coworker relations influence the interpretation of work events and can also elicit strong, other-oriented affective feeling states, such as pride, shame, guilt, and jealousy. Social relations and the individual's social ties at work can also contribute to an individual's work identity. Social power is also likely to influence the success of job crafting efforts. In the modern workplace, coworker relations are typically embedded in a social network that can affect motivation for coming to work and for behavior at work (e.g., Bowler & Brass, 2006). Research is needed to examine how attributes of an individual's social network and changes in relationships with key members of the network influence an individual's goals and methods for task accomplishment.

Motivation and Leadership

Motivation is an integral part of leadership theory and practice. Advances during the twentieth century focused on the behaviors and processes by which supervisors and leaders win the "mind" of their subordinates and followers. Investigations of how leaders motivate workers in the team context represent a fertile area for investigating the impact of implicit leader behaviors on subordinate motivation, as well as the role of affectively driven leader behaviors on winning the "hearts" of followers through goal orientation and commitment processes.

Work Motivation over Time

As noted previously, we still know relatively little about the determinants of work motivation cycles or their natural timescales. Studies of within-subject variability have focused largely on affect and mood states. Within-subject studies to identify the impact of personality traits and occupational demands on variability in the direction of resource allocations, motivational state, and goal revision cycles will help

to inform the relative contribution of situational strength and implicit motivation processes on work behavior. Findings from this line of research also have practical implications for work design.

Motivation in Training and Development

The development of dynamic models of learning and investigations of motivation within these models reflect the renaissance that is taking place in this domain. Although there has been substantial progress made in specifying the motivational processes involved in self-regulated learning, organizations and social policy makers continue to raise important research questions in this area. For example, new instructional technologies and e-learning opportunities raise many questions about how these structures may affect situational strength and the self-regulatory strategies used during learning and for transfer. With tens of millions of adults currently engaged in online skill learning, a better understanding of the motivational implications of these environments on learning, behavior, and performance is crucial.

Research on motivation in training would also benefit from closer attention to the trainee's learning environment. Increasingly, individuals complete training in groups and classes characterized by diversity in age, gender, and ethnicity. Training is often conducted online during non-work time. Anecdotal stories by trainees suggest that trainee class diversity, limited social interactions with other students and the teacher, evaluation apprehension, and the cost of training on non-work activities may exert deleterious effects on training motivation. Research to identify best practices for sustaining motivation during training, particularly among mid- and late-life trainees, is urgently needed.

Putting Back the "I" in Work Motivation

Theory and research in work motivation continue to focus on the role that self-related variables, such as self-efficacy and core self-evaluations, play in goal choice, goal pursuit, and job performance. A logical next step in this direction is to consider the role of broader self-constructs, such as work identity on motivation.

Work identity refers to self-concept that is grounded in the tasks that individuals perform, the work roles that they adopt, the organizations in which they work, the occupations with which they identify, and the ways in which they perform their work (Walsch & Gordon, 2008). As such, work identity is a developmental process that likely creates a work schema which may show greater resistance to change with age.

A small but growing number of researchers have begun to study work motivation from an identity perspective. Research by Wrzesniewski (2003; Wrzesniewski, McCauley, Rozin, & Schwartz, 1997), for example, distinguishes between individuals who view their work as a job (focused on attainment of extrinsic rewards, such as pay), a career (focused on advancement), or a calling (intrinsically motivated engagement, for the purpose of performing socially useful work). In a related vein, Wrzesniewski and Dutton (2001) introduced the term *job crafting* to refer to the ways in which individuals attempt to shape the job in a way to provide greater opportunities for satisfaction of intrinsic and social motives (similar to accommodation strategies discussed previously). Although the main focus of work motivation theory and research will likely remain on proximal influences on work behavior and job performance, identity theories offer a higher level conceptualization of motivational orientation that may be particularly helpful in identifying patterns of goal choice, goal pursuit, job crafting, affective reactions, and work outcomes associated with individuals with different perceptions of the purpose for their work.

Work Motivation and Well-being

Self-concordance theory (Sheldon, 2002; Sheldon & Elliot, 1999) posits that individuals who pursue goals and activities that they enjoy and believe in experience higher levels of subjective well-being. As applied to work, this theory suggests that work motivation plays an important role in worker well-being. Although work motivation has been rarely studied in terms of worker well-being beyond that of job satisfaction (for an exception, Judge, Bono, Erez, & Locke, 2005), mounting societal and organizational concern about worker well-being suggests that more attention be given to the factors that promote self-concordant motivation and the consequences of self-concordant motivation for worker well-being. Findings by Bono and Judge (2003) indicate the role of transformational leadership in promoting self-concordant motivation among subordinates. Further research is needed to extend these findings and to more precisely delineate the motivational processes that enhance worker well-being.

Summary and Discussion

Although work motivation remains an area of scientific and practical importance, this review suggests that there has been substantial change in the key constructs, processes, and issues that currently command the attention of motivational scientists and practitioners. In contrast to prior theories that emphasized rational models of goal choice, explicit personal motives, and self-management processes, emerging formulations focus on the determinants and consequences of the individual's goal orientation, and the impact of non-conscious processes and implicit motives on goal choice, goal pursuit, affective states, and performance. Although self-efficacy, goals, and personality traits continue to be studied in work motivation, the focus of attention has subtly shifted toward understanding the dynamics by which these inputs change over time. And affect, long accorded a subordinate role in motivational processing, continues to garner research attention as an independent influence on behavior and a major determinant of self-regulatory processing. Scientific advances, the changing nature of work, and the growing emphasis on worker adjustment has, in turn, shifted research attention to different aspects of content, context, and change influences on work motivation. As discussed previously in this chapter, Table 14.2 highlights some of the current gaps in our knowledge and potentially fruitful areas for future research.

At a more general level, two themes permeate recent theory and research in work motivation. The first theme pertains to the increasing use of person-centric rather than performance-centric approaches. Performance-centric approaches minimize within-person dynamics and emphasize how changes in work design, managerial practices, and organization-level variables (e.g., climate) affect motivation and performance of different individuals at a particular point in time. Accordingly, performance-centric approaches tend to bias investigations about the determinants of motivation and performance toward the study of stable personal traits and changes in the environment. Such approaches have been quite useful, particularly in the study of motivation in production environments where job structure is often high, an individual's goal choice can be accomplished through an immediate increase in allocations of effort (rather than prolonged goal pursuit), and behavior is often closely coupled to job performance.

In contrast to performance-centric approaches, person-centric approaches emphasize the role of adult development and ongoing person-situation interactions in work motivation. Personal characteristics, goals, and experiences are posited to influence

Table 14.2 Examples of Current Knowledge Gaps in Work Motivation Research

Content (Person) Influences:

Worker well-being (e.g., health)

Non-conscious/affective motives (e.g., hostility)

Motivational signatures of discrete emotions

Trait complexes

Context (Environment) Influences:

Situational strength

Intra-team processes (e.g., conflict)

Multi-team processes (e.g., cultural differences, social networks, goal coordination demands)

E-learning

Change-Related Influences:

Intrinsic motivation processes

Resource depletion, recovery, and fatigue

Adult development (aging)

Work transitions (e.g., reemployment, retirement and career change)

what features of the environment are salient to the individual, the interpretation of these perceptions, and their translation into motivational variables, such as self-efficacy. Person-centric approaches also assume that changes in motivation and work behavior bring about changes in both the individual and the environment.

The adoption of a person-centric approach to work motivation offers several distinct theoretical and practical advantages. Person-centric approaches encourage multilevel, longitudinal research designs that can illuminate potential differences in the impact of context both across persons and within persons over time, as well as the potential impact of person traits on context and within-person motivation over time. From a practical perspective, person-centric approaches provide organizations with information about age-normed influences on work motivation and how different interventions affect different aspects of work behavior over time. This is particularly important in the modern workplace, where organizations may not be able to precisely predict which behaviors and work outcomes are going to have the greatest importance for job

performance in the future. The many advantages of person-centric approaches for studying personal and situational factors that influence goal formulation and goal pursuit in the workplace are likely to increase the dominance of this perspective for some time.

A second theme that runs through much of the recent work in the field pertains to the growing interest in the role that affect and social relations play in work motivation. For most of the twentieth century, theories of work motivation viewed affect as a static influence on performance, either in terms of the valence that individuals attach to different work outcomes, or as a work attitude (Weiss & Cropanzano, 1996). However, research on implicit motives, non-conscious motivational processes, and events that trigger non-consciously mediated behaviors (such as anger) maintain a very different view of affect. These approaches generally view affect as dynamic and as distinct, biologically driven, non-conscious processes associated with behavior tendencies that activate during action in much the same way that explicit traits influence cognitively mediated motivational processes. This conceptualization puts motivation and affect on a more equal footing, and suggests that motives and non-conscious affective tendencies operate in unison to influence goal choice and goal pursuit (i.e., work motivation). Indeed, newer theories suggest that explicit self-regulatory activities largely operate in the service of managing non-conscious affective tendencies that conflict with explicit goal accomplishment (e.g., Kehr, 2004), and the existence of a non-conscious goal and regulatory system for these affectively driven action tendencies (Bargh, 2008).

Work motivation researchers are also devoting more attention to how social interactions and interpersonal dynamics influence affective states and non-conscious affective action tendencies. The rich social medium in which modern work is performed increases the likelihood that different emotions will be activated, either as a direct consequence of social interactions or in the anticipation of social interactions (e.g., anxiety). Research currently in progress to investigate the relationship between social interactions and the stream of emotions that occur over the workday can be expected to importantly contribute to further progress in understanding the impact of affect on work motivation.

The adoption of person-centric approaches and the emphasis on social relations and affective processes increase the salience of several thorny questions in motivational science, such as how individuals prioritize resource allocations in multiple goal/task settings, why and how individuals adjust resource allocations to multiple goals/tasks over time, and how individuals resolve goal conflicts, when individuals abandon goals, and factors that affect strategy choice for regulation of implicit motive tendencies and negative emotions. As this review attests, there is good reason to be optimistic that the field will continue to make progress answering these and other central questions about work motivation. Theory and research advances over the past two decades also show that work motivation researchers are equally inspired by pressing practical problems in the workplace. Examples of emerging research streams inspired by real-world issues include studies on motivation in and of teams, the impact of culture and work unit diversity on motivation and performance, the antecedents and consequences of different motivational strategies during job search, the effects of motivation on successful aging in the workplace, the influence of motivational conflicts on self-regulated job performance, and motivational influences on creativity and innovation. The nature of recent advances, driven equally by the goal of translating basic research for practical use, and the goal of translating organizational and worker motivation concerns into workable research questions bode well for the field.

References

Ackerman, P. L. (1996). A theory of adult intellectual development: Process, personality, interests, and knowledge. *Intelligence, 22*, 229–259.

Ackerman, P. L. (1997). Personality, self-concept, interests, and intelligence: Which construct doesn't fit? *Journal of Personality, 65*, 171–204.

Ackerman, P. L. (2011). 100 years without resting. In P. L. Ackerman (Ed.), *Cognitive fatigue: Multidisciplinary perspectives on current research and future applications* (pp. 11–43). Washington, DC: American Psychological Association.

Adams, J. S. (1965). Inequity in social exchange. *Advanced Experimental Social Psychology, 62*, 335–343.

Ajzen, I. (1991). The theory of planned behavior. *Organizational Behavior and Human Decision Processes, 50*, 179–211.

Ambrose, M. L., & Kulik, C. T. (1999). Old friends, new faces: Motivation research in the 1990s. *Journal of Management, 25*, 231–292.

Armitage, C. J., & Conner, M. (2001). Efficacy of the theory of planned behaviour: A meta-analytic review. *British Journal of Social Psychology, 40*, 471–499.

Armor, D. A., & Taylor, S. E. (2003). The effects of mindset on behavior: Self-regulation in deliberative and implemental frames of mind. *Personality and Social Psychology Bulletin, 20*, 86–95.

Ashford, S. J., & Cummings, L. L. (1983). Feedback as an individual resource: Personal strategies for creating information. *Organizational Behavior and Human Performance, 32*, 370–389.

Atkinson, J. W., & Birch, D. (1970). *The dynamics of action*. New York: Wiley.

Austin, J. T., & Klein, H. J. (1996). Work motivation and goal striving. In K. R. Murphy (Ed.), *Individual differences and behavior in organizations* (pp. 209–257). San Francisco: Jossey-Bass.

Bakker, A. B., Hakanen, J. J., Demerouti, E., & Xanthopoulou, D. (2007). Job resources boost work engagement, particularly when job demands are high. *Journal of Educational Psychology, 99*, 274–284.

Baldwin, T. T., Magjuka, R. J., & Loher, B. T. (1991). The perils of participation: Effects of choice of training on trainee motivation and learning. *Personnel Psychology, 44*, 51–65.

Bandura, A. (1969). *Principles of behavior modification*. New York: Holt, Rinehart, & Winston.

Bandura, A. (1973). *Aggression: A social learning analysis*. Englewood Cliffs, NJ: Prentice Hall.

Bandura, A., & Locke, E. A. (2003). Negative self-efficacy and goal effects revisited. *Journal of Applied Psychology, 88*, 87–99.

Bargh, J. A. (2008). Free will is un-natural. In J. Baer, J. Kaufman, & R. Baumeister (Eds.), *Are we free? The psychology of free will* (pp. 128–154). New York: Oxford University Press.

Bargh, J. A., Gollwitzer, P. M., & Oettingen, G. (2010). Motivation. In S. Fiske, D. Gilbert, & G. Lindzey (Eds.), *Handbook of social psychology* (5th ed., pp. 268–316). New York: Wiley.

Barrick, M. R., & Mount, M. K. (1991). The big five personality dimensions and job performance: A meta-analysis. *Personnel Psychology, 44*, 1–26.

Barrick, M. R., Mount, M. K., & Strauss, J. P. (1993). Conscientiousness and performance of sales representatives: Tests of the mediating effects of goal setting. *Journal of Applied Psychology, 78*, 715–722.

Barrick, M. R., Stewart, G. L., & Piotrowski, M. (2002). Personality and job performance: Test of the mediating effects of motivation among sales representatives. *Journal of Applied Psychology, 87*, 43–51.

Baumeister, R. F., Bratslavsky, E., Muraven, M., & Tice, D. M. (1998). Ego-depletion: Is the active self a limited resource? *Journal of Personality and Social Psychology, 74*, 1252–1265.

Beach, L. R., & Mitchell, T. R. (1987). Image theory: Principles, goals, and plans in decision-making. *Acta Psychologica, 66*, 201–220.

Beier, M. E., & Kanfer, R. (2009). Motivation in training and development: A phase perspective. In S. W. J. Kozlowski & E. Salas (Eds.), *Learning, training, and development in organizations* (pp. 65–97). New York: Psychology Press.

Bell, B. S., & Kozlowski, S. W. J. (2002). Adaptive guidance: Enhancing self-regulation, knowledge, and performance in technology-based training. *Personnel Psychology, 55*, 267–306.

Bell, B. S., & Kozlowski, S. W. J. (2008). Active learning: Effects of core training design elements on self-regulatory processes, learning, and adaptability. *Journal of Applied Psychology, 93*, 296–316.

Binnewies, C., Sonnentag, S., & Mojza, E. J. (2009). Daily performance at work: Feeling recovered in the morning as a predictor of day-level job performance. *Journal of Organizational Behavior, 30*, 67–93.

Bono, J. E., & Judge, T. A. (2003). Self-concordance at work: Toward understanding the motivational effects of transformational leaders. *Academy of Management Journal, 46*, 554–571.

Bowler, W. M., & Brass, D. J. (2006). Relational correlates of interpersonal citizenship behavior: A social network perspective. *Journal of Applied Psychology, 91*, 70–82.

Brunstein, J. C., & Maier, G. W. (2005). Implicit and self-attributed motives to achieve: Two separate but interacting needs. *Journal of Personality and Social Psychology, 89*, 205–222.

Button, S. B., Mathieu, J. E., & Zajac, D. M. (1996). Goal orientation in organizational research: A conceptual and empirical foundation. *Organizational Behavior and Human Decision Processes, 67*, 26–48.

Campbell, J. P., & Pritchard, R. D. (1976). Motivation theory in industrial and organizational psychology. In M. D. Dunnette (Ed.), *Handbook of industrial and organizational Psychology* (pp. 63–130). Chicago: Rand McNally.

Carr, J. Z., DeShon, R. P., & Dobbins, H. W. (2001). A process model of goal orientation. In R. P. DeShon (Chair), *New directions in goal orientation: Exploring the construct and its measurement*. Presented at 16th Annual Meeting of the Society for Industrial and Organizational Psychology, San Diego, CA.

Carstensen, L. L. (1992). Motivation for social contact across the life span: A theory of socioemotional selectivity. *Nebraska Symposium on Motivation, 40*, 209–254..

Chen, G., Bliese, P. D., & Mathieu, J. E. (2005). Conceptual framework and statistical procedures for delineating and testing multilevel theories of homology. *Organizational Research Methods, 8*, 375–409.

Chen, G., & Gogus, C. (2008). Motivation in and of work teams: A multilevel perspective. In R. Kanfer, G. Chen, & R. D. Pritchard (Eds.), *Motivation: Past, present, and future* (pp. 285–318). New York: Routledge.

Chen, G., Gully, S. M., Whiteman, J. A., & Kilcullen, R. N. (2000). Examination of relationships among trait-like individual differences, state-like individual differences, and learning performance. *Journal of Applied Psychology, 85*, 835–847.

Chen, G., & Kanfer, R. (2006). Toward a systems theory of motivated behavior in work teams. *Research in Organizational Behavior, 27*, 223–267.

Chen, G., Kanfer, R., DeShon, R. P., Mathieu, J. E., & Kozlowski, S. W. J. (2009). The motivating potential of teams: Test and extension of Chen and Kanfer's (2006) cross-level model of motivation in teams. *Organizational Behavior and Human Decision Processes, 110*, 45–55.

Chen, G., Kirkman, B. L., Kanfer, R., Allen, D., & Rosen, B. (2007). A multilevel study of leadership, empowerment, and performance in teams. *Journal of Applied Psychology, 92*, 331–346.

Chen, G., Webber, S. S., Bliese, P. D., Mathieu, J. E., Payne, S. C., Born, D. H., & Zaccaro, S. J. (2002). Simultaneous examination of the antecedents and consequences of efficacy beliefs at multiple levels of analysis. *Human Performance, 15*, 381–409.

Chiaburu, D. S., & Marinova, S. V. (2005). What predicts skill transfer? Exploratory study of goal orientation, training, self-efficacy, and organizational supports. *International Journal of Training and Development, 9*, 110–123.

Colquitt, J. A., Conlon, D. E., Wesson, M. J., Porter, C., & Ng, K. Y. (2001). Justice at the millenium: A meta-analytic review of 25 years of organizational justice research. *Journal of Applied Psychology, 86*, 425–445.

Colquitt, J. A., LePine, J. A., & Noe, R. A. (2000). Toward an integrative theory of training motivation: A meta-analytic path analysis of 20 years of research. *Journal of Applied Psychology, 85*, 678–707.

Colquitt, J. A., & Simmering, M. J. (1998). Conscientiousness, goal orientation, and motivation to learn during the learning processes: A longitudinal study. *Journal of Applied Psychology, 83*, 654–665.

Cox, C. B., & Beier, M. E. (2009). The moderating effect of individual differences on the relationship between the framing of training and interest in training. *International Journal of Training and Development, 13*, 247–261.

Creed, P. A., King, V., Hood, M., & McKenzie, R. (2009). Goal orientation, self-regulation strategies, and job-seeking intensity in unemployed adults. *Journal of Applied Psychology, 94*, 806–813.

Dalal, R. S., & Hulin, C. L. (2008). Motivation for what: A multivariate, dynamic perspective of the criterion. In R. Kanfer, G. Chen, & R. D. Pritchard (Eds.), *Motivation: Past, present, and future* (pp. 63–100). New York: Routledge.

Dawis, R. V., & Lofquist, L. H. (1984). *A psychological theory of work adjustment: An individual-differences model and its applications*. Minneapolis: University of Minnesota Press.

Day, E. A., Yeo, S., & Radosevich, D. J. (2003). Comparing two- and three-factor models of goal orientation: A meta-analysis. Paper Presented at the 18th Annual Meeting of the Society for Industrial and Organizational Psychology, Orlando, FL.

DeChurch, L. A., & Mesmer-Magnus, J. R. (2010) Measuring shared team mental models: A meta-analysis. *Group Dynamics: Theory, Research, and Practice, 14*, 1–14.

Deci, E. L. (1975). *Intrinsic motivation*. New York: Plenum Publishing.

Deci, E. L., & Ryan, R. M. (2000). The "what" and "why" of goals pursuits: Human needs and the self-determination of behavior. *Psychological Inquiry, 11*, 227–268.

Deci, E. L., & Ryan, R. M. (2002). Self-determination research: Reflections and future directions. In E. L. Deci & R. M. Ryan (Eds.), *Handbook of self-determination research* (pp. 431–441). Rochester, NY: University of Rochester Press.

DeShon, R. P., & Gillespie, J. Z. (2005). A motivated action theory account of goal orientation. *Journal of Applied Psychology, 90*, 1096–1127.

DeShon, R. P., Kozlowski, S. W. J., Schmidt, A. M., Milner, K. R., & Wiechmann, D. (2004). A multiple-goal, multilevel model of feedback effects on the regulation of individual and team performance. *Journal of Applied Psychology, 89*, 1035–1056.

Diefendorff, J. M., & Lord, R. G. (2008). Goal striving and self-regulation processes. In R. Kanfer, G. Chen, & R. D. Pritchard (Eds.), *Motivation: Past, present, and future* (pp. 151–196). New York: Routledge.

Diefendorff, J. M., & Mehta, K. (2007). The relations of motivational traits with workplace deviance. *Journal of Applied Psychology, 92*, 967–977.

Dweck, C. S. (1986). Motivational processes affecting learning. *American Psychologist, 41*, 1040–1048.

Dweck, C. S., & Leggett, E. L. (1988). A social-cognitive approach to motivation and personality. *Psychological Review, 95*, 256–273.

Edwards, J. R. (1996). An examination of competing versions of the person-environment fit approach to stress. *Academy of Management Journal, 39*, 292–339.

Elliot, A. J. (2008). *Handbook of approach and avoidance motivation*. Mahwah, NJ: Lawrence Erlbaum Associates.

Elliot, A. J., & Harackiewicz, J. M. (1996). Approach and avoidance achievement goals and intrinsic motivation: A mediational analysis. *Journal of Personality and Social Psychology, 70*, 461–475.

Elliot, A. J., & McGregor, H. A. (2001). A 2 X 2 achievement goal framework. *Journal of Personality and Social Psychology, 80*, 501–519.

Elliot, A. J., & Thrash, T. M. (2001). Approach-avoidance motivation in personality: Approach and avoidance temperaments and goals. *Journal of Personality and Social Psychology, 82*, 804–818.

Erez, M. (2008). Social-cultural influences on work motivation. In R. Kanfer, G. Chen, & R. D. Pritchard (Eds.), *Motivation: Past, present, and future* (pp. 501–538). New York: Routledge.

Ferguson, M. J., Hassin, R., & Bargh, J. A. (2008). Implicit motivation. In J. Y. Shah & W. L. Gardner (Eds.), *Handbook of motivation science* (pp. 150–166). New York: Guilford Press.

Fishbein, M., & Ajzen, I. (1975). *Belief, attitude, intention, and behavior: An introduction to theory and research.* Reading, MA: Addison-Wesley.

Fishbein, M., & Ajzen, I. (2010). *Predicting and changing behavior: The reasoned action approach.* New York: Psychology Press.

Flavell, J. H. (1979). Metacognition and cognitive monitoring: A new area of cognitive-developmental inquiry. *American Psychologist, 34*, 906–911.

Folger, R., & Cropanzano, R. (1998). *Organizational justice and human resource management.* Thousand Oaks, CA: Sage.

Ford, J. K., Smith, E. M., Weissbein, D. A., Gully, S. M., & Salas, E. (1998). Relationships of goal orientation, metacognitive activity, and practice strategies with learning outcomes and transfer. *Journal of Applied Psychology, 83*(2), 218–233.

Frayne, C. A., & Latham, G. P. (1987). The application of social learning theory to employee self management of attendance. *Journal of Applied Psychology, 72*, 387–392.

French, J. R. P., Caplan, R. D., & Van Harrison, R. (1982). The *mechanisms of job stress and strain.* New York: Wiley.

Frese, M., & Fay, D. (2001). Personal initiative (PI): An active performance concept for work in the 21st century. *Research in Organizational Behavior, 23*, 133–187.

Frese, M., Kring, W., Soose, A., & Zempel, J. (1996). Personal initiative at work: Differences between East and West Germany. *Academy of Management Journal, 39*, 37–63.

Frese, M., & Zapf, D. (1994). Action as the core of work psychology: A German approach. In H. C. Triandis, M. D. Dunnette, & L. M. Hough (Eds.), *Handbook of industrial and organizational psychology* (Vol. 4, pp. 271–340). Palo Alto, CA: Consulting Psychologists Press.

Fried, Y., & Ferris, G. R. (1987). The validity of the job characteristics model: A review and meta-analysis. *Personnel Psychology, 40*, 287–322.

Fried, Y., Grant, A. M., Levi, A. S., Hadant, M., & Slowik, L. H. (2007). Job design in temporal context: A career dynamics perspective. *Journal of Organizational Behavior, 28*, 911–927.

Fritz, C., & Sonnentag, S. (2005). Recovery, well-being and job performance: Effects of weekend experiences. *Journal of Occupational Health Psychology, 10*, 187–199.

Fritz, C., & Sonnentag, S. (2006). Recovery, well-being, and performance-related outcomes: The role of workload and vacation experiences. *Journal of Applied Psychology, 91*, 936–945.

Frost, B. C., Ko, C. E., & James, L. R. (2007). Implicit and explicit personality: A test of a channeling hypothesis for aggressive behavior. *Journal of Applied Psychology, 92*, 1299–1319.

Gagne, M., & Deci, E. L. (2005). Self-determination theory and work motivation. *Journal of Organizational Behavior, 26*, 331–362.

Gagne, M., & Forest, J. (2008). The study of compensation systems through the lens of self-determination theory: Reconciling 35 years of debate. *Canadian Psychology, 49*, 225–232.

Gelfand, M. J., Erez, M., & Aycan, Z. (2007). Cross-cultural organizational behavior. *Annual Review of Psychology, 58*, 479–514.

George, J. M., & Brief, A. P. (1996). Motivational agendas in the workplace: The effects of feelings on focus of attention and motivation. *Research in Organizational Behavior, 18*, 75–109.

Gist, M. E., Bavetta, A. G., & Stevens, C. K. (1990). The effectiveness of self-management versus goal setting training in facilitating training transfer. *Academy of Management Best Papers Proceedings*, 117–121.

Goldstein, I. L. (1993). *Training in organizations* (3rd ed.). Pacific Grove, CA: Brooks/Cole.

Gollwitzer, P. M. (1990). Action phases and mind-sets. In E. T. Higgins & R. M. Sorrentino (Eds.), *Handbook of motivation and cognition* (Vol. 2, pp. 53–92). New York: Guilford Press.

Gollwitzer, P. M. (2003). Why we thought that action mind-sets affect illusions of control. *Psychological Inquiry, 14*, 259–267.

Gollwitzer, P. M., & Kinney, R. F. (1989). Effects of deliberative and implemental mind-sets in the control of action. *Journal of Personality and Social Psychology, 59*, 1119–1127.

Greenberg, J., & Cropanzano, R. (1999). *Advances in organizational justice.* Stanford, CA: Stanford Press.

Greenwald, A. G., McGhee, D. E., & Schwartz, J. K. L. (1998). Measuring individual differences in implicit cognition: The implicit association test. *Journal of Personality and Social Psychology, 74*, 1464–1480.

Greguras, G. J., & Diefendorff, J. M., (2009). Different fits satisfy different needs: Linking person-environment fit to employee attitudes and performance using self-determination theory. *Journal of Applied Psychology, 94*, 465–477.

Guion, R. M., & Gottier, R. F. (1965). Validity of personality measures in personnel selection. *Personnel Psychology, 18*, 135–164.

Guerrero, S., & Sire, B. (2001). Motivation to train from the workers' perspective: Example of French companies. *International Journal of Human Resource Management, 12*, 988–1004.

Hackman, J. R., & Oldham, G. R. (1976). Motivation through the design of work: Test of a theory. *Organizational Behavior & Human Performance, 16*, 250–279.

Heckhausen, H. (1991). *Motivation and action.* Berlin: Springer Verlag.

Heckhausen, J., & Schultz, R. (1995). A life-span theory of control. *Psychological Review, 102*, 284–304.

Heggestad, E. D., & Kanfer, R. (2005). The predictive validity of self-efficacy in training performance: Little more than past performance. *Journal of Experimental Psychology: Applied, 11*, 84–97.

Heimerdinger, S. R., & Hinsz, V. B. (2008). Failure avoidance motivation in a goal-setting situation. *Human Performance, 21*, 383–395.

Higgins, E. T. (1998). Promotion and prevention: Regulatory focus as a motivational principle. In M. P. Zanna (Ed.),

Advances in experimental social psychology (Vol. 30, pp. 1–46). New York: Academic Press.

Hobfoll, S. E. (1989). Conservation of resources: A new attempt at conceptualizing stress. *American Psychologist, 44*, 513–524.

Hollenbeck, J. R., & Klein, H. J. (1987). Goal commitment and the goal-setting process: Problems, prospects, and proposals for future research. *Journal of Applied Psychology, 72*, 212–220.

Humphrey, S. E., Nahrgang, J. D., & Morgeson, F. P. (2007). Integrating motivational, social, and contextual work design features: A meta-analytic summary and theoretical extension of the work design literature. *Journal of Applied Psychology, 92*, 1332–1356.

Hurtz, G. M., & Donovan, J. J. (2000). Personality and job performance: The big five revisited. *Journal of Applied Psychology, 85*, 869–879.

Hurtz, G. M., & Williams, K. J. (2009). Attitudinal and motivational antecedents of participation in voluntary employee development activities. *Journal of Applied Psychology, 94*, 635–653.

James, L. R. (1998). Measurement of personality via conditional reasoning. *Organizational Research Methods, 1*, 131–163.

James, L. R., McIntyre, M. D., Glisson, C. A., Green, P. D., Patton, T. W., LeBreton, J. M., Frost, B. C., Russell, S. M., Sablynski, C. J., Mitchell, T. R., & Williams, L. J. (2005). A conditional reasoning measure for aggression. *Organizational Research Methods, 8*, 69–99.

James, L. R., & Rentsch, J. R. (2004). JUSTIFY to explain the reasons why: A conditional reasoning approach to understanding motivated behavior. In B. Schneider & D. B. Smith (Eds.), *Personality and organizations* (pp. 230–250). Mahwah, NJ: Lawrence Erlbaum Associates.

Johns, G. (2006). The essential impact of context on organizational behavior. *Academy of Management Review, 31*, 386–408.

Johnson, R. E., Lord, R. G., Rosen, C. C., & Chang, C. H. (2007). The implicit effects of (un)fairness on motivation: What we aren't aware of might be important! Unpublished manuscript.

Johnson R. E., & Steinman L. (2009). The use of implicit measures for organizational research: An empirical example. *Canadian Journal of Behavioural Science, 41*, 202–212.

Johnson, R. E., Tolentino, A. L., Rodopman, O. B., & Cho, E. (2010). We (sometimes) know not how we feel: Predicting job performance with an implicit measure of trait affectivity. *Personnel Psychology, 63*, 197–219.

Judge, T. A., & Bono, J. E. (2001) Relationship of core self-evaluations traits—self-esteem, generalized self-efficacy, locus of control, and emotional stability—with job satisfaction and job performance: A meta-analysis. *Journal of Applied Psychology, 86*, 80–92.

Judge, T. A., Bono, J. E., Erez, A., & Locke, E. A. (2005). Core self-evaluations and job and life satisfaction: The role of self-concordance and goal attainment. *Journal of Applied Psychology, 90*, 257–268.

Judge, T. A., & Hurst, C. (2007). Capitalizing on one's advantages: Role of core self-evaluations. *Journal of Applied Psychology, 92*, 1212–1227.

Judge, T. A., & Ilies, R. (2002). Relationship of personality to performance motivation: A meta-analytic review. *Journal of Applied Psychology, 87*, 530–541.

Judge, T. A., Locke, E. A., & Durham, C. C. (1997). The dispositional causes of job satisfaction: A core evaluations approach. *Research in Organizational Behavior, 19*, 151–188.

Kanfer, R. (1987). Task specific motivation: An integrative approach to issues of measurement, mechanisms, processes, and determinants. *Journal of Social and Clinical Psychology, 5*, 237–264.

Kanfer, R. (1989). Non-cognitive processes, dispositions, and performance: Connecting the dots within and across paradigms. In R. Kanfer, P. L. Ackerman, & R. Cudeck (Eds.), *Abilities, motivation, and methodology: The Minnesota symposium on learning and individual differences* (pp. 375–388). Hillsdale, NJ: Lawrence Erlbaum Associates.

Kanfer, R. (1990). Motivation theory and industrial and organizational psychology. In M. D. Dunnette (Ed.), *Handbook of industrial and organizational psychology* (Vol. 1, 2nd ed., pp. 75–130). Palo Alto, CA: Consulting Psychologists Press.

Kanfer, R. (1992). Work motivation: New directions in theory and research. In C. L. Cooper & I. T. Robertson (Eds.), *International Review of Industrial and Organizational Psychology* (Vol. 7, pp.1–53). London: John Wiley.

Kanfer, R. (1993). *Education from a workplace perspective: Issues of self-management.* Resources in Education ERIC Document Reproduction Service No. 348–717.

Kanfer, R. (2009). Work and older adults: Motivation and performance. In C. J. Czaja & J. Sharit (Eds.), *The future of work for an aging population.* Baltimore, MD: John Hopkins University Press.

Kanfer, R., & Ackerman, P. L. (1989). Motivation and cognitive abilities: An integrative/aptitude-treatment interaction approach to skill acquisition. [Monograph]. *Journal of Applied Psychology, 74*, 657–690.

Kanfer, R., & Ackerman, P. L. (2004). Aging, adult development, and work motivation. *Academy of Management Review, 29*, 440–458.

Kanfer, R., Ackerman, P. L., & Heggestad, E. (1996). Motivational skills and self-regulation for learning: A trait perspective. *Learning and Individual Differences, 8*, 185–209.

Kanfer, R., Chen, G., & Pritchard, R. D. (2008). The three C's of work motivation: Content, context, and change. In R. Kanfer, G. Chen, & R. D. Pritchard (Eds.), *Motivation: Past, present, and future* (pp. 1–16). New York: Routledge.

Kanfer, R., & Heggestad, E. (1997). Motivational traits and skills: A person-centered approach to work motivation. In L. L. Cummings & B. M. Staw (Eds.), *Research in organizational behavior* (Vol. 19, pp. 1–57). Greenwich, CT: JAI Press.

Kanfer, R., & Kantrowitz, T. M. (2002). Ability and nonability predictors of performance. In S. Sonnentag (Ed.), *Psychological management of individual performance: A handbook in the psychology of management in organizations* (pp. 27–50). Oxford: John Wiley.

Kanfer, F. H., & Phillips, J. S. (1969). *Learning foundations of behavior therapy.* Oxford: John Wiley.

Kanfer, R., Ackerman, P. L., Murtha, T. C., Dugdale, B., & Nelson, L. (1994). Goal setting, conditions of practice, and task performance: A resource allocation perspective. *Journal of Applied Psychology, 79*, 826–835.

Kanfer, R., & Stubblebine, P. (2008). Affect and work motivation. In N. M. Ashkansay & C. L. Cooper (Eds.), *Research companion to emotions in organizations* (pp. 170–182). Cheltenham, UK: Edward Elgar Publishing.

Kanfer, R., Wanberg, C., & Kantrowitz, T. M. (2001). Job search and employment: A personality-motivational analysis and meta-analytic review. *Journal of Applied Psychology, 86*, 837–855.

Kanfer, R., Wolf, M. B., Kantrowitz, T. M., & Ackerman, P. L. (2009). Ability and trait complex predictors of job performance: a person-situation approach. *Applied Psychology: An International Review, 59*, 40–69.

Karasek, R. (1979). Job decision latitude, job demands and mental strain: Implications for job redesign. *Administrative Science Quarterly, 24*, 285–308.

Karasek, R. (1989). The political implications of psychosocial work redesign. *Internet Journal of Health Services, 19*, 481–508.

Katzell, R. A., & Thompson, D. E. (1990). Work motivation: Theory and practice. *American Psychologist, 45*, 144–153.

Kehr, H. (2004). Integrating implicit motives, explicit motives and perceived abilities: The compensatory model of work motivation and volition. *Academy of Management Review, 29*, 479–499.

Keith, N., & Frese, M. (2005). Self-regulation in error management training: Emotion control and metacognition as mediators of performance effects. *Journal of Applied Psychology, 90*(4), 677–691.

Keith, N., & Frese, M. (2008). Effectiveness of error management training: A meta-analysis. *Journal of Applied Psychology, 93*, 59–69.

Klein, H. J., Austin, J. T., & Cooper, J. T. (2008). Goal choice and decision processes. In R. Kanfer, G. Chen, & R. D. Pritchard (Eds.), *Motivation: Past, present, and future* (pp. 101–150). New York: Routledge.

Kooij, D. T. A. M., De Lange, A. H., Jansen, P. G. W., Kanfer, R., & Dikkers, J. S. E. . (2011). Age and work-related motives: Results of a meta-analysis. *Journal of Organizational Behavior, 32*, 197–225..

Kozlowski, S. W. J., & Bell, B. S. (2006). Disentangling achievement orientation and goal setting: Effects on self-regulatory processes. *Journal of Applied Psychology, 91*, 900–916.

Kozlowski, S. W. J., & Ilgen, D. R. (2006). Enhancing the effectiveness of work groups and teams. *Psychological Science in the Public Interest, 7*, 77–124.

Kozlowski, S. W. J., & Salas, E. (Eds.). (2010). *Learning, training, and development in organizations*. New York: Routledge/ Taylor-Francis Group.

Kozlowski, S. W. J., Watola, D. J., Jensen, J. M., Kim, B. H., & Botero, I. C. (2009). Developing adaptive teams: A theory of dynamic team leadership. In E. Salas, G. F. Goodwin, & C. S. Burke (Eds.), *Team effectiveness in complex organizations: Cross-disciplinary perspectives and approaches* (pp. 113–155). New York: Routledge/Taylor & Francis Group.

Kristof, A. L. (1996). Person-organization fit: An integrative review of its conceptualizations, measurement, and implications. *Personnel Psychology, 49*, 1–49.

Kuhl, J. (1986). Human motivation: From decision making to action control. In B. Rehmer, B. Jungermann, P. Laures, & G. Sevon (Eds.), *New directions in research on decision making* (pp. 5–28). Amsterdam: North-Holland.

Lam, C. F., DeRue, D. S., Karam, E. P., & Hollenbeck, J. R. (2011). The impact of feedback frequence on learning and task performance: Challenging the "more is better" assumption. *Organizational Behavior and Human Decision Processes, 116*, 217–228.

Latham, G. P. (2007). *Work motivation: History, theory, research and practice*. Thousand Oaks, CA: Sage

Latham, G. P., & Brown, T. (2006). The effect of learning vs. outcome goals on self-efficacy, satisfaction and performance in an MBA program. *Applied Psychology: An International Review, 55*, 606–623.

Latham, G. P., & Frayne, C. A. (1989). Self management training for increasing job attendance: A follow-up and a replication. *Journal of Applied Psychology, 74*, 411–416.

Latham, G. P., Erez, M., & Locke, E. A. (1988). Resolving scientific disputes by the joint design of crucial experiments by the antagonists: Application to the Erez-Latham dispute re participation in goal setting. *Journal of Applied Psychology, 73*, 753–772.

Latham, G. P., & Pinder, C. C. (2005). Work motivation theory and research at the dawn of the 21st century. *Annual Review of Psychology, 56*, 485–516.

Latham, G. P., Stajkovic, A. D., & Locke, E. A. (2010). The relevance and viability of subconscious goals in the workplace. *Journal of Management, 36*, 234–255.

Lewin, K. (1938). *Conceptual representation and the measurement of psychological forces*. Durham, NC: Duke University Press.

Locke, E. A. (1968). Toward a theory of task motivation and incentives. *Organizational Behavior & Human Performance, 3*, 157–189.

Locke, E. A. (1976). The nature and causes of job satisfaction. In M. D. Dunnette & L. M. Hough (Eds.), *Handbook of industrial and organizational psychology* (pp. 1319–1328). Palo Alto, CA: Consulting Psychologists Press.

Locke, E. A., & Latham, G. P. (1990). *A theory of goal setting and task performance*. Englewood Cliffs, NJ: Prentice-Hall.

Locke, E. A., Shaw, K. N., Saari, L. M., & Latham, G. P. (1981). Goal setting and task performance: 1969–1980. *Psychological Bulletin, 90*, 125–152.

Locke, E. A., & Schweiger, D. M. (1979). Participation in decision-making: One more look. *Research in Organizational Behavior, 1*, 265–340.

Lord, R. G., Diefendorff, J. M., Schmidt, A. M., & Hall, R. J. (2010). Self-regulation at work. *Annual Review of Psychology, 61*, 543–568.

Lord, R. G., & Foti, R. J. (1986). Schema theories, information processing and organizational behavior. In H. P. Sims, Jr., & D. A. Gioia (Eds.), *The thinking organization: Dynamics of organizational social cognitions* (pp. 20–48). San Francisco: Jossey-Bass.

Lord, R. G., & Moon, S. M. (2006). Individual differences in automatic and controlled regulation of emotion and task performance. *Human Performance, 19*, 327–356.

Lubinski, D. (2000). Scientific and social significance of assessing individual differences. "Sinking shafts at a few critical points." *Annual Review of Psychology, 51*, 405–444.

Marks, M. A., DeChurch, L. A., Mathieu, J. E., Panzer, F. J., & Alonso, A. (2005). Teamwork in multiteam systems. *Journal of Applied Psychology, 90*, 964–971.

Marks, M. A., Mathieu, J. E., & Zaccaro, S. J. (2001). A temporally based framework and taxonomy of team processes. *Academy of Management Review, 26*, 35–376.

Mathieu, J. E., & Martineau, J. W. (1997). Individual and situational influences on training motivation. In J. K. Ford & Associates (Eds.), *Improving training effectiveness in work organizations* (pp. 193–222). Mahwah, NJ: Lawrence Erlbaum Associates.

McClelland, D. C. (1987). *Human motivation*. New York: Cambridge University Press.

Meyer, J. P., & Allen, N. J. (1991). A three-component conceptualization of organizational commitment. *Human Resources Management Review, 1*, 61–89.

Meyer, J. P., & Allen, N. J. (1997). *Commitment in the workplace: Theory, research, and application*. Thousand Oaks, CA: Sage.

Meyer, J. P., Becker, T. E., & Vandenberghe, C. (2004). Employee commitment and motivation: A conceptual analysis and integrative model. *Journal of Applied Psychology, 89*, 992–1007.

Meyer, J. P., & Herscovitch, L. (2001). Commitment in the workplace: Toward a general model. *Human Resource Management Review, 11*, 299–326.

Meyer, R. D., & Dalal, R. S. (2009). Situational strength as a means of conceptualizing context. *Industrial and Organizational Psychology: Perspectives on Science and Practice, 2*, 99–102.

Meyer, R. D., Dalal, R. S., & Bonaccio, S. (2009). A meta-analytic investigation into the moderating effects of situational strength on the conscientiousness-performance relationship. *Journal of Organizational Behavior, 30*, 1077–1102.

Meyer, R. D., Dalal, R. S., & Hermida, R. (2010). A review and synthesis of situational strength in the organizational sciences. *Journal of Management, 36*, 121–140.

Michalak, J., Puschel, O., Joormann, J., & Schulte, D. (2006). Implicit motives and explicit goals: Two distinctive modes of motivational functioning and their relations to psychopathology. *Clinical Psychology and Psychotherapy, 13*, 81–96.

Mischel, W. (1968). *Personality and assessment*. New York: Wiley.

Mischel, W., & Ebbesen, E. B. (1970). Attention in delay of gratification. *Journal of Personality and Social Psychology, 16*, 329–337.

Mitchell, T. R. (1974). Expectancy models of job satisfaction, occupational preference, and effort: A theoretical, methodological, and empirical appraisal. *Psychological Bulletin, 81*, 1053–1077.

Mitchell, T. R. (1980). Expectancy-value models in organizational psychology. In N. Feather (Ed.), *Expectancy, incentive and action* (pp. 293–312). Hillsdale, NJ: Lawrence Erlbaum Associates.

Mitchell, T. R. (1982). Motivation: New directions for theory, research, and practice. *Academy of Management Review, 7*, 80–88.

Mitchell, T. R., & Daniels, D. (2003). Motivation. In W. C. Borman, D. R. Ilgen, & R. J. Klimoski (Eds.), *Handbook of psychology*, Volume 12, *Industrial psychology* (pp. 225–254). New York: Wiley.

Mitchell, T. R., Harmon, W. S., Lee, T. W., & Lee, D-Y. (2008). Self-regulation and multiple deadline goals. In R. Kanfer, G. Chen, & R. D. Pritchard (Eds.), *Motivation: Past, present, and future* (pp. 197–232). New York: Routledge.

Mitchell, T. R., Hopper, H., Daniels, D., George-Falvy, J., & James, L. R. (1994). Predicting self-efficacy and performance during skill acquisition. *Journal of Applied Psychology, 79*, 506–517.

Muraven, M., Tice, D. M., & Baumeister, R. F. (1998). Self-control as a limited resource: Regulatory depletion patterns. *Journal of Personality and Social Psychology, 74*, 774–789.

Naylor, J. C., Pritchard, R. D., & Ilgen, D. R. (1980). *A theory of behavior in organizations*. New York: Academic Press.

Nicholls, J. G. (1984). Conceptions of ability and achievement motivation. In R. Ames & C. Ames (Eds.), *Research on motivation in education* (Vol. 1., pp. 39–73). San Diego, CA: Academic Press.

Noe, R. A. (1986). Trainees' attributes and attitudes: Neglected influences on training effectiveness. *Academy of Management Review, 11*, 736–749.

Parker, S. K., & Ohly, S. (2008). Designing motivating jobs: An expanded framework for linking work characteristics and motivation. In R. Kanfer, G. Chen, & R. D. Pritchard (Eds.), *Motivation: Past, present, and future* (pp. 233–284). New York: Routledge.

Payne, S. C., Youngcourt, S. S., & Beaubien, J. M. (2007). A meta-analytic examination of the goal orientation nomological net. *Journal of Applied Psychology, 92*, 128–150.

Pearsall, M. J., Christian, M. S., & Ellis, A. P. J. (2010). Motivating interdependent teams: Individual rewards, shared rewards, or something in between? *Journal of Applied Psychology, 95*, 183–191.

Pinder, C. C. (1998). *Work motivation in organizational behavior*. Saddle River, NJ: Prentice Hall.

Pinder, C. C. (2008). *Work motivation in organizational behavior* (2nd ed.). New York: Psychology Press.

Porter, C. O. L. H., Webb, J. W., & Gogus, C. I. (2010). When goal orientations collide: Effects of learning and performance orientation on team adaptability in response to workload imbalance. *Journal of Applied Psychology, 95*, 935–943.

Pritchard, R. D., Harrell, M. M., DiazGranados, D., & Guzman, M. J. (2008). The productivity measurement and enhancement system: A meta-analysis. *Journal of Applied Psychology, 93*, 540–567.

Randel, A. E., & Ranft, A. L. (2007). Motivations to maintain social ties with coworkers: The moderating role of turnover intentions on information exchange. *Group and Organization Management, 32*, 208–232.

Rawsthorne, L. J., & Elliot, A. J. (1999). Achievement goals and intrinsic motivation: A meta-analytic review. *Personality and Social Psychology Review, 3*, 326–344.

Raynor, J. O., & Entin, E. E. (1982). Theory and research on future orientation and achievement motivation. In J. O. Raynor & E. E. Entin (Eds.), *Motivation, career striving, and aging* (pp. 13–82). Washington, DC: Hemisphere.

Rico, R., Sanchez-Manzanares, M., Gil, F., & Gibson, C. (2008). Team implicit coordination processes: A team knowledge-based approach. *Academy of Management Review, 33*, 163–184.

Ruud, C., & Aarts, H. (2010). The unconscious will: How the pursuit of goals operates outside of conscious awareness. *Science, 329*, 47–50.

Salancik, G. R., & Pfeffer, J. (1978). A social information processing approach to job attitudes and task design. *Administrative Science Quarterly, 23*(2), 224–253

Salas, E., Cooke, N. J., & Rosen, M. A. (2008). On teams, teamwork, and team performance: Discoveries and developments. *Human Factors, 50*, 540–547.

Schmidt, A. M., & DeShon, R. P. (2007). What to do? The effects of discrepancies, incentives, and time on dynamic goal prioritization. *Journal of Applied Psychology, 92*, 928–941.

Schmidt, A. M., & DeShon, R. P. (2009). Prior performance and goal progress as moderators of the relationship between self-efficacy and performance. *Human Performance, 22*, 191–203.

Schmidt, A. M., & DeShon, R. P. (2010). The moderating effects of performance ambiguity on the relationship between self-efficacy and performance. *Journal of Applied Psychology, 95*, 572–581.

Schmidt, A. M., Dolis, C. M., & Tolli, A. P. (2009). A matter of time: Individual differences, contextual dynamics, and goal progress effects on multiple goal self-regulation. *Journal of Applied Psychology, 94*, 692–709.

Schultheiss, O. C., & Brunstein, J. C. (2001). Assessment of implicit motives with a research version of the TAT: Picture profiles, gender differences, and relations to other personality measures. *Journal of Personality Assessment, 77*, 71–86.

Schultheiss, O. C., & Pang, J. H. (2007). Measuring implicit motives. In R. W. Robins, R. C. Fraley, & R. F. Krueger (Eds.), *Handbook of research methods in personality psychology* (pp. 322–344). New York: Guilford Press.

Seo, M., Feldman-Barrett, L. F., & Bartunek, J. M. (2004). The role of affective experience in work motivation. *Academy of Management, 29*, 423–439.

Seijts, G. H., & Latham, G. P. (2005). Learning versus performance goals: When should each be used? *Academy of Management Executive, 19*, 124–131.

Shaw, J. D., & Gupta, N. (2004). Job complexity, performance, and well-being: When does supplies-values fit matter? *Personnel Psychology, 57*, 847–879.

Sheldon, K. M. (2002). The self-concordance model of healthy goal-striving: When personal goals correctly represent the person. In E. L. Deci & R. M. Ryan (Eds.), *Handbook of self-determination theory* (pp. 65–86). Rochester, NY: University of Rochester Press.

Sheldon, K. M., & Elliot, A. J. (1999). Goal striving, need-satisfaction, and longitudinal well-being: The self-concordance model. *Journal of Personality and Social Psychology, 76*, 482–497.

Sheppard, B. H., Hartwick, J., & Warshaw, P. R. (1988). The theory of reasoned action: A meta-analysis of past research with recommendations for modifications and future research. *Journal of Consumer Research, 15*, 325–343.

Shi, J., Lin, H., Wang, L., & Wang, M. (2009). Linking the big five constructs to organizational justice. *Social Behavior and Personality: An International Journal, 37*(2), 209–222.

Shultz, K., & Adams, G. A. (2007). *Aging and work in the 21st century.* Mahwah, NJ: Lawrence Erlbaum Associates.

Simons, J., Dewitte, S., & Lens, W. (2004). The role of different types of instrumentality in motivation, study strategies, and performance: Know why you learn, so you'll know what you learn! *British Journal of Educational Psychology, 74*, 343–360.

Simons, J., Vansteenkiste, M., Lens, W., & Lacante, M. (2004). Placing motivation and future time perspective theory in a temporal perspective. *Educational Psychology Review, 16*, 121–139.

Simpson, P. A., Greller, M. M., & Stroh, L. K. (2002). Variations in human capital investment activity by age. *Journal of Vocational Behavior, 61*, 109–138.

Sitzmann, T., Bell, B. S., Kraiger, K., & Kanar, A. M. (2009). A multilevel analysis of the effect of prompting self-regulation in technology-delivered instruction. *Personnel Psychology, 62*(4), 697–734.

Sitzmann, T., & Ely, K. (2010). Sometimes you need a reminder: The effects of prompting self-regulatory processes, learning and attrition. *Journal of Applied Psychology, 95*, 132–144.

Sonnentag, S., & Frese, M. (2003). Stress in organizations. In W. C. Borman, D. R. Ilgen, & R. J. Klimoski (Eds.), *Handbook of psychology* (Vol. 12, pp. 453–491). Hoboken, NJ: Wiley.

Sonnentag, S., & Fritz, C. (2007). The Recovery Experience Questionnaire: Development and validation of a measure for assessing recuperation and unwinding from work. *Journal of Occupational Health Psychology, 12*, 204–221.

Sonnentag, S., & Kruel, U. (2006). Psychological detachment from work during off-job time: The role of job stressors, job involvement, and recovery-related self-efficacy. *European Journal of Work and Organizational Psychology, 15*, 197–217.

Spangler, W. D. (1992). Validity of questionnaire and TAT measures of need for achievement: Two meta-analyses. *Psychological Bulletin, 112*, 140–154.

Stajkovic, A. D., Locke, E. A., & Blair, E. S. (2006). A first examination of the relationships between primed subconscious goals, assigned conscious goals, and task performance. *Journal of Applied Psychology, 91*, 1172–1180.

Steel, P., & Konig, C. J. (2006). Integrating theories of motivation. *Academy of Management Review, 31*, 889–913.

Stokes, D. E. (1997). *Pasteur's quadrant.* Washington, DC: Brookings Institution Press.

Taylor, S. E., & Gollwitzer, P. M. (1995). Effects of mindset on positive illusions. *Journal of Personality and Social Psychology, 69*, 213–226.

Thorndike, R. L. (Ed.). (1947). *Research problems and techniques* (Rep. No. 3). Washington, DC: U.S. Printing Office.

Tice, D. M., Baumeister, R. F., Shmueli, D., & Muraven, M. (2007). Restoring the self: Positive affect helps improve self-regulation following ego depletion. *Journal of Experimental Social Psychology, 43*(2), 379–384.

Tolli, A. P., & Schmidt, A. M. (2008). The role of feedback, causal attributions, and self-efficacy in goal revision. *Journal of Applied Psychology, 93*, 692–701.

Triandis, H. C. (1980). Values, attitudes, and interpersonal behavior. *Nebraska Symposium on Motivation 1979: Beliefs, Attitudes and Values* (pp. 195–259). Lincoln: University of Nebraska Press.

Truxillo, D. M., Bauer, T. N., Campion, M. A., & Paronto, M. E. (2006). A field study of the role of big five personality in applicant perceptions of selection fairness, self, and the hiring organization. *International Journal of Selection and Assessment, 14*, 269–277.

Utman, C. H. (1997). Performance effects of motivational state: A meta-analysis. *Personality and Social Psychology Review, 1*, 170–182.

Van Hooft, E. A., & Noordzij, G. (2009). The effects of goal orientation on job search and reemployment: A field experiment among unemployed job seekers. *Journal of Applied Psychology, 94*, 1581–1590.

Vancouver, J. B., More, K. M., & Yoder, R. J. (2008). Self-efficacy and resource allocation: Support for a nonmonotonic, discontinuous model. *Journal of Applied Psychology, 93*, 35–47.

Vancouver, J. B., & Schmitt, N. (1991). An exploratory examination of person-organization fit: Organizational goal congruence. *Personnel Psychology, 44*, 333–352.

Vancouver, J. B., Thompson, C. M., Tischner, E. C., & Putka, D. J. (2002). Two studies examining the negative effect of self-efficacy on performance. *Journal of Applied Psychology, 87*, 506–516.

Vancouver, J. B., Thompson, C. M., & Williams, A. A. (2001). The changing signs in the relationships between self-efficacy, personal goals, and performance. *Journal of Applied Psychology, 86*, 605–620.

VandeWalle, D. (1997). Development and validation of a work domain goal orientation instrument. *Educational and Psychological Measurement, 8*, 995–1015.

Vroom, V. (1964). *Work and motivation.* New York: Wiley.

Walsch, K., & Gordon, J. R. (2008). Creating an individual work identity. *Human Resource Management Review, 18*, 46–61.

Warr, P. B. (2008). Work values: Some demographic and cultural correlates. *Journal of Occupational and Organizational Psychology, 81*, 751–775.

Webb, T. L., & Sheeran, P. (2008). Mechanisms of implementation intention effects: The role of goal intentions, self-efficacy, and accessibility of plan components. *British Journal of Social Psychology, 47*, 373–395.

Weiss, H. M., & Cropanzano, R. (1996). Affective events theory: A theoretical discussion of the structure, causes, and consequences of affective experiences at work. *Research in Organizational Behavior, 18*, 1–74.

Whitford, T., & Moss, S. A. (2009). Transformational leadership in distributed work groups: The moderating role of follower regulatory focus and goal orientation. *Communication Research, 35*, 1026–1046.

Winters, D., & Latham, G. P. (1996). The effect of learning versus outcome goals on a simple versus a complex task. *Group and Organization Management, 21*, 235–250.

Wood, R. E., Mento, A. J., & Locke, E. A. (1987). Task complexity as a moderator of goal effects: A meta-analysis. *Journal of Applied Psychology, 72*, 416–425.

Wrzesniewski, A. (2003). Finding positive meaning in work. In K. S. Cameron, J. E. Dutton, & R. E. Quinn (Eds.), *Positive organizational scholarship* (pp. 296–308). San Francisco: Berrett-Koehler.

Wrzesniewski, A., & Dutton, J. E. (2001). Crafting a job: Revisioning employees as active crafters of their work. *Academy of Management Review, 26*, 179–201.

Wrzesniewski, A., McCauley, C., Rozin, P., & Schwartz, B. (1997). Jobs, careers, and callings: People's relations to their work. *Journal of Research in Personality, 31*, 21–33.

Yeo, G., Loft, S., Xiao, T., & Kiewitz, C. (2009). Goal orientations and performance: Differential relationships across levels of analysis and as a function of task demands. *Journal of Applied Psychology, 94*, 710–726.

Yeo, G., & Neal, A. (2006). An examination of the dynamic relationship between self-efficacy and performance across levels of analysis and levels of specificity. *Journal of Applied Psychology, 91*, 1088–1101.

Zaccaro, S. J., Ely, K., & Nelson, J. (2008). Leadership processes and work motivation. In R. Kanfer, G. Chen, & R. D. Pritchard (Eds.), *Motivation: Past, present, and future* (pp. 319–360). New York: Routledge.

Zimmerman, B. J., & Schunk, D. H. (2001). *Self-regulated learning and academic achievement: Theoretical perspectives* (2nd ed.). Mahwah, NJ: Lawrence Erlbaum Associates.

Job Satisfaction and Job Affect

Timothy A. Judge, Charles L. Hulin, *and* Reeshad S. Dalal

Abstract

Job satisfactions—multidimensional psychological responses to one's job—have a long and rich tradition of research in psychology. Comparing and contrasting job attitudes with social attitudes, the present chapter presents various theoretical models of job attitudes. These theoretical approaches give rise to an integrative model which draws most heavily from the Cornell model of job attitudes. We then consider newer theoretical approaches, including engagement, affective events, personality, and unit-level satisfaction. Capitalizing on recent trends in personality, affect, and multilevel research, we also present a core self-evaluations multilevel model. We conclude with a discussion of measurement issues in job satisfaction research.

Key Words: Satisfaction, attitudes, job satisfaction, work attitudes, affect

Employees may and often do have many attitudes about their job and their work. These attitudes vary along many dimensions, including target, specificity, intensity, salience, and stability. In this chapter we discuss portions of the theoretical and empirical literature on one job attitude: job satisfaction. Job satisfaction is an application of the original conceptual definitions of social attitudes, although the deviations that job attitudes have taken from these beginnings are as important as the direct linear connections. We discuss theoretical models of antecedents of job satisfactions. Our discussion of these theoretical models emphasizes constructs (e.g., frames of reference, organizational withdrawal), rather than individual variables, as manifestations of the constructs (e.g., local unemployment, turnover); there are more individual variables that may be regarded as antecedents or consequences of job attitudes than can be reasonably discussed in this chapter. We focus our discussion on three general areas: the theoretically necessary breadth of measures of constructs, the strength and generality

of the job satisfaction/job behavior relationship, and new directions of job attitude research.

We discuss differences and similarities between social attitudes and job satisfactions in terms of their relations with individual job behaviors and general behavioral constructs. Our juxtaposition of job satisfactions with social attitudes is important for several reasons. First, though it is reasonable, perhaps even necessary, to view job satisfactions as social attitudes, there are important differences between these concepts; the differences may tell us as much about social attitudes as they do about job satisfactions. Second, the differences may also suggest questions about the ecological validity of investigations of social attitudes that have studied a limited range of populations, settings, and content or targets of the attitudes. In short, the social attitudes literature has revealed many insights into psychology, but it is often limited by *what* (e.g., overwhelmingly, political or cultural attitudes or identities, as opposed to contextual attitudes about one's job, one's life, one's family, etc.), with *whom* (e.g., a heavy reliance on college undergraduates, which may limit the scope and nature of the investigations), and *how* (e.g., behavior is often not studied, or is studied in a sterile, though well-controlled, experimental context) attitudes are studied. That the job satisfaction literature often addresses these issues suggests that social attitudes researchers would benefit as much from reading the job attitudes literature as the converse. Finally, and as we note immediately below, although theorizing about the nature of social attitudes has served job attitudes research well, some of these theoretical concepts are increasingly being challenged, usually implicitly, by new developments from many areas of psychological research.

We address the departure of the study of job attitudes from the original tripartite definitions of social attitudes that emphasized *cognitive*, *affective*, and *behavioral* elements of attitude space (Campbell, 1963; Thurstone, 1928). Past studies of job satisfaction have focused on judgment-based, cognitive evaluations of jobs, or on characteristics or features of jobs, and have generally ignored affective antecedents of evaluations of jobs, as well as the episodic events that happen on jobs. Accordingly, we devote considerable space in this review to the affective nature of job satisfaction, and how consideration of job affect necessitates revision in how we conceptualize and measure job satisfaction, how we relate the concept to other variables, and how we study job attitudes and affect. Other topics—such as job satisfaction at the between-unit level of analysis, and the contrast between job satisfaction and employee engagement—are also discussed.

Definition and Nature of Job Satisfaction

We define job satisfaction as follows: job satisfactions are multidimensional psychological responses to one's job. These responses have cognitive (evaluative) and affective (emotional) components.[1] Although cognitions are easier to separate from affect in theory than in practice (Adolphs & Damasio, 2001), isolating the two components conceptually does not deny their close—at certain levels inseparable—connections. Job satisfactions refer to internal evaluations of the favorability of one's job. These evaluations are revealed by outward (i.e., verbalized) and inward (i.e., felt) emotional responses. The multidimensional responses can be arrayed along good/bad, positive/negative continua. They may be quantified using assessment techniques that assess evaluations of features or characteristics of the job, emotional responses to events that occur on the job, and, depending on how one defines attitudes,

behavioral dispositions, intentions, and enacted behaviors. We intentionally define job satisfactions in the plural to recognize that while it is meaningful to consider job satisfaction in a global or general sense, it is no less meaningful to consider satisfactions with more specific aspects of one's job (one's pay, one's coworkers, and so on).

Our definition is consistent with definitions of social attitudes offered by Campbell (1963), Eagley and Chaiken (1993), Fishbein (1980), Fishbein and Ajzen (1972, 1975), Thurstone (1928), Triandis (1980), and others. These definitions stress the role of cognitive evaluations in social attitudes but also include affect and behaviors as components of attitudes. Eagley and Chaiken (1993), for example, define an attitude as a psychological tendency that is expressed by evaluating a particular entity with some degree of favor or disfavor. However, they include overt and covert (subconscious) cognitive, affective, and behavioral classes of responding as well.

The original tripartite conceptual definition of attitudes comprising cognitive, affective, and behavioral elements has eroded in industrial and organizational (I/O) psychology, until we are left with assessments of attitudes as cognitive evaluations of social objects. This change seems to have occurred almost by default, perhaps as a result of the *Zeitgeist* in American psychology that has led to the adoption of theoretical positions favoring cognitions even in the absence of definitive data (Zajonc, 1980, 1984). The "cognitive revolution" served psychology well. The many contributions of this revolution—and there have been many—notwithstanding, we are in the midst of another revolution.

This "affective revolution" (Barsade, Brief, & Spataro, 2003) does not deny cognition. It is less oppositional than augmentative. It acknowledges that affective reactions have an evaluative component. Affective responses are more than evaluations, just as all evaluative judgments are not affective, although affect may influence cognitive evaluations. Evaluations of an object very likely influence emotional responses to the object to an unknown degree; the two types of responses are not the same.

Cranny, Smith, and Stone (1992) stated that "Although a review of published works shows that constitutive definitions of the construct vary somewhat from one work to the next, there appears to be general agreement that job satisfaction is an *affective (that is emotional) reaction* to a job that results from the incumbent's comparison of actual outcomes with those that are desired (expected, deserved, and so on)" (p. 1, emphasis added). This definition appears to assume that comparisons of actual outcomes with those desired from a job will reflect variance due to *emotional* reactions and that these emotional reactions can be captured using structured, paper-and-pencil measures of judgments and evaluations. There is little doubt that, until very recently, this was the generally agreed-upon definition; comparisons of job outcomes with desired outcomes were treated as a reasonable basis for measurement of job attitudes.

As a result of the focus of research on satisfaction as a stable individual difference variable, we have a good picture of a network of relations, with job attitudes—assessed as cognitive-affective evaluations of job characteristics—as its core construct. These relations are useful and reliable (Roznowski & Hulin, 1992). This network, however, is a deficient view of the broader construct of job attitudes that includes affective or emotional reactions.

Weiss and Cropanzano (1996) and George (1989) have argued that affect and mood on the job are important components of job attitudes and are potentially important predictors of some job behaviors. The possibility that on-the-job affect will spill over, more generally than do job attitudes, to non-job behaviors that reflect "emotional well-being" cannot be overlooked. Testing a theory that includes affect, however, requires assessments that capture the dynamic, within-person manifestations of affect and emotional reactions. Otherwise, we become enmeshed in a methodological stalemate (Larson & Csikszentmihalyi, 1983), whereby researchers attempt to study propositions of newly developed theories with methods and analyses appropriate only to the needs of an older generation of theoretical models. Weiss, Nicholas, and Daus (1999), Totterdell (2000), Miner (2001), Miner, Glomb, and Hulin (2005), Ilies and Judge (2002), and Dalal, Lam, Weiss, Welch, and Hulin (in press) have assessed affective responses on the job using assessments and analyses that handle the within-person and multilevel demands of conceptualizations and assessments of affect as a dynamic variable.

Summary

The foregoing indicates that the inclusion of affect into definitions of job satisfactions is well-grounded historically (consistent with definitions of social attitudes), but the measurement and theoretical meaning of this grounding is only beginning to be understood and exploited. It is now clear that traditional research designs, historical causal models, and characteristic measurement strategies may do a poor job of capturing the affective nature of job satisfactions. The conceptual and empirical efforts required to capture the essence of job affect will be emphasized at several points later in this chapter.

Conceptual Similarity and Empirical Differences Between Social and Job Attitudes

If we define attitudes as psychological tendencies expressed by cognitive, affective, and behavioral evaluations of a particular entity, then, in the study of job satisfaction, different aspects of the job or the job as a whole become the target of the evaluations. The conceptual overlap between social attitudes and job satisfactions is apparent. Empirical differences are also apparent. Relations between social attitudes and behaviors and between job satisfactions and behaviors are an important difference. At the risk of oversimplification, job attitudes often correlate more strongly with specific job behaviors than social attitudes correlate with specific behaviors (Ajzen & Fishbein, 2005; Campbell, 1963; Eagley & Chaiken, 1993; Fishbein, 1980; Fishbein & Ajzen, 1972, 1974, 1975; Wicker, 1969). Reasons for the lack of reliable relations between social attitudes and specific behaviors have been discussed by Campbell (1963), Doob (1947), Hull, (1943), Fishbein and Ajzen (1974), and Thurstone (1928). Eagley and Chaiken (1993), on the other hand, conclude that the relationship between attitudes and specific behaviors is reliable if a number of other variables are taken into consideration.

Doob (1947), Hull (1943), Thurstone (1928), and Fishbein and Ajzen (1974) have argued that when we identify an individual's attitude toward an object, we have only identified that person's general orientation toward the object; we have not identified if or how they may choose to enact a specific behavior regarding that object. Their attitude will, however, correspond to the centroid of a broad behavioral construct comprising many specific behaviors. Correlations between general attitudes toward an object and specific, isolated behaviors toward that construct are subject to many sources of variance having much to do with behavioral thresholds, distributions, base rates, opportunities, norms, and so on, that may overwhelm any underlying relationship between an attitude and a behavioral orientation toward the object. Moreover, all too often the specific behavior in question may not even be an appropriate operationalization of the behavioral construct of interest. For example, many purportedly "aggressive" responses in popular experimental designs may equally plausibly be interpreted as compliant or conforming responses (Ritter & Eslea, 2005). To assess attitude/behavior correspondence properly, the correspondence between a general attitude toward object and the general value, positive or negative, of a broad family of enacted behaviors should be assessed (Fishbein, 1980; Fishbein & Ajzen, 1972, 1974). Regrettably, however, the content and measurement of important behavioral families (constructs) have been not been the focus of adequate research in social psychology; arguably, the "criterion problem" (Austin & Villanova, 1992) is more severe in social psychology than in I/O psychology.

Fishbein and Ajzen (1974, 1975) have further argued that we need to distinguish among attitudes toward an object, attitudes toward a behavior, and behavioral intentions to carry out that act. The first two constructs predict the last, but behavioral intentions establish the correspondence between attitudes and an act. Relations between attitudes toward acts and behavioral intentions are generally high; relations between attitudes toward an object and intentions to engage in specific behaviors related to that object are occasionally moderately large but are generally modest. Intentions, however, are related to behaviors. This argument shifted the focus from studies of general attitudes and a variety of relevant behaviors and behavioral constructs to analyses of the antecedents of specific behavioral intentions. In this research strategy, every behavior requires the analysis of a different behavioral intention. Behavioral intentions are the *idiot savants* of social and I/O psychology; they do one thing very well, but that is all they do. Dawes and Smith (1985) refer to relations between intentions and behaviors as a *reductio ad absurdum*.

Job Satisfaction and Job Behaviors

Research on relations between job satisfaction and specific behaviors has generated a set of generally positive results. Job attitudes are reliably related to a variety of specific job behaviors (Hulin, 1991; Roznowski & Hulin, 1992). Relations between general job satisfaction and multiple-act behavioral families are stronger and theoretically more useful than relations between general job satisfaction and specific behaviors (Fisher & Locke, 1992; Roznowski & Hulin, 1992). Nonetheless, the general finding is that a wide variety of important specific behaviors are consistently related to job satisfactions. If one has an applied goal predicting a specific behavior, then a measure of intentions to engage in that behavior during the time period of interest is the predictor of choice. However, if corrections for attenuation, sampling variance, and restrictions due to base rates of infrequent behaviors are applied to the observed relations between job attitudes (satisfactions) and specific job behaviors, the resulting estimates of population correlations are noteworthy and may provide a better basis for understanding the attitude/behavior nexus (Hulin, 1991, 2001).

Scientists in other fields of study rarely study variables; they typically study theoretical constructs. The reliable relations between general job attitudes and specific behaviors should not distract us from the scientific goal of establishing relations between general constructs. The practical benefit for applied endeavors can be found by disentangling the relations involving specific behaviors.

Roznowski and Hulin (1992) have concluded that once an individual joins an organization, a vector of scores on a well-constructed, validated set of job satisfaction scales is the most informative data that an organizational psychologist or manager can have about an individual employee and his or her likely behaviors. As evidence for this, they cite a range of empirical relations between job satisfactions and specific job behaviors that include attendance at work (Smith, 1977; Scott & Taylor, 1985), turnover decisions (Carsten & Spector, 1987; Hom, 2001; Hom, Katerberg, & Hulin, 1979; Hulin, 1966b, 1968; Miller, Katerberg, & Hulin, 1979; Mobley, Horner, & Hollingsworth, 1978), decisions to retire (Hanisch & Hulin, 1990, 1991; Schmitt & McCune, 1981), psychological withdrawal behaviors (Roznowski, Miller, & Rosse, 1992), pro-social and organizational citizenship behaviors (Bateman & Organ, 1983; Farrell, 1983; Roznowski et al., 1992), union representation votes (Getman, Goldberg, & Herman, 1976; Schriesheim, 1978; Zalesny, 1985), hostile or punitive behaviors directed toward coworkers or supervisors (Hershcovis et al., 2007), and customers' perceptions of the service provided by employees (Snipes, Oswald, LaTour, & Armenakis, 2005).

Attendance at work, psychological withdrawal, and pro-social behaviors appear to be manifestations of a general family of responses, labeled *work withdrawal*, that reflect attempts to withdraw from the quotidian work tasks that make up a job while maintaining organizational and work-role memberships. Turnover and retirement decisions are manifestations of a family of behaviors labeled *job withdrawal* (Hanisch & Hulin, 1990, 1991). Voting patterns in union representation elections and pre-vote activity may be manifestations of a family of behaviors that represent formal attempts to change characteristics of a work situation (Hulin, 1991). A focus on general behavioral families, rather than on individual behavioral manifestations of the underlying constructs, should generate more reliable relations and greater understanding of the behavioral responses to job satisfactions.

There are many conceptual similarities between social attitudes and job satisfactions. There are also important differences between these constructs as studied. Job attitudes, *qua* evaluations of the job, may be more salient and accessible for workers than the social attitudes typically assessed in social attitude research. Having a dissatisfying job is nearly inescapable from first awakening until the return home. A job is not something we think of only occasionally, as most do about religion, capital punishment, an honor system on campus, people of another race or country, or donating blood. We experience jobs on a nearly constant basis during our working hours; stress caused by job dissatisfaction is our constant companion at work and even on daily commutes. Individuals are also aware of strongly positive job attitudes or job affect throughout the day. The salience and importance of jobs and job attitudes may ensure that job attitudes and job behaviors are more nearly congruent than are many social attitudes and social behaviors.

Job attitudes are also highly personal; one's job intimately involves the self. Job satisfactions represent evaluations of the respondent's own job, the activity that serves to identify us, not an evaluation of an abstract concept or object, as social attitudes typically are. We are what we do. We no longer wear our occupation as our name, as did Archer, Baker, Bowman, Butcher, Brewer, Carpenter, Cartwright, Chandler, Clark, Cooper, Cook, Currier, Dalal, Farrier, Fletcher, Gandhi, Guerrero, Hunter, Jagger, Judge, Mason, Miller, Miner, Porter, Sawyer, Scribner, Shoemaker, Smith, Sodawaterbottleopenerwala, Squire, Tailor, Tanner, Tinker, Wagner, Weaver, and others among our ancestors, but our job remains a major source of our self-identity. We are defined privately and socially by what we do (Green, 1993; Hulin, 2001). Work is a source of autonomy. In individualist cultures, autonomy is among the most strongly held values. In the United States and other individualistic cultures, our autonomy often rests on the foundation of a job, the money it provides, the goods that can be purchased with that money, and the abstract value of "standing on one's own two feet." Attitudes toward that part of ourselves that

one evaluates in a standard job attitude scale cannot be divorced from the individual respondent whose attitudes are being assessed. This degree of personal investment in the attitude object is typically absent from social attitudes assessed in most attitude studies.

Job Satisfaction and Job Performance

Recent evidence suggests that job satisfaction is related to job performance. Judge, Thoresen, Bono, and Patton (2001) have provided an updated meta-analysis of this literature. Their meta-analysis addressed several potential problems with an earlier meta-analysis (Iaffaldano & Muchinsky, 1985) that reported a non-significant relationship. Iaffaldano and Muchinsky (1985) averaged results from specific facets of job satisfaction. Their estimated .17 corrected (.146 uncorrected) correlation between satisfaction and performance was based on the average of the correlations between specific job satisfaction facets and job performance. A composite of the facets or other estimate of the shared variance among the facets is a stronger basis for the relation between general job attitudes with job performance. Addressing these limitations and correcting the estimate for inter-rater unreliability, Judge et al. (2001) estimated the corrected correlation to be .30 (the uncorrected average correlation was .19; the average corrected correlation was .24 when correcting based on intra-rater [internal consistency] reliability). Table 15.1 provides a comparison of these findings with other meta-analytic estimates relating overall job satisfaction to other work outcomes. Readers will differ in how they evaluate the strength of these correlations, and of course the outcomes are not monolithic in either their breadth or measurement. These caveats notwithstanding, the consistency of the estimates is rather remarkable. We would also note that these correlations are underestimates of the *cumulative impact* of job satisfaction for reasons both statistical (the low base rates of withdrawal behaviors downwardly bias correlations; Hulin, 1991) and conceptual (job satisfaction is not related to only one of these behaviors, but is related to families of behaviors).

An important area for research is the nature of job performance (Borman, 1991; Campbell, 1992). It is a broad construct, not a behavior. Job performance comprises many specific behaviors, typically measured through a subjective supervisory evaluation. That job performance is composed of many behaviors is an advantage in terms of its psychometric breadth. It is a disadvantage in terms of isolating its antecedents,

Table 15.1 Summary of Meta-Analyses on Relationship of Job Satisfaction to Work Outcomes

Study	Criterion	$\bar{r}$	$\bar{r}_c$
Judge, Thoresen, Bono, & Patton (2001)[†]	Job performance	.19	.30/.24
Fassina, Jones, & Uggerslev (2008)[*]	Citizenship behavior	.22	.27
Dalal (2005)	Citizenship behavior	.12	.16
LePine, Erez, & Johnson (2002)	Citizenship behavior	.20	.24
Kinicki, McKee-Ryan, Schriesheim, & Carson (2002)	Motivation	.22	.27
Cass, Siu, Faragher, & Cooper (2003)	Employee health	.27	.32
Dalal (2005)	Counterproductive/ deviant behavior	−.29	−.37
Scott & Taylor (1985)	Absenteeism	−.15	−.29
Hackett & Guion (1985)	Absenteeism	−.10	−.14
Hackett (1989)	Absence frequency	−.09	−.15
Hackett (1989)	Absence duration	−.15	−.23
Koslowsky, Sagie, Krausz, & Singer (1997)[*]	Lateness	−.12	−.15
Kinicki, McKee-Ryan, Schriesheim, & Carson (2002)	Days of sick leave	−.10	−.12
Hershcovis et al. (2007)	Coworker aggression	−.14	−.18
Tett & Meyer (1993)	Turnover	−.14	−.25
Griffeth, Hom, & Gaertner (2000)	Turnover	−.17	−.22
Mean		**|.16|**	**|.22|**
Standard deviation		**.05**	**.06**

Notes. $\bar{r}$ = average uncorrected correlation. $\bar{r}_c$ = average correlation corrected for unreliability.

[†] $\bar{r}_c$ = .30 when correcting correlation based on inter-rater reliability; $\bar{r}_c$ = .24 when correcting based on intra-rater (internal consistency) reliability.

[*] Application of composite formula needed for exact estimate.

consequences, and correlates. Research on the job satisfaction–job performance relationship will continue, but we are unlikely to understand the nature of the relationship without knowledge of the myriad antecedent behaviors of job performance and how these behaviors combine and interact with exogenous factors to generate overall job performance. Judge et al. (2001) found similar correlations regardless of the gross nature of the measure of job performance (supervisory evaluations, objective output, etc.), but even objective output is a result of many behaviors by an employee, technological influences, group contributions, feedback from managers, and opportunities.

Moreover, it has been suggested that the more "discretionary" or "contextual"—rather than task-oriented—aspects of job performance are driven primarily by motivational processes, including job attitudes (e.g., Smith, Organ, & Near, 1983). Extrapolating from this, one might predict that job satisfaction's meta-analytic relationships with "discretionary" forms of performance, such as organizational citizenship behavior (OCB) and counterproductive work behavior (CWB), should be somewhat stronger (in absolute value) than the .30 relationship estimated by Judge et al. for overall performance. Although this does appear to be the case for CWB, it does not appear to be so for OCB (see Dalal, 2005).

Further progress on this front was provided by Harrison, Newman, and Roth (2006). Their path analysis based on meta-analytic data supported very broad job attitude (indicated by overall job satisfaction and organizational commitment) and individual effectiveness factors indicated by specific job behaviors (task and interpersonal aspects of job performance, and withdrawal behaviors of lateness, absenteeism, and turnover). When so broadly aggregated, the estimated correlation between job satisfaction and job performance was .50. The model that fit the data best included a progression of withdrawal from lateness to absence to turnover.

Teasing apart the causal nature of satisfaction-performance relationships, investigating mediators and moderators of the relationship, and disaggregating performance to understand what specific behaviors typically compose it may be illuminating. Some job behaviors may result from job satisfaction; others may cause job satisfaction. Still others may be both causes and effects of job satisfaction. The temporal dynamic relations among these constructs and behaviors remain to be explicated. If job performance is disaggregated, behavioral families can be reconstructed, as have behavioral families in the withdrawal area, to highlight relations with antecedents and advance theoretical understanding.

Summary

Reliable relations between job satisfactions and job behaviors may reflect the unavoidability of feelings about jobs, and the salience of jobs to most employees. If we cannot avoid the negative feelings engendered by a job, we avoid as much of the job as we can; we engage in work withdrawal. Job attitudes, if strong enough, may lead to job withdrawal in the form of retirement or quitting. Voting in favor of union representation is an attempt to permanently change the nature of one's job. Positive job attitudes are less likely to engender withdrawal behaviors or attempts to change the work situation.

Theoretical Models of Job Attitudes

In this section we provide a review of the theoretical models of job attitudes.[2] These models attempt to account for the antecedents and complexity of job attitudes among individual workers. The models, for the most part, are not alternative explanations for these attitudes because they focus on different aspects of the general construct. Some specify the characteristics of jobs that workers attend to and evaluate or affectively react to; others specify the process by which job characteristics are evaluated; and still others focus on individual needs as the basis for job reactions. Direct tests of the comparative validity of the models are generally not possible. We offer a description of the models to provide an introduction to the theoretical bases of some of the research in this area.

The Cornell Model

The Cornell model of job attitudes (Hulin, 1991; Smith, Kendall, & Hulin, 1969) was the theoretical foundation of a series of studies of job and retirement attitudes. Two products of this research effort were the Job Descriptive Index (JDI), the most widely used scientific measure of job satisfaction in use today (Cranny, Smith, & Stone, 1992, p. 2; DeMeuse, 1985) and the Retirement Descriptive Index (RDI). A modified version of the Cornell model is depicted in Figure 15.1. This figure depicts sources of influence on frames of reference and how they might influence the *costs* of work role membership and the *value* of work role outcomes to job incumbents, with hypothesized effects on relations between job inputs, job outcomes, and job attitudes.

The Cornell model is differentiated from other theories of job attitudes by the influences of frames of reference on evaluations of job outcomes, as initially formulated (Smith, Kendall, & Hulin, 1969), and also on job inputs, as modified by Hulin (1991), incorporating March and Simon's (1958) input/outcome economic model of job attitudes. Frames of reference can be defined simply as the relative standards that individuals use in evaluating their job outcomes. As shown in Figure 15.1, frames of reference are posited as moderators of the effect of job outcomes on job satisfactions in the sense that whether a certain level of outcomes is judged satisfying depends rather fundamentally on one's standards. These individual standards are influenced by what one has experienced in the past as well as one's immediate economy, living standards, and jobs.

Frame of reference influence on standards for evaluating job outcomes was adapted from Helson's (1948, 1964) work on adaptation-level theory. The concept of frames of reference as generated and modified by individuals' experience was used to account in part for differences in job satisfactions of individuals on objectively identical jobs. Some employees working on objectively unpleasant jobs, with few positive outcomes, express positive evaluations of their work and working conditions, while some employees on objectively desirable jobs evaluate their jobs quite negatively.

Data supporting the influence of frames of reference were provided by Kendall (1963) and Hulin (1966a). Kendall reported an analysis of data from employees of 21 organizations in 21 different communities. Significant negative correlations between

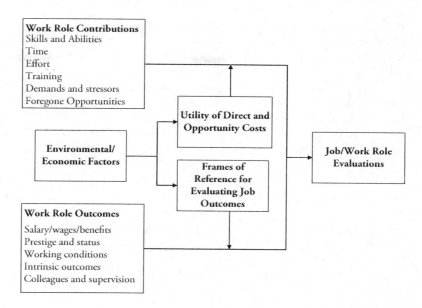

Figure 15.1 Modified Cornell Model of Job Attitudes

Work Role Contributions
Skills and Abilities
Time
Effort
Training
Demands and stressors
Foregone Opportunities

Environmental/ Economic Factors

Work Role Outcomes
Salary/wages/benefits
Prestige and status
Working conditions
Intrinsic outcomes
Colleagues and supervision

Utility of Direct and Opportunity Costs

Frames of Reference for Evaluating Job Outcomes

Job/Work Role Evaluations

community prosperity and job satisfactions were obtained. Hulin (1966a) extended Kendall's (1963) study on a sample of 1950 employees working in 300 different communities employed by the same organization, doing the same work, at the same wage rates. The results confirmed the effects of frames of reference, indexed by economic conditions of communities, extent of substandard housing, and productive farming in the area on job satisfactions. There were consistent negative correlations between economic conditions in communities (scored positively) and job attitudes, and positive correlations between percentage of substandard housing and job attitudes. These results were interpreted as meaning that prosperous communities with few slums, as well as the jobs of other workers in the community, influenced employees' frames of reference for evaluating work, working conditions, and pay; prosperous conditions led to higher frames of reference and lower job satisfactions. Workers living in poor communities tend to positively evaluate their job because the alternative may be a worse job or no job at all.

Utility of direct and opportunity costs is similarly a moderating variable, but of the effect of job inputs on job satisfactions. Utility of direct and opportunity costs can be defined as how individuals evaluate, and value, the costs or investments that represent work role inputs. Utilities in this case are similar to frames of reference in that each often reflects local labor market conditions. They are not, however, the same. As noted previously, utilities concern inputs whereas frames of reference concern outcomes, and this is not a distinction with little difference. Even more than frames of

reference, utilities are tied to one's labor market experiences. As noted by Hulin, Roznowski, and Hachiya (1985, p. 242), "During times when a large number of alternative jobs are available, the utility of alternative activities forgone in order to occupy any specific position with an organization increases. The more abundant and desirable the alternatives, and the greater the expected utility of these other activities to a worker, the less the satisfaction experienced with the present job." As for the other side of the coin, when the labor market is slack (high local unemployment, few positions open in one's area), individuals will attach less relative value to their inputs and, all else equal, experience more satisfaction with the work role.

SUMMARY

The Cornell model highlights the influences of factors exogenous to the individual and the organization on job attitudes and how these factors are translated into evaluations of jobs through their influence on individual differences. This inclusion of factors that characterize broader social and economic settings of organizations and jobs emphasizes limitations of the study of employees removed from their social, organizational, and economic contexts. Additional direct tests of the model, while difficult, would prove worthwhile, and would provide a relevant economic perspective to job attitude research.

Thibaut and Kelley's Comparison Level Model of Satisfaction

Thibaut and Kelley's (1959) comparison level model was developed to account for satisfactions that an individual derived from a dyadic relationship or membership in a group. The core of the model involves comparisons of outcomes from a focal role with outcomes directly or vicariously experienced by the individual in past dyadic roles. The distribution of role outcomes establishes the *comparison level, CL*. Roles that provide outcomes less than the *CL* are dissatisfying; those with role outcomes greater than the *CL* are satisfying. Generalizing Thibaut and Kelley's (1959) model to job satisfactions assumes that group or dyadic membership and work roles are analogous (vis-à-vis attitudes) and that the influence of other roles is from outcomes directly or vicariously experienced.

A second comparison level, *comparison level for alternatives*, denoted as CL_{ALT}, is also important in the Thibaut and Kelley (1959) model. CL_{ALT} refers to the outcomes that one could receive from the best alternative role available to the person. These alternative role outcomes are conceptually related to opportunity costs of holding a given job. The difference between the outcomes from the current role and CL_{ALT} determines the likelihood of the individual changing roles. These relationships, hypothesized by Thibaut and Kelley (1959), are shown in Table 15.2.

The situations depicted in Table 15.2 show the relations among current role outcomes, *CL*, comparisons for alternatives, CL_{ALT}, satisfaction, and likely role withdrawal behaviors. > or < indicates a situation in which the outcomes from the focal role are greater or less, respectively, than *CL* and CL_{ALT}. Satisfaction is influenced by *CL*, behavior by CL_{ALT}. The relations among *CL*, CL_{ALT}, satisfactions, and role withdrawal are complex. The empirical literature suggests that satisfaction is correlated with job withdrawal—leaving a job—operationalized by a number of behaviors. However, local economic conditions may reduce job withdrawal through the operation of CL_{ALT} because there are few alternatives available with superior outcomes. We expect relations between job attitudes and organizational, both work and job, withdrawal (Hanisch & Hulin, 1990, 1991; Hulin, 1991). *The specific withdrawal behaviors enacted may differ, depending on situational constraints* (Hanisch, Hulin, & Seitz, 1996).

SUMMARY

Thibaut and Kelley's (1959) comparison level model highlights interactions of factors exogenous to the individual or the job in the determination of job attitudes and the consequent job behaviors. The bases for *CL* and satisfactions are outcomes from past roles; the bases for withdrawal behaviors are outcomes from currently available alternative work roles. Past roles and currently available alternative roles are exogenous factors that limit relationships between endogenous factors and job satisfactions and constrain the effectiveness of organizational interventions designed to influence job attitudes or control organizational withdrawal behaviors.

Value-Percept Model

Locke (1976) defines *values* as that which one desires or considers important. His value-percept model holds that job satisfaction results from the attainment of important values. The model expresses job satisfaction as follows: satisfaction with a job characteristic = (want − have) × importance, or:

$$S_i = (V_{ci} - P_i) \times V_i$$

Where S_i is satisfaction with the *i-th* job characteristic, V_{ci} is value content (amount wanted) of the *i-th* characteristic, P_i is the perceived amount of the *i-th* characteristic provided by the job, and V_i is the importance of the *i-th* characteristic to the individual. Locke hypothesizes that discrepancies between

Table 15.2 Relations between CL, CL_{ALT}, Satisfaction, and Behavior

	CL	CL_{ALT}	Satisfaction	Behavior
Current role outcomes				
Situation A	>	>	Satisfied	Stay
Situation B	>	<	Satisfied	Leave
Situation C	<	>	Dissatisfied	Stay
Situation D	<	<	Dissatisfied	Leave

Notes. CL = Comparison Level. CL_{ALT} = Comparison Level for Alternatives. The ">" and "<" entries denote comparisons between an individual's appraisal of work role outcomes currently received with CL and CL_{ALT}.

what is desired by the person and what is received from the job are dissatisfying only if the job attribute is important to the individual. A discrepancy between the pay level wanted and the pay provided, for example, is assumed to be more dissatisfying to individuals who value pay highly than those who value pay to a lesser degree. Because individuals consider multiple facets when evaluating their job satisfaction, the cognitive calculus is repeated for each job facet. Overall satisfaction is estimated by aggregating across all contents of a job, weighted by their importance to the individual.

Wainer (1976, 1978) and others (e.g., Aiken, 1966; Ree, Carretta, & Earles, 1998) have discussed the general issue of weighting (multiplying by importance or other variables) and combining correlated facets of any general construct. As long as the facets are correlated and the variability of importance weights (i.e., V_js) is not very large, linear restraints make considerable improvement in the weighted linear combination over a unit weighting of standardized scores of the facets unlikely. Moreover, the reliability of weighted discrepancy scores, generated by multiplying a difference between two unreliable variables by a third unreliable variable, may be problematical. In spite of the theoretical information in importance, empirical gains from weighting deficiencies by importance may not be realized (Mikes & Hulin, 1968).

Despite these psychometric considerations, Rice, Gentile, and McFarlin (1991) found that facet importance moderated the relationships between facet amount and facet satisfaction. They also found that facet importance did not moderate the relationship between facet satisfaction and overall job satisfaction. Simple aggregations of facet satisfactions may predict overall satisfaction because facet importance (intensity) is already reflected in each facet extensity (satisfaction score). Another issue is that without substantial individual differences in values, Locke's (1976) theory loses its cogency. Although individuals may differ in what they value in a job, some attributes are generally more valued and others less valued. Cross-cultural research on populations of workers differing substantially in values could address this issue. Dispositional research showing personality traits underlying values might also contribute to understanding individual differences in values as defined by the Locke model.

SUMMARY

The value-percept model expresses job satisfactions in terms of employees' values and job outcomes. The model highlights the role of individual differences in values, but its use of weighting may be problematic. The model would benefit from additional tests, and research on the cultural, dispositional, as well as other exogenous factors that might explain value differences.

Job Characteristics Model

The job characteristics model (JCM) argues that enrichment of specified job characteristics is the core factor in making employees satisfied with their jobs. The model, formulated by Hackman and Oldham (1976), specifies five core job characteristics that make work challenging and fulfilling, and make jobs that provide them more satisfying and motivating than jobs that provide them to a lesser degree:

Task identity—degree to which one can see one's work from beginning to end;

Task significance—degree to which one's work is seen as important and significant;

Skill variety—extent to which job allows employees to perform different tasks;

Autonomy—degree to which employee has control and discretion for how to conduct his or her job; and

Feedback—degree to which the work itself provides feedback concerning how the employee is performing the job.

The JCM has received direct and indirect support. When individuals are asked to evaluate the importance of different facets of work such as pay, promotion opportunities, coworkers, and so forth, the nature of the work itself consistently emerges as the most important job facet (Jurgensen, 1978). This is not surprising because job satisfaction researchers have known for some time that of the major job satisfaction facets—pay, promotion opportunities, coworkers, supervision, the overall organization, and the work itself—satisfaction with the work itself is generally the facet most strongly correlated with overall job satisfaction (e.g., Rentsch & Steel, 1992) or the factor regarded as the most important (Herzberg, Mausner, Peterson, & Capwell, 1957). That work satisfaction is the facet of job satisfaction that correlates most strongly with overall satisfaction, and is the facet with the strongest correlations with outcomes, suggests that this focus of the JCM, the nature of the work itself, is on a solid foundation. Meta-analyses of relationships between workers' reports of job characteristics and job satisfaction have produced generally positive results (Fried &

Ferris, 1987; Loher, Noe, Moeller, & Fitzgerald, 1985). However, facets of jobs other than the work itself have been shown to be reliably related to behaviors important to employees and organizations (Getman et al., 1976). Satisfaction with pay and supervision was shown to be related to union representation votes; satisfaction with the work itself was not. Satisfaction with supervision was related to attendance at work on a day when a severe snowstorm made attendance optional (Smith, 1977).

Although direct tests of the JCM have been supportive, they have not supported the algebraic combination of the intrinsic factors. Specifically, in the original formulation, the five intrinsic job characteristics were combined into what Hackman and Oldham (1980) called a motivating potential score (MPS). According to the authors, the five job characteristics were combined in the following manner:

$$MPS = \frac{(SV + TI + TS)}{3} \partial \times A \times F$$

where SV = skill variety, TI = task identity, TS = task significance, A = autonomy, and F = feedback.

This weighted combination of the five core characteristics has not been supported. An additive (unit-weighted) combination better predicts satisfaction (e.g., Fried & Ferris, 1987). While important, we do not believe that this problem represents a "fatal flaw" in the scientific integrity or practical utility of the theory. As our previous reviews have shown, complex algebraic formulations of unreliable assessments do not accurately model human psychology. However, that statement does not render irrelevant the concepts that gave rise to the formulation.

Growth need strength (GNS) is a component of the model that accounts for individual differences in receptiveness to challenging job characteristics. According to Hackman and Oldham (1976), GNS is employees' desire for personal development, especially as it applies to work. High-GNS employees want their jobs to contribute to their personal growth; work characteristics are especially important to individuals who score high on GNS. The relationship between work characteristics and job satisfaction is stronger for high-GNS employees (average r = .68) than for low-GNS employees (average r = .38; Frye, 1996). However, task characteristics are related to job satisfaction, even for those who score low on GNS.

Despite empirical support, there are limitations to the theory, beyond the aforementioned issue, involving the algebraic combination of assessments of job characteristics. Specifically, a serious limitation with the JCM is that most of the studies have used self-reports of job characteristics, which have garnered a well-deserved share of criticism (Roberts & Glick, 1981).

Another limitation concerns the GNS construct. It is not clear what this construct measures; little construct validity evidence is available. Are other individual differences involved in the job characteristics/job attitude relationship? Empirical research by Turner and Lawrence (1965) and a review by Hulin and Blood (1968) highlighted the role of differences in cultural background in reactions to job characteristics. Is GNS a reflection of cultural background? Or of personality traits such as conscientiousness? In the research on JCM, the construct validity of GNS has been neglected.

In addition, the direction of causal arrows linking job satisfaction and perceptions of job characteristics are not clear. The relationship between perceptions of job characteristics and job satisfaction may be bidirectional (James & Tetrick, 1986; James & Jones, 1980) or perhaps from satisfaction to perceptions of task characteristics. Finally, there is little evidence that GNS moderates the relationship between job characteristics and outcomes as proposed.

SUMMARY

JCM hypothesizes that job satisfactions depend on characteristics of the work itself and, as does the value-percept model, that the roots of job satisfactions are within the individual and the job and their nexus. GNS may be influenced by individuals' cultural backgrounds, as these lead to individual differences in need configurations; other influences are minimized.

Dispositional Influences

The earliest writings on job satisfaction recognized the importance of dispositional influences on job satisfaction. Hoppock (1935) found that questions about levels of emotional adjustment substantially separated satisfied and dissatisfied employees. This replicated earlier results by Fisher and Hanna (1931). Weitz (1952) developed a "gripe index" to take into account individuals' tendencies to feel negatively, or positively, about many aspects of their lives, to gauge more accurately relative dissatisfaction with one's job. Smith (1955) found that individuals prone to poor emotional adjustment were more susceptible to feelings of monotony. The Cornell model was based in part on the idea that there existed very satisfied garbage collectors and very dissatisfied executives, and that these "anomalous" satisfaction levels could be explained.

However, of the thousands of studies published on the topic of job satisfaction prior to 1985, few considered individual differences as the *sources* of job satisfactions. Even fewer focused on personality. This state of affairs began to change with the publication of two seminal studies by Staw and colleagues, a study by Arvey and colleagues, and an integrative piece by Adler and Weiss (1988) on the benefits of developing and using personality measures designed specifically to be applied to normal, working adults, as opposed to residents of Minnesota mental hospitals or their visitors (for many years, personality was assessed most commonly with the Minnesota Multiphasic Personality Inventory [MMPI], a measure well-validated for diagnosing psychological disorders but poorly suited for assessing employees' personalities). Staw and Ross (1985) found that measures of job satisfaction were reasonably stable over time, even when individuals changed employers or occupations. The Staw and Ross (1985) study has been criticized (e.g., Davis-Blake & Pfeffer, 1989; Gerhart, 1987; Gutek & Winter, 1992; Newton & Keenan, 1991) on the grounds that it is difficult to establish a dispositional basis of job satisfaction unless one actually measures dispositions, and that other, non-dispositional factors might explain job attitude stability. Staw, Bell, and Clausen (1986) corrected this deficiency; using a unique longitudinal data set and childhood ratings of personality, Staw et al. (1986) reported results showing that affective disposition assessed at ages 12–14 correlated .34 ($p < .05$) with overall job satisfaction assessed at ages 54–62. In a similarly provocative study, Arvey, Bouchard, Segal, and Abraham (1989) found significant consistency in job satisfaction levels between 34 pairs of monozygotic twins reared apart from early childhood. Judged from the vantage point of today, these studies may seem less revolutionary than they were at the time. It is not much of an overstatement to argue that in the late 1980s, dispositional explanations were eschewed or, more likely, ignored entirely, in the literature.

The Staw and Arvey et al. studies are as significant for the stimulus they provided as for their substantive findings (Arvey et al., 1989; Staw et al., 1986). Judge and Hulin (1993) attempted to develop an improved measure of the dispositional influence on job satisfaction. Drawing from Weitz's (1952) "gripe" checklist, which asked individuals to indicate their satisfaction with a list of objectively neutral objects

common to everyday life (your telephone number, your first name, 8½" × 11" paper), Judge and Hulin (1993) found that employees' responses to neutral objects were correlated with job satisfaction, a finding replicated by Judge and Locke (1993). Judge and Hulin (1993) also found that the scores on this instrument had an independent path to job turnover four months after the initial assessment *after controlling for job satisfaction*. Despite favorable psychometric evidence for the measure (Judge & Bretz, 1993; Judge & Hulin, 1993), it remains unclear what construct this measure assesses. Other research found support for other dispositional taxonomies, including positive affectivity and negative affectivity (PA and NA; Watson & Slack, 1993) and the five-factor model of personality (Judge, Heller, & Mount, 2002).

In a different approach to dispositional influences on job attitudes, Judge, Locke, and Durham (1997) focus on core self-evaluations, fundamental beliefs that individuals hold about themselves, their functioning, and the world. Core self-evaluations (CSEs) are hierarchical with a broad, general trait comprising specific traits. They argue that core self-evaluations are assessed by traits that meet three criteria: (a) evaluation-focus (the degree to which a trait involves evaluation, as opposed to description); (b) fundamentality (in Cattell's [1965] personality theory, fundamental or source traits underlie surface traits); and (c) breadth or scope (according to Allport [1961], cardinal traits are broader in scope than secondary traits). Judge et al. (1997) identified four specific traits as indicators of CSEs, based on these evaluative criteria: (a) self-esteem, (b) generalized self-efficacy, (c) neuroticism, and (d) locus of control. Questions remain about the degree to which locus of control can be represented by this broad factor (Bono & Judge, 2003). Increasingly, research has utilized direct measures of core self-evaluations. However, the use of such measures does not obviate, entirely, the need to determine the degree to which locus of control belongs in the taxonomy.

In the 12 years since it was first introduced, core self-evaluations (CSE) have been the subject of more than 350 studies (according to a PsycINFO search completed in October 2008). Although the Judge et al. (1997) paper introduced CSE to explain job satisfaction, most of these studies have linked CSE to applied behaviors, including both subjective (e.g., performance ratings) and objective (e.g., sales volume) measures of job performance (Erez & Judge, 2001), responses to performance feedback (Bono & Colbert, 2005), interpersonal interactions with customers (Salvaggio et al., 2007), job search persistence after unemployment (Wanberg, Glomb, Song, & Sorenson, 2005), adjustment to foreign assignments (Johnson, Kristof-Brown, Van Vianen, De Pater, & Klein, 2003), and translating early life advantages (e.g., childhood socioeconomic status, education attainment of one's parents) into later earnings (Judge & Hurst, 2007).

Though CSE research has expanded well beyond job satisfaction research, there have been more than 50 studies of the link between CSEs and job satisfaction. Judge and Bono (2001) completed a meta-analysis of 169 independent correlations (combined N = 59,871) between each of the four core traits and job satisfaction. When the four meta-analyses were combined into a single composite measure, the overall core trait correlates .37 with job satisfaction. Given the various ways of considering affective disposition noted in this review, one might ask what either taxonomy adds beyond PA/NA (Watson, 2000), the affective predisposition scale (Judge & Hulin, 1993, Judge & Locke, 1993), or the Big Five (five-factor) personality model (Goldberg, 1990; McCrae & Costa, 1997). This is a particularly relevant question, given that CSEs are not uncorrelated with traits from either taxonomy (Judge, Erez, Bono, & Thoresen, 2002).

Judge, Heller, and Klinger (2008) found that of the three taxonomic structures (five-factor model, PA/NA, core self-evaluations), core self-evaluations were the most useful predictor of job satisfaction. Altogether, the three frameworks explained 36% of the variance in self-reported job satisfaction and 18% of the variance when using reports by significant others. Judge et al. (2008) further showed that these frameworks could be reduced to three sets of factors for the purposes of predicting job satisfaction: (a) core self-evaluations/neuroticism (all four core traits, plus NA), (b) extraversion (including PA), and (c) conscientiousness. Their results showed that when these three factors were related to job satisfaction, however, only the first factor—CSE—consistently influenced job satisfaction across studies. This study—and several others like it, conducted using multiple methods and statistical approaches—suggests that CSE has the most robust associations with job satisfaction.

Best, Stapleton, and Downey (2005) presented further evidence for the influence of CSE on job satisfaction via appraisals of the work environment. In a study of Veterans Administration employees in a wide range of positions, the authors found that core self-evaluations were negatively related to perceptions of organizational obstacles to goal fulfillment (perceived organizational constraint; β = -.32, $p < .05$). Perceived organizational constraint mediated between CSE and burnout, which negatively predicted job satisfaction (β = -.44, $p < .05$). CSE, furthermore, had a direct negative effect on burnout (β = -.31, $p < .05$). These results suggest that employees high in CSE are less likely to view their job tasks and organizational environment as stressful, shielding them from burnout and its deleterious effects on job satisfaction.

Studies that focus only on perceptual measures of job characteristics make it impossible to distinguish whether high-CSE individuals simply hold a rosier picture of objective attributes or whether they actually select into jobs with better attributes. To address this drawback in earlier research, Judge, Bono, and Locke (2000) examined the mediating role of objective job complexity, ascertained by coding job titles, as well as subjective job characteristics. They found that both subjective and objective indicators of job complexity were partial mediators of the relationship between CSE—measured in childhood and early adulthood—and later job satisfaction for individuals between the ages 41–50. These results suggest that core self-evaluations influence not only how favorably people view their jobs, but also the actual level of complexity of the jobs that they obtain.

In addition to selecting into more challenging jobs, people with high CSE may find their work more satisfying because they choose personally meaningful goals. Self-concordance theory posits that goals pursued for fun or on the basis of personally relevant values increase subjective well-being and goal attainment (Sheldon & Elliot, 1998). Judge, Bono, Erez, and Locke (2005) proposed that individuals with positive self-concept should be less vulnerable to external pressures and, therefore, more likely to set self-concordant goals. In longitudinal studies of college students and employees of several different firms, participants disclosed goals that they had set for the following two months and answered questions that captured the level of self-concordance of each goal. In both studies, self-concordant goals partially mediated between core self-evaluations and life satisfaction and between core self-evaluations and goal attainment. It appears that core self-evaluations do lead to the pursuit of self-concordant goals, which increases life satisfaction and goal attainment. However, the influence of goal attainment on life satisfaction was mixed. The authors concluded that core self-evaluations "may serve more like a trigger than an anchor. People with positive core self-evaluations strive for 'the right reasons,' and therefore 'get the right results'" (p. 266).

SUMMARY

Though organizational psychologists have productively studied numerous traits in relation to job satisfaction, it appears that CSE has the most robust associations with the concept (Judge et al., 2008). Although we can be confident of the predictive validity of CSE, it is a complex concept, and research fully elucidating the process by which it influences job satisfaction remains to be conducted.

Comparisons of Theoretical Approaches

In Figure 15.2 we provide an integration of the job satisfaction models just discussed. There is much similarity among the models. Job outcomes are typically judged in relation to a set of standards. There are a number of hypothesized influences on the standards involved in evaluating job outcomes. These influences range from exogenous economic/environmental influences that affect employees' frames of reference for evaluating specific job outcomes to individuals' personality characteristics or values, and perhaps biological factors. Job outcomes (and perhaps inputs) and standards are processed through a comparator, and the result of these cognitive processes is an evaluation of one's job: job satisfaction.

This integrative model is, for good reason, similar to the Cornell model. Although the Cornell model has never been directly tested in its entirety,

the absence of evidence has not diminished our belief in the merits of the model. Tests of the model are needed. What the integrative model does, however, is add to the Cornell model in two respects. First, it recognizes that work role contributions and outcomes do not exist in a vacuum. They are products of one's personality and one's environment. Accordingly, the integrative model adds personality (core self-evaluations or other traits), and includes links from personality and environmental factors to work role contributions and outcomes. It also includes links from personality to utilities and frames of reference. Personality impacts both the opportunities available to individuals, and how they appraise those opportunities. Similarly, personality may impact individuals' alternatives, and how these alternatives translate into frames of reference. Second, we explicitly include the comparison process as a unique variable in the model. This reflects the important (arguably central) role that such comparisons play in the Cornell model, Thibaut and Kelly's comparison level model, and the value-percept model.

One way to summarize these models of job attitudes is to highlight the sources of the influences on job attitudes. The JCM and Locke's value-percept model emphasize the influence of job characteristics, with the influence of each job characteristic hypothesized to be moderated by the values or GNS of the employees. Core self-evaluations and the other dispositional models stress direct influences from personal and other micro-variables. The Cornell and the Thibaut and Kelley models, the

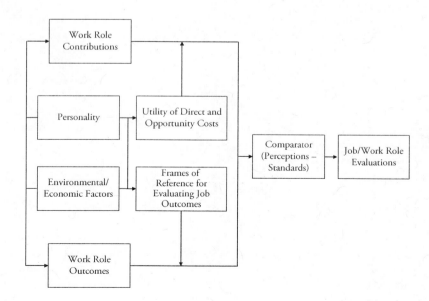

Figure 15.2 Integrative Model of Job Attitudes

most macro of the models, both include substantial influences of variables external to the person/job nexus. Both are relatively balanced in terms of their hypothesized influences of job and person characteristics on job attitudes. Only two, the Thibaut and Kelley and the Cornell models, emphasize macro, exogenous variables external to the individual and his or her job.

The structure and content of the theoretical explanations of the antecedents of job attitudes are also similar in terms of what is omitted. First, unlike social psychological theories of attitudes, none of the aforementioned organizational theories explicitly discusses attitude *formation* (i.e., the establishment of an attitude where none previously existed). Previously, we argued that a job is likely to be much more salient to a person than many topics—such as blood donation or capital punishment—studied by social psychologists. Thus, we believe that forming an attitude toward one's job (unlike, say, toward blood donation) is simply unavoidable. The study of job satisfaction therefore focuses, appropriately enough, on determinants of its level rather than determinants of its existence per se.

Second, and more importantly, none of these theories that link a variety of antecedents and satisfactions through the mechanism of cognitive evaluations and comparisons of one's standards and job outcomes (or inputs) includes on-the-job affect or emotions that may arise from dispositions or from transient events. Affect has been deemphasized to such an extent that this component of attitude space has nearly disappeared. We do not imply that cognitive evaluations of one's job are free of feelings. We do suggest that assessments and inclusions of affect, assessed using methods that capture this dynamic source of variance, might provide unique insights in our attempts to understand job attitudes and predict important behaviors. This idea is developed in a subsequent section.

New Theoretical Developments

In this section, we discuss theoretical (and empirical) developments that seek to augment the traditional view of job attitudes. One such development is the proposition that job attitudes other than job satisfaction are important. In this regard, we discuss the most recently suggested attitudinal construct—employee engagement—and contrast it to job satisfaction. The remaining two developments challenge the conventional wisdom that the between-person level of analysis is the sole level of importance vis-à-vis job satisfaction: they argue that

the within-person level (at which state affect is of focal importance) and the between-organization level should also be considered. These latter two developments, in conjunction, argue for multilevel conceptualizations of job satisfaction.

Employee Engagement and Job Satisfaction

A PsycINFO search in October 2008 revealed more than 23,500 hits for the term "job satisfaction." Additional searches revealed that job satisfaction has been studied much more heavily than all the other job attitudes *combined*. Nonetheless, due perhaps to the "disappointing" observed relationships between job attitudes and job performance (though see Judge et al., 2001), organizational psychologists persist in the quest for new job attitudes. Describing—and decrying—this tendency, Roznowski and Hulin (1992) wrote: "Job satisfaction...has been around in scientific psychology for so long that it gets treated by some researchers as a comfortable 'old shoe,' one that is unfashionable and unworthy of continued research" (p. 124). This admonition notwithstanding, yet another job attitude, "employee engagement," has recently been suggested. The impetus for this construct has come largely from practitioners, with academia playing catch-up.

In the context of employee engagement, Macey and Schneider (2008) have proposed a distinction between, on the one hand, absorption in and enthusiasm for the work tasks, and, on the other, satiation or contentment. It is the former, they contend, that drives job performance. Although the proposed distinction is intuitively appealing, any new job attitude such as employee engagement faces (or at least ought to face) significant barriers to entry.[3]

Specifically, the observed empirical relationships among the various job attitudes are quite strong, especially after controlling for measurement error (e.g., Harrison et al., 2006). This suggests that employees do not make the fine-grained conceptual distinctions among these attitudes emphasized by researchers. Thus, construct redundancy among the job attitudes is a major concern.[4] This concern is heightened in the case of employee engagement, because construct definitions of employee engagement frequently include words related to other job attitudes (e.g., the words "involvement" and "commitment"), and because inventories used to measure employee engagement frequently contain items similar to those in inventories used to measure other job attitudes, as well as positive affect (Dalal, Baysinger, Brummel, & LeBreton, in press).

Construct redundancy leads directly to a lack of incremental validity vis-à-vis criteria. It is unclear whether employee engagement can explain significant incremental variance in behavior/performance criteria, over and above the variance explained by job satisfaction and the other extant responses made by incumbents to their jobs.

A related concern is that any observed incremental effects of employee engagement may be at least partly artifactual. This concern is motivated by another form of construct redundancy, in this case the redundancy between employee engagement (the putative predictor variable) and various behavior/performance criteria. For example, inventories used to measure employee engagement contain items similar to those in inventories used to measure organizational citizenship behavior (Dalal, Brummel, Wee, & Thomas, 2008). It is therefore unclear to what extent the incremental validity claimed for employee engagement over and above job satisfaction and other job attitudes is due to predictor-criterion redundancy versus genuine conceptual advances regarding the construct space of job attitudes.

Thus, Macey and Schneider's (2008) potentially promising distinction between absorption/enthusiasm and satiation/contentment notwithstanding, considerable obstacles remain to be overcome before the construct of employee engagement can be argued to add significantly to our knowledge about employees' attitudinal reactions to their jobs. We note that, although the aforementioned problems may be most severe in the case of employee engagement, they are hardly unique to that construct. For example, many items in popular organizational commitment inventories are clearly redundant with items in inventories measuring withdrawal cognitions (e.g., Bozeman & Perrewé, 2001).

These problems seem to highlight the continued importance of job satisfaction. There is little reason to suspect predictor-criterion redundancy in the case of job satisfaction's relationships with behavior/performance criteria. Moreover, although—or rather because—there is certainly reason to suspect predictor-predictor redundancy among the various job attitudes, the onus is on proponents of the newer job attitudes to distinguish these attitudes conceptually and empirically from job satisfaction. Until such time as this occurs, practitioners seeking to assess job attitudes are advised to begin with job satisfaction.

Work Role Affect

The tripartite view of job attitudes—cognitive, affective, and behavioral components—may have kept attitude research as one of the most active research areas in social science for the past several decades. Whatever the current research emphasis in social science—behaviors, cognitions, or emotions—attitudes, as originally defined, met the criteria for "relevant" research. The de-emphasis of an affect component of social attitudes has been paralleled by a similar treatment of affect or emotions in job attitudes. Weiss and Brief (2001) note the neglect of affect in the history of job satisfaction research. Weiss and Cropanzano (1996) have also drawn attention to the field's neglect of affect and have proposed a theory of job attitudes that emphasizes affect on an equal footing with cognitive evaluations, hypothesizes different antecedents for cognitive evaluations versus affect, and hypothesizes different sets of behaviors as consequences of individual differences in affect as contrasted with cognitive evaluations.

This theory, affective events theory (AET), emphasizes links between job events and job affect, and hypothesizes links between job affect and job behaviors that are independent of the links between traditional job attitudes (cognitive evaluations of jobs) and job behaviors. AET hypothesizes links between job affect and spontaneous, short-term behaviors, such as work withdrawal and organizational citizenship behaviors, rather than the more reasoned long-term behaviors, such as turnover or retirement, that have been related to job satisfactions. These two fuzzy sets of behaviors are identified by Weiss and Cropanzano (1996) as affect- and judgment-driven behaviors. Figure 15.3 depicts our rendition of AET.

Affect is defined conceptually as individuals' emotional reactions to their jobs and to the events that happen on their jobs. It refers to how an individual *feels on the job*. This is in contrast to the cognitive representation of job attitudes—evaluations of stable features and characteristics of jobs. How we conceptualize our job in the morning when we arrive at work is very likely relatively stable and consistent with how we view the job at the end of the day. Empirically, the correlations between affect on adjacent days range from .50 to .65, depending on the scale (PA, NA, or hedonic tone) across 12 days in two studies (Miner, 2001; Miner et al., 2005). These morning, pre-workday, feelings may be influenced by longer than normal commuting delays caused by heavy traffic or construction, an incident of road rage, a blizzard in April, an overnight spike in gas prices, a warm sunny day in February, and other positive and negative exogenous factors.

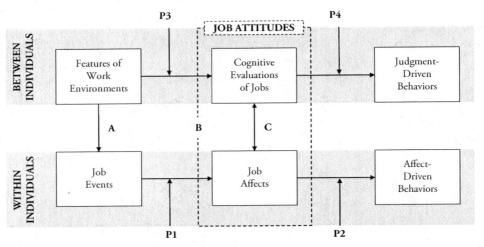

P3   JOB ATTITUDES   P4

A: Influence on distribution of events
B: Fuzzy boundaries between events and features of work environments
C: Reciprocal relationship between cognition and affect
P: Personality variables as moderators of between- and within-individual relationships

Figure 15.3 Modified Version of Affective Events Theory

These feelings are further modified by events that occur on the job during the day. An argument with a coworker, unexpected praise from a supervisor, or a comment by someone about the availability of jobs and starting salaries at another organization will influence our feelings on the job (Miner et al., 2005). These events and the changes in affect that they trigger may be ephemeral but may also have long-term influences on how we evaluate our jobs. Feelings and affect levels triggered by job events, for all their ephemerality, however, have consequences for behaviors on the job: (not) helping our coworkers, getting somebody to cover for us so we can attend a meeting called by our supervisor, or how long we spend on the phone with a customer needing assistance, and so forth (Miner, 2001). Within a framework of stable evaluations of one's job, it is possible to feel anger, frustration, elation, and unhappiness on a job that one evaluates positively and to feel all these emotions in one day and to respond behaviorally, both positively and negatively, to episodes of positive and negative affect.

AET is differentiated from other current approaches by: (a) the distinctions between job structure or features and job events, although job features (e.g., HR policies) are likely to influence *distributions* of job events; (b) an emphasis on affect as a component of job attitudes (see also Clore & Schnall, 2005); and (c) the hypothesized independent links between job affect and affect-driven behaviors, on the one hand, and between

job satisfactions (cognitive evaluations of jobs) and judgment-driven behaviors, on the other. Dispositions are hypothesized to moderate the link between events and affect.

Job features and job events should be treated as fuzzy sets. Features differentiating between these two sets of variables would be permanence, frequency, and predictability; job events are more transient and less predictable than stable job features. A subset of job events that becomes sufficiently frequent and predictable may cross the boundary between features and events. Affect- and judgment-driven behaviors are fuzzy sets; they do not yield crisp classification of all job behaviors into one category or the other. The fuzziness of the boundaries does not invalidate AET as a useful framework. All classes of events in social science are fuzzy sets to some degree.

Job affect is inherently dynamic. We should expect significant within-person co-fluctuations in affect and exogenous events. Job events serve as stochastic shocks to an underlying affect level and cycle. Job events are individually unpredictable and infrequent; their influence contributes to the dynamic nature of job affect. This problem is illustrated by Organ and Ryan (1995), who note that predictions of organizational citizenship behaviors (OCBs) from affective states "...will somehow have to reckon with the problem of *detecting discrete episodes of OCB* (rather than subjective reactions that presumably reflect aggregations or trends of OCB over time) *and the psychological states antecedent to or concurrent with those episodes*" (p. 781, emphasis added). This problem has been addressed, and partially solved, by event signal methods (ESM), or ecological momentary assessments (EMA), and multilevel statistical analyses that combine within- and between-person effects (Beal & Weiss, 2003; Hofman, Griffin, & Gavin, 2000; Raudenbush & Bryk, 2002).

The demands of studying affect levels as dynamic variables have been explored and discussed by Totterdell (1999) and by Weiss et al. (1999). Miner et al. (2005) assessed affect on the job using palm-top/handheld computers to administer mood checklists at four random times during the work day. The within-person, dynamic nature of affect and mood on the job is highlighted by the intraclass correlations that revealed that approximately 60% of the variance in mood or job affect scores resided within persons; approximately 40% of the variance in mood scores could be attributed to between-person differences. Similarly high percentages of within-person variance were obtained by Dalal et al. (2009), across two studies and several conceptualizations of affect (i.e., global happiness-versus-unhappiness, positive affect, and negative affect). This within-person variance would be treated as error in most studies of job attitudes based on static, cross-sectional designs. Relations involving within-person differences and other variables would be impossible to study if affect assessments were aggregated and studied as stable, between-person individual differences. Near real-time assessments of job affect permit analyses of within-person relations between negative and positive job events and mood on the job after controlling for mood assessed at the beginning of each work day (Miner et al., 2005).

One important aspect of this new approach to job attitudes is the possibility of within-person relations between, say, affect and behaviors, that are independent of affect/behavior relations found between individuals. One example of this comes from the medical literature assessing the relationship between exercise and blood pressure (Schwartz & Stone, 1998). When assessed between individuals, we find a negative relationship: those who exercise frequently have lower blood pressure than those who exercise rarely. The same relationship, assessed within individuals, is positive: a person's blood pressure is higher *when* he or she is exercising than when he or she is not. Similarly, Miner (2001) has found that, between individuals, those with more positive affect levels are more likely to exhibit citizenship and helping behaviors. Within persons the relationship

is negative; individuals report lower levels of positive affect while they are helping coworkers.

The overall point is not that we should necessarily expect relationships to operate in different directions, or even to operate in the same direction but with dramatically different magnitudes, at the within-person versus between-person levels of analysis. Rather, the point is simply that no inferences about the within-person level should be made solely on the basis of data collected at the between-person level. Indeed, Chen, Bliese, and Mathieu (2005) maintain that, because researchers know so little about how constructs operate at levels of analysis other than the one at which they are typically studied, assessments of the similarity of relationships between analogous constructs across levels "can and should play an integral role in the validation of multilevel constructs and theories" (p. 376).

In this vein, AET offers a new approach to the study of job attitudes. It emphasizes a source of variance in job attitudes—within-person variance—that has been largely ignored in the past. It represents more than adding a variable—affect—to the study of job attitudes. Appropriate definitions of affect and within-person relations require changed research directions and methods if we are to avoid methodological stalemates that occur when (within-person) hypotheses derived from newer theories are inappropriately tested using data and methods derived to test older (between-person) hypotheses. Analyses of affective events, affect, and the on-the-job consequences of affect may answer some questions about job attitudes and behaviors on the job that are unanswered by the traditional studies of relations between cognitive evaluations and job performance (see, for example, Beal, Weiss, Barros, & MacDermid, 2005).

We recognize that our distinction between cognition and affect is imperfect, as is our decision to identify affect as within-individual and cognition as between-individual. In evaluating our jobs, both cognition and affect are likely involved and, though we assume that cognition is less ephemeral than affect, we realize that this, if true, is a relative rather than absolute distinction that at times is false. It is also the case that much of the conceptual development of affect has emphasized the ephemeral event basis of affect, while similar developments of job attitudes have emphasized their more stable organizational characteristic basis.

At a neurological level, affect and cognition may well be inseparable. Higher level cognition, Damasio (1994) argues, relies on evaluative input in the form of emotion; cognition and emotion are interwoven in our psychological architecture. When we think about our jobs, we have feelings about what we think. When we have feelings while at work, we think about these feelings. Some cognitive effort may be required to deal with these feelings so that we can work effectively. Cognition and affect are thus closely related, in our psychology and even in our psychobiology. Evidence indicates that when individuals perform specific mental operations, a reciprocal relationship exists between cerebral areas specialized for processing emotions and those specialized for processing cognitions (Drevets & Raichle, 1998). There are cognitive theories of emotion (Reisenzein & Schoenpflug, 1992), and emotional theories of cognition (Smith-Lovin, 1991). Moreover, partly for this reason (that cognition and affect are inextricably linked), and partly because cognitions change as the situations upon which the appraisals are based change, cognitions are neither wholly between-individual, nor is affect entirely within-individual. Individuals' cognitions do change, and there are between-individual (i.e., trait) differences in characteristic affect experienced. That being said, an imperfect and probabilistic/fuzzy distinction is not the same as no distinction whatsoever; partial overlap does not necessarily imply redundancy.

A modified version of AET includes personality as a moderator of both the cognitive, between-individual links and the affective, within-individual links. Job events may produce one kind of affect for one kind of person (in the figure as well as its discussion here, P denotes personality traits of the individual), and a different kind of affect for another

(P1). A discussion of politics may be stimulating and enjoyable for an open person and irritating for a closed one. A social interaction may be positive-mood inducing for an extravert and stressful for an introvert. Impulsive people (those low on conscientiousness, high on neuroticism, high on extraversion, or all three) may be more likely to act on their affects (P2) than others. Similarly, prudent individuals (those high on conscientiousness) may be more cognitively driven in their behaviors, or more resolute in acting on cognitions (P4). Some individuals, such as those high in need for cognition or low in openness, may be more likely to make judgments/evaluations about their jobs based on workplace features (P3).

Personality, Within-Individual Variation, and Core Self-Evaluations

Thus far, we have reviewed three recent, distinct contributions to job satisfaction and job affect research: (a) growing acceptance that job satisfaction is, to a substantial degree, rooted in individuals' dispositions in general, and individuals' personalities, including core self-evaluations in particular; (b) the study of job affect as a point of departure from the relatively cognitively oriented nature of past job satisfaction research; and (c) the growing recognition that job satisfaction and job affect both have transient qualities that can only be discovered (and predicted) using ESM designs that focus on within-individual variation.

Putting these streams of thought together, Figure 15.4 represents an integrative model focused on core self-evaluations as both a state-like, within-individual variable, and a trait-like individual-difference

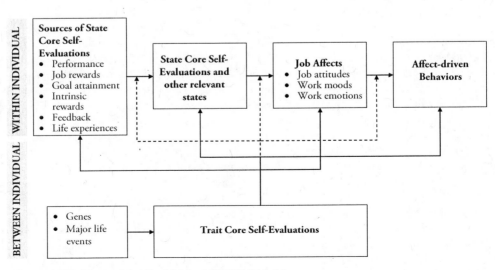

Figure 15.4 Core Self-Evaluations: Job Affect Multilevel (CSEJAM) Model

variable. We label this model the Core Self-Evaluations Job Affect Multilevel (CSEJAM) model. Dealing first with the within-individual portion of the CSEJAM model, we posit that various aspects of one's work and life environment are sources of state core self-evaluations. Performing one's job well, achieving valued outcomes, attaining success in one's occupation, meeting or exceeding important work, job, and career goals, performing interesting, challenging, and meaningful work, obtaining worthwhile and positive job feedback (whether from the work itself or from others), and positive or affirming non-job experiences all might augment one's state core self-evaluations. Conversely, failing at one's work, losing one's job, reaching a dead-end in one's occupation, failing to meet goals, performing stultifying or disappointing work, receiving negative feedback, and isolating or dispiriting life experiences should dampen one's state CSE. State CSE should, in turn, be associated with job affect. That job affect might be moods at work, discrete emotions at work, or job satisfaction. Consistent with Figure 15.3, such job affects should lead to episodic, affect-driven behaviors.

We should note that the within-individual portion of the model is flexible as to the time-frame involved. Within-individual variation may occur over minutes, hours, days, and even years. Within-individual changes in the Big Five personality traits have been considered from intervals ranging from diurnal (Fleeson, 2004) to life course (Roberts, Walton, & Viechtbauer, 2006); there is no reason to believe that variation in self-concept should not be similarly considered.

Turning to the between-individual part of the CSEJAM model in Figure 15.4, the model includes, denoted by solid lines, effects of trait CSE on intercepts of the four within-individual variables. With appropriate (group-mean) centering, this means that trait CSE should predict average levels of the concepts (averaged across within-individual observations). For example, if a study were conducted in which a measure of trait CSE was administered at the onset of the study, and state CSE and job affects were measured on a daily basis for two weeks (or a weekly basis for, say, six weeks, or a yearly basis for, say, six years), individuals with high scores on the trait CSE measure at the onset of the study would be predicted to have higher average levels of state CSE and the job affects. More noteworthy are the moderating effects, denoted by dotted lines, of trait CSE on the within-individual relationships in the model. These predict that the degree to which,

say, outcomes translate into state CSE varies by individuals' trait CSE levels. One would hypothesize that job rewards would be more likely to bolster the self-confidence (state CSE) of those who have characteristically high (trait CSE) levels, because such individuals would be more likely to believe themselves deserving of such rewards. Similarly, job affects might be more likely to translate into action (affect-driven behaviors) for those with high trait CSE levels, because such individuals are more likely to believe that their actions matter.

Unit-Level Job Satisfaction

Thus far, we have discussed job satisfaction at the conventional, between-person level of analysis. We have also discussed job satisfaction (and affect) at the within-person level of analysis. Recently, however, researchers have been interested in job satisfaction at aggregate levels of analysis, such as the organization, work-unit, or work-group. Except where specifically noted, for reasons of parsimony we subsequently refer to all these levels as the "unit" level.

In speaking of unit-level job satisfaction, we seek not to anthropomorphize the organization (obviously, organizations themselves cannot be satisfied or dissatisfied) but rather to discuss an aggregate of the satisfaction of employees within the organization. Specifically, unit-level job satisfaction is typically conceptualized as the mean job satisfaction score of employees within the organization. However, there is an important distinction to be made in what this mean score tells us about the nature of job satisfaction in its aggregated form.

For example, a unit-level satisfaction score of 3 on a 1–5 scale could be due to several individual-level distributions, including (but not limited to): (a) a rectangular distribution, in which equal numbers of employees report scores of 1, 2, 3, 4 and 5 (in which case the unit's score reflects the score of 20% of individual employees); (b) a bimodal distribution, in which half of all employees report a score of 1 whereas the other half report a score of 5 (in which case the unit's score does not reflect the score of any employee); and (c) a "distribution" in which all employees report a score of 3 (in which case the unit's score reflects every employee's score). Only in the last of these cases is within-unit consensus (as measured by indices of inter-individual agreement) high. Thus, in the former two cases, the average would represent *average individual-level job satisfaction,* whereas the latter case might appropriately be considered *unit-level satisfaction.* The broader point—that consensus is needed in order to properly consider job satisfaction as a unit-level phenomenon—is, of course, fully consistent with both theory and empirical demonstrations in the multilevel literature (Chan, 1998; Klein, Dansereau, & Hall, 1994; Kozlowski & Klein, 2000; Morgeson & Hofmann, 1999).

Defining unit-level job satisfaction is, of course, a prelude to assessing its relationship with other same-level constructs. Previously, we noted that relationships at one level of analysis could differ from analogous relationships at a different level of analysis. Two recent meta-analyses (Kokkinou & Dalal, 2008; Van Rooy, Whitman, & Viswesvaran, 2007) investigated the satisfaction-performance relationship at the organization level; they assessed the relationship between organization-level job satisfaction and organization-level performance. However, several potential moderators of the relationship need to be taken into account. Whether the level of analysis was the organization versus work-unit versus work-group, whether the study was conducted in the field versus in a classroom or laboratory setting, and whether organizational performance was measured by financial metrics versus by aggregated ratings of individual employee performance may all make a difference. Both meta-analyses found results virtually identical to each other as well as to the results obtained by Judge et al. (2001) at the individual-employee level: in other words, a corrected satisfaction-performance correlation of approximately 0.30. Moreover, similar to the individual-employee level, temporal precedence remains an open question at the organization or unit level: the lagged satisfaction-performance and performance-satisfaction relationships examined by Kokkinou and Dalal (2008) were of very similar magnitude.

We offer these meta-analyses as an example of a specific avenue of research on organization or unit-level job satisfaction, rather than to indicate that research at this level of analysis is already a "closed shop." On the contrary, such research is in its early stages, and provides opportunities for empirical and theoretical contributions. For instance, little is known thus far about the organization-level antecedents of organization-level satisfaction, although high-performance Human Resource Management practices (e.g., Huselid, 1995) may play a role.

Studying job satisfaction at aggregate levels also serves to connect research in organizational psychology with research in economics, which has examined the satisfaction-performance relationship at the level of *countries*. This research (e.g., Bruni & Porta, 2005), which itself builds on psychological research concerning subjective well-being or life satisfaction, has related country-mean well-being/satisfaction scores to country-GDP per capita scores, in order to test the assumption that a country's economic performance influences the satisfaction of its citizens (interestingly, investigating the reverse causal direction—namely, the idea that satisfied countries perform better economically—does not appear to be a major focus of economic research).

Measurement of Job Attitudes
Job Satisfactions

Measurement of job affect creates problems for researchers. Affective reactions are likely to be fleeting and episodic—state variables rather than consistent chronic, trait-like variables (Tellegen, Watson, & Clark, 1999a; Watson, 2000). Measurement of affect should reflect its state-like, episodic nature.

Triandis (1980), Fishbein (1980), Eagley and Chaiken (1993) and others have included affective responses in the assessments of social attitudes. Emotional or affective responses to objects or entities assessed as stable variables have typically not improved predictions of behavioral intentions or behaviors. One may regard social and job attitudes as "acquired behavioral dispositions" (Campbell, 1963) without treating relations with behavioral intentions or behaviors as the touchstone of the usefulness of an affective component of attitudes. Further, typical assessments of affect—as stable, chronic responses—may not adequately reflect true affect or emotional responses toward objects.

Much satisfaction research has been based on homegrown, unvalidated measures consisting of, generally, a collection of Likert-type items that ask the respondents to evaluate their pay, the work they do, their supervision, and so on. Some scales have been based on collections of items asking respondents how satisfied they were with different features of their jobs. Other scales have been based on items asking about how well the respondents' jobs fulfilled their needs. The Job Descriptive Index (JDI; Smith, Kendall, & Hulin, 1969), modified by Roznowski (1989), the Job Diagnostic Survey (JDS; Hackman & Oldham, 1976), the Minnesota Satisfaction Questionnaire (MNSQ; Weiss, Dawis, England, & Lofquist, 1967), and the Index of Organizational Reactions (IOR; Dunham & Smith, 1979; Dunham, Smith, & Blackburn, 1977) represent significant exceptions to this use of unvalidated scales purporting to assess job attitudes. The JDI appears to be the most widely applied measure of job satisfaction in use today (Cranny, Smith, & Stone, 1992, p. 2; DeMeuse, 1985); the JDS, MNSQ, and the IOR have been used collectively on an additional several thousands of employees. Unfortunately, these four standardized, validated instruments together may account for only a slight majority of the published research on job satisfaction.

The standardized instruments listed above have been evaluated psychometrically; they converge dimensionally with each other when they assess satisfaction with similar job characteristics (Dunham et al., 1977), are related to appropriate individual differences and job characteristics, and have reasonable levels of temporal stability or internal consistency. The four instruments, however, differ substantially. The MSQ assesses the extent to which jobs are evaluated as providing need fulfillment of a number of "basic" needs. The JDS assesses the degree to which jobs provide core characteristics (responsibility, task feed back, task significance, etc.) to the employee. The IOR asks respondents to evaluate job features and scores these into eight facets of job satisfaction (work itself, the organization, career future and security, pay, etc.). The JDI assesses five facets of job satisfaction (work itself, pay, promotional opportunities and policies, supervision, coworkers) by asking respondents to describe their job in terms of the presence or absence of 72 characteristics of the work itself, coworkers, and so on. A complete evaluation of the psychometric properties of all available scales requires more space than we have available.

Investigators interested in research on job attitudes have access to several standardized and validated measures that provide information on different aspects of individuals' job attitudes. In spite of the dimensional convergence, the instruments are not equivalent; the use of one rather than another will generate marginally to significantly different results. The choice of a measure of job attitudes in any study is not an irrelevant detail. The widespread use of the JDI may reflect the extensive psychometric research that accompanied its initial publication (Smith et al., 1969) and that has appeared in the 30+ years since (e.g., Balzer et al., 1997; Hanisch, 1992; Roznowski, 1989). For example, the unusually careful (for organizational psychologists) attention devoted by the JDI's developers to item comprehensibility/readability allows the JDI to be administered without modification to employees with less education and/or lower reading ability (Stone, Stone, & Gueutal, 1990). The five scales that compose the JDI also have been used

extensively as antecedents and outcomes of varying levels of job attitudes in studies ranging from community characteristics and their effects on job attitudes (Hulin, 1969; Kendall, 1963) to longitudinal studies of the effects of sexual harassment (Glomb, Munson, Hulin, Bergman, & Drasgow, 1999). This database provides researchers with the evidence necessary to evaluate the properties and functioning of this set of scales, including relations with behavioral variables, and may account for its wide use.

For researchers and practitioners interested in a single score representing overall job satisfaction, one option is to use measures like the JDI and simply calculate the mean (or sum) of scores on various facets. However, this approach could suffer from errors of omission (i.e., omitting facets important to the employee) and errors of commission (i.e., including facets unimportant to the employee). A preferable approach is to directly measure employees' perceptions of the job as a whole. Several such "global" job satisfaction measures exist. The Job in General scale (JIG; Ironson, Smith, Brannick, Gibson, & Paul, 1989), for example, is the global equivalent of the JDI.

Job Affect, Mood, and Emotions

Job affect or emotions experienced on the job present a different set of conceptual and assessment problems. Job affect and emotions are influenced by events that occur on the job. Individual job events are likely to be infrequent and difficult to predict. Praise from a supervisor, an overheard conversation in the hallway about a coworker's evaluation, a just-in-time delivery that was not-quite-in-time, a pilot being given an extensive holding instruction to await departing traffic, or a surly customer are all job events and are generally unpredictable. Yet they occur, and their occurrences often trigger job emotions. Assessments of emotions on the job, carried out in near real-time several times during a workday, are necessary to tap into event-affect-behavior cycles and capitalize on the dynamic state nature of affect.

The dynamic nature of job affect makes it difficult to use research practices that rely on one-shot, paper-and-pencil assessments of employees' attitudes. Computerized assessments—in which research participants complete measures several times during a day or daily over a week or several weeks—facilitate the collection of such data. In many cases, ESM studies have been carried out in which individuals are required to complete an online survey during a certain period of time, either several times a day or each day of the week for several weeks.

Other studies have used handheld devices (often with an interval contingent method), where such devices signal the participants, present items with clickable response formats, store the data, and maintain an acceptable degree of data security. These devices can control the timing of the response within temporal intervals desired by the researcher as opposed to a signal and diary method in which researchers have no such control (diaries can be completed by the participants any time during the observation period). Items can be sampled randomly at each signal from the pool of items defining the content of the scales (see Dalal et al., 2009). Such sampling may reduce tendencies of respondents to focus on specific emotions that have been assessed at previous signals. It, moreover, allows for the assessment of a broader construct space without an increase in items on any given survey. However, such sampling also has the potential to artifactually increase the within-person variance in affect and to decrease the obtained correlation between a construct assessed at time t and the same construct assessed at time $t+1$.

Several studies of affect and mood that have used ESM or signal contingent methods at work (Alliger & Williams, 1993; Dalal et al., 2009; Fisher, 2000; Ilies & Judge, 2002; Judge & Ilies, 2004; Judge, Scott, & Ilies, 2006; Totterdell, 1999, 2000; Weiss et al., 1999; Zohar, 1999) generally support the hypothesized importance of affect and mood at work and document the promise of ESM to generate assessments of emotions and affect at work. It is not premature to conclude that ESM has become an expected element of the research. Beal and Weiss (2003) provide a thorough overview of ESM, and discuss how such methods can be used effectively in organizational research.

Another issue that must be resolved is the specification of the content of affect and emotion assessments. Should on-the-job affect be assessed as two orthogonal unipolar dimensions of positive affect (PA) and negative affect (NA), or as two orthogonal bipolar dimensions of hedonic tone and arousal/activation? These different rotations of the mood/emotion circumplex (Tellegen, Watson, & Clark, 1999a) are shown in Figure 15.5. Either the PA/NA rotation, indicated by dotted axes, or the hedonic tone/arousal rotation, indicated by solid axes, adequately accounts for the correlations among affective or emotional terms and responses.

The potential contributions of affect to understanding variance in job satisfactions (or anything else, for that matter) may not be realized until the rotation of axes in the mood circumplex is resolved. Although the two rotations may be mathematically equivalent, the use of one rather than the other has significant implications for the study of job affect.

At a conceptual level, it is difficult to comprehend a person who exhibits high scores on both PA and NA. Although this pattern of scores is theoretically possible if PA and NA are independent dimensions, it seems especially problematic with regard to *state* affect, because then such a person would have to exhibit high scores on both PA and NA *simultaneously* or at least within a very short time interval. Moreover, researchers have found it difficult to

Figure 15.5 Mood Circumplex

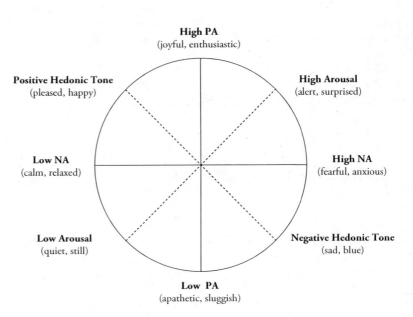

High PA
(joyful, enthusiastic)

Positive Hedonic Tone
(pleased, happy)

High Arousal
(alert, surprised)

Low NA
(calm, relaxed)

High NA
(fearful, anxious)

Low Arousal
(quiet, still)

Negative Hedonic Tone
(sad, blue)

Low PA
(apathetic, sluggish)

distinguish empirically—that is, based on the actual responses of subjects—between the descriptors of low-PA states (e.g., "sluggish") and those of low-NA states (e.g., "at ease"); therefore, though PA and NA seem to be relatively orthogonal at their high poles, they do not seem to be orthogonal at their low poles (Weiss & Cropanzano, 1996). Both these lines of argument favor the rotation that yields the hedonic tone and arousal factors. However, there is some evidence to indicate that PA and NA are the affective manifestations of two relatively independent bio-behavioral systems (i.e., an approach system and an avoidance/withdrawal system; Watson, Wiese, Vaidya, & Tellegen, 1999). Moreover, with regard to the alternative conceptualization of affect, the arousal dimension may explain relatively little variance in relevant criteria (Ilies & Judge, 2002; Miner et al., 2005). Both these lines of argument favor the rotation that yields the PA and NA factors. A possible resolution was proposed by Tellegen, Watson, and Clark (1999b), who argued that, at a higher level of abstraction, the PA and NA factors (and, in all likelihood, the hedonic tone and activation factors) are subsumed by a single, bipolar factor that Tellegen et al. (1999b) referred to as "global happiness-versus-unhappiness." Although this proposed resolution seems reasonable, it has not yet been widely accepted.

There is also the issue of whether one should favor the measurement of discrete (specific) emotions as opposed to the broad mood dimensions. One of the challenges in measuring discrete emotions is deciding which emotions should be studied. Individuals experience myriad emotions in a workday, which range in their stimulus, generality, duration, and intensity. Emotion researchers have struggled in vain to delineate an accepted taxonomy of "core" emotions (see Izard, 1992; Ortony & Turner, 1990; Power, 2006). Another challenge is that discrete emotions, while theoretically separable, are empirically less so. This is especially true with respect to positive emotions (Watson, 2000).

Repeated event-signaled assessments of employees' affect at work should extend our database of job attitudes and add to our knowledge of affect, mood, emotion, and social attitudes in general. The use of event-signal methods in populations of working individuals will correct problems of reliance on relatively uncontrolled static assessments of ongoing organizational and psychological processes at arbitrarily chosen times and will permit generalizations to broader populations of constructs. Both developments should contribute to information about job and social attitudes.

Conclusion

Regardless of whether a person considers his or her job a source of unremitting drudgery, acute frustration, or deep (even spiritual) fulfillment, it seems that job satisfaction is among the most important attitudes that a person holds. In the present chapter, we defined job satisfaction in the context of the term "attitude," described the relationship between job attitudes and job performance while contrasting job attitudes and social attitudes, summarized the more important theoretical models of job attitudes, and discussed several new theoretical developments. These developments include the new job attitude of employee engagement (which we contrasted somewhat unfavorably with job satisfaction), state affect (and within-person approaches more generally) as an important frontier in job attitude research, and the between-unit level as another important frontier. Finally, we discussed issues related to the measurement of job attitudes and job affect. Overall, our review demonstrates that job satisfaction is alive and well, although it is increasingly to be found at different levels of analysis (e.g., within-person or between-unit) and in different forms (e.g., mood or discrete emotions).

We, therefore, continue to maintain that, if one wishes to understand human functioning in the workplace, job satisfaction represents as logical a starting place as any. In this context, perhaps the most unfortunate consequence of the Human Relations movement was the spawning of the "business case" for job satisfaction, which holds that job satisfaction is important because it is a major cause of job performance (and other important job-related behavior, such as turnover). As we have illustrated, research on this contention continues vigorously at multiple levels of analysis. Nonetheless, considering the importance of a person's job in his or her life, viewing job satisfaction *solely*, or even primarily, as a means to the end of job performance loses sight of the fact that job satisfaction is also a means to another end, overall life satisfaction (e.g., Judge & Watanabe, 1993), as well as an important end in and of itself. We did not sufficiently emphasize this idea in the body of the current chapter. However, in an effort to capitalize on the recency effect (Robinson & Brown, 1926), this is the idea with which we conclude.

Notes

1. Although the classic definition of attitudes includes cognition, affect, and behavior, we might be well advised to consider behavior a consequence, rather than a component, of attitudes (including job attitudes). In discussing this issue, Chaiken and Stangor (1987, p. 577) comment: "The tripartite

model…assumes that attitudes have an affective, cognitive, and behavioral component.…Criticisms that this model obscures the attitude-behavior relation…have led some researchers to delete the behavioral component and to regard attitude as a two-dimensional construct." Though we consider behaviors to be essential to the complete conceptualization of attitudes, it may be more productive for future research to define attitudes without an inherent behavioral component.

2. We do not review every theory on the formation of job satisfaction. For example, Herzberg's (1967) two-factor theory is one of the best-known job satisfaction theories, but we do not review it here. Numerous reviews have effectively laid the theory to rest (e.g., Hulin & Smith, 1967; Locke, 1969; Wernimont, 1966), and we see little reason to toil further in what is essentially barren ground. We also do not review the social information approach to job attitudes. This approach to attitude formation accounts for attitudes in information-impoverished laboratory conditions. It has not been applied extensively to account for attitudes of organizational employees in normal working situations.

3. Macey and Schneider (2008) conceptualize employee engagement (or, rather, what they refer to as "state engagement") as a composite construct that contains aspects of several other job attitude constructs, including job satisfaction. However, the predominant position in the literature is to conceptualize employee engagement as a distinct (albeit not orthogonal) attitudinal construct—and it is the predominant position that is adopted here.

4. However, we do note that, in spite of the covariance among the dimensions of job satisfaction, research has shown that employees' scores on different dimensions of job attitudes appear to be reliably related to "appropriate" behaviors. For example, Getman et al. (1976) reported that satisfaction with pay and supervision, two job characteristics that could be changed by union representation, were the dimensions most strongly related to votes for union representation. However, Zalesny (1985) found that satisfaction with the work itself was most strongly related to voting in favor of union representation in a sample of teachers. In this latter sample, working conditions in the form of class sizes could be affected by union representation. Employees make distinctions among job characteristics and act appropriately on the basis of their evaluations with these characteristics.

References

Adler, S., & Weiss, H. M. (1988). Recent developments in the study of personality and organizational behavior. In C. L. Cooper & I. T. Robertson (Eds.), *International review of industrial and organizational psychology* (pp. 307330). Chichester, UK: Wiley.

Adolphs, R., & Damasio, A. R. (2001). The interaction of affect and cognition: A neurobiological perspective. In J. P. Forgas (Ed.), *Handbook of affect and social cognition* (pp. 27–49). Mahwah, NJ: Erlbaum.

Aiken, L. R. (1966). Another look at weighting test items. *Journal of Educational Measurement, 3*, 183–185.

Ajzen, I., & Fishbein, M. (2005). The influence of attitudes on behavior. In D. Albarracín, B. T. Johnson, & M. P. Zanna (Eds.), *The handbook of attitudes* (pp. 173–221). Mahwah, NJ: Erlbaum.

Alliger, G. M., & Williams, K. J. (1993). Using signal-contingent experience sampling methodology to study work in the field: A discussion and illustration examining task perceptions and mood. *Personnel Psychology, 46*, 525–549.

Allport, G. W. (1961). *Pattern and growth in personality.* New York: Holt, Rinehart, & Winston.

Arvey, R. D., Bouchard, T. J., Segal, N. L., & Abraham, L. M. (1989). Job satisfaction: Environmental and genetic components. *Journal of Applied Psychology, 74*, 187–192.

Austin, J. T., & Villanova, P. (1992). The criterion problem: 1917–1992. *Journal of Applied Psychology, 77*, 836–874.

Balzer, W. K., Kihm, J. A., Smith, P. C., Irwin, J. L., Bachiochi, P. D., Robie, C., Sinar, E. F., & Parra, L. F. (1997). *Users' manual for the Job Descriptive Index (JDI, 1997 revision) and the Job In General scales.* Bowling Green, OH: Bowling Green State University.

Barsade, S. G., Brief, A. P., & Spataro, S. E. (2003). The affective revolution in organizational behavior: The emergence of a paradigm. In J. Greenberg (Ed.), *Organizational behavior: The state of the science* (2nd ed., pp. 3–52). Mahwah, NJ: Erlbaum.

Bateman, T. S., & Organ, D. W. (1983). Job satisfaction and the good soldier: The relationship between affect and employee "citizenship." *Academy of Management Journal, 26*, 587–595.

Beal, D. J., & Weiss, H. M. (2003). Methods of ecological momentary assessment in organizational research. *Organizational Research Methods, 6*, 440–464.

Beal, D. J., Weiss, H. M., Barros, E., & MacDermid, S. M. (2005). An episodic process model of affective influences on performance. *Journal of Applied Psychology, 90*, 1054–1068.

Best, R. G., Stapleton, L. M., & Downey, R. G. (2005). Core self-evaluations and job burnout: The test of alternative models. *Journal of Occupational Health Psychology, 10*, 441–451.

Bono, J. E., & Colbert, A. E. (2005). Understanding responses to multi-source feedback: The role of core self-evaluations. *Personnel Psychology, 58*, 171–203.

Bono, J. E., & Judge, T. A. (2003). Core self-evaluations: A review of the trait and its role in job satisfaction and job performance. *European Journal of Personality, 17*, S5–S18.

Borman, W. C. (1991). Job behavior, performance, and effectiveness. In M. D. Dunnette & L. M. Hough (Eds.), *Handbook of industrial and organizational psychology* (2nd ed., Vol. 2, pp. 445–505). Palo Alto, CA: Consulting Psychologist Press.

Bozeman, D. P., & Perrewé, P. L. (2001). The effect of item content overlap on Organizational Commitment Questionnaire-Turnover Cognitions relationships. *Journal of Applied Psychology, 86*, 161–173.

Bruni, L., & Porta, P. L. (2005). *Economics and happiness.* Oxford: Oxford University Press.

Campbell, D. T. (1963). Social attitudes and other acquired behavioral dispositions. In S. Koch (Ed.), *Psychology: A study of a science* (Vol. 6, pp. 94–171). New York: McGraw-Hill.

Campbell, J. P. (1992). Modeling the performance prediction problem in industrial and organizational psychology. In M. D. Dunnette & L. M. Hough (Eds.), *Handbook of industrial and organizational psychology* (2nd ed., Vol. 1, pp. 687–732). Palo Alto, CA: Consulting Psychologists Press.

Carsten, J. M., & Spector, P. W. (1987). Unemployment, job satisfaction, and employee turnover: A meta-analytic test of the Muchinsky model. *Journal of Applied Psychology, 72*, 374–381.

Cass, M. H., Siu, O. L., Faragher, E. B., & Cooper, C. L. (2003). A meta-analysis of the relationship between job satisfaction and employee health in Hong Kong. *Stress and Health, 19*, 79–95.

Cattell, R. B. (1965). *The scientific analysis of personality.* Baltimore, MD: Penguin.

Chaiken, S., & Stangor, C. (1987). Attitudes and attitude change. *Annual Review of Psychology, 38*, 575–630.

Chan, D. (1998). Functional relations among constructs in the same content domain at different levels of analysis: A typology of composition models. *Journal of Applied Psychology, 83*, 234–246.

Chen, G., Bliese, P. D., & Mathieu, J. E. (2005). Conceptual framework and statistical procedures for delineating and testing multilevel theories of homology. *Organizational Research Methods, 8*, 375–409.

Clore, G. L., & Schnall, S. (2005). The influence of affect on attitude. In D. Albarracín, B. T. Johnson, & M. P. Zanna (Eds.), *The handbook of attitudes* (pp. 437–489). Mahwah, NJ: Erlbaum.

Cranny, C. J., Smith, P. C., & Stone, E. F. (Eds.). (1992). *Job satisfaction.* New York: Lexington Books.

Dalal, R. S. (2005). A meta-analysis of the relationship between organizational citizenship behavior and counterproductive work behavior. *Journal of Applied Psychology, 90*, 1241–1255.

Dalal, R. S., Baysinger, M., Brummel, B. J., & LeBreton, J. M. (in press). The relative importance of employee engagement, other job attitudes, and trait affect as predictors of overall employee job performance. In press, *Journal of Applied Social Psychology.*

Dalal, R. S., Brummel, B. J., Wee, S., & Thomas, L. L. (2008). Defining employee engagement for productive research and practice. *Industrial and Organizational Psychology, 1*, 52–55.

Dalal, R. S., Lam, H., Weiss, H. M., Welch, E., & Hulin, C. L. (2009). A within-person approach to work behavior and performance: Concurrent and lagged citizenship-counterproductivity associations, and dynamic relationships with affect and overall job performance. *Academy of Management Journal, 52*, 1051–1066.

Damasio, A. R. (1994). *Descartes' error: Emotion, reason and the human brain.* New York: Grossett/Putnam & Sons.

Davis-Blake, A., & Pfeffer, J. (1989). Just a mirage: The search for dispositional effects in organizational research. *Academy of Management Review, 14*, 385–400.

Dawes, R. M., & Smith, T. L. (1985). Attitude and opinion measurement. In G. Lindzey & E. Aronson (Eds.), *The handbook of social psychology* (3rd ed., pp. 509–566). New York: Random House.

DeMeuse, K. P. (1985). A compendium of frequently used measures in industrial-organizational psychology. *The Industrial-Organizational Psychologist, 2*, 53–59.

Doob, L. W. (1947). The behavior of attitudes. *Psychological Review, 54*, 135–156.

Drevets, W. C., & Raichle, M. E. (1998). Reciprocal suppression of regional cerebral blood flow during emotional versus higher cognitive processes: Implications for interactions between emotion and cognition. *Cognition & Emotion, 12*, 353–385.

Dunham, R. B., & Smith, F. J. (1979). Organizational surveys: An internal assessment of organizational health. Glenview, IL: Scott-Foresman.

Dunham, R. B., Smith, F. J., & Blackburn, R. S. (1977). Validation of the Index of Organizational Reactions with the JDI, the MSQ, and Faces Scales. *Academy of Management Journal, 20*, 420–432.

Eagley, A. H., & Chaiken, S. (1993). *The psychology of attitudes.* New York: Harcourt.

Erez, A., & Judge, T. A. (2001). Relationship of core self-evaluations to goal setting, motivation, and performance. *Journal of Applied Psychology, 86*, 1270–1279.

Farrell, D. (1983). Exit, voice, loyalty, and neglect as responses to job dissatisfaction: A multidimensional scaling study. *Academy of Management Journal, 26*, 596–607.

Fassina, N. E., Jones, D. A., & Uggerslev, K. L. (2008). Relationship clean-up time: Using meta-analysis and path analysis to clarify relationships among job satisfaction, perceived fairness, and citizenship behaviors. *Journal of Management, 34*, 161–188.

Fishbein, M. (1980). A theory of reasoned action: Some applications and implications. In H. Howe & M. M. Page (Eds.), *Nebraska symposium on motivation: Beliefs, attitudes, and values* (pp. 65–116). Lincoln: University of Nebraska Press.

Fishbein, M., & Ajzen, I. (1972). Attitudes and opinions. *Annual Review of Psychology, 81*, 487–544.

Fishbein, M., & Ajzen, I. (1974). Attitudes towards objects as predictors of single and multiple behavioral criteria. *Psychological Review, 81*, 59–74.

Fishbein, M., & Ajzen, I. (1975). Belief, attitudes, intentions, and behavior: An introduction to theory and research. Reading, MA: Addison-Wesley.

Fisher, C. (2000). Mood and emotions while working: Missing pieces of job satisfaction? *Journal of Organizational Behavior, 21*, 185–202.

Fisher, C. D., & Locke, E. A. (1992). The new look in job satisfaction research and theory. In C. J. Cranny, P. C. Smith, & E. F. Stone (Eds.), *Job satisfaction* (pp. 165–194). New York: Lexington.

Fisher, V. E., & Hanna, J. V. (1931). *The dissatisfied worker.* New York: Macmillan.

Fleeson, W. (2004). Moving personality beyond the person-situation debate. *Current Directions in Psychological Science, 13*, 83–87.

Fried, Y., & Ferris, G. R. (1987). The validity of the job characteristics model: A review and meta-analysis. *Personnel Psychology, 40*, 287–322.

Frye, C. M. (1996). New evidence for the Job Characteristics Model: A meta-analysis of the job characteristics-job satisfaction relationship using composite correlations. Paper presented at the Eleventh Annual Meeting of the Society for Industrial and Organizational Psychology, San Diego, CA.

George, J. M. (1989). Mood and absence. *Journal of Applied Psychology, 74*, 317–324.

Gerhart, B. (1987). How important are dispositional factors as determinants of job satisfaction? Implications for job design and other personnel programs. *Journal of Applied Psychology, 72*, 366–373.

Getman, J. G., Goldberg, S. B., & Herman, J. B. (1976). *Union representation elections: Law and reality.* New York: Sage.

Glomb, T. M., Munson, L. J., Hulin, C. L., Bergman, M. E., & Drasgow, F. (1999). Structural equation models of sexual harassment: Longitudinal explorations and cross-sectional generalizations. *Journal of Applied Psychology, 84*, 14–28.

Goldberg, L. R. (1990). An alternative "description of personality": The Big-Five factor structure. *Journal of Personality and Social Psychology, 59*, 1216–1229.

Green, A. (1993). *Wobblies, pilebutts, and other heroes.* Urbana: University of Illinois Press.

Griffeth, R. W., Hom, P. W., & Gaertner, S. (2000). A meta-analysis of antecedents and correlates of employee turnover: Update, moderator tests, and research implications for the next millennium. *Journal of Management, 26*, 463–488.

Gutek, B. A., & Winter, S. J. (1992). Consistency of job satisfaction across situations: Fact or framing artifact? *Journal of Vocational Behavior, 41*, 61–78.

Hackett, R. D. (1989). Work attitudes and employee absenteeism: A synthesis of the literature. *Journal of Occupational Psychology, 62*, 235–248.

Hackett, R. D., & Guion, R. M. (1985). A reevaluation of the absenteeism-job satisfaction relationship. *Organizational Behavior and Human Decision Processes, 35*, 340–381.

Hackman, J. R., & Oldham, G. R. (1976). Motivation through the design of work: Test of a theory. *Organizational Behavior and Human Performance, 16*, 250–279.

Hackman, J. R., & Oldham, G. R. (1980). *Work redesign.* Reading, MA: Addison-Wesley.

Hanisch, K. A. (1992). The Job Descriptive Index revisited: Questions about the question mark. *Journal of Applied Psychology, 77*, 377–382.

Hanisch, K. A., & Hulin, C. L. (1990). Retirement as a voluntary organizational withdrawal behavior. *Journal of Vocational Behavior, 37*, 60–78.

Hanisch, K. A., & Hulin, C. L. (1991). General attitudes and organizational withdrawal: An evaluation of a causal model. *Journal of Vocational Behavior, 39*, 110–128.

Hanisch, K. A., Hulin, C. L., & Seitz, S. T. (1996). Mathematical/computational modeling of organizational withdrawal processes: Benefits, methods, and results. *Research in Personnel and Human Resources Management, 14*, 91–142.

Harrison, D. A., Newman, D. A., & Roth, P. L. (2006). How important are job attitudes? Meta-analytic comparisons of integrative behavioral outcomes and time sequences. *Academy of Management Journal, 49*, 305–325.

Helson, H. (1948). Adaptation-level as a basis for a quantitative theory of frames of reference. *Psychological Review, 55*, 297–313.

Helson, H. (1964). *Adaptation-level theory.* New York: Harper & Row.

Hershcovis, M. S., Turner, N., Barling, J., Arnold, K. A., Dupré, K. E., Inness, M., LeBlanc, M. M., & Sivanathan, N. (2007). Predicting workplace aggression: A meta-analysis. *Journal of Applied Psychology, 92*, 228–238.

Herzberg, F. (1967). *Work and the nature of man.* Cleveland, OH: World Book.

Herzberg, F., Mausner, B., Peterson, R. O., & Capwell, D. F. (1957). *Job attitudes: A review of research and opinions.* Pittsburgh: Psychological Services of Pittsburgh.

Hofmann, D. A., Griffin, M. A., & Gavin, M. B. (2000). The application of hierarchical linear modeling to organizational research. In K. J. Klein & S. W. J. Kozlowski (Eds.), *Multilevel theory, research, and methods in organizations* (pp. 467–511). San Francisco, CA: Jossey-Bass.

Hom, P. W. (2001). The legacy of Hulin's work on turnover thinking and research. In F. D. Drasgow & J. M. Brett (Eds.), *Psychology of work: Theoretically based empirical research* (pp. 169–187). Mahwah, NJ: Erlbaum.

Hom, P. W., Katerberg, R., & Hulin, C. L. (1979). A comparative examination of three approaches to the prediction of turnover. *Journal of Applied Psychology, 64*, 280–290.

Hoppock, R. (1935). *Job satisfaction.* New York: Harper.

Hulin, C. L. (1966a). The effects of community characteristics on measures of job satisfaction. *Journal of Applied Psychology, 50*, 185–192.

Hulin, C. L. (1966b). Job satisfaction and turnover in a female clerical population. *Journal of Applied Psychology, 50*, 280–285.

Hulin, C. L. (1968). The effects of changes in job satisfaction levels on turnover. *Journal of Applied Psychology, 52*, 122–126.

Hulin, C. L. (1969). Sources of variation in job and life satisfaction: The role of community and job-related variables. *Journal of Applied Psychology, 53*, 279–291.

Hulin, C. L. (1991). Adaptation, persistence, and commitment in organizations. In M. D. Dunnette & L. M. Hough (Eds.), *Handbook of industrial and organizational psychology* (2nd ed., Vol. 2, pp. 445–505). Palo Alto, CA: Consulting Psychologist Press.

Hulin, C. L. (2001). Lessons from I/O psychology. In F. D. Drasgow & J. M. Brett (Eds.), *Psychology of work: Theoretically based empirical research* (pp. 3–22). Mahwah, NJ: Erlbaum.

Hulin, C. L., & Blood, M. R. (1968). Job enlargement, individual differences, and work responses. *Psychological Bulletin, 69*, 41–55.

Hulin, C. L., Roznowski, M., & Hachiya, D. (1985). Alternative opportunities and withdrawal decisions: Empirical and theoretical discrepancies and an integration. *Psychological Bulletin, 97*, 233–250.

Hulin, C. L., & Smith, P. A. (1967). An empirical investigation of two implications of the two-factor theory of job satisfaction. *Journal of Applied Psychology, 51*, 396–402.

Hull, C. L. (1943). *Principles of behavior: An introduction to behavior theory.* New York: Appleton-Century-Crofts.

Huselid, M. A. (1995). The impact of human resource management practices on turnover, productivity, and corporate financial performance. *Academy of Management Journal, 38*, 635–672.

Iaffaldano, M. T., & Muchinsky, P. M. (1985). Job satisfaction and job performance: A meta-analysis. *Psychological Bulletin, 97*, 251–273.

Ilies, R., & Judge, T. A. (2002). Understanding the dynamic relationships among personality, mood, and job satisfaction: A field experience sampling study. *Organizational Behavior and Human Decision Processes, 89*, 1119–1139.

Ironson, G. H., Smith, P. C., Brannick, M. T., Gibson, W. M., & Paul, K. B. (1989). Construction of a Job in General scale: A comparison of global, composite, and specific measures. *Journal of Applied Psychology, 74*, 193–200.

Izard, C. E. (1992). Basic emotions, relations among emotions, and emotion-cognition relations. *Psychological Review, 99*, 561–565.

James, J. R., & Tetrick, L. E. (1986). Confirmatory analytic tests of three causal models relating job perceptions to job satisfaction. *Journal of Applied Psychology, 71*, 77–82.

James, L. R., & Jones, A. P. (1980). Perceived job characteristics and job satisfaction: An examination of reciprocal causation. *Personnel Psychology, 33*, 97–135.

Johnson, E. C., Kristof-Brown, A. J., Van Vianen, A. E. M., De Pater, I. E., & Klein, M. R. (2003). Expatriate social ties: Personality antecedents and consequences for adjustment. *International Journal of Selection and Assessment, 11*, 277–288.

Judge, T. A., & Bono, J. E. (2001). Relationship of core self-evaluations traits—self-esteem, generalized self-efficacy, locus of control, and emotional stability—with job satisfaction and job performance: A meta-analysis. *Journal of Applied Psychology, 86*, 80–92.

Judge, T. A., Bono, J. E., Erez, A., & Locke, E. A. (2005). Core self-evaluations and job and life satisfaction: The role of self-concordance and goal attainment. *Journal of Applied Psychology, 90*, 257–268.

Judge, T. A., Bono, J. E., & Locke, E. A. (2000). Personality and job satisfaction: The mediating role of job characteristics. *Journal of Applied Psychology, 85*, 237–249.

Judge, T. A., & Bretz, R. D. (1993). Report on an alternative measure of affective disposition. *Educational and Psychological Measurement, 53*, 1095–1104.

Judge, T. A., Erez, A., Bono, J. E., & Thoresen, C. J. (2002). Are measures of self-esteem, neuroticism, locus of control, and generalized self-efficacy indicators of a common core construct? *Journal of Personality and Social Psychology, 83*, 693–710.

Judge, T. A., Heller, D., & Klinger, R. (2008). The dispositional sources of job satisfaction: A comparative test. *Applied Psychology: An International Review, 57*, 361–372.

Judge, T. A., Heller, D., & Mount, M. K. (2002). Five-factor model of personality and job satisfaction: A meta-analysis. *Journal of Applied Psychology, 87*, 530–541.

Judge, T. A., & Hulin, C. L. (1993). Job satisfaction as a reflection of disposition: A multiple source casual analysis. *Organizational Behavior and Human Decision Processes, 56*, 388–421.

Judge, T. A., & Hurst, C. (2007). Capitalizing on one's advantages: Role of core self-evaluations. *Journal of Applied Psychology, 92*, 1212–1227.

Judge, T. A., & Ilies, R. (2004). Affect and job satisfaction: A study of their relationship at work and at home. *Journal of Applied Psychology, 89*, 661–673.

Judge, T. A., & Locke, E. A. (1993). Effect of dysfunctional thought processes on subjective well-being and job satisfaction. *Journal of Applied Psychology, 78*, 475–490.

Judge, T. A., Locke, E. A., & Durham, C. C. (1997). The dispositional causes of job satisfaction: A core evaluations approach. *Research in Organizational Behavior, 19*, 151–188.

Judge, T. A., Scott, B. A., & Ilies, R. (2006). Hostility, job attitudes, and workplace deviance: Test of a multilevel model. *Journal of Applied Psychology, 91*, 126–138.

Judge, T. A., Thoresen, C. J., Bono, J. E., & Patton, G. K. (2001). The job satisfaction-job performance relationship: A qualitative and quantitative review. *Psychological Bulletin, 127*, 376–407.

Judge, T. A., & Watanabe, S. (1993). Another look at the job satisfaction-life satisfaction relationship. *Journal of Applied Psychology, 78*, 939–948.

Jurgensen, C. E. (1978). Job preferences (What makes a job good or bad?). *Journal of Applied Psychology, 50*, 479–487.

Kendall, L. M. (1963). Canonical analysis of job satisfaction and behavioral, personal background, and situational data. Unpublished Ph.D. dissertation, Cornell University.

Kinicki, A. J., McKee-Ryan, F. M., Schriesheim, C. A., & Carson, K. P. (2002). Assessing the construct validity of the Job Descriptive Index: A review and meta-analysis. *Journal of Applied Psychology, 87*, 14–32.

Klein, K. J., Dansereau, F., & Hall, R. J. (1994). Levels issues in theory development, data collection, and analysis. *Academy of Management Review, 19*, 195–229.

Kokkinou, I., & Dalal, R. S. (2008). *The relationship between organization-level satisfaction and performance: A meta-analysis.* Paper presented at the meeting of the Academy of Management, Anaheim, CA.

Koslowsky, M., Sagie, A., Krausz, M., Singer, A. D. (1997). Correlates of employee lateness: Some theoretical considerations. *Journal of Applied Psychology, 82*, 79–88.

Kozlowski, S. W. J., & Klein, K. J. (2000). A levels approach to theory and research in organizations. In K. J. Klein & S. W. J. Kozlowski (Eds.), *Multilevel theory, research and methods in organizations* (pp. 3–90). San Francisco: Jossey-Bass.

Larson, R., & Csikszentmihalyi, M. (1983). The experience sampling method. In H. T. Reis (Ed.), *Naturalistic approaches to studying social interaction* (pp. 41–56). San Francisco: Jossey-Bass.

LePine, J. A., Erez, A., & Johnson, D. E. (2002). The nature and dimensionality of organizational citizenship behavior: A critical review and meta-analysis. *Journal of Applied Psychology, 87*, 52–65.

Locke, E. A. (1969). What is job satisfaction? *Organizational Behavior and Human Performance, 4*, 309–336.

Locke, E. A. (1976). The nature and causes of job satisfaction. In M. D. Dunnette (Ed.), *Handbook of industrial and organizational psychology* (pp. 1297–1343). Chicago: Rand McNally.

Loher, B. T., Noe, R. A., Moeller, N. L., & Fitzgerald, M. P. (1985). A meta-analysis of the relation of job characteristics to job satisfaction. *Journal of Applied Psychology, 70*, 280–289.

Macey, W. H., & Schneider, B. (2008). The meaning of employee engagement. *Industrial and Organizational Psychology, 1*, 3–30.

March, J. G., & Simon, H. A. (1958). *Organizations.* New York: Wiley.

McCrae, R. R., & Costa, P. T., Jr. (1997). Personality trait structure as a human universal. *American Psychologist, 52*, 509–516.

Mikes, P. S., & Hulin, C. L. (1968). The use of importance as a weighting component of job satisfaction. *Journal of Applied Psychology, 52*, 394–398.

Miller, H. E., Katerberg, R., & Hulin, C. L. (1979). Evaluation of the Mobley, Horner, and Hollingsworth model of employee turnover. *Journal of Applied Psychology, 64*, 509–517.

Miner, A. G. (2001). Antecedents, behavioral outcomes, and performance implications of mood at work: An experience sampling study. Unpublished Ph.D. dissertation, University of Illinois at Urbana-Champaign.

Miner, A. G., Glomb, T. M., & Hulin, C. (2005). Experience sampling mood and its correlates at work. *Journal of Occupational and Organizational Psychology, 78*, 171–193.

Mobley, W. H., Horner, S. O., & Hollingsworth, A. T. (1978). An evaluation of precursors of hospital employee turnover. *Journal of Applied Psychology, 63*, 408–414.

Morgeson, F. P., & Hofmann, D. A. (1999). The structure and function of collective constructs: Implications for multilevel research and theory development. *Academy of Management Review, 24*, 249–265.

Newton, T., & Keenan, T. (1991). Further analyses of the dispositional argument in organizational behavior. *Journal of Applied Psychology, 76*, 781–787.

Organ, D. W., & Ryan, K. (1995). A meta-analytic review of attitudinal and dispositional predictors of organizational citizenship behavior. *Personnel Psychology, 48*, 775–802.

Ortony, A., & Turner, T. J. (1990). What's basic about basic emotions? *Psychological Review, 97*, 315–331.

Power, M. J. (2006). The structure of emotion: An empirical comparison of six models. *Cognition & Emotion, 20*, 694–713.

Raudenbush, S. W., & Bryk, A. S. (2002). *Hierarchical linear models: Applications and data analysis methods.* Thousand Oaks, CA: Sage.

Ree, M. J., Carretta, T. R., & Earles, J. A. (1998). In top-down decisions, weighting variables does not matter: A consequence of Wilks' theorem. *Organizational Research Methods, 1*, 407–420.

Reisenzein, R., & Schoenpflug, W. (1992). Stumpf's cognitive-evaluative theory of emotion. *American Psychologist, 47,* 34–45.

Rentsch, J. R., & Steel, R. P. (1992). Construct and concurrent validation of the Andrews and Withey job satisfaction questionnaire. *Educational and Psychological Measurement, 52,* 357–367.

Rice, R. W., Gentile, D. A., & McFarlin, D. B. (1991). Facet importance and job satisfaction. *Journal of Applied Psychology, 76,* 31–39.

Ritter, D., & Eslea, M. (2005). Hot sauce, toy guns, and graffiti: A critical account of current laboratory aggression paradigms. *Aggressive Behavior, 31,* 407–419.

Roberts, B. W., Walton, K. E., & Viechtbauer, W. (2006). Patterns of mean-level change in personality traits across the life course: A meta-analysis of longitudinal studies. *Psychological Bulletin, 132,* 1–25.

Roberts, K. H., & Glick, W. (1981). The job characteristics approach to task design: A critical review. *Journal of Applied Psychology, 66,* 193–217.

Robinson, E. S., & Brown, M. A. (1926). Effect of serial position on memorization. *American Journal of Psychology, 37,* 538–552.

Roznowski, M. (1989). Examination of the measurement properties of the Job Descriptive Index with experimental items. *Journal of Applied Psychology, 74,* 805–814.

Roznowski, M., & Hulin, C. (1992). The scientific merit of valid measures of general constructs with special reference to job satisfaction and job withdrawal. In C. J. Cranny, P. C. Smith, & E. F. Stone (Eds.), *Job satisfaction* (pp. 123–163). New York: Lexington.

Roznowski, M., Miller, H. E., & Rosse, J. G. (1992). *On the utility of broad-band measures of employee behavior: The case for employee adaptation and citizenship.* Presented at the annual meeting of the Academy of Management, Las Vegas.

Salvaggio, A. N., Schneider, B., Nishii, L. H., Mayer, D. M., Ramesh, A., & Lyon, J. S. (2007). Manager personality, manager service quality orientation, and service climate: Test of a model. *Journal of Applied Psychology, 92,* 1741–1750.

Schmitt, N., & McCune, J. T. (1981). The relationship between job attitudes and the decision to retire. *Academy of Management Journal, 24,* 795–802.

Schriesheim, C. (1978). Job satisfaction, attitudes toward unions, and voting in a union representation election. *Journal of Applied Psychology, 63,* 548–552.

Schwartz, J. E., & Stone, A. A. (1998). Strategies for analyzing ecological momentary assessment data. *Health Psychology, 17,* 6–16.

Scott, K. D., & Taylor, G. S. (1985). An examination of conflicting findings on the relationship between job satisfaction and absenteeism: A meta-analysis. *Academy of Management Journal, 28,* 599–612.

Sheldon, K. M., & Elliot, A. J. (1998). Not all personal goals are personal: Comparing autonomous and controlled reasons for goals as predictors of effort and attainment. *Personality and Social Psychology Bulletin, 24,* 546–557.

Smith, C. A., Organ, D. W., & Near, J. P. (1983). Organizational citizenship behavior: Its nature and antecedents. *Journal of Applied Psychology, 68,* 653–663.

Smith, F. J. (1977). Work attitudes as predictors of attendance on a specific day. *Journal of Applied Psychology, 62,* 16–19.

Smith, P. C. (1955). The prediction of individual differences in susceptibility to industrial monotony. *Journal of Applied Psychology, 39,* 322–329.

Smith, P. C., Kendall, L. M., & Hulin, C. L. (1969). *Measurement of satisfaction in work and retirement.* Chicago: Rand-McNally.

Smith-Lovin, L. (1991). An affect control view of cognition and emotion. In J. A. Howard & P. L. Callero (Eds.), *The self-society dynamic: Cognition, emotion, and action* (pp. 143–169). New York: Cambridge University Press.

Snipes, R. L., Oswald, S. L., LaTour, M., & Armenakis, A. A. (2005). The effects of specific job satisfaction facets on customer perceptions of service quality: An employee-level analysis. *Journal of Business Research, 58,* 1330–1339.

Staw, B. M., Bell, N. E., & Clausen, J. A. (1986). The dispositional approach to job attitudes: A lifetime longitudinal test. *Administrative Science Quarterly, 31,* 437–453.

Staw, B. M., & Ross, J. (1985). Stability in the midst of change: A dispositional approach to job attitudes. *Journal of Applied Psychology, 70,* 469–480.

Stone, E. F., Stone, D. L., & Gueutal, H. G. (1990). Influence of cognitive ability on responses to questionnaire measures: Measurement precision and missing response problems. *Journal of Applied Psychology, 75,* 418–427.

Tellegen, A., Watson, D., & Clark, L. A. (1999a). On the dimensionality and hierarchical structure of affect. *Psychological Science, 10,* 297–303.

Tellegen, A., Watson, D., & Clark, L. A. (1999b). Further support for a hierarchical model of affect: Reply to Green and Salovey. *Psychological Science, 10,* 307–309.

Tett, R. P., & Meyer, J. P. (1993). Job satisfaction, organizational commitment, turnover intention, and turnover: Path analyses based on meta-analytic findings. *Personnel Psychology, 46,* 259–293.

Thibaut, J. W., & Kelley, H. H. (1959). *The social psychology of groups.* New York: Wiley.

Thurstone, L. L. (1928). Attitudes can be measured. *American Journal of Sociology, 33,* 529–554.

Totterdell, P. (1999). Mood scores: Mood and performance in professional cricketers. *British Journal of Psychology, 90,* 317–332.

Totterdell, P. (2000). Catching moods and hitting runs: Mood linkage and subjective performance in professional sports teams. *Journal of Applied Psychology, 85,* 848–859.

Triandis, H. C. (1980). Values, attitudes, and interpersonal behavior. In H. Howe & M. M. Page (Eds.), *Nebraska symposium on motivation: Beliefs, attitudes, and values* (Vol. 27, pp. 195–259). Lincoln: University of Nebraska Press.

Turner, A. N., & Lawrence, P. R. (1965). *Industrial jobs and the worker.* Cambridge, MA: Harvard University Press.

Van Rooy, D. L., Whitman, D. S., & Viswesvaran, C. (2007). *A meta-analytic investigation of the unit-level employee satisfaction–performance link.* Paper presented at the meeting of the Society for Industrial and Organizational Psychology, New York.

Wainer, H. (1976). Estimating coefficients in linear models: It don't make no nevermind. *Psychological Bulletin, 83,* 213–217.

Wainer, H. (1978). On the sensitivity of regression and regressors. *Psychological Bulletin, 85,* 267–273.

Wanberg, C. R., Glomb, T. M., Song, Z., & Sorenson, S. (2005). Job-search persistence during unemployment: A 10-wave longitudinal study. *Journal of Applied Psychology, 90,* 411–430.

Watson, D. (2000). *Mood and temperament.* New York: Guilford.

Watson, D., & Slack, A. K. (1993). General factors of affective temperament and their relation to job satisfaction over time.

Organizational Behavior and Human Decision Processes, 54, 181–202.

Watson, D., Wiese, D., Vaidya, J., & Tellegen, A. (1999). The two general activation systems of affect: Structural findings, evolutionary considerations, and psychobiological evidence. *Journal of Personality and Social Psychology, 76*, 820–838.

Weiss, H. M., & Brief, A. P. (2001). Affect at work: An historical perspective. In R. L. Payne & C. L. Cooper (Eds.), *Emotions at work* (pp. 133–172). Chichester, UK: Wiley.

Weiss, H. M., & Cropanzano, R. (1996). Affective events theory: A theoretical discussion of the structure, causes and consequences of affective experiences at work. *Research in Organizational Behavior, 19*, 1–74.

Weiss, D. J., Dawis, R. V., England, G. W., & Lofquist, L. H. (1967). *Manual for the Minnesota Satisfaction Questionnaire.* Minneapolis: University of Minnesota.

Weiss, H. M., Nicholas, J. P., & Daus, C. S. (1999). An examination of the joint effects of affective experiences and job satisfaction and variations in affective experiences over time.

Organizational Behavior and Human Decision Processes, 78, 1–24.

Weitz, J. (1952). A neglected concept in the study of job satisfaction. *Personnel Psychology, 5*, 201–205.

Wernimont, P. F. (1966). Intrinsic and extrinsic factors in job satisfaction. *Journal of Applied Psychology, 50*, 41–50.

Wicker, A. W. (1969). Attitudes versus actions: The relationship of verbal and overt behavioral responses to attitude objects. *Journal of Social Issues, 25*, 41–78.

Zajonc, R. B. (1980). Feeling and thinking: Preferences need no inferences. *American Psychologist, 35*, 151–175.

Zajonc, R. B. (1984). On the primacy of affect. *American Psychologist, 39*, 117–123.

Zalesny, M. D. (1985). Comparison of economic and non-economic factors in predicting faculty vote preference in a union representation election. *Journal of Applied Psychology, 70*, 243–256.

Zohar, D. (1999). When things go wrong: The effect of daily work hassles on effort, exertion and negative mood. *Journal of Occupational and Organizational Psychology, 72*, 265–283.

Organizational Justice

Jason A. Colquitt

Abstract

This chapter frames the development of the justice literature around three literature-level trends: differentiation, cognition, and exogeneity. The differentiation trend has impacted how justice is conceptualized, with additional justice dimensions being further segmented into different sources. The cognition trend has created a rational, calculative theme to the most visible justice theories. The exogeneity trend has resulted in justice occupying the independent variable position in most empirical studies. Taken together, these trends have resulted in a vibrant and active literature. However, I will argue that the next phase of the literature's evolution will benefit from a relaxation—or even reversal—of these trends. Path-breaking contributions may be more likely to result from the aggregation of justice concepts, a focus on affect, and the identification of predictors of justice.

Key Words: Justice, fairness, attitudes, cognition, emotion

Introduction

For some four decades, scholars interested in justice have been examining individuals' reactions to decisions, procedures, and relevant authorities (for a historical review, see Colquitt, Greenberg, & Zapata-Phelan, 2005). One of the central themes of this research is that individuals do not merely react to events by asking "Was that good?" or "Was that satisfying?" Instead, they also ask "Was that fair?" Hundreds of studies have shown that perceptions of fairness are distinct from feelings of outcome favorability or outcome satisfaction (Cohen-Charash & Spector, 2001; Colquitt, Conlon, Wesson, Porter, & Ng, 2001; Skitka, Winquist, & Hutchinson, 2003). Many of those same studies have further shown that fairness perceptions explain unique variance in key attitudes and behaviors, including organizational commitment, trust in management, citizenship behavior, counterproductive behavior, and task performance (Cohen-Charash & Spector, 2001; Colquitt et al., 2001).

In the early years of the literature, justice scholars focused solely on the fairness of decision outcomes, termed *distributive justice*. Drawing on earlier work by Homans (1961), Adams (1965) showed that individuals react to outcome allocations by comparing their ratio of outcomes to inputs to some relevant comparison other. If those ratios match, the individual feels a sense of equity. Although equity is typically viewed as the most appropriate allocation norm in organizations, theorizing suggests that other norms can be viewed as fair in some situations. For example, allocating outcomes according to equality and need norms are perceived to be fair when group harmony or personal welfare are the relevant goals (Deutsch, 1975; Leventhal, 1976). Integrating these perspectives, distributive justice has been defined as the degree to which the appropriate allocation norm is followed in a given decision-making context.

Working at the intersection of social psychology and law, Thibaut and Walker (1975) conducted a series of studies on the fairness of decision-making processes, termed *procedural justice*. The authors recognized that the disputants in legal proceedings judge both the fairness of the verdict and the fairness of the courtroom procedures. Thibaut and Walker (1975) argued that procedures were viewed as fair when disputants possessed process control, meaning that they could voice their concerns in an effort to influence the decision outcome. A separate stream of work by Leventhal (1980) broadened the conceptualization of procedural justice in the context of resource allocation decisions. Specifically, Leventhal (1980) argued that allocation procedures would be viewed as fair when they adhered to several "rules," including consistency, bias suppression, accuracy, correctability, and ethicality.

While examining fairness in a recruitment context, Bies and Moag (1986) observed that decision events actually have three facets: a decision, a procedure, and an interpersonal interaction during which that procedure is implemented. The authors used the term *interactional justice* to capture the fairness of that interpersonal interaction. They further argued that interactional justice was fostered when relevant authorities communicated procedural details in a respectful and proper manner, and justified decisions using honest and truthful information. In a subsequent chapter, Greenberg (1993b) argued that the respect and propriety rules are distinct from the justification and truthfulness rules, labeling the former criteria *interpersonal justice* and the latter criteria *informational justice*.

Adopting an umbrella term first coined by Greenberg (1987), the dimensions reviewed above have come to define the "organizational justice" landscape. In a series of reviews, Greenberg charted the development of the organizational justice literature from its intellectual adolescence to its status as a more adult literature (Colquitt & Greenberg, 2003; Greenberg, 1990b; Greenberg, 1993a). That maturation saw articles on organizational justice gain an ever-expanding presence in academic journals, scholarly book series, and conference programs in organizational behavior and industrial/organizational (I/O) psychology. Indeed, the top ten journals in organizational behavior included 50 or more articles on organizational justice in 2001, 2003, and 2006—up from single digits throughout the 1980s (Colquitt, 2008).

The current review will argue that the development of the organizational justice literature has been shaped by three major trends: differentiation, cognition, and exogeneity. The trend toward *differentiation* has impacted the ways in which justice is conceptualized and measured, with specific justice dimensions being further segmented into different sources or "foci." The trend toward *cognition* has created a rational, calculative theme in many of the most visible theories in the justice literature. Finally, the trend toward *exogeneity* has resulted in justice occupying the independent variable position in most empirical studies, resulting in an emphasis on its predictive validity. Taken together, these trends have influenced the typical study in the justice literature in a number of ways, including its research question, its conceptual lens, and its methods and procedures.

The sections to follow will review each of these trends in some detail, focusing on the key articles that helped to trigger and shape those trends. Perhaps more importantly, the sections will explore the following premise: that the "next steps" in the development of the justice literature would benefit from a reversal, or at least a stemming, of the trends that have dominated the literature. Although Greenberg (2007) argued that there are still many "conceptual parking spaces" available to study in the justice literature, progress in mature fields inevitably takes on a more incremental and nuanced nature. Studies that strive for a more significant impact may need to "go against the grain" of the literature to examine research questions in a novel and innovative manner. With that in mind, this chapter will explore the merits of the obverses of the three literature forces: a trend toward *aggregation* of justice concepts, a trend toward *affect* in justice theorizing, and a trend toward *endogeneity* in causal models.

Trend One: Differentiation

Many of the earliest studies on justice in the mainstream organizational behavior and industrial/organizational psychology literature were focused on differentiating procedural justice from distributive justice. For example, Greenberg (1986) asked managers to think of a time when they received a particularly fair or unfair performance evaluation rating, and to write down the single most important factor that contributed to that fairness level. After the responses were typed on a set of index cards, another set of managers participated in a Q-sort in which shared responses were identified and fit into categories. After the categories were cross-validated, another sample of managers were given a survey that included the categories and were asked to rate how important they were as determinants of fair performance evaluations. Importantly, a factor analysis of those ratings resulted in a two-factor solution with procedural factors (e.g., consistent application of standards, soliciting input, ability to challenge evaluation) loading separately from distributive factors (e.g., rating based on performance, recommendation for raise or promotion). Importantly, the procedural factors were similar to the rules that Thibaut and Walker (1975) and Leventhal (1980) had identified in their theorizing.

Once evidence had been established that procedural justice and distributive justice could be differentiated in Q-sorts and factor analyses, scholars began examining whether the two constructs varied in their predictive validity. Folger and Konovsky (1989) gave employees in a manufacturing plant a survey about their most recent salary increase. Twenty-six survey items were written to assess procedural justice, including Leventhal's (1980) rules, Thibaut and Walker's (1975) concepts, and—in a foreshadowing of a looming debate in the literature—Bies and Moag's (1986) concepts. These 26 items wound up loading on five factors, four of which were retained in the analyses. Another four items were included to assess distributive justice and outcome favorability, and the survey also included measures of organizational commitment, trust in supervisor, and pay satisfaction. Regression analyses revealed that the procedural justice variables were stronger predictors of organizational commitment and trust in supervisor, whereas the distributive justice and outcome favorability variables were stronger predictors of pay satisfaction. This pattern—where procedural justice was a stronger predictor of system-referenced attitudes and distributive justice was a stronger predictor of outcome-referenced attitudes—came to be termed the *two-factor model* (Sweeney & McFarlin, 1993; see also McFarlin & Sweeney, 1992).

After the publication of Bies and Moag (1986) and some initial studies on the interactional justice construct (e.g., Bies & Shapiro, 1988), justice scholars turned their attention to differentiating interactional justice from procedural and distributive justice. In a study of citizenship behavior in the paint and coatings industry, Moorman (1991) created a 13-item measure that included procedural and interactional justice dimensions. Whereas Folger and Konovsky (1989) had included "procedural justice" items that tapped Bies and Moag's (1986) concepts, Moorman included "interactional justice" items that tapped Leventhal's (1980) and Thibaut and Walker's (1975) rules (e.g., bias suppression, process control). Such items were actually consistent with chapters that provided a somewhat

revised conceptualization of interactional justice—defining the construct in terms that went beyond respect, propriety, truthfulness, and justification to include manager-originating versions of Leventhal's rules (Folger & Bies, 1989; Greenberg, Bies, & Eskew, 1991; Tyler & Bies, 1990).

Moorman's (1991) results showed that interactional justice was distinct from procedural justice in a confirmatory factor analysis. It was also distinct from a measure of distributive justice taken from Price and Mueller's (1986) work. From a predictive validity perspective, the results also showed that interactional justice was a better predictor of citizenship behaviors than either procedural or distributive justice. Moorman's (1991) study had a lasting impact on the justice literature in two respects. First, it helped to establish citizenship behavior as the most common behavioral outcome in the justice literature (for a review, see Moorman & Byrne, 2005). Second, it introduced one of the most commonly used measures in the literature, reducing the tendency for scholars to construct ad hoc measures in a given study.

Although Moorman's (1991) measure brought an increased amount of attention to interactional justice, the remainder of the decade was characterized by a debate about whether that justice form could truly be differentiated from procedural justice. The chapters that had reconceptualized the new justice form seemed to suggest—either explicitly or implicitly—that interactional justice was merely a manager-originating version of procedural justice (Folger & Bies, 1989; Greenberg et al., 1991; Tyler & Bies, 1990). Moreover, the fact that Moorman's (1991) interactional justice scale included concepts from Thibaut and Walker's (1975) and Leventhal's (1980) theorizing seemed to result in inflated correlations between interactional and procedural justice. As a result, scholars who utilized Moorman's (1991) scale sometimes wound up combining the interactional and procedural dimensions due to high intercorrelations (e.g., Mansour-Cole & Scott, 1998; Skarlicki & Latham, 1997).

In an attempt to clarify these issues, Colquitt (2001) validated a new justice measure whose items were based on more literal interpretations of Thibaut and Walker (1975), Leventhal (1980), and Bies and Moag (1986). Thus, the interactional items assessed respect, propriety, truthfulness, and justification, not procedural concepts such as process control or consideration. Drawing on Greenberg's (1993b) earlier conceptual work, Colquitt (2001) also examined the merits of further differentiating interactional justice into interpersonal (respect and propriety) and informational (truthfulness and justification) facets. Confirmatory factor analyses in two independent samples showed that a four-factor structure fit the data significantly better than one-, two-, or three-factor versions. In addition, structural equation modeling results revealed that the four justice dimensions had unique relationships with various outcome measures.

At its core, the differentiation of interpersonal and informational justice acknowledges that the politeness and respectfulness of communication is distinct from its honesty and truthfulness. Indeed, that differentiation is not at all controversial in the literature on explanations and causal accounts, where scholars routinely separate the sensitivity of an account from the truthfulness or comprehensiveness of its content (e.g., Bobocel, Agar, & Meyer, 1998; Gilliland & Beckstein, 1996; Greenberg, 1993c). Several of the studies that have utilized Colquitt's (2001) scales have provided factor-analytic support for the interpersonal-informational distinction (e.g., Ambrose, Hess, & Ganesan, 2007; Bell, Wiechmann, & Ryan, 2006; Camerman, Cropanzano, & Vandenberghe, 2007; Choi, 2008; Jawahar, 2007; Judge & Colquitt, 2004; Mayer, Nishii, Schneider, & Goldstein, 2007; Scott, Colquitt, & Zapata-Phelan, 2007; Streicher et al., 2008). Of course, several other studies have included only one of the interactional facets, depending on which is most relevant to the research question. For example, Roberson and Stewart's (2006) study of the motivational effects of feedback focused on informational justice but not interpersonal justice. As another example, Judge, Scott, and Ilies's (2006) study of hostility and deviance focused on interpersonal justice but not informational justice.

Even as the organizational justice dimensions were being differentiated into three and then four dimensions, scholars were drawing additional distinctions. For example, scholars argued that the justice dimensions could be distinguished by their *focus*, not just their *content* (Blader & Tyler, 2003; Colquitt, 2001; Rupp & Cropanzano, 2002). Just as formal organizational procedures could be perceived as consistent and unbiased, so too could managers' own decision-making styles (Folger & Bies, 1989; Greenberg et al., 1991; Tyler & Bies, 1990). Just as managerial accounts could be perceived as respectful and candid, so too could an organization's more formal communications. Blader and Tyler referred to this organization- versus manager-originating distinction as *formal justice* versus *informal justice*,

whereas Rupp and Cropanzano (2002) utilized the terms *organizational justice* versus *supervisory justice*.

The distinction between justice "foci" (to utilize Rupp and Cropanzano's (2002) terminology) serves to complement one of the dominant theoretical lenses in the literature: social exchange theory (Blau, 1964). This theory suggests that supportive behaviors by an authority can be viewed as a benefit to an employee that should trigger an obligation to reciprocate. That obligation to reciprocate can then be expressed through positive discretionary behaviors. As applied in the justice literature, this core theoretical premise can be used to explain findings such as the positive relationship between justice perceptions and citizenship behavior (Masterson, Lewis, Goldman, & Taylor, 2000; Organ, 1990). Differentiating organization and manager-originating justice can allow scholars to examine this exchange dynamic with more nuance (Lavelle, Rupp, & Brockner, 2007). For example, organization-originating justice should be a stronger predictor of organization-directed citizenship (e.g., attending optional meetings). In contrast, supervisor-originating justice should be a stronger predictor of supervisor-directed citizenship (e.g., helping one's supervisor with a heavy workload).

These sorts of propositions have been tested in three studies, beginning with Rupp and Cropanzano (2002) and continuing in Liao and Rupp (2005) and Horvath and Andrews (2007). Support for the propositions can be examined by contrasting the size of "focus matching" correlations (e.g., supervisor-originating procedural justice and supervisor-directed citizenship, organization-originating procedural justice and organization-directed citizenship) with their non-matching analogs. Rupp and Cropanzano (2002) and Horvath and Andrews (2007) examined procedural and interpersonal justice, whereas Liao and Rupp (2005) included procedural, interpersonal, and informational justice. Taken together, the correlation matrices in the three studies yielded 28 different matching versus non-matching contrasts. Of those, 18 contrasts revealed the predicted pattern. Interestingly, all three studies suggested that supervisor-originating justice (whether procedural, interpersonal, or informational) was actually a stronger predictor of organization-directed citizenship than was organization-originating justice. Indeed, supervisor-originating justice always explained more variance in the citizenship outcomes, regardless of their target, than organization-originating justice.

Advantages and Disadvantages of the Differentiation Trend

The trend toward differentiation has benefited the literature in many ways. Differentiating procedural justice from distributive justice has allowed scholars to distinguish between the effects of the decision-making process and the effects of the ultimate outcome, while also exploring the interaction of the two (Brockner, 2002; Brockner & Wiesenfeld, 1996). Differentiating interactional justice from procedural justice has highlighted the critical role that the agents of the organization can play when communicating procedural and distributive details (e.g., Greenberg, 1990a; Schaubroeck, May, & Brown, 1994). Decomposing interactional justice into its interpersonal and informational facets has helped to clarify that those agents have dual responsibilities during such communications—to be respectful but also to be honest and informative—and that both of those responsibilities are uniquely relevant to employee reactions (Ambrose et al., 2007; Greenberg, 1993b; Kernan & Hanges, 2002). The end result of these streams of research is that justice scholars can offer managers four distinct strategies for improving fairness perceptions in their organizations.

Differentiating the focus of the justice perceptions has brought a more careful analysis to the examination of justice effects. For example, consider a study demonstrating that procedural justice was more strongly related to organizational commitment than was interpersonal justice. A tempting takeaway from that sort of study would be that concepts like consistency, bias suppression, and accuracy are more salient drivers of attachment than concepts like respect or propriety. However, if the procedural justice scale was focused on the organization and the interpersonal justice scale was focused on a supervisor, the result may instead show that organization-originating justice is more relevant to organization-focused attitudes. Indeed, Liao and Rupp's (2005) study actually showed that organization-originating interpersonal justice was a stronger predictor of organizational commitment than organization-originating procedural justice. This nuance can therefore provide cleaner interpretations of the relative importance of the justice rules that have been identified by scholars (Adams, 1965; Bies & Moag, 1986; Leventhal, 1976, 1980; Thibaut & Walker, 1975).

However, the trend toward differentiation brings significant costs as well. One of those costs is multicollinearity (Ambrose & Arnaud, 2005; Colquitt & Shaw, 2005; Fassina, Jones, & Uggerslev,

2008). Studies using Colquitt's (2001) scales to measure the justice dimensions tend to yield distributive-procedural correlations in the .50s, procedural-informational correlations in the .60s, and interpersonal-informational correlations in the .60s, with other correlations tending to fall in the .40 range (e.g., Ambrose et al., 2007; Bell et al., 2006; Camerman et al., 2007; Choi, 2008; Jawahar, 2007; Johnson, Selenta, & Lord, 2006; Judge & Colquitt, 2004; Mayer et al., 2007; Roberson & Stewart, 2006; Scott et al., 2007; Siers, 2007; Spell & Arnold, 2007; Streicher et al., 2008). Studies using multifoci justice scales tend to yield "within-focus correlations" (e.g., supervisor-originating procedural justice with supervisor-originating interpersonal justice) in the .70s, with other correlations falling in the .40 area (Blader & Tyler, 2003; Horvath & Andrews, 2007; Liao & Rupp, 2005; Rupp & Cropanzano, 2002).

Of course, most justice scholars would argue that such strong correlations are to be expected, especially given that meta-analyses place even the distributive-procedural justice correlation in the .50–.60 range (Cohen-Charash & Spector, 2001; Colquitt et al., 2001; Hauenstein, McGonigle, & Flinder, 2001). Still, when it comes to multicollinearity, most scholars "prefer less to more" (Schwab, 2005, p. 257). After all, multicollinearity inflates the standard errors around regression coefficients, harming statistical power and resulting in "bouncing betas" from one study to the next (Cohen, Cohen, West, & Aiken, 2003; Schwab, 2005). Moreover, because the formula for beta subtracts some portion of predictor covariation from a given correlation, multicollinearity results in circumstances in which a given predictor's beta can be near-zero, or even opposite in sign from its correlation. Finally, shared covariance between a set of predictors and an outcome creates interpretational difficulties, given that no one predictor receives "credit" for the effect.

Another cost of the differentiation trend is decreased parsimony. In his discussion of theory evaluation, Bacharach (1989) argued that useful theories have constructs that sufficiently—although parsimoniously—tap the phenomenon of interest. The parsimony of justice models is hindered when several variables (and degrees of freedom) are required to adequately capture justice perceptions—particularly when each of those variables winds up having its own mediator in a structural equation model. Although scholars within the literature have become used to such models, they may constrain the integration of justice concepts into other literatures. For example, a scholar wanting to incorporate justice concepts into a model of job satisfaction might be fine measuring two justice variables, yet may balk at the idea of measuring four, or even eight.

The Merits of Aggregation

One potential course of action to address these issues is to aggregate justice, rather than differentiate it. Two different approaches are possible in this vein. One approach is to treat justice as a multidimensional construct, viewing "organizational justice" as a construct rather than a literature label (see Figure 16.1). Law, Wong, and colleagues have noted that many literatures possess "pseudo-multidimensional constructs," in which authors are vague about whether their labels reflect true constructs or merely useful umbrella terms (Law, Wong, & Mobley, 1998; Wong, Law, & Huang, 2008). Indeed, the authors list the justice literature as an example of this problem, noting that scholars sometimes draw conclusions about justice, in a general sense, from findings that focus specifically on particular dimensions.

Law, Wong, and colleagues describe multiple types of multidimensional constructs, noting that sound theory is needed to guide one's choice of the most appropriate type (Law et al., 1998; Wong et al., 2008). The most familiar type is the "latent model," in which the construct is viewed as a higher order, unobservable abstraction underlying the specific dimensions. In a latent model, specific dimensions serve as different manifestations or realizations of the construct, with each representing the construct with varying degrees of accuracy. The specific dimensions tend to be functionally similar and more or less substitutable. Moreover, the specific dimensions are highly correlated, as the latent construct is defined solely by the common variance shared by the dimensions.

Do theories in the justice literature support a latent model conceptualization? Unfortunately, the answer is likely "sometimes," as the justice literature includes a number of theories and models that do not necessarily converge in their implications for that question. As it is applied in the justice literature, social exchange theory does seem consistent with a latent model conceptualization, at least on a "within-focus" basis (Lavelle et al., 2007; Rupp & Cropanzano, 2002). The application of the theory tends to view the specific justice dimensions as more or less substitutable examples of a "benefits" construct (Blau, 1964). The key distinction is one of focus, as supervisor-originating benefits should trigger supervisor-directed reciprocation, whereas organization-originating benefits should trigger organization-directed reciprocation. No differential predictions are made for the distributive, procedural, interpersonal, and informational justice dimensions when focus is held constant (Lavelle et al., 2007; Liao & Rupp, 2005; Rupp & Cropanzano, 2002).

Fairness heuristic theory represents another theory that would be consistent with a latent model conceptualization. This theory argues that

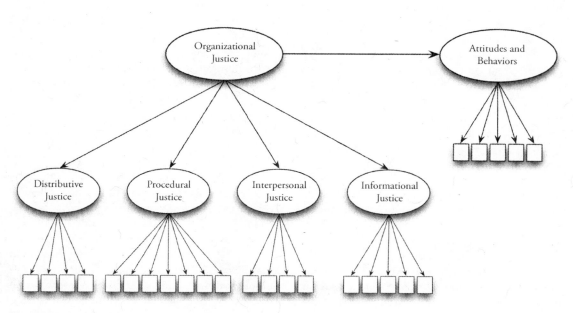

Figure 16.1 Aggregating Justice Using a Higher-Order Latent Variable.

newcomers in an organization are motivated to form a "fairness heuristic" quickly, so that the heuristic can be used to inform decisions about whether to cooperate with authorities (Lind, 2001a; Van den Bos, 2001). The newcomers draw on whatever justice-relevant information is first encountered or is most interpretable, regardless of whether it is of a procedural, distributive, interpersonal, or informational nature. During this initial judgmental phase, the justice-relevant information is used to form a general fairness impression. However, after this initial phase, it is actually that general impression that drives judgments of the specific justice dimensions (Lind, 2001a). At that point, judgments of procedural, distributive, interpersonal, or informational justice merely serve as different manifestations of the same fairness heuristic construct.

A third theory in the literature would not be consistent with a latent model conceptualization, however. Fairness theory argues that individuals react to decision events by engaging in counterfactual thinking (Folger & Cropanzano, 1998, 2001). "Could" counterfactuals consider whether the decision event could have played out differently. "Should" counterfactuals consider whether moral standards were violated during the event. "Would" counterfactuals consider whether one's well-being would have been better if events had played out differently. The theory suggests that individuals will blame an authority for an event when it could have (and should have) occurred differently, and when well-being would have been better had the alternative scenario played out. Importantly, the different justice dimensions are most relevant to different counterfactuals (Shaw, Wild, & Colquitt, 2003). For example, distributive justice is most relevant to the "would" counterfactual because well-being is often defined in outcome terms. Procedural and interpersonal concepts such as bias suppression, ethicality, and propriety are most relevant to the "should" counterfactual because they are more "morally charged." Informational justice is most relevant to the "could" counterfactual if explanations are used to excuse the event in question. Thus, the justice dimensions are less substitutable in this theory's formulations, and do not appear to be different manifestations of some common construct.

The appropriateness of a latent model conceptualization would therefore seem to depend on the theoretical grounding for a given study and the nature of its specific predictions. If predictions are focused on the independent or interactive effects of specific justice dimensions, such an approach is obviously inappropriate. If predictions are focused on the effects of shared justice variance, however, then a latent model approach would be suitable (Fassina et al., 2008). At this point, however, examples of a latent model approach are very rare. In their chapter on justice measurement, Colquitt and Shaw (2005) showed that Colquitt's (2001) four scales had strong factor loadings if used as latent indicators of a higher order "organizational justice" construct. The only refereed example of a latent model approach is Liao's (2007) study of how customer service employees respond to product complaints. Liao noted that the approach was utilized in the interest of parsimony in that differential predictions were not offered for the specific justice dimensions. As in Colquitt and Shaw (2005), Liao's (2007) results showed that the four justice dimensions had strong loadings on a higher order organizational justice factor. In addition, because the specific dimensions were measured and included in the study as indicators, the reader could peruse the correlation matrix to examine any differential relationships that might be evident.

Another approach to aggregation would be to include an actual scale devoted to an overall sense of fairness. Although this overall fairness could serve a number of roles, it is often discussed as "theoretically downstream" from the specific justice dimensions (Ambrose & Arnaud, 2005; Ambrose & Schminke, 2009; Colquitt, Greenberg, & Scott, 2005; Colquitt & Shaw, 2005; Leventhal, 1980). From this perspective, distributive, procedural, interpersonal, and informational justice serve as antecedents of overall fairness, with overall fairness then serving as an antecedent of attitudinal and behavioral outcomes (see Figure 16.2). The positioning of overall fairness in Figure 16.2 is similar to the positioning of overall satisfaction scales in the job satisfaction literature, which often view overall satisfaction as a consequence of more specific satisfaction facets (e.g., Bowling & Hammond, 2008; Ironson, Smith, Brannick, Gibson, & Paul, 1989).

The use of an overall fairness measure has a number of potential benefits. Perhaps most importantly, it explicitly captures the "that's not fair!" response that is expected to accompany violations of rules like equity, consistency, accuracy, respect, truthfulness, and so forth. It also allows scholars to verify that it is that sense of fairness or unfairness that explains why distributive, procedural, interpersonal, and informational justice are predictive of key organizational outcomes. The relationship between overall fairness and those outcomes is also devoid of multicollinearity (though multicollinearity would still

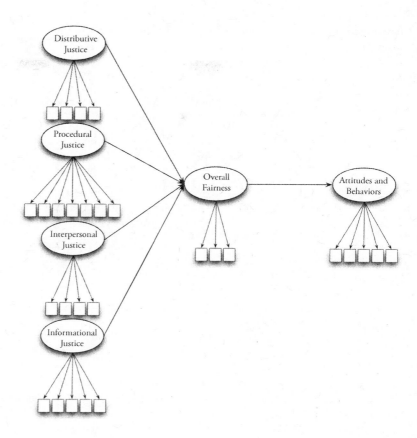

Figure 16.2 Aggregating Justice Using Overall Fairness Perceptions.

become problematic if Figure 16.2 were replaced by a partially mediated structure that included direct effects of the specific justice dimensions on the outcomes of interest). Moreover, because of its brevity, overall fairness could serve as a useful construct for inclusion in studies that are not focused on organizational justice per se.

At least six studies have included measures of overall fairness (Ambrose & Schminke, 2009; Choi, 2008; Kim & Leung, 2007; Masterson, 2001; Rodell & Colquitt, 2009; Zapata-Phelan, Colquitt, Scott, & Livingston, 2009). One challenge in constructing such measures is to avoid item wording or content that seems to reflect some justice dimensions more than others. The measures shown in Table 16.1 attempt to strike that balance by utilizing broad, all-encompassing terms like *is* or *acts*. In contrast, measures by Ambrose and Schminke (2009) and Kim and Leung (2007) sometimes utilize the word *treats*, which may reflect interpersonal justice more than the other justice dimensions. Another challenge in constructing such measures is that perceptions of overall fairness may be driven by more than just the specific justice dimensions. Such judgments

may also be colored by the perceiver's affect or by other qualities of the target, such as supportiveness or flexibility (Colquitt & Shaw, 2005; Hollensbe, Khazanchi, & Masterson, 2008).

Interestingly, of the six studies that have operationalized overall fairness, only two cast overall fairness as a mediator of the effects of the specific justice dimensions. Kim and Leung's (2007) results suggested that overall fairness mediated the effects of the specific justice dimensions on job satisfaction and turnover intentions. Ambrose and Schminke's (2009) results revealed the same pattern for both attitudinal and behavioral outcomes, including citizenship and counterproductive behavior. In contrast, Choi (2008) cast overall fairness as a moderator of the relationship between specific justice dimensions and attitudinal and behavioral outcomes, consistent with Cropanzano, Byrne, Bobocel, and Rupp's (2001) model of "event versus entity" justice judgments. Rodell and Colquitt (2009) cast overall fairness as an antecedent of the specific justice dimensions, consistent with Lind's (2001a) description of fairness heuristic theory. As in the discussion of the latent model, such variations reveal the

Table 16.1 Examples of Measures of Overall Fairness

Author String	Items
Choi (2008)[a]	1. My supervisor always gives me a fair deal. 2. My supervisor is a fair person. 3. Fairness is the word that best describes my supervisor.
Masterson (2001)[a]	1. Overall, I believe the university is a fair organization. 2. I do not believe that the university is a fair organization. (R) 3. In general, I believe the university is just. 4. On the whole, the university is a fair organization.
Rodell & Colquitt (2009)[b]	1. How often does your immediate supervisor act fairly toward you? 2. To what extent do you believe that your immediate supervisor is fair to you? 3. How fair do you think your immediate supervisor is to you?
Zapata-Phelan, Colquitt, Scott, & Livingston (2009)[c]	1. In general, the experiment was fair. 2. Overall, I felt that this experiment was done fairly. 3. If asked, I would tell other students that this experiment was fair.

[a] Item anchors range from 1 = *Strongly Disagree* to 7 = *Strongly Agree*.
[b] Item anchors are as follows: (1) 1 = Almost Never to 5 = Almost Always, (2) 1 = To a Very Small Extent to 5 = To a Very Large Extent, (3) 1 = Very Unfair to 5 = Very Fair.
[c] Item anchors range from 1 = *Strongly Disagree* to 5 = *Strongly Agree*.

differing predictions that justice theories make for overall assessments of fairness.

Trend Two: Cognition

Many of the earliest models of justice were cognitive in nature, viewing justice through a lens of mental deliberation and/or intuition. Some models have stressed the controlled or calculative end of the cognitive continuum, whereas others have stressed the automatic or heuristic end (see Cropanzano et al., 2001, and Lind, 2001b, for a discussion of such issues). Regardless of these differences, the trend toward cognition can be seen in a number of research streams within the literature. Those streams include research focused on why individuals care about justice issues, how individuals form justice perceptions, and why justice is predictive of attitudes and behaviors.

Beginning with the "Why do individuals care?" question, a review by Gillespie and Greenberg (2005) noted that justice is assumed to fulfill a number of key goals, where goals are defined as cognitive representations of desired states. Similarly, Cropanzano et al.'s (2001) review argued that justice is assumed to fulfill multiple needs, where needs can be defined as cognitive groupings of outcomes that have critical consequences to the individual. One goal (or need) that was emphasized in early justice research is control. In what has come to be known as the instrumental model (Lind & Tyler, 1988), Thibaut and

Walker (1975) argued that justice is valued because it provides a sense of control and predictability for outcomes over the long term. From this perspective, individuals value and consider justice rules because justice is instrumental—it helps in the attainment of valued outcomes.

Partially in response to the instrumental model, Lind and Tyler (1988) suggested that individuals also attend to justice issues because fairness satisfies a goal (or need) for positive self-regard or belonging. The relational model argues that individuals are motivated to belong to groups and that they look for signals about the extent to which those groups value them (Lind & Tyler, 1988; Tyler & Lind, 1992). When authorities are neutral and unbiased, or when they implement procedures with dignity and respect, they convey to the relevant individuals a sense of status in the group. This model is capable of explaining why fair treatment is associated with more favorable reactions, even when it does not enhance actual control over outcomes or resources (Tyler, 1994).

A more recent model emphasizes a third goal (or need). The deontic model (Cropanzano, Goldman, & Folger, 2003; Folger, 1998, 2001), sometimes also termed the *moral virtue model* (Cropanzano et al., 2001), argues that individuals attend to justice issues because they signal a respect for principled moral obligations. That is, rather than merely signaling a sense of control or esteem, justice is valued because "virtue serves as its own reward" (Folger, 1998, p. 32). The deontic model is able to explain why individuals value justice, even when it does not benefit their own outcomes, and even when it does not improve their standing in some relevant social group (Turillo, Folger, Lavelle, Umphress, & Gee, 2002).

As with the goals and needs used by the models above, justice theories also use cognitive mechanisms to explain how individuals form justice judgments. As described in the discussion of the differentiation trend, fairness heuristic theory argues that justice-relevant information is quickly aggregated into a "fairness heuristic" that is used to guide subsequent attitudes and behaviors (Lind, 2001a; Van den Bos, 2001). The theory views distributive, procedural, interpersonal, and informational justice information as substitutable inputs into that heuristic creation process. Because organizational newcomers will often experience decision-making procedures before the outcomes become apparent, and because information about outcome comparisons may not be available, procedural information often has a particularly strong impact on the heuristic. Regardless of which justice dimension winds up being experienced first or being viewed as most interpretable, this theory portrays the development of justice judgments as less deliberate and effortful.

A different portrayal is offered by fairness theory (Folger & Cropanzano, 1998, 2001). The counterfactual thinking described by this theory brings a more structured and careful analysis to the justice judgment process, as individuals ask whether events "could" have played out differently, whether authorities "should" have acted differently, and whether well-being "would" have been enhanced if events had occurred differently. Although there is no one order in which these counterfactual cognitions must be considered, all three seem necessary to ultimately decide how to react to the authority in terms of perceived fairness, perceived accountability, and potential for blame. As a result, fairness theory requires a more extensive consideration of the justice dimensions than does fairness heuristic theory.

Although it has gained less research attention than fairness theory and fairness heuristic theory, another model provides a third example of explaining the justice judgment process with cognitive mechanisms. Ambrose and Kulik's (2001) categorization approach relies on categories to describe how fairness perceptions are formed. Categories are cognitive structures that represent the features of a given stimulus. Category prototypes are special structures that include all of the essential features of a given category. Ambrose and Kulik (2001) suggest that the justice rules identified by Thibaut and Walker (1975), Leventhal (1976, 1980), Bies and Moag (1986), and others represent the features of a category prototype for justice, though some rules may be more essential to the prototype, with others being more peripheral. From this perspective, a given decision event is judged to be fair when the event's features match the central elements of the justice category prototype.

Finally, explanations about why justice is predictive of attitudes and behaviors have also been largely cognitive in nature. Consider the social exchange-based explanation described in the prior section—that fair behaviors serve as a benefit to an employee, with attitudes and behaviors that support the organization offered in reciprocation (Blau, 1964). Blau's description of the social exchange dynamic emphasizes the concept of obligation. When fair treatment is received, a general expectation of future return is triggered, though the form or time frame for that return is left unspecified. Blau (1964) also emphasizes the important of trust to the establishment and expansion of the social exchange dynamic. Reciprocation may not be offered if the exchange partner is not deemed trustworthy, and reciprocation will not deepen if trust does not expand commensurately. Those descriptions highlight the calculated rationality used to explain the relationship between justice and employee reactions.

Advantages and Disadvantages of the Cognition Trend

The trend toward cognition has benefited the literature in a number of ways. It has, for example, enabled scholars to look inside the "black box" of justice perceptions to explain how and why individuals come to view decision events and authorities as fair or unfair. In so doing, the theories that introduced the cognitive mechanisms helped to fill a void in the literature. Literature reviews near the beginning of the 1990s pointed to a dearth of integrative theories in the justice literature (Greenberg, 1990b; Lind & Tyler, 1988). The relational model, fairness theory, and fairness heuristic theory joined social exchange theory to give the justice literature a level of conceptual richness that other literatures may not enjoy. Those theories have also served as conceptual "jumping-off points" for other theorizing that has identified mediators and moderators of justice relationships (Colquitt & Greenberg, 2003; Cropanzano et al., 2001).

However, the trend toward cognition has important limitations as well. First and foremost, it has created somewhat of a disconnect between how employees describe fairness and how academics study it. Bies and Tripp (2002) note that employees *feel* injustice on an emotional basis—reporting anger, bitterness, and fear in connection with violations of justice rules. The authors suggested that the justice literature has focused more on the cognitive "high ground" than the emotional "valley of darkness" associated with experiences of injustice. Similarly, Folger, Cropanzano, and Goldman's (2005) discussion of fairness theory and the deontic model notes that the capacity to reason about justice operates simultaneously with a sense of anger that results from violations of moral standards.

The neglect of affective mechanisms creates an unmeasured variables problem in many of the models in the justice literature. Consider the notion that biased procedures result in a less favorable justice judgment, which then results in a scaling back of reciprocation behaviors on the job. Explicitly considering the role of affect could change "what we know" about the links in that presumed causal chain. It may be that the unfavorable justice judgment triggers a negative emotion and gives that emotion its depth and resonance. However, it may also be that the experience of bias itself triggers the emotion, with a justice-relevant label ascribed to make sense of the feeling post hoc (Bies & Tripp, 2002; Colquitt, Greenberg, & Scott, 2005). Moreover, it may be that the emotional reactions fully mediate the effects of the bias on subsequent behaviors, with the justice judgment having no unique mediating role. The only way to ascertain the relative effects of cognitive and affective mechanisms is to integrate affect into the justice literature more fully.

The Merits of Affect

A number of affective variables and mechanisms are potentially relevant to justice theorizing (Cohen-Charash & Byrne, 2008). That list includes emotions, mood, and trait affectivity (for a review, see Grandey, 2008). Emotions are short-term feeling states that are referenced to a particular target. A number of emotions are relevant to justice models, including positive emotions (e.g., happiness, pride, gratitude) and negative emotions (e.g., anger, sadness, fear, envy). Moods are feeling states that are weaker in intensity and longer in duration than emotions, and lack a salient target.

Moods are typically operationalized on a more aggregate basis, with positive moods reflecting pleasant and active forms of state affect and negative moods reflecting unpleasant and active forms of state affect. Finally, trait affectivity reflects a dispositional tendency to experience positive or negative feeling states. As with mood, trait affectivity is typically operationalized on a more aggregate basis, in the form of positive affectivity and negative affectivity. Those dimensions are functionally similar (if not identical) to the personality dimensions of extraversion and neuroticism, respectively (Clark & Watson, 1999).

Figure 16.3 illustrates some of the emotions, mood, and trait affectivity effects that have begun to be examined by justice scholars. For example, Van den Bos (2003) examined the effects of mood on fairness perceptions when information on justice criteria was clear versus unclear. In two studies, the author manipulated the degree to which Thibaut and Walker's (1975) process-control criterion was clearly and unambiguously fulfilled by comparing three conditions: (a) process control explicitly granted, (b) process control explicitly denied, and (c) process control not mentioned. The author also manipulated mood by asking participants to describe and write about the experience of being either happy or angry. The results of the study showed that mood had little impact on fairness perceptions when information about process control was clear and unambiguous. However, when information on that procedural justice rule was omitted, participants in the positive mood condition perceived more fairness than participants in the negative mood condition. Essentially, mood "filled in the gaps" left by the absence of clear information on relevant justice rules.

Barsky and Kaplan (2007) examining the effects of both mood and trait affectivity on measures of procedural, distributive, and interactional justice. More specifically, the authors conducted a meta-analysis of 57 samples that included measures of the justice dimensions, mood, and/or trait affectivity. The results yielded moderately strong correlations between mood and the justice dimensions. Positive mood was associated with more favorable justice perceptions, and negative mood was associated with less favorable justice perceptions. Interestingly, the magnitude of the positive and negative mood effects were quite similar. The results yielded somewhat weaker, but still significant correlations between trait affectivity and the justice dimensions. As with the mood results, the magnitude of the positive and negative

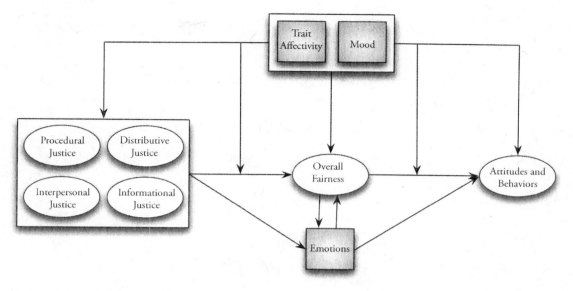

Figure 16.3 Integrating Justice and Affect.

affectivity effects were similar. It therefore appears that positive affect and negative affect can "move the needle" on justice perceptions to a similar degree.

Barsky and Kaplan's (2007) review raises a number of questions about the role of affect in forming justice perceptions. For example, given that most of the articles included in the review were field studies that utilized self-report measures of both affect and justice, it may be that the meta-analytic correlations are inflated by common method bias (Podsakoff, MacKenzie, Lee, & Podsakoff, 2003). It would therefore be useful to compare Barsky and Kaplan's (2007) results with studies that utilize multiple sources. For example, Rodell and Colquitt (2009) showed that ratings of neuroticism by significant others were negatively correlated with a number of justice dimensions. Even here, however, the interpretation of the findings is ambiguous, as individuals who are rated high in negative affectivity should themselves exhibit a strictness bias on many self-report measures (justice included). Moreover, as Barsky and Kaplan (2007) note, it may be that the affect exhibited by individuals leads to "objectively" different treatment by organizational authorities. For example, an individual who frequently exhibits feelings of hostility may actually experience more disrespectful treatment by a supervisor as a direct result (the subsequent section of this review discusses this possibility in more detail).

Whereas the studies reviewed above cast affect as an antecedent of justice perceptions, other work has focused on affect as a consequence of them. This stream of research focuses on emotions rather than mood or trait affectivity, given that emotions can be referenced to a particular agent, action, or event. Drawing on appraisal theories of emotions, Weiss, Suckow, and Cropanzano (1999) conducted one of the earliest studies in this stream. The authors noted that events first trigger a primary appraisal, which is a gross evaluation of whether an event is harmful or beneficial to relevant goals or values. This appraisal determines the general valence of the state affect, in terms of whether it is positive or negative. A secondary appraisal then follows, which includes an assessment of whether the outcome is attributed to the self or some other. It is this secondary appraisal that typically results in the differentiation of positive or negative state affect into more discrete emotions.

In a laboratory study, Weiss et al. (1999) paired participants with a confederate in order to compete with another pair of confederates on a decision-making task. Two procedurally unjust conditions were created: a favorably biased condition in which the confederate mentioned that a friend had already done the study and provided some answers, and an unfavorably biased condition in which the participant overheard the other pair mentioning the same advantage. No such information was given in a third condition, reflecting a more procedurally just circumstance. The study crossed these conditions with outcome favorability, with participants winning the competition in some conditions and losing it in other conditions. Participants then filled out a survey that asked, "Please indicate how you feel about what just happened," with items included to represent happiness, pride, anger, and guilt.

Weiss et al.'s (1999) results showed that happiness was driven solely by outcome favorability, suggesting that it depends only on primary appraisals of harm or benefit. The authors had expected that pride would be highest when the outcome was favorable and the procedure was either just or unfavorably biased. However, as with happiness, pride was driven primarily by outcome favorability, with the predicted procedural pattern failing to emerge. With respect to the negative emotions, anger was highest when the outcome was unfavorable and the procedure was unfavorably biased. Guilt, in contrast, was highest when the outcome was favorable and the procedure was favorably biased. The two negative emotions therefore seemed to depend on both primary and secondary appraisal, with the gross evaluation of harm or benefit needing to be supplemented with information about whether the outcome could be attributed to oneself or another.

In a subsequent study, Krehbiel and Cropanzano (2000) replicated the above findings for happiness and pride, while also showing that a negative emotion—disappointment—was solely driven by outcome favorability. Other emotions again depended on particular combinations of outcome favorability and procedural justice, including anger, guilt, and anxiety. Barclay, Skarlicki, and Pugh (2005) conducted a field study of reactions to a layoff event, focusing primarily on the negative emotions of guilt and anger. As in Weiss et al. (1999), their results showed that those emotions were an interactive function of outcome favorability (i.e., the quality of the severance package) and the justice of the layoff process (i.e., procedural justice and interactional justice).

Given the distinction between outcome favorability and distributive justice, an important issue is whether the same sort of interactive pattern exists when the outcome is expressed in equity terms. A field study by Goldman (2003) examined this issue in a study of reactions to a termination event. The results of the study showed that anger was predicted by a three-way interaction of distributive justice, procedural justice, and interactional justice. The pattern of this interaction revealed that the procedural and interactional justice combinations had stronger relationships with anger when distributive justice was low than when it was high. In addition, the highest levels of anger were felt when all three justice dimensions were low. Thus, as in Weiss et al. (1999), anger seemed to depend on both the primary appraisal and the secondary appraisal.

Goldman's (2003) study also examined two other affective influences from Figure 16.3. First, he examined whether anger served to mediate the negative relationship between justice perceptions and whether the terminated individual filed a legal claim against the company. The results revealed the same three-way interaction for legal claiming that was described above, and the results further showed that the effect was mediated by anger. Second, he examined whether trait anger—a more specific facet of trait negative affectivity—moderated the relationship between the justice dimensions and legal claiming. The results showed that the three-way interaction for legal claiming was more pronounced for individuals who experience anger more frequently, as a function of their disposition.

A field study by Fox, Spector, and Miles (2001) examined a similar set of relationships, though it differed from Goldman's (2003) study in two key respects. First, it focused on the main effects of the justice dimensions rather than their interactive effects. Second, it did not focus on a specific decision event, instead surveying a variety of employees about more general perceptions of distributive and procedural justice (with the latter also containing interactional items). As a result of this second difference, the emotion measures also differed from the studies reviewed above. Rather than asking how the participants felt at a specific point in time, Fox et al. (2001) assessed the degree to which their jobs have made them feel particular emotions during the past 30 days (Van Katwyk, Fox, Spector, and Kelloway [2000] termed this "affective well-being"). The results showed that negative affective well-being (an amalgam of fear, anger, disgust, and sadness) mediated the relationship between procedural justice and counterproductive behaviors. Positive affective well-being (an amalgam of enthusiasm, pride, happiness, and contentment) was also included, though it exhibited weaker relationships with counterproductive behaviors. Fox et al. (2001) also included two measures of trait affectivity—trait anger and trait anxiety—but neither was shown to be a significant moderator of the justice-counterproductive behavior relationships.

A more recent study relied on an experience sampling methodology (ESM) to examine the mediating and moderating effects of emotions and trait affectivity. Judge et al. (2006) surveyed employees at the end of each workday for a three-week time period. The participants completed self-report measures of interpersonal justice, anger, job satisfaction, and counterproductive behavior each day, and a significant other completed a measure of trait anger. The ESM results showed that more than half of the variation in counterproductive behavior was within-person variance (as opposed to between-person variance). The results suggested that the relationship between interpersonal justice and counterproductive behavior was mediated by state anger and job satisfaction. Moreover, trait anger moderated the interpersonal justice–state anger relationship, such that the linkage was stronger for individuals who were more prone to experience feelings of anger and hostility.

Trend Three: Exogeneity

In his review that coined the "organizational justice" term, Greenberg (1987) introduced a 2 × 2 taxonomy to organize the models in the nascent literature. One of the taxonomy dimensions was process versus outcome, reflecting the distinction between procedural and distributive justice. The other dimension was reactive versus proactive, with the former focusing on reactions to just and unjust events, and the latter focused on the behaviors that can create just events. For example, Adam's (1965) work on equity theory exemplified the outcome-reactive cell, because it focused on reactions to inequitable outcome distributions. In contrast, Leventhal's (1976) work on allocation norms was proactive, because it focused on the effects of certain goals (e.g., individual productivity as opposed to group harmony or personal welfare) on the decision to utilize an equity norm.

In reflecting on the 1987 taxonomy, Greenberg and Wiethoff (2001) noted that reactive research explores this focal question: "How do people respond to fair and unfair conditions?" (p. 272). In contrast, proactive research explores a different focal question: "How can fair conditions be created?" (p. 272). At the time of Greenberg's (1987) review, the justice literature was still focused on the specific procedural rules that could be used to promote perceptions of fairness. For example, Greenberg's (1986) Q-sort study supported the notion that process control, consistency, bias suppression, accuracy, correctability, and so forth could be used to create a fair decision-making process (Leventhal, 1980; Thibaut & Walker, 1975). As another example,

initial studies on interactional justice (e.g., Bies & Shapiro, 1988) were focused on supporting the notion that respect, propriety, truthfulness, and justification could be used to create a fair procedural enactment (Bies & Moag, 1986). These sorts of early studies would fall under Greenberg's (1987) proactive label because they are focused on the creation of fairness.

Once the constitutive elements of the justice dimensions became clear, however, the literature began to move in a decidedly reactive direction. Many of the studies spotlighted in the prior sections of this review are indicative of that trend. Early work on the distributive and procedural justice distinction cast justice as the independent variable, with job attitudes (job satisfaction, trust, organizational commitment) serving as the outcomes (Folger & Konovsky, 1989; McFarlin & Sweeney, 1992; Sweeney & McFarlin, 1993). The advent of the social exchange lens brought a new set of variables for justice to predict, including citizenship and other reciprocation-oriented behaviors (Blau, 1964; Masterson et al., 2000; Organ, 1990). Even the studies linking justice to affect have tended to adopt a reactive structure, with the justice dimensions serving as predictors of emotions and emotion-driven behaviors (Barclay et al., 2005; Fox et al., 2001; Goldman, 2003; Krehbiel & Cropanzano, 2000; Judge et al., 2006; Weiss et al., 1999).

The end result of this reactive focus is that justice is exogenous in most of the empirical studies in the literature. That is, scales like Colquitt's (2001) or Moorman's (1991) are utilized as the independent variables, with direct and indirect effects on attitudinal, affective, and behavioral variables. It is true that measures of fairness perceptions, similar to the type shown in Table 16.1, may be endogenous in some studies. However, the focal independent variables in those studies are often manipulations or measures of the rules included in Colquitt's (2001) and Moorman's (1991) measures. Moreover, such studies may still ultimately be focused on the prediction of some attitudinal, affective, or behavioral reaction.

Advantages and Disadvantages of the Exogeneity Trend

The trend toward exogeneity has benefited the literature in a number of ways. Perhaps most importantly, it helped establish the organizational justice literature as a worthy area of study. Within a few years of the construct's introduction to the organizational sciences, reactive research had shown that justice was as predictive, or more predictive, of relevant criteria than other job attitudes or other leader variables. Those findings brought a practical relevance to the literature, providing an incentive to conduct field research that could benefit the host organization. Those findings also brought a theoretical relevance to the literature, encouraging scholars in other literatures to "import" justice concepts into their work. Indeed, were it not for that reactive focus, it would be difficult to conceive of the literature's rapid growth in the past two decades (Colquitt, 2008).

However, a consequence of this focus is that scholars know little about the circumstances that result in an adherence to the justice rules described by Leventhal (1976, 1980), Thibaut and Walker (1975), Bies and Moag (1986), and others. Presumably, there are features of the organization, the manager, or the employee that decrease the likelihood that those justice rules will be violated (Gilliland, Steiner, Skarlicki, & Van den Bos, 2005). As Greenberg and Wiethoff (2001) describe, proactive research treats justice as a motive—it seeks to explain why individuals strive to create just states. Organizational, managerial, and employee factors may predict that motive, or they may create a circumstance in which the motive is easier to act upon. In either event, identifying the factors that foster justice rule adherence requires making the justice dimensions endogenous within empirical studies.

The Merits of Endogeneity

An emerging set of empirical studies has begun to examine antecedents of the justice dimensions. Some of those antecedents are characteristics of the organization. Schminke, Ambrose, and Cropanzano (2000) linked aspects of the organization's structure to adherence to the process control and bias suppression rules of procedural justice. For example, employees reported less adherence to those rules when the organization had a centralized authority hierarchy, meaning that even small decisions had to be referred to a "higher up" for approval. Such results suggest that managers need to be given enough of their own authority to maximize justice rule adherence within their work units. Schminke et al. (2000) also included interactional justice, but it was operationalized using general perceptions of fair treatment, rather than adherence to the specific rules of respect, propriety, truthfulness, and justification.

Gilliland and Schepers (2003) conducted a survey of human resources managers in a study of adherence to interpersonal and informational justice rules during layoff events. One aspect of the organization, whether or not it was unionized, predicted the number of days notice that employees were given—an aspect of informational justice. That variable was not related to the amount of information that was shared, however, nor was it related to the demeanor used to communicate the layoff—an aspect of interpersonal justice. The authors also assessed managerial variables, including past experience conducting layoffs and the number of employees personally laid off. Past experience was actually negatively related to days notice, whereas the number laid off was positively related to the amount of information shared. Neither variable predicted the demeanor used to communicate the layoff, however.

A different set of managerial variables was examined by Mayer et al. (2007) in a sample of grocery store employees. The authors measured managerial personality in terms of the five-factor model, attempting to link those dimensions to procedural, interpersonal, and informational justice rule adherence. The results of the study depended on whether the Big Five were examined separately or in tandem. However, the results seemed to support a negative relationship between neuroticism and interpersonal justice rule adherence and a positive relationship between agreeableness and informational justice rule adherence. Neurotic managers tended to communicate less respectfully, and agreeable managers tended to be more candid and forthcoming. None of the Big Five variables predicted adherence to procedural justice rules, however.

Although the studies reviewed above revealed some linkages between organizational and managerial variables and the justice dimensions, it may also be that the employee has some impact on the treatment that he or she receives. Korsgaard, Roberson, and Rymph (1998) examined this possibility in two studies. They reasoned that assertive employees would receive more extensive justifications from their managers because of their tendency to use confident posture and eye contact and to ask questions of clarification. A laboratory study supported the relationship between employee assertiveness and adherence to informational justice rules, but the linkage was not supported in a field study.

In a more recent study, Scott et al. (2007) examined the effects of employee charisma on managers' adherence to justice rules. The authors argued that charismatic employees have a "personal magnetism" that inspires affective responses on the part of their managers. Those affective responses were operationalized using positive and negative sentiments (i.e., tendencies to experience positive or negative emotions when around specific individuals). Scott et al. (2007) argued that positive sentiments would prompt managers to be more courteous and friendly to employees and to engage in more frequent instances of information sharing with them. Indeed, a field study of insurance company employees revealed a significant relationship between charisma and interpersonal justice, with both positive and negative sentiments mediating that relationship. Contrary to expectations, no relationship was observed for informational justice.

Conclusion

There is little doubt that the three trends spotlighted in this review—differentiation, cognition, and exogeneity—have fueled the growth of the justice literature and have brought a cohesion and structure to the domain. There is also little doubt that the trends have impacted how a given justice study "looks," in terms of the models it tests, the conceptual lenses it uses, and the methods and statistics it employs. As the literature reaches a more mature stage of its life cycle, however, one potential concern is that the significant advances of the past will give way to more incremental or marginal advances. This chapter has argued that justice scholars should consider the merits of the obverses of these literature trends—aggregation, affect, and endogeneity—in order to tap into their potential for creating new directions for justice research. By "breaking the mold" that has come to define justice studies, efforts focused on aggregation, affect, and endogeneity could result in more novel, innovative, and significant advances.

Future Directions

Of course, going against the trends that have shaped the literature could be viewed as risky by the potential authors of such studies. On the one hand, many top-tier journals explicitly emphasize novelty in their mission statements and information for contributors. On the other hand, many editors and reviewers use the characteristics of more typical justice studies to create a sort of template for judging the theoretical and empirical adequacy of new submissions. This chapter therefore closes with some research directions that can be used to guide future steps down the aggregation, affect, and endogeneity paths. These suggested directions are meant to be contributions that are novel but that are still grounded in established or emerging areas of the literature. I begin with suggestions that focus on

one specific trend before moving to directions that involve a combination of the trends.

Aggregation

Future research needs to critically explore whether aggregate or differentiated operationalizations are appropriate with the dominant theoretical lenses in the literature. The social exchange lens has emerged as the dominant framework for understanding the effects of justice on job attitudes and behaviors (Blau, 1964; Masterson et al., 2000; Organ, 1990). As noted above, that lens seems suitable for an aggregate approach, as justice scholars rarely draw distinctions among the justice dimensions when predicting attitudes supportive of reciprocation (e.g., trust, commitment, felt obligation) or behaviors indicative of reciprocation (e.g., citizenship). Instead, the only distinctions that tend to be made concern the source of the justice and the target of the reciprocation. However, discussions of social exchange theory describe a number of benefits that can be used to foster exchange relationships, including information, advice, assistance, social acceptance, status, and appreciation (Blau, 1964; Foa & Foa, 1980). It may be that specific justice rules are more relevant to some of those benefits than others, creating distinctions in the specific nature of the resulting exchange dynamic.

Testing the viability of an aggregate approach to social exchange theorizing could be done in a number of ways. For example, the variance explained in reciprocation attitudes and behaviors by the four justice dimensions could be compared to the variance explained by a higher order justice dimension or a measure of overall fairness. Presumably, some decrement in variance-explained would result from an aggregate approach. The question would be how much was lost, and whether that decrement was justifiable given the gain in parsimony. As another example, the pattern of correlations between aggregate justice (whether a higher order dimension or an overall measure) and a set of reciprocation attitudes and behaviors could be compared to the corresponding patterns for the specific justice dimensions. If the dimensional nuance matters, the distributive, procedural, interpersonal, and informational patterns will differ from one another, and will also differ from the aggregate pattern. Westen and Rosenthal (2003) describe methods for quantifying similarities in correlation patterns that could prove useful in this regard. Regardless of the approach that is utilized, it is important to note that such studies should hold the source of the justice and the target of the reciprocation constant, so that differences in relationships can be interpreted unambiguously.

Affect

Research integrating justice and affect should begin to explore whether emotions mediate justice effects when more cognitive mediators are also modeled. Existing research has been more focused on identifying and clarifying the justice-emotion linkages (Barclay et al., 2005; Fox et al., 2001; Goldman, 2003; Krehbiel & Cropanzano, 2000; Weiss et al., 1999), omitting the kinds of mediators that would flow out of more cognitive justice theorizing. Do positive and negative emotions mediate the relationships between justice and behavioral reactions when mediators like trust and felt obligation are also modeled? Examining this question requires the integration of more cognitive theories, such as social exchange theory (Blau, 1964), with more affective theories, such as affective events theory (Weiss & Cropanzano, 1996).

One challenge in conducting such research is balancing the differing time horizons for emotion-based mediators and cognition-based mediators. Studies that examine the mediating effects of trust or felt obligation would typically be between-individual studies of either a cross-sectional or longitudinal nature. Because emotions are short-term feeling states, it may be inappropriate to operationalize them in such studies. Instead, scholars may need to utilize more long-term feeling states that still possess a particular target, such as affective well-being (Fox et al., 2001; Van Katwyk et al., 2000) or sentiments (Scott et al., 2007). Alternatively, scholars could utilize ESM studies to model within-individual changes in emotions as a function of daily justice experiences. This approach would involve measuring mediators such as trust or felt obligation on a daily basis, so that within-person changes in those mechanisms could also be assessed. It may be, however, that the within-person variation in those more cognitive mediators will be limited, especially relative to the emotional mediators.

Endogeneity

With respect to the endogeneity trend, future research should continue to examine the organizational, managerial, and employee variables that can help predict the adherence to justice rules. At this point, the list of potential antecedents is quite short and varied, including organizational structure (Schminke et al., 2000), unionization (Gilliland & Schepers, 2003), managerial

personality (Mayer et al., 2007), employee assertiveness (Korsgaard et al., 1998), and employee charisma (Scott et al., 2007). Although it is difficult to draw conclusions from so few studies, two trends seem notable. First, several of the studies have yielded either small effect sizes or effects that are not statistically significant. Second, most of the hypotheses have focused on adherence to interpersonal and informational justice rules, such as respect, propriety, justification, and truthfulness (Bies & Moag, 1986; Greenberg, 1993b).

Recent theorizing by Scott, Colquitt, and Paddock (2009) can shed some light on these emerging trends. In their actor-focused model of justice rule adherence, the authors argued that it would be easier for managers to adhere to justice rules when they had more discretion over the actions inherent in those rules. They further argued that discretion over justice-relevant actions could be arrayed on a continuum, with the most discretion afforded to interpersonal justice, followed by informational, procedural, and distributive justice, respectively. The rationale for that rank order was that the interactional justice forms were less constrained by formal systems, that they could be acted upon more frequently, and that they were less costly to managers in an economic sense. If that continuum is correct, it may be more difficult to identify significant predictors of procedural and distributive justice. In the case of procedural justice, a good starting point might involve examining adherence to specific rules. For example, one study could focus on predictors of voice provision, another could focus on predictors of bias suppression, and another could focus on predictors of consistency.

Multiple Trends in Combination

Other future directions lie at the intersection of multiple trends. In the case of aggregation and affect, it is instructive to note that both justice and affect can be conceptualized at higher or lower levels of abstraction. In the case of justice, specific rules can be grouped into the four justice dimensions, which can themselves be modeled as a higher order organizational justice variable. In the case of affect, positive and negative forms of both state and trait affect can be examined at a specific level (e.g., state happiness and trait anger; trait happiness and state anger) or an aggregate level (e.g., positive and negative state affect, positive and negative affectivity). From a bandwidth-fidelity perspective (e.g., Cronbach, 1990), it may be that the strongest justice-affect relationships will be observed when the level of aggregation is consistent across the variables—either both broad or both narrow. That premise is consistent with past research showing that specific combinations of individual justice dimensions may be needed to predict specific emotions (Barclay et al., 2005; Goldman, 2003; Krehbiel & Cropanzano, 2000; Weiss et al., 1999).

In the case of aggregation and endogeneity, it may be the case that the merits of aggregation diminish when justice is cast as the dependent variable. One justification for employing a higher order organizational justice factor is to avoid the multicollinearity that comes with multiple independent variables being highly correlated. However, multicollinearity is not an issue when it is the dependent variables that are correlated (though correlated outcomes can create concerns about the family-wise error rate for hypothesis tests). Moreover, the studies that have examined justice in an endogenous manner have found very different results across the justice dimensions. For example, Gilliland and Schepers (2003) linked organizational unionization to informational justice but not interpersonal justice. Mayer et al. (2007) linked managerial neuroticism to interpersonal justice but not informational or procedural justice. Scott et al. (2007) linked subordinate charisma to interpersonal justice but not informational justice. Further studies should proceed in a differentiated manner to see whether those distinctions are replicated.

Affect and Endogeneity

In the case of affect and endogeneity, future research should explore whether managerial affect encourages or discourages adherence to justice rules. In their actor-focused model, Scott et al. (2009) suggested that positive affect could encourage justice rule adherence, as managers look to maintain that affect by acting prosocially. Negative affect, in turn, could discourage justice rule adherence, as aversive feelings cloud moral judgment and trigger venting behaviors. Tests of those propositions could involve trait affectivity or mood, as the affect need not be targeted to a given employee for justice-relevant actions to be affected. Indeed, Mayer et al.'s (2007) result linking higher managerial neuroticism to lower interpersonal justice rule adherence is supportive of Scott et al.'s theorizing. Those could also involve emotions if an ESM approach is utilized. For example, a study could link within-individual variation in positive emotions (e.g., happiness, enthusiasm, pride, compassion, gratitude) and negative emotions (e.g., anger, sadness, guilt, anxiety, envy)

to within-manager variation in justice rule adherence. That sort of research could reveal that organizational justice varies significantly within managers, not just between managers.

References

Adams, J. S. (1965). Inequity in social exchange. In L. Berkowitz (Ed.), *Advances in experimental social psychology* (Vol. 2, pp. 267–299). New York: Academic Press.

Ambrose, M., & Arnaud, A. (2005). Are procedural justice and distributive justice conceptually distinct? In J. Greenberg & J. A. Colquitt (Eds.), *The handbook of organizational justice* (pp. 59–84). Mahwah, NJ: Erlbaum.

Ambrose, M., Hess, R. L., & Ganesan, S. (2007). The relationship between justice and attitudes: An examination of justice effects on event and system-related attitudes. *Organizational Behavior and Human Decision Processes, 103*, 21–36.

Ambrose, M., & Kulik, C. T. (2001). How do I know that's fair? A categorization approach to fairness judgments. In S. Gilliland, D. Steiner, & D. Skarlicki (Eds.), *Theoretical and cultural perspectives on organizational justice* (pp. 35–61). Greenwich, CT: Information Age Publishing.

Ambrose, M. L., & Schminke, M. (2009). The role of overall justice judgments in organizational justice research: A test of mediation. *Journal of Applied Psychology, 94*, 491–500.

Bacharach, S. B. (1989). Organizational theories: Some criteria for evaluation. *Academy of Management Review, 14*, 496–515.

Barclay, L. J., & Skarlicki, D. P., & Pugh, S. D. (2005). Exploring the role of emotions in injustice perceptions and retaliation. *Journal of Applied Psychology, 90*, 629–643.

Barsky, A., & Kaplan, S. A. (2007). If you feel bad, it's unfair: A quantitative synthesis of affect and organizational justice perceptions. *Journal of Applied Psychology, 92*, 286–295.

Bell, B. S., Wiechmann, D., & Ryan, A. M. (2006). Consequences of organizational justice expectations in a selection system. *Journal of Applied Psychology, 91*, 455–466.

Bies, R. J., & Moag, J. F. (1986). Interactional justice: Communication criteria of fairness. In R. J. Lewicki, B. H. Sheppard, & M. H. Bazerman (Eds.), *Research on negotiations in organizations* (Vol. 1, pp. 43–55). Greenwich, CT: JAI Press.

Bies, R. J. & Shapiro, D. L (1988). Voice and justification: Their influence on procedural fairness judgments. *Academy of Management Journal, 31*, 676–685.

Bies, R. J., & Tripp, T. M. (2002). "Hot flashes, open wounds": Injustice and the tyranny of its emotions. In S. W. Gilliland, D. D. Steiner, & D. P. Skarlicki (Eds.), *Emerging perspectives on managing organizational justice* (pp. 203–221). Greenwich, CT: Information Age Publishing.

Blader, S. L., & Tyler, T. R. (2003). What constitutes fairness in work settings? A four-component model of procedural justice. *Human Resource Management Review, 13*, 107–126.

Blau, P. (1964). *Exchange and power in social life*. New York: Wiley.

Bobocel, D. R., Agar, S. E., & Meyer, J. P. (1998). Managerial accounts and fairness perceptions in conflict resolution: Differentiating the effects of minimizing responsibility and providing justification. *Basic and Applied Social Psychology, 20*, 133–143.

Bowling, N. A., & Hammond, G. D. (2008). A meta-analytic examination of the construct validity of the Michigan Organizational Assessment Questionnaire job satisfaction subscale. *Journal of Vocational Behavior, 73*, 63–77.

Brockner, J. (2002). Making sense of procedural fairness: How high procedural fairness can reduce or heighten the influence of outcome favorability. *Academy of Management Review, 27*, 58–76.

Brockner, J., & Wiesenfeld, B. M. (1996). An integrative framework for explaining reactions to decisions: Interactive effects of outcomes and procedures. *Psychological Bulletin, 120*, 189–208.

Camerman, J., Cropanzano, R., & Vandenberghe, C. (2007). The benefits of justice for temporary workers. *Group and Organization Management, 32*, 176–207.

Choi, J. (2008). Event justice perceptions and employees' reactions: Perceptions of social entity justice as a moderator. *Journal of Applied Psychology, 93*, 513–528.

Clark, L. A., & Watson, D. (1999). Temperament: A new paradigm for trait psychology. In L. A. Pervin & O. P. John (Eds.), *Handbook of personality: Theory and research* (pp. 399–423). New York: Guilford Press.

Cohen, J., Cohen, P., West, S. G., & Aiken, L. S. (2003). *Applied multiple regression/correlation analysis for the behavioral sciences.* Mahwah, NJ: Erlbaum.

Cohen-Charash, Y., & Byrne, Z. S. (2008). Affect and justice: Current knowledge and future directions. In N. M. Ashkanasy & C. L. Cooper (Eds.), *Research companion to emotion in organizations* (pp. 360–391). Northampton, MA: Edward Elgar.

Cohen-Charash, Y., & Spector, P. E. (2001). The role of justice in organizations: A meta-analysis. *Organizational Behavior and Human Decision Processes, 86*, 278–324.

Colquitt, J. A. (2001). On the dimensionality of organizational justice: A construct validation of a measure. *Journal of Applied Psychology, 86*, 386–400.

Colquitt, J. A. (2008). Two decades of organizational justice: Findings, controversies, and future directions. In C. L. Cooper & J. Barling (Eds.), *The Sage handbook of organizational behavior,* Volume 1, *Micro approaches* (pp. 73–88). Newbury Park, CA: Sage.

Colquitt, J. A., Conlon, D. E., Wesson, M. J., Porter, C. O. L. H., & Ng, K. Y. (2001). Justice at the millennium: A meta-analytic review of 25 years of organizational justice research. *Journal of Applied Psychology, 86*, 425–445.

Colquitt, J. A., & Greenberg, J. (2003). Organizational justice: A fair assessment of the state of the literature. In J. Greenberg (Ed.), *Organizational behavior: The state of the science* (pp. 165–210). Mahwah, NJ: Erlbaum.

Colquitt, J. A., Greenberg, J., & Scott, B. A. (2005). Organizational justice? Where do we stand? In J. Greenberg & J. A. Colquitt (Eds.), *The handbook of organizational justice* (pp. 589–619). Mahwah, NJ: Erlbaum.

Colquitt, J. A., Greenberg, J., & Zapata-Phelan, C. P. (2005). What is organizational justice? A historical overview. In J. Greenberg & J. A. Colquitt (Eds.), *The handbook of organizational justice* (pp. 3–56). Mahwah, NJ: Erlbaum.

Colquitt, J. A., & Shaw, J. C. (2005). How should organizational justice be measured? In J. Greenberg & J. A. Colquitt (Eds.), *The handbook of organizational justice* (pp. 113–152). Mahwah, NJ: Erlbaum.

Cronbach, L. J. (1990). *Essentials of psychological testing.* New York: HarperCollins.

Cropanzano, R., Byrne, Z. S., Bobocel, D. R., & Rupp, D. E. (2001). Moral virtues, fairness heuristics, social entities, and other denizens of organizational justice. *Journal of Vocational Behavior, 58*, 164–209.

Cropanzano, R., Goldman, B., & Folger, R. (2003). Deontic justice: The role of moral principles in workplace fairness. *Journal of Organizational Behavior, 24*, 1019–1024.

Deutsch, M. (1975). Equity, equality, and need: What determines which value will be used as the basis for distributive justice? *Journal of Social Issues, 31*, 137–149.

Fassina, N. E., Jones, D. A., & Uggerslev, K. L. (2008). Meta-analytic tests of relationships between organizational justice and citizenship behavior: Testing agent-system and shared-variance models. *Journal of Organizational Behavior, 29*, 805–828.

Foa, U. G., & Foa, E. B. (1980). Resource theory: Interpersonal behavior as exchange. In K. J. Gergen, M. S. Greenberg, & R. H. Willis (Eds.), *Social exchange: Advances in theory and research* (pp. 77–94). New York: Plenum.

Folger, R. (1998). Fairness as a moral virtue. In M. Schminke (Ed.), *Managerial ethics: Morally managing people and processes* (pp. 13–34). Mahwah, NJ: Erlbaum.

Folger, R. (2001). Fairness as deonance. In S. W. Gilliland, D. D. Steiner, & D. P. Skarlicki (Eds.), *Theoretical and cultural perspectives on organizational justice* (pp. 3–34). Greenwich, CT: Information Age Publishing.

Folger, R., & Bies, R. J. (1989). Managerial responsibilities and procedural justice. *Responsibilities and Rights Journal, 2*, 79–89.

Folger, R., & Cropanzano, R. (1998). *Organizational justice and human resource management.* Thousand Oaks, CA: Sage.

Folger, R., & Cropanzano, R. (2001). Fairness theory: Justice as accountability. In J. Greenberg & R. Cropanzano (Eds.), *Advances in organizational justice* (pp. 89–118). Stanford, CA: Stanford University Press.

Folger, R., Cropanzano, R., & Goldman, B. (2005). What is the relationship between justice and morality? In J. Greenberg & J. A. Colquitt (Eds.), *The handbook of organizational justice* (pp. 215–245). Mahwah, NJ: Erlbaum.

Folger, R., & Konovsky, M. A. (1989). Effects of procedural and distributive justice on reactions to pay raise decisions. *Academy of Management Journal, 32*, 115–130.

Fox, S., Spector, P. E., & Miles, D. (2001). Counterproductive work behavior (CWB) in response to job stressors and organizational justice: Some mediator and moderator tests for autonomy and emotions. *Journal of Vocational Behavior, 59*, 291–309.

Gillespie, J. Z., & Greenberg, J. (2005). Are the goals of organizational justice self-interested? In J. Greenberg & J. A. Colquitt (Eds.), *The handbook of organizational justice* (pp. 179–213). Mahwah, NJ: Erlbaum.

Gilliland, S. W., & Beckstein, B. A. (1996). Procedural and distributive justice in the editorial review process. *Personnel Psychology, 49*, 669–691.

Gilliland, S. W., & Schepers, D. H. (2003). Why we do the things we do: A discussion and analysis of determinants of just treatment in layoff implementation decisions. *Human Resource Management Review, 13*, 59–83.

Gilliland, S. W., Steiner, D. D., Skarlicki, D. P., & Van den Bos, K. (2005). *What motivates fairness in organizations?* Greenwich, CT: Information Age Publishing.

Goldman, B. M. (2003). The application of referent cognitions theory to legal claiming by terminated workers: The role of organizational justice and anger. *Journal of Management, 29*, 705–728.

Grandey, A. A. (2008). Emotions at work: A review and research agenda. In C. L. Cooper & J. Barling (Eds.), *The*

Sage handbook of organizational behavior, Volume 1, *Micro approaches* (pp. 235–261). Newbury Park, CA: Sage.

Greenberg, J. (1986). Determinants of perceived fairness of performance evaluations. *Journal of Applied Psychology, 71*, 340–342.

Greenberg, J. (1987). A taxonomy of organizational justice theories. *Academy of Management Review, 12*, 9–22.

Greenberg, J. (1990a). Employee theft as a reaction to underpayment inequity: The hidden cost of paycuts. *Journal of Applied Psychology, 75*, 561–568.

Greenberg, J. (1990b). Organizational justice: Yesterday, today, and tomorrow. *Journal of Management, 16*, 399–432.

Greenberg, J. (1993a). The intellectual adolescence of organizational justice: You've come a long way, maybe. *Social Justice Research, 6*, 135–148.

Greenberg, J. (1993b). The social side of fairness: Interpersonal and informational classes of organizational justice. In R. Cropanzano (Ed.), *Justice in the workplace: Approaching fairness in human resource management* (pp. 79–103). Hillsdale, NJ: Erlbaum.

Greenberg, J. (1993c). Stealing in the name of justice: Informational and interpersonal moderators of theft reactions to underpayment inequity. *Organizational Behavior and Human Decision Processes, 54*, 81–103.

Greenberg, J. (2007). Ten good reasons why everyone needs to know about and study organizational justice. In I. Glendon, B. Myors, & B. Thompson (Eds.), *Advances in organisational psychology: An Asia-Pacific perspective* (pp. 181–297). Bowen Hills, Queensland, Australia: Australian Academic Press.

Greenberg, J., Bies, R. J., & Eskew, D. E. (1991). Establishing fairness in the eye of the beholder: Managing impressions of organizational justice. In R. Giacalone & P. Rosenfeld (Eds.), *Applied impression management: How image making affects managerial decisions* (pp. 111–132). Newbury Park, CA: Sage.

Greenberg, J., & Wiethoff, C. (2001). Organizational justice as proaction and reaction: Implications for research and application. *Justice in the workplace: From theory to practice* (Vol. 2, pp. 271–302). Mahwah, NJ: Erlbaum.

Hauenstein, N. M. A., McGonigle, T., & Flinder, S. W. (2001). A meta-analysis of the relationship between procedural justice and distributive justice: Implications for justice research. *Employee Responsibilities and Rights Journal, 13*, 39–56.

Hollensbe, E. C., Khazanchi, S., & Masterson, S. S. (2008). How do I assess if my supervisor and organization are fair? Identifying the rules underlying entity-based justice perceptions. *Academy of Management Journal, 51*, 1099–1116.

Homans, G. C. (1961). *Social behaviour: Its elementary forms*. London: Routledge & Kegan Paul.

Horvath, M., & Andrews, S. B. (2007). The role of fairness perceptions and accountability attributions in predicting reactions to organizational events. *Journal of Psychology, 141*, 203–222.

Ironson, G. H., Smith, P. C., Brannick, M. T., Gibson, W. M., & Paul, K. B. (1989). Construction of a job in general scale: A comparison of global, composite, and specific measures. *Journal of Applied Psychology, 74*, 193–200.

Jawahar, I. M. (2007). The influence of perceptions of fairness on performance appraisal reactions. *Journal of Labor Research, 28*, 735–754.

Johnson, R. E., Selenta, C., & Lord, R. G. (2006). When organizational justice and the self-concept meet: Consequences for the organization and its members. *Organizational Behavior and Human Decision Processes, 99*, 175–201.

Judge, T. A., & Colquitt, J. A. (2004). Organizational justice and stress: The mediating role of work-family conflict. *Journal of Applied Psychology, 89*, 395–404.

Judge, T. A., Scott, B. A., & Ilies, R. (2006). Hostility, job attitudes, and workplace deviance: Test of a multilevel model. *Journal of Applied Psychology, 91*, 126–138.

Kernan, M. C., & Hanges, P. J. (2002). Survivor reactions to reorganization: Antecedents and consequences of procedural, interpersonal, and informational justice. *Journal of Applied Psychology, 87*, 916–928.

Kim, T. Y., & Leung, K. (2007). Forming and reacting to overall fairness: A cross-cultural comparison. *Organizational Behavior and Human Decision Processes, 104*, 83–95.

Korsgaard, M. A., Roberson, L., & Rymph, R. D. (1998). What motivates fairness? The role of subordinate assertiveness behavior on managers' interactional fairness. *Journal of Applied Psychology, 83*, 731–744.

Krehbiel, P. J., & Cropanzano, R. (2000). Procedural justice, outcome favorability, and emotion. *Social Justice Research, 13*, 339–360.

Lavelle, J. J., Rupp, D. E., & Brockner, J. (2007). Taking a multifoci approach to the study of justice, social exchange, and citizenship behavior: The target similarity model. *Journal of Management, 33*, 841–866.

Law, K. S., Wong, C. S., & Mobley, W. H. (1998). Toward a taxonomy of multidimensional constructs. *Academy of Management Review, 23*, 741–755.

Leventhal, G. S. (1976). The distribution of rewards and resources in groups and organizations. In L. Berkowitz & W. Walster (Eds.), *Advances in experimental social psychology* (Vol. 9, pp. 91–131). New York: Academic Press.

Leventhal, G. S. (1980). What should be done with equity theory? New approaches to the study of fairness in social relationships. In K. Gergen, M. Greenberg, and R. Willis (Eds.), *Social exchange: Advances in theory and research* (pp. 27–55). New York: Plenum Press.

Liao, H. (2007). Do it right this time: The role of employee service recovery performance in customer-perceived justice and customer loyalty after service failures. *Journal of Applied Psychology, 92*, 475–489.

Liao, H., & Rupp, D. E. (2005). The impact of justice climate and justice orientation on work outcomes: A cross-level multifoci framework. *Journal of Applied Psychology, 90*, 242–256.

Lind, E. A. (2001a). Fairness heuristic theory: Justice judgments as pivotal cognitions in organizational relations. In J. Greenberg & R. Cropanzano (Eds.), *Advances in organizational justice* (pp. 56–88). Stanford, CA: Stanford University Press.

Lind, E. A. (2001b). Thinking critically about justice judgments. *Journal of Vocational Behavior, 58*, 220–226.

Lind, E. A., & Tyler, T. R. (1988). *The social psychology of procedural justice*. New York: Plenum Press.

Mansour-Cole, D. M., & Scott, S. G. (1998). Hearing it through the grapevine: The influence of source, leader-relations, and legitimacy on survivors' fairness perceptions. *Personnel Psychology, 51*, 25–54.

Masterson, S. S. (2001). A trickle-down model of organizational justice: Relating employees' and customers' perceptions of and reactions to fairness. *Journal of Applied Psychology, 86*, 594–604.

Masterson, S. S., Lewis, K., Goldman, B. M., & Taylor, M. S. (2000). Integrating justice and social exchange: The differing effects of fair procedures and treatment on work relationships. *Academy of Management Journal*, *43*, 738–748.

Mayer, D., Nishii, L., Schneider, B., & Goldstein, H. (2007). The precursors and products of justice climates: Group leader antecedents and employee attitudinal consequences. *Personnel Psychology*, *60*, 929–963.

McFarlin, D. B., & Sweeney, P. D. (1992). Distributive and procedural justice as predictors of satisfaction with personal and organizational outcomes. *Academy of Management Journal*, *35*, 626–637.

Moorman, R. H. (1991). Relationship between organizational justice and organizational citizenship behaviors: Do fairness perceptions influence employee citizenship? *Journal of Applied Psychology*, *76*, 845–855.

Moorman, R. H., & Byrne, Z. S. (2005). How does organizational justice affect organizational citizenship behavior? In J. Greenberg & J. A. Colquitt (Eds.), *The handbook of organizational justice* (pp. 355–380). Mahwah, NJ: Erlbaum.

Organ, D. W. (1990). The motivational basis of organizational citizenship behavior. In L. L. Cummings & B. M. Staw (Eds.), *Research in organizational behavior* (Vol. 12, pp. 43–72). Greenwich, CT: JAI Press.

Podsakoff, P. M., MacKenzie, S. B., Lee, J., & Podsakoff, N. P. (2003). Common method bias in behavioral research: A critical review of the literature and recommended remedies. *Journal of Applied Psychology*, *88*, 879–903.

Price, J. L., & Mueller, C. (1986). *Handbook of organizational measurement*. Marshfield, MA: Pittman.

Roberson, Q. M., & Stewart, M. M. (2006). Understanding the motivational effects of procedural and informational justice in feedback processes. *British Journal of Psychology*, *97*, 281–298.

Rodell, J. B., & Colquitt, J. A. (2009). Looking ahead in times of uncertainty: The role of anticipatory justice in an organizational change context. *Journal of Applied Psychology*, *94*, 989–1002.

Rupp, D. E., & Cropanzano, R. (2002). The mediating effects of social exchange relationships in predicting workplace outcomes from multifoci organizational justice. *Organizational Behavior and Human Decision Processes*, *89*, 925–946.

Schaubroeck, J., May, D. R., & Brown, F. W. (1994). Procedural justice explanations and employee reactions to economic hardship: A field experiment. *Journal of Applied Psychology*, *79*, 455–460.

Schminke, M., Ambrose, M. L., & Cropanzano, R. S. (2000). The effect of organizational structure on perceptions of procedural fairness. *Journal of Applied Psychology*, *85*, 294–304.

Schwab, D. P. (2005). *Research methods for organizational studies*. Mahwah, NJ: Erlbaum.

Scott, B. A., Colquitt, J. A., & Paddock, E. L. (2009). An actor-focused model of justice rule adherence and violation: The role of managerial motives and discretion. *Journal of Applied Psychology*, *94*, 756–769.

Scott, B. A., Colquitt, J. A., & Zapata-Phelan, C. P. (2007). Justice as a dependent variable: Subordinate charisma as a predictor of interpersonal and informational justice perceptions. *Journal of Applied Psychology*, *92*, 1597–1609.

Shaw, J. C., Wild, R. E., & Colquitt, J. A. (2003). To justify or excuse? A meta-analysis of the effects of explanations. *Journal of Applied Psychology*, *88*, 444–458.

Siers, B. (2007). Relationships among organisational justice perceptions, adjustment, and turnover of United States-based expatriates. *Applied Psychology: An International Review*, *56*, 437–459.

Skarlicki, D. P., & Latham, G. P. (1997). Leadership training in organizational justice to increase citizenship behavior within a labor union: A replication. *Personnel Psychology*, *50*, 617–633.

Skitka, L. J., Winquist, J., & Hutchinson, S. (2003). Are outcome fairness and outcome favorability distinguishable psychological constructs? A meta-analytic review. *Social Justice Research*, *16*, 309–341.

Spell, C. S., & Arnold, T. (2007). An appraisal perspective of justice, structure, and job control as antecedents of psychological distress. *Journal of Organizational Behavior*, *28*, 729–751.

Streicher, B., Jonas, E., Maier, G. W., Frey, D., Woschée, & Waßmer, B. (2008). Test of the construct and criteria validity of a German measure of organizational justice. *European Journal of Psychological Assessment*, *24*, 131–139.

Sweeney, P. D., & McFarlin, D. B. (1993). Workers' evaluations of the "ends" and the "means": An examination of four models of distributive and procedural justice. *Organizational Behavior and Human Decision Processes*, *55*, 23–40.

Thibaut, J., & Walker, L. (1975). *Procedural justice: A psychological analysis*. Hillsdale, NJ: Erlbaum.

Turillo, C. J., Folger, R., Lavelle, J. J., Umphress, E. E., & Gee, J. O. (2002). Is virtue its own reward? Self-sacrificial decisions for the sake of fairness. *Organizational Behavior and Human Decision Processes*, *89*, 839–865.

Tyler, T. R. (1994). Psychological models of the justice motive: Antecedents of distributive and procedural justice. *Journal of Personality and Social Psychology*, *67*, 850–863.

Tyler, T. R., & Bies, R. J. (1990). Beyond formal procedures: The interpersonal context of procedural justice. In J. Carroll (Ed.), *Applied social psychology and organizational settings* (pp. 77–98). Hillsdale, NJ: Erlbaum.

Tyler, T. R., & Lind, E. A. (1992). A relational model of authority in groups. In M. P. Zanna (Ed.), *Advances in experimental social psychology* (Vol. 25, pp. 115–191). San Diego, CA: Academic Press.

Van den Bos, K. (2001). Fairness heuristic theory: Assessing the information to which people are reacting has a pivotal role in understanding organizational justice. In S. Gilliland, D. Steiner, & D. Skarlicki (Eds.), *Theoretical and cultural perspectives on organizational justice* (pp. 63–84). Greenwich, CT: Information Age Publishing.

Van den Bos, K. (2003). On the subjective quality of social justice: The role of affect as information in the psychology of justice judgments. *Journal of Personality and Social Psychology*, *85*, 482–498.

Van Katwyk, P. T., Fox, S., Spector, P. E., & Kelloway, E. K. (2000). Using the job-related affective well-being scale (JAWS) to investigate affective responses to work stressors. *Journal of Occupational Health Psychology*, *5*, 219–230.

Weiss, H. M., & Cropanzano, R. (1996). Affective events theory: A theoretical discussion of the structure, causes, and consequences of affective experiences at work. In B. M. Staw and L. L. Cummings (Eds.), *Research in organizational behavior* (Vol. 18, pp. 1–74). Greenwich, CT: JAI Press.

Weiss, H. M., Suckow, K., & Cropanzano, R. (1999). Effects of justice conditions on discrete emotions. *Journal of Applied Psychology, 84,* 786–794.

Westen, D., & Rosenthal, R. (2003). Quantifying construct validity: Two simple measures. *Journal of Personality and Social Psychology, 84,* 608–618.

Wong, C. S., Law, K. S., & Huang, G. (2008). On the importance of conducting construct-level analysis for multidimensional constructs in theory development and testing. *Journal of Management, 34,* 744–764.

Zapata-Phelan, C. P., Colquitt, J. A., Scott, B. A., & Livingston, B. (2009). Procedural justice, interactional justice, and task performance: The mediating role of intrinsic motivation. *Organizational Behavior and Human Decision Processes, 108,* 93–105.

Dynamic Performance

Sabine Sonnentag, *and* Michael Frese

Abstract

This chapter reviews research on dynamic job performance. It summarizes the empirical literature and presents conceptual and theoretical approaches of conceptualizing performance change and performance fluctuations over time. It addresses longer term performance changes, describes predictors (e.g., ability, personality) and outcomes of individual differences in these changes, and incorporates a life-span perspective. It discusses vicious and positive cycles in which performance and its outcomes reinforce one another. It presents a within-person approach that focuses on short-term performance variability within persons and describes action-related and self-regulation process models of dynamic performance. The chapter closes with a taxonomy of dynamic performance processes and a research agenda for the future.

Key Words: Performance, change, stability, variability, trajectory, skill acquisition, self-regulation, action theory, life span

Introduction

Performance is a core concept within industrial and organizational (I/O) psychology. Various theories in this domain aim at predicting high job performance, and human resource management endeavors center around the goal of improving performance in work organizations.

A "convenient" assumption of selection research and other areas of industrial and organizational psychology has been that performance is rather stable. This assumption is convenient: if predictors of performance and the criterion of performance do not show stability, it is difficult to predict later performance from earlier attributes. Such an assumption is not only convenient, it is also partially true because meta-analyses showed that attributes, behaviors and performance are rather stable across time (Ouellette & Wood, 1998). However, this assumption is only half-true because stability across time clearly never even approaches 1.0 (even after correcting for

attenuation). Depending upon the circumstances, stability across time is sometimes high and sometimes low (Sturman, Cheramie, & Cashen, 2005). A person's performance level may increase due to learning processes and practice and may decrease due to transient (e.g., fatigue) and more enduring (e.g., aging) processes. In addition, performance may also fluctuate within persons within short time intervals. If such fluctuations were random, they might not justify much attention; however, if they are more systematic, it will be important to identify factors that predict a particularly high performance level within a person.

To develop a comprehensive theory of performance, it is necessary to address the stable and the dynamic aspects of performance. Given the emphasis on selection issues in I/O psychology, the stable part of performance has usually been emphasized. In this chapter, we approach the topic of performance from a dynamic point of view; thus, we see our approach to be compensatory to the usual approach taken in I/O psychology. The dynamics of performance is particularly evident in the following areas of performance: learning and forgetting, temporal vigor and fatigue, engagement and burnout—to give just a few examples. These various temporal processes may actually feed upon each other—they then lead to positive or negative cycles, or they may level off, or even have a curvilinear effect over time. Dynamic performance effects may also unfold differentially across time, for example, the effect of job redesign may lead to changes only after a certain period of time. Performance effects may appear at a later period and may not directly after the implementation of a new job design (e.g., Wall & Clegg, 1981). Other predictor changes may have an immediate effect on performance, such as reinforcement (Luthans, Paul, & Baker, 1981). Finally, there may be fluctuations of performance around a mean across time.

One major research approach that addresses changes in performance is the area of training and education. Training and education lead to changing levels of knowledge and skills (Lipsey & Wilson, 1993); however, although interesting approaches have been proposed regarding learning and change of performance (Kozlowski et al., 2001) and on conceptualizing how self-regulatory processes stimulated in training interventions bring about performance change and adaptation (Bell & Kozlowski, 2008; Smith, Ford, & Kozlowski, 1997), instructional interventions are not the focus of this article. Similarly, during recent years, studies have increased our understanding about how people adapt to changes at their workplace or changes in the tasks that they have to perform (Lang & Bliese, 2009; LePine, 2003; LePine, Colquitt, & Erez, 2000). In the present chapter, we look at the dynamics of performance in the sense of changes that do not take place as a direct result of outside interventions (such as training, or changes in the job, task, or organizational design), but that take place as a result of time or time on task (time x task interactions), as well as changing task structures over time because of self-regulatory processes. However, we should hasten to add that time per se is not the important variable—rather, there are processes within time that produce the effects of dynamic performance. "Although we analyzed the effects of time on validity, we do not imply that time per se was the causal factor in the observed validity decrements. Those things that occur while individuals are learning and performing jobs and during skill acquisition are the

assumed causal agents" (Hulin, Henry, & Noon, 1990, p. 336).

This chapter focuses on the dynamics of individual performance. Performance dynamism occurs also at other levels within organizations, for example, at the team level or the organizational level (for research in these areas, cf. Chen, Thomas, & Wallace, 2005; Kozlowski, Gully, McHugh, Salas, & Cannon-Bowers, 1996; Kozlowski, Gully, Nason, & Smith, 1999; LePine et al., 2000; Marks, Mathieu, & Zaccaro, 2001).

We begin our chapter with definitions of performance and of dynamic performance. In the second section, we briefly describe the relevance of the topic. The sections that follow are devoted to (a) long-term performance trajectories, (b) performance cycles, (c) short-term performance variability within persons, and (d) dynamism within performance action phases. We conclude with a discussion that provides an integrative theoretical overview of dynamic performance and suggests avenues for future research.

Definitions and Conceptualizations
Definition of Job Performance
Job performance is a broad concept comprising multiple dimensions. On a basic level, job performance comprises a process aspect (i.e., *behavior*) and an *outcome* aspect (Campbell, McCloy, Oppler, & Sager, 1993; Motowidlo, 2003; Roe, 1999). The process aspect refers to multiple, discrete behaviors that people *do* at work (Campbell, 1990). It focuses on the action itself—as opposed to the results or outcomes of this action. It limits itself to behaviors that contribute to the goals of the organization and that are under the control of the acting person (Campbell et al., 1993). The outcome aspect refers to the *results* of behavior and comprises states or conditions that are only partially under people's control.

At the conceptual level, many researchers agree to focus on the behavioral aspect of performance (Campbell et al., 1993; Motowidlo, Borman, & Schmit, 1997), but empirical research often operationalizes performance from a results-oriented perspective (Sturman, 2007), particularly when examining performance changes over time (e.g., Ployhart & Hakel, 1998). The behavioral and outcome aspect are related, but they are conceptually and empirically distinct: while the performance process aims to achieve positive performance outcomes, the performance outcomes (i.e., results) are usually influenced by other processes in addition to a person's performance behavior (e.g., situational and organizational constraints, market conditions, random processes). This observation implies that studies that only examine performance outcomes (instead of the performance processes) are seriously underestimating and mis-specifying the effect of predictors of process performance. However, we must acknowledge that performance outcomes matter more to most business organizations and are often more readily measured than performance processes.

There is broad consensus in the literature that the performance process comprises aspects of task and contextual performance (Borman & Motowidlo, 1993; Hoffman, Blair, Meriac, & Woehr, 2007; Rotundo & Sackett, 2002). Task performance refers to activities that directly transform materials or information into goods or services and to activities that directly support the organization's core activities (e.g., by delivery activities or planning and coordination; Motowidlo, 2003). Contextual performance refers to discretionary behaviors that add to organizational effectiveness by improving the functioning of the social and organizational context of work.

Recently, additional differentiations were suggested. The two most important ones are: adaptive and proactive performance (Griffin, Neal, & Parker, 2007). The core of the adaptive performance concept is that people cope with and support organizational change (Griffin et al., 2007; Pulakos, Arad, Donovan, & Plamondon, 2000). The proactive performance concept (Grant & Ashford, 2008) refers to behaviors that initiate change, are self-starting, and are future oriented (Frese & Fay, 2001; Griffin et al., 2007). It includes personal initiative (Frese, Kring, Soose, & Zempel, 1996; Thompson, 2005), taking charge (McAllister, Kamdar, Morrison, & Turban, 2007; Morrison & Phelps, 1999), voice (LePine & Van Dyne, 2001), active feedback seeking (Ashford & Tsui, 1991), and some forms of engagement (Macey & Schneider, 2008). Table 17.1 describes the four dimensions of performance, defines them and cites some representative authors.

The majority of studies that examined dynamic performance focused on task performance; but there are a few studies that also looked at the dynamic nature of performance in the areas of contextual (Ilies, Scott, & Judge, 2006) and proactive performance (Frese, Garst, & Fay, 2007; Seibert, Crant, & Kraimer, 1999).

Definitions and Conceptualizations of Dynamic Performance

Performance is considered to be dynamic if it changes over time without outside and directed interventions; changes over time can imply changes in mean values, changes in correlations between performance dimensions, and lack of stability of job performance over time (Deadrick, Bennett, & Russell, 1997; Hanges, Schneider, & Niles, 1990). According to Sturman (2007), lack of stability refers to the behavioral aspect of performance, not to the results or utility of performance. One implication of this specification is that individuals' rank order of performance scores change over time. Change may refer to intraindividual change and to interindividual differences in intraindividual change (Hofmann, Jacobs, & Baratta, 1993).

Performance dynamism can refer to both long-term and short-term changes in individual performance. Reb and Cropanzano (2007) characterized the long-term changes as performance trends. Such long-term changes result—among others—from changes in knowledge, skills, and experience. In organizational settings, these trends may cover periods of months or even years (Deadrick et al., 1997; Ployhart & Hakel, 1998); in laboratory research, such trends occur over periods of some hours (Ackerman, 1988). From such performance trends, short-term performance fluctuations can be differentiated, reflecting performance variations around a constant mean (Reb & Cropanzano, 2007). These variations are not random but may be influenced by momentary affective states (Beal, Weiss, Barros, & MacDermid, 2005). In this chapter, we address both the long- and short-term changes in performance.

Relevance of Performance Dynamism

Looking at job performance from a dynamic perspective is important for a number of reasons. First, to arrive at a better understanding of job performance at the conceptual level, research attention must be paid to the dynamic aspects of performance. Although there was a lively debate during the past four or five decades about whether performance is dynamic or static (for an overview, see Sturman, 2007), researchers now largely agree that performance and performance criteria change over time. Thus, performance must not be seen as stable, but rather as a highly dynamic concept. Second, taking a dynamic approach to performance enables researchers to make predictions about performance trajectories over time. Such an approach enhances our predictive knowledge about how performance increases (or decreases) over time and about the pattern of such performance changes (linear, cubic, etc). In addition, we can develop more realistic concepts

Table 17.1 The Four Dimensions of Process Performance

Concept	Definition	Differentiation from other Constructs	Dominant operationalization	Authors
Task performance	Task performance refers to activities that directly transform materials or information into goods or services and to activities that directly support the organization's core activities	Task performance is the primary necessity of doing one's job well	Supervisor ratings	Murphy & Cleveland, 1995
Contextual performance or organizational citizenship behavior (OCB)	Contextual performance refers to discretionary behaviors that add to organizational effectiveness by improving the functioning of the social and organizational context of work: Aspects are altruism, compliance, sportsmanship, courtesy, civic virtue	Contextual performance is oriented toward helping others with their jobs, supporting the smooth social functioning of the organization (Borman, Penner, Allen, & Motowidlo, 2001)	Questionnaire filled out by supervisor or colleague	Organ 1988 Borman & Motowidlo, 1993; Motowidlo & Van Scotter, 1994
Adaptive performance	Coping and supporting organizational change, adapting to new job conditions or requirements.	Deals with the dynamic, unpredictable nature of work that necessitates change	Questionnaire (and experimental approach)	Smith, Ford, & Kozlowski, 1997; Pulakos et al., 2000; Joung, Hesketh, & Neal, 2006; Ployhart & Bliese, 2006
Active performance	Self-starting, proactive approach, and persistent in overcoming difficulties (Frese & Fay, 2001, p. 134).	Active forms of performance can appear in the areas of task, contextual, and adaptive performance	Self-reported and peer reported questionnaire, interview, situational judgment test	Frese & Fay, 2001; Griffin et al., 2007; Grant & Ashford, 2008; Morrison & Phelps, 1999; Van Dyne & LePine, 1998

about when a performance plateau is reached and can identify individual characteristics and situational features that predict performance changes over time (e.g., who will show stronger increases in performance early in his or her career?).

Third, taking a dynamic approach to performance makes it possible to combine research on performance with research on lifelong development, thus, integrating knowledge about performance changes across the lifetime into work and organizational psychology (Kanfer & Ackerman, 2004; Schalk et al., 2010).

Fourth, acknowledging the dynamics of performance makes it possible to examine fluctuations of performance around a person-specific mean level (Reb & Cropanzano, 2007). We are then able to develop indicators about the degree of these performance fluctuations (e.g., within a week, a month,

or a year) and whether they are still in a "normal" range or not.

Fifth, the dynamic perspective of performance is also relevant for practical issues such as personnel selection. Traditionally, selection procedures assume that the rank order of individuals tested for selection purposes does not change over time. However, as research on dynamic performance has shown, rank orders are not completely invariant over time (e.g., (Hofmann, Jacobs, & Gerras, 1992). Thus, the utility of such traditional selection approaches that assume an unchanged rank order of individuals' performance over time cannot remain unquestioned. To improve selection procedures, research may identify factors that predict interindividual differences in performance trajectories (i.e., individual differences in performance change over time; cf., Ployhart & Hakel, 1998).

Long-Term Dynamic Performance Trajectories

Evidence for Performance Dynamism

Early research on dynamic performance originated from a discussion of the stability of performance and whether performance ratings are reliable over time (Barrick & Alexander, 1987; Ghiselli & Haire, 1960; Humphreys, 1960). An example for this type of study is that performance scores at various points in time follow a simplex pattern, characterized by a decrease in the size of correlations as the time lag between the performance measurements increases (Humphreys, 1960). Despite this evidence that performance measures are not completely stable over time, it remained unclear from this early research whether changes in performance measures are attributable to true changes in performance or to unreliability of the measures. Sturman et al. (2005) addressed these issues in a meta-analysis and examined the extent of job performance changes over time. Specifically, they aimed at separating stability (the extent to which the true score does not change over time) from temporal consistency (the extent to which observed performance measures correlate over time) and test-retest reliability (the degree of convergence between the observed and the true score). This meta-analysis, based on 22 independent samples with an overall sample size of 4,294 individuals, made use of a total of 309 correlations, with time lags ranging between one week (Rothe, 1970) and 72 months (Hanges et al., 1990). Overall, this meta-analysis showed that temporal consistency decreased as time between measurement points increased and that objective performance measures (as opposed to subjective measures) and greater job complexity were associated with lower test-retest reliability, with job complexity moderating the effects of time. A breakdown of the results for specific subgroups of measures and time lags revealed that average stability of performance ranged between 0.44 (objective measure, low complexity, three-year time lag) and 0.96 (subjective measure, high complexity, 0.5-year time lag). Average temporal consistency ranged between 0.14 (objective measure, high complexity, three-year time lag) and 0.69 (subjective measure, low complexity, 0.5-year time lag). Average test-retest reliability ranged between 0.50 (objective measure, high complexity) and 0.83 (subjective measure, low complexity). Overall, these findings demonstrate that performance is far from being stable over time, but nevertheless seems to have a stable "component," as the stability coefficients decreased but did not approach zero. Interestingly, stability tended to be lower in highly complex jobs, a fact that can be attributed to a greater change in specific job requirements over time and an increased difficulty to assess performance when jobs are more complex.

Evidence for Interindividual Differences in Performance Trajectories

Sturman et al. (2005) showed that performance is not stable over time. An additional issue of a dynamic view of performance relates to the fact that performance instability may not be uniform for all individuals, and individuals may differ in their changes over time. For example, after starting a new job, some people increase their performance rather quickly, whereas others need more time. Several studies have examined predictors of interindividual differences in performance trajectories and whether performance trends are systematic.

Hofmann and his coworkers (Hofmann et al., 1993; Hofmann et al., 1992) addressed the questions of whether individuals differ in their performance trajectories over time and whether different patterns of performance trajectories can be detected. The first study (Hofmann et al., 1992) analyzed performance data from two groups of professional baseball players (128 batters and 76 pitchers) over a 10-year period; it found a quadratic trend in one of the groups, and a quadratic and cubic trend in the other groups. Moreover, baseball players differed in their performance trajectories over time; subgroups with positive versus negative linear trends could be clearly differentiated.

In the second study, 12 subsequent quarters of insurance sales were examined; Hofmann et al. (1993) found that individuals differed in their performance trajectories; that is, the change in performance over time was not uniform across individuals. More specifically, 69% of the variance of linear growth parameter and 30% of the variance of the quadratic growth parameter were systematic, indicating that linear and quadratic parameters differed between individuals; however, there were no differences between individuals for a cubic parameter. Hofmann et al. (1993) suggested that differences in individual skills, knowledge, or goal orientations might influence differences in performance trajectories.

Hofmann et al.'s (1993) findings were confirmed by a number of subsequent studies demonstrating systematic differences in people's performance trends (Day, Sin, & Chen, 2004; Deadrick et al., 1997; Ployhart & Hakel, 1998). Some of these studies demonstrated that interindividual differences exist not only in the linear growth parameter (i.e., slope) of performance trajectories but also in higher order parameters of the performance curve, such as quadratic (Ployhart & Hakel, 1998; Thoresen, Bradley, Bliese, & Thoreson, 2004; Zickar & Slaughter, 1999) and cubic (Ployhart & Hakel, 1998; Thoresen et al., 2004) parameters. Quadratic trends imply that the increase in performance decreases over time (i.e., "flattens out"); cubic trends refer to more complex patterns that often can only be interpreted in light of the specific research setting and the specific time frame (cf., Thoresen et al., 2004).

Taken together, there is rather consistent evidence that individuals differ in performance trends (cf. also, Zyphur, Bradley, Landis, & Thoresen, 2008), with the most obvious differences in the linear trends. Conclusions that differences in quadratic or cubic trends are less relevant might be premature because these higher order trends have been analyzed only in a few studies.

Studies conducted since the mid-1990s addressed the question of whether predictors of these individual differences in performance trajectories can be identified. Deadrick et al. (1997) examined performance trajectories of sewing machine operators over a relatively short period of 24 weeks. The authors identified job experience and abilities as predictors of the linear growth parameter. Specifically, job experience was negatively related to the linear growth parameter, indicating that workers with previous experience in the specific domain improved more slowly than workers with no previous experience. Cognitive ability predicted a fast increase in performance. Interestingly, only 5% of the variance in the linear performance trend was explained by the predictors included in this analysis.

While Deadrick et al. (1997) examined performance changes within a relatively small time span, most of the other studies on performance trajectories looked at longer time intervals. Ployhart and Hakel (1998) analyzed gross sales commissions of salespeople over a period of eight quarters and examined individual difference variables (past salary and future expected earning, persuasion, empathy) as predictors of mean performance levels and growth parameters. Latent growth curve modeling demonstrated that past salary and future expected earning predicted interindividual performance differences at the first measurement occasion. Self-reported persuasion and self-reported empathy were related to the linear growth parameter, indicating that those who think of themselves as persuasive

and empathetic increased their sales performance at a faster pace than those who rate themselves lower in these dimensions. The predictors were not related to a quadratic growth parameter (i.e., acceleration in performance over time).

Thoresen et al. (2004) also examined predictors of sales performance and sales performance trajectories and extended Ployhart and Hakel's (1998) research by including Big Five personality variables as potential moderators and by differentiating between two job stages. More specifically, Thoresen and his coauthors built on the work of Murphy (1989) and distinguished between maintenance and transitional job stages. When people are in a maintenance stage, they have learned well to perform all major job tasks and are no longer facing situations characterized by novel or unpredictable demands. When people are in a transitional stage, they are confronted with undefined methods of operation, and they must learn new skills and make decisions about topics that are unfamiliar to them (Murphy, 1989). In other words, during transitional stages, employees do not yet have routines available for accomplishing their tasks (Frese & Zapf, 1994). For the maintenance sample, the authors found the following: there was a significant linear and cubic trend, indicating an overall increase in performance over time, with a large increase in performance from Quarter 1 to Quarter 2, relative stability from Quarter 2 to Quarter 3, and another increase from Quarter 3 to Quarter 4. Also, job tenure and conscientiousness were significantly related to mean levels of performance; extraversion was a marginally significant predictor of performance. Additionally, in this maintenance sample, there were no significant interactions between Big Five personality variables and the linear and quadratic trends in the performance trajectories, suggesting that broad personality constructs did not matter much with respect to performance increase and acceleration over time during the maintenance stage. However, there was a significant interaction between conscientiousness and the cubic trend of sales performance, indicating that higher-order patterns of performance trajectories may depend on conscientiousness in the sample that had already developed a certain number of routines.

For the transitional sample, analyses revealed: there was a strong positive linear trend and a significant negative quadratic trend (but no cubic trend), indicating a strong general increase in performance and a plateauing of this increase over time. Also, agreeableness and openness to experience were significantly related to mean performance when job tenure was controlled for. Moreover, agreeableness was positively and emotional stability was negatively related to the linear growth parameter. This unexpected finding with respect to emotional stability might indicate that employees low on emotional stability react more strongly to disturbances and unforeseen changes, which in turn might help to increase performance. Openness to experience was negatively related to the quadratic growth parameter, indicating that persons high on openness were less likely to show plateauing of their performance level over the study period.

Overall, this study showed that personality factors as predictors of performance growth trajectories differ between maintenance and transitional job stages. Personality seems to matter for changes in the transitional stage, but not for changes in the maintenance stage. Thus, this study demonstrated that it can be very important to differentiate between various job stages when examining long-term performance trajectories (Thoresen et al., 2004).

Other studies examined performance trajectories in more specific samples, such as film directors and sports professionals. Using performance data from film directors, Zickar and Slaughter (1999) aimed at predicting individual differences in performance trajectories. In this study, performance was operationalized by critics' ratings of the directors' films. The number of films that a director produced per year throughout his or her career predicted the linear and the quadratic trends of critics' ratings. Directors who produced many films per year showed an improvement in critics' ratings over their careers and had an accelerating performance trajectory.

Day et al. (2004) studied performance trajectories of players of the U.S. National Hockey League over the course of nine seasons. Overall, the authors observed a negative linear trend. Performance trajectories differed between persons, whereas position within the team and age were important factors. For example, offensive and older players had a flatter performance trajectory than defensive and younger players.

While the studies presented so far concentrated on individual performance, Chen (2005) explicitly linked individual performance trajectories to team-level processes. More specifically, he analyzed performance change of knowledge workers after they joined a project team. Performance was assessed via peer and team leader ratings. As predictors of newcomers' performance change, empowerment, team expectations, and initial team performance were examined. Analysis showed that initial team performance predicted change in newcomers' performance over a period of six weeks. Although empowerment and team expectations predicted newcomers' initial performance levels, there were no significant predictors for performance change. This study is noteworthy, as it included situational variables (e.g., team performance) as potential predictors of performance change. In combination with the other studies, it suggests that not only individual-difference variables, but also environmental variables play a major role for explaining differences in performance trajectories.

Dynamic Changes of Performance Predictors Over the Life Span

Lifelong developmental psychology has shown that the two most important predictors of performance—cognitive ability and conscientiousness—change across the life span. In particular, fluid intelligence decreases over time, while crystallized intelligence does not decrease (Baltes, Staudinger, & Lindenberger, 1999; Verhaeghen & Salthouse, 1997). The biological process of a sharp reduction of all parts of intelligence comes at a very high age (when most people are retired from work; Baltes et al., 1999). However, there is a certain degree of plasticity even in the decrement of intelligence over the life span (Baltes et al., 1999). Work psychology also produced evidence that the reduction of cognitive ability is dependent upon the complexity of work done; employees in highly complex jobs show few signs of reduction of cognitive ability with age, in contrast to employees in less complex jobs (Kohn & Schooler, 1978; Schallberger, 1988; Schleicher, 1973; Schooler, Mulatu, & Oates, 1999). This effect of complexity of work is more pronounced in older than in younger workers (Schooler et al., 1999).

Decrements in cognitive ability do not translate immediately into decrements in performance. As a matter of fact, meta-analysis show that there is a zero relationship between age and core task performance (Ng & Feldman, 2008). A more differentiated analysis shows even some positive effects of age on reduced absenteeism, reduced tardiness, some forms of organizational citizenship behavior, and small positive effects on safety behavior; counterproductive behavior and work place aggression are reduced with age (Ng & Feldman, 2008). The fact that age has no substantial effect on core job performance—in spite of decreased fluid intelligence as a function of age—can be explained by the complex nature of the performance dynamics. First, some of the jobs may require little fluid intelligence, even though crystalline intelligence requirements may be high (e.g., managers; Kanfer & Ackerman, 2004). Thus, there may be little reason to expect performance decrements in such jobs over time. Second, there are compensatory mechanisms. People at work may compensate memory loss by taking notes, may optimize their approaches to the tasks (effort, time allocation, etc.), and may select (if possible) those tasks at which they excel (or reduce the number of tasks); all of this suggests an SOC (selection/optimization/compensation) approach to performance (Baltes, 1997; Zacher & Frese, 2011). Selection (selecting those activities and goals that are central), optimization (e.g., seizing the right moment, investing resources, honing skills, knowledge, and attention for those activities that were selected), and compensation (maintaining good performance in spite of loss by making good use of alternative means) are functional, particularly at old age. A good example is a quote on Rubinstein by Baltes (1997, p. 371):

> When the concert pianist Arthur Rubinstein, as an 80-year-old, was asked in a television interview how he managed to maintain such a high level of expert piano playing, he hinted at the coordination of three strategies. First, Rubinstein said that he played fewer pieces (selection); second, he indicated that he now practiced these pieces more often (optimization); and third, he suggested that to counteract his loss in mechanical speed, he now used a kind of impression management, such as introducing slower play before fast segments, so to make the latter appear faster (compensation).

Third, workers may be able to compensate for memory losses with increased levels of conscientiousness. There is evidence that older workers become more conscientious across the life span (Roberts, Walton, & Viechtbauer, 2006). Conscientious older workers use SOC approaches (Baltes, 1997) to keep up good performance (Bajor & Baltes, 2003). Thus, good predictors of performance (such as conscientiousness) tend to change over time. It is useful to think of the motivational effects of these various changes as mediating mechanisms of performance change over time (Kanfer & Ackerman, 2004).

Consequences of Individual Differences in Performance Trajectories

Most studies that examined individual differences in performance growth parameters focused on predictors of these differences. In addition, a few studies examined possible outcomes of such differences in performance trajectories (Harrison, Virick, & William, 1996; Sturman & Trevor, 2001).

Sturman and Trevor (2001) analyzed the performance trends of 1413 employees of a financial services organization: Hierarchical linear modeling revealed that persons who stayed in the organization during the eight-month study period showed a positive performance trend over time; however, persons who left the organization during the study period had not increased their performance. When current performance level was controlled, longer term negative performance trends in the past predicted turnover. Moreover, longer term performance trends in the past interacted with current performance in predicting turnover: employees with low current performance levels showed an increased tendency to voluntary turnover when their performance trend in the past was negative, but not when their performance trend in the past was positive; for employees with high current performance, past performance trends did not matter with respect to voluntary turnover.

This study is informative, as it demonstrates that performance trends over time can result in outcomes that are highly relevant for organizations and individuals alike. Moreover, Sturman and Trevor (2001) showed how important it is to examine performance trends for practical and theoretical purposes. The evidence on non-dynamic models of turnover may point to conclusions that are only related to the current performance levels to be predictors of turnover (Williams & Livingstone, 1994) and not to past trajectories of performance. However, it makes sense from a practical point of view that current performance level is not the only predictor of turnover, but that one looks at one's development in much more detail to decide whether to leave. Similarly, managers may observe their subordinates' performance trajectories when they ask someone to leave.

It would be an interesting avenue for future research to examine performance trends related to other variables, such as job attitudes, or to motivational constructs, including self-efficacy. For example, research within a control theory framework suggests that affective outcomes are predicted not only by a person's current performance level and progress toward a goal, but also by the velocity of goal attainment (Lawrence, Carver, & Scheier, 2002). Similarly, longer term performance trends that reflect these velocity aspects might be relevant for job satisfaction and similar constructs.

Theoretical Models

In addition to answering the empirical questions of whether performance is dynamic over time and to identify predictors of specific performance trajectories, researchers aim at explaining why performance is dynamic. Among the most prominent theoretical models that try to account to performance dynamism are the changing-subject and the changing-task model (Alvares & Hulin, 1972; Henry & Hulin, 1987), the skill acquisition model (Ackerman, 1987, 1988), and the employment stage model (Murphy, 1989). It has been argued that models from other disciplines, such as learning curve theory, might be applied to develop a model of individual dynamic performance (Sturman, 2007).

Changing-Subject and Changing-Task Model

The changing-subject model (changing-person model, as described by Keil & Cortina, 2001) proposed that individual characteristics relevant for performance change over time as the individual gains more experience with the task. One specific formulation of this approach referred to changing levels of abilities (Adams, 1957). Later, it was argued that it might be more appropriate to specify changes in skills because skills are conceptualized to be more changeable than abilities (Keil & Cortina, 2001). Sturman (2007) argued that also motivation and job knowledge may change over time and could therefore be incorporated in changing-subject models. It is important to note that this model assumes that the causes of performance change over time, but that the contribution of these causes to performance may remain stable. The changing-task model states that the contribution of specific abilities to performance changes over time, but the individual's level of these abilities remains stable. The relative contribution of specific abilities may change over time because of job changes, assignment of new roles and tasks, and revised organizational requirements such as changes in technology (Sturman, 2007). Keil and Cortina (2001) have argued that these two models should be seen as complementary rather than competing.

We agree with Keil and Cortina (2001) that these two models can be integrated—as a matter of fact, we think that there are sometimes interactions of changes in individuals and the task environment. Moreover, industrial and organizational psychology has tended to underestimate the plasticity of traits and abilities across the life span. Abilities (e.g., cognitive abilities) and personality traits

change, as shown above. Moreover, there are likely interactions of these changes with task environments. We suggest that it is useful to think of traits, abilities, and skills as being changeable over time, and these changing traits, abilities, and skills may interact with the task structure to produce changes in performance. There may be differential rates of change—with some factors changing very slowly, even as a result of direct interventions (slow-changing traits) and some others changing more quickly (e.g., skills). The rate of change of predictors needs to be determined empirically and should not be assumed to be either all or nothing (Nesselroade, 1991; Srivastava, John, Gosling, & Potter, 2003).

Skill-Acquisition Model and Self-Regulation

Several theoretical models have suggested different stages of skill acquisition—all of them assuming a stage in which conscious attention to the relevant parameters play an important role, a stage in which various parts of the skills are integrated, and a stage in which the skill becomes routinized (Ackerman & Cianciolo, 2000; Anderson, 1982; Frese & Zapf, 1994; Hacker, 1998). Ackerman's (1987, 1988) skill-acquisition model is particularly relevant for performance dynamism. This model differentiates between three stages of skill acquisition; each stage is associated with a certain type of abilities that predicts performance during this phase. Ackerman proposed that during a first phase of skill acquisition (cognitive phase) when the demands on the cognitive-attentional system are high, general mental ability is crucial for performance. During the second phase (associative phase) when the stimulus-response connections are refined, perceptual speed abilities are most relevant. Perceptual speed abilities refer to the "speed of consistent encoding and comparing symbols" (Ackerman, 1988, p. 290). During the third and final phase (autonomous phase), when tasks can be completed without full attention, psychomotor ability is most important for performance. Psychomotor ability describes the speed of responding to stimuli that involve only little or no cognitive-processing demands. Thus, during the continuous process of skill acquisition, the importance of general mental ability is high at the beginning and then decreases over time. Perceptual speed ability is low at the beginning, increases over time, and decreases again as task completion becomes more automatized. Finally, psychomotor ability is low at the beginning and increases over time.

Ackerman (1988) further argued that the skill-acquisition process is dependent on the complexity and consistency of the task. *Complexity* refers to memory load, number of response choices, amount of information provided to the learner, and other aspects of the cognitive demands of the task. More complex tasks require more attention, reduce the accuracy of task performance, and increase the amount of time needed to complete a trial. *Task consistency* refers to invariant rules for information processing, invariant components of processing, and invariant sequences of information-processing components (Ackerman, 1987). It therefore determines the degree to which automaticity of task completion can be achieved during skill acquisition. Consistent tasks can become automatic, fast, effortless within rather short periods of time, whereas inconsistent tasks cannot be processed with automaticity and, therefore, remain largely resource dependent. Task consistency has an effect on the relevance of the various abilities over time. During the first phase, general mental ability is highly important, irrespective of task consistency. Consistent tasks become dependent on perceptual speed ability and psychomotor ability as practice increases; inconsistent tasks, however, remain largely dependent on general mental abilities because attention is needed for successful task completion.

Ackerman and coworkers tested the core propositions of the theory in a series of experiments with various types of tasks. Overall, data provided support for the assumptions (Ackerman, 1988). However, although skill acquisition was assessed over hundred trials of practice, the experiments nevertheless spanned only a relatively short period of time and therefore the generalizability to real-life work situations has been questioned (Keil & Cortina, 2001). Farrell and McDaniel (2001) aimed at testing the Ackerman (1988) model for real jobs. They relied on cross-sectional data from the GATB database and examined the correlations between the different types of ability and supervisor performance ratings by different levels of job experience (ranging between 6 months and 12 years). Graphic plots of correlations over time suggest that for highly consistent jobs, the correlations between cognitive ability and performance decreased over time, whereas they remained rather stable for inconsistent jobs. The correlations between psychomotor ability and performance substantially increased over time for consistent jobs, but increased only slowly for inconsistent jobs. With respect to perceptual speed ability, the findings were less clear and did not challenge the superior importance of cognitive ability. Overall, this study provides partial support for the Ackerman model in the field;

possibly, the use of cross-sectional data may not be fully suitable for testing changes within individuals over time (Sturman, 2007).

Keil and Cortina (2001) tested the Ackerman (1987, 1988) model by using 1,157 correlations from 49 independent studies. Keil and Cortina (2001) categorized the predictors used in the original studies as predictors representing cognitive ability, perceptual speed ability, and psychomotor ability. Tasks were categorized either as consistent or inconsistent. Moreover, they differentiated between studies covering a short time span (one day or less) and studies covering a longer time span (up to five years and even longer). Regression analyses predicting performance from the linear, quadratic, and cubic time component showed that overall the ability-performance correlations decreased over time, irrespective of type of ability and type of task. In addition, there was rather strong evidence for curvilinear, particularly cubic, trends (with a decrease in the correlation between ability and performance in early time periods, a plateauing during intermediate time periods, and a further decrease in late time periods). Keil and Cortina (2001) interpreted such a cubic pattern as a Eureka effect that refers to an insight that causes sudden "jumps" in performance. They concluded that empirical data do not match very well with the specific patterns proposed for different abilities and different type of tasks; they suggested that the relationships between abilities and performance over time might be even more complex than modeled in Ackerman's approach.

Murphy (1989) developed a dynamic model of job performance that overlaps to some degree with Ackerman's work (1987, 1988), but puts more emphasis on job performance (as opposed to task performance). Murphy (1989) suggested two specific stages: a transition stage and a maintenance stage. During *transition stages* (for example, after entering a new job or when major changes of the job occur), job duties, procedures, and methods of operation are new or unknown to the employee. The employee must learn new skills and make decisions in domains with which he or she is not familiar. During such transition stages, job performance depends largely on cognitive ability. During *maintenance stages*, job tasks are well learned and can be performed with little effort by relying on well-learned procedures. Therefore, interindividual differences in cognitive ability are of only minor importance for predicting differences in job performance. Murphy (1989) suggested that personality and motivational factors become more important during maintenance stages. The length of the transitional stage differs between various types of jobs (e.g., it is rather short in traditional assembly line jobs and can last months or even years in more complex jobs) and is also influenced by individual and situational characteristics. Transition stages are not unique phases when entering a new job or when major organizational changes occur; in many jobs, they may happen from time to time when some changes at the workplace happen.

Other Approaches

Sturman (2007) suggested that learning curve theory, used in operations research, could be applied to model dynamic performance over time. This modeling approach states that when a task is repeatedly executed over time, task performance improves and that this improvement can be represented by specific mathematical models. Although learning curve theory has been developed to predict organizational productivity, it might be useful for specifying also the shape of individual performance over time. Sturman (2007) discussed necessary steps to be undertaken before learning curve theory can be fully applied to the prediction of individual performance changes over time. These steps include the development of the appropriate functional form for modeling performance over time, the extension to non-routine tasks, and including the effects of management efforts to increase performance.

Conclusion

Overall, the models of dynamic performance described in this section offer some explanation about how performance develops over time and which individual characteristics predict such performance trends. Empirical research is encouraging for these theoretical models (e.g., Farrell & McDaniel, 2001; Keil & Cortina, 2001); however, the discussion about how to theoretically explain performance trends over time is far from being resolved. Future research will certainly need to rely more on longitudinal designs, try to capture performance in real jobs (as opposed to task performance in comparatively short-term experiments), and be more specific about the type of tasks (or combinations of tasks) within these jobs.

Vicious and Positive Cycles

We have examined predictors of performance trajectories. However, performance may also have an effect on predictors. The literature often assumes that only the predictor of performance

affects performance and that there is no further effect of performance on these predictors. However, hypotheses can be developed in both directions. If high performance has positive effects and low performance has negative effects on these predictors, then positive (virtuous) or negative (vicious) cycles will appear. An example would be that positive emotions have an effect on performance and that performance leads to more positive emotions, for example, job satisfaction (Judge, Thoresen, Bono, & Patton, 2001).

The theoretical starting point for such cycles is reciprocal determinism (Bandura, 1983). Reciprocal determinism implies that "people are both, producers and products of social systems" (Bandura, 1997, p. 6). People have an influence on the social systems surrounding them (e.g., the work group, the organization, the supervisor, the division of labor and workplace) which, in turn, has an influence on how they behave. Performance cycles should appear whenever performance changes those conditions that have an influence on performance. This is particularly so for psychological constructs, which are instrumental in changing conditions. Thus, active forms of performance are more likely to lead to such changes in conditions which, in turn, change the active form of performance. A good example is the effect of self-efficacy on performance and, vice versa, the effect of performance on self-efficacy (Lindsley, Brass, & Thomas, 1995; Shea & Howell, 2000).

A variant of the self-efficacy–performance cycle is the high-performance cycle described by Latham and Locke (2007). High and specific goals plus self-efficacy lead—via the mediators of direction, effort, persistence, and task-specific strategies—to high performance, rewards, and satisfaction, which, in turn, lead to higher commitment to the organization and to an increased willingness to accept challenges, which in turn influence goal setting.

A somewhat similar cycle has also been shown for personal initiative—personal initiative means that people are self-starting (goals are developed and pursued without external pressure, role requirements, or instruction), proactive (prepared for future negative or positive events), and are persistent in overcoming barriers and problems (Frese & Fay, 2001). One set of studies examined longitudinally the effects of job resources on work engagement (composed of vigor, dedication, absorption), of work engagement on personal initiative and of personal initiative on work engagement, and of work engagement on job resources (Hakanen, Perhoniemi, & Toppinen-Tanner, 2008). Most studies have only examined the effect of work engagement on personal initiative—this aspect has been found in several studies, both with daily survey (Sonnentag, 2003) as well as with a longitudinal study design (Lisbona, Palací, Salanova, & Frese, 2008) that was similar to the study of Hakanen et al. (2008). The overall results imply that job resources increase the level of work engagement and that there are reciprocal influences of work engagement and personal initiative.

A second cycle approach examined the interplay between work characteristics—mainly the resources of control and complexity—and personal initiative (Frese et al., 2007). People are supposed to show personal initiative when they can influence conditions at work (control) and when they have the required competencies (resulting from complexity). Thus, control and complexity at work should increase personal initiative. In turn, personal initiative should also lead to increasing control and complexity, because people with high personal initiative may generate some added control and complexity in their given jobs; the tasks of a job are not completely fixed, once and for all, because of emergent elements in a job (Ilgen & Hollenbeck, 1991). For example, if a person develops initiatives to improve productivity, his or her job is changed, and control and complexity are increased; superiors may give high personal initiative employees more responsibilities, which translate into more complex and controllable work tasks. A second mechanism involves job change. People high in personal initiative are likely to look for and make use of opportunities for getting more challenging jobs and for increasing their career success. These predictions were borne out by the data in a longitudinal study with four measurement points (Frese et al., 2007)—this process is mediated by control aspiration (desire to exercise control), perceived opportunity for control (expectation to have control), and self-efficacy (belief in own competence).

The performance cycles may have virtuous or vicious forms. Whenever conditions are low (e.g., control and complexity), they lead to lower active performance. In turn, a low degree of active performance may lead to lower positive conditions. An example may be a study of small business owners: lack of planning contributed to lower success levels (or higher failure rates) of these small businesses. Lack of success also led to a lower degree of planning (Van Gelderen, Frese, & Thurik, 2000). Theoretically, this kind of process can be explained with the threat-rigidity cycle, which was conceptualized to exist on the individual, group, and organizational levels (Staw, Sandelands, & Dutton, 1981). A threatening situation leads to more rigidity in the behavior; however, a higher degree of rigidity also leads to a lower level of performance, because rigidity reduces good information seeking and increases being reactive to the situation rather than attempting to actively influence the situation. Such a reactive approach leads to low performance and is not a very effective strategy for dealing with major problems at work (Van Gelderen et al., 2000).

A positive cycle was also shown by Van Gelderen et al. (2000): good action planning by business owners leads to higher firm performance, but higher firm performance leads to better (and more) planning. This result has been confirmed in a study in Africa (Krauss, Frese, & Friedrich, 2009).

Two of the more controversial hypotheses on cycles are the hypotheses by Lindsley et al. (1995) that spirals lead to a deviation amplification and to an ever increasing (or decreasing) performance. A deviation-amplifying loop exists because "a deviation in one variable (decrease in self-efficacy) leads to a similar deviation in another variable (lower performance), which, in turn, continues to amplify. Thus, the cyclic nature of the self-efficacy–performance relationship can result in a downward (decreasing self-efficacy and performance) or upward (increasing self-efficacy and performance) spiral." (Lindsley et al., 1995, pp. 645). There are two issues here. First, as Shea and Howell (2000, p. 791) point out, the self-efficacy–performance cycle is probably not a never-ending positive cycle upward, because "the pattern of changes in self-efficacy and performance from trial-to-trial contained self-corrections, suggesting that the efficacy-performance relationship does not necessarily proceed in a monotonic, deviation-amplifying spiral." Thus, there are self-correcting, self-regulating processes that lead to asymptotes rather than to never-ending positive or negative cycles. Second, as of yet, there are no good data that suggest a variance increase across time. For example, the study on the cycle of control and complexity at work and personal initiative did not show any increase in variance of performance (and in the predictors) over time (Frese et al., 2007). An action theory analysis may help to understand why this is so (Frese & Zapf, 1994): performance is not only determined by goals, action models of the task and the task environment, action plans, and feedback, but high (and low) performance has an influence on these goals, action models, action plans, and feedback. When there is high performance, people achieve their goals in the action area A. As a result, they turn to other goals (often higher goals; Bandura, 1997) or to goals that are not in the same area. Thus, people may turn to an action area B. Once people turn to the other action area, they reduce attention to action area A; therefore, there is less learning in action area A, and the action plans may become less adaptive to the situation, because attention to feedback is reduced. This may lead to a performance plateau and may actually even reduce performance in action area A over time (Vancouver, 1997). The opposite effect appears when there is low performance, but high or medium aspirations: in this case, attention to achieving the goals in action area A is increased, including the development of better plans and better models of the environment and task structure, and better feedback processing. All of these changes lead to higher performance, which may be stopped when the goal of good (or adequate) performance is reached (and not higher aspirations appear).

Another mechanism that limits upward and downward spirals is caused by over- and underconfidence. Overconfidence may be the result of high performance (Lindsley et al., 1995), but it may lead to risky strategies that reduce performance again (Bandura & Locke, 2003; Vancouver & Kendall, 2006). Similarly, underconfidence is the result of low performance and may lead people to take extra care in preparing for an action (Sonnentag & Volmer, 2009), leading to higher performance. Of course, in any case, there must be a high aspiration level or strong incentives for high performance so that there is striving for high performance.

This section has been on the cycles only; however, it is also possible that dynamic processes lead to some kind of equilibrium or some pendulum movement. For example, if high performance has negative effects on the predictors of performance and if low performance has positive effects on these predictors, some equilibrium or possibly a pendulum movement will appear (Vancouver, 1997). An example would be that job satisfaction leads to higher performance, but performance reduces job satisfaction because too much motivated effort is necessary to keep up high performance, which may have detrimental effects on job satisfaction.

Thus, there is some evidence that cycles or spirals exist. These spirals are probably higher whenever active forms of performance are measured. It is more likely that conditions are changed; when active forms of performance are measured, one of the prerequisites is that both the conditions change active performance, and active performance changes the conditions.

Short-Term Performance Variability Within Persons

Another important aspect of dynamic performance refers to performance variations around a constant mean (Reb & Cropanzano, 2007). An individual's performance does not only change over longer periods of time, but also fluctuates within certain time intervals. Empirical studies have addressed these fluctuations of individual performance not only with respect to task performance (Fisher & Noble, 2004; Stewart & Nandkeolyar, 2006; Trougakos, Beal, Green, & Weiss, 2008), but also with respect to contextual performance dimensions including organizational citizenship behavior (OCB; Ilies et al., 2006) and personal initiative behavior (Binnewies, Sonnentag, & Mojza, 2009; Sonnentag, 2003).

Degree to Which Performance Fluctuates Within Persons

Research using experience-sampling methodology (Beal & Weiss, 2003; Reis & Gable, 2000) and similar approaches (including daily and weekly surveys) provide rather consistent evidence that performance fluctuates substantially within persons. For example, Stewart and Nandkeolyar (2006) examined weekly sales performance of 167 sales persons over a period of 26 weeks and found that 73% of the variance in performance resided within persons. Similarly, a study on the performance of professional football players revealed that 63% of the week-to-week variance in performance was within persons (Stewart & Nandkeolyar, 2007). Trougakos et al. (2008) found that even within small time units, performance varies largely within persons. Within-persons variance in observed performance during a total of eight performance episodes during three days was 48%. Also, Fisher and Noble (2004) reported substantial fluctuation of performance within persons. Specifically, in an experience-sampling study with five measurement occasions per day, these authors found that subjectively rated performance at a given point in time only predicted 3% of subjectively rated performance at the following measurement occasion.

Within-person variability in performance is not limited to task performance; also, contextual performance varies substantially within a person. Ilies et al. (2006) analyzed 825 experience-sampling data points collected from 62 persons over a period of 15 working days. They found that 29% of the total variance in OCB resided within persons. Binnewies et al. (2009), using day-level data from 99 persons, reported that even 50% of the total variance in OCB was within-person variance. Also, proactive behavior such as personal initiative fluctuates within person. In a day-level study on personal initiative as a specific type of proactive behavior, Sonnentag (2003) found that 46% of the total variance was within-person variance. In the study by Binnewies et al. (2009), 56% of the total variance of personal initiative behavior resided within persons.

Taken together, task and contextual performance fluctuate within persons. Interestingly, these within-person fluctuations were found for self-ratings of performance (Fisher & Noble, 2004; Binnewies et al., 2009), as well as for objective performance measures (Stewart & Nandkeolyar, 2006; Trougakos et al., 2008). Analysis of within-persons variance demonstrates that performance is not only dynamic within larger time frames (as demonstrated by research on performance trajectories over months or years; e.g., Ployhart & Hakel, 1998), but varies largely from day to day and from week to week.

A special case of within-day fluctuations of performance around a mean is the circadian rhythm. This 24-hour rhythm has been shown to be biologically based and entrained via social *zeitgebers* (conditions, agents, or events that provide cues to set the biological clock), which regulate the sleep-wake cycle of humans (Aschoff, 1981). Research has shown that performance parameters fluctuate across the day (Daniel & Potašová, 1989; Folkard, 1990). One of the earliest studies of the circadian rhythm was on errors (often conceptualized as the converse of performance; Bjerner, Holm, & Swensson, 1955).

Predictors of Within-Person Fluctuation of Performance

Empirical studies demonstrated that the day-to-day and week-to-week variation in performance within persons can be explained by within-person predictors. In their study using an experience-sampling methodology with a total of more than 3,500 measurement occasions from 114 persons, Fisher and Noble (2004) found that momentary task performance was predicted by perceived skill level (with respect to the specific task), task difficulty, interest, and effort. Effort partially mediated the effect of interest on task performance. Ilies et al. (2006) showed that momentarily experienced states (positive affect, job satisfaction) predicted day-specific organizational citizenship behavior (OCB). On days when employees experienced high levels of positive affect and job satisfaction, they engaged more in OCB. Ilies and his coworkers (2006) further

tested interaction effects between the experienced states and personality variables. A test of cross-level interactions showed that high levels of agreeableness attenuated the effects of positive affect on OCB. Persons with high agreeableness showed relatively high levels of OCB irrespective of their momentary affect, whereas persons with low agreeableness showed OCB when experiencing high levels of positive affect, but not when experiencing low levels of positive affect.

Whereas Fisher and Noble (2004) and Ilies et al. (2006) examined job-domain variables as predictors of short-term performance fluctuations, other authors included experiences from the non-work domain in their analyses. Specifically, Sonnentag (2003) and Binnewies et al. (2009) tested whether feeling recovered (i.e., well-rested; assessed in the morning before work) predicted day-level performance during the working day. Using a daily-survey design, the studies showed that feeling recovered in the morning predicted task performance (Binnewies et al., 2009), OCB (Binnewies et al., 2009), and personal initiative (Binnewies et al., 2009; Sonnentag, 2003) throughout the day. Mediation analysis identified day-specific work engagement (Schaufeli & Bakker, 2004) as the mediator between feeling recovered in the morning and personal initiative behavior. Probably, feeling recovered indicates that regulatory resources are available, which can be invested in the task accomplishment process. A study by Trougakos et al. (2008) supports this view. This study focused on one specific type of task performance, namely affective display in cheerleaders. Using an experience-sampling design, Trougakos and his coauthors showed that positive emotions and respites (i.e., breaks) from previous work efforts were positively related to subsequent task performance.

Studies by Stewart and Nandkeolyar (2006, 2007) demonstrate that not only factors within the performing person, but also influences from other persons impact a person's performance variability. In their study of sales performance, Stewart and Nandkeolyar (2006) identified referrals (i.e., specific information about sales opportunities) from a central office as an important predictor of a salesperson's week-level performance. More than 60% of the variance in a salesperson's weekly performance was explained by referrals from the central office. Moreover, personality variables moderated the relationship between referrals and performance; the relationship was stronger for persons high on conscientiousness and lower for persons high on openness for experience. Following this line of research, Stewart and Nandkeolyar (2007) examined weekly performance of professional football players and found that in this domain, performance fluctuation also can be explained by constraints from outside the focal performing person. More specifically, teammate constraints (i.e., teammates competing for individual performance) and opposition strength were negatively related to weekly performance.

Taken together, research identified affective states, states related to recovery and respites, as well as constraints external to the performing person, as the core predictors of shorter term fluctuations of job performance. This research is not only important for understanding performance dynamics, it is also highly relevant for managing performance in organizations. Of course, one might argue that variations within persons might not matter in the long run, as long as a person's mean performance level is sufficiently high. However, in many modern workplaces it is not enough to show high performance on average, but to perform reliably well on specific days (Sonnentag, Dormann, & Demerouti, 2010). Examples for the importance of having to perform reliably are the implementation of a new technological system within a very short time, or a presentation to be delivered to a very important customer. If individual employees' performance is low on these days, negative consequences, both for the organization and the individual, may be severe—no matter how good the employees' average performance is. Thus, it is crucial that on such days, individuals perform at a high level (i.e., better than their mean level). Moreover, with the increasing importance of customer service quality, it is crucial that employees show good performance at the day level. Poor performance on specific days may directly impact customer satisfaction and cannot be compensated by an overall acceptable performance level averaged across longer periods of time.

Theoretical Models Explaining Within-Person Variability of Performance

Theoretical accounts for within-person fluctuations of performance refer to fluctuating affective states as the core cause of performance variability. Two models received substantial attention during the past decade: affective events theory (Weiss & Cropanzano, 1996) and the episodic process model of performance (Beal et al., 2005).

Affective events theory (Weiss & Cropanzano, 1996) explains fluctuations in job performance by fluctuations in employee affect. More broadly, affective events theory focuses on the structure, causes, and consequences of affective experiences and thereby explicitly acknowledges that affect fluctuates within the person. Work events are regarded as proximal causes of affective reactions that in turn influence behavior and attitudes. Thus, performance as behavior is seen as a consequence of affective experiences resulting from events encountered at work (along with mood cycles and dispositions to experience specific affective states). Weiss and Cropanzano (1996) summarized broad empirical evidence that affect predicts processes relevant for performance. More recent research that tested the theory's propositions about the correspondence between fluctuations in affect and fluctuations in performance is still rare, but generally supports the theoretical assumptions (Ilies et al., 2006; Rothbard & Wilk, 2006).

To explain within-person fluctuations of performance, Beal et al. (2005) proposed a theoretical model that focuses on episodic performance. Performance episodes are relatively short units of behavior that are naturally segmented and organized around rather proximal work-related goals. Typically, one workday comprises several performance episodes. By building on resource allocation models (Kanfer, Ackerman, Murtha, Dugdale, & Nelson, 1994), Beal et al. (2005) suggested that performance within each episode is influenced by the person's general resource level (e.g., cognitive ability, task-relevant skills) and the momentary allocation of resources. Performance within an episode is impaired when the person does not succeed in allocating all necessary resources to the primary work task and when attention is diverted by off-task demands. Affective experiences—along with distractions and interruptions causing specific affective states—are a core source of attentional demands that interfere with the attentional demands of the primary work tasks. Beal et al. (2005) argued that affective experiences reduce episodic performance because these affective experiences call for affect regulation which, in turn, depletes resources that otherwise could be devoted to the task. A recent empirical study provided support for the core assumptions of this model (Beal, Trougakos, Weiss, & Green, 2006). Specifically, it was found that when experiencing negative emotions, persons find it more difficult to regulate their emotions and to follow display rules which, in turn, decreases job performance. More studies are needed that test other facets of the model.

Dynamism Within Performance Action Phases

When describing performance from a dynamic perspective, it is important to not only examine performance trajectories over time, but also to describe performance cycles and pay attention to performance fluctuations within a given period of time. A behavioral performance unit in itself can be viewed as a dynamic process, ranging from setting a goal via planning and executing to feedback processing. Such a perspective on performance is, for example, suggested by action theory (DeShon & Gillespie, 2005; Frese & Zapf, 1994) and control theory (Carver & Scheier, 1998; Vancouver & Day, 2005). These approaches aim at describing the cognitive and motivational processes involved in goal choice and goal pursuit (Chen et al., 2005; DeShon, Kozlowski, Schmidt, Milner, & Wiechman, 2004).

At the conceptual level, phases such as (a) goal development and goal setting, (b) problem analysis and orientation within the problem space, (c) planning, (d) executing and monitoring, and (e) feedback processing can be clearly differentiated. In real-task completion processes, the several phases are very closely intertwined (Sonnentag, 1998). Field studies of performance from such an action perspective require specific process-tracing methods, such as thinking-aloud approaches (Ericsson & Simon, 1993); alternatively, experimental setups help in differentiating between the various phases. There is some empirical support for the idea that action cycles that comprise of all important phases contribute to better performance outcomes than do action processes that are incomplete (Tschan, 2002).

DeShon et al. (2004) proposed a multilevel model of individual performance processes nested in team processes. These authors suggested that situational factors, such as feedback and individual characteristics (for example, mastery and performance orientation), impact individual-level intentions (including individual goals, individual goal commitment, and self-efficacy), which, in turn, influence individual strategies and self-focused effort. An empirical study conducted in a training context provided support for the model, with good individual strategy emerging as the most potent predictor of individual-level performance. Moreover, in support of their multilevel conceptualization, parallel processes emerged at the individual and at the team level. Chen and Kanfer (2006) also addressed individual performance processes within teams and suggested cross-level linkages between team-level and individual-level processes (cf. also Chen, Kirkman, Kanfer, Allen, & Rosen, 2007).

Engagement in action phases (e.g., planning, feedback processing) can also be regarded from a performance trajectory perspective. For example, over time when a person accumulates experience with a specific task or in a specific domain, planning activities will be reduced and feedback processing will be limited to a small set of features (Frese & Zapf, 1994). Research on expertise supports this idea and shows that, compared to beginners, persons with long years of experience in a specific domain show a different approach to task accomplishment (Ericsson & Lehmann, 1996). These studies, however, basically follow cross-sectional designs, and conclusions about real changes over time remain premature (Sturman, 2007). Following changes in action processes over longer periods of times (e.g., months or years) puts great challenges on researchers because it requires good measures of the action phases. Such measures, however, are most often not available in real-world job settings.

Moreover, it would be interesting to examine within-person fluctuations in engagement in action phases (Frese & Zapf, 1994). Fluctuations in task requirements and in affect might be responsible for such fluctuations. For example, goals may change when they are achieved, plans are adjusted when barriers, problems, or errors appear, and feedback processing changes with environmental conditions. Also, when people are in a negative affective state, they tend to process information more systematically than in a more positive affective state (Schwarz & Bohner, 1996). Therefore, one can assume that planning or feedback processing will increase with negative affective states.

Discussion

In this chapter we have looked at issues related to dynamic performance. The term *dynamic performance* seems to imply that two performance concepts exist: (*stable*) *performance* and *dynamic performance*. We do not share this view, but rather maintain that performance is an essentially dynamic process. We believe that all performance research should take into account the concept of time and ask how it relates to the specific research question and how performance may change over time.

We also have consciously restricted ourselves to the individual level of analysis because it seemed too big a task to produce this chapter for other levels of analyses as well. We believe, however, that it is particularly important to think of the dynamic nature of performance also at higher levels of analyses. It is likely that the dynamic nature of performance is highly applicable to groups and organizations (Hackman, 1990; Hambrick & D'Aveni, 1988; Lindsley et al., 1995). We also have not discussed other processes that may be of importance for performance cycles and the dynamics of performance, such as attribution of failure and success (Lindsley et al., 1995). However, as far as we know, there has been little research on propositions involving attributional processes in this area.

Summary of Research Evidence

Research summarized in this chapter showed that performance is not stable over time (see Table 17.2 for an overview). More specifically, studies looking at performance changes within longer periods of time demonstrated that performance scores do not only increase as tenure on the job increases (Quiñones, Ford, & Teachout, 1995; Sturman, 2003; Tesluk & Jacobs, 1998); also, the rank order of individuals' performance scores changes over time (Sturman et al., 2005). This finding implies that an individual, for instance, who performs above average at the beginning of his or her career may show below-average performance after a few years. Studies that explicitly tested performance trends over time largely agree that individuals differ in these trends

(Day et al., 2004; Deadrick et al., 1997). Abilities and personality factors were identified as predictors of the differences in performance trends (Deadrick et al., 1997; Ployhart & Hakel, 1998; Thoresen et al., 2004). Interestingly, performance trends were shown to have implications for employee turnover and for performance ratings (Reb & Cropanzano, 2007; Sturman & Trevor, 2001). Theoretical models aiming at explaining individual differences in performance trends (Ackerman, 1988; Murphy, 1989) have emphasized that it is important to differentiate between various stages within performance trajectories and that individual characteristics differ in their relevance within the various stages.

Taken together, the crucial question of whether performance is dynamic or stable is resolved (Chen & Mathieu, 2008)—performance is both stable to some extent, as well as dynamic. But the knowledge that performance is also dynamic has led to a broad range of further questions that are far from being answered. Until now, theoretical models and empirical studies on performance trends remain largely un-integrated—although there are some important exceptions (e.g., Keil & Cortina, 2001). Furthermore, time frames chosen in the various empirical studies differ greatly, ranging from several hours to months and years. In addition, potential predictors of individual differences in performance

Table 17.2 Summary of Research Evidence on Dynamic Performance

Core Findings and Processes	Predictors of Core Processes	Relevant Theoretical Concepts and Models
Performance is not stable over time, but has a stable component	Time lag between measures Job complexity	Simplex pattern
Persons differ in performance trajectories	Job experience Cognitive ability Personality Team performance Age	Changing-subject, changing-task model skill acquisition model (including distinction between transitional and maintenance stages) Selection-optimization-compensation
Performance and its predictors constitute a cycle	Self-efficacy Work engagement Job complexity Job control	High performance cycle
Performance fluctuates within persons across days and weeks	Affect State of being recovered Task-specific skill Effort Performance opportunities	Affective events theory Episodic process model
Behavioral performance units combine into a dynamic process	Task requirements Affect	Action theory Control theory

trends have not been studied very systematically and differ largely between studies. This situation is understandable if one thinks of the practical difficulties of gathering longitudinal data suitable for modeling performance trends. It seems that researchers often have to use the data that are made available to them—and they do not have substantial say in the decisions about time lags and predictor variables. As a consequence, knowledge remains scattered and scientific progress is slow.

The situation becomes even more complicated if one thinks of the large changes occurring in today's work situations, where tasks and job requirements change rapidly—and maybe not at the same pace for all individuals. These circumstances make it very difficult to disentangle task-related and person-related reasons for performance changes. Moreover, because employees change jobs rather quickly, data for performance trajectories over longer periods of time might be increasingly difficult to gather—and available data (that are often company based) might only reflect performance trends for a relatively small (and nonrepresentative) part of the workforce (i.e., individuals who stay in one company, who may not change jobs frequently, and who may not be very active).

Performance cycles have been shown in three main areas. First, the high performance cycle of goal-setting research has been shown to exist. Here, high and specific goals and high self-efficacy lead to high performance, which, in turn, affects rewards and satisfaction, which, in turn, increase commitment, which in turn affects the willingness to take on challenges of high and specific goals (Latham & Locke, 2007). Second, there is good data showing that self-efficacy leads to higher performance which, in turn, leads to higher self-efficacy (Lindsley et al., 1995, Frese et al., 2007). Finally, personal initiative and engagement as active performance strategies have been shown to affect the work environment so that higher challenges appear. This in turn then leads to higher personal initiative and engagement (Frese et al., 2007). The common theoretical concept of all performance cycles is that an active form of performance or high performance either changes the challenges posed by the work environment, or increases the readiness to accept challenges, which in turn has an influence on these active approaches to performance.

Studies on performance variability within persons have shown that performance fluctuates substantially within persons (Ilies et al., 2006; Stewart & Nandkeolyar, 2006), both from day to day and from week to week. Fluctuating performance levels can be partly explained by factors outside the performing person and partly by factors within the persons. Here, in particular, affective states and other states resulting from recovery and respite experiences play a role. Theoretical models explaining performance fluctuations also largely focused on affective processes.

Toward a Taxonomy of Dynamic Performance

Table 17.3 presents a taxonomy of dynamic performance. On the left vertical side (the y-axis), we describe short- and long-term changes that constitute the forms of the performance changes. Horizontally (the x-axis), we describe the most important factors that produce dynamic performance changes. Not every taxon of this table can be filled (therefore, we call it a partial taxonomy); some can probably be filled with new research, and in a few cases we suggest the building blocks of such new research. Other taxons may not exist (e.g., curvilinear changes in knowledge)—although we should be open to the idea even in such cases (e.g., as a function of age, including very old age). We believe that most taxons could attract a smaller or even larger research tract—in any case, this part of our chapter should contribute to the development of new research ideas. In the following, we describe Table 17.3 by discussing the taxons line by line, starting with long-term changes.

LONG-TERM CHANGES—INCREASING

Long-term changes that increase or lead to a stronger expression of a personality trait or an emotion may appear in knowledge, skills, ability and personality, emotion, and motivation. Knowledge increases as a result of learning processes. At this point, it is necessary to maintain a difference between learning processes and training. While we are not concerned about training interventions in this chapter (because it constitutes direct interventions meant to introduce learning), we should concentrate on those learning processes that take place regardless of training interventions. Much as expertise is developed over time, so is knowledge developed as a result of doing something for a longer period of time (Tesluk & Jacobs, 1998). However, research has persuaded us that expertise is not purely a function of time (in the sense that people increase their knowledge because they are doing something longer), but rather, expertise develops as a function of the time that people spend in processing knowledge in depth. For example, it is not true that purely spending time as a programmer produces expertise in programming; rather, intensity, breadth, and depth of programming leads people to

Table 17.3 A Partial Taxonomy of Dynamic Performance

	Knowledge	Skills	Ability and Personality	Emotion	Motivation
Long-term changes					
Increasing	Learning Deliberate practice	Learning Deliberate practice	Maturation Personality enhancing workplace	Maturation	Maturation
Decreasing	Forgetting	Non-use of skills	Aging Burnout	Aging	Aging
Cycles					
Upward cycle	Self-efficacy–performance	Self-efficacy-performance	Self-efficacy-performance	"Broaden and build"–positive affect	Self-efficacy-performance personal initiative-work characteristics
Downward cycle				Reactive–low performance threat-rigidity cycle	Threat-rigidity cycle
Curvilinear Changes		Relapse to prior habits		Opponent-process	Opponent-process relapse
Short-term changes					
Increasing	Attention and memory		Attention and memory	Affective events–emotion, performance	Extrinsic motivation, escalation of commitment
Decreasing	Forgetting Fatigue	Monotony Fatigue	Attention reduction Fatigue	Fatigue	Fatigue
Daily fluctuation	Circadian rhythm	Circadian rhythm	Circadian rhythm		Circadian rhythm

be called experts by their peers (Sonnentag, 1996, 1998). This type of expertise can be developed by deliberate practice, for example, with the help of a coach (Ericsson & Lehmann, 1996), or when people force themselves to work on issues that are difficult and that lead to a maximal increase of knowledge and expertise (Sonnentag, 2000; Sonnentag & Kleine, 2000; Unger, Keith, Hilling, Gielnik, & Frese, 2009).

A similar process to the development of knowledge also appears in skill development; the increase of skills is an important part of expertise, and there are interactions of skills and knowledge (Chase & Simon, 1973). An additional issue here is, however, that skill development if often developed in a tacit

way (Myers & Davids, 1993) and, therefore, cannot be verbalized.

Ability can increase and decrease depending upon the complexity of work. Age-dependent reductions of cognitive ability occur more frequently in non-complex work (Schallberger, 1988; Schleicher, 1973; Schooler et al., 1999). Personality traits also change with age. Often, such a change seems to be related to maturity—older people tend to take fewer risks and are less open to experience. However, they are more likely to be conscientious and emotionally stable. "People become more socially dominant, conscientious, and emotionally stable mostly in young adulthood, but in several cases also in middle and old age. We found that individuals demonstrated gains in social vitality and openness to experience early in life and then decreases in these two trait domains in old age" (Roberts, Walton, & Viechtbauer, 2006). Also, wisdom increases with age (Baltes & Staudinger, 1993). Thus, maturation may be a natural process of time that affects both ability and personality. Maturation also plays a role in emotional and motivational long-term changes.

LONG-TERM CHANGES—DECREASING

The second row discusses decreases of knowledge, skills, ability, emotions, and motivation—here, aging plays a pivotal role. Forgetting is an important process that leads to a reduction of knowledge and skills. Forgetting may be a function of time-decay (Portrat, Barrouillet, & Camos, 2008) or of interference of new information (Oberauer & Kliegl, 2006). For skills, non-use may be most important for its loss. Finally, burnout effects in the sense of exhaustion (in contrast to energy), cynicism (in contrast to involvement), and inefficacy (in contrast to efficacy) may also be a function of time in a specific and stressful environment (Maslach & Leiter, 2008).

CYCLES UPWARD AND DOWNWARD

Upward and downward cycles appear in nearly all areas. We have already discussed the self-efficacy–performance cycle as an example. A specific instance of such a cycle is the cycle described by Frese et al. (2007): self-efficacy leads to higher performance; it also leads to an increase in the complexity and controllability of the work tasks, which, in turn, leads to higher self-efficacy (Frese et al., 2007, among others, have shown such job enrichment as a result of control orientation, which includes self-efficacy).

Upward and downward cycles also exist in the areas of ability and motivation. The "broaden and build" theory of positive emotions is related to such a cycle; it shows positive emotions to have a positive influence on that type of performance that needs to incorporate new information (such as innovation tasks; Fredrickson & Losada, 2005). The emotional-cycle view assumes that the "broaden and build" theory of emotion leads to more challenging work (because people are open to innovations); good performance in innovative tasks leads to positive affect, which, in turn, would increase openness to innovation tasks (Fredrickson & Losada, 2005). In the field of motivation, there is both the self-efficacy–performance cycle as well as the personal-initiative–work characteristics cycle (control and complexity). Both of these have been described above.

The downward cycles can all be the obverse of the above effects—thus, low self-efficacy can cycle downward because people do not take up challenges, do not work hard on complex and controllable tasks and, therefore, the challenges are reduced, which leads to low self-efficacy. The opposite of personal initiative is a reactive strategy, which leads to lack of success, which, in turn, leads to a higher degree of reactive strategy in small business (Van Gelderen et al., 2000). A specific negative cycle is the threat-rigidity cycle: individual or organizational threat leads to individual or organizational rigidity, which produces reactive approaches, which, in turn, lead to higher threat (Staw et al., 1981).

CURVILINEAR CHANGES

The area of curvilinear changes is more difficult to discuss. One of the curvilinear changes that appear in skills is reverting back to old habits. Psychoanalytic and behaviorist theorists have called this phenomenon habit regression (Mowrer, 1940). Habit regression appears when two conflicting habits have been developed sequentially (one habit is older than the other) and some frustration or conflicting environmental cues are added. This often leads to regressing (reverting back) to the older habits (Mowrer, 1940). This is important at work when workers revert back to older habits under time pressure or when people are again in the environment in which old habits had developed. This phenomenon is similar to regression because the old habits were originally developed in the work environment; in this case, the new behavior may also not have been developed into a habit yet (i.e., these newly acquired behaviors have not been routinized yet). In this case, the conscious decision to use the new behaviors learned in the training program cannot be put into effect because of cognitive interference due to double tasks or time pressure. Thus, relapse to old habits ensues. Relapse has been a topic of high importance in clinical psychology (Semmer & Frese, 1985), and treatments have been discussed as to how well they prevent relapse—developing explicit skills against relapse may function particularly well (Hollon et al., 2005; Strunk, DeRubeis, Chiu, & Alvarez, 2007). The issue of relapse has not been an important topic in industrial and organizational psychology; however, similar concepts, such as rigidity, resistance toward change in organizational development (Cummings & Worley, 1993), structural inertia of organizations (Aldrich, 1999), and entropy in system theory (Katz & Kahn, 1978) have attempted to describe something similar—the tendencies of individuals and organizations not to change, although the need to change may be accepted. Probably, there is a large overlap of these terms regarding relapse to prior habits and routines.

In motivation, this relapse to older habits plays a large role as well (e.g., if one is not really motivated to show the new behavior at the workplace). In addition, a motivational theory, called the opponent process theory of motivation, might be used to explain curvilinear changes as inherent processes of motivation and emotion: "The theory assumes that many hedonic, affective, or emotional states are automatically opposed by central nervous system mechanisms which reduce the intensity of hedonic feelings, both pleasant and aversive. The opponent processes for most hedonic states are strengthened by use and are weakened by disuse" (Solomon & Corbit, 1974, p. 119). This theory can also explain how adaptation processes appear so that cycles do not continue forever.

SHORT-TERM CHANGES—INCREASING

Short term increases of attention may have an influence on the development of knowledge. What we attend to can be stored in memory, and what we attend to will be rehearsed enough to be kept in memory. Emotional processes are a function of affective events, as described above (Weiss & Cropanzano, 1996). Motivational theory is full of descriptions of how motivation can be increased on a short-term basis by changes at work—usually via extrinsic motivation. Often positive reinforcement is seen to produce short-term changes (that are also reduced again, if reinforcements are withdrawn; Eisenberger, Pierce, & Cameron, 1999). Motivational processes may be enhanced too much in the sense of escalation of commitment (Staw & Ross, 1987). While escalation of commitment has positive effects on performance that is the target of motivation (in the sense of working harder, but not in the sense of working smarter), alternative routes and plans for goal achievement may also get rejected, or they are not attended to. Thus, a state of over-motivation for one approach can be observed.

SHORT-TERM CHANGES—DECREASING

A short-term decrease of knowledge, skills, ability, motivation, and so on, can be observed as a result of fatigue. Mental fatigue can be defined as "a psychophysiological state resulting from sustained performance on cognitively demanding tasks and coinciding with changes in motivation, information processing, and mood" (van der Linden, Frese, &

Sonnentag, 2003, p. 484). Fatigue leads to higher rigidity, a lower degree of planning, and a higher degree of errors, as well as to a lower degree of motivation (Lorist et al., 2000; van der Linden, Frese, & Meijman, 2003). One of the results of fatigue is a reduction of attention (van der Linden & Eling, 2006). All of this leads to decreased performance. However, this decrease of performance is not absolute (and often not observable at work), because people often compensate the effects of fatigue with different strategies or enhanced effort (Meijman & Mulder, 1998; Sperandio, 1971).

PERFORMANCE FLUCTUATION

Performance fluctuations within days are tied to the circadian rhythm. We have discussed the circadian rhythm above and do not need to repeat it here. The important issue is that performance fluctuations are regulated by the circadian rhythm; this means that humans typically show a higher performance at certain times across the day (e.g., between 6:00 and 9:00 A.M. or at around 6:00 P.M.). The lowest level of performance is likely to be at around 3:00 A.M. The interesting finding here is that these effects appear regardless of whether people have already worked for eight hours or are just starting their workday; there seems to be a seamless performance cycle as a result of the circadian rhythm (Bjerner et al., 1955).

Further Avenues for Future Research

As described above, research on dynamic performance still appears rather unsystematic and sometimes lacks a clear theoretical focus. This is particularly the case for performance trajectories over longer periods of time, but also applies to other aspects of dynamic performance. We propose an agenda for future research on dynamic performance that addresses four core issues: (a) advancing theory on dynamic performance, (b) using a more systematic approach for studying performance trajectories over time, (c) including contextual performance in the study of performance trajectories, and (d) paying more attention to performance fluctuation within persons.

With respect to advancement in theory building, it seems reasonable to build on existing models of performance change over time (Ackerman, 1988; Murphy, 1989) and to continue the differentiation between various stages of performance trajectories. Moreover, it is necessary that the time frames for performance changes are specified in some detail—taking into account that the time frames might differ largely between various types of jobs. Although the existing models on performance change over time are already reasonably complex, even more comprehensive theoretical approaches might be useful. For example, these approaches should aim at combining abilities and skills with personality factors in predicting individual differences in performance trajectories. Moreover, better integration of theory and empirical research is necessary.

When it comes to empirical studies, a more systematic approach, which includes longitudinal data sets, is highly needed—and these longitudinal data sets probably also need longer time frames than is typical of research at the moment (cf. the longitudinal studies surveyed by Ng and Feldman, 2008, covered an average time period of only 11 months). This can be achieved by designing studies more systematically with respect to type of jobs, time frames, and type of predictor variables. It is also useful to do studies in critical transition stages, as suggested by Ng and Feldman (2008).

Another option might be to achieve some systematization by meta-analytical approaches that summarize findings from a large database of studies. However, at this moment in time, we do not have sufficient primary studies that qualify for inclusion in such a quantitative review. For increasing our understanding of longer term performance dynamics (i.e., performance trajectories over time), longitudinal studies are essential. Sturman (2007) suggested that such studies, using hierarchical linear modeling or latent growth curve approaches, might want to build on learning curve theory developed in operations research. When implementing these suggestions, researchers have to develop innovative approaches about how to deal with problems typical for longitudinal research, such as missing data. Often, it is not known whether missing data are random or non-random. This difficulty becomes evident when looking at the relationship between performance trends and turnover (Harrison et al., 1996; Sturman & Trevor, 2001) suggesting that turnover does not represent random dropout of study participants, but that it is closely intertwined with performance changes over time.

Interestingly, research on performance trends over time has largely focused on task performance. Other aspects of performance (OCB, proactive behavior) have been neglected (an exception is the meta-analysis by Ng and Feldman [2008] on aging and performance). For example, it is more than plausible to assume that within specific work settings, individual citizenship behaviors increase (or decrease) over time. Similarly, proactive behaviors such as personal initiative might not be stable over one's career, but the increase might be influenced by features of the job situation. For example, job control and supportive supervision might increase personal initiative over time (i.e., predict a positive trend), whereas lack of control and discouragement from the supervisor might predict a negative trend.

The degree to which performance fluctuates within a person has not received much research attention. Therefore, future research should address such performance fluctuations more thoroughly. For example, employees may differ in the degree to which their performance fluctuates from day to day or from week to week. Of course, from the perspective of an organization, it is preferable to have as little fluctuation in employees' performance as possible. Life-span development research showed performance variability within persons to increase with age (MacDonald, Hultsch, & Dixon, 2003; Murphy, West, Armilio, Craik, & Stuss, 2007). However, very little is known about predictors of performance variability within persons who are still participating within the workforce. Thus, studies are needed that treat performance variability within person as an *outcome*. Here, it might be also interesting to link research on performance trends with research on performance variability within persons. For example, performance variability might decrease at later stages of performance trajectories.

In addition to these core issues to be addressed in future research, other research questions are also important and seem promising. First, it would be interesting to examine how engagement in various performance phases (e.g., planning, feedback processing) unfolds its dynamics. For example, explicit planning probably decreases over time. Moreover, changes in the performance process might be related differently to performance outcomes at various stages of a performance trajectory. Second, most studies on performance trajectories did not provide much information about HR interventions that might have occurred during the study time. For example, trainings and other HR practices might boost performance levels over time. Sturman (2007) suggested that future studies might want to explicitly look at the effects of HR interventions on performance trajectories. Third, in this chapter we focused on the "positive" aspects of performance. Scholars have argued that a broad performance concept should also incorporate counterproductive behavior (Penney & Spector, 2005; Rotundo & Sackett, 2002). Therefore, it would be an exiting endeavor to examine also counterproductive behavior from a dynamic perspective. Fourth, very little is known about the boundary conditions of performance variability within persons. For example, in highly structured work settings with low levels of job control performance, variability might be much smaller than in settings where employees can decide themselves about how to do their jobs (cf., Binnewies et al., 2009).

Conclusion

Overall, research on dynamic performance is a very exciting area within industrial and organizational psychology. It is a particularly interesting and challenging topic because it tries to disentangle the processes underlying performance and because it promises to add to our understanding of how high job performance comes about. Many questions are still unresolved, and the various aspects of dynamic-performance research still remain un-integrated. However, we are optimistic that in this research area much progress will be made within the years to come.

References

Ackerman, P. L. (1987). Individual differences in skill learning: An integration of psychometric and information processing perspectives. *Psychological Bulletin, 102,* 3–27.

Ackerman, P. L. (1988). Determinants of individual differences during skill acquisition: Cognitive abilities and information processing. *Journal of Experimental Psychology: General, 117,* 288–318.

Ackerman, P. L., & Cianciolo, A. T. (2000). Cognitive, perceptual-speed, and psychomotor determinants of individual differences during skill acquisition. *Journal of Experimental Psychology: Applied, 6,* 259–290.

Adams, J. A. (1957). The relationship between certain measures of ability and the acquisition of a psychomotor criterion response. *The Journal of General Psychology, 56,* 121–134.

Aldrich, H. E. (1999). *Organizations evolving.* London: Sage.

Alvares, K. M., & Hulin, C. L. (1972). Two explanations of temporal changes in ability-skill relationships: A literature review and theoretical analysis. *Human Factors, 14,* 295–308.

Anderson, J. R. (1982). Acquisition of cognitive skill. *Psychological Review, 89,* 369–406.

Aschoff, J. (1981). Circadian rhythms: Interference with and dependency: On work rest schedules. In L. Johnson, D. I. Tepas, W. P. Caolquoun, & M. J. Colligan (Eds.), *The twenty four hour workday: Proceedings of a symposium on variations in work sleep schedules* (pp. 13–50). Cincinnati, OH: National Institute of Occupational Safety and Health.

Ashford, S. J., & Tsui, A. S. (1991). Self-regulation for managerial effectiveness: The role of active feedback seeking. *The Academy of Management Journal, 34,* 251–280.

Bajor, J. K., & Baltes, B. B. (2003). The relationship between selection optimization with compensation, conscientiousness, motivation, and performance. *Journal of Vocational Behavior, 63,* 347–367.

Baltes, P. B. (1997). On the incomplete architecture of human ontogeny: Selection, optimization, and compensation as foundation of developmental theory. *American Psychologist, 52,* 366–380.

Baltes, P. B., & Staudinger, U. M. (1993). The search for a psychology of wisdom. *Current Directions in Psychological Science, 2,* 1–6.

Baltes, P. B., Staudinger, U. M., & Lindenberger, U. (1999). Lifespan psychology: Theory and application to intellectual functioning. *Annual Review of Psychology, 50,* 471–507.

Bandura, A. (1983). Temporal dynamics and decomposition of reciprocal determinism: A reply to Phillips and Orton. *Psychological Review, 90,* 166–170.

Bandura, A. (1997). *Self-efficacy: The exercise of control.* New York: Freeman.

Bandura, A., & Locke, E. A. (2003). Negative self-efficacy and goal effects revisited. *Journal of Applied Psychology, 88,* 87–99.

Barrick, M. R., & Alexander, R. A. (1987). A review of quality circle efficacy and the existence of positive findings bias. *Personnel Psychology, 40,* 579–592.

Beal, D. J., Trougakos, J. P., Weiss, H. M., & Green, S. G. (2006). Episodic processes in emotional labor: Perceptions of affective delivery and regulation strategies. *Journal of Applied Psychology, 91,* 1053–1065.

Beal, D. J., & Weiss, H. M. (2003). Methods of ecological momentary assessment in organizational research. *Organizational Research Methods, 6,* 440–464.

Beal, D., J., Weiss, H. M., Barros, E., & MacDermid, S. M. (2005). An episodic process model of affective influences on performance. *Journal of Applied Psychology, 90,* 1054–1068.

Bell, B. S., & Kozlowski, S. W. J. (2008). Active learning: Effects of core training design elements on self-regulatory processes, learning, and adaptability. *Journal of Applied Psychology, 93,* 296–316.

Binnewies, C., Sonnentag, S., & Mojza, E. J. (2009). Daily performance at work: Feeling recovered in the morning as a predictor of day-level job performance. *Journal of Organizational Behavior, 30,* 67–93.

Bjerner, B., Holm, A., & Swensson, A. (1955). Diurnal variation in mental performance: A study of three-shift workers. *British Journal of Industrial Medicine, 12,* 103–110.

Borman, W. C., & Motowidlo, S. J. (1993). Expanding the criterion domain to include elements of contextual performance. In N. Schmitt & W. Borman (Eds.), *Personnel selection in organizations* (pp. 71–98). New York: Jossey-Bass.

Borman, W. C., Penner, L. A., Allen, T. D., & Motowidlo, S. J. (2001). Personality predictors of citizenship performance. *International Journal of Selection and Assessment, 9,* 52–59.

Campbell, J. P. (1990). Modeling the performance prediction problem in industrial and organizational psychology. In M. D. Dunnette & L. M. Hough (Eds.), *Handbook of industrial and organizational psychology* (Vol. 1, pp. 687–732). Palo Alto, CA: Consulting Psychologists Press.

Campbell, J. P., McCloy, R. A., Oppler, S. H., & Sager, C. E. (1993). A theory of performance. In N. Schmitt & W. C. Borman (Eds.), *Personnel selection in organizations* (pp. 35–70). San Francisco: Jossey-Bass.

Carver, C. S., & Scheier, M. F. (1998). *On the self-regulation of behavior.* Cambridge: Cambridge University Press.

Chase, W. G., & Simon, H. A. (1973). Perception in chess. *Cognitive Psychology, 4,* 55–81.

Chen, C. C., & Mathieu, J. E. (2008). Goal orientation dispositions and performance trajectories: The roles of supplementary and complementary situational inducements. *Organizational Behavior and Human Decision Processes, 106*, 21–38.

Chen, G. (2005). Newcomer adaptation in teams: Multilevel antecedents and outcomes. *Academy of Management Journal, 48*, 101–116.

Chen, G., & Kanfer, R. (2006). Toward a systems theory of motivated behavior in work teams. *Research in Organizational Behavior, 27*, 223–267.

Chen, G., Kirkman, B. L., Kanfer, R., Allen, D., & Rosen, B. (2007). A multilevel study of leadership, empowerment, and performance in teams. *Journal of Applied Psychology, 92*, 331–346.

Chen, G., Thomas, B., & Wallace, J. C. (2005). A multilevel examination of the relationships among training outcomes, mediating regulatory processes, and adaptive performance. *Journal of Applied Psychology, 90*, 827–841.

Cummings, G., & Worley, C. G. (1993). *Organizational development and change* (5th ed.). Minneapolis, MA: West Publishing.

Daniel, J., & Potašová, A. (1989). Oral temperature and performance in 8 h and 12 h shifts. *Ergonomics, 32*, 689–696.

Day, D. V., Sin, H.-P., & Chen, T. T. (2004). Assessing the burdens of leadership: Effects of formal leadership roles on individual performance over time. *Personnel Psychology, 57*, 573–605.

Deadrick, D. L., Bennett, N., & Russell, C. J. (1997). Using hierarchical linear modeling to examine dynamic performance criteria over time. *Journal of Management, 23*, 745–757.

DeShon, R. D., & Gillespie, J. Z. (2005). A motivated action theory account of goal orientation. *Journal of Applied Psychology, 90*, 1096–1127.

DeShon, R. P., Kozlowski, S. W. J., Schmidt, A. M., Milner, K. R., & Wiechman, D. (2004). A multiple-goal, multilevel model of feedback effects on the regulation of individual and team performance. *Journal of Applied Psychology, 89*, 1035–1056.

Eisenberger, R., Pierce, W. D., & Cameron, J. (1999). Effects of reward on intrinsic motivation—negative, neutral, and positive: Comment on Deci, Koestner, and Ryan (1999). *Psychological Bulletin, 125*, 669–677.

Ericsson, K. A., & Lehmann, A. C. (1996). Expert and exceptional performance: Evidence of maximal adaptation to task constraints. *Annual Review of Psychology, 47*, 273–305.

Ericsson, K. A., & Simon, H. A. (1993). *Protocol analysis: Verbal reports as data* (Rev. ed.). Cambridge, MA: Massachusetts Institute of Technology.

Farrell, J. N., & McDaniel, M. A. (2001). The stability of validity coefficients over time: Ackerman's (1988) model and the General Aptitude Test Battery. *Journal of Applied Psychology, 86*, 60–79.

Fisher, C. D., & Noble, C. S. (2004). A within-person examination of correlates of performance and emotions while working. *Human Performance, 17*, 145–168.

Folkard, S. (1990). Circadian performance rhythms: Some practical and theoretical implications. In D. E. Broadbent, J. T. Reason & A. D. Baddeley (Eds.), *Human factors in hazardous situations* (pp. 95–105). New York: Clarendon Press/Oxford University Press.

Fredrickson, B. L., & Losada, M. F. (2005). Positive affect and the complex dynamics of human flourishing. *American Psychologist, 60*, 678–686.

Frese, M., & Fay, D. (2001). Personal Initiative (PI): A concept for work in the 21st century. *Research in Organizational Behavior, 23*, 133–188.

Frese, M., Garst, H., & Fay, D. (2007). Making things happen: Reciprocal relationships between work characteristics and personal initiative (PI) in a four-wave longitudinal structural equation model. *Journal of Applied Psychology, 92*, 1084–1102.

Frese, M., Kring, W., Soose, A., & Zempel, J. (1996). Personal initiative at work: Differences between East and West Germany. *Academy of Management Journal, 39*, 37–63.

Frese, M., & Zapf, D. (1994). Action as the core of work psychology: A German approach. In H. C. Triandis, M. D. Dunnette & L. Hough (Eds.), *Handbook of industrial and organizational psychology* (Vol. 4, pp. 271–340). Palo Alto, California: Consulting Psychologists Press.

Ghiselli, E. E., & Haire, M. (1960). The validation of selection tests in the light of the dynamic character of criteria. *Personnel Psychology, 13*, 225–231.

Grant, A. M., & Ashford, S. J. (2008). The dynamics of proactivity at work. *Research in Organizational Behavior, 28*, 3–34.

Griffin, M. A., Neal, A., & Parker, S. K. (2007). A new model of work role performance: Positive behavior in uncertain and interdependent contexts. *Academy of Management Journal, 50*, 327–347.

Hacker, W. (1998). *Allgemeine Arbeitspsychologie* [General work psychology]. Bern: Huber.

Hackman, R. (1990). Groups that work (and those that don't): Creating conditions for effective teamwork. San Francisco: Jossey-Bass.

Hakanen, J. J., Perhoniemi, R., & Toppinen-Tanner, S. (2008). Positive gain spirals at work: From job resources to work engagement, personal initiative and work-unit innovativeness. *Journal of Vocational Behavior, 73*, 78–91.

Hambrick, D. C., & D'Aveni, R. A. (1988). Large corporate failures as downward spirals. *Administrative Science Quarterly, 33*, 1–23.

Hanges, P. J., Schneider, B., & Niles, K. (1990). Stability of performance: An interactionist perspective. *Journal of Applied Psychology, 75*, 658–667.

Harrison, D. A., Virick, M., & William, S. (1996). Working without a net: Time, performance, and turnover under maximally contingent rewards. *Journal of Applied Psychology, 81*, 331–345.

Henry, R. A., & Hulin, C. L. (1987). Stability of skilled performance across time: Some generalizations and limitations on utilities. *Journal of Applied Psychology, 72*, 457–462.

Hoffman, B. J., Blair, C. A., Meriac, J. P., & Woehr, D. J. (2007). Expanding the criterion domain? A quantitative review of the OCB literature. *Journal of Applied Psychology, 92*, 555–566.

Hofmann, D. A., Jacobs, R., & Baratta, J. E. (1993). Dynamic criteria and the measurement of change. *Journal of Applied Psychology, 78*, 194–204.

Hofmann, D. A., Jacobs, R., & Gerras, S. J. (1992). Mapping individual performance over time. *Journal of Applied Psychology, 77*, 185–195.

Hollon, S. D., DeRubeis, R. J., Shelton, R. C., Amsterdam, J. D., Salomon, R. M., O'Reardon, J. P., et al. (2005). Prevention of relapse following cognitive therapy vs. medications in moderate to severe depression. *Archives of General Psychiatry, 62*, 417–422.

Hulin, C. L., Henry, R. A., & Noon, S. L. (1990). Adding a dimension: Time as a factor in the generalizability of predictive relationships. *Psychological Bulletin, 107*, 328–340.

Humphreys, L. G. (1960). Investigating the simplex. *Psychometrika, 25*, 313–323.

Ilgen, D. R., & Hollenbeck, J. R. (1991). The structure of work: Job design and roles. In M. D. Dunnette & L. M. Hough (Eds.), *Handbook of industrial and organizational psychology* (Vol. 2, pp. 165–208). Palo Alto, CA: Consulting Psychologists Press.

Ilies, R., Scott, B. A., & Judge, T. A. (2006). The interactive effects of personal traits and experienced states on intraindividual patterns of citizenship behavior. *Academy of Management Journal, 49*, 561–575.

Judge, T. A., Thoresen, C. J., Bono, J. E., & Patton, G. K. (2001). The job satisfaction-performance relationship: A qualitative and quantitative review. *Psychological Bulletin, 127*, 376–407.

Joung, W., Hesketh, B., & Neal, A. (2006). Using war stories to train for adaptive performance: Is it better to learn from error or success? *Applied Psychology: An International Review, 55*, 282–302.

Kanfer, R., & Ackerman, P. L. (2004). Aging, adult development, and work motivation. *Academy of Management Review, 29*, 440–458.

Kanfer, R., Ackerman, P. L., Murtha, T. C., Dugdale, B., & Nelson, L. (1994). Goal setting, conditions of practice, and task performance: A resource allocation perspective. *Journal of Applied Psychology, 79*, 826–835.

Katz, D., & Kahn, R. L. (1978). *Social psychology of organizations* (2nd ed.). New York: Wiley.

Keil, C. T., & Cortina, J. M. (2001). Degradation of validity over time: A test and extension of Ackerman's model. *Psychological Bulletin, 127*, 673–697.

Kohn, M. L., & Schooler, C. (1978). The reciprocal effects of the substantive complexity of work and intellectual flexibility: A longitudinal assessment. *American Journal of Sociology, 84*, 24–52.

Kozlowski, S. W. J., Gully, S. M., McHugh, P. P., Salas, E., & Cannon-Bowers, J. A. (1996). A dynamic theory of leadership and team effectiveness: Developmental and task contingent leader roles. In G. R. Ferris (Ed.), *Research in personnel and human resource management* (Vol. 14, pp. 253–305). Greenwich, CT: JAI Press.

Kozlowski, S. W. J., Gully, S. M., Nason, E. R., & Smith, E. M. (1999). Developing adaptive teams: A theory of compilation and performance across levels and time. In D. R. Ilgen & E. D. Pulakos (Eds.), *The changing nature of work performance: Implications for staffing, personnel actions, and development* (pp. 240–292). San Francisco: Jossey-Bass.

Kozlowski, S. W. J., Gully, S. M., Brown, K. G., Salas, E., Smith, E. M., & Nason, E. R. (2001). Effects of training goals and goal orientation traits on multidimensional training outcomes and performance adaptability. *Organizational Behavior and Human Decision Making Processes, 85*, 1–31.

Krauss, S. I., Frese, M., & Friedrich, C. (2009). Longitudinal effects of planning and entrepreneurial orientation on performance and vice versa: The case of performance cycles. National University of Singapore: Manuscript.

Lang, J. W. B., & Bliese, P. D. (2009). General mental ability and two types of adaptation to unforeseen change: Applying discontinuous growth models to the task-change paradigm. *Journal of Applied Psychology, 94*, 411–428.

Latham, G. P., & Locke, E, A, (2007). New developments in and directions for goal-setting research. *European Psychologist, 12*, 290–300.

Lawrence, J. W., Carver, C. S., & Scheier, M. F. (2002). Velocity toward goal attainment in immediate experience as a determinant of affect. *Journal of Applied Social Psychology, 32*, 788–802.

LePine, J. A. (2003). Team adaptation and postchange performance: Effects of team composition in terms of members' cognitive ability and personality. *Journal of Applied Psychology, 88*, 27–39.

LePine, J. A., Colquitt, J. A., & Erez, A. (2000). Adaptability to changing task contexts: Effects of general cognitive ability, conscientiousness, and openness to experience. *Personnel Psychology, 53*, 563–593.

LePine, J. A., & Van Dyne, L. (2001). Voice and cooperative behavior as contrasting forms of contextual performance: Evidence of differential relationships with Big Five personality characteristics and cognitive ability. *Journal of Applied Psychology, 86*(2), 326–336.

Lindsley, D. H., Brass, D. J., & Thomas, J. B. (1995). Efficacy-performance spirals: A multilevel perspective. *Academy of Management Review, 20*, 645–678.

Lipsey, M. W., & Wilson, D. B. (1993). The efficacy of psychological, educational, and behavioral treatment. *American Psychologist, 48*, 1181–1209.

Lisbona, A., Palací, F. J., Salanova, M., & Frese, M. (2008). The effects of work engagement and self-efficacy on personal initiative and performance. *submitted for publication.*

Lorist, M. M., Klein, M., Nieuwenhuis, S., De Jong, R., Mulder, G., & Meijman, T. F. (2000). Mental fatigue and task control: Planning and preparation. *Psychophysiology, 37*, 614–625.

Luthans, R., Paul, R., & Baker, D. (1981). An experimental analysis of the impact of contingent reinforcement on sales persons' performance behavior. *Journal of Applied Psychology, 66*, 314–323.

MacDonald, S. W. S., Hultsch, D. F., & Dixon, R. A. (2003). Performance variability is related to change in cognition: Evidence from the Victoria Longitudinal Study. *Psychology and Aging, 18*, 510–523.

Macey, W. H., & Schneider, B. (2008). The meaning of employee engagement. *Industrial and Organizational Psychology: Perspectives on Science and Practice, 1*, 3–30.

Marks, M. A., Mathieu, J. E., & Zaccaro, S. J. (2001). A temporally based framework and taxonomy of team processes. *Academy of Management Review, 26*, 356–376.

Maslach, C., & Leiter, M. P. (2008). Early predictors of job burnout and engagement. *Journal of Applied Psychology, 93*, 498–512.

McAllister, D. J., Kamdar, D., Morrison, E. W., & Turban, D. B. (2007). Disentangling role perceptions: How perceived role breadth, discretion, instrumentality, and efficacy relate to helping and taking charge. *Journal of Applied Psychology, 92*, 1200–1211.

Meijman, T. F., & Mulder, G. (1998). Psychological aspects of workload. In P. J. D. Drenth, H. Thierry & C. J. De Wolff (Eds.), *Handbook of work and organizational psychology* (2nd ed., Vol. 1, pp. 5–33). London: Psychology Press.

Morrison, E. W., & Phelps, C. C. (1999). Taking charge at work: Extrarole efforts to initiative workplace change. *Academy of Management Journal, 42*, 403–419.

Motowidlo, S. J. (2003). Job performance. In W. C. Borman, D. R. Ilgen & R. J. Klimoski (Eds.), *Handbook of psychology*, Volume 12, *Industrial and organizational psychology* (pp. 39–53). Hoboken, NJ: Wiley.

Motowidlo, S. J., Borman, W. C., & Schmit, M. J. (1997). A theory of individual differences in task and contextual performance. *Human Performance, 10*, 71–83.

Motowidlo, S. J., & Van Scotter, J. R. (1994). Evidence that task performance should be distinguished from contextual performance. *Journal of Applied Psychology, 79*, 475–480.

Mowrer, O. H. (1940). An experimental analogue of "regression" with incidental observations on "reaction-formation." *The Journal of Abnormal and Social Psychology, 35*, 56–87.

Murphy, K. R. (1989). Is the relationship between cognitive ability and job performance stable over time? *Human Performance, 2*, 183–200.

Murphy, K. R., & Cleveland, J. N. (1995). *Understanding performance appraisal: Social, organizational, and goal-based perspectives.* Thousand Oaks, CA: Sage.

Murphy, K. J., West, R., Armilio, M. L., Craik, F. I. M., & Stuss, D. T. (2007). Word-list-learning performance in younger and older adults: Intra-individual performance variability and false memory. *Aging, Neuropsychology, and Cognition, 14*, 70–94.

Myers, C., & Davids, K. (1993). Tacit skill and performance at work. *Applied Psychology: An International Review, 42*, 117–137.

Nesselroade, J. R. (1991). Interindividual differences in intraindividual change. In L. M. Collins & J. L. Horn (Eds.), *Best methods for the analysis of change: Recent advances, unanswered questions, future directions* (pp. 95–105). Washington, DC: American Psychological Association.

Ng, T. W. H., & Feldman, D. C. (2008). The relationship of age to ten dimensions of job performance. *Journal of Applied Psychology, 93*, 392–423.

Oberauer, K., & Kliegl, R. (2006). A formal model of capacity limits in working memory. *Journal of Memory and Language, 55*, 601–626.

Organ, D. W. (1988). *Organizational citizenship behavior: The good soldier syndrome.* Lexington, MA: Lexington.

Ouellette, J. A., & Wood, W. (1998). Habit and intention in everyday life: The multiple processes by which past behavior predicts future behavior. *Psychological Bulletin, 124*, 54–74.

Penney, L. M., & Spector, P. E. (2005). Job stress, incivility, and counterproductive work behavior (CWB): The moderating role of negative affectivity. *Journal of Organizational Behavior, 26*, 777–796.

Ployhart, R. E., & Bliese, P. D. (2006). Individual Adaptability (I-ADAPT) Theory: Conceptualizing the antecedents, consequences, and measurement of individual differences in adaptability. *Advances in Human Performance and Cognitive Engineering Research, 6*, 3–39.

Ployhart, R. E., & Hakel, M. D. (1998). The substantive nature of performance variability: Predicting interindividual differences in intraindividual performance. *Personnel Psychology, 51*, 859–901.

Portrat, S., Barrouillet, P., & Camos, V. (2008). Time-related decay or interference-based forgetting in working memory? *Journal of Experimental Psychology: Learning, Memory, and Cognition, 34*, 1561–1564.

Pulakos, E. D., Arad, S., Donovan, M. A., & Plamondon, K. E. (2000). Adaptability in the workplace: Development of a taxonomy of adaptive performance. *Journal of Applied Psychology, 85*, 612–624.

Quiñones, M. A., Ford, J. K., & Teachout, M. S. (1995). The relationship between work experience and job performance: A conceptual and meta-analytic review. *Personnel Psychology, 48*, 887–910.

Reb, J., & Cropanzano, R. (2007). Evaluating dynamic performance: The influence of salient Gestalt characteristics on performance ratings. *Journal of Applied Psychology, 92*, 490–499.

Reis, H. T., & Gable, S. L. (2000). Event-sampling and other methods for studying everyday experience. In T. H. Reis & M. C. Judd (Eds.), *Handbook of research methods in social and personality psychology* (pp. 190–222). New York: Cambridge University Press.

Roberts, B. W., Walton, K. E., & Viechtbauer, W. (2006). Patterns of mean-level change in personality traits across the life course: A meta-analysis of longitudinal studies. *Psychological Bulletin, 132*, 1–25.

Roe, R. A. (1999). Work performance: A multiple regulation perspective. In C. L. Cooper & I. T. Robertson (Eds.), *International review of industrial and organizational psychology* (Vol. 14, pp. 231–335). Chichester, UK: Wiley.

Rothbard, N. P., & Wilk, S. L. (2006). *Waking up on the right side of the bed: The influence of mood on work attitudes and performance.* Paper presented at the 21st Annual Conference of the Society of Industrial and Organizational Psychology, May 2006, Dallas, Texas.

Rothe, H. F. (1970). Output rates among welders: Productivity and consistency of following removal of a financial incentive system. *Journal of Applied Psychology, 54*, 549–551.

Rotundo, M., & Sackett, P. R. (2002). The relative importance of task, citizenship, and counterproductive performance to global ratings of job performance: A policy-capturing approach. *Journal of Applied Psychology, 87*, 66–80.

Schalk, R., van Veldhoven, M., de Lange, A. H., De Witte, H., Kraus, K., et al. (2010). Moving European research on work and ageing forward: Overview and agenda. *European Journal of Work and Organizational Psychology, 19*, 76–101.

Schallberger, U. (1988). Berufsausbildung und Intelligenzentwicklung (Vocational training and the development of intelligence). In K. Huafeli, U. Kraft & U. Schallberger (Eds.), *Berufsausbildung und Persönlichkeitsentwicklung. Eine Längsschnittuntersuchung* (pp. 148–167). Bern: Huber.

Schaufeli, W. B., & Bakker, A. B. (2004). Job demands, job resources, and their relationship with burnout and engagement: A multi-sample study. *Journal of Organizational Behavior, 25*, 293–315.

Schleicher, R. (1973). Intelligenzleistungen Erwachsener in Abhängigkeit vom Niveau beruflicher Tätigkeit. *Probleme und Ergebnisse der Psychologie, 44*, 24–25.

Schooler, C., Mulatu, M. S., & Oates, G. (1999). The continuing effects of substantively complex work on the intellectual functioning of older workers. *Psychology and Aging, 14*, 483–506.

Schwarz, N., & Bohner, G. (1996). Feelings and their motivational implications: Moods and the action sequence. In P. M. Gollwitzer & J. A. Bargh (Eds.), *The psychology of action: Linking cognition and motivation to behavior* (pp. 119–145). New York: Guilford.

Seibert, S. E., Crant, J. M., & Kraimer, M. L. (1999). Proactive personality and career success. *Journal of Applied Psychology, 84*, 416–427.

Semmer, N., & Frese, M. (1985). Action theory in clinical psychology. In M. Frese & J. Sabini (Eds.), *Goal directed behavior: The concept of action in psychology* (pp. 296–310). Hillsdale, NJ: Lawrence Erlbaum.

Shea, C. M., & Howell, J. M. (2000). Efficacy-performance spirals: An empirical test. *Journal of Management, 26*, 791–812.

Smith, E. M., Ford, J. K., & Kozlowski, S. W. J. (1997). Building adaptive expertise: Implications for training design strategies.

In M. A. Quiñones & A. Ehrenstein (Eds.), *Training for a rapidly changing workplace: Applications of psychological research* (pp. 89–118). Washington, DC: American Psychological Association.

Solomon, R. L., & Corbit, J. D. (1974). An opponent-process theory of motivation: I. Temporal dynamics of affect. *Psychological Review, 81*, 119–145.

Sonnentag, S. (1996). Planning and knowledge about strategies: Their relationship to work characteristics in software design. *Behaviour and Information Technology, 15*, 213–225.

Sonnentag, S. (1998). Expertise in professional software design: A process study. *Journal of Applied Psychology, 83*, 703–715.

Sonnentag, S. (2000). Expertise at work: Experience and excellent performance. *International Review of Industrial and Organizational Psychology, 15*, 223–264.

Sonnentag, S. (2003). Recovery, work engagement, and proactive behavior: A new look at the interface between non-work and work. *Journal of Applied Psychology, 88*, 518–528.

Sonnentag, S., Dormann, C., & Demerouti, E. (2010). Not all days are created equal: The concept of state work engagement. In A. B. Bakker & M. P. Leiter (Eds.), *Work engagement: Recent developments in theory and research* (pp. 25–38). New York: Psychology Press.

Sonnentag, S., & Kleine, B. M. (2000). Deliberate practice at work: A study with insurance agents. *Journal of Occupational and Organizational Psychology, 73*, 87–102.

Sonnentag, S. & Volmer, J. (2009). Individual-level predictors of task-related teamwork processes: The role of expertise and self-efficacy in team meetings. *Group and Organization Management, 34*, 37–66.

Sperandio, J. C. (1971). Variation of operator's strategies and regulating effects on workload. *Ergonomics, 14*, 571–577.

Srivastava, S., John, O. P., Gosling, S. D., & Potter, J. (2003). Development of personality in early and middle adulthood: Set like plaster or persistent change? *Journal of Personality and Social Psychology, 84*, 1041–1053.

Staw, B. M., & Ross, J. (1987). Behavior in escalation situations: Antecedents, prototypes and solutions. *Research in Organizational Behavior, 9*, 39–78.

Staw, B. M., Sandelands, L. E., & Dutton, J. E. (1981). Threat-rigidity effects in organizational behavior: A multilevel analysis. *Administrative Science Quarterly, 26*, 501–524.

Stewart, G. L., & Nandkeolyar, A. K. (2006). Adaptation and intraindividual variation in sales outcomes: Exploring the interactive effect of personality and environmental opportunity. *Personnel Psychology, 59*, 307–332.

Stewart, G. L., & Nandkeolyar, A. K. (2007). Exploring how constraints created by other people influence intraindividual variation in objective performance measures. *Journal of Applied Psychology, 92*, 1149–1158.

Strunk, D. R., DeRubeis, R. J., Chiu, A. W., & Alvarez, J. (2007). Patients' competence in and performance of cognitive therapy skills: Relation to the reduction of relapse risk following treatment for depression. *Journal of Consulting and Clinical Psychology, 75*, 523–530.

Sturman, M. C. (2003). Searching for the inverted U-shaped relationship between time and performance: Meta-analyses of the experience/performance, tenure/performance, and age/performance relationships. *Journal of Management, 29*, 609–640.

Sturman, M. C. (2007). The past, present, and future of dynamic performance research. *Research in Personnel and Human Resources Management, 26*, 49–110.

Sturman, M. C., Cheramie, R. A., & Cashen, L. H. (2005). The impact of job complexity and performance measurement on the temporal consistency, stability, and test-retest reliability of employee job performance ratings. *Journal of Applied Psychology, 90*, 269–283.

Sturman, M. C., & Trevor, C. O. (2001). The implications of linking the dynamic performance and employee turnover literatures. *Journal of Applied Psychology, 86*, 684–696.

Tesluk, P. E., & Jacobs, R. R. (1998). Towards an integrated model of work experience. *Personnel Psychology, 51*, 321–355.

Thompson, J. A. (2005). Proactive personality and job performance: A social capital perspective. *Journal of Applied Psychology, 90*, 1011–1017.

Thoresen, C. J., Bradley, J. C., Bliese, P. B., & Thoreson, J. D. (2004). The Big Five personality traits and individual job performance growth trajectories in maintenance and transitional job stages. *Journal of Applied Psychology, 89*, 835–853.

Trougakos, J. P., Beal, D. J., Green, S. G., & Weiss, H. M. (2008). Making the break count: An episodic examination of recovery activities, emotional experiences, and positive affective displays. *Academy of Management Journal, 51*, 131–146.

Tschan, F. (2002). Ideal cycles of communication (or cognitions) in triads, dyads, and individuals. *Small Group Research, 33*, 615–643.

Unger, J. M., Keith, N., Hilling, C., Gielnik, M., & Frese, M. (2009). Deliberate practice among South African small business owners: Relationships with education, cognitive ability, knowledge, and success. *Journal of Occupational and Organizational Psychology, 82*, 21–44.

Vancouver, J. B. (1997). The application of HLM to the analysis of the dynamic interaction of environment, person and behavior. *Journal of Management, 23*, 795–818.

Vancouver, J. B., & Day, D. V. (2005). Industrial and organisation research on self-regulation: From constructs to applications. *Applied Psychology: An International Review, 54*, 155–185.

Vancouver, J. B., & Kendall, L. N. (2006). When self-efficacy negatively relates to motivation and performance in a learning context. *Journal of Applied Psychology, 91*, 1146–1153.

van der Linden, D., & Eling, P. (2006). Mental fatigue disturbs local processing more than global processing. *Psychological Research/Psychologische Forschung, 70*, 395–402.

van der Linden, D., Frese, M., & Meijman, T. F. (2003). Mental fatigue and the control of cognitive processes: Effects on perseveration and planning. *Acta Psychologica, 113*, 45–65.

van der Linden, D., Frese, M., & Sonnentag, S. (2003). The impact of mental fatigue on exploration in a complex computer task: Rigidity and loss of systematic strategies. *Human Factors, 45*, 483–494.

Van Dyne, L., & LePine, J. A. (1998). Helping and voice extra-role behaviors: Evidence of construct and predictive validity. *Academy of Management Journal, 41*, 108–119.

Van Gelderen, M., Frese, M., & Thurik, R. (2000). Strategies, uncertainty and performance of small business startups. *Small Business Economics, 15*, 165–181.

Verhaeghen, P., & Salthouse, T. A. (1997). Meta-analyses of age-cognition relations in adulthood: Estimates of linear and nonlinear age effects and structural models. *Psychological Bulletin, 122*, 231–249.

Wall, T. D., & Clegg, C. W. (1981). A longitudinal study of group work redesign. *Journal of Occupational Psychology, 2*, 31–49.

Weiss, H. M., & Cropanzano, R. (1996). Affective Events Theory: A theoretical discussion of the structure, causes and consequences of affective experiences at work. In B. M. Staw & L. L. Cummings (Eds.), *Research in organizational behavior* (Vol. 18, pp. 1–74). Stamford, CT: JAI Press.

Williams, C. R., & Livingstone, L. P. (1994). Another look at the relationship between performance and voluntary turnover. *Academy of Management Journal, 37,* 269–298.

Zacher, H., & Frese, M. (2011). Maintaining a focus on future opportunities at work: The interplay of age, work characteristics, and selection, optimization, and compensation strategies. *Journal of Organizational Behavior, 32,* 291–318.

Zickar, M. J., & Slaughter, J. E. (1999). Examining creative performance over time using hierarchical linear modeling: An illustration using film directors. *Human Performance, 12,* 211–230.

Zyphur, M. J., Bradley, J. C., Landis, R. S., & Thoresen, C. J. (2008). The effects of cognitive ability and conscientiousness on performance over time: A censored latent growth model. *Human Performance, 21,* 1–27.

PART 5

Informal Learning, Meaning Creation, and Social Influence

Organizational Socialization: Background, Basics, and a Blueprint for Adjustment at Work

Georgia T. Chao

Abstract

Organizational socialization is defined as a learning and adjustment process that enables an individual to assume an organizational role that fits both organizational and individual needs. It is a dynamic process that occurs when an individual assumes a new or changing role within an organization. A description of general socialization within the field of psychology is presented as a background for the study of organizational socialization. Four theories: uncertainty reduction theory, the need to belong, social exchange theory, and social identity theory are presented as theoretical foundations for organizational socialization. Against this background, the basic components of organizational socialization—its processes, content, and outcomes—are reviewed. Emphasis is given to organizational and individual tactics used to facilitate socialization, as well as to the specific content of what is learned. Finally, a blueprint for future research directions is presented to address current gaps in a general model of organizational socialization. In particular, a call for research to understand how organizations learn from the socialization process is presented to balance the study of work adjustment from individual and organizational perspectives.

Key Words: organizational socialization, newcomers, person-organization fit, work adjustment

In 1914, Henry Ford announced an experiment in a new wage and profit-sharing plan that would double the income of his factory workers. The new $5/day plan created a media sensation, made Ford a celebrity, and ushered in a new era of human resources management. The plan was part of a cultural change effort to reduce turnover, increase productivity, and maximize profits. With considerably less fanfare, another part of the cultural change was the establishment of the Ford Sociological Department. This department employed about 200 investigators who were charged with the mission of determining which factory workers were eligible for the profit sharing plan. Only "good Ford men" would qualify for profit sharing (Hooker, 1997). Investigators entered employee homes, interviewing family members and neighbors, to ascertain whether a worker would "show himself sober, steady, industrious and must satisfy the superintendent and staff that his money will not be wasted in riotous living" (Meyer, 1981, p. 125). Men who did not satisfy company expectations were given six months to comply, or risked termination.

Ford justified these actions on the premise that a good company culture rested on a foundation built by good home conditions (Lacey, 1986). Employees who did not speak English were enrolled in an Americanization Campaign that included the Ford English School as well as American work values. An example of Ford's changes may be found in one worker's New Year's resolution, which declared: "Of my own free will and accord, I sincerely covenant with myself...To exalt the Gospel of Work...To keep head, heart, and hand so busy that I won't have time to think of my troubles. Because idleness is a disgrace, low aim is criminal, and work minus its spiritual quality becomes drudgery" (Hooker, 1997, p. 49).

Henry Ford's efforts to create and enforce his new vision for Ford Motor Company's culture can be viewed as a classic case of organizational socialization. Ford wanted employees with proper values, who would work hard, and would save their money to buy Ford cars. Socialization efforts included formal instruction on work-related matters such as industry and efficiency, as well as formal courses on personal values related to domestic relations, thrift and economy, and community relations. Ford's Americanization Campaign served as a model for other employers. Despite criticisms that the Sociological Department was infringing on workers' personal lives, the changes in human resources management were associated with dramatic decreases in turnover and significant increases in profit. Hooker (1997) reports that one investigator of Ford's alleged abuses of paternalism concluded, "I don't care what you call it—philanthropy, paternalism, autocracy – the results which are being obtained are worth all you can set against them, and the errors in the plan will provoke their own remedies" (p. 51).

The Ford case illustrates how organizations can manage role expectations for their members. Organizational socialization is the process of learning a new role in an organization. It is a particular form of socialization that has developed into a field of study over the past 40 years. This chapter grounds the study of organizational socialization within the larger field of socialization research. Following this background, a review of key theoretical perspectives on socialization and the basic components of organizational socialization are presented, along with a discussion of what we know and what remains to be investigated.

A Background on Socialization Theory and Research

Socialization is generally defined as a learning process by which an individual develops as a social being and a member of a society or group (Brim, 1966). Clausen (1968) noted that philosophers have long considered how children should be developed into proper members of a society; thus a historical beginning for the study of socialization might be traced back to early civilizations. Although philosophical classics, from Confucius's *Analects* to Plato's *Republic*, offer early theories of socialization; scientific examinations did not emerge until the end of the nineteenth century (Clausen, 1968). The term *socialization* was first used in the emerging discipline of sociology, and it was a subject of study in psychology and anthropology as well. A history of socialization theory and treatment in these three disciplines is described by Clausen (1968). While there is some cross-fertilization of socialization concepts across the disciplines, this chapter focuses on the psychological aspects of socialization and describes how these treatments of socialization provide the foundation for the study of organizational socialization.

Psychology and Socialization

In the twentieth century, socialization was a prominent subject of research in three psychological disciplines: developmental, personality, and social psychology (Clausen, 1968). In developmental psychology, Baldwin (1911) wrote: "The social custom, belief, and practice are absorbed by the individual through his acceptance of the instruction and discipline of his group; thus the mass of tradition and the accumulated knowledge of his ancestors becomes his social heritage" (p. 66). In personality psychology, Murray (1938) associated socialization with cultural norms and recognized socialization's role in personality development. Finally, much of social psychology is characterized by socialization themes. Early work by Allport (1924) viewed socialization as instruction in a social context to help individuals adapt to civilized society. Later developments in social learning theory (Bandura, 1977) and social identification theory (Tajfel, 1981) provided theoretical frameworks for empirical examinations of socialization.

Much of the socialization research in psychology has focused on socialization content and processes within specific contexts (Goslin, 1969). Table 18.1 is drawn from work by Brim (1966) and Mortimer and Simmons (1978) and shows how socialization content and processes differ for two broad populations: children and adults. An overview of how children and adults might be socialized can shed light on how socialization processes unfold in organizations. Childhood socialization is generally viewed as primary socialization, with a major impact on personality development; whereas adult socialization is viewed as secondary socialization, with impact on social identities. A child generally has less power than his or her adult socializers and learns appropriate sex roles, family roles, and student roles, often from an explicit position as learner. Conversely, an adult may have comparable power with his or her socializers and may not take or accept a learner or subservient position. Children generally have little choice or control over their socializing environments, whereas

Table 18.1 Comparison of Childhood and Adult Socialization

Comparison dimension	Childhood socialization	Adult socialization
Impact - extent of socialization	Socialization is a major factor in shaping a child's personality. Primary socialization involves the internalization of core values and behaviors within a general society or culture.	Socialization is a major factor in shaping an adult's social identities. Secondary socialization involves the adoption of values and behaviors associated with a specific subgroup.
Focal Person –who gets socialized	A child is generally more malleable than an adult. Socialization experiences are often imposed on a child without choice, consent, or latitude for negotiation.	An adult may have resources to initiate, negotiate, resist, or withdraw from socialization experiences. Socialization may be more voluntary.
Agents –who acts as socializers	Primary socialization involves significant others as socializing agents. The focal person has important relationships with these agents and intense feelings toward them.	Secondary socialization involves agents who hold special roles in a group or organization. The focal person may not have close relationships or intense feelings toward them.
Content –what is learned	Basic knowledge relevant for a member of a society: language, cultural values, and behaviors related to primary roles, such as the regulation of biological drives and appropriate sex roles. Values may be learned within an idealistic frame of how things should be. Early socialization experiences help a child's personality development.	Specific knowledge relevant to be a member of a specific group: organizational values, lexicon, and behaviors for appropriate roles in the group. Values may be learned within a realistic frame of how things actually work. Previous socialization experiences serve as a filter to interpret new socialization experiences.
Context – where learning takes place	Learning is ubiquitous and lessons generalize to other contexts.	Learning may be confined to specific groups with limited generalizability.

adults are better positioned to select, negotiate with, or leave specific groups. Finally, children are generally quite malleable in primary socialization because their new social roles are learned *ex nihilo*; there are no existing roles to interfere with this learning. In contrast, adults draw on a wide variety of previous roles that influence the motivation, learning, negotiation, and acceptance of any new role (Berger, 1979; Berger & Luckmann, 1966).

Table 18.1 presents a wide spectrum of socialization issues that serve as a foundation for the understanding of where organizational socialization is positioned within this broad perspective. For most people, organizational socialization is a type of adult socialization that involves secondary socialization content and processes. However, Table 18.1 reminds us that the adult socialization experiences take meaning from a wide base of childhood socialization experiences. Berger and Luckmann (1966) note that secondary socialization poses a fundamental problem because internalized values, attitudes, and social behaviors learned during primary socialization tend

to persist. Incongruencies between primary and secondary socialization experiences are likely to impede effective socialization to new roles. Furthermore, organizational socialization is but one type of socialization context that adults may experience in simultaneous and/or sequential streams. Acquiring new roles related to marriage, parenthood, new technology, and life interests may enhance or detract from an individual's organizational socialization.

The comparison between primary and secondary socialization processes provides insight as to how and why some organizational socialization processes prove to be powerful experiences for change within individuals. Some organizations can incorporate aspects of primary socialization by totally immersing the individual in the organization. Examples of this institutional socialization can be found in military units and religious orders (Hall & Schneider, 1972), where newcomers leave their former life roles and enter a new lifestyle that consumes almost all of their time, attention, and energy. In these contexts, characteristics of primary socialization are likely:

the new recruit is malleable, basic knowledge and values are taught, socialization agents are organizational superiors with power to reward and punish recruits, and the learning is ubiquitous because the recruit lives within the organization continuously or for significant time periods.

Defining Organizational Socialization

Although there have been several sociological studies on occupational socialization (cf. Huntington, 1957), the study of organizational socialization did not emerge until the 1960s with chapters in general books on socialization. These early discussions of organizational socialization were seated in larger treatises on self-image (Brim, 1968), roles (Manning, 1970), and occupational identification (Moore, 1969). Most notable are Schein's publications that are classics in organizational psychology and have influenced much of the organizational socialization research to date (Schein, 1965, 1968). His essay on "Organizational Socialization and the Profession of Management" (1968) defines organizational socialization as "the process by which a new member learns the value system, the norms, and the required behavior patterns of the society, organization, or group which he is entering" (p. 2). It is a ubiquitous process that individuals experience as their careers unfold over several job and organizational changes. Although these early articles clearly took a broad view of new roles as any organizational role associated with formal or informal job changes, much of the empirical literature focuses on new roles associated with organizational entry.

There are several later definitions of organizational socialization that narrow the construct from Schein's early definition. Most notably, there were efforts to distinguish *socialization* from *individualization*; the former refers to organizational attempts to change individuals to meet organizational needs, whereas the latter refers to individual attempts to change organizations to meet the individual's needs (Kramer & Miller, 1999). Jablin (1982, 1987) described *assimilation* as the interaction between socialization and individualization. However, the individualization and assimilation labels did not prove to be popular. The term *individualization* has been used in a variety of contexts, ranging from individualistic cultural values to a focus on the individual level for attention or application. An electronic search of scholarly articles on *organizational assimilation* located only 12 articles, whereas a similar search on *organizational socialization* yielded 165 scholarly articles. These articles often merged

organizational and individual attempts to define organizational roles under the socialization label.

More recently, definitions of organizational socialization have focused on organizational newcomers, and the term *onboarding* has been equated with organizational socialization. Bauer and Erdogan (2010) take this approach when they define organizational socialization as "a process through which new employees move from being organizational outsiders to becoming organizational insiders" (p. 51). Though this trend reflects most of the empirical research that has used organizational newcomers as subjects, *onboarding* does not seem to apply to socialization processes as individuals change jobs within an organization, or as individuals change the job or work environment to fit their needs. Moreover, that term is often used to describe human resource administration processes (e.g., enrollment in payroll and benefit plans) that are not germane to organizational socialization. There is enough theory and research to justify a more encompassing definition of organizational socialization. Thus, this review seeks to curtail the construct drift and to refocus the definition of organizational socialization on its theoretical roots. Organizational socialization is defined as a learning and adjustment process that enables an individual to assume an organizational role that fits both organizational and individual needs. This definition captures efforts at work adjustment on the part of the organization and the individual. Thus, the adjective *organizational* describes where the socialization occurs, or the context of socialization, rather than who or what is socializing.

This definition also dovetails with Schein's (1978) theory that socialization needs are most salient when individuals cross three types of organizational boundaries. Functional boundaries are associated with organizational functions, such as production, finance, and marketing. Hierarchical boundaries are associated with different ranks, such as executive, middle management, and blue-collar. Lastly, inclusionary boundaries are associated with the centrality of one's position in relation to others. In network terms, someone high on inclusion is a network hub with tight connections to many other people; whereas someone low on inclusion is peripheral to a network and has few ties to others. Van Maanen and Schein (1979) recognize that organizational newcomers generally face the greatest socialization challenges because they cross all three organizational boundaries. However, organizational incumbents who change jobs (functional boundary), who are promoted (hierarchical boundary), or who become more central to getting work done (inclusion boundary) are also likely to face learning and adjustment demands. Thus, they wrote that "organizational socialization is ubiquitous, persistent, and forever problematic" (van Maanen & Schein, 1979, p. 213).

This review begins with an overview of theories that contribute to our understanding of organizational socialization. Against this background, the basic components of organizational socialization—its processes, content, and outcomes—are presented. Finally, the review concludes with a blueprint for future research directions.

Theoretical Foundations for Organizational Socialization

Many theories help explain why and how individuals adjust to new positions in an organization. However, there is no cohesive theory describing the process and content of organizational socialization that has been widely adopted (Ashforth, Sluss & Harrison, 2007; Cooper-Thomas & Anderson, 2006). Thus, the current research on organizational socialization is fragmented. Four general theories on human needs and interpersonal interactions are highlighted below to provide a theoretical foundation for the study of organizational socialization. Two need theories—uncertainty reduction theory and the need to belong—identify why it is important for individuals to fit into their organizational roles. Building on these needs, two theories from social psychology—social exchange theory and social identity theory—address how individuals define and make sense of their organizational role.

Need Theories

UNCERTAINTY REDUCTION THEORY

From the communications field, Berger and Calabrese (1975) advanced uncertainty reduction theory (URT) to explain how interpersonal relationships begin between strangers. A central assumption in URT is the notion that individuals need to reduce uncertainty, or conversely increase predictability, of behaviors unfolding in the initial interaction of two strangers. Understanding what behaviors are appropriate, expected, or rewarded in a relationship can help individuals move beyond cultural social norms or rules for etiquette, and advance to more meaningful interactions. Uncertainty reduction can be a proactive process, when an individual anticipates what a stranger might do, in order to behave appropriately. Furthermore, uncertainty reduction can be a reactive process, when an individual tries to

make sense of a stranger's behavior. Accurate interpretations could increase the individual's ability to anticipate future behaviors from the other person, and to identify the most appropriate responses to those behaviors. Much of the literature on attribution theory (cf. Kelley, 1967) and sense making (cf. Weick, 1995) can be consulted here to derive meanings from a stranger's behavior and to identify behaviors that an individual might select as appropriate responses.

Refinements of URT consider how the anticipated outcomes of an interaction can shape the uncertainty reduction process (Berger, 1986). Valued outcomes are more likely to increase awareness and monitoring of behavioral interactions in order to maximize the likelihood of receiving that valued outcome. For example, a new employee who values raises and promotions in the organization is more likely to be sensitive to his or her interactions with the boss than he or she is to interactions with others. Uncertainty reduction has been extended to established relationships, recognizing the need to reduce new uncertainties as events or situations change individuals and/or their behavior.

In organizational socialization, individuals in a new role face significant uncertainty regarding their ability to succeed in the new position (Lester, 1987). URT identifies this uncertainty as a driver in an individual's socialization behaviors and in an organization's socialization strategies. From the individual's perspective, uncertainty can be reduced by interacting with organizational members who can teach a newcomer about organizational life. These lessons would identify appropriate behaviors and would help the newcomer assess his or her probability of being successful in the organization. From the organization's perspective, a newcomer's uncertainty can be reduced by communicating a coherent organizational identity with clear goals and by providing performance feedback to the newcomer. Organizational activities, such as initiation rituals or the telling of organizational stories, can help newcomers reduce uncertainty by identifying behaviors that are most likely to be valued and rewarded by the organization. Several models of organizational socialization include the need to reduce uncertainty (cf. Miller & Jablin, 1991; Saks & Ashforth, 1997a).

Despite the acknowledgment of URT in organizational socialization, the need to reduce uncertainty has not been directly measured or treated as an individual difference in research (Morrison, 2002a). Instead, it is tied to proximal outcomes of socialization in role ambiguity (role clarity) and role conflict constructs (Ashforth & Saks, 1996). Organizational tactics to socialize newcomers have been found to reduce role ambiguity and role conflict, thus reducing uncertainty for newcomers (Bauer, Bodner, Tucker, Erdogan, & Truxillo, 2007; Saks, Uggerslev, & Fassina, 2007).

NEED TO BELONG

Most need theories of motivation include a need to belong or to maintain positive and significant interpersonal relationships. In organizational psychology, this need is found in Maslow's need hierarchy (Maslow, 1943) and in Alderfer's existence-relatedness-growth theory (Alderfer, 1969). Individuals need to belong to groups in order to share resources, labor, and knowledge. Furthermore, belonging to a group or organization can provide social support and protection against rival groups. Research in social psychology has concluded that there is a fundamental need for people to belong to social groups (Hornsey & Jetten, 2004). The need to belong is demonstrated when people form attachments to groups quickly (Sherif & Sherif, 1969), when people suppress opinions in order to conform with the group (Asch, 1952), and when people favor group members over non-members (Tajfel & Turner, 1979).

There are two general features of the need to belong: (1) the need requires frequent interactions with a specific individual or group, and (2) the relationship is perceived as a stable bond with a foreseeable future (Baumeister & Leary, 1995). Both features are evident for most people who accept new positions in organizations. Employees often form attachments to their organizations, and linkages between the two are central to an individual's commitment to the organization (Mowday, Porter, & Steers, 1982). An individual with a strong need to belong to an organization is more likely to engage in social exchanges with other organizational members and is more likely to value identification with that organization. Thus, the need to belong serves as a theoretical foundation for social exchange theory and social identity theory.

Theories in Social Psychology
SOCIAL EXCHANGE THEORY

Social exchange theory (SET) was primarily developed in the fields of sociology and social psychology (Emerson, 1976). Homans (1958) viewed social behavior as an exchange of goods and services between two actors. Actors can be individuals or corporate groups, embodied by specific people (e.g., your best friend) or by structural positions (e.g., your boss). Goods and services can be material or non-material (e.g., approval or prestige). The nature of these exchanges is dynamic, whereby a current exchange is influenced by the history of past exchanges. Rewarding exchanges lead to positive relationships; conversely, punishing exchanges discourage future interactions (Homans, 1974). Furthermore, networks of exchange partners generate social structures that form group norms. Thus, exchanges between two actors, A and B, may influence their subsequent exchanges with actors C and D, and may even influence how C and D interact outside A and B's relationship. For organizational socialization, these exchange networks provide multiple opportunities for a newcomer to learn about organizational life.

Social exchange theory describes rules for the exchange process (Cropanzano & Mitchell, 2005). Basic rules range from formal negotiations and quid pro quo exchanges to informal and tacit rules of reciprocity in which something is given and something returned between actors without any explicit bargaining (Molm, 2001). Cropanzano and Mitchell (2005) describe how reciprocity rules can help individuals and organizations establish positive exchanges wherein perceived organizational support is met with individual responses related to effort and performance, citizenship behavior, and felt obligation to the organization.

In addition to negotiation and reciprocity rules, Molm (2001) describes exchanges as direct or indirect. Direct exchanges are negotiated and are reciprocal when A provides a value to B, and B provides a value to A. Indirect exchanges, or generalized exchanges, involve more than two actors, with A providing a value to B, B providing a value to C, and C providing a value to A, with all three actors operating within a social unit. Organizations provide a context for all of these exchange rules. New hires directly negotiate terms of their conditions for employment; and employees coordinate activities among themselves in reciprocal or generalized fashions in order to perform tasks at the group level.

As relationships between individuals and organizations develop, the exchanges are likely to become more predictable (uncertainty reduction), allowing individuals to form work identities and to derive meaning from their jobs (Wrzesniewski & Dutton, 2001). Furthermore, positive exchanges are theorized to generate positive emotions such as interest and satisfaction with work, and affective attachment toward the organization (Lawler, 2001). Theories on uncertainty reduction, need to belong, and social exchange drive the formation of social identities.

SOCIAL IDENTITY THEORY

Social identity theory (SIT) is based on the construct of self-categories, or cognitive groupings of a person's perception of him- or herself with a class of stimuli. Self-categories that are unique from other people are termed *personal identities*, whereas self-categories based on shared similarities with groups of people are termed *social identities* (Turner, Oakes, Haslam & McGarty; 1994). Social identities are defined in relational and comparative terms to help us identify who we are and who we are not ("us versus them") (Tajfel & Turner, 1986). Social identities emerge as part of a natural process of self-definition, motivated by needs to reduce uncertainty and to enhance self-esteem (Hogg & Terry, 2001). As individuals, we strive to build positive images of ourselves. Groups are associated with value connotations that can enhance an individual's self-definition if the group is positively valued. Conversely, if an individual belongs to a group that is negatively valued, he or she may be motivated to change groups, change the value connotation, or minimize the strength of identification with that particular group (Peteraf & Shanley, 1997; Tajfel, 1981; Turner, 1975).

Hogg and Terry (2000) posit that uncertainty reduction may be more relevant than the self-enhancement motive when people build social identities in organizations because uncertainty reduction may be more adaptive when defining what values and behaviors are appropriate to a particular organizational role. Within an organizational socialization context, the uncertainty found in new roles and/or new environments is highly salient for the newcomer; thus, the need to reduce uncertainty is linked to the formation of organizational identities.

Tajfel (1981, p. 254–255) wrote: "The acquisition of value differentials between one's own group (or groups) and other groups is part and parcel of the general processes of socialization." Individuals with strong positive organizational identities are more likely to be committed to the organization, to cooperate with others, to internalize organizational values and group norms, and to reinforce an organization's unique culture than individuals with weak organizational identification (Ashforth & Mael, 1989). To complicate matters, individuals may form multiple social identities within an organization (Ashforth & Johnson, 2001) as individuals identify themselves as members of a job class, work

group, department, division, and so forth within the organization. Moreland, Levine, and McMinn (2001) theorized that most organizational socialization occurs within the work group because it represents the immediate environment for an individual to be evaluated in, to be committed to, and to transition into as an accepted member. Within these perspectives, organizational socialization helps an individual define him- or herself as a member of the organization, holding particular roles. Thus, social identities in organizations are powerful influences on an employee's affect and behavior.

Summary

When a person joins an organization, accepts a new job, and/or moves into a new position, these events are typically formal and discrete. The first day on the job is recognized by the newcomer, the organization, and any observers as evidence that the newcomer is an organizational member in a particular role. When the role is new and unfamiliar, the newcomer's need to reduce uncertainty and the need to belong to a group initiate the socialization process. However, these need theories do not explain *how* the needs are fulfilled.

Social exchange theory provides a general framework that can explain how a newcomer can reduce uncertainty and form an attachment to a group or organization. Reichers (1987) described how symbolic interactionism helps a newcomer establish situational identities. Relationships emerge from a series of social exchanges, and the meanings derived from these relationships help form a social identity with a particular group. Furthermore, socialization within a group or organization is expedited when an organizational newcomer and organizational insiders are proactive in their social interactions, providing more opportunities to acquire role-appropriate behaviors and to make sense of the newcomer's role (Reichers, 1987).

Social identities with an organization or unit generally emerge when relationships develop and stabilize into a community-of-practice. Uncertainty is reduced when group norms are learned, and a newcomer becomes attached to a group when these norms are accepted and internalized. The four theoretical perspectives—URT, need to belong, SET and SIT—provide a foundation for understanding organizational socialization. The need theories address the question, "Why do people engage in organizational socialization?" SET helps us understand "How do people become socialized in an organization?," whereas SIT helps us understand "Why is organizational socialization important?" Although there are many other theories that can be tapped to help understand organizational socialization, these four were selected to provide a broad-based theoretical foundation for most socialization contexts.

Despite these theoretical underpinnings, there is no cogent theory of organizational socialization. URT and the need to belong are often mentioned in the organizational socialization literature; however, I did not find any empirical studies that directly measured these needs and their effects on socialization. Perhaps this was due to the field's early focus on organizational attempts to socialize individuals, and these need theories were associated with organizational constructs like role ambiguity or person-organization fit, as opposed to an individual's proaction to socialization. However, it would be interesting to explore organizational needs to reduce uncertainty with a new hire, or organizational needs to bond with particular employees. Cultural values like uncertainty avoidance describe how organizational members collectively need to structure activities in order to reduce stress or anxiety caused by uncertainty (Hofstede, 1980). Needs at the organizational level may be more salient when specific performance standards exist or when the organization's culture strongly values its members. Uncertainty reduction is facilitated when organizations train and evaluate new employee performance against clear standards. In addition, when organizations value their human capital as a competitive advantage, the need to form rewarding relationships with employees is relevant. The sustainability of an organization may depend on how well new members support the continuity of the organization's mission, values, and performance.

In a similar vein, SET and SIT are generally used to explain how work groups and organizations might interact with newcomers in order to gain positive outcomes such as organizational loyalty and commitment. Examination of the organizational socialization process from multiple perspectives (individual, group and organization) could help build a more coherent theory for organizational socialization.

Organizational Socialization Processes

Early discussions on the organizational socialization process are generally formulated around two themes. First, stage models of organizational socialization describe how an individual evolves from a naïve new member to an accepted and adjusted organizational member. Second, organizational

tactics describe how an organization can design socialization experiences in order to process people effectively into the types of organizational members who are desired.

Stage Models of Organizational Socialization

In the late 1970s and early 1980s, several stage models were published in the organizational literature to identify distinct phases of the adjustment process (Feldman, 1981; Graen, 1976; Schein, 1978; Van Maanen, 1976). Direct comparisons of these models are provided by Ashforth, Sluss, and Harrison (2007), Fisher (1986), and Wanous, Reichers, and Malik (1984). Although the labels of the stages vary, these models generally describe a three-phase process that begins when an individual forms expectations about a future role in an organization, attempts to adjust to that role, and settles into that role. Feldman's (1976) labels for these stages are used here, describing the three as: (1) anticipatory socialization, (2) accommodation, and (3) role management, respectively. Successful organizational socialization is generally recognized when both the individual and the organization perceive a fit between that individual and the expectations of his or her organizational role.

STAGE 1: ANTICIPATORY SOCIALIZATION

The first stage begins before the individual enters a new job, organization, or work environment. It is the accumulation of knowledge and experiences that shape the individual's expectations about a particular role in an organization. For people entering new careers, this knowledge includes self-images related to a chosen career, as well as expectations about the new organizational role that the individual has agreed to assume. Formal education and training for a chosen profession help shape these expectations. Informal guidance from role models, mentors, family, friends, and colleagues provides additional perspectives to help the individual learn about a particular occupational role. General learning and preparation for an occupation or career is also known as *vocational socialization* (Jablin, 1987). This type of socialization complements Holland's (1985) theory of vocational psychology that describes how individuals are attracted to certain vocational environments that match an individual's personality.

Beyond vocational socialization, the anticipatory socialization stage recognizes that an individual is looking for an organizational position with desired characteristics. Most people do not look for any job in any organization. There are certain aspects about jobs, organizations, and careers that help define an individual's identity and self-concept. Schneider (1987) extends Holland's theory with his attraction-selection-attrition (ASA) framework, arguing that similar people are attracted to an organization and are more likely to be selected into that organization. Those who were selected but later are determined to be dissimilar with the status quo are likely to leave that organization. Together, these processes result in a relatively homogeneous organization where "people make the place." Later, Schneider and his colleagues incorporated organizational socialization processes as additional mechanisms whereby an organization polishes the fit between a newcomer and the modal personality that characterizes most organizational members (Schneider, Smith, Taylor, & Fleenor, 1998). Thus, the ASA framework may be better described as an ASSA framework, recognizing attraction-selection-socialization-attrition cycles of people processing.

Feldman (1976) described two process variables in the anticipatory socialization stage: realism and congruence. Realism addresses the accuracy of the information accumulated by the individual, whereas congruence addresses the fit between the organization's resources and the individual's needs. Expectations based on inaccurate or incomplete information are likely to be unmet as reality offers a different picture from that which a newcomer envisioned. Organizations can improve the accuracy of these expectations by providing realistic job previews during the selection process (Wanous, 1992). This information helps an applicant accept/reject a job offer and inoculates a new hire against some negative experiences after organizational entry. When an individual takes on a new role, the expectations formed during the anticipatory socialization phase are tested. How the individual makes sense of the new role and how the individual adapts to the new realities of that role will transition the individual into the accommodation phase.

STAGE 2: ACCOMMODATION

The heart of organizational socialization lies in the second stage. The accommodation stage embodies the learning, sense making, and adjustment of an individual to a new or changed organizational role. Dean (1983) defined "reality shock" as the discrepancy between a new employee's expectations before starting a job and the experienced realities after job entry.[1] Expectations from the anticipatory

socialization stage are often nebulous, operating at a tacit level of knowledge. Myriad new organizational experiences could overwhelm newcomers, putting them in a state of shock as they struggle to make sense of work demands, delights, discoveries, and disappointments. Louis (1980) describes how newcomers make sense of a new role through filters of concurrent and previous roles. A unique role will place higher learning demands on a newcomer than a role that shares aspects with that newcomer's role repertoire. The contrast between new and established roles may facilitate adaptation to the new role when previously learned behavioral scripts are appropriate. Conversely, old roles may invoke inappropriate scripts or may cause a newcomer to resist new ways of doing things, thus making the adjustment process problematic. Finally, disparities between initial expectations and early experiences represent surprises to newcomers. The adjustment process is a sense-making process as newcomers evaluate the changes, contrasts, and surprises against their accumulated knowledge base of roles, conscious and non-conscious predispositions for sense making, and the sense-making interpretations of others. The adjustment process results in revised expectations of the new role, and initiates another round of comparisons between new expectations and subsequent experiences.

The theory of met expectations (Porter & Steers, 1973) has been used to predict outcomes of the accommodation stage (Wanous, 1992). Unmet expectations that are important to a newcomer are likely to cause low job satisfaction and subsequent turnover. Conversely, met expectations are linked with job satisfaction, organizational commitment, and intentions to remain with the organization (Major, Kozlowski, Chao, & Gardner, 1995; Premack & Wanous, 1985).

Feldman (1981) describes three process variables during the accommodation stage: (1) initiation to the task (learning how to master new work tasks), (2) initiation to the group (building positive interpersonal relationships), and (3) role definition (negotiating a psychological contract that identifies employee and employer obligations to one another). Two additional process variables—managing conflict with work-nonwork and managing conflict between organizational units—are more specialized processes that do not apply to all newcomers; thus they will not be discussed here. The focus on learning how to perform one's job, learning how to get along with others, and learning one's role in the organization can be extrapolated to job content, job context, and career categories. Learning and adjusting to required job content, within a specific job context, are immediate concerns for a newcomer's successful accommodation. Learning one's role in the organization can also include learning how that role may lead to future roles and opportunities (e.g., promotions and career outlook). This perspective provides depth to the sense-making process: to see how one fits in now, and how one might fit into the organization's future.

Much of the literature on person-organization fit adds depth and breadth to organizational socialization. Good overviews of this literature are provided by Kristof-Brown and Guay (2010) and Ostroff and Schulte (2007). Kristof (1996) defines person-organization fit as "the compatibility between people and organizations that occurs when: (a) at least one entity provides what the other needs, or (b) they share similar fundamental characteristics, or (c) both" (pp. 4–5). Fundamental characteristics shared by individuals and organizations are generally values that guide goals, preferences, and behavioral norms. Chatman (1989) identified selection and socialization as the primary processes for an organization to admit and shape new employees to fit that organization's dominant value structure. Good person-organization fit would be positively related to outcomes such as job satisfaction and organizational citizenship behaviors, and negatively related to outcomes such as stress and turnover (Kristof-Brown & Guay, 2010).

Organizational socialization during the accommodation stage is generally linked to early or proximal outcomes for the newcomer. Proximal outcomes of socialization are associated with immediate needs to reduce uncertainty and/or to increase a sense of belonging. Chao, O'Leary-Kelly, Wolf, Klein, & Gardner (1994) argued that the most immediate outcomes are the lessons learned during the socialization process. If a newcomer is unwilling or unable to learn the lessons needed to assume a new role within an organization, it may be difficult for the organization to accept that newcomer as a permanent member. These lessons can be represented not only by the content of what is learned, but also by reduced uncertainties defined by role ambiguity or role conflict. In addition, actions to fulfill the need to belong would affect a proximal outcome of social acceptance of a newcomer or of perceived fit with the organization. Finally, fulfillment of both needs would affect a proximal outcome of self-efficacy as reduced uncertainties and increased bonds with the organization should enhance a newcomer's perceptions of being a capable organizational member.

STAGE 3: ROLE MANAGEMENT

The last stage follows the accommodation stage for newcomers and focuses on the learning and adjustment that is required to become a fully accepted member of the organization. Learning in the role management stage adds detail and clarity to learning from previous stages. A deeper level of understanding of the organization and work role is learned when supervisors and other organizational members stop treating the individual as a newcomer. Mistakes are less easily forgiven, and conflicts between people and/or tasks are realized, as greater familiarity reveals who is friendly, competent, and trustworthy. This stage of organizational socialization has received the least amount of research attention, mostly likely due to the various names and descriptions for the final stage of socialization. Other names for this stage include: *change and acquisition* (Porter, Lawler, & Hackman, 1975; Feldman, 1981), *performance* (Buchanan, 1974), *integrating* (Graen, 1976), *mutual acceptance* (Schein, 1978), and *adaptation* (Louis, 1980).

Schein (1968) described how an organization might use events to symbolize organizational acceptance of a new employee. Such events include: positive performance appraisals, salary increases, permanent or challenging job assignments, sharing of organizational "secrets" or privileged information for trusted employees, initiation rites, and formal promotions. These events communicate to the new employee and to his or her coworkers that the new employee's status has changed from newcomer, or someone on probation, to an accepted organizational member. In return, the new employee fulfills his or her part of a psychological contract with the organization by deciding to remain with the organization, showing high levels of motivation and commitment to the work/organization, and by accepting some temporary constraints, delays, or undesirable work assignments that might arise. Van Maanen (1976) noted that the transition to full-fledged organizational membership may take a long time after entry. Examples may be found in professions such as academia, accounting, or law, where tenure or partnership is not granted until several years of evaluated service.

Van Maanen (1976) described this stage as a metamorphosis in which the individual's newly learned behaviors and attitudes have changed him or her into a different person. The new role may be assumed with varying levels of acceptance, ranging from reluctant compliance to full internalization of the organization's values and role demands. Social identity theory has been used to explain why organizational socialization can change an individual's self-definitions (Ashforth & Mael, 1989). A new social identity based on a work group or organization can enhance an individual's self-esteem and provide a distinct set of values and practices for the new member to draw upon.

Louis (1980) described how newcomers make sense of their experiences and how these lessons, in turn, influence behavioral responses and future expectations. Thus, the final stage of organizational socialization is associated with more distal outcomes of the socialization process, as compared to more proximal outcomes in the accommodation stage. Whereas the proximal outcomes of socialization are focused on what is learned and early reactions from those lessons, more distal outcomes are focused on attitudes and behaviors that have stabilized after initial adjustments. Successful socialization is described by lessons that are acquired, accepted, and applied to improve subsequent actions and attitudes toward the organization. Distal outcomes include behaviors such as job performance and turnover, as well as attitudes such as job satisfaction and organizational commitment.

I used Feldman's (1976) label for this stage, *role management*, to emphasize that roles are continuously affected by temporal, technological, and personnel changes; thus, individuals need to manage and adjust their roles as these changes emerge. Within the person-environment fit literature, Ostroff and Schulte (2007) describe how individuals adapt to progressive and sudden changes in the environment. Progressive changes are gradual and might prompt an individual to adapt to an emerging dominant behavioral pattern, drawing on explicit and implicit knowledge bases to guide their changes. In contrast, sudden changes may be characterized by a punctuated equilibrium that demands rapid adjustments for survival. A growing accumulation of stressors ultimately reaches a tipping point, and a critical mass of change agents identify a new set of behaviors or values to accommodate the new environment. Thus, fit may be a moving target when an individual confronts a new supervisor, new job requirements, new group members, or any significant change to that individual's role within the organization. Such changes in fit would demand resocialization or role management.

Summary

Stage models of organizational socialization generally describe three distinct learning stages: (1) job/career content and anticipations of a work role prior to new role entry; (2) accommodation of work role requirements and fitting in an organization and work group after entry; and (3) role management with deeper understanding of role conflicts and adjustment needs due to changes in personnel, work requirements, or the organizational environment. Although some early research supported different stages of socialization (e.g., Graen, Orris, & Johnson, 1973; Toffler, 1981), Fisher (1986) concluded that there was no research to support a universal stage model for all jobs, organizations, or people. In addition, Bauer, Morrison, and Callister (1998) note that these stage models focus on socialization content, or what characterizes each stage, rather than socialization process, or how learning and adjustment changes occur. Finally, all of the stage models are focused on how an individual acquires a new role without any consideration for the likelihood that this acquisition may be linked to the abandonment of an old role. Louis (1980) criticized the socialization stage models for failing to consider how old socialization lessons may need to be unfrozen in order to accommodate the new lessons.

Despite the fact that socialization stage models have not attracted much research attention (Ashforth, Sluss, & Harrison, 2007), they remain valuable because they recognize that organizational socialization is a dynamic process that changes over time. It begins before an individual joins a particular organization. There is no definitive end because changes in the work environment often provoke needs for further adjustments. Van Maanen (1984) wrote that "socialization takes place from womb to tomb" (p. 213), whereby socialization episodes form a chain of lessons learned through time. In this chain, early lessons construct a foundation of knowledge that informs, interprets, and influences subsequent socialization experiences.

Drawing from the initial discussion of childhood and adult socialization, it is easy to see how chains of socialization experiences are linked together. Our understanding of organizational socialization could benefit from research that examines how early socialization experiences influence later ones, and how non-organizational socialization influences organizational socialization, and vice versa. This review next examines organizational socialization tactics as specific mechanisms by which individuals learn new roles.

Tactics in Organizational Socialization

Tactics are processes by which organizations structure socialization experiences or by which individuals gather information to learn and adjust to a new role. Chronologically, research on organizational socialization first examined organizational tactics, then moved on to investigations of individual tactics. These categories are described in separate sections, but it should be noted that both types of tactics and their interactions should be considered for a comprehensive understanding of organizational socialization.

Organizational Tactics

Much of the empirical research on organizational socialization processes is centered on six tactics introduced by Van Maanen and Schein (1979); however, they note that their list is not exhaustive, and they speculate that an infinite number of tactics may exist, since tactics are cultural forms that change with new ideas and circumstances. Table 18.2 presents tactics in the organizational socialization literature with a brief description. This list is not intended to be a comprehensive list, but is presented as a resource for future examinations of socialization processes.

Van Maanen and Schein's (1979) theory of organizational socialization rests on the notion that "*what* people learn about their work roles in organizations is often a direct result of *how* they learn it" (Van Maanen & Schein, 1979, p. 209). Their description of six socialization tactics, coupled with Jones's (1986) measure for these tactics, generated a large portion of the empirical research on organizational socialization during the last 25 years.

The six tactics are described as organizational teaching methods for individuals who are learning a new organizational role. They may be purposefully designed by organizations, or they may evolve without formal thought or control. Each tactic is described on a continuum, anchored at each end by distinct processes to help individuals assume a target role. First, *collective versus individual* socialization tactics describe whether newcomers are processed in a group, with common experiences, or individually, with more unique experiences tailored to that person. Second, *formal versus informal* socialization tactics describe the extent to which newcomers are distinguished and segregated from other organizational members. Formal tactics are characterized by probationary or trial periods and evaluation, whereas informal tactics make few distinctions between newcomers and established members. Third, *sequential versus random* socialization tactics describe the extent to which a distinct sequence of hurdles must be passed before the newcomer is accepted as a member. Hurdles in sequential tactics

may include passing training programs in the classroom and on the job, whereas steps for acceptance in random tactics are unknown or unclear. Fourth, *fixed versus variable* socialization tactics are described by a distinct or ambiguous timetable for assuming a full organizational role. Fixed tactics specify the maximum time that it will take for a newcomer to be accepted as a full member with formal recognition in the form of promotion, partnership, or tenure. Variable tactics do not have a formal deadline or recognition of successful role assumption. Fifth, *serial versus disjunctive* socialization tactics describe the extent to which an experienced member or role model helps the newcomer assume a similar role in the organization. Serial tactics provide role models, whereas disjunctive tactics require newcomers to learn more on their own because there are no role predecessors or job incumbents available. Finally, *investiture versus divestiture* socialization tactics describe the extent to which a newcomer's personal characteristics are welcomed by the organization. Investiture tactics affirm the newcomer's knowledge, skill, and abilities, embracing this diversity, whereas divestiture tactics seek to mold the newcomer to be like everyone else. Divestiture tactics may require the newcomer to disconfirm preexisting personal characteristics (e.g., attitudes, values, relationships with organizational outsiders) in order to rebuild the newcomer's self-image to an organizational identity.

Van Maanen and Schein (1979) theorized that the sequential, variable, serial, and divestiture tactics would most likely be associated with a *custodial* role orientation, in which the newcomer accepts an organizational role and the status quo, without challenge or change. In contrast, collective, formal, random, fixed, and disjunctive tactics are most likely associated with a *content innovation* role orientation, in which the newcomer takes the initiative to make changes or improvements to a role's knowledge base or behavioral practices. Finally, more extreme changes to an organizational role's mission and purpose, or a *role innovation* orientation, are most likely found in organizations that use individual, informal, random, disjunctive, and investiture tactics.

Jones (1986) was the first to empirically study the relationship between these socialization tactics and newcomer adjustment. He classified the tactics under *institutionalized* and *individualized* headings that roughly parallel Van Maanen and Schein's custodial and innovative responses to socialization, respectively. However, in contrast to Van Maanen and Schein, Jones reversed the placement of two

Table 18.2 Descriptions of Organizational and Individual Tactics of Organizational Socialization

Organizational Tactics – General Processes	Description and Reference
Collective vs. individual	Collective tactics are conducted in group contexts with similar newcomers; individual tactics are not (Van Maanen, 1978; Van Maanen & Schein, 1979).
Formal vs. informal	Formal tactics segregate and differentiate newcomer from established organizational members. Informal tactics are less structured by the organization. (Van Maanen, 1978; Van Maanen & Schein, 1979)
Sequential vs. random	Sequential tactics are designed to engage the newcomer in a series of stages or experiences that must be passed before full acceptance into the organization is granted. Random or non-sequential tactics are characterized by one transitional stage or an ambiguous sequence of steps. (Van Maanen, 1978; Van Maanen & Schein, 1979).
Fixed vs. variable	Fixed tactics specify a timetable for transition from probationary status to accepted member. Variable tactics do not communicate any time expectations for newcomers to achieve member status (Van Maanen, 1978; Van Maanen & Schein, 1979).
Serial vs. disjunctive	Serial tactics involve job incumbents who serve as role models and help the newcomer adjust. Disjunctive tactics do not provide any role models or job predecessors (Van Maanen, 1978; Van Maanen & Schein, 1979).
Investiture vs. divestiture	Investiture tactics affirm the newcomer's individuality and his/her needs are addressed. Divestiture tactics strip the newcomer's individuality so he/she is like all others. Individual needs are subordinate to the organization (Van Maanen, 1978; Van Maanen & Schein, 1979).
Tournament vs. contest	Tournament tactics track different newcomers based on ability or potential. Newcomers who fail to meet expectations in one track are demoted to a lower track permanently. Contest tactics do not track newcomers in different categories; thus one setback does not impair future considerations (Van Maanen, 1978).

Organizational Tactics – Specific Interventions	Description and Reference
Formal orientation program	Formal orientation programs are training programs designed to introduce newcomers to their job and coworkers. Orientation programs can also provide information about the organization's mission, culture, and general processes (Klein & Weaver, 2000; Wesson & Gogus, 2005).
Training	Training programs can range from off-site formal programs to on-site informal programs that provide newcomers with specific instructions on how to perform a task (Chao, 1997a; Louis, Posner & Powell, 1983).
Social/recreational activities	Social and recreational activities are generally not related to a newcomer's job or work unit. Instead, these tactics provide fun activities that can help the newcomer identify him/herself as an organizational member (Louis, Posner & Powell, 1983).
Business trips	Business trips away from the newcomer's typical location can help the newcomer learn about the job and organization in a larger context. Different situations and relationships with people outside the organization (customers, suppliers, competitors, etc.) provide different contexts for sense making (Louis, Posner & Powell, 1983).

(Continued)

Table 18.2 (continued)

Individual Tactics	Description and Reference
Monitoring	Monitoring or observing others can yield information on normative standards. Discrete observations minimize social costs for this information seeking tactic. Self-monitoring or observations of how people react to the newcomer can also aid adjustment. (Ashford & Cummings, 1993; Miller & Jablin, 1991)
Inquiry	Inquiries can be direct questions for information or feedback, or inquiries can be more covert, involving indirect questions, hinting, or general conversation. Covert inquiries are more likely when the newcomer is uncomfortable asking direct questions or is not sure what questions should be asked (Ashford & Black, 1996; Miller & Jablin, 1991).
Written and electronic sources	Written sources (e.g., manuals, handbooks, annual reports, etc.) are non-interpersonal tactics that provide information to newcomers. Electronic sources (e.g., web sites, e-mail) also provide information and can involve interactions with other organizational members (Morrison, 1993a; Ostroff & Kozlowski, 1992).
Job changes	Job changes include active experimentation and/or negotiation for different tasks, responsibilities, and/or expectations of performance. Experimentation can include trial-and-error behaviors and testing limits of current rules to learn more about what the organization values and tolerates (Miller & Jablin, 1991; Ostroff & Kozlowski, 1992; Saks et al., 2011).
Social influence	Social influence tactics help newcomers build positive relationships with others. Tactics include general networking as well as impression management tactics such as ingratiation, exchange of benefits, and rationality (Ashford & Black, 1996; Morrison, 2002b; Su, 2010).

tactics within this classification scheme. First, Van Maanen and Schein believed that fixed socialization tactics would produce innovative responses, and variable tactics would produce custodial responses; whereas Jones predicted that fixed tactics would be associated with institutionalized socialization and variable tactics with individualized socialization. Explanations are based on different lines of logic. Van Maanen and Schein thought that the uncertainty in variable tactics would maximize a newcomer's anxiety, thus motivating that person to conform to organizational norms in order to reduce uncertainty and anxiety. In contrast, Jones thought that variable tactics were more likely to promote innovative responses, with the individual taking the initiative to reduce uncertainty and anxiety.

Second, Van Maanen and Schein thought that divestiture tactics would lead to a custodial response because divestiture, by definition, strips away an individual's uniqueness to mold that person to the organizational norm. In addition, investiture tactics would lead to innovative responses because the organization accepts the individual "as is," and is willing to consider that individual's new ideas and innovations.

Jones questioned this logic and suggested that divestiture tactics could motivate individuals to question the status quo and could stimulate innovative responses to improve the situation. Furthermore, Jones reasoned that early acceptance of newcomers with investiture tactics may motivate them toward custodial responses in order to demonstrate acceptance of the organization "as is." Empirical studies have been mixed, with some supporting investiture with a custodial response (e.g., Allen & Meyer, 1990; Ashforth & Saks, 1996), and others supporting investiture with an innovative response (Saks & Ashforth 1997a; Laker & Steffy, 1995). Both lines of logic for the discrepancies between Van Maanen and Schein's and Jones's classifications are plausible, and they illustrate the distinction between *what* people learn and *how* they learn it. A more comprehensive theory on organizational socialization should advance beyond Van Maanen and Schein's original premise and recognize both process and content aspects.

Although the idea of grouping the six tactics along two broader dimensions is appealing, features between these tactics and responses make too many assumptions to support a simple binary taxonomy. Inherent in the assignment of a particular tactic to a custodial or innovative response is the content of what is learned. A tactic describes *how* an organization processes its people. In contrast, a custodial or innovative response describes *what* the individual does to conform to or rebel against the organization's status quo. A particular method is not always associated with a particular behavior or outcome. Like the old adage "You can lead a horse to water, but you can't make it drink," these socialization tactics can provide specific experiences for newcomers, but cannot ensure that newcomers will learn and accept intended lessons from these experiences.

Two meta-analyses examining the relationships between these tactics and outcomes (Bauer et al., 2007; Saks et al., 2007) drew similar conclusions. All six socialization tactics reflecting institutionalized tactics were positively related to job satisfaction and negatively related to role ambiguity and intentions to quit. Fewer tactics were significantly related to behavioral outcomes of performance and actual turnover. Furthermore, both meta-analyses found proximal socialization outcomes (e.g., role ambiguity and fit) to partially mediate relationships between socialization tactics and distal outcomes (e.g., satisfaction and commitment). Lastly, stronger relationships between tactics and outcomes were found in both meta-analyses for recent graduates transitioning from school to work, as compared to experienced workers, and for cross-sectional studies, as compared with longitudinal research.

In addition to the six organizational tactics introduced by Van Maanen and Schein (1979), Van Maanen (1978) describes *tournament versus contest* socialization tactics. Tournament strategies place employees on different tracks based on their performance or potential to the organization. High-potential employees are on fast tracks, with resources and opportunities that are unavailable to other employees. Like an athletic tournament, these strategies remove members from a track when they fail at a particular round of assessment. These employees either leave the organization or cascade down to lower level tracks. In contrast, contest strategies consider all qualified employees for a particular round of promotions, regardless of their failure or success in earlier rounds. These tactics tend to socialize employees to be more competitive in tournaments and more cooperative in contest environments. There are no empirical studies that directly assess tournament and contest socialization tactics, most likely because of the challenges in measuring a practice that organizations and individuals may not formally recognize or accurately observe over time.

The organizational socialization tactics described thus far tap general ways in which to process people. More specific tactics have been identified in subsequent research, and they are described in Table 18.2. Ostroff and Kozlowski (1992) examined six information sources that could aid the learning process for newcomers. One source is identified here as an organizational tactic, whereas the other five are described later, in the section on individual tactics. Manuals are created by organizations to help employees learn about policies, procedures, and the job. For example, employee handbooks are intentionally designed to help employees understand organizational policies and common practices. Furthermore, organizational publications, web sites, and social media networks can provide information on company goals, values, and future directions. Thus, these forms of print and electronic media can provide information to help newcomers learn and adjust to their new roles. Despite the potential for manuals to help socialization, Ostroff and Kozlowski found that this tactic was rated low by new hires as a source of information, and it was unrelated to new hire reports of knowledge gained and to socialization outcomes like satisfaction, adjustment, and stress. These results may be linked to fundamental differences between the realities of work and the ways that organizations formally describe work in manuals, organizational charts, and job descriptions (Brown & Duguid, 1991).

Louis, Posner, and Powell (1983) examined ten specific organizational interventions. These organizational practices were identified by professionals in human resources and college placement, as well as new hires, for being common socialization tactics. Four of these tactics tap specific experiences for newcomers. *Formal orientation programs* are formal tactics intentionally designed to help new hires learn about organizational life. Klein and Weaver (2000) found that newcomers who completed a formal orientation program learned more about the organization's goals/values, history, and people, and were subsequently more committed to the organization than newcomers who opted out of this orientation. In addition, Wesson and Gogus (2005) found that newcomers who completed a group, social-based orientation program showed higher levels of organizational socialization, commitment, and satisfaction than newcomers who completed an individual, computer-based orientation program.

A second formal tactic, *off-site training,* helps newcomers prepare for their work roles. Fan and Wanous (2008) evaluated an orientation program for international graduate students that combined realistic information and coping skills training. Students who completed this orientation program reported better adjustments to academic and social life than students who completed a traditional orientation program without any skills training. Aside from orientation training, the general training literature supports positive effects of training programs on individual job performance and organizational financial performance, but few distinctions are drawn between on-site and off-site programs (Aguinis and Kraiger, 2009). Chao (1997a) stated that unstructured or informal training is generally more often used than formal training programs. She noted that the effectiveness of formal training programs can be enhanced or inhibited by informal training; thus lessons from these two modes of training should be designed to reinforce one another. Louis et al. (1983) found that a sample of young adults rated these tactics as moderately helpful in learning to become effective organizational members.

Two additional organizational tactics were rated as less helpful for socialization than the ones discussed above. *Social/recreational activities* represent non-work attempts to help a newcomer identify with the organization. Finally, *business trips* offer unique work experiences that may accentuate a newcomer's organizational membership as he or she deals with people outside the organization and/or outside a newcomer's typical work environment. These four types of experiences can provide different learning opportunities to help newcomers adjust to their roles. Like the more general tactics, these experiences do not describe *what* is learned, but *how* one learns.

The remaining six tactics identify socialization agents or specific organizational members as resources to help newcomers learn to be effective organizational members themselves. Louis et al. found that interactions with other newcomers, peers, senior coworkers, supervisor, mentor, and support staff were generally rated as more helpful than the previous four experiential tactics, with one exception. Help from secretary/support staff was not perceived to be as helpful as the other tactics. In contrast, help from peers, senior coworkers, and supervisors were rated most helpful, and they were also significantly related to newcomer attitudes like job satisfaction and commitment. However, the extent to which these tactics represent ways that an organization manages the socialization of its newcomers is open for debate. Interactions with supervisors and mentors are more likely to be aligned with organizational goals than are interactions with members of less status and power. Most interpersonal relationships within an organization are not monitored, supervised, or evaluated; hence the interpersonal tactics may not suit organizational needs. Therefore, the formal organization may not sanction ways by which other newcomers, peers, coworkers, and support staff help a newcomer to learn his or her role.

In addition to the recognition that interpersonal tactics may not support organizational goals and values, these tactics may not be initiated or controlled by established organizational members. Instead, the newcomer may initiate and direct the ways in which relationships with organizational insiders develop. Individual tactics are described in the next section as a complement to organizational tactics; however, it should be recognized that the two groups are not mutually exclusive. The interaction between newcomers and organizational sources of information are likely to be two-way and dynamic, evolving and building upon previous exchanges as relationships develop and the adjustment process unfolds.

Individual Tactics

There is no commonly accepted taxonomy of individual tactics in organizational socialization; however, there is clear recognition of the importance of newcomer proaction in the socialization process (Miller & Jablin, 1991; Morrison, 1993a; Nicholson, 1984; Ostroff & Kozlowski, 1992; Reichers, 1987). Grant and Ashford (2008) define proactive behavior as "anticipatory action that employees take to impact themselves and/or their environments" (p. 8). Thus, proactive behavior is focused on the future, with an expected impact. Within an organizational socialization context, proactive behaviors can change a newcomer's role or environment to better fit the person, can change the newcomer to adapt to the organization, or can result in mutual development of both parties (Cooper-Thomas & Burke, in press). Proactive behaviors that are related to organizational socialization are labeled here as *individual tactics* for two reasons. First, not all proactive behaviors are related to work behavior or person-environment fit (Parker & Collins, 2010); thus, *individual tactics* differentiate only proactive behaviors related to organizational socialization. Second, *individual tactics* provides a linguistic counterpart to *organizational tactics* and may facilitate recognition of both organizational and individual attempts toward work role adaptation. Five general tactics—monitoring, inquiry, written and electronic sources, job changes, and social influence—are presented to illustrate individual tactics in organizational socialization.

MONITORING

Monitoring involves attending to one's environment and learning through observation. Ashford and Cummings (1983) described monitoring as a personal strategy to create information. By monitoring supervisors, coworkers, subordinates, and others involved with the organization, newcomers can learn how their roles fit within a larger context and can benchmark their own behaviors to normative standards. By monitoring interactions among organizational members, newcomers can learn about power and reward structures, as well as reactions to their own behaviors. Discrete observations on focused targets or on serendipitous targets generally provide information with little social cost to the observer (Miller & Jablin, 1991). A newcomer who inconspicuously monitors others and the work environment does not draw attention to him- or herself, and it may not be known to others that the newcomer is seeking information from these observations. Finally, newcomers who engage in self-observation monitor themselves as they learn to adjust to a new role (Saks & Ashforth, 1996).

Ostroff and Kozlowski (1992) and Morrison (1993b, 1995) found that newcomers relied on monitoring tactics more often than other methods of information acquisition, such as direct inquiries or experimentation. Furthermore, Morrison (1993b) found that monitoring was positively associated with favorable outcomes such as satisfaction and performance, and was negatively associated with unfavorable outcomes, such as intentions to quit. In addition, Ostroff and Kozlowski found significant correlations between monitoring and stress, suggesting that this tactic may stress a newcomer who has to observe and interpret organizational experiences with little support from the organization. Saks and Ashforth (1996) found that newcomers' self-observation was positively related to their internal motivation and ability to cope, negatively related to task-specific anxiety, but unrelated to satisfaction, commitment, intentions to quit or to job performance. Furthermore, observations of coworkers and supervisors were not found to be related to supervisor ratings of overall job performance, but these observations were related to newcomers' self-ratings of their task mastery (Saks & Ashforth, 1997b).

Monitoring tactics can vary in effort costs, from high proactivity, when newcomers intentionally shadow particular targets to gain specific knowledge, to spontaneous monitoring of events that happen before the newcomer (Miller & Jablin, 1991). Although observations of the work environment can be easily accomplished, the lessons learned from those observations may be prone to misinterpretation. The meaning from observations is drawn from the environmental cues that are noticed by the individual and his or her interpretive framework, based on prior knowledge and experiences, as well as goals, values, and expectations for that environment. Without specific questions and answers, observations may not address pertinent needs for information. Also, the sense making from monitoring may be bound by what others are willing to let a newcomer see and hear. Newcomers who are unproven and have yet to earn the trust of organizational members may sensitize others to their presence, resulting in censorship or impression management that provides a biased picture. Thus, monitoring tactics may not provide all the information that a newcomer needs to adjust to an organizational role.

INQUIRY

Inquiry tactics involve direct interactions with others for solicitation of information. Miller and Jablin (1991) described three types of inquiry tactics: overt questions, indirect questions, and disguising conversations. Overt questions are direct questions posed to a target in order to get information openly and efficiently. Social costs to this tactic may be high when a newcomer exposes his or her ignorance to the target (i.e., face loss costs) and/or when the response taxes the target's effort and knowledge. Indirect questions and disguising conversations generally reduce this risk of exposure; however, the target may not understand the implied questions and may fail to address the newcomer's learning needs. Indirect questions may involve non-interrogative questions or hints about a topic, whereas disguising conversations are more discursive, with an initial goal of establishing a rapport with the target and then encouraging the target to provide information. Indirect questions may be used when newcomers are embarrassed to ask direct questions, or when the targets are viewed as intimidating. Disguising conversations also may be used under these circumstances, or when the newcomer is not sure of what questions to ask. Finkelstein, Kulas, and Dages (2003) found that covert information seeking (e.g., hinting for information) was negatively related to role clarity and job satisfaction. They speculated that indirect inquiries may not yield good information that meet a newcomer's needs.

Inquiries are directed at targets who are defined by their relative position to the newcomer. Studies on information seeking in organizational socialization have generally identified support staff, other newcomers, peers, senior coworkers, supervisors, and mentors as targets for inquiries (Louis, Posner & Powell, 1983). Target selection will vary on social costs and usefulness of information; however, the research results are mixed. Morrison (1993b) found that newcomers were more likely to approach supervisors for technical information (e.g., how to perform job tasks), but they tended to approach other newcomers and coworkers for referent information (e.g., role demands and expectations). In contrast, Chan and Schmitt (2000) and van der Velde, Ardts, and Jansen (2005) found that newcomers preferred coworkers over their supervisors for technical information, and Ostroff and Kozlowski (1992) found no differences between information acquired from supervisors and coworkers with regard to task and organizational content domains. However, newcomers acquired more information from supervisors for role information, and they acquired more information from coworkers for group information. Thus, different sources were targeted for different kinds of information seeking. Furthermore, Chan and Schmitt (2000) found intraindividual changes in inquiries over time. Newcomers constantly sought technical information from their supervisors, but inquiries to coworkers for this information declined over time. In addition, newcomer inquiries on referent information increased over time for supervisors, but remained constant over time for coworkers. These studies illustrate the dynamic complexity of information seeking. Different kinds of information are needed at different times from different sources.

Results from research examining the effects of inquiries on outcomes are also mixed. With regard to performance or task mastery outcomes, inquiries soliciting information about how to perform the job were positively related to performance (Ashford & Black, 1996; Morrison, 1993b), negatively related to performance (Settoon & Adkins, 1997), or unrelated to task mastery (Gruman, Saks, & Zweig, 2006). In addition, inquiries soliciting feedback on the newcomer's performance are generally positively related to performance (Ashford & Black, 1996, Gruman et al., 2006), but not always (Morrison, 1993b). Results looking at relationships between inquiries and role clarity have found strong support (Callister, Kramer, &

Turban, 1999; Gruman et al, 2006; Saks, Gruman, & Cooper-Thomas, 2011), some support (Wanberg & Kammeyer-Mueller, 2000; Holder, 1996), or no support (Settoon & Adkins, 1997). Finally, research examining the relationship between inquiries and job satisfaction or organizational commitment generally find a positive relationship (Gruman et al, 2006; Morrison, 1993b; Saks et al, 2011; Wanberg & Kammeyer-Mueller, 2000); although Ashford and Black (1996) found no significant correlations between either information-seeking inquiries or feedback-seeking inquiries and satisfaction.

WRITTEN OR ELECTRONIC SOURCES

In contrast with inquiry tactics, written or electronic sources are generally non-interpersonal tactics. Written sources include technical manuals and employee handbooks that may address specific questions that a newcomer has about the job or about employee conduct. Additional written sources, such as annual reports, memos, house organs, or newsletters, can help inform newcomers about the organization in general. Furthermore, electronic resources, such as organizational web sites and organizational accounts to social networking sites (e.g., Facebook, Twitter, LinkedIn, etc.), can provide information about organizational life. Some electronic resources are similar to written sources, with little to no user interaction, whereas other resources are designed for personal interactions with others. For example, the U.S. Army maintains a web site exclusive for company commanders (Dixon, Allen, Burgess, Kilner & Schweitzer, 2005). New commanders can post questions on a wide variety of topics, seeking guidance from more experienced commanders. The web site also allows commanders to create professional forums for discussions on specific topics, and it houses a reading program for commanders to read common books and articles and hold online discussions of them. CompanyCommand.com is an important vehicle for past, present, and future company commanders to connect with one another and to hold conversations that improve their leadership and job performance. The web site was originally informally established by company commanders; however, the success of the site prompted the Army to formally manage it and to protect the security of its communications. Interactive web sites blur the distinction between proactive tactics like inquiry and electronic resources, as well as distinctions between organizational and individual tactics.

Ostroff and Kozlowski (1992) found that newcomers did not acquire as much information from manuals as they did from interpersonal sources or from experimentation; however, there was a significant correlation between acquiring information from manuals at Time 1 and organizational commitment at Time 2. Similarly, Morrison (1993a) found that newcomers did not use "memos, annual reports, or other written material" as often as inquiry or monitoring tactics to seek information. In general, these written sources had no effect on outcomes such as role clarity, acculturation, and social integration, but consulting written sources for performance feedback was related to task mastery at a later time period. In contrast, van der Velde, Ardts, and Jansen (2005) found written materials to be an important predictor of organizational knowledge and commitment. The empirical research on written sources is limited and, to date, there is no research examining the effects of electronic or Internet sources on organizational socialization. Given the popularity of social network sites and the growing presence of organizations in these networks, these sources of information for newcomers should be researched. Like monitoring tactics, consulting written or electronic sources of information can be easy and involve no social costs, unless the newcomer engages in virtual interpersonal exchanges.

In addition to organizationally sanctioned electronic resources, non-sanctioned sources (e.g., informal chat rooms, individual blogs, web sites from disgruntled former employees, etc.) can provide contrasting information to newcomers. Access to written and electronic sources will vary by effort to locate pertinent information, interpersonal contact to obtain information, and the quality of the information to newcomer socialization. These sources of information may help the newcomer learn the boundaries of behavior that is rewarded, tolerated, or punished by the organization. Further understanding of these boundaries may be accomplished by a newcomer's own testing and experimentation.

JOB CHANGES

Proactive behaviors to change the conditions of a newcomer's job may involve experimentation or negotiation. Experimentation tactics involve a newcomer's proactive changes in behavior and learning from the consequences of that behavior. Ostroff and Kozlowski (1992) describe *trying* as an information acquisition tactic in which a newcomer learns through trial and error or learns from experimenting with different behaviors. Reactions from these types of behaviors can help reduce uncertainty and better define what is valued in the organization. Miller and

Jablin (1991) describe a specific type of experimentation tactic, *testing limits*, that involves a newcomer deliberately violating a rule or normative practice. The purpose of this testing is to force specific targets, generally a supervisor and/or colleagues, to react to the violation. Tolerance of the behavior may signal low importance of a particular rule or acceptance of different behaviors from the newcomer; whereas disapproval and efforts to make the newcomer conform to rules and behavioral norms signal more rigid expectations for socialization.

Saks and Ashforth (1996) examined self-management strategies and proactive socialization. Of these strategies, self-goal-setting can be construed as a form of trying or experimentation when a newcomer defines specific directions and standards of performance for him- or herself. These self-set goals may be presented to others as a test of what is important, or as a check on whether the newcomer's perceptions of performance goals are in line with organizational expectations. Saks and Ashforth found that self-set goals were positively related to ability to cope and negatively related to anxiety and stress. However, self-set goals were not related to intention to quit or to job performance. In contrast, Holder (1996) found no significant relationship between testing and socialization outcomes for a sample of female newcomers in non-traditional occupations. Results from open-ended probes indicted that these newcomers often perceived heightened scrutiny of their performance; thus, they were less likely to take risks involved in testing limits.

Direct negotiations with others, particularly supervisors and coworkers, can help newcomers change performance expectations, task assignments, or other job characteristics (Ashford & Black, 1996). Negotiating job changes has been found to be positively related to role clarity, but unrelated to job satisfaction or turnover intention (Gruman et al., 2006; Saks et al., 2011). These mixed results may be due to the fact that these studies measured the extent to which newcomers engaged in job-change negotiations, but did not measure whether the negotiations were successful or whether any negotiated changes were evaluated favorably by the newcomer.

The variety of proactive behaviors that can be used to change the newcomer's environment is infinite. What matters are the reactions to these behaviors by important others and the newcomer's responses or adjustments to these initial reactions. The reactions of others can be shaped by the types of relationships that a newcomer can form with these targets.

SOCIAL INFLUENCE

Social influence tactics refer to proactive attempts to build relationships with others. Goffman (1959) describes how first impressions are critical for an individual to communicate, to a particular audience, the type of person that he or she is. Efforts to manage the impression that an audience has about an individual could significantly affect subsequent interactions and long-term relationships. Parallels between the literatures on organizational socialization and impression management can be drawn in numerous ways. First, both constructs share the goal of defining a situation for a focal person. Consistent with URT and SET, information about an individual enables others to know what to expect from him or her and what that person may expect from them. The person can influence an audience via conscious efforts with influence tactics, or via non-conscious efforts through scripts and overlearned habits (Gardner & Martinko, 1988). Second, individual and organizational efforts in the socialization process are mirrored by the exchange of roles between an actor and audience in the impression-management process. During initial interactions, it may be difficult to determine who is actor and who is audience, as both parties attempt to influence each other. Lastly, both processes involve individual behaviors, audience or organizational reactions to that behavior, interpretations or sense making of those reactions, and learning and adjustments for future behaviors.

Organizational newcomers are likely to be motivated to create favorable impressions with their supervisors in order to gain positive performance evaluations and rewards (Rao, Schmidt, & Murray, 1995). Examples of upward influence tactics include ingratiation (being humble and making the target person feel important), exchange of benefits (personal favors in exchange for something), rationality (use of facts or logic to influence the target), assertiveness (demanding actions), upward appeal (obtaining support from superiors), and coalitions (using alliances with others to strengthen influence) (Kipnis, Schmidt, & Wilkinson, 1980; Yukl & Falbe, 1990). Su (2010) found significant correlations between two of these tactics, ingratiation and rationality, with organizational socialization for a sample of hotel employees in Taiwan. Furthermore, consistent with a high power distance culture, employees who rated themselves high on organizational socialization were less likely to be rated by their supervisors as using assertiveness tactics. Thus, for a Chinese sample, subordinates who understood their work role were less likely to be assertive with their supervisors.

At a general level, building social relationships can also be viewed as social influence tactics as newcomers establish bonds with organizational members. Fang, Duffy, and Shaw (2011) posit that successful organizational socialization is achieved through access and mobilization of social capital. Accessibility to social capital is influenced by network locations and resources, whereas mobilization of social capital involves purposive or instrumental actions with a newcomer's network to gain economic, political, and/or social outcomes (Lin, 1999). Theoretical explanations for social networking parallel several arguments for organizational socialization. Lin (1999) describes four reasons for social ties: they facilitate information acquisition; they facilitate influence on others; they help define roles or social credentials; and they reinforce social identities. Newcomers who build more social capital within an organization are more likely to learn and adjust to their new roles.

Ashford and Black (1996) developed scales to measure three relationship-building tactics: *general socializing*, *networking* (building relationships with interdepartmental colleagues), and *building relationships with the boss*. Only the last scale was related to newcomer performance, whereas *general socializing* and *networking* were unrelated to performance (Ashford & Black, 1996; Gruman et al., 2006). In addition, these scales were found to be significantly related to role clarity, satisfaction, and commitment, although the *networking* scale was sometimes not found to be significantly correlated with these outcomes (Gruman et al., 2006; Saks et al., 2011; Wanberg & Kammeyer-Mueller, 2000). Lastly, the general socializing scale was found to be consistently related to turnover intentions (Gruman et al., 2006; Saks et al., 2011; Wanberg & Kammeyer-Mueller, 2000), although it was not related to actual turnover (Wanberg & Kammeyer-Mueller, 2000).

Morrison (2002b) examined relationships between social network structures and socialization outcomes. She found that newcomers' informational networks were more strongly related to learning outcomes than assimilation outcomes, but the newcomers' friendship networks were more strongly related to assimilation outcomes than learning outcomes. Furthermore, structural characteristics of these networks, such as size, density, and strength, were differentially related to socialization outcomes. For example, information network size was associated with organizational knowledge, whereas information network density and strength were associated with task mastery and role clarity.

Thus, patterns of organizational relationships affect newcomer learning and assimilation.

Summary

Our understanding of socialization tactics has advanced from a one-sided perspective of how organizations process people, to recognition of individual and organizational efforts in learning and adjustment (Nicholson, 1984). Both types of tactics range from general processes (e.g., individual versus group socialization) to specific interventions (e.g., interactive web sites). Although some tactics may be classified as both individual and organizational methods (e.g., interactions with supervisor), the purpose of identifying organizational and individual socialization tactics is to emphasize the active role that each party plays in the socialization process. Organizational and individual tactics can converge to help a newcomer identify and learn from role models in the organization (Filstad, 2004). Furthermore, different tactics can solicit different types of information (Morrison, 1993b), resulting in a variety of lessons, adjustments, and outcomes.

Conceptually, both individual and organizational tactics are featured in socialization models (cf. Ashforth, Sluss, & Harrison, 2007; Bauer, et al., 2007; Fang et al, 2011; Griffin, Colella, & Goparaju, 2000; Klein & Heuser, 2008; Saks & Ashforth, 1997a); however, there are relatively few empirical studies of both. Saks and Ashforth (1997b) found that both information acquisition and organizational tactics were significantly related to socialization outcomes for newly hired accountants. Furthermore, information acquisition partially mediated the relationships between institutional organizational tactics and outcomes such as task mastery, satisfaction, and commitment. They concluded that organizational tactics may influence the types of individual tactics that are used by newcomers. Other studies found individual tactics to moderate the relationships between organizational tactics and socialization outcomes (Gruman et al., 2006; Kim et al., 2005). In contrast, Griffin, Colella, and Goparaju (2000) provide theoretical arguments for organizational tactics to moderate the relationships between individual tactics and socialization outcomes.

Atzori, Lombardi, Fraccaroli, Battistelli, and Zaniboni (2008) examined organizational tactics and individual proactivity on the organizational socialization of women in the Italian army. They found that individual proactivity (i.e., general socializing) was more strongly related to learning than organizational tactics (i.e., tutoring/mentoring and granting time to adjust). Interestingly, a second proactive tactic, information seeking, was not related to any learning or outcomes. Atzori et al. speculated that the hierarchical and formal nature of the army did not encourage information seeking, particularly from women. Furthermore, they found that learning organizational goals and values and learning organizational politics mediated the relationships between both individual proactivity and organizational tactics and socialization outcomes of team cohesion and organizational identification.

Ashforth, Sluss, and Saks (2007) examined organizational tactics and proactive behavior on socialization learning and outcomes for new hires who entered their first full-time jobs after college graduation. The organizational tactics were based on Van Maanen and Schein's taxonomy, but the investiture tactic was considered separately from all the other tactics that were combined to form an institutionalized tactic scale. Results showed that newcomer proactive behavior was more predictive of learning than institutionalized tactics; furthermore, the investiture tactic was not related to newcomer learning. In addition, they found that all tactics were associated with some socialization outcomes (i.e., institutionalized tactics were negatively related to intentions to quit and role innovation), independent of newcomer learning. Thus, Ashforth et al. concluded that socialization processes or tactics could have direct impact on socialization outcomes, independent of any learning content.

Both the Atzori et al. and Ashforth et al. studies found individual tactics to be more strongly related to learning, compared with organizational tactics. This may not be surprising, given that individual tactics can be purposively used to address a specific learning need. However, the types of tactics, learning content, and outcomes varied greatly between the two studies, and more research is needed to examine differential effects of organizational and individual tactics on organizational socialization.

Another common component of the two studies is the use of socialization learning content to mediate the relationships between socialization tactics and outcomes. Contrary to what Van Maanen and Schein stated in 1979, *how* people learn may not directly affect *what* they learn. During the 1990s, several researchers began to measure socialization content directly, instead of having this content inferred from knowledge about socialization tactics. A review of socialization content—*what* newcomers learn—is presented as the core component of organizational socialization.

Organizational Socialization Content

People who are new to an organization or position have a lot to learn. Learning content can range from boring minutiae related to a specific task, to grand conjectures on future career potential in the organization. However, not all learning is related to organizational socialization, nor are all lessons effectively applied to an individual's adjustment within that organization. Learning new knowledge, skills, or capabilities in order to position oneself for a new job or career may be unrelated to socialization or adjustment to the current position, particularly if new career moves take place outside the current organization. Thus, the study of organizational socialization content, *what* is learned, needs to be considered within the bounds of a current socialization episode, *what* is learned to help adjust to *which* organizational role. Our current understanding of chains of socialization episodes and the dynamic stages of any one socialization process highlights the links between what we learn as we adjust to one position, and how we might use those lessons to help us make sense of what we learn as we adjust to a subsequent position. Experiences today shape anticipations for the future.

Measuring Organizational Socialization Content

Researchers have developed several scales to measure the content of learning in organizational socialization. A description of some of the more prominent scales in the socialization literature is summarized in Table 18.3. Each scale's dimensions are briefly described with a representative item. As one might expect, there is considerable conceptual overlap of content across scales; however, the variety of definitions and nuances within and between scales preclude clean match-ups of content domains, (see Ashforth, Sluss, & Harrison, 2007 for a comparison). These scales have generally followed two forms of structure: socialization content structured by specific knowledge areas (e.g., learning how to perform a task/job), or socialization content structured by specific reference areas (e.g., learning at the job, group, and organization levels). Examples of each type are described, followed by an integrated discussion of socialization content.

The Chao et al. (1994) scales are currently the most widely used (Ashforth, Sluss, & Harrison, 2007; Bauer et al., 2007; Klein & Heuser, 2008)

and are described here as an example of socialization content structured by specific knowledge subjects. Their six content dimensions are: performance proficiency, language, people, politics, organizational goals and values, and history. Each content area was drawn from the theoretical literature on organizational socialization, with the proviso that only content areas related to organizational interventions and outcomes were considered. Thus, learning related to an individual's self-concept, or personal learning (Fisher, 1986), was not included. The *performance proficiency* dimension is described as learning how to perform tasks required on the job. Obviously, learning how to perform the job proficiently is a fundamental requirement for most individuals interested in keeping that job; thus performance proficiency is a primary content dimension that needs to be learned before or shortly after a new job has begun. A second content dimension, *people*, is also fundamental in most organizational contexts. The *people* dimension involves learning how to get along with others in the work unit and may involve work-related and nonwork-related social interactions. Third, knowledge about the *organization's goals and values* is often found in definitions of organizational socialization. These goals and values reflect an organization's culture, linking a newcomer to the larger organization, beyond his or her immediate work unit. Fourth, the *politics* content dimension concerns learning about informal relationships and power structures. The knowledge of who is more powerful than others can help a newcomer learn effective behavior patterns for a new role. Fifth, the *history* content dimension taps knowledge about the organization's past, including personal backgrounds of key organizational figures. Finally, the sixth content area, *language*, is the narrowest dimension, concerned with learning technical language, slang, and acronyms unique to a profession or organization. Not all jobs and organizations have unique language terms; therefore this dimension may have limited applications. However, learning company-specific acronyms and jargon can facilitate communications with other organizational members.

Chao et al. (1994) found different response patterns across these six content dimensions for samples of employees who kept their jobs, changed jobs within an organization, or changed jobs and organizations, over the course of five years. Some of these dimensions of organizational socialization content were also found to be related to the amount of standardized procedures on the job (Hsiung &

Table 18.3 Content Dimensions of Organizational Socialization

Source	Content Areas and Sample Items
Ostroff & Kozlowski, (1992) 33 items on 5 point Likert-type scale ranging from "not very knowledgeable" to "extremely knowledgeable"	Task domain: task mastery and how to do the job— "*How to perform the basic job tasks and duties.*" (alpha = .84) Role domain: boundaries of responsibility for the position – "*What is expected on my job*" (alpha = .83) Group domain: how to get along with coworkers – "*The objectives and goals of my group*" (alpha = .76) Organizational domain: politics, power, culture, and values – "*Who has power and authority in the organization.*" (alpha = .83)
Chao et al. (1994) 34 items rated on a 5 point Likert-type scale ranging from "strongly disagree" to "strongly agree"	Performance proficiency: learning to perform required job tasks – "*I understand what all the duties of my job entail.*" (5 items; alpha = .80) Language: learning a profession's technical language as well as organization-specific acronyms, slang and jargon – "*I have not mastered this organization's slang and special jargon.*" (reverse scored item) (5 items; alpha = .81) Politics: learning formal and informal work relationships and power structures – "*I have learned how things 'really work' on the inside of this organization.*" (6 items; alpha = .81) People: learning to build successful and satisfying work relationships – "*Within my work group, I would be easily identified as 'one of the gang.'*" (6 items; alpha = .80) Organizational goals and values: learning rules or principles and goals that characterize the organization – "*I understand the goals of my organization.*" (7 items; alpha = .81) History: learning about the organization's traditions and customs as well as the background of a work group – "*I know the organization's long-held traditions.*" (5 items; alpha = .85)
Morrison, (1995) 40 items for 7 categories of information. Rating on a 5 point Likert-type scale, ranging from "very useful" to "not useful"; items repeated with ratings from "to a great extent" to "not at all" for 3 sets of additional ratings on: Inquiry, Monitoring, and Passive Receipt. Reliabilities ranged from .74 to .91. Note: Ashforth, Sluss & Saks (2007) used Morrison's items but with a different rating scale to measure socialization content learning. 5 point Likert-type scale ranging from "To a very little extent" to "To a very large extent," rating "extent to which they have learned in these areas" (p. 455) alpha for 40-item scale = .96	Technical information: how to perform required job tasks – "*How to perform specific aspects of one's job*" (5 items) Referent Information: what others expect (role demands) from the newcomer – "*Performance standards associated with one's job position*" (6 items) Social Information: how to interact with others in acceptable ways – "*How to get along with people in the organization*" (7 items) Appraisal Information: how others perceive a newcomer's performance – "*Feedback on the adequacy of one's job skills and abilities*" (5 items) Normative Information: information about expected attitudes and behaviors – "*The history of the organization*" (7 items) Organizational Information: information about the organization's structure, procedures and performance – "*Organizational policies and procedures*" (6 items) Political Information: how power is distributed in the organization – "*Who makes the important decisions in the organization*" (4 items)
Thomas & Anderson (1998) 21 items on 7 point Likert-type scale, ranging from "not at all" to "totally."	Role information: understanding performance expectations—"*I understand what my personal responsibilities are*" (6 items, alpha = .88) Social information: integration with colleagues—"*I can easily be identified as 'one of the team'*" (8 items, alpha = .93) Interpersonal resources: establish network for help—"*I have someone I feel comfortable going to if I need help with personal problems*" (3 items, alpha = .81) Organization information: understanding organizational structure and culture—"*I am familiar with the unwritten rules of how things are done at this organization*" (4 items, alpha = .76)

(Continued)

Table 18.3 (continued)

Source	Content Areas and Sample Items
Haueter, Macan & Winter (2003) 35 items rated on a 7 point Likert-type scale, ranging from "strongly disagree" to "strongly agree."	Organizational socialization: history, goals, policies, politics at organizational level – "*I know the specific names of the products/services produced/provided by this organization.*" (12 items, alpha = .88) Group socialization: understanding work group role, group values, politics; relation of own group to other groups,—"*I understand how my particular work group contributes to the organization's goals.*" (12 items; alpha = .92) Task socialization: understanding how to perform tasks, tools, responsibilities, how to meet customer needs – "*I know the responsibilities, tasks and projects for which I was hired.*" (11 items; alpha = .89)
Taormina (1994), revised scale (2004) 20 items rated on a 7 point Likert-type scale, ranging from "strongly disagree" to "strongly agree." Note: Only one item is identical in both the 1994 and 2004 measures.	Training: learning through job training – "*This company offers thorough training to improve employee job skills.*" (5 items, alpha = .76) Understanding: learning about organizational objectives, processes, and goals – "*This organization's objectives are understood by almost everyone who works here.*" (5 items; alpha = .79) Coworker support: emotional support and help from coworkers – "*My co-workers are usually willing to offer their assistance or advice.*" (5 items; alpha = .81) Future prospects: learning about the probabilities for future promotions and a secure career in the organization – "*I am happy with the rewards offered by this organization.*" (5 items; alpha = .76)

Hsieh 2003), attitudes (Mitus, 2006; Moon, 2006) and to cross-cultural adjustment (Liu & Lee, 2008). Furthermore, socialization content was found to mediate relationships between early socialization experiences and later affective outcomes (Atzori et al., 2008; Hart & Miller, 2005; Klein & Weaver, 2000; Klein, Fan, & Preacher, 2006; Wesson & Gogus, 2005).

In a similar vein, Morrison (1995) identified seven types of information that newcomers may need to learn. They are: technical information (how to perform the job), referent information (expectations and role requirements), social information (how to get along with others), appraisal information (feedback), normative information (organizational history, goals), organizational information (structure, policies), and political information (authority over others). Although Morrison developed her scales to examine the usefulness of the information types during the socialization process, Ashforth, Sluss, and Saks (2007) adopted her scales to measure the extent to which newcomers learned in each content area. They found that newcomer learning mediated some relationships between socialization tactics and socialization outcomes such as performance and job satisfaction, but some organizational and individual tactics were also found to be directly related to

outcomes such as role innovation and intentions to quit.

Taormina's Organizational Socialization Inventory (OSI) taps four dimensions: *training, understanding one's job and organization, coworker support,* and *future prospects* in the employing organization (Taormina, 1997). The OSI differs from previous scales by combining a specific socialization tactic, training programs, with job learning content in the *training* dimension, and by including a *future prospects* dimension that may be more relevant to anticipatory socialization for the next job, as opposed to organizational socialization in the current position.

Three scales are structured by reference domains or are hybrids of reference domains and subject areas. Ostroff and Kozlowski's (1992) scales are structured in four dimensions: *task, role, group,* and *organization.* The *task* and *role* dimensions are focused on specific knowledge related to task performance and role expectations, respectively. In contrast, the *group* and *organization* dimensions tap a wider base of knowledge that incorporates several of Chao et al.'s content dimensions. Items related to goals, authority, and socializing can be found in both dimensions, and the focus is on a particular reference group. In a similar vein, Haueter, Macan, and Winter (2003) developed a three-dimension Newcomer Socialization Questionnaire (NSQ) that focused on job/task, group, and organizational domains. Finally, Thomas and Anderson's (1998) scale consists of four dimensions: *role information, social information, interpersonal resources,* and *organization information.* The addition of the *interpersonal resources* dimension is unique, addressing the availability of other people to help the newcomer in work or personal matters. The *organization* dimension contains items from different knowledge domains (e.g., values, history, structure), similar to the previous two measures. Cooper-Thomas and Anderson (2002, 2005) found that learning content mediated the relationship between socialization tactics and affective outcomes.

Critique and Extensions of Socialization Content

The Chao et al. measure is often used in abbreviated versions (Bauer et al., 2007), and it has been criticized for a number of shortcomings. Klein and Heuser (2008) note that some scales are multidimensional (e.g., goals and values), some combine learning and proximal outcomes that are the results of learning (e.g., performance proficiency scale and task mastery), and the scales do not differentiate socialization at the job, group, and organization levels. Criticisms have also been leveled at other scales, and Klein and Heuser concluded, "Despite these limitations, the Chao et al. (1994) typology is the least problematic, contains the fewest dimensions that confound outcomes with learning content, and has been the most widely used of the frameworks currently available within the literature" (p. 300).

Klein and Heuser further note that current measures structured along job, group, and organization levels combine a variety of learning content that make it problematic to examine specific content areas. Thus, current measures are either deficient in identifying precise knowledge domains (*what* needs to be learned), or they are deficient in identifying precise reference levels (*what* needs to be learned by *level*). Building from Chao et al.'s work, Klein and Heuser propose a new taxonomy of socialization content that identifies 12 knowledge domains; they are introduced here with the dimension labels noted in italics. *Language, history,* and performance proficiency were generally retained from Chao et al., but the last dimension was renamed *task proficiency* for conceptual clarity. The people dimension was subdivided to differentiate *working relationships* and *social relationships;* the politics dimension was subdivided

to differentiate formal *structure* and informal *politics;* and the organizational goals and values was subdivided to differentiate *goals and strategy* from *culture and values.* In addition, three new dimensions were related to learning formal *rules and policies,* implicit rules and norms (*navigation*), and learning about *inducements* or rewards that are tied to newcomer contributions. They propose that these dimensions of socialization content should be measured at different levels within the organization, and at different times during the socialization process in order to capture what is learned, at which level, and when.

The dimensions of socialization content identified by Klein and Heuser represent a good foundation for the next generation of socialization measures. The 12 dimensions can assess knowledge domains related to a particular socialization level. Inherent in this perspective is a focus on the organization, and all its levels, as the context for socialization content. However, learning and sense making from organizational experiences also contribute to learning about the newcomer's own capabilities, vulnerabilities, and expectations for the future. Future measures may consider knowledge domains in personal growth and change that might support or challenge lessons learned in traditional socialization content domains. Davey and Arnold (2000) identified different themes of personal change from multiple methods and discussed the challenges of research in this area.

One limitation of all the current socialization measures is their inability to assess the tacit knowledge that a newcomer learns. Tacit knowledge is personal knowledge gained from implicit learning (Reber, 1995). It is largely non-conscious and cannot be articulated; thus it cannot be captured by traditional paper-and-pencil measures. However, tactic knowledge is likely to be learned through a socialization process of shared experiences (Nonanka, 1994). Chao (1997b) draws parallels between organizational socialization and implicit learning, noting that the two are both context-bound and involve incidental learning events. Thus, newcomers may not be aware that they are learning anything when they observe and interact with others in the organization. Knowledge acquisition can be influenced by any and all experiences, whether they are initiated by the organization or the newcomer, and whether they are intended lessons or unintended revelations. Given the primacy and ubiquity of implicit learning (Lewicki, Hill, & Czyzewska, 1992), *what* is learned may need to be assessed by measures that capture more than subjects' conscious perceptions.

Three studies tested a mediation model, examining the socialization tactics → socialization content → socialization outcomes relationship (Ashforth, Sluss, & Saks, 2007; Cooper-Thomas & Anderson, 2002; Kammeyer-Mueller & Wanberg, 2003). Kammeyer-Mueller and Wanberg examined three sources of influence: organizational (orientation and training), leader, and coworkers on newcomer learning. These sources can be viewed as organizational tactics, but Kammeyer-Muller and Wanberg found little support for socialization content to mediate the relationships between these tactics and outcomes such as organizational commitment and work withdrawal. In contrast, the other two studies (Ashforth, Sluss, & Saks, 2007; Cooper-Thomas & Anderson, 2002) found support for socialization content, or learning to fully mediate some relationships between socialization tactics and outcomes. For example, Cooper-Thomas and Anderson found that the positive relationships between institutionalized tactics and attitudes like job satisfaction and organizational commitment were fully mediated by their measure of information acquisition. Ashforth et al. also found that newcomer learning fully mediated positive relationships between institutionalized tactics and outcomes such as performance, job satisfaction, and organizational commitment. In addition, they found that the investiture tactic was unrelated to learning content but was directly and positively related to organizational identification, job satisfaction, and negatively related to turnover intention. Moreover, institutionalized tactics and newcomer proactivity were directly related to role innovation and turnover intention, independent of newcomer learning. They concluded that "*how* newcomers are socialized has substantive and symbolic value over and above *what* they actually learn" (p. 447). However, given the limitations of current socialization content measures, an alternative conclusion could be that additional content domains may be required to examine the mediation model. Clearly, more research is needed to understand what is learned, how it is learned, and the impact of those lessons.

A Blueprint for Future Research

Over the past 40 years, the field of organizational socialization has developed from descriptions of how people adjust to their occupations (e.g., Hughes, 1958) to meta-analyses of a growing body of empirical research (e.g., Bauer et al., 2007; Saks et al., 2007). The study of organizational socialization has progressed from a one-sided view of

organizational tactics that process people, to a more dynamic view of proactive individuals and organizations interacting to help newcomers adjust to a new organizational role. Much has been learned; yet much remains to be investigated. As a guide for future research, Figure 18.1 presents a blueprint of organizational socialization, its components and primary relationships.

The model depicts a socialization process roughly in chronological order, starting from the left, at a time prior to job/organization entry (anticipatory socialization), and progressing to the right, through the encounter and role management phases. Before an individual assumes a new position, the organizational context and individual differences "set the stage" for socialization. The organization's context—its culture, mission, physical properties, and managerial practices—establish characteristics that influence how the organization attracts applicants (both internal and external), and selects them for new positions. Saks and Ashforth (1997a) include extra-organizational variables as part of the context for organizational socialization. National cultures and employment laws affect organizational structures and practices that may be important features for newcomers entering a foreign work environment. Similarly, Kammeyer-Mueller (2007) includes the organization's competitive environment as an important contextual feature that affects the kind of newcomer that it wants to attract and hire.

When organizations are attracting and selecting new hires, individuals also exercise strategies as they look for new positions. From the individual's perspective, general personality traits can affect which jobs are selected for application and the types of tactics that he or she is likely to use to appear as an attractive candidate and as a valued employee. Schneider et al. (1998) found evidence for modal organizational personalities, thus supporting the attraction-selection-socialization-attrition process. In addition, personality traits and individual differences such as extroversion and openness to experience (Wanberg & Kammeyer-Mueller, 2000), self-efficacy (Major & Kozlowski, 1997; Saks & Ashforth, 1997b), and curiosity (Harrison, Sluss, & Ashforth, 2011) have been found to predict newcomer proactive behaviors. Similarly, expectations formed from the anticipatory socialization phase can also drive newcomer attitudes and behaviors (Riordan, Weatherly, Vandenberg, & Self, 2001; Scholarios, Lockyer, & Johnson, 2003; Wanous, 1992).

Organizational tactics and individual tactics are likely to interact with one another during

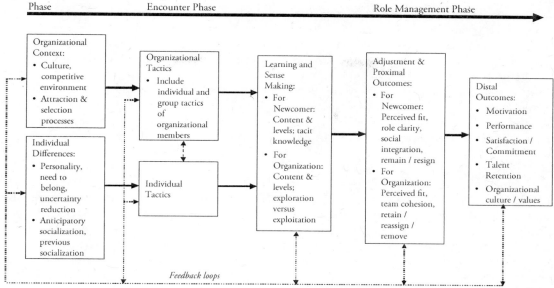

Figure 18.1 A Blueprint for Organizational Socialization.

the learning and sense-making process, but more research is needed to understand how specific tactics can reinforce or contradict lessons learned. Current research in organizational socialization has focused on what the newcomer learns; solid progress has been achieved identifying learning content, and future research can improve on existing measures and distinguish specific content across socialization levels. Furthermore, research examining tacit knowledge that is learned during the socialization process might fill in some of the gaps or missing variables in current research.

Along with lessons learned from tactics and early experiences, newcomers go through a sense-making process to make these lessons sensible. Weick (1995) described sense making as a process with seven distinguishing characteristics. Applied to an organizational socialization context, these characteristics are as follows. Sense making is (1) grounded in identity construction as an organizational member. It is (2) retrospective because newcomers can observe or experiment with behaviors on a new job, but then try to make sense of those behaviors after the fact. Sense making involves (3) actions in dynamic environments. It is (4) social, (5) ongoing, and (6) focuses on extracted cues or those events that are perceived by newcomers as important. Finally, sense making may (7) settle for plausibility, which may not be accurate. These characteristics of sense

making share common ground with many of the aspects of organizational socialization described in this chapter. Some of the socialization research that examines positive framing can be viewed as examples of sense making. Ashford and Black (1996) argued that newcomer efforts to regard their experiences as positive (i.e., positively frame their work environments) can affect how they understand their new roles.

Alongside future research that examines newcomer learning and sense making, it is now time to also address organizational learning and sense making. Kozlowski, Chao, and Jensen (2010) describe how organizations learn at multiple levels and how learning can be a two-way process between newcomers and organizational members/teams during organizational socialization. March (1991) contrasts two adaptive systems in organizational learning: *exploration* applies organizational learning toward innovation and new possibilities, whereas *exploitation* applies organizational learning toward improvements of current products and operations. Organizations engage in both exploration and exploitation, but these adaptive systems compete for scarce resources, forcing organizations to make choices or priorities between the two. Mutual learning between the organization and newcomers affect the social context of organizational learning. Organizations that socialize their newcomers slowly may have more opportunities to learn from these newcomers than organizations with newcomers who quickly adopt current, and potentially stagnant, values and practices. Organizational learning, particularly in exploration, is more likely when organizations can capitalize on the diversity that newcomers bring. Thus, March cautions that the gains from quick socialization may be offset by losses from missed opportunities for organizational learning and concludes that "rapid socialization may hurt the socializers even as it helps the socialized" (p. 86). This concern is echoed by Schneider et al. (1998), who noted that the homogeneity resulting from attraction-selection-socialization-attrition processes is unlikely to foster the adaptability needed for creativity, innovation, and long-term organizational effectiveness.

Organizational learning can take place at the individual (e.g., leader), group, or organizational level. Like the calls for newcomer learning to recognize different socialization levels, examinations of organizational learning should also recognize these differences. Moreland and Levine (2001) argue that socialization at the work group level is more important than socialization at the organizational level because a work group generally has more power over their members, making a newcomer more committed to a work group than to the organization as a whole. Very little research has been conducted in this area (Kozlowski & Bell, 2003). One exception is Chen and Klimoski's (2003) study that examined team leader and team member expectations of newcomer performance approximately three weeks after a newcomer joins the team. They found that these combined expectations predicted newcomer performance about six weeks later. Subsequent analyses showed that these expectations of newcomer performance also predicted newcomer performance and team performance around three months after the newcomer's entry (Chen, 2005). More research is needed to understand how leaders and team members form expectations about newcomers, how these expectations may change as organizational members learn more about a newcomer, and how they adjust as a team after members make sense of their learned lessons.

Organizational learning is important to organizational socialization because the knowledge gained can directly change tactics designed to socialize newcomers. An example of these links can be found in the U.S. Army's restructure of its basic boot camp. Jaffe (2006) describes the Army's concern when fewer young adults were joining the Army and the attrition rate of new recruits was around 18% during the first six months of basic training. The new training program takes a softer approach than traditional boot camp, including less yelling, more mentoring, and making available experienced soldiers to answer recruits' questions. Early results with the new socialization tactics were promising, with the attrition rate declining to 11%. The Army learned about the latest generation of recruits and concluded that a more positive socialization approach would be more effective.

The learning and sense making that newcomers and organizational members experience will affect proximal socialization outcomes for all parties. Proximal outcomes may be viewed as proxies for sense making. For example, a newcomer who perceives a good fit with the job or organization may have concluded that the job or organization "makes sense" to him- or herself. Conversely, a newcomer who does not perceive a good fit may have concluded that the job or organization "does not make sense." Likewise, a newcomer who makes sense of the job is more likely to perceive role clarity than a newcomer who cannot make sense of the job.

The proximal outcomes should be considered at both the individual and organization's perspectives. Parallel to the newcomer's perceived fit with the group and organization are the organizational units' perceived fit with the newcomer. Parallel to the newcomer's decision to remain or resign from the organization are the organization's decisions to retain, reassign, or remove the newcomer. In turn, these proximal outcomes will affect more distal outcomes related to motivation, commitment, values, and performance at the individual, group, and organization levels.

The model presented in Figure 18.1 can serve as a general blueprint for future research. Key to our understanding of how individuals and organizations adjust within the context of organizational socialization is the recognition of the active efforts of both parties, their learning and sense making, and the effects of that learning on proximal and distal outcomes. Furthermore, feedback loops represented by dotted lines connect model components as the socialization process unfolds over time. This is an area for more research; there is a need to better capture how experiences and learning affect subsequent knowledge gains, sense making, and adjustments. As a recent example, Kammeyer-Mueller, Livingston, and Liao (2011) found that newcomer proactive behavior could be influenced by the degree to which they perceived themselves as similar to their work groups; thus, the work group context can influence individual socialization tactics. Finally, the entire model itself repeats as a new socialization episode is anticipated, encountered, and managed. Thus, links between model components within one socialization episode or across multiple models in chains of socialization can be fruitful areas for future research.

A final area for future research is not captured in Figure 18.1. Little attention has been paid to those individuals who cannot or will not fully adapt to their work environments. Schneider (1987) posits that people who do not fit in the places where they work are likely to leave the organization, thus making up the third feature in his attraction-selection-attrition model. However, under conditions of high unemployment, there may be substantial numbers of people who "don't fit, but don't 'attrit.'" Some may utilize their differences to make positive contributions to the organization (March, 1991), though for most, the outcomes may not be healthy for the person or the place. Despite the negative consequences, a job is better than no job, and functional employees are better than a labor shortage; thus these situations can persist. Future research can examine how these individuals and organizations cope with one another, what can be done to improve these situations, and what can be done to prevent these situations.

Table 18.4 summarizes the recommendations for future research. Some of these initiatives will require different populations of subjects (e.g., newcomers who refuse to be socialized), methodologies (e.g., assessing tacit knowledge), and constructs (e.g., organizational learning) that are new to our current examination of organizational socialization. However, the outcomes of these future research directions are likely to help individuals, teams, and organizations as they negotiate new and changing roles.

Conclusions

This chapter opened with an account of Henry Ford's experiment to create and enforce a company culture. Ford's Sociological Department was charged with the mission to "explain opportunity, teach American ways and customs, English language, duties of citizenship...counsel and help unsophisticated employees to obtain and maintain comfortable, congenial and sanitary living conditions" (Meyer, 1981, p. 126). These lessons were believed to help employees at work and at home. Initial reactions were favorable, with thousands of men migrating to Detroit to apply for Ford jobs. Meyer reports turnover declined from an unbelievable 370% in 1913

to 16% in 1915. However, sanctioned "American" ways evolved to include anti-German and anti-union attitudes during World War I. Workers and the general public expressed disapproval and hostility toward the program's ultimatums to change worker lives on and off the job. In an effort to tone down the Sociological Department, it was renamed the Educational Department in 1915, and in 1917 the title of "investigators" was changed to "advisers" (Meyer, 1981); but the old names persisted. Problems with the demands to conform to Ford's primary socialization attempts continued, with negative consequences. Turnover rose to 51% in 1918 and the Socialist-led Auto Workers Union began attracting workers (Meyer, 1981; Wood, 2004). The temporary gains did not justify the costs of the program; in 1921, Ford eliminated the Sociology Department and scaled back the profit-sharing plan. The experiment was a failure. Ford's paternalism and efforts to socialize his workforce failed for a variety of reasons; perhaps foremost among them was the failure to enforce Ford values with $5 a day.

The Ford case showed that organizational efforts to socialize its workforce can fail despite a strong mandate from top management and generous resources. Research and theory development in organizational socialization has generated a great deal of understanding about how individuals adjust to new roles in organizations. It builds on basic psychological theories related to uncertainty reduction, need to belong, social exchanges, and social identities to understand why newcomers need to adjust to their new roles and how this adjustment adds to a newcomer's own sense of identity. Future research could benefit from a better grounding of organizational socialization with its theoretical foundations. As a recent example, Vancouver, Tamanini, and Yoder (2010) used dynamic computational modeling to examine proactive newcomer information seeking and uncertainty reduction theory.

We also know that organizational tactics and individual tactics directly influence *what* is learned during the socialization process. In turn, the learning and implied sense making from these tactics influence proximal outcomes that, in turn, influence more distal outcomes. What we do not know is how these tactics affect organizational learning at the leader, group, and organizational levels, and how that learning influences subsequent actions and outcomes from those organizational units. We also do not know how implicit learning—the primary learning process, and tacit knowledge—influence the socialization process for newcomers and for

Table 18.4 Research Recommendations

Research area	Research recommendations
Organizational context and tactics for socialization	• Research examining links between organizational/environmental characteristics and organizational practices for attracting, selecting, and socializing people can provide a more comprehensive understanding for human resources management.
Individual differences and tactics for socialization	• More research is needed to understand how previous socialization experiences affect a current socialization episode. • More research is needed to tie basic theoretical foundations of socialization (e.g., uncertainty reduction theory, need to belong, social exchange theory, social identity theory) to individual usage of particular socialization tactics.
Organizational and individual socialization tactics	• More research is needed to examine how organizational and individual tactics interact to reinforce or contradict lessons learned. • Research is needed to identify conditions that might cause organizations and individuals to initiate, change, or terminate tactics.
Individual learning and sense making	• Better measures of socialization content, across levels of an organization are needed. • Research is needed to identify what tacit knowledge is learned during the socialization process and how this learning might mediate relationships between socialization tactics and outcomes. • Characteristics of sense making can be applied to help understand how learning is interpreted to affect adjustment attitudes and behavior.
Organizational learning and sense making	• More research is needed to examine how leaders and teams form expectations about newcomers, how these expectations may change as organizational members learn more about a newcomer, and how they adjust as a team after members make sense of their learned lessons. • Research is needed to link newcomer learning and organizational learning. How can organizations learn from newcomers to promote exploration and exploitation goals? • Research is needed to link lessons learned from previous socialization episodes to the design and implementation of subsequent organizational socialization tactics.
Learning and proximal outcomes	• Research is needed to examine parallel processes of newcomers and organizational members' perceptions of fit between the newcomer and job, supervisor, team, and organization
Proximal and distal outcomes	• Much of the current literature shows strong ties between proximal and distal outcomes; new research may involve additional outcomes. For example, organizations with high turnover may present research challenges as their culture and values change with critical masses of newcomers.
Feedback loops	• Feedback loops recognize the dynamic nature of the socialization process. Future research can examine how proximal and distal outcomes can affect the need to use additional socialization tactics and subsequent learning and sense making. • Research is needed to examine how early socialization episodes influence later socialization. • Research is needed to address the practical problems that individuals and organizations face when people do not adjust or fit well with current organizational situations.

organizations. Finally, research is needed to examine the impact of previous socialization experiences on current and future socialization.

Advances in research on organizational socialization will benefit both science and practice. Scientific contributions can be made with better understanding of a theory of organizational socialization. We have begun to study why and how people adjust to new work environments, and progress has been made with research on what organizations and people do throughout this adjustment process. Results not only inform our knowledge of organizational socialization, but can be used to inform psychological science (e.g., motivation and satisfaction) and managerial science (e.g., organizational effectiveness).

Practical benefits from research on organizational socialization are found at many levels. Most people who work in organizations experience a number of changes that require adjustments in order to maintain or improve their performance. New positions, changes in leadership, and technological innovations are common catalysts for changing the way in which people approach their work. Thus, the socialization process is ubiquitous for individuals, teams, leaders, and organizations as they learn, influence, and adjust to one another. Research results can help all involved in a socialization process to find the right balance of adjustments to satisfy needs for an individual's work life as well as needs for an organization's workforce and sustainability.

The study of organizational socialization itself is adjusting to new knowledge gained from current research, new challenges with the next generation of workers, and new ways of doing business. These adjustments should advance theory and practice, to help individuals develop satisfying and successful careers, and to help organizations develop a committed and productive workforce. Henry Ford would have paid big bucks for this.

Acknowledgment

Georgia T. Chao gratefully acknowledges the Office of Naval Research (ONR), Command Decision Making Program (N00014–09–1–0519, S. W. J. Kozlowski and G. T. Chao, Principal Investigators) for support that, in part, assisted the composition of this chapter. Any opinions, findings, and conclusions or recommendations expressed are those of the author and do not necessarily reflect the views of ONR.

Note

1. Although many publications in the socialization literature cite Everett C. Hughes's 1958 book, *Men and their Work*, as a source for "reality shock," that book does not contain any reference to or discussion of reality shock. However, Miriam Wagenschein, a student of Hughes, authored an unpublished master's thesis entitled "Reality Shock: A Study of Beginning School Teachers" in 1950 at the University of Chicago (Goffman, 1952). In that thesis, she wrote that people "are often surprised or disillusioned with what they find when they enter an occupation. For practical purposes of analysis, we have termed this surprise as 'reality shock'" (Wagenschein, 1950, p. 1).

References

Aguinis, H. & Kraiger, K. (2009). Benefits of training and development for individuals and teams, organizations, and society. *Annual Review of Psychology, 60,* 451–474.

Alderfer, C. P. (1969). An empirical test of a new theory of human needs. *Organizational Behavior and Human Performance, 4,* 142–175.

Allen, N. J., & Meyer, J. P. (1990). Organizational socialization tactics: A longitudinal anaysis of links to newcomers' commitment and role orientation. *Academy of Management Journal, 33,* 847–858.

Allport, F. H. (1924). *Social psychology.* New York: Houghton Mifflin.

Asch, S. E. (1952). Effects of group pressures upon the modification and distortion of judgments. In G. E. Swanson, T. M. Newcomb, & E. L. Hartley (Eds.), *Readings in social psychology* (pp. 393–401). New York: Holt, Reinhart & Winston.

Ashford, S. J. & Black, J. S. (1996). Proactivity during organizational entry: The role of desire for control. *Journal of Applied Psychology, 81(2),* 199–214.

Ashford, S. J., & Cummings, L. L. (1983). Feedback as an individual resource: Personal strategies of creating information. *Organizational Behavior & Human Performance, 32,* 370–398.

Ashforth, B. E. & Mael, F. (1989). Social identity theory and the organization. *Academy of Management Review, 14,* 20–39.

Ashforth, B. E., & Johnson, S. A. (2001). Which hat to wear? The relative salience of multiple identities in organizational contexts. In M. A. Hogg & D. J. Terry (Eds.), *Social identity processes in organizational contexts* (pp. 31–48). Philadelphia: Psychology Press.

Ashforth, B. E. & Saks, A. M. (1996). Socialization tactics: Longitudinal effects on newcomer adjustment. *Academy of Management Journal, 39,* 149–178.

Ashforth, B. E., Sluss, D. M., & Harrison, S. H. (2007). Socialization in organizational contexts. In G. P. Hodgkinson & J. K. Ford (Eds.), *International review of industrial and organizational psychology,* (pp. 1–70). West Sussex, UK: John Wiley & Sons.

Ashforth, B. E., Sluss, D. M., & Saks, A. M. (2007). Socialization tactics, proactive behavior, and newcomer learning: Integrating socialization models. *Journal of Vocational Behavior, 70,* 447–462.

Atzori, M., Lombardi, L., Fraccaroli, F., Battistelli, A., & Zaniboni, S. (2008). Organizational socilization of women in the Italian army: Learning processes and proactive tactics. *Journal of Workplace Learning. 20,* 327–347.

Baldwin, J. M. (1911). *The individual and society.* Boston: Richard G. Badger, The Gorham Press.

Bandura, A. (1977). *Social learning theory.* Englewood Cliffs, NJ: Prentice-Hall.

Bauer, T. N., Bodner, T., Tucker, J. S., Erdogan, B., & Truxillo, D. M. (2007). Newcomer adjustment during organizational socialization: A meta-analytic review of antecedents, outcomes, and methods. *Journal of Applied Psychology, 92,* 707–721.

Bauer, T. N., & Erdogan, B. (2010). Organizational socialization: The effective onboarding of new employees. In S. Zedeck, H. Aguinis, W. Cascio, M. Gelfand, K. Leung, S. Parker, & J. Zhou (Eds.). *APA Handbook of I/O Psychology* (Vol. III, pp. 51–64). Washington, DC: APA Press.

Bauer, T. N., Morrison, E. W., & Callister, R. R. (1998). Organizational socialization: A review and directions for future research. In G. R. Ferris (Ed.), *Research in Personnel and Human Resource Management, 16,* 149–214.

Baumeister, R. F. & Leary, M. R. (1995). The need to belong: Desire for interpersonal attachments as a fundamental human motivation. *Psychological Bulletin, 117,* 497–529.

Berger, C. R. (1979). Beyond initial interaction: Uncertainty, understanding, and the development of interpersonal relationships. In. H. Giles & R. N. St Clair (Eds.). *Language and social psychology* (pp. 122–144). Baltimore: University Park Press.

Berger, C. R. (1986). Uncertain outcome values in predicted relationships: Uncertainty reduction theory then and now. *Human Communication Research, 13,* 34–38.

Berger, C. R., & Calabrese, R. J. (1975). Some explorations in initial interaction and beyond: Toward a developmental theory of interpersonal communication. *Human Communication Research, 1,* 99–112.

Berger, P. L., & Luckmann, T. (1966). *The social construction of reality: A treatise in the sociology of knowledge.* Garden City, NY: Doubleday.

Brim, O. G., Jr. (1966). Socialization through the life cycle. In O. G. Brim, Jr., & S. Wheeler (Ed.), *Socialization after childhood.* New York: Wiley.

Brim, O. G., Jr. (1968). Adult socialization. In J. A. Clausen (Ed.), *Socialization and society* (pp. 184–226). Boston: Little, Brown.

Brown, J. S., & Duguid, P. (1991). Organizational learning and communities-of-practice: Toward a unified view of working, learning, and innovation. *Organization Science, 2,* 40–57.

Buchanan, B., II (1974). Building organizational commitment: The socialization of managers in work organizations. *Administrative Science Quarterly, 19,* 533–546.

Callister, R. R., Kramer, M. W., & Turban, D. B. (1999). Feedback seeking following career transitions. *Academy of Management Journal, 42,* 429–438.

Chan, D., & Schmitt, N. (2000). Interindividual differences in intraindividual changes in proactivity during organizational entry: A latent growth modeling approach to understanding newcomer adaptation. *Journal of Applied Psychology, 85,* 190–210.

Chao, G. T. (1997a). Unstructured training and development: The role of organizational socialization. In J. K. Ford, S. W. J. Kozlowski, K. Kraiger, E. Salas, & M. S. Teachout (Eds.), *Improving training effectiveness in work organizations* (pp. 129–151). Mahwah, NJ: Lawrence Erlbaum.

Chao, G. T. (1997b). Organizational socialization in multinational corporations: The role of implicit learning. In C. L. Cooper & S. E. Jackson (Eds.) *Creating tomorrow's organizations: A handbook for future research in organizational behavior,* (pp. 43–57). New York: John Wiley & Sons.

Chao, G. T., O'Leary-Kelly, A. M., Wolf, S., Klein, H. J., & Gardner, P. D. (1994). Organizational socialization: Its content and consequences. *Journal of Applied Psychology, 79,* 730–743.

Chatman, J. A. (1989). Improving interactional organizational research: A model of person-organization fit. *Academy of Management Review, 14,* 333–349.

Chen, G. (2005). Newcomer adaptation in teams: Multilevel antecedents and outcomes. *Academy of Management Journal, 48(1),* 101–116.

Chen, G., & Klimoski, R. J. (2003). The impact of expectations on newcomer performance in teams as mediated by work characteristics, social exchanges, and empowerment. *Academy of Management Journal, 46(5),* 591–607.

Clausen, J. A. (1968). A historical and comparative view of socialization theory and research. In J. A. Clausen, O. G. Brim, Jr., A. Inkeles, R. Lippitt, E. E. Maccoby, & M. B. Smith (Eds.), *Socialization and society* (pp. 18–72). Boston: Little, Brown.

Cooper-Thomas, H. D., & Anderson, N. (2002). Newcomer adjustment: The relationship between organizational socialization tactics, information acquisition, and attitudes. *Journal of Occupational and Organizational Psychology, 75,* 423–437.

Cooper-Thomas, H. D., & Anderson, N. (2005). Organizational socialization: A field study into socialization success and rate. *International Journal of Selection and Assessment, 13(2),* 116–128.

Cooper-Thomas, H. D., & Anderson, N. (2006). Organizational socialization: A new theoretical model and recommendations for future research and HRM practices in organizations. *Journal of Managerial Psychology, 21,* 492–516.

Cooper-Thomas, H. D., & Burke, S. E. (in press). Newcomer proactive behavior: chan there be too much of a good thing? In C. Wanberg (Ed.) *Handbook of organizational socialization,*

Cropanzano, R., & Mitchell, M. S. (2005). Social exchange theory: An interdisciplinary review. *Journal of Management, 31,* 874–900.

Davey, K. M. & Arnold, J. (2000). A multi-method study of accounts of personal change by graduates starting work: Self-ratings, categories and women's discourses. *Journal of Occupational and Organizational Psychology, 73,* 461–486.

Dean, R. A. (1983). Reality shock: The link between socialization and organizational commitment. *Journal of Management Development, 2(3),* 55–65.

Dixon, N. M., Allen, N., Burgess, T., Kilner, P., & Schweitzer, S. (2005). *CompanyCommand: Unleasing the power of the Army profession.* West Point, NY: Center for the Advancement of Leader Development and Organizational Learning.

Emerson, R. M. (1976). Social exchange theory. *Annual Review of Sociology, 2,* 335–362.

Fan, J., & Wanous, J. P. (2008). Organizational and cultural entry: A new type of orientation program for multiple boundary crossings. *Journal of Applied Psychology, 93(6),* 1390–1400.

Fang, R., Duffy, M. K., & Shaw, J. D. (2011). The organizational socialization process: Review and development of a social capital model. *Journal of Management, 37,* 127–152.

Feldman, D. C. (1976). A contingency theory of socialization. *Administrative Science Quarterly, 21,* 433–452.

Feldman, D. C. (1981). The multiple socialization of organization members. *Academy of Management Review, 6,* 309–318.

Filstad, C. (2004). How newcomers use role models in organizational socialization. *Journal of Workplace Learning, 16,* 396–409.

Finkelstein, L. M., Kulas, J. T., & Dages, K. D. (2003). Age differences in proactive newcomer socialization strategies in two populations. *Journal of Business and Psychology, 17,* 473–502.

Fisher, C. D. (1986). Organizational socialization: An integrative review. *Research in Personnel and Human Resource Management, 4*, 101–145.

Gardner, W. L., & Martinko, M. J. (1988). Impression management in organizations. *Journal of Management, 14*, 321–338.

Goffman, E. (1952). On cooling the mark out: Some aspects of adaptation to failure. *Psychiatry, 15*, 451–463.

Goffman, E. (1959). *The presentation of self in everyday life.* Garden City, NY: Doubleday Anchor.

Goslin, D. A. (1969). Introduction. In D. A. Goslin (Ed.), *Handbook of socialization theory and research* (pp. 1–21). Chicago: Rand McNally.

Graen, G. (1976). Role making processes within complex organizations. In M. D. Dunette (Ed.), *The handbook of industrial and organizational psychology* (pp. 1201–1245). Chicago: Rand McNally.

Graen, G. B., Orris, J. B., & Johnson, T. W. (1973). Role assimilation processes in a complex organization. *Journal of Vocational Behavior, 3*, 395–420.

Grant, A. M., & Ashford, S. J. (2008). The dynamics of proactivity at work. *Research in Organizational Behavior, 28*, 3–34.

Griffin, A. E. C., Colella, A., & Goparaju, S. (2000). Newcomer and organizational socialization tactics: An interactionist perspective. *Human Resource Management Review, 10*, 453–474.

Gruman, J. A., Saks, A. M., & Zweig, D. I. (2006). Organizational socialization tactics and newcomer proactive behaviors: An integrative study. *Journal of Vocational Behavior, 69*, 90–104.

Hall, D. T. & Schneider, B. (1972). Correlates of organizational identification as a function of career pattern and organizational type. *Administrative Science Quarterly, 17*, 340–350.

Harrison, S. H., Sluss, D. M. & Ashforth, B. E. (2011). Curiosity adapted the cat: The role of trait curiosity in newcomer adaptation. *Journal of Applied Psychology, 96*, 211–220.

Hart, Z. P., & Miller, V. D. (2005). Context and message content during organizational socialization: A research note. *Human Communication Research, 31(2)*, 295–309.

Haueter, J. A., Macan, T. H., & Winter, J. (2003). Measurement of newcomer socialization: Construct validation of a multidimensional scale. *Journal of Vocational Behavior, 63*, 20–39.

Hofstede, G. (1980). *Culture's consequences.* Beverly Hills, CA: Sage.

Hogg, M. A., & Terry, D. J. (2000). Social identity and self-categorization processes in organizational contexts. *Academy of Management Review, 25*, 121–140.

Hogg, M. A., & Terry, D. J. (2001). Social identity theory and organizational processes. In M. A. Hogg & D. J. Terry (Eds.), *Social identity processes in organizational contexts* (pp. 1–12). Philadelphia: Psychology Press.

Holder, T. (1996). Women in nontraditional occupations: Information-seeking during organizational entry. *The Journal of Business Communication, 33*, 9–26.

Holland, J. L. (1985). *Making vocational choices: A theory of vocational personalities and work environments.* Odessa, FL: Psychological Assessment Resources.

Homans, G. C. (1958). Social behavior as exchange. *American Journal of Sociology, 63(6)*, 597–606.

Homans, G. C. (1974). *Social behavior: Its elementary forms* (Rev. ed.). New York: Harcourt Brace Jovanovich.

Hooker, C. (1997). Ford's sociology department and the Americanization campaign and the manufacture of popular culture among assembly line workers c. 1910–1917. *Journal of American Culture, 20*, 47–53.

Hornsey, M. J., & Jetten, J. (2004). The individual within the group: Balancing the need to belong with the need to be different. *Personality and Social Psychology Review, 8*, 248–264.

Hsiung, T. L., & Hsieh, A. T. (2003). Newcomer socialization: The role of job standardization. *Public Personnel Management, 32*, 579–589.

Hughes, E. C. (1958). *Men and their work.* Glencoe, IL: Free Press.

Huntington, M. J. (1957). The development of a professional self-image. In R. K. Merton, G. G. Reader, & P. L. Kendall (Eds.), *The student-physician: Introductory studies in the sociology of medical education* (pp. 179–187). Cambridge, MA: Harvard University Press.

Jablin, F. M. (1982). Organizational communication: An assimilation approach. In M. E. Roloff & C. R. Berger (Eds.), *Social cognition and communication* (pp. 255–286). Beverly Hills, CA: Sage Publications.

Jablin, F. M. (1987). Organizational entry, assimilation, and exit. In F. M. Jablin, L. L. Putnam, K. H. Roberts, & L. W. Porter (Eds.), *Handbook of organizational communication.* (pp. 679–740). Beverly Hills, CA: Sage Publications.

Jaffe, G. (February 15, 2006). Marching orders: To keep recruits, boot camp gets a gentle revamp; Army offers more support, sleep, second helpings; drill sergeants' worries; 'It would look so much nicer.' *Wall Street Journal.* Retrieved from http://search.proquest.com.proxy1.cl.msu.edu/docview/399003370/fulltext?accountid=12598.

Jones, G. R. (1986). Socialization tactics, self-efficacy, and newcomers' adjustments to organizations. *Academy of Management Journal, 29(2)*, 262–279.

Kammeyer-Mueller, J. D. (2007). The dynamics of newcomer adjustment: Dispositions, context, interaction, and fit. In C. Ostroff & T. A. Judge (Eds.). *Perspectives on organizational fit* (pp. 99–122). London: Psychology Press.

Kammeyer-Mueller, J. D., Livingston, B. A., & Liao, H. (2011). Perceived similarity, proactive adjustment, and organizational socialization. *Journal of Vocational Behavior, 78*, 225–236.

Kammeyer-Mueller, J. D. & Wanberg, C. R. (2003). Unwrapping the organizational entry process: Disentangling multiple antecedents and their pathways to adjustment. *Journal of Applied Psychology, 88(5)*, 779–794.

Kelley, H. H. (1967). Attribution theory in social psychology. In D. Levine (Ed.), *Nebraska symposium on motivation* (pp. 192–240). Lincoln: University of Nebraska Press.

Kim, T., Cable, D. M., & Kim, S. (2005). Socialization tactics, employee proactivity, and person-organization fit. *Journal of Applied Psychology, 90(2)*, 232–241.

Kipnis, D., Schmidt, S. M., & Wilkinson, I. (1980). Intraorganizational influence tactics: Explorations in getting one's way. *Journal of Applied Psychology, 65(4)*, 440–452.

Klein, H. J., Fan, J., & Preacher, K. J. (2006). The effects of early socialization experiences on content mastery and outcomes: A mediational approach. *Journal of Vocational Behavior, 68*, 96–115.

Klein, H. J., & Heuser, A. E. (2008). The learning of socialization content: A framework for researching orienting practices. *Research in Personnel and Human Resources Management, 27*, 279–336.

Klein, H. J., & Weaver, N. A. (2000). The effectiveness of an organizational-level orientation training program in the socialization of new hires. *Personnel Psychology, 53*, 47–66.

Kozlowski, S. W. J., & Bell, B. S. (2003). Work groups and teams in organizations. In W. C. Borman, D. R. Ilgen, & R. J. Klimoski (Eds.), *Handbook of psychology: industrial and organizational psychology* (Vol. 12, pp. 333–375). London: Wiley.

Kozlowski, S. W. J., Chao, G. T., & Jensen, J. M. (2010). Building an infrastructure for organizational learning: A multilevel approach. In S. W. J. Kozlowski & E. Salas (Eds.), *Learning, training, and development in organizations* (pp. 363–403). New York: Routledge.

Kramer, M. W., & Miller, V. D. (1999). A response to criticisms of organizational socialization research: In support of contemporary conceptualizations of organizational assimilation. *Communication Monographs, 66,* 358–367.

Kristof, A. L. (1996). Person-organization fit: An integrative review of its conceptualizations, measurement, and implications. *Personnel Psychology, 49,* 1–49.

Kristof-Brown, A. L. & Guay, R. P. (2010). Person-environment fit. In S. Zedeck, H. Aguinis, W. Cascio, M. Gelfand, K. Leung, S. Parker, & J. Zhou (Eds.), *APA handbook of I/O psychology* (Vol. III, pp. 3–50). Washington, DC: APA Press.

Lacey, R. (1986). *Ford: The men and the machine.* Boston, MA: Little Brown.

Laker, D. R., & Steffy, B. D. (1995). The impact of alternative socialization tactics on self-managing behavior and organizational commitment. *Journal of Social Behavior and Personality, 10,* 645–660.

Lawler, E. J. (2001). An affect theory of social exchange. *American Journal of Sociology, 107,* 321–352.

Lester, R. E. (1987). Organizational culture, uncertainty reduction, and the socialization of new organizational members. In S. Thomas (Ed.), *Culture and communication: Methodology, behavior, artifacts, and institutions* (pp. 105–113). Norwood, NJ: Ablex.

Lewicki, P., Hill, T., & Czyzewska, M. (1992). Non-conscious acquisition of information. *American Psychologist, 47,* 796–801.

Lin, N. (1999). Building a network theory of social capital. *Connections, 22,* 28–51.

Liu, C., & Lee, H. (2008). A proposed model of expatriates in multinational corporations. *Cross Cultural Management, 15,* 176–193.

Louis, M. R. (1980). Surprise and sense making: What newcomers experience in entering unfamiliar organizational settings. *Administrative Science Quarterly, 25,* 226–251.

Louis, M. R., Posner, B. Z., & Powell, G. N. (1983). The availability and helpfulness of socialization practices. *Personnel Psychology, 36,* 857–866.

Major, D. A. & Kozlowski, S. W. J. (1997). Newcomer information seeking: Individual and contextual influences. *International Journal of Selection and Assessment, 5,* 16–28.

Major, D. A., Kozlowski, S. W. J., Chao, G. T., & Gardner, P. D. (1995). A longitudinal investigation of newcomer expectations, early socialization outcomes, and the moderating effects of role development factors. *Journal of Applied Psychology, 80,* 418–431.

Manning, P. K. (1970). Talking and becoming: A view of organizational socialization. In J. D. Douglas (Ed.), *Understanding everyday life* (pp. 239–256). Chicago: Aldine.

March, J. G. (1991). Exploration and exploitation in organizational learning. *Organization Science, 2,* 71–87.

Maslow, A. H. (1943). A theory of human motivation. *Psychological Review, 50,* 370–396.

Meyer, S. (1981). *The five dollar day: Labor management and social control in the Ford Motor Company, 1908–1921.* Albany: State University of New York Press.

Miller, V. D., & Jablin, F. M. (1991). Information seeking during organizational entry: Influences, tactics, and a model of the process. *Academy of Management Review, 16,* 92–120.

Mitus, J. S. (2006). Organizational socialization from a content perspective and its effect on the affective commitment of newly hired rehabilitation counselors. *Journal of Rehabilitation, 72,* 12–20.

Molm, L. D. (2001). Theories of social exchange and exchange networks. In G. Ritzer & B. Smart (Eds.), *Handbook of social theory* (pp. 260–272). Thousand Oaks, CA: Sage.

Moon, B. (2006). The influence of organizational socialization on police officers' acceptance of community policing. *Policing: An international journal of police strategies & management, 29,* 704–722.

Moore, W. E. (1969). Occupational socialization. In D. A. Goslin (Ed.), *Handbook of socialization theory and research.* (pp. 861–883). Chicago: Rand McNally.

Moreland, R. L., & Levine, J. M. (2001). Socialization in organizations and work groups. In M. E. Turner (Ed.) *Groups at work: Theory and research* (pp. 69–112). Mahwah, NJ: Lawrence Erlbaum Associates.

Moreland, R. L., Levine, J. M., & McMinn, J. G. (2001). Self-categorization and work group socialization. In M. A. Hogg & D. J. Terry (Eds.), *Social identity processes in organizational contexts* (pp. 87–100). Philadelphia: Psychology Press.

Morrison, E. W. (1993a). Longitudinal study of the effects of information seeking on newcomer socialization. *Journal of Applied Psychology, 78*(2), 173–183.

Morrison, E. W., (1993b). Newcomer information seeking: Exploring types, modes, sources, and outcomes. *Academy of Management Journal, 36,* 557–589.

Morrison, E. W. (1995). Information usefulness and acquisition during organizational encounter. *Management Communication Quarterly, 9,* 131–155.

Morrison, E. W. (2002a). Information seeking within organizations. *Human Communication Research, 28,* 229–242.

Morrison, E. W. (2002b). Newcomers' relationships: The role of social network ties during socialization. *Academy of Management Journal, 45,* 1149–1160.

Mortimer, J. T., & Simmons, R. G. (1978). Adult socialization. *Annual Review of Sociology, 4,* 421–454.

Mowday, R. T., Porter, L., & Steers, R. M. (1982). *Employee-organization linkages: The psychology of commitment, absenteeism & turnover.* New York: Academic Press.

Murray, H. L. (1938). *Explorations in personality.* New York: Oxford University Press.

Nicholson, N. (1984). A theory of work-role transitions. *Administrative Science Quarterly, 29,* 172–191.

Nonanka, I. (1994). A dynamic theory of organizational knowledge creation. *Organization Science, 5,* 14–37.

Ostroff, C., & Kozlowski, S. W. J. (1992). Organizational socialization as a learning process: The role of information acquisition. *Personnel Psychology, 45,* 849–874.

Ostroff, C., & Schulte, M. (2007). Multiple perspectives of fit in organizations across levels of analysis. In C. Ostroff & T. A. Judge (Eds.), *Perspectives on organizational fit.* (pp. 3–69). London: Psychology Press.

Parker, S. K., & Collins, C. G. (2010). Taking stock: Integrating and differentiating multiple proactive behaviors. *Journal of Management, 36,* 633–662.

Peteraf, M., & Shanley, M. (1997). Getting to know you: A theory of strategic group identity. *Strategic Management Journal, 18,* 165–186.

Porter, L. W., Lawler, E. E., III, & Hackman, J. R. (1975). *Behavior in organizations*, New York: McGraw-Hill.

Porter, L. W., & Steers, R. M. (1973). Organizational, work, and personal factors in employee turnover and absenteeism. *Psychological Bulletin, 80,* 151–176.

Premack, S. L., & Wanous, J. P. (1985). A meta-analysis of realistic job preview experiments. *Journal of Applied Psychology, 70,* 706–719.

Rao, A., Schmidt, S. M., & Murray, L. H. (1995). Upward impression management: Goals, influence strategies, and consequences. *Human Relations, 48,* 147–167.

Reber, A. (1995). *Implicit learning and tacit knowledge: An essay on the cognitive unconscious.* New York: Oxford University Press.

Reichers, A. E. (1987). An interactionist perspective on newcomer socialization rates. *Academy of Management Review, 12,* 278–287.

Riordan, C. M., Weatherly, E. W., Vandenberg, R. J., & Self, R. M. (2001). The effects of pre-entry experiences and socialization tactics on newcomer attitudes and turnover. *Journal of Managerial Issues, 13*(2), 159–176.

Saks, A. M., & Ashforth, B. E. (1996). Proactive socialization and behavioral self-management. *Journal of Vocational Behavior, 48,* 301–323.

Saks, A. M., & Ashforth, B. E. (1997a). Organizational socialization: Making sense of the past and present as a prologue for the future. *Journal of Vocational Behavior, 51,* 234–279.

Saks, A. M., & Ashforth, B. E. (1997b). Socialization tactics and newcomer information acquisition. *International Journal of Selection and Assessment, 5,* 48–61.

Saks, A. M., Gruman, J. A., & Cooper-Thomas, H. (2011). The neglected role of proactive behavior and outcomes in newcomer socialization. *Journal of Vocational Behavior, 79*(1), 36–46.

Saks, A. M., Uggerslev, K. L. & Fassina, N. E. (2007). Socialization tactics and newcomer adjustment: A meta-analytic review and test of a model. *Journal of Vocational Behavior, 70,* 413–446.

Schein, E. H. (1965). *Organizational psychology.* Englewood Cliffs, NJ: Prentice-Hall.

Schein, E. H. (1968). Organizational socialization and the profession of management. *Industrial Management Review, 2,* 1–16.

Schein, E. H. (1978). *Career dynamics: Matching individual and organizational needs.* Reading, MA: Addison-Wesley.

Schneider, B. (1987). The people make the place. *Personnel Psychology, 40,* 437–454.

Schneider, B., Smith, D. B., Taylor, S., & Fleenor, J. (1998). Personality and organizations: A test of the homogeneity of personality hypothesis. *Journal of Applied Psychology, 83(3),* 462–470.

Scholarios, D., Lockyer, C., & Johnson, H. (2003). Anticipatory socialization: The effect of recruitment and selection experiences on career expectations. *Career Development International, 8(4),* 182–197.

Settoon, R. P., & Adkins, C. L. (1997). Newcomer socialization: The role of supervisors, coworkers, friends, and family members. *Journal of Business and Psychology,* 11, 507–516.

Sherif, M., & Sherif, C. W. (1969). *Social psychology.* New York: Harper & Row.

Su, C. (2010). An examination of the usage and impact of upward influence tactics by workers in the hospitality sector of Taiwan: Expanding the framework of Rao, Schmidt, and Murray (1995). *Canadian Journal of Administrative Sciences, 27,* 306–319.

Tajfel, H. (1981). *Human groups and social categories: Studies in social psychology.* Cambridge: Cambridge University Press.

Tajfel, H., & Turner, J. C. (1979). An integrative theory of intergroup conflict. In W. G. Austin & S. Worchel (Eds.), *The social psychology of intergroup relations* (pp. 33–47). Monterey, CA: Brooks/Cole.

Tajfel, H., & Turner, J. C. (1986). The social identity theory of inter-group behavior. In S. Worchel & L. W. Austin (Eds.), *Psychology of intergroup relations.* Chicago: Nelson-Hall.

Taormina, R. J. (1994). The Organizational Socialization Inventory. *International Journal of Selection and Assessment, 2,* 133–145.

Taormina, R. J. (1997). Organizational socialization: A multi-domain, continuous process model. *International Journal of Selection and Assessment, 5,* 29–47.

Taormina, R. J. (2004). Convergent validation of two measures of organizational socialization. *International Journal of Human Resource Management, 15,* 76–94.

Thomas, H. D. C., & Anderson, N. (1998). Changes in newcomers' psychological contracts during organizational socialization: A study of recruits entering the british army. *Journal of Organizational Behavior, 19,* 745–767.

Toffler, B. L. (1981). Occupational role development: The changing determinants of outcomes for the individual. *Administrative Science Quarterly, 26,* 396–418.

Turner, J. C. (1975). Social comparison and social identity: Some prospects for intergroup behaviour. *European Journal of Social Psychology, 5,* 5–34.

Turner, J. C., Oakes, P. J., Haslam, S. A., & McGarty, C. (1994). Self and collective: Cognition and social context. *Personality and Social Psychology Bulletin, 20,* 454–463.

van der Velde, M. E. G., Ardts, J. C. A., & Jansen, P. G. W. (2005). The longitudinal effect of information seeking on socialization and development in three organizations: Filling the research gaps. *Canadian Journal of Career Development, 4,* 32–42.

Van Maanen, J. (1976). Breaking-in: Socialization to work. In R. Dubin (Ed.) *Handbook of work, organization, and society* (pp. 67–130). Chicago: Rand McNally.

Van Maanen, J. (1978). People processing: Strategies of organizational socialization. *Organizational Dynamics, 7*(1), 18–36.

Van Maanen, J. (1984). Doing new things in old ways: Chains of socialization. In J. Bess (Ed.), *Education and organization theory* (pp. 211–246). New York: New York University Press.

Van Maanen, J. & Schein, E. (1979). Toward a theory of organizational socialization. *Research in Organizational Behavior, 1,* 209–264.

Vancouver, J. B., Tamanini, K. B., & Yoder, R. J. (2010). Using dynamic computational models to reconnect theory and research: Socialization by the proactive newcomer as example. *Journal of Management, 36*(3), 764–793.

Wagenschein, M. (1950). *"Reality shock": A study of beginning elementary school teachers.* Unpublished master's thesis, University of Chicago.

Wanberg, C. R., & Kammeyer-Mueller, J. D. (2000). Predictors and outcomes of proactivity in the socialization process. *Journal of Applied Psychology, 85,* 373–385.

Wanous, J. P. (1992). Organizational entry: Recruitment, selection and socialization of newcomers (2nd ed.). Reading MA: Addison-Wesley.

Wanous, J. P., Reichers, A. E., & Malik, S. D. (1984). Organizational socialization and group development: Toward an integrative perspective. *Academy of Management Review, 9,* 670–683.

Weick, K. E. (1995). *Sensemaking in organizations.* Thousand Oaks, CA: Sage.

Wesson, M. J., & Gogus, C. I. (2005). Shaking hands with a computer: An examination of two methods of organizational newcomer orientation. *Journal of Applied Psychology, 90,* 1018–1026.

Wood, G. (2004). "The paralysis of the labor movement": Men, masculinity, and unions in 1920s Detroit. *Michigan Historical Review, 30,* 59–91.

Wrzesniewski, A., & Dutton, J. E. (2001). Crafting a job: Revisioning employees as active crafters of their work. *Academy of Management Review, 26,* 179–201.

Yukl, G., & Falbe, C. M. (1990). Influence tactics and objectives in upward, downward, and lateral influence attempts. *Journal of Applied Psychology, 75*(2), 132–140.

Workplace Mentoring: Past, Present, and Future Perspectives

Lillian T. Eby

Abstract

This chapter reviews the existing research on workplace mentoring from the perspective of both the protégé and the mentor. Factors related to the initiation, maturation, and decline of mentoring relationships are discussed, along with the major theoretical frameworks that have been used to study mentoring relationships and that show promise in pushing mentoring scholarship in new directions. Consistent with emerging research workplace mentoring, both the positive and potentially negative aspects of mentoring are highlighted in order to present a comprehensive perspective on this unique type of work relationship. The organizational context is also considered in terms of its influence on the initiation of workplace mentoring relationships, as well as the relational patterns that emerge in workplace mentoring relationships. Finally, methodological challenges associated with the study of mentoring are outlined and considered in terms of important avenues for future research on the topic.

Key Words: Mentoring, mentor, protégé, work relationships, interpersonal relationships

Mentoring refers to a developmentally oriented interpersonal relationship between two individuals: a more senior or experienced organizational insider (the mentor) and a more junior or less experienced organizational member (the protégé; Kram, 1985). Experience as a protégé is associated with a wide range of positive work attitudes (e.g., job satisfaction, organizational commitment), career attitudes (e.g., career satisfaction, career expectations), work behaviors (e.g., lower turnover), and career outcomes (e.g., pay, promotion rate; Allen, Eby, Poteet, Lentz, & Lima, 2004; Eby, Allen, Evans, Ng, & DuBois, 2008). Mentoring is also related to a variety of positive attitudinal and career-related outcomes for the mentor (for a review see Allen, 2007). Notwithstanding the positive aspects of mentoring, there is increasing evidence that, like other types of close relationships, mentoring can also be marked by negative experiences for both the mentor and the protégé (for a review see Eby, 2007). These negative

experiences run the gamut from minor difficulties, such as mismatched attitudes and values, to more serious problems like deception, jealousy, and betrayal. To fully understand workplace mentoring, it is important to consider the full range of relational experiences that can occur in these relationships. Therefore, the present chapter considers both the positive and negative aspects of mentoring, from the perspective of both the mentor and the protégé.

Workplace mentoring relationships can take many forms (Eby, 1997). The most commonly studied type of relationship is hierarchical, non-supervisory mentoring, in which a more experienced individual serves as a mentor to a less experienced individual who is outside the mentor's immediate chain of command (Kram, 1985). A variation on hierarchical mentoring occurs when an immediate supervisor assumes the role of mentor for a subordinate (e.g., Payne & Huffman, 2005; Scandura & Schriescheim, 1994). Peers can also serve as mentors to one another, although the support provided is different from that found in hierarchical mentoring relationships (Ensher, Thomas, & Murphy, 2001; Kram & Isabella, 1985). Most research on workplace mentoring focuses on the relationship that a protégé has with a particular mentor, although there is some research on multiple mentoring relationships in which the protégé reports on his or her experiences with multiple mentors or networks of supportive developmental relationships (e.g., Higgins & Thomas, 2001). A final important distinguishing feature of a mentoring relationship is whether it develops spontaneously on the basis of mutual attraction and shared interests (informal mentoring) or is formally arranged and sanctioned by the organization (formal mentoring).

This chapter provides an in-depth, comprehensive summary of what we know about one-on-one, hierarchical mentoring relationships. Because peer and multiple mentoring relationships vary in important ways from one-on-one, hierarchical mentoring relationships, they are not reviewed here. The chapter is organized using a developmental perspective, recognizing that mentoring is a time-bound relationship that progresses through distinct stages or phases (Kram, 1985; Phillips-Jones, 1982). Adopting such a perspective facilitates a deeper understanding of the unique issues associated with *relationship initiation* (e.g., who enters into mentoring relationships and why; do individuals with mentoring experience have more positive work, career, and personal experiences than those without such experience; what influences motivation to mentor others), *relationship maturation* (e.g., what predicts the quality and quantity of mentoring received/provided; how does the relational experience relate to protégé and mentor outcomes), and *relationship decline* (e.g., how and why do mentoring relationships deteriorate; what predicts the termination of mentoring relationships).

A Developmental Perspective on Mentoring in the Workplace

While developmental theories are diverse in origin and offer varying perspectives on the human experience, they share several common features.[1] First, a developmental approach assumes systematic, organized, and successive change over time (Levinson, 1986; Vondracek, Lerner, & Schulenberg, 1986). This means that development is a dynamic yet predictable process. Second, development is typically characterized as a goal-directed process whereby the end state is adaptation or maturity (Reese &

Overton, 1970; Vondracek et al., 1986). This implies that development is purposive and that development is a lifelong journey. Third, developmental approaches assume that everyone progresses through the same stages of development, although an individual's experience in a particular stage is idiosyncratic (Vondracek et al., 1986). Fourth, individuals are not passive agents in the process of development (Reese & Overton, 1970). In other words, an individual's behavioral choices influence how effectively he or she deals with the major tasks to be accomplished at a particular stage of development (Levinson, 1986). Fifth, the developmental perspective recognizes that the context in which an individual is embedded both constrains and directly affects one's developmental trajectory (Chickering, 1969; Vondracek et al.). Finally, in many developmental theories (e.g., Ainsworth, 1989; Chickering, 1969; Erickson, 1950; Freud, 1954; Levinson, 1986), close relationships are essential for human growth and development. As Levinson (1986) notes, "...relationships are the stuff our lives are made of...they are the vehicle by which we live out—or bury—various aspects of ourselves and by which we participate, for better or worse, in the world around us" (p. 6).

Phases of the Mentoring Relationship

One way to think about workplace mentoring from a developmental perspective is to recognize that these relationships progress through a series of phases, each characterized by unique attributes and relational patterns (Kram, 1985; Phillips-Jones, 1982). The first phase is relationship initiation. During this phase, the mentor and protégé come together informally, or through some formal process such as participation in a formal mentoring program. Through repeated interactions, the two individuals become acquainted and develop a sense of whether or not there is a good relational fit. During relationship initiation, both mentors and protégés develop expectations about whether or not the relationship will meet their unique needs, based on the idealized expectations that they bring into the relationship. As such, this phase is often discussed in terms of fantasies that each individual has about the relationship, which become tested against reality as the relationship moves into the second phase of cultivation (Kram, 1985). In many ways, initiation is the "make or break" phase of the mentoring relationship. In other words, in some situations a mentoring relationship may never progresses beyond initiation. A mentoring relationship may end before it ever develops into a true mentorship, or it might never progress beyond superficial interpersonal interactions (Eby, Butts, Lockwood, & Simon, 2004).

Assuming that the relationship makes it past initiation, the next phase is cultivation (Kram, 1985). In this phase, individuals discover the value (or lack thereof) of relating to one another. While there is variability in the quantity and quality of mentoring support provided during this phase, the provision of mentoring support should be at its highest during cultivation (Kram, 1985). The finding that the length of the mentoring relationship is related to the amount of mentoring reported by protégés generally supports this assumption (Burke, 1984; Chao, Walz, & Gardner, 1992; Eby, Lockwood, & Butts, 2006; Egan, 2005). As the cultivation phase continues, the relationship may shift from a one-way helping relationship to a mutually beneficial partnership. Because benefits and mutuality should be at their height during this phase, uncertainty and conflict are expected to be the lowest during the cultivation phase (Kram, 1985). Moreover, in some mentoring relationships, the cultivation phase is associated with the development of a close, trusting relationship between mentor and protégé—one that is based on mutual respect and admiration. Notwithstanding the possibility that a deep emotional bond develops between mentor and protégé, like any other type of relationship the level of emotional intensity, commitment, and engagement that develops in the cultivation phase can vary substantially from relationship to relationship (Ragins, Cotton, & Miller, 2000).

Since mentoring is a developmentally oriented relationship, a time will come when the relationship has outlived its usefulness for one or both individuals. This marks the third phase of the mentoring relationship—separation (Kram, 1985). During this phase, the mentor may start to withdraw support, the protégé may be less likely to seek support from the mentor, or both. The separation phase can be difficult because one individual may not be ready for the relationship to end; the mentor may want to continue on as an important counsel to the protégé, or the protégé may not feel ready to go out on his or her own. This stage is discussed as the most tumultuous and can result in feelings of loss and anxiety by one or both individuals (Kram, 1985). There may be both structural and emotional separation during this phase, whereby interaction decreases and relational closeness starts to dissipate. Although not discussed by Kram (1985) in her initial theorizing about the separation phase, it is also possible

that separation can occur prematurely in situations in which the mentor or protégé reports relational problems in the mentorship. For instance, a serious breach of trust on the part of the protégé or perceived sabotage on the part of the mentor may lead to the abrupt dissolution of what was otherwise a healthy mentoring relationship (Eby, 2007).

The final phase of the mentoring relationship is redefinition. During redefinition, the relationship takes on a new meaning (Kram, 1985). Some mentoring relationships evolve into peer-like friendships. Other mentoring relationships may be marked by hostility and resentment. Yet another possibility is that the relationship will never be replaced with a new one. In this situation, the mentor may continue to provide guidance and support in a way that is responsive to his or her protégé's changing developmental needs. A common characteristic of the redefinition phase is a sense of indebtedness on the part of the former protégé (Kram, 1985). This provides one explanation for the finding that those who have been mentored in the past tend to express more willingness to mentor others in the future (Allen, Poteet, & Burroughs, 1997; Ragins & Cotton, 1993).

Developmental Tasks in Adulthood

Another way to think about developmental issues in mentoring is to examine the major developmental tasks associated with adulthood. While developmental theories are diverse in orientation and focus on a wide range of issues, such as personality development (e.g., Erickson, 1950; Freud, 1954), emotional development (e.g., Ainsworth, 1989), cognitive development (e.g., Kohlberg, 1969; Piaget, 1970), and career development (e.g., Super, 1980), there is a common emphasis on the milestones or tasks associated with an individual's developmental progression. Specific tasks to be accomplished in adulthood include: developing competence; learning how to effectively manage one's emotions; developing autonomy; establishing identity; developing a sense of purpose; developing integrity; learning how to cultivate intimate, trusting interpersonal relationships; experiencing occupational success; avoiding stagnation; and experiencing generativity (Ainsworth, 1989; Chickering, 1969; Erickson, 1950; Greenhaus, Callanan, & Godshalk, 2000; Levinson, Darrow, Levinson, Klein, & McKee, 1978).

Workplace mentoring relationships are one way that individuals can accomplish some of the major tasks associated with adult development (Greenhaus et al., 2000; Levinson et al., 1978). A major goal of a mentoring relationship is the personal and professional development of the protégé. A mentor can provide the protégé with the opportunity to develop specific competencies and can help facilitate early career success experiences (Kram, 1985). Over time, this should foster a sense of autonomy in the protégé as he or she develops both self-confidence and professional skills. Mentoring support can also help the protégé develop a sense of personal and professional identity (Kram, 1985). Elevating the importance of mentoring to good parenting, Levinson et al. (1978) discusses how the mentor can play a critical role in helping the young adult develop a sense of purpose and meaning in life. Moreover, a mentor often becomes an influential role model for his or her protégé. As such, through the process of being mentored, a protégé may learn effective interpersonal skills (including emotion management), as well as develop a stronger sense of his or her own personal values and ethics. Finally, in high-quality mentoring relationships, both individuals can obtain the experience of being in a mature, deeply connected, mutually beneficial interpersonal relationship (Ragins & Verbos, 2007).

Mentoring others can also fulfill developmental needs in adulthood. One of the commonly reported benefits reported by mentors is generativity—feeling as if one has improved society by developing others and believing that one has left a lasting legacy for future generations (Levinson et al., 1978; Ragins & Scandura, 1999). A mentor can also develop new competencies by mentoring others, both in terms of honing his or her own technical skills and further developing his or her own interpersonal skills (Allen, Poteet, & Burroughs, 1997; Eby & Lockwood, 2005). There is also some evidence that serving as a mentor to others can reduce perceptions of being plateaued (Lentz & Allen, 2005) and can enhance perceptions of career success (Allen, Lentz, & Day, 2006). Finally, serving as a mentor can give mid-career employees a renewed sense of purpose and identity in their jobs (Hunt & Michael, 1983).

Literature Review of Workplace Mentoring: A Developmental Perspective

A developmental perspective is adopted as a way to understand the initiation, maturation, and decline of workplace mentoring relationships. Focusing on universal developmental tasks that individuals face in adulthood provides a platform to understand how mentoring experiences, either as a protégé or as a mentor, may help (or hinder) individual development. This perspective also provides a useful organizing framework for summarizing

the existing literature. In the sections that follow, empirical research on mentoring is reviewed in the context of each phase of the mentoring relationship: relationship initiation, relationship maturation, and relationship decline. Since mentoring relationships are inherently dyadic, research from both the mentor and the protégé perspective is reviewed and integrated in order to provide a comprehensive perspective on this unique type of workplace relationship.

Research on Relationship Initiation

The first phase of the mentoring relationship involves the process whereby two individuals come together and a mentoring relationship is formed. In informal mentoring, the initiation process involves the protégé, mentor, or both approaching one other and establishing a relationship (Scandura & Williams, 2001). The spontaneous and volitional nature of informal mentoring suggests that interpersonal attraction probably underlies relationship initiation. In formal mentoring, the relationship initiation process is markedly different. Although some formal programs attempt to match mentor and protégé on individual characteristics that should engender interpersonal attraction (e.g., sex, race, functional area), this is not always the case. In fact, some mentoring programs match on *dissimilarity* since this may actually maximize learning and development (Eddy, Tannenbaum, Alliger, D'Abate, & Givens, 2001). In other formal mentoring programs, there may not be the luxury of matching mentor and protégé due to a limited pool of potential mentors. Another factor that may influence match fit is whether or not the protégé voluntarily participates in the formal mentoring program. Formal mentoring programs that are part of a new employee socialization program or a high potential development program may expect employees to assume the role of protégé. If would-be protégés do not participate voluntarily in a formal mentoring program, this may reduce their interest in, or commitment to, the relationship, which in turn may negatively influence relational fit. While participation is typically voluntary for would-be mentors (Allen, Eby, & Lentz, 2006a), some individuals may feel subtly coerced into assuming the role of mentor in a formal program. Mismatches may be more likely to occur in these situations due to low mentor motivation or lack of mentor commitment to the formal mentoring program or the mentoring relationship.

Various streams of mentoring scholarship inform the relationship initiation process. One line of research compares individuals with and without mentoring experience. This provides insight into the characteristics of those who enter into mentoring relationships as a protégé or as a mentor. This line of research also tells us something about the value of the mentoring experience by comparing those with and without such experience on a wide range of personal and professional outcomes. A related area of research examines willingness to mentor and motives for mentoring in an effort to understand the factors associated with the decision to become a mentor to others.

PREDICTORS OF RELATIONSHIP INITIATION

Mentoring is typically viewed as a positive career-enhancing experience. Decades of research finds differences in career outcomes as a function of race (Avery, 2006) and gender (Eby, 2006). Perhaps because of these disparities, numerous studies have examined whether there are race or gender differences in the experience of being a protégé. In terms of race, several studies find that non-whites are just as likely to have experience as a protégé as are whites (Blake-Beard, 1999; Mobley, Jaret, Marsh, & Lim, 1994; Thomas, 1990; but see Dreher & Cox, 1996, for an exception). Likewise, there is little evidence that women are less likely to be mentored compared to men (Broadbridge, 1999; Dreher & Ash, 1990; Dreher & Cox, 1996; Horgan & Simeon, 1990; Viator & Scandura, 1991). In fact, several studies find that women are actually *more likely* to be mentored than are men (Hubbard & Robinson, 1998; Mobley et al., 1994). However, an important caveat is that non-whites (Cox & Nkomo, 1991) and women (Ragins & Cotton, 1991) tend to report less access to mentors and perceive greater barriers to finding a mentor. This suggests that non-whites and women may have to work harder to secure a mentoring relationship than their white or male counterparts, respectively. There is also some evidence that women prefer same-sex mentors and believe that cross-sex relationships pose some unique challenges (e.g., greater tension, public image concerns; Burke & McKeen, 1990). Cross-race relationships can also be more complicated, given that the issue of race is often viewed as taboo in organizational settings (Thomas, 1990), with the preferred strategy for dealing with race in a mentoring relationship being denial rather than open discussion (Thomas 1993).

While there is little evidence that the base-rate of mentoring varies by sex or race, there is some evidence that the *type* of individual one has as a mentor differs across these groups. For example, whites

are more likely to be in informal relationships than are non-whites (Dreher & Cox, 1996), which is potentially important, since informal relationships tend to be more effective than formal ones (e.g., Allen, Day, & Lentz, 2005; Chao et al., 1992; Eby, Lockwood, & Butts, 2006; Fagenson-Eland, Marks, & Amendola, 1997; Viator, 2001). In addition, both racial minorities (Dreher & Cox, 1996; Turban, Dougherty, & Lee, 2002) and women (Dreher & Chargois, 1998) are less likely to have white mentors. Furthermore, women are less likely to have male mentors than are men (Burke, McKeen, & McKenna, 1990; Turban et al., 2002). The different composition of mentoring relationships for non-whites and women may have downstream career implications, since having white and/or male mentors is positively related to objective indicators of career success such as pay (e.g., Dreher & Chargois, 1998; Ragins & Cotton, 1999; Wallace, 2001). Finally, research finds that non-whites are more likely to have mentors who are outside their immediate chain of command (Thomas, 1990). While research is mixed as to whether having an external mentor is more or less advantageous for a protégé (cf. Baugh & Fagenson-Eland, 2005; Brashear, Bellenger, Boles, & Barksdale, 2006; Peluchette & Jeanquart, 2000), having mentors outside one's chain of command may restrict some of the important career-enhancing functions of mentoring, such as challenging assignments and sponsorship.

Other predictors of experience as a protégé include being at an early stage in one's career (Burke, 1984; Hubbard & Robinson, 1998), having a more androgynous or masculine sex-role orientation (Scandura & Ragins, 1993), and possessing personality traits associated with positive self-perceptions, sociability, and achievement striving (Aryee, Lo, & Kang, 1999; Fagenson, 1992; Fagenson-Eland & Baugh, 2001; Turban & Dougherty, 1994). Research from the mentor's perspective reveals some similar findings. Protégé characteristics that are viewed as desirable by mentors include high performance, potential, and motivation (Allen, Poteet, & Burroughs, 1997; Allen, Poteet, & Russell, 2000; Gaskill, 1991; Olian, Carroll, & Giannantonio, 1993), learning orientation (Allen, 2004; Allen, Poteet, & Burroughs, 1997), and personality traits indicative of interpersonal skills and self-confidence (Allen, Poteet, & Burroughs, 1997; Gaskill, 1991). Mentor characteristics that are viewed as important include strong interpersonal skills (Allen & Poteet, 1999; Olian, Carroll, Giannantonio, & Feren, 1988), strong character skills (e.g., patience, honesty), a genuine motivation to help others, and a strong knowledge base upon which to draw (Allen & Poteet, 1999). Interestingly, gender similarity does not appear to be a strong predictor of willingness to initiate a mentoring relationship from the perspective of either the mentor (Allen, 2004; Olian et al., 1993) or the protégé (Olian et al., 1988), although mentors report that perceived similarity is important (Allen, Poteet, & Burroughs, 1997).

CORRELATES AND OUTCOMES OF RELATIONSHIP INITIATION

Experience as a protégé is related to a variety of work attitudes. This includes higher job satisfaction (Chao, 1997; Corzine, Buntzman, & Busch, 1994; Mobley et al., 1994; Prevosto, 2001; Seibert, 1999; Van Emmerik, 2004), more positive work experiences (Baugh, Lankau, & Scandura, 1996; Viator, 2001), lower turnover intentions (Barker, Monks, & Buckley, 1999; Brashear et al., 2006; Broadbridge, 1999; Prevosto, 2001; Viator & Scandura, 1991), higher job and career motivation (Aryee & Chay, 1994; Chao, 1997; Day & Allen, 2004; Gaskill & Sibley, 1990), less work-family conflict (Nielson, Carlson, & Lankau, 2001), stronger perceptions of a family-friendly work climate (Forret & de Janasz, 2005), and greater performance (Brashear et al., 2006; Kirchmeyer, 2005; Peluchette & Jeanquart, 2000; Viator, 2001). There is also some evidence that having a mentor may buffer the negative effects of adverse work conditions on protégé work attitudes and burnout (Van Emmerik, 2004).

Experience as a protégé is also related to career outcomes, including faster promotion rates (Baugh et al., 1996; Bozionelos, 2006; Fagenson, 1989; Gaskill & Sibley, 1990; Wallace, 2001), more favorable career mobility perceptions (Corzine et al., 1994; Fagenson, 1989; Friedman, Kane, & Cornfield, 1998), greater perceived career success (Aryee & Chay, 1994; Bozionelos, 2006; Collins, 1994; Peluchette & Jeanquart, 2000; Riley & Wrench, 1985; Van Emmerik, 2004), and stronger career commitment (Aryee & Chay, 1994; Colarelli & Bishop, 1990). There is also some research demonstrating that protégés report higher self-esteem (Fagenson-Eland & Baugh, 2001), more effective learning and socialization experiences (Broadbridge, 1999; Chao, 1997; Lankau & Scandura, 2002; Ostroff & Kozlowski, 1993; Schrodt, Cawyer, & Sanders, 2003; Wallace, 2001), higher continuance commitment (Brashear et al., 2006), and greater perceptions of power within the organization (Fagenson, 1988) than do non-protégés.

The findings are mixed in terms of whether or not protégés report higher salaries (cf. Brown & Scandura, 2001; Chao, 1997; Collins, 1994; Corzine et al., 1994; Dreher & Chargois, 1998; Dreher & Cox, 1996; Wallace, 2001), greater organizational commitment (cf. Aryee & Chay, 1994; Brashear et al., 2006; Seibert, 1999), and fewer strain reactions (cf. Bozionelos, 2006; Seibert, 1999; Van Emmerik, 2004) compared to non-protégés. In terms of benefits of experience as a mentor, some research finds higher salaries (Allen, Lentz, & Day, 2006), higher performance ratings (Gentry, Weber, & Sadri, 2008), and greater perceived career success (Collins, 1994) among those with experience as a mentor, compared to those without such experience. In contrast, Burke, McKeen, and McKenna (1994) found no difference in promotion rates among those with experience as a mentor and those without such experience.

WILLINGNESS TO MENTOR OTHERS

Mentors play a pivotal role in the mentoring process and often initiate informal mentoring relationships. The motivation for mentoring others can be self-focused (e.g., gratification seeing others grow and develop) or other-focused (e.g., desire to help others; Allen, Poteet, & Burroughs, 1997). As a consequence, the expected costs and benefits of mentoring are likely to influence whether or not someone takes on the role of mentor (Olian et al., 1993; Ragins & Scandura, 1999). Higher ranking organizational members are more likely to assume the role of a mentor (Ragins & Cotton, 1993). In addition, previous mentoring experience reliably predicts future willingness to mentor (Allen, 2003; Allen, Poteet, Russell, & Dobbins, 1997; Bozionelos, 2004; Eby, Lockwood, & Butts, 2006; Ragins & Cotton, 1993; Ragins & Scandura, 1994, 1999; Van Emmerik, Baugh, Euwema, & Martin, 2005) and helps to prepare individuals for assuming the role of mentor (Allen, Poteet, et al., 1997). A limited number of studies have examined the personal characteristics of individuals who assume the role of a mentor, although there is evidence that trait-based helpfulness, other-oriented empathy, perceived competence, positive career attitudes, and positive affectivity may be important (Allen, 2003; Aryee, Chay, & Chew, 1996; Horgan & Simeon, 1990; Van Emmerik et al., 2005). Protégés prefer mentors with strong interpersonal competence (Gaskill, 1991; Olian et al., 1988) and strong technical skills (Gaskill, 1991).

In terms of the personal characteristics of those willing to assume the role of mentor, the findings are largely inconclusive. Age has been examined in relation to willingness to mentor, and few consistent effects have emerged (Allen, Poteet, et al., 1997; Ragins & Cotton, 1993; Van Emmerik et al., 2005). The findings are also mixed regarding gender differences in willingness to mentor others (cf. Eby, Lockwood, & Butts, 2006; Ragins & Cotton, 1993; Ragins & Scandura, 1994; Van Emmerik et al., 2005), as well as gender differences in the expected drawbacks of mentoring (cf. Ragins & Scandura, 1994; Ragins & Cotton, 1993). However, there is initial evidence that women are more likely to select protégés on the basis of ability than are men (Allen et al., 2000). Individuals with more of an internal locus of control and a stronger achievement orientation also report greater willingness to mentor others (Allen, Poteet, Russell, et al., 1997; Van Emmerik et al., 2005).

SUMMARY

Table 19.1 summarizes the research findings on relationship initiation. As the literature reviewed in this section illustrates, individuals often enter into mentoring relationships, as either protégés and as mentors, in an effort to accomplish some of the developmental tasks associated with adulthood. Those seeking out mentoring relationships tend to be less experienced, younger individuals who have the most to gain from a developmental relationship with a more experienced and higher ranking organizational member. The finding that women and non-whites report less access to mentors and more barriers to relationship initiation is consistent with the finding that these groups face some unique developmental challenges in the workplace (see Avery, 2006; Eby, 2006). It is also telling that individuals who enter into mentoring relationships as protégés tend to be those who have a stronger desire for self-development, as well as greater capacity for learning and self-improvement. Likewise, the personal and professional characteristics that individuals look for in a mentor suggest that would-be protégés are seeking assistance from others who have the capacity to help them successfully navigate the developmental tasks associated with adulthood. In terms of the mentor's perspective, the literature reviewed in this section clearly points to how the experience of being a mentor can also fulfill developmental needs associated with late adulthood (e.g., passing on the torch, career rejuvenation). Like protégés, mentors appear to seek out relational partners who are most likely to provide them with benefits and are most likely to be receptive to the mentoring assistance that they want to provide.

Research on Relationship Maturation

As the relationship matures, mentors provide various forms of support to protégés. Kram (1985) differentiates two general types of mentor support: career-related support and psychosocial support. Career-related support includes mentor behaviors that help the protégé understand how the organization operates and that prepare the protégé for advancement. This includes providing sponsorship, exposure and visibility, coaching, challenging assignments, and protection to the protégé. Psychosocial support is oriented toward building protégé self-efficacy, self-worth, and professional identity. This type of support includes offering unconditional acceptance and confirmation, providing counseling and friendship, and serving as a role model for the protégé. Even though mentoring can be associated with positive experiences for protégés, negative relational events can occur, and when they do, the mentoring relationship can be affected (for a review see Eby, 2007). Research on the quantity and quality of relational experiences provides a different vantage point to understand mentoring relationships than does research on relationship initiation, since the latter simply compares those with and without experience in a mentoring relationship.

While less frequently studied, mentors can also reap rewards for serving as a mentor to others (Kram, 1985). This includes both instrumental rewards (e.g., improved job performance, recognition by the organization) and relational rewards (e.g., self-satisfaction, the development of a loyal base of support; Eby, Durley, Evans, & Ragins, 2006). Mentors may also reap benefits in terms of more favorable work attitudes and career outcomes (for a review, see Allen, 2007). Notwithstanding the potential for a mentoring experience to be positive for the mentor, it is also possible that as the relationship matures, relational problems may surface which thwart the maturation process and perhaps even lead to premature relationship termination (for a review, see Eby, 2007).

Insight into the relationship maturation process can be obtained from research examining the predictors, correlates, and outcomes associated with protégés' receipt of mentoring support as well as mentors' provision of mentoring support. Research on the predictors, correlates, and outcomes associated with mentors' receipt of mentoring benefits also tell us something about the maturation of mentoring relationships. Finally, research on problems in mentoring relationships from the perspective of both protégé and mentor highlights important

Table 19.1 Summary of Research Findings on Relationship Initiation

Predictors of Experience as a Protégé

Demographic variables	No difference in the base-rate of mentoring between non-whites and whites or between men and women. Both non-whites and women are more likely to be in formal mentoring relationships, have less access to mentors, and are less likely to have white male mentors.
Experience-based factors	Early career individuals are more likely to be mentored. Mentors generally desire protégés with greater performance and potential.
Personality traits	Individuals with greater positive self-regard, sociability and achievement striving are more likely to report being mentored. Mentors prefer protégés with self-confidence, strong interpersonal skills, and similarity to themselves. Protégés prefer mentors who display strong interpersonal skills, altruistic tendencies, strong character, and job-related knowledge.

Correlates of Experience as a Protégé

Work attitudes	Individuals with experience as a protégé report higher job satisfaction, stronger career motivation, greater job motivation, more favorable perceptions of the work environment, lower turnover intentions, stronger continuance commitment, and greater perceptions of power within the organization. The research findings are mixed when comparing protégés to non-protégés on affective commitment, pay, and strain reactions.
Career outcomes	Experience as a protégé is related to faster promotion rates, more favorable career mobility perceptions, greater perceived career success, and stronger career commitment. Some initial evidence that experience as a mentor is associated with higher pay, greater perceived career success, and higher performance ratings.
Job performance	Individuals with experience as a protégé report higher job performance as well as more effective learning and socialization experiences.

Willingness to Mentor Others

Demographic variables	No consistent age or gender effects in relation to willingness to mentor others. Some evidence than women are more likely to select protégés on the basis of ability than are men.
Experience-based factors	Those with previous mentoring experience and higher organizational rank report greater willingness to assume the role of a mentor.
Personality traits & attitudes	Individuals higher on trait-based helpfulness, other-oriented empathy, positive affectivity, internal locus of control, and achievement striving, as well as those who hold more positive career attitudes report greater willingness to mentor others. Protégés prefer mentors with strong interpersonal and technical skills.

differences in the extent to which mentoring relationships develop into emotionally close and trusting relationships.

PREDICTORS OF RELATIONSHIP MATURATION

An extensive body of research exists on the predictors of career-related and psychosocial mentoring. Greater mentoring tends to be reported in supervisory mentoring relationships (Fagenson-Eland et al., 1997; Payne & Huffman, 2005; Ragins & McFarlin, 1990; Scandura & Viator, 1994) among protégés who initiate the mentoring relationship (Aryee et al., 1999; Turban & Dougherty, 1994; but see Scandura & Williams, 2001, for differences by protégé sex) and among those with less previous mentoring experience (Ragins & McFarlin, 1990). Mentoring relationships characterized by more frequent mentor-protégé contact (Arnold & Johnson, 1997; Burke, McKeen, & McKenna, 1993; Lankau & Scandura, 2002; Mullen, 1998; Waters, McCabe,

Kiellerup, & Kiellerup, 2002) and an initiation process that is informal rather than formal (Allen et al., 2005; Chao et al., 1992; Eby, Lockwood, & Butts, 2006; Fagneson-Eland et al., 1997; Ragins & Cotton, 1999; Viator, 2001) are also associated with greater mentoring support for protégés. In terms of position characteristics, protégés who are newer to the organization or job (Koberg, Boss, & Goodman, 1998; Sosik & Godshalk, 2000a) and higher in rank (Koberg et al., 1998; Sosik & Godshalk, 2000a; Whitely, Dougherty, & Dreher, 1992) report receiving more mentoring support.

Various protégé motivational, attitudinal, and personality characteristics are associated with the receipt of mentoring support. These include having higher ability or potential (Green & Bauer, 1995), higher motivation and commitment (Green & Bauer, 1995; Koberg et al., 1998; Noe, 1988; Whitely et al., 1992), personality characteristics indicative of strong interpersonal skills (Eby, Lockwood, & Butts, 2006; Kalbfleisch & Davies, 1993), and positive self-regard (Kalbfleisch & Davies, 1993; Koberg et al., 1998; Noe, 1988). In addition, protégé achievement orientation is positively associated with greater learning for both the mentor and the protégé (Hirschfeld, Thomas, & Lankau, 2006) as well as protégé expectations regarding the receipt of mentoring support (Young & Perrewé, 2004). In terms of mentor characteristics, there is some evidence that mentor proactivity (Wanberg, Kammeyer-Mueller, & Marchese, 2006), openness to experience (Bozionelos, 2004), organizational status (Arnold & Johnson, 1997; Burke et al., 1993), previous experience as a mentor (Fagenson-Eland et al., 1997), and various aspects of a more transformational leadership style (Sosik & Godshalk, 2000a, 2004; Sosik, Godshalk, & Yammarino, 2004) positively relate to protégé perceptions of mentoring support.

Several protégé background characteristics are associated with greater mentoring support, including being younger (Finkelstein, Allen, & Rhoton, 2003; Scandura & Williams, 2001; Sosik & Godshalk, 2000a; Whitely et al., 1992), more educated (Koberg et al., 1998; Noe, 1988; Okurame & Balogun, 2005; but see Sosik & Godshalk, 2000a, for an exception), and of higher socioeconomic status (Whitely et al., 1992). Mentor and protégé gender have also been examined extensively as predictors of the receipt of mentoring support. The findings here are mixed, with some studies finding no effect for protégé sex (Barker et al., 1999; Fagenson, 1992; Ragins & McFarlin, 1990;

Scandura & Ragins, 1993; Whitely et al., 1992) or mentor sex (Arnold & Johnson, 1997; Burke & McKeen, 1996; Johnson, Holmes, Huwe, & Norlund, 2001; Ragins & McFarlin, 1990). Other studies find some sex differences in mentoring support, although the nature of these differences varies from study to study (for protégé sex, see Cianni & Romberger, 1995; Goh, 1991; Koberg, Boss, Chappell, & Ringer, 1994; Noe, 1988; for mentor sex, see Allen & Eby, 2004; Burke et al., 1990; Burke et al., 1993). Research examining protégé race is more limited, but likewise inconclusive. In one study, Koberg et al. (1994) found greater career-related mentoring among non-whites, whereas a later study found more psychosocial mentoring support among white protégés (Koberg et al., 1998). Cianni and Romberger (1995) also reports mixed results comparing mentoring received among Asian, black, Hispanic, and white protégés; across seven specific mentoring functions, only two significant differences were found. In both cases, white protégés reported greater mentoring support than did non-white protégés.

Owing to the interpersonal nature of mentoring, mentor-protégé similarity has also been examined. The evidence strongly suggests that both mentor and protégé perceptions of similarity positively relate to the amount of mentoring support (Burke et al., 1993; Ensher, Grant-Vallone, & Marelich, 2002; Wanberg et al., 2006, for mentor similarity perceptions; Ensher & Murphy, 1997; Lankau, Riordan & Thomas, 2005; Turban et al., 2002; Wanberg et al., 2006, for protégé similarity perceptions) and relationship quality (Ensher & Murphy, 1997, for protégé similarity perceptions; Lankau et al., 2005, for both mentor and protégé perceptions of similarity). Moreover, the more a mentor perceives the protégé as similar early in the relationship, the greater the relational learning reported by the mentor (Allen & Eby, 2003).

The evidence is less conclusive in terms of actual similarity. Several studies find no differences in mentoring received on the basis of sex similarity (Noe, 1988; Turban et al., 2002) and no differences in relational quality from the protégé's perspective (Lankau et al., 2005). In contrast, several studies find higher rates of some psychosocial mentoring functions (Ensher et al., 2002; Ragins & Cotton, 1999; Ragins & McFarlin, 1990; Scandura & Viator, 1994; Thomas, 1990), including role modeling (Barker et al., 1999; Burke, Burgess, & Fallon, 2006; Lankau et al., 2005, mentor's perspective only; Scandura & Williams, 2001) in same-sex relationships. In terms of career-related support, only Thomas (1990) reports greater mentoring received in same-sex relationships.

Taking a more fine-grained perspective on sex similarity by considering all four gender combinations, Ragins and Cotton (1999) found the lowest amount of career-related support and lowest relationship quality among male protégés with female mentors. This is generally consistent with Sosik and Godshalk's (2000b) finding that the lowest level of career development support was found among protégés with female mentors. Although the cell sizes were very small, Burke et al. (1990) further found that female mentors provided significantly more psychosocial forms of support, such as friendship and counseling, as well as more sponsorship, to female protégés than did mentors in the other sex combinations. It is also worth noting that a number of studies find higher relationship quality in same-sex relationships compared to cross-sex relationship (Allen, Day & Lentz, 2005; Ensher & Murphy, 1997; Lankau et al., 2005, protégé perspective only; Thomas 1990). It may also be important to consider relationship length when examining differences in mentoring received as a function of sex similarity. Turban et al. (2002) found that while early in the relationship sex dissimilarity was detrimental, later in the relationship protégés reported greater mentoring in cross-sex relationships than same-sex relationships.

Fewer studies have examined race similarity, and the findings are inconclusive. Several studies find no differences in career-related (Thomas, 1990; Turban et al., 2002), psychosocial (Ensher & Murphy, 1997; Turban et al., 2002), or overall (Blake-Beard, 1999) mentoring received on the basis of race similarity. Other studies report greater psychosocial (Koberg et al., 1998; Lankau et al., 2005, mentor perspective only; Thomas, 1990) or career-related (Ensher & Murphy, 1997) mentoring in same-race dyads. There are also mixed findings with respect to the effect of race similarity on perceptions of liking. Ensher and Murphy (1997) found significantly greater liking reported by mentors in same-race relationships, but no such differences among protégés.

CORRELATES AND OUTCOMES OF RELATIONSHIP MATURATION

As the mentoring relationship matures and greater mentoring support is received, protégés tend to report more satisfaction with the relationship (Ensher et al., 2001; Johnson et al., 2001; Lankau et al., 2005), greater self-disclosure (Wanberg, Welsh, & Kammeyer-Mueller, 2007), and stronger perceptions that the mentor had a positive effect on one's career (Burke, 1984). Likewise, mentors and protégés who expect more out of the relationship tend to report receiving more benefits (Young & Perrewé, 2004). The provision of mentoring support may also build protégé trust and strengthen the perception that the relationship is effective (Young & Perrewé, 2000). For mentors, trust and relationship effectiveness is associated with the protégé putting forth noticeable effort into the mentorship (Young & Perrewé, 2000).

Mentoring support has also been examined in relation to a wide range of work attitudes. The receipt of mentoring is related to higher job satisfaction (Bahniuk, Dobos, & Hill, 1990; Burke et al., 2006; Ensher et al., 2001; Higgins & Thomas, 2001; Koberg et al., 1994; Lankau, Carlson, & Nielson, 2006; Lankau & Scandura, 2002; Murphy & Ensher, 2001; Seibert, 1999; Whitely & Coetsier, 1993), stronger job involvement (Aryee & Chay, 1994; Cox & Nkomo, 1991), greater perceptions of career success (Aryee & Chay, 1994; Aryee et al., 1996; Bahniuk et al., 1990; Bozionelos & Wang, 2006; Burke et al., 2006; Cox & Nkomo, 1991; Ensher et al., 2001; Murphy & Ensher, 2001; Okurame & Balogun, 2005; Seibert, Kraimer, & Liden, 2001; Turban & Dougherty, 1994; Waters et al., 2002; Whitely & Coetsier, 1993; for an exception, see Wayne, Liden, Kraimer, & Graf, 1999), and lower turnover intentions (Harris, Winskowski, & Engdahl, 2007; Higgins & Thomas, 2001; Koberg et al., 1998; Lankau & Scandura, 2002; Scandura & Viator, 1994; Viator & Scandura, 1991; for exceptions, see Raabe & Beehr, 2003; Wanberg et al., 2006). In terms of the association between mentoring and organizational commitment, research has found both positive (Aryee & Chay, 1994; Donaldson, Ensher, & Grant-Vallone, 2000; Payne & Huffman, 2005; Seibert, 1999) and non-significant (Green & Bauer, 1995; Raabe & Beehr, 2003; Wanberg et al., 2006) effects. One explanation may be that the effects of mentoring on organizational commitment are indirect, perhaps operating through reduced role conflict or role ambiguity (Lankau et al., 2006). Likewise, the evidence linking the receipt of mentoring to various types of role stressors is mixed and inconclusive (cf. Lankau & Scandura, 2002; Nielson et al., 2001; Seibert, 1999; Sosik & Godshalk, 2000a; Viator, 2001).

In terms of career attainment, most studies find that mentoring is positively related to protégé promotion rate (Aryee, Wyatt, & Stone, 1996; Cox & Nkomo, 1991; Dreher & Ash, 1990; Orpen,

1995; Scandura & Schriescheim, 1994; Seibert et al., 2001; Turban & Dougherty, 1994; Whitely & Coetsier, 1993; Whitely et al., 1991; for exceptions, see Bozionelos & Wang, 2006; Higgins & Thomas, 2001; Scandura, 1992) and salary (Bahniuk et al., 1990; Dreher & Ash, 1990; Orpen, 1995; Scandura, 1992; Scandura & Schriescheim, 1994; Seibert et al., 2001; Turban & Dougherty, 1994; Whitely et al., 1991; for exceptions, see Aryee et al., 1996; Wayne et al., 1999; Whitely & Coetsier, 1993). The receipt of mentoring support is also positively related to protégé self-esteem (Seibert, 1999; Waters et al., 2002), promotability (Wayne et al., 1999), goal clarity (Wanberg et al., 2006), future career prospects (Burke et al., 2006), and socialization (Feldman, Folks, & Turnley, 1999; Schrodt et al., 2003).

The evidence linking mentoring to protégé behavior is less conclusive. For example, the results are mixed as to whether mentoring is related to actual turnover (cf. Higgins & Thomas, 2001; Payne & Huffman, 2005) or performance (cf. Green & Bauer, 1995; Scandura & Schriescheim, 1994; Wanberg et al., 2006). One explanation for these inconsistent results may be that mentoring is only associated with higher protégé performance when the mentor is a high performer and the relationship is of longer duration (Tonidandel, Avery, & Phillips, 2007). In terms of extra-role behavior, Donaldson et al. (2000) found initial evidence that the receipt of mentoring is positively related to protégé organizational citizenship behavior.

Finally, a limited number of studies have examined the relationship between mentoring and outcomes for the mentor. For example, Gentry et al. (2008) found that mentors who provided greater career-related support to protégés received higher performance ratings from their bosses, particularly if the mentor worked in a performance-oriented cultural context. Other research finds that as mentors provide more psychosocial mentoring support to protégés, they tend to report more positive mentoring experiences (Wanberg et al., 2006). Likewise, Eby, Durley, et al. (2006) found that mentors who report more short-term instrumental and relational benefits from the mentoring relationship tend to have more positive work attitudes and stronger future intentions to mentor. In a study examining the conditions under which mentors are more likely to seek information from their protégés, Mullen and Noe (1999) found that this occurs more often in situations in which the protégé is perceived as competent and the mentor provides more career-related mentoring to the protégé.

PROBLEMS IN MENTORING RELATIONSHIPS

While mentoring relationships are presumed to be positive developmental experiences, several recent meta-analyses find that the effect sizes associated with the relationship between mentoring and protégé outcomes tend to be small to moderate in magnitude (Allen et al., 2004; Eby, Allen, et al., 2008; Kammeyer-Mueller & Judge, 2008; Underhill, 2006). This begs the question as to whether mentoring relationships might sometimes be marked by relationship difficulties. The idea that a close relationship is likely to have both relational "ups and downs" is well accepted in the social-psychological literature on close relationships (see Huston & Burgess, 1979), but has only recently been the focus of research on workplace mentoring. Interestingly, seminal work on mentoring by Kram (1985) and Levinson et al. (1978) discuss how mentoring relationships can become destructive for one or both individuals over time. However, only recently have scholars started to discuss the various ways that mentoring relationships can run into trouble, issuing a call for empirical research on the topic (Feldman, 1999; Scandura, 1998).

A series of studies by Eby and colleagues investigated the problems that can occur in mentoring relationships and offered some initial evidence on the antecedents, correlates, and consequences of relational problems in mentoring. In a qualitative study of 84 protégés, Eby, McManus, Simon, and Russell (2000) identified five distinct types of negative mentoring experiences for protégés: mismatch within the mentor-protégé dyad, mentor neglect, mentor manipulative behavior, lack of mentor expertise, and general dysfunctionality on the part of the mentor. The most commonly reported relational problem was a mismatch in values, work styles, or personality (i.e., mismatch within the mentor-protégé dyad). Mismatches were also the most commonly reported problem by protégés participating in a formal mentoring program, although a unique aspect of mismatches in this sample was the sense of interpersonal discomfort and awkwardness associated with being matched by a third party (Eby & Lockwood, 2005). Other relationship problems associated specifically with formal mentoring include scheduling difficulties, geographic distance, unmet expectations, and mentor neglect (Eby & Lockwood, 2005).

Negative experiences with mentors are not uncommon; over half of the study participants in the Eby et al. (2000) study reported at least one negative experience with their mentors and many reported more than one distinct type of relational problem (also see Kalbfleisch, 1997; Rosser, 2005). A follow-up multidimensional scaling study found that individuals conceptualize protégé negative relational experiences in terms of outcome severity (i.e., minor versus serious), behavioral specificity (i.e., mentor behavior targeted toward a particular protégé versus mentor behavior that is more diffuse in nature), and mentoring function (i.e., negative experiences oriented more toward the career-related versus the psychosocial aspects of mentoring; Simon & Eby, 2003). Research indicates that protégé reports of relational problems with mentors are also distinct from positive relational experiences, both substantively and empirically (Eby et al., 2004).

Certain types of protégés appear more likely to report relational problems. For instance, protégés with lower self-esteem and higher negative affect tend to report greater relational problems with their mentors (Eby, Lockwood, & Butts, 2006). Two studies have examined protégé gender. Eby, Lockwood, and Butts (2006) found that female protégés reported more negative experiences than male protégés. In terms of direct conflict situations with mentors, Kalbfleisch (1997) found that male protégés reported more conflicts than did female protégés. The strategies used to deal with mentor conflicts also varied by protégé gender (Kalbfleisch, 1997). Male protégés were more likely to appease their mentor and to comply with their mentors' wishes than were women. Women were more likely to respond to conflict situations by crying. There is also evidence that mentor neglect and lack of mentor expertise may be more common in formally arranged mentoring relationships than in informal mentorships (Eby et al., 2004). Eby and Allen (2002) further found that protégés reported that the most negative experiences with their mentor had more of an effect on turnover intentions and strain when protégés reported being in formal as opposed to informal mentoring relationships.

In terms of protégé outcomes, negative relational experiences with one's mentor are related to less favorable social exchange perceptions in the relationship, less learning, lower job satisfaction, stronger intentions to leave the organization, greater reports of depressed mood at work, higher work role stress, and greater psychological job withdrawal (Eby & Allen, 2002; Eby et al., 2004). Along these same lines, Ragins et al. (2000) found that relationship quality is important to consider in understanding the benefits of mentoring for protégés. Protégés in highly satisfying formal *or* informal

mentoring relationships reported greater work satisfaction, organizational and career commitment, organization-based self-esteem, procedural justice, and lower turnover intentions than did protégés in marginal or dissatisfying relationships. In addition, protégés in highly satisfying informal relationships reported more favorable work and career attitudes than non-mentored individuals. However, no differences were found between the non-mentored group and protégés in *dissatisfying* formal or informal mentoring relationships.

Mentors can also have difficulties with protégés. A qualitative study of 90 mentors identified a wide range of relational problems with protégés, some of which were similar to problems reported by protégés (e.g., difficulty relating interpersonally, manipulative behavior) and other problems which were quite different (e.g., protégé unwillingness to learn, protégé submissiveness; Eby & McManus, 2004). Another study by Eby and colleagues (Eby, Durley, et al., 2008) found support for three higher order categories of negative experiences with protégés (i.e., protégé performance problems, interpersonal problems, destructive relational patterns) and provided evidence that relational problems with protégés were positively related to mentor burnout, and negatively related to mentor reports of relationship quality and social exchange perceptions. Mentors' reports of problems with protégés were also negatively related to their protégés' reports of mentoring received, relationship quality, and social exchange perceptions. In terms of formal mentoring relationships, mentors report some other types of relational problems including feelings of personal inadequacy as a mentor and unmet expectations (Eby & Lockwood, 2005).

SUMMARY

The research reviewed in this section on relationship maturation is summarized in Table 19.2. This body of literature also demonstrates the value of taking a developmental perspective on mentoring. Consistent with research comparing those with and without mentoring experience, the research reviewed in this section reveals that individuals who are at an early stage in their journey to adulthood, as well as those newer to the job or organization, tend to receive greater mentoring support. Moreover, protégés who get more out of the mentoring relationship tend to be those who invest more in the relationship, both emotionally and behaviorally. They also tend to be those who express greater potential for development and who demonstrate a greater desire for personal growth.

Table 19.2 Summary of Research Findings on Relationship Maturation

Predictors of Mentoring Received

Socio-demographic variables	Protégés who are younger, more educated, and higher in socioeconomic status report more mentoring support. Mixed findings regarding differences in mentoring received as a function of protégé gender, protégé race, gender mix of the dyad, and racial mix of the dyads.
Experience-based factors	Protégés with less mentoring experience, greater organizational rank, and less tenure report greater mentoring received. Protégés who have mentors with more mentoring experience report receiving more mentoring support.
Personality traits & attitudes	Protégés with higher ability or potential, greater motivation or commitment, stronger interpersonal skills, more positive self-regard, and higher achievement orientation report receiving more mentoring. Mentors higher in proactivity, openness to experience, and transformational leadership characteristics have protégés who report more mentoring support.
Relationship characteristics	Greater mentoring received in supervisory mentoring relationships, formal mentoring relationships, and if the protégé initiates the relationship. More frequent mentor-protégé contact is associated with more mentoring received. Mentor-protégé perceived similarity is related to greater mentoring support as reported by the protégé.

Correlates of Mentoring Received

Work and relationship attitudes	Greater mentoring received is associated with higher job satisfaction, stronger job involvement, higher relationship quality, greater socialization, and lower turnover intentions. Inconclusive findings regarding organizational commitment and role stressors. Some evidence that mentors who provide more mentoring support report higher relationship quality, more favorable work attitudes, and stronger intentions to mentor in the future.
Career outcomes	Those who receive more mentoring support report stronger perceptions of career success, faster promotion rates, greater promotability, and salary.
Behavioral outcomes	Some initial evidence that greater mentoring received is related to protégé organizational citizenship behavior. Mixed evidence regarding the relationship between mentoring received and turnover or performance. Some evidence linking the provision of mentoring to mentor job performance.

Predictors and Correlates of Relational Problems

Personality traits, attitudes, & gender	Protégés with lower self-esteem and higher negative affect report more relational problems. Findings are mixed regarding protégé gender and relational problems.
Relationship characteristics	Some types of relational problems are more common in formally arranged mentoring relationships.
Work attitudes & strain reactions	Protégés indicating more problems with their mentors report lower relationship quality, less job satisfaction, more strain reactions, and stronger intentions to leave the organization. Protégés in lower quality relationships report less favorable work and career attitudes, regardless of relationship formality. Mentors who report more problems with protégés report higher burnout and lower relationship quality.

Also consistent with a developmental perspective, as the mentorship matures it has the potential to provide greater career-related and psychosocial support to protégés. In turn, mentoring support reliably predicts a whole host of positive protégé outcomes, many of which are indicative of increased protégé maturity and successful adaptation. Specifically, as mentoring support increases, protégés report greater professional success, greater investment in their occupation, greater integration into the workplace, and positive work experiences. Mentors can also benefit from the mentoring relationships, both personally and professionally. Moreover, if a mentoring relationship runs into relational trouble, one or both individuals may find that their developmental needs are not being met. This may lead to disengagement from the relationship, psychologically and/or behaviorally, suggesting that the developmental sequence has come to an end.

Research on Relationship Decline

When a mentoring relationship begins, the protégé is a novice and the mentor is an experienced insider. In an effective mentoring relationship, the protégé should develop personally as well as professionally. Thus a time will come when the protégé no longer needs the mentor's guidance and support, and/or the mentor believes that he or she has done all that is possible to develop the protégé (Kram, 1985). This is consistent with the finding that protégés are more likely to perceive their mentor as lacking expertise in later stages of the mentoring relationship (Eby, Lockwood, & Butts, 2006). Formal mentoring relationships are also time-bound. Most formal relationships officially terminate after some predetermined length of time, typically around one year (Allen, Day, & Lentz, 2001).

Compared to other phases of the mentoring relationship, far less research exists on relationship decline. The research that does exist offers some interesting insights into this phase, which are largely consistent with theory. As Kram (1985) suggests, there is evidence that some relational problems may be more common in the separation phase compared to other phases of the mentoring relationship (Eby et al., 2004). In addition, tension created during the separation phase is associated with less job satisfaction and lower organizational commitment, which in turn predicts turnover intentions (Viator & Pasewark, 2005). While relationship decline is a natural part of a mentoring relationship, it may also happen prematurely if the relationship is viewed as ineffective or dysfunctional by one or both individuals (Eby & McManus, 2004; Eby et al., 2000). In terms of the relational processes found during the separation phase, only a few studies exist on the topic. Bouquillon, Sosik, and Lee (2005) found that while levels of trust and identification were constant across mentoring stages, as expected, protégés did report less role modeling and career-related support during the separation phase compared to other phases. However, this runs counter to Chao's (1997) finding of no significant differences in career-related

or psychosocial mentoring support in the cultivation phase compared to the separation and redefinition phases.

Though empirical research comparing mentoring phases is sparse, some inferences can be drawn about relationship decline from research on relationship termination and the predictors of intentions to leave the mentoring relationship. Several studies find that protégés report greater intentions to leave the relationship if they perceive themselves as more dissimilar to their mentors (Ensher & Murphy, 1997) or if they report greater relational problems with their mentors (Eby et al., 2004). There is also some evidence that as mentors report greater problems with protégés, both mentors and their protégés report stronger intentions to leave the relationship (Eby, Durley, et al., 2008). A related area of research focuses specifically on relationship termination. Ragins and Scandura (1997) found a wide range of reasons that protégés leave mentoring relationships, including jealousy, overdependence on the mentor, lack of support, and outgrowing the relationship. Many of these reasons for exiting the mentoring relationship are similar to the mentoring problems discussed in the previous section. Other researchers have found that structural separation from the mentor (e.g., mentor leaving the organization or moving into another job function) can be a catalyst for relationship termination and may be viewed as a relationship problem since this can restrict the availability of mentoring support (Burke, 1984; Eby & Lockwood, 2005). Taken together, these findings are consistent with Kram's (1985) discussion of the difficulties associated with the separation phase.

REDEFINITION

Kram (1985) discusses the redefinition phase as the final phase of a mentoring relationship. During this phase, the relationship takes on new meaning for both the mentor and the protégé. Very little research has compared protégé attitudes and reactions during the redefinition phase to other phases of the mentoring relationship. Bouquillon et al. (2005) found similar levels of trust and identification in this phase compared to other relationship phases, along with higher levels of psychosocial mentoring. This runs counter to Kram's (1985) characterization of the redefinition phase. However, consistent with the notion that protégés are generally independent of their mentor and have established their own professional identity in the redefinition phase (Kram, 1985), Bouquillon et al. (2005) found less role modeling and career-related mentoring in the redefinition phase compared to the initiation phase.

SUMMARY

The literature on relationship decline is in its infancy. As such, it is not prudent to summarize the findings in table form, as was done for relationship initiation and relationship maturation. However, a few summary comments are in order. Consistent with the developmental perspective, relationship decline signals the stage at which either the relationship has met its goals or the relationship is unable to fulfill one or both individuals' needs. Since mentoring relationships are dynamic yet predictable, this represents a natural phase of the mentoring relationship, albeit one that is often marked by turmoil and anxiety. Both mentor and protégé behavior influence how the decline phase plays out, as well as what the redefinition phase holds for the relationship.

Contextual Influences on Workplace Mentoring Relationships

There is a long-standing tradition in psychology to view organizational behavior from an interactionist perspective in which both the individual and the situation influence behavior (Lewin, 1951). Consideration of situational or contextual factors is also a key element in the developmental perspective since individuals interact with their environment and contextually embedded experiences influence one's developmental trajectory (Vondracek et al., 1986). A major contextual factor for workplace mentoring is the organizational setting in which the relationship is embedded. Organizations have a vested interest in mentoring relationships, since many of the positive outcomes associated with mentoring reflect attitudes and behaviors that are of interest to the organization (e.g., positive work attitudes, effective socialization, lower turnover). As such, organizations informally encourage or even actively facilitate mentoring relationships. Conversely, there may be some organizational contexts that make it difficult for individuals to initiate and maintain effective mentoring relationships.

Organization-level research on contextual influences on mentoring is virtually nonexistent. However, several studies have examined *individual perceptions* of organizational attributes in relation to mentoring. For example, perceptions of a learning and development climate within the organization are viewed by mentors as important in facilitating effective mentoring relationships (Allen, Poteet, & Burroughs, 1997). Other perceived organizational attributes associated with effective mentoring relationships include a cooperative, team-oriented approach to work, decentralized decision making, employee development-linked reward system, and a climate where innovation is encouraged and where tolerance for employee mistakes is high (Allen, Poteet, & Burroughs, 1997; Aryee, Chay, & Chew, 1996; Aryee, Lo, & Kang, 1999). Interestingly, O'Neill (2005) found differences in the level of career-related and psychosocial support provided as a function of the organizational climate; competitive organizational climates were associated with greater career-oriented mentoring support, whereas participative climates were associated with more psychosocial mentoring support.

Employee perceptions of top management support for mentoring also appears to be important, given that it is positively related to the receipt of mentoring and negatively related to protégé reports of relational problems (Eby, Lockwood, & Butts, 2006). Perceived management support for mentoring has also been linked to positive mentoring outcomes for mentors (Parise & Forret, 2008). Finally, in an experimental study of organizational attraction, Allen and O'Brien (2006) found that the mere presence of a formal mentoring program positively influenced applicants' organizational attraction. This attraction effect was particularly strong among those higher in learning goal orientation, suggesting that formal mentoring programs may help recruit the type of applicants that organizations are most interested in hiring.

Another contextual vantage point to understand mentoring is the manner in which organizations design and deliver formal mentoring programs. Programs vary considerably in terms of program design (e.g., mentor-protégé matching, program purpose, selection criteria to identify participants) and program structure (e.g., training provided, guidelines for interaction, program monitoring; see Eddy et al., 2001). Recent research finds that some of these program features relate to participant reactions to participation in formal mentoring programs, and to the amount of mentoring that occurs in formally arranged mentoring relationships.

Allowing participants to have input into the process of being matched with a mentoring partner is viewed favorably by both mentors and protégés (Eby & Lockwood, 2005). In fact, input into the matching process is positively correlated with the overall quality of the relational experiences for protégés (Allen et al., 2006a; Lyons & Oppler, 2004) and perceived program effectiveness from the perspective of both mentor and protégé (Allen et al., 2006b). Mentors also report fewer perceived costs associated with mentoring others if they have greater input into the matching process (Parise & Forret, 2008). One reason that having a voice in the matching process may be important is that it may increase perceptions of similarity with one's relational partner (Smith-Jentsch, Hudson, & Peuler, 2008) and, as discussed previously, perceived similarity is consistently related to positive mentoring outcomes. Interestingly, the effects of matching on *actual* similarity are far less conclusive (cf. Allen et al., 2006a; Eby & Lockwood, 2005; Donovan & Battista, 2008; Ragins et al., 2000). The selection criteria for program participation may also influence the quality of formal mentoring relationships. For instance, selecting mentors who are genuinely interested in serving as a mentor and are committed to the mentoring relationship should increase the likelihood of a high-quality relationship (Allen & Eby, 2008). Another variable that has been examined is voluntary participation in formal mentoring programs. Interestingly, voluntary participation on the part of the protégé has not been linked to protégé outcomes (Allen et al., 2006a; Ragins et al., 2000). In contrast, voluntary mentor participation relates positively to mentor outcomes (Parise & Forret, 2008).

While formal mentoring programs can be designed for many different purposes (e.g., new employee socialization, diversity enhancement, high potential development), only one published study has examined how program purpose relates to protégé outcomes. Ragins et al. (2000) compared protégé attitudes based on whether individuals participated in a formal mentoring program designed to promote career development or one geared toward employee socialization. Only one significant difference was found across a wide range of work and career attitudes; mentoring programs designed primarily to promote career development were associated with greater satisfaction with promotions than programs where the primary purpose was employee socialization. One explanation for the lack of findings in this study may be that mentoring programs may often have more than one stated purpose (Eddy et al., 2001). Another possibility is that some programs may not do a good job of communicating the purpose of the formal mentoring program for participants, so there is often confusion regarding the goals of the program (Eby & Lockwood, 2005).

Another mentoring program feature that may relate to participant outcomes is program structure.

This includes the use of training to prepare individuals for their respective roles in the relationship, the provision of interaction guidelines (e.g., meeting frequency, discussion topics), relationship contracting, program monitoring, and program evaluation (Allen et al., 2001). A common complaint by formal mentoring program participants is lack of program structure (e.g., lack of training, unclear role expectations, uncertainty about meeting frequency; Eby & Lockwood, 2005). Empirical research finds that participants report more positive outcomes in formal programs when greater structure is provided in the form of pre-participation training for protégés (Allen et al., 2006a, 2006b) and for mentors (Allen et al., 2006a, 2006b; Parise & Forret, 2008), and when meetings with the mentor are more frequent (Donovan & Battista, 2008; Lyons & Oppler, 2004).

SUMMARY

Like other types of organizational programs and practices, formal mentoring programs can send a message about the value of employee development, the mobility norms within the organization, and the importance placed on relationships in the workplace. The literature reviewed in this section clearly points to how contextual factors relate to both mentor and protégé perceptions of the mentoring relationship as well as the quality of the relational exchange.

Major Theoretical Frameworks in Mentoring Scholarship

With a comprehensive review of empirical research on mentoring behind us, we can now turn our attention to the major theoretical frameworks that have been used to study workplace mentoring. This segues into a discussion of how other existing theories can be drawn upon to better understand mentoring relationships at work. Kram's (1985) groundbreaking qualitative research on mentoring at work remains a mainstay for mentoring scholarship. This influential research provided an in-depth description of mentoring from the perspective of both the protégé and the mentor, outlined the developmental phases associated with mentoring relationships, and discussed the psychological and behavioral dynamics of organizational mentoring.

Other theoretical frameworks have been utilized to understand organizational mentoring. The similarity-attraction paradigm (Byrne, 1971) has been repeatedly applied to understand both relationship initiation and relationship development in formal and informal mentoring. Byrne (1971) proposes that perceptions of similarity are strong forces that attract individuals to one another and increase the likelihood of a successful relationship. Consistent with the major tenets of this paradigm, numerous studies find that the effect of similarity on mentoring outcomes is partially or fully mediated by liking (Armstrong, Allinson, & Hayes, 2002; Ensher & Murphy, 1997; Lankau et al., 2005). Notwithstanding its utility for understanding mentoring relationship, one limitation of the similarity-attraction paradigm is that in a mentoring relationship the protégé may specifically seek out a mentor who has skills or attributes that he or she lacks, yet wants to develop. This suggests that mentor-protégé *dissimilarity* may influence relationship initiation in some situations. In fact, there is some evidence that protégés may receive *more* mentoring in heterogeneous relationships (Noe, 1988; Turban et al., 2002), perhaps because the opportunity for learning is greater. It is also important to recognize that similarity is not a static property of a mentoring relationship. Mentor and protégé may become increasingly similar over time through the process of role modeling and identification. The similarity-attraction paradigm is not well suited to understand how dissimilarity may be advantageous or the dynamic nature of similarity in mentoring relationships.

Social exchange theory (Blau, 1964; Thibaut & Kelly, 1959) is also frequently applied to the study of workplace mentoring. The premise of this theory is that an individual's relational attitudes and behaviors are influenced by the rewards and costs associated with a particular relationship. More specifically, a norm of reciprocity develops in relationships such that as one individual provides support and resources, the other individual feels compelled to reciprocate or "pay back" his or her relational partner (Gouldner, 1960). Over time, this presumably creates high-quality exchanges between mentor and protégé, facilitating positive affective reactions to the mentoring relationship. The social exchange perspective has also been used to understand relational problems in mentoring; lack of reciprocity may be one reason that both mentors and protégés report problems in mentoring relationships (Eby et al., 2004; Eby, Durley, et al., 2008).

Notwithstanding its applicability to workplace mentoring, the social exchange perspective has been criticized for placing too much emphasis on the instrumental gains of mentoring and for not considering the possibility that communal norms are used in mentoring relationships (Ragins & Verbos,

2007). In high-quality mentoring relationships, individuals may not "keep score" as social exchange theory suggests (Ragins & Verbos, 2007). Rather, individuals may give resources to one another without the expectation of repayment, being motivated instead by genuine concern for the other individual (Clark & Mills, 1979). This alternative perspective on the exchange relationship has important implications for understanding motives for mentoring and the development of high-quality mentoring relationships. It also suggests that existing research may not be capturing the full range of positive experiences that individuals can experience in a mentoring relationship, such as an enhanced sense of self-worth, vitality, and the desire to establish a growth-fostering relationship with another person (Fletcher & Ragins, 2007). Research and theory from positive psychology (Seligman & Csikszentmihalyi, 2000) and positive organizational scholarship (Luthans, 2002) may be particularly useful theoretical bridges to understand mentoring relationships at their very best.

Other established theoretical perspectives may be applied to the study of mentoring in an effort to move the field forward. Social-psychological theories about the development of close relationships seem particularly well suited in this regard and, with the exception of social exchange theory, have not been integrated into workplace mentoring research. For example, Rusbult's (1980a, 1980b, 1983) investment theory proposes that relationships are evaluated not just in terms of their potential benefits, but also in terms of their costs. Perceptions of benefits and costs in turn influence satisfaction with the relationship. Investment theory further predicts that it is not just relationship satisfaction that predicts how committed one is to a relationship. Rather, "sunk costs" or investments in the relationship (e.g., time, energy), as well as whether or not there are alternative relational partners, influences relationship commitment and ultimately whether or not one remains in a relationship. With its emphasis on both benefits and costs, this framework may be particularly useful in understanding the interplay between positive and negative mentoring experiences (Eby & McManus, 2004; Ragins & Scandura 1997).

Mentoring relationships may also help to fulfill a fundamental human need to belong—a desire to develop and maintain relationships with others that is fulfilled through a sense of affiliation with, and acceptance from, other people (Baumeister & Leary, 1995). Allen and Eby (2008) discuss this possibility and propose that mentoring scholarship may benefit from examining research and theorizing on the construct of belongingness. Doing so may help us to better understand how and why mentoring relates to positive mentor and protégé outcomes. It may also shed light on how negative mentoring experiences may in part reflect the failure to meet essential belongingness needs on the part of the protégé and/or the mentor.

Methodological Issues in the Study of Mentoring

Examining the current state of mentoring scholarship puts some of the methodological concerns with this body of research in sharp relief. Focusing on the methods used to study a phenomenon is important since methodological choices impact the accumulation of knowledge over time (Scandura & Williams, 2000) and influence both the breadth and depth of knowledge on a topic (Allen, Eby, O'Brien, & Lentz, 2008). Therefore, examining methodological issues in mentoring scholarship has utility for advancing the progressive theoretical development of mentoring scholarship and can help pinpoint specific gaps in existing research on organizational mentoring.

The vast majority of research on mentoring utilizes cross-sectional field studies (Allen et al., 2008). Very little research examines mentoring using experimental (for exceptions, see Allen, 2004; Olian, Carroll, & Giannantonio, 1993; Olian, Carroll, Giannantonio, & Feren, 1988) or quasi-experimental (for exceptions, see Ensher & Murphy, 1997; Seibert, 1999) designs, or examines mentoring longitudinally (for exceptions, see Donaldson et al., 2000; Green & Bauer, 1995, Lankau et al., 2005; Payne & Huffman, 2005). This is problematic for several reasons. First, cross-sectional designs do not allow for cause-and-effect inferences about mentoring, meaning that fundamental questions about mentoring remain unanswered. For example, does mentoring lead to higher job performance and career outcomes for protégés? Or do those who are more successful in their careers obtain more mentoring because they are more desirable mentoring partners? Does performance actually change over time as individuals experience high-quality mentoring? Or would those who experience mentoring do as well in their career without high-quality mentoring? As another illustration, does the experience of being a mentor affect subsequent work and career outcomes? Or, are those with more positive work attitudes and career potential those who choose to become mentors in the first place?

Second, cross-sectional research only provides a snapshot of a mentoring relationship. In addition

to Kram's (1985) own work on mentoring, social psychologists lament the importance of studying change over time to fully understand close relationships (Duck, 1992). The developmental perspective used to frame the current chapter further supports the importance of taking a longitudinal perspective on mentoring. Currently, we have virtually no understanding of the dynamic nature of mentoring relationships or how critical events in a mentoring relationship influence the trajectory of the relationship. This omission is especially noteworthy in light of emerging research on relational problems in mentoring. Research on other types of close relationships, such as marriages and friendships, argues that some negative relational events can be turning points that lead to the ultimate demise of a close relationship, whereas other times the relationship can recover from relational setbacks and perhaps even grow stronger because of them (Duck, 1992; Graziano & Musser, 1982). Longitudinal designs are clearly needed to examine systematic patterns in the unfolding of relational problems over time and the effect that negative mentoring experiences have on the course of a mentoring relationship.

A related methodological concern is the heavy reliance on single-source data (Allen et al., 2008). The most commonly discussed problem here is the possibility that research findings are influenced by common method bias. It is hard to precisely estimate the extent to which common method bias represents a threat to validity in mentoring scholarship, since few studies of mentoring statistically examine whether common method bias is a likely threat (for exceptions, see Eby et al., 2004, 2008). However, because many of the constructs of interest are subjective perceptions and attitudinal reactions, concerns regarding social desirability and consistency motifs should not be taken lightly. Another specific concern with the use of single-source data is that most research has focused on the protégé's perspective (Allen et al., 2008). However, both the protégé and the mentor are active participants in a mentoring relationship, so both individuals' perspectives are important to consider. Underscoring the importance this issue, numerous studies find that the pattern of relationships among study variables varies considerably across mentors and protégés (Ensher & Murphy, 1997; Fagenson-Eland et al., 1997; Hirschfeld et al., 2006; Lankau et al., 2005; Wanberg et al., 2006), particularly when mentor and protégé differ from one another in age or tenure (Fagenson-Eland, Baugh, & Lankau, 2005). Moreover, the correlation between mentor and protégé reports of the same relational phenomenon (e.g., mentoring support, relationship quality) is often only moderate in magnitude (Eby, Durley, et al., 2008; Fagenson-Eland et al., 2005; Raabe & Beehr, 2003). Studies that examine the perspective of both protégé and mentor are essential to gain a complete understanding of mentoring relationships.

Research that focuses on the protégé perspective leads to another concern, namely the limited research examining crossover effects among mentor-protégé dyads and the lack of research examining organization-level effects. While dyadic composition variables such as race (e.g., Ensher et al., 2002; Ensher & Murphy, 1997; Turban et al., 2002) and gender (e.g., Ensher et al., 2002; Lankau et al., 2005; Ragins & McFarlin, 1990; Turban et al., 2002) have been the subject of inquiry, little research has examined how a mentor's attitudes and behaviors relate to his or her protégé's attitudes and behaviors. This limits our understanding of mentoring since it makes both intuitive and theoretical sense that relational partners are likely to influence one another. Recent research on intact mentor-protégé dyads lends credence to the importance of examining crossover effects. Among individuals in formal mentoring relationships, Allen et al. (2006a) found that protégé (mentor) input into the matching process predicted mentor (protégé) perceptions of relationship quality and the amount of mentoring provided by the mentor. In another study, Allen et al. (2006b) found that the protégé's perception of his or her mentor's commitment to the relationship and the extent to which the protégé had a clear understanding of the mentoring program predicted the mentor's perception of program effectiveness (Allen et al., 2006b). Likewise, Eby, Durley, et al. (2008) found that mentors' reports of relational problems with protégés were related to protégés' perceptions of the amount of mentoring received, intentions to leave the mentoring relationship, and various indicators of relational quality.

A final methodological concern is the dearth of research on organization-level variables in mentoring scholarship. As reviewed above, several studies have examined individual perceptions of organizational attributes, such as perceived organizational support for mentoring (e.g., Eby, Lockwood, & Butts, 2006). However, no published research exists on mentoring as a group-level or organization-level phenomenon. This is surprising, since both social information-processing theory (Salancik & Pfeffer, 1978) and social learning theory (Bandura, 1977)

suggest that individuals develop expectations about appropriate behavior based on the attitudes and behaviors of others in their social environment, particularly those in positions of authority. Since mentoring is a highly visible and discretionary work behavior on the part of managers, it seems reasonable to expect that in work groups or organizations where more mentoring occurs, members may have stronger shared perceptions of a "positive mentoring climate." These shared climate perceptions may influence individual-level attitudes and behaviors at work (for an illustration, see Zohar, 2000) as well as organization-level outcomes such as business unit performance, morale, or retention rates. This type of research is particularly important given the common, yet currently unsubstantiated claim that mentoring can improve organizational effectiveness (see Wilson & Elman, 1990).

Future Directions

In this section, several specific avenues for future research are proposed in an effort to direct future research on organizational mentoring. Based on the methodological concerns discussed in the previous section, a high priority area for future research is examining the developmental, dynamic nature of mentoring relationships. Of particular importance is longitudinal research that investigates the psychological and behavioral processes that influence how mentoring relationships develop and change over time. This line of research should examine both positive and negative relational experiences to understand the additive and interactive effects of relational benefits and costs on attitudinal, career, and behavioral outcomes for both the mentor and the protégé. Several mentoring scholars (Eby, 2007; Ragins & Verbos, 2007) discuss the theoretical value of examining specific relationship episodes in terms of predicting the future course of a mentoring relationship, yet no published research to date has tackled this important issue.

Along these same lines, process-oriented research that examines the "black box" of mentoring is essential for mentoring research to advance. While mentoring scholars generally agree that mentoring is related to both protégé and mentor outcomes, little is known about *why* mentoring works (Wanberg, Welsh, & Hezlett, 2003). A high-priority area for future research is developing and testing multivariate models that specify the psychological, cognitive, and behavioral mechanisms linking the experience of mentoring to personal and professional outcomes. This is absolutely essential for theory building since

"...the primary goal of theory is to answer the questions of *how, when* and *why*" (Bacharach, 1989, p. 498, original emphasis).

Three recent works provide excellent starting points in this regard. Ramasawami and Dreher's (2007) conceptual model of the consequences of mentoring for protégés proposes various affective and cognitive pathways by which specific types of career-related mentoring (e.g., sponsorship, role modeling, coaching) relate to individual and organizational outcomes. Focal mediating mechanisms identified by Ramasawami and Dreher (2007) include self-efficacy, instrumentality and expectancy perceptions, knowledge gains, and values clarification. Bearman, Blake-Beard, Hunt, and Crosby (2007) also discuss the importance of better understanding why mentoring works and suggest two key developmental mechanisms. The first is scaffolding (Wood, Bruner, & Ross, 1976), which describes an incremental process in which the assistance of a more experienced individual elevates an individual's developmental capacity to a point where it would not be otherwise. Scaffolding occurs gradually over time through a series of low-level interactions between two individuals. This makes it conceptually similar to the idea of mentoring episodes (Ragins & Verbos, 2007) and episodic mentor-protégé interactions (Eby, 2007): specific relational exchanges that, when cumulated over time, affect the quality of a mentoring relationship. A second developmental mechanism offered by Bearman et al. (2007) to explain why mentoring works is self-efficacy. Through the process of providing mentoring support, mentors can facilitate graduated mastery experiences, provide vicarious role modeling, engage in verbal persuasion, and create heightened arousal among protégés. All of these experiences should increase protégé self-efficacy and positively impact protégé performance (Bandura, 1977). Focusing more on the psychological value of mentoring, Allen and Eby (2007) propose that it can fulfill a fundamental need to belong for both mentors and protégés. As this need for belonging is fulfilled, individuals experience positive affective, cognitive, and behavioral outcomes. Also focusing on psychological processes linking the experience of mentoring to protégé outcomes is the notion that mentoring support may serve to reduce protégé work role stressors (Lankau et al., 2006) and may increase protégé career motivation (Day & Allen, 2004).

Mentoring scholarship can also be pushed in new directions by considering a wider range of motives in mentoring relationships. The idea that communal norms may operate in some mentoring relationships may help to explain why individuals invest in relationships when no immediate gain is likely. Research is needed that investigates the extent to which communal norms exist in mentoring relationships, and if they do exist, the factors that give rise to such norms. For example, women tend to adopt a more communal approach to relationships than do men (Heilman & Chen, 2005), and social expectations of women include characteristics such as empathy, interpersonal warmth, and compassion (Beehr, Farmer, Glazer, Gudanowski, & Nair, 2003). This suggests that there may be important gender differences in the use of communal norms in mentoring relationships. Communal norms may also be more likely in later phases of a mentoring relationship, when emotional intimacy is higher and relational partners develop a sense of shared goals. Social-psychological research on close relationships support this idea by noting that individuals develop a sense of interlocking goals over time in close relationships (Huston & Burgess, 1979). In the presence of synchronized goals it is difficult, if not impossible, for individuals to use social exchange heuristics in judging what is given and received in close relationships.

Additional research is also needed on the "darker" motives in mentoring relationships given the growing evidence that both protégés and mentors report relational problems. Two specific lines of research seem particularly important there. One involves examining the interplay between positive and negative relational events. Rather than viewing mentoring experiences as *either good or bad*, it seems more realistic to examine *both the good and the bad* associated with mentoring. This is consistent with research on other types of close relationships which acknowledges that all relationships have positive and negative aspects. There is also a well-established body of research demonstrating that bad relational experiences may actually be more predictive of individual outcomes than good relational experiences (see Baumeister, Bratslavsky, Finkenauer, & Vohs, 2001; Gottman & Krokoff, 1989). Theoretical explanations for this effect include the evolutionary value of paying close attention to potentially harmful or threatening information (Baumeister et al., 2001) and a general positive-negative asymmetry effect in which negative information is processed more systematically and contributes more to one's impression than does positive information (Peeters & Czapinski, 1990). A second line of research involves examining the possible interactive effects of positive and negative relational experiences on individual outcomes. For example, a protégé might remain in a relationship with a manipulative mentor if that mentor also provides substantial career-related support and sponsorship. Likewise, a protégé may remain in a mentoring relationship in which the mentor is not highly skilled technically if that mentor is able to provide support, encouragement, and acceptance.

Another recommendation for future research is the consideration of mentoring as a multilevel phenomenon. Organizational scholars are increasingly recognizing the value of developing integrated multilevel frameworks to understand complex organizational phenomena such as mentoring (Kozlowski & Klein, 2000). One approach is to simply extend the study of mentoring from the individual level to the dyad, work group, and perhaps even organizational level. As an illustration, belongingness can be conceptualized as an individual-level perception, characteristic of the mentor-protégé dyad, or shared perception within a department or business unit (see Allen & Eby, 2007). These various conceptualizations of belongingness may have different meanings and may relate to different outcomes. For example, protégé perceptions of belongingness may be positively related to satisfaction with the mentoring relationship and protégé work attitudes, whereas shared perceptions of belongingness may demonstrate a positive relationship with the average organizational tenure of protégés in the work group. One can also envision organization-level research that examines fundamental questions about mentoring, such as whether or not there is a relationship between the amount or average quality of mentoring in an organization and aggregate measures of organizational performance (e.g., profitability, return on investment, customer service ratings).

A variation on this theme is to examine crossover effects among intact mentor-protégé dyads. This is critically important given the dearth of such research and the logical expectation of a reciprocal relationship between mentoring attitudes and behaviors among members of a mentoring dyad. For instance, the phenomenon of social contagion (Latané, 2000) suggests that enthusiasm and the display of professional commitment on the part of a protégé is likely to engender helping behavior on the part of the mentor. Similarly, a mentor's lack of engagement in a mentoring relationship, whether due to neglect or poor fit, may lead to protégé withdrawal behavior or disappointment in the relationship. It would also be informative to examine cross-over effects among mentor and protégé perceptions of positive and negative relational experiences. This would start to answer important questions such as whether mentors' reports of problems with protégés are related to protégés' reports of problems with mentors. If so, on which types of relational problems do we see more or less concordance? Another important area for future research is whether protégés who report more problems with mentors have mentors who report receiving fewer benefits from the mentoring relationship. If so, this might help explain some of the underlying reasons for relational problems in mentoring.

Finally, research at the dyadic level has much to offer in terms of enhancing our understanding of mentoring relationships. One area where this could be particularly useful involves better understanding the role of mentor-protégé similarity in mentoring relationships. Most research has examined overall perceptions of similarity or actual similarity in terms of race or gender. The results here generally find stronger and more consistent effects for perceived similarity, although few studies have unpacked the construct of perceived similarity to understand what is driving these findings. In addition, mentoring research has not considered the possibility that it may be a combination of *similarity* (e.g., attitudes, values, beliefs) *and dissimilarity* (e.g., skills and expertise, functional area) that leads to the most effective mentoring relationships. This moves us beyond "either-or" thinking on similarity and allows for a more nuanced examination of what makes for an effective mentoring relationship. Social-psychological research on the assortative mating (Buss, 1984) may be a useful theoretical bridge here, since it considers how positive assortment (attraction based on similarity) and negative assortment (attraction based on dissimilarity) influence relationship initiation, maturation, and decline. While two individuals may be similar to one another on a variety of characteristics, research finds considerable variability in terms of the extent to which such similarity predicts relational processes and outcomes (Luo & Klohnen, 2005). Moreover, some research finds that those in arranged marriages (in which the mating process is less based on similarity) are either similarly satisfied (Myers, Madathil, & Tingle, 2005) or more satisfied (Yelsma & Athappilly, 1988) with their marriages than those in marriages of choice. This research suggests that not all aspects of similarity may be equally important in the process of developing and sustaining a mentoring relationship.

In closing, the present chapter provides a comprehensive summary of organizational mentoring from the perspective of both the protégé and the mentor. Like other types of relationships, mentoring is dynamic and unfolds over time as relational partners negotiate their respective roles, develop relational expectations, and develop, both personally and professionally. Decades of research on mentoring clearly points to the potential value of mentoring for both mentor and protégé, although the effect sizes associated with mentoring outcomes tend to be small to moderate in magnitude. This reinforces the notion that mentoring relationships may sometimes run into difficulties over time. The literature reviewed in this chapter further suggests that developing and sustaining effective mentoring relationships may require careful consideration of the complex interplay between mentor, protégé, and the organizational context. It is hoped that this chapter, by providing a critical analysis of mentoring scholarship, leads to the charting of new theoretical and empirical territory on organizational mentoring.

Note

1. Developmental approaches vary considerably in their core assumptions. There is also considerable controversy regarding the meaning of the term *development*. It is beyond the scope of the present chapter to discuss these issues. The interested reader is referred to Vondracek, Lerner, and Schulenberg (1986) for an excellent discussion of these issues in the context of career development, or to Reese and Overton (1970) for a more general discussion and comparison of various theoretical approaches to the study of human development.

References

Ainsworth, M. S. (1989). Attachments beyond infancy. *American Psychologist, 44*, 709–716.

Allen, T. D. (2003). Mentoring others: A dispositional and motivational approach. *Journal of Vocational Behavior, 62*, 134–154.

Allen, T. D. (2004). Protégé selection by mentors: Contributing individual and organizational factors. *Journal of Vocational Behavior, 65*, 469–483.

Allen, T. D. (2007). Mentoring relationships from the perspective of the mentor. In B. R. Ragins & K. E. Kram (Eds.), *The handbook of mentoring: Theory, research and practice* (pp. 123–147). Thousand Oaks, CA: Sage.

Allen, T. D., Day, R., & Lentz, E. (2001, April). *Formal mentoring programs: A review and survey of design features and recommendations.* Paper presented at the annual meeting of the Society for Industrial and Organizational Psychology, San Diego, CA.

Allen, T. D., Day, R., & Lentz, E. (2005). The role of interpersonal comfort in mentoring relationships. *Journal of Career Development, 31*, 155–169.

Allen, T. D., & Eby, L. T. (2003). Relationship effectiveness for mentors: Factors associated with learning and quality. *Journal of Management, 29*, 469–486.

Allen, T. D., & Eby, L. T. (2004). Factors related to mentor reports of mentoring functions provided: Gender and relational characteristics. *Sex Roles, 50*, 129–139.

Allen T. D., & Eby, L. T. (2007). *Blackwell handbook of mentoring: A multiple perspectives appraoch.* Oxford: Blackwell.

Allen, T. D., & Eby, L. T. (2008). Mentor commitment in formal mentoring relationsihps. *Journal of Vocational Behavior, 72*, 309–316.

Allen, T. D., Eby, L. T., & Lentz, E. (2006a). Mentorship behaviors and mentorship quality associated with mentoring programs: Closing the gap between research and practice. *Journal of Applied Psychology, 91*, 567–578.

Allen, T. D., Eby, L. T., & Lentz, E. (2006b). The relationship between formal mentoring program characteristics and perceived program effectiveness. *Personnel Psychology, 59*, 125–153.

Allen, T. D., Eby, L. T., O'Brien, K. E., & Lentz, E. (2008). The state of mentoring research: A qualitative review and future research implications. *Journal of Vocational Behavior, 73*, 343–357.

Allen, T. D., Eby, L. T., Poteet, M. L., Lentz, E., & Lima, L. (2004). Outcomes associated with mentoring protégés: A meta-analysis. *Journal of Applied Psychology, 89*, 127–136.

Allen, T. D., Lentz, E., & Day, R. (2006). Career success outcomes associated with mentoring others: A comparison of mentors and nonmentors. *Journal of Career Development, 32*, 272–285.

Allen, T. D., & O'Brien, K. E. (2006). Formal mentoring programs and organizational attraction. *Human Resource Development Quarterly, 17*, 43–58.

Allen, T. D. & Poteet, M. L. (1999). Developing effective mentoring relationships: Strategies from the mentor's viewpoint. *The Career Development Quarterly, 48*, 59–73.

Allen, T. D., Poteet, M. L., & Burroughs, S. M. (1997). The mentor's perspective: A qualitative inquiry and future research agenda. *Journal of Vocational Behavior, 51*, 70–89.

Allen, T., Poteet, M. L., Russell, J. (2000). Protégé selection by mentors: What makes the difference? *Journal of Organizational Behavior, 21*, 271–282.

Allen, T. D., Poteet, M. L., Russell, J. E. A., & Dobbins, G. H. (1997). A field study of factors related to supervisors' willingness to mentor others. *Journal of Vocational Behavior, 50*, 1–22.

Armstrong, S. J., Allinson, S. W., & Hayes, J. (2002). Formal mentoring systems: An examination of the effects of mentor/protégé cognitive styles on the mentoring process. *Journal of Management, 39*, 1111–1137.

Arnold, J., & Johnson, K. (1997). Mentoring in early career. *Human Resource Management Journal, 7*, 61–70

Aryee, S., & Chay, Y. W. (1994). An examination of the impact of career-oriented mentoring on work commitment attitudes and career satisfaction among professionals and managerial employees. *British Journal of Management, 5*, 241–249.

Aryee, S., Chay, Y. W., & Chew, J. (1996). The motivation to mentor among managerial employees: An interactionist approach. *Group and Organization Management, 21*, 261–277.

Aryee, S., Lo, S., & Kang, I-E. (1999). Antecedents of early career stage mentoring among Chinese employees. *Journal of Organizational Behavior, 20*, 563–576.

Aryee, S., Wyatt, T., & Stone, R. (1996). Early career outcomes of graduate employees: The effect of mentoring and ingratiation. *Journal of Management Studies, 33*, 95–118.

Avery, D. R. (2006). Racial discrimination. In J. H. Greenhaus & G. A. Callanan (Eds.), *Encyclopedia of career development* (pp. 667–671). Thousand Oaks, CA: Sage.

Bacharach, S. B. (1989). Organizational theories: Some criteria for evaluation. *Academy of Management Review, 14*, 496–515.

Bahniuk, M. H., Dobos, J., & Hill, S. K. (1990). The impact of mentoring, collegial support, and information adequacy on career success: A replication. *Journal of Social Behavior and Personality, 5*, 431–451.

Bandura, A. (1977). *Social learning theory*. Englewood Cliffs, NJ: Prentice Hall.

Barker, P., Monks, K., & Buckley, F. (1999). The role of mentoring in the career progression of chartered accountants. *British Accounting Review, 31*, 297–312.

Baugh, S. G., & Fagenson-Eland, E. A. (2005). Boundaryless mentoring: An exploratory study of the functions provided by internal versus external organizational mentors. *Journal of Applied Social Psychology, 35*, 939–955.

Baugh, S. G., Lankau, M. J., & Scandura, T. A. (1996). An investigation of the effects of protégé gender on responses to mentoring. *Journal of Vocational Behavior, 49*, 309–323.

Baumeister, R. F., Bratslavsky, E., Finkenauer, C., & Vohs, K. D. (2001). Bad is stronger than good. *Review of General Psychology, 5*, 323–370.

Baumeister, R. F., & Leary, M. R. (1995). The need to belong: Desire for interpersonal attachment as a fundamental human emotion. *Psychological Bulletin, 117*, 497–529.

Bearman, S., Blake-Beard, S., Hunt, L., & Crosby, F. J. (2007). New directions in mentoring. In T. D. Allen & L. T. Eby (Eds.), *Blackwell handbook of mentoring: A multiple perspectives approach* (pp. 375–395). Oxford: Blackwell.

Beehr, T. A., Farmer, S. J., Glazer, S., Gudanowski, D. M., & Nair, V. N. (2003). The enigma of social support and occupational stress: Source congruence and gender role effects. *Journal of Occupational Health Psychology, 8*, 220–231.

Blake-Beard, S. D. (1999). The costs of living as an outsider within: An analysis of the mentoring relationships and career success of black and white women in the corporate sector. *Journal of Career Development, 26*, 21–36.

Blau, P. M. (1964). *Exchange and power in social life*. New York: Wiley,

Bouquillon, E., Sosik, J., & Lee, D. (2005). "It's only a phase": Examining trust, identification and mentoring functions receiving across the mentoring phases. *Mentoring and Tutoring, 13*, 239–258.

Bozionelos, N. (2004). Mentoring provided: Relation to mentor's career success, personality, and mentoring received. *Journal of Vocational Behavior, 64*, 24–46.

Bozionelos, N. (2006). Mentoring and expressive network resources: Their relationship with career success and emotional exhaustion among Hellenes employees involved in emotion work. *International Journal of Human Resource Management, 17*(2), 362–378.

Bozionelos, N., & Wang, L. (2006). The relationship of mentoring and network resources with career success in the Chinese organizational environment. *International Journal of Human Resource Management, 17*(9), 1531–1546.

Brashear, T. G., Bellenger, D. N., Boles, J. S., & Barksdale, H. C. (2006). An exploratory study of the relative effectiveness of different types of sales force mentors. *Journal of Personal Selling and Sales Management, 26*, 7–18.

Broadbridge, A. (1999). Mentoring in retailing: A tool for success? *Personnel Review, 28*, 336–355.

Brown, N., & Scandura, T. A. (2001). The effect of mentorship and sex-role style on male-female earnings. *Industrial Relations, 33*, 263–274.

Burke, R. J. (1984). Mentors in organizations. *Group and Organization Studies, 9*, 353–372.

Burke, R. J., Burgess, Z., & Fallon, B. (2006). Benefits of mentoring to Australian early career women managers and professionals. *Equal Opportunities International, 25*, 71–79.

Burke, R. J., & McKeen, C. A. (1990). Mentoring in organization: Implications for women. *Journal of Business Ethics, 9*, 317–332.

Burke, R. J., & McKeen, C. A. (1996). Gender effects in mentoring relationships. *Journal of Social Behavior and Personality, 11*, 91–104.

Burke, R. J., McKeen, C. A., & McKenna, C. S. (1990). Sex differences and cross-sex effects on mentoring: Some preliminary data. *Psychological Reports, 67*, 1011–1023.

Burke, R. J., McKeen, C. A., & McKenna, C. S. (1993). Correlates of mentoring in organizations: The mentor's perspective. *Psychological Reports, 72*, 883–896.

Burke, R. J., McKeen, C. A., & McKenna, C. (1994). Benefits of mentoring in organizations. *Journal of Managerial Psychology, 9*, 23–32.

Buss, D. M. (1984). Evolutionary biology and personality psychology: Toward a conception of human nature and individual differences. *American Psychology, 39*, 1135–1147.

Byrne, D. (1971). *The attraction paradigm*. New York: Academic Press.

Chao, G. T. (1997). Mentoring phases and outcomes. *Journal of Vocational Behavior, 51*, 15–28.

Chao, G. T., Walz, P. M., & Gardner, P. D. (1992). Formal and informal mentorships: A comparison on mentoring functions and contrast with nonmentored counterparts. *Personnel Psychology, 45*, 619–636.

Chickering, A. W. (1969). *Education and identity*. San Francisco: Jossey-Bass.

Cianni, M., & Romberger, B. (1995). Perceived racial, ethnic, and gender differences in access to developmental experiences. *Group & Organization Management, 20*, 440–459.

Clark, M. S., & Mills, J. (1979). Interpersonal attraction in exchange and communal relationships. *Journal of Personality and Social Psychology, 37*, 12–24.

Colarelli, S. M., & Bishop, R. C. (1990). Career commitment: Functions, correlates, and management. *Group & Organization Studies, 15*, 158–176.

Collins, P. M. (1994). Does mentorship among social workers make a difference? An empirical investigation of career outcomes. *Social Work, 39*, 413–419.

Corzine, J. B., Buntzman, G. F., & Busch, E. T. (1994). Mentoring, downsizing, gender, and career outcomes. *Journal of Social Behavior and Personality, 9*, 517–528.

Cox, T. H., & Nkomo, S. M. (1991). A race and gender-group analysis of the early career experience of MBAs. *Work and Occupations, 18*, 431–446.

Day, R., & Allen, T. D. (2004). The relationship between career motivation and self-efficacy with protégé career success. *Journal of Vocational Behavior, 64*, 72–91.

Donaldson, S. I., Ensher, E. A., & Grant-Vallone, E. J. (2000). Longitudinal examination of mentoring relationships on organizational commitment and citizenship behavior. *Journal of Career Development, 26*, 233–247.

Donovan, C. B., & Battista, M. (2008, April). *Mentoring program relationship to mentor and protégé intent to remain*. Paper presented at the annual meeting of the Society for Industrial and Organizational Psychology, San Francisco.

Dreher, G. F., & Ash, R. A. (1990). A comparative study of mentoring among men and women in managerial, professional, and technical positions. *Journal of Applied Psychology, 75,* 539–546.

Dreher, G. F., & Chargois, J. A. (1998). Gender, mentoring experiences, and salary attainment among graduates of an historically black university. *Journal of Vocational Behavior, 53,* 401–416.

Dreher, G. F., & Cox, T. H. (1996). Race, gender, and opportunity: A study of compensation attainment and the establishment of mentoring relationships. *Journal of Applied Psychology, 81,* 297–308.

Duck, S. (1992). The role of theory in the examination of relationship loss. In T. L. Orbuch (Ed.), *Close relationship loss: Theoretical approaches* (pp. 3–27). New York: Springer-Verlang.

Eby, L. T. (1997). Alternative forms of mentoring in changing organizational environments: A conceptual extension of the mentoring literature. *Journal of Vocational Behavior, 51,* 125–144.

Eby, L. T. (2006). Gender and careers. In J. H. Greenhaus & G. A. Callanan (Eds.), *Encyclopedia of career development* (pp. 325–331). Thousand Oaks, CA: Sage.

Eby, L. T. (2007). Understanding problems in mentoring: A review and proposed investment model. In B. R. Ragins & K. E. Kram (Eds.), *Handbook of mentoring at work: Theory, research and practice* (pp. 323–344). Thousand Oaks, CA: Sage.

Eby, L. T., & Allen, T. D. (2002). Further investigation of protégés' negative mentoring experiences: Patterns and outcomes. *Group and Organization Management, 27,* 456–479.

Eby, L. T., Allen, T. D., Evans, S. C., Ng, T., & DuBois, D. L. (2008). Does mentoring matter? A multidisciplinary meta-analysis comparing mentored and non-mentored individuals. *Journal of Vocational Behavior, 72,* 254–267.

Eby, L. T., Butts, M. M., Lockwood, A., & Simon, S. A. (2004). Protégés' negative mentoring experiences: Construct development and nomological validation. *Personnel Psychology, 57,* 411–447.

Eby, L. T., Durley, J., Carr, S. E., & Ragins, B. R. (2006). The relationship between short-term mentoring benefits and long-term mentor outcomes. *Journal of Vocational Behavior, 69,* 424–444.

Eby, L. T., Durley, J., Evans, S. C., & Ragins, B. R. (2008). Mentors' perceptions of negative mentoring experiences: Scale development and nomological validation. *Journal of Applied Psychology, 93,* 358–373.

Eby, L. T., & Lockwood, A. (2005). Protégés' and mentors' reactions to participating in formal mentoring programs: A qualitative investigation. *Journal of Vocational Behavior, 67,* 441–458.

Eby, L. T., Lockwood, A. L., & Butts, M. (2006). Perceived support for mentoring: A multiple perspectives approach. *Journal of Vocational Behavior, 68,* 267–291.

Eby, L. T., & McManus, S. E. (2004). The protégé's role in negative mentoring experiences. *Journal of Vocational Behavior, 65,* 255–275.

Eby, L. T., McManus, S. E., Simon, S. A., & Russell, J. E. A. (2000). The protégé's perspective regarding negative mentoring experiences: The development of a taxonomy. *Journal of Vocational Behavior, 57,* 1–21.

Eddy, E., Tannenbaum, S., Alliger, G., D'Abate, C., & Givens, S. (2001). *Mentoring in industry: The top 10 issues when building and supporting a mentoring program.* (Tech. rep. Contract No. N61339–99-D-0012). Prepared for the Naval Air Warfare Training Systems Division.

Egan, T. M. (2005). The impact of learning goal orientation similarity on formal mentoring relationships. *Advances in Developing Human Resources, 7,* 489–504.

Ensher, E. A., Grant-Vallone, E. J., & Marelich, W. D. (2002). Effects of perceived attitudinal and demographic similarity on protégés' support and satisfaction gained from their mentoring relationships. *Journal of Applied Social Psychology, 32,* 1407–1430.

Ensher, E. A., & Murphy S. E. (1997). Effects of race, gender, and perceived similarity, and contact on mentor relationships. *Journal of Vocational Behavior, 50,* 460–481.

Ensher, E. A., Thomas, C., & Murphy, S. E. (2001). Comparison of traditional, step-ahead, and peer mentoring on protégés' support, satisfaction and perceptions of career success: A social exchange perspective. *Journal of Business and Psychology, 15,* 415–433.

Erickson, E. H. (1950). *Childhood and society.* New York: Norton.

Fagenson, E. A. (1988). The power of a mentor: Protégés' and nonproteges perceptions of their own power in organizations. *Group and Organizational Studies, 13,* 182–194.

Fagenson, E. A. (1989). The mentor advantage: Perceived career/job experiences of protégés versus non-protégés. *Journal of Organizational Behavior, 10,* 309–320.

Fagenson, E. A. (1992). Mentoring—who needs it? A comparison of protégés and nonproteges need for power, achievement, affiliation, and autonomy. *Journal of Vocational Behavior, 41,* 48–60.

Fagenson-Eland, E. A., & Baugh, S. G. (2001). Personality predictors of protégé mentoring history. *Journal of Applied Social Psychology, 31,* 2502–2517.

Fagenson-Eland, E. A., Baugh, S. G., & Lankau, M. J. (2005). Seeing eye to eye: A dyadic investigation of the effect of relational demography on perceptions of mentoring activities. *Career Development International, 10,* 460–477.

Fagenson-Eland, E. A., Marks, M. A., & Amendola, K. L. (1997). Perceptions of mentoring relationships. *Journal of Vocational Behavior, 51,* 29–42.

Feldman, D. (1999). Toxic mentors of toxic protégés? A critical re-examination of dysfunctional mentoring. *Human Resource Management Review, 9,* 247–278.

Feldman, D. C., Folks, W. R., & Turnley, W. H. (1999). Mentor-protégé diversity and its impact on international internship experiences. *Journal of Organizational Behavior, 20,* 597–611.

Finkelstein, L., Allen, T., & Rhoton, L. (2003). An examination of the role of age in mentoring relationships. *Group & Organization Management, 28,* 249–281.

Fletcher, J. K., & Ragins, B. R. (2007). Stone Center Relational Cultural Theory: A window on relational mentoring. In B. R. Ragins & K. E. Kram (Eds.), *Handbook of mentoring at work: Theory, research and practice* (pp. 373–399). Thousand Oaks, CA: Sage.

Forret, M., & de Janasz, S. (2005). Perceptions of an organization's culture for work and family: Do mentors make a difference? *Career Development International, 10,* 478–492.

Freud, S. (1954). *Collected works* (Standard ed.). London: Hogarth Press.

Friedman, R., Kane, M., & Cornfield, D. B. (1998). Social support and career optimism: Examining the effectiveness of network groups among black managers. *Human Relations, 51,* 1155–1176.

Gaskill, L. R. (1991). Same-sex and cross-sex mentoring of female protégés: A comparative analysis. *Career Development Quarterly, 40*, 48–63.

Gaskill, L. R., & Sibley, L. R. (1990). Mentoring relationships for women in retailing: Prevalence, perceived importance, and characteristics. *The Clothing and Textiles Research Journal, 9*, 1–10.

Gentry, W. A., Weber, T. J., & Sadri, G. (2008). Examining career-related mentoring and managerial performance across cultures: A multilevel analysis, *Journal of Vocational Behavior, 72*, 241–253.

Goh, S. C. (1991). Sex differences in perceptions of interpersonal work style, career emphasis, supervisory mentoring behavior, and job satisfaction. *Sex Roles, 24*, 701–710.

Gottman, J. M., & Krokoff, L. J. (1989). Marital interaction and satisfaction: A longitudinal view. *Journal of Consulting and Clinical Psychology, 57*, 47–52.

Gouldner, A. W. (1960). The norm of reciprocity. *American Sociological Review, 25*, 165–167.

Graziano, W. G., & Musser, L. M. (1982). The joining and parting of ways. In S. Duck (Ed.), *Personal relationships 4: Dissolving personal relationships* (pp. 75–106). London: Academic Press.

Green, S. G., & Bauer, T. N. (1995). Supervisory mentoring by advisers: Relationships with doctoral student potential, productivity, and commitment. *Personnel Psychology, 48*, 537–560.

Greenhaus, J. H., Callanan, G. A., & Godshalk, V. M. (2000). *Career management*. Fort Worth, TX: Dryden Press.

Harris, J. I., Winskowski, A. M., & Engdahl, B. E. (2007). Types of workplace social support in the prediction of job satisfaction. *The Career Development Quarterly, 56*, 150–156.

Heilman, M. E., & Chen, J. J. (2005). Same behavior, different consequences: Reactions to men's and women's altruistic citizenship behavior. *Journal of Applied Psychology, 90*, 431–441.

Higgins, M. C., & Thomas, D. A. (2001). Constellations and careers: Toward understanding the effects of multiple developmental relationships. *Journal of Organizational Behavior, 22*, 223–247.

Hirschfeld, R. R., Thomas, C. H., & Lankau M. J. (2006). Achievement and avoidance motivational orientations in the domain of mentoring. *Journal of Vocational Behavior, 68*, 524–537.

Horgan, D. D., & Simeon, R. J. (1990). Gender, mentoring, and tacit knowledge. *Journal of Social Behavior and Personality, 5*, 453–471.

Hubbard, S. S., & Robinson, J. P. (1998). Mentoring: A catalyst for advancement in administration. *Journal o f Career Development, 24*, 289–299.

Hunt, D. M., & Michael, C. (1983). Mentorship: A career and development tool. *Academy of Management Review, 8*, 475–485.

Huston, T. L., & Burgess, R. L. (1979). Social exchange in developing relationships: An overview. In T. L. Huston & R. L. Burgess (Eds.), *Social exchanges in developing relationships* (pp. 3–28). New York: Academic Press.

Johnson, B. W., Holmes, E. K., Huwe, J. M., & Norlund, M. D. (2001). Mentoring experiences among Navy midshipmen. *Military Medicine, 166*, 27–31.

Kalbfleisch. P. J. (1997). Appeasing the mentor. *Aggressive Behavior, 23*, 389–403

Kalbfleisch. P. J., & Davies, A. B. (1993). An interpersonal model for participation in mentoring relationships. *Western Journal of Communication, 57*, 399–415.

Kammeyer-Mueller, J. D., & Judge, T. A. (2008). A quantitative review of mentoring research: Test of a model. *Journal of Vocational Behavior, 27*, 269–283.

Kirchmeyer, C. (2005). The effects of mentoring on academic careers over time: Testing performance and political perspectives. *Human Relations, 58*, 637–660.

Koberg, C. S., Boss, R. W., & Goodman, E. (1998). Factors and outcomes associated with mentoring among health-care professionals. *Journal of Vocational Behavior, 53*, 58–72.

Koberg, C. S., Boss, R. W., Chappell, D., & Ringer, R. C. (1994). Correlates and consequences of protégé mentoring in a large hospital. *Group & Organization Management, 19*, 219–239.

Kohlberg, L. (1969). Stage and sequence: A cognitive-developmental approach to socialization. In J. G. Goslin (Ed.), *Handbook of socialization theory and research* (pp. 347–480). Chicago: Rand McNally.

Kozlowski, S. W. J., & Klein, K. J. (2000). A multilevel approach to theory and research in organizations: Contextual, temporal, and emergent processes. In K. J. Klein & S. W. J. Kozlowski (Eds.), *Multilevel theory, research, and methods in organizations* (pp. 3–90). San Francisco: Jossey Bass.

Kram, K. E. (1985). *Mentoring at work*. Glenview, IL: Scott, Foresman.

Kram, K. E., & Isabella, L. A. (1985). Mentoring alternatives: The role of peer relationships in career development. *Academy of Management Journal, 28*, 110–132.

Lankau, M. J., Carlson, D. S., & Nielson, T. R. (2006). The mediating influence of role stressors in the relationship between mentoring and job attitudes. *Journal of Vocational Behavior, 68*, 308–322.

Lankau, M., Riordan, C., & Thomas, C. (2005). The effects of similarity and liking in formal relationships between mentors and protégés. *Journal of Vocational Behavior, 67*, 252–265.

Lankau, M. J., & Scandura, T. A. (2002). An investigation of personal learning in mentoring relationships: Content, antecedents and consequences. *Academy of Management Journal, 45*, 779–790.

Latané, B. (2000). Pressures to uniformity and the evolution of cultural norms: Modeling dynamic social impact. In D. R. Ilgen & C. L. Hulin (Ed.), *Computational modeling in organizations* (pp. 189–220). Washington, DC: American Psychological Association.

Lentz, E., & Allen, T. D. (2005). *The link between mentoring and the career plateau: Addressing the empirical gap*. Paper presented at the annual meeting of the Society for Industrial and Organizational Psychology, Los Angeles, CA.

Levinson, D. J. (1986). A conception of adult development. *American Psychologist, 41*, 3–13.

Levinson, D. J., Darrow, D., Levinson, M., Klein, E. B., & McKee, B. (1978). *Seasons of a man's life*. New York: Academic Press.

Lewin, K. (1951). *Field theory in the social sciences*. New York: Harper Collins.

Luo, S., & Klohnen, E. C. (2005). Assortative mating and marital quality in newlyweds: A couple centered approach. *Journal of Personality and Social Psychology, 88*, 304–326.

Luthans, F. (2002). The need for and meaning of positive organizational behavior. *Journal of Organizational Behavior, 23*, 695–706.

Lyons, B. D., & Oppler, E. S. (2004). The effects of structural attributes and demographic characteristics on protégé satisfaction in mentoring programs. *Journal of Career Development, 30*, 215–229.

Mobley, G. M., Jaret, C., Marsh, K., & Lim, Y. Y. (1994). Mentoring, job satisfaction, gender and the legal profession. *Sex Roles, 31*, 79–98.

Mullen, E. J. (1998). Vocational and psychosocial mentoring functions: Identifying mentors who serve both. *Human Resources Development Quarterly, 9*, 319–331.

Mullen, E. J., & Noe, R. A. (1999). The mentoring information exchange: When do mentors seek information from their protégés? *Journal of Organizational Behavior, 20*, 233–242.

Murphy, S. E., & Ensher, E. A. (2001). The role of mentoring support and self-management strategies on reported career outcomes. *Journal of Career Development, 27*, 229–246.

Myers, J. E., Madathil, J., & Tingle, L. R. (2005). Marriage satisfaction and wellness in India and the United States: A preliminary comparison of arranged marriages and marriages of choice. *Journal of Counseling and Development, 83*, 183–190.

Nielson, T. R., Carlson, D. S., & Lankau, M. J. (2001). The supportive mentor as a means of reducing work-family conflict. *Journal of Vocational Behavior, 59*, 364–381.

Noe, R. A. (1988). An investigation of the determinants of successful assigned mentoring relationships. *Personnel Psychology, 41*, 457–479.

O'Neill, R. M. (2005). An examination of organizational predictors of mentoring functions. *Journal of Managerial Issues, 17*, 439–460.

Okurame, D. E., & Balogun, S. K. (2005). Role of informal mentoring in the career success of first-line bank managers: A Nigerian case study. *Career Development International, 10*, 512–521.

Olian, J. D., Carroll, S. J., & Giannantonio, C. M. (1993). Mentor reactions to protégés: An experiment with managers. *Journal of Vocational Behavior, 43*, 266–278.

Olian, J. D., Carroll, S. J., Giannantonio, C. M., & Feren, D. B. (1988). What do protégés look for in a mentor? Results of three experimental studies. *Journal of Vocational Behavior, 33*, 15–37.

Orpen, C. (1995). The effect of mentoring on employees' career success. *The Journal of Social Psychology, 135*, 667–668.

Ostroff, C., & Kozlowski, S. W. J. (1993). The role of mentoring in the information gathering processes of newcomers during early organizational socialization. *Journal of Vocational Behavior, 42*, 170–183.

Parise, M. R., & Forret, M. L. (2008). Formal mentoring programs: The relationship of program design and support to mentors' perceptions of benefits and costs. *Journal of Vocational Behavior, 72*, 225–240.

Payne, S. C., & Huffman, A. H. (2005). A longitudinal examination of the influence of mentoring on organizational commitment and turnover. *Academy of Management Journal, 48*, 158–168.

Peeters, G., & Czapinski, J. (1990). Positive-negative asymmetry in evaluations: The distinction between affective and information negativity social ties, and psychological distress among older adults. *Gerontologist, 30*, 193–199.

Peluchette, J., & Jeanquart, S. (2000). Professionals' use of different mentor sources at various career stages: Implications for career success. *Journal of Social Psychology, 140*, 549–564.

Phillips-Jones, L. (1982). *Mentors and protégés*. New York: Arbor House.

Piaget, J. (1970). Piaget's theory. In P. H. Mussen (Ed.), *Carmichael's manual of child psychology* (3rd ed., Vol. 1, pp. 703–732). New York: Wiley.

Prevosto, P. (2001). The effect of "mentored" relationships on satisfaction and intent to stay of company-grade U.S. Army Reserve nurses. *Military Medicine, 166*, 21–26.

Raabe, B., & Beehr, T. A. (2003). Formal mentoring versus supervisor and coworker relationships: Differences in perceptions and impact. *Journal of Organizational Behavior, 24*, 271–293.

Ragins, B. R., & Cotton, J. L. (1991). Easier said than done: Gender differences in perceived barriers to gaining a mentor. *Academy of Management Journal, 34*, 939–951.

Ragins, B. R., & Cotton, J. L. (1993). Gender and willingness to mentor in organizations. *Journal of Management, 19*, 97–111.

Ragins, B. R., & Cotton, J. L. (1999). Mentor functions and outcomes: A comparison of men and women in formal and informal mentoring relationships. *Journal of Applied Psychology, 84*, 529–550.

Ragins, B. R., Cotton, J. L., & Miller, J. S. (2000). Marginal mentoring: The effects of type of mentor, quality of relationship, and program design on work and career attitudes. *Academy of Management Journal, 43*, 1177–1194.

Ragins, B. R., & McFarlin, D. B. (1990). Perceptions of mentor roles in cross-gender mentoring relationships. *Journal of Vocational Behavior, 37*, 321–339.

Ragins, B. R., & Scandura, T. A. (1994). Gender differences in expected outcomes of mentoring relationships. *Academy of Management Journal, 37*, 957–972.

Ragins, B. R., & Scandura, T. A. (1997). The way we were: Gender and the termination of mentoring relationships. *Journal of Applied Psychology, 82*, 945–953.

Ragins, B. R., & Scandura, T. A. (1999). Burden or blessing? Expected costs and benefits of being a mentor. *Journal of Organizational Behavior, 20*, 493–509.

Ragins, B. R., & Verbos, A. K. (2007). Positive relationships in action: Relational mentoring and mentoring schemas in the workplace. In J. E. Dutton & B. R. Ragins (Eds.), *Exploring positive relationship at work: Building a theoretical and research foundation* (pp. 91–116). Mahwah, NJ: Erlbaum.

Ramasawami, A., & Dreher, G. F. (2007). The benefits associated with workplace mentoring relationships. In T. D. Allen & L. T. Eby (Eds.), *Blackwell handbook of mentoring* (pp. 211–231). Malden, MA: Blackwell.

Reese, H. W., & Overton, W. F. (1970). Models of development and theories of development. In. L. R. Coulet & P. B. Baltes (Eds.), *Life-span developmental psychology: Research and theory* (pp. 116–145). New York: Academic Press.

Riley, S., & Wrench, D. (1985). Mentoring among women lawyers. *Journal of Applied Social Psychology, 15*, 374–386.

Rosser, M. H. (2005). Mentoring from the top: CEO perspectives. *Advances in Developing Human Resources, 7*, 527–539.

Rusbult, C. E. (1980a). Commitment and satisfaction in romantic associations: A test of the Investment Model. *Journal of Experimental Social Psychology, 16*, 172–186.

Rusbult, C. E. (1980b). Satisfaction and commitment in friendships. *Representative Research in Social Psychology, 11*, 96–105.

Rusbult, C. E. (1983). A longitudinal test of the Investment Model: The development (and deterioration) of satisfaction and commitment in heterosexual involvements. *Journal of Personality and Social Psychology, 45*, 101–117.

Salancik, G. J., & Pfeffer, J. (1978). A social information processing approach to job attitudes and task design. *Administrative Science Quarterly, 23*, 224–253.

Scandura, T. A. (1992). Mentoring and career mobility: An empirical investigation. *Journal of Organizational Behavior, 13*, 169–174.

Scandura, T. A. (1998). Dysfunctional mentoring relationships and outcomes. *Journal of Management, 24*, 449–467.

Scandura, T. A., & Ragins, B. R. (1993). The effects of sex and gender role orientation on mentorship in male-dominated occupations. *Journal of Vocational Behavior, 43*, 251–265.

Scandura, T. A., & Schriescheim, C. A. (1994). Leader-member exchange and supervisor career mentoring as complementary constructs in leadership research. *Academy of Management Journal, 37*, 1588–1602.

Scandura, T. A., & Viator, R. E. (1994). Mentoring in public accounting firms: An analysis of mentor-protégé relationships, mentorship functions, and protégé turnover intentions. *Accounting, Organizations, and Society, 19*, 717–734.

Scandura, T. A., & Williams, E. A. (2000). Research methodology in management: Current practices, trends, and implications for future research. *Academy of Management Review, 18*, 377–391.

Scandura, T. A., & Williams, E. A. (2001). An investigation of the moderating effects of gender on the relationships between mentorship initiation and protégé perceptions of mentoring functions. *Journal of Vocational Behavior, 59*, 342–363.

Schrodt, P., Cawyer, C. S., & Sanders, R. (2003). An examination of academic mentoring behaviors and new faculty members' satisfaction with socialization and tenure and promotion process. *Communication Education, 52*, 17–29.

Seibert, S. (1999). The effectiveness of facilitated mentoring: A longitudinal quasi-experiment. *Journal of Vocational Behavior, 54*, 483–502.

Seibert, S. E., Kraimer, M. L., & Liden, R. C. (2001). A social capital theory of career success. *Academy of Management Journal, 44*(2), 219–237.

Seligman, M. E. P., & Csikszentmihalyi, M. (2000). Positive psychology: An introduction. *American Psychologist, 55*, 5–14.

Simon, S. A., & Eby, L. T. (2003). A typology of negative mentoring experiences: A multidimensional scaling study. *Human Relations, 56*, 1083–1106.

Smith-Jentsch, K., Hudson, N., & Peuler, M. (2008, April). *The impact of protégé choice on mentoring processes.* Paper presented at the annual meeting of the Society for Industrial and Organizational Psychology, San Francisco, CA.

Sosik, J. J., & Godshalk, V. M. (2000a). Leadership styles, mentoring functions received, and job-related stress: A conceptual model and preliminary study. *Journal of Organizational Behavior, 21*, 365–390.

Sosik, J.J., & Godshalk, V. M. (2000b). The role of gender in mentoring: Implications for diversified and homogenous mentoring relationships. *Journal of Vocational Behavior, 57*, 102–222.

Sosik, J. J., & Godshalk, V. M. (2004). Self-other rating agreement in mentoring. *Group of Organization Management, 29*, 442–469.

Sosik, J. J., Godshalk, V. M., & Yammarino, F. (2004). Transformational leadership, leaning goal orientation, and expectations for career success in mentor-protégé

relationships: A multiple levels of analysis perspective. *The Leadership Quarterly, 15*, 241–261.

Super, D. E. (1980). A life-span, life-space approach to career development. *Journal of Vocational Behavior, 16*, 282–298.

Thibaut, J. W., & Kelley, H. H. (1959). *The social psychology of groups.* New York: Wiley.

Thomas, D. A. (1990). The impact of race on managers' experiences of developmental relationships (mentoring and sponsorship): An intra-organizational study. *Journal of Organizational Behavior, 11*, 479–492.

Thomas, D. A. (1993). Mentoring and irrationality: The role of racial taboos. In L. Hirschhorn & K. C. Barnett (Eds.), *The psychodynamics of organizations* (pp. 191–202). Philadelphia: Temple University Press.

Tonidandel, S., Avery, D. R., & Phillips, M. G. (2007). Maximizing returns on mentoring: Factors affecting subsequent protégé performance. *Journal of Organizational Behavior, 28*, 89–110.

Turban, D. B., & Dougherty, T. W. (1994). Role of protégé personality in receipt of mentoring and career success. *Academy of Management Journal, 37*, 688–702.

Turban, D. B., Dougherty, T. W., & Lee, F. K. (2002). Gender, race, and perceived similarity effects in developmental relationships: The moderating role of relationship duration. *Journal of Vocational Behavior, 61*, 240–262.

Underhill, C. M. (2006). The effectiveness of mentoring programs in corporate settings: A meta-analytical review of the literature *Journal of Vocational Behavior, 68*, 292–307.

Van Emmerik, H. (2004). For better or for worse: Adverse working conditions and the beneficial effects of mentoring. *Career Development International, 9*, 358–373.

Van Emmerik, H., Baugh, G. S., Euwema, M. C., & Martin C. (2005). Who wants to be a mentor? An examination of attitudinal, instrumental, and social motivational components. *Career Development International, 10*, 310–324.

Viator, R. E. (2001). The association of formal and informal public accounting mentoring with role stress and related job outcomes. *Accounting Organizations and Society, 26*, 73–93.

Viator, R., & Pasewark, W. (2005). Mentorship separation tension in the accounting profession: The consequences of delayed structural separation. *Accounting Organizations and Society, 30*, 371–387.

Viator, R. E., & Scandura, T. A. (1991). A study of mentor-protégé relationships in large public accounting firms. *Accounting Horizons, 5*, 20–30.

Vondracek, F. W., Lerner, R. M., & Schulenberg, J. E. (1986). *Career development: A life-span developmental approach.* Hillsdale, NJ: Erlbaum.

Wallace, J. E. (2001). The benefits of mentoring female lawyers. *Journal of Vocational Behavior, 58*, 366–391.

Wanberg, C. R., Kammeyer-Mueller, J., & Marchese, M. (2006). Mentor and protégé predictors and outcomes of mentoring in a formal mentoring program. *Journal of Vocational Behavior, 69*, 410–423.

Wanberg, C. R., Welsh, E. T., & Hezlett, S. A. (2003). Mentoring research: A review and dynamic process model. *Research in Personnel and Human Resource Management, 22*, 39–124.

Wanberg, C. R., Welsh, E. T., & Kammeyer-Mueller, J. (2007). Protégé and mentor self-disclosure: Levels and outcomes within formal mentoring dyads in a corporate context. *Journal of Vocational Behavior, 70*, 398–412.

Waters, L., McCabe, M., Kiellerup, D., & Kiellerup, S. (2002). The role of formal mentoring on business success and self-esteem in participants of a new business start-up program. *Journal of Business and Psychology, 17,* 107–121.

Wayne, S. J., Liden, R. C., Kraimer, M. L., & Graf, I. K. (1999). The role of human capital, motivation, and supervising sponsorship in predicting career success. *Journal of Organizational Behavior, 20,* 577–595.

Whitely, W. T., & Coetsier, P. (1993). The relationship of career mentoring to early career outcomes. *Organization Studies, 14,* 419–441.

Whitely, W. T., Dougherty, T. W., & Dreher, G. F. (1991). Relationship of career mentoring and socioeconomic origin to managers' and professionals early career progress. *Academy of Management Journal, 2,* 331–351.

Whitely, W. T., Dougherty, T. W., & Dreher, G. F. (1992). Correlates of career-oriented mentoring for early career managers and professionals. *Journal of Organizational Behavior, 13,* 141–154.

Wilson, J. A., & Elman, N. S. (1990). Organizational benefits of mentoring. *Academy of Management Executive, 4,* 88–94.

Wood, D., Bruner, J. S., & Ross, G. (1976). The role of tutoring in problem solving. *Journal of Child Psychology and Psychiatry, 17,* 89–100.

Yelsma, P., & Athappilly, K. (1988). Marital satisfaction and communication *Journal of Comparative Family Studies, 19,* 37–54.

Young, M. A., & Perrewé, P. L. (2000). What did you expect? An examination of career-related support and social support among mentors and protégés. *Journal of Management, 26,* 611–632.

Young, M. A., & Perrewé, P. L. (2004). The role of expectations in the mentoring exchange: An analysis of mentor and protégé expectations in relation to perceived support. *Journal of Managerial Issues, 16,* 103–126.

Zohar, D. (2000). A group-level model of safety climate: Testing the effect of group climate on microaccidents in manufacturing jobs. *Journal of Applied Psychology, 85,* 587–596.

Organizational Culture and Climate

Dov Zohar, *and* David A. Hofmann

Abstract

Although there have been several attempts to address the conceptual ambiguities in the literature discussing organizational climate, organizational culture, and their interrelationship, there remains much confusion and a general lack of clarity about what these two constructs represent, as well as how they may interrelate. In order to provide some clarity, we provide a comprehensive review of both constructs and conclude with a model describing how organizational climate can be viewed as a bottom-up (i.e., flowing from employee perceptions) indicator of the underlying core values and assumptions that form the organization's culture. Recommendations for researchers seeking to investigate organizational climate and culture, as well as suggestions for future research, are discussed throughout the chapter.

Key Words: Espoused values, enacted values, multiple strategic climates, organizational culture, organizational climate, and organizational systems and processes

Despite attempts to reconcile the conceptual ambiguity permeating the relationship between organizational climate and culture, there remains a lack of clarity and much confusion over definitions, measurement and the interrelationship between these two constructs. As just one example, Verbeke, Volgering, and Hessels (1998) reviewed 25 years of research and identified 32 different definitions of organizational climate and 54 different definitions of organizational culture. As much as we would like to say that the ensuing decade resolved all of this ambiguity, that is unfortunately not the case. The purpose of this chapter, hopefully, is to provide some much needed clarity. In order to accomplish this, we first start with the construct of organizational climate and discuss its defining features and seek to clarify several conceptual ambiguities. We then do the same for the construct of organizational culture. Finally, we conclude by describing an integrative model discussing how organizational climate can serve as a window through which organizational culture can be viewed.

Organizational Climate

Perhaps the best place to begin our discussion of organizational climate is by focusing on the principal components cutting across the various definitions in the literature. Fortunately, this has been done for us. Specifically, Verbeke et al. (1998) found that the various definitions of organizational climate virtually all identified climate as socially shared perceptions of organizational members regarding key characteristics of their organization. This defining feature is both good news and bad news. The good news is that, despite there being 32 different definitions of organizational climate, one can identify commonalities across all of these definitions. The bad news, however, is that this defining feature is so broad as to perhaps lose any potential for usefulness. Organizational behavior research is characterized, in fact, by a large number of perception-based measures referring to key organizational characteristics or features—such as work monotony (Melamed, Ben-Avi, Luz, & Green, 1995), routinization and formalization (Bacharach, Bamberger, & Conley, 1990), or job control and complexity (Frese, Kring, Soose, & Zempel, 1996)—which are all based on employee perceptions. Similarly, assessments of supervisory supportiveness (Oldham & Cummings, 1996), team cohesion (Chang & Bordia, 2001), and deviant organizational behavior (Vardi & Weitz, 2004) are also based on employee perceptions. This leaves unanswered the question of how perceptions of organizational climate are conceptually distinct from these other perceptions of key organizational characteristics and features. The following sections contain our attempt at clarifying these differences.

We begin with perhaps one of the most agreed upon areas of conceptual ambiguity—recognizing that agreement on an area of conceptual ambiguity may very well be an oxymoron—that climate perceptions can vary in breadth from a single, multidimensional global perception to much more narrow perceptions focused on a particular strategic element (e.g., Glick, 1985; Ostroff, Kinicki, & Tamkins, 2003; Schneider, Bowen, Ehrhart, & Holcombe, 2000).

Climate as Global Perceptions

Early work on global climate perceptions suffered from a lack of discriminant validity in terms of the underlying dimensions comprising the overall global perceptions. Given the presumption that organizational climate represents a summary of the manner by which employees experience their organization, climate scholars have taken the liberty of including almost any conceivable dimension, resulting in a proliferating set of dimensions and lack of uniformity among alternative climate scales. There, however, have been several notable exceptions where specific, theoretically driven inclusion criteria have been specified.

One such example is the global organizational climate discussion based on person-environment (P-E) fit (Ostroff, 1993). Following previous work on P-E fit, Ostroff (1993) identified three higher order climate dimensions (i.e., affective, cognitive, and instrumental), each subdivided into four lower order dimensions. From this theoretical frame, employees are assumed to assess the psychological meaning of their environment in terms of fit to key personal factors. Shared assessments focusing on such personal factors identify respective climate dimensions. Recently, Carr, Schmidt, Ford, and

DeShon (2003) adopted this taxonomy as a conceptual model for global organizational climate. Using meta-analytic techniques, they analyzed the results of 51 studies, reporting significant relationships between the three higher order climate dimensions and three generic outcome criteria: job performance, psychological well-being, and withdrawal. These relationships were mediated by job satisfaction and organizational commitment, constituting proximal outcomes of this global climate.

A second exception is the Organizational Climate Measure (OCM) published recently by Patterson et al. (2005). The theoretical framework in this case involves the competing values model (Quinn & McGrath, 1985; Quinn & Rohrbaugh, 1983). The competing values model has as its foundation the organizational structure dimensions of internal integration and external flexibility (adaption), where these dimensions are viewed as competing values (i.e., flexibility vs. control; internal vs. external orientation). The dimensionality of OCM is thus structured in terms of the four competing values' quadrants, which are subdivided into 12 lower order dimensions or subscales as follows: (a) human relations (e.g., employee welfare, autonomy, participation, supervisory support); (b) internal process (e.g., formalization, tradition); (c) open systems (e.g., flexibility, innovation, outward focus); and (d) rational goals (e.g., efficiency, quality, performance feedback). Based on a large validation study, Patterson et al. (2005) reported that subscales in each quadrant exhibited concurrent and predictive validity with a number of content-related outcome criteria.

These theory-based approaches to global climate seem to advance organizational climate research by offering a strategy for dealing with the problem of ill-defined boundaries or ever-expanding climate dimensions. However, it is noteworthy that the theoretical frameworks for global climates, such as the ones described above, have been developed for purposes other than organizational climate. In other words, in both of the examples above, existing theoretical frameworks were used to then formulate a climate assessment. This is a much different approach than developing a theoretical framework for *organizational climate* and then developing measures based on this frame. In addition, this approach does not really answer the question of what constitutes a climate perception. Is it the case that any individual-level theory focused on employee perceptions of organizational characteristics can become part of a global climate measure as long as the perceptions become shared?

Answering such questions would not only offer a foundation for climate theory, but it should also allow for the integration of other theoretical models and constructs into climate research.

Climate as Domain-Specific Perceptions

The other perspective on organizational climate is that climate should be "for something," where the something should be a strategic focus of the organization (e.g., climate for customer service, quality, safety). Within this approach, organizational climate is made up of shared perceptions among employees concerning the procedures, practices, and kinds of behaviors that get rewarded and supported with regard to a specific strategic focus (Schneider, 1990). While this view of climate involves shared perceptions—as do all approaches to organizational climate—this view of climate clearly puts in place an important boundary condition. Implicit in this approach to climate is that the shared perceptions are limited to specific organizational facets or domains (e.g., climate for service, innovation, ethics, safety; Schneider, Bowen, Ehrhart, & Holcombe, 2000). Thus, rather than having universal referents such as supervisory support or procedural formalization, this perspective on organizational climate focuses climate perceptions on a specific strategic focus of the organization, in which the climate informs employees of the kinds of role behavior likely to be supported and rewarded. Two good examples of this approach to organizational climate are service climate (Schneider, White, & Paul, 1998) and safety climate (Zohar, 1980, 2003).

In addition to the theoretical benefits of being clear in terms of focus and boundary conditions, facet-specific climates offer some methodological refinement by creating congruent linkages between predictor and outcome criteria, which are operationalized at the same level of specificity (Schneider & Reichers, 1983). For example, recent meta-analyses of safety climate research, covering 202 studies, identified significant corrected correlations between safety climate and outcomes such as employee safety behavior and accident/injury rate (Beus, Payne, Bergman, & Arthur, 2010; Christian, Bradley, Wallace, & Burke, 2009; Nahrgang, Morgeson, & Hofmann, 2009). Similar data were presented for service climate as a predictor of customer satisfaction and perceptions of service quality (Schneider et al., 1998). This type of equal specificity of predictor and criteria has not always been observed within the global climate perspective (Schneider & Reichers, 1983). The advantages associated with domain-specific climates notwithstanding, further development of climate theory requires the specification of additional conceptual boundaries as qualifiers of the unique attributes of climate perceptions. It is to this task that we turn next.

ATTRIBUTES OF DOMAIN-SPECIFIC CLIMATE PERCEPTIONS

An examination of early discussions of organizational climate reveals that one of its qualifying attributes is that of apprehending the (implicit) order in the organizational environment as a means for better adapting or adjusting to that environment (Schneider, 1975). Assuming that the building blocks of the organizational environment consist largely of policies, procedures, and practices, climate perceptions as order-seeking interpretations of the environment refer to the nature of *relationships between or the relative priorities among* these elements, rather than to the consideration of individual elements in isolation. This process is equivalent to pattern recognition, whereby raw data are classified into recognizable patterns whose characteristics transcend those of the individual elements making up the pattern. The main practical advantage of this higher level of analysis stems from the fact that once patterns are recognized and the relationships between and relative priorities among these elements are perceived, individuals will have a more informed and comprehensive perspective on the kinds of behaviors that are likely to be supported and rewarded.

This adds an additional criterion to climate perceptions. Climate perceptions should not only be domain specific, but they should also focus on the configurations, relationships, or relative priorities among several strategically focused domains. Unlike other perception-based constructs in organizational behavior, the referents of climate perceptions relate to system- or pattern-level properties characterizing specific domains of the organizational environment and strategy. Thus, safety climate perceptions focus on the nature of relationships between safety policies, procedures, and practices, taking into account additional characteristics such as discrepancies or misalignments between words and deeds. Added to this perception of safety in isolation, however, is the notion that often rules and procedures associated with one domain compete with those associated with other domains (e.g., safety vs. productivity or efficiency). From an employee standpoint, it is the overall pattern and signals sent by this complex web of rules and policies across competing domains that ultimately must be sorted out in order to discern what role behavior is expected, rewarded, and supported. Our argument is that domain-specific climate perceptions should move beyond a focus on a specific domain in isolation toward a more comprehensive evaluation that captures at least some of these competing domains. We now turn to this and other pattern-level attributes that we believe should begin to constitute both theoretical discussions of organizational climate, as well as measurement operationalizations of climate.

RELATIVE PRIORITIES

As noted above, one system-level attribute that differentiates climate from other types of perceptual measures is the notion of relative priority among competing strategic goals or operational demands. Organizations and organizational leaders have been long recognized as having to deal with competing demands. For example, Lawrence and Lorsch (1967) identified the competing structural demands of integration versus differentiation, and Quinn and Rohrbaugh (1983) identified the dual polarities of flexibility versus stability and internal versus external orientations as primary dimensions of organizational structure. Such structural complexity requires organizational leaders to exhibit cognitive and behavioral complexity in an effort to not only understand these competing demands but also manage them (Denison, Hooijberg, & Quinn, 1995). One basic element of leading and managing in this environment is determining and communicating to employees relative priorities among these competing operational demands.

Take safety climate as an exemplar: one expression of competing demands arises in manufacturing organizations where production speed or profitability tend to compete with non-productive investments in workers' health and safety. Facing such competing demands, organizational leaders are likely to (formally or informally) assign relative priorities to each facet (Humphrey, Moon, Conlon, & Hofmann, 2004). Given this, a rational response by employees is to evaluate these (implicit) signals regarding relative priorities so that they can align their role behavior with the expectations of organizational leaders. This evaluation of relative priorities can be based on a comparison of safety versus production policies, procedures, and practices and the implied signals regarding the importance of each domain. Obviously, how organizational leaders trade off these policies and procedures when situations arise in which they are in direct conflict will provide the clearest message to employees regarding which is most important. Practically speaking, if productivity is favored across a variety of situations, it implies a higher priority, and employees will align their behaviors accordingly.

The operationalization of safety climate, therefore, should involve employees evaluating the relative priority of safety such that the overall level of safety climate represents the shared perceptions of the priority of safety compared to other competing priorities (Zohar, 2003). Using a modified safety climate scale in which safety considerations were contextualized by the presence of different competing demands, Zohar and Luria (2004) demonstrated that supervisory decisions in situations in which they had to choose between safety and accomplishing the mission were predictive of employee perceptions of safety climate. A similar logic would apply with other types of organizational climates as well. Service climate, for example, has been shown to compete with productivity and/or efficiency goals (Schneider & Bowen, 1995), and the climate for creativity or innovation (Anderson & West, 1998) would compete with organizational demands for stability and control (Quinn & Rohrbaugh, 1983). Irrespective of the climate domain, we believe that organizational climate perceptions should be viewed from the perspective of "procedures-as-pattern" rather than to individual procedures viewed in isolation. In other words, climate—irrespective of domain—should be operationalized in the context of other competing domains.

ALIGNMENT BETWEEN ESPOUSALS AND ENACTMENTS

A second pattern-level attribute of organizational climate is the alignment between espoused and enacted priorities. This attribute refers to the extent of convergence or divergence (i.e., alignment or misalignment) between words and deeds on behalf of managers at different levels of the organizational hierarchy (Argyris & Schon, 1996; Simons, 2002). For example, it has been documented that, despite the espousal of employee safety as a high-priority issue, safety procedures are often compromised under competing operational demands such as production pressures or costs, thus resulting in a gap between enacted and espoused priorities (Eakin, 1992; Pate-Cornell, 1990; Wright, 1986). In keeping with our general discussion of organizational climate, espoused and enacted priorities must have a particular referent (e.g., a certain policy or some goal) such that they are domain specific (Lewicki, McAllister, & Bies, 1998). For example, a unit manager might espouse a strong emphasis on service quality, even though her daily practices might suggest that this is true for only a small group of customers (e.g., business-class customers). Simultaneously, this same manager's espoused attitudes regarding employee empowerment could line up nicely with her daily actions regarding empowerment.

This alignment between enacted and espoused priorities is an important attribute of climate perceptions because it is only the *enacted* policies that provide reliable information regarding the kinds of behavior likely to be rewarded and supported (Zohar, 2003). In other words, the distinction between espoused and enacted priorities is of key adaptive significance because only the latter informs employees of behavior-outcome expectancies (Zohar, 2000, 2003).

This alignment between enacted and espoused priorities is not always an easy thing for employees to evaluate. As noted by Simons (2002), the assessment of alignment requires multiple observations, across multiple situations. Over time and across situations, a pattern will emerge that will inform employees how large the gap is between enacted and espoused priorities. As this gap becomes clearer, climate perceptions will be adjusted accordingly.

The evaluation of espoused versus enacted priorities will also include supplementary assessments involving the situational demands contributing to alignment (or the lack thereof). For example, if managers act inconsistently with their espoused priorities only under extreme circumstances, this signifies a higher priority for the focal domain, as opposed to gaps occurring under ordinary conditions. Espoused priorities regarding service quality, for example, might be compromised for certain customer types (e.g., one-time or low-volume customers) or certain product categories, where the justifying logic is that the organization must focus its limited resources on key customers or products. Similarly, the espoused priorities regarding employee safety might be compromised under conditions in which production has fallen a certain number of days behind schedule or if safety changes cost more than a certain amount of money. Such compromises and the situational characteristics that trigger them create for employees a discrepancy between enacted and espoused priorities which, in turn, help to inform their overall climate perceptions.

INTERNAL CONSISTENCY

A third pattern-level attribute of climate perceptions is the internal consistency among policies, procedures, and practices. Whereas the previous attribute referred to discrepancies between leaders' words and actions, this attribute refers to potential inconsistencies nested among organizational policies, procedures, and practices. Although the bureaucratic, or rational, view of organizations suggests an internal consistency and stability among policies, procedures, and practices (Blau & Scott, 1962; Weber, 1968), other views characterize organizations as "organized anarchies" (Cohen, March, & Olsen, 1972) and "loosely coupled systems" (Weick, 1979). These various views of organizations suggest that internal consistency among organizational elements and processes may vary considerably. In other words, as almost every reader has probably experienced, organizations can create rules and policies that seem logically inconsistent and/or mutually exclusive.

Adopting a level-of-analysis perspective, it is possible to identify cross-level inconsistencies. A recent multilevel model of climate (Zohar, 2000, 2003; Zohar & Luria, 2005), suggested that organizational policies define strategic goals and the means of their attainment, whereas procedures provide tactical guidelines for actions related to these goals and means. Practices, on the other hand, relate to the implementation of policies and procedures in each subunit. In other words, top managers are concerned with policy making and the establishment of procedures to facilitate policy implementation, while at lower organizational levels, supervisors execute these procedures by turning them into predictable, situation-specific action directives (identified as supervisory practice). A potential area for inconsistencies to arise is through supervisory discretion in policy implementation. Supervisory discretion stems from a number of sources, such as the presence of competing operational demands, and the fact that procedures rarely cover all situations (Zohar & Luria, 2005). As members of both individual units and the organization as a whole, employees will perceive signals both from senior management regarding policies and from their local supervisor regarding how these practices are operationalized in their immediate job context. The result is perceptions regarding both an overall organizational climate as well as a local group-level climate in which these two climates may be well aligned and consistent, or quite inconsistent and discrepant. As these discrepancies arise, employees perceive a lack of internal consistency among policies, procedures, and local practices. This inconsistency will further inform climate perceptions.

As an example, consider a supervisor who directs workers to disregard certain safety procedures whenever production falls behind schedule, thus creating a gap between company procedures and subunit practices. This local practice, which departs from organizational policy, helps to inform employee perceptions regarding the level of safety climate within the subunit. If the procedurally inconsistent supervisory practices are accompanied by aligned supervisory words and deeds, this will further strengthen the discrepancy between group- and organization-level climates (Zohar & Luria, 2005).

Reexamination of Existing Climate Scales

Given the qualification of climate perceptions as adaptively oriented order-seeking interpretations of the organizational environment, focusing on system-level attributes and priorities among policies, procedures, and practices; it is possible to examine the extent to which available climate scales are actually capturing the distinctive aspects of organizational climate. An examination of a number of existing scales suggests that most scales include a mix of items, some of which meet these climate qualifications and some of which do not. For example, one recently developed scale—the Organizational Climate Measure (Patterson et al., 2005)—includes many procedure- and practice-based items that agree with our central attributes of climate (e.g., management lets people make their own decisions much of the time; people are suspicious of other departments; and everything has to be done by the book). Items that do not capture the distinctive aspects of organizational climate include general perceptions of organizational operations (e.g., time and money could be saved if work were better organized; the organization is continually looking for new opportunities in the marketplace; and the way that this organization does things has never changed very much). Although these latter items refer to perceived organizational policies and practices, they bear little relationship to adaptive challenges and relative priorities, both of which signal the kinds of behavior likely to be rewarded and supported. In contrast, items from the former group inform employees of priorities (e.g., making one's own decisions, operating by the book), or misalignments (e.g., holding back rather than cooperating with other departments).

Many of the domain-specific measures of organizational climate include the same sort of item mix. For example, the climate for creativity (Amabile, Conti, Coon, Lazenby, & Herron, 1996) includes 10 subscales in which some items address climate attributes (e.g., people are encouraged to solve problems creatively; I have the freedom to decide how I am going to carry out my projects; and there is free and open communication within my work group); whereas other items capture more general perceptions (e.g., I have too much work to do in too little time; my area of this organization is effective; there are many political problems in this organization; my supervisor serves as a good work model; and I feel challenged by the work I am currently doing).

Although we have cited a few examples above, we believe that many of the existing climate scales—both general and domain-specific—do not sufficiently distinguish between climate perceptions and other more generalized employee perceptions. This failure to adequately distinguish climate from other perceptions raises issues with respect to discriminant validity and conceptual clarity—both of which impede the development of a clear and concise theory of organizational climate. Although domain-specific climates (i.e., safety climate, service climate) help to eliminate potential conceptual ambiguity, assessing "climates-for-something" does not necessarily ensure that the other attributes of climate are being assessed (e.g., patterns of policies, relative priorities). The following sections, associated with the etiology of climate, offer several additional features that can qualify organizational climate as a unique construct.

Although clarifying climate measures will go a long way in helping to reduce the conceptual ambiguity currently existing within the field, measures alone will not address all the issues. Another issue occurs after individual perceptions are measured: climate perceptions must be shared among employees in order for a "climate" to exist. It is to this issue that we now turn.

Measuring Individual Perceptions Is Not Enough: They Must Be Shared

Organizational climate is an emergent construct such that it consists of *shared* employee perceptions regarding psychologically meaningful attributes of the organizational environment. From a levels-of-analysis perspective, organizational climate originates with individual members' experiences and perceptions, which gradually become socially shared through a variety of mechanisms, thus emerging as a group-level property (Kozlowski & Klein, 2000).

One key theoretical question relates to the process through which these perceptions become shared and, therefore, climate emerges. How do individual perceptions become shared? Why do groups engage in activities resulting in this emergence? These questions—focused on the antecedents of climate—have not received much attention in the literature, yet this is another key factor distinguishing climate perceptions from other, more general, employee perceptions.

How Do Climate Perceptions Become Shared?

Previous reviews identified a number of antecedents likely to promote the emergence of shared climate perceptions (Ostroff et al., 2003; Schneider & Reichers, 1983). Given the limited empirical evidence for most of them, they will be used to highlight a research agenda for the continued development of climate theory.

STRUCTURALIST VIEW

The structuralist explanation for climate emergence is based on research suggesting that organizational settings create environmental features influencing employees' attitudes and perceptions. Early research in this area investigated the relationship between objective settings (e.g., size, hierarchal levels, technology type, and formalization) and global organizational climates (James & Jones, 1974; Payne & Pugh, 1976). Reviews of this literature have found, however, a lack of consistent results between objective structural attributes and organizational climates (Berger & Cummings, 1979; Ouchi & Wilkins, 1985). Other studies, using less tangible structural attributes, resulted in different outcomes. For example, Kozlowski and Hults (1987) tested the effects of standardization, centralization, specialization, and reward procedures on the climate for technical updating among support and R&D engineers. Technological complexity, less emphasis on formal procedures, and greater opportunities for internal rewards were associated with a more positive updating climate.

This research suggests that structural features may influence climate perceptions, but they do not dictate climate perceptions. In other words, since structural features are things that every employee can observe or experience, they create a mechanism for shared perceptions to emerge. Yet, as noted above, individual supervisors can exhibit a great deal of discretion in the local unit in terms of how they enact day-to-day practices related to these structural features. Given the distinction between espoused and enacted policies and procedures, as well as variations in the consistency between formal policies and group-level operationalization, it follows that structural features may be predictive of between-situational variance in climates, yet there is

likely to be significant variability unaccounted for by these structural features. Thus, even though the formal structure will influence employee perceptions, we argue that the main predictors of climate perceptions will be the more proximal characteristics such as supervisory decisions made when two competing operational demands come head-to-head.

SYMBOLIC INTERACTIONISM

Symbolic interactionism is the philosophical view that meaning and reality are socially construed, arising from cognitive exchanges among people seeking to comprehend their environment (Blumer, 1969; Stryker, 2008). In other words, the meaning of things and the interpretation of events arise from the interplay between one's own perceptions and those of others in the same situation. During such a process, one's perceptions are being checked and modified in light of others' observations and assessments. Symbolic interaction involves comparing bits of information and cues, discussing possible interpretations, and attempting to reach consensual interpretation of the meaning of events, procedures, and practices at the workplace. As a result of such a process, over time, group members' perceptions are expected to converge, resembling processes of newcomer socialization (Schneider & Reichers, 1983). Such convergence promotes the emergence of climate because group members come to share the meanings of their organizational environment. Because group members interact more often with each other than with employees from other groups, they are likely to develop shared perceptions of the local, subunit climate as well as more global organizational climate perceptions.

SENSE MAKING

Similar to symbolic interactionism, sense making refers to an ongoing interpretative process in which the meaning of daily events and changing circumstances is construed through social exchanges among the individuals experiencing it (Weick, 1995, 2005). Sense making is typically discussed in the context of individuals facing complex and ambiguous work situations. When this occurs, individuals discuss possible meanings and interpretations and, through this process, develop a shared understanding of the situation and possible responses (Weick, Sutcliffe, & Obstfeld, 1999). Sense making is, therefore, an ongoing, socially based interpretive process directed at the construction of plausible interpretations or accounts of ambiguous situations requiring action on behalf of the participating actors (Brown, 2000).

The role of sense making or symbolic interactions as antecedents to climate has not been well studied, despite the long-standing proposition regarding its key role in climate emergence (Schneider & Reichers, 1983). The few available studies on this subject used social-interaction rating scales (Gonzalez-Roma, Peiro, & Tordera, 2002; Klein, Conn, Smith, & Sorra, 2001), or social-network techniques (Rentsch, 1990; Zohar & Tenne-Gazit, 2008), as proxies for sense-making processes. Using a variety of specific climates, these studies reported positive relationships between the frequency of social exchanges and density of group communication networks and climate strength (i.e., the degree of within-unit agreement among unit members' climate perceptions; Zohar & Tenne-Gazit, 2008).

LEADERSHIP

Throughout much of the history of climate research, there has been a long-held proposition that "leaders create climate" (Lewin, Lippitt, & White, 1939). The notion of leadership as a climate antecedent has hardly changed since, although this has resulted in limited empirical work (Dragoni, 2005; Kozlowski & Doherty, 1989; Ostroff et al., 2003). Much of the available work focuses on safety climate, consistently supporting the climate-leadership relationship (Barling, Loughlin, & Kelloway, 2002; Gonzalez-Roma et al., 2002; Hofmann & Morgeson, 1999; Hofmann, Morgeson, & Gerras, 2003; Zohar, 2002; Zohar & Luria, 2004; Zohar & Tenne-Gazit, 2008).

This relationship can be explained as a social learning process in which group members repeatedly observe and exchange information with their leader as a means for interpreting the organizational environment (Dragoni, 2005). Supervisory practices are relatively easy to observe due to their proximity and availability, and they routinely inform group members as to relative priorities as well as behavior that is valued and supported by both the leader and the organization at large (Ashforth, 1985; Zohar, 2003). When such perceptions are shared due to the commonality of the leader's messages and practices, they constitute the core meaning of domain-specific climate.

Transformational leadership, in particular, is likely to be quite influential in the development of climate perceptions. Transformational leaders foster closer relationships with group members (Bass, 1990; Yukl, 2006), characterized by mutual trust and openness (House & Shamir, 1993), and by rich two-way interpersonal communication (Klauss & Bass,

1982). This type of leadership creates opportunities for sharing and clarifying task cues and perceptions (Kirkpatrick & Locke, 1996). Transformational leaders are also expected to exhibit greater consistency across situations in terms of their leadership practices due to reliance on values and visions as the main driver of their behavior (Bass, 1990; Burke et al., 2006; Shamir, House, & Arthur, 1993).

Transformational leadership, therefore, will directly influence climate through the articulation of long-term goals and objectives and the ongoing two-way communication that will serve to clarify expected and supported behaviors as well as the relative priorities within the unit. Transformational leaders are also likely to affect climate emergence indirectly through their influence on the nature of communication among group members. For example, a recent meta-analysis found that transformational leadership is predictive of group cohesion (Bass, Avolio, Jung, & Berson, 2003; Burke et al., 2006). This increased cohesion, since it increases communication and group identity, will result in stronger shared climate perceptions. More direct evidence of this relationship has been provided recently by Zohar and Tenne-Gazit (2008). They found that the relationship between transformational leadership and safety climate strength was mediated by the density of the communication network among group members.

These antecedents imply that shared climate perceptions evolve as a result of ongoing member-leader and member-member interactions (see also Kozlowski & Doherty, 1989). Although there is much evidence suggesting that these interactions do result in shared climate perceptions, less consideration has been given as to why individuals engage in this collective investment of cognitive effort. In other words, a less asked question is: Where does the motivation for engaging in such social information processing—as opposed to individually searching for the requisite answers—come from?

The Motivation for Climate Perceptions: Social Verification

Given that organizational climate qualifies as *shared* perceptions of the organizational environment, it is important to explicate possible reasons for the shared quality of climate perceptions. Namely, why do group members strive for shared perceptions? We believe that a key reason for the creation of shared perceptions lies in the complexity and equivocality of the organizational environment. As noted above, there are a variety of sources for such complexity, including the presence of competing values (Quinn & Rohrbaugh, 1983), competing operational demands (Lawrence & Lorsch, 1967), discrepancies between espousals and enactments (Simons, 2002), and cross-level variations in policy implementations (Zohar & Luria, 2005). Other sources relate to the multiplicity of organizational policies and procedures, accompanied by the fact that they are often little known or understood by relevant employees (Hargie & Dickson, 2007; Stevens, Steensma, Harrison, & Cochran, 2005). Given the lack of a simple and rational structure, employees need to engage in interpretive and sense-making activities that involve a social-, interpersonal-based process (Weick, 1995).

This is consistent with other theoretical perspectives suggesting that when contextual cues are ambiguous, individuals turn to others for social verification (Festinger, 1954). One such perspective—the shared-reality model (Hardin & Higgins, 1996)—postulates that subjective experiences survive as reliable and valid interpretations by virtue of being reproduced in others and accepted by them as the veridical interpretation of the group's external world.

In the context of organizational climate, these theories suggest that the formation of shared climate perceptions is motivated by the need to interpret the complex pattern of signals existing within the organizational context regarding what issues are of high priority and what behaviors are likely to be rewarded and supported. Given the complexity of the organizational environment, individuals will be motivated to test their understanding with others in order to determine if it is a reliable and valid understanding of the organizational context. We believe that it is this social verification process that motivates the formation or emergence of organizational climate.

Not One, But Multiple Climates

Now that we have explored the attributes of organizational climate as well as the process through which they come about, we turn our attention to looking across multiple climates. The domain-specific climate perspective implies the existence of multiple coexisting climates in an organization. For example, financial institutions such as bank branches should have climates for business ethics, customer service, and professional updating. Manufacturing companies should have climates for innovation, quality, and safety. Despite the obviousness of this possibility, there has not been much consideration of this theoretically nor many investigations empirically. Theoretically, it is possible to argue for three possible models describing the nature of relationships between coexisting climates, identified in terms of independent, interactive, and causal effects.

INDEPENDENT CLIMATES

A model postulating independent climates in organizations assumes that specific climates can coexist, exerting independent effects on employees' work behavior. In statistical terms, this is equivalent to a main effects model in which independent climates are unaffected by each other (i.e., when the level of one climate is expected to exert no effect on the other climates).

An example of such a model is provided in a study testing the effects of the climates for initiative and psychological safety on firm performance and profitability outcomes (Baer & Frese, 2003). Both climates were positively related to the firm performance outcomes of return on assets and goal achievement, acting also as two independent moderators of the relationship between firm-level innovation (i.e., use of lean manufacturing, simultaneous engineering, and JIT production) and its performance outcomes. Across all analyses, both climates were investigated independently. Another example is Ostroff's (1993) global climate perspective in which three dimensions—identified as cognitive, affective, and instrumental climates—were tested with meta-analytic techniques by Carr et al. (2003). The results revealed that the three subclimates exerted independent effects on job satisfaction and organizational commitment.

INTERACTIVE CLIMATES

The interactive climate model assumes that coexisting climates either influence each other's level or that their effect on outcome criteria reveals an interaction effect. An example for the former is offered by the Organizational Climate Measure (OCM), based on the competing values framework (Patterson et al., 2005). As noted above, this global climate measure is based on four subclimates associated with the organizational domains of: (a) human relations, (b) internal processes, (c) open systems, and (d) rational goals. Rather than being independent, these domains are assumed to exert competing strategic and operational demands, requiring senior and lower level managers to cope with the resultant complexity (Quinn & Rohrbaugh, 1983). In statistical terms, such competition implies interaction because the higher the priority of one domain or quadrant, the lower should be the priority of the competing domain. In their validation study, Patterson and colleagues (2005) tested the relationships between each subclimate and its relevant outcome criteria (e.g., open-systems climate was tested with the company's market-research and innovation activities, whereas internal-process climate was tested with use of performance appraisals and cross-functional teams); however, no statistical tests of interaction effects were reported.

CAUSAL CLIMATES

The causal climates model extends the interactive model with the assumption that some climates are more fundamental than others because they refer to contextual factors in the organizational environment that are likely to influence or interact with a variety of specific climates. Schneider and colleagues refer to them as foundational climates and particularly highlight two (Schneider, White, & Paul, 1998). The first foundational climate is focused on work facilitation, referring to the removal of obstacles and the introduction of facilitators such as supportive supervisory practices, sharing information, giving feedback, and offering training. The second foundational climate is focused on internal organizational service, referring to interdepartmental cooperation practices, shared job knowledge, and the quality of internal service. Because these climates reflect the availability of resources for performing the work, as well as the extent of managerial concern for employees' well-being, they were expected to influence relevant facet-specific climates such as the climate for service. Using a longitudinal design, Schneider and colleagues (1998) reported data supporting a causal relationship between the foundation climates and the service climate which predicted, in turn, customer-satisfaction level. A similar study tested the effects of the foundational climates for management-employee relations and organizational support of employees on safety climate in a transportation company (Wallace, Popp, & Mondore, 2006). Results indicated that safety climate mediated the effect of the foundation climates on driving accident rates during the following year.

Similar ideas were discussed more recently by Zohar (2008) regarding the climates of safety and work ownership. The climate for work ownership concerns the extent to which employees see opportunities and managerial support for psychologically owning aspects of their work. Such psychological ownership means that aspects of the work become

part of, or an extension of, one's identity (Pierce, Kostova, & Dirks, 2003), which results in greater commitment to the owned objects, increased professional self-esteem, and a proactive orientation toward work (Van Dyne & Pierce, 2004). This climate can be considered a foundational climate by virtue of its relationship to the fundamental issues of prevention versus promotion (Higgins, 2002), or passivity versus (pro)activity as primary work orientations. This underlying orientation, in turn, should influence domain-specific climate perceptions associated with facets such as service, innovation, ethics, or safety.

For example, if work-ownership climate is high, resulting in a proactive orientation to work, and safety is considered a high-priority issue (i.e., high safety climate), employees are expected to consider safety as an ownership target. This combination would result in safety citizenship behavior, characterized by initiating change, offering help, and exhibiting stewardship (Hofmann et al., 2003). If, however, high work ownership is accompanied by a low safety climate, ownership targets are likely to exclude safety considerations, resulting in safety defiance. Such situations are often described in post-accident reports, indicating that production or profit goals may lead managers and employees to overlook substantial risks while striving to achieve other higher priority goals (Hopkins, 2006). A low work-ownership climate would result in safety compliance under conditions in which safety is considered important, but workers are only expected to follow rules and procedures when getting the work done.

Climate as Multilevel Perceptions

In addition to multiple domain-specific climates occurring within the organizational context, climate perceptions will also be influenced by the hierarchical nature of organizations. As noted above, the variety of unique situations accompanying task execution will leave the door open for supervisors to exercise discretion in the implementation of various policies and procedures. Between-unit variability relating to different ways of implementing company policies and procedures is, therefore, to be expected. That said, however, there is also between-organization variability in the overall climate level (Zohar & Luria, 2005). Think about it this way. The overall organizational climate sets the general level of climate (i.e., overall mean), whereas the discretion exercised in the various subunits establishes the variability around this mean. Between-organization variance exists at the level of the overall mean and between-unit variance exists within the organization across subunits. The customer service climate of fast food restaurants are a good example. McDonalds, Hardees, Wendy's, and Chick-fil-a differ in their overall levels of customer service climate. Yet, within each of these organizations, there would be variability across each of the locations in terms of service climate.

Given this between-organization and between-subunit variability, employee climate perceptions will be constructed at multiple levels of analysis. Corporate policies, procedures, and the gap between espoused and enacted priorities constitute the primary target or referent for organizational level climate perceptions. Supervisory practices and daily decisions made between competing operational demands constitute the target or reference for subunit climate. Consistent with this theoretical level, organization-level climate perceptions should be aggregated to the organizational level, and subunit climate perceptions should be aggregated to the subunit level—assuming homogeneity or consensus in perceptions exists at the appropriate level of analysis (Kozlowski & Klein, 2000).

There is evidence validating this multilevel view of climate perceptions. Specifically, Zohar and Luria (2005) found that there was significant variance across subunits in group climate and significant variance between organizations in organizational climate. In addition, they found that subunit climate mediated the effect of organizational climate on employee safety behavior, and that stronger organizational climates reduced the between subunit variance in group climate. These results suggest that, despite the challenge of formulating climate perceptions, employees were able to develop multilevel climate perceptions that varied systematically between organizations and across subunits within an organization. A summary of the above discussion is presented in Table 20.1.

Organizational Culture

Organizational culture, like climate, has suffered from conceptual ambiguity and varying definitions. A content analysis of the 54 available definitions of culture revealed that, at its foundation, it consists of a system of shared behavioral norms and underlying beliefs and values that shape the way of doing things in the organization (Verbeke et al., 1998). Most scholars also agree that organizational culture consists of different elements (e.g., assumptions, stories, behavioral regularities) that are hierarchically

ordered from deeper to more surface levels (behavioral regularities; Detert, Schroeder, & Mauriel, 2000; Furnham & Gunter, 1993; Rousseau, 1990; Schein, 2004). Deep-level elements typically include basic assumptions, values, and/or beliefs about the organizational context that have shown to be successful in the past and are, therefore, now ingrained, taken for granted, and unquestioned (Allaire & Firsirotu, 1984; Detert et al., 2000; Schein, 2004). Surface-level elements include observable artifacts or manifestations of the underlying, deep-level elements. Artifacts include a large variety of objects such as structures and processes, myths and stories, language and signals, and policies and procedures that are more easily observable than deep-level elements (Allaire & Firsirotu, 1984; Trice & Beyer, 1993). Because each deep-level element can express itself by a large variety of artifacts, there is a few-to-many mapping such that a very few deep-level elements can produce a much greater number of surface-level elements.

A subset of these artifacts—namely, espoused beliefs, values, and ideologies—are often viewed as guiding role behaviors and organizational practices, leading Schein (2004) to consider this as an intermediate culture level. Espoused beliefs can consist of public declarations during meetings or ceremonies, written documents describing the company and its strategy, or symbols and stories. If the espoused beliefs and values are congruent with the underlying assumptions, they can establish clearer links across the deep and surface culture levels. However, as has been noted above, because of misalignment between espoused beliefs and enacted beliefs, such congruence cannot be assumed, leaving the core of culture hard to decipher or delineate by organizational members and/or observers.

Culture's Syntax

Although an organization's culture can be characterized by only a few basic assumptions, beliefs, or core values, the diversity of their manifestations through surface-level artifacts can result in large cultural variations. By analogy, even though the syntactic structure of a legitimate sentence can be defined by a very few elements (e.g., subject, predicate, adjective, and adverb), the elements can result in an endless number of specific manifestations that communicate quite different ideas. One way to deal with this complexity of different manifestations of culture is to organize the deeper level elements into basic content categories. One such categorization included the following dimensions (Schein, 2004):

Table 20.1 Key Observations and Research Needs

Organizational Climate

Key Observations

Organizational members are motivated to understand the organizational context in order to clarify behavioral expectations and to ensure their success. Yet, organizational contexts are complex, with competing demands, goals, and priorities. Thus, understanding this environment requires a complex pattern-matching process in which organizational members decipher the relative priorities of various strategic initiatives. This view of organizational climate suggests:

1. Organizational climate should be conceptualized and measured as domain-specific, shared perceptions regarding key strategic initiatives of the organization (e.g., safety, customer service, quality).

2. Organizational climate should be conceptualized and measured as a relative priority. For example, safety climate should be conceptualized and measured as the relative priority of safety compared to production. Climate for service should be conceptualized and measured as the relative priority of service versus other competing demands (costs, efficiency).

3. The pattern-level attributes of organizational climate consist of:

    a. The relative priority of different objectives—particularly in situations where two (or more) strategic objectives compete with one other (safety versus productivity, service versus costs).

    b. Alignment (or gaps) between espoused and enacted priorities.

    c. Internal consistency of priorities among policies/strategic initiatives at the top of the organization and localized practices within subunits.

4. Organizational climate should be viewed as a multilevel construct. The policies and strategic focus of top management establishes the broad, organizational-level climate, whereas local practices within the subunit establish the more localized, subunit climate.

Recommendations/Future Research

Our recommendations for organizational climate include:

1. Measures of organizational climate need to be focused on domain-specific climates (i.e., climate for "something") and vary by organizational level:

    a. Climate measures designed to assess the overall organizational climate should be focused on policies and strategic initiatives.

    b. Climate measures designed to assess localized, subunit climate should be focused on localized practices (i.e., how policies get enacted through localized behavioral practices).

2. Future research needs to further explore how climate perceptions become shared both at the subunit and organizational levels.

3. There has been virtually no research investigating the interrelationships among different climates. We proposed three possibilities—independent, interactive, and causal. Much more research is needed here.

Organizational Culture

Key Observations

Over time, organizational members develop a system of shared assumptions, values, underlying beliefs, and behavioral norms that have been shown to help the organization with external adaptation and internal integration. These shared perceptions represent the organization's culture. This view of organizational culture suggests that:

1. Organizational culture is hierarchically structured, with basic assumptions, core values, and beliefs residing in the "deep core layer" of organizational culture. Behavioral norms and organizational artifacts offer surface-level manifestations of culture. Such a structure suggests that similar basic assumptions and core values may result in a number of different behavioral norms and artifacts (few-to-many mapping).

2. Although many researchers have used the foundations of organizational culture—basic assumptions and core values—interchangeably, they are fundamentally different starting points and, therefore, should lead to different endpoints. These differences relate to their respective referents:

(Continued)

Table 20.1 (Continued)

a. The referent of basic assumptions is a shared history of success in solving the fundamental organizational problems of external adaptation and internal integration. Organizational responses that have proven successful time and again assume a taken-for-granted status, making it difficult to think of any other alternative.

b. The referent of core values is a shared moral criterion or action standard that defines what is good, desirable, and right. Such criteria or standards frequently become socially shared by means of social learning, often using the organization's founder and/or figure heads as role models. Jointly, they describe the right way to act in pursuing the ultimate human goal of "best possible living," and, as such, act as socially shared guiding principles or an internal moral compass. These socially shared values constitute the value-based elements of organizational culture.

3. Given that the two referent categories are conceptually different, it follows that they cannot be used as interchangeable culture constructs. Available culture categorization models use either basic assumptions (e.g., Hofstede, 1998; Schein, 2004), or core values (e.g., Schwartz, 1992) as their conceptual framework. At the current time, the mapping of elements belonging to one framework onto the other remains an open question.

4. Given the hierarchical nature of culture elements, deep-level elements are, by definition, more difficult to measure than surface-level elements. Yet, only the former can define the essence of culture. Although there has been progress in the measurement of values (e.g., Schwartz's 1992 circumplex model), the same is not true for the measurement of basic assumptions and/or beliefs. We suggest that the integration of climate and culture constructs offers some promise in this regard.

5. Organizational culture, like climate, should be viewed as a multilevel construct. Using values as the requisite referent, it has been shown that employees compare their individual values with group- and organization-level value systems, which are amenable to subsequent comparisons with professional and national value systems. Likewise, basic assumptions have been shown to exist at various levels of analysis, allowing cross-level comparisons.

Recommendations/Future Research

1. Organizational culture must be measured and described in terms of its underlying assumption- and value-based elements. In other words, there is a need for measuring culture in terms of both primary components.

2. Future models of organizational culture should conceptualize the nature of relationships or mapping between the two element categories, developing an integrated framework. Because the respective referents belong to different conceptual categories, they should no longer be used as interchangeable constructs, a practice that has increased conceptual ambiguity associated with the culture construct.

Integration of Organizational Climate and Culture

Key Observations

Our perspective on organizational climate—that it represents shared perceptions of the relative priorities enacted within the organization—suggests that organizational climate could be used as a bottom-up indicator of organizational culture. Specifically:

1. The shared assumptions and core values forming the foundation of the organization's culture will inform the strategic initiatives and policies enacted by senior management.

2. As these strategic initiatives and polices are enacted, gaps can develop between these espoused and enacted values and practices. Organizational members—motivated to understand the organizational context—decipher these gaps and other patters of enacted behavior, which forms their perceptions of the relative priorities among competing goals and objectives.

3. In this way, climate is a bottom-up, inductive way to learn about the underlying values and core assumptions of the organization. This is considered a bottom-up process because it is flowing from the perceptions of organizational members regarding what is actually done, as opposed to the top-down process (driven by core values and assumptions) focused on what should be done.

Recommendations/Future Research

There has been virtually no research using organizational climate perceptions as a way to bridge enacted practices with the deeper, underlying core values and assumptions forming the deep structure of organizational culture. Much work is still to be done.

external adaptation, internal integration, reality and truth, nature of time, and human nature and relationships. Each of these dimensions is further subdivided into a number of subcategories. For example, the external adaptation category includes shared basic assumptions about the core mission and primary tasks of the organization, goals and means for achieving this mission, how results will be measured, and potential corrective actions that will need to be taken in response to feedback. The nature-of-time category includes assumptions about the definition and measurement modes of time, kinds of time, and its importance in the organization. Once culture is conceived as a combination of assumptions in each of these categories, it can be measured or described in terms of qualitative descriptions or quantitative analysis of employees' shared cognitions regarding the nature of the assumptions within each category.

Another well-known categorization of culture is Hofstede's (1980; 1998) five-category bipolar list of assumptions associated with the world of work: (a) large versus small power distance, (b) strong versus weak uncertainty avoidance, (c) individualism versus collectivism, (d) masculinity versus femininity, and (e) long versus short-term orientation. Using cross-organizational data, Hofstede (1980) used these five categories to identify varying cultural assumptions across different countries (e.g., process vs. results orientation, employee vs. job orientation, parochial vs. professional orientation, open system vs. closed system, loose vs. tight control, and normative vs. pragmatic orientation).

The above examples highlight the fact that alternative classifications of culture have used non-overlapping categories for describing organizational culture. Such a lack of uniformity makes the operationalization of culture more challenging. This lack of uniformity also has been compounded by the lack of standard measurement procedures as will be discussed below.

Culture Typologies

Instead of starting with the notion of culture and attempting to identify its underlying content, an alternative approach is to identify different types of cultures based on other a priori theoretical frameworks. A well-known example is the competing values framework for organizational culture (Cameron & Quinn, 1999). As noted above, this framework specifies two dimensions of organizational effectiveness criteria (flexibility vs. stability; internal vs. external orientation), resulting in four quadrants that represent different basic assumptions

and core values. Because the quadrants represent opposite poles of the underlying dimensions, they identify competing assumptions and values (i.e., competing culture types). The four culture types are labeled as: hierarchy (internally focused and stable organization), market (external focus and stability), clan (internally focused and flexible organization), and adhocracy (external focus and flexibility). Since these different cultural types are assumed to compete one with the other, organizations will have a certain level of each culture. Organizational effectiveness will result from different patterns of cultures that are congruent with environmental demands.

A similar typology, based on the same two underlying dimensions, has been discussed by Denison and colleagues (Denison, 2001; Denison & Mishra, 1995). Their four cultural types were described in terms of adaptability, involvement, consistency, and mission (Denison, 2001; Denison & Mishra, 1995). Each quadrant is operationalized with three attributes as follows: involvement (empowerment, team orientation, and capability development); consistency (core values identifying primary expectations, interpersonal agreement, and coordination and integration); adaptability (creating change, customer focus, organizational learning); and mission (vision, goals and objectives, strategic direction).

Notably, both typologies are based on structural dimensions of organizations; in this sense, they are similar to Schein's (2004) categories of external adaptation and internal integration. Although it is easy to view Schein's typology as subsuming the typologies of Cameron and Quinn and Denison, these latter authors argue that each of the four culture types implicates congruent basic assumptions associated with the other content categories in Schein's system (e.g., nature of human beings, social relations, leadership, and management). These arguments obviously need empirical validation.

Goffee and Jones (1998, 2001) suggested another typology, based on the social-interaction dimensions of solidarity (i.e., cooperation between different or unlike individuals or groups) and sociability (i.e., affective or friendly relations at work). Again, these two dimensions result in four different cultural types: mercenary (high on solidarity, low on sociability), communal (high on sociability, low on solidarity), networked (high on both), and fragmented (low on both). This framework construes the foundation of organizational culture as assumptions about the nature of social relationships within the organization. The authors further explore additional assumptions connected to each of their four culture types (e.g., assumptions related to the physical world, nature of time, individual identity, and social communication).

A different typology, focusing on behavior norms, was offered by Cooke and Szumal (1993, 2000). The two bipolar dimensions underlying this typology are people versus task, and satisfaction versus security. The first orientation (people vs. task) is associated with primary leadership dimensions (Blake & Mouton, 1964), and the second with the self-regulatory dimensions of promotion versus prevention (Higgins, 1997, 2002). Jointly, they result in four behavioral norms, which have been empirically found to formulate three types of culture: constructive culture (achievement, self-actualizing, humanistic, and affiliative norms), passive/defensive culture (approval, conventional, dependent, and avoidance norms), and aggressive/defensive culture (oppositional, power, competitive, and perfectionist norms). Based on this framework, Cooke and Szumal (2000) developed the Organizational Culture Inventory (OCI), which assesses both the ideal and currently operationalized culture (i.e., normative behavior).

The idealized culture is viewed as being driven by basic assumptions and values. The operationalized culture—or the behavior norms currently existing within the organization—are viewed as driven by not only these basic assumptions and beliefs, but also by other attributes of the organization (e.g., role hierarchy, procedural formalization, employee participation, and leadership style) which, in turn, are influenced by the broader resources of and demands placed upon the organization (e.g., financial reserves, technical expertise, performance pressures, technological change). When these attributes of the organization exert a greater influence on the culture than the underlying assumptions and values, then gaps can emerge between the deeper-level aspects of culture (values, assumptions) and the surface-level manifestations of this culture (behavioral norms).

The above examples demonstrate that there is little agreement among culture scholars regarding the categories comprising culture or the resultant types of organizational culture. Whereas some scholars base the elements of culture on organizational structure (e.g., external vs. internal orientation or flexibility vs. stability), others focus on social interaction (e.g., solidarity and sociability), or behavioral orientations (e.g., task vs. people and satisfaction vs. security orientations). Not surprisingly, the resulting typologies are qualitatively different. Despite these differences, most of the available models of culture preserve the basic distinction between deep-and surface-level cultural layers. At the same time, however, an examination of the elements comprising the deep layer of culture reveals potential sources of ambiguity that need to be clarified in order to enhance the development of organizational culture research. It is to this issue that we turn next.

Values as Culture Elements

As noted above, the deep layer of culture includes basic assumptions and values as key elements. Assuming internal consistency between the two element classes, they offer complementary perspectives for construing and classifying culture. Whereas most discussions and measures of organizational culture relate to basic assumptions, values can offer some advantages.

As noted by several authors, the development of value theory has lingered for several decades due to conceptual ambiguity associated with the construct (Hitlin & Piliavin, 2004; Rohan, 2000). Recent developments, however, have served to resolve some of this ambiguity. A value system is a meta-cognitive structure guiding the way in which social actors behave, evaluate others' actions, and explain their own actions (Schwartz, 1994). The organizing principle of the value system is that of relative priorities among individual values or their relative importance. In Aristotelian terms, value priorities serve as guides to the ultimate human goal of "best possible living" through the actualization of human potential. Each value within the larger system can be conceptualized as a desirable outcome of actions, which guides the selection and evaluation of actions and events (Schwartz & Bilsky, 1987). Values form criteria or referents for the desirable or preferable, ordered by relative importance (Rokeach, 1973).

Schwartz (1992) offered a value classification system based on the two dimensions of openness to change versus conservation, and self-enhancement versus self-transcendence. Ten value types, representing the full range of human values, are arranged in this space, forming a circumplex model. The distance between value locations indicates intraindividual differences in value priorities and opposite locations along the circumplex indicate competing values. For example, one person's value system might give high priority to the values of stimulation and self-direction, whereas another person's value system would prioritize security and traditional values. Using the Schwartz Value Inventory, it has been shown that the ten value types and their spatial locations remain stable across national cultures around the world, suggesting that it can be used as a universal classification system (Schwartz, 1994, 1999, 2004).

Schwartz's (1992) circumplex model has been shown to not only adequately represent personal value systems, but it also has been shown to represent socially shared value systems (Rohan, 2000). A socially shared value system within an organizational context reflects that organization's culture. Individuals have been shown to be able to construe several concurrent value systems and to be able to compare these different value systems. In the case of organizational culture, this suggests that individuals will be able to compare and contrast their personal value system to the socially shared value system of the organization and experience the degree of fit. Layered upon these individual and organizational value systems could also be value systems that operate at the national cultural level. Taken together, this suggests a multilevel values model in which individuals construe and compare several structurally compatible value systems, comparing their personal values with their group- and organization-level values and, possibly, their professional and/or national value priorities. Rohan (2000), for example, reported that a better fit between personal and organizational values resulted in greater organizational commitment and job satisfaction. This model is akin to the multilevel climate model as described above, suggesting that culture, like climate, is based on individual assessments that turn into shared social assessments, which operate at different levels of analysis (e.g. group, organization, or profession).

Culture as Basic Assumptions or Core Values

Conceiving culture as a pattern of shared basic assumptions or core values offers complementary perspectives for the culture construct. Both elements can serve as guiding principles for action and adaptation and, therefore, help to define appropriate behavior across situations. They do, however, differ in terms of how they define and operationalize appropriate behavior.

The referent of basic assumptions is a shared history of success in solving the fundamental organizational problems of external adaptation and internal integration (Detert et al., 2000; Schein, 2004). Assumptions that have proven successful time and again assume a taken-for-granted status, making it inconceivable to think of any other alternative. Philosophically and theoretically, the problems presented by issues of external adaption and internal integration lead to a process of sense making and the construction of reality utilizing an inquiry

process (e.g., What is the problem here? What does this mean? How should we respond?; see also Dewey, 1938; Weick 1995, 2005). When this sensemaking process is consistently successful, it creates underlying schemas or mental models that become accepted as true and valid (DiMaggio, 1997; Gioia & Poole, 1984). Because this process of inquiry has to do with ongoing organizational adaptation issues, it starts with the founders of the company, establishing the original organizational culture, and continues with subsequent leaders in their ongoing process of coping with the issues of external adaptation and internal integration.

In contrast to basic assumptions that are based on successful organizational responses, the referent for core values is an ideal action in terms of desirability, based on the goal of the best possible living (Rohan, 2000). They are oriented toward the self-concept of individuals and social concept of groups, serving as an internal moral compass. Thus, in contrast to being built on past successful actions, values offer a more abstract reference point for the self-regulation of one's own behavior and the social regulation of others' behavior (Smith, 1991). At its most basic level of understanding, values provide the criteria or standards that define what is good, desirable, and right (Hitlin & Piliavin, 2004). The referents of value systems, therefore, relate to the good, desirable, and right way to achieve the best possible living.

Although individuals and organizations develop basic assumptions based on their successful past behavior, it is more of an open question as to why an individual or organization would adopt certain values over others. Hitlin and Piliavin (2004) suggested that a number of different factors—socialization, education, occupation, parental (and founders') values, and national culture—can lead to the formation of core values. Once identified and adopted, the maintenance and sustainability of shared values is assumed to depend on: (a) the bottom-up influence of surface-level artifacts that reinforce the core values (e.g., formal procedures, informal expectations, and organizational practices; Markus & Kitayama, 1994), and (b) ongoing processes subsumed in the attraction-selection-attrition model (Goodman & Svyantek, 1999; O'Reilly, Chatman, & Caldwell, 1991; Schneider et al., 1995).

Basic Assumptions and Core Values: Two Very Different Roads to Organizational Culture

The notion of organizational culture, at its deepest level, comprising basic, unquestioned assumptions and core values, has been long acknowledged in the literature. Yet the fundamental differences between these two foundations and the implications of these two different starting points have been rarely acknowledged. In fact, much of the literature has used core values and basic assumptions interchangeably. For example, as described above, the OCI model provides two culture profiles identified as OCI-Ideal and OCI-Norms (Cooke & Szumal, 1993, 2000). The former describes deep-level values and assumptions whereas the latter describes surface-level norms and practices. The strength of relationships between the two levels depends on external situational attributes, resulting in possible culture disconnects. A similar distinction has been applied for the Competing Values model (Cameron & Quinn, 1999), in which the quadrant-based culture profile is measured by reference to the current and preferred organizational practices. In both cases, the measurement of (current) culture is based on observable artifacts, whereas the measurement of (ideal or preferred) culture is assumed to be driven by underlying values and assumptions. Such conceptualizations of culture overlook the inherent differences between basic assumptions and core values.

Core values represent moral and "best-possible-living" criteria as guiding principles for life of individuals and organizations, whereas basic assumptions represent schema developed from successful past behavior. Arguably, however, because these referents belong to different conceptual categories, they are not necessarily synonymous or interchangeable, nor can one be deduced from the other. For example, in the Competing Values model, a clan culture is founded upon the basic assumptions of internal maintenance, coupled with flexibility and concern for people (Cameron & Quinn, 1999). Such a culture is characterized by the artifacts of loyalty, commitment, teamwork, and mentoring. Using the Schwartz (1992) model, it is possible to infer that this culture is based on the core values of benevolence (whose artifacts include helpfulness, honesty, and loyalty) and universalism (expressed by artifacts such as equality, broad-mindedness, and social justice), emerging out the underlying dimensions of self-transcendence and conservatism (Schwartz, 1992)—two dimensions that are semantically quite different from the internal maintenance and flexibility/concern for people dimensions of the Competing Values model. This means that, although the assumptions and values of the clan culture overlap with core values in the Schwartz (1992) model, these values are manifestations

of different underlying dimensions that are not interchangeable.

The three-culture typology of constructive, passive/defensive, and aggressive/defensive cultures (Cooke & Szumal, 2000) offers even poorer mapping with the values model. By way of example, the constructive culture is associated with the norms of achievement, self-actualization, humanistic encouragement, and social affiliation. An examination of the circumplex values model reveals that these norms are scattered all over the model, violating its empirically derived organization whereby similar values must be located adjacent to each other.

The lack of one-to-one mapping between assumption-based and value-based culture typologies carries two important implications. First, a complete description of culture requires the separation of basic assumptions and core values as deep-level elements. Each of these element types should be measured separately, and culture ought to be described in terms of both. Second, future models of organizational culture should conceptualize the nature of relationships between the two dimensions, developing an integrated framework.

Measurement Issues Related to Organizational Culture

Despite repeated calls for the development of better (quantitative) culture measurement methodologies, there has been little progress over the last decades (Ashkanasy, Broadfoot, & Falkus, 2000; Ostroff et al., 2003). One of the major challenges in this regard stems from the dominance of the multilayered model of culture, stipulating a distinction between deep and surface layers. This distinction poses measurement problems because the model assumes complex, moderated mixed-effect relationships between its layers. Any basic assumption can result in a variety of (espoused) values and beliefs, giving rise, in turn, to a variety of observable or reportable artifacts. Because cross-layer relationships are moderated by situational attributes, there is a one-to-many mapping problem that prohibits a simple deductive process in which observable artifacts can be used to uncover the underlying assumptions or core values.

This difficulty has led to the ongoing debate between etic versus emic approaches, or qualitative versus quantitative measurement of culture, which has been well discussed in previous reviews (Allaire & Firsirotu, 1984). Furthermore, the available quantitative scales—favored by organizational psychologists—tend to focus on observable or reportable artifacts (e.g., behavior norms or espoused values; Ashkanasy et al., 2000; Hofmann & Jones, 2004). Consequently, the available culture measurement scales deduce the nature of underlying assumptions associated with each of its possible profiles. For example, Cameron and Quinn's (1999) clan culture—emerging from an internal focus coupled with high flexibility—is postulated to signify a series of basic assumptions, such as: the organization is like an extended family, leaders are mentors or parent figures, the organization is held together by loyalty and tradition, and employees perform best through participation and teamwork. Although these are logical deductions, they assume a one-to-one mapping between cultural layers, resulting in an operationalization of culture that does not adequately capture the underlying complexity of the theoretical construct.

One of the few attempts to develop a non-linear, induction-based framework for the cross-layer measurement of culture was done by Schein (2004), who utilized a 10-step clinical assessment methodology. This methodology, as outlined by Schein (2004), involves a structured process of qualitative inquiry that focuses on cross-layer transformations as a mechanism for discovering the underlying basic assumptions of the organization's culture. The process is based on group interviews in which culture is first described in terms of artifacts and espoused values, and then any observed conflicts and discrepancies between these elements are discussed. Using intuitive reasoning and brainstorming techniques, group members search for the underlying factors that could have resulted in such inconsistencies, framing them as tentative basic assumptions. Notably, this process is guided by an informed consultant/researcher who is knowledgeable about the theory of culture and relevant classifications of culture elements at each of its layers. A summary of the above discussion is presented in Table 20.1.

Integration of Organizational Culture and Climate

The challenges of measuring and conceptualizing organizational culture as a multilayered construct in which the deepest layer represents core values and unquestioned assumptions must also be viewed from the perspective of employees within the organization (i.e., members of the culture itself). In fact, the issues of organizational culture interpretation on behalf of the individuals who live in that culture has remained little discussed or studied (Erez & Early, 1993). Yet, if the deepest layers of organizational

culture take on an unconscious or taken-for-granted/unquestioned nature, then it seems that employees may only be aware of the more surface-layer elements (e.g., cultural artifacts, espoused values, organizational structures, behavioral routines), and it is these elements that influence their behavior. From this vantage point, organizational culture is assumed to shape the way of doing things in the organization primarily through its surface-layer attributes. This further implies an integrative conceptual framework in which climate constitutes a cognitive mechanism for the interpretation of culture by organizational employees (Ostroff et al., 2003).

An examination of the organizational climate literature reveals three relevant attributes of climate theory. First, climate perceptions focus on the surface-layer attributes of culture (e.g., policies, procedures, and practices). Second, due to the multiplicity of policies, procedures, and other artifacts, employees focus on those associated with key performance facets or job domains. Third, climate perceptions concern artifact patterns—drawing on symbolic interactionism (Blumer, 1969; Stryker, 2008) and sense-making processes (Weick, 1995, 2005)—that identify any gaps between espoused and enacted priorities, internal inconsistencies between policies and practices, and relative priorities of competing goals as indicators of the underlying values and beliefs. Organizational climate was thus redefined as shared assessments of the true (vs. espoused) priorities among competing demands (e.g., customer service vs. transaction efficiency), misalignments between espoused and enacted priorities and goals, and cross-level discrepancies between formally declared organizational policies and informal supervisory practices.

Our climate model presumes that organizational employees focus on alignments, misfits, and priorities among observable artifacts as a means for identifying the kinds of behavior likely to be rewarded and supported with regard to key facets. In fact, the identification of true priorities and/or misalignments between espousals and enactments offers a parsimonious strategy or solution for the challenges imposed by organizational complexity. This is equivalent to the identification of the tacit organizational theory-in-use, which is often at odds with the espoused theory that is being used for explaining or justifying organizational policies and practices (Argyris & Schon, 1996). In both cases, the goal is to structure multiple artifacts into a meaningful pattern indicative of the implicit payoff structure (i.e., behaviors that get rewarded) in organizations where this is often at odds with the espoused payoffs. Organizational climate, according to this model, structures the variety of domain-specific artifacts into recognizable patterns whose attributes inform employees of the true payoffs for alternative role behaviors.

Climate perceptions, resulting in shared cognitions of enacted (vs. espoused) priorities and values at the workplace, provide an important, if little used, step in deciphering the deep layer of organizational culture. In fact, such perceptions offer similar information to that offered by Schein's clinical assessment methodology for organizational culture. However, rather than relying on an expert consultant or researcher for conducting the assessment process, our climate model presumes that organizational employees engage in functionally equivalent processes, focusing on alignments, misfits, and priorities among observable artifacts as a means for inferring the nature of underlying elements driving these artifacts.

As noted above, the specificity of climates implies the emergence of several concurrent climates with which employees assess key domains in their organizational environment (i.e., a multiclimate model). Once the implicit priorities and enacted values associated with each climate domain are combined or integrated, their joint meaning can be considered as forming an interim layer of culture whose specification should make it easier to map observable artifacts with basic assumptions and core values. For example, a poor safety climate (indicative of low priority for operator safety in situations in which it competes with productivity or efficiency considerations) coupled with a poor ethics climate (indicative of little concern for employee welfare and customer rights) suggest core values of power and dominance and/or basic assumptions associated with a Darwinist perspective on organizational survival and success.

This line of reasoning suggests a bottom-up process in which the demonstrated efficacy of employees in developing shared climate perceptions results in socially verified patterning of artifacts in terms of true priorities and enacted values. Such patterning identifies implicit attributes of the organizational environment, whose combined meaning can be used for mapping cultural artifacts with deep layer elements. The referents of climate perceptions thus offer an intermediate level of culture analysis whose metrics (i.e., pattern attributes) can be used for enhancing the mapping of relationships between observable artifacts and deeper layer elements.

This intermediate level of analysis differs from Schein's (2004) intermediate level in several ways. Schein's (2004) model postulates that the intermediate level of culture refers to *espoused* beliefs and values or formally declared strategies and action philosophies, serving to justify organizational policies and actions. Because espousals originate with senior management, it follows that this is a top-down model. Our intermediate level refers to *enacted* beliefs and values, whose detection or identification results from sense-making processes conducted by organizational employees. Consequently, this is a bottom-up model. Theoretically speaking, the recorded prevalence of espousal and enactment misalignments in organizations (Argyris & Schon, 1996; Simons, 2002) suggests that enacted beliefs and values offer more valid information regarding deep-layer assumptions and values than their espoused counterparts. Although such information does not allow linear mapping with the deep-layer elements, it is postulated to constitute a more proximal indicator than the espoused counterparts. Further development of climate theory and research, focusing on multiclimate issues and the integration of multiple climates as indicators of underlying assumptions and core values, offers a promising agenda for organizational culture and climate research. This model is presented graphically in Figure 20.1.

The organizational culture model that we are proposing includes organizational climate as an integral element, incorporating top-down and bottom-up processes in culture conceptualization and measurement. Conceiving climate as a socially based inquiry of the implicit structure of the organizational environment suggests that it is possible to use an insider perspective for studying organizational culture. Contrary to the traditional use of the external perspective, associating it with qualitative analysis by participant expert observers (Allaire & Firsirotu, 1984), climate methodology allows quantitative analysis of standard surveys whose items are designed according to the criteria listed above. Once this analysis is expanded, covering the major specific climates for an organization, it should be possible to collect more complex, employee-based descriptions of enacted beliefs and values. The analysis of multiclimate perceptions should thus offer richer information for deducing the nature of underlying assumptions and core values (i.e., the organization's culture).

This integrative framework posits that organizational employees are more capable of interpreting

Graphic description of the theoretical model

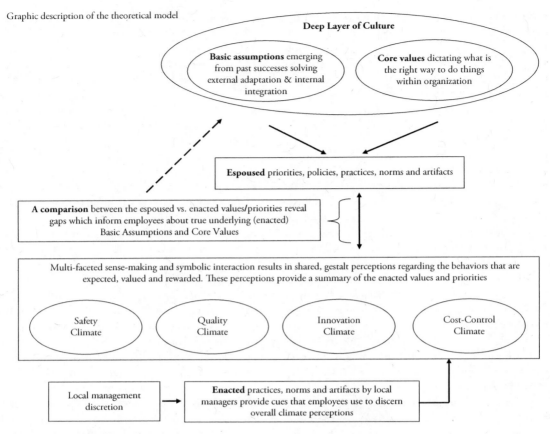

Figure 20.1 Graphic Description of the Theoretical Model

the deep layer of their organizational culture than is commonly assumed. Using climate-based cognitions as leverage for inquiring about implicit properties of their organizational environment, organizational employees may have developed greater capacity for conceptualizing the culture they live in than has been assumed. This perspective is consistent with other cognitive approaches to organizational culture (DiMaggio, 1997) and organizational behavior at large (Erez & Early, 1993), highlighting the complex architecture of cognitive structures and processes. In fact, the extent of requisite cognitive variety and complexity is seemingly greater than has been hitherto implicated, considering that each of the specific climates has a multilevel structure, resulting in organization- and group-level climates (Zohar, 2000). The resultant variation between group climates is expected to result in concordant variations in organizational culture perceptions (see Martin, 2002). The challenge in moving forward is to align the theoretical perspective discussed here with the measurement and assessment of both organizational climate and culture. Once the

measurement approaches are aligned, then researchers will be in a much better position to investigate the interrelationship between climate and culture. We are optimistic that these interrelationships will begin to bridge the gap between these two literatures such that they are eventually viewed as integrative concepts in which one (organizational climate) is viewed as a lens through which to view the other (the deep layers of organizational culture).

Conclusions

In this chapter, we have attempted to provide a comprehensive analysis of both the organizational climate and culture literatures, as well as providing thoughts on the integration of culture and climate. Our hope is that we have provided much needed clarity in terms of what constitutes climate perceptions and how they differ from other perceptions studied in organizational behavior. We also hope that we have provided some needed analysis of the deep structure of organizational culture, the two pathways through which it comes about, and the difficulty of one-to-one mapping of deep layers of culture with more observable artifacts. By viewing the overall pattern-level interpretation aspects of *multiple* domain-specific climates as a window through which to assist in the mapping of cultural artifacts—one of which is organizational climate—with deeper, tightly held organizational assumptions and values, we have proposed a model linking these two constructs together in a new way. This new linkage, of course, needs to be the focus of much empirical research moving forward. Because we have covered so much ground, we thought that it might be useful for us to pull together our key observations, recommendations, and ideas for the future in one place. Table 20.1 provides a high-level map to our key observations.

References

Allaire, Y., & Firsirotu, M. E. (1984). Theories of organizational culture. *Organization Studies, 5*, 193–226.

Amabile, T. M., Conti, R., Coon, H., Lazenby, J., & Herron, M. (1996). Assessing the work environment for creativity. *Academy of Management Journal, 39*, 1154–1184.

Anderson, N. R., & West, M. A. (1998). Measuring climate for work group innovation: Development and validation of the team climate inventory. *Journal of Organizational Behavior, 19*, 235–258.

Argyris, C., & Schon, D. A. (1996). *Organizational learning: Theory, method, and practice* (2nd ed.). Reading, MA: Addison-Wesley.

Ashforth, B. E. (1985). Climate formation: Issues and extensions. *Academy of Management Review, 10*, 837–847.

Ashkanasy, N. M., Broadfoot, L. E., & Falkus, S. (2000). Questionnaire measures of organizational culture. In N. M. Ashkanasy, C. P. Wilderom, & M. F. Peterson (Eds.), *Handbook of organizational culture and climate* (pp. 131–145). Thousand Oaks, CA: Sage.

Bacharach, S. B., Bamberger, P. R., & Conley, S. C. (1990). Work processes, role conflict, and role overload. *Work and Occupations, 17*, 199–229.

Baer, M., & Frese, M. (2003). Innovation is not enough: Climates for initiative and psychological safety, process innovations, and firm performance. *Journal of Organizational Behavior, 24*, 45–68.

Barling, J., Loughlin, C., & Kelloway, E. K. (2002). Development and test of a model linking safety-specific transformational leadership and occupational safety. *Journal of Applied Psychology, 87*, 488–496.

Bass, B. M. (1990). *Bass and Stodgill's handbook of leadership* (3rd ed.). New York: Free Press.

Bass, B. M., Avolio, B. J., Jung, D. I., & Berson, Y. (2003). Predicting unit performance by assessing transformational and transactional leadership. *Journal of Applied Psychology, 88*, 207–218.

Berger, C. J., & Cummings, L. L. (1979). Organizational structure, attitudes, and behaviors. In B. M. Staw (Ed.), *Research in organizational behavior* (Vol. 1, pp. 169–208). Greenwich, CT: JAI Press.

Beus, J. M., Payne, S. C., Bergman, M. E., & Arthur, W. (2010). Safety climate and injuries: An examination of theoretical and empirical relationships. *Journal of Applied Psychology, 95*, 713–727.

Blake, R. R., & Mouton, J. S. (1964). *The managerial grid*. Houston, TX: Gulf.

Blau, P., & Scott, W. R. (1962). *Formal organizations: A comparative approach*. San Francisco: Chandler.

Blumer, H. (1969). *Symbolic interactionism: Perspective and method*. Englewood Cliffs, NJ: Prentice-Hall.

Brown, A. (2000). Making sense of inquiry sensemaking. *Journal of Management Studies, 37*, 45–75.

Burke, S., Stagl, K., Klein, C., Goodwin, G., Salas, E., & Halpin, S. (2006). What type of leadership behaviors are functional in teams: A meta-analysis. *Leadership Quarterly, 17*, 288–307.

Cameron, K. S., & Quinn, R. E. (1999). *Diagnosing and changing organizational culture*. Reading, MA: Addison-Wesley.

Carr, J. Z., Schmidt, A. M., Ford, J. K., & DeShon, R. P. (2003). Climate perceptions matter: A meta-analytic path analysis relating molar climate, cognitive and affective states, and individual level work outcomes. *Journal of Applied Psychology, 88*, 605–619.

Chang, A., & Bordia, P. (2001). A multidimensional approach to the group cohesion-group performance relationship. *Small Group Research, 32*, 379–405.

Christian, M. S., Bradley, J. C., Wallace, J. C., & Burke, M. J. (2009). Workplace safety: A meta-analysis of the roles of person and situation factors. *Journal of Applied Psychology, 94*, 1103–1127.

Cohen, M., March, J., & Olsen, J. (1972). A garbage can model of organizational choice. *Administrative Science Quarterly, 17*, 1–25.

Cooke, R. A., & Szumal, J. L. (1993). Measuring normative beliefs and shared behavioral expectations in organizations. *Psychological Reports, 72*, 1299–1330.

Cooke, R. A., & Szumal, J. L. (2000). Using the Organizational Culture Inventory to understand the operating cultures of organizations. In N. M. Ashkanasy, C. P. Wilderom, & M. F. Peterson (Eds.), *Handbook of organizational culture and climate* (pp. 147–162). Thousand Oaks, CA: Sage.

Denison, D. R. (2001). Organizational culture: Can it be a key lever for driving organizational change? In: C. L. Cooper, S. Cartwright, & P. C. Early (Eds.), *The international handbook of organizational culture and climate* (pp. 347–372). New York: John Wiley.

Denison, D. R., & Mishra, A. (1995). Toward a theory of organizational culture and effectiveness. *Organizational Science, 6*, 204–223.

Denison, D. R., Hooijberg, R., & Quinn, R. E. (1995). Paradox and performance: Toward a theory of behavioral complexity in managerial leadership. *Organization Science, 6*, 524–540.

Detert, J. R., Schroeder, R. G., & Mauriel, J. J. (2000). A framework for linking culture and improvement initiatives in organizations. *Academy of Management Review, 25*, 850–863.

Dewey, J. (1938). *Logic: The theory of inquiry*. New York: Holt, Rinehart, & Winston.

DiMaggio, P. (1997). Culture and cognition. *Annual Review of Sociology, 23*, 263–287.

Dragoni, L. (2005). Understanding the emergence of state goal-orientation in organizational work groups: The role of leadership and multilevel climate perceptions. *Journal of Applied Psychology, 90*, 1084–1095.

Eakin, J. M. (1992). Leaving it up to the workers: Sociological perspective on the management of health and safety in small workplaces. *International Journal of Health Services, 22*, 689–704.

Erez, M., & Early, P. C. (1993). *Culture, self-identity, and work.* New York: Oxford University Press.

Festinger, L. (1954). A theory of social comparison processes. *Human Relations, 7,* 117–140.

Frese, M., Kring, W., Soose, A., & Zempel, J. (1996). Personal initiative at work: Differences between East and West Germany. *Academy of Management Journal, 39,* 37–64.

Furnham, A., & Gunter, B. (1993). Corporate culture: Definition, diagnosis and change. *International Review of I/O Psychology, 8,* 233–261.

Gioia, D. A., & Poole, P. P. (1984). Scripts in organizational behavior. *Academy of Management Review, 9,* 449–459.

Glick, W. H. (1985). Conceptualizing and measuring organizational and psychological climate: Pitfalls in multilevel research. *Academy of Management Review, 10,* 601–616.

Goffee, R., & Jones, G. (1998). *The character of a corporation.* New York: Doubleday.

Goffee, R., & Jones, G. (2001). Organizational culture: A sociological perspective. In: C. L. Cooper, S. Cartwright, & P. C. Early (Eds.), *The international handbook of organizational culture and climate* (pp. 3–20). New York: John Wiley.

Gonzalez-Roma, V., Peiro, J. M., & Tordera, N. (2002). An examination of the antecedents and moderator influences of climate strength. *Journal of Applied Psychology, 87,* 465–473.

Goodman, S. A., & Svyantek, D. J. (1999). Person-organization fit and contextual performance: Do shared values matter? *Journal of Vocational Behavior, 55,* 254–275.

Hardin, C., & Higgins, E. T. (1996). Shared reality: How social verification makes the subjective objective. In R. M. Sorrentino & E. T. Higgins (Eds.), *Handbook of motivation and cognition: Foundations of social behavior* (3rd ed., pp. 28–42). New York: Guilford.

Hargie, O., & Dickson, D. (2007). Are important corporate policies understood by employees? *Journal of Communication Management, 11,* 9–28.

Higgins, E. T. (1997). Beyond pleasure and pain. *American Psychologist, 52,* 1280–1300.

Higgins, E. T. (2002). How self-regulation creates distinct values: The case of promotion and prevention decision making. *Journal of Consumer Psychology, 12,* 177–191.

Hitlin, S., & Piliavin, J. A. (2004). Values: Reviving a dormant concept. *Annual Review of Sociology, 30,* 359–393.

Hofmann, D. A., & Jones, L. M. (2004). Some foundational and guiding questions for multi-level construct validation. In F. J. Yammarino & F. Dansereau (Eds.), *Research in multi-level issues* (Vol. 3, pp. 305–315). Bingley, UK: Emerald Publishing.

Hofmann, D. A., & Morgeson, F. P. (1999). Safety-related behavior as a social exchange: The role of perceived organizational support and leader-member exchange. *Journal of Applied Psychology, 84,* 286–296.

Hofmann, D. A., Morgeson, F. P., & Gerras, S. J. (2003). Climate as a moderator of the relationship between LMX and content-specific citizenship behavior: Safety climate as an exemplar. *Journal of Applied Psychology, 88,* 170–178.

Hofstede, G. (1980). *Culture's consequences: International differences in work-related values.* Beverly Hills, CA: Sage.

Hofstede, G. (1998). Attitudes, values and organizational culture: Disentangling the concepts. *Organization Studies, 19,* 477–492.

Hopkins, A. (2006). Studying organizational cultures and their effects on safety. *Safety Science, 44,* 875–889.

House, R. J., & Shamir, B. (1993). Toward the integration of transformational, charismatic, and visionary theories. In

M. M. Chemers & R. Ayman (Eds.), *Leadership theory and research: Perspectives and directions* (pp. 81–103). San Diego, CA: Academic Press.

Humphrey, S. E., Moon, H., Conlon, D. E., & Hofmann, D. A. (2004). Decision-making and behavior fluidity: How focus on completion and emphasis on safety changes over the course of projects. *Organizational Behavior and Human Decision Processes, 94,* 14–27.

James, L. R., & Jones, A. P. (1974). Organizational climate: A review of theory and research. *Psychological Bulletin, 81,* 1096–1112.

Kirkpatrick, S. A., & Locke, E. A. (1996). Direct and indirect effects of three core charismatic leadership components on performance and attitudes. *Journal of Applied Psychology, 81,* 36–51.

Klauss, R., & Bass, B. M. (1982). *Interpersonal communication in organizations.* New York: Academic Press.

Klein, K. J., Conn, A. B., Smith, D. B., & Sorra, J. S. (2001). Is everyone in agreement? An exploration of within-group agreement in employee perceptions of the work environment. *Journal of Applied Psychology, 86,* 3–16.

Kozlowski, S. W. J., & Doherty, M. L. (1989). Integration of climate and leadership: Examination of a neglected issue. *Journal of Applied Psychology, 74,* 546–553.

Kozlowski, S. W. J., & Hults, B. M. (1987). An exploration of climates for technical upgrading and performance. *Personnel Psychology, 40,* 539–563.

Kozlowski, S. W. J., & Klein, K. J. (2000). A multilevel approach to theory and research in organizations. In K. J. Klein & S. W. J. Kozlowski (Eds.), *Multilevel theory, research, and methods in organizations* (pp. 4–90). San Francisco: Jossey-Bass.

Lawrence, P. R., & Lorsch, J. W. (1967). *Organization and environment.* Boston: Harvard Business School.

Lewicki, R. J., McAllister, D. J., & Bies, R. J. (1998). Trust and distrust: New relationships and realities. *Academy of Management Review, 23,* 438–458.

Lewin, K., Lippitt, R., & White, R. K. (1939). Patterns of aggressive behavior in experimentally created social climates. *Journal of Social Psychology, 10,* 271–299.

Markus, H. R., & Kitayama, S. (1994). A collective fear of the collective: Implications for selves and theories of selves. *Personality and Social Psychology Bulletin, 20,* 568–579.

Martin, J. (2002). *Organizational culture: Mapping the terrain.* Thousand Oaks, CA: Sage.

Melamed, S., Ben-Avi, I., Luz, J., & Green, M. S. (1995). Objective and subjective work monotony. *Journal of Applied Psychology, 80,* 29–42.

Nahrgang, J. D., Morgeson, F. P., & Hofmann, D. A. (2011). Safety at work: A meta-analytic investigation of the link between job demands, job resources, burnout, engagement, and safety outcomes. *Journal of Applied Psychology, 96,* 71–94.

Oldham, G. R., & Cummings, A. (1996). Employee creativity: Personal and contextual factors at work. *Academy of Management Journal, 39,* 607–634.

O'Reilly, C. A., Chatman, J., & Caldwell, D. F. (1991). People and organizational culture: A profile comparison approach to assessing person-organization fit. *Academy of Management Journal, 34,* 487–516.

Ostroff, C. (1993). The effects of climate and personal influences on individual behavior and attitudes in organizations. *Organizational Behavior and Human Decision Processes, 56,* 56–90.

Ostroff, C., Kinicki, A. J., & Tamkins, M. M. (2003). Organizational culture and climate. In W. C. Borman, D. R. Ilgen, & R. J. Klimoski (Eds.), *Handbook of psychology* (Vol. 12, pp. 565–593). New York: Wiley.

Ouchi, W. G., & Wilkins, A. L. (1985). Organizational culture. *Annual Review of Sociology, 11*, 457–483.

Pate-Cornell, M. E. (1990). Organizational aspects of engineering system safety: The case of offshore platforms. *Science, 250*, 1210–1217.

Patterson, M., West, M., Shackleton, V., Dawson, J., Lawthom, R., Maitlis, S., Robinson, D., & Wallace, A. (2005). Validating the organizational climate measure: Links to managerial practices, productivity, and innovation. *Journal of Organizational Behavior, 26*, 379–408.

Payne, R. L., & Pugh, S. S. (1976). Organizational structure and organization climate. In M. D. Dunnette (Ed.), *Handbook of industrial and organizational psychology* (pp. 1125–1173). Chicago: Rand McNally.

Pierce, J. L., Kostova, T., & Dirks, K. T. (2003). The state of psychological ownership: Integrating and extending a century of research. *Review of General Psychology, 7*, 84–107.

Quinn, R. E., & McGrath, M. R. (1985). The transformation of organizational culture: A competing values perspective. In P. J. Frost, L. F. Moore, M. R. Louis, C. C. Lundberg, & J. Martin (Eds.), *Organizational culture* (pp. 315–344). Beverly Hills, CA: Sage.

Quinn, R. E., & Rohrbaugh, J. (1983). A spatial model of effectiveness criteria: Towards a competing values approach to organizational analysis. *Management Science, 29*, 363–377.

Rentsch, J. R. (1990). Climate and culture: Interaction and qualitative differences in organizational meanings. *Journal of Applied Psychology, 75*, 668–681.

Rohan, M. J. (2000). A rose by any name? The values construct. *Personality and Social Psychology Review, 4*, 255–277.

Rokeach, M. (1973). *The nature of human values.* New York: Free Press.

Rousseau, D. M. (1990). Assessing organizational culture: The case for multiple methods. In B. Schneider (Ed.), *Organizational climate and culture* (pp. 153–192). San Francisco: Jossey-Bass.

Schein, E. H. (2004). *Organizational culture and leadership* (3rd ed.). San Francisco: Jossey-Bass.

Schneider, B. (1975). Organizational climates: An essay. *Personnel Psychology, 28*, 447–479.

Schneider, B. (1990). The climate for service: An application of the climate construct. In B. Schneider (Ed.), *Organizational climate and culture* (pp. 383–412). San Francisco: Jossey-Bass.

Schneider, B., & Bowen, D. (1995). *Winning the service game.* Boston: Harvard Business School Press.

Schneider, B., Bowen, D. E., Ehrhart, M. G., & Holcombe, K. M. (2000). The climate for service: Evolution of the construct. In N. M. Ashkanasy, C. P. Wilderom, & M. F. Peterson (Eds.), *Handbook of organizational culture and climate* (pp. 21–36). Thousand Oaks, CA: Sage.

Schneider, B., & Reichers, A. E. (1983). On the etiology of climates. *Personnel Psychology, 36*, 19–39.

Schneider, B., Goldstein, H. W., & Smith, D. B. (1995). The ASA framework: An update. *Personnel Psychology, 48*, 747–773.

Schneider, B., White, S. S., & Paul, M. C. (1998). Linking service climate and customer perceptions of service quality: Test of a causal model. *Journal of Applied Psychology, 83*, 150–163.

Schneider, B., Bowen, D. E., Ehrhart, M. G., & Holcombe, K. M. (2000). The climate for service: Evolution of the construct. In N. M. Ashkanasy, C. P. Wilderom, & M. F. Peterson (Eds.), *Handbook of organizational culture and climate* (pp. 21–36). Thousand Oaks, CA: Sage.

Schwartz, S. (1992). Universals in the content and structure of values: Theoretical advances and empirical tests in 20 countries. In M. P. Zanna (Ed.), *Advances in experimental social psychology* (Vol. 24, pp. 1–65). San Diego, CA: Academic.

Schwartz, S. (1994). Are there universal aspects in the structure and content of human values? *Journal of Social Issues, 50*, 19–45.

Schwartz, S. (1999). Cultural value differences: Some implications for work. *Applied Psychology: An International Journal, 48*, 23–47.

Schwartz, S. (2004). Mapping and interpreting cultural differences around the world. In H. Vinken, J. Soeters, & P. Ester (Eds.), *Comparing cultures: Dimensions of culture in a comparative perspective* (pp. 232–243). Leiden, The Netherlands: Brill.

Schwartz, S., & Bilsky, W. (1987). Toward a psychological structure of human values. *Journal of Personality and Social Psychology, 53*, 550–562.

Shamir, B., House, R. J., & Arthur, M. B. (1993). The motivational effects of charismatic leadership: A self-concept based theory. *Organization Science, 4*, 577–594.

Simons, T. (2002). Behavioral integrity: The perceived alignment between managers' words and deeds as a research focus. *Organization Science, 13*, 18–35.

Smith, M. B. (1991). *Values, self, and society: Toward a humanist social psychology.* New Brunswick, NJ: Transaction.

Stevens, J. M., Steensma, H. K., Harrison, D. A., & Cochran, P. L. (2005). Symbolic or substantive document? The influence of ethics codes on financial executives' decisions. *Strategic Management Journal, 26*, 181–195.

Stryker, S. (2008). From Mead to structural symbolic interactionism and beyond. *Annual Review of Sociology, 34*, 15–31.

Trice, H. M., & Beyer, J. M. (1993). *The cultures of work organizations.* Englewood Cliffs, NJ: Prentice-Hall.

Van Dyne, L., & Pierce, J. L., (2004). Psychological ownership and feelings of possession: Three field studies predicting employee attitudes and organizational citizenship behavior. *Journal of Organizational Behavior, 25*, 439–459.

Vardi, Y., & Weitz, E. (2004). *Misbehavior in organizations.* Mahwah, NJ: Erlbaum.

Verbeke, W., Volgering, M., & Hessels, M. (1998). Exploring the conceptual expansion within the field of organizational behavior: Organizational climate and organizational culture. *Journal of Management Studies, 35*, 303–329.

Wallace, J. C., Popp, E., & Mondore, S. (2006). Safety climate as a mediator between foundation climates and occupational accidents: A group-level investigation. *Journal of Applied Psychology, 91*, 681–688.

Weber, M. (1968). *Economy and society.* Berkeley: University of California Press.

Weick, K. E. (1979). *The social psychology of organizing.* Reading, MA: Addison-Wesley.

Weick, K. E. (1995). *Sensemaking in organizations.* Thousand Oaks, CA: Sage.

Weick, K. E. (2005). Managing the unexpected: Complexity as distributed sensemaking. In R. R. McDaniel & D. J. Driebe (Eds.), *Uncertainty and surprises in complex systems* (pp. 51–65). Berlin: Springer-Verlag.

Weick, K. E., Sutcliffe, K. M., & Obstfeld, D. (1999). Organizing for high reliability: Processes of collective mindfulness. *Research in Organizational Behavior, 21*, 81–123.

Wright, C. (1986). Routine deaths: Fatal accidents in the oil industry. *Sociological Review, 4,* 265–289.

Yukl, G. (2006). *Leadership in organizations* (6th ed.). Upper Saddle River, NJ: Prentice-Hall.

Zohar, D. (1980). Safety climate in industrial organizations: Theoretical and applied implications. *Journal of Applied Psychology, 65,* 96–102.

Zohar, D. (2000). A group-level model of safety climate: Testing the effect of group climate on micro-accidents in manufacturing jobs. *Journal of Applied Psychology, 85,* 587–596.

Zohar, D. (2002). The effects of leadership dimensions, safety climate, and assigned priorities on minor injuries in work groups. *Journal of Organizational Behavior, 23,* 75–92.

Zohar, D. (2003). The influence of leadership and climate on occupational health and safety. In D. A. Hofmann & L. E. Tetrick (Eds.), *Health and safety in organizations: A Multilevel perspective* (pp. 201–230). San Francisco: Jossey-Bass.

Zohar, D. (2008). Safety climate and beyond: A multi-level multi-climate framework. *Safety Science, 46,* 376–387.

Zohar, D., & Luria, G. (2004). Climate as a social-cognitive construction of supervisory safety practices: Scripts as proxy of behavior patterns. *Journal of Applied Psychology, 89,* 322–333.

Zohar, D., & Luria, G. (2005). A multilevel model of safety climate: Cross-level relationships between organization and group-level climates. *Journal of Applied Psychology, 90,* 616–628.

Zohar, D., & Tenne-Gazit, O. (2008). Transformational leadership and group interaction as climate antecedents: A social network analysis. *Journal of Applied Psychology, 93,* 744–757.

A Social Network Perspective on Organizational Psychology

Daniel J. Brass

Abstract

This paper applies a social network perspective to the study of organizational psychology. Complementing the traditional focus on individual attributes, the social network perspective focuses on the relationships among actors. The perspective assumes that actors (whether they be individuals, groups, or organizations) are embedded within a network of interrelationships with other actors. It is this intersection of relationships that defines an actor's position in the social structure, and provides opportunities and constraints on behavior. A brief introduction to social networks is provided, typical measures are described, and research focusing on the antecedents and consequences of networks is reviewed. The social network framework is applied to organizational behavior topics such as recruitment and selection, performance, power, justice, and leadership, with a focus on research results obtained and directions for future research.

Key Words: social networks, social network measures, organizational psychology, methodological issues, structural holes, social capital

Introduction

In the fall of 1932, the Hudson School for Girls in upstate New York experienced a flood of runaways in a two-week period of time. The staff, who thought they had a good idea of the type of girl who usually ran away, was baffled trying to explain the epidemic. Using a new technique that he called *sociometry*, Jacob Moreno graphically showed how the girls' social relationships with each other, rather than their personalities or motivations, resulted in the contagious runaways (Moreno, 1934). More than 50 years later, Krackhardt and Porter (1986) showed how turnover occurred among clusters of friends working at fast-food restaurants.

During the 1920s, the researchers of the famous Hawthorne studies at the Western Electric Plant in Chicago diagramed the observed interaction patterns of the workers in the bank wiring room. Their diagrams resembled electrical wiring plans and showed how the informal relationships were different from the formally prescribed organizational chart. Today, many studies have investigated employee interaction patterns in organizations (see Brass, Galaskiewicz, Greve, & Tsai, 2004, for a review).

What these studies have in the common is a focus on the relationships among people in organizations, rather than the attributes of the individuals. It is, of course, highly appropriate that the study of organizational behavior focuses on the attributes of individuals in organizations; and, it is to the credit of my organizational psychology colleagues that so much progress has occurred. However, to focus on the individual in isolation, to search in perpetuity for the elusive personality or demographic characteristic that defines the successful employee is, at best, failing to see the entire picture. At worst, it is misdirected effort continued by the overwhelming desire to develop the perfect measurement instrument. There is little doubt (at least in my mind) that the traditional study of industrial/organizational psychology (or organizational behavior) has been dominated by a perspective that focuses on the individual or the organization in isolation. We are of course continually reminded of the need for an interactionist perspective: that the responses of actors are a function of both the attributes of the actors and their environments. Even with attempts to match the individual with the organization, the environment is little more than a context for individual interests, needs, values, motivation, and behavior.

I do not mean to suggest that individuals do not differ in their skills and abilities and their willingness to use them. I too revel in the tradition of American individualism. I will not suggest that individuals are merely the "actees" rather than the actors (Mayhew, 1980). Rather, I wish to suggest an alternative perspective, that of social networks, which does not focus on attributes of individuals (or of organizations). The social network perspective instead focuses on relationships rather than (or in addition to) actors—the links in addition to the nodes. It assumes that social actors (whether they be individuals, groups, or organizations) are embedded within a web (or network) of interrelationships with other actors. It is this intersection of relationships that defines an individual's role, an organization's niche in the market, or simply an actor's position in the social structure. It is these networks of relationships that provide opportunities and constraints that are as much, or more, the causal forces, as the attributes of the actors.

Given the rapid rise of social network articles in the organizational journals, it may be unnecessary to familiarize readers with basics (Borgatti & Foster, 2003). However, the popularity can create confusion and threaten the coherence of the approach (see Kilduff & Brass, 2010, for a discussion of core ideas and key debates). I begin with a brief, general primer on social networks, including tables that illustrate the various social network measures typically used in organizational behavior research. I will not begin at the beginning (excellent histories of social network analysis are available; see Freeman, 2004), nor will I attempt to reference every social network article that has ever appeared in an organizational behavior journal. Reference to my own work is more a matter of familiarity than self-promotion. I will focus on the design of social network research with attention to findings regarding the antecedents and consequences of social

networks from an interpersonal perspective (a micro approach) with only occasional references to interorganizational research when appropriate. I attempt to note the research that has been done and suggest directions for future research, also noting the criticisms and challenges of this approach. My overall goal is to provide readers enough information to conduct social network research and enough ideas to encourage research on social networks in organizational behavior.

Social Networks

I define a network as a set of nodes and the set of ties representing some relationship or absence of relationship between the nodes. In this most abstract definition, networks can be used to represent many different things, resulting in the adoption of the perspective across a wide range of disciplines (see Borgatti, Mehra, Brass, & Labianca, 2009). Even researchers in the hard sciences of physics and biology have applied networks to their favorite theories. Thus, we find no universal theory of networks. Rather, we find a perspective that applies many of the network concepts and measures to a variety of theories.

In the case of social networks, the nodes represent actors (i.e., individuals, groups, organizations). Actors can be connected on the basis of (a) similarities (same location, membership in the same group, or similar attributes such as gender); (b) social relations (kinship, roles, affective relations such as friendship, or cognitive relations such as "knows about"); (c) interactions (talks with, gives advice to); or (d) flows (information; Borgatti et al., 2009). In organizational behavior research, the links typically involve some form of interaction, such as communication, or represent a more abstract connection, such as trust, friendship, or influence. They may also be used to represent physical proximity or affiliations in groups, such as CEOs who sit on the same boards of directors (e.g., Mizruchi, 1996). Although the particular content of the relationships represented by the ties is limited only by the researcher's interest, typically studied are flows of information (communication, advice) and expressions of affect (friendship). I will refer to a focal actor in a network as *ego*; the other actors with whom ego has direct relationships are called *alters*.

Although the dyadic relationship is the basic building block of networks, dyadic relationships have for many years been studied by social psychologists. The idea of a network (if not the technical graph-theoretic definition) implies more than one link. Indeed, the added value of the network perspective, the unique contribution, is that it goes beyond the dyad and provides a way of considering the structural arrangement of many nodes. The unit of analysis is not the dyad. As Wellman (1988) notes, "It is not assumed that network members engage only in multiple duets with separate alters." Indeed, it might be said that the triad is the basic building block of networks (Krackhardt, 1998; Simmel, 1950). The focus is on the relationships among the dyadic relationships (i.e., the network). Typically, a minimum of two links connecting three actors is implicitly assumed in order to have a network and to establish such notions as indirect links and paths.

The importance of indirect ties and paths is illustrated in Travers and Milgram's (1969) experimental study of "the small world problem." They asked 296 volunteers in Nebraska to attempt to reach by mail a target person living in the Boston area. They were instructed, "If you do not know the target person on a personal basis, do not try to contact him directly. Instead, mail this folder to a personal acquaintance who is more likely than you to know the target person," (Travers & Milgram, 1969, p. 420). Recipients of the mailings were asked to return a postcard to the researchers and to mail the folder on to the target (if known personally) or to someone more likely to know the target. Of the folders that eventually reached the target, the average number of intermediaries (path length) was approximately six, leading to the notion of "six degrees of separation" and providing empirical evidence for the common expression, "It's a small world" (see Watts, 2003, for a more refined and updated thesis on small worlds).

Closely connected to the assumption of the importance of indirect ties and paths is the assumption that something (often information, influence, or affect) is transmitted or flows through the connections. Although other mechanisms for explaining the results of network connections have been provided (Borgatti et al., 2009), most organizational researchers explain the outcomes of social networks by reference to flows of resources. For example, a central actor in the network may benefit because of access to information. Podolny (2001) coined the term *pipes* to refer to the "flow" aspect of networks, but also noted that networks can serve as *prisms*, conveying mental images of status, for example, to observers.

The final assumption of most social network research is that the network provides the opportunities and constraints that affect the outcomes of individuals and groups. Often included is the assumption that these linkages as a whole may be used to interpret the social responses of the actors (Mitchell, 1969). While this assumption does not exclude the possible causal effects of human capital, it assigns primacy to network relationships and leads logically to the concept of social capital.

Social Capital

As differentiated from human capital (an individual's skills, ability, intelligence, personality, etc.) or financial capital (money), the popularized concept of social capital refers to benefits derived from relationships with others. The task of precisely defining and measuring social capital has received much attention and has resulted in considerable disagreement (see Adler & Kwon, 2002, for a cogent discussion of the history of usage of the term). Definitions have generally followed two perspectives. One perspective focuses on individuals and how they might access and control resources exchanged through relationships with others in order to gain benefits or acquire social capital. This approach is exemplified by the studies that suggest that an actor's position in the network provides benefits to the actor. Burt's (1992) work on the advantages of "structural holes" in one's network (ego is connected to alters who are not themselves connected) is an example. The other perspective focuses on the collective and assesses how groups of actors collectively build relationships that provide benefits to the group (e.g., Oh, Labianca, & Chung, 2006). This approach is exemplified by Coleman's (1990) often cited reference to social capital as norms and sanctions, trust, and mutual obligations that result from "closed" networks (a high number of interconnections between members of a group; ego's alters are connected to each other). Putnam's (1995) "Bowling Alone" work on the demise of social capital in the United States is another example of this collective approach. Putnam's (1995) statistics show a steady decline in membership in bowling leagues, bridge clubs, and community and church groups since the 1950s. The collective, group-level approach does not forgo the individual entirely, as it suggests how collective social capital may benefit the individual members of the group as well as the group. Indeed, both approaches suggest individual- and group-level benefits.

The difference in the focus is amplified by seemingly contradictory predictions concerning the acquisition of social capital. At the individual level, connecting to disconnected others results in social capital; at the collective level, connecting to others who are themselves connected results in closure in the network and the social capital associated with trust, norms, and group sanctions. Such networks can provide social support and a sense of identity (Halgin, 2009). However, one can be "trapped in your own net," as closed networks can constrain action (Gargiulo & Benassi, 2000). Indeed, both approaches are based on the underlying network proposition that densely connected networks constrain attitudes and behavior. In one case (Coleman, 1990; Putnam, 1995), this constraint promotes good outcomes (trust, norms of reciprocity, monitoring and sanctioning of inappropriate behavior); in the other case (Burt, 1992), constraint produces bad outcomes (redundant information, a lack of novel ideas). When the network is extended outward (enlarged), it is typically the bridges (structural hole positions) that provide the closure for the larger network.

Attempts have been made both to test one approach versus the other, as well as to reconcile both approaches (Burt, 2005). However, as Lin (2001, p. 8) points out, "Whether social capital is seen from the societal-group level or the relational (individual) level, all scholars remain committed to the view that it is the interacting members who make the maintenance and reproduction of this social asset possible." Nahapiet & Ghoshal, (1998, p. 243) offer a comprehensive definition: "The sum of the actual and potential resources embedded within, available through, and derived from the network of relationships possessed by an individual or social unit." One can view social capital, like other forms of capital, from an investment perspective with the expectation of future (often times uncertain) benefits (Adler & Kwon, 2002). We invest in relationships with the hoped-for return of benefits. These benefits may be in the form of human capital, financial capital, physical capital, or additional social capital.

Some network researchers have dismissed the definitional battles surrounding social capital as irrelevant to their research. They note that the definitions have become so broad as to be meaningless. As Coleman (1990) notes, social capital is like a "chair"—it comes in many different shapes and sizes but is defined by its function. And it is important to note that much social network research focuses on how actors become similar (e.g., diffusion studies), rather than on how actors differentially benefit from networks. Nevertheless, the seemingly contradictory hypotheses of structural holes versus closure have generated a furious deluge of research. In addition,

the concept of social capital has provided a legitimizing label that reinforces many of the underlying assumptions of social network analysis.

Social Network Approaches and Measures

Social network research can be categorized in many ways; I choose to organize around four approaches or research foci: (a) structure, (b) relationships, (c) resources, and (d) cognition. To these four, I add the traditional organizational behavior focus on the attributes of actors and note that these approaches can be, and often are, combined (e.g., Seibert, Kraimer, & Liden, 2001). Associated with each approach, I list network measures that have typically been used in organizational research.

Focus on Structure

Consider the diagrams in Figure 21.1. Almost everyone would predict that the center node (position A) in Figure 21.1a is the most powerful position. Most people make this prediction without asking whether the nodes represent individuals or groups, or whether the lines represent communications, friendship, or buy-sell transactions. Nor does anyone ask if the lines are of differing strengths or intensities, or whether they represent directional or reciprocated interactions. Most people simply look at the diagram and predict that node A is the most powerful.

We make these judgments based simply on the pattern or structure of the nodes and ties; Figure 21.1 provides no information other than the structural arrangement of positions. We do not know the values, attitudes, personalities, or abilities of any of the nodes. From a purely structural perspective, a tie is a tie is a tie, and a node is a node is a node (differentiated only on the basis of its structural position in the network).

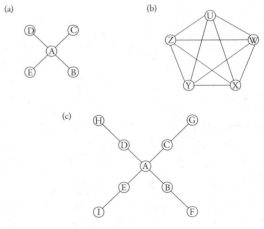

Figure 21.1 Network Diagrams

It is the *pattern* of relationships that provide the opportunities and constraints that affect outcomes.

The structural focus is at the heart of social network analysis, and the abstract nature of patterns of nodes and ties have led to the wide application of networks to a variety of different disciplines. It has also led to a search for universal patterns that may be applied to such diverse topics as atoms and molecules, transportation networks, and electrical grids. For example, researchers have noted small-world patterns (dense clusters connected by a small number of bridges) in nematodes, electrical power transmission systems, and Hollywood actors (Watts, 2003).

A purely structural explanation for the advantage of A over the other nodes in Figure 21.1a would simply note that A is the most central position in the network. Period. However, purely structural explanations are rarely acceptable to reviewers for organizational behavior journals (for the extreme structural perspective, see Mayhew, 1980). Rather, reviewers and authors exhibit a tendency toward reductionism and theoretical explanations based on human agency. These tendencies represent a metaphysical preference, masquerading as a debatable point (Mehra, 2009).

In explaining their choice in Figure 21.1a, most people could articulate an intuitive notion of centrality. They might suggest that position A is at the "center" of the group, that position A has access to all the other positions, or that the other positions are dependent on position A—they must "go through" position A in order to reach each other. They might conclude that position A controls the group; A is not dependent on any one other node, and all the other nodes are dependent on A. Thus, most people have an intuitive idea of what social networks are, what centrality is, and how both might relate to power. Consequently, few people would be surprised to learn that their intuitive prediction has been supported in a number of settings (see Brass, 1992).

Table 21.1 (adapted from Brass, 1995a) presents typical measures used to describe structural positions in the network (see also Kilduff & Brass, 2010, for a glossary of network terms). It is important to keep in mind that these measures are not attributes of isolated individual actors; rather, they represent the actor's relationship within the network. If any aspect of the network changes, the actor's relationship within the network also changes. For example, in Figure 21.1a, adding an additional tie and node to each of the four nodes B, C, D, and E (21.1c) will substantially decrease A's power. In addition to describing positions within the network, several structural measures have been developed to describe the entire network.

For example, network 1a could be described as more centralized than network 1b. Some typical structural measures used to describe entire networks are listed in Table 21.2 (adapted from Brass, 1995a).

Structural measures have also been developed for identifying groups or clusters of nodes (actors) within the network. For example, a network is sometimes described as having single or multiple components (all nodes in a component are connected by either direct or indirect links). Any actor in a component can reach all other actors in the component directly or through a path of indirect ties. One large component is typical of networks within organizations.

There are two typical methods of grouping actors within components, a relational method often called *cohesion,* and a structural method referred to as *structural equivalence*. The relational cohesion approach clusters actors based on their ties to each other. For example, a clique is a group of actors in which every actor is connected to every other actor (network 21.1b represent a clique). Other measures have been developed to relax the clique criteria for grouping actors. For example, n-clique groups all actors who are connected by a maximum of n links. A k-plex is a group of actors in which each actor is directly connected to all except k of the other actors (Scott, 2000).

The structural equivalence approach is based on the notion that actors may occupy similar positions within the network structure, although they may not be directly connected to each other. For example, two organizations in the same industry may have similar patterns of links to suppliers and customers but may not have any direct connection between themselves. The two organizations are structurally equivalent, as they occupy similar structural positions in the network. In a communication network, structurally equivalent actors may communicate with similar others but not necessarily communicate with each other. In network 21.1a, actors B, C, D, and E are structurally equivalent. A technique called *block modeling* is used to group actors on the basis of structural equivalence (DiMaggio, 1986).

Because actors in organizations are typically formally grouped via hierarchy and work function, it is difficult to find organizational behavior research that uses network measures to group people. For an extensive and detailed description of grouping measures, see Scott (2000, pp. 100–145) or Wasserman and Faust (1994, pp. 249–423).

Focus on Relationships

Rather than assuming that all relationships are the same (a tie is a tie is a tie), social network researchers

Table 21.1 Typical Structural Social Network Measures Assigned to Individual Actors

Measure	Definition
Degree	Number of direct links with other actors.
In-degree	Number of directional links to the actor from other actors (in-coming links).
Out-degree	Number of directional links form the actor to other actors (out-going links).
Range (Diversity)	Number of links to different others (others are defined as different to the extent that they are not themselves linked to each other, or represent different groups or statuses).
Closeness	Extent to which an actor is close to, or can easily reach, all the other actors in the network. Usually measured by averaging the path distances (direct and indirect links) to all others. A direct link is counted as 1, indirect links receive proportionately less weight.
Betweenness	Extent to which an actor mediates, or falls between any other two actors on the shortest path between those two actors. Usually averaged across all possible pairs in the network.
Centrality	Extent to which an actor is central to a network. Various measures (including degree, closeness, and betweenness) have been used as indicators of centrality. Some measures of centrality (eigenvector, Bonacich) weight an actor's links to others by the centrality of those others.
Prestige	Based on asymmetric relationships, prestigious actors are the object rather than the source of relations. Measures similar to centrality are calculated by accounting for the direction of the relationship (i.e., in-degree).
Structural holes	Extent to which an actor is connected to alters who are not themselves connected. Various measures include ego-network density and constraint as well as betweenness centrality.
Ego-network density	Number of direct ties among other actors to whom ego is directly connected divided by the number of possible connections among these alters. Often used as a measure of structural holes when controlling for the size of ego's network.
Constraint	Extent to which an actor (ego) is invested in alters who are themselves invested in ego's other alters. Burt's (1992, p. 55) measure of structural holes; constraint is the inverse of structural holes.
Liaison	An actor who has links to two or more groups that would otherwise not be linked, but is not a member of either group.
Bridge	An actor who is a member of two or more groups.

often attempt to differentiate the ties. Focusing on the content of the relationships (what type of tie the lines in the network diagram represent) is a boundary specification issue (see below). Rather than focus on the particular content, several other ways to characterize the ties have been measured by social network researchers. While the structural approach typically treats ties as binary (present or absent) and directional (ego seeks advice from alter), the focus on relationships typically assigns values to ties (such as frequency or intensity). Table 21.3 (adapted from Brass, 1995a) indicates typical measures of links, or ties. Although each of the measures in Table 21.3 can be used to describe a particular link between two actors, the measures can be aggregated and assigned to a particular actor or can be used to describe the

entire network. For example, we might note that 70% of the ties in a network are reciprocated.

The focus on relationships in social networks has been dominated by Granovetter's (1973) theory of the "strength of weak ties." Granovetter (1973) argued that job search is embedded in social relations which he defined as strong or weak ties. Tie strength is a function of time, intimacy, emotional intensity (mutual confiding), and reciprocity (Granovetter, 1973, p. 348). Strong ties are often characterized as friends and family; weak ties are acquaintances. Granovetter (1973) found that weak ties were more often the source of helpful job information than strong ties.

Although the research exemplified the relational approach, it was Granovetter's (1973) structural

Table 21.2 Typical Structural Social Network Measures Used to Describe Entire Networks

Measure	Definition
Size	Number of actors in the network.
Inclusiveness	Total number of actors in a network minus the number of isolated actors (not connected to any other actors). Also measured as the ratio of connected actors to the total number of actors.
Component	Largest connected subset of network nodes and links. All nodes in the component are connected (either direct or indirect links) and no nodes have links to nodes outside the component. Number of components or size of the largest component is measured.
Connectivity (Reachability)	Minimum number of actors or ties that must be removed to disconnect the network. Reachability is 1 if two actors can reach each other, otherwise 0. Average reachability equals connectedness.
Connectedness/ fragmentation	Ratio of pairs of nodes that are mutually reachable to total number of pairs of nodes.
Density	Ratio of the number of actual links to the number of possible links in the network.
Centralization	Difference between the centrality scores of the most central actor and those of other actors in a network is calculated, and used to form ratio of the actual sum of the differences to the maximum sum of the differences.
Core-peripheriness	Degree to which network is structured such that core members connect to everyone, while periphery members connect only to core members and not other members of the periphery.
Transitivity	Three actors (A, B, C) are transitive if whenever A is linked to B and B is linked to C, then C is linked to A. Transitivity is the number of transitive triples divided by the number of potential transitive triples (number of paths of length 2). Also known as the weighted clustering coefficient.
Small-worldness	Extent to which a network structure is both clumpy (actors are clustered into small clumps) yet having a short average distance between actors.

explanation for the "strength of weak ties" that generated research interest in networks. Focusing on the indirect ties in the network, Granovetter (1973) argued that strong ties tend to be themselves connected (part of the same social circle) and provide the job seeker with redundant information. Weak ties, on the other hand, tend to not be connected themselves; they represent ties to disconnected social circles (bridges) that provide useful, non-redundant information in finding jobs. Thus, "social structure can dominate motivation" (Granovetter, 2005, p. 34). While strong-tie friends may be more motivated to help than weak-tie acquaintances, it is likely to be acquaintances who provide information concerning new jobs. Although subsequent research refined and modified these results (cf., Bian, 1997; Lin, 1999; Wegener, 1991), Granovetter's (1973) notion that weak ties can be useful bridges connecting otherwise disconnected social circles is one of the most referenced ideas in the social sciences.

Strong ties have also received research attention, as they are often thought to be more influential, more motivated to provide information, and of easier access than weak ties. For example, Krackhardt (1992) showed that strong ties were influential in determining the outcome of a union election. Hansen (1999) found that while weak ties were more useful in searching out information, strong ties were more useful for the effective transfer of information. Uzzi (1997) found that "embedded ties" were characterized by higher levels of trust, richer transfers of information, and greater problem-solving capabilities when compared to "arms-length" ties. On the downside, strong ties require more time and energy to maintain and come with stronger obligations to reciprocate.

In addition, negative ties have recently drawn research attention (Labianca & Brass, 2006). Defined as "dislike," "prefer to avoid," or "difficult to work with," Labianca and Brass (2006, p. 597) propose that these "social liabilities" are a function

Table 21.3 Typical Relational Social Network Measures of Ties

Measure	Definition	Example
Indirect links	Path between two actors is mediated by one or more others.	A is linked to B, B is linked to C, thus A is indirectly linked to C through B.
Frequency	How many times, or how often the link occurs.	A talks to B 10 times per week.
Duration (stability)	Existence of link over time.	A has been friends with B for 5 years.
Multiplexity	Extent to which two actors are linked together by more than one relationship.	A and B are friends, they seek out each other for advice, and they work together.
Strength	Amount of time, emotional intensity, intimacy, or reciprocal services (frequency or multiplexity sometimes used as measures of strength of tie).	A and B are close friends, or spend much time together.
Direction	Extent to which link is from one actor to another.	Work flows from A to B, but not from B to A.
Symmetry (reciprocity)	Extent to which relationship is bi-directional.	A asks for B for advice, and B asks A for advice.

of four characteristics: strength (mild distaste to intense hatred), reciprocity (one or both parties dislike the other), cognition (awareness by each party of dislike by the other), and social distance. Social distance refers to whether the negative relationship is direct or whether it involves being connected to someone who has a negative tie to a third party (or extended distance in the network). Being friends with someone who is disliked by others can be a social liability, but disliking a person who is disliked by many others may mitigate social liabilities. Research on negative asymmetry suggests that negative relationships may be more powerful predictors of outcomes than positive relationships. For example, Labianca, Brass, and Gray (1998) found that positive relationships (friends in the other groups) were not related to perception of intergroup conflict, but negative relationships were (someone disliked in the other group).

Focus on Resources

Rather than assume that all nodes (in particular, alters) are the same, some social network researchers have focused on the resources of alters. Lin (1999) has argued that tie strength and the disconnection among alters is of little importance if the alters do not possess resources useful to ego. In response to Granovetter's (1973) findings, Lin, Ensel, and Vaughn (1981) found that weak ties reached higher status alters and that alters' occupational prestige was the key to ego obtaining a high-status job. Lin (1999) reviewed research supporting this resource-based approach to status attainment across a variety

of samples in different countries. While a more complete focus might address the complementarity of ego's and alters' resources, this approach has primarily relied on status indicators. For example, Brass (1984) found that links to the dominant coalition of executives in a company were related to power and promotions for non-managerial employees.

Focus on Attributes

As Kilduff and Tsai (2003, p. 68) note, the study of individual attributes "calls forth various degrees of scorn and dismissal from network researchers." In carving out their structural niche, network researchers have largely ignored individual attributes, with the exception of controlling for various demographic characteristics such as gender. Similarly, the effects of human agency in emerging networks and the ability or motivation of individuals to take advantage of structural positions is missing from most network research. From a structural perspective, individual characteristics such as personality are the result of a historical accumulation of positions in the network structure. Thus, there is ample opportunity for research that investigates how individual characteristics affect network structure (e.g., Mehra, Kilduff, & Brass, 2001) or how individual abilities and motivations might interact with the opportunities and constraints presented by network structures (e.g., Zhou, Shin, Brass, Choi, & Zhang, 2009). Rather than arguing about the relative importance of structure and agency, it may be more useful to determine which structures maximize individual agency. While the centralized structure in Figure 21.1a presents a strong situation and an easy structural prediction, it is difficult to predict the most powerful node in Figure 21.1b without reference to individual attributes.

Focus on Cognition

Rather than viewing networks as "pipes" through which resources flow, the cognitive approach to social networks has focused on networks as "prisms." As reported by Kilduff and Krackhardt (1994), when approached for a loan, the wealthy Baron de Rothschild replied, "I won't give you a loan myself, but I will walk arm-in-arm with you across the floor of the Stock Exchange, and you will soon have willing lenders to spare" (Cialdini, 1989, p. 45). As exemplified by this quote, the cognitive approach to networks focuses on individuals' cognitive interpretations of the network. Kilduff and Krackhardt (1994) found that being perceived to have a prominent friend had more effect on one's reputation for high performance than actually having a prominent friend in the organization. Likewise, Podolny (2001) notes how the market relations between firms are not only affected by the transfer of resources, but also by how third parties perceive the quality of the relationship. You are known by the company you keep. But, cognitive interpretations are not only made by third party observers. Relationships hinge on the cognitive interpretations of actions by the parties involved. For example, we are not likely to form relationships with people whom we perceive as trying to use us. Calculated self-interest in building relationships, if perceived, is self-defeating. Brokers may be perceived as less trustworthy than closely connected members of the groups they connect. I also include in this category studies that focus on individuals' mental maps of networks (e.g., Krackhardt, 1990). The focus on cognition also poses the question of whether the enhanced awareness of social networks (through social networking sites such as Facebook and management consultants offering network workshops) may alter the way people form, maintain, and terminate ties. Such awareness also challenges self-reports as valid sources of network data. Kilduff and Tsai (2003) and Kilduff and Krackhardt (2008) provide more extended discussions of cognition and networks.

Methodological Issues

Social network data may be collected from archival records (interorganizational alliances, e-mail, membership in groups), observations, informant perceptions (interviews or questionnaires), or a combination of these methods. While archival records provide accuracy, it is often difficult to determine what is being exchanged or how to interpret the ties. Observation is very time-consuming, and the chances of missing an important link or misinterpreting an interaction are high. At the interpersonal level, most organizational behavior researchers have used questionnaires to obtain self-reports from actors. People are asked whom they talk with, trust, are friends with, and so forth. Although research has shown that people are not very accurate in reporting specific interactions (Bernard, Killworth, Kronenfeld, & Sailer, 1984), reports of typical, recurrent interactions are reliable and valid (Freeman, Romney, & Freeman, 1987). While recurrent interactions provide a stable picture of the underlying network, recent research (Sasovova, Mehra, Borgatti, & Schippers, 2010) suggests that there may be more "churn" in the network than previously thought.

People can be asked to *list* the names of alters in response to name generators or can be asked to select their alters from a *roster* of all names in the network of interest. While the list method relies on people remembering all important alters and having the time and motivation to list them all, the roster method assumes that the researcher can identify all possible alters prior to data collection. People are more likely to remember their strong ties, so the roster method may be preferable when attempting to tap weak ties, and vice versa. The roster method will almost always result in larger reported networks.

Researchers can collect *ego network* data (typically used when sampling unrelated egos from a large population) or *whole network* data (typically used when collecting data from every ego within a specified network, such as one particular organization). An ego network consists of ego, his direct-link alters, and ties among those alters (Borgatti, 2006). Ego is typically asked to list his direct-link alters and to indicate whether the alters are themselves connected. Such data is limited by ego's ability to accurately describe the connections among direct-tie alters, and many structural network measures cannot be applied to ego network data (i.e., centrality). No attempt is made to collect data on path lengths beyond direct-tie alters. Whole network data consists of archival, observational, or informant reports of all nodes and ties within a specified network (e.g., all organizational alliances within an industry, all friendship relations among employees within a group or an organization). All participants are asked to report their direct ties, and all reports are combined to form the whole network. While the whole network approach does not rely on a single informant and allows the researcher to calculate extended paths and additional structural measures, the danger arises from the possibility of mis-specifying the network (important nodes and links are not included).

Boundary Specification

If it is indeed a small world, bounding the network for research purposes is an important, if seldom addressed, issue. Given the research question, what is the appropriate membership of the network? This involves specifying the number of different types of networks to include, as well as the number of links removed from ego (indirect links) that should be considered. Both decisions have conceptual as well as methodological implications.

In organizational research, formal boundaries exist: work groups, departments, organizations, industries. Seldom have researchers even addressed the issue of how many links (direct and indirect) to include, as the network may extend well beyond ego's direct ties. The importance of this boundary specification is emphasized by Brass's (1984) finding that centrality within departments was positively related to power and promotions, while centrality within the entire organization produced a negative finding. The appropriate number of links has recently garnered renewed attention with the publication of Burt's (2007) findings. He found that second-hand brokerage (structural holes beyond ego's local direct-tie network) did not significantly add to variance in outcomes in three samples from different organizations, justifying his use of data focusing on ego's local, direct-tie network (ego network data). Unlike sexually transmitted diseases, information in organizations tends to decay across paths and including ties three or four steps removed from ego may be unnecessary. As Burt (2007) notes, people may not have the ability or energy to think through the complexity of brokerage in an extended network. He also notes that his results are limited to the brokerage-performance relationship, as several examples exist of the importance of third-party ties (two steps removed from ego): Bian (1997) in finding jobs; Gargiulo (1993) in gaining two-step leverage; Labianca et al. (1998) in perceptions of conflict; and Bowler and Brass (2006) in organizational citizenship behavior.

Whole network measures of structural holes (accounting for longer paths) also have been shown to be significant in predicting power and promotions

(Brass, 1984, 1985a) and performance (Mehra et al., 2001), although Burt (2007) suggests these results may hinge on a strong relationship between direct-tie brokerage and extended brokerage. Although experimental studies of exchange networks have shown that an actor's structural hole power to negotiate (play one alter off against the other) is significantly weakened if the two alters each have an additional link to an alternative negotiating partner (Cook, Emerson, Gilmore, & Yamagishi, 1983), Brass and Burkhardt (1992) found no evidence of this effect in a field study. In sum, there is considerable evidence for both a local and the more extended network approach, and it is likely that debate will ensue and continue. Including the appropriate number of links is likely a function of the research question and the mechanism involved in the flow, but assuredly, researchers will need to attend to and justify their boundaries more explicitly in the future.

The conceptual implications concern the issue of structural determinism and individual agency. Direct relationships are jointly controlled by both parties, and motivation by one party may not be reciprocated. All dance invitations are not accepted. If important outcomes are affected by indirect links (over which ego has even less control), the effects of agency become inversely related to the path distance of alters whose relationships may affect ego. Structural determinism increases to the extent that distant relationships affect ego. For example, a highly publicized study by Fowler and Christakis (2008) found that ego's happiness was predicted by the happiness of people up to three links removed from ego.

Identifying the domain of possible types of relationships (network content) is equally troublesome (see Borgatti & Halgin, 2011, for an extended discussion of network content). Burt (1983) noted that people tend to organize their relationships around four categories: friendship, acquaintance, work, and kinship. Types of networks (the content of the relationships) are sometimes classified as informal versus formal, or instrumental versus expressive (Ibarra, 1992). For example, Grosser, Lopez-Kidwell, and Labianca (2010) found that negative gossip was primarily transmitted through expressive friendship ties, while positive gossip flowed through instrumental ties. However, interpersonal ties often tend to overlap, and it is sometimes difficult to exclusively separate ties on the basis of content.

Conceptually, the issue is one of appropriability. Coleman (1990) included appropriability as a key concept in his notion of social capital. One type of tie may be appropriated for a different use. For example, friendship and workplace ties are often used to sell Girl Scout cookies. Indeed, Granovetter's (1985) critique of economics argued that economic transactions are embedded in, and are affected by, networks of interpersonal relationships (see also Uzzi, 1997). Although the concept of "embeddedness" has been confused in a number of ways, the idea that different types of relationships overlap and that one type of tie may be appropriated for another use casts doubt on the notion that different types of networks produce different outcomes. If different ties are appropriable, the danger of focusing on only one type of tie (e.g., advice) is that other important ties (e.g., friendship) may be missing from the data. Thus, researchers like Burt (1997) typically measure several different types of content and aggregate across content networks. On the other hand, Podolny and Baron's (1997) findings suggest different outcomes from different types of networks, and there is evidence that people prefer their affective and instrumental ties to be embedded in different networks (Ingram & Zou, 2008), as they represent contrasting norms of reciprocity (see also Casciaro & Lobo, 2008). Of course, it is unlikely that negative ties (Labianca & Brass, 2006) can be appropriated for positive use; centrality in a conflict network will certainly lead to different results than centrality in a friendship network.

Levels of Analysis

Social networks are often touted for their ability to integrate micro and macro approaches (Wellman, 1988); they provide the opportunity to simultaneously investigate the whole as well as the parts (Ibarra, Kilduff, & Tsai, 2005). The dyadic relationships are used to compose the network; they are the parts that form the whole. Network measures assigned to individual actors (Table 21.1) are cross-level because they represent the relative position of a part within the whole. Actors also can be clustered into groups or cliques based on their relationships within the network. Thus, it is possible to study the effects of whole network characteristics (e.g., core-periphery structure) on group (e.g., clique formation) and individual (e.g., centrality) characteristics. Combining measures at different levels, researchers might ask how individual centrality within the group interacts with the centralization of the group to affect important outcomes such as power. Although possible, such analyses have rarely been undertaken (see Sasidharen, Santhanam, Brass, & Sambamurthy, 2012, for an exception).

Breiger (1974) notes that when two people interact, they not only represent themselves, but also any formal or informal group/organization of which they are a member. Thus, individual interaction is often assumed to also represent group interaction. For example, CEOs who sit on the same boards of directors are assumed to exchange information that is subsequently diffused through their respective organizations and affects organization outcomes (e.g., Galaskiewicz & Burt, 1991). While the assumptions are not directly tested (Zaheer & Soda, 2009), they provide a convenient compositional model for moving across levels of analysis.

Social Network Theory

Despite reference to an amorphous "social network theory" in the management literature, perhaps the most frequent criticism of the approach is that it represents a set of techniques and measures devoid of theory (but see Borgatti & Halgin, 2011, and Borgatti & Lopez-Kidwell, 2011). Just as Tables 21.1, 21.2, and 21.3 illustrate, it is often easier to catalog the measures than to provide a theoretical explanation for the emergence and persistence of social networks. More often, the measures are used to operationalize constructs suggested by the researcher's favorite theory. Rather than a weakness, the development of sophisticated measures of social structure is a distinctive strength of social network analysis that has allowed researchers from many different disciplines to mathematically represent concepts that were previously only loose metaphors (Wellman, 1988). In the chronology of networks, the first step was to develop mathematical measures to represent structural patterns. Such measures abound and new measures are constantly being developed. For example, the social network software program UCINet (Borgatti, Everett, & Freeman, 2002) includes nine different measures of the concept of positional centrality. With the measures in hand, it was then necessary to show that they relate to important outcomes. Without this step, it made little sense to investigate the emergence of networks (antecedents) or how networks develop and change over time.

Social networks are often equated with social structure (Wellman, 1988). Attitudes and behavior are interpreted in terms of social structure rather than the human capital of the actors. Similar structures produce similar outcomes. At the extreme, "the pattern of relationships is substantially the same as the content" (Wellman, 1988, p. 25). Rather than adopting this extreme position, I rely on structuration theory (Giddens, 1976).

As outlined in Brass (1995a), interaction and communication can be intended and purposeful, or can be unintended, and more or less constrained by factors external to the actors. As Barley (1990) notes, "...while people's actions are undoubtedly constrained by forces beyond their control and outside their immediate present, it is difficult to see how any social structure can be produced or reproduced except through ongoing action and interaction" (pp. 64–65). Whether to satisfy social or instrumental needs, in a general sense, people interact in order to make sense of, and successfully operate on, their environment. As Darwin noted, survival may have gradually nudged humans toward cooperative groups that benefit survival. When the interaction is helpful in this regard, the interaction continues and a relationship is formed. Although interactions may be initially coincidental, repeated interaction is not. Repeated interaction leads to social structure: relatively stable patterns of behavior, interaction, and interpretation. As these patterns emerge from recurrent interaction, they take on the status of predictable "taken-for-granted facts" (Barley, 1990, p. 67). Institutionalized patterns of interaction become external to individuals and constrain their behavior. The constrained behavior in turn further reinforces the socially shared social structure that facilitates future interaction, just as language facilitates communication. However, interactions that occur within the constraints of structure can gradually modify that structure. For example, those persons disadvantaged by the current structural constraints may actively seek to change them, or exogenous shocks may provide the occasion for major restructuring. In attempting to merge the individual and the social structure, I do not ignore individual agency or the structural constraints that may at times render it useless. Structure and behavior are intertwined, each affecting the other. Thus, I proceed to explore the antecedents and outcomes of networks in relation to organizations. I underscore the dynamic nature of structuration theory, noting that antecedents can at times be outcomes and vice versa.

Social Networks: Antecedents
Spatial, Temporal, and Social Proximity

Although the advent of e-mail and social networking sites such as Facebook may moderate the effects of proximity on relationships, the same might have been said for telephones. However, being in the same place at the same time fosters relationships that are easier to maintain and are more likely to be strong, stable links (Borgatti & Cross, 2003;

Festinger, Schachter, & Back, 1950; see Krackhardt, 1994, for the "law of propinquity"). In addition to spatial and temporal proximity, social proximity also fosters relationships. A person is more likely to form a relationship with an alter two links removed (e.g., acquaintance of a friend) than three or more links removed. To the extent that organizational workflow and hierarchy locate employees in physical and temporal space, we can expect additional effects on social networks. Because it would be difficult for a superior and subordinate directly linked by the formal hierarchy to avoid interacting, it would not be surprising for the "informal" social network to shadow the formal hierarchy of authority (or workflow). For example, Tichy and Fombrun (1979) found higher density and connectedness in the interpersonal interaction network in an organic organization than a mechanistic organization. Similarly, Shrader, Lincoln, and Hoffman (1989) found networks of high density, connectivity, multiplexity, and symmetry, and a low number of clusters in organic organizations. Confirming this intuition, Burkhardt and Brass (1990) and Barley (1990) found that communication patterns in an organization changed when the organization adopted a new technology.

Homophily

Spatial, temporal, and social proximity provide opportunities to form relationships, but we do not form relationships with everyone we meet. Social psychologists and sociologists are quite familiar with homophily: a preference for interaction with similar others. A good deal of research has supported this proposition, and it is a basic assumption in many theories (see McPherson, Smith-Lovin, & Cook, 2001, for a cogent review). Similarity has been operationalized on such dimensions as race and ethnicity, age, religion, education, occupation, and gender (roughly in order of importance). People can be similar on many different dimensions. Distinctiveness theory suggests that the salient dimension is the one most distinctive, relative to others in the group (Leonard, Mehra, & Katerberg, 2008; Mehra, Kilduff, & Brass, 1998). As McPherson et al. (2001, p. 415) summarize, similarity breeds connections of every type: marriage, friendship, work, advice, support, information transfer, and co-membership in groups. "The result is that people's personal networks are homogeneous with regard to many sociodemographic, behavioral, and interpersonal characteristics." Similarity is thought to ease communication, to increase predictability of behavior, to foster trust and reciprocity, and to reinforce self-identity. Using electronic name tags to trace interactions at a business mixer, Ingram and Morris (2007) found evidence of associative homophily: a tendency to join conversations when someone in the group was similar. We would expect the characteristics of the links between actors to be related to the degree of actor similarity. Interaction between two similar actors is likely to be more frequent, reciprocated, salient, symmetric, stable, multiplex, strong, and to decay less quickly than interaction between dissimilar actors. Similarity of actors also may be positively related to the density or connectedness of the network. Homophily is not a perfect predictor of relationships, as similarity can also lead to rivalry for scarce resources, and differences may be complementary and combined for successful outcomes. Exceptions can also occur as people aspire to make connections with higher status alters. However, there is little incentive for the higher status person to reciprocate, absent homophily on other characteristics. For example, Brass and Burkhardt (1992) found that interaction patterns were correlated with similar levels of power.

Focusing on gender homophily, Brass (1985a) found two largely segregated networks (one predominately men, the other women) in an organization. Ibarra (1992) also found evidence for homophily in her study of men's and women's networks in an advertising agency. In distinguishing types of networks, she found that women had social support and friendship network ties with other women, but they had instrumental network ties (e.g., communication, advice, influence) with men. Men, on the other hand, had homophilous ties (with other men) across multiple networks, and these ties were stronger. Gibbons and Olk (2003) found that similar ethnic identification led to friendship and similar centrality. Perceived similarity (religion, age, ethnic and racial background, and professional affiliation) among executives has been shown to influence interorganizational linkages (Galaskiewicz. 1979). Although social network measures were not included, research on relational and organizational demography (e.g., Williams & O'Reilly, 1998) has employed the similarity/attraction assumptions. We also would expect similarity of personality and ability to be related to the interpersonal network patterns of interaction.

Due to culture, selection, socialization processes, and reward systems, an organization may exhibit a modal demographic or personality pattern. Kanter (1977) has referred to this process as "homosocial reproduction," consistent with attraction-selection-attrition research (Schneider,

Goldstein, & Smith, 1995). Thus, an individual's similarity in relation to the modal attributes of the organization (or the group) may determine the extent to which he or she is central or integrated in the interpersonal network. This suggests that minorities may be marginalized, and peripheral status and homophily may result in large rather than small world networks for minorities in organizations (Mehra et al., 1998; Singh, Hansen, & Podolny, 2010).

The above discussion implies that interaction in organizations is emergent and unrestricted. However, organizations are by definition organized. Labor is divided. Positions are formally differentiated, both horizontally (by technology. work flow, task design) and vertically (by administrative hierarchy), and the means for coordinating among differentiated positions are specified. Similarity is a relational concept, and organizational coordination requirements may provide opportunities or restrictions on the extent to which a person is similar or dissimilar to others.

Balance

Early studies (DeSoto, 1960) showed that transitive, reciprocal relationships were easier to learn, an indication of how people organize relationships in their minds, with an apparent preference for balance. More recently, Krackhardt and Kilduff (1999) found similar perceptual notions of balance based on distance from ego. Indeed, cognitive balance (Heider, 1958) is often at the heart of network explanations (see Kilduff & Tsai, 2003, for a more complete exploration). A friend of a friend is my friend; a friend of an enemy is my enemy. Granovetter's theory of weak ties assumes a relationship between alters who are both strongly tied to ego. Structurally, balance is seen as transitivity, and efforts have been made to extend the triadic notion of balance to larger networks (Hummon & Doreian, 2003). However, we know that balance is not the sole mechanism for explaining network structure. In a perfectly balanced world, everyone would be part of one giant positive cluster, or two opposing clusters linked by negative ties. The adage "two's company, three's a crowd," also suggests that strong ties to alters do not guarantee that the alters will become friends themselves; rather, they may become rivals for ego's time and attention.

Human and Social Capital

As Lin's (1999) theory of social resources suggests, actors who possess more human capital (skills, abilities, resources, expertise) are going to be more attractive partners than those with less human capital. Indeed, centrality in the advice network may provide a good proxy for expertise. However, affect plays an important role. Casciaro and Lobo (2008) found that when faced with the choice of "competent jerk" or a "lovable fool" as a work partner, people were more likely to choose positive affect over ability. Of course, relationships with persons with more human capital (e.g., status) are tempered by the high-status person's possible reluctance to form a relationship with lower status people. However, in general, it is probably accurate to say that human capital creates social capital. In addition to human capital, those who possess more social capital may be more attractive than those who possess less. For example, forming a relationship with a person with many connections creates opportunities for indirect flows of information and other resources. While Coleman (1990) famously noted that social capital creates human capital, human capital can create social capital, and social capital can create even more social capital.

Personality

Due to the structural aversion to individual attributes, until recently few studies had investigated the effects of personality on network patterns. Mehra et al. (2001) found that high self-monitors were more likely to occupy structural holes in the network (connect to alters who were not themselves connected), and Oh and Kilduff (2008) reinforced these findings in a Korean sample. Self-monitoring refers to an individual's inherent tendency to monitor social cues and to present the image suggested by the audience. Using a battery of personality traits, Kalish and Robins (2006) found that individualism, high locus of control, and neuroticism were related to structural holes, and Klein, Lim, Saltz, and Mayer (2004) found a variety of personality factors related to in-degree centrality in advice, friendship, and adversarial networks. Yet, the results indicated relatively few correlates and minimal, although significant, variance explained. While many other network measures and personality traits might be correlated, the results suggest that strong theoretical rationale is needed.

Culture

Organizational and national culture also may be reflected in social network patterns. For example, French employees prefer weak links at work, whereas Japanese workers tend to form strong,

multiplex ties (Monge & Eisenberg, 1987). Lincoln, Hanada, and Olson (1981) found that vertical differentiation was positively related to personal ties and work satisfaction for Japanese and Japanese Americans. Horizontal differentiation had negative effects on these workers. In addition, in Chinese cooperative high-tech firms, Xiao and Tsui (2007) found that bridging structural holes could be likened to "standing in two boats." More research is needed to fully understand how culture may affect social networks (see Pachucki & Breiger, 2010 for an extended discussion of networks and culture). In particular, research suggests that cooperative versus competitive cultures may be an important moderator of network effects.

Clusters and Bridges

Proximity, homophily, and balance predict that the world will be organized into clusters of close friends with similar demographics and values. Indeed, it is nice to be surrounded by people with the same values, whom you can trust and upon whom you can rely for social support. We add to this the tendency for friends to reinforce each other and become even more similar. As Feld (1981) notes, activities are often organized around "social foci"—actors with similar demographics, attitudes, and behaviors will meet in similar settings, interact with each other, and enhance that similarity. In-group/out-group biases foster tightly knit cliques. Yet, it is the bridges—people who connect different clusters—that make it a "small world." Figure 21.2 represents the clusters and bridges thought to portray the way in which the world's relationships are organized.

Whether these clusters represent the volunteers in Nebraska and lawyers in Boston, different departments in an organization, different ethnic groups, or, as is the case in this diagram from Rob Cross, an organization's R&D departments in different countries (Cross, Parker, & Sasson, 2003), it is the bridges that make it possible for information or resources to flow from one cluster to another. As Travers and Milgram (1969) noted, letters that circulated among friends within the same cluster did not reach the lawyer in Boston. The letter reached its destination only when it was sent to a bridge that allowed it to move away from the cluster.

With the strong preferences for homophily and balance, what then motivates a person to connect with a different cluster? As Granovetter (1973) and Burt (1992) argue, there are advantages to connecting to those who are not themselves connected. Information circulates within a cluster and soon

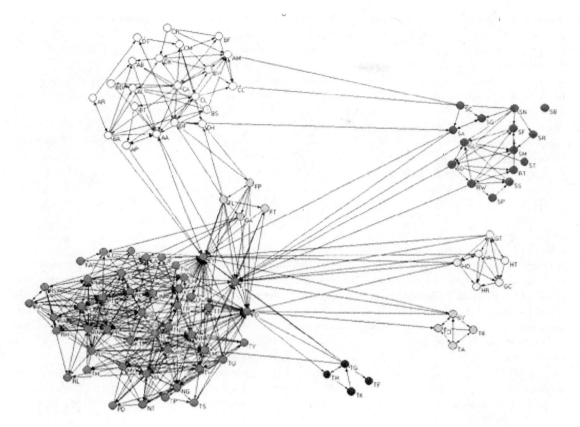

Figure 21.2 Cluster and Bridges

becomes redundant. Connecting to diverse clusters provides novel information and different perspectives, which can lead to creativity and innovation (as well as finding a better job).

A variety of factors can affect social networks. Obviously, the influences are complex and the effects cross levels of analysis. Additional influences remain to be explored. In addition, few studies have examined more than one influence. Multivariate studies encompassing multiple theories and multiple levels of analysis are needed to begin to understand the complex interactions involved among the factors (Monge & Contractor, 2003).

Social Networks: Outcomes

Returning to structuration theory, network patterns emerge and become routinized and act as both constraints on, and facilitators of, behavior. I now turn to the outcomes of these networks, noting that the antecedents are only of interest if the networks affect important outcomes. I focus on traditional I/O topics and outcomes. Network research has followed two classes of outcomes: how people are the same (e.g., contagion/diffusion studies) and how people are different (e.g., performance studies) based on their networks. I begin with attitude similarity.

Attitude Similarity: Contagion

Just as I noted the propensity for similar actors to interact, theory and research have also noted that those who interact become more similar (sometimes referred to as induced homophily). Asch's (1951) classic experiments on conformity demonstrate how individuals can be influenced by others. Erickson (1988) provides the theory and research concerning the "relational basis of attitudes." People are not born with their attitudes, nor do they develop them in isolation. Attitude formation occurs primarily through social interaction—people attempt to make sense of reality by comparing their own perceptions with those of others—in particular, similar others. Attitudes of dissimilar others have little effect, and may even be used to reinforce one's own attitudes.

Attitude similarity has received much research attention under the general heading of "contagion."

Much writing has focused on the role of social networks in adoption and diffusion of innovations (cf. Burt, 1982; Rogers, 1971). These studies generally show that cosmopolitans (i.e., actors with external ties that cross social boundaries) are more likely to introduce innovations than are locals (Rogers, 1971). Likewise, central actors, sometimes identified as "opinion leaders," are unlikely to be early adopters of innovations when the innovation is not consistent with the established norms of the group (Rogers, 1971). The network studies focus on the spread of diseases as well as new ideas.

The classic study of the diffusion of tetracycline among physicians (Coleman, Katz, & Menzel, 1957) showed the influence of networks on the prescriptions written for the new drug. However, reanalysis of the original data indicated that adoption was more a matter of occupying similar positions in the network (structural equivalence) than direct interaction. According to Burt (1987), actors cognitively compare their own attitudes and behaviors with those of others occupying similar roles, rather than being influenced by direct communications from others in dissimilar roles. Likewise, Galaskiewicz and Burt (1991) found similar evaluations of nonprofit organizations among structurally equivalent contributions officers, and structural equivalence explained these contagion effects better than the direct contact "cohesion" approach. Walker (1985) found that structurally equivalent individuals had similar cognitive judgments of means-ends relationships regarding product success.

However, supporting a direct connection, cohesion approach, Davis (1991) showed how the "poison pill" diffused through the network of intercorporate ties. Likewise, Rice and Aydin (1991) found that attitudes about new technology were similar to those with whom employees communicated frequently and immediate supervisors. However, estimates of others' attitudes were not correlated with others' actual (reported) attitudes. In another study, Rentsch (1990) found that members of an accounting firm who interacted with each other had similar interpretations of organizational events, and that these meanings differed qualitatively across different interaction groups. Krackhardt and Kilduff (1990) found that friends had similar perceptions of others in the organization, even when controlling for demographic and positional similarities. In a longitudinal study following a technological change, Burkhardt (1994) found attitude similarity among both structurally equivalent actors and those with direct links. While the debate about structural equivalence versus direct interaction generated several studies, research interest decreased as it became apparent that both have an effect. In addition, the Coleman et al. (1957) data that generated the original debate has been reanalyzed several times, with each reanalysis refuting the previous one (see Kilduff & Oh, 2006, for an in-depth history and summary of results). Recent similarity studies have been more concerned with the topics of leadership (Pastor, Meindl, & Mayo, 2002), perceptions of justice (Umphress, Labianca, Brass, Kass, & Scholten, 2003) and affect (Totterdell, Wall, Holman, Diamond, & Epitropaki, 2004) than with the previous structural equivalence/cohesion debate.

The small-world model of bridges to disconnected clusters provides the underlying theory for the far-reaching and rapid spread of information. While this model works well when considering contagious diseases, or information about job openings, where a single contact is all that is needed for diffusion, the adoption of social behavior (such as innovations) may be more complex than the spread of disease (Centola, 2010). A change in social behavior may require redundant exposure from multiple contacts providing the reinforcement necessary to promote adoption. In an Internet experimental study, Centola (2010) found that adoption was more likely when participants received "redundant" encouragement from multiple ties. In addition to fostering behavioral change, redundant ties also provide credibility or verification of information and make one less dependent on single sources of such information or other resources (Brass & Halgin, 2012). While strong ties and the inverse of structural holes may provide good proxies for redundant ties, friends may be sources of non-redundant information, and disconnected contacts may provide the same redundant information. Brass and Halgin (2011) propose a focus on redundant *content* (what flows through the connections) in place of, or in addition to, redundant *positions* in the network. While everyone needs to know a doctor or a car mechanic, having a redundant backup mechanic provides a second opinion that we often find useful. Rather than avoiding redundancy, redundant contacts may represent an additional source of social capital.

Job Satisfaction

Early laboratory studies (see Shaw, 1964, for review) found that central actors were more satisfied than peripheral actors in these small (typically five-person) groups, and Roberts and O'Reilly (1979) found that relative isolates (zero or one link) in the communication network were less satisfied than participants (two or more links). However, Brass (1981) found no relationship between satisfaction and centrality (closeness) in the work flow of work groups or departments and a negative relationship to centrality within the entire organization's work flow. Brass (1981) suggested that this latter finding may be due to the routine jobs associated with the core technology of the organization. Job characteristics mediated the relationship between work flow network measures and job satisfaction (Brass, 1981; Ibarra & Andrews, 1993).

Although more research is needed, these limited results suggest that there may be a curvilinear relationship such that isolation is probably negatively related to satisfaction, while a high degree of centrality may lead to conflicting expectations, communication overload, and stress. In addition, interaction is not always positive. When possible, we tend to avoid interaction with people we dislike, thereby producing a positive correlation between interaction and friendship. However, work requirements place constraints on the voluntary nature of social interaction in organizations. The possibility that such required interaction may involve negative outcomes suggests the need for further research on the negative side of social interaction (Labianca & Brass, 2006).

Affect

Focusing on affect rather than job satisfaction, Totterdell et al. (2004) found that membership in a densely connected group was negatively related to negative affective states, and reductions in network density (due to a merger) were related to negative changes in affect. While interest in job satisfaction has waned, research on affect in organizations has dramatically increased (Barsade, Brief, & Spataro, 2003; George & Brief, 1992). Of particular interest to network researchers is emotional contagion: the transfer and diffusion of moods and emotions within work groups to the point of suggesting constructs such as group emotion (Barsade, 2002).

Power

A variety of studies and setting have noted that central network positions are associated with power (Brass, 1984, 1985a; Brass & Burkhardt, 1993; Burkhardt & Brass, 1990; Fombrun, 1983; Krackhardt, 1990; Shaw, 1964; Sparrowe & Liden, 2005). Theoretically, actors in central network positions have greater access to relevant resources (decreasing their dependence on others), and

potential control over such resources (increasing others' dependence on them). Thus, two measures of centrality—closeness (representing access), and betweenness (representing control)—correspond to resource dependence notions (Brass, 1984; Brass, 2002). Both measures have been shown to contribute to the variance in reputational measures of power, and to promotions in organizations (Brass, 1984, 1985a). In addition, simple degree centrality measures of the size of one's ego network (symmetric and asymmetric) have been associated with power (Brass & Burkhardt, 1992, 1993; Burkhardt & Brass, 1990), including degree centrality in the gossip network (Grosser, Lopez-Kidwell, Labianca, & Ellwardt (2011).

Studying non-supervisory employees, Brass (1984) found that links beyond the work group and work flow requirements were related to influence. In particular, closeness to the dominant coalition in the organization was strongly related to power and promotions. The dominant coalition was identified by a clique analysis of the interaction patterns of the top executives in the company. In a follow-up study (Brass, 1985a), men were more closely linked to the dominant coalition (composed of four men) and were perceived as more influential than women, even when controlling for performance. Assuming male domination of powerful executive positions in many organizations, women may be forced to forgo any preference for homophily in order to build connections with the dominant coalition. Thus, the organizational context places constraints on preferences for homophily, especially for women and minorities (Ibarra, 1993). Women in integrated work groups (at least two men and two women) and who were closely connected to the men's network (only male employees considered) were perceived as more powerful than women who were not. However, there were also power benefits for men who had links (closeness centrality) to the women's network (only women employees considered; Brass, 1985a).

Sparrowe and Liden (2005) related betweenness centrality in the advice network to power and also found a three-way interaction between leader-member exchange relationships (LMX), supervisor centrality, and overlap between supervisor and subordinate network. Subordinates benefited from trusting LMX relationships with central supervisors who shared their network connections (sponsorship). When leaders were low in centrality, sharing ties in their trust network was detrimental.

In integrating the structural perspective with the behavioral perspective, Brass and Burkhardt (1993) found that network position was related to behavioral tactics used, that both network position and behavioral tactics were independently related to perceptions of power, and that each mediated the relationship between the other and power. While network position may represent potential power, behavioral tactics represent the strategic use of resources. Behavioral tactics increased in importance as network position decreased in strength.

One such tactic, building coalitions, has been investigated from a network perspective (Murnighan & Brass, 1991; Stevenson, Pearce, & Porter, 1985). Murnighan and Brass (1991) suggest that coalitions form around issues; actors are connected on the basis of common attitudes about, or mutual support, of an issue, and networks change as issues change. Although recurring interactions based on affect, advice, or work flow may provide a probable template for coalition activity, issue networks are more fleeting. Forming successful coalitions requires an accurate knowledge of the network. Adopting a cognitive approach, Krackhardt (1990) found that the accuracy of individual cognitive maps of the social network in an organization was related to perceptions of influence. In a case analysis, Krackhardt (1992) also demonstrated how a lack of knowledge of the social networks in a firm prevented a union from successfully organizing employees.

Recruitment and Selection

In the classic example of the strength of weak ties, people were able to find jobs more effectively through weak ties (acquaintances) than strong ties or formal listings (Granovetter, 1982). Subsequent studies reinforced and modified those results (Lin et al., 1981; Wegener, 1991). Weak ties used in finding jobs led to higher status jobs when the weak ties connected the job seekers to those of higher occupational status, forming the foundation for Lin's (1999) theory focusing on the resources of alters. For example, Halgin (2009) found effects for connections to high-status others on hiring decisions, even when controlling for previous performance.

Focusing on the employer side of the labor market, Fernandez and colleagues (Fernandez, Castilla, & Moore, 2000; Fernandez & Weinberg, 1997) investigated the use of employee referral networks in recruitment and selection of bank employees. Organizations often provide monetary bonuses to employees who provide referrals who are eventually hired by the company and who remain for a specified period of time. Using employee networks for recruitment and selection is thought to provide a richer pool of applicants, a better match between referred applicants and job requirements, and social enrichment (referred applicants when hired have already established social connections to the referring employee). All three mechanisms suggest that referred hires are less likely to quit. Fernandez and Weinberg (1997) found that referred applicants had more appropriate resumes and timing, but these did not explain referrals' advantage in hiring. Fernandez et al. (2000) also found support for the richer pool explanation, but did not find that referred applicants were better informed of job requirements (better match argument). There was some evidence of the social enrichment mechanism at work (interdependence of turnover between referrers and referrals). In a cost analysis, they found that the $250 monetary bonus resulted in a return of $416 in reduced recruiting costs. They also found evidence of homophily in hiring referrals, suggesting the danger of homosocial reproduction in organizations (Kanter, 1977). However, a diverse pool of existing employees can lead to continued diversity in the workforce. Consistent with the referral hiring advantage, Seidel, Polzer, and Stewart (2000) found that hires with previous connections in the organization were able to negotiate higher salaries than those with no previous connections. Likewise, Williamson and Cable (2003) found that firms hired top management team members from sources with whom they shared network ties. They also noted social contagion effects among firms in their hiring practices. Similarly, in a qualitative study, Leung (2003) found that entrepreneurial firms tended to rely on strong, direct ties in the recruitment and selection of employees.

As in the case of recruiting via the use of networks, selection may also depend on network ties, particularly when the qualified applicant pool is large or when hiring standards are ambiguous. In such cases, similarity between applicant and recruiter may be an important basis of the selection choice. Because of the overlap between social networks and actor and attitude similarity, selection research might fruitfully pursue the effects of patterns of social relationships on hiring decisions.

In a case study, Burt and Ronchi (1990) analyzed hiring practices in an organization in which conflict had escalated to the point of shootings and bomb threats. Using archival data provided in the application forms of current employees, they matched the pattern of hiring with the warring factions in the company. The network analyses showed how a manager had virtually taken control of the company years earlier by hiring family, friends, and friends of friends, from a close geographical location surrounding his community. The conflicts arose between those people obligated to the manager and others hired from a rival community. The network structure was also used to identify employees with links to both groups who could serve as mediators of the conflict (Burt & Ronchi, 1990).

Socialization

Following selection, network involvement may play a key role in the socialization and commitment of new employees (Eisenberg, Monge, & Miller, 1984; Jablin & Krone, 1987; Sherman, Smith, & Mansfield, 1986). Similarly, Morrison (2002) found that network size, density, tie strength, and range were related to organizational knowledge, task mastery, and role clarity. Newcomers' friendship networks related to their social integration and organizational commitment. However, because network integration and socialization and commitment may be reciprocally causal, it is impossible to know from these correlational studies whether integration into the network leads to commitment, or vice versa.

Training

Few studies address social networks or provide a structural perspective on training (Brass, 1995a). If training is viewed as acquiring new and innovative ideas and skills, once training is introduced or adopted, the diffusion of the training (or the spread of new ideas and skills) can be predicted by social network relationships. For example, Burkhardt and Brass (1990) investigated the introduction, training, and diffusion of a major technological change in an organization. The diffusion process closely followed the network patterns following the change, with structurally equivalent employees adopting it at similar times.

In a similar study of the introduction of a new computer technology, Papa (1990) found that productivity following the change, as well as speed of learning the new technology, was positively related to interaction frequency, network size, and network diversity (i.e., number of different departments and hierarchical levels contacted). While formal training programs can provide basic operating information, much of the learning about a new technology occurs in on-the-job exchange of information as employees attempt to apply the training (Sasidharen et al., 2012). Exchanging information with others had a positive effect on productivity, even when controlling for past performance (Papa, 1990).

Training may also be viewed as an opportunity to build social connections among participants. Deep and lasting relationships can be formed when cohorts proceed through intense training experiences (e.g., military training) or through life experiences in college (Brass, 1995a). Organizations may form cross-functional training groups that promote network connections across diverse, heterogeneous groups, or may encourage "staff swaps" to integrate distinct subcultures in organizations (Krackhardt & Hanson, 1993). However, mandated interaction does not always lead to stable links, and longitudinal research is needed to map network connections formed during training.

Career Development: Getting Ahead

Subsequent to Granovetter's strength of weak ties, Burt's 1992 book, *Structural Holes,* was perhaps the most influential research in propelling studies of social networks. Burt (1992) argued that the size of one's network is not as important as the pattern of relationships; in particular, the extent to which your contacts are not themselves connected (creating a "structural hole" in your network). Based on Simmel's (1950) analysis of triads, Burt (1992) noted the advantages of the *tertius gaudens* (i.e., "the third who benefits"). Not only does the tertius gain non-redundant information from the contacts (i.e., the strength of weak ties argument), but the tertius is in a position to control the information flow between the two (i.e., broker the relationship), or to play the two off against each other. The tertius profits from the disunion of others. However, in order to play one off against the other, the two alters need to be somewhat redundant, offsetting any advantage gained from non-redundant information. In addition, the irony of the structural hole strategy is that connecting to any previously disconnected alter creates brokerage opportunities for the alter as well as for ego (Brass, 2009). Without entirely ignoring the strength of ties, Burt (1992) argued that a direct, structural measure of disconnection among alters was preferable to the weak-tie proxy. Contrasted with Coleman's (1990) and Putnam's (1995) conceptualization of social capital as trust generated by closed networks, Burt's (1992) focus on the social capital of structural holes led to a tremendous number of research studies.

Using the criterion of rate of previous early promotions, Burt (1992) found the presence of structural holes to be effective for a sample of 284 managers in a large, high-technology firm, except in the case of women and newly hired managers. For women and newcomers, a strong tie pattern of connecting to well-connected sponsors worked best. Burt, Hogarth, and Michaud (2000) replicated the benefits of structural holes for French managers using salary as the dependent variable. Often cited in support of Burt's (1992) structural hole hypothesis, Podolny and Baron (1997) found that an upward change in grade shift during the previous year (mobility) was related to large, sparse networks. Unlike Burt (1992), who aggregated across five different networks, Podolny and Baron (1997) found that in one of the five networks (the "buy-in" network) dense connections were advantageous, providing what Podolny and Baron (1997) suggested was an identity advantage of closed networks. They argue that the content of the network makes a difference. Because the network data in each of the above studies were not longitudinal, it is difficult to discern whether the networks were the result of promotions or the cause of promotions (although Podolny & Baron, 1997, eliminated ties formed following promotions). However, previous studies by Brass (1984, 1985a) support Burt's (1992) contention, finding that betweenness centrality (a whole network measure of structural holes within departments) led to promotions for both men and women three years following the network data collection. Supporting Lin's (1999) resource approach, Brass (1984) also found that connections to the dominant coalition (a highly connected group of top executives) were significantly related to promotions.

In a study of 1,359 Dutch managers, Boxman, De Graaf, and Flap (1991) found that external work contacts and memberships related to income attainment and level of position (number of subordinates) for both men and women when controlling for human capital (education and experience). The return on human capital decreased as social capital increased. In a study combining different network approaches (structural, relational, resource, and attribute) and measuring flows, Seibert et al. (2001) found that both weak ties and structural holes in career advice network were related to social resources, which, in turn, were related to salary, promotions over one's career, and career satisfaction.

Individual Performance

As with promotions, Burt's (1992) structural hole theory has also been applied to individual performance in organizations. Supporting this approach, Mehra et al. (2001) found that betweenness centrality was related to supervisors' ratings of performance. Likewise, Mizruchi and Stearns

(2001) found that density (few structural holes) and hierarchy (dominated by one or a few persons) in approval networks negatively related to closing bank deals. Network size was positively related, and strength of tie was negative. Also supporting structural holes, Cross and Cummings (2004) found that ties to diverse others related to performance in knowledge-intensive work. Finally, Burt (2007) reports relationships between structural holes and performance for three samples: supply chain managers (salary and performance evaluations), investment bankers (annual compensation), and financial analysts (election to the Institutional Investor All-American Research Team). Sparrowe, Liden, Wayne, and Kraimer (2001) found that in-degree centrality in the advice network was positively related to supervisor ratings of performance, but they did not include measures of structural holes in their analysis. Different findings were reported in one study (Lazega, 2001), indicating that constraint (lack of structural holes) positively related to performance (billings) in a U.S. law firm. Lazega (2001) extensively describes the cooperative, sharing culture in the law firm, suggesting a cooperation/competition contingency. Supporting the notion of a cooperation contingency, Xiao and Tsui (2007) found that structural holes had a negative effect on salary and bonuses in high-commitment organizations in the collectivist culture of China. They liken the structural hole position to a Chinese cultural interpretation of "standing in two boats." Noting the difference in being the object of directional relationships, rather than the source (Burt & Knez, 1995), Gargiulo, Ertug, and Galunic (2009) found that closed networks were beneficial (bonus) for information seekers, but not information providers. Although the data in the above studies are cross-sectional, and some evidence suggests a cooperation/competition contingency, there seems to be solid support for the structural hole–performance relationship.

Adopting a cognitive focus on performance, Kilduff and Krackhardt (1994) found that being perceived as having a powerful friend in the organization related to one's reputation for good performance, although actually having a powerful friend was not related to reputation. While being closely linked to a powerful other may result in "basking in the reflected glory," it may also result in being perceived as "second fiddle" or "riding the coattails" of a powerful other. Strong connections to a mentor may be perceived as an indication of potential success early in one's career, but as second fiddle late in one's career. The reliance on a mentor's network creates a dependency on the mentor to mediate the flow of resources; thus, a strong tie to the mentor (or high LMX with one's supervisor) may be required (Sparrowe & Liden, 2005).

Group Performance

A variety of studies have investigated the effects of interpersonal network patterns on group performance. Uzzi (1997) described how embedded relationships characterized by trust, fine-grain information, and joint problem solving can have both positive and negative economic outcomes for small firms in the garment industry. Firms can become over-embedded and miss economic opportunities presented by "arms-length" transactions. Hansen (1999) found that weak interunit ties speed up group project completion times when needed information is simple, but slow them down when knowledge to be transferred is complex. He concludes that weak ties help search activities; strong ties help knowledge transfer. Of course, employees must know who knows what in the organization (Borgatti & Cross, 2003). Tsai (2001) noted that in-degree centrality in knowledge-transfer network (among units) interacted with absorptive capacity to predict business unit innovation and performance.

Much of the work on interpersonal networks and group performance has been done by Reagans, Zuckerman, and McEvily (2004), who conclude that internal density and external range in knowledge-sharing networks related to group performance (as measured by project duration). Similarly, Oh, Chung, and Labianca (2004) found that internal density (inverted U relationship) and number of bridging relationships to external groups in an informal socializing network related to group performance (as rated by executives). A meta-analysis by Balkundi and Harrison (2006) showed that density within teams, leader centrality in teams, and team centrality in intergroup networks related to various performance measures. These studies provide a solution to the debate about structural holes and cohesion. Teams benefit from internal cohesion and external links to other groups that are not themselves connected.

Leadership

Despite early laboratory studies showing that central actors in centralized group structures were overwhelmingly chosen as leaders (Leavitt, 1951; see Shaw, 1964, for a review), there have been few empirical studies of networks and leadership (see Balkundi & Kilduff, 2005, Brass & Krackhardt,

1999, and Sparrowe & Liden, 1997, for theoretical articles). An exception is Mehra, Dixon, Brass, and Robertson (2006), who found that leaders' centrality in external and internal friendship networks was related to objective measures of group performance and to their personal reputations for leadership among different organizational constituencies.

Job Design

Although traditional research on job design (e.g., Hackman & Oldham, 1976) waned in the 1990s, an early study by Brass (1981) found that job characteristics (e.g., task variety and autonomy) mediated relationships between workflow centrality in the work group and employee satisfaction and performance. Centrality within the entire organization's work flow network (rather than the smaller work groups) was negatively related to job characteristics (Brass, 1981). These latter jobs in the organization's technical core were routinized, while the jobs on the boundary of the organization were more complex. In a follow-up study, Brass (1985b) used network techniques to identify pooled, sequential, and reciprocal interdependencies within work groups. Performance varied according to combinations of technological uncertainty, job characteristics, and network patterns. The results suggest that performance is best when the networks match the task and work flow requirements, possible contingency factors noted by Burt (2000). For example, laboratory studies (see Shaw, 1964, for a review) found that centralized communication networks (e.g., Figure 21.1a) resulted in more efficient performance when tasks were simple and routine. For complex, uncertain tasks, decentralized networks (e.g., Figure lb) were better. For a summary of the recent resurgence in job design from a social perspective, see Grant and Parker (2009).

Turnover

While job satisfaction is often related to turnover, Mossholder, Settoon, and Heneghan (2005) found that in-degree centrality (combined advice and communication networks) added significant variance to satisfaction in predicting turnover over a five-year study window. Krackhardt and Porter (1986) found that turnover in fast-food restaurants did not occur randomly, but in structurally equivalent clusters in the perceived interpersonal communication network. In a longitudinal study, Krackhardt and Porter (1985) also investigated the effects of turnover on the attitudes of those who remained in the organization. The closer the employee was to those who left, the more satisfied and committed the remaining employee became, suggesting that the remaining employees cognitively justified their decision to stay by increasing their satisfaction and commitment. Although Krackhardt & Porter (1985, 1986) used cognitive network data, they did not focus on the extent to which turnover in the network provides a signal (prism effect) that activates or justifies additional turnover or whether a threshold effect leads to massive exits detrimental to the organization's survival. Focusing on organizational performance, Shaw, Duffy, Johnson, and Lockhart (2005) investigated the effects of turnover of key network actors (above and beyond turnover rate and individual performance) on the organizational performance of 38 restaurants. They found support for a curvilinear relationship between the loss of employees who occupied structural holes in the network and organizational performance.

Justice

According to equity theory (Adams, 1965), employees compare their perceived input outcome ratios with their perceptions of others' input/outcome ratios. The problem of testing equity predictions outside the laboratory has been the large number of possible "others" that might be considered for possible comparison. Noting this problem, Shah (1998) found that people rely on structurally equivalent others in making task-related comparisons and friends when making social comparisons.

Although justice research has always been relational, few studies have progressed past the dyadic comparison. Degoey (2000, p. 51) notes that the "often ambiguous and emotionally charged nature of justice-related events" compels actors to make sense of these events through social interaction. He provides an extensive review and hypotheses concerning "storytelling" and the social construction and maintenance of shared justice perceptions over time. Building on this work, Shapiro, Brass, and Labianca (2008) theorize about how network patterns might affect the diffusion and durability of perceptions of inequity.

Negotiations

Few topics have generated as much research over the past 40 years as negotiations (see Bazerman, Curhan, Moore, & Valley, 2000, for a review). Despite the many empirical studies, social relationships have been relatively neglected (Valley, Neale, & Mannix, 1995), and even fewer studies have gone beyond the negotiating dyad (Valley, White,

& Iacobucci, 1992) to consider triadic relations or the entire network. Yet, it is likely that the social networks of negotiators will affect both the process and outcomes of negotiations. To the extent that negotiations involve the exercise of power, the network findings regarding centrality should provide some clues as to asymmetric advantages. Structural holes may provide useful, non-redundant information or may tap into transaction alternatives that can be played off against each other, while overlaps in negotiators' networks may provide the closure necessary for trust, reciprocity, and mutually beneficial outcomes. While Granovetter (1985) and Uzzi (1997) have demonstrated how economic transactions are embedded in social relations, McGinn and Keros (2002) have shown how such social ties ease coordination within a negotiation and allow for an improvised shared logic of exchange that facilitates negotiation. Thus, the structural results of network analysis may add predictive power to negotiation research, while the more cognitive and behavioral insights from negotiation research may provide the understanding of the process mechanisms often missing from network analysis.

Conflict

Focusing on the overall pattern of ties in 20 organizations, Nelson (1989) found that low-conflict organizations were characterized by more strong ties between members of different groups than in high-conflict organizations. However, when including negative ties, Labianca et al. (1998) found that friendship ties across groups were not related to perceptions of intergroup conflict, but negative relationships (measured as "prefer to avoid" a person) were related to higher perceived conflict. Third-party relationships (having friends who reported negative relationships across groups) also related to perceptions of intergroup conflict. While psychologists have studied dyadic conflict, the third-party results suggest that future research might investigate the contagion effects of conflict—how it escalates and moves (or is dampened or resolved) through social networks.

Citizenship Behavior

Despite a tremendous amount of research on organizational citizenship behavior (e.g., Bateman & Organ, 1983; Podsakoff, MacKenzie, Paine, & Bachrach, 2000), very few studies of this topic have adopted a social network perspective. Many of the studies focus on a perceived equity exchange between the employee and the organization.

Rather than focusing on the employee/organization exchange, Bowler and Brass (2006) investigated affective exchange between employees. Interpersonal citizenship behavior (as reported by recipients of the behavior) was significantly related to friendship, even when controlling for job satisfaction, commitment, procedural justice, hierarchical level, demographic similarity, and job similarity. People also performed helping behavior for more powerful others and friends of more powerful others. Settoon and Mossholder (2002) found that indegree centrality related to supervisors' ratings of person- and task-focused interpersonal citizenship behavior. Reversing the causality, Bolino, Turnley, and Bloodgood (2002) argue that organizational citizenship behavior can result in the creation of social capital within an organization. They provide a theoretical model of how Van Dyne, Graham, and Dienesch's (1994) five OCB dimensions can foster ties that can be appropriated for other uses, can foster relationships characterized by liking, trust, and identification, and can promote shared narratives and language.

Creativity/Innovation

Fueled by the notion that creativity often involves the synthesis or recombination of different ideas or perspectives, researchers have looked beyond individual cognitive processes for social sources of diverse knowledge (Amabile, 1996), such as an individual's network (Perry-Smith & Shalley, 2003). Following Granovetter (1973), Brass (1995b) proposed that weak ties should provide non-redundant information and thereby increase creativity. Burt (2004) found that ideas submitted by managers with structural holes were judged by top executives to be more creative than managers with few structural holes. Perry-Smith (2006) found effects for weak ties, but not structural holes (using the whole network measure of betweenness centrality) on supervisor ratings of employee creativity. Using a similar measure of employee creativity in a Chinese sample, Zhou et al. (2009) found a curvilinear relationship between weak ties and creativity, but no relationship for structural holes. They argue that weak ties not only capture non-redundant information between alters but also capture homophily effects between ego and alters. This is also one of the few studies to investigate an interaction between individual attributes and networks. They found an interaction between conformity values and weak ties. People with low conformity values were able to take advantage of the opportunities presented by weak ties.

Viewing innovation as the implementation of creative ideas, Obstfeld (2005) focused on a *tertius iugens* orientation: the tendency to bring people together by closing structural holes. Ego network density (few structural holes) aggregated across several networks related to involvement in innovation. Density positively related to structural holes suggesting that closing holes may lead to reciprocation. Obstfeld's (2005) findings were consistent with an earlier study (Ibarra, 1993) that found centrality (asymmetric Bonacich measure) across five networks related to involvement in technical and administrative innovations. Obstfeld (2005) argued that structural holes may lead to creative ideas, but innovation requires the cooperation of closed networks. Focusing on utility patents, Fleming, Mingo, and Chen (2007) found that collaborative brokerage (structural holes) helped generate patents but hampered their diffusion and use by others.

Unethical Behavior

In his critique of economics, Granovetter (1985) noted how social relationships and structure affect trust and malfeasance. Economic transactions are embedded in social relationships, and actors do not always pursue self-interests to the detriment of social relationships. Brass, Butterfield, and Skaggs (1998) built on these ideas within the context of ethics research. They argue that the constraints of various types of relationships (strength, status, multiplexity, asymmetry) and the network structure of relationships (density, cliques, structural holes, centrality) on unethical behavior will increase as the constraints of characteristics of individuals, organizations, and issues decrease, and vice versa. However, such predictions are extremely difficult to test in natural settings. One exceptional paper, Baker and Faulkner (1993), focused on price-fixing conspiracies (illegal networks) in the heavy electrical equipment industry. In this network study, convictions, sentences, and fines related to personal centrality, network structure (decentralized), and management level (middle).

Conclusion: Challenges and Opportunities

Overall, I have attempted to demonstrate how a social network perspective might contribute to our understanding of organizational psychology. In the process, I have tried to note challenges and opportunities for future research. While the structural perspective has provided a useful niche for social network research, measuring the pattern of nodes and ties challenges the researcher to provide explanations of why these patterns of social relations lead to organizational outcomes. While the network provides a map of the highways, seldom is the traffic measured (Brass, 1984; Stevenson & Gilly, 1991). For example, various explanations are provided for the benefits of structural holes (Burt, 1992). Ego may play one alter off against another, ego may acquire non-redundant information or other helpful resources, ego may recognize a synergistic opportunity and act on it herself, or ego may refer one alter to the other and benefit from future reciprocation. Or, ego may simply be mediating a conflict between the two alters. Similarly, network closure is assumed to provide trust and norms of reciprocation, but seldom are these explanatory mechanisms verified. Future network research will need to measure the processes and mechanisms to get a fuller understanding of the value of particular structural patterns.

In establishing the predictive value of a structural perspective, network researchers have emphasized the importance of relationships to the detriment of individual agency. Although few organizational network scholars deny the importance of human capital and individual agency, few efforts have been made to tap the hallmark of industrial/organizational psychology: the ability and motivation of actors. While network researchers have begun to include personality variables, it was previously assumed that, other things being equal, actors would be capable and motivated to take advantage of network opportunities (or equally constrained by existing structures). Researchers will not only need to account for ability and motivation, but also identify strong structures that overwhelm individual agency (i.e., Figure 21.1a) and weak structures that maximize individual differences (i.e., Figure 21.1b). It is likely that individual attributes will interact with network structure to affects outcomes (e.g., Zhou et al., 2009).

The next logical growth in network research is the evolution of networks—how they change over time. Although there are few longitudinal studies of network change at the individual level (e.g., Barley, 1990; Burkhardt & Brass, 1990), interorganizational scholars are now leading the boom via the use of archival, longitudinal, alliance data (e.g., Gulati, 2007). In addition, network scholars have actively devised computer simulations of network change (e.g., Buskens & van de Rijt, 2008; Gilbert & Abbott, 2005). Several questions beg for research. How are ties maintained, and what causes them to decay or be severed (Burt, 2002; Shah, 2000)? What are the effects of past ties, and can dormant, inactive, past ties be reactivated (Levin, Walter, & Murnighan, 2011)? Does the formation of new ties affect existing ties, and vice versa? Can external agents (i.e., managers) affect the network formation and change of others? How do endogenous factors contribute to network change? For example, it is likely that network centrality leads to success and that success in turn leads to greater network centrality. Many opportunities exist for research on the dynamics of networks.

It has become popular to apply network thinking to various established lines of research, much as I have done in this chapter. Equally profitable would a reverse process of applying findings from organizational behavior research to social network analysis. What can social network researchers learn from organizational psychology? It is a small world of organizational psychologists and social network researchers if bridges exist across these disciplinary clusters. Hopefully, this chapter will foster such bridges by energizing collaborative research.

Note

I am indebted to Steve Borgatti, Dan Halgin, Joe Labianca, Ajay Mehra and the other faculty and Ph.D. students at the Links Center (linkscenter.org) for the many interesting and insightful discussions that form the basis for chapters such as this. Equally helpful have been dialogues over the years with my network colleagues and long-time friends Martin Kilduff and David Krackhardt.

References

Adams, J. S. (1965). Inequity in social change. In L. Berkowitz (Ed.), *Advances in experimental social psychology* (pp. 267–300). New York: Academic Press.

Adler, P. S., & Kwon, S. (2002). Social capital: Prospects for a new concept. *Academy of Management Review, 27*, 17–40.

Amabile, T. M. (1996). *Creativity in context: Update to the social psychology of creativity.* Boulder, CO: Westview.

Asch, S. E. (1951). Effects of group pressure upon the modification and distortion of judgments. In H. Guetzkow (Ed.), *Groups, leadership, and men* (pp. 151–162). Pittsburgh: Carnegie Press

Baker, W. E., & Faulkner, R. R. (1993). The social organization of conspiracy: Illegal networks in the heavy electrical equipment industry. *American Sociological Review, 58*, 837–860.

Balkundi, P., & Harrison, D. A. (2006). Ties, leaders, and time in teams: Strong inference about network structure's effects on team viability and performance. *Academy of Management Journal, 49*, 49–68.

Balkundi, P., & Kilduff, M. (2005). The ties that lead: a social network approach to leadership. *The Leadership Quarterly, 16*, 941–961.

Barley, S. R. (1990). The alignment of technology and structure through roles and networks. *Administrative Science Quarterly, 35*, 61–103.

Barsade, S. G. (2002). The ripple effect: Emotional contagion and its influence on group behavior. *Administrative Science Quarterly, 47*, 644–675.

Barsade, S. G., Brief, A. P., & Spataro, E. (2003). The affective revolution in organizational behavior: The emergence of a paradigm. In J. Greenberg (Ed.), *Organizational behavior: The state of the science* (pp. 3–52). Mahwah, NJ: Erlbaum.

Bateman, T. S., & Organ, D. W. (1983). Job satisfaction and the good soldier: The relationship between affect and employee "citizenship." *Academy of Management Journal, 26*, 587–595.

Bazerman, M. H., Curhan, J. R., Moore, D. A., & Valley, K. L. (2000). Negotiations. *Annual Review of Psychology, 51*, 279–314.

Bernard, H. R., Killworth, P., Kronenfeld, D., & Sailer, L. (1984). The problem of informant accuracy: The validity of retrospective data. *Annual Review of Anthropology, 13*, 495–517.

Bian, Y. (1997). Bringing strong ties back in: Indirect ties, network bridges, and job searches in China. *American Sociological Review, 62*, 366–385.

Bolino, M. C., Turnley, W. H., & Bloodgood, J. M. (2002). Citizenship behavior and the creation of social capital in organizations. *Academy of Management Review, 27*, 505–522.

Borgatti, S. P. (2006). *E-NET Software for the Analysis of Ego-Network Data*. Needham, MA: Analytic Technologies.

Borgatti, S. P., & Cross, R. (2003). A relational view of information seeking and learning in social networks. *Management Science, 49*, 432–445.

Borgatti, S. P., Everett, M. G., & Freeman, L. C. (2002). *UCInet for Windows: Software for Social Network Analysis*. Harvard, MA: Analytic Technologies

Borgatti, S. P., & Foster, P. C. (2003). The network paradigm in organizational research: A review and typology. *Journal of Management, 29*, 991–1013.

Borgatti, S. P., & Halgin, D. S. (2011). On network theory. *Organization Science, 22*, 1168–1181.

Borgatti, S. P., & Lopez-Kidwell, V. (2011). Network theory. In P. Carrington & J. Scott, (Eds.), *Handbook of social network analysis*,(pp. 40–54). Thousand Oaks, CA: Sage.

Borgatti, S. P., Mehra, A., Brass, D. J., & Labianca, G. (2009). Network analysis in the social sciences. *Science, 323*, 892–895.

Bowler, M., & Brass, D. J. (2006). Relational correlates of interpersonal citizenship behavior: A social network perspective. *Journal of Applied Psychology, 91*, 70–82.

Boxman, E. A. W., De Graaf, P. M., & Flap, H. D. (1991). The impact of social and human capital on the income attainment of Dutch managers. *Social Networks, 13*, 51–73.

Brass, D. J. (1981). Structural relationships, job characteristics, and worker satisfaction and performance. *Administrative Science Quarterly, 26*, 331–348.

Brass, D. J. (1984). Being in the right place: A structural analysis of individual influence in an organization. *Administrative Science Quarterly, 29*, 518–539.

Brass, D. J. (1985a). Men's and women's networks: A study of interaction patterns and influence in an organization. *Academy of Management Journal, 28*, 327–343.

Brass, D. J. (1985b). Technology and the structuring of jobs: Employee satisfaction, performance, and influence. *Organizational Behavior and Human Decision Processes, 35*, 216–240.

Brass, D. J. (1992). Power in organizations: A social network perspective. In G. Moore & J. A. Whitt (Eds.), *Research in politics and society* (pp. 295–323). Greenwich, CT: JAI Press.

Brass, D. J. (1995a). A social network perspective on human resources management. In G. R. Ferris (Ed.), *Research in personnel and human resources management* (Vol. 13, pp. 39–79). Greenwich, CT: JAI Press.

Brass, D. J. (1995b). Creativity: It's all in your social network. In C. M. Ford & D. A. Gioia (Eds.), *Creative action in organizations* (pp. 94–99). Thousand Oaks, CA: Sage.

Brass, D. J. (2002). Intraorganizational power and dependence. In J. A. C. Baum (Ed.), *Companion to organizations* (pp. 138–157). Oxford: Blackwell.

Brass, D. J. (2009). Connecting to brokers: Strategies for acquiring social capital. In V. O. Bartkus & J. H. Davis (Eds.), *Social capital: Reaching out, reaching in* (pp. 260–274). Northhampton, MA: Elgar Publishing.

Brass, D. J., & Burkhardt. M. E. (1992). Centrality and power in organizations. In N. Nohria & R. Eccles (Eds.), *Networks and organizations: Structure, form, and action* (pp. 191–215). Boston: Harvard Business School Press.

Brass, D. J., & Burkhardt. M. E. (1993). Potential power and power use: An investigation of structure and behavior. *Academy of Management Journal, 36*, 441–470.

Brass, D. J., Butterfield, K. D., & Skaggs, B. C. (1998). Relationships and unethical behavior: A social network perspective. *Academy of Management Review, 23*, 14–31.

Brass, D. J., Galaskiewicz, J., Greve, H. R., & Tsai, W. (2004). Taking stock of networks and organizations: A multilevel perspective. *Academy of Management Journal, 47*, 795–819.

Brass, D. J. & Halgin, D. S. (2012). Social networks: The structure of relationships. In L. Eby & T. Allen (Eds.), *Personal relationships: The effect of supervisory, co-worker, team, customer and nonwork exchanges on employee attitudes, behavior, and well-being*. New York: Wiley.

Brass, D. J., & Krackhardt, D. (1999). The social capital of 21st century leaders. In J. G. Hunt, G. E. Dodge, & L. Wong (Eds.), *Out-of-the-box leadership* (pp. 179–194). Stamford, CT: JAI Press.

Breiger, R. L. (1974). The duality of persons and groups. *Social Forces, 53*, 181–190.

Burkhardt, M. E. (1994). Social interaction effects following a technological change: A longitudinal investigation. *Academy of Management Journal, 37*, 869–898.

Burkhardt, M. E., & Brass, D. J. (1990). Changing patterns or patterns of change: The effect of a change in technology on social network structure and power. *Administrative Science Quarterly, 35*, 104–127.

Burt, R. S. (1982). *Toward a structural theory of action*. New York: Academic Press.

Burt, R. S. (1983). Distinguishing relational content. In R. S. Burt & M. J. Minor (Eds.), *Applied network analysis: A methodological introduction* (pp. 35–74). Beverly Hills, CA: Sage.

Burt, R. S. (1987). Social contagion and innovation: Cohesion versus structural equivalence. *American Journal of Sociology, 92*, 1287–1335.

Burt, R. S. (1992). *Structural holes: The social structure of competition*. Cambridge, MA: Harvard University Press.

Burt, R. S. (1997). A note on social capital and network content. *Social Networks, 19*, 355–373.

Burt, R. S. (2000). The network structure of social capital. In B. M. Staw & R. L. Sutton (Eds.), *Research in organizational behavior* (Vol. 4, pp. 31–56). New York: Elsevier.

Burt, R. S. (2002). Bridge decay. *Social Networks, 24*, 333–363.

Burt, R. S. (2004). Structural holes and good ideas. *American Journal of Sociology, 110*, 349–399.

Burt, R. S. (2005). *Brokerage and closure: An introduction to social capital*. Oxford: Oxford University Press.

Burt, R. S. (2007). Second-hand brokerage: Evidence on the importance of local structure on managers, bankers, and analysts. *Academy of Management Journal, 50,* 110–145.

Burt, R. S., Hogarth, R. M., & Michaud, C. (2000). The social capital of French and American managers. *Organization Science, 11,* 123–147.

Burt, R. S., & Knez, M. (1995). Kinds of third-party effects on trust. *Rationality and Society, 7,* 255–292.

Burt, R. S., & Ronchi. D. (1990). Contested control in a large manufacturing plant. In J. Wessie & H. Flap (Eds.), *Social networks through time* (pp. 121–157). Utrecht, Netherlands: ISOR.

Buskens, V., & van de Rijt, A. (2008). Dynamics of networks if everyone strives for structural holes. *American Journal of Sociology, 114,* 371–407.

Casciaro, T., & Lobo, M. S. (2008). When competence is irrelevant: The role of interpersonal affect in task-related ties. *Administrative Science Quarterly, 53,* 655–684.

Centola, D. (2010). The spread of behavior in an online social network experiment. *Science, 329,* 1194–1197.

Cialdini, R. B. (1989). Indirect tactics of impression management: Beyond basking. In R. A. Giacalone & P. Rosenfield (Eds.), *Impression management in the organization* (pp. 45–56). Hillsdale, NJ: Erlbaum.

Coleman, J., Katz, E., & Menzel, H. (1957). The diffusion of innovation among physicians. *Sociometry, 20,* 253–270.

Coleman, J. S. (1990). *Foundations of social theory.* Cambridge, MA: Harvard University Press.

Cook, K. S., Emerson, R. M., Gilmore, M. R., & Yamagishi, T. (1983). The distribution of power in exchange networks: Theory and experimental results. *American Journal of Sociology, 89,* 275–305.

Cross, R., & Cummings, J. N. (2004). Tie and network correlates of individual performance in knowledge intensive work. *Academy of Management Journal, 47,* 928–937.

Cross, R., Parker, A., & Sasson, L. (2003). *Networks in the knowledge economy.* New York: Oxford University Press.

Davis, G. F. (1991). Agents without principles? The spread of the poison pill through the intercorporate network. *Administrative Science Quarterly, 36,* 583–613.

Degoey, P. (2000). Contagious justice: Exploring the social construction of justice in organizations. In B. M. Staw & R. Kramer (Eds.), *Research in organizational behavior* (Vol. 22, pp. 51–102). Greenwich, CT: JAI Press.

DeSoto, C. B. (1960). Learning a social structure. *Journal of Abnormal and Social Psychology, 60,* 417–421.

DiMaggio, P. (1986). Structural analysis of organizational fields: A blockmodel approach. In B. M. Staw & L. L. Cummings (Eds.), *Research in organizational behavior* (Vol. 8, pp. 335–370). Greenwich, CT: JAI Press.

Eisenberg, E. M., Monge, P. R., & Miller, K. I. (1984). Involvement in communication networks as a predictor of organizational commitment. *Human Communication Research, 10,* 179–201.

Erickson, B. H. (1988). The relational basis of attitudes. In B. Wellman & S. D. Berkowitz (Eds.), *Social structures: A network approach* (pp. 99–121). New York: Cambridge University Press.

Feld, S. L. (1981). The focused organization of social ties. *American Journal of Sociology, 86,* 1015–1035.

Fernandez, R. M., Castilla, E., & Moore, P. (2000). Social capital at work: Networks and hiring at a phone center. *American Journal of Sociology, 105,* 1288–1356.

Fernandez, R. M., & Weinberg, N. (1997). Sifting and sorting: Personal contacts and hiring in a retail bank. *American Sociological Review, 62,* 883–902.

Festinger, L., Schachter, S., & Back, K. (1950). *Social pressures in informal groups: A study of human factors in housing.* Palo Alto, CA: Stanford University Press.

Fleming, L., Mingo, S., & Chen, D. (2007). Collaborative brokerage, generative creativity, and creative success. *Administrative Science Quarterly, 52,* 443–475.

Fombrun, C. J. (1983). Attributions of power across a social network. *Human Relations, 36,* 493–508.

Fowler, J. H., & Christakis, N. A. (2008). The dynamic spread of happiness in a large social network. *British Journal of Medicine, 337,* 1–9.

Freeman, L. C. (2004). *The development of social network analysis: A study in the sociology of science.* Vancouver: Empirical Press.

Freeman, L., Romney, K., & Freeman, S. (1987). Cognitive structure and informant accuracy. *American Anthropologist, 89,* 310–325.

Galaskiewicz, J. (1979). *Exchange networks and community politics.* Beverly Hills, CA: Sage.

Galaskiewicz, J., & Burt, R. S. (1991). Interorganizational contagion in corporate philanthropy. *Administrative Science Quarterly, 36,* 88–105.

Gargiulo, M. (1993). Two-step leverage: Managing constraint in organizational politics. *Administrative Science Quarterly, 38,* 1–19.

Gargiulo, M., & Benassi, M. (2000). Trapped in your own net: Cohesion, structural holes and the adaptation of social capital. *Organization Science, 11,* 183–196.

Gargiulo, M., Ertug, G., & Galunic, C. (2009). The two faces of control: Network closure and individual performance among knowledge workers. *Administrative Science Quarterly, 54,* 299–333.

George, J. M., & Brief, A. P. (1992). Feeling good-doing good: A conceptual analysis of the mood at work-organizational spontaneity relationship. *Psychological Bulletin, 112,* 310–329.

Gibbons, D. E., & Olk, P. M. (2003). Individual and structural origins of friendship and social position among professionals. *Journal of Personality and Social Psychology, 84,* 340–351.

Giddens, A. (1976). *New rules of sociological method.* London: Hutchinson.

Gilbert, N., & Abbott, A. (2005). Introduction. *American Journal of Sociology, 110,* 859–863.

Granovetter, M. S. (1973). The strength of weak ties. *American Journal of Sociology, 6,* 1360–1380.

Granovetter, M. S. (1982). The strength of weak lies: A network theory revisited. In P. V. Marsden & N. Lin (Eds.), *Social structure and network analysis* (pp. 105–130). Beverly Hills. CA: Sage.

Granovetter, M. S. (1985). Economic action and social structure: The problem of embeddedness. *American Journal of Sociology, 91,* 481–510.

Granovetter, M. S. (2005). The impact of social structure on economic outcomes. *The Journal of Economic Perspective, 19,* 33–50.

Grant, A. M., & Parker, S. K. (2009). Redesigning work design theories: The rise of relational and proactive perspectives. *Academy of Management Annals, 3,* 317–375.

Grosser, T. J., Lopez-Kidwell, V., & Labianca, G. (2010). A social network analysis of gossip in organizational life. *Group and Organization Management, 35,* 177–212.

Grosser, T. J., Lopez-Kidwell, V., Labianca, G., & Ellwardt, L. (2011). Hearing it through the grapevine: Positive and negative workplace gossip. *Organizational Dynamics,* forthcoming.

Gulati, R. (2007). *Managing network resources: Alliances, affiliations and other relational assets.* Oxford: Oxford University Press.

Hackman, J. R., & Oldham, G. R. (1976). Motivation through the design of work: Test of a theory. *Organizational Behavior and Human Performance, 16,* 250–279.

Halgin, D. S. (2009). *The effects of social identity on career progression: A study of NCAA basketball coaches.* Best Paper Proceedings, Academy of Management meetings, Chicago.

Hansen, M. T. (1999). The search-transfer problem: The role of weak ties in sharing knowledge across organization subunits. *Administrative Science Quarterly, 44,* 82–111.

Heider, R. (1958). *The psychology of interpersonal relations.* New York: Wiley.

Hummon, N. P., & Doreian, P. (2003). Some dynamics of social balance processes: Bringing Heider back into balance theory. *Social Networks, 25,* 17–49.

Ibarra, H. (1992). Homophily and differential returns: Sex differences in network structure and access in an advertising firm. *Administrative Science Quarterly, 37,* 422–447.

Ibarra, H. (1993). Personal networks of women and minorities in management: A conceptual framework. *Academy of Management Review, 18,* 56–87.

Ibarra, H., & Andrews, S. B. (1993). Power, social influence and sense-making: Effects of network centrality and proximity on employee perceptions. *Administrative Science Quarterly, 38,* 277–303.

Ibarra, H., Kilduff, M., & Tsai, W. (2005). Zooming in and out: Connecting individuals and collectivities at the frontiers of organizational network research. *Organization Science, 16,* 359–371.

Ingram, P., & Morris, M. W. (2007). Do people mix at mixers? Structure, homophily, and the "life of the party." *Administrative Science Quarterly, 52,* 558–585.

Ingram, P., & Zou, X. (2008). Business friendships. *Research in Organizational Behavior, 28,* 167–184.

Jablin, F. M., & Krone, K. J. (1987). Organizational assimilation. In C. Berger & S. H. Chaffee (Eds.), *Handbook of communication science* (pp. 711–746). Newbury Park, CA: Sage.

Kalish, Y., & Robins, G. (2006). Psychological predispositions and network structure: The relationship between individual predispositions, structural holes and network closure. *Social Networks, 28,* 56–84.

Kanter, R. M. (1977). *Men and women of the corporation.* New York: Basic Books.

Kilduff, M., & Brass, D. J. (2010). Organizational social network research: Core ideas and key debates. In J. P. Walsh & A. P. Brief (Eds.), *Academy of Management Annuals* (Vol. 4, pp. 317–357). London: Routledge.

Kilduff, M., & Krackhardt, D. (1994). Bringing the individual back in: A structural analysis of the internal market for reputation in organizations. *Academy of Management Journal, 37,* 87–108.

Kilduff, M., & Krackhardt, D. (2008). *Interpersonal networks in organizations.* Cambridge: Cambridge University Press

Kilduff, M., & Oh, H. (2006). Deconstructing diffusion: An ethnostatistical examination of *Medical Innovation* network data reanalyses. *Organizational Research Methods, 9,* 432–455.

Kilduff, M., & Tsai, W. (2003). *Social networks and organizations.* London: Sage.

Klein, K. J., Lim, B., Saltz, J. L., & Mayer, D. M. (2004). How do they get there? An examination of the antecedents of centrality in team networks. *Academy of Management Journal, 47,* 952–963.

Krackhardt, D. (1990). Assessing the political landscape: Structure, cognition, and power in organizations. *Administrative Science Quarterly, 35,* 342–369.

Krackhardt. D. (1992). The strength of strong ties: The importance of Philos. In N. Nohria & R. Eccles (Eds.), *Networks and organizations: Structure, form, and action* (pp. 216–239). Boston: Harvard Business School Press.

Krackhardt, D. (1994). Constraints on the interactive organization as an ideal type. In C. Hecksher & A. Donnellon (Eds.), *The post-bureaucratic organization: New perspectives on organizational change,* 211–222. Thousand Oaks, CA: Sage.

Krackhardt, D. (1998). Simmelian ties: Super strong and sticky. In R. M. Kramer & M. A. Neale (Eds.), *Power and influence in organizations* (pp. 21–38). Thousand Oaks, CA: Sage.

Krackhardt, D., & Hanson, J. R. (1993). Informal networks: The company behind the chart. *Harvard Business Review, 104*(July–August), 111.

Krackhardt, D., & Kilduff, M. (1990). Friendship patterns and culture: The control of organizational diversity. *American Anthropologist, 92,* 142–154.

Krackhardt, D., & Kilduff, M. (1999). Whether close or far: Social distance effects on perceived balance in friendship networks. *Journal of Personality and Social Psychology, 76,* 770–782.

Krackhardt, D., & Porter, L. W. (1985). When friends leave: A structural analysis of the relationship between turnover and stayers' attitudes. *Administrative Science Quarterly, 30,* 242–261.

Krackhardt, D., & Porter, L. W. (1986). The snowball effect: Turnover embedded in communication networks. *Journal of Applied Psychology, 71,* 50–55.

Labianca, G., & Brass, D. J. (2006). Exploring the social ledger: Negative relationships and negative asymmetry in social networks in organizations. *Academy of Management Review, 31,* 596–614.

Labianca, G., Brass, D. J., & Gray, B. (1998). Social networks and perceptions of intergroup conflict: The role of negative relationships and third parties. *Academy of Management Journal, 41,* 55–67.

Lazega, E. (2001). *The collegial phenomenon: The social mechanisms of cooperation among peers in a corporate law partnership.* Oxford: Oxford University Press.

Leavitt, H. J. (1951). Some effects of certain communication patterns on group performance. *Journal of Abnormal and Social Psychology, 46,* 38–50.

Leonard, S. A., Mehra, A., & Katerberg, R. (2008). The social identity and social networks of ethnic minority groups in organizations: A crucial test of distinctiveness theory. *Journal of Organizational Behavior, 29,* 573–589.

Leung, A. (2003). Different ties for different needs: Recruitment practices of entrepreneurial firms at different development phases. *Human Resource Management, 42,* 303–320.

Levin, D. Z., Walter, J., & Murnighan, J. K. (2011). Dormant ties: The value of reconnecting. *Organizational Science, 22,* 923–939.

Lin, N. (1999). Social networks and status attainment. *Annual Review of Sociology, 25,* 467–487.

Lin, N. (2001). Building a network theory of social capital. In N. Lin, K. Cook, & R. S. Burt (Eds.), *Social capital* (pp. 3–30). New York: Aldine de Gruyter.

Lin, N., Ensel, W. M., & Vaughn, J. C. (1981). Social resources and strength of ties: Structural factors in occupational status attainment. *American Sociological Review, 46*, 393–405.

Lincoln, J. R., Hanada, M., & Olson, J. (1981). Cultural orientation and individual reactions to organizations: A study of employees of Japanese-owned firms. *Administrative Science Quarterly, 26*, 93–115.

Mayhew, B. H. (1980). Structuralism versus individualism: Part I, Shadowboxing in the dark. *Social Forces, 59*, 335–375.

McGinn, K. L., & Keros, A. T. (2002). Improvisation and the logic of exchange in socially embedded transactions. *Administrative Science Quarterly, 47*, 442–473.

McPherson, J. M., Smith-Lovin, L., & Cook, J. M. (2001). Birds of a feather: Homophily in social networks. *Annual Review of Sociology, 27*, 415–444.

Mehra, A. (2009). *Personal communications*. Lexington: University of Kentucky.

Mehra, A., Dixon, A. L., Brass, D. J., & Robertson, B. (2006). The social network ties of group leaders: Implications for group performance and leader reputation. *Organization Science, 17*, 64–79.

Mehra, A., Kilduff, M., & Brass, D. J. (1998). At the margins: A distinctiveness approach to the social identity and social networks of underrepresented groups. *Academy of Management Journal, 41*, 441–452.

Mehra, A., Kilduff, M., & Brass, D. J. (2001). The social networks of high and low self-monitors: Implications for workplace performance. *Administrative Science Quarterly, 46*, 121–146.

Mitchell. J. C. (1969) *Social networks in urban situations*. Manchester: University of Manchester Press.

Mizruchi, M. (1996). What do interlocks do? An analysis, critique, and assessment of research on interlocking directorates. In J. Hagan & K. S. Cook (Eds.), *Annual review of sociology* (Vol. 22, pp. 271–298), Palo Alto, CA: Annual Reviews.

Mizruchi, M. S., & Stearns, L. B. (2001). Getting deals done: The use of social networks in bank decision making. *American Journal of Sociology, 66*, 647–671.

Monge, P. R., & Contractor, N. S. (2003). Theories of communication networks. Oxford: Oxford University Press.

Monge, P. R., & Eisenberg, F. M. (1987). Emergent communication networks. In F. M. Jablin, L. L. Putman, K. H. Roberts, & L. W. Porter (Eds.), *Handbook of organizational communication: An interdisciplinary perspective* (pp. 304–342). Newbury Park. CA: Sage.

Moreno, J. L. (1934). *Who shall survive?* Washington, DC: Publishing Company.

Morrison, E. W. (2002). Newcomers' relationships: The role of social network ties during socialization. *Academy of Management Journal, 45*, 1149–1160.

Mossholder, K. W., Settoon, R. P., & Henaghan, S. C. (2005). A relational perspective on turnover: Examining structural, attitudinal, and behavioral predictors. *Academy of Management Journal, 48*, 507–618.

Murnighan, J. K., & Brass, D. J. (1991). Intraorganizational coalitions. In M. Bazerman, B. Sheppard, & R. Lewicki (Eds.), *Research on negotiations in organizations* (Vol. 3, pp. 283–307). Greenwich, CT: JAI Press.

Nahapiet, J., & Ghoshal, S. (1998). Social capital, intellectual capital, and the organizational advantage. *Academy of Management Review, 23*, 242–266.

Nelson, R. E. (1989). The strength of strong ties: Social networks and intergroup conflict in organizations. *Academy of Management Journal, 32*, 377–401.

Oh, H., Chung, M-H., & Labianca, G. (2004). Group social capital and group effectiveness: The role of informal socializing ties. *Academy of Management Journal, 47*, 860–875.

Oh, H., & Kilduff, M. (2008). The ripple effect of personality on social structure: Self-monitoring origins of network brokerage. *Journal of Applied Psychology, 93*, 1155–1164.

Oh, H., Labianca, G., & Chung, M-H. (2006). A multilevel model of group social capital. *Academy of Management Review, 31*, 569–582

Obstfeld, D. (2005). Social networks, the tertius iungens orientation, and involvement in innovation. *Administrative Science Quarterly, 50*, 100–130.

Pachucki, M. A. & Breiger, R. L. (2010). Cultural holes: Beyond relationality in social networks and culture. *Annual Review of Sociology, 36*, 205–224.

Papa, M. J. (1990). Communication network patterns and employee performance with a new technology. *Communication Research, 17*, 344–368.

Pastor, J. C., Meindl, J. R., & Mayo, M. C. (2002). A networks effects model of charisma attributions. *Academy of Management Journal, 45*, 410–420.

Perry-Smith, J. E. (2006). Social yet creative: The role of social relationships in facilitating individual creativity. *Academy of Management Journal, 49*, 85–101.

Perry-Smith, J. E., & Shalley, C. E. (2003). The social side of creativity: A static and dynamic social network perspective. *Academy of Management Review, 28*, 89–106.

Podolny, J. M. (2001). Networks as the pipes and prisms of the market. *American Journal of Sociology, 107*, 33–60.

Podolny, J. M., & Baron, J. N. (1997). Relationships and resources: Social networks and mobility in the workplace. *American Sociological Review, 62*, 673–693.

Podsakoff, P. M., MacKenzie, S. B., Paine, J. B., & Bachrach, D. G. (2000). Organizational citizenship behavior and the quantity and quality of work group performance. *Journal of Management, 26*, 513–563.

Putnam, R. D. (1995). Bowling alone: America's declining social capital. *Journal of Democracy, 6*, 65–78.

Reagans, R., Zuckerman, E., & McEvily, B. (2004). How to make the team: Social networks vs. demography as criteria for designing effective teams. *Administrative Science Quarterly, 49*, 101–133.

Rentsch, J. R. (1990). Climate and culture: Interaction and qualitative differences in organizational meanings. *Journal of Applied Psychology, 75*, 668–681.

Rice, R. E., & Aydin, C. (1991). Attitudes toward new organizational technology: Network proximity as a mechanism for social information processing. *Administrative Science Quarterly, 36*, 219–244.

Roberts, K. H., & O'Reilly, C. A., III. (1979). Some correlates of communication roles in organizations. *Academy of Management Journal, 22*, 42–57.

Rogers, E. M. (1971). *Communication of innovations*. New York: Free Press.

Sasidharen, D., Santhanam, R., Brass, D. J., & Sambamurthy, V. (2012). Effects of social network structure on the post-implementation of enterprise systems: A longitudinal, multilevel analysis. *Information Systems Resarch*, in press.

Sasovova, Z., Mehra, A., Borgatti, S. P., & Schippers, M. C. (2010). Network churn: The effects of self-monitoring personality on brokerage dynamics. *Administrative Science Quarterly, 55*, 639–670.

Schneider, B., Goldstein, H. W., & Smith, D. B. (1995). The ASA framework: An update. *Personnel Psychology, 48*(4), 747.

Scott, J. (2000). *Social network analysis: A handbook*. London: Sage.

Seibert, S. E., Kraimer, M. L., & Liden, R. C. (2001). A social capital theory of career success. *Academy of Management Journal, 44*, 219–237.

Seidel, M-D. L., Polzer, J. T., & Stewart, K. J. (2000). Friends in high places: The effects of social networks on discrimination in salary negotiations. *Administrative Science Quarterly, 45*, 1–24.

Settoon, R. P., & Mossholder, K. W. (2002). Relationship quality and relationship context as antecedents of person- and task-focused interpersonal citizenship behavior. *Journal of Applied Psychology, 87*, 255–267.

Shah, P. P. (1998). Who are employees' referents? Using a network perspective to determine referent others. *Academy of Management Journal, 41*, 249–268.

Shah, P. P. (2000). Network destruction: The structural implications of downsizing. *Academy of Management Journal, 43*, 101–112.

Shapiro, D., Brass, D. J., & Labianca, G. (2008). Examining justice from a social network perspective. *Research in Social Issues in Management: Justice, Morality, and Social Responsibility, 6*, 201–215.

Shaw, J. D., Duffy, M. K., Johnson, J. L., & Lockhart, D. E. (2005). Turnover, social capital losses, and performance. *Academy of Management Journal, 48*, 594–606.

Shaw, M. E. (1964). Communication networks. In L. Berkowitz (Ed.), *Advances in experimental social psychology* (Vol. 1, pp. 111–147). New York: Academic Press.

Sherman, J. D., Smith, H. L., & Mansfield, E. R. (1986). The impact of emergent network structure on organizational socialization. *Journal of Applied Behavioral Science, 22*, 53–63.

Shrader, C. B., Lincoln, J. R., & Hoffman, A. (1989). The network structures of organizations: Effects of task contingencies and distributional form. *Human Relations, 42*, 43–66.

Simmel, G. (1950). *The sociology of Georg Simmel*. New York: Free Press.

Singh, J., Hansen, M. T., & Podolny, J. M. (2010). The world is not small for everyone: Inequality in searching for knowledge in organizations. *Management Science, 56*, 1415–1438.

Sparrowe, R. T., & Liden, R. C. (1997). Process and structure in leader-member exchange. *Academy of Management Review, 22*, 522–552.

Sparrowe, R. T., & Liden, R. C. (2005). Two routes to influence: Integrating leader-member exchange and network perspectives. *Administrative Science Quarterly, 50*, 505–535.

Sparrowe, R. T., Liden, R. C., Wayne, S. J., & Kraimer, M. L. (2001). Social networks and the performance of individuals and groups. *Academy of Management Journal, 44*, 316–325.

Stevenson, W. B., & Gilly, M. C. (1991). Information processing and problem solving: The migration of problems through formal positions and networks of ties. *Academy of Management Journal, 34*, 918–929.

Stevenson, W. B., Pearce, J. L., & Porter, L. W. (1985). The concept of coalition in organization theory and research. *Academy of Management Review, 10*, 256–268.

Tichy, N., & Fombrun, C. (1979). Network analysis in organizational settings. *Human Relations, 32*, 923–965.

Totterdell, P., Wall, T., Holman, D., Diamond, H., & Epitropaki, O. (2004). Affect networks: A structural analysis of the relationship between work ties and job-related affect. *Journal of Applied Psychology, 89*, 854–867.

Travers, J., & Milgram, S. (1969). An experimental study of the "small world" problem. *Sociometry, 32*, 425–443.

Tsai, W. (2001). Knowledge transfer in intraorganizational networks: Effects of network position and absorptive capacity on business unit innovation and performance. *Academy of Management Journal, 44*, 996–1004.

Umphress, E. E., Labianca, G., Brass, D. J., Kass, E., & Scholten, L. (2003). The role of instrumental and expressive social ties in employees' perceptions of organizational justice. *Organization Science, 14*, 738–753.

Uzzi, B. (1997). Social structure and competition in interfirm networks: The paradox of embeddedness. *Administrative Science Quarterly, 42*, 35–67.

Valley, K. L., Neale, M. A., & Mannix, E. A. (1995). Friends, lovers, colleagues, strangers: The effects of relationships on the process and outcome of dyadic negotiations. *Research on Negotiation in Organizations, 5*, 65–93.

Valley, K. L., White, S. B., & Iacobucci, D. (1992). The process of assisted negotiations: A network analysis. *Group Decision and Negotiation, 2*, 117–135.

Van Dyne, L., Graham, J. W., & Dienesch, R. M. (1994). Organizational citizenship behavior: Construct redefinition, measurement, and validation. *Academy of Management Journal, 37*, 765–802.

Walker, G. (1985). Network position and cognition in a computer firm. *Administrative Science Quarterly, 30*, 103–130.

Wasserman, S., & Faust, K. (1994). *Social network analysis: Methods and applications*. Cambridge: Cambridge University Press.

Watts, D. J. (2003). *Six degrees: The science of a connected age*. New York: W. W. Norton.

Wegener, B. (1991). Job mobility and social ties: Social resources, prior job, and status attainment. *American Sociological Review, 56*, 60–71.

Wellman, B. (1988). Structural analysis: From method and metaphor to theory and substance. In B. Wellman & S. D. Berkowitz (Eds.), *Social structures: A network approach* (pp. 19–61). New York: Cambridge University Press.

Williams, K. Y., & O'Reilly, C. A. (1998). Demography and diversity in organizations: A review of 40 years of research. *Research in Organizational Behavior, 20*, 77–140.

Williamson, I. O., & Cable, D. M. (2003). Organizational hiring practices, interfirm network ties and interorganizational imitation. *Academy of Management Journal, 46*, 349–358.

Xiao, Z., & Tsui, A. S. (2007). When brokers may not work: The cultural contingency of social capital in Chinese high-tech firms. *Administrative Science Quarterly, 52*, 1–31.

Zaheer, A., & Soda, G. (2009). Network evolution: The origins of structural holes. *Administrative Science Quarterly, 54*, 1–31.

Zhou, J., Shin, S. J., Brass, D. J., Choi, J., & Zhang, Z-H. (2009). Social networks, personal values, and creativity: Evidence for curvilinear effects and interaction effects. *Journal of Applied Psychology, 94*(6), 1544–1552.

Leadership

David V. Day

Abstract

Issues related to leadership theory, research, and practices within the field of industrial/organizational (I/O) psychology are examined. Several special circumstances with regard to leadership are first considered, including the varied domains in which leadership is relevant, its multilevel nature, the multiple sources of origin for leadership, and the multiple outcomes in terms of leader emergence and effectiveness. Various leadership theories and frameworks are reviewed, organized around classical theories (evolutionary, trait, behavior, and contingency), bridging theories (charismatic/transformational, leader-member exchange, and leadership perceptions), and emerging approaches (team, shared, and capacity approaches). Future directions in terms of leadership theory, research, and practice are proposed, concluding with a summary of what I/O psychologists know about leadership and speculation as to what has yet to be learned.

Key Words: Leadership, evolution, traits, behaviors, contingency, charisma, transformational, leader-member exchange, leadership perceptions, shared leadership

Introduction

Leadership has a long and checkered history in industrial/organizational (I/O) psychology. Despite its longevity, the leadership field has been characterized as "curiously unformed" (Hackman & Wageman, 2007, p. 43). The pessimistic sentiment stems from factors such as the lack of a standard operational definition of the construct, an overly narrow focus of study, and the tendency to theorize about leadership in ways that make it too esoteric to understand (Locke, 2003; Schriesheim, 2003). These criticisms have raised concerns that perhaps leadership is not a scientific construct at all. In a well-known quote about the many different ways that leadership has been conceptualized and defined, Bass (1990) noted that "there are almost as many definitions of leadership as there are persons who have attempted to define the concept" (p. 11). Indeed, early applied psychologists did not consider

leadership to be a relevant scientific construct and it was not until the 1940s that leadership began to be covered consistently in industrial psychology textbooks (Day & Zaccaro, 2007). Some of the criticisms leveled against the field of leadership are justified; however, one difficulty with attempting to provide a concise leadership definition is that it invariably leaves something out or otherwise oversimplifies a complex, dynamic, and evolving process.

A good place to begin when attempting to review and make sense of the leadership field is with this notion of process, which can be defined as a series of actions or operations conducing to an end or desired outcome. What makes the leadership process especially difficult to define and study cleanly is that leadership is "a complex interaction between the leader and the social and organizational environment" (Fiedler, 1996, p. 241). This view includes the followers as part of the social environment. It is evident from this perspective that leadership is not just about the leader, which reflects an entity rather than process perspective (Uhl-Bien, 2006); however, that is how leadership has tended to be conceptualized and studied in I/O psychology. Although the field attempted to move away from this limited perspective with contingency theories, more recent attention on charismatic and transformational leadership have brought the focus of research squarely back on the leader.

This brief introduction illustrates one of the historical and yet continuing challenges in the field of leadership, which is to "... distinguish it as a process from the *leader* as a person who occupies a central role in that process" (Hollander & Julian, 1969, p. 388, italics in original). A primary goal of this chapter is to trace the development of the leadership field from one that is highly heroic and "leader-centric" (i.e., all about the leader as an entity) to one that recognizes leadership as a more inclusive process with regard to followers and factors in the broader social and organizational environment. In accomplishing this objective, it is necessary to keep in mind that leadership, ultimately, is a process and not a person (Hollander, 1992).

It is not just leadership research that continues to mature; the construct itself is evolving (see Drath et al., 2008, for a good example of this ongoing construct evolution). This is a source of irritation and frustration to some I/O psychologists who would prefer a set, agreed upon, and universal definition of leadership (e.g., Locke, 2003). Despite this hard-nosed scientific perspective, it is an unreasonable expectation, given that leadership is dynamic, interpersonal, multifunctional, and multilevel in nature. It is also the case that the advances in our conceptual frameworks and analytical tools have contributed to changes in the way that I/O psychologists think about and study leadership.

Another important force behind these changes is the increasingly complex challenges that require leadership. No matter how smart or experienced, leaders are more often and more quickly reaching their limits in terms of being able to figure things out and provide ready solutions (Bennis, 2007). One of the more provocative assertions made in the leadership field is that organizations not only need more highly developed leaders to address these complex challenges, but that they need more leaders, period. Indeed, there have been calls to develop everyone as a leader. Critics have countered: If everyone is a leader, then who will follow?

Unfortunately, this demonstrates a very narrow understanding of leadership because leadership is a highly dynamic process that is not restricted to a particular person or position. Someone who is leading at one point in time by influencing others on the team may take on a role of follower subsequently while being influenced by someone else on the team. This is not a new perspective, but it is one that has been widely overlooked. Everyone needs to be prepared as fully as possible to contribute to effective leadership processes when those leadership moments arrive. Complex challenges now and in the future are unlikely to be addressed successfully by any one leader. For these reasons, successful leadership will likely require a more inclusive orientation (Hollander, 2009).

Before reviewing specific theories of leadership in tracing the development of the field and the corresponding construct evolution, this chapter will address several issues that contribute to leadership as a somewhat unique construct within I/O psychology. These include the varied domains in which leadership is relevant, its multilevel nature, the multiple sources of origin for leadership, and the multiple outcomes in terms of leader emergence and effectiveness. To better prepare the background for understanding the various theories that will be presented, a brief introduction to each of these issues is provided.

Domains of Leadership

I/O psychology is a discipline that is guided by a focus on both science and practice (Koppes & Pickren, 2007). Because of this dual focus, I/O psychologists are considered to be scientist-practitioners. This is a particular point of relevance when the focal topic is leadership because the domains in which leadership is practiced are so varied. Leadership is relevant in business, politics, military, sports, education, and religion, among other contexts. But what it takes to be a successful leader or to bring about effective leadership may vary considerably across contexts. Put into somewhat more technical terms, the particular domain may serve as a boundary condition to the research findings that seek to enhance understanding and be of practical value in improving leadership in a given context (Johns, 2006).

An area of long-standing research interest concerns what it takes to be perceived as a leader (i.e., leader emergence). This is considered to be of importance both theoretically and practically, because being seen as a leader provides someone with extra power and influence, especially in situations in which a leader emerges informally in a group rather than being formally appointed. A perceiver is more likely to allow influence from another if that person is seen to have certain characteristics associated with a stored impression of a leader (called a *prototype*). That is, the degree that someone matches a prototype of a leader, the more likely that person will be allowed by others to emerge as a leader and to exercise influence over them (Lord, Foti, & Phillips, 1982).

Research in the topic area of leadership perceptions has shown that there is some degree of commonality across the various context domains in terms of the prototype that people hold in memory about a leader (defined in terms of leader traits); however, there are also important differences (Lord, Foti, & De Vader, 1984). This has practical implications for a leader who may want to move across career domains from business to politics or military to education. What it takes to be perceived as a leader in terms of personal characteristics will be different to some extent across different context domains, and this includes cultural contexts. Because leadership is relevant across so many different contexts, it is important to keep this potential boundary condition in mind. Context matters, especially with leadership.

As another example—or perhaps *caveat* is the more appropriate word—pertains to a distinction between leader and boss (or supervisor). Is there one? The question may appear to be trivial, but there is a continuing controversy about the difference between leaders and managers, and between leadership and management. Most people would recognize that someone could be a manager without being a leader, or be a leader without exercising sound management. But what is the difference between a leader and a manager? The ongoing debate about this difference will not be resolved here, but that is not the point. Rather, in evaluating the research that has been conducted purportedly about leadership, it is sobering to see just how many of these studies have actually sampled managers or other study participants in positions of authority and management and have assumed that the results apply to leaders and leadership (Bedeian & Hunt, 2006). This may, or may not, be an appropriate inference. As informed consumers of leadership research, readers have a responsibility (along with reviewers and editors) to critically evaluate such potential boundary conditions, rather than assuming, based on researchers' own claims, that they are actually studying leadership.

Multilevel Focus

The study and application (science/practice) of leadership often requires a multilevel lens (Zyphur, Barsky, & Zhang, 2012). It is true that a great deal of leadership research is focused at the level of the individual leader (e.g., attempting to identify the traits or behaviors of effective leaders); however, there are other approaches to leadership that have conceptualized it as a leader-member dyadic exchange (LMX; Dansereau, Graen, & Haga, 1975; Graen & Uhl-Bien, 1995), as group or team processes (Carson, Tesluk, & Marrone, 2007; Day, Gronn, & Salas, 2004; Kozlowski, Watola, Jensen, Kim, & Botero, 2009; Pearce & Conger, 2003b), or even at the organization level of analysis (O'Connor & Quinn, 2004). It is inappropriate to assume that any construct—including leadership—that is conceptualized and measured at one level of analysis would be identical in meaning to a construct at a different level in terms of content or process (Chan, 1998; Kozlowski & Klein, 2000). What is needed is clear thinking and empirical evidence of the appropriate composition model across levels (Lord & Dinh, 2012), as well as the analytical tools to handle this extra complexity. For example, when followers are nested within leaders, as in the typical LMX approach (i.e., multiple followers report to the same leader), the resulting data are likely to be non-independent. This violates one of the basic assumptions regarding the appropriate use of inferential statistics regarding independence of observations.

What has helped to spur the evolution of leadership theory and research in recent years has been the significant advances in multilevel modeling. Leadership can be thought of as inherently multilevel in that it involves leaders, followers, and situations (context) and can range from individual to organizational levels of analysis and anything between, including multiteam systems (DeChurch & Marks, 2006). Furthermore, the target of leadership processes can be directed at the level of the organization, the group or team, or individual follower(s). This opens the possibility for cross-level effects, especially if it is assumed that leaders do not treat all followers identically. Multilevel modeling techniques now allow researchers to test the underlying assumptions directly and to model their effects more accurately. Also, in terms of leadership development, there are issues of within-person and between-person changes that can be addressed using multilevel growth modeling procedures (Day & Lance, 2004). Multilevel approaches to leadership help to build more intricate and realistic pictures of leadership causes and effects in organizations.

Another levels issue pertains to the impact or "reach" of a leader. Much of the leadership research examines the downward influence that the leader has on followers in terms of attitudes, behavior, or performance. But those leaders at middle levels and above in organizations often have more than one level of followers as direct reports. They also have indirect reports two or more levels below that can also be affected by the leader's actions (e.g., Dvir, Eden, Avolio, & Shamir, 2002). Studies have also examined the effects of top-level (e.g., CEO) leadership on organizational performance (Barrick, Day, Lord, & Alexander, 1991; Day & Lord, 1988), as well as upward influence by those lower in the organization directed toward those at higher levels (Mowday, 1978; Schilit & Locke, 1982). These are all relevant approaches to understanding the potential effects of leadership, but it is important to always keep in perspective the appropriate target and degree of leadership reach and to make sure that it matches the theoretical and analytical tools that are used.

Multiple Origins

Where does leadership come from? This is a deceptively tricky question because it goes to some of the fundamental assumptions about the nature of leadership. Far and away the most commonly researched source of leadership in I/O psychology is the individual leader (Day & Zaccaro, 2007). This is not surprising, given the attention paid to individual differences in the field of psychology. In particular, researchers have studied leadership with an eye toward understanding what personality traits, behaviors, and decision-making characteristics are associated with effective leaders. Each of these particular origins will be discussed in more detail in the chapter section that reviews various leadership theories. But even without being completely familiar with the theory, it is possible to appreciate how leadership is conceptualized differently by considering these various origins.

Given that many prominent scholars consider the ultimate source of leadership to be social influence (Hollander & Julian, 1969; Katz & Kahn, 1978), the early research on the personality traits of effective leaders (i.e., "Great Man" [sic] theory) approached leadership in terms of which personal characteristics were likely to be associated with influential individuals. As a result, the focus of the personality approach to leadership was and is tightly

on the individual leader. From this perspective, the essence of leadership resides with an individual leader, and the direction in which leadership flows is only from leader to follower. This is interesting because one of the most prominent of these personal characteristics—charisma—was originally proposed by Max Weber ([1924] 1947) as more of a sociological factor relating to how different societies preferred to be governed or led. It was only later that charisma was reconceptualized as an individual difference related to leadership (House, 1977).

An important implication of this perspective is that if leadership is thought to reside with the traits, behaviors, or cognitions of leaders, then the best way to develop more effective leadership is to focus on developing individual leaders (Day, 2000). But this also reveals one of the weaknesses of this line of thinking: Without followers, associates, or other people in the equation, how can there be any leadership? Leadership involves at least one other person in a mutually shared situation. Thus some of the more recent leadership approaches have widened the lens to consider sources beyond the individual leader.

A modest increment over a completely leader-centric focus is to include the possibility of reciprocal influence between a leader and follower, which was originally framed in terms of how the two parties mutually define the subordinate's role (Dansereau et al., 1975; Graen & Cashman, 1975). This perspective has been developed subsequently to consider the relationship between a leader and a follower (or member) as an important source of leadership in organizations (Graen & Uhl-Bien, 1995; Uhl-Bien, 2006). Specifically, it is thought that relationships generate resources that help to forge mutual respect, commitment, trust, and loyalty (Dienesch & Liden, 1986; Graen & Uhl-Bien, 1995). In this way, it is the resources that are embedded in the shared relationship that are important for leadership, rather than the actions of any one particular individual.

An even more inclusive approach to leadership views it not just as input to getting things done, but as an outcome of effective social processes and structure (Gibb, 1954; Salancik, Calder, Rowland, Leblebici, & Conway, 1975). At the group or team level, such processes serve to build teamwork among members, which enhances overall team learning, and ultimately develops team leadership capacity (Day et al., 2004). From this perspective, leadership is not the property of any single individual but is an emergent property within the system of the group (Hollander & Julian, 1969). When leadership is conceptualized in this manner, effectiveness in leadership becomes more of a product of the connections or relationships among members of the system than the result of any one part of that system (O'Connor & Quinn, 2004).

This illustrates another interesting and perhaps unique aspect of leadership, which is that it can originate from an individual, a dyad, or a broader set of relationships, and can even be possibly replaced by other factors in the social environment (Kerr & Jermier, 1978). The goal from a theoretical and research standpoint is to help illustrate ways in which these various perspectives link together—maybe through the use of multilevel modeling frameworks—rather than to try to identify which is the right approach. They all have merit and work in concert with each other as part of a high-performing system.

Multiple Criteria

There are two key ways in which leadership is operationalized as a criterion construct in research. The first and most prevalent way is in terms of leader *emergence,* or the extent to which someone is perceived as a leader (Lord, De Vader, & Alliger, 1986). The second way is in terms of leader *effectiveness,* with regard to a leader's effect on performance (Hogan, Curphy, & Hogan, 1994). Lord et al. (1986) stressed that much of the early work evaluating the linkages between personality and leadership was misinterpreted as pertaining to effectiveness when it was actually addressing the relationship between personality traits and leader emergence (i.e., perceptions).

Conceptually, there is a clear distinction between leader emergence and leader effectiveness, but when these different criterion variables are typically operationalized in leadership research, the distinction becomes muddled (House & Podsakoff, 1994). Both emergence and effectiveness variables tend to be based on others' ratings. Leader emergence refers to the degree to which a target individual is viewed as a leader by others, whereas leader effectiveness is usually based on ratings made by the leader's supervisor, peers, or subordinates. The point is that these ratings of leader effectiveness are likely contaminated by the raters' perceptions of that person as a leader (Judge, Bono, Ilies, & Gerhardt, 2002). It is impossible to disentangle leader emergence from leader effectiveness when both are based on the perceptually based ratings of observers. Although it might be argued that it would be more desirable to use objective measures of performance instead

of ratings, classic work in the field of performance appraisal has argued that objective performance measures (e.g., quantity, frequency) tend to be deficient as criteria, especially when used as measures of managerial performance (Landy & Farr, 1980). There is also a host of issues that can contaminate objective performance measures by including irrelevant information that potentially bias the data. For example, in assessing the relationship between executive leadership and organizational performance, it is unrealistic to expect immediate results following a change in top leadership. Indeed, it was shown that a three-year lag time (as compared with no lag) demonstrated more than double the effects of executive leadership on the performance outcome of profit margins (Day & Lord, 1988).

The issue is important because it goes to the construct validity of the criterion measures used in the majority of leadership research. Without a clear distinction between emergence and effectiveness, it is difficult to infer from the results of research efforts whether a given predictor variable is related primarily to how an individual is perceived as a leader or to his or her respective level of effectiveness as a leader. These are very different concerns. This is further complicated by research on *implicit leadership theories*, which suggest that effectiveness is an important factor in shaping whether someone is perceived as a leader or not (Binning, Zaba, & Whattam, 1986; Eden & Leviathan, 1975; Epitropaki & Martin, 2004; Lord et al, 1984). It is difficult to be perceived as a leader—especially over time—if the leader is associated with ineffective outcomes. As other authors have noted (House & Podsakoff, 1994), the use of perceptual measures of leadership has blurred the distinction between leader emergence and effectiveness, even though they appear to be conceptually distinct.

Similar confusion has been noted in the literature on organizational effectiveness. Therefore, it might make sense in assessing the criteria used for judging leadership to consider the guidelines recommended for mapping the construct space of effectiveness at the macro or organizational level (Cameron & Whetten, 1983), which include addressing questions such as: (a) From what perspective is effectiveness being judged? (b) On what domain of activity is the judgment focused? (c) What level of analysis is being used? (d) What is the purpose of judging effectiveness? (e) What time frame is being used? (f) What types of data are being used for judgments of effectiveness? and (g) What is the referent against which effectiveness is judged? To be clear, this is not suggesting that the outcome of leadership always be represented in terms of individual, group, or organizational effectiveness; leadership can often shape other important outcomes that deserve consideration in research and theory (Podolny, Khurana, & Hill-Popper, 2005). But when used as guidelines, these questions can help to clarify what is meant by leadership effectiveness in general and how it differs from leadership perceptions and leader emergence.

All of the issues discussed above (process orientation, multidisciplinary domains, multilevel focus, multiple origins, and multiple criteria) contribute to the unique positioning of leadership as a construct within I/O psychology. These issues also contribute significantly to the complexity that continues to challenge leadership researchers. But this does not mean that we are ignorant about leadership from a scientific and empirical standpoint—quite the contrary. As noted by certain leadership scholars (Avolio, Sosik, Jung, & Berson, 2003):

> We have learned an enormous amount about what constitutes leadership, where it comes from, how it can be measured, what contributes to it being ethical or unethical, how people see it differently and why, how the context alters its interpretation, and what happens when it is substituted or replaced.
> (p. 277)

In this spirit, the purpose of this chapter is to review and summarize what it is that we do know about leadership. Evidence from various theoretical approaches will be reviewed and organized around three theoretical themes: classical, bridging, and emerging. The chapter will close with a look to future theoretical, research, and practical directions, summarizing what we know about leadership and speculating on what we have yet to learn. The overall goal is to foster an eventual synthesis of the evidence; as such, it is the first step in effective use of scientific evidence in promoting an evidence-based approach (Rousseau, Manning, & Denyer, 2008) to leadership in I/O psychology.

Classical Leadership Theories/Frameworks
Evolutionary Perspectives on Leadership

A question that is as old as the field of psychology is how much of human behavior is due to nature (inherited characteristics) and how much is due to nurture (environment and learning). A similar question that is as old as the field of leadership is whether leaders are born or made. Unfortunately, these are not very interesting questions because the clear answer is that it is some combination of one's

personal makeup and what has been learned. This position was espoused even by the early pioneers of I/O psychology (Bingham, 1927). The empirical evidence supports an "and/both" rather than "either/or" perspective with regard to the importance of both nature and nurture in the development of leaders.

Using a sample of fraternal ($n = 178$) and identical ($n = 214$) female twins, it was estimated that 32% of the variance in leadership role occupancy was associated with heritability or nature (Arvey, Zhang, Avolio, & Krueger, 2007). Furthermore, another 10–15% of the variance was attributable directly to work and life experiences, and the remaining 50% "is as yet undiscovered" (p. 704). A previous study by some of these same authors demonstrated similar results—approximately 30% of the variance in leadership role occupancy could be accounted for by genetics—among a sample of fraternal ($n = 188$) and identical ($n = 238$) male twins (Arvey, Rotundo, Johnson, Zhang, & McGue, 2006). These results illustrate an important point with regard to leadership development: everyone has the potential for leadership, but some will need to work harder to develop it than others.

Ilies, Gerhardt, and Huy (2004) also investigated the extent to which leader emergence could be explained by genetic differences between individuals (i.e., heritability). Rather than comparing fraternal and identical twins directly, the researchers estimated the relationship between personality traits and intelligence with leader emergence, and the relative influence of heritability on personality and intelligence, using previously published estimates of the various components. The results indicated that approximately 17% of the variance in leader emergence could be explained by genetic effects, which are mediated by personality traits and intelligence. Again, these results support the conclusion that some amount of leadership (or emergence as a leader) is due to genetic factors, but the majority of the variance is shaped by non-genetic (e.g., environmental) influences.

There have even been empirical studies of the relationship between inherited physical characteristics (i.e., height) and career outcomes, including the ascendance into leadership (Judge & Cable, 2004). Across a meta-analysis and four large-sample studies, height was shown to be correlated significantly with leader emergence and work performance as well as annual earnings. It is a somewhat remarkable finding that, regardless of sex or occupation, height was positively and significantly related to annual pre-tax earnings. A theoretical model proposed and tested by the authors suggested that height is positively related to self- and social-esteem, which enhances both objective and subjective performance, which in turn contributes to career success in terms of ascendancy into leadership positions and superior job earnings. The authors chose to forgo an evolutionary explanation for their results, but it is clear that the perceptions of other people play an important role in leader emergence, and those individuals who are tall are more likely to be salient and potentially better suited to protect the group by virtue of their physical presence.

Rather than focus on the nature/nurture issue in attempting to estimate the extent that leadership is attributable to each of these sources, others have taken a more intentional and explicit evolutionary perspective on the topic of leadership. It should be noted that evolutionary psychology is an approach to understanding a given psychological construct and not a field of study on its own (Cosmides & Tooby, 1997). It is also helpful to consider that one of the guiding principles of evolutionary psychology is that the neural circuits in human brains were designed by natural selection to solve problems that human ancestors faced during the species' evolutionary history. Thus, from the perspective of evolutionary psychology, a relevant question to consider is: Why is leadership important?

The interrelationship between leadership, followership, and evolution was recently examined. Among the conclusions drawn from their analyses, Van Vugt, Hogan, and Kaiser (2008) assert that leading and following were adaptive strategies for dealing with social coordination problems in early group life, such as group movement, as well as conflict and competition within and between groups. But in order to capitalize on the benefits of leadership for social adaptation, it is necessary for individuals to recognize and identify leadership potential, which is something that "humans possess in abundance" (p. 184).

Although it is important from an evolutionary perspective to be able to identify potential leaders in a group, it is less clear why people would willingly put themselves in a subordinate follower position. Given the fitness and reproductive benefits associated with social status, leaders are generally better off than followers in those important evolutionary ways. The answer to the riddle appears to be that, although followers are generally less well-off than leaders, they are better off than individuals in poorly led groups. Nonetheless, the relationship between leaders and followers is "inherently ambiguous" (p. 182) due to followers' vulnerability and potential exploitation by leaders.

Perhaps most revealing of all in this evolutionary analysis are the insights gleaned about the evolution of leadership throughout history. Beginning with pre-human society and a leadership structure based on "alpha leaders" in dominance-oriented hierarchies, leadership has evolved through prestige-based "big men" (tribal leadership) to formalized and hereditary-based leadership (chiefs, kings, and warlords) to a centralized but democratic leadership structure that is hierarchical but also participatory (state and business leadership). What is particularly interesting about these various leadership structures is the mismatch hypothesis, which posits on the possible lack of fit between the evolved leadership psychology of present-day humans and the way in which leadership is practiced in many modern organizations (Van Vugt, 2012; Van Vugt, Johnson, Kaiser, & O'Gorman, 2008). This hypothesis might help to explain why leaders become abusive or why leadership practices revert to more primal forms in times of crises.

What has been learned from taking an evolutionary perspective on leadership is that heredity plays a role, but the environment and learning play even larger roles in shaping leaders. It also illustrates the role that dominance plays in leadership, emerging as the earliest leadership structure in pre-human society, but that aspects of dominance (e.g., height) may still today partly influence who ascends into leadership roles. Furthermore, the leadership structure of modern organizations may be poorly matched at times to "our advanced leadership psychology, which might explain the alienation and frustration of many citizens and employees" (Van Vugt, Hogan, & Kaiser, 2008, p. 182).

Trait-based Perspectives on Leadership

The question of how leaders might be different—which has usually meant superior—to followers has been of long-standing interest to researchers and practitioners in the field of leadership. The initial approaches that addressed this question were greatly influenced by heritability perspectives on exceptional individuals (e.g., Galton, 1869), focusing on personality traits as innate or heritable qualities of leaders and followers (Zaccaro, 2007). But rather than continuing to be confined to innate and immutable personality characteristics, the meaning of the term *trait* has evolved away from purely heritable qualities.

Leader traits have been defined as "relatively stable and coherent integrations of personal characteristics that foster a consistent pattern of leadership performance across a variety of group and organizational situations" (Zaccaro, Kemp, & Bader, 2004, p. 104). From this perspective, traits can be considered more broadly to include any type of a stable individual difference, including personality, affect, motives, cognitive abilities, skills, and expertise.

The first empirically based treatment of the personal characteristics thought to be associated with leadership was published in 1925; it proposed 15 qualities that were inductively determined through interviews conducted with 110 successful business executives (Craig & Charters, 1925). Another early book that was grounded in industrial psychology (and dedicated to Walter Van Dyke Bingham) listed 10 desirable leader qualities, including enthusiasm, integrity, decisiveness, intelligence, and faith (Tead, 1935). It is difficult to argue with such a list, but that was part of the problem. Lists of plausible leader traits became increasingly prevalent and lengthy. Stogdill (1948) listed 32 personal factors associated with leadership, whereas Bird (1940) listed 70 potential leader attributes. Coupled with a lack of psychometrically sound measures for many of these proposed attributes, the field became mired in trying to deal with the sheer number of plausible leader traits.

The field reached a tipping point of sorts when several prominent researchers began examining the empirical evidence for the trait-based perspective of leadership. Stogdill (1948), Gibb (1947), and Mann (1959) all seemed to provide pessimistic assessments of the field and were widely quoted in subsequent textbooks as "sounding the death knell for the leader trait perspective" (Zaccaro, 2007, p. 10). Other approaches based on leader behaviors and situational contingencies began to emerge and replace the leader trait perspective.

What transpired to revive the leader trait perspective is largely attributable to advances in research methodology and statistical analysis. One of Stogdill's (1948) criticisms of the leader trait field concerned the lack of evidence for the cross-situational consistency of leadership. Specifically, he stated that "... persons who are leaders in one situation may not necessarily be leaders in other situations" (p. 65). A study designed to test this assertion (Barnlund, 1962) apparently supported Stogdill's much-quoted conclusion that leaders in one group situation did not emerge as leaders in other group situations. Later still, these data were reanalyzed using more sophisticated statistical models and were shown to support an entirely different perspective: Between 49% and 82% of the variance in leader emergence could be attributed to stable leader attributes (Kenny & Zaccaro, 1983).

The other methodological advance that brought about a reconsideration of the role of personality traits and leadership was meta-analysis. A now well-known limitation of trying to aggregate findings across studies to reach some overall estimate of effect size is that these estimates can be biased due to sampling error associated with small sample sizes, as well as measurement error due to imperfect reliability among other artifacts (Hunter & Schmidt, 1990). As a result, merely averaging effects or trying otherwise to ascertain their consistency across studies is biased unless procedures are taken to adjust for these potential problems. Meta-analysis revolutionized I/O psychology and reenergized a number of areas of study, including that of leader traits, which had been written off as a result of weak findings using traditional narrative or other flawed review approaches.

Some of the first researchers to apply meta-analytic procedures to leadership studies were Lord and colleagues (Lord et al., 1986). These researchers noted a least two major weaknesses with the previous reviews of the relationship between personality traits and leadership (e.g., Mann, 1959; Stogdill, 1948). The first was that inferior methods were used in reaching these previous conclusions, and the second was that this previous research had been misinterpreted as applying to a leader's effect on performance (i.e., effectiveness), when the criteria in most of the studies in these reviews pertained to leadership emergence. Lord et al. (1986) subsequently reanalyzed the studies reviewed by Mann (1959) via meta-analysis and found that the traits of intelligence, masculinity-femininity, and dominance were significantly related to leadership perceptions (i.e., emergence). These effects held, even after updating their database with studies published subsequent to Mann's (1959) review.

Additional meta-analytic work has further supported the general conclusion that personality traits matter when it comes to leadership. A qualitative and quantitative review of the relationship between personality and leadership focused on the five-factor model of personality (Judge et al., 2002). The so-called Big Five personality model was another advance that sparked resurgent interest in personality research in I/O psychology. The analyses were based on 222 correlations from 73 independent samples and demonstrated an overall multiple correlation of .48 between the Big Five personality factors and leadership. Results from the individual meta-analyses on the specific trait factors showed that *extraversion* was the most consistent correlate of leadership across settings and relevant criteria (emergence and effectiveness). *Conscientiousness*, *openness*, and *neuroticism* (reversed) all demonstrated non-zero relationships with leadership. Only the Big Five factor of *agreeableness* was shown to be unrelated to leadership. From these generally robust results, Judge et al. (2002) concluded that their findings "provide strong evidence in favor of the trait approach…" (p. 776) and urged future researchers to develop process models to help illuminate the dispositional source of leadership.

In yet another application of meta-analysis, researchers examined the relationships between the personality factor of self-monitoring and a number of work-related outcomes including leadership (Day, Schleicher, Unckless, & Hiller, 2002). Self-monitoring personality pertains to individual differences in the extent to which people observe, regulate, and control the public appearances of self that they display (Snyder, 1987). The meta-analytic results indicated an overall correlation between self-monitoring and leadership outcomes across 23 samples (N = 2,777) to be .21 corrected only for sampling and measurement error. These results suggest that those individuals who tend to monitor and control the images that they present to better fit with the social environment around them (i.e., high self-monitors) are more likely to be seen as leaders and to be rated more effectively than individuals who tend to be true to themselves and display more consistent behaviors across situations. Although several explanations have been offered with regard to this finding, it remains the source of ongoing debate (Bedeian & Day, 2004). Specifically, if high self-monitors are social chameleons, as some have suggested (Kilduff & Day, 1994), then why would they make for better leaders than the more consistent and principled low self-monitors?

What is needed is a framework or process model that might help to better understand the dispositional approach to leadership. Zaccaro et al. (2004) offered one such model of leader attributes and leader performance, positing that more distal attributes (traits) such as personality, motive values (e.g., motivation to lead; Chan & Drasgow, 2001), and cognitive abilities directly influence more proximal attributes such as problem-solving skills, social appraisal skills, and expertise. The proximal attributes serve as input to leadership processes at the next stage operating in a leader's environment, which ultimately influence leader emergence,

effectiveness, and advancement. This general framework offers researchers a way to conceptualize and then examine how combinations of traits and attributes, integrated in meaningful ways, are likely to better predict leadership outcomes than are the independent contributions of multiple traits (Foti & Hauenstein, 2007; Zaccaro, 2007).

In summary, the trait-based approach to leadership has seen a resurgence of research interest in the early part of the twenty-first century. Although it is one of the oldest systematic approaches to leadership, and had fallen out of favor following several critical reviews of the available evidence in the mid-twentieth century, the consolidating influence of the five-factor personality model, along with the use and acceptance of meta-analysis, have contributed significantly to this interest.

Behavioral Perspectives on Leadership

Beginning in the 1950s and continuing through to the present, there has been strong research interest in leadership behavior. The focal question from this approach is: What is it that effective leaders do that distinguishes them from less effective leaders or from followers? This shift in perspectives from leader traits to behaviors corresponds roughly with the ascendancy of behaviorism as the dominant theoretical voice in psychology. Rather than consider unobservable dispositional motive forces, the proponents of behaviorism maintained that only observable variables were worthy of scientific study. Ralph Stogdill is often credited with being a driving force behind the abandonment of the trait approach in favor of the leader behavior movement, even though accounts from a former student and collaborator (Ed Fleishman) suggest that Stogdill never intended for his 1948 review to be a rejection of trait approaches; rather, his conclusions were widely misinterpreted in an overly pessimistic manner by other leadership researchers (Day & Zaccaro, 2007).

One factor that had a profound effect on the rise of the behavioral approach to leadership was the widespread acceptance of survey research in the social sciences and psychology in particular. As noted by one prominent leadership scholar: "Survey research with questionnaires is by far the most common method to study the relationship between leadership behavior and various antecedents…or outcomes of this behavior" (Yukl, 2006, p. 57). But questions remain as to whether a construct with such phenomenological origins such as leadership (Calder, 1977) can be legitimately studied using questionnaires. What do the resulting data actually reflect? This is a question without a clear answer, even today.

OHIO STATE AND MICHIGAN STUDIES

The leader behavior approach was radical for its time because it was the first such research program to rely on a statistical technique. The approach taken by a team of researchers at Ohio State University (led by Stogdill) compiled a list of around 1,800 specific leadership behaviors, ultimately reduced to 150 examples of important behaviors for effective leaders. Ratings from civilian and military personnel were gathered whereby respondents rated their respective supervisors (who were assumed to also be leaders) on these behavioral items, which were then subjected to a relatively new statistical procedure called factor analysis. The procedure is used to explain the variability of relationships among observed variables in terms of a smaller number of unobserved dimensions or factors. From these 150 observed behaviors, factor analytic techniques were used to derive (through hand calculations) two broad categories of leader behavior: *consideration* (concern for people) and *initiating structure* (concern for task accomplishment; Halpin & Winer, 1957). The resulting questionnaire went through several revisions before being published as the Leader Behavior Description Questionnaire, Form XII or LBDQ XII (Stogdill, Goode, & Day, 1962). It is probably one of the most famous—or infamous—survey measures in the field of leadership.

Around this same time, researchers at the University of Michigan were also investigating leadership behaviors. In addition to task-oriented and relations-oriented behavior, the Michigan researchers also identified participative leadership and peer leadership as significant factors for group effectiveness (Bowers & Seashore, 1966). These are important additions in that they recognized the role of peer leadership in addition to supervisor-based leadership behavior. As such, participative and peer leadership were precursors to forms of shared leadership that are gaining interest with contemporary leadership researchers (Pearce & Conger, 2003a). The Michigan group authored their own leader behavior questionnaire called the Survey of Organizations (Taylor & Bowers, 1972), which measured multiple aspects of task- and relations-oriented behavior enacted by supervisors and peers.

It is difficult to overestimate the influence of the factors of *consideration* and *initiating structure* on the leadership field. The dimensions reappear in a number of other leadership theories across the years (e.g., contingency theories, transformational leadership) and have generated scores of research studies. A recent meta-analysis on the validity of *consideration* and *initiating structure* in leadership research (Judge, Piccolo, & Ilies, 2004) identified 159 and 163 correlations with leadership outcomes, respectively, for the factors. Furthermore, results indicated that across all criteria evaluated (e.g., follower job satisfaction, follower satisfaction with leader, follower motivation, leader job performance, group/organization performance, leader effectives) the average sample-weighted correlation was .41 for *consideration* and .24 for *initiating structure*, with credibility and confidence intervals excluding zero for both constructs. Because of the surprising strength of these results, Judge et al. (2004) referred to these classic leadership factors as the "forgotten ones" (p. 36) and argued "that it is inadvisable, at this point, to abandon Consideration and Initiating Structure in leadership research" (p. 47).

LIMITATIONS WITH LEADERSHIP QUESTIONNAIRES

Despite this cautionary advice from Judge et al. (2004), there are serious concerns associated with the use of leadership questionnaires, which is how these factors are typically measured. One of the assumptions underpinning the use of questionnaires to measure leader behavior is that the respondents completing those behavioral ratings store in memory and recall observed behaviors. The research evidence suggests that this is an erroneous assumption. When forming impressions of another, observers tend to quickly categorize and characterize (i.e., attach trait labels) to observed behaviors and then go back and correct those trait-based inferences in an effortful manner if there are adequate cognitive resources to do so (Gilbert, 1998). An important implication of this aspect of person perception is that behaviors consistent with an impression of a target person will be endorsed (i.e., rated favorably) even if they never occurred (Sulsky & Day, 1992). Researchers are fooling themselves if they believe that responses to questionnaires accurately reflect observed leader behavior and only leader behavior.

Another factor that has been shown to influence questionnaire ratings of leader behavior is related to a reverse causality issue. Psychology students are trained from their earliest university days to understand that correlation does not mean causation. An assumption with using leadership surveys is that the rated leader behaviors are the cause of individual, group, or organizational outcomes. Unfortunately, most of the questionnaire-based leadership research has used cross-sectional designs, making an alternative inference that performance causes the ratings impossible to rule out (not to mention third variable confounds).

This is not just speculation. Research going back to the 1970s has shown that group members who received bogus group performance feedback distorted their group process ratings in the direction of that feedback (Downey, Chacko, & McElroy, 1979; Staw, 1975). More squarely in the leadership domain, individuals who were told that the videotaped group they had watched was either one of the best or one of the worst of all the groups studied were later shown to provide LBDQ ratings of the group leader biased in the direction of that performance cue feedback—despite seeing identical leader behaviors (e.g., Lord, Binning, Rush, & Thomas, 1978; Mitchell, Larson, & Green, 1977). Put simply, raters infer effective leadership from good group performance and ineffective leadership from poor performance, regardless of what they actually see.

The notion that there are behaviors that distinguish effective from ineffective leaders or leaders from followers has merit. Unfortunately, any such insights about leader behavior have been undermined by the predominantly cross-sectional, questionnaire-based research methodology. Given the dynamic nature of leadership and the various factors that can bias how raters see and evaluate it, there are serious concerns that should be taken into account before attempting to draw any meaningful causal conclusions from research conducted in this manner using survey questionnaires (Antonakis, Bendahan, Jacquart, & Lalive, 2010). All of the evidence suggests that it may be unrealistic to assume that we can measure leadership with a questionnaire. But there is one thing about leadership questionnaires that appears to be beyond dispute: design a brief, easy-to-administer survey questionnaire and researchers will use it. Nonetheless, we should not lose sight of the fact that a map is not the territory, and simply labeling a survey questionnaire a "leadership measure" does not mean that it actually measures leadership.

Situational and Contingency Approaches to Leadership

The next wave of leadership research focused on factors in the situation that might alter the effects of a leader's behavior on relevant outcomes. In other words, the most appropriate leadership "style"

(e.g., behavior, decision-making approach, or other action) was thought to be contingent on situational factors. The motivation behind the rise of contingency leadership theories was the conflicting results with regard to whether *consideration* or *initiating structure* (or a combination) was the preferred leadership style. Although the approach appears to be straightforward in its origins, it ultimately did not have long-standing influence, mainly because the factors that can be used to describe any situation are so varied and difficult to measure—especially with a questionnaire.

The situational or contingency approach is built on the assumption that leadership depends on the situation (Fiedler, 1996; Vroom & Jago, 2007); however, much of the evidence that the effects of leadership vary with the situation was gathered prior to the development of contemporary meta-analytic techniques. And, as noted previously, relatively recent meta-analytic findings have suggested that the predictive validity of the "forgotten ones" of *consideration* and *initiating structure* might be more robust than earlier researchers had concluded (Judge et al., 2004). Despite this reassessment of the robustness of these leader behaviors, the contingency movement helped to bring attention to the role of the situation in leadership processes, if only to demonstrate the difficulties of such endeavors.

The overall goal of contingency theories is to optimally match the source of leadership with particular aspects of the situation in order to enhance desired outcomes, such as follower satisfaction or performance. Although there are a number of different theories from this perspective, the classic contingency theories can be generally classified into those that focused on matching leader traits and those that focused on fitting leader behavior with aspects of the situation (Ayman & Adams, 2012). Situational variables have been conceptualized around a variety of factors, including the quality of leader-member relations, task structure, and position power (Fiedler's contingency theory); stress associated with the boss, coworkers, and the task (cognitive resource theory); availability of information, team support and cohesion, available time, and other factors (normative decision model); as well as subordinate characteristics such as needs, values, and ability (path-goal theory) and follower maturity level (situational leadership theory).

Brief descriptions of each of these five contingency theories (or models) are presented next, including an overall assessment of the respective research support for each. But this is not an exhaustive overview of leadership contingency theories. There are others, such as the multiple linkage model (Yukl, 1971) and substitutes for leadership (Kerr & Jermier, 1978); however, the five discussed below have garnered the most research attention.

FIEDLER'S CONTINGENCY THEORY

Fiedler (1964, 1967) is credited with formulating the first theory combining leader traits with situational variables. Leaders were thought to manifest either a task-motivated or relationship-motivated style, which was measured by the least preferred coworker (LPC) scale. Scale respondents were instructed to think of their least preferred coworker (the person with whom the respondent least preferred to work) and to rate this person on a set of bipolar adjectives. Those who described their least preferred coworker in more positive terms were thought to have a high level of relationship motivation (desire to have close coworker relations), whereas those using more negative terms were classified as holding a high task motivation (desire to achieve task objectives).

The model predicted that relationship-oriented or high LPC leaders would be more effective in situations that were moderately favorable for the leader, whereas task-oriented or low LPC leaders would be more effective in either highly unfavorable or highly favorable situations. The degree of situational favorableness was defined in terms of leader-member relations (good/poor), position power (strong/weak), and task structure (structured/unstructured). Considering all the possible situational combinations provides eight levels, or octants, of favorability.

There was considerable research activity around Fiedler's contingency theory, most of it conducted by Fiedler and his students, resulting in three published meta-analyses (Peters, Hartke, & Pohlmann, 1985; Schriesheim, Tepper, & Tetrault, 1994; Strube & Garcia, 1981), each using different analytic techniques and yielding somewhat different results. Although the overall results have suggested some cautious support for the model, there are lingering concerns with the fundamentals of the LPC measure—specifically, what exactly it might be measuring (Schriesheim & Kerr, 1977)—as well as the amount of empirical support that there is across all of the situational octants.

There is a final point with regard to this contingency approach, and that has to do with a trait-based perspective on the leaders. Given that traits are thought to be generally stable across time, Fiedler did not believe that leaders could alter their style of leadership. Instead, leaders should be selected for situations that fit with their style, or they should diagnose and engineer the job situation to better fit with their particular style. The foundation of this approach is based on the concept of leader match (Fiedler, Chemers, & Mahar, 1976), which has been heavily criticized. The most serious of the critics argued that Fiedler's contingency theory, on which the leader match concept is based, suffers from a number of serious inadequacies that "...render the concept meaningless at best, at worst, downright dangerous" (Hosking & Schriesheim, 1978, p. 498), in that some leaders could suffer serious career harm as a result of its application.

In an ironic twist, subsequent meta-analyses of various managerial training interventions concluded that the results of leader match generalize across situations and because of its demonstrated effectiveness and utility that "...compared with...other leadership training programs, this method of leadership training is encouraged" (Burke & Day, 1986, p. 242). Despite this recommendation, neither Fiedler's theory nor the leader match concept is the focus of much research or practice today.

COGNITIVE RESOURCE THEORY (CRT)

This is an extension of sorts of Fiedler's earlier work on contingency theories of leadership effectiveness. CRT examines the interaction of leader intelligence and experience in conjunction with the amount of stress in a given situation (Fiedler & Garcia, 1987). Specifically, CRT proposed that when under stress the leader's effectiveness will be positively related to his or her experience and negatively related to intelligence. The reverse was predicted for low-stress situations: intelligence rather than experience predicts effectiveness. Although research has provided some support for these contingency hypotheses (e.g., Gibson, Fiedler, & Barrett, 1993; Potter & Fiedler, 1981), CRT has not attracted much of a research following, other than Fiedler and his students.

NORMATIVE MODEL OF LEADERSHIP DECISION MAKING

This approach conceptualizes leadership entirely in terms of leaders' decision making (Vroom & Jago, 1988; Vroom & Yetton, 1973). In particular, it focuses on the amount of decision-making participation or involvement that a leader extends to subordinates. This is a prescriptive model in that by following a set of decision rules, a leader can be advised of a recommended feasible set of process orientations for a given decision (Vroom & Jago, 2007). The types of prescribed decisions range on a continuum of subordinate involvement from fully autocratic (no involvement) to consultative (moderate) to full group participation (high involvement). Within the model there are various decision heuristics that characterize the situation around four possible decision criteria: (a) improve the decision quality, (b) enhance subordinate involvement, (c) reduce decision-making time, and (d) develop subordinates.

Research conducted on the model has shown general support for it, especially when the data regarding the ultimate decision outcomes in terms of quality, involvement, time, and subordinate development are collected from the leader's perspective (Field & House, 1990). It is an open question as to whether this model is used much by practicing leaders to enhance their decision-making effectiveness. It does not appear to be the case.

PATH-GOAL THEORY

The focus of this theory is on how leaders can help motivate subordinates to better reach their goals (Evans, 1970; House, 1971). The theoretical foundation is based on the expectancy theory of motivation. The functions of the leader include increasing extrinsic rewards to subordinates for achieving work goals, clarifying the paths to these rewards, removing obstacles that impede goal attainment, and increasing opportunities for subordinate satisfaction. Path-goal theory is a contingency model because it proposes that the effects of the leader on subordinate outcomes are moderated by situational variables, of which there are two kinds: (a) environment, and (b) subordinate characteristics (House & Mitchell, 1974). The gist of the model is that leaders need to adapt their behavioral style to fit with the situation in order to maximize subordinates' motivation (effort) to attain the desired outcomes. There are four classes of leader behavior: (a) *supportive* (showing consideration), (b) *directive* (setting direction and providing structure), (c) *participative* (consulting with subordinates), and (d) *achievement-oriented* (setting challenging goals for subordinates and showing confidence in their success).

Leadership style influences subordinate motivation and effort through a number of different channels. Supportive leadership is thought to reduce subordinate boredom, increase self-confidence, and lower anxiety, which increases the intrinsic value of the job and the effort-performance expectancy. Directive leadership reduces role ambiguity,

increases incentives, and strengthens reward contingencies, which increases the effort-performance and performance-reward expectancies, and enhances the reward valence for task success. Participative leadership is hypothesized to increase role clarity with unstructured tasks, which increases subordinate effort and satisfaction but has little effect when the task is structured. Achievement-oriented leadership is thought to increase subordinates' self-confidence and the effort-performance expectancy when the task is unstructured, but will have little effect with simple and repetitive tasks.

Most of the conceptual and empirical work has been conducted on supportive and directive leadership using subordinate questionnaires and cross-sectional designs, which makes it difficult to fully evaluate the theory or interpret results of research testing the theory. A published meta-analysis evaluated the evidence for over 30 hypotheses stemming from path-goal theory across 120 studies (Wofford & Liska, 1993). Support for the theory was mixed, but the overall conclusion was that many of the studies designed to test aspects of the theory were seriously flawed, precluding a conclusive evaluation of the merits of the theory.

A conceptual weakness of path-goal theory is its foundation in the expectancy theory of motivation, which is overly complex and perhaps too rational as a human decision-making model (Yukl, 2006). A subsequent reformulation of the theory attempted to address some of these concerns by making the theory more comprehensive (House, 1996); however, with the resulting 10 classes of leader behavior, subordinate individual differences, and task moderator variables organized around 26 different propositions, the enhanced comprehensiveness appears to come at a cost of reduced parsimony. In addition, the evidence is fairly weak for the overall validity of the model (Schriesheim, Castro, Zhou, & DeChurch, 2006). The conclusion of researchers who conducted a thorough review of the purported moderators of leader behavior (Podsakoff, MacKenize, Ahearne, & Bommer, 1995) was that: "...we find the lack of support for the moderating effects predicted by path-goal...leadership models both shocking and disappointing. It is hard to believe that so much research, by so many...over such a long period of time, could have produced such meager results" (p. 465).

SITUATIONAL LEADERSHIP THEORY (SLT)

This approach proposes that the appropriate type of leader behavior (task- or relationship-oriented) depends on the level of follower maturity, conceptualized in terms of ability and self-confidence (Hersey & Blanchard, 1969a, 1969b). As subordinates develop from immature (low ability and low confidence) to fully mature (high ability and high confidence), the amount of task-oriented leader behavior decreases in a linear function from high to low. On the same developmental continuum, relationship-oriented leader behavior is proposed to demonstrate an inverted-U function in which the most support and concern on the part of the leader is provided around the middle of the developmental continuum (high ability and low self-confidence, or low ability and high confidence). When dealing with fully mature subordinates, the prescribed leadership approach is delegation. Leadership style is assessed with a self-report instrument called the Leadership Effectiveness Adaptability Description (LEAD), although many researchers have used the LBDQ XII (Stogdill et al., 1962).

The SLT model is intuitively appealing and was at one time very popular with leadership development consultants (Graeff, 1983); however, empirical support for the approach is weak. An examination of the assumptions underlying SLT suggested little support for the theoretical foundations of the theory (Blank, Weitzel, & Green, 1990). Specifically, there was little evidence that subordinate performance and satisfaction were significantly predicted by the interaction between leader behavior (task and relationship) and follower maturity. Despite the positive aspects of the theory—in theory—such as the focus on follower development and that followers need to be treated differently depending on their maturity levels, there is only a weak empirical foundation for it, and its use in leadership development programs appears to have waned.

CONCLUSIONS

The general contingency theory proposition that leadership is a function of the leader (traits and behaviors), followers, and the situation makes good conceptual sense; however, the research support for the various theories is modest at best and generally mixed. Why is there such a disconnection between what at one level appears to be sound theory and at another provides little evidence-based direction? Part of the problem has to do with the difficulties associated with trying to parse a complex and multifaceted construct, such as the situation, into a core set of measurable variables. Invariably, there is some (probably large) degree of criterion deficiency in which potentially important aspects of the situation are overlooked.

There are also basic measurement problems and the overuse of weak research designs that preclude the ability to make strong causal inferences (Korman & Tanofsky, 1975). Another problem is the overreliance on testing statistical interactions (cross-product or moderator variables) based on correlational data collected using cross-sectional designs. It may also be that researchers are conceptualizing the situation in overly micro ways and that they might be better conceptualized as meso-level constructs that influence leader-follower effects in a cross-level fashion. This would call for the use of multilevel research designs and analytical tools such as hierarchical liner modeling (Raudenbush & Bryk, 2002), which would make sense given that multiple followers are nested typically within leaders who are nested in situations. It is possible that the entire contingency theory approach is based on an inappropriate consideration of these important multilevel issues.

Finally, there has been the tendency to overcomplicate all leadership theory (Schriesheim, 2003) and contingency theories in particular. Even if stronger empirical support were readily available for some of the predictions from various contingency theories, would practicing managers use them? It seems unlikely that the average manager would be able to put into place or act on something that requires such extensive deliberation. Remember that I/O psychology is grounded in the scientist-practitioner model, so the development of theories that would be of little applied relevance to practitioners—even if scientifically valid—is at odds with the core values of the field.

As indicated by the publication dates of many of the references in this section, the classical models of leadership originated in the 1940s or slightly before and reached their heyday in the 1980s. The possible exception is leadership trait theories, which are experiencing resurgent interest. It is also evident that many contingency theories were influenced by the Ohio State factors of *consideration* (concern for people and relationships) and *initiating structure* (concern for task and goal accomplishment). Unfortunately, the vast amount of research directed at finding under what conditions each leadership factor would be most effective failed to provide robust and clear-cut answers. And as suggested by recent meta-analytic findings (Judge et al., 2004), the evidence suggests that the main effects of *consideration* and *initiating structure* on relevant leadership outcomes may be worthy of reconsideration.

The next set of leadership theories to be reviewed began their ascendancy around the last quarter of the twentieth century and bridge with those just emerging in the first decade of the twenty-first century. For that reason, these are termed *bridging theories*, although they could have just as easily been labeled *post-classical theories*.

Bridging Leadership Theories
Charismatic/Transformational Leadership

The term *charisma* has been used to describe a particular type of inspirational leadership, thanks primarily to the work of sociologist Max Weber ([1924] 1947). Bass (2008) provides a detailed overview on the origins of charisma in the leadership literature. But it was through the efforts of Robert House and colleagues (House, 1977; Shamir, House, & Arthur, 1993) that a fully formed, psychologically based theory of charismatic leadership was developed. Around this same time, James MacGregor Burns published a best-selling book on political leadership in which he compared *transforming leadership,* based on higher moral values for social reform, with *transactional leadership,* based on self-interest and the exchange of benefits (Burns, 1978). Bernard Bass and colleagues further developed the theory with an emphasis on leadership in settings other than politics, such as business, government, and military organizations (Bass, 1985; Bass & Riggio, 2006). Further advances were made with the integration of transformational, charismatic, and visionary theories of leadership (House & Shamir, 1993), but what really propelled the theory forward in terms of attracting researchers to the topic was the development of the Multifactor Leadership Questionnaire (MLQ; Bass & Avolio, 2000).

Taken together, the emergence of charismatic, transformational, and visionary leadership theories collectively define what some have termed the New Leadership School (Bass, 2008; Bryman, 1992), representing a potential paradigm shift in the field of leadership theory and research (Hunt, 1999). The leadership field was on the verge of scholarly collapse and practical irrelevance prior to the development of these streams of thinking. What the approaches added to the study of leadership was an emphasis on important and overlooked aspects of inspiration, identification, and vision. Most leadership scholars today discuss charisma and transformational leadership together, in large part to the influence of Bass, who incorporated it into a multidimensional theory of transactional and transformational leadership,

as well as to the integrative focus of House and Shamir (1993). Before reviewing the components of this theory and summarizing the research findings to date, it is of historical interest to note that Bass was a former graduate student of Ralph Stogdill at Ohio State.

The most recent conceptualization of transformational leadership theory is as the full range leadership model (Avolio, 1999, 2004; Bass & Riggio, 2006). A foundation for leadership is set with transactional factors such as *contingent reward* (CR) and *management-by-exception* (MBE; active/passive), which some have attributed more to management than leadership. According to Bass (1985), world-class leadership transcends these transactional factors to also address aspects of *idealized influence* (II; serving as role models that enhance trust, respect, and identification, which includes attributed charisma), *inspirational motivation* (IM; behaving in ways that motivate and inspire others), *intellectual stimulation* (IS; stimulating creativity and innovation in the thinking of others), and *individualized consideration* (IC; paying attention to the special needs of each follower). A non-leadership dimension of *laissez-faire leadership* (LF; avoidant or inactive leadership) describes a dimension in which leadership responsibilities are ignored, actions are delayed, and decisions go unmade.

It is important to emphasize that world-class leaders are thought to go beyond the use of transactional leadership to also exemplify the various components of transformational leadership, which has been termed the *augmentation effect* (Bass & Avolio, 1993). From a research perspective, this means that the effects of transformational leadership should be examined incrementally to determine what is explained by the transactional leadership components. Thus it would be theoretically inappropriate to examine only the effects of the transformational leadership factors without first determining what was predicted by transactional leadership. Bass has even gone on record in stating directly that "the best leaders are both transformational and transactional" (Bass, 1999, p. 21).

As mentioned, a notable feature of the theory is the development of the MLQ for use in measuring the various theory components. Typically, subordinates rate various leadership "behaviors" of their leader or supervisor that are indicative of the different dimensions. The following are example items for each of the components, beginning with the most ineffective and progressing to the so-called 4Is of transformational leadership (from Bass & Riggio, 2006, pp. 6–9):

LF: The leader avoids getting involved when important issues arise.

MBE-passive: The leader takes no action until complaints are received.

MBE-active: The leader directs attention toward failures to meet standards.

CR: The leader makes clear what one can expect to receive when performance goals are achieved.

II: The leader emphasizes the importance of having a collective sense of mission.

IM: The leader articulates a compelling vision of the future.

IS: The leader gets others to look at problems from many different angles.

IC: The leader spends time teaching and coaching.

The typical measurement approach is to have one or more subordinates rate the leader on his or her behavioral style using the MLQ. As such, it is not a direct rating of leader behavior as much as it is the overall evaluation on the various subcomponents of each leadership factor. Early meta-analytic work on 39 published and unpublished studies using the MLQ, designed around an earlier version of the theory, demonstrated overall positive and generalizable relationships with effectiveness outcomes for every component except for MBE (Lowe, Kroeck, & Sivasubramanian, 1996). Indeed, the average corrected (i.e., true score) correlation with effectiveness outcomes was .73 across the transformational leadership dimensions. Despite these encouraging results, there were concerns regarding the potential effects of same-source ratings biases inflating the primary study correlations with effectiveness, in that subordinates tended to provide the leadership as well as the outcome ratings. Also, Lowe et al. were unable to test for the hypothesized augmentation effects because insufficient numbers of studies had adopted this research approach.

A subsequent meta-analysis on transformational and transactional leadership was able to address both of these issues. Across 626 correlations from 87 sources, it was shown that transformational leadership had an overall validity (corrected for statistical artifacts) of .44, whereas CR showed an average corrected validity of .39, LZ leadership correlated on average -.37 with outcomes, and the MBE components were inconsistently related to the criteria (Judge & Piccolo, 2004). Nonetheless, the average validity for transformational leadership was substantially lower than that found in the Lowe et al.

(1996) meta-analysis, possibly reflecting the use of more rigorous research designs as the theory gained wider acceptance over the years. Indeed, moderator analyses examining the influence of using independent data sources showed substantial divergence in effects when comparing same-source with different-source ratings. In tests of the augmentation effect, transformational leadership was shown to have overall significant incremental effects over what was predicted by the transactional and LF leadership components, as well as for the components of follower motivation and satisfaction with the leader, leader effectiveness, but not for leader job performance.

On a somewhat more troubling note, the transactional leadership component of CR was found to relate to overall transformational leadership at an exceptionally high level (corrected true correlation of .80). LF leadership was also strongly correlated with transformational leadership (true correlation of -.65). Both of these findings illustrate potential concerns about the conceptual independence of transformational leadership from some of the other factors in the theory, and empirically it "makes it difficult to separate their unique effects" (Judge & Piccolo, 2004, p. 765).

In conclusion, transformational-transactional leadership theory has had a substantial influence on leadership research and practice over the past two decades. Part of this influence is no doubt due to the compelling features of the theory and the gaps that it filled relative to earlier leadership theories. But this influence is also attributable to the development of a questionnaire measure that can be used to measure "leadership" in a fairly easy and straightforward manner. Despite its prominence in the leadership field, it remains to be seen what the future holds for transformational leadership theory. With the death of Bass in 2008 and Avolio's current focus on different leadership issues, transformational leadership theory will need to continue without two of its pioneering champions. In addition, the theory will need to develop a longitudinal research focus that transcends the predominant use of single-shot, cross-sectional survey designs in demonstrating unequivocally that transformational leaders actually transform individuals and organizations (Antonakis, 2012). In short, charismatic and transformational leadership theory is at a crossroads, and the next few years will be telling in terms of whether the theory will continue its dominance of the field or will fall by the wayside, like so many other leadership theories before it.

Leader-Member Exchange (LMX)

This theoretical approach to leadership focuses on the quality of the exchange relationship that develops between a leader and a particular follower. It was first introduced into the literature as the *vertical dyad linkage* theory of leadership (Dansereau et al., 1975; Graen, Cashman, Ginsburgh, & Schiemann, 1977), which is descriptive of the focus on the leader-follower (supervisor-subordinate) dyad. The theory developed beyond the dyadic linkage to more deeply explore the role-making processes between a leader and different followers (Graen & Cashman, 1975). One of the fundamental tenets of LMX theory is that leaders develop potentially different exchange relationships with their respective subordinates and develop high-quality exchanges with just a few. As such, the theory avoids addressing a leader's overall style or behavioral orientation because that style will vary across followers. Thus, a leader's *average leadership style* is the incorrect unit of analysis in leadership because the leader-follower dyad, not the leader or follower alone, is the appropriate unit of leadership.

At the core of LMX theory is the role-making process that is negotiated between a leader and a follower. Over time, it is thought that their relationship quality can develop from that of a stranger to an acquaintance to a mature partnership (Graen & Uhl-Bien, 1995). Any relationship has the potential to develop to maturity, but not every relationship does. The exact reasons behind these differences in the quality of exchanges that develop are unknown, although it may have partly to due with the leader's limited temporal, social, and affective resources that restrict the number of followers who can be accorded "in-group" status (high-quality LMX relationship). This shapes an orientation that attempts to maximize limited resources by investing them into only the most promising associates. Those relationships that fail to develop into a mature partnership are relegated to some degree of "out-group" status.

Research has been conducted on both the predictors of LMX quality as well as the outcomes. In a longitudinal study across the first six months of employment, it was found that perceived similarity and liking from both the leader's and follower's perspectives predicted LMX quality across time periods (Liden, Wayne, & Stilwell, 1993). Demographic similarity was found to have no significant effects on LMX development. Follower performance and competence have also been shown to be related to LMX quality, although the findings of Liden et al.

suggest that it is less important than were affective variables.

Several meta-analyses have been published examining various LMX issues and outcomes. In the first published meta-analysis of LMX correlates across 85 independent samples (Gerstner & Day, 1997), the strongest relationships with LMX were found for follower job performance, satisfaction (overall and supervisory), commitment, role perceptions, and turnover intentions. It was also noted that the average leader-member agreement in LMX ratings was estimated to be only .29 (average sample-weighted correlation). This is somewhat perplexing, given that both parties supposedly are rating their shared experience, although it is clear from these findings that the meaning of mutually shared events and situations is not necessarily the same. The surprising lack of agreement is something that has been of interest to researchers for decades (Graen & Schiemann, 1978) with little real understanding, even today. A recent meta-analysis and primary study focusing on leader-member agreement in LMX ratings (Sin, Nahrgang, & Morgeson, 2009) concluded, based on data from 64 independent samples (N = 10,884 dyads), that longer relationship tenure and ratings on affectively oriented relationship dimensions were associated with greater levels of agreement. The primary study conducted across 98 matched dyads also showed that the extent of LMX agreement increased as a positive function of the intensity of dyadic interaction. These are promising insights into potential sources of leader-member (dis)agreement; however, it is an area where more research is needed.

Another published meta-analysis focused on the relationship between LMX quality and the citizenship behaviors of followers (Ilies, Nahrgang, & Morgeson, 2007). Results were analyzed across 50 independent samples, suggesting a moderately large and positive relationship between LMX and follower citizenship behavior. Also as hypothesized, LMX predicted individual-targeted citizenship behaviors significantly more strongly than organizational-targeted behaviors.

Taken together, the results of these meta-analytic studies suggest that LMX is significantly related to a number of organizationally relevant outcomes. Nonetheless, there have been criticisms of the theory across the years. One review of the LMX literature concluded that many different definitions of LMX and scales used to measure it have clouded the overall picture as to the meaning of the construct (Schriesheim, Castro, & Cogliser, 1999). Others have noted that much is still unknown about the evolution of LMX and how the role-making process actually occurs (Yukl, 2006), although there has been some recent progress in understanding how personality and performance influence the development of LMX relationships over time (Nahrgang, Morgeson, & Ilies, 2009). Despite these concerns—or maybe because of them—LMX continues to be the focus of research interest more than 30 years after its introduction into the leadership literature. There are several reasons for this long-lived interest, including: (a) the dynamic and developmental nature of LMX; (b) the focus on the relationship between a leader and follower, which has spurred interest in broader theories of relational leadership (Uhl-Bien, 2006; Uhl-Bien, Maslyn, & Ospina, 2012), and especially for I/O psychologists; (c) the importance of followers' relationships with their respective leaders "as a lens through which the entire work experience is viewed" (Gerstner & Day, 1997, p. 840).

There is one final methodological note with regard to LMX. Because, in most studies, followers are nested within leaders (i.e., multiple followers report to the same leader), there are potential problems with non-independent data. One of the basic assumptions of the inferential statistics often used by I/O psychologists is that observations are independent; thus, if that assumption is violated, then the resulting significance tests are in question. Fortunately, there are multilevel analytical techniques (e.g., HLM; Raudenbush & Bryk, 2002) that can be used with these types of non-independent data. Although appropriate analytic techniques exist, researchers do not always use them, or use them appropriately (Antonakis et al., 2010). Furthermore, the kind of theory that is needed to understand higher level (i.e., supervisor) effects on followers' LMX perceptions has lagged behind other research investigating the correlates and outcomes associated with LMX.

Leadership Perceptions

Some researchers have approached leadership as mainly a socio-perceptual phenomenon. In other words, leadership is in the eye of the beholder. Lord and Maher (1991) even defined leadership as "the process of being perceived by others as a leader" (p. 11), although it might be legitimately argued that this is too extreme and overlooks important aspects of what a leader does in terms of behaviors and other goal-related activities. But what makes this perceptual approach compelling in terms of its influence on the leadership field is its recognition of the essential role that followers play in the leadership process. It is ultimately through follower reactions and behaviors that leadership succeeds or fails (Lord & Brown, 2004), and being perceived as a leader by others enhances the likelihood that the leader will be allowed to exercise appropriate influence over others (Lord et al., 1982). It was the first systematic approach to redirect the leadership field from a leader-centric to more of a follower-centric perspective (Brown, 2012), first introduced through the work of Hollander and colleagues (Hollander, 1992; Hollander & Julian, 1969; Hollander & Webb, 1955).

The role of perceptions in leadership has evolved since it was first proclaimed that leadership "*exists only as perception*" (Calder, 1977, p. 202, italics in original). Calder's point was that leadership is primarily a phenomenological construct, and as such, it is difficult to study scientifically but extremely important as naïve psychology. What has occurred over the years is greater attention to, and advances in, the field of social cognition and the subdiscipline of person perception. Contrary to Calder's assertions, it has been demonstrated that perceptual processes (including leadership perceptions) can be studied scientifically and that there are at least two socio-cognitive routes to seeing someone as a leader.

ATTRIBUTIONS AND LEADERSHIP CATEGORIZATION THEORY

One approach, summarized in the thinking of Calder (1977), Pfeffer (1977), and Meindl (Meindl & Ehrlich, 1987; Meindl, Ehrlich, & Dukerich, 1985), portrayed leadership as a type of attributional error or perceptual bias resulting from individuals' needs to easily explain observed outcomes. In this manner, something like organizational performance is attributed to either good or bad leadership, depending on the level of that performance. Leadership is a convenient causal label used to make sense of what is seen and experienced in the world.

Building on research from the fields of information processing and social cognition, Lord and colleagues offered another possible way that people are perceived and labeled as leaders. Based in personality research showing that traits were not very good predictors of behavior across situations but that they are important constructions of perceivers in making sense of social situations (e.g., Mischel, 1973), *leadership categorization theory* was proposed and tested (Lord et al., 1982, 1984). The theory demonstrated that perceivers hold in memory trait-based leadership prototypes that are used to guide whom they are likely to see as a leader. The extent to which behavior could be characterized in ways that matched attributes of the perceiver's implicit prototype for a leader (e.g., honest, intelligent, determined), the greater the chance that the target individual would be perceived as leader-like.

Subsequent work by Lord and Maher (1991) demonstrated how both kinds of processing are used in shaping leadership perceptions. When first encountering a potential leader, perceivers use relatively spontaneous and effortless prototype-matching processes in coming to some initial impression regarding how leader-like the target individual appears. This is a type of "bottom-up" or recognition-based process in which perceived leader attributes (traits) are matched against an implicitly held leadership prototype. The better the prototype match the stronger the leadership perception. A second way in which perceptions are shaped is through more effortful and attribution-based reasoning. This is more of a "top-down" process in which perceivers reason backward from some outcome (successful team performance) to a possible cause (effective leadership). It is important to note that this mode of processing occurs only when there are adequate cognitive resources available and the motivation exists to better understand why something occurred (i.e., to infer causality). In this manner, someone who does not fit the prototype of a leader can still be perceived as one if he or she is associated with successful outcomes. Success is a core feature of the *implicit leadership theories* that people hold about the nature of leadership (Epitropaki & Martin, 2004; Rush, Thomas, & Lord, 1977). Simply put, it is difficult to maintain the perception of a leader if you continue to be unsuccessful—even if you look the part.

PROJECT GLOBE

One of the questions raised by the work of Lord and others in the area of leadership perceptions is to what degree such perceptions might vary as a function of societal culture (Den Hartog & Dickson, 2012). At least one early study addressed this issue directly, finding that leadership prototypes differed in ways that would be expected based on presumed cultural values (Gerstner & Day, 1994). One limitation of this study, however, was that it was based on a sample of college students from different cultures who were studying at a university in the United States (i.e., convenience sample). Despite the interesting study findings, the sampling issues raised

potential concerns regarding the extent to which responses were biased as a function of familiarity with U.S. culture. What would be preferable are respondent samples from various cultures that had little or no firsthand exposure to the United States.

Around the time that the Gerstner and Day (1994) study was published, House was bulding a team of researchers to study issues of culture, leadership, and organizations. What resulted from this initial organizing activity was a coordinating team of 10 researchers overseen by House that coordinated the research activities of approximately 170 country co-investigators across 62 societies. Ultimately, this became the Project GLOBE study, a 10-year research program on Global Leadership and Organizational Behavior Effectiveness (i.e., GLOBE; House, Hanges, Javidan, Dorfman, & Gupta, 2004). The project can be described as a multimethod, multiphase research program with the goals of conceptualizing, operationalizing, testing, and validating a cross-level theory of the relationships among culture and societal, organizational, and leadership effectiveness (House & Javidan, 2004). It was described by pioneering culture researcher Harry Triandis in the foreword to the Project GLOBE book as "the Manhattan Project of the relationship of culture to conceptions of leadership" (p. xv).

Project GLOBE examined culture as practices (how things are done) and values (how things should be done) with regard to leadership. The research team tested a number of hypotheses linking culture with various outcomes, using data collected from 17,300 managers across 951 different organizations. Measurement scales were developed, translated, and back-translated to ensure equivalence in meaning across cultures, and the resulting psychometric properties of these measures were subjected to rigorous scrutiny (see Hanges & Dickson, 2004). Given the scope of such a large, longitudinal study, it is difficult to summarize it or its substantial impact on the field in a concise manner. Therefore, I will focus on just one aspect of this immense study: leadership perceptions across societal cultures.

House and colleagues devised the term of *culturally endorsed implicit leadership theories* (CLT) that were characterized through six global leader behaviors identified in preliminary analyses: (a) charismatic/values-based leadership, (b) team-oriented leadership, (c) participative leadership, (d) humane-oriented leadership, (e) autonomous leadership, and (f) self-protective leadership. The CLT offered ways to potentially differentiate among cultural values and practices and ways in which leadership was perceived in a respective culture. The CLT measure was very much a type of leadership prototype measure that was used to compare perceptions across societal cultures.

The results found some similarities across cultures, as well as specific and hypothesized differences. In general, it was found that cultural values (how things should be done) but not practices (how things are done) were related to the CLT leadership dimensions listed above. There were 22 different leadership attributes that were found to be universally desirable (e.g., decisiveness, foresight), eight leadership dimensions identified as universally undesirable (e.g., irritable, ruthless), and many others that were culturally contingent in that they were desirable in some cultures and undesirable in others (e.g., ambitious, elitist). Overall, the Project GLOBE researchers were able to conclude that "members of cultures share common observations and values concerning what constitutes effective and ineffective leadership" (Javidan, House, & Dorfman, 2004), p. 40). Put somewhat differently, they were able to establish that there are culturally based shared conceptions (i.e., prototypes) of leadership.

Project GLOBE was a landmark study in the examination of the relationships between culture and leadership. A third phase of the project has focused on gathering more detailed qualitative and quantitative information about culture-specific aspects of leadership at the organizational level. There is still apparently much to learn from this very ambitious global project. Of course, it is easy to criticize some aspects of the research, such as how it is possible to represent very large and diverse countries, such as China and India, with relatively small samples. Nonetheless, Project GLOBE represents a major stride forward in better understanding leadership from a cross-cultural or global perspective.

Emerging Leadership Theories

The next section focuses on those leadership theories and approaches that have begun to set the future direction for research and practice. Given that these are relatively new additions to the leadership literature, there is less research available to evaluate their respective contributions as compared with classical and bridging theories. Thus, these approaches represent various degrees of works in progress.

If there is an overarching perspective on these emerging leadership approaches, it is around the notion of enhancing more inclusive forms of leadership. As witnessed with the previous description of so-called bridging theories of leadership, there was a widening of the theoretical lens to consider the important role that followers and followership (Hollander & Webb, 1955) play in leadership processes. The emerging leadership approaches go even further in terms of legitimizing leader as well as follower roles as necessary and important to effective leadership (Riggio, Chaleff, & Lipman-Blumen, 2008). As noted by Hollander (2009):

> The major point . . . is to show how followers can be included actively in leadership, with a role in the mutual process. The overarching goal is to improve the understanding and practice of effective leadership. Leaders usually do have greater initiative, but followers are vital to success, and they too can become leaders. Leadership benefits from active followers, in a unity, including "upward influence" on a two-way rather than a one-way street. . . .
> (p. 3)

The notion of reciprocal influence was mentioned with the bridging theory of leader-member exchange (LMX). Whereas LMX adopts mainly a dyadic focus, the emerging approaches consider the entire work group or team. It should be noted that one particular trend in LMX theory and research is in refocusing it away from dyads to more fully consider the effects of the entire social network represented in the group or organization (Graen & Uhl-Bien, 1995; Sparrowe & Liden, 1997, 2005). This illustrates how a particular theory can evolve and contribute to the next generation of emergent leadership theories. In terms of getting a broader perspective with regard to other emerging approaches to leadership, this section will review the contributions to date of team leadership, shared leadership, and leadership capacity and adaptive capability that, taken together, provide more of a team-based perspective on leadership processes.

Team Leadership

It has been observed that, despite the large literatures available with respect to the separate fields of leadership and teams, there is relatively little known about team leadership as compared with leadership in broader organizations (Kozlowski, Gully, McHugh, Salas, & Cannon-Bowers, 1996; Zaccaro, Rittman, & Marks, 2001). In particular, Kozlowski et al. (1996) noted that it is difficult to apply the prescriptions from general leadership research to teams due to the complex and dynamic environments in which teams typically operate. What has transpired in recent years, however, is nothing short of remarkable.

Through integrative reviews, meta-analyses, and other approaches to synthesize what is known about leadership and team effectiveness, a robust picture has begun to emerge. As noted by some researchers, "[T]eam leadership as a discipline appears to be on the cusp of some truly significant breakthroughs" (Day, Gronn, & Salas, 2006, p. 211).

In one notable example, Kozlowski and Ilgen (2006) reviewed over 50 years of psychological research that examined various factors influencing the processes that underlie team effectiveness. The authors concluded that, regarding team leadership, "emerging theory and empirical findings support leaders as a key leverage point for enhancing team effectiveness" (p. 110). In particular, the available research indicates that leaders are instrumental in the specific activities of enhancing team coordination, cooperation, and communication; helping to enhance and otherwise develop team member competencies; and playing a pivotal role in team regulation, performance dynamics, and team adaptation.

Underpinning much of the research in this area is the notion of *team functional leadership*. Specifically, the primary responsibility of team leaders from this perspective is to identify what role functions are missing or are not being handled adequately in the team and either do it or arrange for it to be done by others (Fleishman et al., 1991; Hackman & Walton, 1986; McGrath, 1962; Zaccaro et al., 2001). From this perspective, team leadership is seen as the ongoing process of team need satisfaction (Morgeson, DeRue, & Peterson, 2010).

The available empirical evidence appears to support the merits of this perspective. A meta-analysis of 231 published and unpublished studies revealed that both task- and person-focused functional leadership behaviors were related to perceived team effectiveness and team productivity (Burke et al., 2006). The subgroup analyses revealed an interesting finding: leader empowerment behaviors accounted for approximately 30% of the variance in team learning. This is an especially important finding when considered along with the conclusions of Kozlowski and Ilgen (2006) that team learning is instrumental to fostering team effectiveness.

A recent review of the team leadership literature from a functional perspective (Morgeson et al., 2010) has proposed an organizing framework for better understanding leadership structures and processes in teams. Specifically, Morgeson et al. (2010) identified 15 different team leadership functions organized around different cycles of goal-directed team activity (Marks, Mathieu, & Zaccaro, 2001):

a *transition* phase in which teams engage in evaluation or planning activities, and an *action* phase in which teams perform work activities that contribute directly to goal accomplishment. In the transition phase, important team leadership functions include composing the team, defining the mission, establishing expectations and goals, structuring and planning, training and developing the team, sense making, and providing feedback. In the action phase, important team leadership functions include monitoring the team, managing team boundaries, challenging the team, performing the team task, solving problems, providing resource, encouraging team self-management, and supporting the team social climate.

Despite its many contributions to better understanding team leadership, the functional approach adopts an implicit assumption that leaders and their respective teams agree on which needs of the team must be fulfilled. Contrary to this assumption, recent research has promoted the importance of considering *leader-team perceptual distance* and the role that it plays in shaping team effectiveness (Gibson, Cooper, & Conger, 2009). The concept is defined as differences between a leader and a team in how they respectively perceive the same social stimulus. Results from a sample of 104 teams, incorporating 813 members from five different companies, indicated that leader-team perceptual distance in the areas of goal accomplishment and constructive conflict had a nonlinear relationship with team performance such that greater perceptual distances were associated with larger decreases in team performance. Furthermore, these effects were stronger when the team's perceptions were more positive, as compared with those of the leader. An important implication of these findings for the functional approach to team leadership is that the alignment or congruence of leader-team perceptions regarding the needs of the team could moderate the relationship between what functions are provided by a leader and the team's ultimate performance and effectiveness. Thus, an important team leader function might be working to align perceptions of the team with those of the leader in terms of what the core needs of the team are. Although an interesting and promising possibility, future research is needed to empirically test these ideas.

The functional approach to team leadership also has been expanded recently to include multiteam systems or teams of teams (DeChurch & Marks, 2006). In this research, functional multiteam leadership was defined as actions taken by formally appointed leaders "that enable and direct teams in collectively working together" (p. 313). The specific leader functions of *strategizing* and *coordinating* were examined as potential influences on multiteam system performance. Training interventions were designed and implemented to examine their effects on the processes and performance of multiteam systems. Leader training was found to improve the multiteam processes as well as performance, as hypothesized. An interesting additional finding was that the leader training was found to have no effect on the team's process or performance, only on the multiteam system. Of course it is risky to attempt to interpret null findings. Nonetheless, taken together, the results from this research suggest that leadership functions in multiteam systems differ from those found in single-team settings. In summary, the functional leadership approach has provided numerous process and performance insights across various levels involving individuals, teams, and even multiteam systems. The approach has truly come a long way from its origins as McGrath's (1962) mimeographed report written at the request of the U.S. Civil Service Commission (Hackman & Walton, 1986).

Although this and other work has helped to clarify what we know about how leaders shape and develop effective teams, it also highlights a pervasive bias in the literature that leadership flows from a given leader to followers or team members of lower status. In other words, the traditional perspective is that leaders serve to enhance the leadership *of* teams by *acting on* followers. A different approach that is at the forefront of the next generation of leadership theory is based on the leadership *in* a team, specifically in terms of how leaders *act with* followers in creating team leadership. One particular type of within-team leadership that is helping to shape the future of leadership theory and research is shared leadership.

Shared Leadership and Self-Managed Work Teams

Shared leadership is defined as a "dynamic, interactive influence process among individuals in groups for which the objective is to lead one another to the achievement of group or organizational goals or both" (Pearce & Conger, 2003a, p. 1). The influence processes involved in shared leadership can involve any combination of upward, downward, or lateral (i.e., peer) influence attempts. It is important to note that whereas this particular form of leadership is gaining in popularity among researchers and other leadership scholars, it is not an altogether new

perspective. Pearce and Conger (2003a) trace the roots of shared leadership back to the early twentieth century and the influence of Mary Parker Follet (1924), who is an icon in the fields of management and I/O psychology. We also saw a version of peer leadership included with the behavioral approach to leadership under the auspices of the University of Michigan studies (Bowers & Seashore, 1966).

Despite its historical roots, shared leadership had not attracted much consistent scholarly attention until recently. Part of the reason is attributable to the historical emphasis on studying the leader (i.e., entity and leader-centric approaches), which includes the recent ascendancy of charismatic and transformational leadership. One of the motivating forces for the resurgent interest in shared leadership is the focus on teams as a preferred organizational form for accomplishing work-related goals. Along with the greater use of teams come requisite changes in the division of labor, with new patterns of interdependence and coordination emerging (Gronn, 2002). There is strong interest in studying teams in the field of I/O psychology, and this includes various forms of team-based leadership. Shared leadership is especially relevant for one particular team form, the self-managed work team (SMWT).

The SMWT literature grew originally from theory and research on self-management and personal control (Manz & Sims, 1980; Mills, 1983) that was grounded in the principles of operant conditioning (Luthans & Davis, 1979). This is ironic because, in perhaps its truest form, the SMWT consists of peers who operate without a formally appointed leader. As a result, the leadership responsibilities are shared among all group members or are possibly distributed in systematic ways across members. A more typical approach, however, is to appoint someone to act as the group's leader or to have the traditional supervisor continue in some manner as an external leader who advises the team and intervenes when circumstances dictate, such as when novel or disruptive events occur (Morgeson, 2005; Morgeson & DeRue, 2006). The paradox of this approach regarding SMWT leadership is that the team becomes less "self-managed" and increasingly resembles a traditional work group (Manz & Sims, 1987). In such cases, team leadership reverts back to some form of the classic functional approach. Having a truly self-managed team requires a different way of thinking about and enacting leadership, which can be an obstacle to implementing a shared approach to leadership in some contexts. From this literature it is clear that, at minimum, a distinction must be made between the external and internal leadership processes of SMWT.

Zaccaro and colleagues have proposed that individual leaders in team-based leadership systems can be conceptualized in three ways: (a) internal leaders, (b) external leaders, and (c) executive coordinators (Zaccaro, Heinen, & Shuffler, 2009). Internal leaders often can be found in teams where leadership functions are distributed among members. There is a need for organizational accountability, even when most of the leadership processes occur in a distributed or shared manner. External leaders typically have more distant connections to the team than internal leadership; however, external leaders are thought to focus a good deal of their attention on managing team boundaries, including seeking information from outsiders and obtaining support from external stakeholders (Druskat & Wheeler, 2003). Executive coordinators provide broad strategic direction to teams and help secure necessary staffing and other operational resources needed for success (Kozlowski et al., 1996), but they leave most of the internal team structuring and leadership processes to team members.

There is a tendency to think about these emerging forms of leadership as "either/or" propositions—either there is something like shared leadership or a traditional vertical approach with a formally appointed leader. Contrary to this "either/or" leadership mentality, some of the most compelling research findings to date on shared leadership suggest that the most effective approach in terms of enhancing performance is to use both shared and vertical leadership. In evaluating performance across change management (Pearce & Sims, 2002) as well as new venture teams (Ensley, Hmielski, & Pearce, 2006), it was found that the most effective leadership forms incorporated both a vertical form of leadership stemming from the formal leader (e.g., transformational leadership of the CEO) as well as shared leadership originating from within the team. Other researchers have noted similar findings with student project teams (Avolio, Jung, Murry, & Sivasubramaniam, 1996), along with yet other research demonstrating that shared leadership is positively related to team performance (Carson et al., 2007; Hiller, Day, & Vance, 2006; Taggar, Hackett, & Saha, 1999). These studies provide promising evidence of the value-added of shared leadership with regard to team performance, and that its contribution can be in addition to, not in place of, more traditional forms of vertical leadership.

A relevant question to ask with regard to these research findings is: How is it possible to have both forms of leadership simultaneously within a team? The answer can be found within the history and evolution of leadership theory. Kozlowski and Ilgen (2006) noted the importance of the leader as a key leverage point in terms of enhancing team effectiveness. Thus, there is little doubt that having an effective leader can help facilitate effective team performance. But it is also the case that what is now called shared leadership has its historical roots in related areas such as social exchange theory, participative decision making, leader-member exchange, followership, empowerment, and shared cognition (Pearce & Conger, 2003a). This illustrates an important but often overlooked point: leadership is inherently eclectic, both theoretically and practically. The focus of leadership theory, research, and practice therefore should not be on attempting to prove what the "right" theory is, but rather on building effective leadership practices based on what is known from the empirical evidence. From this perspective, not only can the individual team leader and shared leadership perspectives coexist, but they must coexist in order to maximize team performance potential.

Shared leadership represents a natural theoretical evolution that has emerged because of the greater emphasis on team-based work (Wuchty, Jones, & Uzzi, 2007) and also because of the limits that are reached in relying on a single leader for direction and guidance (Bennis, 2007). As mentioned at the beginning of this chapter, the challenges being faced by groups and organizations are becoming increasingly complex, requiring the application of more and different human and social capital resources to make sense of them and to act adaptively. As the saying goes, none of us is as smart as all of us. And if you believe some of the most vocal proponents of the theory, "shared leadership will not merely be another blip on the radar screen of organizational science.... Its time has arrived" (Pearce & Conger, 2003a, p. 14).

Leadership Capacity and Dynamic Team Leadership

Another perspective on team leadership takes the least leader-centric approach of all. From this perspective, leadership is thought to emerge through the patterned interactions of group members, instead of flowing from a solitary leader to a team or a set of individual team members. In this way, leadership "exists" as an outcome of effective social processes and structures (Gibb, 1954; Salancik et al., 1975), rather than solely as an input from the individual leader helping a team perform more effectively. This form of team leadership capacity is conceptualized as an emergent state that develops over time; is dynamic in nature (i.e., continually evolving or devolving); and varies as a function of team inputs (e.g., team member resources and capabilities), processes (e.g., teamwork), and outcomes (e.g., team learning; Day et al., 2004; Kozlowski & Bell, 2008). This is shared leadership in its purest form, in that there is no single recognized leader. Leadership is located in the connections and interrelationships among team members rather than with the actions or behaviors of any one individual (also see Carson et al., 2007). In this manner, leadership serves as a resource that is drawn from the team to address complex challenges requiring adaptability, learning, or different forms of sense making (O'Connor & Quinn, 2004).

Among the advantages of having a developed level of team leadership capacity is that it frees up the formal leader to focus on other things such as identifying external threats and opportunities, and it also broadens the overall leadership repertoire of a team. Members of the team are no longer dependent on a single leader to solve their problems or to set the direction for the team. Enhanced team leadership capacity should therefore also contribute to the resiliency of teams under conditions that contribute to disorganization and the collapse of sense making (Weick, 1993).

In the model of team leadership capacity proposed by Day et al. (2004), individual team member resources in the form of knowledge, skills, and abilities shape the level of teamwork that develops, depending on available leader resources and opportunities for formal team training and development activities. Teamwork is subsequently influential in the development of team learning, which in turn, helps to enhance team leadership capacity in the form of shared, distributed, and connective processes. This capacity is then available as an input for the team in handling the leadership challenges being faced. Although this model is in line with the evolution of team theory away from relatively simplistic input-process-output models to those that are more sophisticated and recognize ongoing feedback loops (Ilgen, Hollenbeck, Johnson, & Jundt, 2005), it awaits empirical scrutiny.

In a related area of investigation, Kozlowski and colleagues have advanced a comprehensive and integrative framework for understanding team leadership and team development. The approach is grounded in the observation that it is difficult to apply prescriptions from existing leadership research to teams operating in complex and dynamic decision-making environments (Kozlowski et al., 1996). Beginning with the initial theory and guidelines for application offered in 1996, the research team has provided additional conceptual insight regarding the processes associated with team development (Kozlowski, Gully, Nason, & Smith, 1999), has empirically examined the effects of feedback on the regulation of individual and team performance across multiple goals and multiple levels (DeShon, Kozlowski, Schmidt, Milner, & Wiechmann, 2004), and has further integrated team development and adaptation with team learning as emergent group phenomena (Kozlowski & Bell, 2008). Their most recent contribution has elaborated more specifically on the role of the leader in the team development process (Kozlowski et al., 2009) in terms of helping the team move from relatively novice to expert status and beyond, building adaptive capability in the team. In these latter stages of team development, the team takes on more responsibility for its learning, leadership, and performance. Taken together, this work provides an impressive theoretical and empirical foundation for understanding team leadership and, in particular, how something like adaptive capability—or leadership capacity—develops in teams.

Summary and Conclusions

This section on emerging theories focused on those approaches that have taken broader and typically more inclusive perspectives on leadership. The three approaches reviewed in this section adopt an explicit focus on the team, but vary in terms of how the core construct of leadership is conceptualized. The functional team leadership approach takes the most traditional perspective in primarily considering the contributions of an individual leader in shaping team effectiveness. Shared leadership offers a more inclusive picture in proposing an alternative to traditional, top-down leadership. From this theoretical vantage point, leadership is viewed as a dynamic, ongoing, mutual influence process in which leadership can be initiated by anyone in the team. Another way that this approach has been characterized is as the "serial emergence" of formal as well as informal leaders (Pearce, 2004, p. 48). This indeed represents a more inclusive form of team leadership but is a natural evolution of the functional approach.

The third way in which leadership was considered in this section was as an overall capacity or adaptive capability of the team to work together, learn, and adjust to significant challenges faced as part of their shared experiences. This approach changes the focus from being on any single individual (leader or so-called follower) to the networked connections of those individuals engaged in shared work. Leadership is therefore not only more inclusive in focus but is considered to operate at a different, more aggregate level of analysis than the traditional leadership approaches. Team leadership capacity is an especially important resource for the team when complex adaptive challenges are experienced in which no single individual is sufficiently smart, experienced, or otherwise capable of guiding the team out of the challenge. Under such conditions, it is thought that team leadership capacity can provide the team with the resources needed to be resilient and adaptive, even under the most trying of circumstances.

Future Directions for Leadership Theory, Research, and Practice
Future Theoretical Directions

A prevalent theme in this chapter has been the ongoing evolution of the leadership field in terms of theory, research, and practice. An important trend has been in moving away from traditional "leader-centric" approaches that focus tightly on the personal characteristics and attributes of the leader to more "follower-centric" approaches. This is a welcome trend, given that the follower has been an underexplored factor in the advancement of a more complete understanding of leadership processes. Another way of characterizing this trend is that of moving from an exclusionary focus, in which leaders are seen as exceptional individuals and leadership is a scarce organizational resource, to one that is more inclusive and that recognizes the role that everyone plays in the leadership process (Hollander, 2009). From this latter perspective, it is not that leadership is scarce in organizations but rather that it has been wasted by focusing on formal leaders as the only source of leadership.

Another way in which leadership resources have been wasted historically is through a traditional emphasis on manager (or leader) as male. Across studies and different historical time periods, it was found that men in general were described as more similar to successful managers than women in general (Heilman, Block, Martell, & Simon, 1989; Schein, 1973). Holding entrenched sex stereotypes that disfavor women as successful managers or effective leaders can be manifested in ways that perpetuate both overt as well as covert sex bias (Butler & Geis, 1990). Such biases hinder organizations from fully developing and accessing their entire portfolios of human capital. But the good news is that some researchers have pointed to changes such as the increase in the proportion of women holding managerial positions, as well as increases in the percentage of women in corporate officer and CEO positions, as indicators of a potential emerging shift to a *female leadership advantage* (Carli & Eagly, 2012; Eagly & Carli, 2003). Although not everyone is convinced that the trend is real (Vecchio, 2002, 2003), there do appear to be changes in leadership roles and organizational practices, as well as broader cultural shifts, that have resulted in greater gender inclusiveness when it comes to leadership, including a decrease in the endorsement of a masculine construal of leadership (i.e., leader stereotypes; Koenig, Eagly, Mitchell, & Risitikari, 2011).

There has also been a call for promoting more integrative strategies for theory-building in the field of leadership. Specifically, Avolio (2007) argues that leadership has reached a developmental plateau and that it needs to move to the next level of integration by more fully considering the dynamic interplay between leaders and followers, as well as taking more fully into account the context in which these interactions occur. Another way of thinking about this proposed integrative strategy is in terms of inclusiveness. For far too long, leadership theory mainly has been about the leader, with some notable exceptions (e.g., Hollander & Julian, 1969; Hollander & Webb, 1955; Lord & Brown, 2004). More integrative theories recognize that the leadership landscape includes leaders, followers, and the situational context as essential ingredients in this dynamic interaction.

Future theoretical direction: Develop integrative theory-building strategies that extend beyond leader-centric approaches to those that include all of the basic ingredients in leadership processes (i.e., leader, follower, and situational context).

Another area of future theoretical interest is in moving toward more integrative and inclusive leadership theories of a different kind. The point has been made repeatedly in this chapter that leadership is a dynamic, evolving process. As such, it incorporates behaviors, perceptions, decision making, and a whole host of other constructs. In short, leadership by nature is an eclectic phenomenon, and attempting to conceptualize and study it from any one theoretical perspective (e.g., motivational, emotional, behavioral) will yield, at best, limited results. What are needed are more inclusive and integrative perspectives that cut across any number of theoretical domains. For example, in the related area of leader development, an integrative theoretical approach has been proposed linking the otherwise apparently disparate domains of adult development, identity and self-regulation, and expertise acquisition (Day, Harrison, & Halpin, 2009). Leadership theory will advance by integrating across multiple domains and disciplines in a more eclectic fashion.

Future theoretical direction: Develop integrative theory-building strategies that connect different domains and scholarly disciplines in advancing more eclectic or integral approaches to leadership.

Leadership is a dynamic process, which inherently involves the consideration of time. Despite the need to consider time as part of leadership theory, there are relatively few attempts to do so. Although some researchers have suggested a minimum of a three-year lag in accurately estimating the effects of formal leadership changes at top (i.e., executive) levels on organizational performance (Day & Lord, 1988), this type of specification when it comes to time and leadership is the exception rather than the rule. The point is that, regardless of level or intended outcome, it is unreasonable to expect that leadership of any sort (e.g., traditional or shared) would have an immediate effect on relevant outcomes. Better theories of leadership processes are needed that explicitly address time and the specification of when things happen. As noted by Mitchell and James (2001), a likely way to "enrich our theories and subject them to falsification is to be more precise theoretically, and methodologically, about when events occur" (p. 543).

Future theoretical direction: Integrative theory-building strategies are needed to more fully consider the role of time in leadership processes and theoretically grounded specifications of when leadership effects are likely to occur.

Future Research Directions

Leadership is a dynamic, multilevel, and multidisciplinary construct. Thus, the research methods used to study it should also reflect these basic features. One particular area to encourage additional research is in the use of multilevel modeling approaches (Raudenbush & Bryk, 2002). Especially as more inclusive leadership theories are developed, researchers will need to adopt research designs and analytical tools that capture the multilevel nature of more inclusive forms of leadership (individuals nested within teams that are nested within broader organizational entities).

Future research direction: More inclusive forms of leadership will involve the multilevel consideration of leaders and followers within teams, which are further nested within broader organizational contexts.

Leadership also unfolds over time in a dynamic manner. The timing of leadership effects is something in particular that needs greater research attention. One example can be found in LMX theory, in which the life cycle of leadership making specifies that the leader-follower relationship evolves from stranger to acquaintance and then possibly to maturity (Graen & Uhl-Bien, 1995). Although time is a fundamental driver of the evolution of this leadership making, there is a general lack of empirically based research exploring the explicit role of time in these developmental processes. Similar concerns exist with shared leadership. It is unrealistic to think that shared leadership emerges fully formed in a team at its inception. Rather, it is likely to take some time to develop and will benefit from factors such as adopting a learning orientation within the team (Edmondson, Bohmer, & Pisano, 2001). But again, little is known about the role of time in the development of shared leadership.

Future research direction: Longitudinal methods are encouraged in leadership research, especially in terms of better understanding how and when developmental processes unfold with regard to individuals, teams, and organizations.

The point was raised that leadership theorists and researchers need to better account for the role of context in leadership. This may stipulate a change to different forms of research methods (Zyphur et al., 2012). Typical quantitative or measurement-based leadership approaches generally seek to provide results that can generalize across different contexts. But, as noted at the beginning of this chapter, the type of leadership that occurs in a business context may be quite different from that associated with effective outcomes in a military context where a great deal of personal danger exists. Indeed, some have argued that leadership cannot be fully understood apart from its context (Biggart & Hamilton, 1987).

To more fully understand contextual influences on leadership may require greater use of qualitative research methods such as case studies and designs based on interview data (Bryman, Stephens, & a' Campo, 1996). In order for qualitative studies to add value to the leadership literature, they need to be designed in ways to address questions especially with regard to context. Merely adding more qualitative studies without consideration of the appropriateness of the approach to answer the research question at hand is unlikely to provide much insight. But also unlikely to provide much insight are future studies based on leadership questionnaires used in single-session, cross-sectional designs.

Future research direction: The use of qualitative methods is encouraged to better understand the relationships between leadership and the context in which it occurs or develops.

Future Practice Directions

The field of I/O psychology is grounded in the scientist-practitioner model; thus, suggestions for future practice directions are also needed. It is ironic in some ways that leadership per se is not something that attracts a lot of practice attention, but leadership *development* is a key concern to many organizations. Indeed, there is an entire industry devoted to developing leaders, and this interest appears to cut across business, education, military, and other private and public domains.

Despite the interest and the sheer number of leadership development providers working in the private and public sectors, one recent report claimed that "leadership development is going nowhere fast" (Howard & Wellins, 2008, p. 4). Specific areas that were identified as troublesome include a lack of satisfaction with regard to the development offerings in organizations, that confidence in leaders has declined steadily over the previous eight years, and that on average 37% of those who fill leadership positions fail (i.e., either by leaving the position or failing to achieve the objectives of the position). This last observation is not new. Drucker (1985) noted some time ago: "At most one-third of such [executive selection] decisions turn out right; one-third are minimally effective; and one-third are outright failures" (p. 22). Thus, even though leadership development is a strategic human capital concern of many organizations, data suggest that it is not being done very effectively.

An issue that has challenged the effectiveness of leadership development initiatives is the focus on relatively short-term, episodic-based thinking in terms of how development occurs. Traditional thinking about leadership development has viewed it as a series of unconnected, discrete programs with little assistance in integrating across these developmental episodes (Vicere & Fulmer, 1998). Contemporary thinking about leadership development views it as continuous and ongoing throughout the adult lifespan (Day et al., 2009). In short, just about any experience has the potential to contribute to development to the extent that it includes aspects of assessment, challenge, and support (McCauley, Van Velsor, & Ruderman, 2010).

Future practice direction: Development of leaders and leadership is best considered as an ongoing and continuous process that is most effective when it is connected to the overall strategy of the organization.

Most of what has been portrayed as so-called leadership development would be more accurately called leader development (Day, 2000). Although this might seem to be a fairly trivial distinction, it has important developmental implications. The typical focus of most developmental efforts is on developing the individual leader, using practices such as assessment, feedback, coaching, and job assignments/rotation. The focus is on developing individual leader skills; however, there is no certainty that better leadership will result. After all, leadership requires some dynamic social interaction within a specified situational context. Leadership development would likely require intervention at a more macro group, team, or organizational level. But it is not an "either/or" proposition; rather, state-of-the-art practices involve determining how to link leader development with more aggregate leadership development to enhance the overall leadership capacity in a collective (Day et al., 2004).

Future practice direction: The most effective development initiatives link leader development with leadership development in enhancing an overall capacity for leadership.

Conclusions

The leadership field may appear to be curiously unformed to some commentators (Hackman & Wageman, 2007); nonetheless, there is a good deal that we do know about leadership as a result of 100 years of research. The chapter will conclude with a brief listing of what we have learned about leadership over the years and speculation on what we have yet to learn.

What We Have Learned

• Leadership requires a social interaction between people—traditionally labeled as leaders and followers—within a situational context. Focusing on the leader(s), or follower(s), or situation(s) exclusively and in isolation of each other will provide at best an imperfect picture of the leadership process. All three forces must be considered in forging a more complete picture of that process.

- There is no right or wrong leadership theory. Some theories have more support than others, but most have a modicum of empirical support. Rather than attempting to sort out which is the best of the lot, a more fruitful approach will be in developing more integrative theories that combine the best aspects of the most strongly supported approaches with emerging perspectives on the evolving nature of leadership.

- Taking a static approach to leadership is unlikely to provide much, if any, valuable insight. The essence of leadership is its dynamic and process-based nature. Single-shot, cross-sectional, and survey-based approaches to studying leadership have increasingly limited value.

- Leadership can originate from those designated as formal leaders, from individuals who emerge as informal leaders, from those considered to be followers, or from the overall aggregate collective (e.g., team leadership capacity). Leadership is an inclusive rather than exclusive phenomenon.

- Leaders develop through experience, and it appears that the most potent developmental experiences are those that happen on the job (i.e., in context). Key to using developmental experiences effectively is in enhancing a learning focus with regard to the lessons learned from experience.

What We Have Yet to Learn

- How do we disentangle the leadership criteria of emergence from effectiveness? This has proved to be a sticking point in leadership research when both forms of criteria are measured using perceptually based ratings.

- How does organizational context shape the prevailing leadership processes? As noted, individual leaders and followers are nested within teams and organizations, but we have little understanding of how the higher level context shapes the lower level leadership processes.

- The timing of leadership effects is virtually unknown. Although some researchers have demonstrated that agreement between leaders and followers increases over time (Sin et al., 2009) there is little in the way of specific timing on these or other effects of leadership. The question of interest is: What is the relationship between leadership and time?

- Although we have some grounding in understanding how leaders develop, there is relatively little understanding of how leadership develops. For example, it has been shown that shared leadership adds predictive value over vertical or traditional leadership forms, but there is little understanding of how shared leadership develops within a team.

- How does leadership emerge in a grassroots or bottom-up manner? Using new forms of study such as complexity theory (Hazy, Goldstein, & Lichtenstein, 2007) may hold particular promise for better understanding emergent leadership from what appear to be random or chaotic conditions.

In conclusion, leadership has endured a rocky history in I/O psychology due to challenges with underlying theory, cross-sectional questionnaire-based research approaches, and the lack of evidence-based practices. Despite these challenges, we have discovered a great deal about the nature of leadership and its evolving character, and the good news is that we have much yet to learn.

References

Antonakis, J. (2012). Transformational and charismatic leadership. In D. V. Day & J. Antonakis (Eds.), *The nature of leadership* (2nd ed., pp. 256–288). Los Angeles: Sage.

Antonakis, J., Bendahan, S., Jacquart, P., & Lalive, R. (2010). On making causal claims: A review and recommendations. *Leadership Quarterly, 21,* 1086–1120.

Arvey, R. D., Rotundo, M., Johnson, W., Zhang, Z., & McGue, M. (2006). The determinants of leadership role occupancy: Genetic and personality factors. *Leadership Quarterly, 17,* 1–20.

Arvey, R. D., Zhang, Z., Avolio, B. J., & Krueger, R. F. (2007). Developmental and genetic determinants of leadership role occupancy among women. *Journal of Applied Psychology, 92,* 693–706.

Avolio, B. J. (1999). *Full leadership development: Building the vital forces in organizations.* Thousand Oaks, CA: Sage.

Avolio, B. J. (2004). Examining the Full Range Model of leadership: Looking back to transform forward. In D. V. Day, S. J. Zaccaro, & S. M. Halpin (Eds.), *Leader development for transforming organizations: Growing leaders for tomorrow* (pp. 71–98). Mahwah, NJ: Erlbaum.

Avolio, B. J. (2007). Promoting more integrative strategies for leadership theory-building. *American Psychologist, 62,* 25–33.

Avolio, B. J., Jung, D. I., Murry, W., & Sivasubramaniam, N. (1996). Building highly developed teams: Focusing on shared leadership processes, efficacy, trust, and performance. *Advances in Interdisciplinary Studies of Work Teams, 3,* 173–209.

Avolio, B. J., Sosik, J. J., Jung, D. I., & Berson, Y. (2003). Leadership models, methods, and applications. In W. C. Borman, D. R. Ilgen, & R. J. Klimoski (Eds.), *Handbook of psychology: Industrial and organizational psychology* (Vol. 12, pp. 277–307). Hoboken, NJ: Wiley.

Ayman, R., & Adams, S. (2012). Contingencies, context, situation, and leadership. In D. V. Day & J. Antonakis (Eds.), *The nature of leadership* (2nd ed., pp. 218–255). Los Angeles: Sage.

Barnlund, D. C. (1962). Consistency of emergent leadership in groups with changing tasks and members. *Speech Monographs, 29*, 45–52.

Barrick, M. R., Day, D. V., Lord, R. G., & Alexander, R. A. (1991). Assessing the utility of executive leadership. *Leadership Quarterly, 2*, 9–22.

Bass, B. M. (1985). *Leadership and performance beyond expectations.* New York: Free Press.

Bass, B. M. (1990). *Bass & Stogdill's handbook of leadership: Theory, research, and managerial applications* (3rd ed.). New York: Free Press.

Bass, B. M. (1999). Two decades of research and development in transformational leadership. *European Journal of Work and Organizational Psychology, 8*, 9–32.

Bass, B. M. (2008). *The Bass handbook of leadership: Theory, research, and managerial applications* (4th ed.). New York: Free Press.

Bass, B. M., & Avolio, B. J. (1993). Transformational leadership: A response to critiques. In M. M. Chemers & R. Ayman (Eds.), *Leadership theory and research: Perspectives and directions* (pp. 49–80). San Diego, CA: Academic Press.

Bass, B. M., & Avolio, B. J. (2000). *MLQ: Multifactor leadership questionnaire* (2nd ed.). Redwood City, CA: Mind Garden.

Bass, B. M., & Riggio, R. E. (2006). *Transformational leadership* (2nd ed.). Mahwah, NJ: Erlbaum.

Bedeian, A. G., & Day, D. V. (2004). Can chameleons lead? *Leadership Quarterly, 15*, 687–718.

Bedeian, A. G., & Hunt, J. G. (2006). Academic amnesia and vestigial assumptions of our forefathers. *Leadership Quarterly, 17*, 190–205.

Bennis, W. (2007). The challenges of leadership in the modern world. *American Psychologist, 62*, 2–5.

Biggart, N. W., & Hamilton, G. G. (1987). An institutional theory of leadership. *Journal of Applied Behavioral Science, 23*, 429–441.

Bingham, W. V. (1927). Leadership. In H. C. Metcalf (Ed.), *The psychological foundations of management* (pp. 244–260). Chicago: A. W. Shaw.

Binning, J. F., Zaba, A. J., & Whattam, J. C. (1986). Explaining the biasing effects of performance cues in terms of cognitive categorization. *Academy of Management Journal, 29*, 521–535.

Bird, C. (1940). *Social psychology.* New York: Appleton-Century.

Blank, W., Weitzel, J. R., & Green, S. G. (1990). A test of situational leadership theory. *Personnel Psychology, 43*, 579–597.

Bowers, D. G., & Seashore, S. E. (1966). Predicting organizational effectiveness with a four-factor theory of leadership. *Administrative Science Quarterly, 11*, 238–263.

Brown, D. J. (2012). In the minds of followers: Follower-centric approaches to leadership. In D. V. Day & J. Antonakis (Eds.), *The nature of leadership* (2nd ed., pp. 331–362). Los Angeles: Sage.

Bryman, A. (1992). *Charisma and leadership in organizations.* Newbury Park, CA: Sage.

Bryman, A., Stephens, M., & a' Campo, C. (1996). The importance of context: Qualitative research and the study of leadership. *Leadership Quarterly, 7*, 353–370.

Burke, C. S., Stagl, K. C., Klein, C., Goodwin, G. F., Salas, E., & Halpin, S. M. (2006). What type of leadership behaviors are functional in teams? A meta-analysis. *Leadership Quarterly, 17*, 288–307.

Burke, M. J., & Day, R. R. (1986). A cumulative study of the effectiveness of managerial training. *Journal of Applied Psychology, 71*, 232–245.

Burns, J. M. (1978). *Leadership.* New York: Harper & Row.

Butler, D., & Geis, F. L. (1990). Nonverbal affect responses to male and female leaders: Implications for leadership evaluations. *Journal of Personality and Social Psychology, 58*, 48–59.

Calder, B. J. (1977). An attribution theory of leadership. In B. M. Staw & G. R. Salancik (Eds.), *New directions in organizational behavior* (pp. 179–204). Chicago: St. Clair Press.

Cameron, K. S., & Whetten, D. A. (1983). Some conclusions about organizational effectiveness. In K. S. Cameron & D. A. Whetten (Eds.), *Organizational effectiveness: A comparison of multiple models* (pp. 261–277). Orlando, FL: Academic Press.

Carli, L. L., & Eagly, A. H. (2012). Leadership and gender. In D. V. Day & J. Antonakis (Eds.), *The nature of leadership* (2nd ed., pp. 437–476). Los Angeles: Sage.

Carson, J. B., Tesluk, P. E., & Marrone, J. A. (2007). Shared leadership in teams: An investigation of antecedent conditions and performance. *Academy of Management Journal, 50*, 1217–1234.

Chan, D. (1998). Functional relations among constructs in the same content domain at different levels of analysis: A typology of composition models. *Journal of Applied Psychology, 83*, 234–246.

Chan, K.-Y., & Drasgow, F. (2001). Toward a theory of individual differences and leadership: Understanding motivation to lead. *Journal of Applied Psychology, 86*, 481–498.

Cosmides, L., & Tooby, J. (1997). *Evolutionary psychology: A primer.* Santa Barbara, CA: Center for Evolutionary Psychology.

Craig, D. R., & Charters, W. W. (1925). *Personal leadership in industry.* New York: McGraw-Hill.

Dansereau, F., Jr., Graen, G., & Haga, W. J. (1975). A vertical dyad linkage approach to leadership within formal organizations: A longitudinal investigation of the role making process. *Organizational Behavior and Human Performance, 13*, 46–78.

Day, D. V. (2000). Leadership development: A review in context. *Leadership Quarterly, 11*, 581–613.

Day, D. V., Gronn, P., & Salas, E. (2004). Leadership capacity in teams. *Leadership Quarterly, 15*, 857–880.

Day, D. V., Gronn, P., & Salas, E. (2006). Leadership in team-based organizations: On the threshold of a new era. *Leadership Quarterly, 17*, 211–216.

Day, D. V., Harrison, M. M., & Halpin, S. M. (2009). *An integrative approach to leader development: Connecting adult development, identity, and expertise.* New York: Routledge.

Day, D. V., & Lance, C. E. (2004). Understanding the development of leadership complexity through latent growth modeling. In D. V. Day, S. J. Zaccaro, & S. M. Halpin (Eds.), *Leader development for transforming organizations: Growing leaders for tomorrow* (pp. 41–69). Mahwah, NJ: Erlbaum.

Day, D. V., & Lord, R. G. (1988). Executive leadership and organizational performance: Suggestions for a new theory and methodology. *Journal of Management, 14*, 453–464.

Day, D. V., Schleicher, D. J., Unckless, A. L., & Hiller, N. J. (2002). Self-monitoring personality at work: A meta-analytic investigation of construct validity. *Journal of Applied Psychology, 87*, 390–401.

Day, D. V., & Zaccaro, S. J. (2007). Leadership: A critical historical analysis of the influence of leader traits. In L. L. Koppes (Ed.), *Historical perspectives in industrial and organizational psychology* (pp. 383–405). Mahwah, NJ: Erlbaum.

DeChurch, L. A., & Marks, M. A. (2006). Leadership in multi-team systems. *Journal of Applied Psychology, 91,* 311–329.

Den Hartog, D. N., & Dickson, M. W. (2012). Leadership and culture. In D. V. Day & J. Antonakis (Eds.), *The nature of leadership* (2nd ed., pp. 393–436). Los Angeles: Sage.

DeShon, R. P., Kozlowski, S. W. J., Schmidt, A. M., Milner, K. R., & Wiechmann, D. (2004). A multiple-goal, multilevel model of feedback effects on the regulation of individual and team performance. *Journal of Applied Psychology, 89,* 1035–1056.

Dienesch, R. M., & Liden, R. C. (1986). Leader-member exchange model of leadership: A critique and further development. *Academy of Management Review, 11,* 618–634.

Downey, H. K., Chacko, T., & McElroy, J. C. (1979). Attribution of the "causes" of performance: A constructive, quasi-longitudinal replication of the Staw study (1975). *Organizational Behavior and Human Performance, 24,* 287–299.

Drath, W. H., McCauley, C. D., Palus, C. J., Van Velsor, E., O'Connor, P. M. G., & McGuire, J. B. (2008). Direction, alignment, commitment: Toward a more integrative ontology of leadership. *Leadership Quarterly, 19,* 635–653.

Drucker, P. F. (July/August, 1985). How to make people decisions. *Harvard Business Review, 63*(4), 22–25.

Druskat, V., & Wheeler, J. V. (2003). Managing from the boundary: The effective leadership of self-managing work teams. *Academy of Management Review, 46,* 435–457.

Dvir, T., Eden, D., Avolio, B. J., & Shamir, B. (2002). Impact of transformational leadership on follower development and performance: A field experiment. *Academy of Management Journal, 45,* 735–744.

Eagly, A. H., & Carli, L. L. (2003). The female leadership advantage: An evaluation of the evidence. *Leadership Quarterly, 14,* 807–834.

Eden, D., & Leviathan, U. (1975). Implicit leadership theory as a determinant of the factor structure underlying supervisory behavior scales. *Journal of Applied Psychology, 60,* 736–741.

Edmondson, A., Bohmer, R., & Pisano, G. (2001, October). Speeding up team learning. *Harvard Business Review, 79*(9), 125–132.

Ensley, M. D., Hmielski, K. M., & Pearce, C. L. (2006). The importance of vertical and shared leadership within new venture top management teams: Implications for the performance of startups. *Leadership Quarterly, 17,* 217–231.

Epitropaki, O., & Martin, R. (2004). Implicit leadership theories in applied settings: Factor structure, generalizability, and stability over time. *Journal of Applied Psychology, 89,* 293–310.

Evans, M. G. (1970). The effects of supervisory behavior on the path-goal relationship. *Organizational Behavior and Human Performance, 5,* 277–298.

Fiedler, F. E. (1964). A contingency model of leadership effectiveness. *Advances in Experimental Social Psychology, 1,* 149–190.

Fiedler, F. E. (1967). *A theory of leadership effectiveness.* New York: McGraw-Hill.

Fiedler, F. E. (1996). Research on leadership selection and training: One view of the future. *Administrative Science Quarterly, 41,* 241–250.

Fiedler, F. E., Chemers, M. M., & Mahar, L. (1976). *Improving leader effectiveness: The Leader Match concept.* New York: Wiley.

Fiedler, F. E., & Garcia, J. E. (1987). *New approaches to effective leadership effectiveness: Cognitive resources and organizational performance.* New York: Wiley.

Field, R. H. G., & House, R. J. (1990). A test of the Vroom-Yetton model using manager and subordinate reports. *Journal of Applied Psychology, 75,* 95–102.

Fleishman, E. A., Mumford, M. D., Zaccaro, S. J., Levin, K. Y., Korotkin, A. L., & Hein, M. B. (1991). Taxonomic efforts in the description of leader behavior: A synthesis and functional interpretation. *Leadership Quarterly, 2,* 245–287.

Follett, M. P. (1924). *Creative experience.* New York: Longmans Green.

Foti, R. J., & Hauenstein, N. M. A. (2007). Pattern and variable approaches in leadership emergence and effectiveness. *Journal of Applied Psychology, 92,* 347–355.

Galton, F. (1869). *Hereditary genius.* New York: Appleton.

Gerstner, C. R., & Day, D. V. (1994). Cross-cultural comparison of leadership prototypes. *Leadership Quarterly, 5,* 121–134.

Gerstner, C. R., & Day, D. V. (1997). Meta-analytic review of leader-member exchange theory: Correlates and construct issues. *Journal of Applied Psychology, 82,* 827–844.

Gibb, C. A. (1947). The principles and traits of leadership. *Journal of Abnormal and Social Psychology, 42,* 267–284.

Gibb, C. A. (1954). Leadership. In G. Lindzey (Ed.), *Handbook of social psychology* (Vol. 2, pp. 877–920). Cambridge, MA: Addison-Wesley.

Gibson, C. B., Cooper, C. D., & Conger, J. A. (2009). Do you see what we see? The complex effects of perceptual distance between leaders and teams. *Journal of Applied Psychology, 94,* 62–76.

Gibson, F. W., Fiedler, F. E., & Barrett, K. M. (1993). Stress, babble, and the utilization of the leader's intellectual abilities. *Leadership Quarterly, 4,* 189–208.

Gilbert, D. T. (1998). Ordinary personology. In D. T. Gilbert, S. T. Fiske, & G. Lindzey (Eds.), *The handbook of social psychology* (4th ed., Vol. 2, pp. 89–150). Boston, MA: McGraw-Hill.

Graeff, C. L. (1983). The situational leadership theory: A critical review. *Academy of Management Review, 8,* 285–291.

Graen, G. B., & Cashman, J. F. (1975). A role making model of leadership in formal organizations. In J. G. Hunt & L. L. Larson (Eds.), *Leadership frontiers* (pp. 143–165). Kent, OH: Kent State University.

Graen, G. B., Cashman, J. F., Ginsburgh, S., & Schiemann, W. (1977). Effects of linking-pin quality on the quality of working life of lower participants. *Administrative Science Quarterly, 22,* 491–504.

Graen, G. B., & Schiemann, W. (1978). Leader-member agreement: A vertical dyad linkage approach. *Journal of Applied Psychology, 63,* 206–212.

Graen, G. B., & Uhl-Bien, M. (1995). Relationship-based approach to leadership: Development of leader-member exchange (LMX) theory of leadership over 25 years: Applying a multi-level multi-domain perspective. *Leadership Quarterly, 6,* 219–247.

Gronn, P. (2002). Distributed leadership as a unit of analysis. *Leadership Quarterly, 13,* 423–451.

Hackman, J. R., & Wageman, R. (2007). Asking the right questions about leadership. *American Psychologist, 62,* 43–47.

Hackman, J. R., & Walton, R. E. (1986). Leading groups in organizations. In P. S. Goodman & Associates (Eds.), *Designing effective work groups* (pp. 72–119). San Francisco: Jossey-Bass.

Halpin, A. W., & Winer, B. J. (1957). A factorial study of the leader behavior descriptions. In R. M. Stogdill & A. E. Coons (Eds.), *Leader behavior: Its description and measurement* (pp. 39–51). Columbus: Bureau of Business Research, Ohio State University.

Hanges, P. J., & Dickson, M. W. (2004). The development and validation of the GLOBE culture and leadership scales. In R. J. House, P. J. Hanges, M. Javidan, P. W. Dorfman, & V. Gupta (Eds.), *Culture, leadership, and organizations: The GLOBE study of 62 societies* (pp. 122–151). Thousand Oaks, CA: Sage.

Hazy, J. K., Goldstein, J. A., & Lichtenstein, B. B. (Eds.). (2007). *Complex systems leadership theory: New perspectives from complexity science on social and organizational effectiveness.* Mansfield, MA: ISCE Publishing.

Heilman, M. E., Block, C. J., Martell, R. F., & Simon, M. C. (1989). Has anything changed? Current characterizations of men, women, and managers. *Journal of Applied Psychology, 74*, 935–942.

Hersey, P., & Blanchard, K. H. (1969a). Life cycle theory of leadership. *Training and Development Journal, 2*, 6–34.

Hersey, P., & Blanchard, K. H. (1969b). *Management of organizational behavior.* Englewood Cliffs, NJ: Prentice-Hall.

Hiller, N. J., Day, D. V., & Vance, R. J. (2006). Collective enactment of leadership roles and team effectiveness: A field study. *Leadership Quarterly, 17*, 387–397.

Hogan, R., Curphy, G. J., & Hogan, J. (1994). What we know about leadership: Effectiveness and personality. *American Psychologist, 49*, 493–504.

Hollander, E. P. (1992). The essential interdependence of leadership and followership. *Current Directions in Psychological Science, 1*, 71–75.

Hollander, E. P. (2009). *Inclusive leadership: The essential leader-follower relationship.* New York: Routledge.

Hollander, E. P., & Julian, J. W. (1969). Contemporary trends in the analysis of leadership processes. *Psychological Bulletin, 71*, 387–397.

Hollander, E. P., & Webb, W. B. (1955). Leadership, followership, and friendship: An analysis of peer nominations. *Journal of Abnormal and Social Psychology, 50*, 163–167.

Hosking, D., & Schriesheim, C. A. (1978). Review of "Improving leadership effectiveness: The Leader Match concept." *Administrative Science Quarterly, 23*, 496–505.

House, R. J. (1971). A path-goal theory of leader effectiveness. *Administrative Science Quarterly, 16*, 321–338.

House, R. J. (1977). A 1976 theory of charismatic leadership. In J. G. Hunt & L. L. Larson (Eds.), *Leadership: The cutting edge* (pp. 189–207). Carbondale: Southern Illinois University.

House, R. J. (1996). Path-goal theory of leadership: Lessons, legacy, and a reformulated theory. *Leadership Quarterly, 7*, 323–352.

House, R. J., Hanges, P. J., Javidan, M., Dorfman, P. W., & Gupta, V. (Eds.). (2004). *Culture, leadership, and organizations: The GLOBE study of 62 societies.* Thousand Oaks, CA: Sage.

House, R. J., & Javidan, M. (2004). Overview of GLOBE. In R. J. House, P. J. Hanges, M. Javidan, P. W. Dorfman, & V. Gupta (Eds.), *Culture, leadership, and organizations: The GLOBE study of 62 societies* (pp. 9–28). Thousand Oaks, CA: Sage.

House, R. J., & Mitchell, T. R. (1974). Path-goal theory of leadership. *Journal of Contemporary Business, 3*, 81–97.

House, R. J., & Podsakoff, P. M. (1994). Leadership effectiveness. In J. Greenberg (Ed.), *Organizational behavior: The state of the science* (pp. 45–82). Hillsdale, NJ: Erlbaum.

House, R. J., & Shamir, B. (1993). Towards an integration of transformational, charismatic, and visionary theories of leadership. In M. M. Chemers & R. Ayman (Eds.), *Leadership: Perspectives and research directions* (pp. 81–107). New York: Academic Press.

Howard, A., & Wellins, R. S. (2008). *Global leadership forecast 2008/2009: Overcoming the shortfalls in developing leaders.* Pittsburgh, PA: Development Dimensions International.

Hunt, J. G. (1999). Transformational/charismatic leadership's transformation of the field: An historical essay. *Leadership Quarterly, 10*, 129–144.

Hunter, J. E., & Schmidt, F. L. (1990). *Methods of meta-analysis: Correcting error and bias in research findings.* Newbury Park, CA: Sage.

Ilgen, D. R., Hollenbeck, J. R., Johnson, M., & Jundt, J. (2005). Teams in organizations: From I-P-O models to IMOI models. *Annual Review of Psychology, 56*, 517–543.

Ilies, R., Gerhardt, M. W., & Huy, L. (2004). Individual differences in leadership emergence: Integrating meta-analytic findings and behavioral genetics estimates. *International Journal of Selection & Assessment, 12*, 207–219.

Ilies, R., Nahrgang, J. D., & Morgeson, F. P. (2007). Leader-member exchange and citizenship behaviors: A meta-analysis. *Journal of Applied Psychology, 92*, 269–277.

Javidan, M., House, R. J., & Dorfman, P. W. (2004). A non-technical summary of GLOBE findings. In R. J. House, P. J. Hanges, M. Javidan, P. W. Dorfman, & V. Gupta (Eds.), *Culture, leadership, and organizations: The GLOBE study of 62 societies* (pp. 29–50). Thousand Oaks, CA: Sage.

Johns, G. (2006). The essential impact of context on organizational behavior. *Academy of Management Review, 31*, 386–408.

Judge, T. A., Bono, J. E., Ilies, R., & Gerhardt, M. W. (2002). Personality and leadership: A qualitative and quantitative review. *Journal of Applied Psychology, 87*, 765–780.

Judge, T. A., & Cable, D. M. (2004). The effect of physical height on workplace success and income: Preliminary test of a theoretical model. *Journal of Applied Psychology, 89*, 428–441.

Judge, T. A., & Piccolo, R. F. (2004). Transformational and transactional leadership: A meta-analytic test of their relative validity. *Journal of Applied Psychology, 89*, 755–768.

Judge, T. A., Piccolo, R. F., & Ilies, R. (2004). The forgotten ones? The validity of consideration and initiating structure in leadership research. *Journal of Applied Psychology, 89*, 36–51.

Katz, D., & Kahn, R. L. (1978). *The social psychology of organizations* (2nd ed.). New York: Wiley.

Kenny, D. A., & Zaccaro, S. J. (1983). An estimate of variance due to traits in leadership. *Journal of Applied Psychology, 68*, 678–685.

Kerr, S., & Jermier, J. (1978). Substitutes for leadership: Their meaning and measurement. *Organizational Behavior and Human Performance, 22*, 375–403.

Kilduff, M., & Day, D. V. (1994). Do chameleons get ahead? The effects of self-monitoring on managerial careers. *Academy of Management Journal, 37*, 1047–1060.

Koenig, A. M., Eagly, A. H., Mitchell, A. A., & Risitkari, T. (2011). Are leader stereotypes masculine? A meta-analysis of three research paradigms. *Psychological Bulletin, 137*, 616–642.

Koppes, L. L., & Pickren, W. (2007). Industrial and organizational psychology: An evolving science and practice. In L. L. Koppes (Ed.), *Historical perspectives in industrial and organizational psychology* (pp. 3–35). Mahwah, NJ: Erlbaum.

Korman, A. K., & Tanofsky, R. (1975). Statistical problems of contingency models in organizational behavior. *Academy of Management Journal, 18*, 393–397.

Kozlowski, S. W. J., & Bell, B. S. (2008). Team learning, development, and adaptation. In V. I. Sessa & M. London (Eds.), *Work group learning: Understanding, improving & assessing how groups learn in organizations* (pp. 15–44). New York: Erlbaum.

Kozlowski, S. W. J., Gully, S. M., McHugh, P. P., Salas, E., & Cannon-Bowers, J. A. (1996). A dynamic theory of leadership and team effectiveness: Developmental and task contingent leader roles. *Research in Personnel and Human Resources Management, 4*, 253–305.

Kozlowski, S. W. J., Gully, S. M., Nason, E. R., & Smith, E. M. (1999). Developing adaptive teams: A theory of compilation and performance across levels and time. In D. R. Ilgen & E. D. Pulakos (Eds.), *The changing nature of work performance: Implications for staffing, personnel actions, and development* (pp. 240–292). San Francisco: Jossey-Bass.

Kozlowski, S. W. J., & Ilgen, D. R. (2006). Enhancing the effectiveness of work groups and teams (Monograph). *Psychological Science in the Public Interest, 7*, 77–124.

Kozlowski, S. W. J., & Klein, K. J. (2000). A multilevel approach to theory and research in organizations: Contextual, temporal, and emergent processes. In K. J. Klein & S. W. J. Kozlowski (Eds.), *Multilevel theory, research and methods in organizations: Foundations, extensions, and new directions* (pp. 467–511). San Francisco: Jossey-Bass.

Kozlowski, S. W. J., Watola, D. J., Jensen, J. M., Kim, B. H., & Botero, I. C. (2009). Developing adaptive teams: A theory of dynamic team leadership. In E. Salas, G. F. Goodwin, & C. S. Burke (Eds.), *Team effectiveness in complex organizations: Cross-disciplinary perspectives and approaches* (pp. 113–155). New York: Routledge.

Landy, F. J., & Farr, J., L. (1980). Performance rating. *Psychological Bulletin, 87*, 72–107.

Liden, R. C., Wayne, S. J., & Stilwell, D. (1993). A longitudinal study on the early development of leader-member exchange. *Journal of Applied Psychology, 78*, 662–674.

Locke, E. A. (2003). Foundations for a theory of leadership. In S. E. Murphy & R. E. Riggio (Eds.), *The future of leadership development* (pp. 29–46). Mahwah, NJ: Erlbaum.

Lord, R. G., Binning, J. F., Rush, M. C., & Thomas, J. C. (1978). The effect of performance cues and leader behavior on questionnaire ratings of leadership behavior. *Organizational Behavior and Human Performance, 21*, 27–39.

Lord, R. G., & Brown, D. J. (2004). *Leadership processes and follower self-identity.* Mahwah, NJ: Erlbaum.

Lord, R. G., De Vader, C. L., & Alliger, G. M. (1986). A meta-analysis of the relation between personality traits and leadership perceptions: An application of validity generalization procedures. *Journal of Applied Psychology, 71*, 402–409.

Lord, R. G., & Dinh, J. E. (2012). Aggregation processes and levels of analysis as organizing structures for leadership theory. In D. V. Day & J. Antonakis (Eds.), *The nature of leadership* (2nd ed., pp. 29–65). Los Angeles: Sage.

Lord, R., G., Foti, R. J., & De Vader, C. L. (1984). A test of leadership categorization theory: Internal structure, information processing, and leadership perceptions. *Organizational Behavior and Human Performance, 34*, 343–378.

Lord, R. G., Foti, R. J., & Phillips, J. S. (1982). A theory of leadership categorization. In J. G. Hunt, U. Sekaran, & C. Schriesheim (Eds.), *Leadership: Beyond establishment views* (pp. 104–121). Carbondale: Southern Illinois University.

Lord, R. G., & Maher, K. J. (1991). *Leadership and information processing: Linking perceptions and performance.* Boston: Unwin Hyman.

Lowe, K. B., Kroeck, K. G., & Sivasubramanian, N. (1996). Effectiveness correlates of transformational and transactional leadership: A meta-analytic review. *Leadership Quarterly, 7*, 385–425.

Luthans, F., & Davis, T. (1979). Behavioral self-management (BSM): The missing link in managerial effectiveness. *Organizational Dynamics, 8*, 42–60.

Mann, R. D. (1959). A review of the relationships between personality and performance in small groups. *Psychological Bulletin, 56*, 241–270.

Manz, C. C., & Sims, H. P., Jr. (1980). Self-management as a substitute for leadership: A social learning theory perspective. *Academy of Management Review, 5*, 361–367.

Manz, C. C., & Sims, H. P., Jr. (1987). Leading workers to lead themselves: The external leadership of self-managing work teams. *Administrative Science Quarterly, 32*, 106–129.

Marks, M. A., Mathieu, J. E., & Zaccaro, S. J. (2001). A temporally based framework and taxonomy of team processes. *Academy of Management Review, 26*, 356–376.

McCauley, C. D., Van Velsor, E., & Ruderman, M. N. (2010). Introduction: Our view of leadership development. In E. Van Velsor, C. D. McCauley, & M. N. Ruderman (Eds.), *The Center for Creative Leadership handbook of leadership development* (3rd ed., pp. 1–26). San Francisco: Jossey-Bass.

McGrath, J. E. (1962). *Leadership behavior: Some requirements for leadership training.* Washington, DC: U.S. Civil Service Commission, Office of Career Development.

Meindl, J. R., & Ehrlich, S. B. (1987). The romance of leadership and the evaluation of organizational performance. *Academy of Management Journal, 30*, 90–109.

Meindl, J. R., Ehrlich, S. B., & Dukerich, J. M. (1985). The romance of leadership. *Administrative Science Quarterly, 30*, 78–102.

Mills, P. K. (1983). Self-management: Its control and relationship to other organizational properties. *Academy of Management Review, 8*, 445–453.

Mischel, W. (1973). Toward a cognitive social learning reconceptualization of personality. *Psychological Review, 80*, 252–283.

Mitchell, T. R., & James, L. R. (2001). Building better theory: Time and the specification of when things happen. *Academy of Management Review, 26*, 530–547.

Mitchell, T. R., Larson, J. R., Jr., & Green, S. G. (1977). Leader behavior, situational moderators, and group performance: An attributional analysis. *Organizational Behavior and Human Performance, 18*, 254–268.

Morgeson, F. P. (2005). The external leadership of self-managing teams: Intervening in the context of novel and disruptive events. *Journal of Applied Psychology, 90*, 497–508.

Morgeson, F. P., & DeRue, D. S. (2006). Event criticality, urgency, and duration: Understanding how events disrupt teams and influence team leader intervention. *Leadership Quarterly, 17*, 271–287.

Morgeson, F. P., DeRue, D. S., & Peterson, E. (2010). Leadership in teams: A functional approach to understanding leadership structures and processes. *Journal of Management, 36*, 5–39.

Mowday, R. T. (1978). The exercise of upward influence in organizations. *Administrative Science Quarterly, 23*, 137–156.

Nahrgang, J. D., Morgeson, F. P., & Ilies, R. (2009). The development of leader-member exchanges: Exploring how personality and performance influence leader and member relationships over time. *Organizational Behavior and Human Decision Processes, 108*, 256–266.

O'Connor, P. M. G., & Quinn, L. (2004). Organizational capacity for leadership. In C. D. McCauley & E. Van Velsor (Eds.), *The Center for Creative Leadership handbook of leadership development* (2nd ed., pp. 417–437). San Francisco: Jossey-Bass.

Pearce, C. L. (2004). The future of leadership: Combining vertical and shared leadership to transform knowledge work. *Academy of Management Executive, 18*(1), 47–57.

Pearce, C. L., & Conger, J. A. (2003a). All those years ago: The historical underpinnings of shared leadership. In C. L. Pearce & J. A. Conger (Eds.), *Shared leadership: Reframing the hows and whys of leadership* (pp. 1–18). Thousand Oaks, CA: Sage.

Pearce, C. L., & Conger, J. A. (Eds.). (2003b). *Shared leadership: Reframing the hows and whys of leadership*. Thousand Oaks, CA: Sage.

Pearce, C. L., & Sims, H. P., Jr. (2002). Vertical versus shared leadership as predictors of the effectiveness of change management teams: An examination of aversive, directive, transactional, transformational, and empowering leader behaviors. *Group Dynamics: Theory, Research, and Practice, 6*, 172–197.

Peters, L. H., Hartke, D. D., & Pohlmann, J. T. (1985). Fiedler's contingency theory of leadership: An application of the meta-analysis procedures of Schmidt and Hunter. *Psychological Bulletin, 97*, 274–285.

Pfeffer, J. (1977). The ambiguity of leadership. *Academy of Management Review, 2*, 104–112.

Podolny, J. M., Khurana, R., & Hill-Popper, M. (2005). Revisiting the meaning of leadership. *Research in Organizational Behavior, 26*, 1–36.

Podsakoff, P. M., MacKenize, S. B., Ahearne, M., & Bommer, W. H. (1995). Searching for a needle in a haystack: Trying to identify the illusive moderators of leadership behaviors. *Journal of Management, 21*, 422–470.

Potter, E. H., & Fiedler, F. E. (1981). The utilization of staff member intelligence and experience under high and low stress. *Academy of Management Journal, 24*, 361–376.

Raudenbush, S. W., & Bryk, A. S. (2002). *Hierarchical linear models: Applications and data analysis methods* (2nd ed.). Thousand Oaks, CA: Sage.

Riggio, R. E., Chaleff, I., & Lipman-Blumen, J. (Eds.). (2008). *The art of followership: How great followers create great leaders and organizations*. San Francisco: Jossey-Bass.

Rousseau, D. M., Manning, J., & Denyer, D. (2008). Evidence in management and organizational science: Assembling the field's full weight of scientific knowledge through syntheses. *Academy of Management Annals, 2*, 475–515.

Rush, M. C., Thomas, J. C., & Lord, R. G. (1977). Implicit leadership theory: A potential threat to the internal validity of leader behavior questionnaires. *Organizational Behavior and Human Performance, 20*, 756–765.

Salancik, G. R., Calder, B. J., Rowland, K. M., Leblebici, H., & Conway, M. (1975). Leadership as an outcome of social structure and process: A multidimensional analysis. In J. G. Hunt & L. L. Larson (Eds.), *Leadership frontiers* (pp. 81–101). Kent, OH: Kent State University.

Schein, V. E. (1973). The relationship between sex role stereotypes and requisite management characteristics. *Journal of Applied Psychology, 57*, 95–100.

Schilit, W. K., & Locke, E. A. (1982). A study of upward influence in organizations. *Administrative Science Quarterly, 27*, 304–316.

Schriesheim, C. A. (2003). Why leadership research is generally irrelevant for leadership development. In S. E. Murphy & R. E. Riggio (Eds.), *The future of leadership development* (pp. 181–197). Mahwah, NJ: Erlbaum.

Schriesheim, C. A., Castro, S. L., & Cogliser, C. C. (1999). Leader-member exchange (LMX) research: A comprehensive review of theory, measurement, and data-analytic practices. *Leadership Quarterly, 10*, 63–113.

Schriesheim, C. A., Castro, S. L., Zhou, X., & DeChurch, L. A. (2006). An investigation of path-goal and transformational leadership theory predictions at the individual level of analysis. *Leadership Quarterly, 17*, 21–38.

Schriesheim, C. A., & Kerr, S. (1977). Theories and measures of leadership: A critical appraisal. In J. G. Hunt & L. L. Larson (Eds.), *Leadership: The cutting edge* (pp. 9–45). Carbondale: Southern Illinois University.

Schriesheim, C. A., Tepper, B. J., & Tetrault, L. A. (1994). Least preferred co-worker score, situational control, and leadership effectiveness: A meta-analysis of contingency model performance predictions. *Journal of Applied Psychology, 79*, 561–573.

Shamir, B., House, R. J., & Arthur, M. B. (1993). The motivational effects of charismatic leadership: A self-concept based theory. *Organization Science, 4*, 577–594.

Sin, H.-P., Nahrgang, J. D., & Morgeson, F. P. (2009). Understanding why they don't see eye-to-eye: An examination of leader-member exchange (LMX) agreement. *Journal of Applied Psychology, 94*, 1048–1057.

Snyder, M. (1987). *Public appearances, private realities: The psychology of self-monitoring*. New York: W. H. Freeman.

Sparrowe, R. T., & Liden, R. C. (1997). Process and structure in leader-member exchange. *Academy of Management Review, 22*, 522–552.

Sparrowe, R. T., & Liden, R. C. (2005). Two routes to influence: Integrating leader-member exchange and social network perspectives. *Administrative Science Quarterly, 50*, 505–535.

Staw, B. M. (1975). Attribution of the "causes" of performance: A general alternative interpretation of non-sectional research on organizations. *Organizational Behavior and Human Performance, 13*, 414–432.

Stogdill, R. M. (1948). Personal factors associated with leadership: A survey of the literature. *Journal of Psychology, 25*, 35–71.

Stogdill, R. M., Goode, O. S., & Day, D. R. (1962). New leader behavior description subscales. *Journal of Psychology, 54*, 259–269.

Strube, M. J., & Garcia, J. E. (1981). A meta-analytic investigation of Fiedler's contingency model of leadership effectiveness. *Psychological Bulletin, 90*, 307–321.

Sulsky, L. M., & Day, D. V. (1992). Frame-of-reference training and cognitive categorization: An empirical investigation of rater memory issues. *Journal of Applied Psychology, 77*, 501–510.

Taggar, S., Hackett, R., & Saha, S. (1999). Leadership emergence in autonomous work teams: Antecedents and outcomes. *Personnel Psychology, 52*, 899–926.

Taylor, J., & Bowers, D. (1972). *The survey of organizations: A machine-scored standardized questionnaire instrument*. Ann Arbor: University of Michigan, Institute for Social Research.

Tead, O. (1935). *The art of leadership*. New York: McGraw-Hill.

Uhl-Bien, M. (2006). Relational leadership theory: Exploring the social processes of leadership and organizing. *Leadership Quarterly, 17*, 654–676.

Uhl-Bien, M., Maslyn, J., & Ospina, S. (2012). The nature of relational leadership: A multitheoretical lens on leadership relationships and processes. In D. V. Day & J. Antonakis

(Eds.), *The nature of leadership* (2nd ed., pp. 289–330). Los Angeles: Sage.

Van Vugt, M. (2012). The nature in leadership: Evolutionary, biological, and social neuroscience perspectives. In D. V. Day & J. Antonakis (Eds.), *The nature of leadership* (2nd ed., pp. 141–175). Los Angeles: Sage.

Van Vugt, M., Hogan, R., & Kaiser, R. B. (2008). Leadership, followership, and evolution: Some lessons from the past. *American Psychologist, 63*, 182–196.

Van Vugt, M., Johnson, D. D. P., Kaiser, R. B., & O'Gorman, R. (2008). Evolution and the social psychology of leadership: The mismatch hypothesis. In C. Hoyt, G. R. Giethals, & D. R. Forsyth (Eds.), *Leadership at the crossroads: Leadership and psychology* (Vol. 1, pp. 267–282). London: Praeger.

Vecchio, R. P. (2002). Leadership and gender advantage. *Leadership Quarterly, 13*, 643–671.

Vecchio, R. P. (2003). In search of gender advantage. *Leadership Quarterly, 14*, 835–850.

Vicere, A. A., & Fulmer, R. M. (1998). *Leadership by design.* Boston: Harvard Business School.

Vroom, V. H., & Jago, A. G. (1988). *The new leadership: Managing participation in organizations.* Englewood Cliffs, NJ: Prentice Hall.

Vroom, V. H., & Jago, A. G. (2007). The role of the situation in leadership. *American Psychologist, 62*, 17–24.

Vroom, V. H., & Yetton, P. W. (1973). *Leadership and decision making.* Pittsburgh, PA: University of Pittsburgh.

Weber, M. (1924/1947). *The theory of social and economic organization* (T. Parsons & A. M. Henderson, Trans.). New York: Oxford University Press.

Weick, K. E. (1993). The collapse of sensemaking in organizations: The Mann Gulch disaster. *Administrative Science Quarterly, 38*, 628–652.

Wofford, J. C., & Liska, L. Z. (1993). Path-goal theories of leadership: A meta-analysis. *Journal of Management, 19*, 857–876.

Wuchty, S., Jones, B. F., & Uzzi, B. (2007). The increasing dominance of teams in the production of knowledge. *Science, 316*, 1036–1038.

Yukl, G. (1971). Toward a behavioral theory of leadership. *Organizational Behavior and Human Performance, 6*, 414–440.

Yukl, G. (2006). *Leadership in organizations* (6th ed.). Upper Saddle River, NJ: Prentice-Hall.

Zaccaro, S. J. (2007). Trait-based perspectives of leadership. *American Psychologist, 62*, 6–16.

Zaccaro, S. J., Heinen, B., & Shuffler, M. (2009). Team leadership and team effectiveness. In E. Salas, G. F. Goodwin, & C. S. Burke (Eds.), *Team effectiveness in complex organizations: Cross-disciplinary perspectives and approaches* (pp. 83–111). New York: Routledge.

Zaccaro, S. J., Kemp, C., & Bader, P. (2004). Leader traits and attributes. In J. Antonakis, A. T. Cianciolo, & R. J. Sternberg (Eds.), *The nature of leadership* (pp. 104–124). Thousand Oaks, CA: Sage.

Zaccaro, S. J., Rittman, A. L., & Marks, M. A. (2001). Team leadership. *Leadership Quarterly, 12*, 451–483.

Zyphur, M. J., Barsky, A. P., & Zhang, Z. (2012). Advances in leadership research methods. In D. V. Day & J. Antonakis (Eds.), *The nature of leadership* (2nd ed., pp. 66–107). Los Angeles: Sage.

INDEX

Note: Page numbers followed by "f" and "t" refer to figures and tables, respectively.

National Labor Relations Act, 39, 309
National Labor Standards Act, 39
national origin, discrimination by, 1041
National Research Council (NRC), 44, 45, 1036
National Training Laboratory for Group Development (NTL), 26t, 48
National Transportation Safety Bureau (NTSB), 920
natural experiments, on discrimination, 1037
naturalistic decision making (NDM), 19–20, 1349–75
 adaptation and, 1359
 apprenticeship and, 1371–72
 automaticity and, 1366
 content in, 1369–70
 CTA and, 1361–64, 1361t–1362t
 debriefings and, 1367–68
 embeddedness and, 1359–60
 expertise and, 1352–55, 1353f, 1364–66, 1365t
 frugality and, 1360
 future directions for, 1373–75, 1374t
 individuals and, 1364–66
 interdependence and, 1360
 leadership and, 1357–59, 1368
 macrocognition and, 1374
 memory and, 1365–66
 mentoring and, 1371–72
 metacognition and, 1366
 methodological approaches to, 1361–64
 performance with, 1368–69
 research in, 1351–52
 roles and, 1367
 roots of, 1350–51
 SBT for, 1371
 self-regulation and, 1366
 specialization and, 1359
 STS and, 1368
 teams and, 1366–68, 1366f
 training and, 1369–71
Naval Personnel Research, Studies, and Technology (NPRST), 55
Navy Personnel Research and Development Center (NPRDC), 55
NDM. See naturalistic decision making
need for achievement (nAch), 206, 270
need for affiliation, 270
need-press model, 374, 375
needs analysis
 aging and, 1270
 for training, 338–40
needs-supply theory, 375, 376–77, 379
negative affect (NA), 518–19, 1168
negative coaching, 297–98
negative emotions, 536
negotiation
 affect in, 1132
 confrontation/negotiation, 1066
 cross-cultural psychology and, 1105
 culture and, 1107, 1130–34

intercultural, 1133
 motivation in, 1131–32
 situations and, 1132–33
 socialization and, 597
 social networks and, 688
 in virtual teams, 802
neobehaviorism, 39
networks, 598. See also social networks
 breadth of, 757–59
 centrality of, 757
 diagrams, 670f
 in spatial interdependence, 757–59
neuroticism, 150, 507, 540, 704
newcomers, 596–97
Newcomer Socialization Questionnaire (NSQ), 603
New York State Association of Consulting Psychologists, 25t, 40
Neyman, Jerzy, 91
NHST. See Null Hypothesis Significance Testing
nicotine, 1235
NIH. See National Institutes of Health
NIIP. See National Institute for Industrial Psychology
9/11, 56
Nixon, Richard, 51
nomological noise, 99
non-commensurate dimension, of PE, 377–78
non-conscious motivation, 460
Non-directional Causal Models, 83
Non-Linear Systems, Inc., 53
non-recursive causal models, 83
Non-recursive Relationship, 84, 84f
norepinephrine, 1182
Norman, Donald, 1293
normative decision theory, 1137
notifications, for training, 344–45
NPRDC. See Navy Personnel Research and Development Center
NPRST. See Naval Personnel Research, Studies, and Technology
NRC. See National Research Council
NSQ. See Newcomer Socialization Questionnaire
NTL. See National Training Laboratory for Group Development
NTSB. See National Transportation Safety Bureau
nuisance variable, 88, 103
Null Hypothesis Significance Testing (NHST), 91–95
numerical distinctiveness, discrimination and, 1053

O

OB. See organizational behavior
Obama, Barack, 56
obesity
 discrimination by, 1042–43
 performance appraisal discrimination by, 1074

OBHDP. See Organizational Behavior and Human Decision Processes
objective culture, 1111
objective fit, 380–81
 outcomes and, 383–84, 383f
 subjective fit and, 388–92
OC. See organizational commitment
OCB. See organizational citizenship behavior
Occupational Analysis Inventory, 27t
occupational health psychology (OHP), 1228–41
 future directions for, 1240–41
 health and, 1235–39
 origins of, 1229–30
 safety and, 1230–36
Occupational Information Network (O*Net), 27t, 58, 180, 225
 task statements by, 339–40
 WFC and, 1182
Occupational Psychology, 55
Occupational Safety and Health Act of 1970, 1230
Occupational Safety and Health Administration (OSHA), 51
Occupational Work Inventory, 58
OCI. See Organizational Culture Inventory
OCI-Ideal, 659
OCI-Norms, 659
OCM. See Organizational Climate Measure
OCoPs. See organizational communities of practice
OCP. See Organizational Culture Profile
OD. See organizational development
ODC. See organizational development and change
ODM. See organizational decision making
ODT. See optimal distinctiveness theory
Oedipal complex, 1106
Offerman, Lynn, 61
Office of Strategic Services (OSS), 25t, 45
off-site training, 594
Ohio State Leadership Studies, 26t, 705
OHP. See occupational health psychology
oikos (Greek aristocratic family), 5
OJT. See on-the-job training
OLS. See ordinary least squares
Olson, Gary, 1324
Olson, Judy, 1324
O*Net. See Occupational Information Network
online recruitment, 204–5
on-the-job coaching, 296–98
on-the-job training (OJT), 1371–72
On the Witness Stand (Münsterberg), 1309
Open Courseware, at MIT, 1205–6
openness, 657, 704
 adverse impact and, 1056
 aging and, 1260
 CQ and, 1134
 readiness to learn and, 1215

misfits and, 393
reputation and, 207–8
in virtual teams, 812, 815, 816
social identity theory (SIT), 585, 847, 848, 1050–51, 1062
social influence, 16–17
culture and, 1129–30
leadership and, 699, 1137
socialization and, 598–99
in virtual teams, 815, 817, 838, 847
social information processing theory, 818, 819, 822, 824, 846, 849
social information theory, 818
social-interaction, in organizational culture, 656–57
socialization, 16–17, 579–609
accommodation in, 587–88
anticipatory, 586–87
change in, 597
of children, 580–81, 581t
content in, 580–81, 600–604, 601t–602t
definition of, 582–83
electronic sources for, 596–97
fit and, 390
fixed *versus* variable, 590
formal *versus* informal, 590
future research on, 604–7, 605f, 608t
groups and, 602–3
of individuals, 594–99
inquiry and, 595–96
investiture *versus* divestiture, 590
mentoring and, 629
meta-analysis for, 593
monitoring and, 595
negotiation and, 597
organizational learning and, 605–7
proactive behavior in, 597
psychology and, 580–82
roles and, 588–89, 602–3
sequential *versus* random, 590
serial *versus* disjunctive, 590
social influence and, 598–99
social networks and, 685
stage models of, 586–89
tactics in, 589–600, 591t–592t
tasks and, 602–3
tournament *versus* contest, 593
in virtual teams, 795, 812
written sources for, 596–97
social justice, 659
social learning theory, 27t, 52, 1220
social liabilities, 532–33
social loafing, 304, 824
social networks, 667–90
absorptive capacity and, 970–71
affect and, 683
appropriability in, 676–77
attitudes and, 681–82
attributes and, 674–75
balance in, 679
boundary specifications for, 676–77
bridges in, 680–81, 681f

career and, 685–86
clusters in, 680–81, 681f
cognition and, 675
conflict and, 688
creativity and, 689
culture and, 680
equity theory and, 688
homophily and, 678–79
human capital and, 679–80
indirect ties in, 669
individuals and, 672t
individual performance and, 686–87
innovation and, 689
job design and, 687
leadership and, 687
levels of analysis for, 677
measures of, 670–77, 672t, 673t, 674f
methodological issues with, 675–76
negotiation and, 688
OCB and, 688–89
organizational justice and, 688
outcomes and, 681–85
personality and, 680
power and, 683–84
recruitment and, 684–85
relationships and, 671–74, 676
resources and, 674
satisfaction and, 682–83
selection and, 684–85
social capital and, 669–70, 679–80
socialization and, 685
social proximity and, 678
spatial proximity and, 678
team performance and, 687
temporal proximity and, 678
theory of, 677–78
ties and, 674f
training and, 685
turnover and, 687–88
unethical behavior and, 689
social-oriented achievement motivation, 1121–22
social-oriented inputs, in teams, 777–78
social penetration theory, 819
social presence theory, 819, 820, 822, 846, 848
social proximity, 678
social psychology, 9, 45, 580
Social Psychology (Allport), 39
social/recreational activities, 594
social skills, 270
social status, in virtual teams, 830
social support, work design and, 263–64
social usefulness, 223
social verification, 650–51
social work design, 256
societal-environmental learning barrier, 975
societal goals, continuous learning and, 1205–6
Society for Applied Psychology, 36
Society for Human Resource Management (SHRM), 411, 1175

Society for Industrial and Organizational Psychology (SIOP), 9, 28t, 62, 411, 428, 430
Society for Occupational Health Psychology, 1230
Society for the Psychological Study of Social Issues, 39
socio-emotional behaviors, 1128
socio-technical systems theory (STS), 251, 1293, 1368
Socrates, 1288
soft systems methodologies (SSM), 981
space psychology, 45
spatial interdependence, 753–59
spatial proximity, 678
specialization
knowledge creation and, 939
NDM and, 1359
work design and, 261
specific level, of PE, 387
speed to market, 289
spillover, 1165, 1166, 1169, 1183
Sportsmanship, 166, 167
SR. *See* selection ratio
SSM. *See* soft systems methodologies
Standard Occupational Classification (SOC), 180
Standards for Educational and Psychological Tests and Manuals, 51
Stanford-Binet scale, 36
Starch, Daniel, 34
state engagement, 520n3
state trajectories, 122–24, 123f
state variation, 147
statistics, 45
distrust of, 422
statistical conclusion validity, 90, 91–95, 92t
statistical control, 89
statistical power, 93–95
status characteristics theory, 838
status closure, 836
steady state equilibrium, 124
stereotypes
with age, 1248, 1264–65
discrimination and, 1044–46
fit and, 1045–46
of gender, 1045–46
in-group/out-group and, 1051
pay discrimination and, 1076–77
Stern, William, 30, 35
stigma of incompetence, 1076–77
stochastic linear dynamic systems, 128–32, 129f, 130f, 131f
Stokes, Donald, 9
strategic human resource management (SHRM), 18, 238, 993–1005
aging and, 1268
diversity and, 1016
future research for, 1000–1004
history of, 993–97
knowledge management and, 1002–3
metrics for, 1000